HORNGREN'S
ACCOUNTING

10TH CANADIAN EDITION

TRACIE L. MILLER-NOBLES
Austin Community College

BRENDA MATTISON
Tri-County Technical College

ELLA MAE MATSUMURA
University of Wisconsin—Madison

CAROL A. MEISSNER
Georgian College

JO-ANN L. JOHNSTON
British Columbia Institute of Technology

PETER R. NORWOOD
Langara College

VOLUME ONE

PEARSON

Toronto

In memory of *Charles T. Horngren* 1926–2011

*Whose vast contributions to the teaching and learning of accounting impacted and
will continue to impact generations of accounting students and professionals.*

*I would like to thank my students for keeping me on my toes. Hearing their new ideas and how they think
about accounting makes teaching such a wonderful job.*

Carol A. Meissner

I would like to thank my husband, Bill, and my family for their encouragement and support.

Jo-Ann L. Johnston

I would like to thank my wife, Helen, and my family very much for their support and encouragement.

Peter R. Norwood

Editorial Director: Claudine O'Donnell
Senior Acquisitions Editor: Megan Farrell
Senior Marketing Manager: Loula March
Program Manager: Patricia Ciardullo
Project Manager: Sarah Lukaweski
Manager of Content Development: Suzanne Schaan
Developmental Editor: Suzanne Simpson Millar
Production Editor: Leanne Rancourt
Media Editor: Anita Smale
Media Developer: Olga Avdyeyeva

Copyeditor: Leanne Rancourt
Proofreaders: Susan Broadhurst and
  Bradley T. Smith
Permissions Project Manager: Joanne Tang
Photo and Text Permissions Research: Integra
  Publishing Services
Compositor: Cenveo® Publisher Service
Interior and Cover Designer: Anthony Leung
Cover Image: © John Kuczala / Getty Images

Vice-President, Cross Media and Publishing Services: Gary Bennett

Library and Archives Canada Cataloguing in Publication
Miller-Nobles, Tracie L., author
    Horngren's accounting / Tracie Nobles (Texas State University-San Marcos), Brenda Mattison
(Tri-County Technical College), Ella Mae Matsumura (University of Wisconsin-Madison),
Carol A. Meissner (Georgian College), Jo-Ann L. Johnston (British Columbia Institute of Technology),
Peter R. Norwood (Langara College). -- Tenth Canadian edition.

Includes indexes.
Issued in print and electronic formats.
ISBN 978-0-13-385537-1 (volume 1 : paperback).—ISBN 978-0-13-414064-3
(volume 1 : loose leaf). ISBN 978-0-13-418033-5 (volume 1 : html)

    1. Accounting—Textbooks. I. Norwood, Peter R., author
II. Matsumura, Ella Mae, 1952-, author III. Johnston, Jo-Ann L., author
IV. Mattison, Brenda, author V. Meissner, Carol A., author VI. Title.
VII. Title: Accounting.

HF5636.M54 2016   657   C2015-904630-0
C2015-904631-9

ISBN 978-0-13-385537-1

BRIEF CONTENTS

CONTENTS

Part 1 The Basic Structure of Accounting 2

1 Accounting and the Business Environment 2

2 Recording Business Transactions 58

3 Measuring Business Income: The Adjusting Process 116

4 Completing the Accounting Cycle 174

iv

ABOUT THE AUTHORS

TRACIE L. MILLER-NOBLES, CPA, received her bachelor's and master's degrees in accounting from Texas A&M University. She is an associate professor at Austin Community College. Previously she served as a senior lecturer at Texas State University, San Marcos, Texas, and has served as department chair of the Accounting, Business, Computer Information Systems, and Marketing/Management Department at Aims Community College, Greeley, Colorado. In addition, Tracie has taught as an adjunct professor at University of Texas and has public accounting experience with Deloitte Tax LLP and Sample & Bailey, CPAs.

Tracie is a recipient of the Texas Society of CPAs Outstanding Accounting Educator Award, NISOD Teaching Excellence Award, and the Aims Community College Excellence in Teaching Award. She is a member of the Teachers of Accounting at Two Year Colleges, the American Accounting Association, the American Institute of Certified Public Accountants, and the Texas State Society of Certified Public Accountants. She is currently serving on the board of directors as secretary/webmaster of Teachers of Accounting at Two Year Colleges, as chair of the American Institute of Certified Public Accountants Pre-certification Executive Education committee, and as program chair for the Teaching, Learning and Curriculum section of the American Accounting Association. In addition, Tracie served on the Commission on Accounting Higher Education: Pathways to a Profession.

Tracie has spoken on such topics as using technology in the classroom, motivating nonbusiness majors to learn accounting, and incorporating active learning in the classroom at numerous conferences. In her spare time she enjoys spending time with her friends and family, and camping, fishing, and quilting.

BRENDA L. MATTISON has a bachelor's degree in education and a master's degree in accounting, both from Clemson University. She is currently an accounting instructor at Tri-County Technical College (TCTC) in Pendleton, South Carolina. Brenda previously served as Accounting Program Coordinator at TCTC and has prior experience teaching accounting at Robeson Community College, Lumberton, North Carolina; University of South Carolina Upstate, Spartanburg, South Carolina; and Rasmussen Business College, Eagan, Minnesota. She also has accounting work experience in retail and manufacturing businesses.

Brenda is a member of Teachers of Accounting at Two Year Colleges and the American Accounting Association. She is currently serving on the board of directors as vice-president of registration of Teachers of Accounting at Two Year Colleges.

Brenda engages in the scholarship of teaching and learning (SOTL). While serving as Faculty Fellow at TCTC, her research project was Using Applied Linguistics in Teaching Accounting, the Language of Business. Brenda has presented her research findings. Other presentations include using active learning and manipulatives, such as building blocks and poker chips, in teaching accounting concepts.

In her spare time, Brenda enjoys reading and spending time with her family, especially touring the United States in their motorhome. She is also an active volunteer in the community, serving her church, local Girl Scouts, and other organizations.

ELLA MAE MATSUMURA is a professor in the Department of Accounting and Information Systems in the School of Business at the University of Wisconsin—Madison, and is affiliated with the university's Center for Quick Response Manufacturing. She received a Bachelor of Arts degree in mathematics from the University of California, Berkeley, and a Master of Science and PhD degree from the University of British Columbia. Ella Mae has won two teaching excellence awards at the University of Wisconsin–Madison and was elected as a lifetime fellow of the university's Teaching Academy, formed to promote effective teaching. She is a member of the university team awarded an IBM Total Quality Management Partnership grant to develop curriculum for total quality management education.

Ella Mae was a co-winner of the 2010 Notable Contributions to Management Accounting Literature Award. She has served in numerous leadership positions in the American Accounting Association (AAA). She was co-editor of *Accounting Horizons* and has chaired and served on numerous AAA committees. She has been secretary–treasurer and president of the AAA's Management Accounting Section. Her past and current research articles focus on decision making, performance evaluation, compensation, supply chain relationships, and sustainability. She co-authored a monograph on customer profitability analysis in credit unions.

CAROL A. MEISSNER is a professor in both the School of Business and the Automotive Business School of Canada at Georgian College in Barrie, Ontario. She teaches in the Accounting Diploma,

Automotive Business Diploma, and Bachelor of Business (Automotive Management) programs. Her favourite courses are introductory financial accounting and dealership financial statement analysis.

In 2014, Carol was awarded the Georgian College Board of Governors' Award of Excellence Academic for outstanding contributions to the college and an ongoing commitment to excellence.

Carol has broad experience in curriculum development. She has been a curriculum chair, program coordinator, member of several curriculum committees, and has been involved in writing and renewing degree, diploma, and graduate certificate programs. She is currently helping to launch the new Automotive Dealership Management graduate certificate program for automotive industry executives.

A self-professed "learning junkie," Carol holds a Bachelor of Commerce degree, a Master of Business Administration degree, a Master of Arts degree in Education (Community College concentration), and a CPA designation. She has also earned Georgian College's Professional Development Teaching Practice Credential and is a graduate of Georgian's Aspiring Leaders program. She is a regular attendee at conferences related to teaching, accounting, and the automotive industry.

Carol has always been a teacher. She started as a part-time college instructor when she completed her first degree and has taught full time since 2005. Her "real world" experience includes car dealership controllership and self-employment as a part-time controller and consultant for a wide variety of businesses. Carol recently worked on several online projects for publishers and OMVIC as a subject matter expert. She is a trustee for OPSEU Local 35 and a member of the Secretary Treasurers Association of Ontario.

JO-ANN JOHNSTON is an instructor in the Accounting, Finance and Insurance Department at the British Columbia Institute of Technology (BCIT). She obtained her Diploma of Technology in Financial Management from BCIT, her Bachelor in Administrative Studies degree from British Columbia Open University, and her Master of Business Administration degree from Simon Fraser University. She is also a certified general accountant and completed the Canadian securities course.

Prior to entering the field of education, Jo-Ann worked in public practice and industry for over 10 years. She is a past member of the board of governors of the Certified General Accountants Association of British Columbia and has served on various committees for the association. She was also a member of the board of directors for the BCIT Faculty and Staff Association, and served as treasurer during that tenure.

In addition to teaching duties and committee work for BCIT, Jo-Ann is the financial officer for a family-owned business.

PETER R. NORWOOD is an instructor in accounting and coordinator of the Accounting program at Langara College in Vancouver. A graduate of the University of Alberta, he received his Master of Business Administration from the University of Western Ontario. He is a CPA, a fellow of the Institute of Chartered Accountants of British Columbia, a certified management accountant, and a fellow of the Society of Management Accountants of Canada.

Before entering the academic community, Peter worked in public practice and industry for over 15 years. He is a past president of the Institute of Chartered Accountants of British Columbia and chair of the Chartered Accountants School of Business (CASB). He is also the chair of the Chartered Accountants Education Foundation for the British Columbia Institute of Chartered Accountants and has been active on many provincial and national committees, including the Board of Evaluators of the Canadian Institute of Chartered Accountants. Peter is also a sessional lecturer in the Sauder School of Business at the University of British Columbia.

HORNGREN'S ACCOUNTING ... REDEFINING TRADITION

MAKING CONNECTIONS

CONNECTING CHAPTER boxes appear at the beginning of each chapter. These features combine the chapter outline with the learning objectives, key questions, and page references.

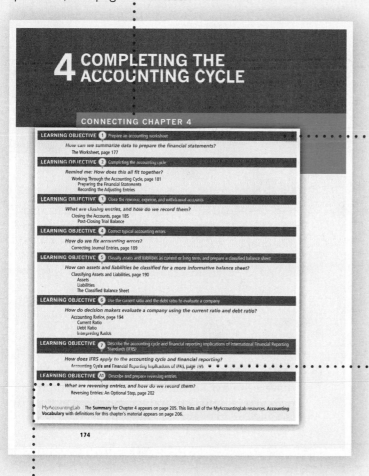

LEARNING OBJECTIVES provide a roadmap showing what will be covered and what is especially important in each chapter.

PAGE REFERENCES give students the ability to quickly connect to the topic they are seeking within the chapter.

KEY QUESTIONS are questions about the important concepts in the chapter, expressed in everyday language.

CHAPTER OPENERS set up the concepts to be covered in the chapter using stories students can relate to. They show why the topics in the chapter are important in the business world. These vignettes are now 100 percent Canadian content.

Kawartha Dairy Limited is a 100% Canadian-owned ice cream and dairy processor located in Bobcaygeon, Ontario, and is still operated by the same family that started it back in 1937. As a business, it is different from many in the food industry because it not only operates its own production facility, but also runs a chain of eight of its own retail stores. It also wholesales its Kawartha Dairy-branded products to other businesses, who in turn offer the products in their own stores. In addition to ice cream and milk, it produces specialized products like buttermilk for the baking industry and private-label items for other companies.

A firm like this has a huge investment in assets. Kawartha Dairy owns buildings, land, production equipment, and office furniture that it uses to run the business. It also has a fleet of trucks to deliver its goods to its own retail outlets, independent specialty shops, grocery stores, and institutional customers.

How does the company record the purchase of these trucks in their accounting records? Do they expense them or set them up as assets? Because they help the company earn revenue over several periods, they are reported as assets.

How should Kawartha Dairy account for the use of the trucks? They record amortization over each truck's useful life. Managers estimate how long they can use the truck and how much they can sell it for when it is taken out of service. They don't amortize this last amount because they get it back when they sell the truck or trade it in for a new one.

Because most companies keep assets for as long as they can, they also need to make repairs and maintain the trucks. *How do you decide when work done on the truck is part of the cost or considered a repair?* Professional judgment is just as important in these decisions as are the generally accepted accounting principles. Managers at Kawartha and other companies need to know how to account for these assets.

This chapter covers these and other matters about property, plant, and equipment, the long-term tangible assets that a business uses to operate, such as airplanes for Air Canada and automobiles for Discount Car and Truck Rentals. It also looks at *intangibles*—those assets with no physical form, such as trademarks and copyrights, and finally, this chapter shows how to account for natural resources such as oil and timber.

559

NEW

INSTRUCTOR TIPS RIGHT IN THE CHAPTER
Found throughout the text, these handwritten notes mimic the experience of having an experienced teacher walk a student through concepts on the board. Many include mnemonic devices or examples to help students remember the rules of accounting.

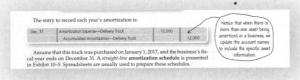

NEW

IFRS/ASPE COMPARISON Each applicable chapter ends with a table comparing how concepts in that chapter are dealt with for those using IFRS and ASPE.

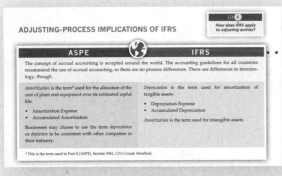

NEW

ANNOTATED EXHIBITS More annotated exhibits have been developed for this edition to improve clarity and reduce related explanations in the text.

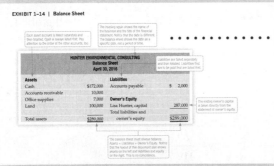

NEW

TRY IT! BOXES Found at the end of each learning objective section in the text, **Try It!** features (formerly Just Checking) give students the opportunity to apply the concepts they just learned to an accounting problem. For this edition, care was taken to streamline this feature to include fewer questions to avoid interrupting the flow of student learning. Deep linking in the eText will allow students to practise in MyAccountingLab without interrupting their interaction with the eText. **Try It! Solutions** are provided at the end of each chapter.

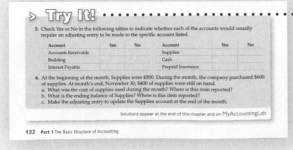

· · · · · **REVISED WHY IT'S DONE THIS WAY BOXES**
Descriptions in these boxes have been shortened to focus on the key new points in the chapter, without referencing levels. For instructors who want longer and more technical notes, these are included in the instructor's material.

REVISED END-OF-CHAPTER MATERIAL
The number of Starters and Exercises provided in each chapter has been increased, while maintaining both A and B Problem sets.

All learning objectives now have consistent coverage in end-of-chapter questions.

There is now more variety of questions provided.

ENGAGING REDESIGN The redesign of this text throughout includes clean and consistent art for T-accounts, journal entries, financial statements, and the accounting equation.

New art types include clear explanations and connection arrows to help students follow the transaction process. Illustrations are updated to be more modern and clean.

Margins have been decluttered, ensuring a smoother, more open and approachable look, while keeping the most important content visible.

Closing entry ❸ would then credit Income Summary to close its debit balance and transfer the net loss to Lisa Hunter, Capital:

❸ May 31	Lisa Hunter, Capital	1,000	
	Income Summary		1,000
	To close the Income Summary account and transfer net loss to the Capital account.		

After posting, these two accounts would appear as follows:

Income Summary			
Clo. ❷ 27,500	Clo. ❶ 26,500		
Bal. 1,000	Clo. ❸ 1,000		

Lisa Hunter, Capital	
Clo. ❸ 1,000	120,100
	Bal. 119,100

Changes to the Tenth Canadian Edition

Additional Starters and Exercises have been added to *all* chapters in Volume 1. Instructors wanted more of these types of questions and more variety in the questions, so the Tenth Canadian Edition has been updated to reflect this.

Chapter 1—Accounting and the Business Environment

- Chapter 1 has been completely reworked and refreshed. The explanation of accounts has been moved from Chapter 2, thus removing duplication and ensuring students have all the information they need to create financial statements.
- Updates to this chapter include information reflecting the changing professional landscape of accountants in Canada, and the history of accounting material has been removed.
- Annotated exhibits for the balance sheet and income statement have been provided to strengthen explanations of the financial statements.

Chapter 2—Recording Business Transactions

- The introduction of the accounting cycle has been moved from Chapter 4 to the start of this chapter because this is where the topic is first introduced.
- The demonstration of posting to a T-account is now covered before introducing a more formal ledger account.
- Exhibits relating to the rules of debits and credits have been improved.
- The explanation of journal entries and calculating the balance of a T-account has been improved with new annotated exhibits.

Chapter 3—Measuring Business Income: The Adjusting Process

- The discussion on cash-basis versus accrual-basis accounting has been reduced since instructors told us that the accrual basis needed to be the focus of the lesson. We moved some cash-basis information to MyAccountingLab for those instructors who still want to cover this topic in more detail.
- There is an expanded alternative presentation example of property, plant, and equipment (where we show rather than tell).
- Again because of instructor requests, we added an additional example of partial pay periods to support student learning of a very difficult concept.
- The flow of the chapter has been improved by moving the order of adjusting entry topics so that they are in the same order as presented in the exhibit.
- The learning objective about using the worksheet to prepare the adjusted trial balance has been removed to make it easier for some schools to skip the topic of worksheets.

Chapter 4—Completing the Accounting Cycle

- Duplicate information about worksheets and the accounting cycle has been removed.
- The complexity of the classified balance sheet example has been reduced.

Chapter 5—Merchandising Operations

- The summary problem has been updated to cover more of the key learning objectives. The Ninth Canadian Edition solved problem, which included a merchandiser's worksheet and closing entries, has been moved to MyAccountingLab, so it is still available for those instructors who teach those topics.
- The information about sales taxes, which was included as Appendix C to this chapter, has been moved to Chapter 11 (Current Liabilities) to remove the additional complexity this adds to the chapter and avoid duplication of topics in the book.

Chapter 6—Accounting for Merchandise Inventory

- The main change to this chapter is the removal of the learning objective, chapter section, and problem material related to the assessment of the impact of IFRS on inventory recording and reporting.

Chapter 7—Accounting Information Systems

- The learning objective that covered special journals with sales taxes (Learning Objective 6 in the Ninth Canadian Edition) has been moved to MyAccountingLab to reduce complexity, since sales taxes are not covered in detail until Chapter 11. Instructors who cover this topic still have the information they need.
- Information has been added on the use of new technology and security, such as the cloud.

Chapter 8—Internal Control and Cash

- All of the internal control information has been merged into one learning objective to streamline the content and reduce duplication.
- The Sarbanes-Oxley Act (SOX) discussion has been updated to include the Frank Dodd Act.

Chapter 9—Receivables

- Duplication of statement presentation information has been removed.
- Online payments have been added to keep the text material current.
- Internal control topics have been removed to keep the chapter focus on the most important topics in the chapter.
- Annotated T-account explanations about how to calculate the Allowance for Doubtful Accounts balance have been added to clarify a difficult topic for students.

Chapter 10—Property, Plant, and Equipment; and Goodwill and Intangible Assets

- The discussions of "construction in progress" and internal control have been removed to focus on key chapter concepts.
- The discussion about operating leases has been removed because this topic is covered in Volume 2.

Chapter 11—Current Liabilities and Payroll

- In order to reduce duplication, information about the presentation of liabilities has been consolidated.
- Payroll and sales tax rates have been updated for consistency with legislation at the time of writing.
- The concept of crowdfunding has been introduced to keep the text current.
- Internal control topics have been removed to keep the chapter focus on the most important topics in the chapter.
- The flow of recording payroll journal entries has been reworked to reduce duplication and improve clarity.

Student and Instructor Resources

The primary goal of the supplements that accompany *Horngren's Accounting*, Tenth Canadian Edition, is to help instructors deliver their course with ease using any delivery method—traditional, self-paced, or online—and for students to learn and practise accounting in a variety of ways that meet their learning needs and study preferences.

MyAccountingLab

MyAccountingLab delivers proven results in helping individual students succeed. It provides engaging experiences that personalize, stimulate, and measure learning for each student, including a personalized study plan, mini-cases, and videos. MyAccountingLab is the portal to an array of learning tools for all learning styles—algorithmic practice questions with guided solutions are only the beginning!

For Students

The following features are **NEW** to MyAccountingLab for the Tenth Canadian Edition:

 Assignable Accounting Cycle Tutorial—MyAccountingLab's new interactive tutorial helps students master the accounting cycle for early and continued success in the introduction to accounting course. The tutorial, accessed by computer, smartphone, or tablet, provides students with brief explanations of each concept of the accounting cycle through engaging videos and/or animations. Students are immediately assessed on their understanding, and their performance is recorded in the MyAccountingLab gradebook. Whether the Accounting Cycle Tutorial is used as a remediation self-study tool or course assignment, students have yet another resource within MyAccountingLab to help them be successful with the accounting cycle.

 Enhanced Pearson eText—The Enhanced eText keeps students engaged in learning on their own time, while helping them achieve greater conceptual understanding of course material. The worked examples bring learning to life, and algorithmic practice allows students to apply the concepts they are reading about. Combining resources that illuminate content with accessible self-assessment, MyAccountingLab with Enhanced eText provides students with a complete digital learning experience—all in one place.

The Pearson eText gives students access to the text whenever and wherever they have online access to the Internet. eText pages look exactly like the printed text, offering powerful new functionality for students and instructors. Users can create notes, highlight text in different colours, create bookmarks, zoom, click hyperlinked words and phrases to view definitions, and view in single-page or two-page view.

Dynamic Study Modules—Canadian study modules allow students to work through groups of questions and check their understanding of foundational accounting topics. As students work through questions, the Dynamic Study Modules assess their knowledge and only show questions that still require practice. Fully Assignable, flowing through the Gradebook, or Self-Directed Dynamic Study Modules can be completed online using a computer, tablet, or mobile device.

Learning Catalytics—A "bring your own device" assessment and classroom activity system that expands the possibilities for student engagement. Using Learning Catalytics, you can deliver a wide range of auto-gradable or open-ended questions that test content knowledge and build critical thinking skills. Eighteen different answer types provide great flexibility, including graphical, numerical, textual input, and more.

Audio Lecture Videos—These pre-class learning aids are available for every learning objective and are professor-narrated PowerPoint summaries that will help students prepare for class. These can be used in an online or flipped classroom experience or simply to get students ready for the lecture.

Adapative Assessment—Integrated directly into the MyAccountingLab Study Plan, Pearson's adaptive assessment is the latest technology for individualized learning and mastery. As students work through each question, they are provided with a custom learning path tailored specifically to the concepts they need to practise and master.

In addition, students will find the following assets to help improve their learning experience:

- Help Me Solve This Guides
- Worked Solutions
- Videos
- DemoDocs
- Check Figures
- Student PowerPoint Presentations
- Audio Chapter Summaries
- Accounting Cycle Tutorial Animations
- Excel Spreadsheet Templates
- General Ledger **(NEW!)**
- Open-Response Questions **(NEW!)**

For Instructors

The following resources are available for Instructors at the Instructor's Resource Centre on the catalogue, at catalogue.pearsoned.ca:

- **Instructor's Solutions Manual.** This manual provides instructors with a complete set of solutions to all the end-of-chapter material in the text. Available in both Word and PDF formats.

- **Computerized Testbank.** The Testbank for *Horngren's Accounting* offers a comprehensive suite of tools for testing and assessment. TestGen allows educators to easily create and distribute tests for their courses, either by printing and distributing through traditional methods or by online delivery. The more than 100 questions per chapter can be sorted by the chapter's Learning Objectives, difficulty ranking, Bloom's Taxonomy, and—new to this edition—applicable Canadian Professional Accounting Standards. Types of questions included are Multiple Choice, True/False, Short Answer, and Essay. One NEW Essay question has been created for each chapter, building on cumulative learning across all previous chapters.

- **Test Item File.** All the test questions from the TestGen testbank are available in Microsoft Word format.
- **Instructor's Teaching Tips in Digital eText Resource:** Instructors can easily locate useful teaching tips and resources throughout the eText, which is annotated by apple icons throughout the chapters. This eText is located in MyAccountingLab.
- **PowerPoint Presentations.** Prepared for each chapter of the text, these presentations offer helpful graphics that illustrate key figures and concepts from the text.
- **Image Library.** We are pleased to provide the exhibits from the text in .jpg format for use in the classroom or for building your own lectures or PowerPoint presentations.

Learning Solutions Managers

Pearson's Learning Solutions Managers work with faculty and campus course designers to ensure that Pearson technology products, assessment tools, and online course materials are tailored to meet your specific needs. This highly qualified team is dedicated to helping schools take full advantage of a wide range of educational resources by assisting in the integration of a variety of instructional materials and media formats. Your local Pearson sales representative can provide you with more details on this service program.

Acknowledgements for *Horngren's Accounting*, Tenth Canadian Edition

Horngren's Accounting, Tenth Canadian Edition, is the product of a rigorous research process that included multiple reviews in the various stages of development to ensure the revision meets the needs of Canadian students and instructors. The extensive feedback from the following reviewers helped shape this edition into a clearer, more readable and streamlined textbook in both the chapter content and assignment material:

- Bharat Aggarwal, Seneca College
- Ionela Bacain, Humber College
- Maria Belanger, Algonquin College
- Robin Day, British Columbia Institute of Technology
- Meredith Delaney, Seneca College
- Denise Dodson, Nova Scotia Community College
- Stanley Faria, Humber College
- Carol Fearon, Seneca College
- Darla Lutness, Northern Alberta Institute of Technology
- Michael Malkoun, St. Clair College
- Vnit Nath, British Columbia Institute of Technology
- Dal Pirot, MacEwan University
- Raymond Sungaila, Humber College
- Selina Tang, Douglas College
- Dan Wong, Southern Alberta Institute of Technology

Special thanks to Brad Witt at Humber College for being a "super reviewer" of this manuscript—his comments helped us improve the end-of-chapter material.

We would also like to thank the late Charles Horngren and Tom Harrison for their support in writing the original material.

We would like to give special thanks to Chris Deresh, CPA, Manager, Curriculum Content, at Chartered Professional Accountants of Canada for his guidance and technical support. His willingness to review and discuss portions of the manuscript was generous and insightful, and it is gratefully acknowledged.

The Chartered Professional Accountants, as the official administrator of generally accepted accounting principles in Canada, and the *CPA Canada Handbook*, are vital to the conduct of business and accounting in Canada. We have made every effort to incorporate the most current *Handbook* recommendations in this new edition of *Accounting* for both private enterprises (ASPE) and for publicly accountable enterprises subject to International Financial Reporting Standards (IFRS).

Thanks are extended to Indigo Books & Music Inc. and TELUS Corporation for permission to use their annual reports in Volumes I and II of this text and on MyAccountingLab. We acknowledge the support provided by the websites of various news organizations and by the annual reports of a large number of public companies.

We would like to acknowledge the people of Pearson Canada, in particular Senior Acquisitions Editor Megan Farrell, who put together a great team for this project, and Marketing Manager Loula March. Special thanks to Suzanne Simpson Millar, Queen Bee at Simpson Editorial Services, who was an awesome Developmental Editor on this edition. Leanne Rancourt as Production Editor also added her many talents as the project neared completion.

We would like to thank Media Editor Anita Smale for her excellent work on the MyAccountingLab that accompanies this textbook.

Our task is to provide educational material in the area of accounting to instructors and students to aid in the understanding of this subject area. We welcome your suggestions and comments on how to serve you better.

1 ACCOUNTING AND THE BUSINESS ENVIRONMENT

Connecting Chapter "X" appears at the beginning of each chapter and gives a guide to the content of the chapter with page references.

CONNECTING CHAPTER 1

**LEARNING OBJECTIVE ① ** Define accounting, and describe the users of accounting information

Learning Objectives are a "roadmap" showing what will be covered and what is especially important in each chapter.

Why is accounting important, and who uses the information?

Accounting: The Language of Business, page 4
  Users of Accounting Information
  Financial Accounting and Management Accounting
  Accountants
  Ethics in Accounting and Business

Key Questions are questions about the important concepts in the chapter expressed in everyday language.

**LEARNING OBJECTIVE ② ** Compare and contrast the forms of business organizations

In what form can we set up a company?

Forms of Business Organizations, page 7
  Proprietorship
  Partnership
  Corporation

**LEARNING OBJECTIVE ③ ** Describe some concepts and principles of accounting

What are some of the guidelines for accounting, and why do we need them?

Accounting Concepts, page 9
  Framework for Financial Reporting

**LEARNING OBJECTIVE ④ ** Use the accounting equation to analyze business transactions

How do business activities affect the accounting records of a company?

The Accounting Equation, page 12
  Assets
  Liabilities
  Owner's Equity
  Accounting for Business Transactions

**LEARNING OBJECTIVE ⑤ ** Prepare financial statements

What financial statements are prepared by a company, and how do we create them?

The Financial Statements, page 21
  Income Statement
  Statement of Owner's Equity
  Balance Sheet
  Cash Flow Statement
  Relationships among the Financial Statements

**LEARNING OBJECTIVE ⑥ ** Briefly explain the different accounting standards

What are IFRS and ASPE?

ASPE vs. IFRS, page 25

MyAccountingLab   The **Summary** for Chapter 1 appears on page 28. This lists all of the MyAccountingLab resources. **Accounting Vocabulary** with definitions for this chapter's material appears on page 29.

Lisa Hunter graduated from university with a degree in environmental studies. She then went to work with an environmental consulting company and gained extensive experience in the area of environmental sustainability. Lisa soon came to realize that many small businesses were starting to recognize the benefits of "going green."

Lisa decided to start her own consulting firm, but she did not have a lot of knowledge about businesses or their record keeping. She had so many questions. What kind of business should she set up? How would she know if the business was making any money? How would she know how much money she could take out of her business? She took some night school courses in accounting and small business management before starting her business to make sure she could answer those questions.

She named her new company "Hunter Environmental Consulting." She was now an entrepreneur! She realized she needed to develop a business plan, secure clients, set up an office, and hire staff.

Lisa's first year in business was stressful and successful. Her work in the first year was in the area of energy efficiency and suggesting how her clients could reduce their energy consumption and their energy costs.

"My previous training and experience gave me the confidence to know that I could be successful in this field. However, I did not realize how carefully you have to watch the books—costs can get out of control in a hurry if you're not careful!"

A **chapter-opening story** shows why the topics in the chapter are important to real companies and businesspeople. We refer to this story throughout the chapter.

> What role does accounting play in Lisa Hunter's situation? Lisa had to decide how to organize her company. She set up her business as a proprietorship—a single-owner company—with herself as the owner. As her business grows, she may decide to expand it by taking on a partner. She might also choose to incorporate—that is, to form a corporation. In this chapter, we discuss all three forms of business organization: proprietorships, partnerships, and corporations.

You may already know various accounting terms and relationships, because accounting affects people's lives in many ways. This first accounting course will help you see this by explaining how accounting works. As you progress through this course, you will see how accounting helps people like Lisa Hunter—and you—achieve business goals.

ACCOUNTING: THE LANGUAGE OF BUSINESS

LO 1

Why is accounting important, and who uses the information?

Learning objectives in the margin signal the beginning of the section that covers the learning-objective topic.

Boldfaced words are new terms that are explained here and defined in the Accounting Vocabulary section at the end of this chapter and the Glossary at the end of the book.

Accounting is the information system that measures **business** financial activities, processes that information into reports, and communicates the results to decision makers. For this reason it is called "the language of business." The better you understand the language, the better your decisions will be, and the better you can manage financial information. And as with any language, there is unique terminology that takes practice to learn. Students must practise using this new language as much as possible. Many business managers believe it is more important for students to learn accounting than any other business subject.

Financial statements are a key product of an accounting system and provide information that helps people make informed business decisions. Financial statements report on a business in monetary terms and help you answer questions such as, Is my business making a **profit**? Should I hire assistants? Who owes me money? Am I earning enough money to expand my business?

Students sometimes mistake bookkeeping for accounting. **Bookkeeping** is a procedural element of accounting, just as arithmetic is a step used when solving a mathematical problem (or just as skating is an important part of hockey). There are many accounting software packages that will handle detailed bookkeeping. Recording the information is important, but understanding what it all means and how it helps you make better decisions is even more important. Exhibit 1–1 illustrates the role of accounting in business.

EXHIBIT 1–1 | The Accounting System: The Flow of Information

Exhibits summarize key ideas in a visual way.

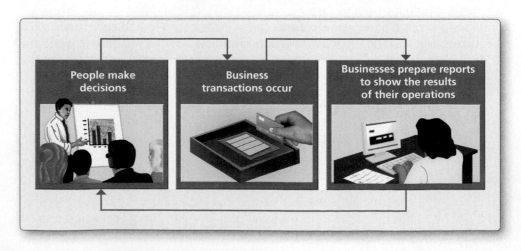

| People make decisions | Business transactions occur | Businesses prepare reports to show the results of their operations |

Users of Accounting Information

It seems that almost everyone uses financial information to make decisions.

Individuals People use accounting information in day-to-day affairs to manage bank accounts, evaluate job prospects, make investments, and decide whether to lease or buy a new car.

Businesses Business owners and managers use accounting information to set goals for their organizations. They evaluate their progress toward those goals, and they make changes when necessary. For example, Lisa Hunter makes decisions based on accounting information. She knows the amount of money that will be earned, since she and her client will agree on a fee for the consulting work she will perform. She needs to determine the scope of the work, how many consultants she will require, and how many hours it will take to complete the project. She needs to make sure that her costs do not exceed the fee she will receive from her client if she wants to make sure that she maintains a profitable business.

Investors and Creditors Investors and creditors provide the money to finance business activities. To decide whether to invest, **investors** predict the amount of income that will be earned on their investment. Before lending money, **creditors** such as banks and suppliers evaluate the borrower's ability to pay them back.

Government and Regulatory Bodies Provincial and federal governments levy taxes on individuals and businesses. Income tax is calculated by using accounting information as a starting point. A business's accounting system is required to keep track of provincial sales tax, goods and services tax, and harmonized sales tax that a business collects from its customers and pays to its suppliers. In addition, some companies are regulated by provincial securities commissions, such as the British Columbia Securities Commission or the Ontario Securities Commission, which dictate that businesses selling their shares to and borrowing money from the public disclose certain financial information.

Not-for-Profit Organizations Organizations such as churches, hospitals, government agencies, universities, and colleges, which operate for purposes other than to earn a profit, use accounting information to make decisions related to the organization in much the same way that profit-oriented businesses do.

Other Users Employees and labour unions may make wage demands based on the accounting information that shows their employer's reported income. Consumer groups and the general public are also interested in the amount of income that businesses earn.

Financial Accounting and Management Accounting

Users of accounting information may be grouped as external users or internal users. This distinction allows us to classify accounting into two fields—financial accounting and management accounting.

Financial accounting provides information primarily to people outside the company. Creditors and outside investors, for example, are not part of the day-to-day management of the company. Likewise, government agencies and the general public are **external users** of a company's accounting information. This book deals primarily with financial accounting.

Management accounting generates information for internal decision makers, such as company executives, department managers, and hospital administrators. **Internal users** ask questions such as, What price should we set for our product in order to make the most money? How much of a raise can we afford to give our employees?

Exhibit 1–2 shows how financial accounting and management accounting are used by Hunter Environmental Consulting's internal and external decision makers.

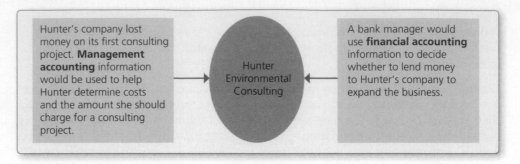

Accountants

Canadian accountants have been going through a period of transition. The largest organization of designated accountants in Canada is now the **Chartered Professional Accountants (CPAs)**. Until recently, there were three **professional designations** for accountants in Canada—Chartered Accountants (CAs), Certified General Accountants (CGAs), and Certified Management Accountants (CMAs). Those accountants who joined the CPA as a result of the merger of these organizations will retain their **legacy designation** on their business cards.

Professional Conduct   Professional accountants are governed by standards of professional conduct. Many of these standards apply whether the members are **public accountants** who perform work for other businesses or **private accountants** who are employed by a particular business. These rules concern the confidentiality of information the accountant is privy to, maintenance of the profession's reputation, the need to work with integrity and due care, competence, refusal to be associated with false or misleading information, and compliance with professional standards. Other rules are applicable only to those members in public practice and deal with things like the need for **independence** and how to advertise, seek clients, and conduct a practice. This helps the public determine its expectations of members' behaviour. However, the rules of professional conduct should be considered a minimum standard of performance; ideally, the members should continually strive to exceed them.

Audits   One type of work done by **designated accountants** is an **audit**. An audit is a financial examination. Audits are conducted by independent accountants who express an opinion on whether or not the financial statements fairly reflect the economic events that occurred during the accounting period. Companies and their auditors must behave in an ethical manner. Exhibit 1–3 illustrates the relationship among accounting and business entities that are public companies (companies that sell shares of stock to investors).

EXHIBIT 1–3 | Relationship among Accounting and Business Entities

CPA Canada Advanced Certificate in Accounting and Finance (ACAF) The ACAF certificate program prepares people for a career in accounting and finance as an alternative to pursuing a professional designation.

Ethics in Accounting and Business

We need to consider **ethics** in all areas of accounting and business. Investors, creditors, and regulatory bodies need reliable information about a company. Naturally, companies want to make themselves look as good as possible to attract investors, so there is a potential for conflict. Unfortunately for the accounting profession, accounting scandals involving both public companies and their auditors have made the headlines over the years. At the turn of this century, Enron Corporation, which was the seventh-largest company in the United States, issued misleading financial statements. Enron was forced into bankruptcy and its auditors' actions were questioned. The impact of the Enron bankruptcy was felt by many different parties, including Enron shareholders, who saw their investments become worthless; employees, who lost their jobs and their pensions; and the accounting profession, which lost some of its integrity and reputation as gatekeepers and stewards for the investing public. This situation shocked the business community and caused investors to question the reliability of financial information.

Since the financial health of a company is important to many different groups of users, these users must be confident that they can rely on the financial information they are given when they are making decisions. To increase users' confidence, the accounting profession and other interested stakeholder groups made important changes over the past decade to improve the quality of the financial information provided.

Try It! questions appear at the end of each learning-objective section, allowing you to test your mastery of the concepts in this learning objective before moving on to the next one. The solutions appear at the end of the chapter and on MyAccountingLab.

1. For each of the following users of accounting information, indicate if the user is an internal or external user.
   a. Supplier
   b. Owner
   c. Marketing manager
   d. Lender
   e. Ontario Securities Commission

Solutions appear at the end of this chapter and on MyAccountingLab

FORMS OF BUSINESS ORGANIZATIONS

A business can be organized as a

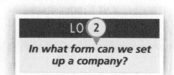

LO **2**

In what form can we set up a company?

- Proprietorship
- Partnership
- Corporation

Exhibit 1–4 summarizes some of the differences between the three forms of business organization.

Proprietorship

A **proprietorship** has a single owner, called the proprietor, who often manages the business. Proprietorships tend to be small retail stores, restaurants, and service businesses, but they can also be very large. From an accounting viewpoint, each proprietorship is distinct from its owner. Thus, the accounting records of

EXHIBIT 1–4 | Comparison of the Forms of Business Organization

	Proprietorship	Partnership	Corporation
Owner(s)	Proprietor—one owner	Partners—two or more owners	Shareholder(s)—one or many owners
Life of organization	Limited by owner's choice or death	Limited by owners' choices or death of one of the partners	Indefinite
Personal liability of owner(s) for business debts	Owner is personally liable	Partners are personally liable*	Shareholders are not personally liable
Legal status	The owner and the business are not legally separate	The partnership is the partners; they are not legally separate	The corporation is separate from the shareholders (owners).
Taxation	The owner pays tax on the proprietorship's earnings; income is added onto the owner's personal tax return	The owners each pay tax on their share of the partnership's earnings; income is added onto each partner's personal tax return	Separate taxable entity; the corporation pays tax on its earnings

*Unless it is a limited-liability partnership (LLP)

the proprietorship do not include the proprietor's personal accounting records. However, from a legal perspective, the business *is* the proprietor, so if the business cannot pay its debts, lenders can take the proprietor's personal assets (cash and belongings) to pay the proprietorship's debt.

Partnership

A **partnership** joins two or more individuals together as co-owners. Each owner is a partner. Many retail stores and professional organizations of physicians, lawyers, and accountants are partnerships. Accounting treats the partnership as a separate organization distinct from the personal affairs of each partner. From a legal perspective, though, a partnership *is* the partners in a manner similar to a proprietorship. If the partnership cannot pay its debts, lenders can take each partner's personal assets to pay the partnership's debts.

Limited-Liability Partnership (LLP) A **limited-liability partnership (LLP)** is a partnership in which one partner cannot create a large liability for the other partners. Each partner is liable only for his or her own actions and those actions under his or her control.

Corporation

A **corporation** is a business owned by **shareholders**. These are the people or other corporations who own shares of ownership in the business. Although proprietorships and partnerships are more numerous, corporations engage in more business and are generally larger in terms of total assets, income, and number of employees. In Canada, corporations generally have *Ltd.* or *Limited, Inc.* or *Incorporated*, or *Corp.* or *Corporation* in their legal name to indicate that they are incorporated. Corporations need not be large; a business with only one owner and only a few assets could be organized as a corporation.

From a legal perspective, a corporation is formed when the federal or provincial government approves its articles of incorporation. Unlike a proprietorship or a partnership, once a corporation is formed it is a legal entity separate and distinct from its owners. The corporation operates as an "artificial person" that exists apart from its owners and that conducts business in its own name. The corporation has many of the rights that a person has. For example, a corporation may buy, own, and sell property; the corporation may enter into contracts and sue and be sued.

Corporations differ significantly from proprietorships and partnerships in another way. If a proprietorship or partnership cannot pay its debts, lenders can take the owners' personal assets to satisfy the business's obligations. But if a corporation goes bankrupt, lenders cannot take the personal assets of the shareholders. This **limited personal liability** of shareholders for corporate debts explains why corporations are so popular compared to proprietorships and partnerships, which have **unlimited personal liability**.

Corporations divide ownership into individual shares. Companies such as WestJet Airlines Ltd. and Canadian Tire Corporation, Limited, have issued millions of shares of stock and have tens of thousands of shareholders. An investor with no personal relationship either to the corporation or to any other shareholder can become an owner by buying 30, 100, 5,000, or any number of shares of its stock. For most corporations, the investor may sell the shares at any time. It is usually harder to sell one's investment in a proprietorship or a partnership than to sell one's investment in a corporation.

Accounting for corporations includes some unique complexities. For this reason, we initially focus on proprietorships. We cover partnerships in Chapter 12 and begin our discussion of corporations in Chapter 13.

> Try It!

2. For each of the following scenarios, indicate the applicable form of business in the space provided.

	Proprietorship	Partnership	Corporation
a. The business is not making enough money to pay its bills. The owners do not have to make up the difference with their personal funds.			
b. Anna and Sui have owned their business together for 5 years. Anna dies. The business must be closed if they chose this form of business.			
c. An unincorporated business with five owners is a …			
d. The profits of Chi's business must be reported on her tax return.			
e. There is a lawsuit against a business and there is not enough money to pay the claim. The owners only lose the amount they have invested into the business.			

Solutions appear at the end of this chapter and on MyAccountingLab

ACCOUNTING CONCEPTS

Earlier in this chapter, we discussed the importance of financial information to various user groups. Users must be confident that they can rely on the financial information they are given when they are making decisions. To increase users' confidence, accounting practices need to follow certain guidelines that govern how accountants measure, process, and communicate financial information. They are known as **generally accepted accounting principles,** or **GAAP**.

Individual countries determine their own GAAP. In the past, the standards used around the world were very different. Over time, as more businesses operated in multiple countries, the preparation of different statements for each country became

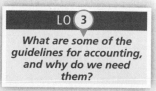

LO 3

What are some of the guidelines for accounting, and why do we need them?

costly and inefficient. For example, a Canadian company that sold its shares on a stock exchange in Germany actually had to prepare one set of financial statements under Canadian GAAP and another under German GAAP or, at least, provide a reconciliation from one to the other. A group of accountants from different countries worked together to develop accounting standards that could be applied anywhere in the world. This group formed the **International Accounting Standards Board (IASB)** and developed **International Financial Reporting Standards**, or **IFRS**. These standards are now recognized, permitted, or under adoption in over 138 countries.

Canadian guidelines are developed by the Accounting Standards Board and published in the *CPA Canada Handbook – Accounting*. There are several parts to this *Handbook* for different types of business entities. Part I covers IFRS for companies that qualify as publicly accountable enterprises. **Publicly accountable enterprises**, generally speaking, are companies that are publicly traded or for which a strong public interest exists. In Canada, they are small in number but contribute heavily to our economy. Canadian Tire Corporation, Limited and Tim Hortons Inc. are examples of these sorts of businesses.

Most Canadian businesses are small to medium in size and are privately owned. The most significant users of their financial information are their creditors (likely their bank) and the government (for computing income taxes and sales taxes). Consequently, a second set of accounting standards, **Accounting Standards for Private Enterprises**, or **ASPE**, was developed for these types of businesses and forms Part II of the *Handbook*. The primary reason for this second standard is related to users' access to a company's financial information. For smaller, **private enterprises**, whether they are proprietorships, partnerships, or corporations, the various user groups that interact with the company typically have better access to the owners and managers of the company. Therefore, the users do not need as much information from the financial statements. If a banker has a question about a private company's purchases of equipment, the banker can ask the owner directly. However, many of the user groups who need financial information about larger, publicly traded companies do not have the same access to the managers and, therefore, need more information, which is included in the IFRS-based financial statements. Because of the large number of businesses in Canada that follow ASPE, and because most later accounting courses focus on IFRS, this textbook will focus on ASPE, with IFRS material appearing as the final learning objective when appropriate.

Both IFRS and ASPE are "principles-based." This means that standards cannot possibly be developed for every accounting transaction a company will encounter, so the accountant must use professional judgment in some circumstances. Professional judgment is an acquired skill—you need a good knowledge of accounting standards and many years of experience in order to exercise sound professional judgment. However, it is important to note that the starting point in acquiring professional judgment is a solid understanding of the concepts of accounting.

Framework for Financial Reporting

Fundamental accounting concepts form the basis of how accounting should be done and reported to users. We will refer to the concepts shown in Exhibit 1–5 throughout the text as they are the reason we do things the way we do. For your convenience, the full exhibit is repeated on the inside back cover of the book. We will discuss the shaded topics in Exhibit 1–5 in later chapters.

As the pyramid shape indicates, the endpoint is the *objective of financial reporting*: to provide *useful* information to investors, creditors, and other users in making investment decisions or assessing the success of a company by looking at the financial statements.

The *qualitative characteristics of accounting information* of relevance, reliability, comparability, and understandability explain what makes information useful to the various users of financial reports. Assume that you have decided that you would like to invest some of your savings in the shares of a company. How would you decide on a company to invest in? Your starting point would likely be the financial statements. You expect that the financial statements include information that is:

- **Relevant:** It provides important information upon which you can base your investment decision.

EXHIBIT 1–5 | A Hierarchy of Financial Statement Concepts

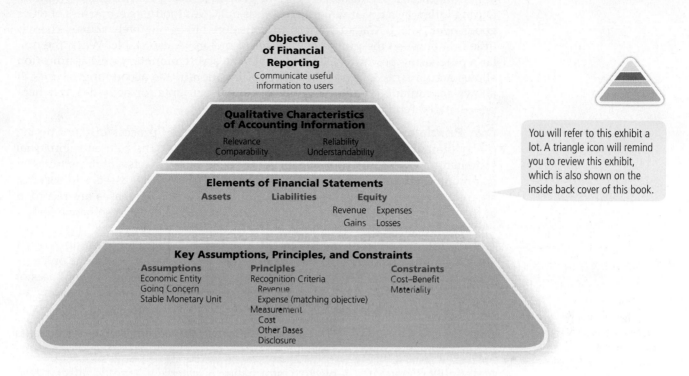

You will refer to this exhibit a lot. A triangle icon will remind you to review this exhibit, which is also shown on the inside back cover of this book.

- **Reliable:** The information reported accurately reflects the business events that affect the company.
- **Comparable:** You should be able to compare the information against the business's own financial results in previous years or against the results of another company in the same industry.
- **Understandable:** Clear and concise so that information is not misunderstood.

Certainly there is other information that you may want to study before you make your decision, but the financial statements are a good starting point.

Elements of financial statements are the accounts that are explained in the next learning objective in this chapter.

The bottom level forms the foundation of understanding financial information, through *assumptions, recognition and measurement criteria*, and *constraints*, some of which are discussed below.

Elements

Foundation: Assumptions, Principles, Constraints

Economic Entity Assumption   In accounting, an *entity* is an organization or a section of an organization that stands apart from other organizations and individuals as a separate economic unit. This is known as the **economic entity assumption**. Each entity keeps separate accounting records. This means you keep your business's accounting separate from your personal accounting so that you can evaluate the success of your business. It also means companies keep each department's accounting separate from all the other departments to assess and evaluate the performance of each department.

Going Concern Assumption   When accountants record financial information, they assume that the entity is going to be in business for the foreseeable future. Under the **going concern assumption**, accountants *assume* that the business will remain in operation long enough to use its resources rather than being forced to accept whatever price it can get because it is going out of business.

Stable Monetary Unit Assumption   In Canada, accountants record transactions in dollars because the dollar is the measure we use when we make purchases and sales. However, unlike other measures like a kilometre or a tonne, the value of a dollar can change over time. A rise in the general level of prices is called **inflation**. During inflation, a dollar will purchase less milk, less toothpaste, and less of other goods over time. In Canada, prices are considered to be relatively stable—there is little inflation—so the purchasing power of money is also stable. When the dollar's purchasing power is relatively stable, the **stable monetary unit assumption** allows accountants to ignore the effect of inflation in the accounting records. It allows accountants to add and subtract dollar amounts for activities that happened at different times.

Cost Principle of Measurement   **Measurement** is the process of determining the amount at which an item is recognized in the financial statements. Financial statements are prepared primarily using the historical-cost basis of measurement, commonly called the *cost principle,* which states that acquired assets and services should be recorded at their actual cost (historical cost). Purchases are recorded at the price actually paid and not at the "expected" cost or what someone feels it might be worth.

The **cost principle of measurement** also holds that the accounting records should continue reporting the historical cost of an asset for as long as the business holds the asset. Why? Because historical cost is a *reliable* measure. Other bases of measurement can be used but only in limited circumstances. In later chapters we will look at them when they are appropriate.

Cost–Benefit Constraint   The **cost–benefit constraint** stipulates that the benefits of the information produced should exceed the costs of producing the information.

Materiality Constraint   A piece of information is *material* if it would affect a decision maker's decision. **Materiality** is not defined in the standards but is a matter of the information preparer's judgment. For example, information about hardware inventory is important to users of RONA Inc.'s financial statements, since a large change in inventory could change a decision about investing in RONA or selling products to RONA. Thus, such information would be provided to decision makers. However, information about the office supplies at RONA would not likely change an investment decision, so details about office supplies are not provided.

These references to **MyAccountingLab** are reminders that you can review these topics using the videos and animations on MyAccountingLab.

MyAccountingLab

Video: Accounting Principles and Concepts

> Try It!

3. Suppose you are considering the purchase of a building. The seller is asking $200,000 for a building that cost her $100,000. An appraisal shows the building has a value of $180,000. You first offer $160,000. The seller counteroffers with $190,000. Finally, you and the seller agree on a price of $185,000. What dollar amount for this building is reported on your financial statements? Which accounting assumption or principle guides your answer?
4. Suppose you own a company that delivers newspapers. The company owns two trucks that are used for delivering the papers. You have decided that you need a new car for mainly personal purposes but you want the company to buy it for you. Is this appropriate? Name the assumption or principle that must be considered.

Solutions appear at the end of this chapter and on MyAccountingLab

THE ACCOUNTING EQUATION

LO 4

How do business activities affect the accounting records of a company?

Financial statements tell us how a business is performing. They are the final product of the accounting process. But how do we arrive at the items and amounts that make up the financial statements? The most basic tool is the **accounting equation**. It measures the resources of a business and the claims to those resources.

The accounting equation in Exhibit 1–6 shows how assets, liabilities, and owner's equity are related. Assets appear on the left side of the equation. The legal and economic claims against the assets—the liabilities and owner's equity—appear on the right side of the equation. As the exhibit shows, *the two sides must be equal.*

MyAccountingLab

Videos:
• The Accounting Equation
• Accounting Equation: Impact on Owner's Equity

EXHIBIT 1–6 | The Accounting Equation

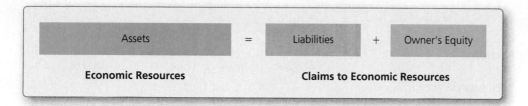

The basic summary device of accounting is the **account**, which is the detailed record of the changes that have occurred in a particular asset, liability, or item of owner's equity during a period of time and the total at any point in time. Business activities cause the changes.

REAL WORLD EXAMPLE

Account names are not the same for all companies. Once an account name is used, then the same name is used all the time for that company.

Assets

Assets are economic resources controlled by an entity that are expected to benefit the business in the future. Most firms use the asset accounts similar to the ones shown in Exhibit 1–7.

EXHIBIT 1–7 | Asset Accounts

Account Name	Explanation
Cash	A business's money. Includes bank balances, bills, coins, and cheques.
Accounts Receivable	A business may sell its goods or services in exchange for an oral or implied promise of future cash receipts. Such sales are made on credit—*on account*—to customers who buy a business's products or services and recorded in the **Accounts Receivable** account.
Notes Receivable	A business may sell its goods or services in exchange for a **promissory note**, which is a written pledge that the customer will pay the business a fixed amount of money by a certain date. A **note receivable** offers more **security** for collection than an account receivable does, and it can require the customer to pay interest on the amount the customer owes.
Prepaid Expenses	A business often pays certain expenses in advance. A **prepaid expense** is an asset because it provides future benefits to the business. The business avoids having to pay cash in the future for the specified expense. Examples include: Prepaid Rent, Prepaid Insurance, and Office Supplies.
Land	The cost of land a business owns and uses in its operations. Land held for sale is accounted for separately—in an investment account.
Building	The cost of a business's buildings—office, warehouse, garage, or store. These are the buildings used in the operation of the business.
Equipment, Furniture, and Fixtures	A business has a separate asset account for each type of equipment—Computer Equipment, Office Equipment, and Store Equipment, for example.

Liabilities

Liabilities are debts that are payable to creditors. For example, a creditor who has lent money to a business has a claim—a legal right—to a part of the assets until the business pays the debt. Many liabilities have the word *payable* in their title. A business generally has fewer liability accounts than asset accounts because a business's liabilities can be summarized under relatively few categories. Some are shown in Exhibit 1–8 while others will be added in later chapters. A more comprehensive list of typical account names for **service proprietorships** is given in Appendix B at the end of this book.

EXHIBIT 1–8 | Liability Accounts

Account Name	Explanation
Accounts Payable	The oral or implied promise to pay off debts arising from credit purchases. Such purchases are said to be made *on account*. **Accounts payable** are usually amounts owed to a business's suppliers for goods or services purchased.
Note Payable	A **note payable** account represents an amount that the business must pay because it signed a promissory note to borrow money. Interest must be paid in addition to the amount borrowed.

Owner's Equity

The equity accounts, as shown in Exhibit 1–9, show the owner's claims to the business assets. Keep this perspective in mind when working through transactions. Always remember to record information from the company's perspective.

EXHIBIT 1–9 | Equity Accounts

Account Name	Explanation
Capital	Owner's claims to the business assets are called **owner's equity** or **capital**. In this book, the account to represent this equity is written as Lisa Hunter, Capital or L. Hunter, Capital, although Hunter, Capital is also considered correct.
Withdrawals	Distributions of cash or other assets to the owner. Withdrawals *decrease equity*. The amounts taken out of the business appear in a separate account entitled Lisa Hunter, Withdrawals. **Owner withdrawals** do not represent a business expense because the cash is used for the owner's personal affairs unrelated to the business.
Revenues	The purpose of business is to *increase owner's equity* through **revenues**, which are amounts earned by delivering goods or services to customers. Typical accounts include Service Revenue, Sales Revenue (see Chapter 5 on the sale of goods), Interest Revenue (if a business lends money), and Rent Revenue.
Expenses	**Expenses** result in a *decrease in owner's equity*. They occur when a business uses or consumes assets or increases liabilities in the course of delivering goods and services to customers. Expenses are often thought of as the "costs of doing business." Examples include Salaries Expense, Office Supplies Expense, Rent Expense, Advertising Expense, and Utilities Expense.

Partnerships and corporations have similar accounts: The owner's equity is called **partners' equity** in a partnership and **shareholders' equity** in a corporation.

Profits paid to owners in a corporation are called **dividends**. We use these accounts in Volume 2 of the textbook.

	Sole Proprietorship	Partnership	Corporation
Equity account	Owner's Equity	Partners' Equity	Shareholders' Equity
Resources removed from the business by the owner	Withdrawals, or Drawings	Withdrawals, or Drawings	Dividends

The accounting equation you first saw in Exhibit 1–6 can be expanded to show details of the Owner's Equity accounts. We will learn shortly that the calculation of revenues less expenses tells us whether the business earns a net income or has incurred a net loss. This means we can further expand the accounting equation as shown in Exhibit 1–10.

EXHIBIT 1–10 | Expanded Accounting Equation

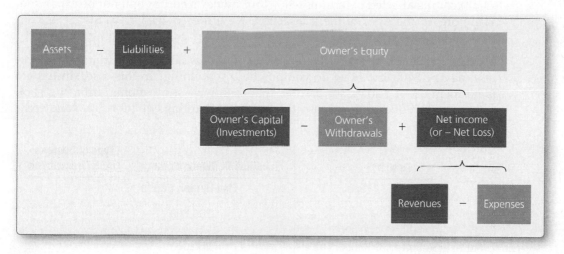

Accounting for Business Transactions

Accounting is based on transactions, not opinions or desires. A **transaction** is any event that affects the financial position of the business entity *and* can be measured reliably. Many events may affect a company, including elections and economic booms, but accountants do not record the effects of these events because they cannot be measured reliably. An accountant records as transactions only events with dollar amounts that can be measured reliably, such as purchases and sales of merchandise inventory, payment of rent, and collection of cash from customers. In Exhibit 1–1 on page 4, transactions are the middle step in the flow of information in an accounting system.

To illustrate accounting for business transactions, let's go back to our opening story and look at the transactions for Lisa Hunter's company, Hunter Environmental Consulting (HEC), in the first month of her business. We will consider 10 events and analyze each in terms of its effect on the accounting equation of HEC.

Transaction 1: Starting the Business Hunter invests $250,000 of her money to start the business. Specifically, she deposits $250,000 in a bank account set up for Hunter Environmental Consulting.

We do not use an account called Bank. Why not? It is just how we do it in this book. Could a real business call this account Bank? Yes! But throughout this book, we always use an account called Cash.

KEY POINTS

A transaction is an event that must always satisfy these two conditions:

1. It affects the financial position of a business entity.
2. It can be measured reliably.

Key Points highlight important details from the text and are good tools for reviewing concepts.

The effect of this transaction on the accounting equation of the HEC business entity is as follows:

	Assets	=	Liabilities	+	Owner's Equity	Type of Owner's Equity Transaction
	Cash				Lisa Hunter, Capital	
(1) +250,000					+250,000	*Owner investment*

For every transaction, the amount on the left side of the equation must equal the amount on the right side. The first transaction increases both the assets (in this case, Cash) and the owner's equity of the business (Lisa Hunter, Capital). When we update the owner's equity, what we are saying is that the business has increased what it owes to its owner. The transaction involves no liabilities of the business because it creates no obligation for HEC to pay an outside party. The assets and liabilities elements of the accounting equation will be expanded to show the specific accounts affected by a transaction, but owner's equity will not be expanded. Therefore, to the right of the transaction, we write "owner investment" to keep track of the reason for the effect on owner's equity.

Transaction 2: Purchase of Land HEC purchases land for a future office location, paying $100,000. How do you purchase something? In this case, since there is no mention of a loan, we assume that cash was used (money from the bank account). The effect of this transaction on the accounting equation is as follows:

LEARNING TIPS

Note that the sums of balances (which we shorten to Bal.) on both sides of the equation are equal. This equality must always exist.

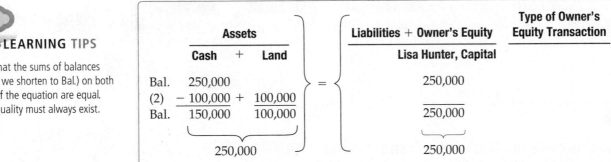

	Assets			=	Liabilities + Owner's Equity	Type of Owner's Equity Transaction
	Cash	+	Land		Lisa Hunter, Capital	
Bal.	250,000				250,000	
(2)	− 100,000	+	100,000			
Bal.	150,000		100,000		250,000	
		250,000			250,000	

The cash purchase of the land increases one asset, Land, and decreases another asset, Cash, by the same amount. After the transaction is completed, HEC has cash of $150,000, land of $100,000, no liabilities, and owner's equity of $250,000.

Transaction 3: Purchase of Office Supplies HEC buys stationery and other office supplies, agreeing to pay $7,000 within 30 days. This transaction increases both the assets and the liabilities of the company, as follows:

LEARNING TIPS

Office Supplies that are held for future use are an asset. When they are used, they become an expense. Because there is a gap in time between buying $7,000 worth of supplies and using them, we record each event separately.

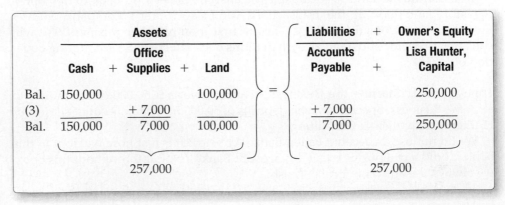

	Assets					=	Liabilities	+	Owner's Equity
			Office				Accounts		Lisa Hunter,
	Cash	+	Supplies	+	Land		Payable	+	Capital
Bal.	150,000				100,000				250,000
(3)			+ 7,000				+ 7,000		
Bal.	150,000		7,000		100,000		7,000		250,000
			257,000					257,000	

The asset increased is Office Supplies, and the liability increased is called Accounts Payable. *A payable is always a liability.* Because HEC is obligated to pay $7,000 in the future but signs no formal promissory note, we record the liability as an account payable. (If a promissory note had been signed, we would have recorded the liability as a note payable.)

Transaction 4: Earning of Service Revenue HEC earns service revenue by providing environmental consulting services for clients. Assume the business earns $30,000 and collects this amount in cash. The effect on the accounting equation is an increase in the asset Cash and an increase in Lisa Hunter, Capital, as follows:

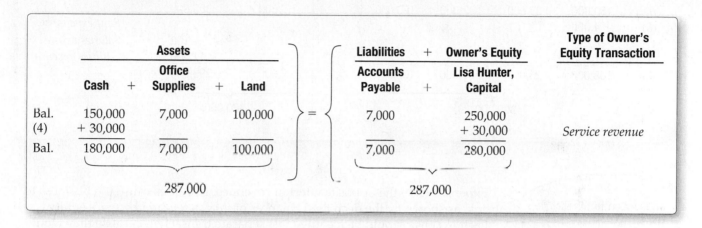

	Assets				=	Liabilities	+	Owner's Equity	Type of Owner's Equity Transaction
	Cash	+	Office Supplies	+ Land		Accounts Payable	+	Lisa Hunter, Capital	
Bal.	150,000		7,000	100,000		7,000		250,000	
(4)	+ 30,000							+ 30,000	Service revenue
Bal.	180,000		7,000	100,000		7,000		280,000	
	287,000						287,000		

A revenue transaction causes the business to grow, as shown by the increase in total assets and owner's equity. A company like RONA or Canadian Tire that sells goods to customers is a **merchandising business**. Its revenue is called **sales revenue**. In contrast, HEC performs services for clients, so HEC's revenue is called **service revenue**.

Transaction 5: Earning of Service Revenue on Account HEC performs consulting services for clients who do not pay immediately. In return for the services, HEC issues an invoice and the clients will pay the $25,000 amount within one month. This amount owed to HEC is an asset to HEC, an account receivable, because the business expects to collect the cash in the future. In accounting, we say that HEC performed this service *on account* and earned the revenue. Performing the service, not collecting the cash, earns the revenue. HEC records an increase in the asset Accounts Receivable and an increase in Service Revenue, which increases Lisa Hunter, Capital, as follows:

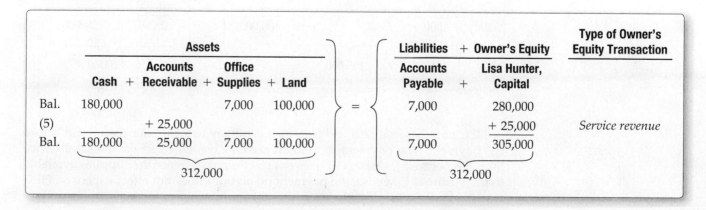

	Assets					=	Liabilities	+	Owner's Equity	Type of Owner's Equity Transaction
	Cash	+	Accounts Receivable	+ Office Supplies	+ Land		Accounts Payable	+	Lisa Hunter, Capital	
Bal.	180,000			7,000	100,000		7,000		280,000	
(5)			+ 25,000						+ 25,000	Service revenue
Bal.	180,000		25,000	7,000	100,000		7,000		305,000	
	312,000							312,000		

Transaction 6: Payment of Expenses During the month, HEC pays $12,000 in cash expenses: office rent, $4,000 (HEC purchased land to build an office in the future [Transaction 2], but the company is renting fully furnished office space in

the meantime); employee salaries, \$6,500 (for a full-time assistant and a junior consultant); and total utilities, \$1,500. The effects on the accounting equation are as follows:

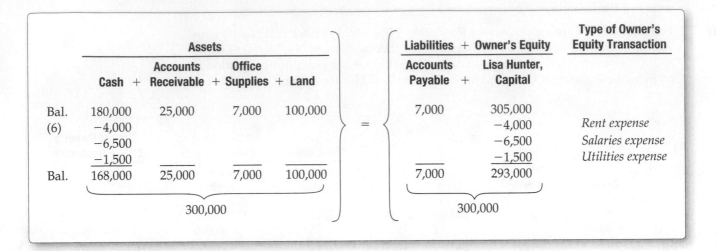

	Assets					Liabilities + Owner's Equity		Type of Owner's Equity Transaction
	Cash +	Accounts Receivable +	Office Supplies +	Land		Accounts Payable +	Lisa Hunter, Capital	
Bal.	180,000	25,000	7,000	100,000		7,000	305,000	
(6)	−4,000				=		−4,000	*Rent expense*
	−6,500						−6,500	*Salaries expense*
	−1,500						−1,500	*Utilities expense*
Bal.	168,000	25,000	7,000	100,000		7,000	293,000	
		300,000					300,000	

Expenses have the opposite effect of revenues. Expenses cause the business to shrink, as shown by the decreased balances of total assets and owner's equity.

Each expense should be recorded in a separate transaction because they would likely be three separate payments (cheques or online payments) to different people or companies. Here, for simplicity, the expenses are listed together.

> Pay attention to the specific words and phrases used. Remember, accounting is the language of business and as such has very specific wording. "Paid" means they "paid using Cash." A "payment on account" means that a prior bill (account) is what got paid.

Transaction 7: Payment on Account HEC pays \$5,000 to the store from which it purchased \$7,000 worth of office supplies in Transaction 3. In accounting, we say that the business pays \$5,000 *on account*. The effect on the accounting equation is a decrease in the asset Cash and a decrease in the liability Accounts Payable as follows:

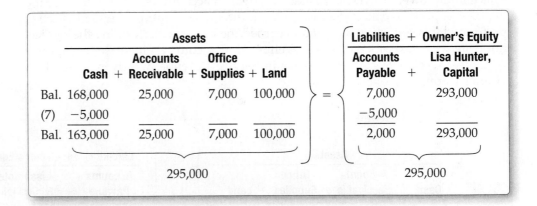

	Assets					Liabilities + Owner's Equity	
	Cash +	Accounts Receivable +	Office Supplies +	Land		Accounts Payable +	Lisa Hunter, Capital
Bal.	168,000	25,000	7,000	100,000		7,000	293,000
(7)	−5,000				=	−5,000	
Bal.	163,000	25,000	7,000	100,000		2,000	293,000
		295,000					295,000

HEC now has less cash and it owes less money to a supplier than it did before the payment. The payment of cash on account has no effect on the asset Office Supplies because the payment does not increase or decrease the supplies available to the business. Likewise, the payment on account does not affect expenses. HEC was paying off a liability (the account), not an expense.

Transaction 8: Personal Transaction Lisa Hunter remodels her home at a cost of \$30,000, paying cash from personal funds. This event is *not* a transaction of HEC. It has no effect on HEC's business affairs and, therefore, is not recorded by the business. It is a transaction of the Hunter *personal* entity, not the HEC business entity. We are focusing solely on the *business* entity, and this event does not affect it. This transaction illustrates the *economic entity assumption*.

Transaction 9: Collection on Account In Transaction 5, HEC performed consulting services for clients on account. We set up our accounting records in Transaction 5 to show that HEC will receive payment "later." Well, now is the time we are receiving that payment. The business collects $15,000 from the client. We say that it collects the cash *on account*. It will record an increase in the asset Cash and a decrease in the asset Accounts Receivable. Should it also record an increase in service revenue? No, because HEC already recorded the revenue when it performed the service in Transaction 5. The effect on the accounting equation is as follows:

LEARNING TIPS

When recording a transaction, always look at what is happening "at the moment" and update only what accounts are affected at that time.

	Assets					Liabilities + Owner's Equity	
	Cash +	Accounts Receivable +	Office Supplies +	Land		Accounts Payable +	Lisa Hunter, Capital
Bal.	163,000	25,000	7,000	100,000	=	2,000	293,000
(9)	+15,000	−15,000					
Bal.	178,000	10,000	7,000	100,000		2,000	293,000
		295,000					295,000

Total assets are unchanged from the preceding transaction's total. Why? Because HEC merely exchanged one asset for another.

Transaction 10: Withdrawing of Cash Lisa withdraws $6,000 cash for her personal use. The difference between this transaction and Transaction 8 is that this money comes from the business's bank account, so this event *does* impact the business and must be recorded in the business's records. The effect on the accounting equation is as follows:

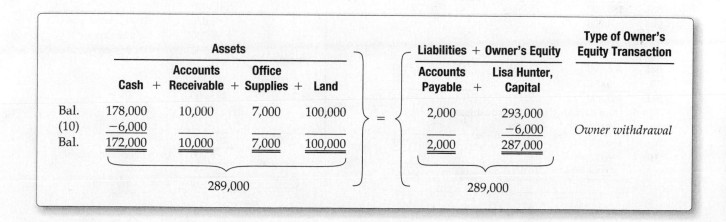

	Assets					Liabilities + Owner's Equity		Type of Owner's Equity Transaction
	Cash +	Accounts Receivable +	Office Supplies +	Land		Accounts Payable +	Lisa Hunter, Capital	
Bal.	178,000	10,000	7,000	100,000	=	2,000	293,000	
(10)	−6,000						−6,000	*Owner withdrawal*
Bal.	172,000	10,000	7,000	100,000		2,000	287,000	
		289,000					289,000	

Hunter's withdrawal of $6,000 decreases the asset Cash and also the owner's equity of the business.

Owner withdrawals do not represent a business expense because the cash is used for the owner's personal affairs unrelated to the business.

The double underlines below each column indicate a final total after the last transaction.

Exhibit 1–11 summarizes the 10 preceding transactions. As you study the exhibit, note that every transaction maintains the equality of the accounting equation:

$$\text{Assets} = \text{Liabilities} + \text{Owner's Equity}$$

EXHIBIT 1–11 | Analysis of Transactions of Hunter Environmental Consulting

PANEL A: DETAILS OF TRANSACTIONS

(1) The business recorded the $250,000 cash investment made by Lisa Hunter.
(2) Paid $100,000 cash for land.
(3) Bought $7,000 of office supplies on account.
(4) Received $30,000 cash from clients for service revenue earned.
(5) Performed services for clients on account, $25,000.
(6) Paid cash expenses: rent, $4,000; employee salaries, $6,500; utilities, $1,500.
(7) Paid $5,000 on the account payable created in Transaction 3.
(8) Remodelled Hunter's personal residence. This is not a transaction of the business.
(9) Collected $15,000 on the account receivable created in Transaction 5.
(10) The business paid $6,000 cash to Hunter as a withdrawal.

PANEL B: ANALYSIS OF TRANSACTIONS

| | | | | | | | | | | Type of Owner's |
| | Assets | | | | | | Liabilities + Owner's Equity | | | Equity Transaction |
	Cash	+ Accounts Receivable	+ Office Supplies	+ Land			Accounts Payable	+ Lisa Hunter, Capital		
(1)	+250,000							+250,000		*Owner investment*
Bal.	250,000							250,000		
(2)	−100,000			+100,000						
Bal.	150,000			100,000				250,000		
(3)			+7,000				+7,000			
Bal.	150,000		7,000	100,000			7,000	250,000		
(4)	+30,000							+30,000		*Service revenue*
Bal.	180,000		7,000	100,000			7,000	280,000		
(5)		+25,000						+25,000		*Service revenue*
Bal.	180,000	25,000	7,000	100,000	=		7,000	305,000		
(6)	−4,000							−4,000		*Rent expense*
	−6,500							−6,500		*Salaries expense*
	−1,500							−1,500		*Utilities expense*
Bal.	168,000	25,000	7,000	100,000			7,000	293,000		
(7)	−5,000						−5,000			
Bal.	163,000	25,000	7,000	100,000			2,000	293,000		
(8)	Not a transaction of the business									
(9)	+15,000	−15,000								
Bal.	178,000	10,000	7,000	100,000			2,000	293,000		
(10)	−6,000							−6,000		*Owner withdrawal*
Bal.	172,000	10,000	7,000	100,000			2,000	287,000		

289,000   289,000

> Try It!

5. a. If the assets of a business are $75,000 and the liabilities total $65,000, how much is the owner's equity?

  b. If the owner's equity in a business is $50,000 and the liabilities are $20,000, how much are the assets?

6. Indicate whether each account listed below is a(n) asset (A), liability (L), owner's equity (OE), revenue (R), or expense (E) account.

Accounts Receivable	_____	Salaries Expense	_____
Computer Equipment	_____	Consulting Service Revenue	_____
S. Scott, Capital	_____	Cash	_____
Rent Expense	_____	Notes Payable	_____
Supplies	_____	Supplies Expense	_____
S. Scott, Withdrawals	_____	Accounts Payable	_____

7. Using the information provided, analyze the effects of Lawlor Lawn Service's transactions on the accounting equation.

May 1	Received $1,700 and gave capital to Eric Lawlor.
May 3	Purchased a mower on account, $1,440.
May 5	Performed lawn services for client on account, $200.
May 17	Paid $60 cash for gas used in mower.
May 28	Eric Lawlor withdrew cash of $300.

Create a chart using the following format to record your answers:

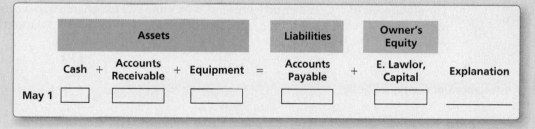

Solutions appear at the end of this chapter and on MyAccountingLab

THE FINANCIAL STATEMENTS

LO 5
What financial statements are prepared by a company, and how do we create them?

Once the analysis of the transactions is complete, how does a business present the results of the transactions? We now look at the *financial statements*, which are the formal reports of an entity's financial information.

In order to create these reports, we use the totals from Exhibit 1–11.

Income Statement

Is the business making any money?

The **income statement**, as shown in Exhibit 1–12, presents a summary of the *revenues* and *expenses* of an entity for a period of time, such as a month or a year. Businesspeople run their businesses with the objective of having more revenues than expenses. An excess of total revenues over total expenses is called **net income**, **net earnings**, or **net profit**. If total expenses exceed total revenues, the result is called a **net loss**.

The income statement, also called the **statement of earnings** or **statement of operations**, is often described as a video of the entity's operations—a moving financial picture of business operations during the period.

MyAccountingLab

Video: Introduction to Financial Statements

EXHIBIT 1–12 | Income Statement

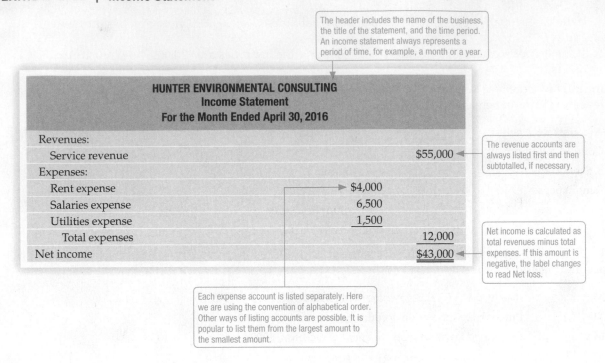

EXHIBIT 1–13 | Statement of Owner's Equity

Statement of Owner's Equity

The **statement of owner's equity** presents a summary of the changes that occurred in the entity's *owner's equity* during a specific period of time, such as a month or a year. Exhibit 1–13 illustrates how to lay it out and calculate the total.

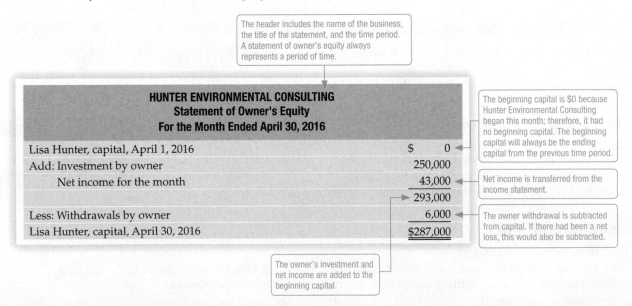

Balance Sheet

The **balance sheet** (or **statement of financial position**) lists all of the assets, liabilities, and owner's equity of an entity as of a specific date, usually the end of a month or a year. The balance sheet is like a snapshot of the entity because it captures values at a moment in time. For HEC, this means the end of the business day on April 30. Exhibit 1–14 shows how this document is typically laid out.

EXHIBIT 1–14 | Balance Sheet

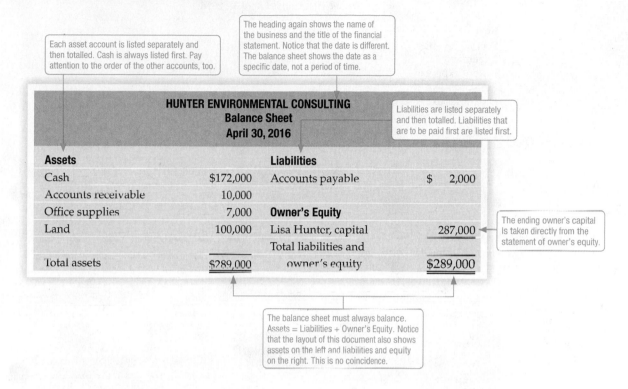

Each asset account is listed separately and then totalled. Cash is always listed first. Pay attention to the order of the other accounts, too.

The heading again shows the name of the business and the title of the financial statement. Notice that the date is different. The balance sheet shows the date as a specific date, not a period of time.

Liabilities are listed separately and then totalled. Liabilities that are to be paid first are listed first.

The ending owner's capital is taken directly from the statement of owner's equity.

HUNTER ENVIRONMENTAL CONSULTING
Balance Sheet
April 30, 2016

Assets		Liabilities	
Cash	$172,000	Accounts payable	$ 2,000
Accounts receivable	10,000		
Office supplies	7,000	**Owner's Equity**	
Land	100,000	Lisa Hunter, capital	287,000
		Total liabilities and	
Total assets	$289,000	owner's equity	$289,000

The balance sheet must always balance. Assets = Liabilities + Owner's Equity. Notice that the layout of this document also shows assets on the left and liabilities and equity on the right. This is no coincidence.

Cash Flow Statement

The **cash flow statement** reports the cash coming in and the cash going out during a period. The cash flow statement shows the net increase or decrease in cash during the period and the cash balance at the end of the period. We devote all of Chapter 17 to the cash flow statement, so here we will only look at it briefly.

If you review the bottom of Exhibit 1–15 found on page 24, you will see that as with other statements there is a three-line heading that indicates the name of the business, the type of financial statement, and the date. A cash flow statement covers a period of time. It explains the change in the balance of the cash account during this period and answers the questions, Where did the money come from and where did it go?

The statement reports cash flows from three types of business activities (*operating, investing*, and *financing* activities) during the month. Each category of cash flow activities includes both cash receipts, which are positive amounts, and cash payments, which are negative amounts (denoted by parentheses). Each category results in a net cash inflow or a net cash outflow for the period.

Relationships among the Financial Statements

Exhibit 1–15 on page 24 illustrates how all four financial statements are connected.

1 The income statement needs to be prepared first. The net income (or net loss) is required in the statement of owner's equity.

2 The balance in the capital account is needed for the balance sheet.

3 The balance in the cash account must be the same on both the balance sheet and the cash flow statement.

MyAccountingLab

Video: Relationships among the Financial Statements
Video: Real World Accounting

EXHIBIT 1–15 | Financial Statements of Hunter Environmental Consulting

HUNTER ENVIRONMENTAL CONSULTING
Income Statement
For the Month Ended April 30, 2016

Revenue:		
Service revenue		$55,000
Expenses:		
Rent expense	$4,000	
Salaries expense	6,500	
Utilities expense	1,500	
Total expenses		12,000
Net income		$43,000

HUNTER ENVIRONMENTAL CONSULTING
Statement of Owner's Equity
For the Month Ended April 30, 2016

Lisa Hunter, capital, April 1, 2016	$ 0
Add: Investment by owner	250,000
Net income for the month	43,000
	293,000
Less: Withdrawals by owner	6,000
Lisa Hunter, capital, April 30, 2016	$287,000

HUNTER ENVIRONMENTAL CONSULTING
Balance Sheet
April 30, 2016

Assets		Liabilities	
Cash	$172,000	Accounts payable	$ 2,000
Accounts receivable	10,000		
Office supplies	7,000	**Owner's Equity**	
Land	100,000	Lisa Hunter, capital	287,000
		Total liabilities and	
Total assets	$289,000	owner's equity	$289,000

HUNTER ENVIRONMENTAL CONSULTING
Cash Flow Statement*
For the Month Ended April 30, 2016

Cash flows from operating activities		
Cash collections from customers**		$ 45,000
Cash payments to suppliers***	$ (10,500)	
Cash payments to employees	(6,500)	(17,000)
Net cash inflow from operating activities		28,000
Cash flows from investing activities		
Acquisition of land	$(100,000)	
Net cash outflow from investing activities		(100,000)
Cash flows from financing activities		
Investment by owner	$ 250,000	
Withdrawal by owner	(6,000)	
Net cash inflow from financing activities		244,000
Net increase in cash		$172,000
Cash balance, April 1, 2016		0
Cash balance, April 30, 2016		$172,000

*Chapter 17 explains how to prepare this statement.
**$30,000 + $15,000 = $45,000
***$4,000 + $1,500 + $5,000 = $10,500

Notes to the Financial Statements The four financial statements are accompanied by *notes* that provide more information about what is presented in the statements. The *CPA Canada Handbook* identifies the information that is required, which varies by the type of business or not-for-profit organization. Preparation of the notes is beyond the scope of this book, but reading and understanding them is a useful skill for all users of financial information.

> *You will look at the notes to the financial statements in many of the Financial Statement Case questions at the end of each chapter.*

> # Try It!

8. Indicate whether each account listed below appears on the balance sheet (B), income statement (I), statement of owner's equity (OE), or cash flow statement (CF). Some items appear on more than one statement.

Accounts Receivable	_____	Salaries Expense	_____
Computer Equipment	_____	Consulting Service Revenue	_____
S. Scott, Capital	_____	Cash	_____
Rent Expense	_____	Notes Payable	_____
Supplies	_____	Supplies Expense	_____
S. Scott, Withdrawals	_____	Accounts Payable	_____

9. Using the following information, complete the income statement, statement of owner's equity, and balance sheet for DR Painting for the month of March, 2017. The business began operations on March 1, 2017.

Accounts receivable	$ 1,400	Salaries expense	800
Accounts payable	1,000	Service revenue	7,000
Cash	22,300	Office supplies	1,800
Owner contribution during March	40,000	Land	20,000
Owner withdrawal during March	1,500	Utilities expense	200
D. Richardson, Capital, March 1, 2017	0		

Solutions appear at the end of this chapter and on MyAccountingLab

This textbook illustrates accounting for businesses that follow Accounting Standards for Private Enterprises (ASPE). When there are differences from International Financial Reporting Standards (IFRS), this information is noted with a chart as the last learning objective for a chapter. Some chapters won't have a chart, because in many cases the standards are the same! In Volume 2, these charts will become more detailed.

LO 6

What are IFRS and ASPE?

ASPE	IFRS
In Canada, both International Financial Reporting Standards (IFRS) and Accounting Standards for Private Enterprises (ASPE) are prepared under the authority of the Accounting Standards Board and are published as part of the *CPA Canada Handbook*.	
Sole proprietorships follow ASPE, which are simpler and less costly to implement. Private corporations can choose to follow ASPE or IFRS.	Publicly accountable enterprises or those planning to become one must follow IFRS.
Financial reports contain less information under ASPE because readers have more access to the details themselves.	Financial reports contain more detailed information than under ASPE because users do not have easy access to the information.
Companies reporting under either method must also provide notes to the financial statements, which include significant accounting policies and explanatory information.	

SUMMARY PROBLEM FOR YOUR REVIEW

The **Summary Problem for Your Review** is an extensive, solved review problem that pulls together the chapter concepts.

Todor Biris opened a website design business in Calgary. He is the sole owner of the proprietorship, which he names Biris Web Design. During the first month of operations, July 2016, the following transactions occurred:

a. Biris invests $50,000 of personal funds to start the business.

b. The business purchases, on account, office supplies costing $2,000.

c. Biris Web Design pays cash of $26,000 to acquire a parcel of land. The business intends to use the land as a future building site for its business office.

d. The business provides services for clients and receives cash of $10,000.

e. The business pays $1,000 on the account payable created in Transaction (b).

f. Biris pays $2,750 of personal funds for a vacation for his family.

g. The business pays cash expenses for office rent, $2,500, and utilities, $500.

h. The business returns to the supplier office supplies that cost $300. The wrong supplies were shipped.

i. Biris withdraws $3,000 cash for personal use.

Required

1. Analyze the preceding transactions in terms of their effects on the accounting equation of Biris Web Design. Use Exhibit 1–11 on page 20 as a guide, but show balances only after the last transaction.

2. Prepare the income statement, statement of owner's equity, and balance sheet of Biris Web Design after recording the transactions. Use Exhibit 1–15 on page 24 as a guide.

SOLUTION

As you review the details of each transaction, think of the parts of the accounting equation that will be affected.

Requirement 1

For each transaction, make sure the accounting equation, Assets = Liabilities + Owner's Equity, balances before going on to the next transaction.

		Assets				Liabilities	+	Owner's Equity	Type of Owner's Equity Transaction
		Cash	+ Office Supplies	+ Land		Accounts Payable		Todor Biris, Capital	
(a)		+ 50,000						+50,000	Owner investment
(b)			+2,000			+2,000			
(c)		− 26,000		+ 26,000					
(d)		+ 10,000						+ 10,000	Service revenue
(e)		− 1,000			=	−1,000			
(f)		Not a business transaction							
(g)		− 2,500						− 2,500	Rent expense
		− 500						− 500	Utilities expense
(h)			− 300			−300			
(i)		− 3,000						− 3,000	Owner withdrawal
Bal		27,000	1,700	26,000		700		54,000	

54,700   54,700

Requirement 2

BIRIS WEB DESIGN		
Income Statement		
For the Month Ended July 31, 2016		
Revenue:		
Service revenue		$10,000
Expenses:		
Rent expense	$2,500	
Utilities expense	500	
Total expenses		3,000
Net income		$ 7,000

The title must include the name of the company, "Income Statement," and the specific period of time covered.

Gather all the revenue and expense account names and amounts from Requirement 1. They appear in the Todor Biris, Capital column.
- List the revenue account first.
- List the expense accounts next. In this book, expenses are usually listed in alphabetical order.

BIRIS WEB DESIGN	
Statement of Owner's Equity	
For the Month Ended July 31, 2016	
Todor Biris, capital, July 1, 2016	$ 0
Add: Investment by owner	50,000
Net income for July	7,000
	57,000
Less: Withdrawal by owner	3,000
Todor Biris, capital, July 31, 2016	$54,000

The title must include the name of the company, "Statement of Owner's Equity," and the specific period of time covered.

The net income amount (or net loss amount) is transferred from the income statement.

The withdrawal amount is found in the solution to Requirement 1 in the Todor Biris, Capital column.

BIRIS WEB DESIGN			
Balance Sheet			
July 31, 2016			
Assets		**Liabilities**	
Cash	$27,000	Accounts payable	$ 700
Office supplies	1,700	**Owner's Equity**	
Land	26,000	Todor Biris, capital	54,000
		Total liabilities and	
Total assets	$54,700	owner's equity	$54,700

The title must include the name of the company, "Balance Sheet," and the date of the balance sheet. It shows the financial position on one specific date.

Gather all the asset and liability accounts and Bal. amounts from the solution to Requirement 1. List assets first, then liabilities. Cash always goes first on the asset side. The owner's equity amount is transferred from the statement of owner's equity.

Check: Total Assets = Total Liabilities + Owner's Equity

SUMMARY

The **Summary** gives a concise description of the material covered in the chapter along with page references, so you can link back into the chapter if you want to review particular material. It is organized by learning objective. In addition, references to MyAccountingLab are included so you can connect to what you need quickly and easily.

LEARNING OBJECTIVE Define accounting, and describe the users of accounting information

Why is accounting important, and who uses the information?   Pg. 4
- Accounting is an information system for measuring, processing, and communicating financial information.
- As the "language of business," accounting helps a wide range of users (such as individual investors, businesses, government agencies, and lenders) make business decisions.
- Ethical considerations affect all areas of accounting and business.

LEARNING OBJECTIVE Compare and contrast the forms of business organizations

In what form can we set up a company?   Pg. 7
- The three basic forms of business organizations are
  - Proprietorship
  - Partnership (a limited-liability partnership is a special form of partnership)
  - Corporation
- See Exhibit 1–4 on page 8 for a comparison of the three forms.

LEARNING OBJECTIVE Describe some concepts and principles of accounting

What are some of the guidelines for accounting, and why do we need them?   Pg. 9
- Accounting concepts guide accountants in their work.
- They are summarized in Exhibit 1–5 on page 11 and on the inside back cover of this book:
  - The primary objective of financial statements is to provide information that is useful for users in their decision making.
  - To be useful, the information must have the qualitative characteristics of understandability, reliability, relevance, and comparability.
  - Key assumptions and principles are the economic entity assumption, the going concern assumption, the stable monetary unit assumption, and the cost principle of measurement. They are subject to both the cost–benefit and materiality constraints.

  MyAccountingLab **Video:** Accounting Principles and Concepts

LEARNING OBJECTIVE Use the accounting equation to analyze business transactions

How do business activities affect the accounting records of a company?   Pg. 12
- The accounting equation is

  Assets = Liabilities + Owner's Equity

- A *transaction* is an event that affects the financial position of an entity *and* can be reliably measured.

  MyAccountingLab **Video:** The Accounting Equation
  Video: Accounting Equation: Impact on Owner's Equity

LEARNING OBJECTIVE Prepare financial statements

What financial statements are prepared by a company, and how do we create them?   Pg. 21
- The *financial statements* communicate information for decision making by an entity's users, including managers, owners, and creditors.
- The *income statement* summarizes the entity's operations in terms of revenues earned and expenses incurred during a specific period of time.

  If revenues > expenses, there is a net income.
  If revenues < expenses, there is a net loss.

- The *statement of owner's equity* reports the changes in owner's equity during the period.

  End Balance Capital = Opening Balance Capital – Withdrawals + Net Income – Net Loss

- The *balance sheet* lists the entity's assets, liabilities, and owner's equity at a specific date.

  Assets = Liabilities + Owner's Equity

- The *cash flow statement* reports the changes in cash during the period.
- See Exhibit 1–15 on page 24 for model statements.

MyAccountingLab **Video:** Relationships among the Financial Statements
Video: Real World Accounting
Video: Introduction to Financial Statements

LEARNING OBJECTIVE ⑥ Briefly explain the different accounting standards

What are IFRS and ASPE?   Pg. 25
- ASPE = Accounting Standards for Private Enterprises
- IFRS = International Financial Reporting Standards

Check **Accounting Vocabulary** for all key terms used in Chapter 1 and the **Glossary** at the back of the book for all key terms used in the textbook.

MORE CHAPTER REVIEW MATERIAL

MyAccountingLab

DemoDoc covering Basic Transactions

Accounting Cycle Tutorial

Student PowerPoint Slides

Audio Chapter Summary

Note: All MyAccountingLab resources can be found in the Chapter Resources section and in the Multimedia Library.

Accounting Vocabulary lists all the new bold-faced terms that were explained in the chapter with their definitions. They are also defined in the Glossary. Page references help you to review the terms.

ACCOUNTING VOCABULARY

Like many other subjects, accounting has a special vocabulary. It is important that you understand the following terms:

Account   The detailed record of the changes that have occurred in a particular asset, liability, or item of owner's equity during a period (*p. 13*).

Accounting   The system that measures business activities, processes that information into reports and financial statements, and communicates the findings to decision makers (*p. 4*).

Accounting equation   The most basic tool of accounting: Assets = Liabilities + Owner's Equity (proprietorship) or Assets = Liabilities + Shareholders' Equity (corporation) (*p. 12*).

Account payable   The oral or implied promise to pay off debts arising from credit purchases. A liability that is backed by the general reputation and credit standing of the debtor (*p. 14*).

Account receivable   An asset; a promise to receive cash in the future from customers to whom the business has sold goods or services (*p. 13*).

Accounting Standards for Private Enterprises (ASPE)   Created by the Accounting Standards Board, guidelines for reporting the financial results of non-publicly accountable enterprises in Canada (*p. 10*).

Asset   An economic resource a business owns that is expected to be of benefit in the future (*p. 13*).

Audit   The examination of financial statements by outside accountants. The conclusion of an audit is the accountant's professional opinion about the financial statements (*p. 6*).

Balance sheet   A list of an entity's assets, liabilities, and owner's equity (proprietorship) or shareholders' equity (corporation) as of a specific date. Also called the *statement of financial position* (*p. 22*).

Bookkeeping   A procedural element of accounting; the keeping of the financial records and the recording of financial information (*p. 4*).

Business   One or more individuals selling goods or services with the intent of making a profit (*p. 4*).

Capital   Another name for the owner's equity of a business (*p. 14*).

Cash flow statement   Reports cash receipts and cash payments classified according to the entity's major activities: operating, investing, and financing (*p. 23*).

Chartered Professional Accountant (CPA)   An accountant who has met the examination and experience requirements of the CPA Canada (*p. 6*).

Comparable   A qualitative characteristic of accounting information that says financial statements should be able to be measured against results in previous years or other businesses in the same industry (*p. 11*).

Corporation   A business owned by shareholders that begins when the federal or provincial government approves its articles of incorporation. A corporation is a legal entity, an "artificial person," in the eyes of the law (p. 8).

Cost–benefit constraint   An accounting constraint that says the benefits of the information produced should not exceed the costs of producing the information (p. 12).

Cost principle of measurement   States that assets and services are recorded at their purchase cost and that the accounting record of the asset continues to be based on cost rather than current market value (p. 12).

Creditors   Businesses or individuals to which payment is owed (p. 5).

Designated accountants   Accountants who have met the education, examination, and experience requirements of an accounting body (p. 6).

Dividends   Distributions by a corporation to its shareholders (p. 15).

Economic entity assumption   The accounting assumption that an organization or a section of an organization stands apart from other organizations and individuals as a separate economic unit for accounting purposes. (p. 11).

Ethics   Rules of behaviour based on what is good or bad (p. 7).

Expenses   Costs incurred when running a business (or the using up of assets). Decrease in owner's equity that occurs in the course of delivering goods or services to customers or clients (p. 14).

External users   Readers of financial information who do not work for the business (p. 5).

Financial accounting   The branch of accounting that provides information to people outside the business (p. 5).

Financial statements   Business documents that report financial information about an entity to persons and organizations outside the business (p. 4).

Generally accepted accounting principles (GAAP) Accounting guidelines, formulated by the Accounting Standards Board, that govern how businesses report their results in financial statements to the public (p. 9).

Going concern assumption   An accounting assumption that the business will continue operating in the forseeable future (p. 11).

Income statement   A list of an entity's revenues, expenses, and net income or net loss for a specific period. Also called the *statement of earnings* or *statement of operations* (p. 21).

Independence   In accounting, this refers to there being no financial interest outside of the current business relationship. Auditors and other accountants must not be influenced by personal or professional gain from their auditing or accounting decisions (p. 6).

Inflation   A rise in the general level of prices (p. 12).

Internal users   Readers of financial information who either own the business or are employed by it (p. 5).

International Accounting Standards Board (IASB)   The body that sets International Financial Reporting Standards (p. 10).

International Financial Reporting Standards (IFRS)   The accounting standards that specify the generally accepted accounting principles that must be applied by publicly accountable enterprises in Canada and over 130 countries (p. 10).

Investors   A person or business that provides capital (usually money) to a business with the expectation of receiving financial gain (p. 5).

Legacy designation   The accounting designation of CPAs who joined as part of the initial merger of accounting bodies. It is the name of their prior accounting designation that must be used in conjunction with the CPA designation for a period of 10 years (p. 6).

Liability   An economic obligation (a debt) payable to an individual or an organization outside the business (p. 14).

Limited-liability partnership (LLP)   A form of partnership in which each partner's personal liability for the business's debts is limited to a certain amount (p. 8).

Limited personal liability   The owner's legal and financial liability is limited to the amount he or she invested into the business (p. 9).

Management accounting   The branch of accounting that generates information for internal decision makers of a business (p. 5).

Materiality   The accounting constraint that says information should be reported if it is material to the user—that is, if knowing it might affect a decision maker's decision (p. 12).

Measurement   The process of determining the amount at which an item is included in the financial statements (p. 12).

Merchandising business   A business that resells products previously bought from suppliers (p. 17).

Net earnings   Excess of total revenues over total expenses. Also called *net income* or *net profit* (p. 21).

Net income   Excess of total revenues over total expenses. Also called *net earnings* or *net profit* (p. 21).

Net loss   Excess of total expenses over total revenues (p. 21).

Net profit   Excess of total revenues over total expenses. Also called *net earnings* or *net income* (p. 21).

Note payable   A liability evidenced by a written promise to make a future payment (p. 14).

Note receivable   An asset evidenced by another party's written promise that entitles you to receive cash in the future (p. 13).

Owner's equity   In a proprietorship, the claim of an owner of a business to the assets of the business. Also called *capital* (p. 14).

Owner withdrawals   Amounts removed from the business by an owner (p. 14).

Partnership   An unincorporated business with two or more owners (p. 8).

Partners' equity   The name for owner's equity when there is more than one owner. In this case, the owners are called partners (p. 14).

Prepaid expense   A category of assets that are paid for first, then expire or get used up in the near future (p. 13).

Private accountants   Accountants that only work for one employer that is not a public accounting firm (p. 6).

Private enterprise   A corporation that does not offer its shares for sale to the public (p. 10).

Professional designations   Acknowledgement of educational achievement from an agency to assure qualification to perform a job. (p. 6).

Profit   Excess of total revenues over total expenses. Also called *net earnings, net income,* or *net profit* (p. 4).

Promissory note   A written promise to pay a specified amount of money at a particular future date (p. 13).

Proprietorship   An unincorporated business with a single owner (p. 7).

Public accountants   Designated accountants that provide services to clients in the practice of public accounting (p. 6).

Publicly accountable enterprise   A corporation that has its shares traded on a stock exchange or for which a strong public interest exists (p. 10).

Relevant   Information that might influence a decision (p. 10).

Reliable   A qualitative characteristic of accounting information that stays financial information is only useful if it accurately represents the impact of transactions—that is, it is free of error and bias (p. 11).

Revenue   Amounts earned from delivering goods or services to customers. The increase in owner's equity that is earned by delivering goods or services to customers or clients (p. 14).

Sales revenue   The amount that a merchandiser earns from selling its inventory before subtracting expenses. Also called *sales* (p. 17).

Security   An asset that will become the property of the lender if the debt that is owed to the lender is not paid (p. 13).

Service proprietorship   An unincorporated business with one owner that earns income from selling services (p. 14).

Service revenue   The amount of revenue that a business earns from selling services (p. 17).

Shareholder   A person or company who owns one or more shares of stock in a corporation (p. 8).

Shareholders' equity   The account name for owner's equity when the business is a corporation. In this case, the owners are called shareholders (p. 14).

Stable monetary unit assumption   Accountants' basis for ignoring the effect of inflation and making no adjustments for the changing value of the dollar (p. 12).

Statement of earnings   Another name for the *income statement* (p. 21).

Statement of financial position   Another name for the *balance sheet* (p. 22).

Statement of operations   Another name for the *income statement*. Also called the *statement of earnings* (p. 21).

Statement of owner's equity   A summary of the changes in an entity's owner's equity during a specific period (p. 22).

Transaction   An event that has a financial impact on a business and that can be reliably measured (p. 15).

Understandable   A qualitative characteristic of accounting information that says users should be able to understand the information in financial statements (p. 11).

Unlimited personal liability   When the debts of a business are greater than its resources, the owner is (owners are) responsible for their payment (p. 9).

SIMILAR ACCOUNTING TERMS

Similar Accounting Terms are a link between the terms used in this book and similar terms you might have heard outside your accounting class in the media or your day-to-day business dealings.

ACAF	Advanced Certificate in Accounting and Finance
Accounting equation	Assets = Liabilities + Owner's Equity
ASPE	Accounting Standards for Private Enterprises
Balance sheet	Statement of financial position
Business	Company; enterprise; firm
Capital	Owner's equity
CPA	Chartered Professional Accountant
GAAP	Generally accepted accounting principles
Historical cost	Cost basis; cost principle
IASB	International Accounting Standards Board
IFRS	International Financial Reporting Standards
Income statement	Statement of operations; statement of earnings
LLP	Limited-liability partnership
Management accounting	Managerial accounting
Net income	Net earnings; net profit; profit
Profit	Income
Sales	Revenue
Statement of owner's equity	Statement of equity
Withdrawals	Drawings

SELF-STUDY QUESTIONS

Test your understanding of the chapter by marking the correct answer for each of the following questions:

1. Which of the following forms of business organization is an "artificial person" and must obtain legal approval from the federal or provincial government to conduct business? (*p. 8*)
   a. Law firm
   b. Proprietorship
   c. Partnership
   d. Corporation

2. What accounting assumption, criteria, or constraint tells an accountant to group small expense accounts together into one subtotal on a financial statement? (*p. 12*)
   a. Going concern assumption
   b. Materiality constraint
   c. Stable monetary unit assumption
   d. Economic entity assumption

3. You have purchased some T-shirts for $6,000 and can sell them immediately for $8,000. What accounting assumption, criteria, or constraint governs the amount at which to record the goods you purchased? (*p. 12*)
   a. Economic entity assumption
   b. Reliability characteristic
   c. Cost principle
   d. Going concern assumption

4. The economic resources of a business are called (*p. 13*)
   a. Assets
   b. Liabilities
   c. Owner's equity
   d. Accounts payable

5. If the assets of a business are $200,000 and the liabilities are $90,000, how much is the owner's equity? (*p. 13*)
   a. $290,000
   b. $110,000
   c. $200,000
   d. $90,000

6. A business has assets of $160,000 and liabilities of $180,000. How much is its owner's equity? (*p. 13*)
   a. $0
   b. ($20,000)

c. $160,000
d. $340,000

7. If the owner's equity in a business is $70,000 and the liabilities are $35,000, how much are the assets? (*p. 13*)
   a. $35,000
   b. $70,000
   c. $105,000
   d. $45,000

8. Purchasing office supplies on account will (*p. 16*)
   a. Increase an asset and increase a liability
   b. Increase an asset and increase owner's equity
   c. Increase one asset and decrease another asset
   d. Increase an asset and decrease a liability

9. Performing a service for a customer or client and receiving the cash immediately will (*p. 17*)
   a. Increase one asset and decrease another asset
   b. Increase an asset and increase owner's equity
   c. Decrease an asset and decrease a liability
   d. Increase an asset and increase a liability

10. Paying an account payable will (*p. 18*)
    a. Increase one asset and decrease another asset
    b. Decrease an asset and decrease owner's equity
    c. Decrease an asset and decrease a liability
    d. Increase an asset and increase a liability

11. The financial statement that summarizes assets, liabilities, and owner's equity is called the (*p. 22*)
    a. Cash flow statement
    b. Balance sheet
    c. Income statement
    d. Statement of owner's equity

12. The financial statements that are dated for a time period (rather than for a specific point in time) are the (*pp. 21–23*)
    a. Balance sheet and income statement
    b. Balance sheet and statement of owner's equity
    c. Income statement, statement of owner's equity, and cash flow statement
    d. All financial statements are dated for a time period

ASSIGNMENT MATERIAL

QUESTIONS

1. Distinguish between accounting and bookkeeping.
2. Identify five users of accounting information and explain how they use it.
3. What is the difference between financial accounting and management accounting?
4. What is an audit and why is it important that it be performed by independent accountants?
5. What organization formulates generally accepted accounting principles in Canada?
6. Explain the differences between proprietorships, partnerships, and corporations based on owners, life of the organization, liability of owners, and legal status.
7. Identify the owner(s) of a proprietorship, a partnership, and a corporation.
8. Identify two advantages of the corporate form of business over a proprietorship.
9. Why is the economic entity assumption so important to accounting?
10. Give four examples of types of accounting entities.
11. Briefly describe the reliability characteristic.
12. Explain why the going concern assumption is important to know when reading a financial statement.
13. What role does the cost principle of measurement play in accounting?
14. If assets = liabilities + owner's equity, then liabilities = ?
15. Explain the difference between an account receivable and an account payable.
16. What role do transactions play in accounting?
17. A company reported monthly revenues of $92,000 and expenses of $96,400. What is the result of operations for the month?
18. Give a more descriptive title for the balance sheet.
19. What feature of the balance sheet gives this financial statement its name?
20. Give another title for the income statement.
21. Which financial statement is like a snapshot of the entity at a specific time? Which financial statement is like a video of the entity's operation during a period of time?
22. What information does the statement of owner's equity report?
23. Give another term for the owner's equity of a proprietorship.
24. What piece of information flows from the income statement to the statement of owner's equity? What information flows from the statement of owner's equity to the balance sheet? What balance sheet item is explained by the cash flow statement?
25. Why does it make sense that Canadian companies whose shares are publicly traded on stock exchanges in Canada follow International Financial Reporting Standards instead of standards developed for private companies in Canada?

A brief description and the learning objectives covered appear beside each Starter, Exercise, and Problem.

STARTERS

Starter 1–1 For each of the following users of accounting, indicate if the user would use financial accounting (FA) or management accounting (MA).

    a. Investor

    b. Banker

    c. Canada Revenue Agency

    d. Owner

    e. Human resources department manager

Financial and management accounting

Starter 1–2 Suppose you need a bank loan to purchase lawn equipment for Ralph's Landscaping Service. In evaluating your loan request, the banker asks about the assets and liabilities of your business. In particular, the banker wants to know the amount of the business's owner's equity.

Users of financial information

1. Is the banker considered an internal or an external user of financial information?

2. Which financial statement would provide the best information to answer the banker's questions?

Internal and external users of financial information

Starter 1–3 For each of the users of accounting information, indicate whether they are an external decision maker (E) or an internal decision maker. (I).

a. Marketing manager _____

b. Canada Revenue Agency _____

c. Investor _____

d. Controller _____

e. Supplier _____

Forms of business organizations

Starter 1–4 Louise Layton plans to open Louise's Floral Designs. She is considering the various types of business organizations and wishes to organize her business with unlimited life and limited-liability features. Which type of business organization will meet Louise's needs best?

Describing accounting assumptions, principles, and constraints

Starter 1–5 Match the assumption, principle, or constraint description with the appropriate term by placing a, b, c, d, e, and f on the appropriate line.

a. Cost principle of measurement   _____ Benefits of the information produced by an accounting system must be greater than the costs

b. Going concern assumption   _____ Amounts may be ignored if the effect on a decision maker's decision is not significant

c. Stable monetary unit assumption   _____ Transactions are recorded based on the cash amount received or paid

d. Economic entity assumption   _____ Ignore the effects of inflation in the accounting records

e. Cost–benefit constraint   _____ Assumes that a business is going to continue operations indefinitely

f. Materiality constraint   _____ A business must keep its accounting records separate from its owner's accounting records

Defining transactions

Starter 1–6 A potential customer is extremely interested in renting a number of kayaks from Mayne Island Kayaks and emails his intention to rent kayaks in the summer. Would an accountant consider this event a transaction to be recorded in the accounting records? Explain.

Explaining revenues and expenses

Starter 1–7 Ralph's Landscaping Service has been open for one year, and Ryan Ralph, the owner, wants to know whether the business earned a net income or a net loss for the year. First, he must identify the revenues earned and the expenses incurred during the year. What are revenues and expenses?

Applying accounting concepts and principles

Starter 1–8 Erin Chan is the proprietor of a property management company near the campus of a local university. The business has cash of $12,000 and furniture that cost $24,000 and has a market value of $30,000. Debts include accounts payable of $10,000. Chan's personal home is valued at $400,000 and her personal bank account contains $12,000.

1. Consider the accounting concepts and principles discussed in the chapter, and identify the principle that best matches each of the following situations:

   a. Chan's personal assets are not recorded on the property management company's balance sheet.

   b. Chan records furniture at its cost of $24,000, not the market value of $30,000.

c. Chan does not make adjustments for inflation.

d. The account payable of $10,000 is documented by a statement from the furniture company showing the property management company still owes $10,000 on the furniture. Chan's friend thinks the property management company should only owe about $6,000. The account payable is recorded at $10,000.

2. How much is the owner's equity of the property management company?

Starter 1-9 Outdoor Adventures Travel recorded revenues of $3,000 earned on account by providing travel service for clients.

Analyzing transactions

1. How much are the business's cash and total assets, assuming this is the only transaction?

2. Name the business asset that was increased as a result of this transaction.

Starter 1-10 Suppose Northern Adventures rents stand up paddleboards to tourists. The company purchased a storage building for the boards for $200,000 and financed the purchase with a loan of $150,000 and an investment by the owner for the remainder. Use the accounting equation to calculate the owner's equity amount.

Using the accounting equation

Starter 1-11 Determine the expenses for September based on the following data:

Understanding accounts

September net income	$10,000
Beginning owner's equity	$25,000
Owner's withdrawals	$ 5,000
Ending owner's equity	$30,000
September revenue	$42,000

Starter 1-12 What four main financial statements are provided in a company's annual report? An example of a company's' annual report is provided in Appendix A at the back of this textbook.

Examples of financial statements

Starter 1-13 Laurel Wedding Planners has just completed operations for the year ended December 31, 2016. This is the third year of operations for the company. As the owner, you want to know how well the company performed during the year. To address this question, you have assembled the data below. Use these data to prepare the income statement of Laurel Wedding Planners for the year ended December 31, 2016.

Preparing the income statement

Net income, $48,000

Insurance Expense	$ 3,000	Salary Expense	$50,000
Service Revenue	120,000	Accounts Payable	8,000
Supplies Expense	1,000	Supplies	2,500
Rent Expense	18,000	Withdrawals	40,000

Check figures appear in the margin when applicable to help you make sure you are "on track."

Starter 1-14 Jacob's Overhead Doors reports the following financial information:

Using the income statement to assess a business

Assets	$45,800
Liabilities	15,230
Owner's Investment	28,700
Owner's Withdrawal	7,000
Revenues	10,890
Expenses	?

1. Use the accounting equation to solve for the missing information.

2. Was it a good year or a bad year for the business?

EXERCISES

MyAccountingLab

Exercise 1-1

Jim and Andrea McGee want to open a restaurant. In need of cash, they meet with their bank manager for a loan. With little knowledge of finance, the McGees don't know how the lending process works. Explain to them what sort of information the lender would review and why.

Users of financial statements

①

Exercise 1–2

Forms of business organizations
②

Indicate whether each statement below applies to a sole proprietorship, a partnership, or a corporation.

a. The life of the business is limited by the death of the owner.

b. Each owner is personally liable for claims against the business.

c. A business in which there is only one owner and "he or she is the business."

d. Owners are not personally liable for claims against the business.

e. The form of business typically used by accountants and lawyers.

f. Ownership is easily transferred in a public exchange.

g. Canadian Tire and Tim Hortons are examples of this form of business.

Exercise 1–3

Describing accounting assumptions, principles, and constraints
③

Match the situation with the best term to explain why things are done this way.

1. Every year a business uses the same account names so it can evaluate results between years.

2. When we prepare a financial statement, we show all assets at the price we paid for them.

3. A business should not spend $1,000 on counting and recounting $500 worth of inventory.

4. If we record a truck on the financial statement at the price we could get for it if we tried to sell it quickly, we are violating this accounting assumption.

5. We try to include information in the accounting records such that financial statements provide enough information for readers to make an investment decision.

6. A car dealership will report profits for the parts department separate from the service department so that senior management can see how well each part of their business is doing.

a. Historic cost principle

b. Going concern assumption

c. Relevance characteristic

d. Cost–benefit constraint

e. Economic entity assumption

f. Comparability characteristic

Exercise 1–4

Business transactions
④

Complete the following chart for the selected transactions for Martha's Muffins shown below.

a. Martha invests $10,000 cash into a business known as Martha's Muffins.

b. Martha purchases baking supplies on account for $500.

c. Martha receives and pays the kitchen's utilities bill amounting to $425.

d. Sales revenue for the current period amounts to $2,000 (all revenue transactions involved cash).

e. Martha purchases a new fridge for $3,500 cash.

	Assets	Liabilities	Owner's Equity
a)			
b)			
c)			
d)			
e)			
Totals			

Exercise 1–5

Using the accounting equation
④

For each of the following independent transactions, indicate the change in total assets.

a. Purchased $750 of supplies on account.

b. Paid cash to employees for their salaries, $5,000.

c. Purchased furniture for $1,600 on account.

d. Received telephone bill for $200, to be paid in the following period.

e. Work performed; customer will pay $150 next month.

f. Earned $800 of revenue by performing a service for cash.

g. Performed $3,000 of services on account.

Exercise 1–6

Compute the missing amount in the accounting equation for each business.

Using the accounting equation

Marpole Dry Cleaners liabilities, $50,000

	Assets	Liabilities	Owner's Equity
Economy Cuts	$?	$120,000	$40,000
Marpole Dry Cleaners	100,000	?	50,000
Dauphin Gift and Cards	145,000	115,000	?

Exercise 1–7

Janice Thorpe owns Grinds Coffee House, near the campus of Western Community College. The company has cash of $18,000 and furniture that cost $40,000. Debts include accounts payable of $7,000 and a $30,000 note payable. Write the accounting equation of Grinds Coffee House. What is the owner's equity of the company?

Using the accounting equation

Owner's equity, $21,000

Exercise 1–8

Indicate the effects of the following business transactions on the accounting equation of a proprietorship. Transaction *a* is answered as a guide.

Transaction analysis

(4)

a. Received $50,000 cash from the owner.

  Answer: Increase asset (Cash)

     Increase owner's equity (Owner, Capital)

b. Paid the current month's office rent of $4,000.

c. Paid $3,500 cash to purchase office supplies.

d. Performed engineering services for a client on account, $6,000.

e. Purchased office furniture on account at a cost of $5,000.

f. Received cash on account, $3,000.

g. Paid cash on account, $2,500.

h. Sold land for $50,000 cash, which was the business's cost of the land.

i. Performed engineering services for a client and received cash of $6,000.

> This margin note reminds you that an Excel template is available in MyAccountingLab to help you answer this question.

Exercise 1–9

Gayle Hayashi, M.D., opens a medical clinic. During her first month of operation, January, the clinic, entitled Hayashi Medical Clinic, experienced the following events:

Excel Spreadsheet Template

Transaction analysis, accounting equation

Total assets, $266,500

Jan.	6	Hayashi invested $250,000 in the clinic by opening a bank account in the name of Hayashi Medical Clinic.
	9	Hayashi Medical Clinic paid cash for land costing $150,000. There are plans to build a clinic on the land. Until then, the business will rent an office.
	12	The clinic purchased medical supplies for $10,000 on account.
	15	On January 15, Hayashi Medical Clinic officially opened for business.
	15–31	During the rest of the month, the clinic earned professional fees of $20,000 and received cash immediately.
	15–31	The clinic paid cash expenses: employee salaries, $5,000; office rent, $4,000; utilities, $500.
	28	The clinic sold supplies to another clinic at cost for $1,000.
	31	The clinic paid $4,000 on the account from January 12.

Required Analyze the effects of these events on the accounting equation of Hayashi Medical Clinic. Use a format similar to that of Exhibit 1–11, Panel B, on page 20 with headings for Cash; Medical Supplies; Land; Accounts Payable; and Gayle Hayashi, Capital.

Exercise 1–10

Using accounting vocabulary

④ ⑤

Match each of the following accounting terms with its correct definition:

Terms:	Definitions:
1. Accounting equation	a. An economic resource that is expected to be of benefit in the future
2. Asset	b. An economic obligation (a debt) payable to an individual or an organization outside the business
3. Balance sheet	c. Excess of total expenses over total revenues
4. Expense	d. Excess of total revenues over total expenses
5. Income statement	e. The basic tool of accounting, stated as Assets = Liabilities + Owner's Equity
6. Liability	f. The decrease in equity that occurs from using assets or increasing liabilities in the course of delivering goods or services to customers
7. Net income	g. Amounts earned by delivering goods or services to customers
8. Net loss	h. Report that shows cash receipts and cash payments during a period
9. Revenue	i. Report that shows an entity's assets, liabilities, and owner's equity as of a specific date
10. Cash flow statement	j. Report that shows an entity's revenues, expenses, and net income or net loss for a period of time
11. Statement of owner's equity	k. Report that shows the changes in owner's equity for a period of time

Exercise 1–11

Classifying accounts, working with financial statements

④ ⑤

The accounting records of Chiang Consulting Services contain the following accounts:

Supplies Expense	Accounts Payable
Accounts Receivable	Rent Expense
J. Chiang, Capital	Cash
Salary Expense	J. Chiang, Withdrawals
Computer Equipment	Supplies
Consulting Service Revenue	Notes Payable

Required

1. Indicate whether each account listed is a(n) asset (A), liability (L), owner's equity (OE), revenue (R), or expense (E) account.

2. Indicate whether each account listed appears on the balance sheet (B), income statement (I), statement of owner's equity (SOE), or cash flow statement (CF). Some accounts can appear on more than one statement.

Exercise 1–12

Using the accounting equation, evaluating business performance

④ ⑤

1. Increase in owner's equity, $4,000

Prairie Snow Removal began 2016 with total assets of $44,000 and total liabilities of $18,000. At the end of 2016, the business's total assets were $50,000 and total liabilities were $20,000.

Required

1. Did the owner's equity of Prairie Snow Removal increase or decrease during 2016? By how much?

2. Identify two possible reasons for the change in owner's equity of Prairie Snow Removal during the year.

Exercise 1–13

Business organizations, transactions, net income

④ ⑤

2. Net income, $4,500

The analysis of the transactions that Oakdale Equipment Rental engaged in during its first month of operations follows. The business buys electronic equipment that it rents out to earn rental revenue. The owner of the business, Gary Oake, made only one investment to start the business and made no withdrawals from Oakdale Equipment Rental.

	Cash	+	Accounts Receivable	+	Rental Equipment	=	Accounts Payable	+	G. Oake, Capital
a.	+50,000								+50,000
b.	+1,000								+1,000
c.					+80,000		+80,000		
d.			+1,000						+1,000
e.	−2,000								−2,000
f.	+4,500								+4,500
g.	+500		−500						
h.	−5,000						−5,000		

Required

1. Describe each transaction of Oakdale Equipment Rental.

2. If these transactions fully describe the operations of Oakdale Equipment Rental during the month, what was the amount of net income or net loss?

Exercise 1–14

Presented below are the balances of the assets and liabilities of Summerland Consulting Services as of September 30, 2017. Also included are the revenue and expense account balances of the business for September.

Consulting Service Revenue..........	$62,000	Computer Equipment......	$80,000
Accounts Receivable.......................	25,000	Supplies	5,000
Accounts Payable............................	16,000	Note Payable.....................	50,000
Salary Expense.................................	10,000	Rent Expense.....................	4,000
M. Hall, Capital	?	Cash......................................	5,000

Business organization,
balance sheet
(2) (5)
2. Total assets, $115,000

Required

1. What type of business entity or organization is Summerland Consulting Services? How can you tell?

2. Prepare the balance sheet of Summerland Consulting Services as of September 30, 2017.

3. What does the balance sheet report—financial position or operating results? Which financial statement reports the other information?

Exercise 1–15

Examine Exhibit 1–11 on page 20. The exhibit summarizes the transactions of Hunter Environmental Consulting for the month of April 2016. Suppose the business completed Transactions 1 to 7 and needed a bank loan on April 21, 2016. The vice-president of the bank requires financial statements to support all loan requests.

Preparing the financial statements
(5)
Total assets, $295,000

Required Prepare the income statement, statement of owner's equity, and balance sheet that Hunter Environmental Consulting would present to the banker on April 21, 2016, after completing the first seven transactions.

Exercise 1–16

The assets, liabilities, owner's equity, revenue, and expenses of Philpott Company, a proprietorship, have the following final balances at December 31, 2017, the end of its first year of business. To start the business, Brian Philpott invested $90,000.

Note Payable............................	$ 50,000	Office Furniture	$ 50,000
Utilities Expense.....................	18,000	Rent Expense...........................	48,000
Accounts Payable..................	12,000	Cash...	15,000
B. Philpott, Capital................	90,000	Office Supplies........................	14,000
Service Revenue	610,000	Salary Expense........................	430,000
Accounts Receivable.............	35,000	Salary Payable.........................	5,000
Supplies Expense...................	30,000	Research Expense..................	27,000
Equipment..............................	100,000		

Excel Spreadsheet Template

Income statement for a proprietorship
(5)
Net income, $57,000

Required Prepare the income statement of Philpott Company for the year ended December 31, 2017. What is Philpott Company's net income or net loss for 2017? (Hint: Ignore balance sheet items.)

SERIAL EXERCISE

The Serial Exercise involves a company that will be revisited throughout relevant chapters in Volume 1 and Volume 2. It begins as a proprietorship in Volume 1, and then grows to a partnership and then a corporation in Volume 2. You can complete the Serial Exercises using MyAccountingLab.

Exercise 1–17

Transaction analysis, accounting equation, financial statements
④ ⑤
Total assets, $31,750

Michael Lee started his new executive coaching business on June 1. Lee Management Consulting completed the following transactions during June 2016:

Jun.	2	Received $25,000 cash from owner Michael Lee. The business gave owner's equity in the business to Lee.
	2	Lee found a great downtown loft from which to operate. He paid cash for rent for the month of June, $3,000.
	3	Paid cash for a laptop, $1,000. The computer is expected to remain in service for four years. (Use the Equipment account for this transaction.)
	4	Purchased office furniture on account, $5,000. The furniture is expected to last for five years.
	5	Purchased supplies on account, $500.
	9	Performed consulting services for a client on account, $3,000.
	12	Paid utility expenses with cash, $250
	18	Performed consulting services for a client and received cash of $2,000.
	21	Received $2,000 in advance for client services to be performed at a rate of $100 per day for a period of 20 days. (Use the liability account Unearned Revenue for this transaction. We will learn more about this account in Chapter 3.)
	22	Hired an office manager on a part-time basis. She will be paid $2,000 per month. She started work on Monday, June 25.
	23	Paid $500 cash for the supplies purchased on June 5.
	26	Collected a partial payment of $1,500 from the consulting client invoiced on June 9.
	28	Michael Lee withdrew $2,000 cash for personal use.

Required Analyze the effects of Lee Management Consulting's transactions on the accounting equation. Use the format of Exhibit 1–11, Panel B, on page 20, and use these headings: Cash; Accounts Receivable; Supplies; Equipment; Furniture; Accounts Payable; Unearned Revenue; and Michael Lee, Capital.

In Chapter 2, we will account for these same transactions in a different way—as the accounting is actually performed in practice.

CHALLENGE EXERCISES

Exercise 1–18

Using the financial statements
④ ⑤
Net income:
Fraser Co., $200,000
Delta Co., $170,000
Pine Co., $225,000

Compute the missing amounts for each of the following businesses:

	Fraser Co.	Delta Co.	Pine Co.
Beginning:			
Assets	$350,000	$300,000	$540,000
Liabilities	200,000	120,000	360,000

	Fraser Co.	Delta Co.	Pine Co.
Ending:			
Assets	$500,000	$360,000	$?
Liabilities	250,000	160,000	480,000
Owner's equity:			
Investments by owner	$?	$ 0	$ 50,000
Withdrawals by owner	250,000	150,000	220,000
Income Statement:			
Revenues	$660,000	$350,000	$900,000
Expenses	460,000	?	675,000

Exercise 1–19

Merit Logistics's balance sheet data are shown below:

Using the accounting equation, preparing the statement of owner's equity

④ ⑤

2. Net income, $20,000

	January 1, 2017	December 31, 2017
Total assets	$300,000	$420,000
Total liabilities	260,000	340,000

Required

1. Compute the amount of net income or net loss for the company during the year ended December 31, 2017, if the owner invested $50,000 in the business and withdrew $30,000 during the year. Show all calculations.

2. Prepare the statement of owner's equity for Sandy Merit, the owner of Merit Logistics, for the year ended December 31, 2017.

BEYOND THE NUMBERS

Beyond the Numbers 1–1

As an analyst for Royal Bank, it is your job to write recommendations to the bank's loan committee. Vernon Engineering Co., a client of the bank, has submitted these summary data to support the company's request for a $150,000 loan:

Analyzing a loan request

① ⑤

Income Statement Data	2017	2016	2015
Total revenues	$550,000	$490,000	$475,000
Total expenses	400,000	345,000	305,000
Net income	$150,000	$145,000	$170,000

Statement of Owner's Equity Data	2017	2016	2015
Beginning capital	$230,000	$205,000	$215,000
Add: Net income	150,000	145,000	170,000
	$380,000	$350,000	$385,000
Less: Withdrawals	(175,000)	(120,000)	(180,000)
Ending capital	$205,000	$230,000	$205,000

Balance Sheet Data	2017	2016	2015
Total assets	$450,000	$425,000	$375,000
Total liabilities	$245,000	$195,000	$170,000
Total owner's equity	205,000	230,000	205,000
Total liabilities and owner's equity	$450,000	$425,000	$375,000

Required   Analyze these financial statement data to decide whether the bank should lend $150,000 to Vernon Engineering Co. Consider the trends in net income and owner's equity and the change in total liabilities in making your decision. Write a one-paragraph recommendation to the bank's loan committee.

Transaction analysis, effects on financial statements

Beyond the Numbers 1–2

Shining Star Camp conducts summer camps for children with physical challenges. Because of the nature of its business, Shining Star Camp experiences many unusual transactions. Evaluate each of the following transactions in terms of its effect on Shining Star Camp's income statement and balance sheet.

a. A camper suffered a dental injury that was not covered by insurance. Shining Star Camp paid $1,000 for the child's dental care.

b. One camper's mother is a physician. Shining Star Camp allows this child to attend camp in return for the mother serving part time in the camp infirmary for the two-week term. The standard fee for a camp term is $1,500. The physician's salary for this part-time work would be $1,500.

c. Lightning during a storm damaged the camp dining hall. The cost to repair the damage will be $5,000 over and above what the insurance company will pay.

ETHICAL ISSUES

Ethical Issue 1

The following excerpt was taken from the 2012 Consolidated Financial Statements of Cash Store Financial:

Note 3 – Restatement of Previously Reported Results

a) These consolidated financial statements for the years ended September 30, 2012 and 2011, as initially reported, have been amended and restated to correct for an error resulting from the misunderstanding of the settlement terms and conditions of the March 5, 2004 British Columbia Class Action claim, which resulted in the application of an accounting principle to measure and record the liability as at September 30, 2010 and subsequent reporting periods that was not appropriate in the circumstances. The restatement impacts the years ended September 30, 2012 and September 30, 2011 and the fifteen months ended September 30, 2010. The restatement resulted in a reduction in net income in the fifteen months ended September 30, 2010 of $6,601, an increase in the net income in the year ended September 30, 2011 of $1,537 and an increase in net loss of $433 in the year ended September 30, 2012.

Required

1. Why is it important that this type of information be disclosed?

2. Suppose you were the chief financial officer responsible for the financial statements. What ethical issues would you face as you consider what to report in 2012?

3. What are the negative consequences to Cash Store Financial of not telling the truth? What are the negative consequences to Cash Store Financial of telling the truth?

Ethical Issue 2

The board of directors of Cloutier Inc. is meeting to discuss the past year's results before releasing financial statements to the public. The discussion includes this exchange:

Sue Cloutier, company president: "Well, this has not been a good year! Revenue is down and expenses are up—way up. If we don't do some fancy stepping, we'll report a loss for the third year in a row. I can temporarily transfer some land that I own into the company's name, and that will beef up our balance sheet. Rob, can you shave $500,000 from expenses? Then we can probably get the bank loan that we need."

Rob Samuels, company chief accountant: "Sue, you are asking too much. Generally accepted accounting principles are designed to keep this sort of thing from happening."

Required

1. What is the fundamental ethical issue in this situation?
2. Discuss how Cloutier's proposals violate generally accepted accounting principles. Identify the specific concept(s) or principle(s) involved.

PROBLEMS (GROUP A)   MyAccountingLab

Problem 1–1A

Tanner Glass had been operating his law practice in Mississauga under the name Tanner Glass, Lawyer, for two years and had the following business assets and liabilities (at their historical costs) on April 30, 2016:

Accounting concepts/principles

Cash	$45,000
Accounts Receivable	30,000
Supplies	2,000
Furniture and Computers	75,000
Accounts Payable	20,000

The following business transactions took place during the month of May 2016:

May 1   Glass deposited $30,000 cash into the business bank account.

      3   Glass completed legal work for a home builder. He charged the builder $5,000, not the $6,000 the work was worth, in order to promote business from the builder.

      5   The business bought furniture from Ajax Furniture for $8,000, paying $2,000 cash and promising to pay $1,000 per month at the beginning of each month starting June 1, 2016, for six months. Glass would like to expense the entire amount to reduce net income for tax reasons.

   10   The company signed a lease to rent additional space at a cost of $2,000 per month. Glass will occupy the premises effective June 1, 2016.

   18   Determining that the business would need more cash in June, Glass went to the bank and borrowed $20,000 on a personal loan and transferred the money to the company.

   25   Glass purchased a painting for his home from one of his clients. He paid for the $3,000 purchase with his personal credit card.

   28   Glass withdrew $5,000 from the business. He used $2,000 of the money to repay a portion of the loan arranged on May 18.

   31   The business did legal work with a value of $10,000 for Apex Computers Ltd. Apex paid for the work by giving the company computer equipment with a selling price of $12,000.

Required   Identify the accounting characteristic, assumption, or principle that would be applicable to each of the transactions and discuss the effects it would have on the transactions of Tanner Glass, Lawyer.

Entity concept, transaction
analysis, accounting equation

③ ④

2. Total assets, $61,000

Problem 1–2A

Jon Conlin was a lawyer and partner in a large firm, a partnership, for five years after graduating from university. Recently, he resigned his position to open his own legal practice, which he operates as a proprietorship. The name of the new company is Conlin & Associates.

Conlin recorded the following events during the organizing phase of his new business and its first month of operations. Some of the events were personal and did not affect the legal practice. Others were business transactions and should be accounted for by the business.

Jul.	4	Conlin received $100,000 cash from his former partners in the firm from which he resigned.
	5	Conlin invested $50,000 cash in his business, Conlin & Associates.
	5	The business paid office rent expense for the month of July, $3,000.
	6	The business paid $1,000 cash for letterhead stationery for the office.
	7	The business purchased office furniture on account for $7,000, promising to pay within six months.
	10	Conlin sold 2,000 shares of Royal Bank stock, which he had owned for several years, receiving $25,000 cash from his stockbroker.
	11	Conlin deposited the $25,000 cash from sale of the Royal Bank shares in his personal bank account.
	12	A representative of a large construction company telephoned Conlin and told him of the company's intention to transfer its legal business to Conlin & Associates.
	29	The business provided legal services for a client and submitted the bill for services, $10,000. The business expected to collect from this client within two weeks.
	31	Conlin withdrew $3,000 cash from the business.

Required

1. Classify each of the preceding events as one of the following (list each date, then choose a, b, or c):

   a. A business transaction to be accounted for by the business, Conlin & Associates.

   b. A business-related event but not a transaction to be accounted for by Conlin & Associates.

   c. A personal transaction not to be accounted for by Conlin & Associates.

2. Analyze the effects of the above events on the accounting equation of Conlin & Associates. Use a format similar to Exhibit 1–11, Panel B, on page 20.

Problem 1–3A

Business transactions and
analysis

④

Tisdale Suppliers was recently formed as a proprietorship. The balance of each item in the business's accounting equation is shown below for June 21 and for each of the nine following business days:

		Cash	Accounts Receivable	Supplies	Land	Accounts Payable	Owner's Equity
June	21	$19,000	$9,000	$3,000	$18,000	$9,000	$40,000
	22	26,000	9,000	3,000	18,000	9,000	47,000
	23	16,000	9,000	3,000	28,000	9,000	47,000
	24	16,000	9,000	7,000	28,000	13,000	47,000
	25	12,000	9,000	7,000	28,000	9,000	47,000
	26	15,000	6,000	7,000	28,000	9,000	47,000
	27	22,000	6,000	7,000	28,000	9,000	54,000
	28	17,000	6,000	7,000	28,000	4,000	54,000
	29	14,000	6,000	10,000	28,000	4,000	54,000
	30	4,000	6,000	10,000	28,000	4,000	44,000

Required Assuming that a single transaction took place on each day, describe briefly the transaction that was most likely to have occurred. Begin with June 22 and complete up to June 30. Indicate which accounts were affected and by what amount. No revenue or expense transactions occurred on these dates.

Problem 1–4A

Shawn Steele is a realtor. He buys and sells properties on his own, and he also earns commission revenue as a real estate agent. He organized his business as a sole proprietorship on November 15, 2016. Consider the following facts as of November 30, 2016:

a. The business owed $30,000 on a note payable for some undeveloped land. This land had been acquired by the business for a total price of $70,000.

b. Steele's business had spent $15,000 for a RE/MAX Ltd. real estate franchise, which entitled him to represent himself as a RE/MAX agent. RE/MAX is a national affiliation of independent real estate agents. This franchise is a business asset.

c. Steele owed $250,000 on a personal mortgage on his personal residence, which he acquired in 2001 for a total price of $500,000.

d. Steele had $25,000 in his personal bank account and $9,000 in his business bank account.

e. Steele owed $1,000 on a personal charge account with Hudson's Bay.

f. The business acquired business furniture for $9,000 on November 25. Of this amount, the company owed $3,000 on account at November 30.

g. The real estate office had $500 worth of office supplies on hand on November 30.

Balance sheet for a proprietorship, entity concept

Total assets, $103,500

Required

1. Steele is concerned about liability exposure. Which proprietorship feature, if any, limits his personal liability?

2. Identify the personal items given in the preceding facts that would not be reported in the financial records of the business.

3. Prepare the balance sheet of the real estate business of Shawn Steele, Realtor, at November 30, 2016.

Problem 1–5A

Presented below are the amounts of (a) the assets and liabilities of Canadian Gardening Consultants as of December 31, 2017, and (b) the revenues and expenses of the company for the year ended December 31, 2017. The items are listed in alphabetical order.

Excel Spreadsheet Template

Income statement, statement of owner's equity, balance sheet, evaluating business performance

1. Net income, $135,000

Accounts Payable	$ 57,000	Insurance Expense	$ 4,500
Accounts Receivable	36,000	Interest Expense	15,000
Advertising Expense	48,500	Land	37,500
Building	300,000	Note Payable	195,000
Cash	15,000	Salary Expense	240,000
Computer Equipment	165,000	Salary Payable	22,500
Courier Expense	7,000	Service Revenue	450,000
Furniture	45,000	Supplies	7,500

The opening balance of owner's equity was $300,000. At year end, after the calculation of net income, the owner, Jin Wu, withdrew $103,500.

Required

1. Prepare the business's income statement for the year ended December 31, 2017.

2. Prepare the statement of owner's equity of the business for the year ended December 31, 2017.

3. Prepare the balance sheet of the business at December 31, 2017.

4. Answer these questions about the business:

a. Was the result of operations for the year a profit or a loss? How much was it?

b. Did the business's owner's equity increase or decrease during the year? How would this affect the business's ability to borrow money from a bank in the future?

c. How much in total economic resources does the business have at December 31, 2017, as it moves into the new year? How much does the business owe? What is the dollar amount of the owner's portion of the business at December 31, 2017?

Problem 1–6A

The bookkeeper of Oliver Services Co., a proprietorship, prepared the balance sheet of the company while the accountant was ill. The balance sheet is not correct. The bookkeeper knew that the balance sheet should balance, so he "plugged in" the owner's equity amount needed to achieve this balance. The owner's equity amount, however, is not correct. All other amounts are accurate except the "Total assets" amount.

OLIVER SERVICES CO.				
Balance Sheet				
For the Month Ended July 31, 2016				
Assets		**Liabilities**		
Cash	$ 70,000	Service revenue		$220,000
Office supplies	5,000	Note payable		55,000
Land	130,000	Accounts payable		45,000
Advertising expense	10,000			
Office furniture	50,000			
Accounts receivable	75,000	**Owner's Equity**		
Rent expense	22,000	J. Enderby, capital		42,000
Total assets	$362,000	Total liabilities and owner's equity		$362,000

Required

1. Prepare the corrected balance sheet, and date it correctly. Compute total assets, total liabilities, and owner's equity.

2. Consider the original balance sheet as presented and the corrected balance sheet you prepared for Requirement 1. Did the total assets presented in your corrected balance sheet increase, decrease, or stay the same compared to the original balance sheet? Why?

Problem 1–7A

Mary Reaney is the proprietor of a career counselling and employee search business, Reaney Personnel Services. The following amounts summarize the financial position of the business on August 31, 2017:

		Assets			=	Liabilities	+	Owner's Equity
	Cash +	Accounts Receivable +	Supplies +	Furniture and Computers =		Accounts Payable +		M. Reaney, Capital
Bal.	40,000	35,000		95,000		55,000		115,000

During September 2017 the following company transactions occurred:

a. Reaney deposited $80,000 cash in the business bank account.

b. Performed services for a client and received cash of $5,000.

c. Paid off the August 31 balance of accounts payable.

d. Purchased supplies on account, $6,000.

e. Collected cash from a customer on account, $7,500.

f. Consulted on a large downsizing by a major corporation and billed the client for services rendered, $48,000.

g. Recorded the following business expenses for the month:
   (1) Paid office rent for September 2017—$5,000.
   (2) Paid advertising—$3,000.

h. Sold supplies to another business for $1,000 cash, which was the cost of the supplies.

i. Reaney withdrew $8,000 cash.

Required

1. Analyze the effects of the above transactions on the accounting equation of Reaney Personnel Services. Adapt the format of Exhibit 1–11, Panel B, on page 20.

2. Prepare the income statement of Reaney Personnel Services for the month ended September 30, 2017. List expenses in decreasing order of amount.

3. Prepare the business's statement of owner's equity for the month ended September 30, 2017.

4. Prepare the balance sheet of Reaney Personnel Services at September 30, 2017.

Problem 1–8A

Terrace Board Rentals was started on January 1, 2016, by Ryan Terrace with an investment of $50,000 cash. The company rents out snowboards and related gear from a small store. During the first 11 months, Terrace made additional investments of $20,000 and borrowed $40,000 from the bank. He did not withdraw any funds. The balance sheet accounts, excluding Terrace's capital account, at November 30, 2016, are as follows:

Transaction analysis, accounting equation, financial statements, evaluation

3. Net income, $54,000

Cash..	$45,000
Accounts Receivable......................................	15,000
Rental Gear..	32,000
Rental Snowboards..	48,000
Store Equipment...	30,000
Accounts Payable..	12,000
Note Payable..	40,000

The following transactions took place during the month of December 2016:

Dec. 1   The business paid $5,000 for the month's rent on the store space.

4   The business signed a one-year lease for the rental of additional store space at a cost of $4,000 per month. The lease is effective January 1. The business will pay the first month's rent in January.

6   Rental revenues for the week were Gear, $4,000; Boards, $10,000. Three-quarters of the fees were paid in cash and the rest on account.

10   The business paid the accounts payable from November 30, 2016.

12   The business purchased gear for $20,000 and boards for $40,000, all on account.

13   Rental revenues for the week were Gear, $7,000; Boards, $14,000. All the fees were paid in cash.

15   The company received payment for the accounts receivable owing at November 30, 2016.

18   The company purchased store equipment for $10,000 by paying $3,000 cash with the balance due in 60 days.

20   Rental revenues for the week were Gear, $8,000; Boards, $14,000. Half the fees were paid in cash and half on account.

21   Terrace withdrew $7,000.

24   The company paid the balance owing for the purchases made on December 12.

27   Rental revenues for the week were Gear, $6,000; Boards, $10,000. All the fees were paid in cash.

27   The company received payment for rental fees on account from December 6.

31   The company paid its employees for the month of December. The total wages expense was $10,000.

31   Terrace paid the utility bill for the month of December, which was $4,000.

Required

1. What is the total net income earned by the business over the period of January 1, 2016, to November 30, 2016?

2. Analyze the effects of the December 2016 transactions on the accounting equation of Terrace Board Rentals. Include the account balances from November 30, 2016.

3. Prepare the income statement for Terrace Board Rentals for the month ended December 31, 2016.

4. Prepare the statement of owner's equity for Terrace Board Rentals for the month ended December 31, 2016.

5. Prepare the balance sheet for Terrace Board Rentals at December 31, 2016.

6. Terrace has expressed concern that although the business seems to be profitable and growing, he constantly seems to be investing additional money into it. Prepare a reply to his concerns.

PROBLEMS (GROUP B)   MyAccountingLab

Problem 1–1B

Accounting concepts/principles ③

John Chang has been operating a plumbing business as a proprietorship (John Chang Plumbing) for four years and had the following business assets and liabilities (at their historical costs) on May 31, 2016:

Cash..	$60,000
Accounts Receivable....................................	30,000
Shop Supplies	10,000
Shop Equipment...	80,000
Accounts Payable..	33,000

The following events took place during the month of June 2016:

Jun. 1   John's brother retired and sold his equipment to John for $30,000. The equipment had cost $50,000 and had a replacement cost of $38,000.

3   The business did some plumbing repairs for a customer. The business would normally have charged $1,500 for the work, but had agreed to do it for $1,000 cash in order to encourage more business from the customer.

10   The business signed a lease to rent additional shop space for the business at a cost of $3,000 per month. The business will occupy the premises effective July 1, 2016.

18   Finding he was low on cash, John went to the bank and borrowed $8,000 on a personal loan.

22   The value of John's equipment has doubled. John does not understand why accountants ignore the effect of inflation in the accounting records.

28   John withdrew $12,000 from the business and used $7,000 to repay the personal bank loan of June 18.

Required Identify the accounting assumption, principle, or characteristic that would be applicable to each of the events, and discuss the effects it would have on the transactions of John Chang Plumbing.

Problem 1–2B

Entity concept, transaction analysis, accounting equation ③ ④

Linda Horowitz is an architect and was a partner with a large firm, a partnership, for 10 years after graduating from university. Recently she resigned her position to open her own architecture office, which she operates as a proprietorship. The name of the new entity is Horowitz Design.

Horowitz recorded the following events during the organizing phase of her new business and its first month of operations. Some of the events were personal and did not affect the practice of architecture. Others were business transactions and should be accounted for by the business.

Jul. 1   Horowitz sold 1,000 shares of Canadian Tire stock, which she had owned for several years, receiving $60,000 cash from her stockbroker.

2   Horowitz deposited the $60,000 cash from the sale of the Canadian Tire shares into her personal bank account.

3   Horowitz received $100,000 cash from her former partners in the architecture firm from which she resigned.

5   Horowitz deposited $80,000 into a bank account in the name of Horowitz Design.

5	Horowitz Design paid office rent for the month of July, $4,000.
6	A representative of a large real estate company telephoned Linda Horowitz and told her of the company's intention to transfer its design business to her business, Horowitz Design.
7	Horowitz Design paid $3,000 cash for office supplies, including letterhead and stationery.
9	Horowitz Design purchased office furniture on account for $10,000, promising to pay in three months.
23	Horowitz Design finished design work for a client and submitted the bill for design services, $12,000. It expects to collect from this client within one month.
31	Horowitz withdrew $5,000 for personal use.

Required

1. Classify each of the preceding events as one of the following (list each date and then choose a, b, or c):
   a. A business transaction to be accounted for by the business, Horowitz Design.
   b. A business-related event but not a transaction to be accounted for by Horowitz Design.
   c. A personal transaction not to be accounted for by Horowitz Design.

2. Analyze the effects of the above events on the accounting equation of Horowitz Design. Use a format similar to Exhibit 1–11, Panel B, on page 20.

Problem 1–3B

Recently, Kate Cameron formed a management accounting practice as a proprietorship. The balance of each item in the proprietorship accounting equation follows for November 16 and for each of the eight following business days:

Business transactions and analysis

	Cash	Accounts Receivable	Office Supplies	Furniture	Accounts Payable	Owner's Equity
Nov. 16	$6,000	$10,000	$ 1,000	$8,000	$6,000	$19,000
17	7,000	9,000	1,000	8,000	6,000	19,000
18	6,000	9,000	1,000	8,000	5,000	19,000
19	6,000	9,000	1,500	8,000	5,500	19,000
20	8,000	9,000	1,500	8,000	5,500	21,000
23	7,000	9,000	1,500	8,000	4,500	21,000
24	9,000	9,000	1,500	6,000	4,500	21,000
25	8,500	9,000	2,000	6,000	4,500	21,000
26	7,500	9,000	2,000	6,000	4,500	20,000

Required Assuming that a single transaction took place on each day, describe briefly the transaction that was most likely to have occurred. Begin with November 17 and complete up to November 26. Indicate which accounts were affected and by what amount. Assume that no revenue or expense transactions occurred on these dates.

Problem 1–4B

Lupita Goodwin is a realtor. She buys and sells properties on her own, and she also earns commission revenue as a real estate agent. She invested $70,000 on March 10, 2017, in the business, Lupita Goodwin Realty. Consider the following facts as of March 31, 2017:

Balance sheet, entity concept

a. Goodwin had $10,000 in her personal bank account and $90,000 in the business bank account.

b. The real estate office had $6,000 of office supplies on hand on March 31, 2017.

c. Lupita Goodwin Realty had spent $25,000 for a Royal LePage franchise, which entitled the company to represent itself as a Royal LePage member firm. This franchise is a business asset.

d. The company owed $130,000 on a note payable for some undeveloped land that had been acquired by the company for a total price of $165,000.

e. Goodwin owed $185,000 on a personal mortgage on her personal residence, which she acquired in 2001 for a total price of $320,000.

f. Goodwin owed $2,000 on a personal charge account with Sears.

g. The company acquired business furniture for $18,000 on March 26. Of this amount, Lupita Goodwin Realty owed $14,000 on account at March 31, 2017.

Required

1. Goodwin is concerned about liability exposure. Which proprietorship feature, if any, limits her personal liability?

2. Identify the personal items given in the preceding facts that would not be reported on the balance sheet of the business.

3. Prepare the balance sheet of the real estate business of Lupita Goodwin Realty at March 31, 2017.

Excel Spreadsheet Template

Income statement, statement of owner's equity, balance sheet

⑤

Problem 1–5B

The amounts of (a) the assets and liabilities of Harada Office Cleaning as of December 31, 2017, and (b) the revenues and expenses of the company for the year ended on December 31, 2017, appear below. The items are listed in alphabetical order.

Accounts Payable	$ 40,000		Land	$100,000
Accounts Receivable	50,000		Notes Payable	200,000
Building	350,000		Property Tax Expense	10,000
Cash	25,000		Repairs Expense	30,000
Equipment	110,000		Salary Expense	280,000
Furniture	18,000		Service Revenue	650,000
Interest Expense	14,000		Supplies	10,000
Interest Payable	3,000		Utilities Expense	25,000

The beginning amount of owner's equity was $200,000. During the year, the owner, Yoshi Harada, withdrew $71,000.

Required

1. Prepare the income statement of Harada Office Cleaning for the year ended December 31, 2017.

2. Prepare the statement of owner's equity of the business for the year ended December 31, 2017.

3. Prepare the balance sheet of the business at December 31, 2017.

4. Answer these questions about Harada Office Cleaning:

   a. Was the result of operations for the year a profit or a loss? How much was it?

   b. Did the business's owner's equity increase or decrease during the year? How would this affect the business's ability to borrow money from a bank in the future?

   c. How much in total economic resources does the company have at December 31, 2017, as it moves into the new year? How much does the company owe? What is the dollar amount of the owner's portion of the business at December 31, 2017?

Problem 1–6B

Correcting a balance sheet

⑤

The bookkeeper of McBride Insurance Agency prepared the balance sheet of the company while the accountant was ill. The balance sheet contains errors. In particular, the bookkeeper knew that the balance sheet should balance, so she "plugged in" the owner's equity amount needed to achieve this balance. The owner's equity amount, however, is not correct. All other amounts are accurate except the "Total assets" amount.

McBRIDE INSURANCE AGENCY
Balance Sheet
For the Month Ended October 31, 2016

Assets		Liabilities	
Cash	$ 24,000	Premium revenue	$ 53,000
Insurance expense	2,000	Accounts payable	23,000
Rent expense	6,000	Note payable	40,000
Salary expense	8,000		
Office furniture	20,000		
Accounts receivable	22,000	**Owner's Equity**	
Utilities expense	2,000	C. McBride, capital	(8,000)
Notes receivable	24,000		
Total assets	$108,000	Total liabilities and owner's equity	$108,000

Required

1. Prepare the corrected balance sheet, and date it correctly. Compute total assets, total liabilities, and owner's equity.
2. Identify the accounts listed above that should *not* be presented on the balance sheet and state why you excluded them from the corrected balance sheet you prepared for Requirement 1.

Problem 1-7B

Miranda Sykes operates an interior design studio called Sykes Design Studio. The following amounts summarize the financial position of the business on April 30, 2017:

Transaction analysis, accounting equation, financial statements

④ ⑤

		Assets					=	Liabilities	+	Owner's Equity
Cash	+	Accounts Receivable	+	Supplies	+	Land	=	Accounts Payable	+	M. Sykes, Capital
Bal. 27,000		26,000				102,000		33,000		122,000

During May 2017, the company did the following:

a. Sykes received $20,000 as a gift and deposited the cash in the business bank account.
b. Paid the beginning balance of accounts payable.
c. Performed services for a client and received cash of $5,000.
d. Collected cash from a customer on account, $4.000.
e. Purchased supplies on account, $3,000.
f. Consulted on the interior design of a major office building and billed the client for services rendered, $16,000.
g. Recorded the following business expenses for the month:
   (1) Paid office rent for May 2017—$6,000.
   (2) Paid advertising—$4,000.
h. Sold supplies to another interior designer for $1,000 cash, which was the cost of the supplies.
i. Sykes withdrew $7,000 cash for personal use.

Required

1. Analyze the effects of the above transactions on the accounting equation of Sykes Design Studio. Adapt the format of Exhibit 1–11, Panel B, on page 20.

2. Prepare the income statement of Sykes Design Studio for the month ended May 31, 2017. List expenses in decreasing order of amount.

3. Prepare the statement of owner's equity of Sykes Design Studio for the month ended May 31, 2017.

4. Prepare the balance sheet of Sykes Design Studio at May 31, 2017.

Problem 1–8B

Transaction analysis, accounting equation, financial statements, evaluation

④ ⑤

Wilson Marketing Consulting, a proprietorship owned by Lin Wilson, was started on January 1, 2016, with an investment of $50,000 cash. The company prepares marketing plans for clients. It has been operating for one year. Business was quite slow in the first year of operations but has steadily increased. Wilson has made additional investments of $30,000 but has not made any withdrawals. The general ledger showed the following balances as of December 31, 2016:

Cash	$ 25,000
Accounts Receivable	30,000
Software	21,000
Office Furniture	15,000
Computer Equipment	32,000
Accounts Payable	18,000
L. Wilson, Capital	105,000

The following transactions took place during the month of January 2017:

Jan.	2	Wilson invested $20,000 in the business.
	2	The business paid $4,000 for the month's rent on the office space.
	4	The business signed a lease for the rental of additional office space at a cost of $3,500 per month. The lease is effective February 1. The business will pay the first month's rent in February.
	6	The business developed a marketing plan for Banting Ltd. and received $10,000 now plus additional $7,000 payments to be received on the 15th of the month for the next three months.
	10	The business paid $1,000 to a courier service.
	12	Wilson signed an agreement to provide a marketing plan to Smith Inc. for $15,000 to be paid upon completion of the work.
	14	The company purchased $5,000 of software that will be required for the Smith assignment. The company paid $3,000 and promised to pay the balance by the end of the month.
	15	The company received $7,000 as the monthly payment from Banting Ltd. from January 6.
	18	The company purchased computer equipment for $10,000 by paying $4,000 cash with the balance due in 60 days.
	23	The company completed a marketing plan for Salem Ltd., which promised to pay $12,000 by the end of the month.
	29	The company paid the balance owing for the software purchased on January 14.
	31	Employees of Wilson Marketing Consulting are paid at the end of each month. The total wages expense for January was $10,000.
	31	Wilson Marketing Consulting paid the utilities expense for January, $1,000.
	31	Lin Wilson withdrew $5,000 for personal use.

Required

1. What is the total net income earned by the business over the period of January 1, 2016, to December 31, 2016?

2. Analyze the effects of the January 2017 transactions on the accounting equation of Wilson Marketing Consulting. Be sure to include the account balances from December 31, 2016.

3. Prepare the income statement for Wilson Marketing Consulting for the month ended January 31, 2017.

4. Prepare the statement of owner's equity for Wilson Marketing Consulting for the month ended January 31, 2017.

5. Prepare the balance sheet for Wilson Marketing Consulting at January 31, 2017.

6. Lin Wilson has expressed concern that although the business seems to be profitable and growing, she constantly seems to be investing additional money into it and has been unable to make many withdrawals for the work she has put into it. Prepare a reply to her concerns.

CHALLENGE PROBLEMS

Problem 1–1C

The going concern assumption is becoming an increasing source of concern for users of financial statements. There are instances of companies filing for bankruptcy several months after issuing their annual audited financial statements. The question is, Why didn't the financial statements predict the problem?

Understanding the going concern assumption
(3)

A friend has just arrived on your doorstep; you realize she is very angry. After calming her down, you ask what the problem is. She tells you that she had inherited $40,000 from an uncle and invested the money in the common shares of Outdoor Sports Equipment Corp. (OSEC). She had carefully examined OSEC's financial statements for the latest year end and had concluded that the company was financially sound. This morning, she had read in the local paper that the company had gone bankrupt and her investment was worthless. She asks you why the financial statements valued the assets at values that are in excess of those the trustee in bankruptcy expects to realize from liquidating the assets. Why have the assets suddenly lost so much of the value they had six months ago?

Required Explain to your friend why assets are valued on a going concern basis in the financial statements and why they are usually worth less when the company goes out of business. Use inventory and accounts receivable as examples.

Problem 1–2C

You and three friends have decided to go into the landscape business for the summer to earn money to pay for your schooling in the fall. Your first step was to sign up customers to satisfy yourselves that the business had the potential to be profitable. Next, you planned to go to the bank to borrow money to buy the equipment you would need.

Accounting for business transactions

After considerable effort, your group obtained contracts from customers for 200 residences for the summer. One of your partners wants to prepare a balance sheet showing the value of the contracts as an asset. She is sure that you will have no trouble with borrowing the necessary funds from the bank on the basis of the proposed balance sheet.

Required Explain to your friend why the commitments (signed contracts) from customers cannot be recognized as assets. What suggestions do you have that might assist your group in borrowing the necessary funds?

EXTENDING YOUR KNOWLEDGE

DECISION PROBLEMS

Decision Problem 1

Using financial statements to
evaluate a request for a loan
① ⑤

Two businesses, Tyler's Bicycle Centre and Ryan's Catering, have sought business loans
from you. To decide whether to make the loans, you have requested their balance sheets.

For a business like Tyler's Bicycle
Centre, "Inventory" is the cost of
the bicycles and accessories the
business has available to sell to
customers.

TYLER'S BICYCLE CENTRE			
Balance Sheet			
December 31, 2016			
Assets		**Liabilities**	
Cash	$ 27,000	Accounts payable	$ 36,000
Accounts receivable	42,000	Notes payable	354,000
Inventory	55,000	Total liabilities	390,000
Store supplies	2,000		
Furniture and fixtures	26,000	**Owner's Equity**	
Building	246,000	T. Jones, capital	230,000
Land	222,000		
Total assets	$620,000	Total liabilities and owner's equity	$620,000

RYAN'S CATERING			
Balance Sheet			
December 31, 2016			
Assets		**Liabilities**	
Cash	$ 30,000	Accounts payable	$ 9,000
Accounts receivable	12,000	Note payable	204,000
Office supplies	6,000	Total liabilities	213,000
Inventory	60,000		
Office furniture	15,000	**Owner's Equity**	
Investments*	600,000	R. Smith, capital	510,000
Total assets	$723,000	Total liabilities and owner's equity	$723,000

*The investments of $600,000 can be sold today for $750,000.

Required

1. Based solely on these balance sheets, which entity would you be more comfortable lending money to? Explain fully, citing specific items and amounts from the balance sheets.
2. In addition to the balance sheet data, what other financial statement information would
   you require? Be specific.

Decision Problem 2

A friend learns that you are taking an accounting course. Knowing that you do not plan a career in accounting, the friend asks why you are "wasting your time." Explain to the friend:

Using accounting information
① ④ ⑤

1. Why you are taking the course.

2. How accounting information is used or will be used:

   a. In your personal life.

   b. In the business life of your friend, who plans to be a farmer.

   c. In the business life of another friend, who plans a career in sales.

FINANCIAL STATEMENT CASES

These and similar cases in later chapters focus on the financial statements of two real Canadian companies—Indigo Books & Music Inc. (Indigo) and TELUS Corporation (TELUS).

Indigo is a Canadian retail bookstore chain. It sells books, music, and gifts both online and in stores. It owns Chapters and Coles as well as a number of other smaller bookstores.

Vancouver-based TELUS Corporation is a national telecommunications company that many people recognize as a wireless communications provider from their friendly and colourful advertising campaigns featuring animals and nature. They also operate a broad variety of services to both consumers and businesses for Internet, data, television, entertainment, and other services.

Using these two companies, you will gradually build the confidence to understand and use financial statements of large corporations in addition to the smaller businesses we look at throughout the textbook.

Financial Statement Case 1

Refer to the Indigo financial statements located in Appendix A at the end of this book and on MyAccountingLab. Notice that all amounts are reported in thousands of Canadian dollars. Also, Indigo has a 52-week fiscal year, so its fiscal year end changes from year to year. In these statements, the year end was March 29 in 2014 and March 30 in 2013.

Identifying items from a company's financial statements
④ ⑤
5. March 29, 2014, net loss of $30,999,000

Required

1. How much accounts receivable did Indigo have at March 29, 2014?

2. What were total assets at March 29, 2014? At March 30, 2013?

3. Write the company's accounting equation at March 29, 2014, by filling in the dollar amounts:

$$\boxed{\text{Assets} = \text{Liabilities} + \text{Equity}}$$

REAL WORLD EXAMPLE

Most companies' financial statements are stated at a month end, but many retail and merchandising companies (companies that sell products rather than services) choose to use a 52-week year instead.

4. Identify total revenue for the year ended March 29, 2014. Indigo presents this information on a "Consolidated Statements of Earnings" report rather than calling it an income statement. What was the revenue for the year ended March 30, 2013? Did revenue increase or decrease during fiscal 2014?

5. How much net income or net loss did Indigo experience for the 52-week period ended March 29, 2014? Was 2014 a good year or bad year compared to 2013?

Financial Statement Case 2

Refer to the TELUS Corporation financial statements located on MyAccountingLab. TELUS calls their balance sheet a "Consolidated Statement of Financial Position" and their income statement is called a "Consolidated Statement of Income."

Identifying items from a company's financial statements
④ ⑤
5. Dec. 31, 2013, net income, $1,294,000,000

Required

1. How much accounts receivable did TELUS have at December 31, 2013?

2. What were total assets at December 31, 2013? At December 31, 2012? Note: There is no title for this amount, but there is a total on the statement.

3. Write the company's accounting equation at December 31, 2013, by filling in the dollar amounts:

> **Assets = Liabilities + Owners' Equity**

4. Identify total operating revenues for the year ended December 31, 2013, and the year ended December 31, 2012. Did revenue increase or decrease during 2013?

5. How much net income or net loss did TELUS experience for the year ended December 31, 2013? Was 2013 a good year or bad year compared to 2012?

IFRS MINI-CASE

IFRS Mini-Cases appear in selected chapters and highlight the similarities and differences between ASPE and IFRS.

Lisa Hunter has been in business for two years and her company, Hunter Environmental Consulting (HEC), has been very successful. Lisa would like to expand the business by opening offices in central and eastern Canada, and eventually in the United States. However, Lisa realizes these plans require more money than she can borrow from a bank. One option she is considering is to make Hunter Environmental Consulting a corporation so she can list the company on a stock exchange and sell shares in the company to the general public. Lisa knows you are studying accounting and asks you whether HEC has to change the way it is reporting—HEC reports under ASPE currently—if HEC becomes a publicly traded company. Answer Lisa's question and explain why there are two sets of reporting standards in Canada.

>Try It! SOLUTIONS FOR CHAPTER 1

1. internal = b, c; external = a, d, e
2.

	Proprietorship	Partnership	Corporation
a.			X
b.		X	
c.		X	
d.	X		
e.			X

3. The measurement criteria in Exhibit 1–5 tell us that the cost principle of measurement should be used. This transaction would be recognized at the amount of cash paid for the building. You paid $185,000 for the building. Therefore, $185,000 is the cost to report on your financial statements.
4. If the car is not going to be used for business purposes, the car should be the personal responsibility of the owner. The economic entity assumption means that the assets of the business should not be mixed with the assets of the owner to ensure that the results of the business can be identified and analyzed accurately.

5. To answer both questions, use the accounting equation:

   a. **Assets − Liabilities = Owner's Equity**
      $75,000 − $65,000 = $10,000

   b. **Assets = Liabilities + Owner's Equity**
      $70,000 = $20,000 + $50,000

6.

Accounts Receivable	A
Computer Equipment	A
S. Scott, Capital	OE
Rent Expense	E
Supplies	A
S. Scott, Withdrawals	OE
Salary Expense	E
Consulting Service Revenue	R
Cash	A
Notes Payable	L
Supplies Expense	E
Accounts Payable	L

7.

	Assets						Liabilities		Owner's Equity	Explanation
	Cash	+	Accounts Receivable	+	Equipment	=	Accounts Payable	+	E. Lawlor, Capital	
May 1	1,700								1,700	Owner investment
May 3					+1,440		+1,440			
May 5			+200						+200	Service revenue
May 17	−60								−60	Gas expense
May 28	−300								−300	Owner's withdrawal
Bal.	1,340		200		1,440		1,440		1,540	
			2,980						2,980	

8.

Accounts Receivable	B
Computer Equipment	B
S. Scott, Capital	B, OE
Rent Expense	I
Supplies	B
S. Scott, Withdrawals	OE
Salary Expense	I
Consulting Service Revenue	I
Cash	B, CF
Notes Payable	B
Supplies Expense	I
Accounts Payable	B

DR PAINTING
Statement of Owner's Equity
For the month ended March 31, 2017

D. Richardson, capital, March 1, 2017	$ 0
Add: Investments	40,000
Net Income	6,000
Less: Withdrawals	(1,500)
D. Richardson, capital, March 31, 2017	$44,500

DR PAINTING
Balance Sheet
March 31, 2017

Assets		Liabilities	
Cash	$22,300	Accounts payable	$ 1,000
Accounts receivable	1,400		
Office supplies	1,800	**Owner's equity**	
Land	20,000	D. Richardson, capital	44,500
Total assets	$45,500	Total liabilities and owner's equity	$45,500

9.

DR PAINTING
Income Statement
For the month ended March 31, 2017

Service revenue		$7,000
Expenses		
Salaries expense	$800	
Utilities expense	200	
Total expenses		1,000
Net income		$6,000

2 RECORDING BUSINESS TRANSACTIONS

CONNECTING CHAPTER 2

MyAccountingLab   The **Summary** for Chapter 2 appears on page 86. This lists all of the MyAccountingLab resources. **Accounting Vocabulary** with definitions for this chapter's material appears on page 87.

A car dealership can be found in almost every town. Some are owned by local businesspeople while others are owned by larger corporations with owners in towns far away. Guelph Toyota is a prime example of a small business that has grown to be a large company. It started in 1983 and is now owned by Barry Dohms. He bought the business in 2005 and also owns three other dealerships.

Guelph Toyota uses financial information to make its business decisions. Its owners and managers rely on the accounting system to provide them with daily and monthly financial statements to run their business. Are the managers accountants? No! They are smart businesspeople who know that they need to understand the daily and monthly revenues and expenses so that the business can survive in the short term and grow in the long term. Guelph Toyota has been around for over 30 years, so it must be doing something right!

The accounting department must provide timely information for decision making by recording transactions as they occur. Most businesses prepare financial reports on a monthly basis. Managers in this dealership get daily financial reports. The managers read them, see how their department is doing, and make changes immediately—reducing expenses and identifying opportunities—based on the statements. The result? Guelph Toyota is profitable. The company's profits are used not only to expand the business, but also to support worthwhile community programs and events. Guelph Toyota and its partners, Kiwanis Club of Guelph and Co-operators Insurance, sponsor the Guelph Police Department's VIP Program, which teaches youth about a number of personal safety issues.

This chapter shows how Guelph Toyota and other companies record their business transactions. The procedures outlined in this chapter are followed by entities ranging from giant multinational corporations like Ford Canada, to regional businesses such as Guelph Toyota, to local owner-managed businesses like Hunter Environmental Consulting.

> Chapter 1

introduced transaction analysis and the financial statements by using a table based on the accounting equation to list all of the transactions. This method of tracking account balances was useful to show how accounts and statements connect, but there are too many transactions in a typical business to record information this way. In this chapter we will look at the way bookkeeping is done in the real world. First we look at the entire process and then we will go back and do it step by step.

THE ACCOUNTING CYCLE

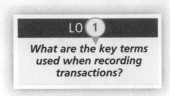

LO 1

What are the key terms used when recording transactions?

The **accounting cycle** is the formal process by which companies produce their financial statements and update their financial records for a specific period of time. Exhibit 2–1 outlines the complete accounting cycle. In this chapter, we will look at steps 1 through 4, which represent what is done *during* the **accounting period**. The next two chapters will introduce the last steps in the cycle, which are done *at the end* of the period.

EXHIBIT 2–1 | The Accounting Cycle

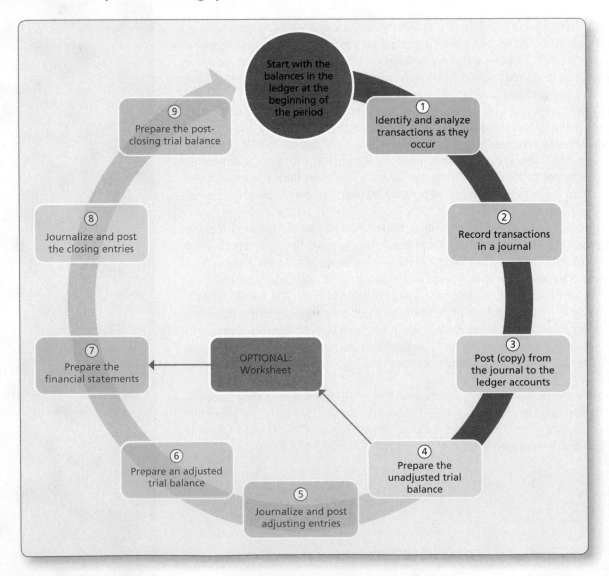

START Recall that the basic summary device of accounting is the account, which is the detailed record of the changes that have occurred in a particular asset, liability, or item of owner's equity during a period of time. Business transactions cause these changes.

For a new business, the cycle begins with setting up (opening) the ledger accounts. Lisa Hunter started Hunter Environmental Consulting (HEC) on April 2, 2016, so the first step in the cycle was to plan and open the accounts.

Account balances carry over from period to period until the accounting cycle is complete, for example, at the end of one year. Therefore, the accounting cycle usually starts with the account balances at the beginning of the period.

1 Our first step is to analyze the transaction to identify changes in accounts.

2 Accountants record transactions first in a **journal**, which is the chronological record of transactions.

3 Accountants then copy (post) the data to a record of all the accounts called the **ledger**. (One way to think of a ledger is as a binder, with each page in the binder representing one account.) In the phrase "keeping the books," *books* refers to the ledger. Exhibit 2–2 shows how asset, liability, and owner's equity accounts can be grouped into the ledger.

EXHIBIT 2–2 | The Ledger (Asset, Liability, and Owner's Equity Accounts)

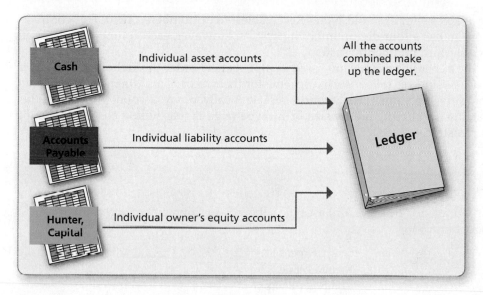

4 Then a list of all the ledger accounts and their balances is prepared. This is called a **trial balance**, or more precisely, an unadjusted trial balance at this stage.

CHART OF ACCOUNTS

Companies use a **chart of accounts** to list all their accounts. This is just a list and not a financial statement. In many cases, the account names are listed along with the account numbers. Account numbers are just shorthand versions of the account names. One number equals one account name—just like your social insurance number is unique to you. This numbering system makes it easy to locate individual accounts in the ledger and to key in entries in an accounting software program.

Accounts are identified by account numbers with two or more digits. Assets are often numbered beginning with 1, liabilities with 2, owner's equity with 3, revenues with 4, and expenses with 5. The second, third, and higher digits in an account number indicate the position of the individual account within the category.

The chart of accounts for Hunter Environmental Consulting appears in Exhibit 2–3. Notice the gap in account numbers between 1200 and 1400. Lisa Hunter realizes that at some later date the business may need to add another category of

LEARNING TIPS

It would be helpful to make your own list of accounts as you learn new account names.

EXHIBIT 2-3 | Chart of Accounts—Hunter Environmental Consulting

REAL WORLD EXAMPLE

Companies do not need to use the numbering system illustrated here. They can develop any system that makes sense to them. For example, a Ford dealership uses account 7630 for Parts Department Advertising Expense and a General Motors dealership uses account number 065-07 for the exact same expense.

Balance Sheet Accounts		
Assets	**Liabilities**	**Owner's Equity**
1100 Cash	2100 Accounts Payable	3000 Lisa Hunter, Capital
1200 Accounts Receivable	2300 Notes Payable	3100 Lisa Hunter, Withdrawals
1400 Office Supplies		
1500 Furniture		
1900 Land		

Income Statement Accounts (part of Owner's Equity)	
Revenues	**Expenses**
4000 Service Revenue	5100 Rent Expense
	5200 Salaries Expense
	5300 Utilities Expense

receivables—for example, Notes Receivable—to be numbered 1210. This company chose to use a four-digit numbering system. However, each company chooses its own account numbering system.

The expense accounts are listed in alphabetical order throughout this chapter. Many businesses follow such a scheme for their records and financial statements. Computer programs list accounts alphabetically or by account number. Other systems of ordering are by size or by type (e.g., listing selling costs then listing administrative costs).

> Try It!

1. Indicate whether each account listed below is a(n) asset (A), liability (L), owner's equity (OE), revenue (R), or expense (E) account.

Salary Payable	_____	Salary Expense	_____
Land	_____	Rent Revenue	_____
L. Graham, Capital	_____	Computer Equipment	_____
Rent Expense	_____	Notes Payable	_____
Supplies	_____	Prepaid Rent	_____
Accounts Payable	_____	L. Graham, Withdrawals	_____

2. Create a chart of accounts by matching each of the following account names with an appropriate account number. Assume this company uses a system similar to that described in the chapter, with asset numbers beginning with 1 and expense numbers beginning with 5.

Accounts Payable	30200
Rent Expense	10100
Furniture and Fixtures	50600
Service Revenue	20100
L. Starks, Capital	40100
Accounts Receivable	10400
Cash	30100
Income Taxes Payable	20500
L. Starks, Withdrawals	10200

Solutions appear at the end of this chapter and on MyAccountingLab

DOUBLE-ENTRY ACCOUNTING

Accounting uses the *double-entry system*, which means that we record the dual, or two, effects of each transaction. As a result, *every transaction affects at least two accounts.*

Consider a cash purchase of supplies. What are the dual effects of this transaction? A cash purchase of supplies:

1. Increases supplies (the business *received* supplies)
2. Decreases cash (the business *gave* cash)

Similarly, a credit purchase of a truck (a purchase made with a bank loan):

1. Increases vehicles (the business *received* the truck)
2. Increases the bank loan payable (the business *gave* a promise to pay in the future)

The T-Account

The form of account used for most illustrations in this book is called the *T-account* because it takes the form of the capital letter "T."

The vertical line divides the account into its left and right sides, with the account title at the top. For example, the Cash account appears in the following T-account format:

Cash	
(Left side)	**(Right side)**
Debit	*Credit*

The left side of the account is called the **debit** side, and the right side is called the **credit** side.

Even though *left side* and *right side* may be more convenient, *debit* and *credit* are what they are called in a business environment.[1] Debit and credit are abbreviated as follows:

Dr = Debit	**Cr = Credit**

Increases and Decreases in the Accounts

The type of an account (asset, liability, owner's equity) determines how we record increases and decreases. For any given type of account, all increases are recorded on one side, and all decreases are recorded on the other side. Increases in *assets* are recorded in the left (debit) side of the account. Decreases in assets are recorded in the right (credit) side of the account. Conversely, increases in liabilities and owner's equity are recorded by *credits*. Decreases in liabilities and owner's equity

LO 2
How do we track changes in accounts?

One way to think about this is to remember the old adage... "you don't get something for nothing." In accounting, money does not just appear and goods are not received without payment. There are always at least two sides to each transaction.

KEY POINTS

A T-account is a quick way to show the effect of transactions on a particular account—a useful shortcut or tool used in accounting. T-accounts are *not* part of the formal accounting records.

Debits are not "good" or "bad." Neither are credits. Debits are not always increases and credits are not always decreases. Debit simply means left side, and credit means right side.

---

[1] The words *debit* and *credit* abbreviate the Latin terms *debitum* and *creditum*. Luca Pacioli, the Italian monk who wrote about accounting in the 15th century, used these terms.

are recorded by *debits*. These are the *rules of debit and credit* and can be summarized as follows:

Assets		Liabilities and Owner's Equity	
Increase = Debit	Decrease = Credit	Decrease = Debit	Increase = Credit

This pattern of recording debits and credits is based on the accounting equation:

> **ASSETS = LIABILITIES + OWNER'S EQUITY**
> **DEBITS = CREDITS**

Assets are on the opposite side of the accounting equation from liabilities and owner's equity. Therefore, increases and decreases in assets are recorded in the opposite manner from increases and decreases in liabilities and owner's equity. Liabilities and owner's equity are on the same side of the equal sign, so they are treated in the same way. Exhibit 2–4 shows the relationship between the accounting equation and the rules of debit and credit.

EXHIBIT 2–4 | The Accounting Equation and the Rules of Debit and Credit (The Effects of Debits and Credits on Assets, Liabilities, and Owner's Equity)

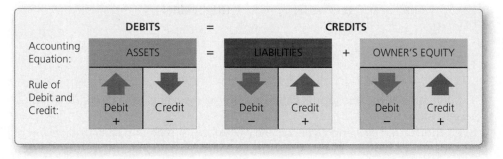

To demonstrate the rules shown in Exhibit 2–4, reconsider Transactions 1 and 2 from Chapter 1 on pages 15–16. In Transaction 1, Lisa Hunter invested $250,000 cash to begin her environmental consulting firm. The company received $250,000 cash from Hunter and gave her the owner's equity. We are accounting for the business entity, Hunter Environmental Consulting (HEC). What accounts of HEC are affected? By what amounts? On what side (debit or credit)? The answer is that assets and owner's equity would increase by $250,000, as the following T-accounts show:

ASSETS   = LIABILITIES + OWNER'S EQUITY

Cash		Lisa Hunter, Capital	
Debit for increase, 250,000			Credit for increase, 250,000

The amount remaining in an account is called its *balance*. Transaction 1 gives Cash a $250,000 debit balance and Lisa Hunter, Capital a $250,000 credit balance.

Transaction 2 is a $100,000 cash purchase of land. This transaction affects two assets: Cash and Land. It decreases (credits) Cash and increases (debits) Land, as shown in the T-accounts:

ASSETS = LIABILITIES + OWNER'S EQUITY

Cash		
Balance	250,000	Credit for decrease, 100,000
Balance	**150,000**	

Lisa Hunter, Capital	
Balance	250,000

Land	
Debit for increase, 100,000	
Balance	**100,000**	

After this transaction, Cash has a $150,000 debit balance ($250,000 debit balance from the previous transaction reduced by the $100,000 credit amount), Land has a debit balance of $100,000, and Lisa Hunter, Capital has a $250,000 credit balance, as shown in the section of Exhibit 2–5 labelled Transaction 2. Notice that the debits still equal the credits, but there are now two accounts on the left side.

EXHIBIT 2–5 | Debits and Credits for the First Two Transactions of Hunter Environmental Consulting

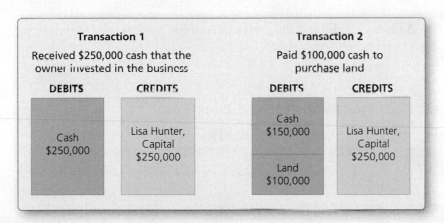

We create accounts as they are needed. The process of creating a new account in preparation for recording a transaction is called *opening the account*. For Transaction 1, we opened the Cash account and the Lisa Hunter, Capital account. For Transaction 2, we opened the Land account.

Expanding the Rules of Debit and Credit: Revenues and Expenses

Owner's equity includes revenues and expenses because revenues and expenses make up net income or net loss, which flows into owner's equity. As we discussed in Chapter 1, *revenues* are increases in owner's equity from providing goods and services to customers. *Expenses* are decreases in owner's equity from using assets or increasing liabilities in the course of operating the business. Therefore, we must expand the accounting equation as we did in Exhibit 1–10 (page 15). Exhibit 2–6 shows revenues and expenses under equity because they directly affect owner's equity.

EXHIBIT 2–6 | **Expanded Accounting Equation**

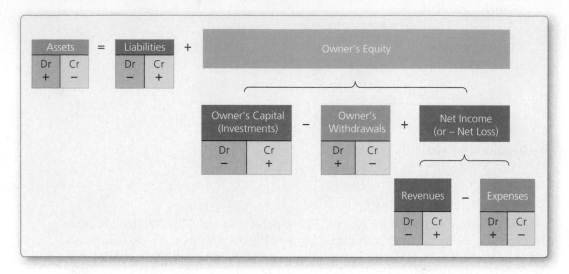

Normal Balance of an Account

An account's **normal balance** appears on the side of the account—debit or credit—where *increases* are recorded. For example, Cash and other assets usually have a debit balance, so the normal balance of assets is on the debit side. Conversely, liabilities and owner's equity usually have a credit balance, so their normal balances are on the credit side. Exhibit 2–7 illustrates the normal balances by highlighting the side where the balance is increased.

One way to memorize this is to use an acronym, such as AWE ROL. In this case, the (A)sset, (W)ithdrawal, and (E)xpense accounts all have debit balances, while the (R)evenue, (O)wner's Equity, and (L)iability accounts all have credit balances.

Or memorize which side has the "+" (increase), and then all the "–" (decreases) are the opposite. This way you only have to memorize half of them!

Try DR. AWE—the debits (dr) belong with the (A)sset, (W)ithdrawal, and (E)xpense accounts.

EXHIBIT 2–7 | **Final Rules of Debit and Credit**

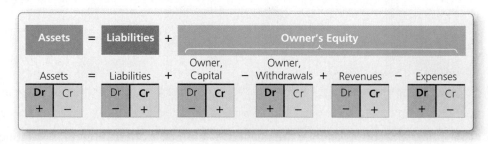

An account that normally has a debit balance may occasionally have a credit balance, which indicates a negative amount of the item. For example, Cash will have a credit balance if the entity **overdraws** its bank account. Similarly, the liability Accounts Payable—normally a credit balance account—will have a debit balance if the entity overpays its accounts payable. In other instances, the shift of a balance amount away from its normal column may indicate an accounting error. For example, a credit balance in Office Supplies, Furniture, or Buildings is an error because negative amounts of these assets cannot exist.

> Try It!

3. Indicate whether each account listed below is a(n) asset (A), liability (L), owner's equity (OE), revenue (R), or expense (E) account. Next to each answer, indicate whether the account's normal balance is a debit (Dr) or a credit (Cr).

Accounts Payable	___ ; ___	Cash	___ ; ___
Service Revenue	___ ; ___	Rent Expense	___ ; ___
K. Lockyer, Withdrawals	___ ; ___	Vehicles	___ ; ___
Rent Revenue	___ ; ___	Notes Payable	___ ; ___
Accounts Receivable	___ ; ___	Land	___ ; ___
Insurance Expense	___ ; ___	K. Lockyer, Capital	___ ; ___

4. a. Indicate on which side of these accounts—debit (Dr) or credit (Cr)—you would record an increase.

_____ Accounts Receivable	_____ Salary Expense
_____ John Ladner, Capital	_____ Interest Payable
_____ Service Revenue	_____ Furniture

b. Indicate on which side of these accounts—debit (Dr) or credit (Cr)—you would record a decrease.

_____ Notes Payable	_____ Land
_____ Cash	_____ Accounts Payable
_____ Income Tax Payable	_____ Income Tax Expense

Solutions appear at the end of this chapter and on MyAccountingLab

SOURCE DOCUMENTS—THE ORIGIN OF TRANSACTIONS

Accounting data come from **source documents**, which are the evidence of a transaction. For example, when Hunter Environmental Consulting (HEC) receives cash or a cheque, it deposits the money into its bank account. The **bank deposit slip** is the document that shows the amount of money received by the business and deposited in its bank account. Based on this document, the company can record this transaction in the accounting records.

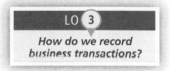

LO 3
How do we record business transactions?

Other source documents that businesses use include:

- **Purchase invoice**: A document that tells the business how much to pay and when to pay the vendor.
- **Bank cheque**: A document that tells the amount and the date of cash payments.
- **Sales invoice**: A document sent to the customer when a business sells goods or services and tells the business how much revenue to record.

RECORDING TRANSACTIONS IN THE JOURNAL

We could record all transactions directly in the ledger accounts, as we have shown for the first two HEC transactions. However, that way of accounting does not leave a clear record of each transaction. You may have to search through all the accounts to find both sides of a particular transaction. To stay organized and keep all information about a transaction in one place, accountants first keep a record of each transaction in a *journal*, the chronological (listed by date) record of the entity's transactions. They then transfer this information from the journal into the accounts.

The process for thinking through how to write a journal entry is as follows:

Transaction: Identify the transactions from source documents.

Analysis: Identify each account affected by the transaction and its type (asset, liability, owner's equity, revenue, or expense). Determine whether each account is increased or decreased by the transaction. Using the rules of debit and credit, determine whether to debit or credit the account to record its increase or decrease.

Accounting Equation: Verify that the increases and decreases result in an accounting equation that is still in balance.

Journal Entry: Record the transaction in the journal, as explained in Exhibit 2–8. Total debits must always equal total credits. This step is also called "making the journal entry" or "journalizing the transaction."

EXHIBIT 2–8 | The Journal

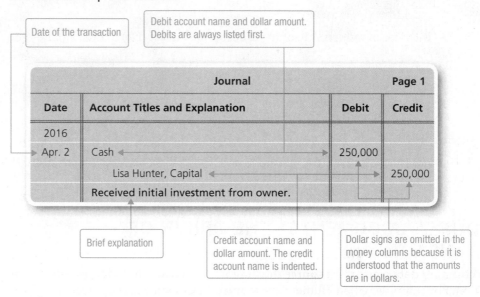

Regardless of the accounting system in use—computerized or manual—an accountant must analyze every business transaction in the manner we are presenting in these opening chapters. Accounting software performs the same actions as accountants do in a manual system. For example, when a sales clerk swipes your VISA card through the credit card reader, the accounting system records both the store's sales revenue and the receivable from VISA. The software automatically records the transaction as a journal entry, but an accountant had to program the computer to do so. A computer's ability to perform routine tasks and mathematical operations quickly and without error frees accountants for decision making.

MyAccountingLab

Video: Journalizing Transactions
Video: Operating Activities and Their Impact on the Accounting Equation
Video: Financing and Investing Activities and Their Impact on the Accounting Equation

> Try It!

5. For each of the following transactions, select the source document that provides the best evidence of the transaction. Choose from these source documents: bank deposit slip, bank cheque, invoice received from a vendor, or invoice sent to a customer.
   a. A company purchases supplies on account.
   b. A company pays for the supplies it purchased in Transaction a.

POSTING (TRANSFERRING INFORMATION) FROM THE JOURNAL TO THE LEDGER

Journalizing a transaction records the data only in the journal—but not in the ledger. Remember, the ledger tracks all transactions related to an account. To appear in the ledger, the data must be copied or transferred there. The process of transferring data from the journal to the ledger is called **posting**.

Posting really just means *copying* a debit in the journal to a debit in the ledger and a credit in the journal to a credit in the ledger. The first transaction of Hunter Environmental Consulting is posted to the ledger as shown in Exhibit 2–9. Here we are using a T-account as a short form for a ledger. In Exhibit 2–11 we illustrate posting the same transaction in a three-column ledger, which is used in formal accounting records.

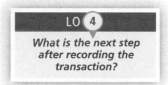

LO 4

What is the next step after recording the transaction?

EXHIBIT 2–9 | Making a Journal Entry and Posting to the Ledger

Panel A – Journal Entry

Journal				Page 1
Date	Account Titles and Explanation	Post. Ref.	Debit	Credit
2016				
Apr. 2	Cash		250,000	
	Lisa Hunter, Capital			250,000
	Received initial investment from owner.			

Panel B – Posting to the Ledger

Cash	
(1) 250,000	

Lisa Hunter, Capital	
	(1) 250,000

ACCOUNTING FOR BUSINESS TRANSACTIONS

So, to recap, steps **❶** – **❸** of the accounting cycle are as follows:

❶ Identify and analyze transactions as they occur.

❷ Record transactions in a journal.

❸ Post (copy) from the journal to the ledger accounts.

In the pages that follow, we record the transactions of Hunter Environmental Consulting (HEC) from Chapter 1. Keep in mind that we are accounting for the business entity and not recording Lisa Hunter's personal transactions.

We temporarily ignore the date of each transaction in order to focus on the accounts and their dollar amounts. We will also post the transactions to T-accounts instead of ledger accounts for the same reason.

---

1. *Transaction:* **Lisa Hunter invested $250,000 cash to begin her environmental consulting business, Hunter Environmental Consulting. The money was deposited in the company's bank account, as shown by the following deposit slip:**

CREDIT ACCOUNT OF:
HUNTER ENVIRONMENTAL CONSULTING
10300 004 06000303600

DATE

DAY	MONTH	YEAR
02	04	16

LIST OF CHEQUES

CHEQUE IDENTIFICATION

1 Lisa Hunter	250,000	0	0
2			
3			
4			
5			
6			
7			
8			
9			
10			
11			
12			
13			

CHEQUE SUBTOTAL $ 250,000 0 0

BUSINESS ACCOUNT DEPOSIT SLIP

BANK OF THE PEOPLE
SHOPPING CONCOURSE BRANCH
VANCOUVER, BC Y2R 2X1

CREDIT ACCOUNT OF:
HUNTER ENVIRONMENTAL CONSULTING
10300 004 06000303600

DATE

DAY	MONTH	YEAR
02	04	16

INITIALS

DEPOSITORS	TELLERS
LH	SM

CASH COUNT

× 5	
× 10	
× 20	
× 50	
× 100	
× $2 COIN	
× $1 COIN	
COIN	
CASH SUBTOTAL	0

DEPOSIT

ENTER CREDIT CARD VOUCHER TOTAL	0	
CASH SUBTOTAL	0	
CHEQUE SUBTOTAL	250,000	0 0

DEPOSIT TOTAL $ 250,000 0 0

⑈10300⑈004⑈ 0600 ⑈0303600⑈

Analysis: Hunter's investment in Hunter Environmental Consulting increased its asset cash; to record this increase, debit Cash. The investment also increased its owner's equity; to record this increase, credit Lisa Hunter, Capital.

Accounting	ASSETS	=	LIABILITIES	+	OWNER'S EQUITY
Equation:	Cash				Lisa Hunter, Capital
	+250,000	=	0	+	250,000

The journal entry records the same information that you learned by using the accounting equation in Chapter 1. Both accounts—Cash and Lisa Hunter, Capital—increased because the business received $250,000 cash and gave Hunter $250,000 of capital (owner's equity) in the business.

Journal Entry:

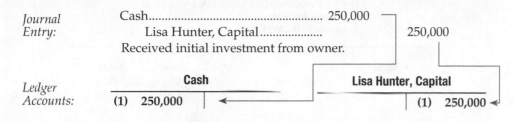

Cash... 250,000
    Lisa Hunter, Capital................... 250,000
Received initial investment from owner.

Ledger Accounts:

Cash		Lisa Hunter, Capital	
(1) 250,000			**(1) 250,000**

---

2. *Transaction*: Hunter Environmental Consulting paid $100,000 cash for land as a future office location.

Analysis: The purchase decreased cash; therefore, credit Cash. The purchase increased the entity's asset, land; to record this increase, debit Land.

Accounting	ASSETS		=	LIABILITIES	+	OWNER'S EQUITY
Equation:	Cash	Land				
	−100,000	+100,000	=	0	+	0

This transaction increased one asset, land, and decreased another asset, cash. The net effect on the business's total assets was zero, and there was no effect on liabilities or owner's equity. We use the term *net* in business to mean an amount after a subtraction.

Journal Entry:

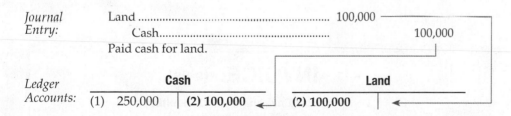

Land 100,000
    Cash... 100,000
Paid cash for land.

Ledger Accounts:

Cash		Land	
(1) 250,000	(2) 100,000	(2) 100,000	

---

3. *Transaction*: The business purchased office supplies for $7,000 on account, as shown by the purchase invoice on the next page.

Analysis: The purchase of office supplies increased this asset, so we debit Office Supplies. The purchase was *on account*, so it also increased a liability; to record this increase, credit Accounts Payable.

Accounting	ASSETS	=	LIABILITIES	+	OWNER'S EQUITY
Equation:	Office Supplies		Accounts Payable		
	+7,000	=	+7,000	+	0

INVOICE (purchase)

WHOLESALE OFFICE SUPPLY
500 HENDERSON ROAD
VANCOUVER, BC

Date: April 3, 2016   Invoice No: 9623
Terms: 30 days
Sold to: **Hunter Environmental Consulting**
281 Wave Avenue
Vancouver, BC V6R 9C8

Quantity	Item	Price	Total
580	Laser paper	$10	$5,800.00
80	Desk calendars	15	1,200.00
	Total amount due:		**$7,000.00**

Journal Entry:

Office Supplies 7,000
        Accounts Payable........................   7,000
Purchased office supplies on account.

Ledger Accounts:

Office Supplies			**Accounts Payable**	
(3) 7,000				(3) 7,000

---

4. *Transaction:* The business provided environmental consulting services for clients and received $30,000 cash. The source document is Hunter Environmental Consulting's sales invoice shown below. There would also be a deposit slip like the one on page 70.

INVOICE (sale)

Hunter Environmental Consulting
281 Wave Avenue
Vancouver, BC V2R 9C8

Date: April 8, 2016
Sold to: **Allied Energy Corporation**
325 Brooks Street
Vancouver, BC

Invoice No: **0001**
Service: 1000 DVD0503 service for all locations

PAID

Total amount due: $30,000

All accounts are due and payable within 30 days.

Analysis: The asset, cash, is increased; therefore, debit Cash. The revenue account, service revenue, is increased; credit Service Revenue.

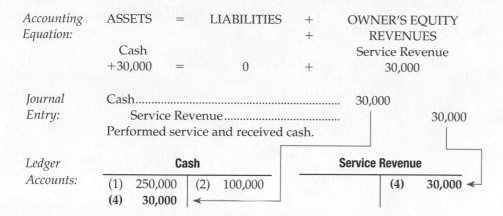

Accounting Equation:

ASSETS	=	LIABILITIES	+	OWNER'S EQUITY
			+	REVENUES
Cash				Service Revenue
+30,000	=	0	+	30,000

Journal Entry:

Cash... 30,000
    Service Revenue... 30,000
Performed service and received cash.

Ledger Accounts:

Cash			Service Revenue	
(1) 250,000	(2) 100,000			(4) 30,000
(4) 30,000				

---

5. *Transaction:* The business provided environmental consulting services of $25,000 to clients who will pay for the services within one month.

Analysis: The asset, accounts receivable, is increased; therefore, debit Accounts Receivable. Service revenue is increased; credit Service Revenue.

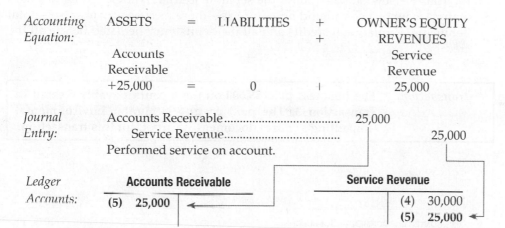

Accounting Equation:

ASSETS	=	LIABILITIES	+	OWNER'S EQUITY
			+	REVENUES
Accounts				Service
Receivable				Revenue
+25,000	=	0	+	25,000

Journal Entry:

Accounts Receivable.................................... 25,000
    Service Revenue... 25,000
Performed service on account.

Ledger Accounts:

Accounts Receivable		Service Revenue	
(5) 25,000		(4) 30,000	
		(5) 25,000	

Notice the differences and the similarities between Transactions 4 and 5. In both transactions, Service Revenue was increased because in both cases the company earned revenue. However, in Transaction 4 the company was paid at the time of service. In Transaction 5 the company will receive cash later (Accounts Receivable). This is key, because the amount of earnings is not determined by when the company receives cash. Earnings (revenue) are recorded when the company does the work, or earns revenue.

---

6. *Transaction:* The business paid the following expenses: office rent, $4,000; employee salaries, $6,500; and utilities, $1,500.

Analysis: The asset cash is decreased; therefore, credit Cash for each of the three expense amounts. The following expenses are increased: Rent Expense, Salaries Expense, and Utilities Expense. Each should be debited for the appropriate amount.

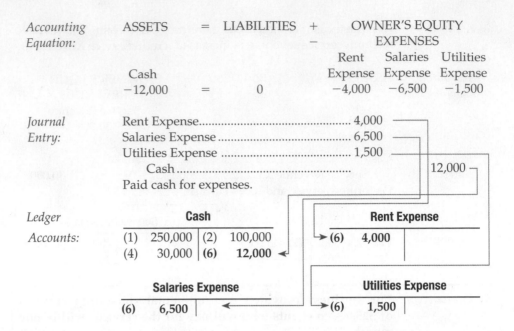

Accounting Equation:	ASSETS	=	LIABILITIES	+ −	OWNER'S EQUITY EXPENSES		
					Rent Expense	Salaries Expense	Utilities Expense
	Cash						
	−12,000	=	0		−4,000	−6,500	−1,500

Journal Entry:

Rent Expense.. 4,000
Salaries Expense 6,500
Utilities Expense 1,500
     Cash..   12,000
Paid cash for expenses.

Ledger Accounts:

Cash				Rent Expense	
(1) 250,000	(2) 100,000			(6) 4,000	
(4) 30,000	(6) 12,000				

Salaries Expense			Utilities Expense	
(6) 6,500			(6) 1,500	

In practice, the business would record these three transactions separately if they are all paid with separate cheques. To save space, we can record them together to illustrate a **compound journal entry**. See the Summary Problem for Your Review on page 82 for the separate journal entries. No matter how many accounts a compound entry affects—there may be any number—total debits must equal total credits and all the debits must be listed before all the credits.

---

7. Transaction: The business paid $5,000 on the account payable created in Transaction 3. The paid cheque is Hunter Environmental Consulting's source document, or proof, for this transaction.

| *Analysis:* | The payment decreased the asset cash; therefore, credit Cash. The payment also decreased the liability accounts payable, so we debit Accounts Payable. |

Accounting	ASSETS	=	LIABILITIES	+	OWNER'S EQUITY
Equation:	Cash		Accounts Payable		
	−5,000	=	−5,000	+	0

Journal Entry:

Accounts Payable... 5,000

    Cash... 5,000

Paid cash on account.

Ledger Accounts:

		Cash					**Accounts Payable**		
(1)	250,000	(2)	100,000		(7)	5,000	(3)	7,000
(4)	30,000	(6)	12,000					
		(7)	5,000					

---

8. Transaction: Lisa Hunter remodelled her personal residence with personal funds. This is not a business transaction of the environmental consulting business, so no journal entry is made.

---

9. Transaction: The business received $15,000 cash from one of the clients discussed in Transaction 5.

| *Analysis:* | The asset cash is increased; therefore, debit Cash. The asset accounts receivable is decreased; therefore, credit Accounts Receivable. |

Accounting	ASSETS		=	LIABILITIES	+	OWNER'S EQUITY
Equation:		Accounts				
	Cash	Receivable				
	+15,000	−15,000	=	0	+	0

Journal Entry: Cash.. 15,000

    Accounts Receivable 15,000

    Received cash on account.

This transaction has no effect on revenue; the related revenue is accounted for in Transaction 5.

Ledger Accounts:

		Cash					**Accounts Receivable**		
(1)	250,000	(2)	100,000		(5)	25,000	(9)	15,000
(4)	30,000	(6)	12,000					
(9)	15,000	(7)	5,000					

---

10. Transaction: Lisa Hunter withdrew $6,000 cash for personal living expenses.

Analysis: The withdrawal decreased the entity's cash; therefore, credit Cash. The transaction also decreased the owner's equity of the entity. Decreases in the owner's equity of a proprietorship that result from owner withdrawals are debited to a separate owner's equity account entitled Withdrawals. Therefore, debit Lisa Hunter, Withdrawals.

LEARNING TIPS

This is an example of the *economic entity assumption*. The personal expenses of the owner are not reported as expenses for the business.

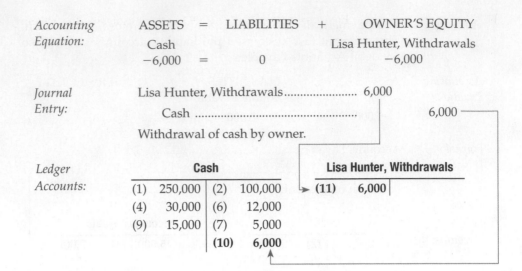

Accounting
Equation:

ASSETS = LIABILITIES + OWNER'S EQUITY

Cash   Lisa Hunter, Withdrawals
−6,000 = 0   −6,000

Journal
Entry:

Lisa Hunter, Withdrawals..................... 6,000
    Cash   6,000
Withdrawal of cash by owner.

Ledger
Accounts:

Cash				Lisa Hunter, Withdrawals	
(1)	250,000	(2)	100,000	(11) 6,000	
(4)	30,000	(6)	12,000		
(9)	15,000	(7)	5,000		
		(10)	**6,000**		

LEARNING TIPS

Since T-accounts are not formal documents, the conventions vary for how they are recorded. Sometimes dates are used (with or without explanations), sometimes numbers or letters, and sometimes there are just amounts. You will see different versions throughout the chapters in this book.

Each journal entry posted to the T-accounts (representing the ledger) is identified by date or by transaction number (in this example, the transaction numbers have been in brackets). In this way any transaction can be traced from the journal to the ledger, and, if need be, back to the journal. This helps to locate efficiently any information you may need.

The T-Accounts after Posting

Exhibit 2–10 shows the accounts of Hunter Environmental Consulting after posting. Each account has a balance that is the difference between the account's total debits and its total credits. We set a balance apart by a horizontal line. If an account has only one entry, you can total the account and label its balance, but you do not have to since the balance is obvious.

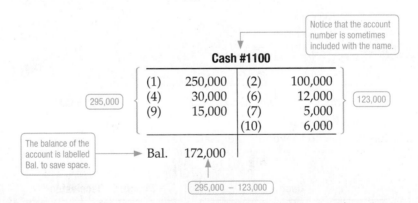

Notice that the account number is sometimes included with the name.

Cash #1100

	(1)	250,000	(2)	100,000	
295,000	(4)	30,000	(6)	12,000	123,000
	(9)	15,000	(7)	5,000	
			(10)	6,000	

The balance of the account is labelled Bal. to save space.

Bal. 172,000

295,000 − 123,000

> Why It's Done This Way

Objective of Financial Reporting

Companies record transactions, summarize them, and report them in a format that is recognizable to user groups and *communicates useful information* for them. The financial statements produced by a company are the end result of the accounting cycle. The starting point, as you have seen in this chapter, is to properly record transactions.

The first question that must be asked is whether the transaction represents a financial event that should be recorded in the company's ledger. If the answer to that question is yes, then we say it is *recognized*.

If the transaction is recognized, then we use the *elements* of the financial statements—the accounts—to record information in a way that is *understandable* to everyone.

Assets	=	Liabilities	+	Owner's Equity

Cash #1100

(1)	250,000	(2)	100,000
(4)	30,000	(6)	12,000
(9)	15,000	(7)	5,000
		(10)	6,000
Bal.	172,000		

Accounts Receivable #1200

(5)	25,000	(9)	15,000
Bal.	10,000		

Office Supplies #1400

(3)	7,000	
Bal.	7,000	

Land #1900

(2)	100,000	
Bal.	100,000	

Accounts Payable #2100

(7)	5,000	(3)	7,000
		Bal.	2,000

Lisa Hunter, Capital #3000

		(1)	250,000
		Bal.	250,000

Lisa Hunter, Withdrawals #3100

(11)	6,000	
Bal.	6,000	

REVENUE
Service Revenue #4000

		(4)	30,000
		(5)	25,000
		Bal.	55,000

EXPENSES
Rent Expense #5100

(6)	4,000	
Bal.	4,000	

Salaries Expense #5200

(6)	6,500	
Bal.	6,500	

Utilities Expense #5300

(6)	1,500	
Bal.	1,500	

> Try It!

7. Refer to Try It #6 on page 69 for the transactions of Peterson Engineering

a. Create the following T-accounts with their September 1 balances: Cash #101, debit balance $3,000; Accounts Receivable #103, $0; Supplies #105, $0; Equipment #107, $0; Land #110, debit balance $29,000; Accounts Payable #201, $0; Notes Payable #205, $0; R. Peterson, Capital #301, credit balance $32,000; Service Revenue #401, $0; Utilities Expense #501, $0.

b. Record the transactions directly in the T-accounts affected. Use dates as posting references in the T-accounts. Journal entries are not required. (Or you may use the answer to Try It #9 and post those journal entries.)

c. Compute the September 30 balance for each account, then add the balances to prove that total debits equal total credits.

(continued)

8. Calculate the account balance for each of the following:

Supplies Expense		Accounts Payable		Cash	
110		150	400	5,000	150
290		800	2,900	12,600	800
544		475	1,600	926	475
			750	6,200	290

9. Compute the missing amount represented by X in each account:

(1) Cash			(2) Accounts Payable	
Bal. 10,000	13,000		X	Bal. 12,800
20,000				45,600
Bal. X				Bal. 23,500

10. Refer to Try It #6 on page 69 for the transactions of Peterson Engineering. Record each transaction on Page 1 of the journal. Include an explanation for each journal entry.

Solutions appear at the end of this chapter and on MyAccountingLab

Details of Journals and Ledgers

Posting means transferring information from the journal to the ledger accounts. We saw how to do this in Exhibit 2–9. In practice, the journal and the ledger provide additional details that create a "trail" through the accounting records for future reference. For example, suppose we wanted to find out where the $250,000 in cash came from that is listed in the ledger of the Cash account of Hunter Environmental Consulting. We would need to know where to find the original journal entry. The system of cross-referencing that is explained in detail in Exhibit 2–11 is how accountants trace through the accounting records to find information.

The Journal Exhibit 2–11, Panel A, describes two transactions, and Panel B presents a widely used *journal* format. Notice the following:

- The journal page number appears in the upper right corner.
- The year appears directly under the Date heading at the top of each journal page or when the year has changed.
- The date of the transaction is recorded for every transaction. ❶
- A blank line is left between journal entries to make it easier to read.
- The **posting reference**, abbreviated Post. Ref. (or sometimes PR) tells the reader in which ledger (and in which account in that ledger) the information was posted. ❹ The account number (1100) indicates that the $250,000 debit to Cash has been posted to the Cash account in the ledger. The account number (3000) for Lisa Hunter, Capital below it shows that the $250,000 amount of the credit has been posted to the ledger. As mentioned earlier, the account numbers come from the chart of accounts, as shown in Exhibit 2–3 on page 62.

The Ledger Exhibit 2–11, Panel C, presents the *ledger* in the **three-column format**. Each account has its own record in the ledger. Our example shows Hunter Environmental Consulting's Cash account; Land account; and Lisa Hunter, Capital account. These are the steps to posting:

- ❶ The date is transferred from the journal to the ledger.
- The Item column is often left blank because special notations are rarely used. Typically, the only item notation used is an indication of an opening balance or a balance brought forward from a previous period.

EXHIBIT 2–11 | Details of Journalizing and Posting

Panel A – Two of Hunter Environmental Consulting's Transactions

Date	Transaction
Apr. 2, 2016	Lisa Hunter invested $250,000 in the business.
	The business received cash and gave Hunter owner's equity in the business.
Apr. 3, 2016	Paid $100,000 cash for land.

MyAccou

Video: The Details of Journalizing and Posting

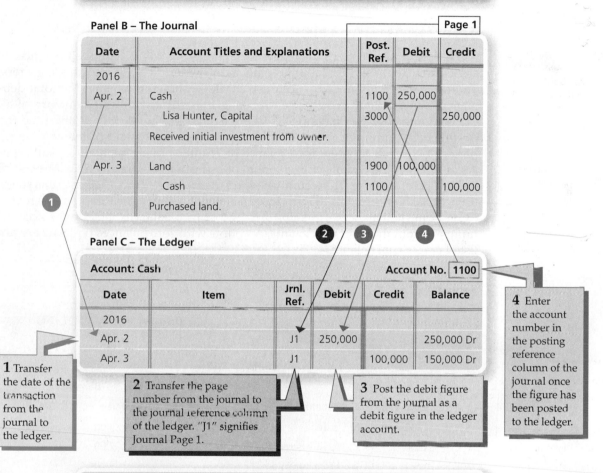

Panel B – The Journal

Page 1

Date	Account Titles and Explanations	Post. Ref.	Debit	Credit
2016				
Apr. 2	Cash	1100	250,000	
	Lisa Hunter, Capital	3000		250,000
	Received initial investment from owner.			
Apr. 3	Land	1900	100,000	
	Cash	1100		100,000
	Purchased land.			

Panel C – The Ledger

Account: Cash Account No. 1100

Date	Item	Jrnl. Ref.	Debit	Credit	Balance
2016					
Apr. 2		J1	250,000		250,000 Dr
Apr. 3		J1		100,000	150,000 Dr

1 Transfer the date of the transaction from the journal to the ledger.

2 Transfer the page number from the journal to the journal reference column of the ledger. "J1" signifies Journal Page 1.

3 Post the debit figure from the journal as a debit figure in the ledger account.

4 Enter the account number in the posting reference column of the journal once the figure has been posted to the ledger.

Account: Land Account No. 1900

Date	Item	Jrnl. Ref.	Debit	Credit	Balance
2016					
Apr. 3		J1	100,000		100,000 Dr

Account: Lisa Hunter, Capital Account No. 3000

Date	Item	Jrnl. Ref.	Debit	Credit	Balance
2016					
Apr. 2		J1		250,000	250,000 Cr

- ❷ The Jrnl. Ref. means Journal Reference. J1 refers to Page 1 of the journal it comes from. In later chapters you will see other journals and cross-reference codes.
- ❸ Post (copy) the debit amount in a journal entry to the debit column of the ledger. A credit amount will get copied to the credit column.
- The balance column keeps a running total of the account balance. The balance can be followed by the letters Dr or Cr (indicating a debit or credit, respectively); however, this is not always required.
- ❹ Now go back to the journal and update the posting reference. This makes a link to show *where* the journal information was posted.

THE TRIAL BALANCE

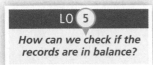

LO 5
How can we check if the records are in balance?

MyAccountingLab

Video: Preparation of a Trial Balance
Video: Real World Accounting

A *trial balance* summarizes the ledger by listing all accounts with their balances—assets first, followed by liabilities, and then owner's equity. Before computers, the trial balance provided an accuracy check by showing whether the total debits equalled the total credits. The trial balance is still useful as a summary of all the accounts and their balances. A trial balance may be created at any time the postings are up to date. The most common time is at the end of the accounting period. Exhibit 2–12 is the trial balance of Hunter Environmental Consulting at April 30, 2016, the end of the first month of operations before any adjustments are made. Therefore it is more accurately called the *unadjusted trial balance* at this stage. (Other trial balances will be introduced in later chapters.) The totals on this report came from the balances in Exhibit 2–10. Most trial balances include the account numbers from the chart of accounts. Accounts with zero balances typically are not listed on the trial balance.

EXHIBIT 2–12 Trial Balance

Note: Do not confuse the trial balance with the balance sheet. A trial balance is an internal document seen only by the company's owners, managers, and accountants. The company reports its financial position—both inside the business and to the public—on the balance sheet, a formal financial statement. The trial balance is merely a step in the preparation of the financial statements.

	HUNTER ENVIRONMENTAL CONSULTING Unadjusted Trial Balance April 30, 2016		
		Balance	
Account Number	**Account**	**Debit**	**Credit**
1100	Cash	$222,000	
1200	Accounts receivable	10,000	
1400	Office supplies	7,000	
1900	Land	50,000	
2100	Accounts payable		$ 2,000
3000	Lisa Hunter, capital		250,000
3100	Lisa Hunter, withdrawals	6,000	
4000	Service revenue		55,000
5100	Rent expense	4,000	
5200	Salaries expense	6,500	
5300	Utilities expense	1,500	
	Total	$307,000	$307,000

Correcting Trial Balance Errors

Throughout the accounting process, total debits should always equal total credits. If they are not equal, then accounting errors exist. Computerized accounting systems eliminate many errors because most software will not let you make a journal entry that doesn't balance. But computers cannot eliminate *all* errors because humans sometimes input the wrong data or input data to the wrong accounts.

If you are working with a manual system—such as in your course work—you might appreciate some strategies to help you figure out errors:

- Search the trial balance for a missing account. For example, suppose the accountant omitted Lisa Hunter, Withdrawals from the trial balance in Exhibit 2–12. Total debits would then be $301,000 ($307,000 – $6,000) and total credits would be $307,000, a difference of $6,000. Look through the ledger to see if all the accounts are listed in the trial balance and if they are showing the correct amounts.

- Search the journal for the amount of the difference. For example, suppose the total credits on Hunter Environmental Consulting's trial balance equal $307,000 and total debits equal $306,000. A $1,000 transaction may have been posted incorrectly to the ledger by omitting the debit entry. Search the journal for a $1,000 transaction and check its posting to the ledger.

- Divide the difference between total debits and total credits by 2. A debit treated as a credit, or vice versa, doubles the amount of error. Suppose the accountant paid $1,000 cash for the utilities expenses. This transaction was recorded correctly in the journal, but was posted as a debit to Cash and a debit to Utilities Expense. Thus, $2,000 appears on the debit side of the trial balance, and there is nothing on the credit side relating to this transaction. The out-of-balance amount is $2,000, and dividing by 2 reveals that the relevant transaction may have had a value of $1,000. Search the journal for a $1,000 transaction and check the posting to the ledger.

- Divide the out-of-balance amount by 9. If the result is evenly divisible by 9, the error may be a **slide**, which is adding or deleting one or several zeros in a figure (e.g., writing $61 as $610), or a **transposition** (e.g., treating $61 as $16). Suppose the accountant listed the $6,000 balance in Lisa Hunter, Withdrawals as $60,000 on the trial balance—a slide-type error. Total debits would differ from total credits by $54,000 (i.e., $60,000 – $6,000 = $54,000). Dividing $54,000 by 9 yields $6,000, the correct amount of the withdrawals. Trace this amount through the ledger until you reach the Lisa Hunter, Withdrawals account with a balance of $6,000. Dividing by 9 can give the correct transaction amount for a slide, but not for a transposition.

> Try It!

11. Shiny Floor Cleaning's accounting records reported the following data on December 31, 2016. Accounts appear in no particular order.

Supplies	$ 7,500	S. Shaw, Withdrawals	$ 5,000
Equipment	2,000	Cash	13,000
Accounts Payable	1,000	Supplies Expense	6,000
S. Shaw, Capital	15,000	Accounts Receivable	12,500
Cleaning Revenue	30,000		

Prepare the trial balance of Shiny Floor Cleaning at December 31, 2016. List the accounts in proper order, as shown in Exhibit 2–12.

12. Refer to the trial balance for Shiny Floor Cleaning created in Try It #11. Suppose Susan Shaw, the owner, accidentally listed equipment as $200 instead of the correct amount of $2,000. Compute the incorrect trial balance totals for debits and credits. Then show how to correct this error, which is called a *slide*.

Solutions appear at the end of this chapter and on MyAccountingLab

SUMMARY PROBLEM FOR YOUR REVIEW

The trial balance of Bancroft Management Consulting on March 1, 2016, lists the company's assets, liabilities, and owner's equity on that date.

	BANCROFT MANAGEMENT CONSULTING		
	Trial Balance		
	March 1, 2016		
Account		Balance	
Number	Account Title	Debit	Credit
1100	Cash	$26,000	
1200	Accounts receivable	4,500	
2100	Accounts payable		$ 2,000
3100	John Cassiar, capital		28,500
	Total	$30,500	$30,500

During March the business engaged in the following transactions:

Mar. 3   Borrowed $45,000 from the bank and signed a note payable in the name of the business.

5   Paid cash of $40,000 to a real estate company to acquire land in the town of Bancroft.

11   Performed service for a customer and received cash of $5,000.

12   Purchased supplies on account, $300.

14   Performed customer service and earned revenue on account, $2,600.

17   Paid $1,200 of the Accounts Payable balance from the March 1, 2017, trial balance.

19   Paid the following cash expenses: salaries, $3,000; rent, $1,500; and interest, $400.

20   Received $3,100 of the Accounts Receivable balance from the March 1, 2017, trial balance.

24   Received a $200 utility bill that will be paid next week.

28   John Cassiar withdrew $1,800 for personal use.

Required

Prepare a ledger account for each account name. Place the opening balance in the ledger account, remembering that the normal balance is a debit for asset and expense accounts, and a credit for liability, equity, and revenue accounts.

1. Open the following accounts, with the balances indicated, in the ledger of Bancroft Management Consulting. Use the three-column ledger format.

Assets: Cash, #1100, $26,000; Accounts Receivable, #1200, $4,500; Supplies, #1400, no balance; Land, #1900, no balance

Liabilities: Accounts Payable, #2100, $2,000; Notes Payable, #2300, no balance

Owner's Equity: John Cassiar, Capital, #3000, $28,500; John Cassiar, Withdrawals, #3100, no balance

Revenues: Service Revenue, #4000, no balance

Expenses: Interest Expense, #5100; Rent Expense, #5200; Salaries Expense, #5300; Utilities Expense, #5400 (none have balances)

Refer to the rules of debit and credit shown in Exhibit 2–7 on page 66.

2. Journalize the preceding transactions on Page 2 of the journal.

3. Post the transactions to the ledger.

4. Prepare the unadjusted trial balance of Bancroft Management Consulting at March 31, 2016.

SOLUTION

Requirement 1 is combined with Requirement 3

Requirement 2

When a transaction involves cash, always first decide whether cash increased or decreased. An increase is a debit to Cash. A decrease is a credit to Cash. Then decide which other accounts are affected.

Ensure total debits equal total credits in each journal entry. Selected journal entries are explained more fully.

				Page 2
Date	Account Titles and Explanations	Post. Ref.	Debit	Credit
Mar. 3	Cash	1100	45,000	
	Notes Payable	2300		45,000
	Borrowed cash on note payable.			
Mar. 5	Land	1900	40,000	
	Cash	1100		40,000
	Purchased land for cash.			
Mar. 11	Cash	1100	5,000	
	Service Revenue	4000		5,000
	Performed service and received cash.			
Mar. 12	Supplies	1400	300	
	Accounts Payable	2100		300
	Purchased supplies on account.			
Mar. 14	Accounts Receivable	1200	2,600	
	Service Revenue	4000		2,600
	Performed service on account.			
Mar. 17	Accounts Payable	2100	1,200	
	Cash	1100		1,200
	Paid cash to reduce accounts payable.			
Mar. 19	Salaries Expense	5300	3,000	
	Cash	1100		3,000
	Issued cheque to pay salaries expense.			
Mar. 19	Rent Expense	5200	1,500	
	Cash	1100		1,500
	Issued cheque to pay rent expense.			
Mar. 19	Interest Expense	5100	400	
	Cash	1100		400
	Issued cheque to pay interest expense.			
Mar. 20	Cash	1100	3,100	
	Accounts Receivable	1200		3,100
	Received cash on account.			

"On account" means no cash was used in the transaction. Therefore, use Accounts Payable or Accounts Receivable since cash will be paid or collected in the future.

"Paid" usually means a cheque was written, so Cash is credited.

			Page 2		
Date	**Account Titles and Explanations**	**Post. Ref.**	**Debit**		**Credit**
Mar. 24	Utilities Expense	5400	200		
	Accounts Payable	2100			200
	Received utility bill.				
Mar. 28	John Cassiar, Withdrawals	3100	1,800		
	Cash	1100			1,800
	Withdrew cash for personal use.				

Receiving a bill indicates an amount is owed for goods or services received. Increase the liability Accounts Payable, since cash will be paid for the utility bill in the future.

Requirements 1 and 3

Account: Cash   **Account No. 1100**

Date	Item	Jrnl. Ref.	Debit	Credit	Balance
Mar. 1	Beginning balance				26,000 Dr
Mar. 3		J2	45,000		71,000 Dr
Mar. 5		J2		40,000	31,000 Dr
Mar. 11		J2	5,000		36,000 Dr
Mar. 17		J2		1,200	34,800 Dr
Mar. 19		J2		3,000	31,800 Dr
Mar. 19		J2		1,500	30,300 Dr
Mar. 19		J2		400	29,900 Dr
Mar. 20		J2	3,100		33,000 Dr
Mar. 28		J2		1,800	31,200 Dr

Transfer amounts from the journal entries in Requirement 2 into the ledger accounts here.

Make sure each transaction is posted to the proper ledger account, and make sure no transactions were missed.

Account: Accounts Receivable   **Account No. 1200**

Date	Item	Jrnl. Ref.	Debit	Credit	Balance
Mar. 1	Beginning balance				4,500 Dr
Mar. 14		J2	2,600		7,100 Dr
Mar. 20		J2		3,100	4,000 Dr

Remember to add up the balance after each transaction. The Accounts Receivable balance is $4,500 + 2,600 = $7,100; $7,100 − 3,100 = $4,000.

Account: Supplies   **Account No. 1400**

Date	Item	Jrnl. Ref.	Debit	Credit	Balance
Mar. 12		J2	300		300 Dr

Account: Land   **Account No. 1900**

Date	Item	Jrnl. Ref.	Debit	Credit	Balance
Mar. 5		J2	40,000		40,000 Dr

Account: Accounts Payable   **Account No. 2100**

Date	Item	Jrnl. Ref.	Debit	Credit	Balance
Mar. 1	Beginning balance				2,000 Cr
Mar. 12		J2		300	2,300 Cr
Mar. 17		J2	1,200		1,100 Cr
Mar. 24		J2		200	1,300 Cr

Account: Notes Payable   **Account No. 2300**

Date	Item	Jrnl. Ref.	Debit	Credit	Balance
Mar. 3		J2		45,000	45,000 Cr

Account: John Cassiar, Capital   **Account No. 3000**

Date	Item	Jrnl. Ref.	Debit	Credit	Balance
Mar. 1	Beginning balance				28,500 Cr

Account: John Cassiar, Withdrawals   **Account No. 3100**

Date	Item	Jrnl. Ref.	Debit	Credit	Balance
Mar. 28		J2	1,800		1,800 Dr

Account: Service Revenue   **Account No. 4000**

Date	Item	Jrnl. Ref.	Debit	Credit	Balance
Mar. 11		J2	5,000		5,000 Cr
Mar. 14		J2	2,600		7,600 Cr

Account: Interest Expense   **Account No. 5100**

Date	Item	Jrnl. Ref.	Debit	Credit	Balance
Mar. 19		J2	400		400 Dr

Account: Rent Expense   **Account No. 5200**

Date	Item	Jrnl. Ref.	Debit	Credit	Balance
Mar. 19		J2	1,500		1,500 Dr

Account: Salaries Expense   **Account No. 5300**

Date	Item	Jrnl. Ref.	Debit	Credit	Balance
Mar. 19		J2	3,000		3,000 Dr

Account: Utilities Expense   **Account No. 5400**

Date	Item	Jrnl. Ref.	Debit	Credit	Balance
Mar. 24		J2	200		200 Dr

Requirement 4

The title must include the name of the company, "Unadjusted Trial Balance," and the date of the trial balance. It shows the account balances on one specific date.

BANCROFT MANAGEMENT CONSULTING Unadjusted Trial Balance March 31, 2016			
		Balance	
Account Number*	**Account Title**	**Debit**	**Credit**
1100	Cash	$31,200	
1200	Accounts receivable	4,000	
1400	Supplies	300	
1900	Land	40,000	
2100	Accounts payable		$ 1,300
2300	Notes payable		45,000
3000	John Cassiar, capital		28,500
3100	John Cassiar, withdrawals	1,800	
4000	Service revenue		7,600
5100	Interest expense	400	
5200	Rent expense	1,500	
5300	Salaries expense	3,000	
5400	Utilities expense	200	
	Total	$82,400	$82,400

List all the accounts that have a balance in their ledger accounts. Accounts with a zero balance typically are not listed on the trial balance. Write the final balance amount for each account from Requirement 3 into the debit or credit column of the trial balance. Make sure that the total of the Debit column equals the total of the Credit column.

Double underline the totals to show that the columns have been added and the totals are final.

* *Note:* Listing the account numbers is optional.

SUMMARY

LEARNING OBJECTIVE ① Define and use key accounting terms

What are the key terms used when recording transactions?   Pg. 60

- A *transaction* is an event that affects the financial position of a particular entity and may be reliably measured.
- A *journal* is a chronological accounting record of transactions.
- The *ledger* contains a record for each account.
- A *chart of accounts* lists all the accounts in the ledger and their account numbers in the following order: assets, liabilities, and owner's equity (and its subparts: revenues and expenses).

LEARNING OBJECTIVE ② Apply the rules of debit and credit

How do we track changes in accounts?   Pg. 63

- Transactions are recorded in accounts, which can be viewed either in the form of the letter "T" or in a three-column format.

Account Name

(left side)	(right side)
debit	credit

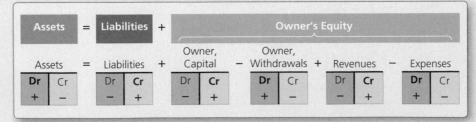

MyAccountingLab **Video:** Rules of Debits and Credits

LEARNING OBJECTIVE ③ Analyze and record transactions in the journal

How do we record business transactions?   Pg. 67

- The accountant begins the recording process by analyzing the transaction, deciding if it is a transaction, and then entering the transaction's information in the *journal*, a chronological list of all the entity's transactions.

MyAccountingLab **Video:** Journalizing Transactions
  Video: Operating Activities and Their Impact on the Accounting Equation
  Video: Financing and Investing Activities and Their Impact on the Accounting Equation

LEARNING OBJECTIVE ④ Post from the journal to the ledger

What is the next step after recording the transaction?   Pg. 69

- *Posting* means transferring information from the journal to the *ledger* accounts. We often use T-accounts as a shortcut to represent ledgers in this book. Posting references are used to trace amounts back and forth between the journal and the ledger.

MyAccountingLab **Video:** The Details of Journalizing and Posting

LEARNING OBJECTIVE ⑤ Prepare and use a trial balance

How can we check if the records are in balance?   Pg. 80

- The *trial balance* is a summary of all the non-zero account balances in the ledger. When *double-entry accounting* has been done correctly, the total debits and the total credits in the trial balance are equal.
- We can now trace the flow of accounting information through these steps: Business Transaction → Source Documents → Journal Entry → Posting to Ledger Accounts → Unadjusted Trial Balance

MyAccountingLab **Video:** Preparation of a Trial Balance
  Video: Real World Accounting

Check **Accounting Vocabulary** for all key terms used in Chapter 2 and the **Glossary** at the back of the book for all key terms used in the textbook.

MORE CHAPTER REVIEW MATERIAL

MyAccountingLab

DemoDoc covering Debit/Credit Transaction Analysis

Accounting Cycle Tutorial

Student PowerPoint Slides

Audio Chapter Summary

Note: All MyAccountingLab resources can be found in the Chapter Resources section and the Multimedia Library.

ACCOUNTING VOCABULARY

Accounting cycle The process by which accountants produce an entity's financial statements and update the financial reports for a period of time *(p. 60)*.

Accounting period The time frame, or period of time, covered by financial statements and other reports *(p. 60)*.

Bank cheque A document that instructs the bank to pay the designated person or business the specified amount of money *(p. 67)*.

Bank deposit slip A document that shows the amount of cash deposited into a person's or business's bank account *(p. 67)*.

Chart of accounts A list of all the accounts and their account numbers in the ledger *(p. 61)*.

Compound journal entry A journal entry with more than one debit and credit *(p. 74)*.

Credit The right side of an account *(p. 63)*.

Debit The left side of an account *(p. 63)*.

Journal The chronological accounting record of an entity's transactions *(p. 61)*.

Ledger The book (or printout) of accounts *(p. 61)*.

Normal balance The balance that appears on the side of an account—debit or credit—where we record increases *(p. 66)*.

Overdraw To remove more money from a bank account than exists in the bank account. This puts the bank account into a negative balance. This becomes a loan from the bank *(p. 66)*.

Posting Transferring of amounts from the journal to the ledger *(p. 69)*.

Posting reference A column in the journal that indicates to the reader to which account the journal entry has been posted *(p. 78)*.

Purchase invoice   A document from a vendor that shows a customer what was purchased, when it was purchased, and how much it cost (p. 67).

Sales invoice   A seller's request for cash from the purchaser. This document gives the seller the amount of revenue to record (p. 67).

Slide   A type of error in which one or several zeros are added or deleted in a figure; for example, writing $30 as $300 (p. 81).

Source document   A document that is evidence of a transaction, such as an invoice (p. 67).

Three-column format   One common type of ledger format that includes three columns for dollar amounts—one for debit amounts, one for credit amounts, and the other for a running balance (p. 78).

Transposition   A type of error in which two digits in a number are shown in reverse order (p. 81).

Trial balance   A list of all the ledger accounts with their balances (p. 61).

SIMILAR ACCOUNTING TERMS

Cr	Credit; right
Dr	Debit; left
Entering the transaction in a journal	Making the journal entry; journalizing the transaction
J1	Page 1 of the journal
Jrnl. Ref.	Journal reference
The Journal	A general journal; a book of original entry
The Ledger	The books; the general ledger
Open the accounts	Set up the accounts; create the ledger accounts
Post. Ref.	Posting reference
P.R.	Posting reference

SELF-STUDY QUESTIONS

Test your understanding of the chapter by marking the correct answer for each of the following questions:

1. A T-account has two sides called the (p. 63)
   a. Debit and credit
   b. Asset and liability
   c. Revenue and expense
   d. Journal and ledger

2. Increases in liabilities are recorded by (p. 64)
   a. Debits
   b. Credits

3. Why do accountants record transactions in the journal? (p. 67)
   a. To ensure that all transactions are posted to the ledger
   b. To ensure that total debits equal total credits
   c. To have a chronological record of all transactions
   d. To help prepare the financial statements

4. Posting is the process of transferring information from the (p. 69)
   a. Journal to the trial balance
   b. Ledger to the trial balance
   c. Ledger to the financial statements
   d. Journal to the ledger

5. The purchase of land for cash is recorded by a (p. 71)
   a. Debit to Cash and a credit to Land
   b. Debit to Cash and a debit to Land
   c. Debit to Land and a credit to Cash
   d. Credit to Cash and a credit to Land

6. The purpose of the trial balance is to (p. 80)
   a. List all accounts with their balances
   b. Ensure that all transactions have been recorded
   c. Speed up the collection of cash receipts from customers
   d. Increase assets and owner's equity

7. What is the normal balance of the Accounts Receivable, Office Supplies, and Rent Expense accounts? (p. 66)
   a. Debit
   b. Credit

8. A business has Cash of $3,000, Notes Payable of $2,500, Accounts Payable of $4,300, Service Revenue of $7,000, and Rent Expense of $2,400. Based on these data, how much are its total liabilities? (p. 64)
   a. $4,600
   b. $6,800
   c. $9,800
   d. $13,800

9. Simpson Transport earned revenue on account. The earning of revenue on account is recorded by a (p. 73)
   a. Debit to Cash and a credit to Revenue
   b. Debit to Accounts Receivable and a credit to Revenue
   c. Debit to Accounts Payable and a credit to Revenue
   d. Debit to Revenue and a credit to Accounts Receivable

10. The account credited for a receipt of cash on account (p. 73)
   a. Cash
   b. Accounts Payable
   c. Service Revenue
   d. Accounts Receivable

ASSIGNMENT MATERIAL

QUESTIONS

1. Name the basic shortcut device or tool used in accounting. What letter of the alphabet does it resemble? Name its two sides.

2. Is the following statement true or false? Debit means decrease and credit means increase. Explain your answer.

3. Explain the rules of debits and credits for each type of account.

4. What are the three basic types of accounts? Name two additional types of accounts. To which one of the three basic types are these two additional types of accounts most closely related?

5. Suppose you are the accountant for Whistler Marketing Enterprises. Keeping in mind double-entry bookkeeping, identify the dual effects of Sasha Chandler's investment of $10,000 cash in her business.

6. Briefly describe the flow of accounting information using the accounting cycle.

7. To what does the normal balance of an account refer?

8. Indicate the normal balance of the five types of accounts.

Account Type	Normal Balance
Assets	_____
Liabilities	_____
Owner's equity	_____
Revenues	_____
Expenses	_____

9. What does posting accomplish? Why is it important? Does it come before or after journalizing?

10. Label each of the following transactions as increasing owner's equity (+), decreasing owner's equity (−), or having no effect on owner's equity (0). Write the appropriate symbol in the space provided.

___ Investment by owner

___ Invoice customer for services

___ Purchase of supplies on credit

___ Pay expenses with cash

___ Cash payment on account

___ Withdrawal of cash by owner

___ Borrowing money on a note payable

___ Sale of services on account

11. What four steps does the posting process include? Which step is the fundamental purpose of posting?

12. Rearrange the following accounts in their logical sequence in the chart of accounts.

Note Payable	Salary Expense
Accounts Receivable	Cash
Sales Revenue	Sam Westman, Capital

13. What is the meaning of the statement "Accounts Payable has a credit balance of $2,800"?

14. Spiffy Cleaners launders the shirts of customer Bobby Ng, who has a charge account at the cleaners. When Ng picks up his clothes and is short of cash, he charges it. Later, when he receives his monthly statement from the cleaners, Ng writes a cheque on his bank account and mails the cheque to the cleaners. Identify the two business transactions described here for Spiffy Cleaners. Which transaction increases the business's owner's equity? Which transaction increases Spiffy Cleaners's cash?

15. Explain the difference between the ledger and the chart of accounts.

16. Why do accountants prepare a trial balance?

17. What is a compound journal entry?

18. The accountant for Wingers Construction mistakenly recorded a $600 purchase of supplies on account as $6,000. He debited Supplies and credited Accounts Payable for $6,000. Does this error cause the trial balance to be out of balance? Explain your answer.

19. What is the effect on total assets of collecting cash on account from customers?

20. Briefly summarize the similarities and differences between manual and computer-based accounting systems in terms of journalizing, posting, and preparing a trial balance.

MyAccountingLab

Make the grade with MyAccountingLab: The Starters, Exercises, and Problems marked in red can be found on MyAccountingLab. You can practise them as often as you want, and most feature step-by-step guided instructions to help you find the right answer.

STARTERS

The accounting cycle
(1)

Starter 2–1 Put the steps in the accounting cycle in the proper sequence by inserting the numbers 1 to 11.

a. Prepare a post-closing trial balance   _____

b. Prepare an adjusted trial balance   _____

c. Identify and analyze the transaction   _____

d. Prepare the unadjusted trial balance   _____

e. Post adjusting journal entries to the ledger _____

f. Post from the journal to the ledger accounts _____

g. Journalize adjusting journal entries   _____

h. Journalize closing entries   _____

i. Prepare financial statements   _____

j. Post closing entries to the ledger   _____

k. Record transaction in a journal   _____

Using accounting terms
(1)

Starter 2–2 Fill in the blanks to review some key definitions.

Josh Stone is describing the accounting process to a friend who is a philosophy major. Josh states, "The basic summary device in accounting is the _____. The left side is called the _____ side, and the right side is called the _____ side. We record transactions first in a _____. Then we post (copy the data) to the _____. It is helpful to list all the accounts with their balances on a _____."

Using accounting terms
(1)

Starter 2–3 Accounting has its own vocabulary and basic relationships. Match the accounting terms at left with the corresponding definitions at right.

_____ 1. Credit	A. Record of transactions
_____ 2. Normal balance	B. Always an asset
_____ 3. Payable	C. Right side of an account
_____ 4. Journal	D. Side of an account where increases are recorded
_____ 5. Receivable	E. Copying data from the journal to the ledger
_____ 6. Capital	F. Increases in equity from providing goods and services
_____ 7. Posting	G. Always a liability
_____ 8. Revenue	H. Revenues – Expenses (where expenses exceed revenues)
_____ 9. Net loss	I. Grouping of accounts
_____ 10. Ledger	J. Owner's equity in the business

Starter 2–4

Jose Suarez is tutoring Blaine McCormick, who is taking introductory accounting. Jose explains to Blaine that *debits* are used to record increases in accounts and *credits* record decreases. Blaine is confused and seeks your advice.

Explaining the rules of debit and credit
(2)

- When are credits increases? When are credits decreases?
- When are debits increases? When are debits decreases?

Starter 2–5

For each of the following changes, indicate whether a debit or credit entry would be made to the balance sheet account:

Explaining the rules of debit and credit
(2)

a. To decrease Accounts Payable
b. To increase Cash
c. To increase Notes Payable
d. To increase Office Supplies

e. To increase Equipment
f. To increase Accounts Payable
g. To increase Land
h. To increase Owner, Capital

Starter 2–6

For each of the following accounts, identify whether the normal balance is a debit or a credit:

Normal balances
(2)

a. Accounts Payable
b. J. Yuen, Withdrawals
c. Utilities Expense
d. Cash

e. Service Revenue
f. Rent Expense
g. Accounts Receivable

Starter 2–7

State the account to be debited and the account to be credited for the following transactions. Choose from the following list of accounts: Cash, Accounts Receivable, Supplies, Equipment, Land, Accounts Payable, Note Payable, Capital, Withdrawals, Service Revenue, Utilities Expense, and Salaries Expense.
(Hint: Not all accounts will be used.)

Identifying accounts
(3)

	Debit	Credit
a. Owner invests cash into the business.	____	____
b. Purchased supplies for cash.	____	____
c. Performed services for cash.	____	____
d. Purchased equipment by issuing a note payable.	____	____
e. Purchased supplies on account.	____	____
f. Performed services on account.	____	____
g. Received cash on account.	____	____
h. Paid a creditor on account.	____	____

Starter 2–8

Lochlan Mystrie opened a wedding planning business. Record the following transactions in the journal of the business. Include an explanation with each journal entry.

Recording transactions
(3)

Sep. 1 Mystrie invested $29,000 cash in a business bank account to start his business. The business received the cash and gave Mystrie owner's equity in the business.
2 Purchased decorating supplies on account, $9,500.
2 Paid cash for September's office rent of $4,100.
3 Recorded $6,800 revenue for services rendered to clients on account.

Starter 2–9

After operating for a month, Lochlan Mystrie's business completed the following transactions during the latter part of September:

Recording transactions
(3)

Sep. 22 Performed service for clients on account, $6,000.
30 Received cash on account from clients, $4,500.
30 Received a telephone bill, $150, which will be paid during November.
30 Paid cash for advertising expense of $900.
30 Paid cash for monthly salary to his assistant, $3,900.

Journalize the business transactions. Include an explanation with each journal entry.

Posting to accounts and
calculating balances

Starter 2–10 Your co-worker wanted the afternoon off and you graciously agreed to
finish up his work for him. Use the completed journal entries provided
and post them to their T-accounts. Assume all accounts start with a zero
balance. Compute the balance of each account and mark it as *Bal*.

	Journal			
Date	**Account Titles and Explanations**	**Post. Ref.**	**Debit**	**Credit**
Apr. 1	Cash		32,000	
	Taylor Moffat, Capital			32,000
	Received investment from owner.			
2	Medical Supplies		9,500	
	Accounts Payable			9,500
	Purchased supplies on account.			
2	Rent Expense		4,100	
	Cash			4,100
	Paid office rent for April.			
3	Cash		6,800	
	Service Revenue			6,800
	Performed service for cash.			
5	Accounts Payable		2,700	
	Cash			2,700
	Partial payment of balance on account.			

Journalizing transactions;
posting to T-accounts

Starter 2–11 Nancy Carpenter Optical Dispensary bought supplies on account for
$10,000 on September 8. On September 22, the company paid half on
account.

1. Journalize the two transactions for Nancy Carpenter Optical Dispensary.
   Include an explanation for each transaction.
2. Open the Accounts Payable T-account and post to Accounts Payable.
   Compute the balance and denote it as *Bal*.

Journalizing transactions;
posting to T-accounts

3. a. Earned $12,000

Starter 2–12 On October 5, Tina Serelio performed legal services for a client who
could not pay immediately. The business expected to collect the $12,000
the following month. On November 18, the business received $5,500 cash
from the client.

1. Record the two transactions for Tina Serelio, Lawyer. Include an explanation for each transaction.
2. Open these T-accounts: Cash; Accounts Receivable; Service Revenue.
   Post to all three accounts. Compute each account's balance and denote
   it as *Bal*.
3. Answer these questions based on your analysis:
   a. How much did the business earn? Which account shows this amount?
   b. How much in total assets did the business acquire as a result of the
      two transactions? Identify each asset and show its amount.

Calculate T-account balances

Starter 2–13 Calculate the account balance for each of the following T-accounts:

Accounts Receivable		**Cash**		**Accounts Payable**	
2,700	2,700	67,500	4,200	1,100	4,600
5,800	1,100	16,800	12,300		700
4,900	850				
	4,090				

Starter 2–14
Compute the missing amount represented by X in each account:

Find missing amounts
(4)

R. Glennie, Capital		
22,000	Bal.	X
		56,000
		15,000
	Bal.	73,000

Accounts Receivable		
Bal.	21,800	X
	55,100	
Bal.	47,000	

Starter 2–15
Use the information shown below to prepare a trial balance for Balzy Indoor Tennis Club at November 30, 2017.

Preparing a trial balance from T-accounts
(4) (5)
Trial balance total, $36,240

Balzy Indoor Tennis Club
General Ledger

Cash	10002
5,000	150
12,600	800
955	475
6,200	290

Furniture	17500
5,500	

Accounts Payable	20001
3,000	9,640
3,000	100

Stan Balzy, Capital	30001
	27,000

Stan Balzy, Withdrawals	30002
1,200	

Sales Revenue	40001
	5,500

Supplies Expense	51200
2,500	

Rent Expense	53200
4,000	

Starter 2–16
Redwing Floor Covering reported the following summarized data at December 31, 2017. Accounts appear in no particular order.

Preparing a trial balance
(5)
Trial bal. total, $75,000

Revenue	$32,000	Other Liabilities	$17,000
Equipment	43,000	Cash	6,000
Accounts Payable	1,000	Expenses	26,000
Capital	25,000		

Prepare the trial balance of Redwing Floor Covering at December 31, 2017. List the accounts in proper order, as in Exhibit 2–12 on page 80.

Starter 2–17
Hunter Environmental Consulting prepared its unadjusted trial balance on page 80. Suppose Lisa Hunter made an error: She listed the Capital balance of $250,000 as a debit rather than a credit by mistake.

Correcting a trial balance
(5)
Incorrect trial bal. total debits, $557,000

Compute the incorrect trial balance totals for debits and credits. Then refer to the discussion of correcting errors on pages 80 and 81 and show how to correct this error.

Starter 2–18
Return to Hunter Environmental Consulting's unadjusted trial balance on page 80. Assume that Lisa Hunter accidentally listed her utilities expense as $150 instead of the correct amount of $1,500. Compute the incorrect trial balance totals for debits and credits. Then show how to correct this error, which is called a *slide*.

Correcting a trial balance
(5)
Incorrect trial bal. total debits, $305,650

EXERCISES

MyAccountingLab

Exercise 2–1

Your employer, Prairie Tours, has just hired an office manager who does not understand accounting. The Prairie Tours trial balance lists Cash of $57,800. Write a short memo to the office manager explaining the accounting process that produced this listing on the trial balance. Mention *debits, credits, journal, ledger, posting,* and *trial balance.*

Using accounting vocabulary
(1)

Exercise 2-2

Using accounting vocabulary
①

Review accounting terms by completing the following crossword puzzle.

Across:

5. Copy data from the journal to the ledger
7. Book of accounts
8. List of accounts with their balances
10. Revenue – net income
11. Records an increase in a liability
12. Left side of an account

Down:

1. Amount collectible from a customer
2. Statement of financial position
3. An economic resource
4. Record of transactions
6. "Bottom line" of an income statement
9. Another word for liability

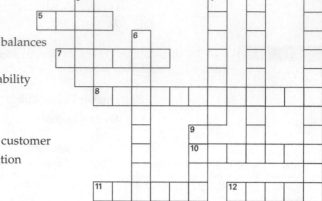

Exercise 2-3

Using debits and credits with the accounting equation
① ②
2. Net income, $2,500

Refer to the Summary Problem for Your Review, specifically the unadjusted trial balance on page 86.

Required

1. Write the company's accounting equation and label each element as a debit amount or a credit amount. If you use $28,500 for the owner's equity, why is the accounting equation out of balance?

2. Write the equation to compute Bancroft Management Consulting's net income or net loss for March 2016. Indicate which element is a debit amount and which element is a credit amount. Does net income represent a net debit or a net credit? Does net loss represent a net debit or a net credit?

3. How much did the owner, John Cassiar, withdraw during March 2016? Did the withdrawal represent a debit amount or a credit amount?

4. Considering both the net income (or net loss) and withdrawal for March 2016, by how much did the company's owner's equity increase or decrease? Was the change in owner's equity a debit amount or a credit amount?

Exercise 2-4

Normal balances
②

For each of the following accounts, indicate the type of account and whether the normal balance of the account is a debit or a credit:

a. Interest Revenue

b. Accounts Payable

c. Chapman Li, Capital

d. Office Supplies

e. Advertising Expense

f. Service Revenue

g. Chapman Li, Withdrawals

Exercise 2-5

Analyzing and journalizing transactions
② ③

The following transactions occurred for London Engineering:

Jul. 2 Received $10,000 contribution from Bill London in exchange for capital

4 Paid utilities expense of $400

5 Purchased equipment on account for $2,100

10	Performed services for a client on account, $2,000
12	Borrowed $7,000 cash, signing a note payable
19	The owner, Bill London, withdrew $500 cash from the business
21	Purchased office supplies for $800 and paid cash.
27	Paid the liability from July 5.

Required Journalize the transactions of London Engineering. Include an explanation with each journal entry. Use the following accounts: Cash; Accounts Receivable; Office Supplies; Equipment; Accounts Payable; Notes Payable; B. London, Capital; B. London, Withdrawals; Service Revenue; Utilities Expense.

Exercise 2–6

Analyze the following transactions of Pretty Party Planners in the manner shown for the December 1 transaction. Also, record each transaction in the journal.

Analyzing and journalizing transactions

Dec.	1	Paid monthly utilities expense of $200.
		(Analysis: The expense, utilities expense, is increased; therefore, debit Utilities Expense. The asset, cash, is decreased; therefore, credit Cash.)
	1	Utilities Expense 200
		Cash 200
	4	Borrowed $20,000 cash, signing a note payable.
	8	Purchased equipment on account, $4,000.
	12	Performed service on account for a customer, $6,000.
	19	Sold land for $24,000 cash that had cost this same amount.
	22	Purchased supplies for $1,200 and paid cash.
	27	Paid the liability created on December 8.

Exercise 2–7

Yula's Yoga engaged in the following transactions during March 2017, its first month of operations:

Excel Spreadsheet Template

Journalizing transactions

Mar.	1	The business received a $15,000 cash investment from Yula Gregore to start Yula's Yoga.
	1	Paid $4,000 cash to rent a yoga studio for the month of March.
	1	Purchased studio supplies for $4,000 on account.
	6	Presented a wellness seminar for a corporate customer and received cash, $3,000.
	9	Paid $1,000 on accounts payable.
	17	Taught yoga classes for customers on account, $800.

Required Record the preceding transactions in the journal of Yula's Yoga. Identify transactions by their date and include an explanation for each entry, as illustrated in the chapter. Use the following accounts: Cash; Accounts Receivable; Studio Supplies; Accounts Payable; Yula Gregore, Capital; Service Revenue; Rent Expense.

Exercise 2–8

Journalize the following transactions for DJ Services:

Journalize transactions

a. Owner, Liam Deresh, invested $2,500 cash into the business.

b. Rented a sound system and paid one month's rent, $1,100.

c. Performed DJ services on account, $1,700.

d. Paid $600 cash for equipment.

e. Owner, Liam Deresh, withdrew $500 cash for personal use.

f. Purchased $40 of supplies for cash.

Exercise 2–9

The first five transactions of Lin's Tai Chi Retreat have been posted to the company's accounts as shown here:

Cash			
(1)	7,500	(3)	5,250
(4)	1,375	(5)	1,500

Supplies	
(2)	275

Exercise Equipment	
(5)	1,500

Land	
(3)	5,250

Accounts Payable	
(2)	275

Note Payable	
(4)	1,375

S. Lin, Capital	
(1)	7,500

Required   Prepare the journal entries that served as the sources for posting the five transactions. Date each entry April 30, 2017, and include an explanation for each entry as illustrated in the chapter.

Exercise 2–10

The journal of Alumet Defensive Driving for July 2016 is shown below:

Journal					Page 5
2016	**Account Titles and Explanations**	**Post. Ref.**	**Debit**	**Credit**	
Jul. 2	Cash		5,600		
	Tomas Misheal, Capital			5,600	
9	Supplies		54		
	Accounts Payable			54	
11	Accounts Receivable		1,620		
	Service Revenue			1,620	
14	Rent Expense		1,400		
	Cash			1,400	
22	Cash		280		
	Accounts Receivable			280	
25	Advertising Expense		590		
	Cash			590	
27	Accounts Payable		54		
	Cash			54	
31	Fuel Expense		564		
	Accounts Payable			564	

Required

1. Describe each transaction.

2. Set up T-accounts using the following account numbers: Cash, #1000; Accounts Receivable, #1200; Supplies, #1400; Accounts Payable, #2000; Tomas Misheal, Capital, #3000; Service Revenue, #4000; Advertising Expense, #5100; Rent Expense, #5600; Fuel Expense, #5800.

3. Post to the T-accounts. Identify each transaction by date. You may write the account numbers as posting references directly in the journal in your book unless directed otherwise by your instructor. Compute the balance in each account after posting.

Exercise 2–11

On July 2, 2017, Efficient Energy Services performed an energy audit for an industrial client and earned $4,000 of revenue on account. On July 14, 2017, the company received a cheque for the entire amount.

Required

1. Journalize the two transactions on the sixth page of the journal. Include an explanation for each transaction.
2. Create the Accounts Receivable three-column ledger and post the two transactions. The account number for Accounts Receivable is 12001.

Exercise 2–12

Open the following three-column ledger accounts for Yarrow Strategic Consulting at May 1, 2017: Cash, #1100; Accounts Receivable, #1300; Office Supplies, #1500; Office Furniture, #1800; Accounts Payable, #2100; Florence Yarrow, Capital, #3100; Florence Yarrow, Withdrawals, #3200; Consulting Revenue, #4100; Rent Expense, #5500; Salary Expense, #5600.

Journalizing and posting transactions to a three-column ledger

③ ④

Journalize the following May 2017 transactions on the ninth page of the journal, then post to the ledger accounts. Use the dates to identify the transactions.

May   2   Florence Yarrow opened a strategic consulting firm by investing $39,200 cash and office furniture valued at $16,200.
2   Paid cash for May's rent of $2,500.
2   Purchased office supplies on account, $1,800.
15   Paid employee salary, $4,000 cash.
17   Paid $1,200 of the account payable from May 2.
19   Performed consulting service on account, $69,000.
30   Withdrew $8,000 cash for personal use.

Exercise 2–13

Refer to Exercise 2–7 for the transactions of Yula's Yoga.

Posting transactions using T-accounts, preparing a trial balance

④ ⑤

2. Trial bal. total, $21,800

Required

1. After journalizing the transactions of Exercise 2–7, post the entries to T-accounts. Identify transactions by their date. Date the ending balance of each account Mar. 31.
2. Prepare the unadjusted trial balance of Yula's Yoga at March 31, 2017.

Exercise 2–14

Prepare the unadjusted trial balance of Lin's Tai Chi Retreat at April 30, 2017, using the account data from Exercise 2–9.

Preparing a trial balance

⑤

Trial bal. total, $8,950

Exercise 2–15

The accounts of Boots Consulting are listed below with their normal balances at October 31, 2017. The accounts are listed in no particular order.

Excel Spreadsheet Template
Preparing a trial balance

⑤

Trial bal. total, $720,600

Account	Balance
M. Boots, capital	$252,800
Advertising expense	9,900
Accounts payable	33,800
Service revenue	161,000
Land	174,000
Notes payable	270,000
Cash	30,000
Salary expense	36,000
Building	390,000
Computer rental expense	2,000
M. Boots, withdrawals	36,000
Utilities expense	2,400
Accounts receivable	35,000
Supplies expense	3,800
Supplies	1,500

Required Prepare the company's trial balance at October 31, 2017, listing accounts in the sequence illustrated in the chapter. (Hints: Supplies comes before Building and Land. List the expenses alphabetically.)

Exercise 2–16

Preparing a trial balance

⑤

Trial bal. total, $125,000

After recording the transactions in Exercise 2–12, prepare the unadjusted trial balance of Yarrow Strategic Consulting at May 31, 2017.

Exercise 2–17

Correcting errors in a trial balance

⑤

Trial bal. total, $35,300

The trial balance of Mia's Memories at February 28, 2017, does not balance.

Cash	$ 3,100	
Accounts receivable	1,900	
Supplies	700	
Land	26,100	
Accounts payable		$11,400
M. Mia, capital		11,900
Service revenue		9,600
Rent expense	900	
Salary expense	1,600	
Utilities expense	500	
Total	$34,800	$32,900

Investigation of the accounting records reveals that the bookkeeper made the following errors:

a. Recorded a $400 cash revenue transaction by debiting Accounts Receivable. The credit entry was correct.

b. Posted a $2,000 credit to Accounts Payable as $200.

c. Did not record utilities expense or the related account payable in the amount of $500.

d. Understated M. Mia, Capital by $100.

Required Prepare the corrected trial balance at February 28, 2017, complete with a heading. Journal entries are not required.

SERIAL EXERCISE

Exercise 2–18 continues with the consulting business of Michael Lee, begun in Serial Exercise 1–17. Here you will account for Lee Management Consulting's transactions as it is actually done in practice.

Exercise 2–18

Recording transactions, preparing a trial balance

② ③ ④ ⑤

4. Trial bal. total, $37,000

Lee Management Consulting began operations and completed the following transactions during June 2016:

Jun.
2   Received $25,000 cash from owner Michael Lee. The business gave owner's equity in the business to Lee.

2   Lee found a great downtown loft from which to operate. He paid cash for rent for the month of June, $3,000.

3   Paid cash for a laptop, $1,000. The computer is expected to remain in service for four years. (Use the Equipment account for this transaction.)

4   Purchased office furniture on account, $5,000. The furniture is expected to last for five years.

5   Purchased supplies on account, $500.

9   Performed consulting services for a client on account, $3,000.

12 Paid utility expenses with cash, $250.

18   Performed consulting services for a client and received cash of $2,000.

21   Received $2,000 in advance for client services to be performed at a rate of $100 per day for a period of 20 days. (Use the liability account Unearned Revenue for this transaction. We will learn more about this account in Chapter 3.)

22   Hired an office manager on a part-time basis. She will be paid $2,000 per month. She started work on Monday, June 25.

23   Paid $500 cash for the account related to supplies purchased on June 5.

26   Collected a partial payment of $1,500 from the consulting client invoiced on June 9.

28   Michael Lee withdrew $2,000 cash for personal use.

Required

1. Open T-accounts in the ledger for Cash; Accounts Receivable; Supplies; Equipment; Furniture; Accounts Payable; Unearned Revenue; Michael Lee, Capital; Michael Lee, Withdrawals; Service Revenue; Rent Expense; Salaries Expense; and Utilities Expense.

2. Journalize the transactions. No explanations are required (to save time).

3. Post to the T-accounts. Identify all items by date and label an account balance as Bal. Formal posting references are not required

4. Prepare an unadjusted trial balance at June 30, 2016.

CHALLENGE EXERCISES

Exercise 2–19

The owner of Fergus Technical Services is an architect with little understanding of accounting. She needs to compute the following summary information from the accounting records:

a. Net income for the month of March

b. Total cash paid during March

c. Cash collections from customers during March

d. Payments on account during March

The quickest way to compute these amounts is to analyze the following accounts:

Computing financial statement amounts

②⑤

b. Cash paid, $10,880

Account	Balance Feb. 28	Mar. 31	Additional Information for the Month of March
a. B. Fergus, Capital......................	$1,440	$2,400	Withdrawals, $640
b. Cash...	1,800	1,640	Cash receipts, $10,720
c. Accounts Receivable	3,840	6,160	Sales on account, $12,160
d. Accounts Payable	2,080	2,560	Purchases on account, $508

The net income for March can be computed as follows:

B. Fergus, Capital

March Withdrawals	640	Feb. 28 Bal.	1,440
		March Net Income	$x = \$1,600$
		March 31 Bal.	2,400

Use a similar approach to compute the other three items.

Exercise 2–20

Bridget Battle has trouble keeping her debits and credits equal. During a recent month, Bridget made the following errors:

Analyzing accounting errors

②③⑤

a. In preparing the trial balance, Bridget omitted a $5,000 note payable.

b. Bridget recorded a $340 purchase of supplies on account by debiting Supplies and crediting Accounts Payable for $430.

c. In recording a $200 payment on account, Bridget debited Supplies instead of Accounts Payable.

d. In journalizing a receipt of cash from service revenue, Bridget debited Cash for $50 instead of the correct amount of $500. The credit was correctly recorded in the amount of $500.

e. Bridget posted a $1,000 utility expense as $100. The credit to Cash was correct.

Required

1. For each of these errors, state whether the total debits equal total credits on the trial balance.

2. Identify each account that has an incorrect balance and indicate the amount and direction of the error (e.g., "Accounts Receivable $500 too high").

BEYOND THE NUMBERS

Beyond the Numbers 2–1

Creating a chart of accounts

Stan Raza asks your advice in setting up the accounting records for his new business, Stan's Bake Shop. The business will be a bakery and will operate in a rented building. Stan's Bake Shop will need office equipment and baking equipment. The business will borrow money using a note payable to buy the needed equipment. Stan's Bake Shop will purchase on account food supplies and office supplies. Each asset has a related expense account, some of which have not yet been discussed. For example, equipment wears out (amortizes) and thus needs an amortization account. As supplies are used up, the business must record a supplies expense.

The business will need an office manager. This person will be paid a weekly salary of $1,800. Other expenses will include advertising and insurance. Since Stan's Bake Shop will want to know which aspects of the business generate the most and the least revenue, it will use separate service revenue accounts for cupcakes (his specialty!), office catering, and wedding cakes. Stan's Bake Shop's better customers will be allowed to open accounts with the business.

Required List all the accounts Stan's Bake Shop will need, starting with the assets and ending with the expenses. Indicate which accounts will be reported on the balance sheet and which accounts will appear on the income statement.

ETHICAL ISSUE

Associated Charities Trust, a charitable organization in Brandon, Manitoba, has a standing agreement with Prairie Bank. The agreement allows Associated Charities Trust to overdraw its cash balance at the bank when donations are running low. In the past, Associated Charities Trust managed funds wisely and rarely used this privilege. Greg Glowa has recently become the president of Associated Charities Trust. To expand operations, Glowa is acquiring office equipment and spending large amounts for fundraising. During his presidency, Associated Charities Trust has maintained a negative bank balance (a credit Cash balance) of approximately $28,000.

Required What is the ethical issue in this situation? State why you approve or disapprove of Glowa's management of Associated Charities Trust's funds.

PROBLEMS (GROUP A)

MyAccountingLab

Problem 2–1A

Baycrest Cinema Company owns movie theatres. Baycrest Cinema engaged in the following transactions in November 2016:

Analyzing and journalizing transactions
② ③

Nov. 1   Darrell Palusky invested $350,000 personal cash in the business by depositing that amount in a bank account titled Baycrest Cinema Company. The business gave capital to Palusky.

1   Paid November's rent on a theatre building with cash, $6,000.

2   Paid $320,000 cash to purchase land for a theatre site.

5   Borrowed $220,000 from the bank to finance the first phase of construction of the new theatre. Palusky signed a note payable to the bank in the name of Baycrest Cinema Company.

10   Purchased theatre supplies on account, $1,000.

16   Paid employees' salaries of $2,900 cash.

22   Paid $600 on account.

28   Palusky withdrew $8,000 cash.

29   Paid property tax expense on the land for the new theatre, cash of $1,400.

30   Received $20,000 cash from service revenue and deposited that amount in the bank.

Baycrest uses the following accounts: Cash; Supplies; Land; Accounts Payable; Notes Payable; Darrell Palusky, Capital; Darrell Palusky, Withdrawals; Service Revenue; Property Tax Expense; Rent Expense; Salaries Expense.

Required

1. Prepare an analysis of each business transaction of Baycrest Cinema Company as shown for the November 1 transaction:

Nov. 1   The asset cash is increased. Increases in assets are recorded by debits; therefore, debit Cash. The owner's equity of the entity is increased. Increases in owner's equity are recorded by credits; therefore, credit Darrell Palusky, Capital.

2. Record each transaction in the journal with an explanation, using the account titles given. Identify each transaction by its date.

Problem 2–2A

Zeb Slipewicz opened a renovation business called WeReDoIt Construction on September 3, 2017. During the first month of operations, the business completed the following transactions:

Journalizing transactions
② ③

Sep. 3   Zeb deposited a cheque for $72,000 into the business bank account to start the business.

4   Purchased supplies, $600, and furniture, $4,400, on account

5   Paid September rent expense, $1,500 cash.

6   Performed design services for a client and received $2,400 cash.

7   Paid $44,000 cash to acquire land for a future office site.

10   Designed a bathroom for a client, billed the client, and received her promise to pay the $5,800 within one week.

14   Paid for the furniture purchased September 4 on account.

15   Paid assistant's salary, $940 cash.

17   Received cash on account, $3,400.

22   Received $5,000 cash from a client for renovation of a cottage.

25   Prepared a recreation room design for a client on account, $1,600.

30   Paid assistant's salary, $940 cash.

30   Zeb withdrew $5,600 cash for personal use.

Required Record each transaction in the journal with an explanation. Identify each transaction by date. Use the following accounts: Cash; Accounts Receivable; Supplies; Furniture; Land; Accounts Payable; Z. Slipewicz, Capital; Z. Slipewicz, Withdrawals; Service Revenue; Rent Expense; Salary Expense.

Problem 2–3A

Journalizing transactions and posting to ledger accounts
② ③ ④

The trial balance of Thomson Engineering at February 28, 2017, is shown below:

	THOMSON ENGINEERING		
	Trial Balance		
	February 28, 2017		
Account Number	Account	Debit	Credit
1100	Cash	$ 4,000	
1200	Accounts receivable	16,000	
1300	Supplies	3,600	
1600	Automobile	37,200	
2000	Accounts payable		$ 8,000
3000	R. Thomson, Capital		50,000
3100	R. Thomson, Withdrawals	4,400	
5000	Service revenue		16,400
6100	Rent expense	2,000	
6200	Salary expense	7,200	
	Total	$74,400	$74,400

During March, Thomson Engineering completed the following transactions:

Mar.	4	Collected $600 cash from a client on account.
	8	Designed a system for a client on account, $580.
	13	Paid cash for items purchased on account, $320.
	18	Purchased supplies on account, $120.
	20	R. Thomson withdrew $200 cash for personal use.
	21	Received a verbal promise of a $2,000 contract.
	22	Received cash of $620 for consulting work just completed.
	31	Paid employees' salaries, $1,300 cash.

Required

1. Record the March transactions in Page 3 of the journal. Include an explanation for each entry.

2. Open three-column ledger accounts for the accounts listed in the trial balance, together with their balances at February 28. Enter Bal. (for previous balance) in the Item column, and place a check mark (✓) in the journal reference column for the February 28 balance in each account.

3. Post the transactions to the ledger, using dates, account numbers, journal references, and posting references.

Problem 2–4A

Recording transactions, using three-column ledger accounts, preparing a trial balance
② ③ ④ ⑤

Sophie Vaillancourt started an investment management business, Vaillancourt Management, on June 1, 2017. During the first month of operations, the business completed the following selected transactions:

a. Sophie began the business with an investment of $20,000 cash, land valued at $60,000, and a building valued at $120,000. The business gave Sophie owner's equity in the business for the value of the cash, land, and building.

b. Purchased office supplies on account, $2,600.

c. Paid $15,000 cash for office furniture.

d. Paid employee salary, $2,200 cash.

e. Performed consulting service on account for clients, $12,100.

f. Paid in cash $800 of the account payable created in Transaction b.

g. Received a $2,000 bill for advertising expense that will be paid in the near future.

h. Performed consulting services for customers and received cash, $5,600.

i. Received cash on account, $2,400.

j. Paid the following cash expenses:

   (1) Rent of photocopier, $1,700.

   (2) Utilities, $400.

k. Sophie withdrew $6,500 cash for personal use.

Required

1. Record each transaction in the journal. Use the letters to identify the transactions.

2. Open the following three-column ledger accounts: Cash, #1100; Accounts Receivable, #1300; Office Supplies, #1400; Office Furniture, #1500; Building, #1700; Land, #1800; Accounts Payable, #2100; Sophie Vaillancourt, Capital, #3100; Sophie Vaillancourt, Withdrawals, #3200; Service Revenue, #4100; Advertising Expense, #5100; Equipment Rental Expense, #5300; Salary Expense, #5500; Utilities Expense, #5700.

3. Post to the accounts and keep a running balance for each account.

4. Prepare the unadjusted trial balance of Vaillancourt Management at June 30, 2017.

Problem 2–5A

The owner of Archer Communications, Nancy Archer, is selling the business. She offers the trial balance shown below to prospective buyers.

Analyzing a trial balance

Net income, $55,000

ARCHER COMMUNICATIONS Trial Balance December 31, 2017		
Cash	$ 28,000	
Accounts receivable	30,500	
Prepaid expenses	6,000	
Land	64,000	
Accounts payable		$ 62,500
Note payable		38,000
N. Archer, capital		45,000
N. Archer, withdrawals	72,000	
Service revenue		151,000
Advertising expense	4,500	
Rent expense	39,000	
Supplies expense	10,500	
Wages expense	42,000	
Total	$296,500	$296,500

Your best friend is considering buying Archer Communications. He seeks your advice in interpreting this information. Specifically, he asks whether this trial balance is the same as a balance sheet and an income statement. He also wonders whether Archer Communications is a sound company because all the accounts are in balance.

Required Write a short note to answer your friend's questions. To aid his decision, state how he can use the information on the trial balance to compute Archer Communications's net income or net loss for the current period. State the amount of net income or net loss in your note.

Problem 2–6A

Correcting errors in a trial balance
② ⑤
Trial bal. total, $70,000

The following trial balance does not balance:

MINTER LANDSCAPE CONSULTING		
Trial Balance		
June 30, 2017		
Cash	$ 1,600	
Accounts receivable	10,000	
Supplies	900	
Office furniture	3,600	
Land	46,600	
Accounts payable		$ 3,800
Notes payable		23,000
R. Minter, capital		31,600
R. Minter, withdrawals	2,000	
Consulting service revenue		7,300
Advertising expense	400	
Rent expense	1,000	
Salary expense	2,100	
Utilities expense	410	
Total	$68,610	$65,700

The following errors were detected:

a. The cash balance is understated by $1,300.

b. The cost of the land was $44,600, not $46,600.

c. A $400 purchase of supplies on account was neither journalized nor posted.

d. A $3,000 credit to Consulting Service Revenue was not posted.

e. Rent Expense of $200 was posted as a credit rather than a debit.

f. The balance of Advertising Expense is $600, but it was listed as $400 on the trial balance.

g. A $300 debit to Accounts Receivable was posted as $30. The credit to Consulting Service Revenue was correct.

h. The balance of Utilities Expense is overstated by $80.

i. A $900 debit to the R. Minter, Withdrawals account was posted as a debit to R. Minter, Capital.

Required   Prepare the corrected trial balance at June 30, 2017. Journal entries are not required.

Problem 2–7A

Journalizing entries, posting to ledger accounts, preparing a trial balance
② ③ ④ ⑤
Trial bal. total, $452,300

CrossCountry Movers had the following account balances, in random order, on December 15, 2017 (all accounts have their "normal" balances):

Moving fees income	$261,600	Cash	$ 17,200
Accounts receivable	17,400	Storage fees income	57,900
Rent expense	47,100	Notes receivable	45,000
H. Martinez, capital	63,000	Utilities expense	2,400
Office supplies expense	2,100	Office supplies	9,600
Mortgage payable	39,000	Accounts payable	33,000
Salaries expense	161,100	Office equipment	12,300
Insurance expense	6,300	Moving equipment	132,200

The following events took place during the final weeks of the year:

Dec. 16   The accountant discovered that an error had been made in posting an entry to the Moving Fees Income account. The entry was correctly journalized, but $2,400 was accidentally posted as $4,200 in the account.

17   Moved a customer's goods to CrossCountry's rented warehouse for storage. The moving fees were $4,000. Storage fees are $600 per month. The customer was billed for one month's storage and the moving fees.

18   Collected a $15,000 note owed to CrossCountry Movers and collected interest income of $1,800 cash.

19   Used a company cheque to pay for Martinez's hydro bill in the amount of $400.

21   Purchased storage racks for $12,000. Paid $3,600 cash, provided moving services for $1,500, and promised to pay the balance in 60 days.

23   Collected $3,000 cash; $2,600 of this was for moving goods on December 15 (recorded as an account receivable at that time) and the balance was for storage fees for the period of December 16 to 23.

24   CrossCountry Movers paid cash of $18,000 owing on the mortgage.

27   Martinez withdrew $5,000 cash for personal use.

29   Provided moving services to a lawyer for $2,400. The lawyer paid CrossCountry Movers $1,500 and provided legal work for the balance.

31   Martinez, the owner of CrossCountry Movers, sold 2,000 shares he held in Brandon Haulage Inc. for $12,000.

Required

1. Where appropriate, record each transaction from December 16 to 31 in the journal. Include an explanation for each journal entry.

2. Post entries in T-accounts and calculate the balance of each one.

3. Prepare the unadjusted trial balance of CrossCountry Movers at December 31, 2017.

PROBLEMS (GROUP B)   MyAccountingLab

Problem 2–1B

Gladys Yuan is a research analyst who operates under the business title Yuan Research. During April 2017, the company engaged in the following transactions:

Analyzing and journalizing transactions

Apr. 1   Yuan deposited $40,000 cash in the business bank account. The business gave Yuan owner's equity in the business.

5   Paid April's rent on a shared office space with cash, $400.

10   Purchased supplies on account, $600.

19   Paid $100 on account for supplies purchased on April 10.

21   Paid $25,000 cash to purchase land for a future office location.

22   Borrowed $15,000 from the bank for business use. Yuan signed a note payable to the bank in the name of the business.

30   Paid cash for employee salaries of $3,500 and utilities of $350.

30   Revenues earned during the month included $1,300 cash and $2,400 on account.

30   Yuan withdrew $1,200 cash from the business for personal use.

Yuan Research uses the following accounts: Cash; Accounts Receivable; Supplies; Land; Accounts Payable; Notes Payable; G. Yuan, Capital; G. Yuan, Withdrawals; Service Revenue; Office Rent Expense; Salaries Expense; Utilities Expense.

Required

1. Prepare an analysis of each business transaction of Yuan Research, as shown for the April 1 transaction:

Apr. 1   The asset cash is increased. Increases in assets are recorded by debits; therefore, debit Cash. The owner's equity is increased. Increases in owner's equity are recorded by credits; therefore, credit G. Yuan, Capital.

2. Record each transaction in the journal with an explanation, using the dates and account titles given.

Problem 2–2B

Journalizing transactions
② ③

Scott Jameson opened a translation business on January 2, 2017. During the first month of operations, the business completed the following transactions:

Jan.	2	The business received $60,000 cash from Jameson, which was deposited in a business bank account entitled Jameson Translation Service.
	3	Purchased supplies, $750, and furniture, $2,800, on account.
	3	Paid January's rent expense with cash, $1,100.
	4	Performed translation services for a client and received cash, $2,250.
	7	Paid $38,000 cash to acquire land for a future office site.
	11	Translated a brochure for a client and billed the client $1,200.
	15	Paid secretary salary, $975 cash.
	16	Paid cash for the furniture purchased January 3 on account.
	18	Received partial payment from a client on account, $600 cash.
	19	Translated legal documents for a client on account, $11,350.
	22	Paid cash for the water and electricity bills, $300.
	29	Received $2,700 cash for translation for a client in an overseas business transaction.
	31	Paid secretary salary, $975 cash.
	31	Jameson withdrew $12,000 cash for personal use.

Required   Record each transaction in the journal with an explanation, using the account titles given. Use the following accounts: Cash; Accounts Receivable; Supplies; Furniture; Land; Accounts Payable; Scott Jameson, Capital; Scott Jameson, Withdrawals; Translation Revenue; Rent Expense; Salary Expense; Utilities Expense.

Problem 2–3B

Journalizing transactions and posting to three-column ledger accounts
② ③ ④

The trial balance of the online book publishing business of Bobbie Singh at November 15, 2017, is shown below:

Account Number	Account	Debit	Credit
	SUNSHINE PUBLISHING		
	Trial Balance		
	November 15, 2017		
1100	Cash	$ 16,000	
1200	Accounts receivable	16,000	
1300	Supplies	1,200	
1900	Equipment	70,000	
2100	Accounts payable		$ 9,200
4000	B. Singh, Capital		90,000
4100	B. Singh, Withdrawals	4,600	
5000	Service revenue		14,200
6000	Rent expense	2,000	
6100	Salaries expense	3,600	
	Total	$113,400	$113,400

During the remainder of November, the business completed the following transactions:

Nov. 16   Collected $6,000 cash from a client on account.
17   Performed publishing services for a client on account, $2,100.
21   Made a payment on account in the amount of $2,600.
22   Purchased supplies on account, $4,600.
23   Singh withdrew $2,100 cash for personal use.
24   Was advised that Desk Top Inc. was prepared to buy all of Sunshine Publishing for $67,800.
26   Received $11,900 cash for design work just completed.
30   Paid employees' salaries, $2,700 cash.

Required

1. Record the transactions that occurred during November 16 through 30 on Page 6 of the journal. Include an explanation for each entry.
2. Post the transactions to three-column accounts in the ledger, using dates, account numbers, journal references, and posting references. Open the ledger accounts listed in the trial balance together with their balances at November 15. Enter *Bal.* (for previous balance) in the Item column, and place a check mark (✓) in the journal reference column for the November 15 balance of each account.

Problem 2–4B

Bill Ronalds started a catering service called Blue Ribbon Catering. During the first month of operations, January 2017, the business completed the following selected transactions:

Recording transactions, using three-column ledger accounts, preparing a trial balance

a. Ronalds began the company with an investment of $50,000 cash and a van (automobile) valued at $26,000. The business gave Ronalds owner's equity in the business.
b. Paid $8,000 cash for food service equipment.
c. Purchased supplies on account, $14,800.
d. Paid employee salary, $12,600 cash.
e. Received $4,000 cash for a catering job.
f. Performed services at a wedding on account, $8,600.
g. Paid $12,000 cash as a partial payment for Transaction c.
h. Received a $1,600 bill for advertising expense that will be paid in the near future.
i. Received cash on account, $2,200.
j. Paid the following cash expenses:
   (1) Rent, $3,000.
   (2) Insurance, $1,600.
k. Ronalds withdrew $12,000 cash for personal use.

Required

1. Record the transactions in the journal. Use the letters to identify the transactions.
2. Open the following three-column ledger accounts: Cash, #1100; Accounts Receivable, #1300; Supplies, #1500; Food Service Equipment, #1600; Automobile, #1700; Accounts Payable, #2100; B. Ronalds, Capital, #3100; B. Ronalds, Withdrawals, #3200; Service Revenue, #4100; Advertising Expense, #5100; Insurance Expense, #5500; Rent Expense, #5700; Salary Expense, #5800.
3. Post to the accounts and keep a running balance for each account.
4. Prepare the unadjusted trial balance of Blue Ribbon Catering at January 31, 2017.

Problem 2–5B

Analyzing a trial balance

Ricky Ricardo, the owner of Online Designs, is selling the business. He offers the trial balance below to prospective buyers.

ONLINE DESIGNS Trial Balance December 31, 2017		
Cash	$ 36,000	
Accounts receivable	10,000	
Prepaid expenses	4,000	
Land	78,000	
Accounts payable		$ 72,000
Note payable		44,000
R. Ricardo, capital		76,000
R. Ricardo, withdrawals	30,000	
Service revenue		130,000
Advertising expense	26,000	
Rent expense	24,000	
Supplies expense	18,000	
Wages expense	96,000	
Total	$322,000	$322,000

Your best friend is considering buying Online Designs. She seeks your advice in interpreting this information. Specifically, she asks whether this trial balance is the same as a balance sheet and an income statement. She also wonders whether Online Designs is a sound company. She thinks it must be because the accounts are in balance.

Required Write a short note to answer your friend's questions. To aid her decision, state how she can use the information on the trial balance to compute Online Designs's net income or net loss for the current period. State the amount of net income or net loss in your note.

Problem 2–6B

Correcting errors in a trial balance

The trial balance for Mackle Fitness, shown below, does not balance.

MACKLE FITNESS Trial Balance July 31, 2017		
Cash	$ 47,000	
Accounts receivable	30,000	
Supplies	7,500	
Office furniture	34,500	
Fitness equipment	600,000	
Accounts payable		$ 30,000
Notes payable		194,500
G. Mackle, Capital		442,500
G. Mackle, Withdrawals	55,500	
Service revenue		73,500
Salary expense	42,500	
Rent expense	9,000	
Advertising expense	6,000	
Utilities expense	3,000	
Total	$835,000	$740,500

The following errors were detected:

a. The cash balance is overstated by $6,000.

b. Rent expense of $3,000 was posted as a credit rather than a debit.

c. The balance of Advertising Expense is $4,500, but it is listed as $6,000 on the trial balance.

d. A $9,000 debit to Accounts Receivable was posted as $900.

e. The balance of Utilities Expense is understated by $900.

f. A $19,500 debit to the G. Mackle, Withdrawals account was posted as a debit to G. Mackle, Capital.

g. A $1,500 purchase of supplies on account was neither journalized nor posted.

h. An $87,000 credit to Service Revenue was not posted.

i. Office furniture should be listed in the amount of $19,500.

Required Prepare the corrected trial balance at July 31, 2017. Journal entries are not required.

Problem 2–7B

Maquina Lodge, owned by Bob Palmiter, had the following account balances, in random order, on December 15, 2017 (all accounts have their "normal" balances):

Journalizing entries, posting to ledger accounts, preparing a trial balance

Guest revenue............................	$309,000	Furniture...............................	$57,800
Accounts receivable................	8,800	Cash......................................	3,800
Equipment rental expense......	11,800	Notes receivable...................	26,000
B. Palmiter, capital...................	209,800	Utilities expense...................	21,000
Supplies expense......................	2,800	Supplies inventory..............	5,800
Mortgage payable....................	30,000	Accounts payable................	12,000
Salaries expense......................	81,000	Office equipment................	10,200
Insurance expense...................	6,800	Boating equipment.............	96,800
Building......................................	200,000	Land..	30,000

The following events also took place during the final weeks of the year:

Dec.	16	The accountant discovered that an error had been made in posting an entry to the Guest Revenue account. The entry was correctly journalized, but $4,200 was accidentally posted as $2,400 in the account.
	17	Signed an agreement to let a retired professor move in during the off season for a long stay, beginning today. The monthly rate is $3,200 payable at the beginning of each month. The professor paid $1,550 cash for the remainder of December.
	18	Collected an $18,000 note owed to Maquina and collected interest of $2,400 cash.
	21	Purchased boating equipment for $14,000 from Boats Unlimited. Maquina Lodge paid $5,000 cash, provided room rentals for $1,600 to Boats Unlimited, and promised to pay the balance in 60 days.
	23	Collected $2,800 cash for rooms for a conference held from December 16 to 23.
	24	Maquina Lodge paid $2,000 cash owing on the mortgage.
	27	Palmiter withdrew $14,000 cash for personal use.
	29	Provided meeting rooms to a lawyer for $2,000. The lawyer paid Maquina Lodge $1,100 cash and provided legal work for the balance.

Required

1. Where appropriate, record each transaction from December 16 to 29 in the journal. Include an explanation for each entry.

2. Post entries in T-accounts and calculate the balance of each one.

3. Prepare the unadjusted trial balance of Maquina Lodge at December 31, 2017.

CHALLENGE PROBLEMS

Problem 2–1C

Understanding the rules of debit and credit

Some individuals, for whatever reason, do not pay income tax or pay less than they should. Often their business transactions are cash transactions, so there is no paper trail to prove how much or how little they actually earned. Canada Revenue Agency, however, has a way of dealing with these individuals; they use a model (based on the accounting equation) to calculate how much the individual must have earned.

Canada Revenue Agency is about to audit Donna Wynn for the period January 1, 2017, to December 31, 2017. Wynn buys and sells collectible coins for cash. Wynn had $8,000 cash and no other assets or liabilities at January 1, 2017.

Required

1. Use the accounting equation (specifically owner's equity) to explain how the Canada Revenue Agency model will be used to audit Donna.

2. What do you think are the accounting concepts underlying the model?

Problem 2–2C

Using a formal accounting system
3 4

Over the years you have become friendly with a farmer, Jack Russell, who raises crops, which he sells, and has small herds of beef cattle and sheep. Russell maintains his basic herds and markets the calves and lambs each fall. His accounting system is quite simple; all his transactions are in cash. Russell pays tax each year on his income, which he estimates. He indicated to you once that he must be doing it right because Canada Revenue Agency audited him recently and assessed no additional tax.

You are taking your first accounting course and are quite impressed with the information one can gain from a formal accounting system.

Required   Explain to Russell why it would be to his advantage to have a more formal accounting system with accounts, ledgers, and journals.

Problem 2–3C

Understanding the rules of debit and credit, preparing a trial balance
2 5
Trial bal. total, $14,981

Cash...	$2,840		Notes Payable..............	$1,200
Accounts Receivable.................	3,331		Fees Income.................	2,380
Supplies.......................................	800		Salaries Expense..........	3,400
Equipment.................................	3,000		Office Expense.............	910
Accounts Payable.....................	2,666			

Each of the above accounts has a normal balance in the ledger of Kala's Kabinet Konnection at December 31, 2017. An examination of the ledger and journal reveals the following errors:

a. Cash received from a customer on account was debited for $570 and Accounts Receivable was credited for the same amount. The actual collection was for $750.

b. The purchase of a computer monitor on account for $350 was recorded as a debit to Supplies for $350 and a credit to Accounts Payable for $350.

c. Services were performed on account for a client for $890. Accounts Receivable was debited for $890 and Fees Income was credited for $89.

d. A debit posting to Salaries Expense of $900 was omitted.

e. A payment on account for $206 was credited to Cash for $206 and credited to Accounts Payable for $260.

f. The withdrawal of $600 cash for Kat Kala's personal use was debited to Salaries Expense for $600 and credited to Cash for $600.

Required

1. For each item above, describe how a correction would be made, either by giving a correcting journal entry or by describing how a posting error would be corrected in the ledger.

2. Prepare the trial balance for Kala's Kabinet Konnection after the corrections are made.

EXTENDING YOUR KNOWLEDGE

DECISION PROBLEMS

Decision Problem 1

Your friend, Amin Akmali, has asked your advice about the effects that certain business transactions will have on his business. His business, Car Finders, finds the best deals on automobiles for clients. Time is short, so you cannot journalize transactions. Instead, you must analyze the transactions and post them directly to T-accounts. Akmali will continue in the business only if he can expect to earn monthly net income of $8,000. The business had the following transactions during March 2017:

a. Akmali deposited $50,000 cash in a business bank account.

b. The business borrowed $8,000 cash from the bank, which is recorded as a note payable due within one year.

c. Purchased for cash a vehicle to drive clients to appointments, $27,000.

d. Paid $1,600 cash for supplies.

e. Paid cash for advertising in the local newspaper, $1,200.

f. Paid the following cash expenses for one month: commission, $12,400; office rent, $800; utilities, $600; gas, $1,000; interest, $200.

g. Earned revenue on account, $20,600.

h. Earned $7,500 revenue and received cash.

i. Collected cash from customers on account, $2,400.

Required

1. Open the following T-accounts: Cash; Accounts Receivable; Supplies; Vehicle; Notes Payable; Amin Akmali, Capital; Advising Revenue; Advertising Expense; Interest Expense; Rent Expense; Commission Expense; Gas Expense; Utilities Expense.

2. Record the transactions directly in the T-accounts without using a journal. Identify each transaction by its letter.

3. Prepare an unadjusted trial balance at March 31, 2017. List expenses alphabetically.

4. Compute the amount of net income or net loss for this first month of operations. Would you recommend Akmali continue in business?

Recording transactions directly in the ledger, preparing a trial balance, measuring net income or loss

② ③ ④ ⑤

3. Trial bal. total, $86,100

Decision Problem 2

Although all the following questions deal with the accounting equation, they are not related:

1. Explain the advantages of double-entry bookkeeping to a friend who is opening a used-book store.

2. When you deposit money in your bank account, the bank credits your account. Is the bank misusing the word *credit* in this context? Why does the bank use the term *credit* to refer to your deposit and not *debit*?

3. Your friend asks, "When revenues increase assets and expenses decrease assets, why are revenues credits and expenses debits and not the other way around?" Explain to your friend why revenues are credits and expenses are debits.

Using the accounting equation

②

FINANCIAL STATEMENT CASES

Financial Statement Case 1

Examining financial statements

Refer to the Indigo Books & Music Inc.'s (Indigo) financial statements in Appendix A at the end of this book or on MyAccountingLab. Answer the following questions:

1. In what currency are Indigo's financial statements presented?
2. How are the dollar amounts on the Indigo financial statements presented?
3. On what exact date were the most recent Indigo financial statements prepared?
4. Does Indigo follow IFRS? How do you know?

Financial Statement Case 2

Journalizing transactions

② ③

This problem helps to develop journalizing skills by using an actual company's account titles for a selected set of accounts. Refer to the TELUS Corporation's (TELUS) financial statements that appear on MyAccountingLab. Assume TELUS completed the following selected (fictitious) transactions during December 2013:

a. Made sales on account, $950.
b. Paid cash for goods, $1,100.
c. Paid annual financing costs of $447.
d. Collected accounts receivable of $2,100.
e. Paid cash for prepaid rent, $24.
f. Purchased equipment on account for $550.
g. Paid cash for services, $1,800.

Required

1. Set up T-accounts for Cash (debit balance of $1,607); Accounts Receivable (debit balance of $2,611); Prepaid Expenses (debit balance of $144); Property, Plant, and Equipment (debit balance of $7,878); Accounts Payable and Accrued Liabilities (credit balance of $1,185); Service Revenue (credit balance of $9,651); Goods and Services Purchased (debit balance of $2,062); Financing Costs ($0 balance).

2. Journalize TELUS's Transactions a to g. Explanations are not required.

3. Post to T-accounts and compute the balance for each account. Identify each posting by its transaction letter.

4. For each of the accounts, compare your balances to TELUS's actual balances as shown on the December 31, 2013, balance sheet and income statement. All your amounts should agree with the actual figures rounded to the nearest dollar.

   Cash

   Accounts receivable

   Prepaid expenses

   Property, plant, and equipment

   Accounts payable and accrued liabilities

   Service revenue

   Goods and services purchased

   Financing costs

5. Balance sheet and income statement accounts listed are really categories representing summarized account balances. List three accounts that would be reflected in each of the following categories:

   a. Property, plant, and equipment
   b. Accounts payable and accrued liabilities
   c. General and administration expenses

1.

Salary Payable	L	Salary Expense	E	
Land	A	Rent Revenue	R	
L. Graham, Capital	OE	Computer Equipment	A	
Rent Expense	E	Notes Payable	L	
Supplies	A	Prepaid Rent	A	
Accounts Payable	L	L. Graham, Withdrawals	OE	

2.

10100	Cash
10200	Accounts Receivable
10400	Furniture and Fixtures
20100	Accounts Payable
20500	Income Taxes Payable
30100	L. Starks, Capital
30200	L. Starks, Withdrawals
40100	Service Revenue
50600	Rent Expense

3.

Accounts Payable	L; Cr	Cash	A; Dr
Service Revenue	R; Cr	Rent Expense	E; Dr
K. Lockyer, Withdrawals	OE; Dr	Vehicles	A; Dr
Rent Revenue	R; Cr	Notes Payable	L; Cr
Accounts Receivable	A; Dr	Land	A; Dr
Insurance Expense	E; Dr	K. Lockyer, Capital	OE; Cr

4. a. Increases

Dr	Accounts Receivable	Dr	Salary Expense
Cr	John Ladner, Capital	Cr	Interest Payable
Cr	Service Revenue	Dr	Furniture

b. Decreases

Dr	Notes Payable	Cr	Land
Cr	Cash	Dr	Accounts Payable
Dr	Income Tax Payable	Cr	Income Tax Expense

5.

a. A company purchases supplies on account—invoice received from a vendor

b. A company pays for the supplies it purchased in Transaction a.—bank cheque

c. A company performs services on account for a college—invoice sent to a customer

d. The college pays the company for the services performed in Transaction c.—bank deposit slip

e. A customer pays the company immediately for services performed—bank deposit slip

f. The company hires a student to provide office support during the summer—no source document since this is not a transaction.

6.

Sep. 4   The asset, cash, is increased; therefore, debit Cash.

The liability, note payable, is increased; therefore, credit Notes Payable.

Sep. 8   The asset, accounts receivable, is increased; therefore, debit Accounts Receivable.

The revenue, service revenue, is increased; therefore, credit Service Revenue.

Sep. 12   The asset, equipment, is increased; therefore, debit Equipment.

The liability, accounts payable, is increased; therefore, credit Accounts Payable.

Sep. 24   The asset, supplies, is increased; therefore, debit Supplies.

The asset, cash, is decreased; therefore, credit Cash.

Sep. 27   The liability, accounts payable, is decreased; therefore, debit Accounts Payable.

The asset, cash, is decreased; therefore, credit Cash.

7. *a., b., and c.*

Cash # 101

Bal.	3,000	Sep. 1	140
Sep. 4	10,000	24	600
		27	2,000
Bal.	10,260		

Accounts Receivable # 103

Sep. 8	3,000		
Bal.	3,000		

Supplies # 105

Sep. 24	600		
Bal.	600		

Equipment # 107

Sep. 12	2,000		
Bal.	2,000		

Land # 110

Bal.	29,000		
Bal.	29,000		

Accounts Payable # 201

Sep. 27	2,000	Sep. 12	2,000
		Bal.	0

Notes Payable # 205			R. Peterson, Capital # 301			Service Revenue # 401		
	Sep. 4	10,000		Bal.	32,000		Sep. 8	3,000
	Bal.	10,000		Bal.	32,000		Bal.	3,000

Utilities Expense # 501		
Sep. 1	140	
Bal.	140	

Total debits: $10,260 + $3,000 + $600 + $2,000 + $29,000 + $140 = $45,000

Total credits: $10,000 + $32,000 + $3,000 = $45,000

8.

Supplies Expense		Accounts Payable		Cash	
110		150	400	5,000	150
290		800	2,900	12,600	800
544		475	1,600	926	475
944			750	6,200	290
			4,225	**23,011**	

Supplies Expense = $110 + 290 + 544 = $944

Accounts Payable = $400 + 2,900 + 1,600 + 750 − 150 − 800 − 475 = $4,225

Cash = $5,000 + 12,600 + 926 + 6,200 − 150 − 800 − 475 − 290 = $23,011

9. (1) The ending balance (X) for Cash is:

$X = \$10,000 + 20,000 - \$13,000$

$X = \$17,000$

(2) We are given the beginning and ending balances. We can compute the debit entry as follows:

$\$12,800 + \$45,600 - X = \$23,500$

$\$12,800 + \$45,600 - \$23,500 = X$

$X = \$34,900$

10.

Journal					Page 1
Date	**Account Titles and Explanations**	**Post. Ref.**	**Debit**	**Credit**	
Sep. 1	Utilities Expense		140		
	Cash			140	
	Paid monthly utilities expense.				
4	Cash		10,000		
	Note Payable			10,000	
	Borrowed cash on a note payable.				
8	Accounts Receivable		3,000		
	Service Revenue			3,000	
	Performed service on account.				
12	Equipment		2,000		
	Accounts Payable			2,000	
	Purchased equipment on account.				
24	Supplies		600		
	Cash			600	
	Purchased supplies and paid cash.				
27	Accounts Payable		2,000		
	Cash			2,000	
	Paid the September 12 liability.				

11.

SHINY FLOOR CLEANING Trial Balance December 31, 2016		
Account	Debit	Credit
Cash	$13,000	
Accounts receivable	12,500	
Supplies	7,500	
Equipment	2,000	
Accounts payable		$ 1,000
S. Shaw, capital		15,000
S. Shaw, withdrawals	5,000	
Cleaning revenue		30,000
Supplies expense	6,000	
Total	$46,000	$46,000

12.

SHINY FLOOR CLEANING Incorrect Trial Balance December 31, 2016		
Account	Debit	Credit
Cash	$13,000	
Accounts receivable	12,500	
Supplies	7,500	
Equipment	200*	
Accounts payable		$ 1,000
S. Shaw, capital		15,000
S. Shaw, withdrawals	5,000	
Cleaning revenue		30,000
Supplies expense	6,000	
Total	$44,200	$46,000

* Incorrect; should be listed as $2,000.

To correct this error:
1. Take the difference between total debits and total credits: $44,200 − $46,000 = $1,800
2. Divide the error by 9: $1,800/9 = $200
3. Locate $200 on the trial balance. Equipment, at $200, holds the error. Trace the Equipment balance back to the ledger account, which shows the correct amount of $2,000.
4. Correct the trial balance.

3 MEASURING BUSINESS INCOME: THE ADJUSTING PROCESS

CONNECTING CHAPTER 3

MyAccountingLab   The **Summary** for Chapter 3 appears on page 144. This lists all of the MyAccountingLab resources. **Accounting Vocabulary** with definitions for this chapter's material appears on page 145.

Tracy Daytona's Trim and Detail is a NASCAR-themed hair salon whose target market is men. Their business model is unique in that it is a salon that does not look like a salon!

How does the owner know if the salon is making money? Can the salon hire another stylist? Would the business be able to get a loan to open a new location? The information to answer these sorts of questions can only come from precise record keeping and the preparation of the financial statements. To produce complete and accurate financial statements, the business needs to account for *all* transactions, even those that may not have typical source documents.

Suppose Tracy Daytona's stylists work today but receive their paycheques next week. If the financial statements need to be prepared before payday next week, wages expense on the income statement would be too low if several days of wages were not recorded. An adjusting entry would ensure that the wages expense and the wages payable liability are included in the accounting records so that the income statement and balance sheet are complete and accurate.

Suppose an order of hair-care supplies arrived today without an invoice. If the financial statements must be prepared tomorrow, the supplies asset and the account payable to the supplier would be too low if this transaction is not recorded. Again, an adjusting entry will make the accounting records complete, which will lead to complete and accurate financial statements. This chapter will look at why and how these (and other) adjusting entries are done.

> **In** Chapter 2 we looked at recording transactions, posting to the ledger, and preparing the unadjusted trial balance. This is shown in Exhibit 3–1 steps 1 to 4 of the accounting cycle. The account balances in the trial balance include the effects of the transactions that occurred during the period—cash collections, purchases of assets, payments of bills, sales of assets, and so on. That certainly takes care of routine transactions. But not all transactions have source documents. It is a normal part of the accounting process to review account balances and bring the balances *up to date*. What does this mean? It will take a whole chapter to explain it.

Whether the business is Tracy Daytona's or Hunter Environmental Consulting, a business must do some *adjusting entries* (step 5) at the end of the period to bring the records up to date before preparing the financial statements. In this chapter, we use the accounting concepts, assumptions, and principles found in the accounting framework (Exhibit 1–5 on page 11 and the inside back cover of this book) to measure income and prepare the financial statements of Hunter Environmental Consulting (HEC) for the month of May.

EXHIBIT 3–1 | The Accounting Cycle

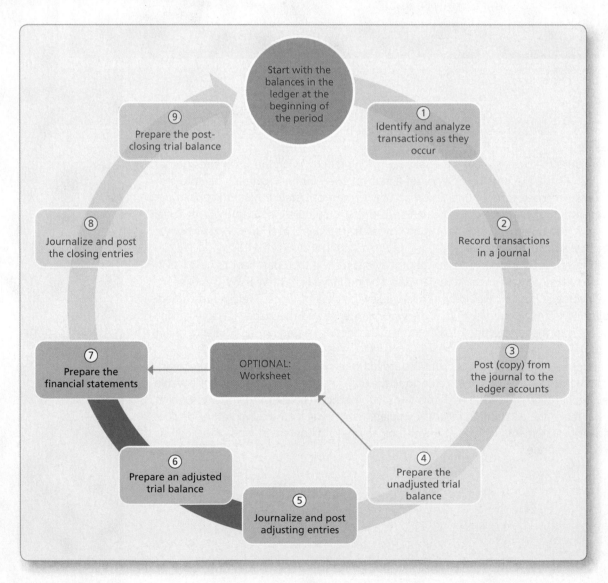

TIME PERIOD ASSUMPTION

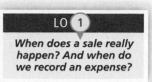

Managers, investors, and creditors make decisions daily and need current information about the business's progress. They want to know how much profit the business has made during the period. The **time period assumption** ensures that accounting information is reported at regular intervals.

The most basic accounting period is one year, and virtually all businesses prepare annual financial statements. For many companies, the annual accounting period is the calendar year from January 1 through December 31. Other companies use a **fiscal year** ending on some date other than December 31. Retailers traditionally make their fiscal year end at the low point in their business activity following the after-Christmas sales in January. The fiscal year end of Hudson's Bay is January 31 for that reason.

Managers and investors cannot wait until the end of the year to analyze a company's progress. Companies, therefore, prepare financial statements for *interim* periods that are less than a year. Statements can be prepared monthly, quarterly (three-month period), and semi-annually (six-month period). Tracy Daytona's managers receive their information on a monthly basis. Given the fast pace of business, some companies such as car dealers (like Guelph Toyota) have accounting systems that produce daily financial reports and weekly summaries so managers can make decisions even more quickly. While many of the adjusting entries in this chapter are based on an annual accounting period, the procedures and statements can be applied to interim periods as well.

RECOGNITION CRITERIA FOR REVENUES AND EXPENSES

Recognition is the process of including an item in the financial statements of a business. First we will discuss the recognition of revenues; then we will discuss the recognition of expenses.

Revenue Recognition

The **recognition criteria for revenues** tell accountants

- *When* to record revenue—that is, when to make a journal entry for a revenue transaction
- The *amount* of revenue to record

Revenue, defined in Chapter 1 (page 14) is the increase in owner's equity from delivering goods and services to customers in the course of operating a business. When we speak of "recording" something in accounting, we mean "to make an entry in the journal." Another way of saying this is to "recognize a transaction." That is where the accounting process starts.

When to Record Revenue   Revenue recognition criteria state that revenue should be recorded when it has been *earned*—but not before. In most cases, revenue is earned when the business has delivered a good or completed a service to the customer. The business has done everything required by the agreement, including transferring the item to the customer.

Exhibit 3–2 shows two situations that provide guidance on when to record revenue. Situation 1 illustrates when *not* to record revenue, because the client merely states her plans. Situation 2 illustrates when revenue should be recorded—after the company has performed the service for the client.

The Amount of Revenue to Record   The general principle is to record revenue equal to the cash value of the goods or the service transferred to the customer. Suppose that, in order to obtain a new client, HEC performs environmental assessment services for the discounted price of $5,000. Ordinarily the business would have charged $7,000 for this service. How much revenue should the business record? The answer is $5,000, because that was the cash value of the transaction.

EXHIBIT 3–2 | Recording Revenue: The Recognition Criteria for Revenues

Recognition Criteria for Expenses

Just as we have criteria that help us determine when to recognize revenue and how much revenue we should record, we also have criteria to help us determine when to recognize expenses. This is commonly referred to as the **matching objective**. Recall that expenses such as utilities and advertising are the costs of assets and services that are consumed when earning revenue. The matching objective directs accountants to

1. Identify all expenses incurred during the accounting period.
2. Measure the expenses.
3. Match the expenses against the revenues earned during that period.

To match expenses against revenues means to subtract the related expenses from the revenues to compute net income or net loss. Exhibit 3–3 illustrates the matching objective.

EXHIBIT 3–3 | Expense Recognition—An Illustration of the Matching Objective

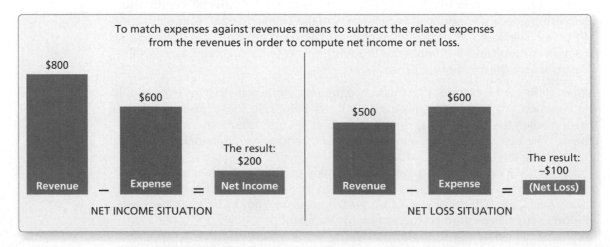

Accountants follow the matching objective by identifying the revenues of a period and then the expenses that can be linked to particular revenues. For example, a business that pays sales commissions to its salespeople will have commission expense if the employees make sales. If they make no sales, the business has no commission expense.

Other expenses are not so easy to link with particular sales. HEC's monthly rent expense occurs, for example, regardless of the revenues earned during the period. The matching objective directs accountants to identify these types of expenses with a particular time period, such as a month or a year. If HEC employs an office assistant at a monthly salary of $2,500, the business will record salary expense of $2,500 each month.

> Try It!

1. On December 20, 2016, Kobe Company receives an order from Windsor Company for products costing $5,000. The order will not be shipped until January 5, 2017. Kobe Company wants to record the revenue on December 20 so it can include it in the current year's financial statements. As Kobe's accountant, you object to this accounting treatment. Why?

2. On December 20, 2016, Kobe Company receives an order from Windsor Company for products costing $5,000. The order is shipped immediately. Kobe Company pays a commission of 5 percent of the selling price to its sales representative who received the order. This commission will not be paid until January 2017. Kobe's fiscal year end is December 31. When should the journal entry needed to account for the sales commission be recorded? Explain.

Solutions appear at the end of this chapter and on MyAccountingLab

ACCRUAL-BASIS ACCOUNTING VERSUS CASH-BASIS ACCOUNTING

We can tie those three accounting principles together now as we look at two different ways to keep accounting records.

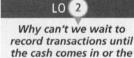

LO 2

Why can't we wait to record transactions until the cash comes in or the cash goes out?

Accrual-basis accounting, frequently called *accrual accounting*, records the effect of every business transaction as it occurs, no matter when cash receipts and cash payments occur. Accrual accounting is based on the time period assumption and recognition criteria for revenues and expenses. Most businesses use the accrual basis because it is required as part of the generally accepted accounting principles (GAAP). Thus, accrual-basis accounting is the method covered in this book, and so far the accounts receivable and accounts payable accounts have helped us record information this way. We will look at a few more accounts to help us keep track of every transaction in the right period later in this chapter. The Canada Revenue Agency (CRA) also requires accrual accounting for income tax purposes except in special cases.

Cash-basis accounting records transactions only when cash receipts and cash payments occur. Only very small businesses tend to use cash-basis accounting for their bookkeeping. Their accountant may later convert their financial records to the accrual basis when their tax returns are prepared.

MyAccountingLab

Video: Cash Basis versus Accrual Basis of Accounting

Exhibit: Accrual-Basis versus Cash-Basis Accounting

Accrual-basis accounting provides more complete information than does cash-basis accounting. This difference is important, because the more complete the data, the better equipped decision makers are to reach accurate conclusions about the firm's financial health and future prospects.

> Try It!

3. Suppose HEC collects $6,000 from customers on January 1. The company will earn the $6,000 evenly during January, February, and March. How much service revenue will HEC report each month under (a) accrual-basis accounting and (b) cash-basis accounting?

4. Suppose HEC prepays $1,500 for Internet advertising on October 1. The ads will run during October, November, and December. How much advertising expense will HEC report each month under (a) accrual-basis accounting and (b) cash-basis accounting?

Solutions appear at the end of this chapter and on MyAccountingLab

ADJUSTING THE ACCOUNTS

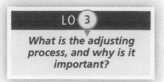

LO 3

What is the adjusting process, and why is it important?

At the end of the period, the accountant prepares the financial statements. This end-of-period process begins with the unadjusted trial balance that lists the accounts and their balances after the period's transactions have been recorded in the journal and posted to the accounts in the ledger. We prepared trial balances in Chapter 2, which is shown as step 4 in Exhibit 3–1.

For illustration purposes, assume Exhibit 3–4 is the unadjusted trial balance of Hunter Environmental Consulting at May 31, 2016. (Account numbers are not shown. The balances and accounts are different from those described in earlier chapters because they reflect additional transactions that occurred during the month of May.) This unadjusted trial balance includes some new accounts that will be explained in this chapter.

EXHIBIT 3–4 | Unadjusted Trial Balance

HUNTER ENVIRONMENTAL CONSULTING		
Unadjusted Trial Balance		
May 31, 2016		
Cash	$ 31,000	
Accounts receivable	14,000	
Office supplies	1,500	
Prepaid insurance	3,600	
Furniture	45,000	
Land	50,000	
Accounts payable		$ 12,000
Unearned service revenue		3,000
Lisa Hunter, capital		120,100
Lisa Hunter, withdrawals	6,000	
Service revenue		24,000
Rent expense	3,000	
Salaries expense	4,000	
Utilities expense	1,000	
Total	$159,100	$159,100

REAL WORLD EXAMPLE

This monthly end-of-period process of updating the accounts is called "month end" and keeps many accounting department staff members very busy!

Accrual-basis accounting requires adjusting entries at the end of the period in order to produce correct balances for the financial statements.

Adjusting entries assign revenues to the period in which they are earned and expenses to the period in which they are incurred. Adjusting entries also update the asset and liability accounts. They are needed to

1. Properly measure the period's income on the income statement
2. Bring related asset and liability accounts to correct balances for the balance sheet

This chapter shows the end-of-period process of updating the accounts, which is called *adjusting the accounts, making the adjusting entries,* or *adjusting the books.* This is step 5 in Exhibit 3–1.

Prepaids and Accruals

Two basic types of adjustments are *prepaids* and *accruals.* In a *prepaid*-type adjustment, the cash is paid or received before the related expense or revenue is recorded. Prepaids are also called *deferrals* because the recording of the expense or the revenue is deferred (delayed) to periods after cash is paid or received. *Accrual*-type adjustments are the opposite of prepaids. For accruals, we record the expense or revenue before the related cash is paid or received. The timeline in Exhibit 3–5 helps to show how you can remember the difference between prepaids and accruals:

EXHIBIT 3–5 | Timeline for Adjusting Entries

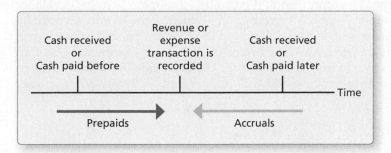

Adjusting entries can be further divided into five categories, as illustrated in Exhibit 3–6 below.

EXHIBIT 3–6 | Adjusting Entries

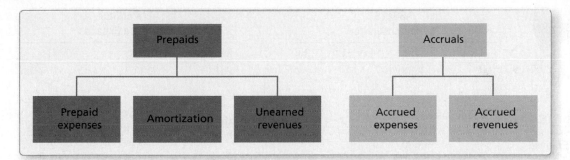

Prepaid Expenses

Prepaid expenses are assets that typically expire or are used up in the near future. They are assets since they represent a potential future economic benefit. Prepaid rent, prepaid insurance, and supplies are examples of prepaid expenses. They are called "prepaid" expenses because they are expenses that are paid in advance. Companies must later make adjustments regarding prepaid expenses to show what has been used up and to reflect an accurate asset balance on the balance sheet. For example, Tracy Daytona's makes prepayments for rent, hair-care supplies, and insurance.

Prepaid Insurance   Business insurance is usually paid in advance. This prepayment creates an asset for the policyholder, because the policyholder has purchased the future benefit of insurance protection. Suppose HEC purchases a business liability insurance policy on May 1, 2016. The cost of the insurance is $3,600 for one year of coverage. The entry to record the payment is a debit to the asset account, Prepaid Insurance, as follows:

May 1	Prepaid Insurance	3,600	
	Cash		3,600
	Paid annual premium for business liability insurance.		

After posting, Prepaid Insurance appears as follows:

ASSETS
Prepaid Insurance

May 1	3,600

LEARNING TIPS

Watch out! Accrual-basis accounting and accruals are not exactly the same thing! *Accrual-basis accounting* means recording transactions as they happen even if no cash is exchanged. There are two types of adjustments required to accomplish accrual-basis accounting: prepaids and *accruals*.

Study this material carefully because it is the most challenging topic in all of introductory accounting.

KEY POINTS
Prepaid expenses are assets, not expenses.

MyAccountingLab

Video: Prepaid Expenses
Interactive Figure: Interact with Prepaid Rent

The unadjusted trial balance at May 31, 2016, shown in Exhibit 3–4 on page 122 lists Prepaid Insurance as an asset with a debit balance of $3,600. Throughout May, the Prepaid Insurance account maintains this balance. But $3,600 is *not* the amount of Prepaid Insurance for HEC's balance sheet at May 31, 2016. Why?

At May 31, Prepaid Insurance should be adjusted to remove from its balance the amount of insurance that has been used up, which is one month's worth. By definition, the amount of an asset that has been used, or has expired, is an *expense*. The adjusting entry transfers one-twelfth, or $300 ($3,600 × $\frac{1}{12}$), of the debit balance from Prepaid Insurance to Insurance Expense. The debit side of the entry records an increase in Insurance Expense and the credit records a decrease in the asset Prepaid Insurance.

May 31	Insurance Expense	300	
	Prepaid Insurance		300
	To record insurance expense ($3,600 × $\frac{1}{12}$)		

After posting, Prepaid Insurance and Insurance Expense show correct ending balances at May 31, 2016, as follows:

	ASSETS Prepaid Insurance				EXPENSES Insurance Expense	
May 1	3,600	May 31	300	**May 31**	300	
Bal.	3,300			Bal.	300	

A = One month's Prepaid Insurance of $300, an asset

E = May's Insurance Expense of $300, an expense

The whole circle represents the full year of insurance coverage divided into 12 monthly pieces.

Correct asset amount is $3,300, which is 11/12 of $3,600 → **Total accounted for, $3,600** ← **Correct expense amount is $300, which is 1/12 of $3,600**

The full $3,600 has been accounted for. As shown in the diagram in the margin, eleven-twelfths measures the asset, and one-twelfth measures the expense. Recording this expense illustrates the matching objective. A similar journal entry would be made at the end of the month for the next 11 months, eventually bringing the Prepaid Insurance balance to zero and the Insurance Expense balance to $3,600 over the life of the policy.

The chapter appendix shows an alternative treatment of prepaid expenses where the expense is recorded first and the adjusting entry sets up the asset. The end result on the financial statements is the same as that for the method given here.

Supplies Supplies are accounted for in the same way as prepaid expenses. Suppose that, on May 2, HEC paid cash of $1,500 for office supplies:

The same analysis applies to a prepayment of 12 months' rent. The only difference is in the account titles, which would be Prepaid Rent and Rent Expense instead of Prepaid Insurance and Insurance Expense.

May 2	Office Supplies	1,500	
	Cash		1,500
	Paid cash for office supplies.		

Assume that the business purchased no additional office supplies during April. The May 31 unadjusted trial balance, therefore, lists Office Supplies with a $1,500 debit balance as shown in Exhibit 3–4. But HEC's May 31 balance sheet should *not* report supplies of $1,500. Why?

During May, HEC used supplies in performing services for clients. The cost of the supplies used is the measure of *supplies expense* for the month. To measure HEC's supplies expense during May, Lisa Hunter counts the supplies on hand at the end of the month. This is the amount of the asset still available to the business. Assume the count indicates that supplies costing $1,000 remain. Subtracting the entity's $1,000 of supplies on hand at the end of May from the cost of supplies available during May ($1,500) measures supplies expense during the month ($500):

Cost of asset available during the period		Cost of asset on hand at the end of the period		Cost of asset used (expense) during the period
$1,500	−	$1,000	=	$500

This same analysis could be done using a T-account:

ASSETS
Office Supplies

May 2	1,500		?
Bal. May 31	1,000		

Solve for the amount used during the period (in this case, $1,500 − $1,000 = $500)

The May 31 adjusting entry updates the Office Supplies account and records the expense for supplies for May as follows:

May 31	Supplies Expense	500	
	Office Supplies		500
	To record supplies expense ($1,500 − $1,000).		

After posting, the Office Supplies and Supplies Expense accounts hold correct ending balances:

ASSETS
Office Supplies

May 2	1,500	**May 31**	**500**
Bal.	1,000		

→

EXPENSES
Supplies Expense

May 31	**500**	
Bal.	500	

Correct asset amount, $1,000 → Total accounted for, $1,500 ← Correct expense amount, $500

The Office Supplies account enters the month of June with a $1,000 balance, and the adjustment process is repeated each month until the asset is used up.

Why It's Done This Way

Objective of Financial Reporting

Let's look at how the accounting framework explains why we need to adjust accounts prior to creating financial statements by looking more closely at prepaid accounts. Assume that a company has purchased its business insurance for the next year.

We can see that this transaction should be *recognized* as a financial transaction and we should *measure* the transaction at its cost.

The company would categorize the insurance as an *asset* since there is future economic benefit to the company—the company has insurance coverage for the next year.

By recording and measuring the transaction in this manner, we have provided information that is *relevant* and *reliable* at the time the insurance is purchased.

The insurance coverage will expire a year from the date it was purchased, so the value of the prepaid asset declines with the passage of time. If we were to prepare the financial statements five months after the insurance was purchased, the balance sheet would not be *relevant* if it still showed the prepaid insurance at its original cost.

By completing the adjustment to expense the used portion, our financial statements remain both *reliable* and *relevant* to users and the balance sheet and income statement will *communicate useful information to users.*

LEARNING TIPS

Don't confuse current (and often increasing) real estate prices (market value) with the historic cost of the asset reported in the accounting records. Amortization expense is an accounting estimate that allocates the cost of the asset to an expense account as it is used over time. It is not intended to reflect current market values.

REAL WORLD EXAMPLE

In the United States, *depreciation* is the term used for amortizing tangible assets. *Amortization* is the term used for intangible assets. Many Canadian companies also use this convention since the *CPA Canada Handbook* uses the term amortization but does not require it.

REAL WORLD EXAMPLE

As with prepaid expenses, in most accounting software programs the adjusting entry for amortization can be programmed to occur automatically each month for the duration of the asset's life.

Amortization

The accrual basis of accounting also applies to how businesses account for capital assets. **Property, plant, and equipment (PPE)** are identifiable **tangible capital assets**, which are physical assets such as land, buildings, furniture, vehicles, machinery, and equipment. All of these tangible capital assets except land decline in usefulness as they age. This decline is an *expense* to the business. Land is the only tangible capital asset that does not decline in usefulness.

Accountants systematically spread the cost of each type of plant and equipment less any residual (or salvage) value over its *estimated* useful life. The *CPA Canada Handbook* calls this process of allocating the cost of plant and equipment to an expense account over its life **amortization**. (Another term for amortization in common usage is *depreciation*.)

Many companies also own **intangible assets**, which are capital assets with no physical form such as patents and trademarks, in their business. Amortization will be discussed in more detail in Chapter 10.

Similarity to Prepaid Expenses The concept of accounting for amortization expense is the same as for prepaid expenses. In a sense, plant and equipment are large prepaid expenses that expire over a number of periods. For both prepaid expenses and plant and equipment, the business purchases an asset that wears out or is used up. As the asset is used, more and more of its cost is transferred from the asset account to the expense account. The major difference between prepaid expenses and capital assets is the length of time it takes for the asset to lose its usefulness (or expire). Prepaid expenses usually expire within a year, whereas plant and equipment assets remain useful for a number of years.

Consider HEC's operations. Suppose that, on May 3, the business purchased furniture for $45,000 and made this journal entry:

May 3	Furniture	45,000	
	Cash		45,000
	Purchased office furniture.		

After posting, the Furniture account appears as follows:

ASSETS
Furniture

May 3	45,000	

In accrual-basis accounting, an asset is recorded when the furniture is acquired. Then, a portion of the asset's cost is transferred from the asset account to Amortization Expense each period that the asset is used. This method matches the asset's expense to the revenue of the period, which is an application of the matching objective.

Straight-Line Method Lisa Hunter believes the furniture will remain useful for five years and be virtually worthless at the end of its life. One common way to calculate the amount of amortization to be recorded is the **straight-line method**. It divides the cost of the asset (less any **residual value** or *salvage value*) by its useful life so that the same amount of amortization is recorded for each full year the asset provides value to its owner:

$$\text{Straight-line Amortization Expense} = \frac{\text{Cost} - \text{Residual value}}{\text{Useful life in years}}$$

$$= \frac{\$45,000 - \$0}{5}$$

$$= \$9,000 \text{ per year}$$

In the case of HEC, the adjusting entries are prepared monthly, so the annual amortization expense must be divided by 12 to get the monthly cost. To find the monthly expense amount:

MyAccountingLab

Video: Fixed Assets and Depreciation

- Divide the annual amount by 12: $9,000 ÷ 12 = $750 per month.

   Alternatively,

- The useful life could be shown as 60 months (5 years × 12 months = 60 months).
- The calculation would be $45,000 ÷ 60 = $750 per month.

Amortization expense for May is recorded by the following adjusting entry:

May 31	Amortization Expense—Furniture	750	
	Accumulated Amortization—Furniture		750
	To record monthly amortization expense on furniture.		

The Accumulated Amortization Account Accumulated Amortization—Furniture is credited—not Furniture—because the original cost of any property, plant, and equipment acquisitions should remain in the asset account as long as the business uses the asset. Accountants and managers may refer to the Furniture account to see how much the asset cost. This information is useful in a decision about whether to replace the furniture and the amount to pay. Accountants use the **Accumulated Amortization** account to show the cumulative sum of all amortization expense from the date of acquiring the tangible capital asset. Therefore, the balance in this account increases over the life of the asset—the account balance continues to "accumulate" over the life of the asset.

Accumulated Amortization is a *contra asset* account. A **contra account** has two main characteristics:

- A contra account has a companion account.
- A contra account's normal balance (debit or credit) is the opposite of (or *contrary* to) the companion account's normal balance. (Recall from Chapter 2, page 66, that the normal balance of an account is the side of the account where increases are recorded.)

In this case, Accumulated Amortization—Furniture is the contra account that accompanies Furniture. It appears in the ledger directly after Furniture. Furniture has a debit balance, and therefore Accumulated Amortization—Furniture, a contra asset, has a credit balance. *All contra asset accounts have credit balances.*

After posting the amortization, the related accounts of HEC are as follows:

KEY POINTS
Use a separate Amortization Expense account and Accumulated Amortization account for each major type of tangible asset (Amortization Expense—Furniture, Amortization Expense—Buildings, and so on). Notice the format of the account names, which are expanded to describe the different assets.

	ASSETS Furniture		CONTRA ASSET Accumulated Amortization—Furniture			EXPENSES Amortization Expense— Furniture	
May 3	45,000			**May 31**	750	**May 31** 750	
Bal.	45,000			Bal.	750	Bal. 750	

Book Value The balance sheet reports both Furniture and Accumulated Amortization—Furniture. Because it is a contra account, the balance of Accumulated Amortization—Furniture is subtracted from the balance of Furniture. This net amount (cost minus accumulated amortization) of a capital asset is called its **book value**, or *net book value*, or **carrying value,** which can be shown on a financial statement this way:

> There is no rule or standard for how this financial information is presented. Some companies show brackets on the amount of a contra account. Other companies do not include the word "Less" in the statement. Everyone is correct.

Furniture	$45,000
Less: Accumulated Amortization—Furniture	750
Furniture, net	$44,250

The balance sheet at May 31 would report HEC's property, plant, and equipment as shown in Exhibit 3–7.

When a business shows this summary level of information in the balance sheet (perhaps they are a large corporation with many accounts) then the details of the assets' cost and accumulated amortization are presented in the notes to the financial statement.

EXHIBIT 3–7 | Property, Plant, and Equipment on the Partial Balance Sheet of Hunter Environmental Consulting

Property, Plant, and Equipment		
Furniture	$45,000	
Less: Accumulated amortization—furniture	750	$44,250
Land		50,000
Property, Plant, and Equipment, Net		$94,250
OR		
Property, Plant, and Equipment		
Furniture, net		$44,250
Land		50,000
Property, Plant, and Equipment, Net		$94,250

Unearned Revenues

Some businesses collect cash from customers in advance of doing work for them. Receiving cash in advance creates a liability called **unearned revenue** or **deferred revenue**. The company owes a product or service to the customer or the money back. Only when the job is completed will the business have earned the revenue.

Suppose a developer, By Me Real Estate, engages HEC to provide consulting services, agreeing to pay $3,000 monthly in advance beginning immediately. Suppose HEC receives the first payment in advance and begins work on May 20. HEC records the cash receipt and the related increase in the business's liabilities as follows:

May 20	Cash	3,000	
	Unearned Service Revenue		3,000
	Received revenue in advance.		

After posting, the account appears as follows:

LIABILITIES
Unearned Service Revenue

| | May 20 | 3,000 |

Unearned Service Revenue is a liability because it represents HEC's obligation to perform a service for the client. The May 31 unadjusted trial balance (Exhibit 3–4, page 122) lists Unearned Service Revenue with a $3,000 credit balance prior to the adjusting entries. During the last 10 days of the month—May 21 through May 31—HEC will have *earned* roughly one-third (10 days divided by May's total 31 days) of the $3,000, or $1,000. Therefore, the accountant makes the following adjustment to decrease the liability, Unearned Service Revenue, and to record an increase in Service Revenue as follows:

May 31	Unearned Service Revenue	1,000	
	Service Revenue		1,000
	To record service revenue earned and paid from the advance ($3,000 × $\frac{1}{3}$).		

MyAccountingLab

Video: Unearned Revenue
Video: Unearned Revenue Adjusting Entries

This adjusting entry shifts $1,000 of the total amount of unearned service revenue from the liability account to the revenue account. After posting, the balance of Service Revenue is increased by $1,000 (10 days of revenue was earned), and the balance of Unearned Service Revenue has been reduced by $1,000 to $2,000 (as less work—only 20 days—is still unearned, or due to be performed). Now both accounts have their correct balances at May 31, as follows:

LIABILITIES					**REVENUES**	
Unearned Service Revenue					**Service Revenue**	
May 31	**1,000**	May 20	3,000			24,000
		Bal.	2,000		May 31	1,500
					May 31	**1,000**
					Bal.	26,500

Correct liability amount, $2,000 (which is 2/3 of $3,000, or 20 days of work due) → Total accounted for, $3,000 ← Correct revenue amount, $1,000 (which is 1/3 of $3,000, or 10 days of revenue earned)

When the revenue is finally earned, debit the Unearned Revenue account (to reduce the liability) and credit the Revenue account (to increase it).

Accrued Expenses

Businesses incur many expenses before they pay cash. Payment is not due until later, but no bill or invoice is provided to signal the payable. Consider an employee's salary. An employee earns pay every day but is not paid daily. The employer's salaries expense and salaries payable grow as the employee works, so the liability is said to *accrue*. Another example is interest expense on a note payable. Interest accumulates over time but, by the terms of the agreement, is only paid at a later date. This interest liability and expense must be shown on the financial statements.

The term **accrued expense** refers to an expense that the business has incurred but has not yet paid. An accrued expense *always* creates a liability. Accrued expenses can be viewed as the opposite of prepaid expenses. A prepaid expense is paid first and expensed later; an accrued expense is expensed first and paid later.

It is time-consuming to make hourly, daily, or even weekly journal entries to accrue expenses. Consequently, the accountant waits until the end of the period. Then an adjusting entry brings each expense (and related liability) up to date just before the financial statements are prepared.

Accruing Salaries Expense   Most companies pay their employees at predetermined times. Suppose HEC pays its two employees $4,000 bi-monthly (on the 15th and on the last day of the month). Suppose, for illustration purposes, that this is the calendar for May (it isn't, but let's pretend it is) with the two paydays circled:

LEARNING TIPS

One way of thinking about an accrued expense is that it is almost like an accounts payable but without an invoice.

MAY

S	M	T	W	T	F	S
				1	2	3
4	5	6	7	8	9	10
11	12	13	14	⑮	16	17
18	19	20	21	22	23	24
25	26	27	28	29	30	㉛

MyAccountingLab

Video: Accrued Expenses

Assume that, if either payday falls on a weekend, HEC pays the employees on the following Monday. Many companies will just pay on the Friday, but HEC doesn't.

During May, HEC paid its employees' salaries of $4,000 on Thursday, May 15, and recorded the following entry:

May 15	Salaries Expense	4,000	
	Cash		4,000
	To pay salaries.		

After posting, the Salaries Expense account is as follows:

EXPENSES
Salaries Expense

May 15	4,000

The unadjusted trial balance at May 31 (Exhibit 3–4, page 122) includes Salaries Expense with a debit balance of $4,000. Because May 31, the second payday of the month, falls on a Saturday, the second $4,000 payment will be made on Monday, June 2. Without an adjusting entry, this second $4,000 amount is not included in the May 31 trial balance amount for Salaries Expense, even though the expense has been incurred. Therefore, at May 31 the business adjusts for additional *salaries expense* and *salaries payable* of $4,000 by recording an increase in each of these accounts as follows:

May 31	Salaries Expense	4,000	
	Salaries Payable		4,000
	To accrue salaries expense.		

> All accrued expenses are recorded with similar entries—a debit to the appropriate expense account and a credit to the related liability account.

After posting, the Salaries Expense and Salaries Payable accounts are updated to May 31:

EXPENSES		**LIABILITIES**	
Salaries Expense		**Salaries Payable**	
May 15	4,000	May 31	4,000
May 31	4,000	Bal.	4,000
Bal.	8,000		

The accounts at May 31 now contain the complete salaries information for the month of May. The expense account has a full month's salaries, and the liability account shows the portion that the business still owes at May 31.

HEC will record the payment of this liability on Monday, June 2 as follows:

Jun. 2	Salaries Payable	4,000	
	Cash		4,000
	To record the payment of the salary payable.		

This payment entry does not affect May or June expenses because the May expense was recorded on May 15 and May 31. This entry only records the payment of the payable. June expense will be recorded in a like manner, starting on June 15.

Accrued Revenues

As we have just seen, expenses can occur before the cash payment, and that creates an accrued expense. Likewise, businesses often earn revenue before they collect the cash. Collection occurs later. Revenue that has been earned but not yet invoiced or collected is called an **accrued revenue**.

Assume HEC is hired on May 15 by Rock Creek Development to provide environmental consulting services on a monthly basis. Under this agreement, Rock Creek will pay HEC $3,000 monthly, with the first payment on June 15. During May, HEC will earn half a month's fee, $1,500, for work performed May 15 through May 31. On May 31, HEC makes the following adjusting entry to record an increase in Accounts Receivable and Service Revenue:

LEARNING TIPS

One way of thinking about an accrued revenue is that it is like an accounts receivable but without an invoice.

In this case, it would be inappropriate to send an invoice for the part of the work completed as the agreement is for payment of a monthly amount on the 15th of the month. Work was completed, so the revenue must be recognized with an adjusting entry.

May 31	Accounts Receivable	1,500	
	Service Revenue		1,500
	To accrue service revenue ($3,000 × $\frac{1}{2}$).		

We see from the unadjusted trial balance in Exhibit 3–4 (page 122) that Accounts Receivable has an unadjusted balance of $14,000. The Service Revenue unadjusted balance is $24,000. Posting the May 31 adjustment has the following effects on these two accounts:

ASSETS		**REVENUES**	
Accounts Receivable		**Service Revenue**	
	14,000		24,000
May 31	**1,500**	**May 31**	**1,500**
Bal.	15,500	Bal.	25,500

This adjusting entry illustrates the concept of revenue recognition. Without the adjustment, HEC's financial statements would be misleading—they would understate Accounts Receivable and Service Revenue by $1,500 each.

Summary of the Adjusting Process

Exhibit 3–8 summarizes the timing of prepaid-type and accrual-type adjusting entries (in blue) and shows the related journal entries made before or after them.

> All accrued revenues are accounted for similarly: Debit a receivable account and credit a revenue account.

EXHIBIT 3–8 | Timing of Prepaid and Accrual Adjustments (Examples and amounts are from pages 123–131)

PREPAIDS—The cash transaction occurs initially. (The expense is incurred or the revenue is earned later.)

	Initially			**Later**		
Prepaid expenses	Pay expense in advance and record an asset:			→ Record the expense later and decrease the asset:		
	Prepaid Expense (e.g., Insurance)	3,600		Expense (e.g., Insurance)	300	
	Cash		3,600	Prepaid Expense (e.g., Insurance)		300
Amortization	Purchase the asset:			→ Record the expense later:		
	Asset (e.g., Furniture)	45,000		Amortization Expense—Asset (e.g., Furniture)	750	
	Cash		45,000	Accum. Amort.—Asset (e.g., Furniture)		750
Unearned revenues	Receive cash in advance and record unearned revenue (a liability):			→ Record the revenue later and decrease unearned revenue:		
	Cash	3,000		Unearned Revenue (e.g., Consulting)	1,000	
	Unearned Revenue (e.g., Consulting)		3,000	Revenue (e.g., Consulting Service)		1,000

(Continued)

EXHIBIT 3–8 | Timing of Prepaid and Accrual Adjustments *(Continued)*

ACCRUALS—The cash transaction occurs later. (The expense is incurred or the revenue is earned first.)

	Initially		**Later**	
Accrued expenses	Record (accrue) an expense first and the related payable:	→	Pay the liability later:	

Expense (e.g., Salaries)	4,000			Payable (e.g., Salaries)	4,000	
Payable (e.g., Salaries)		4,000		Cash		4,000

Accrued revenues	Record (accrue) a revenue first and the related receivable:	→	Collect cash later:

Receivable (e.g., from customer)	1,500			Cash	1,500	
Revenue (e.g., Consulting Service)		1,500		Receivable (e.g., from customer)		1,500

> No adjusting entry debits or credits Cash because the cash transactions are recorded at other times.

The chapter appendix shows an alternative treatment of unearned revenues and prepaid expenses.

The adjusting entries are summarized in Exhibit 3–9. They are necessary to:

1. Accurately measure net income or net loss on the *income statement*. Every adjusting entry affects either a revenue or an expense account.

2. Update the *balance sheet*. Every adjusting entry affects either an asset or a liability account. Note that these are in blue in the exhibit.

MyAccountingLab

Video: Road Map to Adjusting Entries

EXHIBIT 3–9 | Summary of Adjusting Entries

		Type of Account	
	Category of Adjusting Entry	**Debited**	**Credited**
Prepaid-type	Prepaid expense	Expense	Asset
	Amortization	Expense	Contra asset
	Unearned revenue	Liability	Revenue
Accrual-type	Accrued expense	Expense	Liability
	Accrued revenue	Asset	Revenue

➤ Try It!

5. Check Yes or No in the following tables to indicate whether each of the accounts would usually require an adjusting entry to be made to the specific account listed.

Account	Yes	No	Account	Yes	No
Accounts Receivable			Supplies		
Building			Cash		
Interest Payable			Prepaid Insurance		

6. At the beginning of the month, Supplies were $500. During the month, the company purchased $600 of supplies. At month's end, November 30, $400 of supplies were still on hand.
   a. What was the cost of supplies used during the month? Where is this item reported?
   b. What is the ending balance of Supplies? Where is this item reported?
   c. Make the adjusting entry to update the Supplies account at the end of the month.

Solutions appear at the end of this chapter and on MyAccountingLab

Exhibit 3–10 summarizes the adjusting entries of HEC at May 31 and shows the accounts after they have been posted. The adjustments are identified by their letter.

EXHIBIT 3–10 | Journalizing and Posting the Adjusting Entries of Hunter Environmental Consulting

PANEL A: Information for Adjustments at May 31, 2016

a. Prepaid insurance expired during May, $300

b. Supplies remaining on hand at May 31, 2016, $1,000

c. Amortization on furniture for the month of May, $750

d. Accrued salaries expense, $4,000

e. Accrued service revenue, $1,500

f. Amount of unearned service revenue that was earned during May, $1,000

PANEL B: Adjusting Entries

a. Insurance Expense	300	
Prepaid Insurance		300
To record insurance expense.		

b. Supplies Expense	500	
Office Supplies		500
To record supplies used.		

c. Amortization Expense—Furniture	750	
Accumulated Amortization—Furniture		750
To record amortization on furniture.		

d. Salaries Expense	4,000	
Salaries Payable		4,000
To accrue salaries expense.		

e. Accounts Receivable	1,500	
Service Revenue		1,500
To accrue service revenue.		

f. Unearned Service Revenue	1,000	
Service Revenue		1,000
To record unearned revenue that has been earned.		

PANEL C: Amounts Posted to T-Accounts

ASSETS

Cash
Bal. 31,000	

Accounts Receivable
Bal. 14,000	
(e) 1,500	
Bal. 15,500	

Office Supplies
Bal. 1,500	(b) 500
Bal. 1,000	

Prepaid Insurance
Bal. 3,600	(a) 300
Bal. 3,300	

Land
Bal. 50,000	

Furniture
Bal. 45,000	

Accumulated Amortization—Furniture
	(c) 750
	Bal. 750

LIABILITIES

Accounts Payable
	Bal. 12,000

Salary Payable
	(d) 4,000
	Bal. 4,000

Unearned Service Revenue
(f) 1,000	Bal. 3,000
	Bal. 2,000

OWNER'S EQUITY

Lisa Hunter, Capital
	Bal. 120,100

Lisa Hunter, Withdrawals
Bal. 6,000	

REVENUES

Service Revenue
	Bal. 24,000
	(e) 1,500
	(f) 1,000
	Bal. 26,500

EXPENSES

Amortization Expense—Furniture
(c) 750	
Bal. 750	

Insurance Expense
(a) 300	
Bal. 300	

Rent Expense
Bal. 3,000	

Salaries Expense
Bal. 4,000	
(d) 4,000	
Bal. 8,000	

Supplies Expense
(b) 500	
Bal. 500	

Utilities Expense
Bal. 1,000	

THE ADJUSTED TRIAL BALANCE

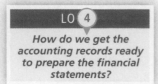

LO 4

How do we get the accounting records ready to prepare the financial statements?

This chapter began with the trial balance before any adjusting entries—the unadjusted trial balance (Exhibit 3–4). After the adjustments are journalized and posted, the accounts appear as shown in Exhibit 3–10, Panel C. A useful step in preparing the financial statements is to list the accounts, along with their adjusted balances, on an **adjusted trial balance.** This is step 6 in Exhibit 3–1 on page 118. This document has the advantage of listing all the accounts and their adjusted balances in a single place. Exhibit 3–11 shows an adjusted trial balance.

EXHIBIT 3–11 | Adjusted Trial Balance

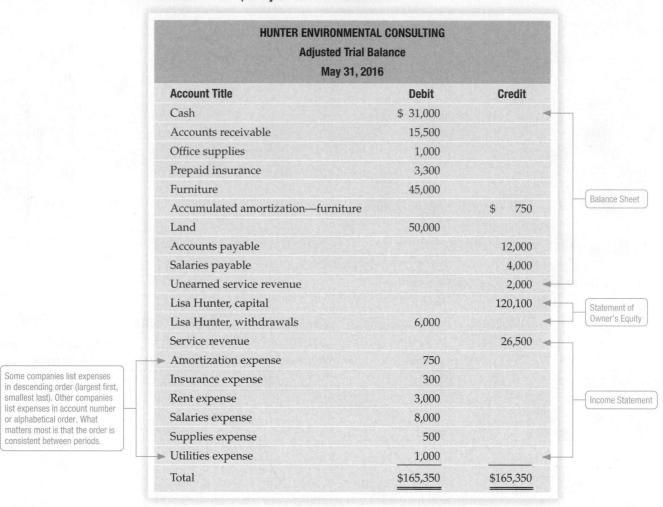

Account Title	Debit	Credit
Cash	$ 31,000	
Accounts receivable	15,500	
Office supplies	1,000	
Prepaid insurance	3,300	
Furniture	45,000	
Accumulated amortization—furniture		$ 750
Land	50,000	
Accounts payable		12,000
Salaries payable		4,000
Unearned service revenue		2,000
Lisa Hunter, capital		120,100
Lisa Hunter, withdrawals	6,000	
Service revenue		26,500
Amortization expense	750	
Insurance expense	300	
Rent expense	3,000	
Salaries expense	8,000	
Supplies expense	500	
Utilities expense	1,000	
Total	$165,350	$165,350

HUNTER ENVIRONMENTAL CONSULTING — Adjusted Trial Balance — May 31, 2016

Balance Sheet

Statement of Owner's Equity

Income Statement

Some companies list expenses in descending order (largest first, smallest last). Other companies list expenses in account number or alphabetical order. What matters most is that the order is consistent between periods.

In Chapter 4 we will look at worksheets as an alterative tool for accountants to use when preparing an adjusted trial balance.

PREPARING THE FINANCIAL STATEMENTS FROM THE ADJUSTED TRIAL BALANCE

LO 5

Remind me: How do we prepare the financial statements?

The May financial statements of Hunter Environmental Consulting (HEC) can be prepared from the adjusted trial balance in Exhibit 3–11. The right margin shows how the accounts are distributed to the financial statements.

- The income statement (Exhibit 3–12) is created using the revenue and expense accounts.

- The statement of owner's equity (Exhibit 3–13) shows the reasons for the change in the owner's capital account during the period.
- The balance sheet (Exhibit 3–14) reports the assets, liabilities, and owner's equity.

EXHIBIT 3–12 | Income Statement

HUNTER ENVIRONMENTAL CONSULTING
Income Statement
For the Month Ended May 31, 2016

Revenue:		
Service revenue		$26,500
Expenses:		
Amortization expense	$ 750	
Insurance expense	300	
Rent expense	3,000	
Salaries expense	8,000	
Supplies expense	500	
Utilities expense	1,000	
Total expenses		13,550
Net income		$12,950

EXHIBIT 3–13 | Statement of Owner's Equity

HUNTER ENVIRONMENTAL CONSULTING
Statement of Owner's Equity
For the Month Ended May 31, 2016

Lisa Hunter, capital, May 1, 2016	$120,100
Add: Net income	12,950
	133,050
Less: Withdrawals	6,000
Lisa Hunter, capital, May 31, 2016	$127,050

❶

EXHIBIT 3–14 | Balance Sheet

HUNTER ENVIRONMENTAL CONSULTING
Balance Sheet
May 31, 2016

Assets			Liabilities		
Cash		$ 31,000	Accounts payable		$ 12,000
Accounts receivable		15,500	Salaries payable		4,000
			Unearned service		
Office supplies		1,000	revenue		2,000
Prepaid insurance		3,300			
Furniture	$45,000		Total liabilities		18,000
Less: Accumulated					
amortization—					
furniture	750	44,250	**Owner's Equity**		
Land		50,000	Lisa Hunter, capital		127,050
			Total liabilities and		
Total assets		$145,050	owner's equity		$145,050

❷

Relationships among the Three Financial Statements

The arrows in Exhibits 3–12, 3–13, and 3–14 illustrate the relationships among the income statement, the statement of owner's equity, and the balance sheet. (This was introduced in Chapter 1, page 23.) Consider why the income statement is prepared first and the balance sheet last.

1 The income statement reports net income or net loss, calculated by subtracting expenses from revenues. Because revenues and expenses are owner's equity accounts, their net figure is then transferred to the statement of owner's equity.

2 Capital is a balance sheet account, so the ending balance in the statement of owner's equity is transferred to the balance sheet.

You may be wondering why the total assets on the balance sheet ($145,050 in Exhibit 3–14) do not equal the total debits on the adjusted trial balance ($165,350 in Exhibit 3–11). Likewise, the total liabilities and owner's equity do not equal the total credits on the adjusted trial balance ($165,350 in Exhibit 3–11). One reason for these differences is that Accumulated Amortization—Furniture and Lisa Hunter, Withdrawals are contra accounts. Recall that contra accounts are *subtracted* from their companion accounts on the balance sheet. However, on the adjusted trial balance, contra accounts are *added* as a debit or credit in their respective columns.

ETHICAL CONSIDERATIONS IN ACCRUAL ACCOUNTING

Like most other aspects of life, accounting poses ethical challenges. At the most basic level, accountants must be honest in their work. Only with honest and complete information, including accounting data, can people expect to make wise decisions. Two examples will illustrate the importance of ethics in accrual accounting.

- Suppose Hunter Environmental Consulting has been quite successful, so Lisa Hunter decides to open a second office. She needs to borrow $50,000 to do some minor renovations and set it up with computers and furniture. Suppose further that HEC understated expenses purposely to make net income higher than it should be on the company's income statement. This could be accomplished by not accruing expenses so that the total expenses are reported at an amount lower than their true amount. A banker could be tricked into lending money to HEC because the company appears to be more profitable than it really is. Then, if HEC could not repay the loan, the bank might lose money if Lisa Hunter cannot repay HEC's loan herself—all because the banker relied on incorrect accounting information.

- Recall from earlier in this chapter that amortization expense is an estimated figure. No business can foresee exactly how long its buildings and equipment will last, so accountants must *estimate* these assets' useful lives. A dishonest proprietor could buy a five-year asset and amortize it over 10 years. For each of the first five years, the company will report less amortization expense and more net income than it should. Or a dishonest business owner could overlook amortization expense altogether. Failing to record amortization would overstate net income. In both these situations, people who rely on the company's financial statements, like bank lenders, can be deceived into doing business with the company.

Accounting information must be honest and complete to serve its intended purpose. As you progress through introductory accounting, you will see other situations that challenge the ethics of accountants.

The cash basis of accounting poses fewer ethical challenges because cash is not an estimated figure. Either the company has the cash or it does not. Therefore, the amount of cash a company reports is rarely disputed. By contrast, adjusting entries must often be estimated. Whenever there is an estimate, the accountant may be asked by managers or owners of the business to use the adjusting process to make the company appear different from its true condition. Even with added ethical challenges, the accrual basis provides more complete accounting information than the cash basis.

> Try It!

7. Prepare just the assets side of a balance sheet given the following accounts and balances, which are presented in random order. Exhibit 3–14 on page 135 can be used as a model for the correct order of accounts.

Furniture	$21,000		Accounts Receivable	11,750
Accumulated Amortization—Furniture	7,500		Land	85,000
Prepaid Insurance	1,450		Supplies	1,100
Cash	63,200			

Solutions appear at the end of this chapter and on MyAccountingLab

ADJUSTING-PROCESS IMPLICATIONS OF IFRS

LO 6

How does IFRS apply to adjusting entries?

ASPE	IFRS

The concept of accrual accounting is accepted around the world. The accounting guidelines for all countries recommend the use of accrual accounting, so there are no process differences. There are differences in terminology, though.

ASPE	IFRS
Amortization is the term* used for the allocation of the cost of plant and equipment over its estimated useful life: • Amortization Expense • Accumulated Amortization Businesses may choose to use the term *depreciation* or *depletion* to be consistent with other companies in their industry.	*Depreciation* is the term used for amortization of tangible assets: • Depreciation Expense • Accumulated Depreciation *Amortization* is the term used for intangible assets.

* This is the term used in Part II (ASPE), Section 3061, *CPA Canada Handbook*.

SUMMARY PROBLEM FOR YOUR REVIEW

The unadjusted trial balance of Smart Touch Learning Centre for November 30, 2016, which is the end of its fiscal accounting period is shown below:

SMART TOUCH LEARNING CENTRE Unadjusted Trial Balance November 30, 2016		
Cash	$ 13,800	
Accounts receivable	10,000	
Supplies	2,000	
Furniture	20,000	
Accumulated amortization—furniture		$ 8,000
Building	100,000	
Accumulated amortization—building		60,000
Land	44,000	
Accounts payable		4,000
Salaries payable		0
Unearned service revenue		16,000
Gina Ho, capital		64,000
Gina Ho, withdrawals	50,000	
Service revenue		120,000
Salaries expense	32,000	
Supplies expense	0	
Amortization expense—furniture	0	
Amortization expense—building	0	
Miscellaneous expense	200	
Total	$272,000	$272,000

Data needed for the adjusting entries include the following:

a. A count of supplies on November 30 shows $400 of supplies on hand.
b. Amortization for the year on furniture, $4,000.
c. Amortization for the year on building, $2,000.
d. Salaries owed at year end but not yet paid, $1,000.
e. Service revenue that must be accrued, $2,600.
f. Of the $16,000 balance of unearned service revenue, $6,000 was earned during the year.

Required

1. Open the ledger accounts with their unadjusted balances using T-account format.
2. Journalize Smart Touch Learning Centre's adjusting entries at November 30, 2016. Identify entries by their letter as in Exhibit 3–10 (page 133) and the date.
3. Post the adjusting entries into the T-accounts.
4. Prepare an adjusted trial balance as at November 30, 2016.

5. Prepare the income statement, the statement of owner's equity for the year ended November 30, 2016, and the balance sheet as at November 30, 2016. Draw the arrows linking these three statements.

SOLUTION

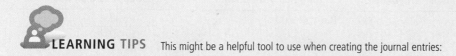

LEARNING TIPS This might be a helpful tool to use when creating the journal entries:

Refer to the rules shown in Exhibit 3–9 on page 132, to assist you with preparing the adjusting entries.

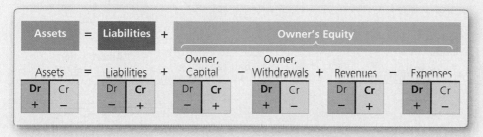

Requirement 2

2016			
a. Nov. 30	Supplies Expense	1,600	
	Supplies		1,600
	To record supplies used ($2,000 – $400).		
b. Nov. 30	Amortization Expense—Furniture	4,000	
	Accumulated Amortization—Furniture		4,000
	To record amortization expense on furniture.		
c. Nov. 30	Amortization Expense—Building	2,000	
	Accumulated Amortization—Building		2,000
	To record amortization expense on building.		
d. Nov. 30	Salaries Expense	1,000	
	Salaries Payable		1,000
	To accrue salary expense.		
e. Nov. 30	Accounts Receivable	2,600	
	Service Revenue		2,600
	To accrue service revenue.		
f. Nov. 30	Unearned Service Revenue	6,000	
	Service Revenue		6,000
	To record unearned service revenue that has been earned.		

Transaction a is explained more fully: On the November 30, 2016, trial balance, Supplies has a balance of $2,000. If the supplies on hand at year end are $400, then make an adjusting entry for the $1,600 of supplies that were used ($2,000 – $400). Increase Supplies Expense (expense) and decrease Supplies (asset).

The remaining transactions do not require further calculations to determine the amounts of the adjustments.

Requirements 1 and 3

For Requirement 1, create a T-account for each account name listed in the November 30, 2016, trial balance on the previous page. Insert the opening balances into the T-accounts from the trial balance, ensuring debit and credit balances on the trial balance are debit and credit balances in the T-accounts.

For Requirement 3, work slowly and check your work to make sure each transaction is posted to the proper T-account and no transactions were missed.

Requirements 1 and 3

ASSETS

Cash

Bal.	13,800	

Accounts Receivable

Bal.	10,000	
(e)	2,600	
Bal.	12,600	

Supplies

Bal.	2,000	(a)	1,600
Bal.	400	

Furniture

Bal.	20,000	

Accumulated Amortization—Furniture

		Bal.	8,000
		(b)	4,000
		Bal.	12,000

Building

Bal.	100,000	

Accumulated Amortization—Building

		Bal.	60,000
		(c)	2,000
		Bal.	62,000

Land

Bal.	44,000	

LIABILITIES

Accounts Payable

		Bal.	4,000

Salaries Payable

		(d)	1,000
		Bal.	1,000

Unearned Service Revenue

(f)	6,000	Bal.	16,000
		Bal.	10,000

OWNER'S EQUITY

Gina Ho, Capital

		Bal.	64,000

Gina Ho, Withdrawals

Bal.	50,000	

REVENUE

Service Revenue

		Bal.	120,000
		(e)	2,600
		(f)	6,000
		Bal.	128,600

EXPENSES

Salaries Expense

Bal.	32,000	
(d)	1,000	
Bal.	33,000	

Supplies Expense

(a)	1,600	
Bal.	1,600	

Amortization Expense—Furniture

(b)	4,000	
Bal.	4,000	

Amortization Expense—Building

(c)	2,000	
Bal.	2,000	

Miscellaneous Expense

Bal.	200	

Requirement 4

The title of each statement must include the name of the company, the name of the statement, and either the specific period of time covered or the date of the statement.

Expenses are listed here from highest to lowest dollar amount, with Miscellaneous Expense always listed as the final expense item. They could also be listed alphabetically.

Miscellaneous Expense is a catch-all account for expenses that do not fit in another category. It is usually reported last. Miscellaneous Expense should be a reasonably low dollar amount. If it is not, new accounts should be created for relevant expenses.

Ensure total debits equal total credits then double underline the totals to show they are final. Refer to Chapter 2 pages 80–81 for help if the totals are not equal on your first try.

SMART TOUCH LEARNING CENTRE
Adjusted Trial Balance
November 30, 2016

Account Title	Debit	Credit
Cash	$ 13,800	
Accounts receivable	12,600	
Supplies	400	
Furniture	20,000	
Accumulated amortization—furniture		$ 12,000
Building	100,000	
Accumulated amortization—building		62,000
Land	44,000	
Accounts payable		4,000
Salaries payable		1,000
Unearned service revenue		10,000
Gina Ho, capital		64,000
Gina Ho, withdrawals	50,000	
Service revenue		128,600
Salaries expense	33,000	
Supplies expense	1,600	
Amortization expense—furniture	4,000	
Amortization expense—building	2,000	
Miscellaneous expense	200	
	$281,600	$281,600

Requirement 5

SMART TOUCH LEARNING CENTRE		
Income Statement		
For the Year Ended November 30, 2016		
Revenues:		
Service revenue		$128,600
Expenses:		
Salaries expense	$33,000	
Supplies expense	1,600	
Amortization expense—furniture	4,000	
Amortization expense—building	2,000	
Miscellaneous expense	200	
Total expenses		40,800
Net income		$ 87,800

Gather all the revenue and expense account names and amounts from the Adjusted Trial Balance.

Expenses are listed in the same order they are found on the Adjusted Trial Balance.

SMART TOUCH LEARNING CENTRE	
Statement of Owner's Equity	
For the Year Ended November 30, 2016	
G. Ho, capital, November 1, 2016	$ 64,000
Add: Net income	87,800
	151,800
Less: Withdrawals	50,000
G. Ho, capital, November 30, 2016	$101,800

1 Beginning owner's equity and withdrawals are from the Adjusted Trial Balance. The net income amount is transferred from the income statement.

SMART TOUCH LEARNING CENTRE				
Balance Sheet				
November 30, 2016				
Assets			**Liabilities**	
Cash		$ 13,800	Accounts payable	$ 4,000
Accounts receivable		12,600	Salaries payable	1,000
			Unearned service	
Supplies		400	revenue	10,000
Furniture	$20,000		Total liabilities	15,000
Less: Accumulated				
amortization	12,000	8,000	**Owner's Equity**	
Building	100,000		G. Ho, capital	101,800
Less: Accumulated				
amortization	62,000	38,000		
Land		44,000		
			Total liabilities and	
Total assets		$116,800	owner's equity	$116,800

Note that the date format is different for the balance sheet. This statement shows the financial position on one specific date.

2 Gather all the asset and liability accounts and amounts from the adjusted trial balance. The owner's equity amount is transferred from the statement of owner's equity.

Check that total assets = total liabilities + owner's equity.

CHAPTER 3 APPENDIX

ALTERNATIVE TREATMENT OF ACCOUNTING FOR PREPAID EXPENSES AND UNEARNED REVENUES

LO **A1**

Is there another way to record prepaids?

Chapters 1 through 3 illustrate the most popular way to account for prepaid expenses and unearned revenues. This appendix illustrates an alternative—and equally appropriate—approach.

Prepaid Expense Recorded Initially as an Expense

Prepaid Insurance, Prepaid Rent, Prepaid Advertising, and Prepaid Legal Cost are all prepaid expenses. Supplies that will be used up in the current period or within one year are also accounted for as prepaid expenses.

In the body of the chapter, we showed that when a business prepays an expense it debits an *asset* account and later, as it is used up, debits an *expense* account.

Alternatively, the business can debit an expense account in the entry to record this cash payment. The thinking here is that the asset may be so short-lived that it will expire in the current accounting period—within one year or less. Let's see what happens when it does not expire before year end. How do we then make an adjustment to ensure that the income statement for the period and the balance sheet at year end are correct? A $4,800 cash payment for an advertising contract (for one year, in advance) on August 1, 2016, may be debited to Advertising Expense:

Aug. 1	Advertising Expense	.	4,800	
	Cash			4,800
	Bought a 12-month advertising contract.			

At December 31, 2016, only five months' prepayment has expired, leaving seven months' advertising still prepaid, which should be shown as an asset. In this case, the accountant must transfer $\frac{7}{12}$ of the original prepayment of $4,800, or $2,800, to Prepaid Advertising. At December 31, 2016, the business still has the benefit of the prepayment for January through July of 2017. The adjusting entry is as follows:

	Adjusting Entries			
Dec. 31	Prepaid Advertising		2,800	
	Advertising Expense			2,800
	Prepaid advertising of $2,800 ($4,800 × $\frac{7}{12}$).			

After posting, the two accounts appear as follows:

ASSETS Prepaid Advertising			EXPENSES Advertising Expense		
Dec. 31	Adj. 2,800		Aug. 1 Payment 4,800	Dec. 31 Adj. 2,800	
Dec. 31	Bal. 2,800		Dec. 31 Bal. 2,000		
7 months remaining			**5 months expired**		

The balance sheet for 2016 reports Prepaid Advertising of $2,800 ($400 per month for seven months), and the income statement for 2016 reports Advertising Expense of $2,000 ($400 per month for five months), regardless of whether the business initially debits the prepayment to an asset account or to an expense account.

Unearned Revenue Recorded Initially as a Revenue

Unearned (deferred) revenues arise when a business collects cash in advance of earning the revenue. The recognition of revenue is *deferred* until later when it is earned. Unearned revenues are liabilities because the business that receives cash owes the other party goods or services to be delivered later. In the chapter we saw that this liability was recognized when the cash was received.

Another way to account for the initial receipt of cash is to credit a *revenue* account when the business receives the cash. If the business then earns all the revenue within the period during which it received the cash, no adjusting entry is needed at the end of the period. However, if the business earns only a part of the revenue during the period, it must make adjusting entries at the end of the period.

Suppose on October 1, 2016, a consulting firm records as consulting revenue the receipt of $18,000 cash for revenue to be earned over nine months. The cash receipt entry is as follows:

LO A2

Is there another way to record unearned revenues?

Oct. 1	Cash	18,000	
	Consulting Revenue		18,000
	Received revenue to be earned over nine months.		

At December 31 the firm has earned only $\frac{3}{9}$ of the $18,000, or $6,000. Accordingly, the firm makes an adjusting entry to transfer the unearned portion ($\frac{6}{9}$ of $18,000, or $12,000) from the revenue account to a liability account as follows:

Adjusting Entries			
Dec. 31	Consulting Revenue	12,000	
	Unearned Consulting Revenue		12,000
	Adjust for consulting revenue still to be earned		

The adjusting entry moves the unearned portion ($\frac{6}{9}$ of $18,000, or $12,000) of the original amount into the liability account because the consulting firm still owes consulting service to the client during January through June of 2017. After posting, the total amount ($18,000), representing nine months of work, is properly divided between the liability account ($12,000, which is six months of work) and the revenue account ($6,000, which is three months of work) as follows:

LIABILITIES		REVENUE	
Unearned Consulting Revenue		**Consulting Revenue**	
	Dec. 31 Adj. 12,000	Dec. 31 Adj. 12,000	Oct. 1 Receipt 18,000
	Dec. 31 Bal. 12,000		Dec. 31 Bal. 6,000

6 months of the balance is still unearned   **3 months of the balance is earned**

The firm's 2016 income statement reports consulting revenue of $6,000, and the balance sheet at December 31, 2016, reports as a liability the unearned consulting revenue of $12,000, regardless of whether the business initially credits a liability account or a revenue account.

SUMMARY

LEARNING OBJECTIVES ① Apply the recognition criteria for revenues and expenses

When does a sale really happen? And when do we record an expense?   Pg. 119
- The *time period assumption* ensures that accounting information is reported at regular intervals.
- The *recognition criteria for revenues* tell accountants when to record revenue and the amount of revenue to record.
- The *matching objective* guides accounting for expenses. It directs accountants to match expenses against the revenues earned during a particular period of time.

LEARNING OBJECTIVES ② Distinguish accrual-basis accounting from cash-basis accounting

Why can't we wait to record transactions until the cash comes in or the cash goes out?   Pg. 121
- *Accrual-basis accounting*: Business events are recorded as they occur. This is part of GAAP and therefore is a basis for ASPE and IFRS.
- *Cash-basis accounting*: Only those events that affect cash are recorded.

    MyAccountingLab **Video:** Cash Basis versus Accrual Basis of Accounting

    Exhibit: Accrual-Basis versus Cash-Basis Accounting

LEARNING OBJECTIVES ③ Prepare adjusting entries

What is the adjusting process, and why is it important?   Pg. 122
- *Adjusting entries* are made at the end of the period to update the accounts for preparation of the financial statements. They can be divided into five categories: *prepaid expenses, amortization, accrued expenses, accrued revenues,* and *unearned revenues.*
- One method to record amortization is the straight-line method:

$$\text{Straight-line amortization} = (\text{Cost} - \text{Residual value}) \div \text{Useful life}$$

    MyAccountingLab **Videos:** Accrued Expenses, Fixed Assets and Depreciation, Prepaid Expenses, Road Map to Adjusting Entries, Unearned Revenue, Unearned Revenue Adjusting Entries

    Interactive Figure: Interact with Prepaid Rent

    Interactive Figure: Interact with Office Supplies

LEARNING OBJECTIVES ④ Prepare an adjusted trial balance

How do we get the accounting records ready to prepare the financial statements?   Pg. 134
- To prepare the *adjusted trial balance,* make a list of accounts and their balances from the ledger (T-account) totals.

LEARNING OBJECTIVES ⑤ Prepare the financial statements from the adjusted trial balance

Remind me: How do we prepare the financial statements?   Pg. 134
- The three financial statements are related as follows: Income, shown on the *income statement,* increases owner's capital, which also appears on the *statement of owner's equity.* The ending balance of capital is the last amount reported on the *balance sheet.*
- We can now trace the flow of accounting information through these steps:

    Business Transaction → Source Documents → Journal Entry → Posting to Ledger Accounts → Unadjusted Trial Balance → Adjusting Entries → Adjusted Trial Balance → Financial Statements

    MyAccountingLab **Video:** Real World Accounting

    Video: Relationships among the Financial Statements

LEARNING OBJECTIVES ⑥ Describe the adjusting-process implications of International Financial Reporting Standards (IFRS)

How does IFRS apply to adjusting entries?   Pg. 137
- There is no significant impact on the adjusting process since accrual accounting is necessary under both IFRS and ASPE.
- Companies reporting under IFRS generally use the term *depreciation* for PPE. ASPE uses the term *amortization,* but *depreciation* is also acceptable.

APPENDIX Ⓐ1 Account for a prepaid expense recorded initially as an expense

Is there another way to record prepaids?   Pg. 142
- Yes! First record the full amount of the payment made as an expense and then, at the end of the period, make an adjusting entry to record the portion of the payment that is still not used up.

Is there another way to record unearned revenues?   Pg. 143

- Yes! First record the full amount of the payment received as a revenue and then, at the end of the period, make an adjusting entry to record the portion of the revenue that is still not earned.

Check **Accounting Vocabulary** for all key terms used in Chapter 3 and the **Glossary** at the back of the book for all key terms used in the textbook.

MORE CHAPTER REVIEW MATERIAL

MyAccountingLab

DemoDoc covering Adjusting Entries for Accrual Accounting

Accounting Cycle Tutorial

Student PowerPoint Slides

Audio Chapter Summary

Note: All MyAccountingLab resources can be found in the Chapter Resources section and the Multimedia Library.

ACCOUNTING VOCABULARY

Accrual-basis accounting   Accounting that recognizes (records) the impact of a business event as it occurs, regardless of whether the transaction affected cash   *(p. 121).*

Accrued expense   An expense that has been incurred but not yet paid in cash. Also called an *accrued liability*   *(p. 129).*

Accrued revenue   A revenue that has been earned but not yet received in cash   *(p. 131).*

Accumulated amortization   The cumulative sum of all amortization expense from the date of acquiring a capital asset   *(p. 127).*

Adjusted trial balance   A list of all the ledger accounts with their adjusted balances   *(p. 134).*

Adjusting entry   An entry made at the end of the period to assign revenues to the period in which they are earned and expenses to the period in which they are incurred. Adjusting entries help measure the period's income and bring the related asset and liability accounts to correct balances for the financial statements   *(p. 122).*

Amortization   The term the *CPA Canada Handbook* uses to describe the writing off that occurs to expense the cost of capital assets; also called *depreciation*   *(p. 126).*

Book value   The asset's cost less accumulated amortization. Also called *carrying value*   *(p. 127).*

Carrying value (of property, plant, and equipment)   The asset's cost less accumulated amortization. Also called *book value*   *(p. 127).*

Cash-basis accounting   Accounting that records only transactions in which cash is received or paid   *(p. 121).*

Contra account   An account that always has a companion account and whose normal balance is opposite that of the companion account   *(p. 127).*

Deferred revenue   Another name for unearned revenue   *(p. 128).*

Fiscal year   An accounting year of any 12 consecutive months that may or may not coincide with the calendar year   *(p. 119).*

Intangible asset   An asset with no physical form giving a special right to current and expected future benefits   *(p. 126).*

Matching objective   The basis for recording expenses. Directs accountants to identify all expenses incurred during the period, measure the expenses, and match them against the revenues earned during that same span of time   *(p. 120).*

Prepaid expense   A category of assets that are paid for first, then expire or get used up in the near future   *(p. 123).*

Property, plant, and equipment (PPE)   Long-lived tangible capital assets, such as land, buildings, and equipment, used to operate a business   *(p. 126).*

Recognition criteria for revenues   The basis for recording revenues; tells accountants when to record revenue and the amount of revenue to record   *(p. 119).*

Residual value   The expected cash value of an asset at the end of its useful life   *(p. 126).*

Straight-line method   An amortization method in which an equal amount of amortization expense is assigned to each year (or period) of asset use   *(p. 126).*

Tangible capital asset   Physical assets expected to be used beyond the current accounting period. Examples include land, building, and equipment   *(p. 126).*

Time period assumption   Ensures that accounting information is reported at regular intervals   *(p. 119).*

Unearned revenue   A liability created when a business collects cash from customers in advance of doing work for the customer. The obligation is to provide a product or a service in the future. Also called *deferred revenue*   *(p. 128).*

SIMILAR ACCOUNTING TERMS

Accounting period	Reporting period
Accrual-basis accounting	Accrual accounting
Adjusting the accounts	Making the adjusting entries, adjusting the books
Amortization	Depreciation, depletion
Capital assets	Property, plant, and equipment
Carrying value	Book value, net carrying value, net book value
Deferred	Delayed
Property, plant, and equipment (PPE)	Capital asset, plant asset, fixed asset, tangible capital asset
Residual value	Scrap value, salvage value

SELF-STUDY QUESTIONS

Test your understanding of the chapter by marking the correct answer for each of the following questions:

1. Accrual-basis accounting (*p. 121*)
   a. Results in higher income than cash-basis accounting
   b. Leads to the reporting of more complete information than does cash-basis accounting
   c. Is not acceptable under GAAP
   d. Omits adjusting entries at the end of the period

2. Under the recognition criteria for revenues, revenue is recorded (*p. 119*)
   a. At the earliest acceptable time
   b. At the latest acceptable time
   c. After it has been earned, but not before
   d. At the end of the accounting period

3. The matching objective provides guidance in accounting for (*p. 120*)
   a. Expenses
   b. Owner's equity
   c. Assets
   d. Liabilities

4. Adjusting entries (*p. 122*)
   a. Assign revenues to the period in which they are earned
   b. Help to properly measure the period's net income or net loss
   c. Bring asset and liability accounts to correct balances
   d. Do all of the above

5. A building-cleaning firm began November with supplies of $210. During the month, the firm purchased supplies of $250. At November 30, supplies on hand total $160. Supplies expense for the period is (*p. 124*)
   a. $160
   b. $340
   c. $300
   d. $500

6. A building that cost $150,000 has accumulated amortization of $70,000. The book value of the building is (*p. 127*)
   a. $70,000
   b. $80,000
   c. $150,000
   d. $190,000

7. The adjusting entry to accrue salaries expense (*p. 130*)
   a. Debits Salaries Expense and credits Cash
   b. Debits Salaries Payable and credits Salaries Expense
   c. Debits Salaries Payable and credits Cash
   d. Debits Salaries Expense and credits Salaries Payable

8. A business received cash of $3,000 in advance for service that will be provided later. The cash receipt entry debited Cash and credited Unearned Revenue for $3,000. At the end of the period, $1,100 is still unearned. The adjusting entry for this situation will (*p. 128*)
   a. Debit Unearned Revenue and credit Revenue for $1,900
   b. Debit Unearned Revenue and credit Revenue for $1,100
   c. Debit Revenue and credit Unearned Revenue for $1,900
   d. Debit Revenue and credit Unearned Revenue for $1,100

9. First Class Maids recorded $2,500 of unearned service revenue being earned and the collection of $5,000 cash for service revenue previously accrued. The impact of these two entries on total service revenue is (*p. 128*)
   a. A decrease of $2,500
   b. An increase of $5,000
   c. An increase of $7,500
   d. An increase of $2,500

10. The links among the financial statements are (p. 136)
    a. Net income from the income statement to the statement of owner's equity
    b. Ending capital from the statement of owner's equity to the balance sheet
    c. Net income from the balance sheet to the income statement.
    d. Both a and b above

11. Accumulated Amortization is reported on (p. 127)
    a. The balance sheet
    b. The income statement
    c. The statement of owner's equity
    d. Both a and b

ASSIGNMENT MATERIAL

QUESTIONS

1. Distinguish accrual-basis accounting from cash-basis accounting.

2. How long is the basic accounting period? What is a fiscal year? What is an interim period?

3. What two questions do the recognition criteria for revenues help answer?

4. Briefly explain the matching objective.

5. What is the purpose of making adjusting entries?

6. Why are adjusting entries usually made at the end of the accounting period, not during the period?

7. Name five categories of adjusting entries and give an example of each.

8. Do all adjusting entries affect the net income or net loss of the period? Include the definition of an adjusting entry.

9. Why must the balance of Supplies be adjusted at the end of the period?

10. Tascona Supply Company pays $4,800 for an insurance policy that covers four years. At the end of the first year, the balance of its Prepaid Insurance account contains two elements. What are the two elements, and what is the correct amount of each?

11. The title Prepaid Expense suggests that this type of account is an expense. If it is, explain why. If it is not, what type of account is it?

12. Special FX purchased a two-year insurance policy on October 1, 2015. On January 1, 2016, the balance in the Prepaid Insurance account was $3,150. What is the amount of expense to record in the year-end adjusting journal entry on December 31, 2016?

13. What is a contra account? Identify the contra account introduced in this chapter, along with the account's normal balance.

14. The manager of Fast-Out, a convenience store, presents the company's balance sheet to a banker to obtain a loan. The balance sheet reports that the company's property, plant, and equipment have a book value of $155,000 and accumulated amortization of $75,000. What does *book value* of property, plant, and equipment mean? What was the cost of the property, plant, and equipment?

15. Give the entry to record accrued interest revenue of $7,200.

16. Why is unearned revenue a liability? Give an example.

17. Identify the types of accounts (assets, liabilities, and so on) debited and credited for each of the five types of adjusting entries.

18. What purposes does the adjusted trial balance serve?

19. Explain the relationships among the income statement, the statement of owner's equity, and the balance sheet.

20. Richardson Auctioneers failed to record the following adjusting entries at December 31, the end of its fiscal year: (a) accrued expenses, $1,500; (b) accrued revenues, $1,700; and (c) amortization, $3,000. Did these omissions cause net income for the year to be understated or overstated, and by what overall amount?

21. What are two possible differences between IFRS and ASPE in the terms used in amortization journal entries?

*22. A company pays $3,000 on February 1 to rent its office for February, March, and April. Make journal entries dated February 1 to illustrate the two ways this company can record its prepayment of rent.

*23. *Diving Masters Magazine* received $3,400 for magazine subscriptions in advance and recorded the cash receipt as Subscription Revenue. At the end of the year, only $1,400 of this revenue has been earned. What is the required year-end adjusting entry?

*These Questions cover Chapter 3 Appendix topics.

STARTERS

Applying the recognition criteria for revenues
①

Starter 3–1 *Sports Online Unlimited* sells annual subscriptions for magazines that are downloaded to customers monthly. The company collects cash in advance and then downloads the magazines to subscribers each month. Suppose the company collected $80,000 for subscriptions for January to December.

Apply the recognition criteria for revenues to determine (a) when the company should record revenue for this situation and (b) the amount of revenue the company should record for the January-through-March downloads.

Recognition criteria
①

Starter 3–2 Momentous Occasions is a photography business that shoots videos at parties. An alumni reunion group pays $1,000 in advance on March 3 to guarantee services for its party to be held April 2. The total cost of the event was to be $2,500. On April 28, the balance of $1,500 was paid. Answer the following questions about the correct application of the revenue recognition criteria:

a. Is the $1,000 reported as revenue on March 3?
b. On what date was the revenue earned?
c. Is the $1,500 reported as revenue on April 28?

Accounting theory
①

Starter 3–3 For each of the following, state whether you agree or disagree with the accounting treatment. What concept supports your view?

a. No utilities expense was recorded in December because the bill did not arrive until January.
b. A company records all revenue when earned, whether it has been collected or not.
c. Management of Tracy Daytona's requires the accountants to prepare weekly financial statements.

Comparing accrual-basis accounting and cash-basis accounting
②

Service revenue:
Cash basis, $600

Starter 3–4 Suppose you work summers house-sitting for people while they are away on vacation. Most of your customers pay you immediately after you finish a job. A few ask you to send them a bill. It is now June 30 and you have collected $600 from cash-paying customers. Your remaining customers owe you $1,400. How much service revenue would you have under the (a) cash basis and (b) accrual basis of accounting? Which method of accounting provides more information about your house-sitting business? Explain your answer.

Accrual-basis accounting versus cash-basis accounting for expenses
②

Starter 3–5 Smith Barnes Designers uses a sophisticated art program for its design work. Suppose the company paid $5,000 for a computer. Describe how the company would account for the $5,000 expenditure under (a) the cash basis and (b) the accrual basis. State in your own words why the accrual basis is more realistic for this situation.

Accrual-basis accounting versus cash-basis accounting
②

Starter 3–6 Starrs Bakery started 12 months ago as a supplier of gluten-free desserts to restaurants all over the province. During its first year of operations it earned $62,000 in revenues and incurred $51,000 in expenses. The business collected $58,000 from its customers and paid all but $2,500 to its suppliers. Starrs also prepaid $7,500 for prepaid rent and other expenses for the next year. Calculate the net income under the cash basis and then under the accrual basis.

Adjusting prepaid expenses
③

Starter 3–7 On April 1, 2017, you prepaid three months of rent for a total of $18,000. Give your adjusting entry to record rent expense at April 30, 2017. Include the date of the entry and an explanation. Then, using T-accounts, post to the two accounts involved and show their balances at April 30, 2017.

Starter 3–8 On May 1 your company paid cash of $27,000 for computers that are expected to remain useful for three years. At the end of three years, the value of the computers is expected to be zero. (Hint: Use the formula found on page 126.)

Make journal entries to record (a) the purchase of the computers on May 1 and (b) amortization on May 31. Include dates and explanations, and use the following accounts: Computer Equipment, Accumulated Amortization—Computer Equipment, and Amortization Expense—Computer Equipment.

Recording amortization

(b) Amort. Expense, $750

Starter 3–9 Refer to the data in Starter 3–8.
1. Using T-accounts, post to the accounts listed in Starter 3–8 and show their balances at May 31.
2. What is the computer equipment's book value at May 31?

Recording amortization

2. Book value, $26,250

Starter 3–10 Suppose Ladner Environmental Services (LES) borrowed $50,000 on March 1 by signing a note payable to Royal Bank. LES's interest expense for the remainder of its fiscal year (March through May) is $450.

1. Make LES's adjusting entry to accrue interest expense at May 31. Date the entry and include its explanation.

2. Using T-accounts, post to the two accounts affected by the adjustment.

Accruing and paying interest expense

Starter 3–11 Employees of Guelph Toyota work Monday through Friday and are paid every Friday for work done that week. The daily payroll is $13,900 and the last payday was Friday, December 28. What is the required adjusting journal entry, if any, on Monday, December 31?

Accruing wages

Starter 3–12 *The Big Clipper Magazine* collects cash from subscribers in advance and then mails the magazines to subscribers over a one-year period. Give the adjusting entry that the company makes to record the earning of $10,000 of subscription revenue that was collected in advance on March 1, 2017. Include an explanation for the entry, as illustrated in the chapter.

Accounting for unearned revenues

Starter 3–13 Identify the accounts affected by each of the following transactions, and state whether each account is debited or credited:

Identify accounts for adjusting entries

Transaction	Income Statement Account (Dr/Cr)	Balance Sheet Account (Dr/Cr)
a. Revenue is earned but not yet billed.		
b. Prepaid rent expired during the month.		
c. Annual amortization is recorded.		
d. Salaries earned by employees have not been paid yet.		
e. Revenue was earned that was paid for by a customer in advance.		

Starter 3–14 Scott Tax Services had the following accounts and account balances after adjusting entries. Assume all accounts have normal balances. Prepare the adjusted trial balance for Scott Tax Services' year end of September 30, 2017.

Preparing an adjusted trial balance

④

Trial Balance total, $84,850

Cash	$18,150	Equipment	$15,000
Land	20,000	Accounts Receivable	2,250
Utilities Payable	350	Office Supplies	200
Accounts Payable	3,100	S. Scott, Capital	18,400
Accumulated Amortization—Equipment	2,400	Utilities Expense	750
Service Revenue	60,000	Unearned Revenue	600
Supplies Expense	800	Amortization Expense—Equipment	1,200
S. Scott, Withdrawals	22,000	Salaries Expense	4,500

Note: Starters 3–15 and 3–16 should be used only after completing Starter 3–14.

Computing net income
⑤

Starter 3–15 Refer to the data in Starter 3–14. Compute Scott Tax Services' net income for the year ended September 30, 2017.

Computing total assets
⑤

Total assets, $53,200

Starter 3–16 Refer to the data in Starter 3–14. Compute Scott Tax Services' total assets at September 30, 2017. Remember that Accumulated Amortization is a contra asset.

IFRS and adjusting entries
⑥

Starter 3–17 Do International Financial Reporting Standards (IFRS) for publicly accountable enterprises in Canada have an impact on the adjusting process for these companies?

Alternative way to record
prepaid expenses
🅐1

*Starter 3–18 On June 30, 2017, Magnus' Muffins paid $18,000 for business insurance for the next year. Record the entries for the purchase of the insurance by recording it as an expense and then making a year-end entry on December 31, 2017, to adjust the accounts.

Alternative way to record
unearned revenues
🅐2

*Starter 3–19 On November 1, 2017, Freya Albatter's orthodontic office received a $2,500 prepayment from a client for dental work to be performed on November 22. The appointment got postponed until January 15, 2018. Prepare the journal entries for November 1, the December 31 year end, and the January 15 appointment dates. Assume that the prepayment was recorded as a revenue because, at that time, it was assumed the work would be performed within the month.

*These Starters cover Chapter 3 Appendix topics.

EXERCISES

MyAccountingLab

Exercise 3–1

Applying accounting assumptions, criteria, and objectives
①

Identify the accounting assumption, criteria, or objective that gives the most direction on how to account for each of the following situations:

a. The owner of a business desires monthly financial statements to measure the financial progress of the business on an ongoing basis.

b. Expenses of $3,000 must be accrued at the end of the period to measure income properly.

c. A customer states her intention to switch travel agencies. Should the new travel agency record revenue based on this intention? Give the reason for your answer.

d. Expenses of the period total $6,000. This amount should be subtracted from revenue to compute the period's net income.

Exercise 3–2

Applying the recognition criteria for revenues and the matching objective
①

1. Net income, $8.6 million

Dominion Storage operates approximately 300 mini-warehouses across Canada. The company's headquarters are in Medicine Hat, Alberta. During 2017, Dominion earned rental revenue of $26.0 million and collected cash of $23.6 million from customers. Total expenses for 2017 were $17.4 million, of which Dominion paid $15.9 million.

Required

1. Apply the recognition criteria for revenues and the matching objective to compute Dominion Storage's net income for 2017.

2. Identify the information that you did not use to compute Dominion Storage's net income. Give the reason for not using the information.

Exercise 3–3

Accrual-basis accounting
②

Severn Snowmobile Rentals had the following selected transactions during January:

Jan. 1   Paid cash for three months' rent on the showroom building (January, February, and March), $4,200.

5   Paid electricity expenses, $600 cash.

9   Received cash for the day's snowmobile rentals, $1,800.

14   Paid cash for a snowmobile, $6,000. It is expected to last three years.

23	Rented snowmobiles to a corporate group for a team-building event, $1,950. The corporation will pay in 30 days.
31	Made an adjusting entry for January's rent (from January 1).
31	Accrued salary expense for January, $850.

Show how each transaction would be handled using the accrual basis of accounting. Assume the company initially records a prepaid expense as an asset. Give the amount of revenue or expense for January. Journal entries are not required. Use the following format for your answer, and show your computations:

Severn Snowmobile Rentals—Amount of Revenue or Expense for January

Date	Revenue or Expense	Amount

Exercise 3–4

Write a memo to your supervisor explaining in your own words the concept of amortization as it is used in accounting. Use the following format:

Date:	(fill in)
To:	Supervisor
From:	(Student Name)
Subject:	The concept of amortization

Exercise 3–5

Compute the amounts indicated by question marks for each of the following Prepaid Insurance situations. For situations A and B, make the needed journal entry. Consider each situation separately.

	Situation				
	A	**B**	**C**	**D**	**E**
Beginning Prepaid Insurance	$ 4,200	$ 5,000	$16,800	$ 5,900	$?
Payments for Prepaid Insurance during the year	19,800	?	15,000	?	2,500
Total amount to account for	?	?	31,800	15,600	?
Ending Prepaid Insurance	19,000	6,000	?	6,000	1,400
Insurance Expense	?	$12,000	$25,000	$ 9,600	$2,600

Exercise 3–6

Check off the two effects of each of the following transactions:

Transaction	Revenue Earned	Expense Incurred	Liability Incurred	Liability Reduced	Asset Created	Asset Used Up
a. *Country Living Magazine* sent magazines to customers who have paid their subscription.						
b. Young and Rubicam completed work on an advertising plan that will be billed and collected next month.						
c. Automotive Imports recorded the fact that it used up some of the cost of its building.						
d. Classic Ideas Consulting received a cellphone invoice that must be paid next month.						

Exercise 3–7

Indicate the amount of the adjustment and the types of accounts affected by each of the following transactions for Phil's Garden Emporium. Complete the chart below with the following April 30 transactions and indicate the amount of each transaction as well as a "+" to indicate that the account increased or a "−" to indicate a decrease to the account.

a. The annual insurance premium of $1,200 was paid on March 1, 2017, for coverage beginning on that date. At the year end of April 30, 2017, an adjusting entry must be made.

b. At April 30, 2017, there was $900 in salary that was earned by employees but not yet paid to them.

c. At April 30, 2017, the Office Supplies account showed a balance of $1,800. A physical count of the supplies indicated that only $1,500 worth of supplies were left. Aside from needing a stern conversation with employees about telling the accounting department when supplies are used, an adjusting entry is required.

d. Customers prepaid for garden services in January and February for a total of $3,700. In April, some of the work was performed and requires an adjusting entry. The accountant was able to verify that $1,800 of work was still left to be completed in May.

e. Work was completed on April 30, 2017, that was worth $150, but no invoice was prepared because the work crew did not return to the office that day. The work should be recorded as complete in the current fiscal period.

	Income Statement			Balance Sheet		
Transaction	Revenues	Expenses		Assets	Liabilities	Owner's Equity
a.						
b.						
c.						
d.						
e.						

Exercise 3–8

Journalize the entries for the following adjustments at January 31, the end of the accounting period:

a. Amortization, $5,000.

b. Prepaid insurance used, $500.

c. Interest expense accrued, $400.

d. Employee salaries owed for Monday through Thursday of a five-day workweek; the weekly payroll is $16,000.

e. Unearned service revenue that becomes earned, $2,000.

Exercise 3–9

Journalize the adjusting entry needed at December 31 for each of the following independent situations:

a. On June 1, when we collected $48,000 rent in advance, we debited Cash and credited Unearned Rent Revenue. The tenant was paying for one year's rent in advance. At December 31, we must account for the amount of rent we have earned.

b. Interest revenue of $2,400 has been earned but not yet received on a $60,000 note receivable held by the business.

c. Salaries expense is $7,500 per day—Monday through Friday—and the business pays employees each Friday. This year December 31 falls on a Wednesday.

d. Equipment was purchased last year at a cost of $200,000. The equipment's useful life is five years. It will have no value after five years. Record the year's amortization.

e. On September 1, when we paid $6,000 for a one-year insurance policy, we debited Prepaid Insurance and credited Cash.

f. The business owes interest expense of $7,200 that it will pay early in the next period.

g. The unadjusted balance of the Supplies account is $13,500. The total cost of supplies remaining on hand on December 31 is $4,500.

Exercise 3–10

Journalizing adjusting entries
(3)

Journalize the following December 31 transactions for College Park Printing Services. No explanations are required.

a. Equipment cost $24,000 and is expected to be useful for 10 years, at which time it will have no residual value. Calculate and record amortization for the current year.

b. Each Monday, College Park pays employees for the previous week's work. The amount of weekly payroll is $5,600 for a seven-day workweek (Monday to Sunday). This year December 31 falls on a Thursday.

c. The beginning balance of Supplies was $2,500. During the year, College Park purchased supplies for $3,000, and at December 31 the supplies on hand totalled $1,700.

d. College Park prepaid one year of insurance coverage on August 1 of the current year, $5,280. Record insurance expense for the year ended December 31.

e. College Park earned $3,200 of unearned revenue.

f. College Park incurred $150 of interest expense on a note payable that will not be paid until February 28.

g. College Park billed customers $6,000 for printing services performed.

Exercise 3–11

Journalizing adjusting entries
and related transactions
(3)

For each of the following independent situations, journalize both the initial transaction and the subsequent adjusting entry:

a. Dec. 1 – business receives $2,000 for a 10-month service contract.
   Dec. 31 – year-end adjusting entry needed to update the balance in the account.

b. Mar. 31 – work performed but not yet billed to customers for the month, $900.
   Apr. 21 – received payment for the work that was completed.

c. Jun. 15 – purchased $3,500 of office supplies on account.
   Dec. 31 – a count of supplies shows that only $1,700 worth is left at year end, so the balance in the account needs to be updated.

d. Feb. 2 – business paid a $450 deposit for the last month's rental of a copier on a 10-month contract.
   Nov. 30 – the rental period for the copier ended, so the balance in the prepaid account must be updated.

Exercise 3–12

Recording adjustments in
T-accounts
(3)
Service Revenue bal., $91,500

The accounting records of Event Planners include the following unadjusted balances at March 31: Accounts Receivable, $5,400; Supplies, $2,700; Salaries Payable, $0; Unearned Service Revenue, $3,000; Service Revenue, $88,000; Salaries Expense, $22,000; Rent Expense, $18,000; Utilities Expense, $12,000; and Supplies Expense, $0.

The company's accountant develops the following data for the March 31, 2017, adjusting entries:

a. Service revenue accrued, $2,500.

b. Unearned service revenue that has been earned, $1,000.

c. Supplies on hand, $800.

d. Salaries owed to employees, $2,100.

Open T-accounts as needed and record the adjustments directly in the accounts, identifying each adjustment amount by its letter. Show each account's adjusted balance. Journal entries are not required.

Exercise 3–13

Explaining unearned revenues
(3)

Write a paragraph to explain why unearned revenues are liabilities rather than revenues. In your explanation, use the following actual example: *Maclean's* magazine collects cash from subscribers in advance and later mails the magazines to subscribers over a one-year period. Explain what happens to the unearned subscription revenue over the course of a year as the magazines are mailed to subscribers. Into what other account does the unearned subscription revenue go? Give the adjusting entry that *Maclean's* would make to record earning $75,000 of subscription revenue. Include an explanation for the entry.

Exercise 3–14

Prepare an adjusted trial balance

(4)

Adjusted trial balance total, $117,900

Refer to the data in Exercise 3-12. Prepare the adjusted trial balance for Event Planners for March 31, 2017. The remaining account balances you require (after adjustments) are as follows:

Cash	$53,200
Accounts payable	9,500
Jin Singh, capital	12,800

Exercise 3–15

Prepare an adjusted trial balance

(4)

Prepare an adjusted trial balance for Nature Valley Cleaners as at June 30, 2017. Assume that all accounts have their normal balances.

Accounts payable	$4,000
Accumulated amortization—equipment	7,000
Amortization expense—equipment	1,000
Cash	2,400
Equipment	40,000
Insurance expense	200
Les Valley, capital	17,000
Les Valley, withdrawals	8,000
Prepaid insurance	1,800
Salaries expense	16,000
Salaries payable	2,000
Service revenue	44,000
Supplies	4,000
Supplies expense	2,000
Unearned service revenue	1,400

Exercise 3–16

Computing financial statement amounts

(5)

Refer to your solution for Exercise 3–14.

a. Compute Event Planners' net income for the period ended March 31, 2017.

b. Compute Event Planners' total liabilities at March 31, 2017.

Exercise 3–17

Preparing the financial statements

(5)

Refer to the data in Exercise 3-15. Prepare Nature Valley Cleaners' income statement and statement of owner's equity for the year ended June 30, 2017. Then prepare the balance sheet on that date.

Exercise 3–18

Effect of errors on financial statements

(5)

b. Net income understated

On December 31, 2015, Grover Company made the following errors:

a. Did not accrue interest of $7,500 owed on loans due next year

b. Did not accrue service revenue in the amount of $9,200

Assuming the financial statements are prepared before the errors are discovered, state the effects of each error on the financial statement elements by completing the chart below.

	Error a		Error b	
	Overstated	Understated	Overstated	Understated
Assets at Dec. 31, 2016, would be				
Liabilities at Dec. 31, 2016, would be				
Net income for 2016 would be				
Owner's equity at Dec. 31, 2016, would be				

*Exercise 3–19

Recording prepaids in two ways

(3) (A1)

At the beginning of the year, supplies of $4,800 were on hand. During the year, the business paid $10,800 for more supplies. At the end of the year, the count of supplies indicates supplies of $3,400 on hand.

Required

1. Assume that the business records supplies by initially debiting an *asset* account. Therefore, place the beginning balance in the Supplies T-account and record the above entries directly in the accounts without using a journal.

2. Assume that the business records supplies by initially debiting an *expense* account. Therefore, place the beginning balance in the Supplies Expense T-account and record the above entries directly in the accounts without using a journal.

3. Compare the ending account balances under both approaches. Are they the same? Explain.

*Exercise 3-20

At the beginning of the year, a business had a liability to customers of $7,500 for unearned service revenue collected in advance. On May 31, the business received advance cash receipts of $20,000. At year end, December 31, the company's liability to customers was $3,500 for unearned service revenue collected in advance.

Recording unearned revenues in two ways

Unearned Service Revenue bal., $3,500

Required

1. Assume that the company records unearned revenues by initially crediting a *liability* account. Open T-accounts for Unearned Service Revenue and Service Revenue, and place the beginning balance in Unearned Service Revenue. Journalize the cash collection and adjusting entries and post their dollar amounts. As references in the T-accounts, label the balance, the cash receipt, and the adjustment.

2. Assume that the company records unearned revenues by initially crediting a *revenue* account. Open T-accounts for Unearned Service Revenue and Service Revenue, and place the beginning balances in Service Revenue and Unearned Service Revenue. Journalize the cash collection and adjusting entries and post their dollar amounts. As references in the T-accounts, label the balance, the cash receipt, and the adjustment.

3. Compare the ending balances in the two accounts. Explain why they are the same or different.

*Exercise 3-21

Fort Services initially records all prepaid expenses as expenses and all unearned revenues as revenues. Given the following information, prepare the necessary adjusting entries at December 31, 2017, the company's year end.

Recording prepaids as expenses and unearned revenues as revenues, adjusting entries

Supplies Expense, Cr $700

a. On January 3, 2017, the company's first day of operations, $2,500 of supplies were purchased. A physical count revealed $700 of supplies still on hand at December 31, 2017.

b. On January 4, 2017, a $15,000 payment for insurance was made to an insurance agency for a 30-month policy.

c. On June 30, 2017, Fort Services received nine months' rent totalling $13,500 in advance from a tenant.

---

*These Exercises cover Chapter 3 Appendix topics.

SERIAL EXERCISE

Exercise 3-22 continues the Lee Management Consulting situation from Exercise 2-18 of Chapter 2. If you did not complete Exercise 2-18 you can complete Exercise 3-22 by following the instructions in the note below.

Adjusting the accounts, preparing an adjusted trial balance, preparing the financial statements

③ ④ ⑤

4. Adjusted trial balance total, $38,109

5. Net income, $1,841; Total assets, $31,541

Exercise 3-22

Refer to Exercise 2-18 of Chapter 2. Start from the unadjusted trial balance and the posted T-accounts that Lee Management Consulting prepared at June 30. Make sure the account balances in your trial balance and T-accounts match those in the trial balance at June 30, 2016, shown on the next page.

LEE MANAGEMENT CONSULTING		
Unadjusted Trial Balance		
June 30, 2016		
	Debits	**Credits**
Cash	$ 23,750	
Accounts receivable	1,500	
Supplies	500	
Equipment	1,000	
Furniture	5,000	
Accounts payable		$ 5,000
Unearned revenue		2,000
Michael Lee, capital		25,000
Michael Lee, withdrawals	2,000	
Service revenue		5,000
Rent expense	3,000	
Utilities expense	250	
Total	$ 37,000	$37,000

At June 30, the company gathers the following information for the adjusting entries:

a. Accrued service revenue, $400.

b. Earned $800 of the service revenue collected in advance on June 21 for eight days of work.

c. Supplies remaining on hand at June 30, $100.

d. Amortization expense—equipment, $42; furniture, $167 (all amounts are rounded to the nearest dollar).

e. Accrued $500 expense for the secretary's salary.

Required

1. Open these new T-accounts: Accumulated Amortization—Equipment; Accumulated Amortization—Furniture; Salaries Payable; Amortization Expense—Equipment; Amortization Expense—Furniture; Salaries Expense; Supplies Expense.

2. Journalize each of the entries.

3. Post the adjusting entries into the T-accounts. Label each adjusting amount as *Adj.* and an account balance as *Bal.*

4. Prepare an adjusted trial balance at June 30, 2016. List expenses in alphabetical order.

5. Prepare the income statement and statement of owner's equity of Lee Management Consulting for the month ended June 30, 2016, then prepare the balance sheet at that date. (Hint: List the expenses in alphabetical order.)

CHALLENGE EXERCISE

Computing the financial statements

Supplies expense, $10,000

Exercise 3–23

The adjusted trial balances of Pacific Services at December 31, 2017, and December 31, 2016, include these amounts:

	2017	2016
Supplies	$ 4,000	$ 2,000
Salaries payable	5,000	8,000
Unearned service revenue	26,000	32,000

Analysis of the accounts at December 31, 2017, reveals these transactions for 2017:

Cash payment for supplies	$ 12,000
Cash payment for salaries	94,000
Cash receipts in advance for service revenue	160,000

Compute the amount of supplies expense, salaries expense, and service revenue to report on the Pacific Services income statement for 2017.

BEYOND THE NUMBERS

Beyond the Numbers 3–1

Suppose a new management team is in charge of Wild Roses Inc., a micro-brewery. Assume Wild Roses Inc.'s new top executives rose through the company ranks in the sales and marketing departments and have little appreciation for the details of accounting. Consider the following conversation between two executives:

Stephen Federer, President:

"I want to avoid the hassle of adjusting the books every time we need financial statements. Sooner or later we receive cash for all our revenues and we pay cash for all our expenses. I can understand cash transactions, but all these accruals confuse me. If I cannot understand our own accounting, I'm fairly certain the average person who invests in our company cannot understand it either. Let's start recording only our cash transactions. I bet it won't make any difference to anyone."

Kate McNamara, Chief Financial Officer:

"Sounds good to me. This will save me lots of headaches. I'll implement the new policy immediately."

Write a business memo to the company president giving your response to the new policy. Identify at least five individual items (such as specific accounts) in the financial statements that will be reported incorrectly. Will outside investors care? Use the format of a business memo given with Problem 3-2A on page 158.

ETHICAL ISSUES

The net income of Antiques Plus decreased sharply during 2017. Mariah Ciccone, owner of the store, anticipates the need for a bank loan in 2018. Late in 2017, she instructs the accountant to record a $35,000 sale of furniture to the Ciccone family, even though the goods will not be shipped from the manufacturer until January 2018. Ciccone also tells the accountant not to make the following December 31, 2017, adjusting entries:

Salaries owed to employees	$27,000
Prepaid insurance that has expired	1,500

Required

1. Compute the overall effect of these transactions on the store's reported income for 2017.

2. Why did Ciccone take this action? Is this action ethical? Give your reason, identifying the parties helped and the parties harmed by Ciccone's action.

3. As a personal friend, what advice would you give to *the accountant*?

PROBLEMS (GROUP A)   MyAccountingLab

Problem 3–1A

Cash-basis versus accrual-basis accounting
(1) (2)
2. Net income, $5,700

Kandi's Office Design had the following transactions during January:

Jan.	1	Paid for insurance for January through March, $2,400. It is company policy to record this sort of transaction in an asset account.
	4	Performed design service on account, $7,000.
	5	Purchased office furniture on account, $2,100.
	8	Paid advertising expense, $2,000 cash.
	15	Purchased office equipment for cash, $4,500.
	19	Performed design services and received cash, $9,000.
	24	Collected $3,500 on account for the January 4 service.
	26	Paid account payable from January 5.
	29	Paid salaries expense, $7,500 cash.
	31	Recorded adjusting entry for January insurance expense (see January 1).

Required

1. Show how each transaction would be accounted for using the accrual basis of accounting. Use the format below for your answer, and show your computations. Give the amount of revenue or expense for January. Journal entries are not required.

Amount of Revenue or Expense for January

Date	Revenue (Expense)	Amount

2. Compute January net income or net loss under the accrual basis of accounting.

3. State why the accrual basis of accounting is preferable to the cash basis.

Problem 3–2A

Applying accounting assumptions, criteria, and objectives
(1) (3)

As the controller of Best Security Systems, you have hired a new bookkeeper, whom you must train. She objects to making an adjusting entry for accrued salaries at the end of the period. She reasons, "We will pay the salaries soon. Why not wait until payment to record the expense? In the end, the result will be the same." Write a business memo to explain to the bookkeeper why the adjusting entry for accrued salaries expense is needed.

This is the format of the business memo:

Date:	(fill in)
To:	New Bookkeeper
From:	(Student Name)
Subject:	Why the adjusting entry for salaries expense is needed

Problem 3–3A

Journalize the adjusting entry needed on December 31, the company's year end, for each of the following independent cases affecting Eagle Communications:

Journalizing adjusting entries

③

c. Supplies Expense, $9,200

a. Each Friday the company pays its employees for the current week's work. The amount of the payroll is $15,000 for a five-day workweek. The current accounting period ends on Wednesday.

b. Eagle has received notes receivable from some clients for professional services. During the current year, Eagle has earned interest revenue of $800, which will be received next year.

c. The beginning balance of Supplies was $4,800. During the year the company purchased supplies costing $7,600, and at December 31 the inventory of supplies remaining on hand is $3,200.

d. The company is developing a wireless communication system for a large company, and the client paid Eagle $120,000 at the start of the project. Eagle recorded this amount as Unearned Consulting Revenue. The development will take several months to complete. Eagle executives estimate that the company has earned three-fourths of the total fee during the current year.

e. Amortization for the current year includes the following: Office Furniture, $8,600, and Design Equipment, $16,000. Make a compound entry. (Hint: This means showing everything in one journal entry and not two.)

f. Details of Prepaid Insurance are shown in the account:

Prepaid Insurance

Jan. 2 Bal.	6,000	

Eagle Communications prepays a full year's insurance on January 2. Record insurance expense for the year ended December 31 as one annual adjustment for what was used for the year.

Problem 3–4A

Laughter Landscaping has collected the following data for the December 31 adjusting entries:

Journalizing adjusting entries and subsequent journal entries

③

b. Insurance Expense, $4,500

a. Each Friday, Laughter pays employees for the current week's work. The amount of the weekly payroll is $7,000 for a five-day workweek. This year December 31 falls on a Wednesday. Laughter will pay its employees on January 2.

b. On January 1 of the current year, Laughter purchased an insurance policy that covers two years, $9,000.

c. The beginning balance of Office Supplies was $4,000. During the year, Laughter purchased office supplies for $5,200, and at December 31 the office supplies on hand total $2,400.

d. During December, Laughter designed a landscape plan and the client prepaid $7,000. Laughter recorded this amount as Unearned Revenue. The job will take two months to complete. Laughter estimates that the company has earned 75 percent of the total revenue in the current year and will finish by January 12.

e. At December 31, Laughter had earned $3,500 for landscape services completed for Turnkey Appliances. Turnkey has stated that they will pay Laughter on January 10.

f. Amortization for the current year includes Equipment, $3,700, and Trucks, $1,300. Make one compound entry to record the amortization, but use separate amortization accounts for each asset.

g. Laughter has incurred $300 of interest expense on a $450 interest payment due on January 15.

Required

1. Journalize the adjusting entry needed on December 31 for each of the previous items affecting Laughter Landscaping. Assume Laughter records adjusting entries only at the end of the year.

2. Journalize the subsequent journal entries for adjusting entries a, d, and g.

Journalizing and posting adjustments to T-accounts, preparing and using the adjusted trial balance

③ ④

3. Adjusted trial bal. total, $74,035

The trial balance of Kaplan Printing at December 31, 2017, appears below. The data needed for the month-end adjustments follow the trial balance.

KAPLAN PRINTING Unadjusted Trial Balance December 31, 2017		
Cash	$ 5,400	
Accounts receivable	18,600	
Prepaid rent	4,500	
Supplies	1,200	
Furniture and equipment	19,200	
Accumulated amortization—furniture and equipment		$ 5,760
Accounts payable		3,400
Salaries payable		0
Unearned printing revenue		2,400
S. Kaplan, capital		23,140
S. Kaplan, withdrawals	6,000	
Printing revenue		36,500
Salaries expense	12,500	
Rent expense	0	
Amortization expense—furniture and equipment	0	
Advertising expense	3,600	
Supplies expense	0	
Miscellaneous expense	200	
Total	$71,200	$71,200

Adjustment data:

a. Unearned printing revenue still remaining to be earned at December 31, $800.

b. Prepaid rent still available at December 31, $2,000.

c. Supplies used during the month, $450.

d. Amortization for the month, $660.

e. Accrued miscellaneous expense at December 31, $200 (credit Accounts Payable).

f. Accrued salaries expense at December 31, $1,975.

Required

1. Open T-accounts for the accounts listed in the trial balance, inserting their December 31 unadjusted balances.

2. Journalize the adjusting entries on December 31 and post them to the T-accounts. Identify the journal entries and posted amounts by their letter.

3. Prepare the adjusted trial balance.

4. How will the company use the adjusted trial balance?

The adjusted trial balance of Cook Antique Auctioneers at the end of its year, December 31, 2017, is shown below:

Excel Spreadsheet Template

Preparing the financial statements from an adjusted trial balance

(5)

1. Net income, $314,800

COOK ANTIQUE AUCTIONEERS
Adjusted Trial Balance
December 31, 2017

Cash	$ 9,400	
Accounts receivable	166,000	
Prepaid rent	8,000	
Supplies	4,200	
Equipment	468,420	
Accumulated amortization—equipment		$ 72,000
Office furniture	96,000	
Accumulated amortization—office furniture		38,400
Accounts payable		56,000
Unearned service revenue		8,000
Interest payable		1,100
Salaries payable		4,200
Notes payable		220,000
A. Cook, capital		129,520
A. Cook, withdrawals	92,000	
Service revenue		780,000
Amortization expense—equipment	36,000	
Amortization expense—office furniture	9,600	
Salaries expense	320,000	
Rent expense	48,000	
Interest expense	13,200	
Utilities expense	21,600	
Insurance expense	13,200	
Supplies expense	3,600	
Total	$1,309,220	$1,309,220

Required

1. Prepare Cook Antique Auctioneers' 2017 income statement, statement of owner's equity, and balance sheet. List expenses in decreasing-balance order on the income statement and show total liabilities on the balance sheet. If your three financial statements appear on one page, draw the arrows linking the three financial statements. If they are on separate pages, write a short paragraph describing how the three financial statements are linked. How will what you have learned in this problem help you manage a business?

2. a. Which financial statement reports Cook's results of operations? Were 2017 operations successful? Cite specifics from the financial statements to support your evaluation.

   b. Which statement reports the company's financial position? Does Cook's financial position look strong or weak? Give the reason for your evaluation.

Preparing an adjusted trial
balance and the financial
statements

③ ④ ⑤

2. Net income, $6,550

Problem 3–7A

Consider the unadjusted trial balance of Burrows Landscaping at December 31, 2017, and the related month-end adjustment data:

BURROWS LANDSCAPING Unadjusted Trial Balance December 31, 2017		
Cash	$ 24,500	
Accounts receivable	22,000	
Prepaid rent	9,000	
Supplies	5,500	
Equipment	66,000	
Accumulated amortization—equipment		$ 12,650
Accounts payable		7,200
Salaries payable		0
A. Burrows, capital		122,700
A. Burrows, withdrawals	25,000	
Landscaping design revenue		126,000
Salaries expense	82,000	
Rent expense	22,500	
Utilities expense	6,000	
Amortization expense—equipment	6,050	
Supplies expense	0	
Total	$268,550	$268,550

The following adjustments need to be made before the financial statements for the year can be prepared:

a. Accrued landscaping design revenue at December 31, $8,500.

b. One month of the prepaid rent had been used. The unadjusted prepaid balance of $9,000 relates to the four-month period December 1, 2017, through March 31, 2018.

c. Supplies remaining on hand at December 31, $900.

d. Amortization on equipment for the month of December. The equipment's expected useful life is 10 years; it will have no value at the end of its useful life, and the straight-line method of amortization is used.

e. Accrued salaries expense at December 31 should be for two days only. The five-day weekly payroll is $10,000.

Required

1. Sketch T-accounts in your notes to calculate the new balances. Prepare the adjusted trial balance of Burrows Landscaping at December 31, 2017.

2. Prepare the income statement (record expenses from largest to smallest on the income statement) and the statement of owner's equity for the year ended December 31, 2017, and the balance sheet at December 31, 2017. Draw the arrows linking the three financial statements, or write a short description of how they are linked.

Problem 3–8A

Pace Employment Counsellors provides counselling services to employees of companies that are downsizing. The business had the following account balances:

Prepare adjusting entries, an adjusted trial balance, and financial statements

③ ④ ⑤

Net income, $158,075

PACE EMPLOYMENT COUNSELLORS Unadjusted Trial Balance December 1, 2017		
Cash	$ 19,000	
Accounts receivable	23,200	
Prepaid advertising	1,500	
Supplies	5,000	
Computer equipment	69,000	
Accumulated amortization—computer equipment		$ 0
Building	288,000	
Accumulated amortization—building		0
Land	144,000	
Accounts payable		93,600
B. Pace, capital		330,000
B. Pace, withdrawals	79,000	
Counselling revenue		342,500
Salaries expense	120,000	
Supplies expense	0	
Utilities expense	17,400	
Total	$766,100	$766,100

The following transactions occurred during December:

a. On December 1, paid cash to a marketing firm for four months of advertising work in advance. The contract was for $2,875 per month.

b. On December 6, supplies in the amount of $3,700 were purchased on account.

c. On December 15, the company received a cash advance of $8,000 for work to be performed starting January 1, 2018.

d. On December 29, the company provided counselling services to a customer for $15,000, to be paid in 30 days.

The following information was available on December 31, 2017:

e. A physical count shows $7,600 of supplies remaining on hand on December 31.

f. The building has an expected useful life of eight years with no expected value after eight years. The building was purchased on January 2, and the straight-line method of amortization is used.

g. The computer equipment, purchased on January 2, is expected to be used for four years with no expected value after four years. The straight-line method of amortization is used.

h. The marketing firm has performed one-quarter of the work on the contract.

i. The company's managing director, who earns $800 per day, worked the last six days of the year and will be paid on January 4, 2018.

Required

1. Journalize the entries. Add new accounts if necessary.

2. Prepare an adjusted trial balance on December 31, 2017.

3. Prepare an income statement for the year ended December 31, 2017. List expenses in the order of dollar amount, from the greatest amount to the smallest.

4. Prepare a statement of owner's equity for the year ended December 31, 2017. Assume there have been no changes to the capital account since January 1.

5. Prepare a balance sheet at December 31, 2017.

*Problem 3–9A

Recording prepaid rent and
service revenue collected in
advance in two ways
③ (A1) (A2)
Rent Expense bal., $10,000

Park Sales and Service completed the following transactions during 2017:

Aug. 31		Paid $15,000 store rent covering the six-month period ending February 28, 2018.
Dec. 1		Collected $6,400 cash in advance from customers. The service revenue earned will be $1,600 each month over the four-month period ending March 31, 2018.

Required

1. Journalize these entries by debiting an asset account for Prepaid Rent and by crediting a liability account for Unearned Service Revenue. Explanations are not required.

2. Journalize the related adjustments at December 31, 2017.

3. Post the entries to T-accounts and show their balances at December 31, 2017. Posting references are not required.

4. Repeat Requirements 1 through 3. This time debit Rent Expense for the rent payment and credit Service Revenue for the collection of revenue in advance.

5. Compare the account balances in Requirements 3 and 4. They should be equal.

_____

*This Problem covers Chapter 3 Appendix topics.

PROBLEMS (GROUP B)   MyAccountingLab

Problem 3–1B

Accrual-basis accounting
① ②

Rajeesh Skin Clinic experienced the following selected transactions during October:

Oct.	1	Paid for insurance for October through December, $9,000. The payment was recorded in an asset account.
	4	Paid utility invoice with cash, $1,200.
	5	Performed services on account, $8,000.
	9	Purchased office equipment for cash, $7,000.
	12	Received cash for services performed, $4,400.
	14	Purchased office equipment on account, $2,400.
	28	Collected $3,000 on account from October 5.
	31	Paid salaries expense, $4,500 cash.
	31	Paid account payable from October 14.
	31	Recorded adjusting entry for October insurance expense (see October 1).

Required

1. Show how each transaction would be accounted for using the accrual basis of accounting. Use the format below for your answer, and show your computations. Give the amount of revenue or expense for October. Journal entries are not required.

Amount of Revenue or Expense for October

Date	Revenue/Expense	Amount

2. Compute October net income or net loss under the accrual basis of accounting.

3. Why is the accrual basis of accounting preferable to the cash basis?

Problem 3–2B

Write a business memo to a new bookkeeper to explain the difference between the cash basis of accounting and the accrual basis. Mention the roles of the recognition criteria for revenues and the matching objective in accrual-basis accounting.

Applying accounting assumptions, criteria, and objectives
①②

This is the format of a business memo:

Date:	(fill in)
To:	New Bookkeeper
From:	(Student Name)
Subject:	Difference between the *cash basis* of accounting and the *accrual basis* of accounting

Problem 3–3B

Journalize the adjusting entry needed on December 31, the company's year end, for each of the following independent cases affecting East Coast Contractors:

Journalizing adjusting entries
③

a. Details of Prepaid Rent are shown in the account:

Prepaid Rent	
Jan. 1 Bal.	4,500
Mar. 31	9,000
Sep. 30	9,000

East Coast Contractors pays office rent semi-annually on March 31 and September 30. At December 31, part of the last payment is still available to cover January to March of the next year. No rent expense was recorded during the year.

b. East Coast Contractors pays its employees each Friday. The amount of the weekly payroll is $5,000 for a five-day workweek, and the daily salary amounts are equal. The current accounting period ends on Wednesday.

c. East Coast Contractors has lent money to help employees find housing, receiving notes receivable in return. During the current year the entity has earned interest revenue of $1,400 from employees' loans, which it will receive next year.

d. The beginning balance of Supplies was $5,100. During the year the company purchased supplies costing $16,500, and at December 31 the inventory of supplies remaining on hand is $5,500.

e. East Coast Contractors is installing cable in a large building, and the owner of the building paid East Coast Contractors $42,000 as the annual service fee. East Coast Contractors recorded this amount as Unearned Service Revenue. Robin Zweig, the general manager, estimates that the company has earned one-fourth of the total fee during the current year.

f. Amortization expenses for the current year are Equipment, $14,000, and Trucks, $33,000. Make a compound entry. (Hint: This means include all the accounts in one journal entry.)

Problem 3–4B

Lindsey Home Staging is almost done its accounting for the year. Lindsey just found the last December 31 adjusting entries that need to be recorded:

Journalizing adjusting entries and subsequent journal entries
③

a. Each Friday Lindsey pays employees for the current week's work. The amount of the weekly payroll is $6,500 for a five-day workweek. This year December 31 falls on a Tuesday. Lindsey will pay the employees on January 3.

b. On January 1 of the current year, Lindsey purchases a business insurance policy that covers two years for $5,500.

c. The beginning balance of her decorating supplies account was $4,200. During the year she purchased more supplies for $5,100, and at December 31 the supplies on hand total $2,900.

d. During December Lindsey prepared a home remodelling plan and the client prepaid $9,000. Lindsey recorded this amount as Unearned Revenue. The job will be completed by January 14. Lindsey estimates that the company earned 70 percent of the total revenue during the current year.

e. At December 31 Lindsey had earned $4,000 for staging services for Tomball Adamsey. Tomball has stated he will pay Lindsey on the closing date of his home, January 10.

f. Amortization for the current year includes Equipment, $3,600, and Vehicles, $1,400. Write this as one compound entry but use separate amortization accounts for each asset.

g. Lindsey incurred $300 of interest expense on a $500 interest payment due on January 18.

Required

1. Journalize the adjusting entries needed on December 31 for each of the items affecting Lindsey's Home Staging. Assume Lindsey only records adjusting entries at the end of the year.

2. Journalize the subsequent journal entries for adjusting entries a, d, and g.

Problem 3–5B

Journalizing and posting adjustments to T-accounts, preparing the adjusted trial balance

The trial balance of Wellwood Realty at December 31, 2017, appears below. The data needed for the month-end adjustments follow the trial balance.

WELLWOOD REALTY Unadjusted Trial Balance December 31, 2017		
Cash	$ 24,180	
Accounts receivable	44,500	
Prepaid rent	8,800	
Supplies	2,100	
Furniture	69,000	
Accumulated amortization—furniture		$ 34,500
Accounts payable		5,800
Salaries payable		0
Unearned commission revenue		6,400
K. Wellwood, capital		75,180
K. Wellwood, withdrawals	12,000	
Commission revenue		48,000
Salaries expense	7,200	
Rent expense	0	
Amortization expense—furniture	0	
Advertising expense	2,100	
Supplies expense	0	
Total	$169,880	$169,880

Adjustment data at December 31:

a. Prepaid rent still available at December 31, $4,400.

b. Supplies used during the month, $1,800.

c. Amortization on furniture for the month, $670.

d. Accrued salaries expense at December 31, $950.

e. Unearned commission revenue still remaining to be earned at December 31, $2,500.

Required

1. Open T-accounts for the accounts listed in the trial balance, inserting their December 31 unadjusted balances.

2. Journalize the adjusting entries and post them to the T-accounts. Key the journal entries and the posted amounts by letter. Show the ending balance of each account.

3. Prepare the adjusted trial balance.

4. How will the company use the adjusted trial balance?

Problem 3–6B

The adjusted trial balance of Georgian Protection at December 31, 2017, is shown below:

Excel Spreadsheet Template

Preparing the financial statements from an adjusted trial balance

GEORGIAN PROTECTION Adjusted Trial Balance December 31, 2017		
Cash	$ 4,200	
Accounts receivable	28,500	
Supplies	5,200	
Prepaid rent	7,500	
Equipment	162,000	
Accumulated amortization—equipment		$ 38,000
Office furniture	70,000	
Accumulated amortization—office furniture		36,000
Accounts payable		14,800
Interest payable		500
Unearned service revenue		13,800
Notes payable		50,000
M. Wrosek, capital		29,300
M. Wrosek, withdrawals	17,000	
Service revenue		291,000
Amortization expense—equipment	19,000	
Amortization expense—office furniture	6,000	
Salaries expense	105,000	
Rent expense	25,000	
Interest expense	3,500	
Utilities expense	7,200	
Insurance expense	4,800	
Supplies expense	8,500	
Total	$473,400	$473,400

Required

1. Prepare Georgian Protection's 2017 income statement, statement of owner's equity, and balance sheet. List expenses in decreasing-balance order on the income statement and show total liabilities on the balance sheet. If your three financial statements appear on one page, draw the arrows linking the three financial statements. If they are on separate pages, write a short paragraph describing how the three financial statements are linked. How will what you have learned in this problem help you manage a business?

2. a. Which financial statement reports Georgian Protection's results of operations? Were operations successful during 2017? Cite specifics from the financial statements to support your evaluation.

   b. Which statement reports the company's financial position? Does Georgian Protection's financial position look strong or weak? Give the reason for your evaluation.

Problem 3-7B

Preparing an adjusted trial balance and the financial statements
③ ④ ⑤

The unadjusted trial balance of LaBarbara Data at December 31 2017, appears below:

LABARBARA DATA Unadjusted Trial Balance December 31, 2017		
Cash	$ 24,200	
Accounts receivable	38,500	
Prepaid rent	12,000	
Supplies	2,400	
Furniture	72,000	
Accumulated amortization—furniture		$ 13,800
Accounts payable		18,400
Salaries payable		0
J. LaBarbara, capital		125,000
J. LaBarbara, withdrawals	46,000	
Consulting revenue		121,500
Salaries expense	32,000	
Rent expense	33,000	
Utilities expense	12,000	
Amortization expense—furniture	6,600	
Supplies expense	0	
Total	$278,700	$278,700

Adjustment data:

a. Accrued consulting revenue at December 31, $3,800.

b. The prepaid balance of $12,000 represented one year of rent. Four months of prepaid rent have been used.

c. Supplies remaining on hand at December 31, $900.

d. The estimated useful life of the furniture is 10 years, it will have no value at the end of the 10 years, and the straight-line method of amortization is used. Amortization expense had only been taken for the first 11 months.

e. Accrue salaries expense at December 31 for three days. The five-day weekly payroll is $6,000.

Required

1. Prepare the adjusted trial balance of LaBarbara Data at December 31, 2017. Sketch T-accounts in your notes to calculate the new balances.

2. Prepare the income statement and the statement of owner's equity for the year ended December 31, 2017, and the balance sheet at December 31, 2017. Draw the arrows linking the three financial statements, or write a short description of how they are linked.

Problem 3–8B

Paris Communications provides telecommunications consulting services. The business had the following account balances:

Prepare adjusting entries, an adjusted trial balance, and financial statements

PARIS COMMUNICATIONS Unadjusted Trial Balance December 1, 2017		
Cash	$ 19,000	
Accounts receivable	17,100	
Prepaid advertising	13,000	
Supplies	3,900	
Computer equipment	54,000	
Accumulated amortization—computer equipment		$ 0
Furniture	120,000	
Accumulated amortization—furniture		0
Accounts payable		28,000
R. Paris, capital		98,000
R. Paris, withdrawals	45,000	
Consulting revenue		260,600
Salaries expense	82,500	
Supplies expense	0	
Travel expense	32,100	
Total	$386,600	$386,600

The following transactions occurred during December:

a. On December 1, paid cash for an Internet advertising consultant for four months of work in advance. The contract was for $3,200 per month. Work will begin on January 1, 2018.

b. On December 10, supplies in the amount of $2,975 were purchased on account.

c. On December 18, the company received a cash advance of $4,000 for work to be performed starting January 1.

d. On December 30, the company provided consulting services to a customer for $12,500; payment will be received in 30 days.

The following adjustments information was available on December 31, 2017:

e. A physical count shows $5,100 of supplies remaining on hand on December 31.

f. The computer equipment has an expected useful life of four years with no residual value after four years. The computers were purchased on January 2, and the straight-line method of amortization is used.

g. The furniture, purchased on January 2, is expected to be used for eight years with no expected value after eight years. The straight-line method of amortization is used.

h. On October 1, Paris hired an advertising firm to prepare a marketing plan and agreed to pay the firm $2,200 per month. Paris paid for five months' work in advance and has made no adjusting entries for this during 2017. Record the portion of the prepayment that has been used to date.

i. The company's office manager, who earns $400 per day, worked the last five days of the year and will be paid on January 5, 2018.

Required

1. Journalize the entries.
2. Prepare an adjusted trial balance on December 31, 2017.

3. Prepare an income statement for the year ended December 31, 2017. List expenses in alphabetical order.

4. Prepare a statement of owner's equity for the year ended December 31, 2017. Assume there have been no changes to the capital account since January 1.

5. Prepare a balance sheet at December 31, 2017.

*Problem 3–9B

Connect Air completed the following transactions during 2017:

Oct. 15	Paid $10,000 for advertising and promotional material covering the four-month period ending February 15, 2018.
Nov. 1	Received $15,600 payment in advance for a series of charter flights. Revenue of $2,600 will be earned each month over the six-month period ending April 30, 2018.

Required

1. Open T-accounts for Advertising Expense, Prepaid Advertising, Unearned Flight Revenue, and Flight Revenue.

2. Journalize these entries by debiting an asset account for Prepaid Advertising and by crediting a liability account for Unearned Flight Revenue. Explanations are not required.

3. Journalize the related adjustments at December 31, 2017.

4. Post the entries to the T-accounts and show their balances at December 31, 2017. Posting references are not required.

5. Repeat Requirements 1 through 4. This time debit Advertising Expense instead of Prepaid Advertising, and credit Flight Revenue instead of Unearned Flight Revenue.

6. Compare the account balances in Requirements 4 and 5. They should be equal.

---

*This Problem covers Chapter 3 Appendix topics.

CHALLENGE PROBLEMS

Problem 3–1C

The matching objective is well established as a basis for recording expenses.

Required

1. New accountants sometimes state the objective as matching revenues against expenses. Explain to a new accountant why matching revenues against expenses is incorrect.

2. It has been suggested that not-for-profit organizations, such as churches and hospitals, should flip their income statements and show revenues as a deduction from expenses. Why do you think that the suggestion has been made?

Problem 3–2C

The basic accounting period is one year and all organizations report on an annual basis. It is common for large companies to report on a semi-annual basis, and some even report monthly. Interim reporting has a cost, however.

You are working part time as an accounting clerk for Hughes Corporation. The company was private and prepared only annual financial statements for its shareholders. Hughes has gone public and now must report quarterly. Joshua Ferguson, your supervisor in the accounting department, is concerned about all the additional work that will be required to produce the quarterly statements.

Required

What does Ferguson mean when he talks about "additional work"?

EXTENDING YOUR KNOWLEDGE

DECISION PROBLEMS

Decision Problem 1

Cameron Masson has owned and operated Alberta Biotech, a management consulting firm, since its beginning 10 years ago. From all appearances the business has prospered. Masson lives in the fast lane—flashy car, home located in an expensive suburb, frequent trips abroad, and other signs of wealth. In the past few years, you have become friends with him through weekly rounds of golf at the country club. Recently, he mentioned that he has lost his zest for the business and would consider selling it for the right price. He claims that his clientele is firmly established and that the business "runs on its own." According to Masson, the consulting procedures are fairly simple and anyone could perform the work.

Assume you are interested in buying this business. You obtain its most recent monthly trial balance, which is shown below. Assume that revenues and expenses vary little from month to month and that April is a typical month.

Your investigation reveals that the trial balance does not include the effects of April's revenues of $3,300 and expenses totalling $6,300. If you were to buy Alberta Biotech, you would hire a manager so you could devote your time to other duties. Assume that this person would require a monthly salary of $6,000.

Valuing a business on the basis of its net income
④ ⑤

ALBERTA BIOTECH Trial Balance April 30, 2017		
Cash	$ 29,100	
Accounts receivable	44,700	
Prepaid expenses	7,800	
Property, plant, and equipment	723,900	
Accumulated amortization—property, plant, and equipment		$568,800
Land	144,000	
Accounts payable		41,400
Salaries payable		0
Unearned consulting revenue		170,100
C. Masson, capital		172,200
C. Masson, withdrawals	27,000	
Consulting revenue		36,900
Salaries expense	10,200	
Rent expense	0	
Utilities expense	2,700	
Amortization expense	0	
Supplies expense	0	
Total	$989,400	$989,400

Required

1. Is this an unadjusted or an adjusted trial balance? How can you tell?

2. Assume that the most you would pay for the business is 40 times the monthly net income you could expect to earn from it. Compute this possible price.

3. Masson states that the lowest price he will accept for the business is $450,000 plus the balance in owner's equity on April 30. Compute this amount.

4. Under these conditions, how much should you offer Masson? Give your reasons.

Decision Problem 2

Understanding the concepts underlying the accrual basis of accounting
① ②

The following independent questions relate to the accrual basis of accounting:

1. It has been said that the only time a company's financial position is known for certain is when the company is wound up and its only asset is cash. Why is this statement true?

2. A friend suggests that the purpose of adjusting entries is to correct errors in the accounts. Is your friend's statement true? What is the purpose of adjusting entries if the statement is wrong?

3. The text suggested that furniture (and the other property, plant, and equipment assets that are amortized) is a form of prepaid expense. Do you agree? Why do you think some accountants view property, plant, and equipment this way?

FINANCIAL STATEMENT CASES

Financial Statement Case 1

Explaining the effects of accruals and deferrals on the financial statements
① ② ③ ④

During the year ended March 29, 2014, Indigo Books & Music Inc. (Indigo) recorded numerous accruals and deferrals. As a long-term employee of Indigo's accounting and finance staff, it is your job to explain the effects of accruals and deferrals on Indigo's financial statements. (Indigo's financial statements appear in Appendix A at the end of this book and on MyAccountingLab.) Suppose the following questions were raised at the shareholders' meeting:

1. "Prepaid expenses" in the amount of $5,184,000 are listed on the March 29, 2014, balance sheet. What items could be included in this balance, and why is this account listed as a balance sheet account instead of an expense account?

2. The balance sheet lists "Cash and cash equivalents" of $157,578,000. Look at Note 6 to see what is included in this amount.

3. "Accounts payable and accrued liabilities" is shown on the balance sheet in the amount of $136,428,000. Define an accrued liability and give an example of items that could be included in this liability.

4. What is "depreciation" and how much depreciation has been recorded so far for the computer equipment at March 29, 2014? (Hint: Refer to Note 8 for this amount.)

Financial Statement Case 2

Explaining the effects of accruals and deferrals on the financial statements
① ② ③ ④

During the year ended December 31, 2013, TELUS Corporation (TELUS) recorded numerous accruals and deferrals. As a long-term employee of TELUS's accounting and finance staff, it is your job to explain the effects of accruals and deferrals on TELUS's 2013 financial statements. (TELUS's 2013 financial statements appear on MyAccountingLab.) Suppose the following questions were raised at the shareholders' meeting:

1. Prepaid expenses are listed on the December 31, 2013, consolidated statements of financial position (balance sheet). What is the balance at this date? What items would be included in this balance, and why is this account listed as a balance sheet account instead of an expense account?

2. "Accounts payable and accrued liabilities" are shown on the December 31, 2013, consolidated statements of financial position in the amount of $1,735,000,000. Define an accrued liability. Use Note 25a to identify what accounts are specifically included in TELUS's statement.

3. What is depreciation and how much would have been recorded for the year ended December 31, 2013, on the consolidated statements of income?

>Try It! SOLUTIONS FOR CHAPTER 3

1. The revenue has not been earned on December 20. The customer could cancel the order, or Kobe may not be able to fill the order. In order to earn the revenue, the order would have to be delivered, which will not happen until 2017. Thus, the revenue should be recognized in 2017, not in 2016.

2. Expense recognition criteria indicate that all expenses associated with a revenue transaction should be reported in the same fiscal period as the revenue. The sales commission that will be paid to the sales representative came about because of the sales order on December 20. The recognition criteria for revenues suggest that the revenue has been earned in the current year. The matching objective (part of the recognition criteria for expenses) tells us that we should recognize all expenses incurred in the same fiscal period as their related revenue. The company should accrue the commission in the current fiscal year.

3. If HEC collects $6,000 from customers on January 1 and will earn the $6,000 evenly during January, February, and March, HEC will report the following service revenue each month under (a) accrual-basis accounting and (b) cash-basis accounting:

		Jan.	Feb.	Mar.
(a) Accrual-basis accounting:	Service revenue	$2,000	$2,000	$2,000
(b) Cash-basis accounting:	Service revenue	$6,000		

Under accrual-basis accounting, HEC records the revenue when the company earns it. This is the correct way to account for revenues.

4. If HEC prepays $1,500 for Internet advertising on October 1 and the ads will run during October, November, and December, HEC will report the following advertising expense each month under (a) accrual-basis accounting and (b) cash-basis accounting:

		Oct.	Nov.	Dec.
(a) Accrual-basis accounting:	Advertising expense	$ 500	$500	$500
(b) Cash-basis accounting:	Advertising expense	$1,500		

The accrual basis is the correct way to account for the expense.

5.

Account	Yes	No	Account	Yes	No
Accounts Receivable	✓		Supplies	✓	
Building		✓*	Cash		✓
Interest Payable	✓		Prepaid Insurance	✓	

*The Building account is not affected directly. Accumulated Amortization—Building (a contra account) is updated during the adjusting process.

6. a.

	Beginning balance	$ 500
+	Purchases	600
=	Supplies available	1,100
−	Ending balance	400
=	Expense (supplies used)	$ 700

Report Supplies Expense among the expenses on the income statement.

b. The ending balance of Supplies is $400.
Report Supplies among the assets on the balance sheet.

c. Adjusting entry:

Nov. 30	Supplies Expense	700	
	Supplies		700
	To record supplies expense.		

7. The adjusted trial balance amounts are shown below:

Cash		$ 63,200
Accounts receivable		11,750
Supplies		1,100
Prepaid insurance		1,450
Furniture	$21,000	
Less: Accumulated amortization—furniture	(7,500)	13,500
Land		85,000
Total assets		$176,000

4 COMPLETING THE ACCOUNTING CYCLE

CONNECTING CHAPTER 4

LEARNING OBJECTIVE 1 Prepare an accounting worksheet

How can we summarize data to prepare the financial statements?

LEARNING OBJECTIVE 2 Completing the accounting cycle

Remind me: How does this all fit together?

LEARNING OBJECTIVE 3 Close the revenue, expense, and withdrawal accounts

What are closing entries, and how do we record them?

LEARNING OBJECTIVE 4 Correct typical accounting errors

How do we fix accounting errors?

LEARNING OBJECTIVE 5 Classify assets and liabilities as current or long term, and prepare a classified balance sheet

How can assets and liabilities be classified for a more informative balance sheet?

LEARNING OBJECTIVE 6 Use the current ratio and the debt ratio to evaluate a company

How do decision makers evaluate a company using the current ratio and debt ratio?

LEARNING OBJECTIVE 7 Describe the accounting cycle and financial reporting implications of International Financial Reporting Standards (IFRS)

How does IFRS apply to the accounting cycle and financial reporting?

LEARNING OBJECTIVE A1 Describe and prepare reversing entries

What are reversing entries, and how do we record them?

MyAccountingLab   The **Summary** for Chapter 4 appears on page 205. This lists all of the MyAccountingLab resources. **Accounting Vocabulary** with definitions for this chapter's material appears on page 206.

It's a beautiful day in late spring in Vancouver, but you are still immersed in hockey as you watch the Vancouver Canucks play the Toronto Maple Leafs in the sixth game of the Stanley Cup Final. The teams are playing a best-of-seven series, and the Leafs lead the series three games to two. The Canucks need to win this game or Toronto will win the Stanley Cup.

The game is tied 1–1 at the end of the second period. Toronto scores early in the third period to take a 2–1 lead. The Canucks fight back and score the tying goal with two minutes to go. There is no more scoring in regulation time, and the final result will be decided in overtime.

The game goes back and forth in overtime before the Canucks finally score to force a seventh game back in Toronto.

When the teams return to Toronto to play the seventh game, what will the scoreboard say at the start of the game? Will it be 3–2 to carry over the score from the previous game, or will the scoreboard be set back to zero? The answer should be obvious no matter what sport is being discussed: After a game is completed, the scoreboard is always set back to zero.

In the same way, the accounting process sets the company's financial scoreboard back to zero at the end of each fiscal year. The process is called *closing the books*, and that is the main topic in this chapter. The logic behind the closing process in accounting is the same as setting the scoreboard back to zero after a game. Companies need to see how well they are doing in each financial period.

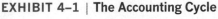 this chapter we take one final look at the accounting cycle and see how the accounting records are completed and made ready to start the next accounting period. We will also look at how to provide more useful information to readers of financial statements by introducing a detailed format for the balance sheet—a classified format. This more detailed format will make it easier to begin our first look at financial analysis at the end of the chapter.

THE ACCOUNTING CYCLE

So far, we have prepared the financial statements from an adjusted trial balance. This is not the final step in the accounting process, nor is it the only way to prepare information for reporting. As part of the process, accountants often use a document known as a worksheet. Worksheets are useful because they summarize a lot of data, allow for changes, and aid decision making. They are shown as an optional step in Exhibit 4–1. They can help accountants prepare financial statements that include adjustments without having to journalize and post all the adjusting entries.

At the end of the accounting cycle, the scoreboard is reset for the next accounting period. These closing entries (step 8) follow the same basic pattern for all

EXHIBIT 4–1 | The Accounting Cycle

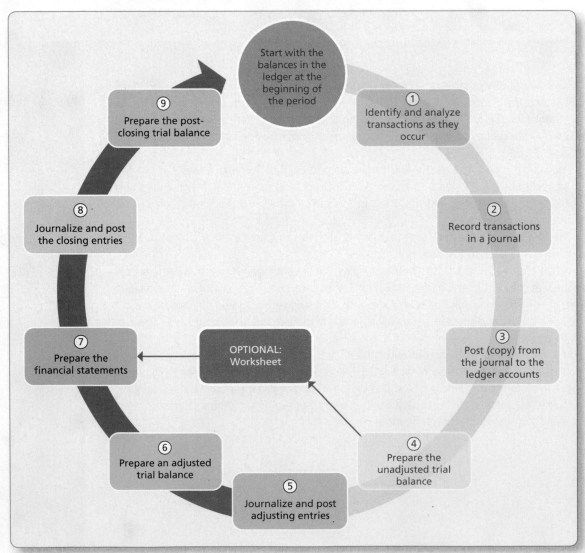

service businesses. In Chapter 5 we will show how a company that earns revenue by selling products rather than services adjusts and closes its books.

THE WORKSHEET

Accountants often use a **worksheet**, a document with many columns, to help summarize data for the financial statements. Listing all the accounts and their unadjusted balances helps identify the accounts that need adjustment. After the adjusting entries are completed, the worksheet aids the closing process by listing the ending adjusted balances of all the accounts.

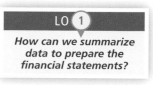

The worksheet is not part of the journal or the ledger, nor is it a financial statement. Therefore, it is not part of the formal accounting system. Instead, it is a summary device that exists for the accountant's convenience. An Excel spreadsheet works well for an accounting worksheet.

Exhibits 4–2 through 4–6 illustrate the development of a worksheet for Hunter Environmental Consulting (HEC).

A step-by-step description of its preparation follows, with all amounts given in Exhibits 4–2 through 4–6. Simply turn the acetate pages to follow from exhibit to exhibit.

Exhibit 4–2   *Step ❶. Print the account titles in the first column and their unadjusted ending balances in the Trial Balance columns of the worksheet, and total the amounts.*

The account titles and balances come directly from the ledger accounts before any adjusting entries are prepared. Accounts are usually listed in the order in which they appear in the ledger (Cash first, Accounts Receivable second, and so on). Total debits must equal total credits. Accounts may have zero balances (for example, Amortization Expense).

Exhibit 4–3   *Step ❷. Enter the adjusting entries in the Adjustments columns, and total the amounts.*

We can identify the accounts that need to be adjusted by scanning the trial balance. Cash needs no adjustment because all cash transactions are recorded as they occur during the period.

Exhibit 4–3 includes the May adjusting entries that we made in Chapter 3 to prepare the adjusted trial balance.

Accounts Receivable is listed next. Has HEC earned revenue that it has not yet recorded? The answer is yes. At May 31, the business has earned $1,500 that must be accrued because the cash will be received during June. Hunter Environmental Consulting debits Accounts Receivable and credits Service Revenue on the worksheet in Exhibit 4–3. A letter is used to link the debit and the credit of each adjusting entry ("e" in this case).

Moving down the trial balance, the accountant identifies other accounts that need adjustment, such as Office Supplies. The business has used supplies during May, so it debits Supplies Expense and credits Office Supplies. The other adjustments are analyzed as you learned in Chapter 3 and entered on the worksheet. After the adjustments are entered on the worksheet, the columns are totalled. Total debits must again equal total credits.

Listing all the accounts in their proper sequence aids the process of identifying accounts that need to be adjusted. But suppose that one or more accounts are omitted from the trial balance. Such accounts can always be written below the first column totals—$159,100. Assume that Supplies Expense was accidentally omitted and thus did not appear on the trial balance. In this case, the accountant can write Supplies Expense on the line beneath the amount totals and enter the debit adjustment—$500—on the Supplies Expense line. Keep in mind that the worksheet is not the finished version of the financial statements, so the order of the accounts on the worksheet is not critical. Supplies Expense will be listed in its proper sequence on the income statement.

LO ❶

How can we summarize data to prepare the financial statements?

LEARNING TIPS

Accounts are grouped on the worksheet by category (assets, liabilities, owner's equity, revenues, expenses).

KEY POINTS

Cash needs no adjusting entry unless there is an error that needs to be corrected. An error in cash is a rare occurrence.

MyAccountingLab

Video: Creating a Worksheet

EXHIBIT 4–2 | Creating an Accounting Worksheet

Notice that even though this is not one of the formal financial statements, it is a report that uses the three-line heading. It shows the name of the business, the name of the document, and the period of time covered.

HUNTER ENVIRONMENTAL CONSULTING

Accounting Worksheet

For the Month Ended May 31, 2016

Account Title	Unadjusted Trial Balance Dr	Cr	Adjustments Dr	Cr	Adjusted Trial Balance Dr	Cr	Income Statement Dr	Cr	Balance Sheet Dr	Cr
Cash	31,000									
Accounts receivable	14,000									
Office supplies	1,500									
Prepaid insurance	3,600									
Furniture	45,000									
Accumulated amortization— furniture		0								
Land	50,000									
Accounts payable		12,000								
Salaries payable		0								
Unearned service revenue		3,000								
Lisa Hunter, capital		120,100								
Lisa Hunter, withdrawals	6,000									
Service revenue		24,000								
Amortization expense	0									
Insurance expense	0									
Rent expense	3,000									
Salaries expense	4,000									
Supplies expense	0									
Utilities expense	1,000									
	159,100	159,100								
Net income										

1 Print the account titles and their unadjusted ending balances in the Trial Balance columns of the work sheet. Total the amounts.

This information comes from Exhibit 3–4.

Exhibit 4–4 *Step ③. Compute each account's adjusted balance by combining the trial balance and the adjustment figures. Enter the adjusted amounts in the Adjusted Trial Balance columns.*

Exhibit 4–4 shows the worksheet with the Adjusted Trial Balance columns completed. For example, Cash is up to date, so it receives no adjustment. Accounts Receivable's adjusted balance of $15,500 is computed by adding the $1,500 debit adjustment to the trial balance debit amount of $14,000. Office Supplies' adjusted balance of $1,000 is determined by subtracting the $500 credit adjustment from the unadjusted debit balance of $1,500. You may want to write out balances in T-accounts to help calculate balances, as shown in the margin. An account may receive more than one adjustment, as in the case of Service Revenue. After all the amounts have been transferred to their appropriate column, calculate the total for each column and verify that total debits equal total credits.

Exhibit 4–5 *Step ④. Transfer the asset, liability, and owner's equity amounts from the Adjusted Trial Balance to the Balance Sheet columns. Transfer the revenue and expense amounts to the Income Statement columns. Total the statement columns.*

Every account is either a balance sheet account or an income statement account. Debits on the adjusted trial balance remain debits in the statement columns, and credits remain credits.

After all the amounts have been transferred to their appropriate column, calculate a subtotal for each income statement and balance sheet column.

Exhibit 4–6 *Step ⑤. On the income statement, compute net income or net loss as the difference between total revenues and total expenses.*

Exhibit 4–6 completes the accounting worksheet, which shows net income of $12,950, computed as follows:

Revenue (total *credits* on the income statement)...................	$26,500
Expenses (total *debits* on the income statement)...................	13,550
Net income..	$12,950

Net Income   Net income of $12,950 is entered as a "plug figure" in the Income Statement *debit* column. This brings total debits up to total credits on the income statement. Net income is also entered as a "plug figure" in the Balance Sheet *credit* column because an excess of revenues over expenses increases capital, and increases in capital are recorded by a credit. After completion, total debits equal total credits in the Income Statement columns and in the Balance Sheet columns.

HUNTER ENVIRONMENTAL CONSULTING
Accounting Worksheet
For the Month Ended May 31, 2016

Account Title	Unadjusted Trial Balance Dr	Cr	Adjustments Dr	Cr	Adjusted Trial Balance Dr	Cr	Income Statement Dr	Cr	Balance Sheet Dr	Cr
Cash	31,000				31,000				31,000	
Accounts receivable	14,000		(e)1,500		15,500				15,500	
Supplies expense	0		(b) 500		500		500			
Utilities expense	1,000				1,000		1,000			
	159,100	159,100	8,050	8,050	165,350	165,350	13,550	26,500	151,800	138,850
Net income							12,950			12,950
							26,500	26,500	151,800	151,800

You have net income when Income Statement credits > Income Statement debits

Net Loss If expenses exceed revenues, the result is a net loss. In that event, *Net loss* is printed on the worksheet. The net loss amount should be entered in the *credit* column of the income statement (to balance out) and in the *debit* column of the balance sheet (to balance out). This is because an excess of expenses over revenue decreases capital, and decreases in capital are recorded by a debit. After completion, total debits equal total credits in the Income Statement columns and in the Balance Sheet columns, as shown below (amounts are assumed).

HUNTER ENVIRONMENTAL CONSULTING

Accounting Worksheet (assumed amounts)

For the Month Ended May 31, 2016

Account Title	Unadjusted Trial Balance		Adjustments		Adjusted Trial Balance		Income Statement		Balance Sheet	
	Dr	Cr	Dr	Cr	Dr	Cr	Dr	Cr	Dr	Cr
Cash	31,000				31,000				31,000	
Accounts receivable	14,000		(e) 1,500		15,500				15,500	
Supplies expense	0		(b) 500		500		500			
Utilities expense	1,000				1,000		1,000			
	186,100	186,100	4,250	4,250	189,100	189,100	19,100	15,000	170,000	174,100
Net loss								4,100	4,100	
							19,100	19,100	174,100	174,100

> You have a net loss when Income Statement debits > Income Statement credits

> Try It!

1. Indicate with a check mark where the final balance for each of the following accounts is extended in a worksheet. Assume each account has a normal balance.

	Income Statement		Balance Sheet	
	Debit	Credit	Debit	Credit
Cash				
Supplies				
Supplies Expense				
Unearned Revenue				
Service Revenue				
Owner's Equity				

2. The unadjusted trial balance of Sigrid's Off Road Adventures at December 31, 2017, the end of its fiscal year, is presented on the next page.

Data needed for the adjusting entries are as follows:

a. Supplies remaining on hand at year end are worth $200.
b. Amortization on furniture, $2,500.
c. Amortization on building, $1,500.
d. Salary owed but not yet paid, $600.
e. Service revenues to be accrued, $1,300.
f. Of the $8,000 balance of Unearned Service Revenue, $2,000 was earned during 2017.

SIGRID'S OFF ROAD ADVENTURES		
Unadjusted Trial Balance		
December 31, 2017		
Cash	$ 6,000	
Accounts receivable	5,000	
Supplies	1,000	
Furniture	10,000	
Accumulated amortization—furniture		$ 4,000
Building	60,000	
Accumulated amortization—building		30,000
Land	20,000	
Accounts payable		2,000
Salary payable		0
Unearned service revenue		8,000
Sigrid Chu, capital		40,000
Sigrid Chu, withdrawals	25,000	
Service revenues		60,000
Salary expense	16,000	
Supplies expense	0	
Amortization expense—furniture	0	
Amortization expense—building	0	
Miscellaneous expense	1,000	
Total	$144,000	$144,000

Prepare the worksheet of Sigrid's Off Road Adventures for the year ended December 31, 2017. Identify each adjusting entry by the letter corresponding to the data given. To plan your worksheet, check the adjusting entries data to see if the same account is affected more than once. If it is, leave one or two blank lines under the account name. Do this for Service Revenues on this worksheet.

Solutions appear at the end of this chapter and on MyAccountingLab

WORKING THROUGH THE ACCOUNTING CYCLE

The worksheet helps to organize accounting data and to compute the net income or net loss for the period. It also helps accountants prepare the financial statements, record the adjusting entries, and close the accounts.

LO 2

Remind me: How does this all fit together?

Preparing the Financial Statements

The worksheet shows the amount of net income or net loss for the period, but it is still necessary to prepare the financial statements. (The financial statements can be prepared directly from the adjusted trial balance, as was shown in Chapter 3. This is why completion of the worksheet is optional and shown in Exhibit 4–1 as an alternative "route" to step 7.) Using the worksheet to sort the accounts to the balance sheet and the income statement eases the preparation of the statements. Exhibit 4–7 presents the May financial statements for Hunter Environmental Consulting, which are based on the data from the worksheet in Exhibit 4–6.

Recording the Adjusting Entries

The adjusting entries are a key element of accrual-basis accounting. The worksheet helps identify the accounts that need adjustments. But the actual adjustment of the accounts requires journal entries that are posted to the ledger accounts. In other

KEY POINTS

Adjusting entries must be journalized and posted prior to closing the accounts.

HUNTER ENVIRONMENTAL CONSULTING
Income Statement
For the Month Ended May 31, 2016

Revenues:		
Service revenue		$26,500
Expenses:		
Amortization expense—furniture	$ 750	
Insurance expense	300	
Rent expense	3,000	
Salaries expense	8,000	
Supplies expense	500	
Utilities expense	1,000	
Total expenses		13,550
Net income		$12,950

HUNTER ENVIRONMENTAL CONSULTING
Statement of Owner's Equity
For the Month Ended May 31, 2016

Lisa Hunter, capital, May 1, 2016	$120,100
Add: Net income	12,950
	133,050
Less: Withdrawals	6,000
Lisa Hunter, capital, May 31, 2016	$127,050

HUNTER ENVIRONMENTAL CONSULTING
Balance Sheet
May 31, 2016

Assets			Liabilities	
Cash		$ 31,000	Accounts payable	$ 12,000
Accounts receivable		15,500	Salaries payable	4,000
Office supplies		1,000	Unearned service revenue	2,000
Prepaid insurance		3,300	Total liabilities	18,000
Furniture	$45,000			
Less: Accumulated			**Owner's Equity**	
amortization—			Lisa Hunter, capital	127,050
furniture	750	44,250		
Land		50,000		
			Total liabilities and	
Total assets		$145,050	owner's equity	$145,050

words, steps 5 and 6 in the accounting cycle are not optional. They may be skipped temporarily to prepare interim statements more quickly, but eventually the adjusting entries must be recorded in the journals. Panel A of Exhibit 4–8 repeats the Hunter Environmental Consulting adjusting entries that we journalized in Chapter 3. Panel B shows the postings to the T-accounts, with "Adj." denoting an amount posted from an adjusting entry. Only the revenue and expense accounts are presented in the exhibit in order to focus on the closing process, which is discussed in the next section. T-accounts, instead of ledger accounts, are used for demonstration purposes.

EXHIBIT 4–8 | Journalizing and Posting the Adjusting Entries and Preparing the Adjusted Trial Balance

Panel A: Journalizing

Adjusting Entries		Page 4
May 31	Insurance Expense	300	
	Prepaid Insurance		300
	To record insurance expense.		
31	Supplies Expense	500	
	Office Supplies		500
	To record supplies used.		
31	Amortization Expense—Furniture	750	
	Accumulated Amortization—Furniture		750
	To record amortization on furniture.		
31	Salaries Expense	4,000	
	Salaries Payable		4,000
	To accrue salaries expense.		
31	Accounts Receivable	1,500	
	Service Revenue		1,500
	To accrue service revenue.		
31	Unearned Service Revenue	1,000	
	Service Revenue		1,000
	To record unearned revenue that has been earned.		

Panel B: Posting the Adjustments to the Revenue and Expense T-Accounts

REVENUE		EXPENSES	

Service Revenue

	24,000
	Adj. 1,500
	Adj. 1,000
	Bal. 26,500

Amortization Expense—Furniture

Adj.	750	
Bal.	750	

Insurance Expense

Adj	300	
Bal.	300	

Rent Expense

	3,000	
Bal.	3,000	

Salaries Expense

	4,000	
Adj.	4,000	
Bal.	8,000	

Supplies Expense

Adj.	500	
Bal.	500	

Utilities Expense

	1,000	
Bal.	1,000	

Adj. = Amount posted from an adjusting entry
Bal. = Balance

(Continued)

Panel C: Adjusted Trial Balance

HUNTER ENVIRONMENTAL CONSULTING Adjusted Trial Balance May 31, 2016		
Cash	$ 31,000	
Accounts receivable	15,500	
Office supplies	1,000	
Prepaid insurance	3,300	
Furniture	45,000	
Accumulated amortization—furniture		$ 750
Land	50,000	
Accounts payable		12,000
Salaries payable		4,000
Unearned service revenue		2,000
Lisa Hunter, capital		120,100
Lisa Hunter, withdrawals	6,000	
Service revenue		26,500
Amortization expense	750	
Insurance expense	300	
Rent expense	3,000	
Salaries expense	8,000	
Supplies expense	500	
Utilities expense	1,000	
Total	$165,350	$165,350

The adjusting entries can be recorded in the journal as they are entered on the worksheet, but it is not necessary to journalize them at the same time. Most accountants prepare the financial statements immediately after completing the worksheet. They can wait to journalize and post the adjusting entries before they make the closing entries.

The next step in the accounting cycle is to prepare the adjusted trial balance. For your convenience, it is presented in Panel C of Exhibit 4–8. This is the same information as in Exhibit 4–4 but having it here lets us look at all the steps in the accounting cycle, and it will make it easier to see where the numbers come from for the closing entries, which are done next.

> Try It!

3. Using the worksheet created in Try It #2 from page 180, prepare the financial statements of Sigrid's Off Road Adventures. Even if you did not complete the worksheet, you can use the solution on page 239 as a starting point for this question.

4. Using the worksheet created in Try It #2, journalize and post using T-accounts the adjusting entries for Sigrid's Off Road Adventures. Provide an explanation for each journal entry. Even if you did not complete the worksheet, you can use the solution on page 239 as a starting point for this question.

Solutions appear at the end of this chapter and on MyAccountingLab

CLOSING THE ACCOUNTS

Closing the accounts occurs at the end of the period. Closing prepares the accounts for recording the transactions of the next period and consists of journalizing and posting the closing entries. Closing results in the balances of the revenue and expense accounts becoming zero in order to clearly measure the net income of each period separately from all other periods. We also close the owner's withdrawals account to reset its balance to zero. This is just like resetting the scoreboard after each game in the hockey playoff series discussed at the beginning of this chapter.

Recall that the income statement reports net income (or net loss) for a specific period. This is the "score" for the year. The revenue and expense accounts represent just what happened in the fiscal period, so they are closed (reset to zero) and are therefore called **temporary (or nominal) accounts**.

The Withdrawals account is also a temporary account because it measures withdrawals taken during a specific period. The Withdrawals account is also closed at the end of the period. *The closing process applies only to temporary accounts.*

To better understand the closing process, contrast the nature of the temporary accounts with the nature of the **permanent (or real) accounts.** They are *not* closed at the end of the period. The permanent accounts represent assets, liabilities, and owner's equity (the Capital account) that are on hand at a specific time. This is why their balances at the end of one accounting period carry over to become the beginning balances of the next period. For example, the Cash balance at December 31, 2016, is also the beginning Cash balance for January 1, 2017.

Closing entries transfer the revenue, expense, and withdrawal balances from their respective accounts to the Capital account. We show this in the statement of owner's equity, but we also need to update the journals and ledgers with the transfer.

It is when we post the closing entries that the Capital account absorbs the impact of the balances in the temporary accounts.

As an intermediate step, however, the revenues and expenses are transferred first to a temporary account entitled **Income Summary**. The Income Summary account is like a temporary "holding tank" that is used only in the closing process. It represents the net income or net loss during the period.

Exhibit 4–9 summarizes the four steps in the closing process.

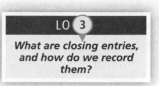

LO 3

What are closing entries, and how do we record them?

MyAccountingLab

Video: Closing Entries

KEY POINTS

There is no account for net income, which is the net result of all revenue and expense accounts. Income Summary combines all revenue and expense amounts into one account, and its balance will equal the net income (or net loss). Income Summary does not appear on financial statements.

EXHIBIT 4–9 | The Closing Process for Net Income

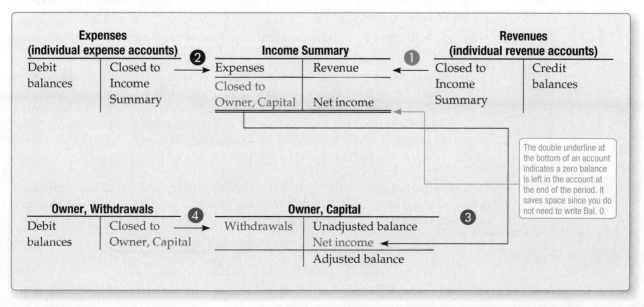

Closing a Net Income   The steps in closing the accounts of a service business like HEC that has a net income are as follows (the circled numbers are keyed to Exhibit 4–9 and Exhibit 4–10):

❶ Revenue account(s)	
	Income Summary

Debit each revenue account for the amount of its credit balance. This closing entry transfers the sum of the revenues to the *credit* side of the Income Summary account.

❷ Income Summary	
	Expense account(s)

Credit each expense account for the amount of its debit balance. This closing entry transfers the sum of the expenses to the *debit* side of the Income Summary account.

❸ Income Summary	
	Capital account

When there is a credit balance in the Income Summary account (net income), the account is closed by debiting the balance.

The Income Summary account now holds the net income of the period, but only for a moment. To close net income, debit Income Summary for the amount of its credit. This closing entry transfers the net income from Income Summary to the Capital account.

❹ Capital account	
	Withdrawals account

This entry transfers the Withdrawals amount to the *debit* side of the Capital account. Withdrawals are not expenses and do not affect net income or net loss.

These steps are best illustrated with an example. Suppose HEC closes the books at the end of May. Exhibit 4–10 presents the complete closing process for the business. The account balances to use are found in the adjusted trial balance (Exhibit 4–8, Panel C, page 184). In Exhibit 4–10, Panel A gives the closing entries; Panel B shows the accounts after the closing entries have been posted.

❶ Transfer Service Revenue's balance of $26,500 to the Income Summary account.

❷ Zero out the expenses and move their total ($13,550) to the debit side of Income Summary. Income Summary's balance is the month's net income ($12,950).

❸ Close the Income Summary account by transferring net income to the credit side of Lisa Hunter, Capital.

❹ Move the owner withdrawals to the debit side of Lisa Hunter, Capital, leaving a zero balance in the Lisa Hunter, Withdrawals account.

The closing entries set the revenues, expenses, and the Withdrawals account back to zero. Now the Capital account includes the full effects of the May revenues, expenses, and withdrawals. These amounts, combined with the beginning Capital account's balance, give Lisa Hunter, Capital an ending balance of $127,050. Trace this ending Capital balance to the statement of owner's equity and also to the balance sheet in Exhibit 4–7 on page 182.

Closing a Net Loss   What would the closing entries be if HEC had suffered a net *loss* during May? Suppose that revenue was still $26,500 but for this example expenses totalled $27,500. The Income Summary account would appear as follows:

Income Summary			
Clo. ❷	27,500	Clo. ❶	26,500
Bal.	1,000		

EXHIBIT 4-10 | **Journalizing and Posting the Closing Entries**

Panel A: Journalizing

		Closing Entries		Page 5
❶ May	31	Service Revenue	26,500	
		Income Summary		26,500
		To close the revenue account and create the Income Summary account.		
❷	31	Income Summary	13,550	
		Amortization Expense—Furniture		750
		Insurance Expense		300
		Rent Expense		3,000
		Salaries Expense		8,000
		Supplies Expense		500
		Utilities Expense		1,000
		To close the expense accounts.		
❸	31	Income Summary	12,950	
		Lisa Hunter, Capital		12,950
		To close the Income Summary account and transfer net income to the Capital account (Income Summary balance = $26,500 − $13,550).		
❹	31	Lisa Hunter, Capital	6,000	
		Lisa Hunter, Withdrawals		6,000
		To close the Withdrawals account and transfer the Withdrawals amount to the Capital account.		

> It is not necessary to make separate closing entries for each revenue and expense account. There is one closing entry for revenues and one closing entry for expenses.

Panel B: Posting

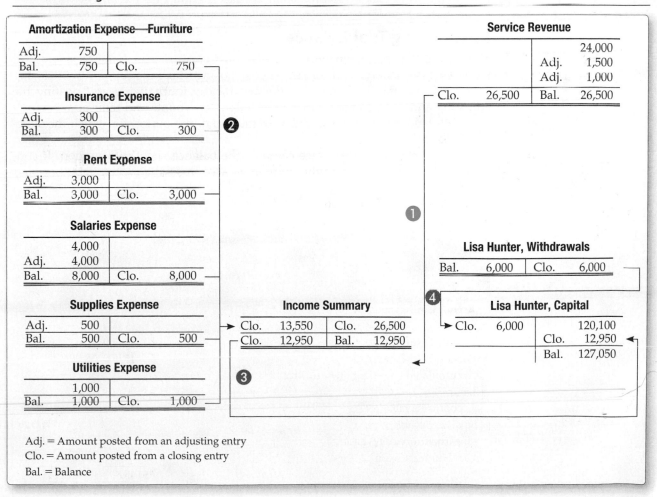

Adj. = Amount posted from an adjusting entry
Clo. = Amount posted from a closing entry
Bal. = Balance

Closing entry ❸ would then credit Income Summary to close its debit balance and transfer the net loss to Lisa Hunter, Capital:

❸ May 31	Lisa Hunter, Capital	1,000	
	Income Summary		1,000
	To close the Income Summary account and transfer net loss to the Capital account.		

After posting, these two accounts would appear as follows:

Income Summary					Lisa Hunter, Capital			
Clo. ❷	27,500	Clo. ❶	26,500		Clo. ❸	1,000		120,100
Bal.	1,000	Clo. ❸	1,000				Bal.	119,100

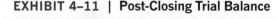

Finally, the Withdrawals balance would be closed to Capital, as before. Notice that the Capital balance is now $119,100. The net loss decreases the Capital balance.

Closing Using Computers   The closing process is fundamentally mechanical and is completely automated in a computerized system. Accounts are identified as either temporary or permanent when they are originally set up. The temporary accounts are closed automatically by selecting that option from the software's menu. Posting also occurs automatically. Many accounting programs allow for records to be open for two accounting periods at the same time. The beginning of a new period is open prior to closing the previous period. The reason for this is because time is needed to accumulate the information to properly adjust and close the accounts, but companies do not want to hold up processing the next period's transactions.

Post-Closing Trial Balance

The accounting cycle can end with the **post-closing trial balance** (step 9 in Exhibit 4-1; see Exhibit 4-11 for HEC's post-closing trial balance). The post-closing trial balance is the final check on the accuracy of journalizing and posting the adjusting and closing entries. It lists the ledger's accounts and their adjusted balances after closing, and it is dated as of the end of the period for which the statements have been prepared.

The post-closing trial balance contains the balance sheet information. It contains the ending balances of the permanent accounts—the assets, liabilities, and

EXHIBIT 4-11 | Post-Closing Trial Balance

HUNTER ENVIRONMENTAL CONSULTING Post-Closing Trial Balance May 31, 2016		
Cash	$ 31,000	
Accounts receivable	15,500	
Office supplies	1,000	
Prepaid insurance	3,300	
Furniture	45,000	
Accumulated amortization—furniture		$ 750
Land	50,000	
Accounts payable		12,000
Salaries payable		4,000
Unearned service revenue		2,000
Lisa Hunter, Capital		127,050
Total	$145,800	$145,800

owner's equity (capital) accounts. No temporary accounts—revenues, expenses, or withdrawal accounts—are included because their balances have been closed. The ledger is up to date and ready for the next period's transactions.

 **Try It!**

5. Using the worksheet created in Try It #2 from page 180, journalize and post using T-accounts the closing entries for Sigrid's Off Road Adventures at December 31, 2017. (Each T-account should carry its balance as shown in the adjusted trial balance.) Provide an explanation for each journal entry. If you did not complete the worksheet you can still do this question by starting with the solution on page 239.

6. Prepare the post-closing trial balance for Sigrid's Off Road Adventures at December 31, 2017, based on the balances in the accounts after completing Try It #5. If you did not complete question #5, you can start using the solution on page 241.

Solutions appear at the end of this chapter and on MyAccountingLab

CORRECTING JOURNAL ENTRIES

In Chapter 2 we discussed errors that affect the trial balance: treating a debit as a credit and vice versa, transpositions, and slides. Here we show how to correct errors in journal entries. Knowing how to detect and correct errors is an important function in the preparation of accurate financial statements.

When the error is detected after posting, the accountant makes a *correcting entry* to correct an error. Correcting entries can appear on the worksheet with the adjusting entries at the end of a period, or they can be journalized and posted as soon as the error is detected.

Suppose HEC paid $10,000 cash for furniture and, in error, debited Office Supplies as follows:

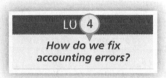

How do we fix accounting errors?

KEY POINTS

Adjusting entries are not the same as correcting entries. Adjustments are made as part of the normal process of accounting. Corrections are made because of errors.

REAL WORLD EXAMPLE

Many software programs allow users to make a correction to the entry by changing the original transaction. The computer reverses the original entry and replaces it with the new, correct entry.

Incorrect Entry			
May 13	Office Supplies	10,000	
	Cash		10,000
	Bought supplies.		

There are two ways to approach this sort of correction: either reverse the original entry and then create the correct journal entry, or create a journal entry that changes only the affected accounts. Exhibit 4–12 shows both approaches.

EXHIBIT 4–12 | Two Approaches for Correcting a Journal Entry Error

Correcting Entry: Reverse original and rewrite			
May 15	Cash	10,000	
	Office Supplies		10,000
	To reverse the original transaction because it was entered incorrectly. Furniture was purchased.		
May 15	Furniture	10,000	
	Cash		10,000
	To correct May 13 journal entry to reflect that furniture was purchased.		

Correcting Entry: One step to change only affected accounts			
May 15	Furniture	10,000	
	Office Supplies		10,000
	To correct May 13 entry. Furniture was purchased.		

The credit to Office Supplies in the correcting entry offsets the incorrect debit of the first entry. The debit to Furniture places the furniture's cost in the correct account. Now both Office Supplies and Furniture are correct.

This method is often preferred because it is easy to do and easy to follow through the journals to see what happened. It has a good *audit trail*—an easy-to-read transaction history to figure out what happened.

Notice that both approaches to correcting this error give the same results: Furniture reflects an increase of $10,000 and Office Supplies reflects an increase of $0, so both account balances are now correct.

> Try It!

7. Suppose a company purchased $200 of supplies on account but in error credited Accounts Receivable for $200. Make the single journal entry to correct this error, then correct the error using two journal entries. Provide an explanation for each journal entry.

Solutions appear at the end of this chapter and on MyAccountingLab

CLASSIFYING ASSETS AND LIABILITIES

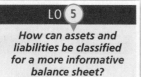

LO 5

How can assets and liabilities be classified for a more informative balance sheet?

Liquidity is a measure of how quickly an item can be converted to cash. All balance sheet accounts are listed in order of their liquidity or their *intended* disposition. Cash is the most liquid asset. Accounts receivable is a relatively liquid asset because the business expects to collect the amount in cash in the near future. Supplies are less liquid than accounts receivable, and furniture and buildings are even less so.

Users of financial statements are interested in liquidity because business difficulties often arise from a shortage of cash. How quickly can the business convert an asset to cash and pay a debt? How soon must a liability be paid? These are questions of liquidity. A **classified balance sheet** lists assets and liabilities in the order of their relative liquidity by introducing subtotals to classify accounts as either *current* or *long term*.

Assets

Current Assets   **Current assets** are assets that are expected to be converted to cash, sold, or consumed during the next 12 months or within the business's normal operating cycle if longer than a year. The **operating cycle** is the time span during which cash is paid for goods and services that are sold to customers, who then pay the business cash:

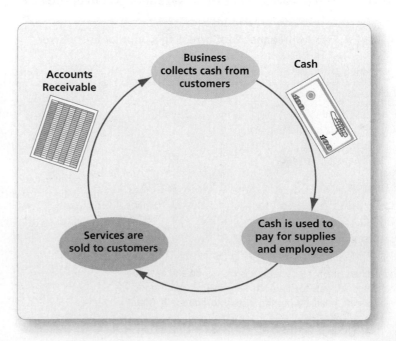

For most businesses, the operating cycle is a few months. Few types of business have operating cycles longer than a year.

Cash, Accounts Receivable, Notes Receivable due within a year or less, Supplies, and Prepaid Expenses are all current assets. **Merchandising entities** such as Hudson's Bay Company and Canadian Tire Corporation and **manufacturing entities** such as Magna International Inc. and Bombardier Inc. have an additional current asset, Inventory. This account shows the cost of goods that are held for sale to customers.

If a note receivable has some part that is due in the current period, the current portion is reported separately as a current asset and the rest of the receivable is reported as a long-term asset. In Exhibit 4–14 we can see that $51,600 is expected to be received in the current period while $48,400 will be received later.

Long-Term Assets   **Long-term assets** are all assets that are not classified as current assets. The term *long-term assets* is not a title on a financial statement—it is just a description of what is not current.

Property, plant, and equipment and intangible assets were introduced in Chapter 3. Two other categories of long-term assets are Long-Term Investments and Other Assets (a catch-all category for assets that are not classified more precisely). We discuss these categories in more detail in later chapters.

Liabilities

Financial statement users (such as creditors) are interested in the due dates of an entity's liabilities. Liabilities that must be paid the soonest create the greatest strain on cash. Therefore, the balance sheet lists liabilities in the order they are due to be paid. Balance sheets usually have at least two liability classifications: *current liabilities* and *long-term liabilities*. Knowing how many of a business's liabilities are current and how many are long term helps creditors assess the likelihood of collecting from the entity.

Current Liabilities   **Current liabilities** are debts that are due to be paid with cash or with goods and services within one year or the entity's operating cycle if the cycle is longer than a year. Accounts Payable, Salaries Payable, Goods and Services Tax Payable, Harmonized Sales Tax Payable, Interest Payable, and Unearned Revenue are all current liabilities.

If the long-term debt such as Notes Payable is paid in instalments, with the first instalment due within one year, the second instalment due the second year, and so on, then the first instalment would be a current liability and the remainder would be shown as a long-term liability. For example, a $100,000 note payable to be paid $10,000 per year over 10 years would include the following:

- A current liability of $10,000 for next year's payment
- A long-term liability of $90,000

Long-Term Liabilities   All liabilities that are not current are classified as **long-term liabilities**. Many notes payable and mortgages payable are long term—payable after the longer of one year or the entity's operating cycle.

The Classified Balance Sheet

Thus far in this book we have presented the *unclassified* balance sheet of Hunter Environmental Consulting. Our purpose was to focus on the main points of assets, liabilities, and owner's equity without the details of *current* assets, *current* liabilities, and so on. Exhibit 4–13 presents HEC's classified balance sheet. Notice that HEC has no long-term liabilities.

Compare HEC's *classified* balance sheet in Exhibit 4–13 with the *unclassified* balance sheet in Exhibit 4–7 (page 182). The classified balance sheet reports totals for current assets and current liabilities, which do not appear on the unclassified balance sheet. These subtotals are extremely handy for financial analysis, as you will see later in this chapter.

**EXHIBIT 4–13 | Classified Balance Sheet of Hunter Environmental Consulting in
Account Format**

HUNTER ENVIRONMENTAL CONSULTING
Balance Sheet
May 31, 2017

Assets			Liabilities		
Current assets:			Current liabilities:		
Cash		$ 31,000	Accounts payable		$ 12,000
Accounts receivable		15,500	Salary payable		4,000
Office supplies		1,000	Unearned service revenue		2,000
Prepaid insurance		3,300	Total current liabilities		18,000
Total current assets		50,800			
Property, plant, and equipment:			**Owner's Equity**		
Furniture	$ 45,000		Lisa Hunter, capital		127,050
Less: Accumulated amortization	750	44,250			
Land		50,000			
Total property, plant, and equipment		94,250			
			Total liabilities and		
Total assets		$145,050	owner's equity		$145,050

The classified balance sheet of CAM Company, is shown in Exhibit 4–14. It shows how a company with many different accounts could present its data on a classified balance sheet.

Formats of Balance Sheets The balance sheet of CAM Company shown in Exhibit 4–14 lists the assets at the top with the liabilities and owner's equity below. This is the *report format*. HEC's balance sheet in Exhibit 4–13 lists the assets at the left with the liabilities and the owner's equity at the right. That is the *account* (or *equation*) *format*. Either format is acceptable.

> Try It!

8. Some of the accounts from the December 31, 2017, trial balance of Mark Wearing Engineers appear here. All accounts have their normal balances.

Mark Wearing, Capital	$ 14,160	Salaries Payable	$ 1,400
Cash	23,600	Accumulated Amortization—	
Furniture	11,200	Furniture	240
Accounts Payable	11,200	Mortgage Payable (current and long term)	20,000
Accumulated Amortization— Equipment	200	Mortgage Payable (current)	1,000
Accounts Receivable	7,600	Unearned Service Revenue	2,400
Equipment	7,000	Supplies	200

Identify the assets (including contra assets) and liabilities, and identify whether each asset and liability is current or long term.

9. Refer to the data in Try It #8. Create the classified balance sheet in report format for Mark Wearing Engineers at December 31, 2017.

Solutions appear at the end of this chapter and on MyAccountingLab

EXHIBIT 4–14 | Classified Balance Sheet of CAM Company in Report Format

CAM COMPANY
Balance Sheet
June 30, 2016

Assets

Current assets:

Cash	$ 26,400	
Short-term investments	57,000	
Accounts receivable	235,000	
Interest receivable	26,800	
Current portion of note receivable	51,600	
Inventory	847,800	
Supplies	5,200	
Prepaid insurance	27,000	
Total current assets		$1,276,800

Long-term investments:

Note receivable	100,000	
Less: Current portion of note receivable	51,600	
Total long-term investments		48,400

Property, plant, and equipment:

Equipment	$ 60,000		
Less: accumulated amortization	18,000	42,000	
Furniture and fixtures	70,000		
Less: accumulated amortization	30,000	40,000	
Buildings	240,000		
Less: accumulated amortization	160,000	80,000	
Land		70,000	
Total property, plant, and equipment		232,000	

Intangible assets:

Trademark		7,000
Total assets		$1,564,200

> Each time more detail is shown, the information is broken down into a column to the left of the total (e.g., $60,000 − $18,000 = $42,000).

> Notice that even though it is the middle of the statement, there is a double underline representing the end of the assets section. This amount is a total of all the amounts directly above it.

Liabilities

Current liabilities:

Accounts payable	$357,000	
Salaries and wages payable	22,400	
Interest payable	24,600	
Goods and services tax payable	64,600	
Current portion of note payable	72,200	
Other current liabilities	23,600	
Total current liabilities		$ 564,400

Long-term liabilities:

Note payable	220,000	
Less: current portion of note payable	72,200	
Total long-term liabilities		147,800
Total liabilities		712,200

Owner's Equity

A. Lannister, capital		852,000
Total liabilities and owner's equity		$1,564,200

> This total is the sum of liabilities ($712,200) and owner's equity ($852,000). It also has a double underline to indicate that it is a final total.

> Why It's Done This Way ▲

The top level of the accounting framework reminds us that financial statements are prepared to provide interested external users with information about the financial health of the company. These users have a variety of relationships with the company—some may be creditors who have lent money to the company, others may be shareholders or investors in the company. These groups want to understand how well the company has done in the past year. As well, they may want to predict how the company will do in the future.

The classified format of the balance sheet is an example of how liquidity information can be provided to help users get a better understanding about the financial condition of a business, which they can use as they calculate and interpret financial ratios.

ACCOUNTING RATIOS

The purpose of accounting is to provide information for decision making. Users of accounting information include managers, investors, and creditors. A creditor considering lending money must predict whether the borrower can repay the loan. If the borrower already has a large amount of debt, the probability of repayment is lower than if the borrower has a small amount of debt. To better understand complex information, decision makers use ratios they compute from a company's financial statements. A ratio is a useful way to show the relationship between numbers. Two of the most widely used decision aids in business are the current ratio and the debt ratio.

Current Ratio

The **current ratio** measures the ability of a business to pay its short-term debt obligations. In other words, it measures the company's ability to pay current liabilities with current assets.

$$\text{Current ratio} = \frac{\text{Total current assets}}{\text{Total current liabilities}}$$

REAL WORLD EXAMPLE

Think of the debt ratio in personal terms to help you remember the guideline that a lower debt ratio is preferred over a higher debt ratio. If you owned a car that is now worth $15,000 (your total assets) but had a loan on it for $17,000 (your total liabilities) this would be "bad." Your debt ratio would be 17,000/15,000 = 1.13.

But if you owned the same $15,000 car and had a $10,000 loan on it, your debt ratio would be 10,000/15,000 = 0.67, which is certainly "better."

A company prefers a high current ratio, which means the business has enough current assets to pay current liabilities when they come due, plus a cushion of additional current assets. An increasing current ratio from period to period generally indicates improvement in ability to pay current debts.

A general rule is that a strong current ratio would be in the range of 2.00, which indicates that the company has approximately $2.00 in current assets for every $1.00 in current liabilities. Such a company would probably have little trouble paying its current liabilities and could probably borrow money on better terms, such as at a lower rate of interest. Most successful businesses operate with current ratios between 1.30 and 2.00. A current ratio of 1.00 is considered quite low.

Let's examine HEC's current ratio, using the company's balance sheet in Exhibit 4–13:

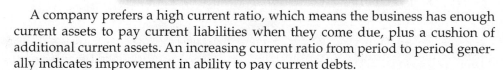

$$\text{Current ratio} = \frac{\text{Total current assets}}{\text{Total current liabilities}} = \frac{\$50,800}{\$18,000} = 2.82$$

HEC has $2.82 in current assets for every dollar the company owes in current liabilities. HEC's current ratio is very high, which makes the business look safe.

Debt Ratio

The **debt ratio** indicates the proportion of a company's assets that are financed with debt, as opposed to the proportion financed by the owner(s) of the company. This ratio measures a company's ability to pay both current and long-term debts—total liabilities.

$$\text{Debt ratio} = \frac{\text{Total liabilities}}{\text{Total assets}}$$

A low debt ratio is safer than a high debt ratio. Why? Because a company with low liabilities has low required payments. Such a company is less likely to get into financial difficulty. A rule of thumb is that a debt ratio below 0.60, or 60 percent, is considered safe for most businesses. Most companies have debt ratios in the range of 0.60 to 0.80. A decreasing ratio indicates improvement over time.

Let's examine HEC's debt ratio, using the company's balance sheet in Exhibit 4–13:

$$\text{Debt ratio} = \frac{\text{Total liabilities}}{\text{Total assets}} = \frac{\$18,000}{\$145,050} = 0.12, \text{ or } 12\%$$

The percentage of HEC's total assets that is financed with debt is 12 percent. A debt ratio of 12 percent is very safe.

KEY POINTS

	Current Ratio	Debt Ratio
Prefer ratio to be	high	low
Improvement means	increasing	decreasing

Interpreting Ratios

Financial ratios are an important aid to decision makers. However, it is unwise to place too much confidence in a single ratio or group of ratios. For example, a company may have a high current ratio, which indicates financial strength, and it may also have a high debt ratio, which suggests weakness. Which ratio gives the more reliable signal about the company? Experienced managers, lenders, and investors evaluate a company by examining a large number of ratios over several years to spot trends and turning points. These people also consider other facts, such as the company's cash position and its trend in net income. No single ratio gives the whole picture about a company.

As you progress through the study of accounting, we will introduce key ratios used for decision making. Chapter 18 (in Volume 2) then summarizes all the ratios discussed in this book and provides an overview of ratios used in decision making.

MyAccountingLab

Video: Real World Accounting

10. Refer to Try It #9, if you completed it, or the solution posted on page 243. Compute and evaluate the current ratio and the debt ratio for Mark Wearing Engineers.

Solutions appear at the end of this chapter and on MyAccountingLab

ACCOUNTING CYCLE AND FINANCIAL REPORTING IMPLICATIONS OF IFRS

LO 7

How does IFRS apply to the accounting cycle and financial reporting?

ASPE		IFRS

The accounting cycle for companies following IFRS is the same as that for companies following ASPE, which we have studied in Chapters 1 to 4. Both systems also allow a company to prepare a balance sheet using either the report format or the accounting equation format. While the approach to recording these transactions has been essentially the same under both reporting systems, the presentation of the information may be quite different.

Terminology

Balance sheet	Choice of name such as statement of financial position or balance sheet. A classified format is required.

(Continued)

ASPE	IFRS
Income statement	Choice of name such as statement of comprehensive income or income statement
	And there is a choice of presentation: Prepare a separate income statement and statement of comprehensive income, or prepare one document that combines both.
Statement of owner's equity (statement of retained earnings for a corporation)	Choice of name such as statement of changes in equity or statement of retained earnings
Cash flow statement	Choice of name such as statement of cash flows or cash flow statement

Format	
Companies use a classified format, which lists the accounts in the order of liquidity in a **current then non-current** order.	Under IFRS, there is a choice between current then non-current OR **non-current then current** order (on the asset side of the balance sheet, they present the long-term assets first followed by the current assets; on the liability and equity side of the balance sheet, they present the equity section, then the long-term liabilities, followed by the current liabilities). The non-current then current order is sometimes called a *reverse order of liquidity*.
	Canadian companies following IFRS will choose the financial statement names and formats that best meet their needs or are favoured by others in their industry.

SUMMARY PROBLEM FOR YOUR REVIEW

The unadjusted trial balance of Cloud Break Consulting at June 30, 2017, the end of its fiscal year, is presented below:

CLOUD BREAK CONSULTING Unadjusted Trial Balance June 30, 2017		
Cash	$131,000	
Accounts receivable	104,000	
Supplies	4,000	
Prepaid rent	27,000	
Building	300,000	
Accumulated amortization—building		$155,000
Land	45,000	
Accounts payable		159,000
Salary payable		0
Unearned service revenue		40,000
Michael Moe, capital		102,000

(Continued)

(Continued)

Michael Moe, withdrawals	7,000	
Service revenue		450,000
Salary expense	255,000	
Supplies expense	0	
Rent expense	25,000	
Amortization expense—building	0	
Miscellaneous expense	8,000	
Total	$906,000	$906,000

Data needed for the adjusting entries include:

a. Supplies remaining on hand at year end are worth $2,000.

b. Nine months of rent ($27,000) were paid in advance on April 1, 2017. No rent expense has been recorded since that date.

c. Amortization expense has not been recorded on the building for the 2017 fiscal year. Amortization is $14,000 per year on the building.

d. Employees work Monday through Friday. The weekly payroll is $5,000 and is paid every Friday. June 30, 2017, is a Monday.

e. Service revenue of $15,000 must be accrued.

f. Cloud Break Consulting received $40,000 in advance for consulting services to be provided evenly from January 1, 2017, through August 31, 2017. None of the revenue from this client has been recorded.

To plan your worksheet, check the adjusting entries data to see if the same account is affected more than once. If it is, leave one or two blank lines under the account name. Do this for Service Revenue on this worksheet.

Required

1. Prepare the worksheet of Cloud Break Consulting for the year ended June 30, 2017. Identify each adjusting entry by the letter corresponding to the data given.

2. Journalize the adjusting entries and post them to T-accounts. (Before posting to the T-accounts, enter into each T-account its balance as shown in the trial balance. For example, enter the $104,000 balance in the Accounts Receivable account before posting its adjusting entry.) Identify adjusting entries by *letter*. Provide explanations. You can take the adjusting entries straight from the worksheet from Requirement 1. Find the ending balances of the permanent accounts.

3. Journalize and post the closing entries. (Each T-account should carry its balance as shown in the adjusted trial balance.) Provide explanations. To distinguish closing entries from adjusting entries, identify the closing entries by *number*. Draw the arrows to illustrate the flow of data, as shown in Exhibit 4–10, page 187. Indicate the balance of the Capital account after the closing entries are posted.

4. Prepare the income statement for the year ended June 30, 2017. List Miscellaneous Expense last among the expenses, which is a common practice.

5. Prepare the statement of owner's equity for the year ended June 30, 2017. Draw the arrow that links the income statement to the statement of owner's equity if both statements are on the same page. Otherwise, explain how they are linked.

6. Prepare the classified balance sheet at June 30, 2017. Use the report format. All liabilities are current. Draw the arrow that links the statement of owner's equity to the balance sheet if both statements are on the same page. Otherwise, explain how they are linked.

SOLUTION

Requirement 1

Using the trial balance given, write the account titles in the first column of the worksheet and the amounts in the Trial Balance columns, ensuring debit and credit balances on the trial balance are debit and credit balances on the worksheet.

When calculating the Adjusted Trial Balance amounts, remember to add and subtract the adjustments properly. For assets, withdrawals, and expenses, add debits and subtract credits. For contra assets, liabilities, owner's equity, and revenues, add credits and subtract debits.

CLOUD BREAK CONSULTING
Worksheet
For the Year Ended June 30, 2017

Account Title	Unadjusted Trial Balance Debit	Unadjusted Trial Balance Credit	Adjustments Debit	Adjustments Credit	Adjusted Trial Balance Debit	Adjusted Trial Balance Credit	Income Statement Debit	Income Statement Credit	Balance Sheet Debit	Balance Sheet Credit
Cash	131,000				131,000				131,000	
Accounts receivable	104,000		(e) 15,000		119,000				119,000	
Supplies	4,000			(a) 2,000	2,000				2,000	
Prepaid rent	27,000			(b) 9,000	18,000				18,000	
Building	300,000				300,000				300,000	
Accum. amort.—building		155,000		(c) 14,000		169,000				169,000
Land	45,000				45,000				45,000	
Accounts payable		159,000				159,000				159,000
Salaries payable		0		(d) 1,000		1,000				1,000
Unearned service revenue		40,000	(f) 30,000			10,000				10,000
Michael Moe, capital		102,000				102,000				102,000
Michael Moe, withdrawals	7,000				7,000				7,000	
Service revenue		450,000		(e)15,000		495,000		495,000		
				(f) 30,000						
Salaries expense	255,000		(d) 1,000		256,000		256,000			
Supplies expense	0		(a) 2,000		2,000		2,000			
Rent expense	25,000		(b) 9,000		34,000		34,000			
Amort. exp.—building	0		(c) 14,000		14,000		14,000			
Miscellaneous expense	8,000				8,000		8,000			
	906,000	906,000	71,000	71,000	936,000	936,000	314,000	495,000	622,000	441,000
Net income							181,000			181,000
							495,000	495,000	622,000	622,000

Selected adjusting entries are explained further:

a. Supplies on hand ($4,000) – supplies still on hand ($2,000) = $2,000 adjustment

b. Of the $27,000 rent paid for nine months (or $3,000 per month), $9,000 should be recorded as rent expense for April, May, and June.

f. Unearned Service Revenue started with a balance of $40,000, and $30,000 was earned for January to June, so that means there is still $10,000 to be earned, which is a liability.

The same "plug figure" ($181,000) must make the final Income Statement column totals equal and the final Balance Sheet column totals equal.

Requirement 2

a.	Jun. 30	Supplies Expense	2,000	
		Supplies		2,000
		To reflect supplies remaining on hand at year end.		
b.	Jun. 30	Rent Expense	9,000	
		Prepaid Rent		9,000
		To record rent expense for April, May, and June (3 × $3,000 = $9,000).		
c.	Jun. 30	Amortization Expense—Building	14,000	
		Accumulated Amortization—Building		14,000
		To record annual amortization expense on building.		
d.	Jun. 30	Salaries Expense	1,000	
		Salaries Payable		1,000
		To record one day's salary owed to employees ($5,000 ÷ 5 = $1,000).		
e.	Jun. 30	Accounts Receivable	15,000	
		Service Revenue		15,000
		To accrue service revenue at year end.		
f.	Jun. 30	Unearned Service Revenue	30,000	
		Service Revenue		30,000
		To record service revenue earned from January to June ($40,000 ÷ 8 = $5,000 revenue per month; six months' revenue is 6 × $5,000 = $30,000).		

Refer to the Adjustments columns of the worksheet. Make journal entries for all the transactions in the Adjustments columns.

Accounts Receivable

	104,000		
(e)	15,000		
Bal.	119,000		

Supplies

	4,000	(a)	2,000
Bal.	2,000		

Prepaid Rent

	27,000		
		(b)	9,000
Bal.	18,000		

Accumulated Amortization— Building

			155,000
		(c)	14,000
		Bal.	169,000

Salaries Payable

		(d)	1,000
		Bal.	1,000

Unearned Service Revenue

(f)	30,000		40,000
		Bal.	10,000

Service Revenue

			450,000
		(e)	15,000
		(f)	30,000
		Bal.	495,000

Salaries Expense

	255,000		
(d)	1,000		
Bal.	256,000		

Supplies Expense

(a)	2,000		
Bal.	2,000		

Rent Expense

	25,000		
(b)	9,000		
Bal.	34,000		

Amortization Expense— Building

(c)	14,000		
Bal.	14,000		

Create T-accounts only for the accounts affected by the adjusting entries.

Remember that the beginning balance in each of these T-accounts is the amount from the Trial Balance columns of the worksheet.

When you post the adjusting entries, use the letters a to f to identify each adjustment. Find the balance of each T-account.

Recall that all the temporary accounts are closed at the end of the period, namely the revenue, expense, and withdrawals accounts.

① To close revenue accounts, debit each revenue account for the amount reported in the Income Statement column of the worksheet. Credit Income Summary for the total of the debits.

② To close expense accounts, credit each expense account for the amount reported in the Income Statement column of the worksheet. Debit Income Summary for the total of the credits.

③ To close the Income Summary account, calculate the difference between the total debits and total credits in the Income Summary account. This should match the net income or net loss amount on the worksheet. In this case, Income Summary has a credit balance. Therefore, debit Income Summary to close it and credit the Capital account. Using an Income Summary T-account may help you close Income Summary more easily.

Requirement 3

① Jun. 30	Service Revenue		495,000	
	Income Summary			495,000
	To close the revenue account and create the Income Summary account.			
② Jun. 30	Income Summary		314,000	
	Salary Expense			256,000
	Supplies Expense			2,000
	Rent Expense			34,000
	Amortization Expense—Building			14,000
	Miscellaneous Expense			8,000
	To close the expense accounts.			
③ Jun. 30	Income Summary		181,000	
	Michael Moe, Capital			181,000
	To close the Income Summary account. (Income Summary balance = $495,000 − $314,000.)			
④ Jun. 30	Michael Moe, Capital		7,000	
	Michael Moe, Withdrawals			7,000
	To close the Withdrawals account and transfer the Withdrawals amount to the Capital account.			

④ To close the Withdrawals account, credit the Withdrawals account for the amounts reported in the Balance Sheet columns of the worksheet, and debit the Capital account.

Identify the closing entries by their journal entry numbers 1, 2, 3, or 4.

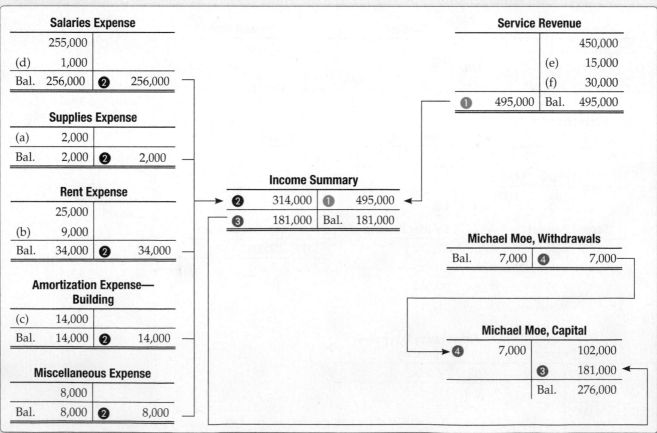

Requirement 4

CLOUD BREAK CONSULTING
Income Statement
For the Year Ended June 30, 2017

Revenues:		
Service revenue		$495,000
Expenses:		
Salaries expense	$256,000	
Rent expense	34,000	
Amortization expense—building	14,000	
Supplies expense	2,000	
Miscellaneous expense	8,000	
Total expenses		314,000
Net income		$181,000

The title must include the name of the company, the name of the document, and the specific period of time covered.

Gather all the revenue and expense account names and amounts from the Income Statement columns of the worksheet.

Requirement 5

CLOUD BREAK CONSULTING
Statement of Owner's Equity
For the Year Ended June 30, 2017

Michael Moe, Capital, July 1, 2016	$102,000
Add: Net income	181,000
	283,000
Less: Withdrawals	7,000
Michael Moe, Capital, June 30, 2017	$276,000

Watch that the line for the date indicates the specific period of time covered.

Beginning owner's equity and withdrawals are from the Balance Sheet columns of the worksheet. The net income amount is transferred from the income statement.

Requirement 6

CLOUD BREAK CONSULTING
Balance Sheet
June 30, 2017

Assets			
Current assets:			
Cash		$131,000	
Accounts receivable		119,000	
Supplies		2,000	
Prepaid rent		18,000	
Total current assets			270,000
Property, plant, and equipment:			
Building	$300,000		
Less: Accumulated amortization	169,000	131,000	
Land		45,000	
Total property, plant, and equipment			176,000
Total assets			$446,000
Liabilities			
Current liabilities:			
Accounts payable		$159,000	
Salaries payable		1,000	
Unearned service revenue		10,000	
Total current liabilities			170,000
Owner's Equity			
Michael Moe, capital			276,000
Total liabilities and owner's equity			$446,000

Notice that the balance sheet shows the financial position on one specific date.

The classified balance sheet uses the accounts and balances that appear in the Balance Sheet columns of the worksheet and includes additional headings and subtotals. Use Exhibit 4–14 as a model.

CHAPTER 4 APPENDIX

REVERSING ENTRIES: AN OPTIONAL STEP

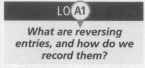

LO A1

What are reversing entries, and how do we record them?

Reversing entries are special types of entries that are used most often in conjunction with accrual-type adjustments such as accrued salary expense and accrued service revenue. Reversing entries are *not* used for adjustments to record amortization and prepayments. *Generally accepted accounting principles (GAAP) do not require reversing entries. They are used only for convenience and to save time.*

Accounting for Accrued Expenses

To see how reversing entries work, return to HEC's unadjusted trial balance at May 31, 2016 (Exhibit 4–2, page 178), for the starting balances:

> Salaries Expense has a debit balance of $4,000 from salaries paid during May. At May 31, the company owes employees an additional $4,000 for the work performed during the last few weeks of the month.

❶ HEC must include the second $4,000 in Salaries Expense for May. To do so, HEC makes the adjusting entry on May 31, which is the starting point in Exhibit 4A–1.

After the adjusting entry,

- The May income statement reports salary expense of $8,000.
- The May 31 balance sheet reports salary payable of $4,000.

❷ The $8,000 debit balance of Salaries Expense is eliminated by a closing entry.

After posting, Salaries Expense has a zero balance.

Assume for this example that on June 4, the next payroll date, HEC will pay $4,000 of accrued salaries plus $200 in salaries that the employees have earned in the first few days of June. HEC's next payroll payment will be $4,200 ($4,000 + $200). There are two ways this next journal entry can be made: with or without the use of a reversing entry.

Accounting without a Reversing Entry

❹ On June 4, the next payday, HEC pays the payroll of $4,200 and can choose to record this journal entry:

Jun. 4	Salaries Payable	4,000	
	Salary Expense	200	
	Cash		4,200

This method of recording the cash payment is correct. However, it wastes time because the company's accountant must refer to the adjusting entries of May 31 to recall how much was accrued. Searching the preceding period's adjusting entries takes time and, in business, time is money. To save time, accountants use reversing entries, which eliminates the need to search the preceding period's adjusting entries.

Making a Reversing Entry

A reversing entry switches the debit and the credit of a previous adjusting entry. *A reversing entry, then, is the exact opposite of a prior adjusting entry.*

The adjusting entry from ❶ was:

May 31	Salaries Expense	4,000	
	Salaries Payable		4,000

❸ This reversing entry is dated the first day of the period following the adjusting entry:

Jun. 1	Salaries Payable	4,000	
	Salaries Expense		4,000

Ordinarily, the accountant who makes the adjusting entry prepares the reversing entry at the same time. HEC dates the reversing entry as of the first day of the next period, however, so that it affects only the new period.

Note how the accounts appear after the company posts the reversing entry:

Salaries Payable				Salaries Expense		
		May 31	4,000		Jun. 1 Rev.	4,000
Jun. 1 Rev.	**4,000**	May 31 Bal.	4,000			
Jun. 1 Bal.	0					

This credit balance in Salaries Expense does not mean that the entity has negative salary expense, as you might think. Instead, the odd credit balance is merely a temporary result of the reversing entry.

❹ The credit balance in the Salaries Expense account is eliminated on June 4. The payment of the payroll does not include an entry to the Salaries Payable account because there is no balance in that account.

Jun. 4	Salaries Expense	4,200	
	Cash		4,200

After posting the journal entry, the Salaries Expense account has its correct debit balance of $200, which is the amount of salaries expense incurred so far in June:

Salaries Expense			
Jun. 4	4,000	Jun. 1 Rev.	4,000
Jun. 4 Bal.	200		

Exhibit 4A–1 shows these transactions side by side to highlight the differences and show that the results are the same whether or not reversing entries are used.

EXHIBIT 4A–1 | Comparison of Two Ways to Record Reversing Entries for Accrued Expenses

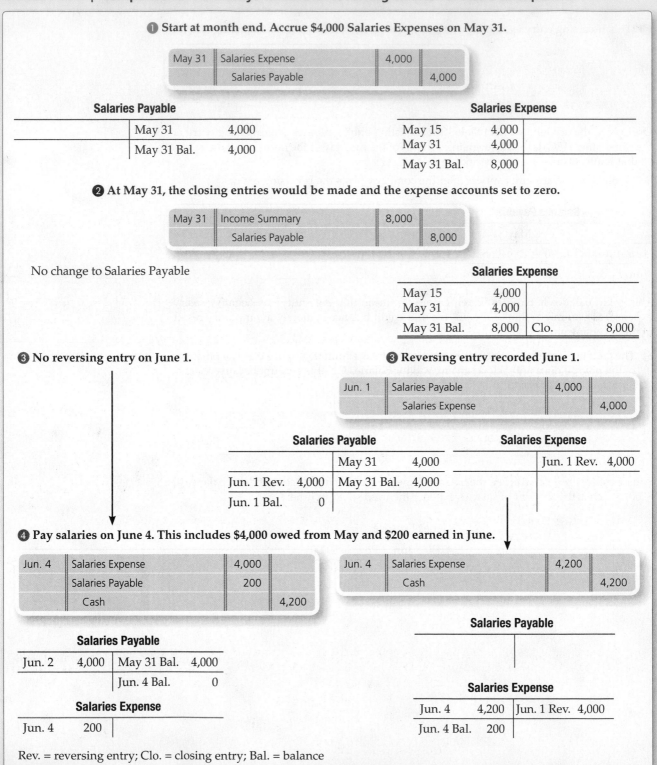

❶ Start at month end. Accrue $4,000 Salaries Expenses on May 31.

May 31	Salaries Expense	4,000	
	Salaries Payable		4,000

Salaries Payable

	May 31	4,000
	May 31 Bal.	4,000

Salaries Expense

May 15	4,000	
May 31	4,000	
May 31 Bal.	8,000	

❷ At May 31, the closing entries would be made and the expense accounts set to zero.

May 31	Income Summary	8,000	
	Salaries Payable		8,000

No change to Salaries Payable

Salaries Expense

May 15	4,000		
May 31	4,000		
May 31 Bal.	8,000	Clo.	8,000

❸ No reversing entry on June 1.

❸ Reversing entry recorded June 1.

Jun. 1	Salaries Payable	4,000	
	Salaries Expense		4,000

Salaries Payable

		May 31	4,000
Jun. 1 Rev.	4,000	May 31 Bal.	4,000
Jun. 1 Bal.	0		

Salaries Expense

	Jun. 1 Rev.	4,000

❹ Pay salaries on June 4. This includes $4,000 owed from May and $200 earned in June.

Jun. 4	Salaries Expense	4,000	
	Salaries Payable	200	
	Cash		4,200

Jun. 4	Salaries Expense	4,200	
	Cash		4,200

Salaries Payable

Jun. 2	4,000	May 31 Bal.	4,000
		Jun. 4 Bal.	0

Salaries Expense

Jun. 4	200	

Salaries Payable

Salaries Expense

Jun. 4	4,200	Jun. 1 Rev.	4,000
Jun. 4 Bal.	200		

Rev. = reversing entry; Clo. = closing entry; Bal. = balance

Accounting for Accrued Revenues

While most reversing entries are made to accrue expenses, reversing entries may be made to accrue revenues. For example, if HEC had completed some consulting work for a client on May 31 and sent the invoice, an entry would be made to debit Accounts Receivable and credit Service Revenue at May 31, 2016. Service Revenue would be closed to the Income Summary account in the usual way. A reversing entry on June 1, 2016, would reduce Accounts Receivable and temporarily create a debit balance in Service Revenue. When the payment is received in June, the accountant would debit Cash and credit Service Revenue.

SUMMARY

LEARNING OBJECTIVE 1 Prepare an accounting worksheet

How can we summarize data to prepare the financial statements? **Pg. 177**

- The accountant's worksheet includes the following columns:

Account Title	Unadjusted Trial Balance		Adjustments		Adjusted Trial Balance		Income Statement		Balance Sheet	
	Dr	Cr	Dr	Cr	Dr	Cr	Dr	Cr	Dr	Cr

LEARNING OBJECTIVE 2 Completing the accounting cycle

Remind me: How does this all fit together? **Pg. 181**

- A worksheet is an optional tool for preparing information used to create financial statements.

  MyAccountingLab **Video:** Creating a Worksheet

LEARNING OBJECTIVE 3 Close the revenue, expense, and withdrawal accounts

What are closing entries, and how do we record them? **Pg. 185**

- The temporary accounts are closed out to zero. Their balances are transferred to the Capital account.
- To remember what is closed, use the acronym REISWC (pronounced rice-wick):

  1. **R**evenues   2. **E**xpenses   3. **I**ncome **S**ummary   4. **W**ithdrawals to **C**apital

- We can now trace the flow of accounting information through these steps:

  - Business Transaction → Source Documents → Journal Entry → Posting to Ledger Accounts → Unadjusted Trial Balance → Adjusting Entries → Adjusted Trial Balance → Financial Statements → Closing Entries → Post-Closing Trial Balance

  MyAccountingLab **Video:** Closing Entries

LEARNING OBJECTIVE 4 Correct typical accounting errors

How do we fix accounting errors? **Pg. 189**

- Accountants use "correcting journal entries" to fix errors. Either reverse the original journal entry and then write a new journal entry, or change only the affected accounts in a new journal entry.

LEARNING OBJECTIVE 5 Classify assets and liabilities as current or long term, and prepare a classified balance sheet

How can assets and liabilities be classified for a more informative balance sheet? **Pg. 190**

- Classify assets and liabilities into one of the following groups:
  - Current (within one year or the company's operating cycle if longer than a year)
  - Long term (non-current)

LEARNING OBJECTIVE 6 Use the current ratio and the debt ratio to evaluate a company

How do decision makers evaluate a company using the current ratio and debt ratio? **Pg. 194**

$$\text{Current ratio} = \frac{\text{Total current assets}}{\text{Total current liabilities}}$$

- The current ratio measures the company's ability to pay current liabilities with current assets.

$$\text{Debt ratio} = \frac{\text{Total liabilities}}{\text{Total assets}}$$

- The debt ratio measures the company's overall ability to pay liabilities. The debt ratio shows the proportion of the entity's assets that are financed with debt.

  MyAccountingLab **Video:** Real World Accounting

How does IFRS apply to the accounting cycle and financial reporting? Pg. 195
- There is no change to the accounting cycle if companies follow IFRS or ASPE.
- Canadian companies reporting under IFRS have several choices in the format of their balance sheet presentation.

LEARNING OBJECTIVE **A1** Describe and prepare reversing entries

What are reversing entries, and how do we record them? Pg. 202
- This convenient step is optional for accrued revenues and accrued expenses.

Check **Accounting Vocabulary** for all key terms used in Chapter 4 and the **Glossary** at the back of the book for all key terms used in the textbook.

MORE CHAPTER REVIEW MATERIAL

MyAccountingLab

DemoDoc covering Closing Entries
Accounting Cycle Tutorial
Student PowerPoint Slides
Audio Chapter Summary

Note: All MyAccountingLab resources can be found in the Chapter Resources section and the Multimedia Library.

ACCOUNTING VOCABULARY

Classified balance sheet A balance sheet that places each asset and liability into a specific category *(p. 190)*.

Closing entries Entries that transfer the revenue, expense, and owner withdrawal balances from these respective accounts to the Capital account *(p. 185)*.

Closing the accounts A step in the accounting cycle at the end of the period that prepares the accounts for recording the transactions of the next period. Closing the accounts consists of journalizing and posting the closing entries to set the balances of the revenue, expense, and owner withdrawal accounts to zero *(p. 185)*.

Current asset An asset that is expected to be converted to cash, sold, or consumed during the next 12 months, or within the business's normal operating cycle if longer than a year *(p. 190)*.

Current liability A debt due to be paid within one year or one of the entity's operating cycles if the cycle is longer than a year *(p. 191)*.

Current ratio Current assets divided by current liabilities. Measures the company's ability to pay current liabilities from current assets *(p. 194)*.

Current then non-current A balance sheet format that reports current assets before long-term assets, and current liabilities before long-term liabilities and equity. This format may be used for reporting under both ASPE and IFRS *(p. 196)*.

Debt ratio Ratio of total liabilities to total assets. Gives the proportion of a company's assets that it has financed with debt *(p. 194)*.

Income Summary A temporary "holding tank" account into which the revenues and expenses are transferred prior to their final transfer to the Capital account *(p. 185)*.

Liquidity A measure of how quickly an item can be converted to cash *(p. 190)*.

Long-term asset An asset not classified as a current asset *(p. 191)*.

Long-term liability A liability not classified as a current liability *(p. 191)*.

Manufacturing entity A company that earns its revenue by making products *(p. 191)*.

Merchandising entity A company that earns its revenue by selling products rather than services *(p. 191)*.

Nominal account Another name for a *temporary account* *(p. 185)*.

Non-current then current A balance sheet format that may be used for companies reporting under IFRS. Accounts are reported in the reverse order of liquidity, for example, long-term assets before current assets *(p. 196)*.

Operating cycle The time span during which cash is paid for goods and services that are sold to customers who then pay the business in cash *(p. 190)*.

Permanent account An asset, liability, or owner's equity account that is not closed at the end of the period. Also called a *real account* *(p. 185)*.

Post-closing trial balance A list of the ledger accounts and their balances at the end of the period after the closing entries have been journalized and posted. The last step of the accounting cycle, it ensures that the ledger is in balance for the start of the next accounting period *(p. 188)*.

Real account   Another name for a *permanent account* *(p. 185)*.

Reversing entry   An entry that switches the debit and the credit of a previous adjusting entry. The reversing entry is dated the first day of the period following the adjusting entry *(p. 202)*.

Temporary account   The revenue and expense accounts that relate to a particular accounting period and are closed at the end of the period. For a proprietorship, the owner withdrawals account is also temporary. Also called a *nominal account (p. 185)*.

Worksheet   A columnar document designed to help move data from the trial balance to the financial statements *(p. 177)*.

SIMILAR ACCOUNTING TERMS

Current ratio	Working capital ratio
Current then non-current	In order of liquidity
Non-current	Long term
Non-current then current	In reverse order of liquidity
Permanent account	Real account
Temporary account	Nominal account

SELF-STUDY QUESTIONS

Test your understanding of the chapter by marking the correct answer to each of the following questions:

1. Arrange the following accounting cycle steps in their proper order, assuming a worksheet is not used. *(p. 176)*
   a. Prepare the unadjusted trial balance
   b. Journalize and post adjusting entries
   c. Prepare the post-closing trial balance
   d. Journalize and post transactions
   e. Prepare the financial statements
   f. Journalize and post closing entries

2. The worksheet is a *(p. 177)*
   a. Journal
   b. Ledger
   c. Financial statement
   d. Device for completing the accounting cycle

3. The usefulness of the worksheet is *(p. 177)*
   a. Identifying the accounts that need to be adjusted
   b. Summarizing the effects of all the transactions of the period
   c. Aiding the preparation of the financial statements
   d. All of the above

4. Which of the following accounts is not closed? *(p. 185)*
   a. Supplies Expense
   b. Prepaid Insurance
   c. Interest Revenue
   d. Withdrawals

5. The closing entry for Salary Expense, with a balance of $322,000, is *(p. 186)*

   a. Salary Expense   322,000
      Income Summary   322,000

   b. Salary Expense   322,000
      Salary Payable   322,000

   c. Income Summary   322,000
      Salary Expense   322,000

   d. Salary Payable   322,000
      Salary Expense   322,000

6. The purpose of the post-closing trial balance is to *(p. 188)*
   a. Provide the account balances for preparation of the balance sheet
   b. Ensure that the ledger is in balance for the start of the next period
   c. Aid the journalizing and posting of the closing entries
   d. Ensure that the ledger is in balance for completion of the worksheet

7. A $500 payment on account to a supplier was recorded by debiting Supplies and crediting Cash. This entry was posted. The correcting entry is *(p. 189)*

   a. Accounts Payable   500
      Supplies   500

   b. Supplies   500
      Accounts Payable   500

   c. Cash   500
      Accounts Payable   500

   d. Cash   500
      Supplies   500

8. The classification of assets and liabilities as current or long term depends on (*pp. 190–191*)
   a. Their order of listing in the ledger
   b. Whether they appear on the balance sheet or the income statement
   c. The relative liquidity of the item
   d. The format of the balance sheet—account format or report format

9. The bookkeeper recorded prepaying insurance in the amount of $2,300 incorrectly as $3,200. Which journal entry will correct the ledger accounts if the business records prepaying expenses by debiting an asset account? (*p. 189*)
   a. Accounts receivable   900
          Prepaid insurance   900

   b. Cash   900
          Prepaid insurance   900

   c. Cash   900
          Insurance expense   900

   d. Insurance expense   900
          Cash   900

10. A classified balance sheet format is required for companies that report under (*p. 196*)
    a. Cash basis of accounting
    b. ASPE
    c. IFRS
    d. Both ASPE and IFRS

ASSIGNMENT MATERIAL

QUESTIONS

1. Identify the steps in the accounting cycle, distinguishing those that occur during the period from those that are performed at the end of the period.

2. Why is the worksheet a valuable accounting tool?

3. Name two advantages the worksheet has over the adjusted trial balance.

4. Why must the adjusting entries be journalized and posted if they have already been entered on the worksheet?

5. Why should the adjusting entries be journalized and posted before the closing entries are made?

6. Which types of accounts are closed?

7. What purpose is served by closing the accounts?

8. State how the worksheet helps with recording the closing entries.

9. Distinguish between permanent accounts and temporary accounts, indicating which type is closed at the end of the period. Give five examples of each type of account.

10. Is Income Summary a permanent account or a temporary account? When and how is it used?

11. Is net income a permanent account, a temporary account, or something else? Explain.

12. Give the closing entries for the following accounts (balances in parentheses): Service Revenue ($5,000), Salary Expense ($1,200), Income Summary (credit balance of $2,000), Withdrawals ($2,500).

13. Why are assets classified as current or long term? On what basis are they classified? Where do the classified amounts appear?

14. Indicate which of the following accounts are current assets and which are long-term assets: Prepaid Rent, Building, Furniture, Accounts Receivable, Cash, Note Receivable (due within one year), Note Receivable (due after one year).

15. In what order are assets and liabilities listed on the balance sheet?

16. Name an outside party that is interested in whether a liability is current or long term. Why would this party be interested in this information?

17. A friend tells you that the difference between a current liability and a long-term liability is that they are payable to different types of creditors. Is your friend correct? Include in your answer the definitions of these two categories of liabilities.

18. Show how to compute the current ratio and the debt ratio. Indicate what ability each ratio measures, and state whether a high value or a low value is safer for each.

19. Capp Company purchased supplies of $120 on account. The accountant debited Inventory and credited Accounts Payable for $120. A week later, after this entry has been posted to the ledger, the accountant discovers the error. Describe two ways the accountant can correct the error.

*20. Why are reversing entries used?

---

*This Question covers Chapter 4 Appendix topics.

STARTERS

Starter 4–1   Scissors Hair Stylists has begun the preparation of its adjusted trial balance as follows:

Start of a worksheet

SCISSORS HAIR STYLISTS						
Preparation of Adjusted Trial Balance						
December 31, 2017						
	Unadjusted Trial Balance		Adjustments		Adjusted Trial Balance	
Account Title	**Debit**	**Credit**	**Debit**	**Credit**	**Debit**	**Credit**
Cash	600					
Supplies	800					
Equipment	16,200					
Accumulated amortization—equipment		1,100				
Accounts payable		500				
Interest payable		0				
Note payable		2,900				
Suzanne Byrd, capital		5,300				
Service revenue		13,000				
Rent expense	4,800					
Supplies expense	0					
Amortization expense	0					
Interest expense	400					
	22,800	22,800				

Year end data:

a. Supplies remaining on hand, $300

b. Amortization, $1,100

c. Accrued interest expense, $700

Complete the company's adjusted trial balance. Identify each adjustment by its letter. To save time, you may write your answer in the spaces provided on the adjusted trial balance.

Starter 4–2   The following accounts appear in the adjusted trial balance columns of a worksheet:

Worksheet columns

a. _____ Service Revenue   f. _____ Supplies
b. _____ Unearned Service Revenue   g. _____ Accumulated Amortization
c. _____ Land   h. _____ Equipment
d. _____ Salaries Expense   i. _____ Owner's Capital
e. _____ Supplies Expense   j. _____ Owner's Withdrawals

State which of the following columns each account balance is extended to:

1. Income statement debit

2. Balance sheet debit

3. Income statement credit

4. Balance sheet credit

Starter 4–3

1. Does this portion of the worksheet show a net income or a net loss? What is the amount of the net income or net loss?

Income Statement		Balance Sheet	
Dr	**Cr**	**Dr**	**Cr**
150,000	120,000	650,850	680,850
	30,000	30,000	
150,000	150,000	680,850	680,850

2. Complete this portion of the worksheet. What is the amount of the net income or net loss?

Income Statement		Balance Sheet	
Dr	**Cr**	**Dr**	**Cr**
194,000	223,500	416,800	387,300

Starter 4–4

Answer the following questions:

1. What type of balance does the Owner, Capital account have—debit or credit?

2. Which income statement account has the same type of balance as the Capital account?

3. Which type of income statement account has the opposite type of balance as the Capital account?

4. What do we call the difference between total debits and total credits on the income statement? Into what account is the difference figure closed at the end of the period?

Starter 4–5

Zhang Insurance started the year with a beginning capital balance of $25,000. During the year the business earned $40,000 of service revenue and incurred $21,000 of expenses. The owner withdrew $8,000 from the business. After the closing entries are recorded and posted, what will be the balance in the Capital account?

Starter 4–6

Indicate whether each of these accounts is permanent (P) or temporary (T):

_____ Accounts Receivable	_____ Equipment
_____ Accumulated Amortization	_____ Taxes Payable
_____ J. Lucas, Withdrawals	_____ J. Lucas, Capital
_____ Furniture	_____ Service Revenue
_____ Interest Expense	_____ Salaries Payable

Starter 4–7

It is December 31, 2017, and time to close the books. Journalize the following closing entries, with explanations, for Kaufman Services:

a. Service revenue, $15,000

b. A compound closing entry for all the expenses: Salaries, $3,500; Rent, $2,000; Advertising, $2,500

c. Income Summary

d. Brett Kaufman, Withdrawals, $3,200

Starter 4–8 This question should be completed by using the information in Starter 4–7.

1. Set up all the T–accounts in Starter 4–7 and insert their adjusted balances (denote as *Bal.*) at December 31, 2017. Also set up a T-account for Brett Kaufman, Capital, $10,500, and for Income Summary. Post the closing entries to the accounts, denoting posted amounts as *Clo.*

2. Compute the ending balance of Brett Kaufman, Capital.

Analyzing the overall effect of the closing entries on the owner's Capital account

③

2. B. Kaufman, Capital, $14,300

Starter 4–9 Lipsky Insurance Agency reported the following items at May 31:

Making closing entries

③

Sales and Marketing		Cash.................................	$1,000
Expense...........................	$1,600	Service Revenue	4,200
Other Assets.......................	500	Accounts Payable..........	300
Amortization Expense......	700	Rent Expense	400
C. Lipsky, Withdrawals....	200	Accounts Receivable.....	1,200
Long-Term Liabilities........	400	C. Lipsky, Capital..........	2,700
Insurance Expense	100		

Make Lipsky Insurance Agency's closing entries, as needed, for these accounts. Include explanations.

Starter 4–10 This starter should be used in conjunction with Starter 4–9. Use the data in Starter 4–9 to set up T-accounts for those accounts that Lipsky Insurance Agency closed on May 31. Insert their account balances prior to closing, post the closing entries to these accounts, and show each account's ending balance after closing. Also show the Income Summary T-account. Label a balance as *Bal.* and a closing entry amount as *Clo.*

Posting closing entries

③

Income Summary credit bal., $3,900

Starter 4–11 After closing its accounts at March 31, 2017, Watts Home Services had the following balances:

Preparing a post-closing trial balance

③

Post-closing trial bal. total, $15,200

Long-Term		Equipment.............................	$8,500
Liabilities	$1,600	Cash..	800
Other Assets.......................	1,600	Service Revenue	0
Accounts Receivable.........	4,000	Will Watts, Capital	8,900
Total Expenses	0	Supplies	300
Accounts Payable..............	1,800	Accumulated Amortization—	
Unearned Service		Equipment...........................	2,000
Revenue..........................	900		

Prepare Watts Home Services' post-closing trial balance at March 31, 2017. List accounts in the order shown in Exhibit 4–11 on page 188.

Starter 4–12 Fred was having a bad day. He was checking his work and discovered that instead of recording the payment of Telephone Expense in the amount of $645 to the right account, he had instead debited Salaries Expense by $465. Fred is unsure how to fix it. Prepare the two journal entries to make the correction on October 22.

Correct an error with two entries

④

Starter 4–13 Suppose a company made the following journal entry to pay for supplies purchased:

Correcting errors

④

Mar. 31	Accounts Receivable	200	
	Cash		200
	To pay for supplies purchased on account.		

Is this an error? If so, correct the error using both methods shown in this chapter. Provide an explanation for each journal entry.

Starter 4–14

Correcting errors

Starter 4–14 Suppose a company made the following journal entry to close its revenue accounts:

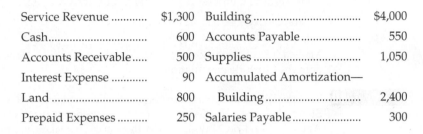

Nov. 30	Income Summary	60,000	
	Service Revenue		55,000
	Other Revenue		5,000
	To close the revenue accounts.		

Make the single journal entry to correct this error, then show the alternative way to correct it. Provide an explanation for each journal entry.

Classifying assets and liabilities as current or long term

Starter 4–15 Ink Jet Printing reported the following partial list of accounts:

Service Revenue	$1,300	Building	$4,000
Cash.................................	600	Accounts Payable	550
Accounts Receivable.....	500	Supplies	1,050
Interest Expense	90	Accumulated Amortization—	
Land	800	Building	2,400
Prepaid Expenses	250	Salaries Payable	300

1. Identify the assets (including contra assets) and liabilities.
2. Classify each asset and each liability as current or long term.

Classify accounts

Starter 4–16 Indicate where each of the following accounts would be reported in the financial statements for the year ended December 31, 2016:

1. _____ Prepaid Rent
2. _____ Unearned Revenue
3. _____ Note Payable (due June 30, 2019)
4. _____ Accounts Receivable
5. _____ Accounts Payable
6. _____ Accumulated Amortization
7. _____ Supplies
8. _____ Company Truck

a. Property, plant, and equipment
b. Current asset
c. Current liability
d. Long-term liability

Calculations involving account classifications

Current liabilities, $850

Starter 4–17 This starter should be used in conjunction with Starter 4–15. Examine Ink Jet Printing's account balances in Starter 4–15. Identify and compute the following amounts for Ink Jet Printing:
a. Total current assets
b. Book value of the building
c. Total current liabilities
d. Total long-term liabilities

Calculate ratios

Debt ratio = 0.30

Starter 4–18 Calculate the current ratio and the debt ratio for JK Consulting at December 31, 2017.

JK Consulting		
Balance Sheet		
December 31, 2017		
Assets		
Current assets:		
Cash		$27,200
Accounts receivable		4,000
Supplies		1,400
Prepaid rent		2,400
Total current assets		35,000
Property, plant, and equipment		
Furniture	31,200	
Less: accumulated amort.	7,800	23,400
Total assets		$58,400
Liabilities		
Current liabilities:		
Accounts payable		$15,800
Unearned service revenue		1,600
Total current liabilities		17,400
Owner's equity		
JK, capital		41,000
Total liabilities and owner's equity		$58,400

Starter 4–19 Daleyza Racing has these account balances at December 31, 2017:

Accounts Payable	$ 8,700	Note Payable,	
Accounts Receivable	12,500	Long-term	$18,000
Cash	6,500	Prepaid Rent	4,000
Accum. Amortization—		Salaries Payable	4,200
Equipment	8,000	Service Revenue	62,000
Equipment	24,000	Supplies	3,000

Compute Daleyza Racing's current ratio and debt ratio.

Computing the current ratio and the debt ratio

(6)

Current ratio = 2.02

Starter 4–20 This starter should be used in conjunction with Starter 4–19.

1. How much in *current* assets does Daleyza Racing have for every dollar of *current* liabilities that it owes? What ratio measures this relationship?
2. What percentage of Daleyza Racing's total assets are financed with debt? What is the name of this ratio?
3. What percentage of Daleyza Racing's total assets does the owner of the company actually own?

Computing and using the current ratio and the debt ratio

(6)

1. $2.02

Starter 4–21 Answer the following questions about IFRS:

1. What are the two main options (those illustrated in the chapter) for balance sheet presentation for companies following IFRS?
2. Explain what is meant by the term "reverse order of liquidity."

Balance sheet presentation under IFRS

(7)

3. What is another name for a balance sheet that may be used by corporations reporting under IFRS?

Canadian reporting
(7)

Starter 4–22 Why would a Canadian company reporting under IFRS choose to follow the traditional current then non-current approach for its balance sheet presentation rather than a non-current then current approach?

EXERCISES

MyAccountingLab

Excel Spreadsheet Template
Preparing a worksheet
(1)

Net income, $12,520

Exercise 4–1

The unadjusted trial balance of Overland Trekkers appears below:

OVERLAND TREKKERS Unadjusted Trial Balance September 30, 2017		
Cash	$ 14,240	
Accounts receivable	11,880	
Prepaid rent	2,400	
Supplies	6,780	
Equipment	65,200	
Accumulated amortization—equipment		$ 5,680
Accounts payable		10,320
Salaries payable		0
R. Puri, capital		72,060
R. Puri, withdrawals	6,000	
Service revenue		23,600
Amortization expense—equipment	0	
Salaries expense	3,600	
Rent expense	0	
Utilities expense	1,560	
Supplies expense	0	
Total	$111,660	$111,660

Additional information at September 30, 2017:

a. The business had sales that were not recorded yet in the amount of $840. It must accrue this service revenue.

b. Equipment Amortization in the amount of $260 needs to be recorded.

c. The business needs to accrue salaries expense of $2,100 for work done but not yet recorded.

d. Prepaid rent used in the amount of $1,200.

e. Supplies worth $3,200 were used up during the period.

Required Complete the Overland Trekkers worksheet for September 2017. What was net income for the month ended September 30, 2017?

Exercise 4–2

Journalizing adjusting and closing entries
(3)

Journalize the adjusting and closing entries for the company in Exercise 4–1. Include explanations.

Exercise 4–3

Set up T-accounts for only those accounts affected by the adjusting and closing entries in Exercise 4–1. Post the adjusting and closing entries from Exercise 4–2 to the accounts, identifying adjustment amounts as *Adj.*, closing amounts as *Clo.*, and balances as *Bal.* Double underline the accounts with zero balances after you close them and show the ending balance in each account.

Posting adjusting and closing entries

R. Puri, Capital bal., $78,580

Exercise 4–4

After completing Exercises 4–2 and 4–3, prepare the post-closing trial balance for Overland Trekkers at September 30, 2017.

Preparing a post-closing trial balance

Exercise 4–5

Hurst Canadian Trucking, a transportation company, reported the following items in a recent financial report:

Identifying and journalizing closing entries

Cash..................................	$ 2,917	Amortization Expense—	
Revenues	28,596	Equipment..............................	$2,090
Accounts Payable.........................	6,866	Equipment..............................	8,043
Accounts Receivable....................	1,692	Interest Expense	726
		Long-term Liabilities	5,647

Prepare Hurst Canadian Trucking's closing entries for the above accounts. Include explanations.

Exercise 4–6

Michael's Tennis reported the following selected accounts in its June 30, 2017, annual financial statements:

Identifying and journalizing closing entries

2. Michael Lucas, Capital bal., $135,600

Michael Lucas, Capital	$118,400	Interest Expense	$ 8,800
Service Revenue	356,400	Accounts Receivable....................	56,000
Unearned Revenues....................	5,400	Salaries Payable..........................	3,400
Salaries Expense	170,000	Amortization Expense................	40,800
Accumulated Amortization.......	140,000	Rent Expense..............................	23,600
Supplies Expense........................	11,800	Michael Lucas, Withdrawals	90,000
Interest Revenue.........................	5,800	Supplies	5,600

Required

1. Prepare the company's closing entries. Include explanations.
2. Prepare a T-account for Michael Lucas, Capital. What is the ending Capital balance at June 30, 2017?

Exercise 4–7

The accountant for Vishal's Sports Consulting has posted adjusting entries (a) through (e) to the accounts at December 31, 2017. All the revenue, expense, and owner's equity accounts of the entity are listed on the next page in T-account form.

Identifying and journalizing closing entries

2. V. Deep, Capital bal., $112,050

Required

1. Journalize Vishal's Sports Consulting's closing entries at December 31, 2017. Include explanations.
2. Determine Vishal's Sports Consulting's ending Capital balance at December 31, 2017.

Accounts Receivable

41,000	
(a) 7,250	

Supplies

6,000	(b)	5,500	

Accumulated Amortization—Furniture

	9,000
	(c) 1,650

Accumulated Amortization—Building

	49,500
	(d) 6,000

Salaries Payable

	(e) 1,050

V. Deep, Capital

	110,600

V. Deep, Withdrawals

122,100	

Service Revenue

	166,500
	(a) 7,250

Salaries Expense

36,000	
(e) 1,050	

Supplies Expense

(b) 5,500	

Amortization Expense—Furniture

(c) 1,650	

Amortization Expense—Building

(d) 6,000	

Exercise 4–8

Making closing entries

③

2. Net loss, $6,900

The adjusted trial balance for Paddy's Cell Systems follows:

PADDY'S CELL SYSTEMS Adjusted Trial Balance March 31, 2017		
Cash	$ 27,600	
Supplies	7,500	
Prepaid rent	3,600	
Office equipment	168,900	
Accumulated amortization—office equipment		$ 26,050
Accounts payable		29,300
Salaries payable		3,250
Unearned service revenue		17,600
P. O'Neill, capital		153,300
P. O'Neill, withdrawals	15,000	
Service revenue		61,000
Salaries expense	45,200	
Rent expense	15,650	
Amortization expense—office equipment	1,200	
Supplies expense	2,650	
Utilities expense	3,200	
	$290,500	$290,500

Required

1. Journalize the closing entries of Paddy's Cell Systems at March 31, 2017. Include explanations.

2. How much net income or net loss did Paddy's Cell Systems earn for March 2017? How can you tell?

Exercise 4-9

Unless your instructor states otherwise, you may use either one or two journal entries, with explanations, to make the following corrections:

Making correcting entries
④

1. Suppose HEC paid an account payable of $2,400 and erroneously debited Supplies. The error correction was recorded on June 5.

2. Suppose HEC made the following adjusting entry to record amortization:

May 31	Amortization Expense—Furniture	4,000	
	Furniture		4,000

3. Suppose, in closing the books to a profitable year, HEC made this closing entry:

Aug. 31	Income Summary	59,200	
	Service Revenue		59,200

Exercise 4-10

Prepare a correcting entry (or entries), with explanations, for each of the following accounting errors:

Correcting accounting errors
④

a. Debited Supplies and credited Accounts Payable for a $9,000 purchase of office equipment on account.

b. Accrued interest revenue of $3,000 by a debit to Accounts Receivable and a credit to Interest Revenue.

c. Adjusted prepaid rent by debiting Prepaid Rent and crediting Rent Expense for $4,000. This adjusting entry should have debited Rent Expense and credited Prepaid Rent for $4,000.

d. Debited Salary Expense and credited Accounts Payable to accrue salary expense of $12,000.

e. Recorded the earning of $7,800 service revenue collected in advance by debiting Accounts Receivable and crediting Service Revenue.

Exercise 4-11

Use the data from your solution to Exercise 4-8 to prepare Paddy's Cell Systems' classified balance sheet at March 31, 2017. Use the report format. You must compute the ending balance of P. O'Neill, Capital first.

Preparing a classified balance sheet
⑤
Total assets, $181,550

Exercise 4-12

Based on the following adjusted trial balance, prepare a classified balance sheet for Rowling Writers on December 31, 2017. (Hint: You will have to compute the owner's capital account balance on December 31, 2017, because the other financial statements are not being prepared.)

Preparing a classified balance sheet
⑤

ROWLING WRITERS Adjusted Trial Balance December 31, 2017		
	Debit	**Credit**
Cash	$29,200	
Accounts receivable	2,000	
Office supplies	1,400	
Prepaid insurance	2,400	
Building	30,100	
Accum. amort.—building		$ 3,900
Accounts payable		16,800

(Continued)

(Continued)

Taxes payable		1,900
Unearned service revenue		3,800
JK Rowling, Capital		41,000
JK Rowling, Withdrawals	9,800	
Service revenue		18,250
Advertising expense	2,800	
Amort. expense—building	1,300	
Supplies expense	1,100	
Insurance expense	2,650	
Utilities expense	2,900	
Total	$85,650	$85,650

Exercise 4–13

Assessing the current ratio and debt ratio
6

Refer to your solution to Exercise 4–11 (and the data in Exercise 4–8).

Required

Compute Paddy's Cell Systems' current ratio and debt ratio at March 31, 2017. One year ago the current ratio was 1.20 and the debt ratio was 0.30. Indicate whether Paddy's Cell Systems' ability to pay its debts has improved or deteriorated during the current year.

Exercise 4–14

Balance sheet presentation choices under International Financial Reporting Standards (IFRS)
7

The adapted balance sheets of two airlines from their 2013 annual reports are shown below. WestJet Airlines Ltd. is a Canadian corporation. British Airways Plc is a British airline. Both businesses follow IFRS. Review each balance sheet and describe at least three differences in their presentation.

WestJet Airlines Ltd. (thousands of Canadian dollars)			
Assets		**Liabilities and shareholders' equity**	
Current assets		**Current liabilities**	
Cash and cash equivalents	1,256,005	Accounts payable	543,167
Restricted cash	58,106	Advance ticket sales	551,022
Accounts receivable	42,164	Non-refundable guest credits	46,975
Prepaid expenses	133,263	Current portion of maintenance provisions	76,105
Inventory	36,722	Current portion of long-term debt	189,191
	1,526,260		1,406,460
Non-current assets		**Non-current liabilities**	
Property and equipment	2,487,734	Maintenance provisions	142,411
Intangible assets	58,691	Long-term debt	689,204
Other assets	70,778	Other liabilities (incl. deferred tax)	315,548
Total assets	4,143,463	**Total liabilities**	2,553,623
		Shareholders' equity	
		Share capital (incl. reserves)	673,045
		Retained earnings	916,795
		Total shareholders' equity	1,589,840
		Total liabilities and shareholders' equity	4,143,463

British Airways Plc
(millions of pounds)

Non-current assets		Shareholders' equity	
Property, plant, & equipment		Issued share capital	290
Fleet	6,456	Share premium	1,512
Property	816	Other reserves	453
Equipment	215	**Total shareholders' equity**	**2,255**
	7,487	Non-controlling interest	200
Intangibles		**Total equity**	**2,455**
Goodwill	40	**Non-current liabilities**	
Landing rights	668	Interest-bearing long-term borrowings	3,453
Emissions allowances	26	Employee benefit obligations	619
Software	147	Provisions for deferred tax	444
	881	Other provisions	185
Investments in associates	115	Derivative financial instruments	11
Available-for-sale financial assets	39	Other long-term liabilities	127
Employee benefit assets	407	**Total non-current liabilities**	**4,839**
Other non-current assets	67	**Current liabilities**	
Total non-current assets	**8,996**	Current portion of long-term borrowings	365
Non-current assets held for sale	**10**	Trade and other payables	4,073
Current assets and receivables		Derivative financial instruments	51
Inventories	110	Current tax payable	1
Trade receivables	533	Short-term provisions	137
Other current assets	338	**Total current liabilities**	**4,627**
Derivative financial instruments	84	**Total equity and liabilities**	**11,921**
Other current interest-bearing deposits	1,220		
Cash and cash equivalents	630		
Total current assets and receivables	**2,915**		
Total assets	**11,921**		

Journalizing reversing entries

Journalizing reversing entries

*Exercise 4–15

On December 31, 2017, Rexall Industries recorded an adjusting entry for $10,000 of accrued interest revenue. On January 15, 2018, the company received interest payments in the amount of $22,000. Assuming Rexall Industries uses reversing entries, prepare the 2017 and 2018 journal entries for these interest transactions.

*Exercise 4–16

On September 30, 2017, its fiscal year end, NS Services recorded an adjusting entry for $2,000 of interest it owes at year end and will include as part of its payment on October 31, 2017. On October 31, 2017, the company paid interest in the amount of $3,000. Assuming NS Services uses reversing entries, prepare the journal entries for these interest transactions.

---

*These Exercises cover Chapter 4 Appendix topics.

SERIAL EXERCISES

These exercises continue the Lee Management Consulting situation from Exercise 3–22 of Chapter 3. If you did not complete Exercise 3–22, you can complete Exercises 4–17 and 4–18 by following the instructions given in the notes below.

Exercise 4–17

Preparing a worksheet

Total balance sheet debits, $33,750

Refer to Exercise 3–22 of Chapter 3. Start from the unadjusted trial balance shown for Lee Management Consulting prepared at June 30, 2016:

LEE MANAGEMENT CONSULTING Unadjusted Trial Balance June 30, 2016		
	Debits	Credits
Cash	$ 23,750	
Accounts receivable	1,500	
Supplies	500	
Equipment	1,000	
Furniture	5,000	
Accounts payable		$ 5,000
Unearned revenue		2,000
Michael Lee, capital		25,000
Michael Lee, withdrawals	2,000	
Service revenue		5,000
Rent expense	3,000	
Utilities expense	250	
Total	$ 37,000	$37,000

At June 30, the company gathers the following information for the adjusting entries:

a. Accrued service revenue, $400.

b. Earned $800 of the service revenue collected in advance on June 21 for eight days of work.

c. Supplies remaining on hand at June 30, $100.

d. Amortization expense—equipment, $42; furniture, $167 (all amounts rounded to the nearest dollar).

e. Accrued $500 expense for the secretary's salary.

Required

1. Set up a worksheet using the unadjusted trial balance figures.

2. Enter the adjusting entries directly into the worksheet.

3. Complete all columns of the worksheet.

Exercise 4-18

Start from the adjusted trial balance shown below that Lee Management Consulting prepared at June 30, 2016:

Completing the accounting cycle and evaluating a business

② ③ ⑤ ⑥

2. Total assets, $31,541

LEE MANAGEMENT CONSULTING		
Adjusted Trial Balance		
June 30, 2016		
Cash	$23,750	
Accounts receivable	1,900	
Supplies	100	
Equipment	1,000	
Accumulated amortization— equipment		$ 42
Furniture	5,000	
Accumulated amortization—furniture		167
Accounts payable		5,000
Salaries payable		500
Unearned revenue		1,200
Michael Lee, capital		25,000
Michael Lee, withdrawals	2,000	
Service revenue		6,200
Amortization expense—equipment	42	
Amortization expense—furniture	167	
Rent expense	3,000	
Salaries expense	500	
Supplies expense	400	
Utilities expense	250	
Total	$38,109	$38,109

Required

1. Journalize, with explanations, and post to T-accounts the closing entries at June 30, 2016. Denote each closing amount as *Clo.* and account balance as *Bal.*

2. Prepare a classified balance sheet in report format at June 30, 2016.

3. Compute the current ratio and the debt ratio of Lee Management Consulting and evaluate these ratio values as indicative of a strong or weak financial position.

4. Prepare a post-closing trial balance at June 30, 2016.

CHALLENGE EXERCISES

Exercise 4-19

The unadjusted account balances of Stinson Consulting follow:

Computing financial statement amounts

② ⑤

1. Net income, $50,000

Cash	$ 1,900	Unearned Service Revenue	$ 5,300
Accounts Receivable	7,200	Scott Stinson, Capital	90,200
Supplies	2,100	Scott Stinson, Withdrawals	46,200
Prepaid Insurance	3,200	Service Revenue	80,600

Furniture......................................	8,400	Salary Expense..........................	22,700
Accumulated Amortization— Furniture................................	1,300	Amortization Expense— Furniture...............................	0
Building.......................................	53,800	Amortization Expense— Building.................................	0
Accumulated Amortization— Building..................................	14,900	Supplies Expense......................	0
Land..	51,200	Insurance Expense	0
Accounts Payable.....................	7,100	Utilities Expense......................	2,700

Adjusting data at the end of the year included the following:

a. Unearned service revenue that has been earned during the year, $4,600.

b. Work was completed but has not been invoiced. The company needs to accrue service revenue in the amount of $2,700.

c. Still need to record the supplies that were used up in operations, $1,900.

d. Employees have worked but have not been paid $2,400. The company needs to accrue salary expense.

e. Prepaid insurance was used up during the accounting period in the amount of $2,800.

f. Amortization expense that has not been recorded yet—furniture, $2,300; building, $3,100.

Scott Stinson, the proprietor of Stinson Consulting, has received an offer to sell his company. He needs to know the following information as soon as possible:

1. Net income for the year covered by these data

2. Total assets

3. Total liabilities

4. Total owner's equity

5. Proof that total assets equal total liabilities plus total owner's equity after all items are updated

Required Without opening any accounts, making any journal entries, or using a worksheet, provide Scott Stinson with the requested information. Show all computations.

*Exercise 4–20

Reversing entries

Refer to Exercise 4–19. Which adjusting entries (a, b, c, d, e, and/or f) can be reversed with reversing journal entries?

_____

*This Exercise covers Chapter 4 Appendix topics.

ETHICAL ISSUES

Discount Hardware wishes to expand its business and has borrowed $200,000 from the Royal Bank. As a condition for making this loan, the bank required Discount Hardware to maintain a current ratio of at least 1.50 and a debt ratio of no more than 0.50 and to submit annual financial statements to the bank.

Business during the third year has been good but not great. Expansion costs have brought the current ratio down to 1.40 and the debt ratio up to 0.51 at December 15. The managers of Discount Hardware are considering the implication of reporting this current ratio to the Royal Bank. One course of action that the managers are considering is to record in December of the third year some revenue on account that Discount Hardware will earn in January of next year. The contract for this job has been signed, and Discount Hardware will deliver the materials during January.

Required

1. Journalize the revenue transaction using your own numbers, and indicate how recording this revenue in December would affect the current ratio and the debt ratio.

2. State whether it is ethical to record the revenue transaction in December. Identify the accounting criteria relevant to this situation.

3. Propose an ethical course of action for Discount Hardware.

PROBLEMS (GROUP A)   MyAccountingLab

Problem 4–1A

The unadjusted trial balance of Dorset Roofing at July 31, 2017, appears below:

Preparing a worksheet
①
Net income, $115,770

DORSET ROOFING		
Unadjusted Trial Balance		
July 31, 2017		
Cash	$ 127,200	
Accounts receivable	226,920	
Supplies	105,960	
Prepaid insurance	23,800	
Equipment	196,140	
Accumulated amortization—equipment		$ 157,440
Building	257,340	
Accumulated amortization—building		63,000
Land	179,800	
Accounts payable		136,140
Interest payable		0
Wages payable		0
Unearned service revenue		63,360
Notes payable, long-term		134,400
T. Jackson, capital		474,780
T. Jackson, withdrawals	25,200	
Service revenue		141,140
Amortization expense—equipment	0	
Amortization expense—building	0	
Wages expense	19,200	
Insurance expense	0	
Interest expense	0	
Utilities expense	6,660	
Advertising expense	2,040	
Supplies expense	0	
Total	$1,170,260	$1,170,260

Additional data at July 31, 2017:

a. Amortization for the period to be recorded: equipment, $2,040; building, $4,210.

b. Wages expense to be recorded because employees worked but have not yet been paid, $3,440.

c. A count of supplies showed that unused supplies amounted to $88,440.

d. During July, $5,000 of prepaid insurance coverage was used.

e. Accrued interest expense, $2,080.

f. Of the $63,360 balance of Unearned Service Revenue, $29,820 was earned during July.

g. Accrued advertising expense, $2,600 (credit Accounts Payable).

h. The company performed $9,600 of services for a client and has not yet been paid.

Required Complete Dorset Roofing's worksheet for July. Identify each adjusting entry by its letter.

Problem 4–2A

The unadjusted trial balance of Silber Insurance Agency at August 31, 2017, appears below:

SILBER INSURANCE AGENCY Unadjusted Trial Balance August 31, 2017		
110 Cash	$142,800	
120 Accounts receivable	83,360	
130 Prepaid rent	7,740	
140 Supplies	5,400	
150 Furniture	92,100	
151 Accumulated amortization—furniture		$ 76,800
170 Building	449,400	
171 Accumulated amortization—building		161,600
180 Land	80,000	
210 Accounts payable		25,440
220 Salaries payable		0
230 Unearned commission revenue		53,400
300 C. Silber, capital		421,520
330 C. Silber, withdrawals	28,800	
400 Commission revenue		163,800
510 Salaries expense	6,600	
520 Rent expense	0	
530 Utilities expense	2,460	
540 Amortization expense—furniture	0	
550 Amortization expense—building	0	
560 Advertising expense	3,900	
570 Supplies expense	0	
Total	$902,560	$902,560

Adjustment data for month-end adjustments:

a. Commission revenue received in advance that had not been earned at August 31, $40,500.

b. Rent still prepaid at August 31, $2,300. (Hint: Calculate the amount of rent that was used up.)

c. Supplies used during the month, $2,040.

d. Amortization on furniture for the month, $2,220.

e. Amortization on building for the month, $2,780.

f. Accrue salary expense at August 31 in the amount of $2,760.

Required

1. Open ledger accounts for the accounts listed in the trial balance and insert their August 31 unadjusted balances. Also open the Income Summary account (account #340). Date the balances of the following accounts as of August 1: Prepaid Rent, Supplies, Furniture, Accumulated Amortization—Furniture, Building, Accumulated Amortization—Building, Unearned Commission Revenue, and C. Silber, Capital.

2. Write the trial balance on a worksheet and complete the worksheet of Silber Insurance Agency for the month ended August 31, 2017.

3. Using the worksheet data, journalize and post the adjusting and closing entries, including explanations. Use dates and posting references. Use Page 7 as the number of the journal page.

Problem 4–3A

The unadjusted T-accounts of Byford Systems at December 31, 2017, and the related year-end adjustment data are given below.

Taking the accounting cycle through the closing entries
① ② ③
2. Net income, $87,000

Cash			Accounts Receivable			Supplies		
Bal.	7,500		Bal.	54,000		Bal.	13,500	

Equipment			Accumulated Amortization—Equipment			Accounts Payable		
Bal.	148,500				Bal. 54,000			Bal. 9,000

Salary Payable			Unearned Service Revenue			Note Payable, Long-term		
		0			Bal. 7,500			Bal. 90,000

T. Byford, Capital			T. Byford, Withdrawals			Service Revenue		
		Bal. 54,000	Bal.	93,000				Bal. 223,500

Salary Expense			Supplies Expense			Rent Expense		
Bal.	79,500			0		Bal.	22,500	

Amortization Expense—Equipment			Interest Expense			Insurance Expense		
	0		Bal.	9,000		Bal.	10,500	

Adjustment data at December 31, 2017, include the following:

a. Of the $7,500 balance of Unearned Service Revenue at the beginning of the year, all of it except $500 was earned during the year.

b. Supplies still unused at year end, $3,000.

c. Amortization for the year, $13,000.

d. Accrued salary expense, $4,000.

e. Accrued service revenue, $5,500.

Required

1. Write the account data in the Trial Balance columns of a worksheet and complete the worksheet. Identify each adjusting entry by the letter corresponding to the data given.

2. Journalize the adjusting and closing entries. Include explanations.

Problem 4–4A

Accountants for Mainland Catering Service encountered the following situations while adjusting and closing the books at December 31. Consider each situation independently.

a. The company bookkeeper made the following entry to record a $4,900 credit purchase of office equipment:

Analyzing and journalizing corrections, adjustments, and closing entries
③ ④
d. Net income understated by $220

Nov. 12	Office Supplies	4,900	
	Accounts Payable		4,900

1. Correct the error by reversing the incorrect entry and preparing the correct entry on December 31. Include an explanation.

2. Prepare the correcting entry, dated December 31, without reversing the incorrect entry. Include an explanation.

b. A $9,000 credit to Accounts Receivable was posted as a debit.
  1. At what stage of the accounting cycle will this error be detected?
  2. Describe the technique for identifying the amount of the error.

c. The $88,500 balance of Equipment was entered as $8,850 on the trial balance.
  1. What is the name of this type of error?
  2. Assume this is the only error in the trial balance. Which will be greater, the total debits or the total credits, and by how much?
  3. How can this type of error be identified?

d. The accountant failed to make the following adjusting entries at December 31:
  1. Accrued property tax expense, $3,400.
  2. Supplies expense, $8,080.
  3. Accrued interest revenue on a note receivable, $7,800.
  4. Amortization of equipment, $11,400.
  5. Earned service revenue that had been collected in advance, $15,300.

  Compute the overall net income effect of these omissions.

e. Record each of the adjusting entries identified in item d. Include an explanation.

f. The revenue and expense accounts, *after* the adjusting entries had been posted, were Service Revenue, $115,200; Interest Revenue, $9,000; Salary Expense, $25,380; Rent Expense, $7,650; and Amortization Expense, $12,320. Two balances prior to closing were S. Jones, Capital, $72,900, and S. Jones, Withdrawals, $45,000. Journalize the closing entries. Include explanations.

Problem 4–5A

Completing the accounting cycle

② ③ ⑤

2. Post-closing trial balance total, $218,500

This problem should be used only in conjunction with Problem 4–3A. It completes the accounting cycle by posting to T-accounts and preparing the post-closing trial balance.

Required

1. Using the data in Problem 4–3A, post the adjusting and closing entries to the T-accounts, identifying adjusting amounts as *Adj.*, closing amounts as *Clo.*, and account balances as *Bal.*, as shown in Exhibit 4–10 (page 187). Double underline all accounts with a zero ending balance.

2. Prepare the post-closing trial balance.

3. Prepare a classified balance sheet at December 31, 2017.

Problem 4–6A

Preparing financial statements from an adjusted trial balance into an account format, journalizing closing entries, and evaluating a business

② ③ ⑤ ⑥

2. Net income, $48,779

The *adjusted* trial balance of Balti Design at June 30, 2017, the end of the company's fiscal year, appears below.

Required

1. Prepare the income statement and statement of owner's equity for the year ended June 30, 2017, and the classified balance sheet on that date. Use the account format for the balance sheet.

2. Journalize the closing entries.

3. Compute Balti Design's current ratio and debt ratio at June 30, 2017. One year ago the current ratio stood at 1.01 and the debt ratio was 0.71. Did Balti Design's ability to pay debts improve or deteriorate during the fiscal year?

BALTI DESIGN Adjusted Trial Balance June 30, 2017	
Cash	$ 12,610
Accounts receivable	15,882
Supplies	18,774
Prepaid insurance	1,920
Equipment	33,480

(*Continued*)

(Continued)

Accumulated amortization—equipment		$ 9,888
Building	68,940	
Accumulated amortization—building		10,110
Land	18,000	
Accounts payable		25,040
Interest payable		1,894
Wages payable		1,462
Unearned service revenue		1,380
Notes payable, long-term		58,200
A. Kapoor, capital		41,034
A. Kapoor, withdrawals	28,180	
Service revenue		83,916
Amortization expense—equipment	4,380	
Amortization expense—building	2,382	
Wages expense	13,882	
Insurance expense	1,860	
Interest expense	7,906	
Utilities expense	2,580	
Supplies expense	2,148	
Total	$232,924	$232,924

Problem 4–7A

The accounts of Bolton Travel at December 31, 2017, are listed below in alphabetical order:

Prepare a classified balance sheet in report format and calculate ratios
⑤ ⑥
Total assets, $388,300

Accounts Payable	$ 15,300		Interest Payable	$ 4,300
Accounts Receivable	19,800		Interest Receivable	1,600
Accumulated			Land	62,500
Amortization—Building	113,400		Notes Payable,	
Accumulated Amortization—			Long-term	91,400
Furniture	34,800		Notes Receivable,	
Advertising Expense	6,600		Long-term	12,500
Amortization Expense	3,900		Other Assets	9,300
Building	313,200		Other Current Liabilities	14,100
Cash	25,000		Prepaid Insurance	3,300
Commission Revenue	280,500		Prepaid Rent	12,700
E. Bolton, Capital	209,400		Salary Expense	73,800
E. Bolton, Withdrawals	143,800		Salary Payable	6,700
Furniture	68,100		Supplies	8,500
Insurance Expense	2,400		Supplies Expense	17,100
			Unearned Commission	
			Revenue	14,200

Required

1. Prepare the company's classified balance sheet in report format at December 31, 2017. *All adjustments have been journalized and posted, but the closing entries have not yet been made.*

2. Compute Bolton Travel's current ratio and debt ratio at December 31, 2017. At December 31, 2016, the current ratio was 1.52 and the debt ratio was 0.37. Did Bolton Travel's ability to pay both current and total debts improve or deteriorate during 2017?

Problem 4–8A

Len Thomas, the accountant for Lancaster Consulting, prepared the worksheet shown on the next page on a computer spreadsheet but has lost much of the data. The only particular item Thomas can recall is that there was an adjustment made to correct an error where $600 of supplies, purchased on credit, had been incorrectly recorded as $600 of equipment.

Preparing a worksheet, journalizing the adjustments, closing the accounts, assessing potential impact of IFRS
① ③ ④ ⑤ ⑥ ⑦
3. Total assets, $205,600

LANCASTER CONSULTING
Worksheet
For the Year Ended December 31, 2017

Account Title	Unadjusted Trial Balance Debit	Unadjusted Trial Balance Credit	Adjustments Debit	Adjustments Credit	Adjusted Trial Balance Debit	Adjusted Trial Balance Credit	Income Statement Debit	Income Statement Credit	Balance Sheet Debit	Balance Sheet Credit
Cash	19,000				19,000					
Accounts receivable	20,400				20,700					
Supplies	2,850			(b) 1,200						
Prepaid insurance	3,000				2,400					
Equipment	41,250				40,650					
Accum. amort.—equip.		3,600				5,400				
Building	90,000				90,000					
Accum. amort.—bldg.		6,000		(e) 3,000						
Land	45,000				45,000					
Accounts payable		7,500								
Interest payable		4,500								
Wages payable		1,800		(f) 900						
Unearned consulting fees		5,250	(g) 750							
Mortgage payable		75,000				75,000				
L. Lancaster, capital		61,500				61,500				
L. Lancaster, withdrawals	9,000				9,000				9,000	
Consulting fees earned		127,450				128,500				
Wages expense	50,250				51,150					
Insurance expense	6,600									
Interest expense	4,500									
Utilities expense	750				750					
Supplies expense			(b) 1,200		1,200					
Amort. exp.—equip.			(d) 1,800		1,800					
Amort. exp.—bldg.										
Totals	292,600	292,600								

Required

1. Complete the worksheet by filling in the missing data.
2. Journalize the closing entries that would be required on December 31, 2017. Include explanations.
3. Prepare the company's classified balance sheet at December 31, 2017, in report format.
4. Compute Lancaster Consulting's current ratio and debt ratio for December 31, 2017. On December 31, 2016, the current ratio was 2.14 and the debt ratio was 0.47. Comment on the changes in the ratios.
5. If this company reported under IFRS, how might the balance sheet presentation differ from that prepared in Requirement 3?

*Problem 4–9A

Refer to the data in Problem 4–2A, page 224.

Using reversing entries
Ⓐ1

Required

1. Open ledger accounts for Salaries Payable and Salaries Expense. Insert their unadjusted balances at August 31, 2017.
2. Journalize adjusting entry f and the closing entry for Salaries Expense at August 31. Include explanations. Post to the accounts.
3. On September 5, Silber Insurance Agency paid the next payroll amount of $3,480. Journalize this cash payment, with explanations, and post to the accounts. Show the balance in each account.
4. Repeat Requirements 1 through 3 using a reversing entry. Compare the balances of Salaries Payable and Salaries Expense computed by using a reversing entry with those balances computed without using a reversing entry (as they appear in your answer to Requirement 3).

*This Problem covers Chapter 4 Appendix topics.

PROBLEMS (GROUP B)   MyAccountingLab

Problem 4–1B

The new office assistant thought he would be helpful and create an alphabetical list of accounts for Aspen Arami Design at May 31, 2017.

Preparing a worksheet
①

	Debit	Credit
Accounts payable		$34,730
Accumulated amortization—building		34,560
Accumulated amortization—furniture		1,480
Advertising expense	$ 1,060	
Amortization expense—building		0
Amortization expense—furniture		0
Aspen Arami, capital		44,290
Aspen Arami, withdrawals	3,800	
Building	53,900	
Cash	18,670	
Design services revenue		26,970
Furniture	27,410	
Insurance expense	0	
Interest payable		0
Interest receivable	0	
Interest revenue		0
Land	43,700	
Notes payable, long-term		18,700
Notes receivable	10,340	
Prepaid insurance	5,790	
Salary expense	3,170	

(Continued)

(Continued)

Salary payable		0
Supplies	560	
Supplies expense	0	
Unearned design services revenue		8,800
Utilities expense	1,130	
Total	$169,530	$169,530

The following additional data at May 31, 2017, was identified and needs to be updated into the accounting records:

a. Amortization for the period, which needs to be recorded: furniture, $480; building, $660.

b. Accrued salary expense, $1,200.

c. A count of supplies showed that unused supplies amounted to $420.

d. During May, $1,390 of prepaid insurance coverage was used.

e. Loan interest expense of $220 was incurred but is not yet paid.

f. Of the $8,800 balance of Unearned Design Services Revenue, $4,000 was earned during May.

g. Advertising expense of $2,060 was incurred but is not yet recorded (credit Accounts Payable).

h. Earned interest revenue in the amount of $150, which had not yet been received.

Required Complete Aspen Arami Design's worksheet for May 2017. Identify each adjusting entry by its letter.

Excel Spreadsheet Template

Practise completing worksheets and closing

② ③

Problem 4–2B

The unadjusted trial balance of Stone Environmental Services at October 31, 2017, is shown below:

STONE ENVIRONMENTAL SERVICES Unadjusted Trial Balance October 31, 2017		
110 Cash	$ 32,050	
120 Accounts receivable	63,895	
130 Prepaid rent	9,900	
140 Supplies	3,780	
150 Furniture	140,735	
151 Accumulated amortization—furniture		$ 25,300
160 Building	307,350	
161 Accumulated amortization—building		49,450
180 Land	76,000	
210 Accounts payable		32,805
220 Salary payable		0
230 Unearned consulting revenue		23,850
300 K. Stone, capital		476,205
330 K. Stone, withdrawals	17,550	
400 Consulting revenue		56,520
510 Salary expense	8,280	
520 Rent expense	0	
530 Utilities expense	4,590	
540 Amortization expense—furniture	0	
550 Amortization expense—building	0	
570 Supplies expense	0	
Total	$664,130	$664,130

The data needed for the month-end adjustments are as follows:

a. Unearned consulting revenue that still had not been earned at October 31, $22,050.
b. Rent still prepaid at October 31, $6,000.
c. Supplies used during the month, $3,465.
d. Amortization on furniture for the month, $11,125.
e. Amortization on building for the month, $1,600.
f. Accrued salary expense at October 31, $4,395.

Required

1. Open ledgers for the accounts listed in the trial balance, inserting their October 31 unadjusted balances. Also open the Income Summary account (account #340). Date the balances of the following accounts October 1: Prepaid Rent, Supplies, Furniture, Accumulated Amortization—Furniture, Building, Accumulated Amortization—Building, Unearned Consulting Revenue, and K. Stone, Capital.

2. Write the trial balance on a worksheet and complete the worksheet of Stone Environmental Services for the month ended October 31, 2017.

3. Using the worksheet data, journalize and post the adjusting and closing entries, including explanations. Use dates and posting references. Use Page 12 as the number of the journal page.

Problem 4–3B

The unadjusted T-accounts of Super Media at December 31, 2017, are shown here. The related year-end adjustment data follow them.

Working through the accounting cycle
①②③

Cash		Accounts Receivable		Supplies	
Bal.	87,000	Bal.	132,000	Bal.	18,000

Equipment		Accumulated Amortization—Equipment		Accounts Payable	
Bal.	171,000		Bal. 36,000		Bal. 48,000

Salary Payable		Unearned Service Revenue		Notes Payable, Long-term	
	0		Bal. 6,000		Bal. 120,000

W. Super, Capital		W. Super, Withdrawals		Service Revenue	
	Bal. 123,000	Bal.	162,000		Bal. 390,000

Supplies Expense		Salary Expense		Insurance Expense	
	0	Bal.	108,000	Bal.	30,000

Amortization Expense—Equipment		Interest Expense	
	0	Bal.	15,000

Adjustment data at December 31, 2017, include the following:

a. Amortization for the year, $7,200.
b. Supplies still unused at year end, $7,000.
c. Accrued service revenue, $12,000.
d. Of the $6,000 balance of Unearned Service Revenue at the beginning of the year, $4,000 was earned during the year.
e. Accrued salary expense, $9,000.

Required

1. Write the account data in the Trial Balance columns of a worksheet and complete the worksheet. Identify each adjusting entry by the letter corresponding to the data given.
2. Journalize the adjusting and closing entries. Include explanations.

Analyzing and journalizing
corrections, adjustments, and
closing entries
③ ④

Problem 4–4B

The auditors of Cohen Logistics encountered the following situations while adjusting and closing the books at February 28. Consider each situation independently.

a. The company bookkeeper made the following entry to record a $2,790 credit purchase of supplies:

Feb. 26	Equipment	2,790	
	Accounts Payable		2,790

    1. Correct the error by reversing the incorrect entry and preparing the correct entry on February 28. Include explanations.

    2. Prepare the correcting entry, dated February 28, without reversing the incorrect entry. Include an explanation.

b. A $540 debit to Accounts Receivable was posted as $450.

    1. At what stage of the accounting cycle will this error be detected?

    2. Describe the technique for identifying the amount of the error.

c. The $3,480 balance of Utilities Expense was entered as $34,800 on the trial balance.

    1. What is the name of this type of error?

    2. Assume this is the only error in the trial balance. Which will be greater, the total debits or the total credits, and by how much?

    3. How can this type of error be identified?

d. The accountant failed to make the following adjusting entries at February 28:

    1. Accrued service revenue, $10,800.

    2. Insurance expense that had been prepaid, $3,160.

    3. Accrued interest expense on a note payable, $6,240.

    4. Amortization of equipment, $22,250.

    5. Earned service revenue that had been collected in advance, $8,130.

    Compute the overall net income effect of these five omissions.

e. Record each of the adjusting entries identified in item d. Include explanations.

f. The revenue and expense accounts after the adjusting entries had been posted were Service Revenue, $199,995; Wages Expense, $78,325; Amortization Expense, $30,540; and Insurance Expense, $1,860. Two balances prior to closing were N. Cohen, Capital, $137,725, and N. Cohen, Withdrawals, $111,000. Journalize the closing entries.

Problem 4–5B

This problem should be used only in conjunction with Problem 4–3B. It completes the accounting cycle by posting to T-accounts and preparing the post-closing trial balance.

Required

1. Using the data in Problem 4–3B, post the adjusting and closing entries to the T-accounts, identifying adjusting amounts as *Adj.*, closing amounts as *Clo.*, and account balances as *Bal.*, as shown in Exhibit 4–10 (page 187). Double underline all accounts with a zero ending balance.

2. Prepare the post-closing trial balance.

3. Prepare the classified balance sheet at December 31, 2017.

Problem 4–6B

Preparing financial statements
from an adjusted trial balance,
journalizing adjusting and
closing entries, evaluating a
business
② ③ ⑤ ⑥

The adjusted trial balance of Musquem Golf School at April 30, 2017, the end of the company's fiscal year, is shown on the next page.

Required

1. Prepare Musquem Golf School's income statement and statement of owner's equity for the year ended April 30, 2017, and the classified balance sheet on that date. Use the account format for the balance sheet.

2. Journalize the closing entries. Include explanations.

3. Compute Musquem Golf School's current ratio and debt ratio at April 30, 2017. One year ago, the current ratio stood at 1.21, and the debt ratio was 0.82. Did Musquem Golf School's ability to pay debts improve or deteriorate during fiscal 2017?

MUSQUEM GOLF SCHOOL
Adjusted Trial Balance
April 30, 2017

Cash	$ 3,740	
Accounts receivable	87,480	
Supplies	7,380	
Prepaid insurance	4,580	
Equipment	127,860	
Accumulated amortization—equipment		$ 56,860
Building	148,660	
Accumulated amortization—building		36,520
Land	40,000	
Accounts payable		41,100
Interest payable		5,560
Wages payable		2,660
Unearned teaching revenue		7,320
Notes payable, long-term		139,800
J. Wilson, capital		128,400
J. Wilson, withdrawals	56,000	
Teaching revenue		197,100
Amortization expense—equipment	13,800	
Amortization expense—building	7,420	
Wages expense	66,620	
Insurance expense	10,740	
Interest expense	17,340	
Utilities expense	9,940	
Supplies expense	13,760	
Total	$615,320	$615,320

Problem 4–7B

The accounts of Wing Telecom Fundamentals at March 31, 2017, are listed in alphabetical order here:

Preparing a classified balance sheet in report format, evaluating a business ⑤ ⑥

Accounts Payable	$31,760	Interest Receivable	$ 720	
Accounts Receivable	9,200	Land	23,000	
Accumulated Amortization—Building	37,840	Notes Payable, Long-term	22,560	
Accumulated Amortization—Furniture	6,160	Notes Receivable, Long-term	5,520	
Advertising Expense	720	Other Assets	16,840	
Amortization Expense	1,520	Other Current Liabilities	880	
A. Wing, Capital	40,560	Prepaid Insurance	480	
A. Wing, Withdrawals	24,960	Prepaid Rent	3,760	
Building	44,720	Salary Expense	14,240	
Cash	27,720	Salary Payable	11,920	
Furniture	34,560	Service Revenue	56,880	
Insurance Expense	480	Supplies	3,040	
Interest Payable	5,240	Supplies Expense	3,680	
		Unearned Service Revenue	1,360	

Required

1. *All adjustments have been journalized and posted, but the closing entries have not yet been made.* Prepare the company's classified balance sheet in report format at March 31, 2017. Use captions for total assets, total liabilities, and total liabilities and owner's equity.
2. Compute Wing Telecom Fundamentals' current ratio and debt ratio at March 31, 2017. At March 31, 2016, the current ratio was 1.28 and the debt ratio was 0.32. Did Wing Telecom Fundamentals' ability to pay both current and total debts improve or deteriorate during fiscal 2017?

Problem 4–8B

Preparing a worksheet, journalizing the adjustments, closing the accounts, assessing the potential impact of IFRS
① ③ ④ ⑤ ⑥ ⑦

Mark Hanson, the accountant for Glenn Graphics, had prepared the worksheet shown below on a computer spreadsheet but has lost much of the data. The only particular item the accountant can recall is that an adjustment was made to correct an error where $900 of supplies, purchased on credit, had been incorrectly recorded as $9,000 of equipment.

GLENN GRAPHICS

Worksheet

For the Year Ended December 31, 2017

Account Title	Unadjusted Trial Balance Dr	Unadjusted Trial Balance Cr	Adjustments Dr	Adjustments Cr	Adjusted Trial Balance Dr	Adjusted Trial Balance Cr	Income Statement Dr	Income Statement Cr	Balance Sheet Dr	Balance Sheet Cr
Cash	18,000				18,000					
Accounts receivable	34,050				34,200					
Supplies	2,100			(b) 1,050						
Prepaid insurance	2,400				2,100					
Equipment	39,000				30,000					
Accum. amort.—equip.		4,500				6,750				
Building	129,000				129,000					
Accum. amort.—bldg.		36,900		(e) 3,450						
Land	36,000				36,000					
Accounts payable		24,000				15,900				
Wages payable		1,350		(f) 600						
Interest payable		3,000								
Unearned revenues		4,050	(g) 600							
Mortgage payable		60,000				60,000				
W. Glenn, capital		118,500				118,500				
W. Glenn, withdrawals	37,000				37,000				37,000	
Graphics fees earned		147,650				148,400				
Wages expense	85,050				85,650					
Insurance expense	3,300									
Interest expense	13,000									
Utilities expense	1,050				1,050					
Supplies expense			(b) 1,050		1,050					
Amort. exp.—equip.			(d) 2,250		2,250					
Amort. exp.—bldg.										
Totals	399,950	399,950								

Required

1. Complete the worksheet by filling in the missing data.

2. Journalize the closing entries that would be required on December 31, 2017. Include explanations.

3. Prepare the company's classified balance sheet as of December 31, 2017, in report format.

4. Compute Glenn Graphics' current ratio and debt ratio for December 31, 2017. On December 31, 2016, the current ratio was 2.25 and the debt ratio was 0.41. Comment on the changes in the ratios.

5. If the company were reporting under IFRS, how might the balance sheet presentation differ from the one prepared in Requirement 3?

*Problem 4–9B

Refer to the data in Problem 4–3B on page 231.

Using reversing entries

Required

1. Open ledger accounts for Accounts Receivable and Service Revenue. Insert their unadjusted balances at December 31, 2017.

2. Journalize the adjusting entry c only and the resulting closing entry for Service Revenue at December 31, 2017. Include explanations. Post to the accounts.

3. On January 10, 2018, Super Media received a payment of $12,000 in settlement of this invoice. Journalize this cash receipt, including an explanation, and post to the accounts. Show the balance in each account.

4. Repeat Requirements 1 through 3 using a reversing entry. Compare the balances of Accounts Receivable and Service Revenue computed by using a reversing entry with those balances computed without using a reversing entry (as they appear in your answer to Requirement 3).

---

*This Problem covers Chapter 4 Appendix topics.

CHALLENGE PROBLEMS

Problem 4–1C

The following errors were made by Classy Catering's new bookkeeper:

Identifying and correcting errors ④

a. A debit of $3,000 was recorded as an account receivable instead of a note receivable.

b. A salary expense accrual in the amount of $14,400 was overlooked when the worksheet was prepared.

c. A catering service revenue accrual of $10,770 was not recorded.

How would you correct these errors if they occurred:

1. After completing the worksheet but before the financial statements were prepared (the accounts have not yet been closed)? Adjust only the accounts affected. (Do not use reversing entries for the corrections.)

2. After closing entries were completed?

Problem 4–2C

It is July 15, 2017. A friend who works in the office of a local company that has four fast-food restaurants has come to you with a question. She knows you are studying accounting and asks if you could help her sort something out. She acknowledges that although she has worked for the company for three years as a general clerk, she really does not understand the accounting work she is doing.

Understanding the current ratio ⑥

The company has a large bank loan and, as your friend understands it, the company has agreed with the bank to maintain a current ratio (she thinks that is what it is called) of 1.8 to 1 (1.8:1). The company's year end is June 30. The owner came to her on July 7, 2017, and asked her to issue a batch of cheques to suppliers but to date them June 30. Your friend recognizes that the cheques will have an effect on the June 30, 2017, financial statements but doesn't think the effect will be too serious.

Required Explain to your friend what the effect of paying invoices after June 30 but dating the cheques prior to June 30 has on the current ratio. Provide an example to illustrate your explanation.

EXTENDING YOUR KNOWLEDGE

DECISION PROBLEMS

Decision Problem 1

Completing the accounting cycle
to develop the information for a
bank loan

④ ⑥

Net income, $65,110; Ending
owner's equity, $42,480

One year ago your friend Don Jenner founded Jenner Consulting Services. The business has prospered. Jenner, who remembers that you took an accounting course while in university, comes to you for advice. He wishes to know how much net income his business earned during the past year. He also wants to know what the entity's total assets, liabilities, and owner's equity are. The accounting records consist of the T-accounts of the company's ledger, which were prepared by a bookkeeper who moved to another city. The ledger at December 31, 2017, appears as follows:

Cash		Accounts Receivable		Prepaid Rent	
Dec. 31 8,745		Dec. 31 18,540		Jan. 2 9,200	

Supplies		Computer Equipment		Accumulated Amortization—Equipment	
Jan. 2 7,800		Jan. 2 65,400			0

Accounts Payable		Unearned Service Revenue		Salaries Payable	
	Dec. 31 27,810		Dec. 31 11,195		0

D. Jenner, Capital		D. Jenner, Withdrawals		Service Revenue	
	Jan. 2 42,500	Dec. 31 65,130			Dec. 31 121,110

Amortization Expense—Equipment		Salaries Expense		Supplies Expense	
0		Dec. 31 25,500		0	

Rent Expense		Utilities Expense	
0		Dec. 31 2,300	

Jenner indicates that at year end customers owe the company $4,800 accrued service revenue, which he expects to collect early next year. These revenues have not been recorded. During the year, the company collected $11,195 service revenue in advance from customers, but the company earned only $1,800 of that amount. Rent expense for the year was $7,200, and the company used up $6,300 in supplies. Jenner estimates that amortization on the equipment was $17,700 for the year. At December 31, Jenner Consulting owes an employee $3,600 accrued salary.

Jenner expresses concern that his withdrawals during the year might have exceeded the business's net income. To get a loan to expand the business, Jenner must show the bank that Jenner Consulting's owner's equity has grown from its original $42,500 balance. Has it? You and Jenner agree that you will meet again in one week. Perform the analysis and prepare the financial statements to answer his questions.

Decision Problem 2

You are preparing the financial statements for the year ended October 31, 2017, for Cusik Publishing Company, a weekly newspaper. You began with the trial balance of the ledger, which balanced, and then made the required adjusting entries. To save time, you omitted preparing an adjusted trial balance. After making the adjustments on the worksheet, you extended the balances from the trial balance, adjusted for the adjusting entries, and computed amounts for the Income Statement and Balance Sheet columns.

Finding an error in the worksheets

a. When you added the debits and credits in the Income Statement columns, you found that the credits exceeded the debits by $15,000. According to your finding, did Cusik Publishing Company have a profit or a loss?

b. You took the balancing amount from the Income Statement columns to the Balance Sheet debit column and found that the total debits exceeded the total credits in the balance sheet. The difference between the total debits and the total credits on the balance sheet is $30,000, which is two times the amount of the difference you calculated for the Income Statement columns. What is the cause of this difference? (Except for these errors, everything else is correct.)

FINANCIAL STATEMENT CASES

Financial Statement Case 1

This case, based on Indigo Books & Music Inc.'s (Indigo's) balance sheet in Appendix A at the end of this book and on MyAccountingLab, will familiarize you with some of the assets and liabilities of this company. Answer these questions, using the company's balance sheet and other information.

Reading a balance sheet of a publicly traded corporation
⑤ ⑥
4. March 29, 2014, current ratio, 1.96

Required

1. Compare Indigo's balance sheet to the balance sheet in Exhibit 4–14 on page 193. What differences in style do you notice between these two balance sheets? Describe these differences.

2. What was the value of Indigo's total current assets in 2014? In 2013?

3. What was the value of the total current liabilities in 2014? In 2013?

4. Compute Indigo's current ratio at March 29, 2014, and at March 30, 2013. Did the ratio improve or deteriorate during the year?

5. Compute Indigo's debt ratio for the fiscal years ended 2014 and 2013. Did the ratio improve or deteriorate during the year?

Financial Statement Case 2

This case, based on TELUS Corporation's balance sheet on MyAccountingLab, will familiarize you with some of the assets and liabilities of this company. Answer these questions, using TELUS Corporation's balance sheet.

Working with a balance sheet for a corporation
⑤ ⑥
7. Dec. 31, 2013, debt ratio, 0.63

Required

1. Compare TELUS's balance sheet (consolidated statement of financial position) to the balance sheet in Exhibit 4–14 on page 193. What differences in style do you notice between these two balance sheets? Describe these differences.

2. What was TELUS's largest current asset in 2013? In 2012?

3. What was the company's largest current liability in 2013? In 2012?

4. What were total current assets in 2013? In 2012?

5. What were total current liabilities in 2013? In 2012?

6. Compute TELUS's current ratio at December 31, 2013, and at December 31, 2012. Did the ratio values improve or deteriorate during the year?

7. Compute TELUS's debt ratio at December 31, 2013, and at December 31, 2012. Did the ratio values improve or deteriorate during the year?

IFRS MINI-CASE

IFRS balance sheet presentation

⑤ ⑦

Prepare the balance sheet for Makincomp Incorporated using the trial balance information provided. Assume that the company follows IFRS and the preferred presentation is the non-current then current format. Use the British Airways Plc balance sheet found on page 219 as your guide.

Hint: The owners' equity of a corporation is the total of two accounts: Common Shares and Retained Earnings.

MAKINCOMP INCORPORATED		
Post-Closing Trial Balance		
May 31, 2017		
Cash	$ 127,200	
Accounts receivable	226,920	
Supplies	105,960	
Prepaid insurance	23,800	
Equipment	196,140	
Accumulated amortization—equipment		$ 157,440
Building	257,340	
Accumulated amortization—building		63,000
Land	179,800	
Accounts payable		136,140
Unearned service revenue		63,360
Notes payable, long-term		134,400
Common shares		449,580
Retained earnings		113,240
Total	$1,117,160	$1,117,160

Try It! SOLUTIONS FOR CHAPTER 4

1.

	Income Statement		Balance Sheet	
	Debit	Credit	Debit	Credit
a. Cash			✓	
b. Supplies			✓	
c. Supplies Expense	✓			
d. Unearned Revenue				✓
e. Service Revenue		✓		
f. Owner's Equity				✓

2. Using the trial balance given, write the account titles in the first column of the worksheet and the amounts in the Trial Balance columns, ensuring debit and credit balances on the trial balance are debit and credit balances on the worksheet. To make sure all the account balances have been entered correctly, trace each worksheet balance back to the December 31, 2017, trial balance.

When calculating the Adjusted Trial Balance amounts, remember to add and subtract the adjustments properly. For assets, withdrawals, and expenses, add debits and subtract credits. For contra assets, liabilities, owner's equity, and revenues, add credits and subtract debits.

SIGRID'S OFF ROAD ADVENTURES										
Worksheet										
December 31, 2017										
	Unadjusted Trial Balance		Adjustments		Adjusted Trial Balance		Income Statement		Balance Sheet	
	Dr	Cr	Dr	Cr	Dr	Cr	Dr	Cr	Dr	Cr
Cash	6,000				6,000				6,000	
Accounts receivable	5,000		(e) 1,300		6,300				6,300	
Supplies	1,000			(a) 800	200				200	
Furniture	10,000				10,000				10,000	
Accum. amort.—furniture		4,000		(b) 2,500		6,500				6,500
Building	60,000				60,000				60,000	
Accum. amort.—building		30,000		(c) 1,500		31,500				31,500
Land	20,000				20,000				20,000	
Accounts payable		2,000				2,000				2,000
Salary payable		0		(d) 600		600				600
Unearned service revenue		8,000	(f) 2,000			6,000				6,000
Sigrid Chu, capital		40,000				40,000				40,000
Sigrid Chu, withdrawals	25,000				25,000				25,000	
Service revenues		60,000		(e) 1,300		63,300		63,300		
				(f) 2,000						
Salary expense	16,000		(d) 600		16,600		16,600			
Supplies expense			(a) 800		800		800			
Amort. exp.—furniture			(b) 2,500		2,500		2,500			
Amort. exp.—building			(c) 1,500		1,500		1,500			
Miscellaneous expense	1,000				1,000		1,000			
Total	144,000	144,000	8,700	8,700	149,900	149,900	22,400	63,300	127,500	86,600
Net income							40,900			40,900
							63,300	63,300	127,500	127,500

3.

SIGRID'S OFF ROAD ADVENTURES
Income Statement
For the Month Ended December 31, 2017

Revenues:		
Service revenue		$63,300
Expenses:		
Amortization expense—furniture	$ 2,500	
Amortization expense—building	1,500	
Miscellaneous expense	1,000	
Salary expense	16,600	
Supplies expense	800	
Total expenses		22,400
Net income		$40,900

SIGRID'S OFF ROAD ADVENTURES
Statement of Owner's Equity
For the Year Ended December 31, 2017

Sigrid Chu, capital, January 1, 2017	$40,000
Add: Net income	40,900
	80,900
Less: Withdrawals	25,000
Sigrid Chu, capital, December 31, 2017	$55,900

SIGRID'S OFF ROAD ADVENTURES
Balance Sheet
December 31, 2017

Assets		
Cash		$ 6,000
Accounts receivable		6,300
Supplies		200
Furniture	$10,000	
Less: Accumulated amortization	6,500	3,500
Building	60,000	
Less: Accumulated amortization	31,500	28,500
Land		20,000
Total assets		$64,500
Liabilities		
Accounts payable		$ 2,000
Salary payable		600
Unearned service revenue		6,000
Total liabilities		8,600
Owner's Equity		
Sigrid Chu, capital		55,900
Total liabilities and owner's equity		$64,500

4. Journalizing Adjusting Entries

Page 4

Dec. 31	Supplies Expense		800	
	Supplies			800
	To record supplies used.			
31	Amortization Expense—Furniture		2,500	
	Accumulated Amortization— Furniture			2,500
	To record amortization on furniture.			
31	Amortization Expense—Building		1,500	
	Accumulated Amortization— Building			1,500
	To record amortization on building.			
31	Salary Expense		600	
	Salary Payable			600
	To accrue salary expense.			
31	Accounts Receivable		1,300	
	Service Revenue			1,300
	To accrue service revenue.			
31	Unearned Service Revenue		2,000	
	Service Revenue			2,000
	To record unearned revenue that has been earned.			

Posting the Adjustments to the Revenue and Expense Accounts

REVENUE

Service Revenue

		Bal.	60,000	
		Adj.	1,300	
		Adj.	2,000	
		Bal.	63,300	

EXPENSES

Salary Expense

Bal.	16,000	
Adj.	600	
Bal.	16,600	

Supplies Expense

Adj.	800	
Bal.	800	

Amort. Exp.—Furniture

Adj.	2,500	
Bal.	2,500	

Amort. Exp.—Building

Adj.	1,500	
Bal.	1,500	

Miscellaneous Expense

Bal.	1,000	
Bal.	1,000	

Adj. = Amount posted from
     an adjusting entry

Bal. = Balance

5. Journalizing and Posting the Closing Entries

Dec.	31	Service Revenue	63,300	
		Income Summary		63,300
		To close the revenue account and create the Income Summary account.		
	31	Income Summary	22,400	
		Salary Expense		16,600
		Supplies Expense		800
		Amortization Expense—Furniture		2,500
		Amortization Expense—Building		1,500
		Miscellaneous Expense		1,000
		To close the expense accounts.		
	31	Income Summary	40,900	
		Sigrid Chu, Capital		40,900
		To close the Income Summary account and transfer net income to the Capital account (Income Summary balance = $63,300 − $22,400).		
	31	Sigrid Chu, Capital	25,000	
		Sigrid Chu, Withdrawals		25,000
		To close the Withdrawals account and transfer the Withdrawals amount to the Capital account.		

Service Revenue

			Bal.	60,000
			Adj.	1,300
			Adj.	2,000
Clo.	63,300		Bal.	63,300

Salary Expense

Bal.	16,000		
Adj.	500		
Bal.	16,500	Clo.	16,500

Supplies Expense

Adj.	800		
Bal.	800	Clo.	800

Amort. Exp.—Furniture

Adj.	2,000		
Bal.	2,000	Clo.	2,000

Amort. Exp.—Building

Adj.	1,000		
Bal.	1,000	Clo.	1,000

Miscellaneous Expense

Bal.	1,000		
Bal.	1,000	Clo.	1,000

Income Summary

Clo.	22,400	Clo.	63,300
Clo.	40,900	Bal.	40,900

S. Chu, Withdrawals

Bal.	25,000	Clo.	25,000

S. Chu, Capital

Clo.	25,000	Bal.	40,000
		Clo.	40,900
		Bal.	55,900

Adj. = Amount posted from an adjusting entry
Clo. = Amount posted from a closing entry
Bal. = Balance

6.

SIGRID'S OFF ROAD ADVENTURES		
Post-Closing Trial Balance		
December 31, 2017		
Cash	$ 6,000	
Accounts receivable	6,300	
Supplies	200	
Furniture	10,000	
Accumulated amortization—furniture		$ 6,500
Building	60,000	
Accumulated amortization—building		31,500
Land	20,000	
Accounts payable		2,000
Salary payable		600
Unearned service revenue		6,000
Sigrid Chu, Capital		55,900
Totals	$102,500	$102,500

8.

Mark Wearing, capital	$14,160	—
Cash	23,600	current asset
Furniture	11,200	long-term asset
Accounts payable	11,200	current liability
Accumulated amortization— equipment	200	long-term contra asset
Accounts receivable	7,600	current asset
Equipment	7,000	long-term asset
Salaries payable	1,400	current liability
Accumulated amortization— furniture	240	long-term contra asset
Mortgage payable (current)	1,000	current liability
Unearned service revenue	2,400	current liability
Supplies	200	current asset
Mortgage payable (current and long-term)	20,000	long-term liability of $19,000

7. With one entry:

Accounts Receivable	200	
Accounts Payable		200
To correct a previous journal entry. Accounts Receivable had been debited in error for a purchase of supplies on account.		

With two journal entries:

Accounts Receivable	200	
Supplies		200
To reverse incorrect entry.		

Supplies	200	
Accounts Payable		200
To record purchase correctly as supplies.		

9.

MARK WEARING ENGINEERS		
Balance Sheet		
December 31, 2017		
Assets		
Current assets:		
Cash	$23,600	
Accounts receivable	7,600	
Supplies	200	
Total current assets		$31,400
Property, plant, and equipment		
Equipment	7,000	
Less: Accumulated amortization—equipment	200	6,800
Furniture	11,200	
Less: Accumulated amortization—furniture	240	10,960
Total property, plant, and equipment		17,760
Total assets		$49,160
Liabilities		
Current liabilities:		
Accounts payable	$11,200	
Salaries payable	1,400	
Unearned service revenue	2,400	
Current portion of mortgage payable	1,000	
Total current liabilities		16,000
Long-term liabilities:		
Mortgage payable	20,000	
Less: current portion of mortgage payable	1,000	
Total long-term liabilities		19,000
Total liabilities		35,000
Owner's Equity		
Mark Wearing, capital		14,160
Total liabilities and owner's equity		$49,160

10. Current ratio = Total current assets ÷ Total current liabilities
        = $31,400 ÷ $16,000
        = 1.96

   Debt ratio = Total liabilities ÷ Total assets
        = $35,000 ÷ $49,160
        = 0.71

Mark's current ratio would be considered acceptable. It indicates that the business could adequately meet its debt obligations. The debt ratio is acceptable but possibly a little high. This means that lenders are financing 71 percent of Mark's assets.

5 MERCHANDISING OPERATIONS

CONNECTING CHAPTER 5

LEARNING OBJECTIVE (A2) Compute the cost of goods sold under the periodic inventory system

How do we compute the cost of goods sold amount under the periodic inventory system?

Cost of Goods Sold, page 275

LEARNING OBJECTIVE (A3) Adjust and close the accounts of a merchandising business under the periodic inventory system

How do we update inventory using the year-end physical count and begin the next cycle using the periodic inventory system?

Adjusting and Closing the Accounts in a Periodic Inventory System, page 276

LEARNING OBJECTIVE (A4) Prepare a merchandiser's financial statements under the periodic inventory system

How can we prepare financial statements for a company using the periodic inventory system?

Preparing the Financial Statements of a Merchandiser, page 279

LEARNING OBJECTIVE (B1) Compare the perpetual and periodic inventory systems

Chapter 5 APPENDIX B

How do the inventory systems compare?

Comparing the Perpetual and Periodic Inventory Systems, page 283

MyAccountingLab   The **Summary** for Chapter 5 appears on page 285. This lists all of the MyAccountingLab resources. **Accounting Vocabulary** with definitions for this chapter's material appears on page 287.

Security is such an important area of risk management for companies competing in today's business environment. Inventory also plays a central role in the success of a merchandising organization. Avigilon Corporation, founded in 2004, provides an interesting example of a company that successfully combines the businesses of security, technology, and inventory merchandising to provide "end-to-end surveillance solutions."

The company manufactures and sells high-definition video management software, mega-pixel cameras, access control, and video analytics products. This is a growing global industry.

Through innovative security solutions and sound inventory management, Avigilon has continued to grow. The company was named Canada's fastest-growing company by *Profit Magazine* in 2013 and generated revenue in 2012 of $100.3 million with net income of $7.2 million. At that time, its gross margin percentage, which is the profit on selling goods and services before expenses, was 49 percent. By the end of 2014, the company increased sales to more than $270 million and its gross margin percentage improved to 57 percent. And net income? It grew to more than $35 million.

Organizations are evaluated on their ability to increase profits. As you can see from the Avigilon example, buying and selling inventory plays a big part in this success. This chapter will illustrate how to record the purchase and sale of goods as well as evaluating how companies make decisions about pricing and stocking inventory.[1]

> **What** comes to mind when you think of *merchandising?* You are familiar with Canadian retailers who sell you the clothing you purchase at a clothing store, the bread you buy at the grocery store, or the gas you purchase at your local service station. Merchandisers include the Hudson's Bay Company, Canadian Tire Corporation, Avigilon Corporation, Shoppers Drug Mart Corporation, and BlackBerry Limited.

How do the operations of merchandisers differ from those of the businesses we have studied so far? In the first four chapters, Hunter Environmental Consulting (HEC) provided an illustration of a business that earns revenue by selling its services. Service enterprises include hotels, airlines, physicians, lawyers, public accountants, and the 12-year-old who cuts lawns in your neighbourhood. A *merchandising entity* earns its revenue by selling products, called *merchandise inventory* or, simply, **inventory**.

This chapter demonstrates the central role of inventory in a business, which includes all goods that the company owns and expects to sell to customers in the normal course of operations. Some businesses, such as department stores, gas stations, and grocery stores, buy their inventory ready for sale to customers. Others, such as Big Rock Brewery Inc. and BlackBerry Ltd., manufacture their own products. Both groups primarily sell products rather than services.

Chapter 5 introduces merchandising. We show how to account for the purchase and sale of inventory by featuring a small ski clothing shop, and we use business documents to illustrate transactions.

Let's compare service entities, with which you are familiar, with merchandising companies. Exhibit 5–1 below shows how the financial statements of a service entity differ from those of a merchandiser.

---

[1] Avigilon Corporation, "About," accessed May 5, 2015, http://avigilon.com/about/; Jenny Lee, "Avigilon Expands with $17-Million Acquisition of RedCloud Security," *Vancouver Sun*, June 4, 2013, accessed May 5, 2015, www.vancouversun.com/business/Avigilon+expands+with+million+acquisition+RedCloud+Security/8478758/story.html#ixzz36eWxkkh7; "Avigilon Corporation Announces First Quarter 2014 Results," Avigilon Corporation, press release, May 7, 2014, accessed May 5, 2015, http://avigilon.com/press-tools/press-releases/avigilon-corporation-announces-first-quarter-2014-results.

EXHIBIT 5–1 | Financial Statements of a Service Company and a Merchandiser

SERVICE CO.* Income Statement For the Year Ended June 30, 2017		MERCHANDISING CO.** Income Statement For the Year Ended June 30, 2017	
Service revenue	$XXX	Sales revenue	$XXX
Expenses		Cost of goods sold	X
Salary expense	X	Gross margin (or profit)	XX
Amortization expense	X	Operating expenses	
Net income	$ X	Salary expense	X
		Amortization expense	X
		Net income	$ X

Service revenue – Operating expenses

Gross margin – Operating expenses = Net Income

SERVICE CO. Balance Sheet June 30, 2017		MERCHANDISING CO. Balance Sheet June 30, 2017	
Assets		Assets	
Current assets:		Current assets:	
Cash	$X	Cash	$X
Accounts receivable, net	X	Accounts receivable, net	X
Prepaid expenses	X	Inventory	X
		Prepaid expenses	X

Merchandise inventory is included in current assets

*Such as Hunter Environmental Consulting

**Such as Slopes Ski Shop, a small ski clothing store in Vancouver, BC

WHAT ARE MERCHANDISING OPERATIONS?

Merchandising consists of buying and selling products rather than services. Merchandisers have some new balance sheet and income statement items.

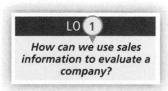

LO **1**

How can we use sales information to evaluate a company?

Balance Sheet	Income Statement
• Inventory, an asset	• Sales revenue
	• Cost of goods sold, an expense
	• Gross margin

These items are bolded in Exhibit 5–1 for Merchandising Co. and explained further here.

The selling price of merchandise sold by a business is called **sales revenue**, often abbreviated as **sales**. The major revenue of a merchandising entity, sales revenue, results in an increase in capital from delivering inventory to customers. When we reference a company's sales we are often referring to **net sales**, defined as follows:

The major expense of a merchandiser is **cost of goods sold** or **cost of sales**. It represents the entity's cost of the goods (the inventory) it sold to customers. While inventory is held by a business it is an asset, because the goods are an economic resource with future value to the company. When the inventory is sold, however, its cost becomes an expense to the seller to match against the revenue from the sale.

Gross margin is a measure of business success. A sufficiently high gross margin is vital to a merchandiser, since all other expenses of the company are deducted from this gross margin.

The following example will clarify the nature of gross margin. Consider Danier Leather Inc., the company that sells leather clothing and accessories across Canada. Suppose Danier Leather's cost for a certain jacket is $250 and Danier sells the jacket to a customer for $600. Danier's gross margin on the jacket is $350 ($600 − $250). The gross margin reported on Danier's year-end income statement is the sum of the gross margins on all the products the company sold during its fiscal year.

What Goes into Inventory Cost?

The cost of inventory on a merchandiser's balance sheet represents all the costs incurred to bring the merchandise to the point of sale. Suppose Danier Leather Inc. purchases handbags from a manufacturer in Asia. Danier's cost of a handbag would include the following:

Item	Explanation	Amount/handbag
Cost of the handbag		$50.00
Customs/duties	Paid to the Canadian government	5.00
Shipping costs (also called freight-in)	From manufacturer in Asia to Danier store	2.50
Insurance	During transportation	1.50
Total Cost		**$59.00**

So Danier Leather's total cost for this handbag is $59.00 ($50.00 + $5.00 + $2.50 + $1.50). The cost principle of measurement applies to all assets, as follows:

> **The cost of any asset is the sum of all the costs incurred to bring the asset to its intended use.**

For merchandise inventory, the intended use is readiness for sale. After the goods are ready for sale, then other costs, such as advertising, display, and sales commissions, are expensed. These costs are *not* included as the cost of inventory.

The Operating Cycle for a Merchandising Business

Some merchandising entities buy inventory, sell the inventory to their customers, and use the cash to purchase more inventory to repeat the cycle. Other merchandisers, like Avigilon Corporation or the Ford Motor Company, manufacture their products and sell them to customers. The balance of this chapter considers the

LEARNING TIPS

The term *cost of goods* sold is often shortened to COGS.

first group of merchandisers, which buys products and resells them. Exhibit 5–2 diagrams the operating cycle for *sales on account*. For a cash sale the cycle is from cash to inventory, which is purchased for resale, and back to cash. For a sale on account the cycle is from cash to inventory to accounts receivable and back to cash. In all lines of business, managers strive to shorten the cycle to keep assets active. The faster the sale of inventory and the collection of cash, the higher the profits, assuming cost and selling price stay the same.

EXHIBIT 5–2 | Operating Cycle of a Merchandiser

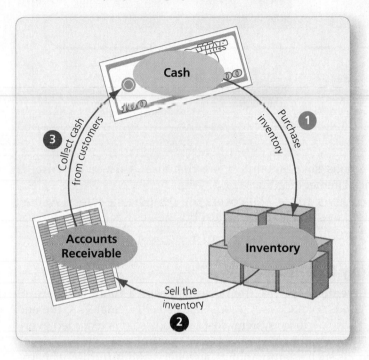

INVENTORY SYSTEMS: PERPETUAL AND PERIODIC

There are two main types of inventory accounting systems:

- Periodic system
- Perpetual system

Periodic Inventory Systems

The **periodic inventory system** is used by businesses that sell relatively inexpensive goods. A very small grocery store without optical-scanning point-of-sale equipment to read UPC or bar codes does not keep a daily running record of every loaf of bread and litre of milk that it buys and sells. The cost of record keeping would be overwhelming. Instead, it counts its inventory periodically—at least once a year—to determine the quantities on hand. The inventory amounts are used to prepare the annual financial statements. Businesses such as restaurants and small retail stores also use the periodic inventory system.

Once the cost of the goods remaining in inventory at the end of the period (ending inventory) is determined by the inventory count, then we can calculate the cost of the inventory sold during the period. To do this, follow these steps:

❶ Determine the cost of the goods that were in inventory at the beginning of the period, which is beginning inventory. This is the same amount as the prior period's ending inventory.

❷ Add the cost of goods purchased during the period. Adding beginning inventory and purchases will give the cost of the goods available for sale during the period.

❸ Subtract the cost of the goods on hand at the end of the period (ending inventory, based on the inventory count).

The formula for cost of goods sold is demonstrated in the graphic below:

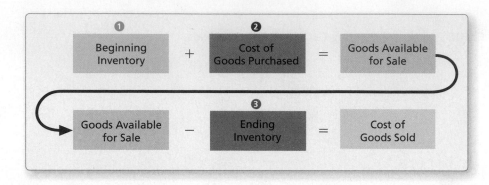

The resulting cost of goods sold amount, a merchandiser's major expense, is included on the income statement for the period.

Appendix A of this chapter (page 273) covers the periodic inventory system. This system is being used less and less since most businesses have computerized their inventory records.

Perpetual Inventory Systems

Under the **perpetual inventory system**, the business keeps a running record of inventory and cost of goods sold. Cost of goods sold is *not* calculated at the end of the period as it is with the periodic system; cost of goods sold is recorded every time a sale is made. The perpetual system achieves control over the inventory, especially expensive goods such as automobiles, jewellery, and furniture. The low cost of automated information systems has increased the use of perpetual systems. This technology reduces the time required to manage inventory and thus increases a company's ability to control its merchandise. But even under a perpetual system, the business counts the inventory on hand at least once a year. The physical count establishes the correct amount of ending inventory for the financial statements (which may have been affected by theft or spoilage) and serves as a check on the perpetual records.

A modern computerized perpetual inventory system records the following:

* Units purchased

* Units sold

* The quantity of inventory on hand

Inventory systems are often integrated with accounts receivable and sales. The computer can keep up-to-the-minute records, so managers can call up current inventory information at any time. For example, in their perpetual system, the point-of-sale equipment at IKEA or Home Depot is a computer terminal that records sales and also updates the inventory records. Bar codes, such as the one shown in the margin, are scanned by a laser. The lines of the bar code represent inventory and cost data that keep track of each item. Most businesses use bar codes, so we focus our inventory discussions on the perpetual system.

GPS tracking technology can be used in a number of ways to manage inventory. You can gain information about where your stock is, such as en route to your location or inside or outside your warehouse.

The following compares the perpetual and periodic systems; Appendix B (page 283) will cover this in more detail:

Perpetual Inventory System	Periodic Inventory System
• Keeps a running record of all inventory as it is bought and sold (units and price)	• Does *not* keep a running record of all goods bought and sold
• Inventory counted at least once a year	• Inventory counted at least once a year

 **Try It!**

1. a. What is the gross margin if net sales are $100,000 and cost of goods sold is $60,000?
   b. If gross margin is $10,000 and cost of goods sold is $30,000, what were net sales?
   c. If net sales are $37,500 and gross margin is $7,500, what was cost of goods sold?

2. Complete the table below:

Beginning Inventory	Cost of Goods Purchased	Goods Available for Sale	Ending Inventory	Cost of Goods Sold
$42,000	$30,000	$ (a)	$24,000	$48,000
(b)	50,000	70,000	40,000	30,000
90,000	(c)	110,000	(d)	40,000
(e)	20,000	130,000	70,000	(f)

Solutions appear at the end of this chapter and on MyAccountingLab

ACCOUNTING FOR INVENTORY PURCHASES IN THE PERPETUAL INVENTORY SYSTEM

The cycle of a merchandising entity begins with the purchase of inventory, as shown in Exhibit 5–2. For example, a menswear store records the purchase of sweaters, shirts, and other items of inventory acquired for resale by debiting the Inventory account. A $40,000 purchase on account is recorded as follows:

LO 2

How can we track the purchase and sale of inventory when we should know how much inventory we have?

May 14	Inventory	40,000	
	Accounts Payable		40,000
	Purchased inventory on account.		

The Inventory account should be used only for purchases of merchandise for resale. Purchases of any other assets are recorded in a different asset account. For example, the purchase of supplies is debited to Supplies, not to Inventory. Inventory is an asset until it is sold.

The Purchase Invoice: A Basic Business Document

Business documents are the tangible evidence of transactions. In this section, we trace the steps that Slopes Ski Shop, a small ski clothing store located in Vancouver, British Columbia, takes to order, receive, and pay for inventory. Slopes Ski Shop

(Slopes) sells ski jackets and other winter wear. Many companies buy and sell their goods electronically—with no invoices, no cheques, and so on. Here we use actual documents to illustrate what takes place behind the scenes.

❶ Suppose Slopes wants to stock ski jackets from Neige Sportswear. Slopes prepares a **purchase order** for ski jackets and transmits it to Neige Sportswear.

❷ On receipt of the purchase order, Neige Sportswear searches its warehouse for the inventory that Slopes has ordered. Neige Sportswear ships the ski jackets and sends the invoice to Slopes on the same day. The **invoice** or **bill** is the seller's request for payment from the purchaser.

❸ Slopes does not pay the invoice immediately. Instead, Slopes waits until the inventory arrives to ensure that it is the correct type and quantity ordered and that it arrives in good condition. After the inventory is inspected and approved, Slopes pays Neige Sportswear the invoice amount according to the terms of payment previously negotiated.

Exhibit 5–3 is a copy of an invoice from Neige Sportswear to Slopes Ski Shop.

EXHIBIT 5–3 | Purchase Invoice

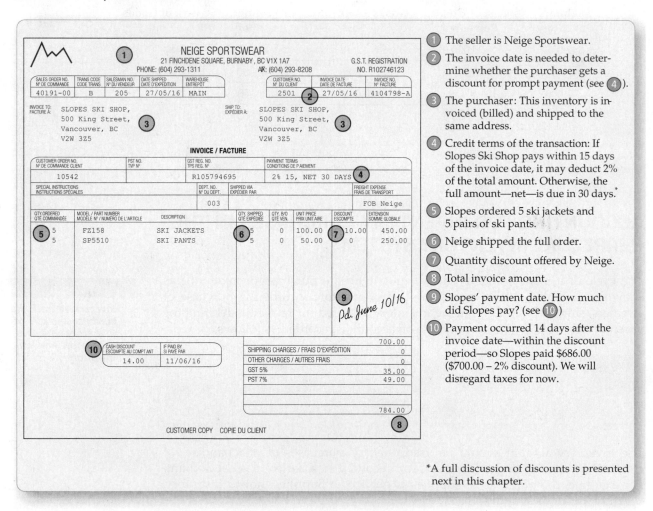

① The seller is Neige Sportswear.

② The invoice date is needed to determine whether the purchaser gets a discount for prompt payment (see ④).

③ The purchaser: This inventory is invoiced (billed) and shipped to the same address.

④ Credit terms of the transaction: If Slopes Ski Shop pays within 15 days of the invoice date, it may deduct 2% of the total amount. Otherwise, the full amount—net—is due in 30 days.*

⑤ Slopes ordered 5 ski jackets and 5 pairs of ski pants.

⑥ Neige shipped the full order.

⑦ Quantity discount offered by Neige.

⑧ Total invoice amount.

⑨ Slopes' payment date. How much did Slopes pay? (see ⑩)

⑩ Payment occurred 14 days after the invoice date—within the discount period—so Slopes paid $686.00 ($700.00 – 2% discount). We will disregard taxes for now.

*A full discussion of discounts is presented next in this chapter.

Discounts from Purchase Prices

There are two major types of discounts from purchase prices: quantity discounts and cash discounts (called *purchase discounts*).

Quantity Discounts A **quantity discount** works this way: The greater the quantity purchased, the lower the price per item. For example, Neige Sportswear may offer no quantity discount for the purchase of only one ski jacket and charge the *list* price—the full price—of $100 per unit. However, Neige Sportswear may offer the following quantity discount terms in order to persuade customers to order more ski jackets:

Quantity	Quantity Discount	Net Price per Unit
Minimum quantity, 2 ski jackets	5%	$95 [$100 − 0.05($100)]
4–9 ski jackets	10%	$90 [$100 − 0.10($100)]
More than 9 ski jackets	20%	$80 [$100 − 0.20($100)]

Suppose Slopes purchases five ski jackets from Neige Sportswear. The cost of each ski jacket is, therefore, $90.00. A purchase of five units on account would be recorded by debiting Inventory and crediting Accounts Payable for the total price of $450.00 ($90.00 per unit × 5 items purchased).

Purchase Discounts Many businesses also offer purchase discounts to their customers. A purchase discount is totally different from a quantity or volume discount. A **purchase discount** (also referred to as a **cash discount**) is a reward for prompt payment. If a quantity discount is also offered, the purchase discount is computed on the net purchase amount after the quantity discount has been subtracted, further reducing the cost of the inventory to the purchaser.

Neige Sportswear's credit terms of "2% 15, net 30 days" can also be expressed as **2/15, n/30**. This means that Slopes Ski Shop may deduct 2 percent of the total amount due if Slopes Ski Shop pays within the **discount period**, which is within 15 days of the invoice date. Otherwise, the full amount—net—is due in 30 days.

Terms of "n/30" indicate that no discount is offered, and payment is due 30 days after the invoice date. Terms of **eom** mean that payment is due by the end of the current month. However, a purchase after the 25th of the current month on terms of *eom* can be paid at the end of the next month.

A computerized accounting system is typically programmed to make the owner aware of invoices as the date for taking the discount approaches so the business can take advantage of the purchase discount.

Let's use the Exhibit 5–3 transaction to illustrate accounting for a purchase discount. For the moment, disregard taxes, which include HST, GST, and PST, and use the balance before taxes of $700.00 when recording purchases and purchase discounts. Slopes records the purchase on account as follows:

May 27	Inventory	700.00	
	Accounts Payable		700.00
	Purchased inventory on account.		

Slopes paid within the discount period of 15 days, so its cash payment entry is:

Jun. 10	Accounts Payable	700.00	
	Cash		686.00
	Inventory		14.00
	Paid on account within discount period.		
	The discount is $14.00 ($700.00 × 0.02).		

KEY POINTS

There is no Quantity Discount account recorded at the time the order is placed. Instead, all accounting entries are based on the net price of a purchase after the quantity discount has been subtracted, as shown on the invoice.

MyAccountingLab

Interactive Figure: Interact with Purchase Discount

KEY POINTS

Whether a company takes the purchase discount or not, the Accounts Payable account for the inventory purchase must always be $0 after final payment is made.

The discount is credited to Inventory. After Slopes has taken its discount, Slopes must adjust the Inventory account to reflect its true cost of the goods. In effect, this inventory cost Slopes $686.00 ($700.00 minus the purchase discount of $14.00), as shown in the following Inventory account:

	Inventory				
(Purchase)	May 27	700.00	Jun. 10	14.00	(Discount)
	Bal.	686.00			

However, if Slopes pays this invoice after the discount period, it must pay the full invoice amount. In this case, the payment entry is:

Jun. 25	Accounts Payable	700.00	
	Cash		700.00
	Paid on account after discount period.		

Without the discount, Slopes' cost of the inventory is the full amount of $700.00, as shown in the following T-account:

	Inventory	
May 27	700.00	

Purchase Returns and Allowances

Most businesses allow their customers to *return* merchandise that is defective, damaged in shipment, or otherwise unsuitable. Or, if the buyer chooses to keep damaged goods, the seller may deduct an *allowance* from the amount the buyer owes. Both purchase returns and purchase allowances decrease the amount that the buyer must pay the seller.

Suppose the $90.00 ski jackets (model FZ158) ordered by Slopes Ski Shop (in Exhibit 5–3) were not the ski jackets received. Slopes returns the merchandise to the seller and records the purchase return as follows:

Jun. 3	Accounts Payable	450.00	
	Inventory		450.00
	Returned inventory to seller.		

Now assume that one pair of the Neige Sportswear ski pants was damaged in shipment to Slopes. The damage is minor, and Slopes decides to keep the ski pants in exchange for a $25.00 allowance from Neige Sportswear. To record this purchase allowance, Slopes makes this entry:

Jun. 4	Accounts Payable	25.00	
	Inventory		25.00
	Received a purchase allowance.		

The return and the allowance had two effects:

- They decreased Slopes' liability, which is why we debit Accounts Payable.
- They decreased the net cost of the inventory, which is why we credit Inventory.

Assume that Slopes has not yet paid its liability to Neige Sportswear. After these return ($450.00) and allowance ($25.00) transactions are posted, Slopes' accounts will show these balances:

Inventory

(Purchase)	May 27	700.00	Jun. 3	450.00	(Return)
			Jun. 4	25.00	(Allowance)
	Bal.	225.00			

Accounts Payable

Jun. 3	450.00	May 27	700.00	
Jun. 4	25.00			
		Bal.	225.00	

Slopes' cost of *inventory* is $225.00, and Slopes owes Neige Sportswear $225.00 on *account payable*. If Slopes pays within the discount period, 2 percent will be deducted from these balances.

Transportation Costs: Who Pays?

The transportation cost of moving inventory from seller to buyer can be significant. Someone must pay this cost. The purchase agreement specifies FOB (*free on board*) terms to indicate who pays the shipping charges. FOB governs:

1. When **legal title**, or ownership, passes from the seller to buyer.
2. Who pays the freight.

- Under **FOB shipping point** terms, legal title passes when the inventory leaves the seller's place of business—the shipping point. The buyer owns the goods while they are in transit, and therefore the buyer pays the transportation cost, or freight.
- Under **FOB destination** terms, legal title passes when the goods reach the destination, so the seller pays the freight.

Exhibit 5–4 summarizes FOB terms.

KEY POINTS

The perpetual method in this text records all discounts, returns, allowances, and freight-in the Inventory account to simplify recording, but most businesses have more detailed records.

REAL WORLD EXAMPLE

Another term used for FOB shipping point is CIF destination, which stands for cost, insurance, and freight.

EXHIBIT 5–4 | FOB Terms Determine Who Pays the Freight

Freight costs are either freight-in or freight-out:

- **Freight-in** is the transportation cost on *purchased goods.*
- **Freight-out** is the transportation cost on *goods sold.*

Freight-in   FOB shipping point terms are the most common. The *buyer* owns the goods while they are in transit, so the buyer pays the freight. In accounting, the cost of an asset includes all costs incurred to bring the asset to its intended use. For inventory, cost therefore includes the following:

- *Net cost* after all discounts, returns, and allowances have been subtracted, plus
- *Freight-in*

Suppose Slopes receives a $100.00 shipping bill directly from the freight company. Slopes' entry to record payment of the freight charge is as follows:

Jun. 1	Inventory	100.00	
	Cash		100.00
	Paid a freight bill.		

The freight charge increases the cost of the inventory to $325.00 as follows:

	Inventory				
(Purchase)	May 27	700.00	Jun. 3	450.00	(Return)
(Freight)	Jun. 1	100.00	Jun. 4	25.00	(Allowance)
(Net cost)	Bal.	325.00			

Under FOB shipping point, the seller sometimes prepays the transportation cost as a convenience and adds this cost on the invoice. The buyer can debit Inventory for the combined cost of the inventory and the shipping cost because both costs apply to the merchandise. A $10,000 purchase of goods, coupled with a related freight charge of $800, would be recorded as follows:

Mar. 12	Inventory	10,800.00	
	Accounts Payable		10,800.00
	Purchased inventory on account, including freight of $800.		

> Normally, no discount is offered on transportation costs.

If the buyer pays within the discount period, the discount will be computed on the $10,000 merchandise cost, not on the $10,800.

Freight-out   The *seller* may pay freight charges to ship goods to customers. This is called *freight-out.* Freight-out is a delivery expense, which is a selling expense, and it is debited to the Delivery Expense account.

Jun. 1	Delivery Expense	100.00	
	Cash		100.00
	Paid a freight bill.		

Summary of Purchase Returns and Allowances, Discounts, and Transportation Costs   Suppose Slopes Ski Shop buys $50,000 of ski wear inventory, takes a discount, and returns some of the goods. Slopes also pays some freight-in. The following summary shows Slopes' **net purchases** of this inventory. All amounts are assumed for this illustration:

Purchases of Inventory						Net Purchases of Inventory
Inventory	−	Purchase Returns and Allowances	−	Purchase Discounts	+ Freight-in =	Inventory
$50,000	−	$2,000	−	$1,000	+ $2,500 =	$49,500

Inventory

Purchases of inventory	50,000	Purchase ret. & allow.	2,000
Freight-in	2,500	Purchase discounts	1,000
Bal.	49,500		

SELLING INVENTORY AND RECORDING COST OF GOODS SOLD

After a company buys inventory, the next step in the operating cycle is to sell the goods. We shift now to the selling side and follow Slopes Ski Shop through a sequence of selling transactions. A sale earns income, Sales Revenue. A sale also requires a cost in the form of an expense, Cost of Goods Sold, as the seller gives up the asset, Inventory.

After making a sale on account, Slopes may experience any of the following:

- A sales return: The customer may return goods to Slopes Ski Shop.
- A sales allowance: Slopes may grant a sales allowance for an error to reduce the amount of cash to be collected from the customer.
- A sales discount: If the customer pays within the discount period—under terms such as 2/10, n/30—Slopes collects the discounted (reduced) amount. No discount is recorded for a quantity, or volume, discount.
- Freight-out: Slopes may have to pay delivery expense to transport the goods to the buyer's location.

The sale of inventory may be for cash or on account, as shown in Exhibit 5–2. Let's begin with a cash sale.

Cash Sale   Assume that Slopes Ski Shop has $60,000 of inventory on hand on January 2. Sales by retailers, such as Slopes, grocery stores, and restaurants, are often for cash. Cash sales of $10,000 would be recorded by debiting Cash and crediting Sales Revenue as follows:

MyAccountingLab

Interactive Figure: Interact with COGS and Merchandise Inventory

Jan. 9	Cash	10,000	
	Sales Revenue		10,000
	Cash sales.		

To update the inventory records for the goods sold, the business also must decrease the Inventory balance. Suppose these goods cost the seller $6,000. An accompanying entry is needed to transfer the $6,000 cost of the goods—*not their selling price of $10,000*—from the Inventory account to the Cost of Goods Sold account as follows:

Jan. 9	Cost of Goods Sold	6,000	
	Inventory		6,000
	Recorded the cost of goods sold.		

The recording of cost of goods sold along with sales revenue is an example of the matching objective (see Chapter 3, page 120)—matching expense against revenue to measure net income.

Cost of goods sold (also called cost of sales) is the largest single expense of most businesses that sell merchandise. It is the cost of the inventory that the business has sold to customers. The Cost of Goods Sold account keeps a current balance as transactions are journalized and posted.

After posting, the Cost of Goods Sold account holds the cost of the merchandise sold ($6,000 in this case):

Inventory				Cost of Goods Sold		
Jan. 2 Bal. 60,000	Jan. 9	6,000		Jan. 9	6,000	

Chapter 5 Merchandising Operations   **257**

For many businesses, the cashier scans the bar code on the product and the computer automatically records the sale and cost of goods sold entry.

Sale on Account   A large amount of sales in Canada are made on account (on credit), using either the seller's credit facility or a credit card such as VISA or MasterCard.

A $12,000 sale on account is recorded by a debit to Accounts Receivable and a credit to Sales Revenue, as follows:

Jan. 2	Accounts Receivable	12,000	
	Sales Revenue		12,000
	Sale on account.		

If we assume that these goods cost the seller $7,200, the accompanying Cost of Goods Sold and Inventory entry is

Jan. 2	Cost of Goods Sold	7,200	
	Inventory		7,200
	Recorded the cost of goods sold.		

When the cash is received, the seller records the cash receipt on account as follows:

Jan. 10	Cash	12,000	
	Accounts Receivable		12,000
	Collection on account.		

Why is there no January 10 entry to Sales Revenue, Cost of Goods Sold, or Inventory? The sales revenue, the related cost of goods sold, and the decrease in inventory for the goods sold were recorded on January 2.

Offering Sales Discounts and Sales Returns and Allowances

We saw that purchase discounts and purchase returns and allowances decrease the cost of inventory purchases. In the same way, **sales discounts** and **sales returns and allowances** decrease the revenue earned on sales. Sales Discounts and Sales Returns and Allowances are contra accounts to Sales Revenue.

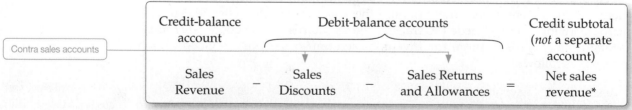

Contra sales accounts

Credit-balance account	Debit-balance accounts		Credit subtotal (*not* a separate account)
Sales Revenue	− Sales Discounts	− Sales Returns and Allowances	= Net sales revenue*

*Often abbreviated as Net sales

This equation calculates net sales. Sales discounts can be given on both goods and services.

Companies keep a close watch on their customers' paying habits and on their own sales of defective and unsuitable merchandise. They maintain separate accounts for Sales Discounts and Sales Returns and Allowances. Let's examine a sequence of Neige Sportswear sale transactions.

Assume Neige Sportswear is now selling to Slopes Ski Shop. On July 7, Neige sells ski wear for $24,000 on credit terms of 2/15, n/30. These goods cost Neige $14,400. Neige's entries to record this credit sale and the related cost of goods sold are as follows:

Jul. 7	Accounts Receivable	24,000	
	Sales Revenue		24,000
	Sale on account.		
7	Cost of Goods Sold	14,400	
	Inventory		14,400
	Recorded the cost of goods sold.		

Sales Returns   Assume the buyer, Slopes Ski Shop, returns goods that were sold by Neige for $3,000. These goods are not damaged and can be resold. Neige, the seller, records the sales return and the related decrease in Accounts Receivable as follows:

Jul. 12	Sales Returns and Allowances	3,000	
	Accounts Receivable		3,000
	Received returned goods.		

Neige receives the returned merchandise and updates the Inventory records. Neige must also decrease Cost of Goods Sold as follows (the returned goods cost Neige $1,800):

Jul. 12	Inventory	1,800	
	Cost of Goods Sold		1,800
	Returned goods to inventory.		

KEY POINTS

The sale of inventory and the return of goods by customers require two separate journal entries.

Sales Allowances   Suppose Neige grants the buyer a $500 sales allowance for damaged goods. Slopes then subtracts $500 from the amount it will pay Neige. Neige journalizes this transaction as follows:

Jul. 15	Sales Returns and Allowances	500	
	Accounts Receivable		500
	Granted a sales allowance for damaged goods.		

No Inventory entry is needed for a sales allowance transaction because the seller, Neige, receives no returned goods from the customer. Instead, Neige will simply receive less cash from the customer.

After the preceding entries are posted, all the accounts have up-to-date balances. Slopes' Accounts Receivable has a $20,500 debit balance, as follows:

Accounts Receivable—Slopes Ski Shop

(Sale)	Jul. 7	24,000	Jul. 12	3,000	(Return)
			Jul. 15	500	(Allowance)
	Bal.	20,500			

On July 22, the last day of the discount period, Neige collects $15,500 of this accounts receivable. Assume Neige allows customers to take discounts on all amounts Neige receives within the discount period (some companies allow purchasers to only take a discount if the invoice is paid in full). The collection entry is as follows:

Jul. 22	Cash*	15,190	
	Sales Discounts**	310	
	Accounts Receivable		15,500
	Cash collection within the discount period.		
	*$15,500 − $310 = $15,190		
	**0.02 × $15,500 = $310		

Suppose Neige collects the remaining amount outstanding of $5,000 on July 28. That date is after the discount period, so there is no sales discount. To record this collection on account, Neige debits Cash and credits Accounts Receivable for the same amount, as follows:

Jul. 28	Cash	5,000	
	Accounts Receivable		5,000
	Cash collection after the discount period.		

Now Slopes' Accounts Receivable balance is zero:

Accounts Receivable—Slopes Ski Shop

(Sale)	Jul. 7	24,000	Jul. 12	3,000	(Return)
			Jul. 15	500	(Allowance)
			Jul. 22	15,500	(Collection)
			Jul. 28	5,000	(Collection)
	Bal.	0			

> Try It!

3. Journalize, without explanations, the following transactions of Royal Fashion Distributors, a wholesaler that uses the perpetual inventory system, during the month of June 2017:

Jun. 3   Purchased $14,500 of inventory from a manufacturer under terms of 1/10, n/eom and FOB shipping point.

7   Returned $2,700 of defective merchandise purchased on June 3.

9   Paid freight bill of $750 on June 3 purchase.

10   Sold inventory for $11,500 to a retail store, collecting cash of $2,400. Payment terms on the remainder were 2/15, n/30. The goods cost Royal Fashion Distributors $6,900.

12   Paid amount owed on credit purchase of June 3.

16   Granted a sales allowance of $1,200 on the portion of the June 10 sale that was on account.

23   Received cash from June 10 customer in full settlement of the debt.

Solutions appear at the end of this chapter and on MyAccountingLab

ADJUSTING AND CLOSING THE ACCOUNTS OF A MERCHANDISING BUSINESS

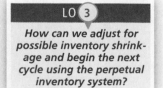

LO 3

How can we adjust for possible inventory shrinkage and begin the next cycle using the perpetual inventory system?

A merchandising business adjusts and closes the accounts the same way a service entity does. If a worksheet is used, the trial balance is entered and the worksheet is completed to determine net income or net loss. The worksheet provides the data for journalizing the adjusting and closing entries and for preparing the financial statements. Since there is very little difference between the worksheet of a service business and that of a merchandising business that uses the perpetual inventory system, we will not cover worksheets here. (However, worksheets are covered in Summary Problems for Your Review 1 and 2 on MyAccountingLab.)

Adjusting Inventory Based on a Physical Count

In theory, the Inventory account remains up to date at all times. However, the actual amount of inventory on hand may differ from what the books show. Losses due to theft and damage can be significant. Also, accounting errors can cause Inventory's balance to need adjustment either upward or, more often, downward. For this reason, virtually all merchandising businesses take a physical count of inventory at least once each year. The most common time for a business to count its inventory is at the end of the fiscal year, before the financial statements are prepared. The business then adjusts the Inventory account to the correct amount based on the physical count.

At year end, Slopes Ski Shop's Inventory account shows an unadjusted balance of $174,000.

Inventory			
Dec. 31	174,000		

With no **shrinkage**—a reduction in the amount of inventory due to theft, spoilage, or error—the business should have on hand inventory costing $174,000. But on December 31, Steve Austin, the owner of Slopes Ski Shop, counts the merchandise in the store, and the total cost of the goods on hand comes to only $168,000.

Inventory Balance Before Adjustment	−	Actual Inventory on Hand	=	Adjusting Entry to Inventory
$174,000	−	$168,000	=	Credit of $6,000

Slopes would record the inventory shrinkage of $6,000 with this adjusting entry:

Dec. 31	Cost of Goods Sold	6,000	
	Inventory		6,000
	Adjustment for inventory shrinkage.		

KEY POINTS

As a result of this inventory adjustment, cost of goods sold is higher and gross margin is lower. The current asset Inventory has been reduced.

This entry brings Inventory to its correct balance.[2]

Inventory				
Dec. 31	174,000	Dec. 31 Adj.	6,000
Dec. 31 Bal.	168,000		

The physical count can also indicate that more inventory is present than the books show. A search of the records may reveal that Slopes Ski Shop received inventory but did not record the corresponding purchase entry. This would be entered the standard way: debit Inventory and credit Cash or Accounts Payable.

---

[2] Some companies record the inventory shrinkage of $6,000 with this adjusting entry:

Dec. 31	Loss on Inventory (or Inventory Shrinkage)	6,000	
	Inventory		6,000
	Adjustment for inventory shrinkage.		

This is done to highlight the shrinkage so that it can be monitored and to identify it as a loss.

If the reason for the excess inventory cannot be identified, the business adjusts the accounts by debiting Inventory and crediting Cost of Goods Sold.

Summary of Merchandising Cost Flows

The Inventory account balance at the end of the period is the amount of beginning inventory in the next period. To summarize the effects of transactions on the Inventory and Cost of Good Sold accounts, Slopes Ski Shop's inventory activities are summarized in Exhibit 5–5. Note that key year-end amounts are shown; other transactions that would have occurred throughout the year are represented as "XXX." These transactions are typical of merchandisers using the perpetual inventory system.

EXHIBIT 5–5 | Summary of Activities Affecting the Inventory and Cost of Goods Sold Accounts

	Inventory		
Dec. 31, 2016, balance	XXX		Entries to record purchase discounts
Entries to record purchases of merchandise		XXX	during 2017
during 2017	XXX		Entries to record purchases returns
Entries to record freight-in costs		XXX	and allowances during 2017
incurred during 2017	XXX		Cost of sales transactions
Entries to record the return of		421,000	during 2017
goods to inventory	XXX		Dec. 31, 2017 adjustment
		6,000	for shrinkage
Dec. 31, 2017, balance	168,000		

	Cost of Goods Sold		
Entries to record the	421,000	XXX	Entries to record the return
cost of sales for 2017			of goods to inventory
Dec. 31, 2017, adjustment	6,000		
for shrinkage			
Dec. 31, 2017, balance	427,000		

> Try It!

4. At December 31, 2017, a merchandising company's year end, the accounting records show a balance of $125,000 in the Inventory account. Suppose a physical count of the goods in the warehouse shows inventory on hand costing $110,000. What journal entry would bring the Inventory account to its correct balance?

5. At December 31, 2017, a merchandising company's year end, the accounting records show a balance of $75,000 in the Inventory account. Suppose a physical count of the goods in the warehouse shows inventory on hand costing $78,000. What journal entry would bring the Inventory account to its correct balance?

6. Using the accounts and balances listed in Exhibit 5–6, calculate the following amounts:
   a. Net sales
   b. Gross margin

Solutions appear at the end of this chapter and on MyAccountingLab

Closing the Accounts of a Merchandising Business

Exhibit 5–6 presents Slopes Ski Shop's closing entries, which are similar to those you have seen previously except for the new accounts highlighted with bold text. All amounts are assumed for demonstration purposes.

EXHIBIT 5–6 | Closing Entries for a Merchandiser

		Closing Entries		
❶ Dec. 31	**Sales Revenue**		**777,000**	
	Interest Revenue		3,000	
	Income Summary			780,000
	To close the revenue accounts and create the Income Summary account.			
❷ Dec. 31	Income Summary		648,000	
	** Cost of Goods Sold**			**427,000**
	** Sales Discounts**			**7,500**
	** Sales Returns and Allowances**			**8,000**
	Operating Expenses			205,500
	To close the expense accounts.			
❸ Dec. 31	Income Summary*		132,000	
	Steve Austin, Capital			132,000
	To close the Income Summary account and transfer net income to the Capital account. *$780,000 − $648,000			
❹ Dec. 31	Steve Austin, Capital		65,000	
	Steve Austin, Withdrawals			65,000
	To close the Withdrawals account and transfer the Withdrawals amount to the Capital account.			

Debit Revenue accounts to close them

Debit Income Summary for total expenses plus contra revenue accounts

LEARNING TIPS

The closing entries here are very similar to those discussed in Chapter 4, pages 185–188. The closing entries also clear the Cost of Goods Sold expense account in order to accumulate costs in the next period.

KEY POINTS

Operating expenses are wages, rent, Insurance, supplies, and so on.

Income Summary			
❷ Closing	648,000	❶ Closing	780,000
❸ Closing	132,000	Balance	0

Steve Austin, Withdrawals			
Balance	65,000	❹ Closing	65,000
		Balance	0

Steve Austin, Capital			
❹ Closing	65,000	Balance (assumed)	90,000
		❸ Closing	132,000
		Balance	157,000

PREPARING A MERCHANDISER'S FINANCIAL STATEMENTS

LO 4
How can we prepare financial statements for a company using the perpetual inventory system?

Exhibit 5–7 presents Slopes Ski Shop's financial statements (prepared after all year-end adjusting entries have been entered).

EXHIBIT 5–7 | Financial Statements of Slopes Ski Shop

SLOPES SKI SHOP
Income Statement
For the Year Ended December 31, 2017

Sales revenue		$777,000
Less: Sales discounts	$ 7,500	
Sales returns and allowances	8,000	15,500
Net sales revenue		761,500
Cost of goods sold		427,000
Gross margin		334,500
Operating expenses		201,000
Income from operations		133,500
Other revenue and (expense):		
Interest revenue	3,000	
Less: Interest expense	4,500	1,500
Net income		$132,000

Gross margin and income from operations are two key measures of operating performance

These are financing activities outside the scope of selling merchandise.

SLOPES SKI SHOP
Statement of Owner's Equity
For the Year Ended December 31, 2017

Steve Austin, capital, January 1, 2017	$ 90,000
Add: Net income	132,000
	222,000
Less: Withdrawals	65,000
Steve Austin, capital, December 31, 2017	$157,000

SLOPES SKI SHOP
Balance Sheet
December 31, 2017
Assets

Current assets:		
Cash	$ 6,000	
Accounts receivable	24,000	
Note receivable	32,000	
Interest receivable	1,000	
Inventory	168,000	
Prepaid insurance	600	
Supplies	500	
Total current assets		232,100
Property, plant, and equipment:		
Furniture and fixtures	120,000	
Less: Accumulated amortization	18,000	
Total Property, plant, and equipment		102,000
Total assets		$334,100

(Continued)

EXHIBIT 5-7 | Financial Statements of Slopes Ski Shop (*Continued*)

Liabilities		
Current liabilities:		
Accounts payable	$128,000	
Unearned sales revenue	1,500	
Wages payable	3,000	
Interest payable	500	
Total current liabilities		133,000
Long-term liabilities:		
Notes payable		44,100
Total liabilities		177,100
Owner's Equity		
Steve Austin, capital		157,000
Total liabilities and owner's equity		$334,100

Income Statement Special presentation is warranted for two items that appear on the income statement: operating expenses and other revenue and expense. **Operating expenses** are those expenses other than cost of goods sold incurred in the entity's major line of business—merchandising. Slopes Ski Shop's operating expenses include wages, rent, insurance, amortization of furniture and fixtures, and supplies.

Many companies report their operating expenses in two categories:

- *Selling expenses* are those expenses related to marketing the company's products—sales salaries; sales commissions; advertising; amortization, rent, utilities, and property taxes on store buildings; amortization on store furniture; delivery expense; and so on.
- *General and administrative expenses* include office expenses, such as the salaries of the executives and office employees; amortization, rent, utilities, property taxes on the home office building; and office supplies.

In this chapter, we will report operating expenses in just one category—operating expenses or simply expenses—to keep the examples simple.

Gross margin minus operating expenses equals **income from operations**, or **operating income**. Many people view operating income as an important indicator of a business's performance because it measures the results of the entity's major ongoing activities.

The last section of Slopes Ski Shop's income statement is **other revenue and expense**. This category reports revenues and expenses that are outside the main operations of the business. Examples include gains and losses on the sale of long-term assets like property, plant, and equipment (not inventory), and gains and losses on lawsuits. Accountants have traditionally viewed Interest Revenue and Interest Expense as "other" items because they arise from lending money and borrowing money.

Statement of Owner's Equity A merchandiser's statement of owner's equity looks exactly like that of a service business. In fact, you cannot determine whether the entity sells merchandise or services from looking at the statement of owner's equity.

Balance Sheet   If the business is a merchandiser, the balance sheet shows inventory as a current asset. In contrast, service businesses usually have no inventory at all or minor amounts of inventory. As we saw in Chapter 4, the classified balance sheet appears in two formats:

- The report format (assets on top, owner's equity at the bottom)
- The account or equation format (assets at left, liabilities and owner's equity at right).

Some examples in this chapter use the equation format to save space. However, in Exhibit 5–7 the report format is used.

MyAccountingLab

Video: Merchandising Income Statement and Transactions

Income Statement Formats

There are also two basic formats for the income statement:

- The multi-step format (Exhibit 5–7)
- The single-step format (Exhibit 5–8)

Multi-Step Income Statement   A **multi-step income statement** shows subtotals to highlight significant relationships and is the most popular format. In addition to net income, it also presents gross margin and operating income, or income from operations. Slopes Ski Shop's multi-step income statement appears in Exhibit 5–7.

Single-Step Income Statement   The **single-step income statement** groups all revenues together, and then lists and deducts all expenses together without drawing any subtotals. Thus it clearly distinguishes revenues from expenses. The income statements in Chapters 1 through 4 were single-step. This format works well for service entities because they have no gross margin to report, and for companies that have several types of revenues. Exhibit 5–8 shows a single-step income statement for Slopes Ski Shop.

EXHIBIT 5–8 | Single-Step Income Statement

SLOPES SKI SHOP Income Statement For the Year Ended December 31, 2017		
Revenues:		
Sales revenue		$777,000
Less: Sales discounts	$7,500	
Sales returns and allowances	8,000	15,500
Net sales revenue		761,500
Interest revenue		3,000
Total revenues		764,500
Expenses:		
Cost of goods sold		427,000
Operating expenses		205,500
Total expenses		632,500
Net income		$132,000

Interest expense of $4,500 is included in operating expenses.

Most published financial statements are highly condensed. Of course, condensed statements can be supplemented with desired details in the notes to the financial statements. For example, notes would disclose which system is being used—periodic or perpetual—as well as if inventory has been pledged as collateral, and so on.

> Try It!

7. The adjusted trial balance of Patti's Party Supplies for the year ended December 31, 2017, appears below. Use this information to prepare the company's single-step income statement for the year ended December 31, 2017.

PATTI'S PARTY SUPPLIES Adjusted Trial Balance December 31, 2017		
Cash	$ 5,600	
Accounts receivable	19,900	
Inventory	25,800	
Furniture	26,500	
Accumulated amortization—furniture		$ 23,800
Accounts payable		4,000
Interest payable		600
Unearned sales revenue		2,400
Note payable, long-term		35,000
Patti Grandy, capital		22,200
Patti Grandy, withdrawals	18,000	
Sales revenue		244,000
Interest revenue		2,000
Sales discounts	10,000	
Sales returns and allowances	8,000	
Cost of goods sold	81,000	
Operating expenses	106,300	
Interest expense	2,900	
Total	$334,000	$334,000

8. Refer to the Patti's Party Supplies adjusted trial balance in Try It #7. Use that information to prepare the company's multi-step income statement for the year ended December 31, 2017.

9. Refer to the Patti's Party Supplies adjusted trial balance in Try It #7. What type of business is Patti's Party Supplies? Which accounts in the adjusted trial balance are unique to this type of business?

Solutions appear at the end of this chapter and on MyAccountingLab

> Why It's Done This Way

Inventory is an asset and an element of the financial statements because it has future economic benefit to the company—the company hopes to sell the inventory for more than it cost to purchase it, creating a positive *gross margin*. When the inventory is sold it becomes an expense referred to as the *cost of goods sold*. The future economic benefit of the inventory is realized when it is sold.

The *multi-step income statement* is an example of the accounting framework's impact on financial reporting and disclosure: Statements must satisfy all the qualitative characteristics (*relevant, reliable, comparable, and understandable*). This form of the income statement communicates useful information to users.

TWO RATIOS FOR DECISION MAKING

LO 5

How can we use ratios to evaluate a business?

Inventory is the most important asset to a merchandising business because it's the reason the business exists. Buying the inventory is risky because if it is not what customers want, it won't sell. If inventory doesn't sell, the merchandiser has invested a lot of its money in purchasing the inventory but has little income. To manage the business, owners and managers focus on the best way to sell the inventory. They use several ratios to evaluate operations, among them *gross margin percentage* and *inventory turnover.*

The Gross Margin Percentage

Gross margin (gross profit) is net sales minus cost of goods sold. Merchandisers strive to increase the **gross margin percentage**, which is computed as follows:

$$\text{Gross margin percentage} = \frac{\text{Gross margin}}{\text{Net sales revenue}} = \frac{\$334{,}500}{\$761{,}500} = 0.439, \text{ or } 43.9\%$$

For Slopes Ski Shop (Exhibit 5–7)

EXHIBIT 5–9

Gross Margin on $1.00 of Sales for Two Merchandisers

A 43.9 percent gross margin means that each dollar of sales generates almost 44 cents of gross profit. On average, the goods cost the seller 56 cents. The gross margin percentage (also called the *gross profit percentage* or the *markup percentage*) is one of the most carefully watched measures of profitability.

Many businesses use the gross margin percentage as a means of determining how profitable a product line is. For example, if too much inventory is purchased and its selling price must be marked down, the gross margin percentage will decline. By monitoring the gross margin percentage, a business can correct problems quickly.

Exhibit 5–9 compares Slopes Ski Shop's gross margin to Walmart Stores Inc.'s most recent gross margin. Walmart's gross margin is $0.24, or 24 percent.

Inventory Turnover

Owners and managers strive to sell inventory as quickly as possible. This is because there is a cost to carrying inventory. If a company purchases inventory on credit (creating an account payable), there is a risk it may buy too much inventory and be unable to sell it before having to pay for the inventory. If this happens, the company either has to borrow funds to pay for the inventory and incur interest expense or use cash that could have been in a bank earning interest. For example, Dell Inc., the computer manufacturer and merchandiser, carries only *two hours* of parts inventory. Why? Prices of parts are continually declining, and Dell does not want to have any more inventory on hand than is absolutely necessary.

Dell is in a unique position in that it sells directly to customers and does not have to keep an inventory of computers on hand. Most retailers, such as Slopes Ski Shop, must keep inventory on hand for customers. Successful merchandisers purchase carefully to keep goods moving through the business at a rapid pace. **Inventory turnover**, the ratio of cost of goods sold to average inventory, indicates how rapidly inventory is sold. Its computation follows:

$$
\begin{array}{l}
\text{Inventory} \\
\text{turnover}
\end{array}
= \frac{\text{Cost of goods sold}}{\text{Average inventory}}
= \frac{\text{Cost of goods sold}}{\begin{array}{c}\text{(Beginning inventory*}\\ \text{+ Ending inventory) / 2}\end{array}}
= \frac{\begin{array}{c}\textbf{For Slopes Ski Shop}\\ \textbf{(Exhibit 5–7)}\end{array}}{}
$$

$$
= \frac{\$427,000}{(\$158,400 + \$168,000) / 2}
$$

= **2.6 times per year (about every 140 days**)**

*Taken from the balance sheet at the end of the preceding period.

**Calculation: 365 days ÷ 2.6 times = approximately 140 days

Inventory turnover is usually computed for an annual period, and the relevant cost of goods sold figure is the amount from the entire year. The resulting inventory turnover statistic shows how many times the average level of inventory was sold during the year. A high rate of turnover is preferable to a low turnover rate. An increase in turnover rate usually means higher profits but may sometimes lead to a shortage of inventory to sell.

Inventory turnover varies from industry to industry. Grocery stores, for example, turn their goods over faster than automobile dealers do. Retailers of specialty sporting goods, such as Slopes Ski Shop, have an average turnover of 3.7 times per year. Exhibit 5–10 compares the inventory turnover rate of Slopes Ski Shop and Walmart Stores, Inc.

Exhibits 5–9 and 5–10 tell an interesting story. Walmart sells lots of inventory at a relatively low gross profit margin. Walmart earns its profits by turning its inventory over rapidly—8.1 times during the year. Slopes Ski Shop, a small business, prices inventory to earn a higher gross margin on each dollar of sales and only turns over its inventory 2.6 times during the year.

Gross margin percentage and rate of inventory turnover do not provide enough information to yield an overall conclusion about a merchandiser, but this example shows how owners and managers can use accounting information to evaluate a company.

MyAccountingLab

Video: Real World Accounting

EXHIBIT 5–10 | Rate of Inventory Turnover for Two Merchandisers

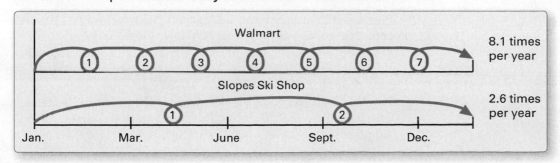

> Try It!

10. Refer to the Patti's Party Supplies adjusted trial balance in Try It #7 on page 267 and the multi-step income statement you created in Try It #8. Calculate the gross margin percentage of this company.

11. Refer to the Patti's Party Supplies adjusted trial balance in Try It #7 on page 267 and the multi-step income statement you created in Try It #8. Ending inventory at December 31, 2016, was $24,000. Calculate the inventory turnover of this company.

Solutions appear at the end of this chapter and on MyAccountingLab

---

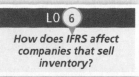

LO **6**

How does IFRS affect companies that sell inventory?

THE EFFECT OF IFRS ON MERCHANDISING OPERATIONS

ASPE		IFRS

The policies are considered converged. However, two concepts are important to note, which apply to both standards: (1) Revenue is recognized only when the likelihood of the return of goods is small. If companies are unable to estimate the amount of inventory that might be returned, the recognition of sales and cost of goods sold should be delayed until the end of the return period. (2) The cost of goods sold and all other expenses related to the sale have to be matched with the revenue earned.

SUMMARY PROBLEM FOR YOUR REVIEW

Another Summary Problem for Your Review for this chapter is available in MyAccountingLab, which covers preparing worksheets, making adjusting and closing entries, preparing financial statements, and computing inventory turnover.

Key Fact: This company is a merchandiser that uses the perpetual inventory system, since the company uses a Cost of Goods Sold account.

Oak Sales Company engaged in the following transactions during September 2017, the first month of the company's fiscal year. Assume the company had no inventory on hand prior to September 3.

Oak Sales Company uses a perpetual inventory system.

Sep. 3	Purchased inventory costing $7,000 on credit terms of 2/10, net eom. The goods were shipped FOB Oak's warehouse.
9	Returned 20 percent of the inventory purchased on September 3. It was defective.
12	Sold goods for cash, $6,000 (cost, $3,000).
15	Purchased inventory of $15,400, less a $400 quantity discount. Credit terms were 2/15, n/30. The goods were shipped FOB the supplier's warehouse.

16	Paid a $1,200 freight bill on the inventory purchased on September 15.
18	Sold inventory for $9,000 on credit terms of 2/10, n/30 (cost, $4,500).
22	Received merchandise returned from the customer from the September 18 sale, $2,000 (cost, $1,000). Merchandise was the wrong size.
24	Borrowed exactly enough money from the bank to pay for the September 15 purchase in time to take advantage of the discount offered. Signed a note payable to the bank for the net amount.
24	Paid supplier for goods purchased on September 15, less all returns and discounts.
28	Received cash in full settlement of the account from the customer who purchased inventory on September 18, less the return on September 22 and less the discount.
29	Paid the amount owed on account from the purchase of September 3, less the September 9 return.
30	Purchased inventory for cash, $4,640, less a quantity discount of $140.

Required

1. Journalize the transactions and include any calculations in the journal entry explanations.
2. Set up T-accounts and post the journal entries to show the ending balances in the Inventory and Cost of Goods Sold accounts.
3. Calculate Oak Sales' gross margin.

SOLUTION

Requirement 1

2017			
Sep. 3	Inventory	7,000	
	Accounts Payable		7,000
	To record purchase on account, terms 2/10, net eom.		
9	Accounts Payable	1,400	
	Inventory		1,400
	Returned 20% of Sep. 3 purchase—goods were defective ($7,000 × 0.20).		
12	Cash	6,000	
	Sales Revenue		6,000
	To record sale of goods for cash.		
12	Cost of Goods Sold	3,000	
	Inventory		3,000
	To record cost of the goods sold for cash on Sep. 12.		
15	Inventory	15,000	
	Accounts Payable		15,000
	To record purchase on account, terms 2/15, n/30. Received a quantity discount of $400 ($15,400 − $400 − $15,000).		

The perpetual method records purchases directly into the inventory account, which always has a running balance.

Notice that freight is not recorded in the Inventory entry because the shipping terms were FOB Oak Sales' (i.e., paid by the seller).

With every sale there is a Cost of Goods Sold/Inventory entry to update the Inventory balance and expense the cost.

The quantity discount is not recorded since it is deducted from the invoice at the time of sale.

(Continued)

(Continued)

Freight is recorded in the Inventory account under the perpetual system; however, it is still tracked for budget purposes. The shipping terms were FOB supplier's warehouse, which means that once they left the supplier title passed and the goods were Oak Sales' responsibility.

16	Inventory	1,200	
	Cash		1,200
	To record payment of the freight bill for the Sep. 15 purchase.		
18	Accounts Receivable	9,000	
	Sales Revenue		9,000
	To record sale of goods on account, terms 2/10, n/30.		
18	Cost of Goods Sold	4,500	
	Inventory		4,500
	To record cost of the goods sold on account on Sep. 18.		
22	Sales Returns and Allowances	2,000	
	Accounts Receivable		2,000
	To record return of goods sold on Sep. 18—wrong size.		

When goods are returned to the supplier, Inventory must also be updated to reflect this.

22	Inventory	1,000	
	Cost of Goods Sold		1,000
	To record cost of the return of goods sold on Sep. 18—wrong size.		
24	Cash	14,700	
	Note Payable		14,700
	Borrowed money from the bank, signing a note payable, to pay for Sep. 15 purchase. Amount borrowed calculated as $14,700 [$15,000 − (0.02 × $15,000)].		

This transaction was eligible for a 2 percent discount, so the amount needed to finance this purchase has a $300 deduction.

A discount is recorded directly to the Inventory account using the perpetual method; however, for management purposes it is coded and tracked.

24	Accounts Payable	15,000	
	Inventory		300
	Cash		14,700
	To record payment of Sep. 15 purchase, taking the 2% discount. Cash payment is calculated as $14,700 [$15,000 − (0.02 × $15,000)]. The discount is $300 ($15,000 × 0.02).		
28	Cash	6,860	
	Sales Discounts	140	
	Accounts Receivable		7,000
	To record receipt of payment from the Sep. 18 sale on account, less the Sep. 22 sales return and the sales discount. The sales discount was $140 [($9,000 − $2,000) × 0.02]. The cash received was $6,860 [($9,000 − $2,000) × 0.98].		
29	Accounts Payable	5,600	
	Cash		5,600
	To record payment of $7,000 Sep. 3 purchase on account, less $1,400 return on Sep. 9. Since the payment is not within the discount period, no discount is taken.		
30	Inventory	4,500	
	Cash		4,500
	To record cash purchase. Received a quantity discount of $140, so final cost was $4,500 ($4,640 − $140).		

Requirement 2

Inventory

Sep. 3	7,000	Sep. 9	1,400
15	15,000	12	3,000
16	1,200	18	4,500
22	1,000	24	300
30	4,500		
Bal	19,500		

Cost of Goods Sold

Sep. 12	3,000	Sep. 22	1,000
18	4,500		
Bal	6,500		

Requirement 3

Sales − Sales returns and discounts − Cost of goods sold = Gross margin

$6,000 + $9,000 − $2,000 − $140 − $6,500 = $6,360

CHAPTER 5 APPENDIX A

ACCOUNTING FOR MERCHANDISE IN A PERIODIC INVENTORY SYSTEM

Purchasing Merchandise in the Periodic Inventory System

Some businesses find it too expensive to invest in a computerized (perpetual) inventory system that keeps up-to-the-minute records of merchandise on hand and cost of goods sold. Sometimes the nature of the inventory makes the perpetual inventory system impractical. These businesses use the periodic inventory system.

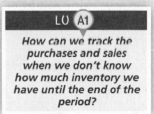

LO A1

How can we track the purchases and sales when we don't know how much inventory we have until the end of the period?

Recording Purchases of Inventory

All inventory systems use the Inventory account. But in a periodic inventory system, purchases, purchase discounts, purchase returns and allowances, and transportation costs are recorded in separate expense accounts bearing these titles. Let's account for the Slopes Ski Shop purchase of the Neige Sportswear goods shown in Exhibit 5–3 on page 252. The following entries record the purchase and payment on account within the discount period:

May 27	Purchases	700.00	
	Accounts Payable		700.00
	Purchased inventory on account.		
Jun. 10	Accounts Payable	700.00	
	Cash		686.00
	Purchase Discounts		14.00
	Paid for inventory on account within the discount period. The discount is $14.00 [$700.00 × 0.02].		

Recording Purchase Returns and Allowances

Suppose instead that, prior to payment, Slopes returned to Neige Sportswear goods costing $60.00 and also received from Neige Sportswear a purchase allowance of $15.00. Slopes would record these transactions as follows:

Jun. 3	Accounts Payable	60.00	
	Purchase Returns and Allowances		60.00
	Returned inventory to seller.		
Jun. 4	Accounts Payable	15.00	
	Purchase Returns and Allowances		15.00
	Received a purchase allowance.		

During the period, the business records the cost of all inventory bought in the Purchases account. The balance of Purchases is the original or gross amount because it does not include subtractions for purchase discounts, returns, or allowances.

	Purchase (*debit* balance account)
(Contra account)	**− Purchase Discounts** (*credit* balance account)
(Contra account)	**− Purchase Returns and Allowances** (*credit* balance account)
	= Net purchases (a *debit* subtotal, not a separate account)

Recording Transportation Costs

Under the periodic system, costs to transport purchased inventory from seller to buyer are debited to a separate expense account, as shown for payment of an $80.00 freight bill:

Jun. 1	Freight-in	80.00	
	Cash		80.00
	Paid a freight bill.		

Recording Sales of Inventory

Recording sales is streamlined in the periodic system. *With no running record of inventory to maintain*, we can record a $5,000 sale as follows:

Jun. 5	Accounts Receivable	5,000	
	Sales Revenue		5,000
	Sale on account.		

No accompanying entry to Inventory and Cost of Goods Sold is required in the periodic system.

Accounting for sales discounts and sales returns and allowances is the same as in the perpetual inventory system (page 258) except that there are no entries to Inventory and Cost of Goods Sold.

> Try It!

12. Refer to the Royal Fashion Distributors transactions in Try It #3 on page 260. Royal engaged in those transactions during June 2017, the first month of the company's fiscal year. Assume the company uses a periodic inventory system and had no inventory on hand prior to June 3. Journalize the transactions.

Solutions appear at the end of this chapter and on MyAccountingLab

COST OF GOODS SOLD

Cost of goods sold (also called cost of sales) is the largest single expense of most businesses that sell merchandise, such as Avigilon, Canadian Tire, Shoppers Drug Mart, and Slopes Ski Shop. It is the cost of the inventory that the business has sold to customers. It is the residual left when we subtract ending inventory from the cost of goods available for sale.

Exhibit 5A–1, Panel A, is an expansion of the cost of goods sold formula introduced on page 250.

LO A2

How do we compute the cost of goods sold amount under the periodic inventory system?

EXHIBIT 5A–1 | Measuring Cost of Goods Sold in the Periodic Inventory System

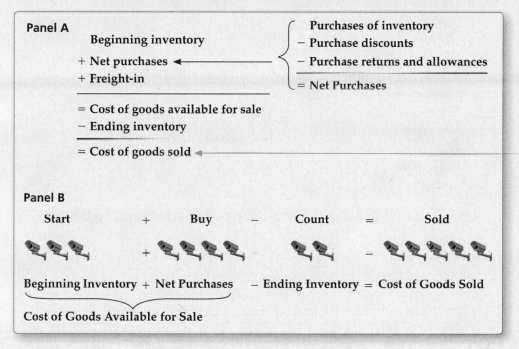

Panel A

Beginning inventory
+ Net purchases ◄——
+ Freight-in
——————————————
= Cost of goods available for sale
− Ending inventory
——————————————
= Cost of goods sold ◄——

Purchases of inventory
− Purchase discounts
− Purchase returns and allowances
——————————————
= Net Purchases

In a periodic system, cost of goods sold must be computed and is not a ledger account.

Panel B

Start	+	Buy	−	Count	=	Sold

Beginning Inventory + Net Purchases − Ending Inventory = Cost of Goods Sold

Cost of Goods Available for Sale

Exhibit 5A–2 on the next page shows Slopes' net sales revenue, cost of goods sold (including net purchases and freight-in) and gross margin on the income statement for the periodic system. (All amounts are assumed.)

> Try It!

13. Refer to Royal Fashion Distributors journal entries created in Try It #12 on page 274. Calculate cost of goods sold and gross profit assuming ending inventory is $11,000 and beginning inventory was $0.

Solutions appear at the end of this chapter and on MyAccountingLab

SLOPES SKI SHOP
Income Statement
For the Year Ended December 31, 2017

PANEL A—Detailed Gross Margin Section—Often Required by Management

Sales revenue			$777,000
Less: Sales discounts		$ 7,500	
Sales returns and allowances		8,000	15,500
Net sales			761,500
Cost of goods sold:			
Beginning inventory		158,400	
Purchases	$422,600		
Less: Purchase discounts	12,000		
Purchase returns and allowances	5,000		
Net purchases		405,600	
Freight-in		31,000	
Cost of goods available for sale		595,000	
Less: Ending inventory		168,000	
Cost of goods sold			427,000
Gross margin			$334,500

Notice that this is the same as the equation in 5A–1, just in statement format

PANEL B—Summary Gross Margin Section—Most Common in Annual Reports to Outsiders

Net sales	$761,500
Cost of goods sold	427,000
Gross margin	$334,500

ADJUSTING AND CLOSING THE ACCOUNTS IN A PERIODIC INVENTORY SYSTEM

LO A3

How do we update inventory using the year-end physical count and begin the next cycle using the periodic inventory system?

A merchandising business adjusts and closes the accounts much like a service entity does. The steps of this end-of-period process are the same: If a worksheet is used, the unadjusted trial balance is entered and the worksheet is completed to determine net income or net loss. The worksheet provides the data for journalizing the adjusting and closing entries and for preparing the financial statements.

The adjusting entries are the same for service entities and merchandisers that use the periodic inventory system. These adjusting entries were described in Chapter 4.

At the end of the period, before any adjusting or closing entries, the Inventory account balance is still the cost of the inventory that was on hand from the beginning of the year. *Closing entries are essential to bring the inventory records up to date.*

To illustrate a merchandiser's closing process under the periodic inventory system, let's use Slopes' December 31, 2017, worksheet shown in Exhibit 5A–3. All the new accounts—Inventory, Purchases, Freight-in, and the contra accounts—are bolded for emphasis. Inventory is the only account that is affected by the new closing procedures. The physical count of inventory gives the ending inventory figure of $168,000.

Preparing and Using the Worksheet in a Periodic Inventory System

Trial Balance Columns   Examine the Inventory account, $158,400 in the trial balance. This $158,400 is the cost of the beginning inventory. The worksheet is designed to replace this outdated amount with the new ending balance, which in our example is $168,000 [additional data item (h)]. As we will see below, this task is accomplished in the columns for the income statement and the balance sheet during the closing process.

Adjusted trial balance columns are optional and are normally only used when the worksheet is introduced (see Chapter 4).

Place beginning inventory here

Place ending inventory here

It is necessary to remove the beginning balance and replace it with the ending inventory count

SLOPES SKI SHOP

Worksheet

For the Year Ended December 31, 2017

Account Title	Unadjusted Trial Balance Dr	Cr	Adjustments Dr	Cr	Income Statement Dr	Cr	Balance Sheet Dr	Cr
Cash	6,000						6,000	
Accounts receivable	24,000						24,000	
Note receivable, current	32,000						32,000	
Interest receivable	0		(a) 1,000				1,000	
Inventory	**158,400**				**158,400**	**168,000**	**168,000**	
Supplies	1,500			(b) 1,000			500	
Prepaid insurance	4,600			(c) 4,000			600	
Furniture and fixtures	120,000						120,000	
Accum. amort.—furn. and fixt.		12,000		(d) 6,000				18,000
Accounts payable		128,000						128,000
Unearned sales revenue		4,100	(e) 2,600					1,500
Wages payable		0		(f) 3,000				3,000
Interest payable		0		(g) 500				500
Note payable, long-term		44,100						44,100
Steve Austin, capital		90,000						90,000
Steve Austin, withdrawals	65,000						65,000	
Sales revenue		774,400		(e) 2,600		777,000		
Sales discounts	**7,500**				**7,500**			
Sales returns and allowances	**8,000**				**8,000**			
Interest revenue		2,000		(a) 1,000		3,000		
Purchases	**422,600**				**422,600**			
Purchase discounts		**12,000**				**12,000**		
Purchase returns and allowances		**5,000**				**5,000**		
Freight-in	**31,000**				**31,000**			
Wages expense	139,000		(f) 3,000		142,000			
Rent expense	48,000				48,000			
Amort. expense—furn. and fixt.	0		(d) 6,000		6,000			
Insurance expense	0		(c) 4,000		4,000			
Supplies expense	0		(b) 1,000		1,000			
Interest expense	4,000		(g) 500		4,500			
	1,071,600	1,071,600	18,100	18,100	833,000	965,000	417,100	285,100
Net income					132,000			132,000
					965,000	965,000	417,100	417,100

Additional data at December 31, 2017:

a. Interest revenue earned but not yet collected, $1,000.
b. Supplies on hand, $500.
c. Prepaid insurance expired during the year, $4,000.
d. Amortization for the year, $6,000.
e. Unearned sales revenue earned during the year, $2,600.
f. Accrued wages expense, $3,000.
g. Accrued interest expense, $500.
h. Ending Inventory on hand based on inventory count, $168,000.

Cost of goods sold can be determined by using the bolded items:

Beginning inventory + Net purchases + Freight-in – Ending Inventory

= $158,400 + $405,600 [$422,600 – $12,000 – $5,000] + $31,000 – $168,000

= $427,000

Journalizing the Closing Entries in the Periodic Inventory System

Exhibit 5A–4 gives Slopes' closing entries. Here is an explanation of each entry:

❶ Debits the revenue accounts and the contra expenses (Purchase Discounts and Purchase Returns and Allowances) and credits income summary for ($797,000).

❷ Debits Income Summary ($674,600) and credits the contra revenue accounts (Sales Discounts and Sales Returns and Allowances) and all the expenses, including Purchases and Freight-in.

Closing entries ❸ and ❹ are new.

❸ Debits Income Summary for the amount of the beginning balance of the Inventory account ($158,400) and credits Inventory.

❹ Debits Inventory for its ending balance, which was determined by the count of inventory at the end of the period ($168,000), and credits Income Summary.

Closing entries ❺ and ❻ finish the closing process.

EXHIBIT 5A–4 | Closing Entries for the Periodic Inventory System

		Closing Entries		
❶ Dec. 31	Sales Revenue		777,000	
	Interest Revenue		3,000	
	Purchase Discounts		12,000	
	Purchase Returns and Allowances		5,000	
	Income Summary			797,000
❷ Dec. 31	Income Summary		674,600	
	Sales Discounts			7,500
	Sales Returns and Allowances			8,000
	Purchases			422,600
	Freight-in			31,000
	Wages Expense			142,000
	Rent Expense			48,000
	Amortization Expense			6,000
	Insurance Expense			4,000
	Supplies Expense			1,000
	Interest Expense			4,500
❸ Dec. 31	Income Summary		158,400	
	Inventory (beginning balance)			158,400
❹ Dec. 31	Inventory (ending balance)		168,000	
	Income Summary			168,000
❺ Dec. 31	Income Summary		132,000	
	Steve Austin, Capital			132,000
	($797,000 − $674,600 − $158,400 + $168,000)			
❻ Dec. 31	Steve Austin, Capital		65,000	
	Steve Austin, Withdrawals			65,000

These entries are essential to update the Inventory ledger account

Now Inventory has its correct ending balance as shown below.

Inventory

Jan. 1 Bal.	158,400	Dec. 31 Clo. ❸	158,400	
Dec. 31 Clo. ❹	168,000			
Dec. 31 Bal.	168,000			

Correct ending balance

The entries to the Inventory account deserve additional explanation. Recall that before the closing process Inventory still has the period's beginning balance. At the end of the period, this balance is one year old and must be replaced with the ending balance so that the financial statements can be prepared at December 31, 2017.

14. Refer to Royal Fashion's journal entries created in Try It #13 on page 275. The inventory count at the end of June 2017 showed an amount of $11,000 on hand. Using this information, prepare the closing entries using the periodic inventory method.

PREPARING THE FINANCIAL STATEMENTS OF A MERCHANDISER

Exhibit 5A–5 presents Slopes Ski Shop's financial statements. The *income statement* through gross margin repeats Exhibit 5A–2. This information is followed by the operating expenses—expenses other than cost of goods sold that are incurred in the entity's major line of business—merchandising.

As mentioned on page 265, many companies report their operating expenses in two categories:

- *Selling expenses* are those expenses related to marketing the company's products.
- *General expenses* include office expenses, such as the salaries of office employees, and amortization, rent, utilities, and property taxes.

The last section of Slopes' income statement is other revenue and expenses, which is handled in the same way in both inventory systems. This category reports revenues and expenses that are outside the company's main line of business.

Net sales, cost of goods sold, operating income, and net income are unaffected by the choice of inventory system. You can prove this by comparing Slopes' financial statements given in Exhibit 5A–5 with the corresponding statements in Exhibit 5–7 on page 264. The only differences appear in the cost of goods sold section of the income statement, and those differences are unimportant. In fact, virtually all companies report cost of goods sold in a streamlined fashion, as shown for Slopes in Exhibit 5–7.

LO A4

How can we prepare financial statements for a company using the periodic inventory system?

SLOPES SKI SHOP
Income Statement
For the Year Ended December 31, 2017

Sales revenue			$777,000
Less: Sales discounts		$ 7,500	
Sales returns and allowances		8,000	15,500
Net sales revenue			761,500
Cost of goods sold:			
Beginning inventory		158,400	
Purchases	$ 422,600		
Less: Purchase discounts	12,000		
Purchase returns and allowances	5,000		
Net purchases		405,600	
Freight-in		31,000	
Cost of goods available for sale		595,000	
Less: Ending inventory		168,000	
Cost of goods sold			427,000
Gross margin			334,500
Operating expenses:			
Wages expense		142,000	
Rent expense		48,000	
Amortization expense		6,000	
Insurance expense		4,000	
Supplies expense		1,000	201,000
Income from operations			133,500
Other revenue and (expense):			
Interest revenue		3,000	
Less: Interest expense		4,500	1,500
Net income			$132,000

SLOPES SKI SHOP
Statement of Owner's Equity
For the Year Ended December 31, 2017

Steve Austin, capital, January 1, 2017	$ 90,000
Add: Net income	132,000
	222,000
Less: Withdrawals	65,000
Steve Austin, capital, December 31, 2017	$157,000

SLOPES SKI SHOP
Balance Sheet
December 31, 2017

Assets			Liabilities		
Current assets:			Current liabilities:		
Cash	$ 6,000		Accounts payable		$128,000
Accounts receivable	24,000		Unearned sales revenue		1,500
Note receivable	32,000		Wages payable		3,000
Interest receivable	1,000		Interest payable		500
Inventory	168,000		Total current liabilities		133,000
Prepaid insurance	600		Long-term liability:		
Supplies	500		Note payable		44,100
Total current assets	232,100		Total liabilities		177,100
Property, plant and equipment:			**Owner's Equity**		
Furniture and fixtures	$120,000		S. Austin, capital		157,000
Less: Accumulated amortization	18,000	102,000			
Total assets		$334,100	Total liabilities and owner's equity		$334,100

SUMMARY PROBLEM FOR YOUR REVIEW

CHAPTER 5 APPENDIX A

Use the data for Oak Sales Company from pages 270–271, except that this time assume that Oak Sales Company uses a periodic inventory system.

Required

1. Journalize the transactions and include any calculations in the journal entry explanations.
2. The inventory count at the end of September 2017 showed $20,050 of inventory on hand. Using this information and the amounts from the journal entries created in Requirement 1, compute the cost of goods sold under the periodic inventory system for Oak Sales Company for the month ended September 30, 2017.
3. Prepare the closing entries under the periodic inventory system for Oak Sales Company for the month ended September 30, 2017. Assume no other transactions took place during September 2017.

SOLUTIONS

Requirement 1

2017			
Sep. 3	Purchases	7,000	
	Accounts Payable		7,000
	To record purchase on account, terms 1/10, net eom.		
9	Accounts Payable	1,400	
	Purchase Returns and Allowances		1,400
	Returned 20% of Sep. 3 purchase—goods were defective ($7,000 × 0.20).		
12	Cash	6,000	
	Sales Revenue		6,000
	To record sale of goods for cash.		
15	Purchases	15,000	
	Accounts Payable		15,000
	To record purchase on account, terms 2/15, n/30. Received a quantity discount of $400 ($15,400 − $400 = $15,000).		
16	Freight-in	1,200	
	Cash		1,200
	To record payment of the freight bill for the Sep. 15 purchase.		
18	Accounts Receivable	9,000	
	Sales Revenue		9,000
	To record sale of goods on account, terms 2/10, n/30.		
22	Sales Returns and Allowances	2,000	
	Accounts Receivable		2,000
	To record return of goods sold on Sep. 18—wrong size.		

Another Summary Problem for Your Review for this appendix is available in MyAccountingLab, which covers preparing worksheets, making adjusting and closing entries, preparing financial statements, and computing inventory turnover.

The Summary Problem for Your Review on pages 270–273 was for a merchandiser using the perpetual inventory system. This Summary Problem uses the same data for the same company, but this time the company uses the periodic inventory system. The only differences are that this problem includes the accounts that make up Cost of Goods Sold.

Using the periodic inventory system, acquisitions are recorded in a separate account and there is no running balance of inventory. Inventory must be counted at the end of each period to verify the balance in stock. The only time that we know the balance in the Inventory account is after the physical count. A separate account is also used for inventory returns.

Using the periodic method, there is no compound entry to record the decrease in inventory from a sale.

A separate account is used for freight-in, which is considered a cost of goods sold account.

(Continued)

(Continued)

24	Cash		14,700	
	Note Payable			14,700
	Borrowed money from the bank, signing a note payable, to pay for Sep. 15 purchase. Amount borrowed calculated as $14,700 [$15,000 − (0.02 × $15,000)].			
24	Accounts Payable		15,000	
	Purchase Discounts			300
	Cash			14,700
	To record payment of Sep. 15 purchase, taking the 2% discount. Cash payment is calculated as $14,700 [$15,000 − (0.02 × $15,000)]. The discount is $300 ($15,000 × 0.02).			
28	Cash		6,860	
	Sales Discounts		140	
	Accounts Receivable			7,000
	To record receipt of payment from the Sep. 18 sale on account, less the Sep. 22 sales return and less the sales discount. The sales discount was $140 [($9,000 − $2,000) × 0.02]. The cash received was $6,860 [($9,000 − $2,000) × 0.98].			
29	Accounts Payable		5,600	
	Cash			5,600
	To record payment of $7,000 Sep. 3 purchase on account, less $1,400 return on Sep. 9. Since the payment is not within the discount period, no discount is taken.			
30	Purchases		4,500	
	Cash			4,500
	To record cash purchase. Received a quantity discount of $140, so final cost was $4,500 ($4,640 − $140).			

Using the periodic method, a separate account is used for inventory discounts and factors into the net purchases calculation.

Requirement 2

Cost of goods sold in the periodic inventory system is calculated as follows:

Beginning inventory (given)		$ 0
+ Net purchases, calculated as:		
Purchases of inventory		
($7,000 + $15,000 + $4,500)	$ 26,500	
− Purchase discounts	300	
− Purchases returns and allowances	1,400	24,800
+ Freight-in		1,200
= Cost of goods available for sale		26,000
− Ending inventory (given)		20,050
= Cost of goods sold		$ 5,950

A physical count is completed at the end of the period.

A company must complete a physical count to enter the ending inventory number.

Using the periodic method, the only way cost of goods sold is calculated is using the formula Beginning inventory + Net purchases − Ending inventory.

Requirement 3

2017			
❶ Sep. 30	Sales Revenue ($6,000 + $9,000)	15,000	
	Purchase Discounts	300	
	Purchase Returns and Allowances	1,400	
	Income Summary		16,700
	To close all revenue and contra expense accounts.		
❷ Sep. 30	Income Summary	29,840	
	Sales Discounts		140
	Sales Returns and Allowances		2,000
	Purchases ($7,000 + $15,000 + $4,500)		26,500
	Freight-in		1,200
	To close all expense and contra revenue accounts.		
❸	No entry required since opening inventory is $0.		
❹ Sep. 30	Inventory	20,050	
	Income Summary		20,050
	To record the ending inventory balance.		
❺ Sep. 30	Income Summary	7,270	
	Capital		7,270
	To close net income ($16,700 − $29,840 + $20,050 − $7,270) from Income Summary to the Capital account.		

Using the periodic method, this closing entry is the only way inventory is updated to carry forward a balance for the next period. This number is derived from a physical count.

CHAPTER 5 APPENDIX B

COMPARING THE PERPETUAL AND PERIODIC INVENTORY SYSTEMS

Exhibit 5B–1 provides a side-by-side comparison of the two inventory accounting systems. It gives the journal entries, the T-accounts, and all financial statement effects of both inventory systems.

LO B1
How do the inventory systems compare?

EXHIBIT 5B–1 | Comparing the Perpetual and Periodic Inventory Systems (amounts assumed)

Not recorded in the Inventory account; use the expense account Purchases instead

Panel A—Recording in the Journal and Posting to the Accounts

Perpetual System			Periodic System		
1. Credit purchases of $600,000:			**1. Credit purchases of $600,000:**		
Inventory	600,000		Purchases ◄	600,000	
Accounts Payable		600,000	Accounts Payable		600,000
2. Credit sales of $1,000,000 (cost $550,000):			**2. Credit sales of $1,000,000:**		
Accounts Receivable	1,000,000		Accounts Receivable	1,000,000	
Sales Revenue		1,000,000	Sales Revenue		1,000,000
Cost of Goods Sold	550,000				
Inventory		550,000			

Note that there is no Cost of Goods Sold entry.

(Continued)

Panel A—Recording in the Journal and Posting to the Accounts

Perpetual System	Periodic System
3. End-of-period entries:	**3. End-of-period entries to update Inventory:**
No entries required. Both Inventory and Cost of Goods Sold are up to date.	**a. Transfer the cost of beginning inventory ($100,000) to Income Summary:**

Income Summary	100,000	
Inventory (beginning balance)		100,000

> Transactions 3a and 3b give the end-of-period entries to update the Inventory account. Transaction 3c closes the Purchases account into Income Summary to complete the periodic process.

b. Record the cost of ending inventory ($150,000) based on a physical count:

Inventory (ending balance)	150,000	
Income Summary		150,000

c. Transfer the cost of purchases to Income Summary:

Income Summary	600,000	
Purchases		600,000

Inventory and Cost of Goods Sold Accounts

Inventory		Cost of Goods Sold	
100,000*	550,000	550,000	
600,000			
150,000			

Inventory and Income Summary Accounts

Inventory		Income Summary	
100,000*	100,000	100,000	150,000
150,000		600,000	
150,000		550,000	

*Beginning inventory was $100,000.

Panel B—Reporting in the Financial Statements

Perpetual System		Periodic System	
Income Statement (partial)			
Sales revenue	$1,000,000	Sales revenue	$1,000,000
Cost of goods sold	550,000 ◄	Cost of goods sold:	
Gross margin	$ 450,000	Beginning inventory	$100,000
		Purchases	600,000
		Cost of goods available for sale	700,000
		Less: Ending inventory	150,000
		► Cost of goods sold	550,000
		Gross margin	$ 450,000
Balance Sheet (partial)			
Current assets:		Current assets:	
Cash	$ XXX	Cash	$ XXX
Accounts receivable	XXX	Accounts receivable	XXX
Inventory	150,000	Inventory	150,000

Note: It was decided to omit consideration of the GST/HST to avoid making the material overly complicated. GST/HST is dealt with in Chapter 11.

SUMMARY

LEARNING OBJECTIVE **1**   Use sales and gross margin to evaluate a company

How can we use sales information to evaluate a company?   **Pg. 247**

- The major revenue of a merchandising business is sales revenue, or net sales. The major expense is cost of goods sold.

  > Net sales − Cost of goods sold = Gross margin, or gross profit

- Gross margin measures the business's success or failure in selling its products at a higher price than it paid for them.

LEARNING OBJECTIVE **2**   Account for the purchase and sale of inventory under the perpetual inventory system

How can we track the purchase and sale of inventory when we should know how much inventory we have?   **Pg. 251**

- For all merchandisers:
  - The major asset is inventory.
  - The accounting cycle is from cash to inventory as the inventory is purchased for resale, and back to cash as the inventory is sold.
  - An invoice is the document generated by a purchase or sale transaction.
  - Most merchandising entities offer purchase returns to their customers to allow them to return unsuitable merchandise and allowances for damaged goods that the buyer chooses to keep.
  - Some suppliers offer merchandising entities (their customers) purchase discounts to encourage them to pay their invoice promptly within the discount period.
- Under the perpetual inventory system, a merchandiser keeps a continuous record for each inventory item to show the inventory on hand at all times.

  MyAccountingLab **Interactive Figure:** Interact with Purchase Discount

  Interactive Figure: Interact with COGS and Merchandise Inventory

LEARNING OBJECTIVE **3**   Adjust and close the accounts of a merchandising business under the perpetual inventory system

How can we adjust for possible inventory shrinkage and begin the next cycle using the perpetual inventory system?   **Pg. 260**

- The end-of-period adjusting and closing process of a merchandising business is similar to that of a service business.
- In addition, a merchandiser using the perpetual inventory system adjusts inventory for theft losses, damage, and accounting errors normally discovered from the physical count of the inventory.

LEARNING OBJECTIVE **4**   Prepare a merchandiser's financial statements under the perpetual inventory system

How can we prepare financial statements for a company using the perpetual inventory system?   **Pg. 264**

- The income statement may appear in the single-step format or the multi-step format.
  - The single-step format has only two sections—one for revenues and the other for expenses—and a single income amount for net income.
  - The multi-step format has subtotals for gross margin and income from operations. (It is the most widely used format.)

  MyAccountingLab **Video:** Merchandising Income Statement and Transactions

LEARNING OBJECTIVE **5**   Use the gross margin percentage and the inventory turnover ratio to evaluate a business

How can we use ratios to evaluate a business?   **Pg. 268**

- Two key decision aids for a merchandiser are:
  - The **gross margin percentage** (Gross margin ÷ Net sales revenue)
  - The **inventory turnover** (Cost of goods sold ÷ Average inventory)
- Increases in these measures usually signal an increase in profits.

  MyAccountingLab **Video:** Real World Accounting

How does IFRS affect companies that sell inventory? Pg. 270

- Income statements for merchandisers following IFRS are not significantly different from those of companies following ASPE. Sales revenue is recognized in the same way at the same time; however, returns are monitored more closely.

LEARNING OBJECTIVE A1 Account for the purchase and sale of inventory under the periodic inventory system

How can we track the purchases and sales when we don't know how much inventory we have until the end of the period? Pg. 273

- Under the periodic inventory system, merchandisers do not keep a continuous record of the inventory on hand. Instead, at the end of the period, the merchandiser makes a physical count of the inventory on hand and applies the cost per item to calculate the cost of the ending inventory.
- During the year, merchandisers using the periodic inventory system:
  - Record purchases of inventory in the Purchases account
  - Record freight-in, purchase discounts, and purchase returns and allowances in separate contra accounts
  - Do not use the Inventory account to record inventory purchases or sales.
  - Record sales in the normal way, but no entry is made to record the cost of the goods sold (as is done under the perpetual system).

LEARNING OBJECTIVE A2 Compute the cost of goods sold under the periodic inventory system

How do we compute the cost of goods sold amount under the periodic inventory system? Pg. 275

- Cost of goods sold is computed at the end of the period using the cost of goods sold formula:

> Beginning inventory
> \+ Net purchases
> \+ Freight-in
> = Cost of goods available for sale
> − Ending inventory
> = Cost of goods sold

- The physical inventory count gives the amount of ending inventory that is required by the cost of goods sold formula.
- Under the periodic inventory system, there is no Cost of Goods Sold account like there is under the perpetual inventory system.

LEARNING OBJECTIVE A3 Adjust and close the accounts of a merchandising business under the periodic inventory system

How do we update inventory using the year-end physical count and begin the next cycle using the periodic inventory system? Pg. 276

- The closing entries for the periodic inventory system are more complicated than those of the perpetual inventory system.
- Purchases, Purchase Returns and Allowances, and Freight-in accounts are all closed to the Income Summary account.
- The opening inventory amount is debited to Income Summary and credited to Inventory to remove opening inventory from the balance sheet.
- The closing inventory amount (based on the inventory count) is debited to Inventory and credited to Income Summary to place closing inventory on the balance sheet.
- The result of these inventory transactions in the Income Summary account is that the cost of goods sold amount appears on the income statement and Inventory on the balance sheet is the closing inventory at year end.

LEARNING OBJECTIVE A4 Prepare a merchandiser's financial statements under the periodic inventory system

How can we prepare financial statements for a company using the periodic inventory system? Pg. 279

- The financial statements report the same results regardless of whether the merchandiser uses the periodic inventory system or the perpetual inventory system.
- The only difference is on the income statement:
  - The cost of goods sold amount is an account balance under the perpetual inventory system.
  - The cost of goods sold amount is a calculation under the periodic inventory system.

How do the inventory systems compare?

- In the perpetual system:
  - Inventory purchases are recorded in the Inventory account.
  - Each sale has a transaction that records the cost of the sale and updates inventory, providing the current level.
- In the periodic system:
  - Inventory purchases are recorded in the Purchases account, which is an expense account.
  - Only the sale is recorded. There is no Inventory update. The cost of goods sold is calculated only at the end of the period.
- Both inventory systems:
  - Require a physical count of inventory at least once per year, usually at the end of the period.
  - Report the same financial results at the end of the period since both adjust Inventory to match the amount based on the physical count.

Check **Accounting Vocabulary** for all key terms used in Chapter 5 and the **Glossary** at the back of the book for all key terms used in the textbook.

MORE CHAPTER REVIEW MATERIAL

MyAccountingLab

DemoDoc covering Inventory Transaction Analysis under the Perpetual System

Student PowerPoint Slides

Audio Chapter Summary

Note: All MyAccountingLab resources can be found in the Chapter Resources section and the Multimedia Library.

ACCOUNTING VOCABULARY

2/15, n30 Credit terms offered by some merchandisers, meaning that if the invoice is paid within 15 days of the invoice date (the *discount period*), a 2 percent discount may be taken. If not, the full amount (net) is due in 30 days *(p. 253)*.

Bill Another term for *invoice* *(p. 252)*.

Cash discount Another name for a purchase discount *(p. 253)*.

Cost of goods sold The cost of the inventory that the business has sold to customers; the largest single expense of most merchandising businesses. Also called *cost of sales* *(p. 248)*.

Cost of sales Another name for *cost of goods sold* (p. 248).

Discount period The time period during which a cash discount is available and a reduced payment can be made by the purchaser *(p. 253)*.

eom A credit term that means an invoice amount is due by the end of the month *(p. 253)*.

FOB destination Legal title passes to the buyer only when the inventory reaches the destination (i.e., the seller pays the freight) *(p. 255)*.

FOB shipping point Legal title passes to the buyer as soon as the inventory leaves the seller's place of business—the shipping point *(p. 255)*.

Freight-in The transportation costs on purchased goods (i.e., from the wholesaler to the retailer) *(p. 256)*.

Freight-out The transportation costs on goods sold (i.e., from the retailer to the customer) *(p. 256)*.

Gross margin Excess of sales revenue over cost of goods sold. Also called *gross profit* *(p. 248)*.

Gross margin percentage Gross margin divided by net sales revenue. A measure of profitability *(p. 268)*.

Income from operations Another name for *operating income* *(p. 265)*.

Inventory All goods that a company owns and expects to sell in the normal course of operation *(p. 246)*.

Inventory turnover The ratio of cost of goods sold to average inventory. Measures the number of times a company sells its average level of inventory during a year *(p. 269)*.

Invoice A seller's request for cash from the purchaser *(p. 252)*.

Legal title The legal ownership of property *(p. 255)*.

Multi-step income statement An income statement format that contains subtotals to highlight significant relationships. In addition to net income, it also presents gross margin and income from operations *(p. 266)*.

Net purchases Purchases plus freight in and less purchase discounts and purchase returns and allowances *(p. 256)*.

Net sales Sales revenue less sales discounts and sales returns and allowances *(p. 248)*.

Operating expense Expense, other than cost of goods sold, that is incurred in the entity's major line of business: rent, amortization, salaries, wages, utilities, property tax, and supplies expense (p. 265).

Operating income Gross margin minus operating expenses plus any other operating revenues. Also called *income from operations* (p. 265).

Other expense Expense that is outside the main operations of a business, such as a loss on the sale of capital assets (p. 265).

Other revenue Revenue that is outside the main operations of a business, such as a gain on the sale of capital assets (p. 265).

Periodic inventory system A type of inventory accounting system in which the business does not keep a continuous record of the inventory on hand. Instead, at the end of the period the business makes a physical count of the on-hand inventory and applies the appropriate unit costs to determine the cost of the ending inventory (p. 249).

Perpetual inventory system A type of accounting inventory system in which the business keeps a continuous record for each inventory item to show the inventory on hand at all times (p. 250).

Purchase discount A reduction in the purchase price granted to the purchaser for paying within the discount period. Also called a *cash discount* (p. 253).

Purchase order A legal document that represents a business's intention to buy goods (p. 252).

Quantity discount A reduction in the purchase price of an item based on the quantity of the item purchased; the greater the quantity purchased, the lower the price per item (p. 252).

Sales Another name for *sales revenue* (p. 247).

Sales discount A reduction in the amount receivable from a customer offered by the seller as an incentive for the customer to pay promptly. A contra account to sales revenue (p. 258).

Sales returns and allowances A decrease in the seller's receivable from a customer's return of merchandise or from granting the customer an allowance from the amount the customer owes the seller. A contra account to sales revenue (p. 258).

Sales revenue The amount that a merchandiser earns from selling inventory before subtracting expenses. Also called *sales* (p. 247).

Shrinkage A reduction in the amount of inventory due to theft, spoilage, or error (p. 261).

Single-step income statement An income statement format that groups all revenues together and then lists and deducts all expenses together without drawing any subtotals (p. 266).

SIMILAR ACCOUNTING TERMS

Cost of goods sold	Cost of sales
FOB destination	CIF destination (CIF stands for cost, insurance, and freight)
Freight-in or Freight-out	Freight; Transportation-in; Transportation costs
Gross margin	Gross profit
Gross margin percentage	Gross profit percentage; Markup percentage
Income from operations	Operating income
Invoice	Bill
List price	Full price; Price with no discounts deducted
Purchase discount	Cash discount; Discount given to reward prompt payment
Quantity discount	Volume discount; Discount given to reward purchase of more than one of a particular item
Sales revenue	Sales

SELF-STUDY QUESTIONS

Test your understanding of the chapter by marking the correct answer for each of the following questions:

1. The major expense of a merchandising business is (p. 248)
   a. Cost of goods sold
   b. Amortization
   c. Rent
   d. Interest

2. Sales total $445,000, cost of goods sold is $220,000, and operating expenses are $175,000. How much is gross margin? (p. 248)
   a. $445,000
   b. $50,000
   c. $270,000
   d. $225,000

3. If a merchandiser's beginning inventory was $60,000, it purchased $125,000 during the period, and a count shows $50,000 of inventory on hand at the end of the period, what was the cost of the goods sold? (*p. 250*)
   a. $110,000
   b. $75,000
   c. $185,000
   d. $135,000

4. A purchase discount results from (*p. 253*)
   a. Returning goods to the seller
   b. Receiving a purchase allowance from the seller
   c. Buying a large enough quantity of merchandise to get the discount
   d. Paying within the discount period

5. Which of the following is *not* an account? (*p. 258*)
   a. Sales Revenue
   b. Net Sales
   c. Inventory
   d. Supplies Expense

6. Which account causes the main difference between a merchandiser's adjusting and closing process and that of a service business? (*p. 261*)
   a. Advertising Expense
   b. Interest Revenue
   c. Cost of Goods Sold
   d. Accounts Receivable

7. The closing entry for Sales Discounts includes (*p. 263*)
   a. Sales Discounts
         Income Summary
   b. Sales Discounts
         Sales Revenue
   c. Income Summary
         Sales Discounts
   d. Not used: Sales Discounts is a permanent account, which is not closed.

8. Which income statement format reports income from operations? (*p. 266*)
   a. Account format
   b. Single-step format
   c. Report format
   d. Multi-step format

9. A company has sales of $375,000, cost of goods sold of $225,000, average inventory during the year of $75,000, and ending inventory of $90,000. The company's inventory turnover for the year is (*p. 269*)
   a. 3.00 times
   b. 2.50 times
   c. 5.00 times
   d. 2.00 times

10. Refer to Self-Study Question 9. About how many days does it take the inventory to turn over? (*p. 269*)
    a. 122
    b. 88
    c. 146
    d. 73

ASSIGNMENT MATERIAL

QUESTIONS

1. Gross margin is often mentioned in the business press as an important measure of success. What does gross margin measure, and why is it important?

2. Describe the operating cycle for (a) the purchase and cash sale of inventory, and (b) the purchase and sale of inventory on account.

3. Identify 10 items of information on an invoice.

4. Indicate which accounts are debited and credited under the perpetual inventory system for (a) a credit purchase of inventory and the subsequent cash payment, and (b) a credit sale of inventory and the subsequent cash collection. Assume no discounts, returns, allowances, or freight.

5. Inventory costing $9,600 is purchased and invoiced on July 28 under terms of 2/10, n/30. Compute the payment amount on August 6. How much would the payment be on August 9? What explains the difference? What is the latest acceptable payment date under the terms of sale?

6. Inventory listed at $80,000 is sold subject to a quantity discount of $6,000 and under payment terms of 1/15, n/45. What is the net sales revenue on this sale if the customer pays within 15 days?

7. Name the new contra accounts introduced in this chapter.

8. Briefly discuss the similarity in computing supplies expense and computing cost of goods sold under the periodic inventory system using the formula shown on page 250.

9. Why is the title of Cost of Goods Sold especially descriptive? What type of account is Cost of Goods Sold?

10. Beginning inventory is $20,000, net purchases total $55,000, and freight-in is $4,000. If ending inventory is $28,000, what is cost of goods sold?

11. You are evaluating two companies as possible investments. One entity sells services; the other entity is a merchandiser. How can you identify the merchandiser by examining the two entities' balance sheets and income statements?

12. You are beginning the adjusting and closing process at the end of your company's fiscal year. Does the trial balance carry the final ending amount of inventory if your company uses the perpetual inventory system? Why or why not?

13. Give the adjusting entry for inventory if shrinkage is $5,000.

14. What is the identifying characteristic of the "other" category of revenues and expenses? Give an example of each.

15. Name and describe two formats for the income statement, and identify the type of business to which each format best applies.

16. List eight different operating expenses.

17. Which financial statement reports sales discounts and sales returns and allowances? Show how they are reported, using any reasonable amounts in your illustration.

18. Does a merchandiser prefer a high or a low rate of inventory turnover? Explain.

19. In general, what does a decreasing gross margin percentage coupled with an increasing rate of inventory turnover suggest about a business's pricing strategy?

*20. In the periodic inventory system, what is meant by the term "cost of goods available for sale"?

*21. In a periodic inventory system, why must inventory be physically counted to determine cost of goods sold?

*22. Why do accountants use a Purchases account when inventory items are acquired in a periodic inventory system?

*23. How are purchase discounts accounted for in a periodic inventory system?

*24. Suppose you are starting a new retail business. What factors would you consider in determining whether to implement a periodic or a perpetual inventory system?

---

*These Questions cover Chapter 5 Appendix A or B topics.

MyAccountingLab

Make the grade with MyAccountingLab: The Starters, Exercises, and Problems marked in red can be found on MyAccountingLab. You can practise them as often as you want, and most feature step-by-step guided instructions to help you find the right answer.

STARTERS

Using the cost of goods sold formula

Starter 5–1 Ending inventory of the previous period was $150,000, and net purchases this period were $750,000. If ending inventory this period is $100,000, how much is cost of goods sold?

Account for the total purchase cost of inventory

②

Starter 5–2 Suppose Puma uses the perpetual inventory system to purchase T-shirts on account for $15,000 from Gildan Activewear Inc. It cost Puma $1,000 FOB Gildan to ship the T-shirts from Gildan to Puma as well as duty and excise fees of $200. Puma was also fined $300 for unloading the inventory in an unauthorized area.

1. Compute the cost of inventory to Puma.

2. Puma pays $500 to deliver the goods to three downtown Sportmart retail outlets. How would this cost be recorded?

Compute inventory balance

②

Starter 5–3 The following data pertain to Corbet Merchandising for the year ended December 31, 2017:

Beginning inventory	$190,300
Purchases of inventory on credit during the year	450,000
Cost of goods sold during the year	65% of sales
Sales (75% on credit) during the year	800,000

a. Prepare entries for the following transactions using a perpetual inventory system:

    i. Purchase of inventory during 2017

    ii. Sales during 2017

    iii. Cost of goods sold during 2017

b. Compute the balance in the Inventory account on December 31, 2017.

Starter 5-4

Suppose Toys Plus uses the perpetual inventory system and buys $100,000 of LEGO toys on credit terms of 2/15, n/45. Some of the goods are damaged in shipment, so Toys Plus returns $12,500 of the merchandise to LEGO. How much must Toys Plus pay LEGO:

a. After the discount period?

b. Within the discount period?

Accounting for the purchase of inventory, purchase discount—perpetual

(2)

b. $85,750

Starter 5-5

Refer to the Toys Plus situation in Starter 5–4 and journalize the following transactions on the books of Toys Plus. Explanations are not required.

a. Purchase of the goods on July 8, 2017.

b. Return of the damaged goods on July 12, 2017.

c. Payment on July 15, 2017.

d. In the end, how much did the inventory cost Toys Plus?

Recording purchase, purchase return, and cash payment transactions—perpetual

(2)

c. Credit Cash, $85,750

Starter 5-6

Details of purchase invoices, including shipping terms, credit terms, and returns, appear below. Compute the total amount to be paid in full settlement of each invoice, assuming that credit for returns is granted before the expiration of the discount period and payment is made within the discount period. (Hint: Assume FOB destination freight is included in the invoice price.)

Purchases including shipping terms

Invoice	Freight and Credit Terms	Transportation Charges	Returns and Allowances
a. $2,000	FOB destination, 3/10, n/45	$ 55	$200
b. $5,500	FOB shipping point, 2/10, n/30	$100	$ 50
c. $6,700	FOB shipping point, 2/10, n/45	$200	$350
d. $9,300	FOB destination, 2/10, n/60	$150	$550

Starter 5-7

Suppose Lululime uses the perpetual inventory system and purchases $160,000 of women's sportswear on account from Spanner Inc. on August 1, 2017. Credit terms are 2/10, net 30. Lululime pays electronically, and Spanner receives the money on August 10, 2017.

Journalize Lululime's (a) purchase and (b) payment transactions. What was Lululime net cost of this inventory?

Note: Starter 5–8 covers this same situation for the seller.

Recording purchase transactions—perpetual

(2)

b. Net inventory cost, $156,800

Starter 5-8

Spanner Inc. sells $160,000 of women's sportswear to Lululime under credit terms of 2/10, net 30 on August 1, 2017. Spanner's cost of the goods is $76,000, and Spanner receives the appropriate amount of cash from Lululime on August 10, 2017. Assume Spanner Inc. uses the perpetual inventory system.

Journalize Spanner's transactions for August 1, 2017, and August 10, 2017.

Note: Starter 5–7 covers the same situation for the buyer.

Recording sales, cost of goods sold, and cash collections—perpetual

(2)

Cash receipt, $156,800

Starter 5-9

Suppose Pearson Education, the publisher, sells 1,000 books on account for $150 each (cost of these books is $100,000) on October 10, 2017. The customer discovered that 100 of these books were the wrong edition, so Pearson later received these books as sales returns on October 13, 2017. Then the customer paid the balance on October 22, 2017. Credit terms were 2/15, net 30.

Journalize Pearson's October 2017 transactions. Pearson uses the perpetual inventory system.

Recording sales, sales return, and collection entries—perpetual

(2)

Cash receipt, $132,300

Starter 5-10

Use the data in Starter 5–9 to compute Pearson Education's:

a. Net sales revenue

b. Gross margin

Computing net sales and gross margin—perpetual

(2)

b. Gross margin, $42,300

Adjusting inventory for
shrinkage—perpetual

Starter 5–11 Beachcombers Inc.'s Inventory account at year end showed a debit balance of $150,000. A physical count of inventory showed goods on hand of $147,000. Journalize the adjusting entry. Beachcombers uses the perpetual inventory system.

Making closing entries—perpetual

Starter 5–12 Murphy RV Accessories' accounting records include the following accounts at December 31, 2017:

Cost of Goods Sold	$310,000	Accumulated Amortization	$300,000
Accounts Payable	24,000	Cash	20,000
Advertising Expense	40,000	Sales Revenue	620,000
Building	400,000	Amortization Expense	30,000
C. Murphy, Capital	355,000	C. Murphy, Withdrawals	30,000
Inventory	380,000	Sales Discounts	17,000
Land	100,000	Accounts Receivable	45,000
Selling Expenses	54,000		

Journalize the required closing entries for Murphy RV Accessories at December 31, 2017. The company uses the perpetual inventory system.

Preparing a merchandiser's
income statement—perpetual

Net income, $23,000

Starter 5–13 Suppose Dawson Communications uses the perpetual inventory system and reported these figures in its December 31, 2017, financial statements:

Accounts payable	$ 8,000
Accounts receivable	5,600
Accrued liabilities	3,200
Cash	7,600
Cost of goods sold	40,000
Equipment, net	17,400
Inventory	800
Long-term notes payable	1,800
Net sales revenue	100,000
Total operating expenses	37,000
V. Dawson, capital	18,400

Prepare Dawson Communications' multi-step income statement for the year ended December 31, 2017.

Shrinkage adjustment and
computing gross profit
⑤

Starter 5–14 Emerson St. Paul Book Shop's accounts at June 30, 2017, included the following unadjusted balances:

Merchandise Inventory	$ 5,400
Cost of Goods Sold	40,300
Sales Revenue	85,300
Sales Discounts	1,400
Sales Returns and Allowances	2,000

St. Paul Book Shop uses a perpetual inventory system. The cost calculated from the physical count of inventory on hand on June 30, 2017, was $5,000.

a. Journalize the adjustment for inventory shrinkage.

b. Compute the gross profit.

Preparing a merchandiser's
balance sheet—perpetual

Starter 5–15 Use the data in Starter 5–13 to prepare Dawson Communications' classified balance sheet at December 31, 2017. Use the report format with all headings. Assume that net income is closed to the capital account.

Starter 5–16 Refer to the Dawson Communications situation in Starters 5–13 and 5–15. Compute the gross margin percentage and rate of inventory turnover for 2017. One year earlier, at December 31, 2016, Dawson's Inventory balance was $600.

Computing the gross margin percentage and the rate of inventory turnover

*Starter 5–17 For each statement below, identify whether the statement applies to the periodic inventory system or the perpetual inventory system:

a. Normally used for relatively inexpensive goods.

b. Keeps a running computerized record of merchandise inventory.

c. Achieves better control over merchandise inventory.

d. Requires a physical count of inventory to determine the quantities on hand.

e. Uses bar codes to keep up-to-the-minute records of inventory.

Compare the perpetual and periodic inventory systems

Starter 5–18 What are two key criteria that merchandisers who report under IFRS must follow? Do these criteria differ from those followed by companies that report under ASPE?

Accounting for a merchandiser using IFRS

*Starter 5–19 Suppose Toys Plus buys $200,000 of LEGO toys on January 15 on credit terms of 2/15, n/45. Some of the goods are damaged in shipment, so on January 20 Toys Plus returns $25,000 of the merchandise to LEGO. Assuming Toys Plus uses a periodic inventory system, how much must Toys Plus pay LEGO:

a. After the discount period?

b. Within the discount period?

c. Journalize the purchase of the goods. An explanation is not required.

d. Journalize the return of the damaged goods. An explanation is not required.

Recording purchase and cash payment transactions—periodic system

b. $171,500

*Starter 5–20 Spanner Inc. sells $160,000 of women's sportswear to Lululime under credit terms of 2/10, net 30 on August 1, 2017. Spanner's cost of goods sold is $76,000, and Spanner receives the appropriate amount of cash from Lululime on August 10, 2017. Assume Spanner Inc. uses a periodic inventory system.

Journalize Spanner's transactions for August 1, 2017, and August 10, 2017.

Recording sales and cash collections—periodic system

Cash receipt, $156,800

*Starter 5–21 Minit Company began the year with inventory of $16,000. During the year Minit purchased $180,000 of goods and returned $12,000 due to damage. Minit also paid freight charges of $1,500 on inventory purchases. At year end, Minit's inventory based on the physical inventory count stood at $32,000. Minit uses the periodic inventory system.

Compute Minit Company's cost of goods sold for the year.

Computing cost of goods sold—periodic system
A2

*Starter 5–22 Suppose Helen's Clothing purchased T-shirts on account for $36,260. Credit terms are 1/15, n/45. Helen's Clothing paid within the discount period.

a. If Helen's Clothing uses a periodic inventory system, when will the purchase of inventory be recorded as an expense—when it is purchased or when it is sold?

b. If Helen's Clothing uses a perpetual inventory system, when will the purchase of inventory be recorded as an expense—when it is purchased or when it is sold?

Comparing periodic and perpetual inventory systems
B1

---

*These Starters cover Chapter 5 Appendix A or B topics.

EXERCISES

Exercise 5-1

Evaluating a company's revenues, gross margin, operating income, and net income

①

2. Gross margin 2017, $2,700 (in thousands)

City Computers reported the information shown below:

CITY COMPUTERS
Income Statement
(Dollars in thousands)

	Fiscal Year Ended	
	January 31, 2017	January 31, 2016
Net sales	$10,000	$9,550
Expenses:		
Cost of goods sold	7,300	7,030
Selling, advertising, general, and administrative	1,830	1,710
Amortization	186	173
Other expenses	54	355
Interest expense	90	94
Other income (expenses)	(17)	(17)
	9,443	9,345
Net earnings	$ 557	$ 205

CITY COMPUTERS
Balance Sheet (partial)
(Dollars in thousands)

	Fiscal Year Ended	
	January 31, 2017	January 31, 2016
Assets		
Current assets:		
Cash	$ 690	$ 185
Accounts and other receivables	130	208
Inventory	1,990	1,800
Prepaid expenses and other current assets	40	80
Total current assets	$2,850	$2,273

Required

1. Is City Computers a merchandising entity, a service business, or both? How can you tell? List the items in City Computers' financial statements that influence your answer.

2. Compute City Computers' gross margin for fiscal years 2017 and 2016. Did the gross margin increase or decrease in 2017? Is this a good sign or a bad sign about the company?

3. Write a brief memo to the owner advising her of City Computers trend of sales, gross margin, and net income. Indicate whether the outlook for City Computers is favourable or unfavourable based on these trends. Use the following memo format:

Date:	_____
To:	The Owner
From:	Student Name
Subject:	Trend of sales, gross margin, and net income for City Computers

Exercise 5-2

Supply the missing income statement amounts in each of the following situations:

Sales	Sales Discounts	Net Sales	Cost of Goods Sold	Gross Margin
$94,500	$2,200	$92,300	$56,700	(a)
99,500	(b)	95,520	(c)	$36,000
68,700	2,100	(d)	37,700	(e)
(f)	3,500	(g)	52,500	18,600

Computing sales, cost of goods sold, and gross margin amounts

①

f. $74,600; g. $71,100

Exercise 5-3

Suppose Sears uses the perpetual inventory system and purchases $300,000 of sporting goods on account from Nike on April 10, 2017. Credit terms are 1/10, net 30. Sears pays electronically, and Nike receives the money on April 20, 2017.

Journalize Sears' (a) purchase and (b) cash payment transactions. What was Sears' net cost of this inventory?

Note: Exercise 5-4 covers this same situation for the seller.

Recording sales, cost of goods sold, and cash collections under the perpetual inventory system

②

Net inventory cost, $297,000

Exercise 5-4

Nike uses the perpetual inventory system and sells $300,000 of sporting goods to Sears under credit terms of 1/10, net 30 on April 10, 2017. Nike's cost of the goods is $210,000, and it receives the appropriate amount of cash from Sears on April 20, 2017.

Journalize Nike's transactions on April 10, 2017, and April 20, 2017. How much gross margin did Nike earn on this sale?

Recording purchase transactions under the perpetual inventory system

②

Gross margin, $87,000

Exercise 5-5

As the proprietor of Willow Auto Service, you receive the invoice below from a supplier (GST has been ignored):

Journalizing transactions from a purchase invoice under the perpetual inventory system

②

3. Net cash paid, $2,197.80

LORDY AUTO PARTS WHOLESALE DISTRIBUTORS

2600 Victoria Avenue

Saskatoon, Saskatchewan S4P 1B3

Invoice date: May 14, 2017   **Payment terms:** 1/10, n/30

Sold to: Willow Auto Service

4219 Cumberland Avenue

Prince Albert, SK S7M 1X3

Quantity Ordered	Description	Quantity Shipped	Price	Amount
6	P135-X4 Radials	6	$90.00	$ 540.00
8	L912 Belted-bias...........	8	100.00	800.00
14	R39 Truck tires	14	120.00	1,680.00
	Total			$3,020.00

Due date: **Amount:**

May 24, 2017 $2,989.80

May 25 through June 13, 2017 $3,020.00

Paid:

Required

1. Journalize the transaction required on May 14, 2017. Willow Auto Services uses the perpetual inventory system.

2. The L912 Belted-bias tires were ordered by mistake and therefore were returned to Lordy. Journalize the return on May 19, 2017.

3. Journalize the payment on May 22, 2017, to Lordy Auto Parts.

Exercise 5–6

Journalizing purchase and sales transactions under the perpetual inventory system

(2)

1. May 14 cash paid, $82,810

On April 30, 2017, Ladysmith Jewellers purchased inventory of $90,000 on account from Northern Gems Ltd., a jewellery importer. Terms were 2/15, n/45. On receiving the goods, Ladysmith checked the order and found $5,500 worth of items that were not ordered but included in the invoice. Therefore, Ladysmith returned this amount of merchandise to Northern on May 4. On May 14, Ladysmith paid Northern.

Required

1. Journalize all necessary transactions for Ladysmith Jewellers, which uses the perpetual inventory system. Explanations are not required.

2. Journalize the transactions of Northern Gems Ltd., which uses the perpetual inventory system. Northern's gross margin is 35 percent, so cost of goods sold is 65 percent of sales. Explanations are not required.

Exercise 5–7

Computing inventory and cost of goods sold amounts

(3)

Inventory bal., $19,000

The following amounts summarize Berloni Company's merchandising activities during 2017. Berloni uses the perpetual inventory system. Set up T-accounts for Inventory and Cost of Goods Sold. Post the amounts below into the accounts and calculate the balances. Briefly discuss the possible causes of the shrinkage amount.

Cost of inventory sold to customers......................	$93,000
Inventory balance, December 31, 2016...................	15,500
Invoice total for inventory purchases	98,000
Cost of freight-in	5,000
Cost of undamaged inventory returned by customers	10,000
Shrinkage calculated on December 31, 2017	12,000
Purchase discounts received.....................................	3,000
Purchase returns and allowances received...........	1,500

Exercise 5–8

Making closing entries under a perpetual inventory system

(3)

2. J. McClelland, Capital bal., $22,200

McClelland Hardware Store's accounting records (partial) carried the following accounts at December 31, 2017:

Accounts Receivable...................	$ 39,500	Selling Expenses...................	$ 87,750
Interest Revenue........................	1,400	Sales Revenue	510,100
Accounts Payable.......................	199,000	Interest Expense	12,000
Other Expense............................	64,500	Inventory...............................	220,500
Cost of Goods Sold....................	210,050	General and Administrative	
J. McClelland, Withdrawals......	168,000	Expenses............................	55,000

Note: For simplicity, all operating expenses have been summarized in the accounts Selling Expenses, and General and Administrative Expenses.

Required

1. Journalize all of this company's closing entries at December 31, 2017. The company uses the perpetual inventory system.

2. Set up T-accounts for the Income Summary account and the J. McClelland, Capital account. Post to these accounts and calculate their ending balances. One year earlier, at December 31, 2016, the Capital balance was $108,000.

Exercise 5–9

Adjusting and closing entries under the perpetual inventory system, computing gross margin

(1) (3)

c. Gross margin, $12,950

Bubble Tea's accounts at December 31, 2017, included these unadjusted balances:

Inventory	$ 4,400
Cost of Goods Sold..	31,200
Sales Revenue	46,800
Sales Discounts..	1,250
Sales Returns and Allowances	700

The physical count of inventory showed $3,700 of inventory on hand. This is the only adjustment needed.

Required

1. Journalize the adjustment for inventory shrinkage. Include an explanation. Bubble Tea uses the perpetual inventory system.
2. Journalize the closing entries for the appropriate accounts.
3. Compute the gross margin.

Exercise 5–10

The Trial Balance and Adjustments columns of the worksheet of Wells Decorating Centre included these accounts and balances at December 31, 2017:

Using worksheet data to make the closing entries under the perpetual inventory system
③
Net income, $93,700

Account Title	Trial Balance Debit	Trial Balance Credit	Adjustments Debit	Adjustments Credit
Cash	17,000			
Accounts receivable	27,500		(a) 2,200	
Inventory	63,500			(b) 1,400
Supplies	18,600			(c) 6,400
Store fixtures	70,000			
Accumulated amortization		35,000		(d) 7,000
Accounts payable		31,200		
Salary payable		0		(e) 3,800
Note payable, long-term		12,500		
B. Wells, capital		41,800		
B. Wells, withdrawals	34,000			
Sales revenue		431,400		(a) 2,200
Sales discounts	4,300			
Cost of goods sold	244,400		(b) 1,400	
Selling expenses	42,800		(c) 5,200	
			(e) 3,800	
General expenses	28,700		(c) 1,200	
			(d) 7,000	
Interest expense	1,100			
Total	551,900	551,900	20,800	20,800

Required

Wells Decorating Centre uses the perpetual inventory system. Compute the adjusted balance for each account that must be closed. Then journalize Wells Decorating Centre's closing entries at December 31, 2017. How much was Wells Decorating Centre's net income or net loss?

Exercise 5–11

Use the data in Exercise 5–10 to prepare the multi-step income statement of Wells Decorating Centre for the year ended December 31, 2017.

Preparing a multi-step income statement under the perpetual inventory system
④
Gross margin, $183,500

Exercise 5–12

Refer to Exercise 5–11. After completing Wells Decorating Centre's income statement for the year ended December 31, 2017, compute these ratios to evaluate Wells Decorating Centre's performance:

1. Gross margin percentage
2. Inventory turnover (ending inventory one year earlier, at December 31, 2016, was $54,500)

Compare your figures with the 2016 gross margin percentage of 40 percent and the inventory turnover rate of 3.82 times. Does the two-year trend suggest that Wells Decorating Centre's profits are increasing or decreasing?

Using the gross margin percentage and the rate of inventory turnover to evaluate profitability
⑤
Gross margin, 42.74%

Exercise 5–13

Selected amounts from the accounting records of Waldron Video Sales for the year ended December 31, 2017, follow:

Journal Entries			
Dec. 31	Sales Revenue	281,400	
	Interest Revenue	1,800	
	Income Summary		283,200
31	Income Summary	254,400	
	Cost of Goods Sold		161,200
	Sales Discounts		12,600
	Sales Returns and Allowances		6,900
	Selling Expenses		57,800
	General Expenses		15,900
31	Income Summary	28,800	
	B. Waldron, Capital		28,800
31	B. Waldron, Capital	28,000	
	B. Waldron, Withdrawals		28,000

Required

1. Waldron Video Sales uses the perpetual inventory system. Prepare the business's multi-step income statement for the year ended December 31, 2017.

2. Compute the rate of inventory turnover for the year. The inventory balance on December 31, 2016, was $25,400 and on December 31, 2017, was $28,600. Last year the turnover rate was 5.42 times. Does this two-year trend suggest improvement or deterioration in inventory turnover?

Exercise 5–14

Prepare Waldron Video Sales' single-step income statement for 2017, using the data from Exercise 5–13. Compute the gross margin percentage and compare it with last year's value of 49 percent for Waldron Video Sales. Does this two-year trend suggest better or worse profitability during the current year?

Exercise 5–15

Networking Systems, which uses the perpetual inventory system, earned sales revenue of $66 million in 2017. Cost of goods sold was $35 million, and net income reached $16 million, Networking's highest ever. Total current assets included inventory of $14.0 million at December 31, 2017. Last year's ending inventory was $13.2 million. The managers of Networking Systems need to know the company's gross margin percentage and rate of inventory turnover for 2017. Compute these amounts.

*Exercise 5–16

Journalize, without explanations, the following transactions of Digbey Auto Parts, a distributor that uses the periodic inventory system, during the month of June 2017:

Jun. 3   Purchased $16,800 of inventory under terms of 2/10, n/eom and FOB shipping point.

7   Returned $1,600 of defective merchandise purchased on June 3.

9   Paid freight bill of $350 on June 3 purchase.

10 Sold inventory for $22,400, collecting cash of $3,600. Payment terms on the remainder were 2/15, n/30.

12 Paid amount owed on credit purchase of June 3.

16 Granted a sales allowance of $1,200 on the June 10 sale.

23 Received cash from the June 10 customer in full settlement of the debt.

*Exercise 5–17

As the proprietor of OK Auto Repair, you receive this invoice from a supplier (GST has been ignored):

Journalizing transactions from a purchase invoice under the periodic inventory system

3. May 22 payment, $2,197.80

LORDY AUTO PARTS WHOLESALE DISTRIBUTORS
2600 Victoria Avenue
Saskatoon, Saskatchewan S4P 1B3

Invoice date: May 14, 2017   **Payment terms:** 1/10, n/30

Sold to: OK Auto Repair

 4245 Cumberland Avenue

 Prince Albert, SK S7M 1X3

Quantity Ordered	Description	Quantity Shipped	Price	Amount
6	P135-X4 Radials	6	$ 90.00	$ 540.00
8	L912 Belted-bias.................................	8	100.00	800.00
14	R39 Truck tires	14	120.00	1,680.00
	Total			$3,020.00

Due date: **Amount:**

May 24, 2017 $2,989.80

May 25 through June 13, 2017 $3,020.00

Paid:

Required

1. Journalize the transaction required on May 14, 2017. OK Auto Repair uses the periodic inventory system.

2. The L912 belted-bias tires were ordered by mistake and therefore were returned to Lordy. Journalize the return on May 19, 2017.

3. Journalize the payment on May 22, 2017, to Lordy Auto Parts.

*Exercise 5–18

On April 30, 2017, Ladysmith Jewellers purchased inventory of $45,000 on account from Northern Gems Ltd., a jewellery importer. Terms were 2/15, net 45. On receiving the goods, Ladysmith checked the order and found $5,500 of unsuitable merchandise. Therefore, Ladysmith returned the merchandise to Northern on May 4, 2017.

 On May 14, 2017, Ladysmith Jewellers paid the net amount owed from April 30.

Journalizing purchase transactions under the periodic inventory system

May 14 cash paid, $38,710

Required

Record the required transactions in the journal of Ladysmith Jewellers. Use the periodic inventory system. Explanations are not required.

*Exercise 5–19

Refer to the business situation in Exercise 5–18. Journalize the transactions of Northern Gems Ltd., which uses the periodic inventory system. Explanations are not required.

Journalizing sale transactions under the periodic inventory system

May 14 cash received, $38,710

---

*These Exercises cover Chapter 5 Appendix A topics.

*Exercise 5–20

Using the cost of goods sold formula in a periodic inventory system

The Wholesale Company began the year with inventory of $24,000. During the year, the company purchased $272,000 of goods and returned $18,000 due to damage. At year end, the Inventory balance was $34,000. The Wholesale Company uses the periodic inventory system.

Compute the Wholesale Company's cost of goods sold for the year.

*Exercise 5–21

Computing inventory purchases

Purchase, $157 million

Suppose MegaSports reported cost of goods sold totalling $150 million. Ending inventory was $65 million, and beginning inventory was $58 million. How much inventory did MegaSports purchase during the year?

*Exercise 5–22

Computing cost of goods sold in a periodic inventory system

Cost of goods sold, $80,600

The periodic inventory records of Presley Video Sales include these accounts at December 31, 2017:

Purchases	$86,250
Purchase Discounts	3,400
Purchase Returns and Allowances	4,300
Freight-in	3,650
Inventory, December 31, 2016	12,700
Inventory, December 31, 2017	14,300

Required

Compute Presley Video's cost of goods sold for 2017.

*Exercise 5–23

Computing inventory and cost of goods sold under the periodic inventory system

a. $700, f. $9,400, j. $20,100

Supply the missing income statement amounts in each of the following situations:

Sales	Sales Discounts	Net Sales	Beginning Inventory	Net Purchases	Ending Inventory	Cost of Goods Sold	Gross Margin
$24,100	(a)	$23,400	$8,800	$16,700	$9,900	(b)	$7,800
20,600	$500	(c)	6,400	10,800	(d)	$11,100	(e)
23,400	400	23,000	(f)	11,200	5,700	14,900	(g)
(h)	800	(i)	10,100	(j)	12,100	18,100	9,700

*Exercise 5–24

Computing cost of goods sold under the periodic inventory system

Net purchases, $219,500

For the year ended December 31, 2017, Home Distributors, a retailer of home-related products, reported net sales of $429,500 and cost of goods sold of $225,000. The company's balance sheets at December 31, 2016 and 2017, reported inventories of $173,000 and $167,500, respectively. What were Home Distributors' net purchases during 2017?

*Exercise 5–25

Cost of goods sold in a periodic inventory system

c. Gross margin, $93,000

Rees Distributors uses the periodic inventory system. Rees reported these amounts at May 31, 2017:

Inventory, May 31, 2016	$29,000
Inventory, May 31, 2017	31,000
Purchases (of inventory)	82,000
Purchase Discounts	2,000
Purchase Returns	3,000
Freight-in	4,000
Sales Revenue	200,000
Sales Discounts	13,000
Sales Returns	15,000

*These Exercises cover Chapter 5 Appendix A topics.

Compute Rees Distributors':

a. Net sales revenue

b. Cost of goods sold

c. Gross margin

*Exercise 5–26

The following characteristics are related to either periodic inventory or perpetual inventory systems.

Describing periodic and perpetual inventory systems

(1) (A1) (B1)

A. Purchases of inventory are journalized to an asset account at the time of purchase.

B. Purchases of inventory are journalized to an expense account at the time of purchase.

C. Inventory records are constantly updated.

D. Sales made require a second entry to be journalized to record cost of goods sold.

E. Bar code scanners that record sales transactions are most often associated with this inventory system.

F. A physical count of goods on hand at year end is performed.

Identify each characteristic as one of the following:

a. Periodic inventory system

b. Perpetual inventory system

c. Both periodic and perpetual inventory systems

d. Neither periodic nor perpetual inventory system

---

*These Exercises cover Chapter 5 Appendix A and B topics.

SERIAL EXERCISE

This exercise continues the Lee Management Consulting situation from Exercise 4–18 of Chapter 4. If you did not complete Exercise 4–18 you can still complete Exercise 5–27 as it is presented.

Exercise 5–27

Lee Management Consulting performs services but also began selling software. Lee Management uses the perpetual inventory system. During July 2016, the business completed these transactions:

Accounting for both merchandising and service transactions under the perpetual inventory system

(2) (3) (4) (5)

4. Net income, $5,351

July	2	Completed a consulting engagement and received cash of $7,200.
	2	Prepaid three months' office rent, $9,000.
	7	Purchased 100 units of software inventory on account, $1,900, plus owed the manufacturer freight-in of $100.
	16	Paid employee salary, $2,000. (Note previous year-end accrual of $500.)
	18	Sold 70 software units on account, $3,100 (cost $1,400).
	19	Consulted with a client for a fee of $900 on account.
	21	Paid on account, $2,000.
	22	Purchased 200 units of software inventory on account, $4,600.
	24	Paid utilities, $300.
	28	Sold 100 units of software for cash, $4,000 (cost $2,210).
	31	Recorded the following adjusting entries:

        Accrued salary expense, $1,000.

        Prepaid rent used, $3,000.

        Amortization of office furniture, $167, and of equipment, $42.

        Physical count of inventory, 120 units, $2,760.

Required

1. Open the following selected T-accounts in the ledger with their normal opening balances as shown: Cash, $23,750; Accounts Receivable, $1,900; Software Inventory, $0; Prepaid Rent, $0; Supplies, $100; Equipment, $1,000; Accumulated Amortization—Equipment, $42; Furniture, $5,000; Accumulated Amortization—Furniture, $167; Accounts Payable, $5,000; Salaries Payable, $500; Unearned Revenue, $1,200; Michael Lee, Capital, $24,841; Income Summary, $0; Service Revenue, $0; Sales Revenue, $0; Cost of Goods Sold, $0; Salaries Expense, $0; Rent Expense, $0; Utilities Expense, $0; Amortization Expense—Equipment, $0; and Amortization Expense—Furniture, $0.

2. Journalize and post to the T-accounts the July transactions. Reference all transactions by date. Total each T-account, where applicable, and denote the balance as *Bal*.

3. Journalize and post the closing entries. Denote each closing amount as *Clo*.

4. Prepare the July 2016 income statement of Lee Management Consulting. Use the single-step format. (*Hint:* List each type of revenue separately in the Revenues section of the income statement.)

BEYOND THE NUMBERS

Beyond the Numbers 5–1

Evaluating a company's profitability

① ⑤

Gross margin percentage in 2017, 26%

Wilson Distributors is a provider of automotive products. The company recently reported the following:

WILSON DISTRIBUTORS		
Consolidated Statements of Operations (Adapted)		
For the Years Ended July 31, 2017 and 2016		
	2017	2016
Sales	$1,320,000	$984,000
Cost of sales	980,000	752,000
Gross margin	340,000	232,000
Cost and expenses:		
Selling, general, and administrative	264,000	204,000
Amortization	34,000	21,000
Restructuring charges	84,000	—
	382,000	225,000
Operating income (loss)	(42,000)	7,000
Other items (summarized)	(7,000)	(16,000)
Net income (loss)	$ (49,000)	$ (9,000)

Required   Evaluate Wilson Distributors' operations during 2017 in comparison with 2016. Consider sales, gross margin, operating income, and net income. Track the gross margin percentage and inventory turnover in both years. Wilson Distributors' inventories at December 31, 2017, 2016, and 2015, were $92,000, $145,000, and $122,000, respectively. In the annual report, management describes the restructuring charges in 2017—the costs of downsizing the company—as a one-time event. How does this additional information affect your evaluation?

ETHICAL ISSUE

Schafer Bearing Company makes all sales of industrial bearings under terms of FOB shipping point. The company usually receives orders for sales approximately one week before shipping inventory to customers. For orders received late in December, Bob Schafer, the owner, decides when to ship the goods. If profits are already at an acceptable level, the company delays shipment until January. If profits are lagging behind expectations, the company ships the goods during December.

Required

1. Under Schafer Bearing Company's FOB or CIF policy, when should the company record a sale?

2. Do you approve or disapprove of Schafer Bearing Company's means of deciding when to ship goods to customers? If you approve, give your reason. If you disapprove, identify a better way to decide when to ship goods. (There is no accounting rule against Schafer Bearing Company's practice.)

PROBLEMS (GROUP A)   MyAccountingLab

Problem 5–1A

Better Homes is a mid-sized retailer in Canada. The kitchen appliances department of Better Homes purchases small appliances such as coffee makers and toasters from many well-known manufacturers. Better Homes uses a sophisticated perpetual inventory system.

Required   You are the manager of a Better Homes store. Write a memo to a new employee in the kitchen appliances department that explains how the company accounts for the purchase and sale of merchandise inventory.

Use the following heading for your memo:

Explaining the perpetual inventory system
① ②

Date:	_____
To:	The Owner
From:	Student Name
Subject:	Better Homes accounting system for inventories

Problem 5–2A

The following transactions occurred between Chao Pharmaceuticals and Hall Drug Store during February of the current year. Both companies use the perpetual inventory system.

Accounting for the purchase and sale of inventory under the perpetual inventory system
②
Feb. 27 Cash amount, $31,000

Feb. 6   Hall purchased $60,000 of merchandise from Chao on credit terms of 1/10, n/30, FOB shipping point. Separately, Hall paid a $1,000 bill for freight-in. Chao invoiced Hall for $60,000 (these goods cost Chao $36,000).

10   Hall returned $5,000 of the merchandise purchased on February 6. Chao issued a credit memo for this amount and returned the goods to inventory (cost, $3,000).

15   Hall paid $24,000 of the invoice amount owed to Chao for the February 6 purchase. Chao allows its customers to take the cash discount on partial payments.

27   Hall paid the remaining amount owed to Chao for the February 6 purchase.

Required   Journalize these transactions, first on the books of Hall Drug Store and second on the books of Chao Pharmaceuticals.

Problem 5–3A

Singh Distributing Company uses the perpetual inventory system and engaged in the following transactions during May of the current year:

Journalizing purchase and sale transactions under the perpetual inventory system
②
2. Inventory balance, $221,170

May   3   Purchased office supplies for cash, $22,000.

7   Purchased inventory on credit terms of 3/10, net eom, $76,000.

8   Returned 25 percent of the inventory purchased on May 7. It was not the inventory ordered.

10	Sold goods for cash, $34,000 (cost, $20,400).
13	Sold inventory on credit terms of 2/15, n/45 for $150,800, less $15,080 quantity discount offered to customers who purchase in large quantities (cost, $90,480).
16	Paid the amount owed on account from the purchase of May 7, less the discount and the return.
17	Received wrong-sized inventory as a sales return from May 13 sale, $12,400, which is the net amount after the quantity discount. Singh's cost of the inventory received was $7,440.
18	Purchased inventory of $164,000 on account. Payment terms were 2/10, net 30.
26	Paid supplier for goods purchased on May 18.
28	Received cash in full settlement of the account from the customer who purchased inventory on May 13.
31	Purchased inventory for cash, $96,000, less a quantity discount of $9,600, plus freight charges of $2,200.

Required

1. Journalize the preceding transactions on the books of Singh Distributing Company.
2. Suppose the balance in Inventory was $20,000 on May 1. What is the balance in inventory on May 31?

Excel Spreadsheet Template

Preparing a merchandiser's worksheet under the perpetual inventory system

③

Net income, $235,600

Problem 5–4A

The trial balance of Marvin's Fine Gems at December 31, 2017, and is shown below:

MARVIN'S FINE GEMS Unadjusted Trial Balance December 31, 2017		
Cash	$ 6,200	
Accounts receivable	57,000	
Inventory	354,800	
Prepaid rent	28,000	
Equipment	108,000	
Accumulated amortization—equipment		$ 43,200
Accounts payable		43,200
Salary payable		0
Interest payable		0
Note payable, long-term		87,000
J. Marvin, capital		270,000
J. Marvin, withdrawals	153,000	
Sales revenue		835,400
Cost of goods sold	328,000	
Salary expense	118,600	
Rent expense	44,000	
Advertising expense	21,600	
Utilities expense	30,800	
Amortization expense—equipment	0	
Insurance expense	13,200	
Interest expense	2,600	
Miscellaneous expense	13,000	
Total	$1,278,800	$1,278,800

Additional data at December 31, 2017:

a. Rent expense for the year, $48,000.

b. The equipment has an estimated useful life of 10 years and is expected to have no value when it is retired from service.

c. Accrued salaries at December 31, $7,000.

d. Accrued interest expense at December 31, $2,600.

e. Inventory based on the inventory count on December 31, $351,200.

Required Complete Marvin's Fine Gems' worksheet for the year ended December 31, 2017. Marvin's Fine Gems uses the perpetual inventory system.

Problem 5–5A

Refer to the data in Problem 5–4A.

Required

1. Journalize the adjusting and closing entries.
2. Determine the December 31, 2017, Capital balance for Marvin's Fine Gems.

Problem 5–6A

Items from the accounts of Marchand Distributors at May 31, 2017, follow, listed in alphabetical order. Marchand Distributors uses the perpetual inventory system. For simplicity, the operating expenses are summarized in the General Expenses and the Selling Expenses accounts.

Accounts Payable	$ 51,000	Interest Payable	$ 2,800	
Accounts Receivable	107,500	Interest Revenue	600	
Accumulated Amortization—		Inventory, May 31, 2017	147,100	
Equipment	96,900	Notes Payable, Long-Term	114,800	
C. Marchand, Capital	167,800	Salaries Payable	7,200	
C. Marchand, Withdrawals	66,900	Sales Discounts	26,500	
Cash	19,900	Sales Returns and		
Cost of Goods Sold	1,086,900	Allowances	45,900	
Equipment	340,800	Sales Revenue	1,991,500	
General Expenses	206,800	Selling Expenses	357,200	
Interest Expense	9,200	Supplies	33,100	
		Unearned Sales Revenue	15,200	

Required

1. Prepare the business's single-step income statement for the year ended May 31, 2017.
2. Prepare the statement of owner's equity for the year ended May 31, 2017.
3. Prepare Marchand Distributors' classified balance sheet in report format at May 31, 2017.

Problem 5–7A

1. Use the data in Problem 5–6A to prepare Marchand Distributors' multi-step income statement for the year ended May 31, 2017.
2. Corry Marchand, owner of the company, strives to earn a gross margin of at least 50 percent and a net income of 20 percent (Net income percentage = Net income ÷ Net sales revenue). Did Marchand Distributors achieve these goals? Show your calculations.

Problem 5–8A

The adjusted trial balance of Propp Products at November 30, 2017, is shown on the next page. Propp Products uses the perpetual inventory system.

Required

1. Journalize Propp Products' closing entries.
2. Compute the gross margin percentage and the rate of inventory turnover for 2017. Inventory on hand one year ago was $10,700. For 2016, Propp Products' gross margin was 32 percent and inventory turnover was 4.9 times during the year. Does the two-year trend in these ratios suggest improvement or deterioration in profitability?

Excel Spreadsheet Template

Journalizing the adjusting and closing entries of a merchandising business under the perpetual inventory system

③

2. Dec. 31, 2017, Capital bal., $352,600

Preparing a single-step income statement and a classified balance sheet under the perpetual inventory system

④

1. Net income, $259,600

Preparing a multi-step income statement and calculating gross margin percentage under the perpetual inventory system

④ ⑤

1. Net income, $259,600

Making closing entries, computing gross margin percentage and inventory turnover under the perpetual inventory system

③ ④ ⑤

2. Gross margin percentage for 2017, 38.4%

PROPP PRODUCTS
Adjusted Trial Balance
November 30, 2017

	Debit	Credit
Cash	$ 4,000	
Accounts receivable	24,250	
Inventory	13,700	
Supplies	700	
Furniture	20,000	
Accumulated amortization—furniture		$ 12,000
Accounts payable		7,250
Salary payable		1,100
Unearned sales revenue		3,600
Note payable, long-term		22,500
A. Propp, capital		20,650
A. Propp, withdrawals	18,000	
Sales revenue		112,500
Sales returns	3,000	
Cost of goods sold	67,500	
Selling expenses	16,850	
General expenses	10,500	
Interest expense	1,100	
Total	$179,600	$179,600

Problem 5–9A

Computing cost of goods sold and gross margin, adjusting and closing the accounts of a merchandising company, preparing a merchandiser's financial statements under the perpetual inventory system

③ ④ ⑤

2. Net loss, $67,500

Buono Adventures, which uses the perpetual inventory system, has the following account balances (in alphabetical order) on July 31, 2017:

Accounts Payable	$ 21,600
Accounts Receivable	23,200
Accumulated Amortization—Equipment	64,600
Cash	8,400
Cost of Goods Sold	687,000
E. Buono, Capital	402,000
E. Buono, Withdrawals	92,000
Equipment	180,000
Interest Earned	4,000
Inventory	143,000
Operating Expenses	355,000
Sales Discounts	10,300
Sales Returns and Allowances	32,900
Sales Revenue	1,045,200
Supplies	14,600
Unearned Sales Revenue	9,000

Note: For simplicity, all operating expenses have been summarized in the account Operating Expenses.

Additional data at July 31, 2017:

a. A physical count of items showed $3,000 of supplies on hand. (Hint: Use the account Operating Expenses in the adjusting journal entry.)

b. An inventory count showed inventory on hand at July 31, 2017, of $140,000.

c. The equipment has an estimated useful life of eight years and is expected to have no value at the end of its life. (Hint: Use the account Operating Expenses in the adjusting journal entry.)

d. Unearned sales revenue of $5,600 was earned by July 31, 2017.

Required

1. Record all adjustments and closing entries that would be required on July 31, 2017.
2. Prepare the financial statements of Buono Adventures for the year ended July 31, 2017.

*Problem 5–10A

The following transactions occurred between Chao Pharmaceuticals and Hall Drug Store during February of the current year.

Accounting for the purchase and sale of inventory under the periodic system

Feb.	6	Hall purchased $50,000 of merchandise from Chao on credit terms 2/10, n/30, FOB shipping point. Separately, Hall paid a $2,000 bill for freight-in. Chao invoiced Hall for $50,000.
	15	Hall returned $7,000 of the merchandise purchased on February 6. Chao issued a credit memo for this amount.
	15	Hall paid $24,000 of the invoice amount owed to Chao for the February 6 purchase. This payment included none of the freight charge.
	27	Hall paid the remaining amount owed to Chao for the February 6 purchase.

Required Journalize these transactions, first on the books of Hall Drug Store and second on the books of Chao Pharmaceuticals. Assume both companies use the periodic inventory system and discounts are allowed on partial payments.

*Problem 5–11A

Singh Distributing Company, which uses the periodic inventory system, engaged in the following transactions during May of the current year:

Journalizing purchase and sale transactions under the periodic inventory system

May	3	Purchased office supplies for cash, $22,000.
	7	Purchased inventory on credit terms of 3/10, net eom, $160,000.
	8	Returned 10 percent of the inventory purchased on May 7. It was not the inventory ordered.
	10	Sold goods for cash, $36,400.
	13	Sold inventory on credit terms of 2/15, n/45 for $60,300, less $8,800 quantity discount offered to customers who purchase in large quantities.
	16	Paid the amount owed on account from the purchase of May 7.
	17	Received wrong-sized inventory returned from May 13 sale, $3,200, which is the net amount after the quantity discount.
	18	Purchased inventory of $76,000 on account. Payment terms were 2/10, net 30.
	26	Paid supplier for goods purchased on May 18.
	28	Received cash in full settlement of the account from the customer who purchased inventory on May 13.
	29	Purchased inventory for cash, $26,000, less a quantity discount of $2,200, and paid freight charges of $600.

Required Journalize the preceding transactions on the books of Singh Distributing Company.

---

*These Problems cover Chapter 5 Appendix A topics.

*Problem 5–12A

The trial balance of Marvin's Fine Gems at December 31, 2017, is shown below:

MARVIN'S FINE GEMS		
Trial Balance		
December 31, 2017		
Cash	$ 6,200	
Accounts receivable	57,000	
Inventory	345,000	
Prepaid rent	28,000	
Equipment	108,000	
Accumulated amortization—equipment		$ 43,200
Accounts payable		43,200
Salary payable		0
Interest payable		0
Note payable, long-term		87,000
J. Marvin, capital		270,000
J. Marvin, withdrawals	153,000	
Sales revenue		835,400
Purchases	337,800	
Salary expense	118,600	
Rent expense	44,000	
Advertising expense	21,600	
Utilities expense	30,800	
Amortization expense—equipment	0	
Insurance expense	13,200	
Interest expense	2,600	
Miscellaneous expense	13,000	
Total	$1,278,800	$1,278,800

Additional data at December 31, 2017:

a. Rent expense for the year, $48,000.

b. The equipment has an estimated useful life of 10 years and is expected to have no value when it is retired from service.

c. Accrued salaries at December 31, $7,000.

d. Accrued interest expense at December 31, $2,600.

e. Inventory based on the inventory count on December 31, 2017, $351,200.

Required Complete Marvin's Fine Gems' worksheet for the year ended December 31, 2017. Marvin's Fine Gems uses the periodic inventory system.

*Problem 5–13A

Refer to the data in Problem 5–12A.

Required

1. Journalize the adjusting and closing entries.
2. Determine the December 31, 2017, balance of Capital for Marvin's Fine Gems.

---

*These Problems cover Chapter 5 Appendix A topics.

*Problem 5–14A

Items from the accounts of Marchand Distributors at May 31, 2017, follow, listed in alphabetical order. Marchand Distributors uses the periodic inventory system. For simplicity, all operating expenses are summarized in the General Expenses and the Selling Expenses account.

Preparing a single-step income statement and a classified balance sheet under the periodic inventory system
(A4)
1. Net income, $259,600

Accounts Payable	$ 71,000	Inventory May 31, 2016	$ 151,800
Accounts Receivable	107,500	Notes Payable,	
Accumulated Amortization—		Long-Term	114,800
Equipment	96,900	Purchases	1,102,200
C. Marchand, Capital	167,800	Salaries Payable	7,200
C. Marchand, Withdrawals	66,900	Sales Discounts	26,500
Cash	19,900	Sales Returns and	
Equipment	340,800	Allowances	45,900
General Expenses	206,800	Sales Revenue	1,991,500
Interest Expense	9,200	Selling Expenses	357,200
Interest Payable	2,800	Supplies	33,100
Interest Revenue	600	Unearned Sales Revenue	15,200

Required

1. Prepare the business's single-step income statement for the year ended May 31, 2017. A physical count of inventory on May 31, 2017, valued it at $167,100.
2. Prepare Marchand Distributors' statement of owner's equity at May 31, 2017.
3. Prepare Marchand Distributors' classified balance sheet in report format at May 31, 2017.

*Problem 5–15A

1. Use the data in Problem 5–14A to prepare Marchand Distributors' multi-step income statement for the year ended May 31, 2017.
2. Corry Marchand, owner of the company, strives to earn a gross margin of at least 50 percent and a net income of 20 percent (Net income percentage = Net income ÷ Net sales revenue). Did Marchand Distributors achieve these goals? Show your calculations.

Preparing a multi-step income statement and calculating gross margin percentage under the periodic inventory system
(5) (A4)
1. Net income, $259,600

*Problem 5–16A

Selected accounts from the accounting records of Boggio Security had the balances shown below at November 30, 2017. Boggio Security uses the periodic inventory system.

Computing cost of goods sold and gross margin in a periodic inventory system, evaluating the business
(1) (5) (A2)
1. Gross margin, $43,600

Purchases	$ 160,000
Selling Expenses	10,000
Furniture and Fixtures	40,000
Purchase Returns and Allowances	1,000
Salaries Payable	1,500
Sales Revenue	205,000
Sales Returns and Allowances	1,900
Inventory: November 30, 2016	36,000
November 30, 2017	37,000
Accounts Payable	9,000
Accounts Receivable	15,000
Cash	3,500
Freight-in	1,400
Accumulated Amortization—Furniture and Fixtures	16,000
Purchase Discounts	1,500
Sales Discounts	1,600
General Expenses	22,000
Amortization Expense—Furniture and Fixtures	4,000
L. Boggio, Capital	81,900
L. Boggio, Withdrawals	20,500

---

*These Problems cover Chapter 5 Appendix A topics.

Required

1. Show the computation of Boggio Security's net sales, cost of goods sold, and gross margin for the year ended November 30, 2017.
2. Len Boggio, the proprietor of Boggio Security, strives to earn a gross margin percentage of 25 percent. Did he achieve this goal?
3. Did the rate of inventory turnover reach the industry average of 3.8 times per year?

*Problem 5–17A

Journalizing, posting to T-accounts, year-end adjusting, preparing financial statements using the periodic inventory system, comparing to the perpetual system.
(A1) (A2) (A3) (A4) (B1)

Mumbai Sales Company engaged in the following transactions during September 2017, the first month of the company's fiscal year. Assume the company had no inventory on hand prior to September 3. Mumbai Sales Company has a periodic inventory system.

Sep.	3	Purchased inventory costing $7,000 on credit terms of 2/10, net eom. The goods were shipped FOB Mumbai's warehouse.
	9	Returned 20 percent of the inventory purchased on September 3. It was defective.
	12	Sold goods for cash, $6,000 (cost, $3,000).
	15	Purchased inventory of $15,400, less a $400 quantity discount. Credit terms were 2/15, n/30. The goods were shipped FOB the supplier's warehouse.
	16	Paid a $1,200 freight bill on the inventory purchased on September 15.
	18	Sold inventory for $9,000 on credit terms of 2/10, n/30 (cost, $4,500).
	22	Received merchandise returned from the customer from the September 18 sale, $2,000 (cost, $1,000). Merchandise was the wrong size.
	24	Borrowed exactly enough money from the bank to pay for the September 15 purchase in time to take advantage of the discount offered. Signed a note payable to the bank for the net amount.
	24	Paid supplier for goods purchased on September 15, less all returns and discounts.
	28	Received cash in full settlement of the account from the customer who purchased inventory on September 18, less the return on September 22 and less the discount.
	29	Paid the amount owed on account from the purchase of September 3, less the September 9 return.
	30	Purchased inventory for cash, $4,640, less a quantity discount of $140.

Required

1. Journalize the transactions and include any calculations in the journal entry explanations.
2. Refer to the Mumbai Sales Company journal entries in Requirement 1 to set up T-accounts, and post the journal entries to calculate the ending balances for the cost of goods sold equation accounts.
3. Calculate cost of good sold using an ending inventory value of $16,000.
4. Assume Mumbai Sales has two year-end adjusting entries: (a) accrue accounting expenses of $1,000, and (b) accrue a sale of $2,000 that was completed on September 30 but unrecorded. Record and post the adjusting entries and closing entries for Mumbai Sales Company.
5. Prepare the financial statements under the periodic inventory system. (Note: Include a statement of owners' equity.)
6. Refer to the Mumbai Sales Company journal entries in Requirement 1 above. Assume that the note payable signed on September 24 requires the payment of $250 interest expense. Was the decision to borrow funds to take advantage of the cash discount wise or unwise?
7. Compare the results of the Summary Problem on page 271 with this solution (periodic). What main differences do you notice?

PROBLEMS (GROUP B)   MyAccountingLab

Problem 5–1B

Explaining the perpetual inventory system
(1) (2)

Clearly Optical is a regional chain of optical shops. The company offers a large selection of eyeglass frames, and Clearly Optical stores provide while-you-wait service. Clearly Optical has launched a vigorous advertising campaign promoting its two-for-the-price-of-one frame sale.

Required Clearly Optical expects to grow rapidly and increase its level of inventory. As chief accountant of the company, you wish to install a perpetual inventory system. Write a memo to the company president to explain how the system would work.

Use the following heading for your memo:

Date:	_____
To:	Company President
From:	Chief Accountant
Subject:	How a perpetual inventory system works

Problem 5–2B

The following transactions occurred between Cloutier Pharmaceuticals and Arnold Drug Stores during June of the current year:

Accounting for the purchase and sale of inventory under the perpetual inventory system ②

Jun. 8 Arnold purchased $29,400 of merchandise from Cloutier on credit terms 2/10, n/30, FOB shipping point. Separately, Arnold paid freight-in of $600. Cloutier invoiced Arnold for $29,400. These goods cost Cloutier $12,600.

11 Arnold returned $3,600 of the merchandise purchased on June 8. Cloutier issued a credit memo for this amount and returned the goods, in excellent condition, to inventory (cost $1,500).

17 Arnold paid $12,000 of the invoice amount owed to Cloutier for the June 8 purchase. This payment included none of the freight charge. Arnold took the purchase discount on the partial payment.

26 Arnold paid the remaining amount owed to Cloutier for the June 8 purchase.

Required Journalize these transactions, first on the books of Arnold Drug Stores, and second on the books of Cloutier Pharmaceuticals. Both companies use the perpetual inventory system.

Problem 5–3B

Coburn Furniture Company engaged in the following transactions during July of the current year:

Journalizing purchase and sale transactions under the perpetual inventory system ②

Jul. 2 Purchased inventory for cash, $12,800, less a quantity discount of $1,800.

5 Purchased store supplies on credit terms of net eom, $6,800.

8 Purchased inventory of $54,000 less a quantity discount of 10 percent, plus freight charges of $2,200. Credit terms are 3/15, n/30.

9 Sold goods for cash, $21,600. Coburn's cost of these goods was $13,000.

11 Returned $2,000 (net amount after the quantity discount) of the inventory purchased on July 8. It was damaged in shipment.

12 Purchased inventory on credit terms of 3/10, n/30, $60,000.

14 Sold inventory on credit terms of 2/10, n/30 for $138,400, less a $13,840 quantity discount (cost, $83,000).

16 Received and paid the electricity bill, $6,400.

20 Received returned inventory from the July 14 sale, $5,000 (net amount after the quantity discount). Coburn shipped the wrong goods by mistake. Coburn's cost of the inventory received was $3,000.

21 Paid supplier for goods purchased on July 8 less the discount and the return.

23 Received $87,120 cash in partial settlement of the account from the customer who purchased inventory on July 14. Granted the customer a 1 percent discount and credited the customer's account receivable for $88,000.

31 Paid for the store supplies purchased on July 5.

Required

1. Journalize the preceding transactions on the books of Coburn Furniture Company. The company uses the perpetual inventory system.
2. Suppose the balance in inventory was $45,500 on July 1. What is the balance in inventory on July 31?

Excel Spreadsheet
Template
Preparing a merchandiser's
worksheet under the perpetual
inventory system
③ ④

Problem 5–4B

Gismondi Produce Company's trial balance below pertains to December 31, 2017. Gismondi Produce Company uses the perpetual inventory system.

GISMONDI PRODUCE COMPANY		
Trial Balance		
December 31, 2017		
Cash	$ 22,150	
Accounts receivable	109,600	
Inventory	119,600	
Store supplies	28,800	
Prepaid insurance	18,000	
Store fixtures	270,000	
Accumulated amortization—store fixtures		$ 162,000
Accounts payable		69,900
Salaries payable		0
Interest payable		0
Notes payable, long-term		47,000
F. Gismondi, capital		119,000
F. Gismondi, withdrawals	52,000	
Sales revenue		1,290,500
Cost of goods sold	726,600	
Salaries expense	238,600	
Rent expense	52,000	
Utilities expense	36,200	
Amortization expense—store fixtures	0	
Insurance expense	6,000	
Store supplies expense	0	
Interest expense	2,350	
Miscellaneous expense	6,500	
Total	$1,688,400	$1,688,400

Additional data at December 31, 2017:

a. Insurance expense for the year should total $21,600.

b. Store fixtures have an estimated useful life of 10 years and are expected to have no value when they are retired from service.

c. Accrued salaries at December 31, $5,500.

d. Accrued interest expense at December 31, $1,600.

e. Store supplies on hand at December 31, $23,800.

f. Inventory based on the inventory count on December 31, $116,500.

Required Complete Gismondi Produce Company's worksheet for the year ended December 31, 2017. Key adjustments by letter.

Problem 5–5B

Refer to the data in Problem 5–4B.

Required

1. Journalize the adjusting and closing entries of Gismondi Produce Company.
2. Determine the December 31, 2017, balance in the Capital account.

Problem 5–6B

Selected accounts of Sterling Building Supplies at July 31, 2017, are listed in alphabetical order below. For simplicity, all operating expenses are summarized in the accounts Selling Expenses and General Expenses. Sterling Building Supplies uses the perpetual inventory system.

Accounts Payable	$ 31,000	Inventory: July 31, 2017	$262,500
Accounts Receivable	78,500	Notes Payable, Long-Term	250,000
Accumulated Amortization—		Salaries Payable	11,500
Store Equipment	30,750	Sales Discounts	12,500
B. Sterling, Capital	451,700	Sales Returns and	
B. Sterling, Withdrawals	41,150	Allowances	26,400
Cash	3,100	Sales Revenue	945,600
Cost of Goods Sold	803,000	Selling Expenses	158,625
General Expenses	122,125	Store Equipment	242,000
Interest Expense	5,100	Supplies	8,100
Interest Payable	4,400	Unearned Sales Revenue	37,400
Interest Revenue	750		

Required

1. Prepare Sterling Building Supplies' single-step income statement for the year ended July 31, 2017.
2. Prepare Sterling Building Supplies' statement of owner's equity.
3. Prepare Sterling Building Supplies' classified balance sheet in report format at July 31, 2017.

Problem 5–7B

1. Use the data in Problem 5–6B to prepare Sterling Building Supplies' multi-step income statement for the year ended July 31, 2017.
2. Bev Sterling, owner of the company, strives to earn a gross margin of at least 50 percent and a net income of 20 percent (Net income percentage = Net income ÷ Net sales revenue). Did Sterling Building Supplies achieve these goals? Show your calculations.

Problem 5–8B

The adjusted trial balance of Harrison Trading Company at September 30, 2017, appears on the next page. Harrison Trading Company uses the perpetual inventory system.

Required

1. Journalize Harrison Trading Company's closing entries.
2. Compute the gross margin percentage and the rate of inventory turnover for 2017. Inventory on hand at September 30, 2016, was $40,000. For 2016, Harrison Trading Company's gross margin percentage was 34.8 percent and the inventory turnover rate was 3.9 times. Does the two-year trend in these ratios suggest improvement or deterioration in profitability?

Excel Spreadsheet Template

Journalizing the adjusting and closing entries of a merchandising business under the perpetual inventory system
③ ④

Preparing a single-step income statement and a classified balance sheet under the perpetual inventory system
④

Preparing a multi-step income statement and calculating gross margin percentage under the perpetual inventory system
④ ⑤

Making closing entries and computing gross margin percentage and inventory turnover under the perpetual inventory system
③ ⑤

HARRISON TRADING COMPANY
Adjusted Trial Balance
September 30, 2017

	Debit	Credit
Cash	$14,000	
Accounts receivable	9,000	
Inventory	42,000	
Supplies	3,000	
Building	280,000	
Accumulated amortization—building		$196,000
Land	70,000	
Accounts payable		11,000
Salary payable		2,400
Unearned sales revenue		1,600
Note payable, long-term		80,000
B. Harrison, capital		70,900
B. Harrison, withdrawals	55,000	
Sales revenue		355,000
Sales returns	14,000	
Cost of goods sold	167,000	
Selling expenses	36,500	
General expenses	22,400	
Interest expense	4,000	
Total	$716,900	$716,900

Problem 5–9B

Computing cost of goods sold and gross margin, adjusting and closing the accounts of a merchandising company, preparing a merchandiser's financial statements under the perpetual inventory system

Singleton Sports Products, which uses the perpetual inventory system, has the following account balances (in alphabetical order) on August 31, 2017:

Accounts Payable	$ 61,500
Accounts Receivable	64,700
Accumulated Amortization—Equipment	124,000
Cash	14,400
C. Singleton, Capital	305,100
C. Singleton, Withdrawals	62,400
Cost of Goods Sold	789,900
Equipment	336,000
Interest Earned	2,600
Inventory	248,400
Operating Expenses	541,200
Sales Discounts	36,200
Sales Returns and Allowances	48,600
Sales Revenue	1,640,000
Supplies	27,600
Unearned Sales Revenue	36,200

Note: For simplicity, all operating expenses have been summarized in the account Operating Expenses.

Additional data at August 31, 2017:

a. A physical count of items showed $14,200 of supplies were on hand. (Hint: Use the account Operating Expenses in the adjusting journal entry.)

b. An inventory count showed inventory on hand at August 31, 2017, of $247,400.

c. The equipment is expected to last five years and to have no value at the end of this time. (Hint: Use the account Operating Expenses in the adjusting journal entry.)

d. Unearned sales of $9,600 were earned by August 31, 2017.

Required

1. Record all adjusting and closing entries required on August 31, 2017.
2. Prepare the financial statements of Singleton Sports Products for the year ended August 31, 2017.

*Problem 5–10B

The following transactions occurred between Wentworth Pharmaceuticals and Arnold Drug Stores during June of the current year:

Accounting for the purchase and sale of inventory under the periodic system

Jun.	6	Arnold purchased $29,400 of merchandise from Wentworth on credit terms 2/10, n/30, FOB shipping point. Separately, Arnold paid freight-in of $300. Wentworth invoiced Arnold for $29,400.
	10	Arnold returned $3,600 of the merchandise purchased on June 6. Wentworth issued a credit memo for this amount.
	15	Arnold paid $12,000 of the invoice amount owed to Wentworth for the June 6 purchase. This payment included none of the freight charge.
	27	Arnold paid the remaining amount owed to Wentworth for the June 6 purchase.

Required Journalize these transactions, first on the books of Arnold Drug Stores and second on the books of Wentworth Pharmaceuticals. Assume both companies use the periodic inventory system.

*Problem 5–11B

Arden Furniture Company, which uses a periodic inventory system, engaged in the following transactions during July of the current year:

Journalizing purchase and sale transactions under the periodic inventory system

Jul.	2	Purchased inventory for cash, $6,400, less a quantity discount of $900.
	5	Purchased store supplies on credit terms of net eom, $3,400.
	8	Purchased inventory of $27,000, less a quantity discount of 10 percent, plus freight charges of $1,100. Credit terms are 2/15, n/30.
	9	Sold goods for cash, $10,800.
	11	Returned $1,000 (net amount after the quantity discount) of the inventory purchased on July 8. It was damaged in shipment.
	12	Purchased inventory on credit terms of 2/10, n/30, for $30,000.
	14	Sold inventory on credit terms of 1/10, n/30, for $69,200, less a $6,920 quantity discount.
	16	Received and paid the electricity bill, $3,200.
	20	Received returned inventory from the July 14 sale, $2,500 (net amount after the quantity discount). Arden shipped the wrong goods by mistake.
	21	Paid supplier for goods purchased on July 8.
	23	Received $43,120 cash in partial settlement of the account from the customer who purchased inventory on July 14. Granted the customer a 2 percent discount and credited the customer's account receivable for $44,000.
	30	Paid for the store supplies purchased on July 5.

Required Journalize the preceding transactions on the books of Arden Furniture Company.

---

*These Problems cover Chapter 5 Appendix A topics.

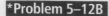
*Problem 5–12B

Gismondi Produce Company's trial balance below pertains to December 31, 2017.

GISMONDI PRODUCE COMPANY		
Trial Balance		
December 31, 2017		
Cash	$ 22,150	
Accounts receivable	109,600	
Inventory	108,300	
Store supplies	28,800	
Prepaid insurance	18,000	
Store fixtures	270,000	
Accumulated amortization—store fixtures		$ 162,000
Accounts payable		69,900
Salaries payable		0
Interest payable		0
Notes payable, long-term		47,000
F. Gismondi, capital		119,000
F. Gismondi, withdrawals	52,000	
Sales revenue		1,290,500
Purchases	737,900	
Salaries expense	238,600	
Rent expense	52,000	
Utilities expense	36,200	
Amortization expense—store fixtures	0	
Insurance expense	6,000	
Store supplies expense	0	
Interest expense	2,350	
Miscellaneous expense	6,500	
Total	$1,688,400	$1,688,400

Additional data at December 31, 2017:

a. Insurance expense for the year should total $21,600.

b. Store fixtures have an estimated useful life of 10 years and are expected to have no value when they are retired from service.

c. Accrued salaries at December 31, $5,500.

d. Accrued interest expense at December 31, $1,600.

e. Store supplies on hand at December 31, $23,800.

f. Inventory based on the inventory count on December 31, $116,500.

Required   Gismondi Produce Company uses the periodic inventory system. Complete Gismondi Produce Company's worksheet for the year ended December 31, 2017. Key adjustments by letter.

*Problem 5–13B

Refer to the data in Problem 5–12B.

Required

1. Journalize the adjusting and closing entries of Gismondi Produce Company.
2. Determine the December 31, 2017, balance in the Capital account.

---

*These Problems cover Chapter 5 Appendix A topics.

*Problem 5–14B

Selected accounts of Olsevik Janitorial Supplies, at July 31, 2017, are listed in alphabetical order below. For simplicity, all operating expenses are summarized in the Selling Expenses account and the General Expenses account. Olsevik Janitorial Supplies uses the periodic inventory system.

Preparing a single-step income statement and a classified balance sheet under the periodic inventory system (A4)

Accounts Payable	$102,000	Inventory: July 31, 2016	$730,000
Accounts Receivable	117,000	Inventory: July 31, 2017	525,000
Accumulated Amortization—		Notes Payable, Long-Term	500,000
Equipment	61,500	Purchases	1,361,000
B. Olsevik, Capital	863,400	Salaries Payable	23,000
B. Olsevik, Withdrawals	42,300	Sales Discounts	25,000
Cash	46,200	Sales Returns and Allowances	52,800
Equipment	484,000	Sales Revenue	1,891,200
General Expenses	284,250	Selling Expenses	317,250
Interest Expense	10,200	Supplies	16,200
Interest Payable	8,800	Unearned Sales Revenue	34,800
Interest Revenue	1,500		

Required

1. Prepare the business's single-step income statement for the year ended July 31, 2017.
2. Prepare Olsevik Janitorial Supplies' statement of owner's equity at July 31, 2017.
3. Prepare Olsevik Janitorial Supplies' classified balance sheet in report format at July 31, 2017.

*Problem 5–15B

1. Use the data in Problem 5–14B to prepare Olsevik Janitorial Supplies' multi-step income statement for the year ended July 31, 2017.
2. Bev Olsevik, owner of the company, strives to earn a gross margin percentage of at least 50 percent and a net income percentage of 20 percent (Net income percentage = Net income ÷ Net sales revenue). Did Olsevik Janitorial Supplies achieve these goals? Show your calculations.

Preparing a multi-step income statement and calculating gross margin percentage under the periodic inventory system

*Problem 5–16B

Selected accounts from the accounting records of Burke Imports at September 30, 2017, are shown below. Burke Imports uses the periodic inventory system.

Computing cost of goods sold and gross margin in a periodic system, evaluating the business

Cash	$28,600
Purchases	206,200
Freight-in	6,200
Sales Revenue	376,400
Purchases Returns and Allowances	3,200
Salaries Payable	4,400
Glen Burke, Capital	66,800
Sales Returns and Allowances	10,600
Inventory: September 30, 2016	46,200
September 30, 2017	51,400
Selling Expense	68,400
Equipment	96,000
Purchase Discounts	2,730
Accumulated Amortization—Equipment	19,200
Sales Discounts	7,200
General Expenses	37,000
Accounts Payable	29,400
Accounts Receivable	34,400

*These Problems cover Chapter 5 Appendix A topics.

Required

1. Using the financial statement format as a guide only, show the computation of Burke Imports' net sales, cost of goods sold, and gross margin for the year ended September 30, 2017.
2. Glen Burke, owner of Burke Imports, strives to earn a gross margin percentage of 40 percent. Did he achieve this goal?
3. Did the rate of inventory turnover reach the industry average of 3.4 times per year?

*Problem 5–17B

Kellet International engaged in the following transactions during November 2017, the first month of the company's fiscal year. Assume the company had no inventory on hand prior to November 3. Kellet International has a periodic inventory system.

Nov. 3	Purchased inventory costing $7,000 on credit terms of 1/10, net eom. The goods were shipped FOB Kellet's warehouse.
9	Returned 20 percent of the inventory purchased on November 3. It was defective.
12	Sold goods for cash, $6,000 (cost, $3,000).
15	Purchased inventory of $15,400, less a $400 quantity discount. Credit terms were 1/15, n/30. The goods were shipped FOB the supplier's warehouse.
16	Paid a $1,200 freight bill on the inventory purchased on November 15.
18	Sold inventory for $9,000 on credit terms of 1/10, n/30 (cost, $4,500).
22	Received merchandise returned from the customer from the November 18 sale, $2,000 (cost, $1,000). Merchandise was the wrong size.
24	Borrowed exactly enough money from the bank to pay for the November 15 purchase in time to take advantage of the discount offered. Signed a note payable to the bank for the net amount.
24	Paid supplier for goods purchased on November 15, less all returns and discounts.
28	Received cash in full settlement of the account from the customer who purchased inventory on November 18, less the return on November 22 and less the discount.
29	Paid the amount owed on account from the purchase of November 3, less the November 9 return.
30	Purchased inventory for cash, $4,640, less a quantity discount of $140.

Required

1. Journalize the transactions and include any calculations in the journal entry explanations.
2. Refer to the Kellet International journal entries in Requirement 1 to set up T-accounts, and post the journal entries to calculate the ending balances for the cost of goods sold equation accounts.
3. Calculate cost of goods sold using an ending inventory value of $16,000.
4. Assume Kellet International has two year-end adjusting entries: (a) accrue accounting expenses of $1,000, and (b) accrue a sale of $2,000 that was completed on November 30 but unrecorded. Record and post the adjusting entries and closing entries for Kellet International.
5. Prepare the financial statements under the periodic inventory system.
6. Refer to the Kellet International journal entries in Requirement 1 above. Assume that the note payable signed on November 24 requires the payment of $250 interest expense. Was the decision to borrow funds to take advantage of the cash discount wise or unwise?
7. Compare the results of the Summary Problem on page 271 with this solution (periodic). What main differences do you notice?

---

*These Problems cover Chapter 5 Appendix A and B topics.

CHALLENGE PROBLEMS

Problem 5–1C

You have been hired recently as an accountant by Apex, a small chain of stores that sells wireless products. One of your first activities is to review the accounting system for Apex.

In your review, you discover that the company determines selling prices by adding a standard markup on cost of 10 percent (i.e., cost plus 10 percent of cost) to the cost of all products. The company uses a perpetual inventory system. You also discover that your predecessor, a bookkeeper, had set up the accounting system so that all purchase discounts and purchase returns and allowances were accumulated in an account that was treated as "other income" for financial statement purposes because he believed that they were financing items and not related to operations.

Sarah Hussey, owner of Apex, uses modern decision-making techniques in running Apex. Two ratios she particularly favours are the gross margin percentage and inventory turnover ratio.

Understanding purchasing and gross margin
①②⑤

Required

1. What is a possible effect of the accounting system described on the pricing of products and thus operations of Apex stores?
2. What is the effect of the accounting system instituted by your predecessor on the two ratios Ms. Hussey favours?

Using an inventory system for control
① Ⓑ①

*Problem 5–2C

Rob Carson is concerned about theft by shoplifters in his chain of three discount stores and has come to your public accounting firm for advice. Specifically, he has several questions he would like you to answer:

a. He wonders if there is any inventory system he can use that will allow him to keep track of products that leave his stores as legitimate sales and will also allow him to determine if inventory has been lost or stolen.

b. He realizes that carrying inventory is expensive. He wants to know if you have any suggestions as to how he can keep close tabs on his inventory at the three stores so he can be sure that the stores don't run out of product or have too much on hand.

c. The space in the stores is limited. Rob wants to install an inventory system that will tell him when a product is slow-moving or obsolete so he can clear it out and replace it with a potentially faster-moving product.

Required Indicate whether a perpetual inventory system or a periodic inventory system will provide Rob with answers to the three questions he has asked. Explain how the inventory system indicated will provide the specific information he has requested.

---

*This Problem covers Chapter 5 Appendix B topics.

EXTENDING YOUR KNOWLEDGE

DECISION PROBLEMS

Decision Problem 1

Mitch Hopkins owns the Happy Valley Drug Store, which has prospered during its second year of operation. To help Hopkins decide whether to open another pharmacy in the area, his bookkeeper has prepared the current income statement of the business.

Using financial statements to decide on a business expansion
④⑤
Net income, $182,200

HAPPY VALLEY DRUG STORE	
Income Statement	
For the Year Ended December 31, 2017	
Sales revenue	$740,000
Interest revenue	30,000
Total revenue	770,000
Cost of goods sold	348,000
Gross margin	422,000
Operating expenses:	
Salary expense	$127,000
Rent expense	32,000
Amortization expense	24,500
Interest expense	10,500
Utilities expense	6,800
Supplies expense	4,000
Total operating expenses	204,800
Income from operations	217,200
Other revenues:	
Sales discounts ($11,000) and returns ($24,000)	35,000
Net income	$252,200

Hopkins recently read in an industry trade journal that a successful two-year-old pharmacy meets these criteria:

a. Gross margin is at least 50 percent.

b. Net income is at least $150,000.

Basing his opinion on the entity's income statement data, Hopkins believes the business meets both criteria. He plans to go ahead with the expansion plan and asks your advice on preparing the pharmacy's income statement in accordance with generally accepted accounting principles. When you point out that the income statement includes errors, Hopkins assures you that all amounts are correct.

Required Prepare a correct multi-step income statement and make a recommendation about whether to undertake the expansion at this time.

Decision Problem 2

Understanding the operating cycle of a merchandiser

Jeremy Chan has come to you for advice. Earlier this year he opened a movie prop rental business with special credit terms for items to be used for less than a month.

Business has been very good. Chan is sure it is because of his competitive prices and the unique credit terms he offers. His problem is that he is short of cash, and his loan with the bank has grown significantly. The bank manager has indicated that he wishes to reduce Chan's line of credit because she is worried that he will get into financial difficulties.

Required

1. Explain to Chan why he, in your opinion, is short of cash.
2. Chan has asked you to explain his problem to the bank manager and to assist in asking for more credit. What might you say to the bank manager to assist Chan?

*Decision Problem 3

Correcting an inventory error

The employees of Olford Furniture Company made an error when they performed the periodic inventory count at year end, October 31, 2017. Part of one warehouse was not

---

*This Problem covers Chapter 5 Appendix A topics.

counted and therefore was not included in inventory. (Assume the error is not material, so the October 31, 2017, financial statements were not corrected.)

Required

1. Indicate the effect of the inventory error on cost of goods sold, gross margin, and net income for the year ended October 31, 2017.
2. Will the error affect cost of goods sold, gross margin, and net income in 2018? If so, what will be the effect?

FINANCIAL STATEMENT CASE

This problem uses both the statement of earnings and the balance sheet of Indigo Books and Music Inc. that appear in Appendix A at the end of this book and on MyAccountingLab.

Closing entries for a corporation that sells merchandise

1. Journalize Indigo's closing entries for the year ended March 29, 2014, up to the line Operating profit (loss). Instead of closing to a Capital account, close to the Retained Earnings account (since Indigo is a corporation, not a proprietorship). What was the amount closed to Retained Earnings?
2. Indigo is Canada's largest book, gift, and specialty toy retailer, operating stores in all 10 provinces and one territory as well as online through its website indigo.ca. What amounts go into the inventory value shown on the balance sheet? Why are online shipping costs excluded from the inventory total? See Note 7 in the annual report for this detail.
3. On the balance sheet the company reports an inventory figure. What amounts are shown on the balance sheet for the Inventory account for March 29, 2014, and March 30, 2013?

IFRS MINI-CASE

Michael Ingolby opened his first The Outdoor Enthusiast sporting goods store in Calgary in 1999. The store was very successful, and Michael realized he had tapped into a market that had long been neglected. He opened his second store in Calgary in 2003 and his third store in Edmonton in 2009.

Assessing the impact of IFRS on a merchandiser

Michael's successes did not go unnoticed. He was approached recently by a venture fund company that is interested in providing cash to open more stores, starting in British Columbia, then targeting the Ontario market. Michael is excited by the possibility of expanding his store concept into other provinces and is very interested in talking to the venture capitalists.

Michael has been the sole owner of The Outdoor Enthusiast. His accounting department keeps the books and prepares the financial statements. Michael also has a public accountant, John Sheppard, who audits the financial statements, prepares the tax returns, and provides financial advice to Michael. John has always ensured that the company follows generally accepted accounting principles. When IFRS came into effect in 2011, the company had to choose between following IFRS or ASPE. Since the company was private with only one shareholder, John recommended that the company follow ASPE.

The venture capitalists have indicated that if the expansion is to take place with their involvement, the company will have to follow IFRS, since the ultimate goal will be to have the company's shares trade on a public stock exchange. The venture capitalists want to review the IFRS financial statements of the company. As a starting point, they are particularly interested in reviewing the income statement.

You are an associate accountant working for John Sheppard. John has asked you to provide a short report focusing on the differences between the income statement prepared under ASPE as opposed to IFRS. He has suggested that you may want to review the financial statements of Canadian Tire Corporation or Loblaw Companies Limited to see what, if any, differences there are compared to an income statement prepared under ASPE.

Required Write a short report outlining the differences in presentation between an income statement prepared using ASPE and one prepared using IFRS.

>Try It! SOLUTIONS FOR CHAPTER 5

1. a. Gross margin = $40,000
   b. Net sales = $40,000
   c. Cost of goods sold = $30,000

2. The missing inventory amounts in each of the following situations are bolded:

Beginning Inventory	Cost of Goods Purchased	Goods Available for Sale	Ending Inventory	Cost of Goods Sold
$42,000	$30,000	**$72,000**	$24,000	$48,000
20,000	50,000	70,000	40,000	30,000
90,000	**20,000**	110,000	**70,000**	40,000
110,000	20,000	130,000	70,000	**60,000**

3.

2017			
Jun. 3	Inventory	14,500	
	Accounts Payable		14,500
7	Accounts Payable	2,700	
	Inventory		2,700
9	Inventory	750	
	Cash		750
10	Cash	2,400	
	Accounts Receivable	9,100	
	Sales Revenue		11,500
10	Cost of Goods Sold	6,900	
	Inventory		6,900
12	Accounts Payable*	11,800	
	Inventory**		118
	Cash***		11,682
16	Sales Return and Allowances	1,200	
	Accounts Receivable		1,200
23	Cash†	7,742	
	Sales Discounts††	158	
	Accounts Receivable†††		7,900

*($14,500 − $2,700)
**($11,800 × 0.01)
***($11,800 − $118)
†($7,900 − $158)
††($7,900 × 0.02)
†††($9,100 − $1,200)

4. The journal entry would be:

2017			
Dec. 31	Cost of Goods Sold	15,000	
	Inventory		15,000
	To record adjustment for inventory shrinkage, calculated as $125,000 − $110,000 = $15,000.		

5. The journal entry would be:

2017			
Dec. 31	Inventory	3,000	
	Cost of Goods Sold		3,000
	To record adjustment to inventory records based on physical count, calculated as $78,000 − $75,000 = $3,000.		

6. a. Net sales = Sales revenue − Sales discounts − Sales Returns and Allowances
   = $777,000 − $7,500 − $8,000
   = $761,500
   b. Gross margin = Net sales − Cost of goods sold
   = $761,500 − $427,000
   = $334,500

7.

PATTI'S PARTY SUPPLIES		
Income Statement		
For the Year Ended December 31, 2017		
Revenues:		
Sales revenue		$244,000
Less: Sales discounts	$ 10,000	
Sales returns and allowances	8,000	18,000
Net sales revenue		226,000
Interest revenue		2,000
Total revenue		228,000
Expenses:		
Cost of goods sold	$ 81,000	
Operating expenses	106,300	
Interest expense	2,900	
Total expenses		190,200
Net income		$ 37,800

8.

PATTI'S PARTY SUPPLIES		
Income Statement		
For the Year Ended December 31, 2017		
Sales revenue		$244,000
Less: Sales discounts	$10,000	
Sales returns and allowances	8,000	18,000
Net sales revenue		226,000
Cost of goods sold		81,000
Gross margin		145,000
Operating expenses		106,300
Operating income		38,700
Other revenue and (expense):		
Interest revenue	2,000	
Less: Interest expense	2,900	(900)
Net income		$ 37,800

9. Patti's Party Supplies is a merchandising company. This is supported by the accounts unique to merchandisers, namely the Cost of Goods Sold, Sales Discounts, and Sales Returns and Allowances accounts on the income statement.

10. Gross margin percentage = Gross margin ÷ Net sales revenue
= $145,000 ÷ $226,000 = 64.2%

11. Inventory turnover = Cost of goods sold ÷ Average inventory
= $81,000 ÷ [($24,000 + $25,800) ÷ 2]
= 3.25 times

12.

2017			
Jun. 3	Purchases	14,500	
	Accounts Payable		14,500
7	Accounts Payable	2,700	
	Purchases Returns & Allowances		2,700
9	Freight-in	750	
	Cash		750
10	Cash	2,400	
	Accounts Receivable	9,100	
	Sales Revenue		11,500
12	Accounts Payable	11,800	
	Purchases Discounts		118
	Cash		11,682
16	Sales Return and Allowances	1,200	
	Accounts Receivable		1,200
23	Cash	7,742	
	Sales Discounts	158	
	Accounts Receivable		7,900

13. Beginning Inventory + Net Purchases − Ending Inventory
= Cost of Goods Sold
$0 + ($14,500 − $2,700 − $118 + $750) − $11,000 = $1,432
Net Sales − COGS = Gross Profit
($11,500 − $1,200 − $158) − $1,432 = $8,710

14. The closing entries are as follows:

2017			
Jun. 30	Sales Revenue	11,500	
	Purchases Returns and Allowances	2,700	
	Purchases Discounts	118	
	Income Summary		14,318
30	Income Summary	16,608	
	Purchases		14,500
	Freight-in		750
	Sales Returns and Allowances		1,200
	Sales Discounts		158
30	Income Summary	0	
	Inventory (Beginning)		0
30	Inventory (Ending)	11,000	
	Income Summary		11,000
30	Income Summary	8,710	
	Capital Account		8,710

6 ACCOUNTING FOR MERCHANDISE INVENTORY

CONNECTING CHAPTER 6

MyAccountingLab   The **Summary** for Chapter 6 appears on page 345. This lists all of the MyAccountingLab resources. **Accounting Vocabulary** with definitions for this chapter's material appears on page 346.

Big B Comics is an Ontario chain of comic book stores established in 1996. There are three stores in the chain located in Niagara Falls, Barrie, and the flagship store in Hamilton. The chain has a well-designed and maintained website with an appealing store atmosphere. Retailers like Big B Comics pay between 30 and 60 cents per comic book and charge on average $3 to $4 per comic book to customers. According to Comichron.com, a resource for comics research, this price is right on target: The weighted-average price in 2014 for a comic book based on the top 300 sold in North America was $4.00.

Every year, Big B Comics hosts a very successful free event that generates a lot of interest among the store's young clientele—Free Comic Book Day, which is held in early May. "The concept of giving away free comics started in 2002 to capitalize on the first *Spider-Man* movie. Most every event since has tied into a comic-themed movie opening in early May." In fact, the event has grown every year and is now a worldwide event and has been described as "Boxing Day on crack." According to John Roma, the owner of Niagara Falls's oldest comic book store, The Neutral Zone, he has to order more free comic books to hand out every year as the event gets better and bigger.

Inventory management and control is a key element of customer satisfaction. Having the right product in place when it is ready to be marketed for sale is crucial to satisfy the needs of these stores' customers. Due to the relatively low value of comic books, retailers like Big B must sell a large volume to make a healthy profit.

The comic book industry is huge and heavily linked to the overall entertainment industry with sales tied to movie and video game releases. According to Comichron.com, sales for May 2014 for the top 300 comics in North America were $25.06 million, with the year to date for this category totalling $121.03 million.[1]

[1]John Law, "Readers Get Ready for Free Comic Book Day," *St. Catharines Standard*, May 1, 2014, accessed May 2, 2015, http://www.stcatharinesstandard.ca/2014/05/01/readers-get-ready-for-free-comic-book-day; Comichron: The Comics Chronicles, "May 2014 Comic Book Sales Figures," accessed May 2, 2015, http://www.comichron.com/monthlycomicssales/2014/2014-05.html.

> **The** last chapter introduced the accounting for merchandise inventory. It showed how Slopes Ski Shop, a sporting goods store, recorded the purchase and sale of its inventory. This chapter completes the accounting for merchandise inventory.

Big B Comics sells comic books and novelties to the young at heart. Big B Comics, like all merchandising companies, may select from several different methods of accounting for its inventory. Inventory is the first area in which a company must pick the accounting method it will use, and it is a key decision for a merchandiser.

This chapter will introduce new vocabulary, including the term *FIFO*. By the end of this chapter, you will also be prepared to decide which accounting method is most appropriate if you ever start your own business.

First, let's review the balance sheet and the income statement, because the financial statements show how merchandise inventory affects a company. Exhibit 6–1 gives the merchandising section of Danier Leather Inc.'s balance sheet and income statement. Inventories, cost of goods sold (sometimes called cost of sales), and gross margin are labelled A, B, and C, respectively, to indicate that, throughout the chapter, we will be computing them using various accounting methods.

EXHIBIT 6–1 | Danier Leather Inc.'s Merchandising Section of the Financial Statements

DANIER LEATHER INC. Balance Sheet (partial, adapted) June 28, 2014	
Assets:	(thousands)
Current assets:	
Cash	$13,507
Accounts receivable	638
Inventories	21,721 Ⓐ
Prepaid expenses	643

DANIER LEATHER INC. Income Statement (partial, adapted) For the Year Ended June 28, 2014	
	(thousands)
Revenue	$141,930
Cost of goods sold	73,697 Ⓑ
Gross margin	$ 68,233 Ⓒ

As you can see in Exhibit 6–1, inventory is the most significant current asset for Danier, as it is for most retail companies. Companies such as Danier and Big B Comics want to make sure that they carry enough inventory to meet customer demand. At the same time, if companies carry too much inventory, they risk "tying up" too much of the company's assets in inventory.

INVENTORY COSTING METHODS

To expand on what we saw in Chapter 5,

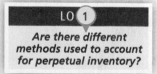

LO 1

Are there different methods used to account for perpetual inventory?

> Ending inventory = Number of units *on hand* × Unit cost
>
> Cost of goods *sold* = Number of units *sold* × Unit cost

Companies determine the number of units from perpetual inventory records that are verified by a physical count. The cost of each unit of inventory is

> **Unit cost = Purchase price − Purchase discounts − Quantity discounts + Any costs necessary to put the unit in a saleable condition, such as freight in, customs duties, and insurance**

Exhibit 6–2 gives the inventory data for a line of skis carried by Slopes Ski Shop.

EXHIBIT 6–2 | Perpetual Inventory Record—Quantities Only

Item: Skis, Model XL			
Date	Quantity Purchased	Quantity Sold	Quantity on Hand
Nov. 1			5 ← Beginning inventory
4	30		35
16		20	15
25	35		50
30		40	10
Totals	65	60	10 ← Ending inventory

In this illustration, Slopes began November with 5 pairs of skis on hand. After buying and selling, Slopes had 10 pairs at the end of the month.

Assume that Slopes's unit cost of each pair is $60. In this case,

> **Ending inventory = Number of units *on hand* (Exhibit 6–2) × Unit cost**
>
> $\qquad = \qquad\qquad 10 \qquad\qquad\qquad × \$60 = \$600$
>
> **Cost of goods sold = Number of units *sold* (Exhibit 6–2) × Unit cost**
>
> $\qquad = \qquad\qquad 60 \qquad\qquad\qquad × \$60 = \$3,600$

What would Slopes's ending inventory and cost of goods sold be if the cost of these skis increased from $60 to $65 or $70 during the period? Companies face price increases like these all the time. A pair of skis that cost Slopes $60 in January may cost $65 in April. Suppose Slopes sells 150 pairs of these skis in November. How many of the skis cost $60? How many cost $65? To compute ending inventory and cost of goods sold, Slopes must assign a unit cost to each item. The accounting profession has developed three costing methods that are compliant with ASPE and acceptable to the Canada Revenue Agency.

- Specific-unit cost
- Weighted-average cost
- First-in, first-out (FIFO) cost

The method chosen will have a direct effect on the balance sheet, the income statement, and cash flows (since it affects the amount of income tax paid). Once it is chosen, however, the company should use this method going forward for consistency and comparability.

The **specific-unit-cost method**, also called the **specific identification method**, uses the specific cost of each unit of inventory for items that have a distinct identity. Some businesses deal in items that differ from unit to unit, such as automobiles,

KEY POINTS

The three inventory costing methods affect the cost of inventory and, consequently, the cost of goods sold. The method used does *not* have to match the physical flow of goods.

jewels, and real estate. For example, Toyota dealers may have two vehicles: a model with vehicle identification number (VIN) 010 that costs $21,000 and a model with VIN 020 that costs $27,000. If the dealer sells the model with VIN 020, cost of goods sold is $27,000, the cost of the specific unit. Suppose the model with VIN 010 is the only unit left in inventory at the end of the period; ending inventory is $21,000, the dealer's cost of that particular car:

Car (VIN) 010 cost $21,000   +   Car (VIN) 020 cost $27,000 = Inventory on hand

Ending inventory = $21,000   Cost of Goods Sold = $27,000

EXHIBIT 6–3 | Cost Flows for the Most Popular Inventory Methods When the Inventory Items Are Identical

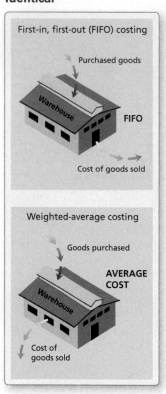

Companies that have units of inventory that can be separately identified because they have a distinctive identity use the specific-unit-cost method to account for their inventory.

Many companies have units of inventory that are exactly the same—they cannot tell one unit of inventory from another. These companies use either the first-in, first-out method or the weighted-average-cost method to value inventory. These methods are *cost flow assumptions* that do not have to match the actual flow of inventory costs. Exhibit 6–3 illustrates how each method works.

- Under the first-in, first-out (FIFO) method, the cost of goods sold is based on the oldest purchases. Perishables are a good example: You have to sell the oldest inventory items first, before they go bad. This is illustrated by the cost of goods sold coming from the *bottom* of the building in Exhibit 6–3.

- Under the weighted-average-cost method, which is discussed in detail in the next section, the cost of goods sold is based on an average cost for the period. This is illustrated by the cost of goods sold coming from the *middle* of the building in Exhibit 6–3.

Exhibit 6–4 summarizes the inventory costing methods with a simple example that shows each method's effects on the income statement (sales, cost of goods sold, and gross margin) and the balance sheet (ending inventory).

EXHIBIT 6–4 | Inventory Costing Methods—An Example

Assume 14 identical units of inventory are purchased in April as shown in Panel A. The inventory sells for $4 per unit. One unit is sold at the end of April. Notice the effects of each inventory costing method—specific-identification, FIFO, and weighted-average-cost methods—on the income statement and balance sheet after the April sale.

Panel A	
Apr. 1	Purchased 1 unit at a cost of $0.600 per unit.
5	Purchased 6 units at a cost of $0.650 per unit.
26	Purchased 7 units at a cost of $0.700 per unit.

(Continued)

EXHIBIT 6-4 | Inventory Costing Methods—An Example (*Continued*)

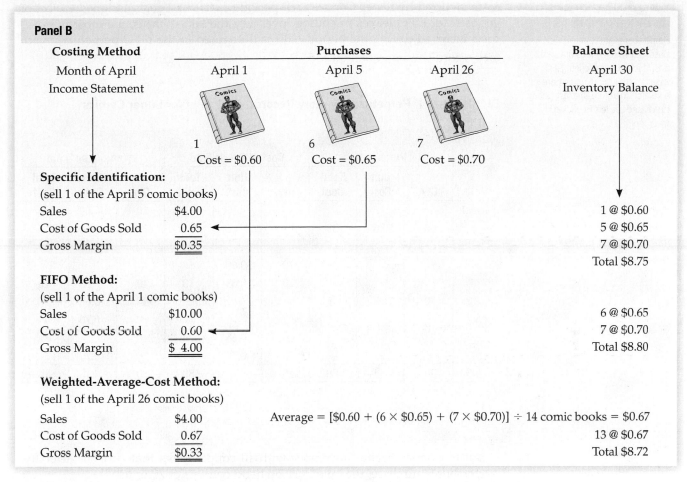

Panel B

Costing Method	Purchases			Balance Sheet
Month of April Income Statement	April 1	April 5	April 26	April 30 Inventory Balance
	1 Cost = $0.60	6 Cost = $0.65	7 Cost = $0.70	

Specific Identification:
(sell 1 of the April 5 comic books)

Sales	$4.00	
Cost of Goods Sold	0.65	
Gross Margin	$0.35	

1 @ $0.60
5 @ $0.65
7 @ $0.70
Total $8.75

FIFO Method:
(sell 1 of the April 1 comic books)

Sales	$10.00	
Cost of Goods Sold	0.60	
Gross Margin	$ 4.00	

6 @ $0.65
7 @ $0.70
Total $8.80

Weighted-Average-Cost Method:
(sell 1 of the April 26 comic books)

Sales	$4.00	Average = [$0.60 + (6 × $0.65) + (7 × $0.70)] ÷ 14 comic books = $0.67
Cost of Goods Sold	0.67	13 @ $0.67
Gross Margin	$0.33	Total $8.72

Now let's see how to compute inventory amounts under the FIFO and weighted-average-cost methods. We use the following transaction data for all the illustrations:

	Comic Book	Number of Units	Unit Cost
Nov. 1	Beginning inventory	10	$6.00
5	Purchase	60	6.50
1	Sale	30	
5	Purchase	70	7.00
1	Sale	90	

We begin with inventory costing in a perpetual system.

INVENTORY COSTING IN A PERPETUAL SYSTEM

The inventory costing methods produce different amounts for:

- Ending inventory
- Cost of goods sold

First-in, First-out Method

Many companies use the **first-in, first-out (FIFO) method** to account for their inventory. FIFO costing is consistent with the physical movement of inventory for most companies. That is, they sell their oldest inventory first.

KEY POINTS

The perpetual inventory record only reflects the cost. The selling price of these units is $4.00.

Remember that the term *FIFO* describes which *goods* are sold, *not* which goods are left. FIFO assumes that goods in first are sold first; therefore, the last goods purchased are left in ending inventory.

Let's look at a comic book store as an example. Under FIFO costing, the first costs incurred by Super Comics each period are the first costs assigned to cost of goods sold. FIFO leaves in ending inventory the last—that is, the most recent—costs incurred during the period. This is illustrated in the FIFO perpetual inventory record shown in Exhibit 6–5.

EXHIBIT 6–5 | Perpetual Inventory Record—FIFO Cost for Super Comics

Comic Books

Date	Purchases Qty.	Unit Cost	Total Cost	COGS Qty.	Unit Cost	Total Cost	Inventory Qty.	Unit Cost	Total Cost
Nov. 1							10	$0.60	$ 6
5	60	$0.65	$39				10	0.60	6
							60	0.65	39
15				10	$0.60	$6			
				20	0.65	13	40	0.65	26
26	70	0.70	49				40	0.65	26
							70	0.70	49
30				40	0.65	26			
				50	0.70	35	20	0.70	14
30	130		$88	120		$80	20		$14

Beginning inventory

Ending inventory

Super Comics began November with 10 comic books that cost $6. After the November 5 purchase, the inventory on hand consists of 70 units.

$$\text{70 units on hand} \begin{cases} \text{10 @ \$0.60} = \$\ 6 \\ \text{60 @ \$0.65} = \underline{39} \end{cases}$$
$$\text{Inventory on hand} = \underline{\underline{\$45}}$$

On November 15, Super Comics sold 30 units. Under FIFO costing, the first 10 units sold are costed at the oldest cost ($0.60 per unit). The next 20 units sold come from the group that cost $0.65 per unit. That leaves 40 units in inventory on hand, and those units cost $0.65 each. The remainder of the inventory record follows that same pattern.

The FIFO monthly summary at November 30 is

- Cost of goods sold: 120 units that cost a total of $80
- Ending inventory: 20 units that cost a total of $14

If Super Comics used the FIFO method, it would measure cost of goods sold and inventory in this manner to prepare its financial statements.

Notice that you can use the familiar cost of goods sold model to check the accuracy of the inventory record, as follows:

Beginning inventory	$ 6
+ Net purchases	88
= Cost of goods available for sale	94
− **Ending inventory**	(14)
= **Cost of goods sold**	$80

Journal Entries under FIFO The journal entries under FIFO costing for the perpetual inventory system follow the data in Exhibit 6–5. For example, on November 5, Super Comics purchased $39 of inventory and made the first journal entry. On November 15, Super Comics sold 30 comic books for the sale price of $4 each, at which time Super Comics recorded the sale ($120) and the cost of goods sold ($19). The remaining journal entries (November 26 and 30) follow the inventory data in Exhibit 6–5. (All purchases and sales are on account. The sale price of the comic books is $4 per unit.)

Nov. 5	Inventory	39	
	Accounts Payable		39
	Purchased inventory on account (60 × $0.65 = $39).		
15	Accounts Receivable	120	
	Sales Revenue		120
	Sale on account (30 × $4 = $120).		
15	Cost of Goods Sold	19	
	Inventory		19
	Cost of goods sold ($0.60 × 10 + 20 × $0.65 = $19).		
26	Inventory	49	
	Accounts Payable		49
	Purchased inventory on account (70 × $0.70 = $49).		
30	Accounts Receivable	360	
	Sales Revenue		360
	Sale on account (90 × $4 = $360).		
30	Cost of Goods Sold	61	
	Inventory		61
	Cost of goods sold ($26 + $35 = $61).		

Moving-Weighted-Average-Cost Method

Suppose Super Comics uses the **moving-weighted-average-cost method** to account for its inventory of comic books. With this method, the business computes a new weighted-average cost per unit after each purchase. Ending inventory and cost of goods sold are then based on the same most-recent weighted-average cost per unit. Exhibit 6–6 shows a perpetual inventory record for the moving-weighted-average-cost method. *We round average unit cost to the nearest cent and total cost to the nearest dollar.*

KEY POINTS

It is possible to round average unit cost to the nearest cent and total cost to the nearest dollar, if necessary.

EXHIBIT 6–6 | Perpetual Inventory Record—Moving-Weighted-Average Cost for Super Comics

Comic Books									
	Purchases			**Cost of Goods Sold**			**Inventory on Hand**		
Date	Qty.	Unit Cost	Total Cost	Qty.	Unit Cost	Total Cost	Qty.	Unit Cost	Total Cost
Nov. 1							10	$0.60	$ 6
5	60	$0.65	$39				70	0.64	44.80
15				30	$0.64	$19.20	40	0.64	25.60
26	70	0.70	49				110	0.68	74.80*
30				90	0.68	61.20	20	0.68	13.60
30	130		$88	120		$80.40	20		$13.60

($6 + 39)/70 units = $0.64

(25.60 + $49.00)/110 = $0.68

*This number is really 74.60 but has changed due to rounding and extending the amount as total cost.

After each purchase, Super Comics computes a new average cost per unit. For example, on November 5, the new weighted-average unit cost combines the cost and quantity of units on hand on November 1 with the November 5 purchase and is calculated as

	Total cost of inventory on hand	÷	Number of units on hand	=	Average cost per unit
Nov. 5	$6 + $39 = $45	÷	70 units	=	$0.64

The goods sold on November 15 are then costed at $0.64 per unit for a total cost of $19.20 (calculated as $0.64/unit × 30 units = $19.20). The total cost of inventory on hand on November 15 is $25.60 (calculated as $44.80 − $19.20 = $25.60) and the unit cost remains as $0.64. Super Comics computes a new average cost after the November 26 purchase, which is why it is called a "moving" weighted-average cost.

The moving-weighted-average-cost summary at November 30 is

- Cost of goods sold: 120 units that cost a total of $80.40
- Ending inventory: 20 units that cost a total of $13.60

If Super Comics used the moving-weighted-average-cost method, it would measure cost of goods sold and inventory in this manner to prepare its financial statements.

Journal Entries under Moving-Weighted-Average Costing   The journal entries under moving-weighted-average costing follow the data in Exhibit 6–6. On November 5, Super Comics purchased $39 of inventory and made the first journal entry. On November 15, Super Comics sold 30 comic books for $4 each. Super Comics recorded the sale ($120) and the cost of goods sold ($19.20). The remaining journal entries (November 26 and 30) follow the data in Exhibit 6–5. (All purchases and sales are on account. The sale price of a comic book is $4 per unit.)

Nov. 5	Inventory	39	
	Accounts Payable		39
	Purchased inventory on account (60 × $0.65 = $39).		
15	Accounts Receivable	120	
	Sales Revenue		120
	Sale on account (30 × $4 = $120).		
15	Cost of Goods Sold	19.20	
	Inventory		19.20
	Cost of goods sold (30 × $0.64 = $19.20).		
26	Inventory	49	
	Accounts Payable		49
	Purchased inventory on account (70 × $0.70 = $49).		
30	Accounts Receivable	360	
	Sales Revenue		360
	Sale on account (90 × $4 = $360).		
30	Cost of Goods Sold	61.20	
	Inventory		61.20
	Cost of goods sold, calculated as:		
	Cost of inventory on hand: $25.60 + $49 = $74.60		
	Moving-weighted-average cost per unit: $74.60/110 = $0.68		
	Cost of goods sold = 90 × $0.68 = $61.20		

> Try It!

1. The Watch Shop carries only watches. Assume The Watch Shop began June with an inventory of 20 wristwatches that cost $60 each. The Watch Shop sells those watches for $100 each. During June, The Watch Shop bought and sold inventory as follows:

Jun.	3	Sold 16 units for $100 each.
	16	Purchased 20 units at $65 each.
	23	Sold 16 units for $100 each.

    Prepare a perpetual inventory record for The Watch Shop under each method:
    - FIFO
    - Moving-weighted-average cost

2. Refer to The Watch Shop data given in the previous question. Journalize all of The Watch Shop's inventory transactions for June for the FIFO and moving-weighted-average-cost methods.

Solutions appear at the end of this chapter and on MyAccountingLab

COMPARING FIFO AND MOVING-WEIGHTED-AVERAGE COST

What leads any company to select the moving-weighted-average-cost method or to use FIFO? The different methods have different benefits.

Exhibit 6–7 summarizes the assumed results for the two inventory methods for Super Comics. It shows sales revenue (assumed) based on $4 per unit and 120 units, cost of goods sold, and gross margin for FIFO and moving-weighted-average costing. All data (except for sales revenue) come from Exhibits 6–5 and 6–6.

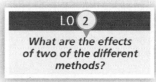

LO 2

What are the effects of two of the different methods?

EXHIBIT 6–7 | Comparative Results for FIFO and Moving-Weighted-Average Cost

	FIFO	Moving-Weighted-Average
Sales revenue (assumed)	$480	$480.00
Cost of goods sold	80	80.40
Gross margin	$400	$399.60
	(from Exhibit 6–5)	(from Exhibit 6–6)

Exhibit 6–7 also shows that when inventory costs are increasing, FIFO costing produces the lower cost of goods sold and the higher gross margin. Net income is also higher under FIFO costing when inventory costs are rising. Many companies prefer high income to attract investors and borrow money on favourable terms. In an environment of increasing costs, FIFO costing offers this benefit.

The moving-weighted-average-cost method generates a gross margin that will be lower than the gross margin generated under FIFO costing when prices are rising. The opposite is true when inventory purchase prices are falling—the moving-weighted-average-cost method would generate a higher gross margin than FIFO costing.

> **Try It!**

3. Refer to the information in Try It #1 on page 333 and your journal entries created for Try It #2. Use that information to show the computation of gross margin for the FIFO and moving-weighted-average-cost methods for The Watch Shop.

4. Refer to Try It #3. Which method maximizes net income? Which method minimizes income taxes?

5. How would your answer to Try It #4 change if inventory purchase prices were falling during June?

Solutions appear at the end of this chapter and on MyAccountingLab

INVENTORY COSTING IN A PERIODIC SYSTEM

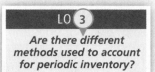

LO 3

Are there different methods used to account for periodic inventory?

KEY POINTS

Hint: To help you with this section, refer to Chapter 5, Appendix A, to review the periodic inventory system, where it is outlined in detail.

Accounting is simpler in a periodic system because the company keeps no daily running record of inventory on hand. The only way to determine the ending inventory and cost of goods sold in a periodic system is to count the goods—usually at the end of the year. The periodic system works well for a small business where the owner can control inventory by visual inspection. Appendix A in Chapter 5 illustrates how the periodic system works.

Cost of goods sold in a periodic inventory system is computed by the following formula (using assumed amounts for this illustration):

Beginning inventory	
(the inventory on hand at the end of the preceding period)	$ 5,000
Net purchases	14,000*
Add: Freight in	6,000
Goods available for sale	25,000
Less: Ending inventory	
(the inventory on hand at the end of the current period)	(7,000)
Cost of goods sold	$18,000
*Purchases	$21,000
Less: Purchase discounts	(2,000)
Purchase returns and allowances	(5,000)
Net purchases	$14,000

The application of the FIFO and weighted-average-cost methods in a periodic inventory system follows the pattern illustrated earlier for the perpetual system. To show how the periodic inventory system works, we use the same Super Comics data that we used for the perpetual system, as follows:

Comic Books		Number of Units	Unit Cost
Nov. 1	Beginning inventory	10	$0.60
5	Purchase	60	$0.65
15	Sale	30	
26	Purchase	70	$0.70
30	Sale	90	

First-in, First-out (FIFO) Method

Super Comics could use the FIFO costing method with a periodic inventory system. The FIFO computations are as follows:

Beginning inventory (10 units at $0.60)	$ 6
Purchases (60 units at $0.65 + 70 units at $0.70)	88
Cost of goods available for sale (140 units)	94
Less: Ending inventory (20 units at $0.70)	(14)
Cost of goods sold (120 units)	$80

The cost of goods available for sale is always the sum of beginning inventory plus purchases. Under FIFO costing, the ending inventory comes from the latest—the most recent—purchases, which cost $0.70 per unit. Ending inventory is therefore $14, and cost of goods sold is $80. These amounts will always be the same as the amounts calculated under the perpetual system.

There are fewer journal entries in the periodic system because Super Comics would record a sale with only a single entry. For example, Super Comics' sale of 40 comic books for $4 each is recorded as follows:

Nov. 15	Accounts Receivable	160	
	Sales Revenue		160
	Sale on account (40 × $4)		

There is no cost of goods sold entry in the periodic inventory system.

Weighted-Average-Cost Method

In the **weighted-average-cost method**, we compute a single weighted-average cost per unit for the entire period as follows:

Cost of goods available for sale	÷	Number of units available for sale	=	Average cost per unit for the entire period
$94	÷	140 units	=	$0.67

This average cost per unit is then used to compute the ending inventory and cost of goods sold as follows (rounded to 2 decimal places):

Beginning inventory (10 units at $0.60)	$ 6.00
Purchases (60 units at $0.65 + 70 units at $0.70)	88.00
Cost of goods available for sale	
(140 units at weighted-average cost of $0.67	93.80
Less: Ending inventory (20 units at $0.67)	(13.40)
Cost of goods sold (120 units at $0.67)	$ 80.40

Using the weighted-average-cost method, ending inventory and cost of goods sold under the periodic system differ from the amounts in a perpetual system. Why? Because under the perpetual system, a new average cost is computed after each purchase (it is a "moving" weighted-average cost). But the periodic system uses a single average cost that is determined at the end of the period.

ACCOUNTING CONCEPTS AND INVENTORIES

Several accounting concepts or constraints have special relevance to inventories. Among them are comparability, disclosure, materiality, and accounting conservatism (which is not part of the framework).

Comparability

The characteristic of **comparability** states that businesses should use the same accounting methods and procedures from period to period. Comparability helps investors compare a company's financial statements from one period to the next.

Suppose you are analyzing a company's net income pattern over a 2-year period. The company switched from moving-weighted-average to FIFO costing during that time. Its net income increased dramatically, but only as a result of the change in inventory method. If you did not know of the change, you might believe that the company's income increased because of improved operations. Therefore, companies must report any changes in the accounting methods they use.

Disclosure

The **disclosure principle** holds that a company's financial statements should report enough information for outsiders to make knowledgeable decisions about the company. In short, the company should report *relevant*, *reliable*, and *comparable* information about itself. This means disclosing the method or methods used to value inventories. Suppose a banker is comparing two companies—one using weighted-average costing and the other using FIFO. The FIFO company reports higher net income, but only because it uses the FIFO inventory method. Without knowledge of these accounting methods, the banker could lend money to the wrong business. In addition, different categories of inventory should be disclosed, such as raw materials, work-in-process, and finished goods inventories.

Materiality

The **materiality constraint** states that a company must perform strictly proper accounting *only* for items that are significant to the business's financial statements. Information is significant—or, in accounting terminology, *material*—when its presentation in the financial statements would influence a decision or cause someone to change a decision. The materiality constraint frees accountants from having to report every item in strict accordance with ASPE. For inventory, this means immaterial items can be expensed rather than included in inventory.

Accounting Conservatism

Conservatism, which is not part of the conceptual framework, in accounting means reporting items in the financial statements at amounts that lead to the most cautious immediate results. Conservatism could be interpreted as:

- "Anticipate no gains, but provide for all probable losses."
- "If in doubt, record an asset at the lowest reasonable amount and a liability at the highest reasonable amount."
- "When there's a question, record as an expense rather than record as an asset."

The goal is for financial statements to report realistic figures. While we want to avoid overstating assets and understating liabilities, we also should not deliberately understate assets, revenues, and gains, nor deliberately overstate liabilities, expenses, and losses. This is an important underlying concept to remember.

6. Pemberton Company began March with 40 units of inventory that cost a total of $800. During March, Pemberton purchased and sold goods as follows:

March	8	Purchase: 60 units at $12.50
	14	Sale: 50 units at $25.00
	22	Purchase: 40 units at $15.00
	27	Sale: 60 units at $30.00

Calculate the gross margin amount using the FIFO method assuming Pemberton uses a periodic inventory system.

7. Refer to the Pemberton Company data in the previous question. Calculate the gross margin amount using the weighted-average method assuming Pemberton uses a periodic inventory system.

Solutions appear at the end of this chapter and on MyAccountingLab

> Why It's Done This Way

In the accounting framework presented in Exhibit 1–5 in Chapter 1 (and on the inside back cover of this book), an asset is described as a resource controlled by the entity with a future economic benefit. Inventory is an asset for a merchandiser because it is presumed that the purchased inventory will be sold at a value higher than the cost of the inventory. At year end, a company needs to count and value its inventory to report it on the balance sheet.

In this chapter, we have studied three flow methods used to account for inventory—specific unit cost; first-in, first-out (FIFO); and moving weighted average. We use these methods to determine the cost of goods sold as well as the inventory value at year end. The specific-unit-cost method tells us the cost of the goods sold and the cost of ending inventory precisely. However, the other two methods are approximations of cost of goods sold and ending inventory. In these inventory situations, how do we ensure, based on the relevancy and reliability aspects of the accounting framework, that these flow methods will be useful to users? If FIFO and weighted-average cost are approximations of inventory value and the cost of goods sold, shouldn't we use only the specific-unit-cost method to get a reliable value for the balance sheet and income statement?

The accounting framework addresses this concern under the constraints section with "materiality." Essentially, materiality allows the accountant to use estimates or approximations of the actual value of an element, like inventory, if the estimate closely reflects the real value. As long as a person reading the financial statements knows the inventory valuation method, this user will not be misled by the use of FIFO or weighted-average cost. The cost of using the specific-unit-cost method would be more than the benefit of having slightly more accurate financial statements, thus violating the cost–benefit constraint. Thus, the financial statements are still considered relevant and reliable even though the inventory value on the balance sheet (and the cost of goods sold expense on the income statement) is estimated, since they lead to statements that communicate useful information to users at a reasonable cost.

OTHER INVENTORY ISSUES

In addition to choosing between the FIFO and weighted-average costing methods for inventory, accountants face other inventory issues. This section covers:

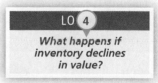

- The lower-of-cost-and-net-realizable-value rule
- Effects of inventory errors
- Ethical issues
- Estimating ending inventory

Note that the matching objective of the cost principle of measurement is applied to ending inventory with LCNRV. The reduction in the value of the inventory is shown in the year the inventory declines in value, *not* in the year the inventory is sold.

Lower-of-Cost-and-Net-Realizable-Value Rule

The **lower-of-cost-and-net-realizable-value** rule (abbreviated as **LCNRV**) shows the principle of accounting conservatism in action. LCNRV requires that inventory be reported in the financial statements at whichever is lower:

- The historical cost of the inventory
- The net realizable value (market value) of the inventory

For inventories, *net realizable value* generally means the expected selling price (i.e., the amount the business could get if it sold the inventory less the costs of selling it). For example, assume the following information:

Item	Quantity	Cost Price/Unit	Market Price/Unit	Selling Costs
001	10	$16	$20	$99

The total cost equals $160 (10 × $16) compared to the net realizable value of $101 (10 × $20 − $99). This would lead to a write-down or impairment of $59 and would require a journal entry to debit Cost of Goods Sold and credit Inventory. If the net realizable value of inventory falls below its historical cost, the business must write down the value of its goods. This write-down is known as an **impairment**. This situation may arise if inventory has become damaged or if it has become obsolete. On the balance sheet, the business reports ending inventory at its LCNRV.

At each year end, a new assessment of the net realizable value is made. If the circumstances that caused inventories to be written down below cost no longer exist, the amount of the write-down is reversed, up to the original cost of the inventory in question, which is called an **impairment reversal**. However, inventory is *never* written up to an amount greater than its original cost, since this would violate the LCNRV rule.

Suppose Super Comics paid $6,000 for comic book inventory on September 26. By December 31, the old comic book inventory can only be sold for $5,000, and the decline in value appears permanent. Net realizable value is below FIFO cost, and the entry to write down the inventory to LCNRV is as follows:

Dec. 31	Costs of Goods Sold*	1,000	
	Inventory		1,000
	To write down inventory to net realizable value.		
	(cost, $6,000 − net realizable value, $5,000)		

*Could also record this in an expense account, such as Holding Loss or Shrinkage.

In this case, Super Comics' balance sheet would report this inventory as follows:

Partial Balance Sheet	
Current assets:	
Inventory, at market	$5,000
(which is lower than $6,000 cost)	

Companies often disclose LCNRV in notes to their financial statements, as shown here for Danier Leather Inc. in its 2014 annual report:

3. Significant Accounting Policies:

(j) Inventories:

Merchandise inventories are valued at the lower of cost, using the weighted average cost method, and net realizable value ... For inventories purchased from third party vendors, cost includes the cost of purchase, duty and brokerage, quality assurance costs, distribution centre costs related to inventories and transportation costs that are directly incurred to bring inventories to their present location and condition.

The Company estimates the net realizable value as the amount at which inventories are expected to be sold, taking into account fluctuations in retail prices due to seasonality, less estimated costs necessary to make the sale. Inventories are written down to net realizable value when the cost of inventories is not estimated to be recoverable due to obsolescence, damage or declining selling prices. When circumstances that previously caused inventories to be written down below cost no longer exist, the amount of the write-down previously recorded is reversed. Storage costs, administrative overheads and selling costs related to the inventories are expensed in the period the costs are incurred.

> Try It!

8. Suppose Luchenko Supplies paid $20,000 for inventory. By its year end, the company had sold 60 percent of the inventory but determined that the remaining inventory could be sold for only 60 percent of its original cost. The company anticipated that this decline was permanent. At what amount would inventory be reported on the year-end balance sheet?

9. Refer to the inventory data in the previous question. Suppose, one month later, a worldwide shortage of this inventory now gives it a net realizable value of $10,000. At what amount would this inventory be reported on the balance sheet one month later?

Solutions appear at the end of this chapter and on MyAccountingLab

EFFECTS OF INVENTORY ERRORS

Businesses count their inventories at the end of the period. For the financial statements to be accurate, it is important to get a correct count of ending inventory. This can be difficult for a company with inventory in many locations.

An error in ending inventory creates a whole string of errors. To illustrate, suppose Super Comics accidentally counted too much ending inventory. Therefore, ending inventory is overstated on the balance sheet. The following chart shows how an overstatement of ending inventory affects cost of goods sold, gross margin, and net income:

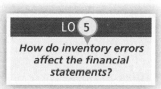

LO 5

How do inventory errors affect the financial statements?

LEARNING TIPS

Use the jingle EI, NI, O to remember the effect on ending inventory. If ending inventory (EI) is overstated or understated, net income (NI) is overstated or understated—that is, it has the same effect.

	Ending Inventory Overstated
Sales revenue	Correct
Cost of goods sold:	
Beginning inventory	Correct
Net purchases	Correct
Cost of goods available for sale	Correct
Ending inventory	**ERROR: Overstated**
Cost of goods sold	**Understated**
Gross margin	**Overstated**
Operating expenses	Correct
Net income	**Overstated**

Understating the ending inventory—reporting the inventory too low—has the opposite effect, as shown here:

	Ending Inventory Understated
Sales revenue	Correct
Cost of goods sold:	
Beginning inventory	Correct
Net purchases	Correct
Cost of goods available for sale	Correct
Ending inventory	**ERROR: Understated**
Cost of goods sold	**Overstated**
Gross margin	**Understated**
Operating expenses	Correct
Net income	**Understated**

KEY POINTS

The effect of inventory errors also affects equity because the Income Summary account is closed to equity. However, by the end of Year 2 after closing entries are posted, the inventory errors have cancelled out in equity.

Recall that one period's ending inventory is the next period's beginning inventory. Thus, an error in ending inventory carries over into the next period. Exhibit 6–8 illustrates the effect of an inventory error. Period 1's ending inventory is overstated by $10,000. The error carries over to Period 2, but Period 3 is correct. In fact, both Period 1 and Period 2 should look like Period 3.

EXHIBIT 6–8 | Inventory Errors: An Example

	Period 1 Ending Inventory Overstated by $10,000		Period 2 Beginning Inventory Overstated by $10,000		Period 3 Correct	
Sales revenue		$100,000		$100,000		$100,000
Cost of goods sold:						
Beginning inventory	$10,000		$20,000		$10,000	
Net purchases	50,000		50,000		50,000	
Cost of goods available for sale	60,000		70,000		60,000	
Ending inventory	(20,000)		(10,000)		(10,000)	
Cost of goods sold		40,000		60,000		50,000
Gross margin		$ 60,000		$ 40,000		$ 50,000
			$100,000			

The correct gross margin is $50,000 for each period.

Ending inventory is *subtracted* in computing cost of goods sold in one period and the same amount is *added* as beginning inventory the next period. Therefore, an inventory error cancels out after two periods. The overstatement of cost of goods sold in Period 2 counterbalances the understatement for Period 1. Thus, the total gross margin for the two periods combined is correct. These effects are summarized in Exhibit 6–9.

EXHIBIT 6–9 | Effects of Inventory Errors

	Period 1		Period 2	
Inventory Error	Cost of Goods Sold	Gross Margin and Net Income	Cost of Goods Sold	Gross Margin and Net Income
Period 1 ending inventory *overstated*	Understated	Overstated	Overstated	Understated
Period 1 ending inventory *understated*	Overstated	Understated	Understated	Overstated

Ethical Issues

Companies whose profits do not meet expectations can be tempted to "cook the books" to increase reported income. The increase in reported income will make the business look more successful than it really is.

There are two main schemes for using inventory to increase reported income. The easier, and the more obvious, is to overstate ending inventory. In Exhibit 6–9, we see how an error in ending inventory affects net income.

The second way of using inventory to increase reported income involves sales. Sales schemes are more complex than simple inventory overstatements. CV Technologies, the producers of COLD FX, had to revise its 2006 consolidated financial statements because of a revenue timing issue in the US market. In a news release, the company reported that sales for two quarterly periods were $8.6 million; however, these were not sales to the consumers but to the retailers to stock the shelves. If the product did not sell, the retailers could return the unsold goods for a refund or credit. The actual sales to consumers during this period were $1.5 to 2.5 million … substantially less than reported. After this incident, based on advice from its auditors, CV Technologies adopted a new policy for recognizing revenue.[2]

In virtually every area, accounting imposes a discipline that brings out the facts sooner or later.

KEY POINTS

Recognize that a dollar change in ending inventory means a dollar change in income. This is one reason auditors examine the ending inventory so carefully. An income statement may be manipulated by altering the amount of ending inventory.

> Try It!

10. Roses Treasures, a craft store, uses a periodic inventory system. The inventory data for the year ended December 31, 2017, are as follows:

Sales revenue	$ 60,000
Cost of goods sold:	
Beginning inventory	11,000
Net purchases	45,000
Cost of goods available for sale	56,000
Less: Ending inventory	(12,000)
Cost of goods sold	44,000
Gross margin	$ 16,000

Suppose it was discovered after the year end that $2,000 of craft supplies had dried up in their packages and should have been destroyed before year end. These supplies had been counted and recorded as ending inventory. What numerical effects did these obsolete craft supplies have on the accounting information above?

11. Refer to the Roses Treasures data in the previous question. What numerical effects will the obsolete craft supplies have on the accounting information for the following year?

Solutions appear at the end of this chapter and on MyAccountingLab

---

[2] "CV Technologies Plans Revisions to Financial Statements in Keeping with Changes to Its Revenue Recognition Policy," *Market Wired*, April 11, 2007, accessed May 3, 2015, http://www.marketwired.com/press-release/cv-technologies-plans-revisions-financial-statements-keeping-with-changes-its-revenue-tsx-cvq-644954.htm.

ESTIMATING ENDING INVENTORY

Often a business must *estimate* the value of its ending inventory. Suppose the company suffers a fire loss and must estimate the value of the inventory destroyed, or suppose a company needs monthly financial statements.

Gross Margin Method

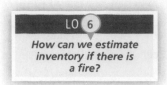

KEY POINTS

Linear equations are equally as effective as income statement models.

The **gross margin method** (also known as the **gross profit method**) provides a way to estimate inventory using the cost of goods sold model (amounts are assumed for illustration):

	Beginning inventory (BI)	$ 20
+	Net purchases (NP)	100
=	Cost of goods available for sale (CGAS)	120
−	**Ending inventory (EI)**	**(40)**
=	**Cost of goods sold (COGS)**	**$ 80**

Rearranging *ending inventory* and *cost of goods sold* makes the model useful for estimating ending inventory (amounts are assumed for illustration):

$$BI + NP - EI = COGS$$
$$BI + NP - COGS = EI$$
$$[20 + 100] - 80 = EI$$
$$40 = EI$$

LEARNING TIPS

Remember that the gross margin % + the cost of goods sold % = 100%. If gross margin is 35% of sales, then cost of goods sold is 65% of sales.

Suppose a fire destroys your inventory. To collect insurance, you must estimate the cost of the ending inventory. Using your normal *gross margin percent* (i.e., gross margin divided by net sales revenue), you can estimate cost of goods sold. Then subtract cost of goods sold from cost of goods available for sale to estimate ending inventory. Exhibit 6–10 illustrates the gross margin method using assumed amounts.

EXHIBIT 6–10 | Gross Margin Method of Estimating Inventory (amounts assumed)

Beginning inventory		$14,000
Purchases		66,000
Cost of goods available for sale		80,000
Estimate cost of goods sold:		
Sales revenue	$100,000	
Less: Estimated gross margin of 40%	(40,000)	
Estimated cost of goods sold (cost is 60% of sales revenue)		(60,000)
Estimated cost of *ending inventory*		$20,000
Equation solution: $14,000 + $66,000 − ($100,000 × 0.60) = $20,000		

Retail Method

The **retail method** of estimating the cost of ending inventory is often used by retail establishments that use the periodic inventory system. This is because it is often easier for retail establishments to calculate the selling price, or retail price, of a wide range of items rather than to look at all the individual invoices to find the costs of each of those items.

Like the gross margin method, the retail method is based on the familiar cost of goods sold model, rearranged to calculate ending inventory:

	Beginning inventory (BI)
+	Net purchases (NP)
=	Cost of goods available for sale
−	Cost of goods sold (COGS)
=	Ending inventory (EI)

However, to use the retail method, a business must know both the total cost and the total selling price of its opening inventory, as well as both the total cost and the total selling price of its net purchases. Total selling price is determined by counting each item of inventory and multiplying it by the item's retail selling price (the price given on the price tag). By summing separately the costs and selling prices of beginning inventory and net purchases, the business knows the cost and retail selling price of the goods it has available for sale.

The business can calculate the total selling price of its sales because this is the sum of the amounts recorded on the cash register when sales are made.

REAL WORLD EXAMPLE

The gross margin and retail methods are also used to estimate inventory for interim periods when it is impractical to take a physical inventory.

> **BI at retail + NP at retail = Selling price of goods for sale**
>
> **Selling price of goods for sale − Actual sales = Ending inventory at selling price**
>
> **Ending inventory at selling price × Retail or cost ratio = Ending inventory at cost**

The retail ratio is the ratio of the cost of goods available for sale at *cost* to the cost of goods available for sale at *selling price*. It is usually expressed as a percentage, as shown in Exhibit 6–11.

EXHIBIT 6–11 | Retail Method of Estimating Inventory (amounts assumed)

	Cost	Selling Price
Beginning inventory	$151,200	$216,000
Purchases	504,000	720,000
Goods available for sale	$655,200	936,000
Net sales, at selling price (retail)		696,000
Ending inventory, at selling price (retail)		$240,000
Estimated ending inventory, at cost ($240,000 × 70%*)	$168,000	

*Retail ratio = ($655,200/$936,000) × 100% = 70%

All of the following amounts are at the retail amount:
BI + NP − Net Sales = EI at retail, but this must be shown at cost, hence it is multiplied by 70%.

KEY POINTS

The reason to calculate goods available for sale at both cost and retail is to find the cost-to-retail percentage, which is 70% in the example.

The retail method can be used to estimate inventory at any point in time, and it is acceptable to use the retail method to calculate year-end inventory cost for financial statement and income tax purposes, although an inventory count must be done at least once per year.

MyAccountingLab

Video: Real World Accounting

12. Beginning inventory is $45,000, net purchases total $160,000, and net sales are $250,000. The normal gross margin is 40 percent of sales. Use the gross margin method to calculate ending inventory.

13. A beachwear shop needs to estimate the cost of its ending inventory for insurance purposes, and since it is summer it cannot close for a physical count of inventory. The insurance company will accept an estimate using the retail method. The shop's owner knows the cost of opening inventory was $25,000 from the previous year end's physical count and its selling price was $60,000. From invoices, the owner knows the cost of purchases was $100,000 and the retail selling prices totalled $240,000. Cash register receipts show that sales from the beginning of the year totalled $250,000. Calculate the cost of ending inventory for the insurance company.

Solutions appear at the end of this chapter and on MyAccountingLab

SUMMARY PROBLEM FOR YOUR REVIEW

Suppose a division of GCA Computers that handles computer parts uses the periodic inventory system and has these inventory records for December 2017:

Date	Item	Quantity	Unit Cost	Sale Price
Dec. 1	Beginning inventory	100 units	$16	
10	Purchase	60 units	18	
15	Sale	70 units		$40
21	Purchase	100 units	20	
30	Sale	90 units		50

Important fact: The periodic inventory system was used during the month of December 2017.

Company accounting records reveal that operating expenses for January were $4,000.

Required

Prepare the December 2017 income statement in multi-step format. Show amounts for FIFO cost and weighted-average cost. Label the bottom line "Operating income." (Round the average cost per unit to three decimal places and all other figures to whole-dollar amounts.) Show your computations, and use the periodic inventory model from pages 334–335 to compute cost of goods sold.

SOLUTION

The best approach to this solution is an organized one. One approach is to complete one income statement line before going to the next, until "Ending inventory." Notice that the amounts for sales revenue, beginning inventory, net purchases, and operating expenses are the same for the two inventory costing methods.

GCA COMPUTERS

Income Statement for Computer Parts Division

For the Month Ended December 31, 2017

	FIFO	Weighted Average	
Sales revenue	$7,300	$7,300	$(70 \times \$40) + (90 \times \$50) = \$7,300$
Cost of goods sold:			$100 \times \$16 = \$1,600$
Beginning inventory	$1,600	$1,600	
Net purchases	3,080	3,080	$(60 \times \$18) + (100 \times \$20) = \$3,080$
Cost of goods available for sale	4,680	4,680	$100 \times \$20 = \$2,000$
Ending inventory	(2,000)	(1,800)*	$100 \times \$18 = \$1,800$
Cost of goods sold	2,680	2,880	
Gross margin	4,620	4,420	
Operating expenses	4,000	4,000	
Operating income	$ 620	$ 420	

SUMMARY

LEARNING OBJECTIVE ① Account for perpetual inventory under the specific-unit-cost, FIFO, and moving-weighted-average-cost methods

Are there different methods used to account for perpetual inventory?   Pg. 326

- In the perpetual inventory system:
  - Inventory is debited immediately at cost when an item is purchased (total number of items purchased × cost per item).
  - Inventory is credited immediately when an item is sold (cost of goods sold = total number of items sold × cost per item)
  - Ending inventory is calculated as the total number of items on hand × cost per item.
- If a company has inventory items that are unique or expensive, they typically use the *specific-unit-cost method* to determine the cost of goods sold and ending inventory.
- If a company has inventory items that are similar, they can assign costs using the *first-in, first-out (FIFO)* or *moving-weighted-average-cost methods* to determine the cost of goods sold and ending inventory.

LEARNING OBJECTIVE ② Compare the effects of the FIFO and moving-weighted-average-cost methods

What are the effects of two of the different methods?   Pg. 333

- FIFO costing reports ending inventory at the most current cost.
- Moving-weighted-average costing reports ending inventory and cost of goods sold at an average amount determined by the value of all relevant units in inventory at the time of the sale.
- When prices are rising, moving-weighted-average costing produces the higher cost of goods sold and the lower income.
- When prices are rising, FIFO costing produces the higher income.

LEARNING OBJECTIVE ③ Account for periodic inventory under the FIFO and weighted-average-cost methods

Are there different methods used to account for periodic inventory?   Pg. 334

- In the periodic inventory system:
  - Purchases are debited immediately at cost when an item is purchased (total number of items purchased × cost per item).
  - The business does not keep an up-to-date balance for ending inventory. Instead, at the end of the period, the business counts the inventory on hand and updates its records.
  - To compute ending inventory and cost of goods sold, a cost is assigned to each inventory item within that category.
- Two methods of assigning costs to similar items are *first-in, first-out (FIFO)* and *weighted average*.
- FIFO costing produces identical balances for ending inventory and cost of goods sold under the periodic and perpetual inventory systems. However, the weighted-average method produces a different result under the periodic and perpetual systems.

What happens if inventory declines in value?   Pg. 337

- The *lower-of-cost-and-net-realizable-value (LCNRV) rule*—an example of accounting conservatism—requires that businesses report inventory on the balance sheet at the lower of its cost and net realizable value or current replacement cost.
- Companies disclose their definition of "net realizable value" for purposes of applying the LCNRV rule in the notes to their financial statements.

LEARNING OBJECTIVE 5 Measure the effects of inventory errors

How do inventory errors affect the financial statements?   Pg. 339

- Although inventory overstatements in one period are counterbalanced by inventory understatements in the next period, effective decision making depends on accurate inventory information.

LEARNING OBJECTIVE 6 Estimate ending inventory by the gross margin method and the retail method

How can we estimate inventory if there is a fire?   Pg. 342

- The *gross margin method* and the *retail method* are techniques for estimating the cost of ending inventory.
- Both methods are useful for preparing interim financial statements and for estimating the cost of inventory destroyed by fire or other disasters.

  MyAccountingLab **Video:** Real World Accounting

Check **Accounting Vocabulary** for all key terms used in Chapter 6 and the **Glossary** at the back of the book for all key terms used in the textbook.

MORE CHAPTER REVIEW MATERIAL

MyAccountingLab

DemoDoc covering Inventory Costing Methods and Lower of Cost and Market

Student PowerPoint Slides

Audio Chapter Summary

Note: All MyAccountingLab resources can be found in the Chapter Resources section and the Multimedia Library.

ACCOUNTING VOCABULARY

Comparability A characteristic of accounting information that states business must use the same accounting methods and procedures from period to period or disclose a change in method (*p. 336*).

Conservatism An accounting concept by which the least favourable figures are presented in the financial statements (*p. 336*).

Disclosure principle An accounting concept that states a business's financial statements must report enough information for outsiders to make knowledgeable decisions about the business (*p. 336*).

First-in, first-out (FIFO) method An inventory costing method by which the first costs into inventory are the first costs out to cost of goods sold. Ending inventory is based on the costs of the most recent purchases (*p. 329*).

Gross margin method A way to estimate inventory based on a rearrangement of the cost of goods sold model: Beginning inventory + Net purchases = Cost of goods available for sale. Cost of goods available for sale − Cost of goods sold = Ending inventory. Also called the *gross profit method* (*p. 342*).

Gross profit method Another name for the *gross margin method* (*p. 342*).

Impairment A write-down in value that occurs when an asset, such as inventory, becomes worth less than its cost (*p. 338*).

Impairment reversal A write-up in value that occurs when an asset that had been written down, such as inventory, increases in value up to the amount of the original write-down (p. 338).

Lower-of-cost-and-net-realizable-value (LCNRV) Requires that an asset be reported in the financial statements at the lower of its historical cost or its market value (current replacement cost for inventory) (p. 338).

Materiality constraint An accounting concept that states a company must perform strictly proper accounting only for items and transactions that are significant to the business's financial statements (p. 336).

Moving-weighted-average-cost method A weighted-average-cost method where unit cost is changed to reflect each new purchase of inventory (p. 331).

Retail method A method of estimating ending inventory based on the total cost and total selling price of opening inventory and net purchases (p. 342).

Specific identification method Another name for the *specific-unit-cost method* (p. 327).

Specific-unit-cost method An inventory costing method based on the specific cost of particular units of inventory. Also called the *specific identification method* (p. 327).

Weighted-average-cost method An inventory costing method used for the periodic inventory system where the average cost is calculated at the end of the period. Weighted-average cost is determined by dividing the cost of goods available for sale by the number of units available for sale (p. 335).

SIMILAR ACCOUNTING TERMS

Cost of goods sold	Cost of sales
Gross margin method	Gross profit method
Moving-weighted-average-cost method	Average-cost method (perpetual)
Weighted-average-cost method	Average-cost method (periodic)

SELF-STUDY QUESTIONS

Test your understanding of the chapter by marking the correct answer to each of the following questions:

1. Suppose a store uses a perpetual inventory system. It made sales of $500,000 and ended the year with inventories totalling $50,000. Cost of goods sold was $300,000, and total operating expenses were $135,000. How much net income did the store earn for the year? (pp. 326–329)
   a. $65,000
   b. $450,000
   c. $200,000
   d. $315,000

2. Which inventory costing method assigns to ending inventory the latest (i.e., the most recent) costs incurred during the period? (p. 330)
   a. Specific-unit cost
   b. First-in, first-out (FIFO)
   c. Moving-weighted-average cost
   d. None of the above

3. Assume Lauder Company began June with 20 units of inventory that cost a total of $760. During June, Lauder purchased and sold goods as follows:

Jun.	8	Purchase:	60 units at $40
	14	Sale:	50 units at $80
	22	Purchase:	40 units at $44
	27	Sale:	60 units at $80

   Assume Lauder uses the FIFO inventory method and a perpetual inventory system. How much is Lauder's cost of goods sold for the transaction on June 14? (p. 330)
   a. $3,160
   b. $4,000
   c. $2,000
   d. $1,960

4. After the purchase on June 22 in question 3, what is Lauder's cost of the inventory on hand if the company is using the FIFO inventory costing method? (p. 330)
   a. $1,200
   b. $1,760
   c. $2,960
   d. $2,880

5. What is Lauder's journal entry on June 14? (p. 331)

   a. Accounts Receivable..... 1,960
      Inventory 1,960

   b. Accounts Receivable..... 4,000
      Sales Revenue 4,000

   c. Cost of Goods Sold........ 1,960
      Inventory 1,960

   d. Both b and c

6. Which inventory costing method results in the lowest net income during a period of rising inventory costs? (p. 333)
   a. Specific-unit cost
   b. First-in, first out (FIFO)
   c. Weighted-average cost
   d. None of the above

7. Suppose Lauder Company used the weighted-average-cost method and a periodic inventory system. Use the Lauder data in question 3 to compute the cost of the company's inventory on hand at June 30. Round unit cost to the nearest cent. (p. 335)
   a. $410.00
   b. $420.80
   c. $820.00
   d. $841.60

8. Which of the following is most closely linked to accounting conservatism? (p. 336)
   a. Comparability characteristic
   b. Disclosure principle
   c. Materiality constraint
   d. Lower-of-cost-and-net-realizable-value rule

9. At December 31, 2017, Malasky Company understated ending inventory by $20,000. How does this error affect cost of goods sold and net income for 2017? (pp. 339–340)
   a. Overstates cost of goods sold, understates net income
   b. Understates cost of goods sold, overstates net income
   c. Overstates both cost of goods sold and net income
   d. Leaves both cost of goods sold and net income correct because the errors cancel each other out

10. Suppose a Super Comics location suffered a fire loss and needs to estimate the cost of the goods destroyed. Beginning inventory was $50,000, net purchases totalled $300,000, and sales came to $500,000. Super Comics' normal gross margin is 45 percent. Use the gross margin method to estimate the cost of the inventory lost in the fire. (p. 342)
    a. $150,000
    b. $125,000
    c. $75,000
    d. $175,000

11. Given the following data, what is the weighted-average cost of ending inventory, rounded to the nearest whole dollar? (p. 332)

Sales revenue:	100 units at $10 per unit
Beginning inventory:	50 units at $8 per unit
Purchases:	90 units at $9 per unit

   a. $400
   b. $360
   c. $346
   d. $864

12. Assume the following data for Burnette Sales for 2017:

Beginning inventory:	10 units at $7 each
Mar. 18 Purchase:	15 units at $9 each
Sale:	20 units at $15 each
Jun. 10 Purchase:	20 units at $10 each
Sale:	12 units at $15 each
Oct. 30 Purchase:	12 units at $11 each
Sale:	10 units at $16 each

   On December 31, a physical count reveals 15 units on hand.

   Under the FIFO method (assuming a perpetual inventory system), what would ending inventory be valued at? (p. 330)
   a. $105
   b. $162
   c. $115
   d. $135

13. Review the following data:

Ending inventory at cost	$24,000
Ending inventory at net realizable value	23,600
Cost of goods sold (before consideration of the lower-of-cost-and-net-realizable-value rule)	37,000

   Which of the following depicts the proper account balance after the application of the lower-of-cost-and-net-realizable-value rule? (p. 338)
   a. Cost of goods sold will be $36,400.
   b. Cost of goods sold will be $37,000.
   c. Cost of goods sold will be $37,400.
   d. Ending inventory will be $24,000.

ASSIGNMENT MATERIAL

QUESTIONS

1. Why is merchandise inventory so important to a retailer or wholesaler?

2. Suppose your business deals in expensive jewellery. Which inventory system and method should you use to achieve good internal control over the inventory? If your business is a hardware store that sells low-cost goods, which inventory system would you most likely use? Why?

3. Identify the accounts debited and credited in the standard purchase and sale entries under (a) the perpetual inventory system and (b) the periodic inventory system.

4. What is the role of the physical count of inventory in (a) the perpetual inventory system and (b) the periodic inventory system?

5. If beginning inventory is $60,000, purchases total $135,000, and ending inventory is $62,500, how much is cost of goods sold?

6. If beginning inventory is $44,000, purchases total $109,000, and cost of goods sold is $115,000, how much is ending inventory?

7. What two items determine the cost of ending inventory?

8. Briefly describe the three perpetual generally accepted inventory costing methods. During a period of rising prices, which method produces the higher reported income? Which produces the lower reported income?

9. Which inventory costing method produces the ending inventory valued at the most current cost?

10. Describe the impact on cost of goods sold of using the FIFO method as opposed to the weighted-average-cost method of valuing ending inventory when the price of inventory purchases is rising. Which method provides a more accurate value of the goods remaining in ending inventory at the end of an accounting period?

11. Your accounting instructor tells you that companies should use the specific identification method to most accurately value items that have been sold and transferred to cost of goods sold, yet most companies do not use this method. Why not?

12. How does the comparability characteristic affect accounting for inventory?

13. Briefly describe the influence that the concept of conservatism has on accounting for inventory.

14. Manley Company's inventory has a cost of $27,000 at the end of the year, and the net realizable value of the inventory is $32,500. At which amount should the company report the inventory on its balance sheet? Suppose the net realizable value of the inventory is $25,500 instead of $32,500. At which amount should Manley Company report the inventory? What rule governs your answers to these questions?

15. Gabriel Products accidentally overstated its ending inventory by $10,000 at the end of Period 1. Is the gross margin of Period 1 overstated or understated? Is the gross margin of Period 2 overstated, understated, or unaffected by the Period 1 error? Is the total gross margin for the two periods overstated, understated, or correct? Give the reason for your answers.

16. Identify two important methods of estimating inventory amounts.

17. A fire destroyed the inventory of Bronk Supplies, but the accounting records were saved. The beginning inventory was $31,500, purchases for the period were $68,250, and sales were $120,000. Bronk's customary gross margin is 30 percent of sales. Use the gross margin method to estimate the cost of the inventory destroyed by the fire.

18. The retail method of estimating inventory seems simple but in reality can be difficult to apply. Why is this so?

MyAccountingLab

Make the grade with MyAccountingLab: The Starters, Exercises, and Problems marked in red can be found on MyAccountingLab. You can practise them as often as you want, and most feature step-by-step guided instructions to help you find the right answer.

STARTERS

Starter 6-1 Terget Company has the following items in its inventory on August 1:

Serial Number	Cost
661	$ 9,100
665	9,300
668	8,700
675	10,950

Computing ending inventory—
specific-unit-cost method

①

Ending inventory, $31,450

The company uses the specific-unit-cost method for costing inventory. During August, it sold units 661 and 668 for $15,000 each and purchased unit 676 for $11,200. What is the value of the ending inventory at August 31?

Starter 6–2 Refer to the information in Starter 6–1. Calculate the gross margin for the month of August.

Starter 6–3 Schwenn Cycles uses the FIFO inventory method. Schwenn started June with five bicycles that cost $190 each. On June 16, Schwenn bought 20 bicycles at $200 each. On June 30, Schwenn sold 15 bicycles. Prepare Schwenn's perpetual inventory record.

Starter 6–4 Use the Schwenn Cycles data in Starter 6–3 to journalize the following transactions:

a. The June 16 purchase of inventory on account
b. The June 30 sale of inventory on account; Schwenn sold each bicycle for $240
c. Cost of goods sold

Starter 6–5 Use the Schwenn Cycles data in Starter 6–3, except assume that Schwenn uses the moving-weighted-average-cost method, and prepare a perpetual inventory record. Round average cost per unit to the nearest cent and all other amounts to the nearest dollar.

Starter 6–6 Use the Schwenn Cycles data in Starter 6–3, except assume that Schwenn uses the moving-weighted-average-cost method, and journalize the following transactions:

a. The June 16 purchase of inventory on account
b. The June 30 sale of inventory on account; Schwenn sold each bicycle for $240
c. Cost of goods sold

Starter 6–7 Examine Starter 6–3 (FIFO costing) and Starter 6–5 (moving-weighted-average costing). Focus on the sale of goods on June 30. Why is cost of goods sold different between FIFO costing and moving-weighted-average costing? Explain.

Starter 6–8 Answer these questions in your own words:

1. Why does FIFO produce the lower cost of goods sold during a period of rising prices?
2. Why does moving-weighted-average costing produce the higher cost of goods sold during a period of rising prices?
3. Which inventory costing method—FIFO or moving weighted average—results in the higher and the lower cost of ending inventory? Prices are rising. Exhibits 6–5 and 6–6 on pages 330 and 331 provide the necessary information.

Starter 6–9 Kim's Dry Goods uses a periodic inventory system. Kim's completed the following inventory transactions during April, its first month of operations:

Apr.	1	Purchased 10 shirts at $50 each
	7	Sold 6 shirts for $80 each
	13	Purchased 6 shirts for $55 each
	21	Sold 3 shirts for $85 each

Compute Kim's ending inventory and cost of goods sold under FIFO costing. Then compute ending inventory and cost of goods sold under the weighted-average-cost method. Round average unit cost to the nearest cent. Compute gross margin under both methods. Which method results in the higher gross margin?

Starter 6–10 On the basis of the following data, determine the value of the inventory at the lower of cost and net realizable value:

Item	Quantity	Cost Price/Unit	Market Price/Unit	Selling Costs
001	5	$29	$30	$100
002	8	$40	$35	$ 50

Starter 6-11 Clinton Cycles uses a periodic inventory system. The inventory data for the year ended December 31, 2016, follow:

Measuring the effects of an inventory error
⑤

Sales revenue	$150,000
Cost of goods sold:	
Beginning inventory	22,000
Net purchases	80,000
Cost of goods available for sale	102,000
Less: Ending inventory	(24,000)
Cost of goods sold	78,000
Gross margin	$ 72,000

Assume that the ending inventory was accidentally overstated by $4,000. What are the correct amounts of cost of goods sold and gross margin after correcting this error?

Starter 6-12 Refer back to the Clinton Cycles inventory data in Starter 6-11. The ending inventory balance is stated correctly at the end of 2017. What effect would the overstatement of ending inventory made in 2016 have on cost of goods sold and gross margin for the year ended December 31, 2017?

Next year's effect of an inventory error
⑤

Starter 6-13 Wesley Carpets began the year with inventory of $1,400,000. Inventory purchases for the year totalled $3,200,000. Sales revenue for the year was $7,000,000 and the gross margin was 40 percent. How much is Wesley Carpets's estimated cost of ending inventory? Use the gross margin method.

Estimating ending inventory by the gross margin method

Estimated cost of ending inventory, $400,000

Starter 6-14 Thorston Industries began the year with inventory of $80,000 and purchased $350,000 of goods during the year. Sales for the year are $600,000, and Thorston Industries' gross margin is 30 percent of sales. Compute the estimated cost of ending inventory by the gross margin method.

Estimating ending inventory by the gross margin method

Ending inventory, $10,000

Starter 6-15 Why are standard setters interested in ensuring that companies use the same inventory costing method from one year to the next?

Explaining inventory policy
④

EXERCISES   MyAccountingLab

Exercise 6-1

Erickson Company buys transformers from manufacturers and sells them to utility companies. The units are costly and the company keeps track of them using serial numbers. On April 1, the company had two transformers in stock:

Computing gross margin— specific-unit-cost method

2. Gross margin, $64,000

Serial Number	Unit Cost
2010901	$55,000
2010905	59,200

During the month, the company purchased the following two transformers:

Serial Number	Unit Cost
20101001	$51,000
20101002	56,800

Erickson Company sold two transformers—serial numbers 2010905 and 20101002—during the month of April. The selling price of the transformers was $90,000 per unit.

Required

1. Erickson Company uses the specific-unit-cost method for costing inventory. Why would the company prefer to use this method?
2. Compute the gross margin for Erickson Company for the month of April.

Measuring ending inventory and
cost of goods sold in a perpetual
system—FIFO

Cost of goods sold, $6,180

Exercise 6–2

Creative Kaos Store carries a large inventory of guitars and other musical instruments. The store uses the FIFO method and a perpetual inventory system. Company records indicate the following for a particular line of guitars:

Date		Item	Quantity	Unit Cost
May	1	Balance	5	$900
	6	Sale	3	
	8	Purchase	10	840
	17	Sale	4	
	30	Purchase	5	840

Required   Prepare a perpetual inventory record for the guitars. Then determine the amounts Creative Kaos Store should report for ending inventory and cost of goods sold under the FIFO method.

Recording perpetual inventory
transactions

Exercise 6–3

After preparing the FIFO perpetual inventory record in Exercise 6–2, journalize Creative Kaos Store's May 8 purchase of inventory on account and the cash sale on May 17 (sale price of each guitar was $1,600).

Applying the moving-weighted-
average-cost method in a
perpetual inventory system

Cost of goods sold, $6,100

Exercise 6–4

Refer to the Creative Kaos Store inventory data in Exercise 6–2, except assume that the store uses the moving-weighted-average-cost method. Prepare Creative Kaos Store's perpetual inventory record for the guitars on the moving-weighted-average-cost basis. Round average cost per unit to the nearest cent and all other amounts to the nearest dollar.

Calculating gross margin under
FIFO and the moving-weighted-
average-cost method in a
perpetual inventory system

Gross margin, moving-weighted-
average-cost method, $4,900

Exercise 6–5

Use your results from Exercises 6–2 and 6–4 to calculate the gross margin for Creative Kaos Store under both the FIFO and the moving-weighted-average-cost methods. Explain why the gross margin is higher under the moving-weighted-average-cost method.

Recording perpetual inventory
transactions

2. Gross margin, $92,000

Exercise 6–6

Atomic Tackle Shop's accounting records yield the following data for the year ended December 31, 2017:

Inventory: January 1, 2017	$ 24,000
Purchases of inventory (on account).................	147,000
Sales of inventory—70 percent on account,	
30 percent for cash (cost $133,000).................	225,000
Inventory at FIFO cost December 31, 2017........	?

Required

1. Journalize Atomic Tackle Shop's inventory transactions for the year in a perpetual system.
2. Report ending inventory, sales, cost of goods sold, and gross margin on the appropriate financial statement.

Recording periodic inventory
transactions

2. Gross margin, $92,000

Exercise 6–7

Refer to the Atomic Tackle Shop data in Exercise 6–6, except assume that Atomic is using a periodic inventory system. Inventory on hand at December 31, 2017, was $38,000, based on a physical count.

Required

1. Journalize Atomic Tackle Shop's inventory transactions for the year in a periodic system.

2. Report ending inventory, sales, cost of goods sold, and gross margin on the appropriate financial statement.

3. How do these amounts compare to the same amounts in the perpetual inventory system calculated in Exercise 6–6, Requirement 2?

Exercise 6–8

Max Office Products markets the ink used in inkjet printers. Max started the year with 10,000 containers of ink (moving-weighted-average cost of $18 each; FIFO cost of $16 each). During the year, Max purchased 80,000 containers of ink at $22 on the first day of its fiscal year and sold 70,000 units for $46 each, with all transactions on account. Max paid a total of $500,000 in operating expenses throughout the year.

Journalize Max's purchases, sales, and operating expense transactions using the following format. Max uses a perpetual inventory system to account for inkjet printer ink.

Applying the moving-weighted-average and FIFO methods in a perpetual inventory system
①
Cost of goods sold, moving-weighted-average cost, $1,509,200

	Debit/Credit Amounts	
Accounts	Moving Weighted Average*	FIFO

*Round moving-weighted-average unit cost to the nearest cent.

Exercise 6–9

Kelso Electrical's inventory records for industrial switches indicate the following at November 30, 2017:

Nov.	1	Beginning inventory	14 units at $160
	8	Purchase	4 units at $170
	15	Purchase	11 units at $180
	26	Purchase	5 units at $190

Excel Spreadsheet Template
Computing ending inventory by applying three inventory costing methods in a periodic inventory system
③
3. FIFO cost of goods sold, $4,720

The physical count of inventory at November 30, 2017, indicates that six units remain in ending inventory and the company owns them.

Required Compute ending inventory and cost of goods sold using each of the following methods, assuming a periodic inventory system is used:

1. Specific-unit cost, assuming three $170 units and three $180 units are on hand on November 30, 2017

2. Weighted-average cost

3. First-in, first-out (FIFO)

Exercise 6–10

1. Supply the missing income statement amounts for each of the following companies for the year ended December 31, 2017:

Determining amounts for the income statement: periodic system
③
(a) $28,000; (c) $10,200

Company	Net Sales	Beginning Inventory	Net Purchases	Ending Inventory	Cost of Goods Sold	Gross Margin
Arc Co.	$46,500	$ 5,300	$31,400	$ 8,700	(a)	$18,500
Bell Co.	(b)	13,700	46,500	(c)	$50,000	26,300
Court Co.	50,000	(d)	27,900	11,300	28,700	(e)
Dolan Co.	51,200	6,400	(f)	4,100	(g)	23,700

2. Prepare the income statement for Bell Co., which uses the periodic inventory system. Bell's operating expenses for the year were $9,700.

Exercise 6–11

This exercise tests your understanding of the three inventory methods. In the space provided, write the name of the inventory method that best fits the description (specific unit, FIFO, or weighted average). Assume that the cost of inventory is rising.

Identifying income and other effects of the three inventory methods

_____ a. Provides the same result for ending inventory in both a periodic and a perpetual inventory system

_____ b. Maximizes reported net income when inventory purchase prices are falling

_____ c. Results in a cost of ending inventory that is close to the current cost of replacing the inventory

_____ d. Maximizes reported net income when inventory purchase prices are rising

_____ e. Used to account for automobiles, jewellery, and art objects

_____ f. Provides a smoother measure of ending inventory and cost of goods sold over time

_____ g. Precisely matches cost of goods sold with net sales revenue.

Exercise 6–12

Applying the lower-of-cost-and-net-realizable-value rule to inventories: perpetual system
① ④

Robertson Garden Supplies, which uses a perpetual inventory system and the FIFO costing method, has these account balances at December 31, 2017, prior to releasing the financial statements for the year:

Inventory		Cost of Goods Sold		Sales Revenue	
Beg. bal.	**50,000**	Bal.	500,000	Bal.	940,000
End. bal.	**84,000**				

The company has determined that the net realizable value of the December 31, 2017, ending inventory is $80,000.

Required Prepare Robertson Garden Supplies's balance sheet at December 31, 2017, to show how Robertson would apply the lower-of-cost-and-net-realizable-value rule to inventories. Include a complete heading for the statement.

Exercise 6–13

Applying the lower-of-cost-and-net-realizable-value rule to inventories: periodic system
③ ④
Gross margin, $90,300

Wire Solutions Company's income statement for the month ended August 31, 2017, reported the following data:

Income Statement		
Sales revenue		$320,000
Cost of goods sold:		
Beginning inventory	$ 82,000	
Net purchases	243,700	
Cost of goods available for sale	325,700	
Ending inventory	105,700	
Cost of goods sold		220,000
Gross margin		$100,000

Before the financial statements were released, it was discovered that the current net realizable value of ending inventory was $96,000.

1. Journalize the entry to apply the lower-of-cost-and-net-realizable-value rule to the inventory.

2. Prepare a revised income statement to adjust the preceding income statement to apply the lower-of-cost-and-net-realizable-value rule to Wire Solutions Company's inventory. Also show the relevant portion of Wire Solutions Company's balance sheet.

Exercise 6–14

Measuring the effect of an inventory error
⑤
1. Gross margin, $60,000

Provence Bakery reported sales revenue of $148,000 and cost of goods sold of $91,000. Compute Provence Bakery's correct gross margin if the company made each of the following independent accounting errors. Show your work.

1. Ending inventory is understated by $3,000.
2. Beginning inventory is understated by $3,000 and ending inventory is overstated by $3,000.

Exercise 6–15

Sportsman Marine Supply reported the comparative income statement for the years ended September 30, 2017, and 2016, shown below:

Correcting an inventory error
(5)

Net income 2016, $34,100

SPORTSMAN MARINE SUPPLY		
Income Statement		
For the Years Ended September 30, 2017 and 2016		
	2017	2016
Sales revenue	$165,000	$146,000
Cost of goods sold:		
Beginning inventory	$ 16,500	$15,400
Net purchases	91,000	78,000
Cost of goods available for sale	107,500	93,400
Ending inventory	23,600	16,500
Cost of goods sold	83,900	76,900
Gross margin	81,100	69,100
Operating expenses	40,000	30,000
Net income	$ 41,100	$ 39,100

During 2017, accountants for the company discovered that ending 2016 inventory was overstated by $5,000. Prepare the corrected comparative income statement for the two-year period, complete with a heading for the statement. What was the effect of the error on net income for the two years combined? Explain your answer.

Exercise 6–16

Janet Chao, accountant of Seaward Electronics Ltd., learned that Seaward Electronics's $24 million cost of inventory at the end of last year was overstated by $3.0 million. She notified the company president, Eric Moffat, of the accounting error and the need to alert the company's lenders that last year's reported net income was incorrect. Moffat explained to Chao that there is no need to report the error to lenders because the error will counterbalance this year. This year's error will affect this year's net income in the opposite direction of last year's error. Even with no correction, Moffat reasons, net income for both years combined will be the same whether or not Seaward Electronics corrects its errors.

Assessing the effect of an inventory error on two years of statements
(5)

Required

1. Was last year's reported net income of $37.0 million overstated, understated, or correct? What was the correct amount of net income last year?
2. Is this year's net income of $41 million overstated, understated, or correct? What is the correct amount of net income for the current year?
3. Whose perspective is better, Chao's or Moffat's? Give your reason. Consider the trend of reported net income both without the correction and with the correction.

Exercise 6–17

Determine whether each of the actions below in buying, selling, and accounting for inventories is ethical or unethical. Give your reason for each answer.

Ethical implications of inventory actions
(3)(5)

1. Spartan Corporation knowingly overstated purchases to produce a high figure for cost of goods sold (and thus a low amount of net income). The real reason was to decrease the company's income tax payments to the government.
2. In applying the lower-of-cost-and-net-realizable-value rule to inventories, Connor Industries recorded an excessively low realizable value for ending inventory. This allowed the company to pay no income tax for the year.

3. In a period of decreasing prices, Sparrow Distributors purchased a lot of inventory shortly before year end to decrease the moving-weighted-average cost of goods sold and increase reported income for the year to reach the level of profit demanded by the company's investors.

4. During a period of rising prices, Callais Electrical Products delayed the purchase of inventory until after December 31, 2017, in order to keep 2017's moving-weighted-average cost of goods sold from growing too large. The delay in purchasing inventory helped net income of 2017 to reach the level of profit demanded by the company's investors.

5. Lacombe Sales Company deliberately overstated ending inventory in order to report higher profits (net income).

Exercise 6–18

Estimating inventory by the gross margin method

Estimated inventory cost, $288,000

Bathurst Company began April with inventory of $200,000. The business made net purchases of $600,000 and had net sales of $800,000 before a fire destroyed the company's inventory. For the past several years, Bathurst Company's gross margin on sales has been 36 percent. Estimate the cost of the inventory destroyed by the fire. Identify another reason owners and managers use the gross margin method to estimate inventory on a regular basis.

Exercise 6–19

Estimating inventory by the retail method

(6)

Estimated ending inventory cost, Teenage line, $67,650

Fabiana's Designs has three lines of women's wear: Teenage, Young Woman, and Mature. On May 18, 2017, Fabiana's Designs had a fire that destroyed the Teenage line of inventory. Sales for the period January 1 to May 18 for the Teenage line were $800,000. Inventory at January 1, 2017, for the Teenage line was $95,000 (cost), $285,000 (retail). Purchases made from January 1 to May 18 for the Teenage line at cost were $240,000, and at retail were $720,000. Use the retail method to calculate the cost of the inventory lost in the fire. Hint: Use the format shown in Exhibit 6–11 to structure each calculation.

SERIAL EXERCISE

This exercise continues the Lee Management Consulting situation from Exercise 5–27 of Chapter 5. If you did not complete Exercise 5–27, you can still complete Exercise 6–20 as it is presented.

Exercise 6–20

Accounting for both merchandising and service transactions under the perpetual inventory system

(2)

1. Trial balance, $52,183

Consider the following July 2016 transactions for Lee Management Consulting, which were also presented in Chapter 5:

Jul.	2	Completed a consulting engagement and received cash of $7,200.
	2	Prepaid three months' office rent, $9,000.
	7	Purchased 100 units of software inventory on account, $1,900, plus owed the manufacturer freight-in of $100.
	16	Paid employee salary, $2,000. (Note previous year-end accrual of $500.)
	18	Sold 70 software units on account, $3,100 (cost $1,400)
	19	Consulted with a client for a fee of $900 on account.
	21	Paid $2,000 on account for the July 7 purchase.
	22	Purchased 200 units of software inventory on account, $4,600.
	24	Paid utilities, $300 cash.
	28	Sold 100 units of software for cash, $4,000.
	31	Recorded the following adjusting entries:

Accrued salary expense, $1,000.
Prepaid rent used, $3,000.
Amortization of office furniture, $167, and of equipment, $42.
Physical count of inventory, 120 units, $2,713.

Required

1. Prepare perpetual inventory records for July for Lee Management Consulting using the moving-weighted-average perpetual method. Round average cost per unit to the

nearest cent and all other amounts to the nearest dollar. (Note: You must calculate cost of goods sold for the July 18, 22, 28, and 31 transactions.)

2. Journalize and post to T-accounts the July transactions using the perpetual inventory record created in Requirement 1. Key all items by date. *Use the opening balances given in Serial Exercise 5–27 on page 301.* Compute each account balance, and denote the balance as *Bal.* (*Adjusting entries are recorded in Requirement 3.*)

3. Journalize and post to T-accounts the adjusting entries. Denote each adjusting amount as *Adj.* After posting all adjusting entries, prove that the debits equal the credits by completing a trial balance.

CHALLENGE EXERCISES

Exercise 6–21

For each of the following situations, identify the inventory method that you are using or would prefer to use or, given the use of a particular method, state the strategy that you would follow to accomplish your goal.

Inventory policy decisions
②

a. Inventory costs are increasing. Your business uses the FIFO method and is having an unexpectedly good year. It is near year end, and you need to keep net income from increasing too much.

b. Inventory costs have been stable for several years, and you expect costs to remain stable for the indefinite future. (Give your reason for your choice of method.)

c. Inventory costs are decreasing and you want to maximize income.

d. Company management prefers an inventory policy that avoids extremes.

e. Your inventory turns over very rapidly, and the business uses a perpetual inventory system. Inventory costs are increasing, and the business prefers to report high income.

Exercise 6–22

Chihooly Glass Products Ltd. is a leading provider of bottles for the brewing industry. Suppose the company recently reported these figures:

Evaluating a company's profitability
②

CHIHOOLY GLASS PRODUCTS LTD.		
Income Statement		
For the Years Ended December 31, 2017, and 2016 (amounts in thousands)		
	2017	2016
Sales	$ 135,000	$103,000
Cost of sales	97,200	77,700
Gross margin	37,800	25,300
Costs and expenses		
Selling, general, and administrative	27,800	21,100
Amortization	2,750	1,170
Restructuring charges	19,050	—
	49,600	22,270
Operating income (loss)	(11,800)	3,030
Other items (summarized)	(800)	(1,700)
Net income (loss)	$ (12,600)	$ 1,330

Required Evaluate Chihooly Glass's operations during 2017 in comparison with 2016. Consider sales, gross margin, operating income, and net income. In the annual report, Chihooly Glass's management describes the restructuring charges in 2017 as a one-time event that is not expected to recur. How does this additional information affect your evaluation?

Comparing the effects of costing
methods under perpetual and
periodic inventory systems

② ③

Exercise 6–23

Shaunessy Auto Supplies made the following purchases and sales of windshield wipers during March:

			Units	Unit Cost	Unit Sale Price
Mar.	1	Beginning	10	$ 6	
	3	Purchase	70	8	
	10	Sale	50		$16
	14	Purchase	25	10	
	20	Purchase	100	11	
	26	Sale	125		16

Required

1. Assuming Shaunessy Auto Supplies uses a perpetual inventory system, calculate the cost of goods sold during March using (a) the moving-weighted-average-cost method and (b) FIFO.

2. Now assume Shaunessy Auto Supplies uses a periodic inventory system. Calculate the cost of goods sold during March using (a) the weighted-average-cost method and (b) FIFO.

3. What do you notice when you compare the FIFO results from Requirement 1 and Requirement 2? Also include a computation of gross margin based on the periodic method in this comparison.

BEYOND THE NUMBERS

Beyond the Numbers 6–1

Assessing the impact of the
inventory costing method on the
financial statements

② ④

The inventory costing method chosen by a company can affect the financial statements and thus the decisions of the users of those statements.

Required

1. A leading accounting researcher stated that one inventory costing method reports the more recent costs in the income statement, while another method reports the more recent costs in the balance sheet. In this person's opinion, this results in one or the other of the statements being "inaccurate" when prices are rising. What did the researcher mean?

2. Conservatism is an accepted accounting concept. Would you want management to be conservative in accounting for inventory if you were (a) a shareholder and (b) a prospective shareholder? Give your reasons.

3. Premier Cycle Shoppe follows conservative accounting and writes the value of its inventory of bicycles down to net realizable value, which has declined below cost. The following year, an unexpected cycling craze results in a demand for bicycles that far exceeds supply, and the net realizable value increases well above the previous cost. What effect will conservatism have on the income of Premier Cycle Shoppe over the two years?

ETHICAL ISSUE

During 2016, Bryant Electronics changed to the weighted-average-cost method of accounting for inventory. Suppose that during 2017 Bryant Electronics changes back to the FIFO method and in the following year switches back to the weighted-average-cost method again.

Required

1. What would you think of a company's ethics if it changed accounting methods every year?
2. What accounting principle would changing methods every year violate?
3. Who can be harmed when a company changes its accounting methods too often? How?

PROBLEMS (GROUP A)　　　　　MyAccountingLab

Problem 6–1A

Markham Leathers, a distributor of leather products, uses the FIFO method for valuing inventories. It began August with 50 units of an inventory item that cost $80 each. During August, the store completed these inventory transactions:

Using the perpetual inventory system—FIFO

①

2. Cost of goods sold, $9,280

		Units	Unit Cost	Unit Sale Price
Aug. 3	Sale	40		$140
8	Purchase	80	$88	
21	Sale	70		150
30	Purchase	10	96	

Required

1. Prepare a perpetual inventory record for this item.
2. Determine the store's cost of goods sold for August.
3. Compute gross margin for August.

Problem 6–2A

Vista Distributors purchases inventory in crates of merchandise. Assume the company began July with an inventory of 30 units that cost $300 each. During the month, the company purchased and sold merchandise on account as shown:

Accounting for inventory using the perpetual system—FIFO

①

1. Cost of goods sold, $37,850

Jul.	10	Purchased 30 units at $320.
	15	Sold 40 units at $700.
	22	Purchased 70 units at $350.
	29	Sold 75 units at $800.

Assume Vista Distributors uses the FIFO cost method for valuing inventories. The company uses a perpetual inventory system. Cash payments on account totalled $15,000. Company operating expenses for the month were $30,000. The company paid one-half in cash, with the rest accrued as Accounts Payable.

Required

1. Prepare a perpetual inventory record, at FIFO cost, for this merchandise.
2. Make journal entries to record the company's transactions.

Problem 6–3A

Refer to the Vista Distributors situation in Problem 6–2A. Keep all the data unchanged, except assume that Vista uses the moving-weighted-average-cost method.

Accounting for inventory in a perpetual system—moving-weighted-average cost

①

1. Cost of goods sold, $37,983

Required

1. Prepared a perpetual inventory record at moving-weighted-average cost. Round the average unit cost to the nearest cent and all other amounts to the nearest dollar.
2. Prepare a multi-step income statement for Vista Distributors for the month of January.

Problem 6–4A

Refer to Problems 6–2A and 6–3A to prepare a table comparing ending inventory, cost of goods sold, and gross margin under both the FIFO and the moving-weighted-average-cost methods. You will need to calculate gross margin for Problem 6–2A. Explain why the gross margin is lower under the moving-weighted-average-cost method.

Problem 6–5A

Sandy's Office Supplies distributes office furniture. The company's fiscal year ends on March 31, 2017. On January 31, 2017, one department in the company had in inventory 20 office suites that cost $1,800 each. During the quarter, the department purchased merchandise on account as follows:

	Units	Unit Cost	Total
January	60	$1,850	$111,000
February	40	1,900	76,000
March	30	1,950	58,500

Sales for each month in the quarter were as follows:

	Units	Unit Selling Price	Total
January	50	$3,600	$180,000
February	20	3,700	74,000
March	34	3,800	129,200

Operating expenses in the quarter were $110,000.

Assume that the company uses a perpetual inventory system. Also assume that monthly purchases of inventory occur on the first day of each month.

Required

1. Determine the cost of the department's ending inventory at March 31, 2017, under (a) moving-weighted-average costing and (b) FIFO costing.

2. Prepare the department's income statement for the quarter ended March 31, 2017, under each method described in Requirement 1. Show gross margin and operating income and note the difference.

Problem 6–6A

Refer to the information in Problem 6-5A, Sandy's Office Supplies. Assume the company uses a periodic inventory system.

Required

1. Determine the cost of the department's ending inventory at March 31, 2017, under (a) weighted-average costing and (b) FIFO costing. Assume the company determines cost of goods sold at the end of each quarter.

2. Prepare the department's income statement for the quarter ended March 31, 2017, under each method described in Requirement 1. Show gross margin and operating income.

Problem 6–7A

Prairie Hardware operates a store in Red Deer, Alberta. The company began 2017 with an inventory of 50 snow blowers that cost $8,000 in total. During the year, the company purchased merchandise on account as follows:

March (60 units at $170)	$ 10,200
August (40 units at $174)	6,960
October (190 units at $180)	34,200
Total purchases	$ 51,360

Cash payments on account during the year totalled $46,000.

During November 2017 the company sold 300 units of merchandise for $85,000, of which $52,000 was for cash and the balance was on account. Prairie uses the FIFO method for inventories.

Required

1. Make summary journal entries to record the company's transactions for the year ended December 31, 2017. The company uses a perpetual inventory system.
2. Determine the FIFO cost of the company's ending inventory at December 31, 2017. Use a T-account.
3. Calculate Prairie Hardware's gross margin for the year ended December 31, 2017.

Problem 6–8A

Fast Framing Co. began March with 73 units of inventory that cost $50 each. During the month, Fast made the following purchases:

Computing inventory by two methods—periodic system
(3)

2. Gross margin, weighted average, $18,942

Mar.	4	113 units at $48
	12	81 units at $49
	19	167 units at $52
	25	34 units at $56

The company uses a periodic inventory system, and the physical count at March 31 shows 51 units of inventory on hand.

Required

1. Determine the ending inventory and cost of goods sold amounts for the March financial statements under (a) weighted-average cost and (b) FIFO cost. Round average cost per unit to the nearest cent and all other amounts to the nearest dollar.
2. Sales revenue for March totalled $40,000. Compute Fast's gross margin for March under each method.
3. Which method will result in lower income taxes for Fast? Why?
4. Which method will result in higher net income for Fast? Why?

Problem 6–9A

Winslow Products, which uses a periodic inventory system, began 2017 with 6,000 units of inventory that cost a total of $90,000. During 2017, Winslow Products purchased merchandise on account as follows:

Using the periodic inventory system—weighted-average and FIFO costing
(3)

3. Gross margin, FIFO, $378,000

Purchase 1 (10,000 units at $14 per unit)	$140,000
Purchase 2 (20,000 units at $12 per unit)	240,000

At year end, the physical count indicated 20,000 units of inventory on hand.

Required

1. How many units did Winslow Products sell during the year? The sale price per unit was $38. Determine Winslow's sales revenue for the year.
2. Compute cost of goods sold by the weighted-average method. Round average cost per unit to the nearest cent and all other amounts to the nearest dollar. Then determine gross margin for the year.
3. Compute cost of goods sold by the FIFO method. Then determine gross margin for the year.
4. Compare the gross margins you calculated for each inventory method in Requirements 2 and 3. What conclusions can you draw when the purchase prices for inventory are falling?

Problem 6–10A

Using the perpetual and periodic
inventory systems

① ③

3. Gross margin, $8,200

Titan Performance Tire began May with 50 units of inventory that cost $264 each. During May Titan Performance Tire completed these inventory transactions:

		Units	Unit Cost	Unit Selling Price
May 2	Purchase	12	$270	
8	Sale	27	264	$360
13	Sale	23	264	360
	Sale	3	270	370
17	Purchase	24	270	
22	Sale	31	270	370
29	Purchase	24	290	

Required

1. The above data are taken from Titan Performance Tire's perpetual inventory records. Which cost method does Titan Performance Tire use?
2. Compute Titan Performance Tire's cost of goods sold for May under the
   a. Perpetual inventory system
   b. Periodic inventory system
3. Compute gross margin for May.

Problem 6–11A

Applying the lower-of-cost-
and-net-realizable-value rule to
inventories

④

Cost of goods sold, $66,700

Hartley Home Furniture has recently been plagued with lacklustre sales. The rate of inventory turnover has dropped, and some of the business's merchandise is gathering dust. At the same time, competition has forced the business to lower the selling prices of its inventory. It is now December 31, 2017. Assume the net realizable value of a Hartley Home Furniture store's ending inventory is $1,500 below what Hartley Home Furniture paid for the goods, which was $10,300. Before any adjustments at the end of the period, assume the store's Cost of Goods Sold account has a balance of $65,200.

Required

1. What action should Hartley Home Furniture take in this situation, if any?
2. Give any journal entry required.
3. At what amount should Hartley Home Furniture report inventory on the balance sheet?
4. At what amount should the business report cost of goods sold on the income statement?
5. Discuss the accounting principle, concept, or constraint that is most relevant to this situation.

Problem 6–12A

Correcting inventory errors over
a three-year period

⑤

1. Net income, 2017,
$32 thousand

The accounting records of Chan Music Stores show these data (in thousands):

	2017		2016		2015	
Net sales revenue		$426		$366		$378
Cost of goods sold:						
Beginning inventory	$ 56		$ 80		$ 96	
Net purchases	276		240		216	
Cost of goods available	332		320		312	
Less: Ending inventory	92		56		80	
Cost of goods sold		240		264		232
Gross margin		186		102		146
Operating expenses		148		92		110
Net income		$ 38		$ 10		$ 36

In early 2018, a team of auditors discovered that the ending inventory of 2015 had been understated by $10 thousand. Also, the ending inventory for 2017 had been overstated by $6 thousand. The ending inventory at December 31, 2016, was correct.

Required

1. Show corrected comparative income statements for the three years.
2. State whether each year's net income as reported here and the related owner's equity amounts are understated or overstated. For each incorrect figure, indicate the amount of the understatement or overstatement.

Problem 6–13A

Sweeney Stores estimates its inventory by the gross margin method when preparing monthly financial statements (Sweeney Stores uses the periodic method otherwise). For the past two years, gross margin has averaged 45 percent of net sales. The business's inventory records for its stores reveal the following data:

Inventory: July 1, 2017	$ 240,000
Transactions during July:	
Purchases	7,890,000
Purchases returns	230,000
Sales	11,250,000
Sales returns	125,000

Excel Spreadsheet Template
Estimating inventory by the gross margin method, preparing the income statement
(6)
2. Gross margin, $5,006,250

Required

1. Estimate the July 31, 2017, inventory using the gross margin method.
2. Prepare the July 2017 income statement through gross margin for Sweeney Stores.

Problem 6–14A

Burrows Shoe Company has a periodic inventory system and uses the gross margin method of estimating inventories for interim financial statements. The company had the following account balances for the fiscal year ended August 31, 2017:

Inventory: Sep. 1, 2016	$ 195,000
Purchases	1,157,000
Purchases returns and allowances	23,000
Freight in	11,000
Sales	1,922,000
Sales returns and allowances	22,000

Accounting for inventory by the periodic system, estimating inventory by the gross margin method
(3)(6)
1. Estimated inventory, Aug. 31, 2017, $200,000

Required

1. Use the gross margin method to estimate the cost of the business's ending inventory, assuming the business has an average cost of 60 percent.
2. The business has done a physical count of the inventory on hand on August 31, 2017. For convenience, this inventory was calculated using the retail selling prices marked on the goods, which amounted to $252,000. Use the information from Requirement 1 and the gross margin method to calculate the cost of the inventory counted.

Problem 6–15A

Toffler Auto Parts uses a perpetual inventory system for the purchase and sale of inventory and had the following information available on November 30, 2017:

Applying the moving-weighted-average and FIFO costing methods, estimating inventory by the gross margin method
(1)(5)(6)
1. Cost of goods sold (a), moving weighted average, $1,352,250

Purchases and Sales		Number of Units	Cost or Selling Price per Unit
Nov.	1	Balance of inventory	3,900	$40
	7	Purchased	6,000	56

(Continued)

(Continued)

8	Sold	4,500	76
12	Purchased	7,500	52
16	Sold	9,000	84
21	Purchased	4,500	52
25	Purchased	10,500	48
29	Sold	13,500	84

Required

1. Calculate the cost of goods sold and the cost of the ending inventory for November under each of the following inventory costing methods: (a) moving-weighted-average cost and (b) FIFO cost.

2. Prepare the journal entries required to record the transactions using the perpetual inventory system with FIFO costing.

3. An internal audit has discovered that a new employee—an accounting clerk—had been stealing merchandise and covering up the shortage by changing the inventory records.

   The external auditors examined the accounting records prior to the employment of the individual and noted that the company has an average gross margin rate of 35 percent. Use the gross margin method to estimate the cost of the inventory shortage (under the FIFO costing method). (Note: The physical count matched the estimate.) Explain the difference between the three inventory values—the accounting records, physical count, and estimates—and their importance in valuing inventory.

4. What would be the effect on the financial statements for the year ending November 30, 2017, if the inventory shortage had not been discovered?

PROBLEMS (GROUP B)   MyAccountingLab

Problem 6–1B

Using the perpetual inventory system—FIFO

①

Barr Lawn Supply, which uses the FIFO method, began March with 200 units of inventory that cost $40 each. During March, Barr completed these inventory transactions:

		Units	Unit Cost	Unit Sale Price
Mar. 2	Purchase	48	$50	
8	Sale	160		$144
17	Purchase	96	60	
22	Sale	124		150

Required

1. Prepare a perpetual inventory record for the lawn supply merchandise.
2. Determine Barr's cost of goods sold for March.
3. Compute gross margin for March.

Problem 6–2B

Accounting for inventory in a perpetual system—FIFO

①

Kamlhani Imports is a furniture distributor. The following information is for one item of inventory, kitchen chairs, for the month of November. The store purchased and sold merchandise on account as follows:

Nov. 1	Opening inventory	50 chairs at $ 50
3	Purchase	60 chairs at $ 55
10	Sale	100 chairs at $120
22	Purchase	90 chairs at $ 60
24	Sale	70 chairs at $140

Assume that Kamlhani Imports uses the FIFO cost method. All sales were made on account. Operating expenses were $14,400, with two-thirds paid in cash and the rest accrued in Accounts Payable.

Required

1. Prepare a perpetual inventory record, at FIFO cost, for this merchandise.
2. Make journal entries to record the company's transactions.

Problem 6–3B

Refer to the Kamlhani Imports situation in Problem 6–2B. Keep all the data unchanged, except that Kamlhani uses the moving-weighted-average-cost method.

Accounting for inventory in a perpetual system—moving-weighted-average cost

Required

1. Prepare a perpetual inventory record at moving-weighted-average cost. Round the average unit cost to the nearest cent and all other amounts to the nearest dollar.
2. Prepare a multi-step income statement for Kamlhani Imports for the month of November.

Problem 6–4B

Refer to Problems 6–2B and 6–3B to prepare a table comparing ending inventory, cost of goods sold, and gross margin under both the FIFO and the moving-weighted-average-cost methods. You will need to calculate gross margin for Problem 6–2B. Explain why the gross margin is lower under the moving-weighted-average-cost method.

Summarize perpetual inventory data and explain

Problem 6–5B

Buntzell Industrial Supplies distributes industrial equipment. The company's fiscal year ends on March 31, 2017. One department in the company had 50 items that cost $540 each on hand at January 1, 2017. During the quarter, the department purchased merchandise on account as follows:

Computing ending inventory by applying two inventory costing methods in a perpetual inventory system

	Units	Unit Cost	Total
January	120	$585	$70,200
February	24	360	8,640
March	48	450	21,600

Sales for each month in the quarter were as follows:

	Units	Unit Selling Price	Total
January	36	$1,260	$ 45,360
February	108	1,080	116,640
March	60	1,020	61,200

Operating expenses in the quarter were $95,000.

Assume that the company uses a perpetual inventory system. Also assume that monthly purchases of inventory occur on the first day of each month.

Required

1. Determine the cost of the department's ending inventory at March 31, 2017, under (a) moving-weighted-average cost and (b) FIFO cost.
2. Prepare the department's income statement for the quarter ended March 31, 2017, under each method described in Requirement 1. Show totals for gross margin and operating income and note the difference, if any.

Problem 6–6B

Refer to the information in Problem 6–5B. Assume that the company uses a periodic inventory system.

Computing ending inventory by applying two inventory costing methods in a periodic inventory system

Required

1. Determine the cost of the department's ending inventory at March 31, 2017, under (a) the weighted-average-cost method and (b) the FIFO method. Assume the company determines cost of goods sold at the end of the quarter.

2. Prepare the department's income statement for the quarter ended March 31, 2017, under each method described in Requirement 1. Show totals for gross margin and operating income.

Problem 6–7B

Accounting for inventory in a perpetual system—FIFO ①

Honjo Hardware Store purchases inventory in crates of merchandise, so each unit of inventory is a crate of tools or building supplies. Assume you are dealing with a single department in the store. Assume the department began the year with an inventory of 40 units that cost a total of $6,000. During the year, the department purchased merchandise on account as follows:

April 30 (60 units at $145)		$ 8,700
July 31 (100 units at $145)		14,500
October 31 (200 units at $140)		28,000
Total purchases		$51,200

Cash payments on account during the year totalled $48,000.

During the year, the department sold 380 units of merchandise for $165,000, as follows:

March 31:	30 units
June 30:	50 units
September 30:	90 units
December 31:	210 units

Of the sales revenue, $93,000 was from cash sales and the balance was on account. Assume Honjo uses the FIFO method for inventories. Department operating expenses for the year were $86,000. The department paid two-thirds of the operating expenses in cash and incurred the rest on account.

Required

1. Make summary journal entries to record the department transactions for the year ended December 31, 2017. Honjo uses a perpetual inventory system.

2. Determine the FIFO cost of the store's ending inventory at December 31, 2017. Use a T-account.

3. Prepare the department's income statement for the year ended December 31, 2017. Include a complete heading, and show totals for the gross margin and net income.

Problem 6–8B

Computing inventory by two methods—periodic system ③

Comet Appliances and Supply began December with 280 units of inventory that cost $90 each. During December, the store made the following purchases:

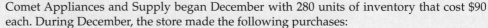

Dec.	3	430 units at $91
	12	190 units at $92
	18	420 units at $93
	27	426 units at $92

The store uses the periodic inventory system, and the physical count at December 31 indicates that 358 units of inventory are on hand.

Required

1. Determine the ending inventory and cost of goods sold amounts for the December financial statements under the weighted-average-cost and FIFO methods. Round the average cost per unit to the nearest cent and all other amounts to the nearest dollar.

2. Sales revenue for December totalled $192,000. Compute Comet Appliances and Supply's gross margin for December under each method.

3. Which method will result in lower income taxes for Comet? Why? Which method will result in higher net income for Comet? Why?

Problem 6–9B

Cloutier Hardware Company, which uses a periodic inventory system, began 2017 with 9,000 units of inventory that cost a total of $90,000. During 2017 Cloutier purchased merchandise on account as follows:

Using the periodic inventory system—FIFO and weighted average
③

Purchase 1 (15,000 units)	$180,000
Purchase 2 (30,000 units)	420,000

At year end, the physical count indicated 10,000 units of inventory on hand.

Required

1. How many units did Cloutier sell during the year? The sale price per unit was $31. Determine Cloutier's sales revenue for the year.

2. Compute cost of goods sold by both the FIFO and the weighted-average-cost method. Then determine gross margin for the year under each method.

Problem 6–10B

The Canvas Company (TCC) began August 2017 with 100 units of inventory that cost $60 each. The sale price of each of those units was $100. During August, TCC completed these inventory transactions:

Using the perpetual and periodic inventory systems
① ③

			Units	Unit Cost	Unit Sale Price
Aug.	3	Sale	32	$60	$100
	8	Purchase	160	62	
	11	Sale	68	60	100
	22	Sale	88	62	104
	30	Purchase	36	64	
	31	Sale	12	62	104

Required

1. The above data are taken from TCC's perpetual inventory records. Which cost method does the company use?

2. Compute TCC's cost of goods sold for August 2017 under the

   a. Perpetual inventory system

   b. Periodic inventory system

3. Compute the gross margin for August 2017.

4. Ignore the unit cost and complete a perpetual inventory record using the moving-weighted-average-cost method.

Problem 6–11B

Senick Building Supplies has recently been plagued with declining sales. The rate of inventory turnover has dropped, and some of the company's merchandise is gathering dust. At the same time, competition has forced Senick to lower the selling prices of its inventory. It is now December 31, 2017, and the net realizable value of Senick's ending inventory is $1,092 below what the business actually paid for the goods, which was $7,644. Before any adjustments at the end of the period, Senick's Cost of Goods Sold account has a balance of $44,928.

What action should Senick Building Supplies take in this situation, if any? Provide any journal entry required. At what amount should Senick report inventory on the balance sheet? At what amount should the company report cost of goods sold on the income statement? Discuss the accounting principle, concept, or constraint that is most relevant to this situation.

Applying the lower-of-cost-and-net-realizable-value rule to inventories

Problem 6–12B

Correcting inventory errors over a three-year period

The books of Hayes Windows and Siding show these data (in thousands):

	2017	2016	2015
Net sales revenue	$410	$345	$320
Cost of goods sold:			
Beginning inventory	$ 49	$ 41	$ 52
Net purchases	146	101	98
Cost of goods available for sale	195	142	150
Less: Ending inventory	52	49	41
Cost of goods sold	143	93	109
Gross margin	267	252	211
Operating expenses	109	102	74
Net income	$158	$150	$137

In early 2018, a team of Canada Revenue Agency auditors discovered that the ending inventory of 2015 had been overstated by $5 thousand. Also, the ending inventory for 2017 had been understated by $7 thousand. The ending inventory at December 31, 2016, was correct.

Required

1. Show corrected comparative income statements for the three years.
2. State whether each year's net income as reported here and the related owner's equity amounts are understated or overstated. For each incorrect figure, indicate the amount of the understatement or overstatement.

Problem 6–13B

Excel Spreadsheet Template

Estimating ending inventory by the gross margin method and preparing the income statement

6

Assume Dresso Linen Stores estimates its inventory by the gross margin method when preparing monthly financial statements (it uses the periodic method otherwise). For the past two years, the cost of goods purchased has averaged 60 percent of net sales. Assume further that the company's inventory records for its stores reveal the following data:

Inventory: June 1, 2017	$ 480,000
Transactions during June:	
Purchases	4,920,000
Sales	8,360,000

Required

1. Estimate the June 30, 2017, inventory using the gross margin method.
2. Prepare the June income statement through gross margin for Dresso Linen Stores.

Problem 6–14B

Accounting for inventory by the periodic system and estimating inventory by the gross margin method

Kenora Supplies has a periodic inventory system and uses the gross margin method of estimating inventories for interim financial statements. The business had the following account balances for the fiscal year ended August 31, 2017:

Inventory: Sep. 1, 2016	$ 136,000
Purchases	1,180,000
Purchases returns and allowances	36,000
Freight in	24,000
Sales	2,100,000
Sales returns and allowances	50,000

Required

1. Use the gross margin method to estimate the cost of the business's ending inventory, assuming the business has an average gross margin rate of 40 percent.

2. The business has done a physical count of the inventory on hand on August 31, 2017. For convenience, this inventory was calculated using the retail selling prices marked on the goods, which amounted to $169,500. Use the information from Requirement 1 and the gross margin method to calculate the cost of the inventory counted.

Problem 6–15B

Booth Sales uses the perpetual inventory system for the purchase and sale of inventory and had the following information available on August 31, 2017:

Applying moving-weighted-average and FIFO costing methods and estimating inventory by the gross margin method ① ⑤ ⑥

Purchases and Sales			Number of Units	Cost or Selling Price per Unit
Aug.	1	Balance of inventory	810	$15
	7	Purchased	2,250	14
	8	Sold	1,800	25
	12	Purchased	1,575	15
	16	Sold	2,600	26
	21	Purchased	1,800	17
	25	Purchased	2,700	20
	29	Sold	3,600	27

Required

1. Calculate the cost of goods sold and the cost of the ending inventory for August under (a) moving-weighted-average cost and (b) FIFO cost.

2. Prepare the journal entries required to record the August transactions using the perpetual inventory system with FIFO costing.

3. An internal audit has discovered that two new employees—an accounting clerk and an employee from the purchasing department—have been stealing merchandise and covering up the shortage by changing the inventory records.

   The external auditors examined the accounting records prior to the employment of the two individuals and noted that the company had an average gross margin rate of 50 percent. The physical count matched the estimate. Use the gross margin method to estimate the cost of the inventory difference (under the FIFO costing method). (Note: The physical count matched the estimate.) Explain the difference between the three inventory values—records, physical count, and estimates—and their importance in valuing inventory.

4. What would be the effect on the financial statements for the year ending August 31, 2017, if the inventory difference had not been discovered?

CHALLENGE PROBLEMS

Problem 6–1C

An anonymous source advised Canada Revenue Agency (CRA) that Jim Mayers, owner of Mayers Grocery Store, has been filing fraudulent tax returns for the past several years. You, a tax auditor with the CRA, are in the process of auditing Mayers Grocery Store for the year ended December 31, 2017. The tax returns for the past five years show a decreasing value for ending inventory from 2014, when Mayers bought the business, to 2016; the return for 2017 shows the same sort of decrease. You have performed a quick survey of the large store and the attached warehouse and observed that both seemed very well stocked.

Measuring inventory and income ②

Required   Does the information set forth above suggest anything to you that might confirm the anonymous tip? What would you do to confirm or deny your suspicions?

Estimating inventory from
incomplete records

It is Monday morning. You heard on the morning news that a client of your public account-ing firm, Kearns and Associates, had a fire the previous Friday night that destroyed its office and warehouse, and you concluded that inventory records as well as inventory prob-ably perished in the fire. Since you had been at Kearns on the previous Friday preparing the monthly income statement for the previous month that ended on Thursday, you realize you probably have the only current financial information available for Kearns.

Upon arrival at your firm's office, you meet your partner, who confirms your suspicions. Kearns and Associates lost its entire inventory and its records. She tells you that the com-pany wants your firm to prepare information for a fire loss claim for Kearns's insurance company for the inventory.

You know the audit file for the fiscal year that ended three months earlier contains a complete section dealing with inventory and the four product lines Kearns carried, includ-ing the most recent gross margin rate for each line. The file will show total inventory and how much inventory there was by product line at year end. You also recall that the file contains an analysis of sales by product line for the past several years and that Kearns used a periodic inventory system.

Required Explain how you would use the information available to you to calculate the fire loss by product line.

EXTENDING YOUR KNOWLEDGE

DECISION PROBLEM

Assessing the impact of a year-end purchase of inventory—periodic system

1. Without purchase: FIFO gross margin, $268,250
Weighted-average gross margin, $259,125

Kao Camping Supplies is nearing the end of its first year of operations. The company uses a periodic inventory system and made inventory purchases of $176,250 during the year as follows:

January	150	units at $165	=	$ 24,750
July	600	units at $195	=	117,000
November	150	units at $230	=	34,500
Totals	900			$176,250

Sales for the year will be 750 units for $410,000 revenue. Expenses other than cost of goods sold will be $105,000. The owner of the company is undecided about whether to adopt FIFO or weighted-average costing as the company's method.

The company has storage capacity for 600 additional units of inventory. Inventory prices are expected to stay at $230 per unit for the next few months. The president is considering purchasing 150 additional units of inventory at $230 each before the end of the year. He wishes to know how the purchase would affect net income before taxes under both the FIFO and weighted-average costing methods.

Required

1. To help the owner make the decision, prepare income statements under FIFO costing and weighted-average costing, both without and with the year-end purchase of 150 units of inventory at $230 per unit.

2. Compare net income before taxes under FIFO costing without and with the year-end purchase. Make the same comparison under weighted-average costing. Under which method does the year-end purchase have the greater effect on net income before taxes?

3. If the company wanted to manipulate net income for the year, is one method more ma-nipulative than the other?

FINANCIAL STATEMENT CASE

The notes are an important part of a company's financial statements, giving valuable details that would clutter the tabular data presented in the statements. This problem will help you learn how to use a company's inventory notes. Refer to the Indigo Books and Music Inc., March 29, 2014, financial statements and the related notes in Appendix A and on MyAccountingLab. Answer the following questions:

Inventories

① ④

1. Refer to Note 7, Inventories. What was the amount of the write-down of inventory as a result of the application of the lower net realizable value policy in 2014 and 2013? What is the reason for using the lower of cost or net realizable value policy?

2. Refer to the significant accounting policies for inventory on page 18 of the annual report.

   a. What were the likely causes of the write-downs in inventory?

   b. What is a vendor settlement accrual?

▷ Try It! SOLUTIONS FOR CHAPTER 6

1. Perpetual inventory records:

FIFO

Wristwatches

Date	Purchases Qty.	Purchases Unit Cost	Purchases Total Cost	Cost of Goods Sold Qty.	Cost of Goods Sold Unit Cost	Cost of Goods Sold Total Cost	Inventory on Hand Qty.	Inventory on Hand Unit Cost	Inventory on Hand Total Cost
Jun. 1							20	$60	$1,200
3				16	$60	$ 960	4	60	240
16	20	$65	$1,300				4	60	240
							20	65	1,300
23				4	60	240			
				12	65	780	8	65	520
30	20		1,300	32		1,980	8		520

Notice that the June 3 items are sold from the opening batch of inventory, which all cost the same amount. However, the June 23 items are sold from two batches of inventory that have different costs. Remember, under FIFO, items from the oldest batch are assumed to be sold first.

Moving-Weighted-Average Costing

Wristwatches

Date	Purchases Qty.	Purchases Unit Cost	Purchases Total Cost	Cost of Goods Sold Qty.	Cost of Goods Sold Unit Cost	Cost of Goods Sold Total Cost	Inventory on Hand Qty.	Inventory on Hand Unit Cost	Inventory on Hand Total Cost
Jun. 1							20	$ 60	$1,200
3				16	$ 60	$ 960	4	60	240
16	20	$65	$1,300				24	64.17	1,540
23				16	64.17	1,027	8	64.17	513
30	20		1,300	32		1,987	8		513

Notice that the June 3 items are sold from the opening batch of inventory, which all cost the same amount. However, the June 23 items are sold from two batches of inventory that have different costs. The moving-weighted-average-cost calculation is given in the solutions for the next question. Under the moving-weighted-average-cost method, both cost of goods sold and ending inventory amounts are calculated using the same moving-weighted-average unit cost.

2. Journal entries:

			FIFO		Moving Weighted Average	
Jun. 3	Accounts Receivable		1,600		1,600	
	Sales Revenue			1,600		1,600
3	Cost of Goods Sold		960		960	
	Inventory			960		960
16	Inventory		1,300		1,300	
	Accounts Payable			1,300		1,300
23	Accounts Receivable		1,600		1,600	
	Sales Revenue			1,600		1,600
23	Cost of Goods Sold		1,020*		1,027**	
	Inventory			1,020		1,027

Notice the following:
- The June 3 and 23 sales entries are the same for both costing methods because the selling price is $100 per unit.
- The June 3 COGS entries are the same because the sale was from beginning inventory.
- The June 16 purchase is recorded as a normal inventory purchase no matter which inventory costing system is used.
- Only the June 23 COGS entries differ. Refer to the calculations provided.

*(4 units × $60) + (12 units × $65) = $1,020

**(4 units × $60) + (20 units × $65) = $1,540; $1,540 / 24 units + $64.17 per unit;
  16 units × $64.17 + $1,027 (rounded)

3.

	FIFO	Moving Weighted Average
Sales revenue ($1,600 + $1,600)	$3,200	$3,200
Cost of goods sold ($960 + $1,020)	1,980	
($960 + $1,027)		1,987
Gross margin	$1,220	$1,213

The sales and COGS amounts are gathered from the journal entries in the previous question.

Gross margin = Sales revenue − COGS

4. The method with:
- The greatest gross margin will maximize net income
- The lowest gross margin will minimize income taxes

When inventory purchase prices are rising, as they are in this question, FIFO maximizes net income. Of the methods allowed in Canada, moving weighted average minimizes income taxes.

5. When inventory purchase prices are falling, moving weighted average maximizes net income and FIFO minimizes income taxes.

6. Under FIFO:

Sales revenue*	$3,050
Cost of goods sold**	1,700
Gross margin	$1,350

*Sales are calculated as (50 × $25) + (60 × $30) = $1,250 + $1,800 = $3,050

(Continued)

(*Continued*)

**Cost of goods sold are calculated as:

Beginning inventory (40 units, total cost given)	$ 800
Purchases (60 units × $12.50) + (40 × $15)	1,350
Cost of goods available for sale (140 units)	2,150
Less: Ending inventory (30 units × $15)	(450)
Cost of goods sold (110 units)	$1,700

7. Under weighted average:

Sales revenue*	$3,050
Cost of goods sold**	1,689
Gross margin	$1,361

*Sales are calculated as (50 × $25) + (60 × $30) = $1,250 + $1,800 = $3,050
**Cost of goods sold are calculated as:

Beginning inventory (40 units, total cost given)	$ 800
Purchases (60 units × $12.50) + (40 × $15)	1,350
Cost of goods available for sale (140 units)	2,150
Less: Ending inventory (30 units × ($2,150 / 140 units))	(461)
Cost of goods sold (110 units × ($2,150 / 140 units))	$1,689

8. Amount of inventory remaining at cost: $20,000 − ($20,000 × 60%) = $8,000
Net realizable value of remaining inventory: $8,000 × 60% = $4,800
Since the net realizable value ($4,800) is lower than the original cost of the remaining inventory ($8,000), the balance sheet should reflect the net realizable amount of $4,800.

9. Amount of inventory at original cost: $20,000 − ($20,000 × 60%) = $8,000
Net realizable value of remaining inventory one month later: $10,000
Current carrying value of this inventory: $4,800
Since the net realizable value ($10,000) is greater than the original cost of the remaining inventory ($8,000) and its current carrying value ($4,800), the balance sheet one month later should reflect the original cost amount of $8,000. The lower-of-cost-and-net-realizable-value rule prevents this inventory from being written up to $10,000 since its original cost is lower than its net realizable value.

10. The ending inventory is overstated by $2,000, which has the following effects:

	Current balance	Effect	Balance should be:
Sales revenue	$ 60,000	correct	$ 60,000
Cost of goods sold:			
Beginning inventory	11,000	correct	11,000
Net purchases	45,000	correct	45,000
Cost of goods available for sale	56,000	correct	56,000
Less: Ending inventory	(12,000)	overstated	(10,000)
Cost of goods sold	44,000	understated	46,000
Gross margin	$ 16,000	overstated	$ 14,000

11. The previous year's ending inventory is overstated by $2,000, which has the following effects on the following year's inventory amounts:

	Current balance	Effect	Balance should be:
Sales revenue	$XX,XXX	correct	$XX,XXX
Cost of goods sold:			
Beginning inventory	12,000	overstated	10,000
Net purchases	XXX	correct	XXX
Cost of goods available for sale	XXX	overstated	XXX
Less: Ending inventory	XXX	correct	XXX
Cost of goods sold	XXX	overstated	XXX
Gross margin	$ XXX	understated	$ XXX

At the end of the second year, the first year's overstatement and the second year's understatement of gross margin cancel each other out, for a net effect of nil. However, both years' balances are still incorrect.

12.

Beginning inventory	$ 45,000
Purchases	160,000
Cost of goods available for sale	205,000
Estimate of cost of goods sold:	
Sales revenue	$ 250,000
Less: Estimated gross margin of 40%	(100,000)
Estimated cost of goods sold	(150,000)
Estimated cost of *ending inventory*	$ 55,000

13. Using the retail method to estimate ending inventory:

	Cost	Selling Price
Beginning inventory	$ 25,000	$ 60,000
Purchases	100,000	240,000
Goods available for sale	$125,000	300,000
Net sales, at selling price (retail)		250,000
Ending inventory, at selling price (retail)		$ 50,000
Ending inventory, at cost ($50,000 × 42%*)	$ 21,000	

*Retail ratio = ($125,000 / $300,000) × 100 = 42%

7 ACCOUNTING INFORMATION SYSTEMS

CONNECTING CHAPTER 7

MyAccountingLab   The **Summary** for Chapter 7 appears on page 405. This lists all of the MyAccountingLab resources. **Accounting Vocabulary** with definitions for this chapter's material appears on page 406.

The last print issue of *SkiNews Magazine* was published in December 2015 by Barry Lanzinger, owner, photographer, and editor in chief, and a team of writers. It was also the first issue published in e-format, which was available as a download to an iPad. In December 2016 Barry and his team relaunched *SkiNews Magazine* in digital format. Over the ensuing months, the website was upgraded to take on the magazine's format. Content followed the magazine's original style and included articles by skiers and coaches written for skiers and coaches.

The magazine reports on the world skiing scene with a focus on Canadian skiing. Barry is not an accountant, but, like many small business owners, he needs an accounting system to track all of his subscription and advertising revenues and his expenses. He needs financial results for his annual income tax return for the Canada Revenue Agency (CRA) and other stakeholders like the provincial government.

Like many small businesses, *SkiNews*'s accounting system began as the classic "shoebox" operation: All the slips for cash received and receipts for payments made were kept in a box, which was then sent to an accountant at year end to prepare the financial statements and tax returns. *SkiNews*'s accounting system had to change when the number of business transactions grew and taxes like the HST arrived in provinces like Ontario. Barry first used QuickBooks but now uses Sage 50—both are accounting software packages that allow him to track all his revenues and expenses on his computer. To ensure he enters all transactions into his accounting system, Barry checks his bank account balances online daily. At the end of the year, he passes over to his accountant all the reports from his accounting system and any backup documents so the accountant can complete the income tax returns.

Barry is delighted that his accounting system is effective and easy to use. It frees him from bookkeeping and allows him to focus his energies on what he does best: tracking ski-meet results and reporting on the world of skiing.

> **Every** organization needs an **accounting information system (AIS)**. An AIS is a set of interrelated components (people, procedures, documents, hardware, software, etc.) that collect, process, store, and disseminate financial information to internal and external users. The system collects information, processes it, and produces reports that meet users' needs. So far in this text we have used a manual general journal and general ledger to create the records in an accounting information system.

Every AIS has a general journal and a general ledger. However, this manual system can efficiently handle a limited number of transactions per accounting period and cannot supply all of the details a company needs, such as which specific customers owe which specific amounts.

Businesses cope with heavy transaction loads in two ways: computerization and specialization. We *computerize* to do the accounting efficiently and more reliably. *Specialization* combines similar transactions to speed up the process. The second half of this chapter covers special journals that can be used for repetitive transactions, as well as subsidiary ledgers that detail amounts owed to a business by specific customers and amounts the business owes to suppliers.

You may be wondering why we cover manual accounting information systems at all, since many businesses use computerized systems. There are four main reasons:

- Learning a manual system will equip you to work with both manual and electronic systems. The accounting is the same regardless of the system.

- Few small businesses have computerized all their accounting. Even companies that use QuickBooks or Sage 50 keep some manual accounting records. For businesses that use manual systems, these systems follow the principles and procedures that we illustrate in this chapter.

- Learning a manual system will help you master accounting. A number of small business owners only know which keys to use in QuickBooks, but if they had accounting knowledge they could better manage their businesses. You will also see how special journals, subsidiary ledgers, and computer modules link to each other to create the final set of financial statements.

- Learning a manual system will help you recognize a computer system that is not set up properly or is not working as intended.

EFFECTIVE ACCOUNTING INFORMATION SYSTEMS

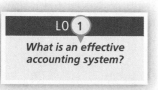

Good personnel are critical to success. Employees must be competent, loyal, and honest. Good design features also make an accounting system run smoothly. An effective system—whether computerized or manual—provides the following:

- Control
- Compatibility
- Flexibility
- Reports that meet users' needs
- A favourable cost–benefit relationship

Features

Control Owners and managers must *control* the business and manage risk. *Internal controls* safeguard assets and eliminate waste. They are the methods and procedures used to authorize transactions, to ensure adherence to management policy, to safeguard assets and records, to prevent and detect error and fraud, to provide security by limiting access to assets and records, and to ensure that information produced is relevant, accurate, and timely. You will see examples of these controls throughout this chapter, such as the use of cheques for all cash payments and the comparison of the **control account** to the subledger listing at the end of the month to reconcile any discrepancies.

For example, in companies such as Indigo Books and Music Inc. or Canadian National Railway Company (CN), managers control cash payments to avoid theft through unauthorized payments. VISA, MasterCard, American Express, and other credit card companies keep accurate records of their accounts receivable to ensure that customers are billed and collections are received on time.

Compatibility A *compatible* system is one that works smoothly with the business's operations, personnel, and organizational structure. For example, branches of the Bank of Nova Scotia report how much revenue is generated and how many bank loans are issued from each branch so that the head office can track these numbers in each region. If revenue and loan numbers in Alberta or Nova Scotia are down, the managers can concentrate their collection efforts in those regions. They may relocate some branch offices, open new branches, or hire new personnel to increase their revenues and net income. A compatible accounting information system conforms to the particular needs of the business.

Flexibility Organizations evolve. They develop new products, sell off unprofitable operations and acquire new ones, adjust employee pay scales, and decide to "go green." Changes in the business often call for changes in the accounting system. A well-designed system is *flexible* if it accommodates changes without needing a complete overhaul. Consider Bombardier's acquisition of Canadair, the aircraft manufacturer. Bombardier's accounting system had the flexibility to fold Canadair's financial statements into those of Bombardier Inc., the parent company.

Reports that Meet Users' Needs If the accounting system processes the information collected but does not produce reports that are usable, then the accounting system is lacking. To address this, most accounting packages allow users to program their preferences for financial statement presentation and allow users to create special reports.

Favourable Cost–Benefit Relationship Achieving control, compatibility, and flexibility costs money. Managers strive for a system that offers maximum benefits at a minimum cost—that is, a system that has a favourable *cost–benefit relationship*. Most small companies use off-the-shelf computerized accounting packages, such as Sage 50 or QuickBooks. Less-expensive accounting software may have limited flexibility and limited capabilities. The very smallest businesses might not computerize at all. But large companies, such as the yoga-wear company lululemon athletica, have specialized needs for information. For them, customized programming is a must because the benefits—in terms of information tailored to the company's needs—far outweigh the cost of the system. The result? Better decisions.

All these features are needed whether the accounting information system is computerized or manual. Let's begin with a computerized system.

Components of a Computerized Accounting Information System

A computerized accounting information system has two basic components (hardware and software) in addition to the personnel and procedures to operate it.

Hardware is the electronic equipment and the network that connects them. Most systems require a **network** to link computers. In a networked system, a **server** stores the program and the data. With the use of technology, a KPMG LLP auditor in Calgary can access the data of a client located in Tokyo, Japan. The result is a speedier audit for the client often at lower cost than if the auditor had to perform all of the work onsite in Tokyo.

Software is the set of programs that drives the computer. Accounting software reads, edits, and stores transaction data. It also generates the reports you can use to run the business. Many software packages are flexible.

Cloud computing, which offers applications and storage services online, are now entering the market to provide businesses and individuals with Internet

REAL WORLD
EXAMPLE

Access to computer information must be strictly controlled. At a Hudson's Bay store, it would be risky for all employees to gain access to customer accounts. An unauthorized employee could change a customer's account balance or learn confidential information about the customer. Hence, access codes limit access to certain information. Source documents should support all sensitive changes to computer files.

options. A cloud provider will offer software, processing, and data storage services via a subscription-based fee or other payment option. The customer accesses these services using the Internet anywhere a connection is available.

For large enterprises, such as the Molson Coors Brewing Company or the Royal Bank of Canada, the accounting software is integrated into the company **database**, or computerized storehouse of information. Many business databases, or *management information systems*, include both accounting and non-accounting data. For example, VIA Rail Canada, in negotiating a union contract, often needs to examine the relationship between the employment history and salary levels of company employees. VIA's database provides the data that managers need to negotiate effectively with their labour unions. During negotiations, both parties carry laptops so that they can access the database and analyze data on the spot.

Personnel who operate the system must be properly trained. In addition, management of a computerized accounting information system requires careful consideration of data security and screening of the people in the organization who will have access to the data. Security is usually achieved with *passwords,* codes that restrict access to computerized records.

> Try It!

1. Why does every business need an accounting information system (AIS)?
   a. It is mandatory to set up a company bank account.
   b. The Canada Revenue Agency requires every business to have an AIS.
   c. Owners and managers of businesses must make decisions, and they need information to run the organization.
   d. The provincial corporation of finance may audit your business.

2. Suppose you are the controller for a small industrial ventilation company that wants to change its accounting information system. The new system you are considering will not accept the current alpha characters in the job-order numbers. Each job is assigned a number and then, as extras are added to the job, an alpha character is added to the job-order number, for example, job 1645a. Which feature of a good accounting information system is being compromised, and what could you do to solve this dilemma?

Solutions appear at the end of this chapter and on MyAccountingLab

HOW ACCOUNTING SYSTEMS WORK

LO **2**

How do accounting systems work?

As we discuss the stages of data processing, observe the differences between a computerized system and a manual system. The relationship among the three stages of data processing—inputs, processing, and outputs—is shown in Exhibit 7–1.

EXHIBIT 7–1 | The Three Stages of Data Processing

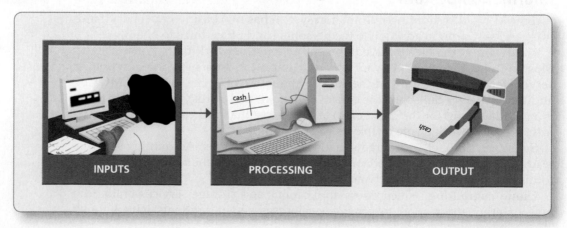

INPUTS   PROCESSING   OUTPUT

Inputs Inputs come from source documents, such as orders received from customers, sales receipts, and bank deposit slips. Inputs are usually grouped by type. For example, a firm would enter cash sales separately from credit sales and purchases.

Processing In a manual system, *processing* includes journalizing transactions, posting to the accounts, and preparing the financial statements. In a computerized system, the initial data entered will be posted automatically to the ledger and then processed into reports (including the journal and account details) and financial statements. Often account numbers or the first letters of a name are used to quickly enter the data into the correct accounts.

Outputs *Outputs* are the reports used for decision making, including the financial statements. Business owners can make better decisions with the reports produced by a good accounting system. In a computerized accounting system, a trial balance is a report (an output). But a manual system would treat the trial balance as a *processing* step leading to the preparation of financial statements. Exhibit 7–2 is an overview of a computerized accounting system. Start with data inputs in the bottom left corner.

KEY POINTS

The output (financial reports) are only as reliable as the input. If the input is incorrect or incomplete, the output will be flawed.

REAL WORLD EXAMPLE

Often a cash register doubles as a computer terminal, called a point-of-sale terminal. The cashier passes the Universal Product Code (UPC) of merchandise over the scanner, which identifies the merchandise to the computer. The use of a scanner eliminates errors in recording sales and automatically updates inventory records (costs and units) in a perpetual inventory system, as discussed in Chapter 5.

EXHIBIT 7–2 | Overview of a Computerized Accounting System

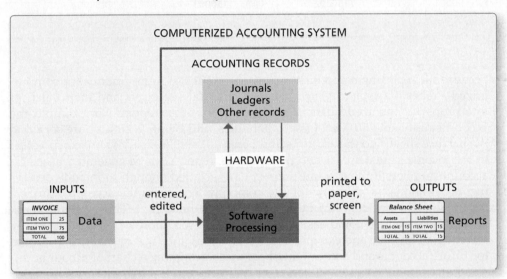

Designing an Accounting System: The Chart of Accounts

An accounting system begins with the chart of accounts. Recall from Chapter 2, page 61, that the chart of accounts lists all accounts in the general ledger and their account numbers. In the accounting system of most companies, the account *numbers* take on added importance. It is efficient to represent a complex account title, such as Accumulated Amortization—Photographic Equipment, with a concise account number (e.g., 16570).

Recall that asset accounts generally begin with the digit 1, liabilities with the digit 2, owner's equity accounts with the digit 3, revenues with 4, and expenses with 5. Exhibit 7–3 diagrams one structure for computerized accounts. Assets in this case are divided into current assets; property, plant, and equipment; and other assets. Among the current assets we illustrate only three general ledger accounts: Cash (Account No. 111), Accounts Receivable (No. 115), and Inventory (No. 120)—there are others that are not shown. Accounts Receivable holds the *total* dollar amount receivable from customers A, B, C, and D.

The importance of a well-structured chart of accounts cannot be overemphasized. Many computer systems have account numbers of fixed length, such as 100000 for Assets, 110000 for Current Assets, 111000 for Cash, and so on. This is

EXHIBIT 7–3 | Structure for Computerized Accounts

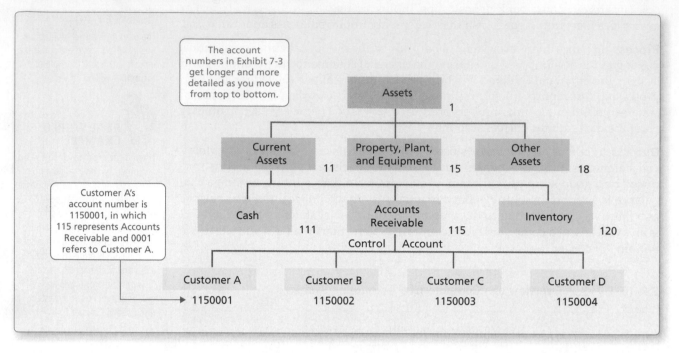

because the reporting component of any accounting system—manual or computerized—relies on *account number ranges* to translate accounts and their balances into properly organized financial statements and other reports. For example, the accounts numbered 101–399 (assets, liabilities, and owner's equity) are sorted to the balance sheet, and the accounts numbered 401–599 (revenues and expenses) go to the income statement. As another example, reports can be generated based on account numbers if the account numbers are detailed enough to include departments, locations, or divisions of the company. For example, account numbers for the housewares department might end with the digit 2. Thus, a departmental income statement could easily be prepared for the housewares department by selecting all revenue and expense accounts that end in 2. It is crucial to leave room for future accounts and account numbers when designing a chart of accounts.

Processing Transactions: Manual and Menu-Driven Accounting Systems

Recording transactions in an actual accounting system requires an additional step that we have skipped thus far. A business of any size *classifies transactions by type* for efficient handling. In an expanded manual system, credit sales, purchases on account, cash receipts, and cash payments are treated as four separate categories. Each category of transactions has its own special journal. (We discuss these journals in detail later in this chapter.) For example:

Payroll payments are another category of transactions and are recorded in the *payroll journal or payroll register,* which we discuss in detail in Chapter 11. Companies can create other special journals for categories of transactions that are important to their own operations or are specific to their industry. The special journals shown here tend to be used most often.

Transactions that do not fit any of the special journals, such as the adjusting and closing entries at the end of the period, are recorded in the *general journal*, which serves as the "journal of last resort."

Computerized systems are organized by function, or task. You can select a function, such as recording sales on account, from a menu. A **menu** is a list of options for choosing computer functions. In such a *menu-driven* system, you first access the main menu. You then choose from a submenu until you reach the function you want. Some accounting packages call these submenu items **modules**.

Posting in a computerized system can be performed continuously (**online processing** or **real-time processing**) or later for a group of similar transactions (**batch processing**). The posting then updates the account balances automatically. Outputs—accounting reports—are the final stage of data processing. In a computerized system, the financial statements can be printed automatically. Spreadsheets can be linked to accounting packages to help prepare more complex reports.

Exhibit 7–4 summarizes the accounting cycle in a computerized system and in a manual system. As you study the exhibit, compare and contrast the two types of systems.

KEY POINTS

You may think a computer skips steps when data are entered because the computer performs some of the steps internally. However, a computerized accounting system performs all the steps a manual system does, except for the worksheet. Even if you never keep a manual set of books, you still need to understand the entire accounting system.

EXHIBIT 7–4 | Comparison of the Accounting Cycle in a Computerized and a Manual System

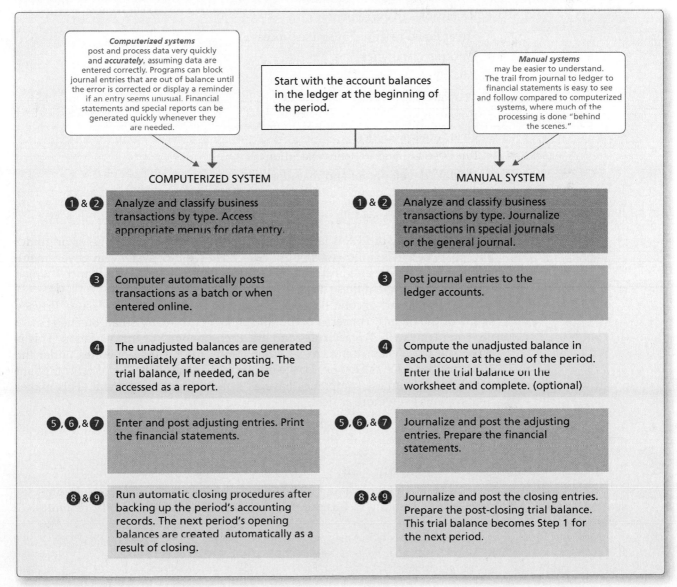

Enterprise Resource Planning

Many small and medium-sized businesses use accounting software such as QuickBooks or Sage 50. However, many large, global companies use **enterprise resource planning (ERP)** systems that feed accounting and other data into software for all company activities—from purchasing to production and customer service. These systems can be expensive to implement but can save money in the long run by integrating all of a company's data and systems.

The larger ERP systems, such as SAP, Sage ERP, Epicor, Oracle, and IQMS (there are many more), are popular for a number of reasons, including the wide range of functionality they offer. Some of the largest providers of ERP software also have financial packages developed specifically for certain industries; they spend a great deal of time discussing what specific industries require and then target those needs. For example, SAP provides the following and more with their ERP software:

- Accounting
- Financial management
- Treasury and financial risk management
- Travel management
- Talent management
- Service delivery
- Receivables management
- Streamlined essential business processes
- Workforce analytics
- Payroll
- Strategic workforce management
- E-recruiting
- Operations analytics
- Procurement and logistics execution
- Product development and manufacturing
- Sales and service
- Integrated modules

The popularity of ERP is largely driven by compliance requirements or guidelines that need to be followed. For this reason we see ERP systems in government, military, health care, and any other enterprises that deal with compliance—which is virtually all of them these days.

Of course, a part of compliance is the need to deal with privacy issues. Privacy is one of the biggest concerns corporations have, but many small businesses are not complaint with privacy rules and are often unaware of this violation. This is especially true when doing cross-border commerce. Canada operates under the same privacy rules as Europe, for the most part, but the US rules are *not* compliant with Canada's unless companies have a "safe harbour" agreement. This makes ERP systems even more critical.

> **Try It!**

3. Create a chart of accounts by matching the account name with the most appropriate account number. Assume the company lists its accounts in this order: assets, liabilities, owner's equity, revenues, expenses.

(Continued)

(Continued)

T. Pioneer, Capital	11001
Advertising Expense	12001
Building	17001
Accounts Payable	18001
Sales Revenue	21001
Miscellaneous Expenses	25001
Cash	30001
T. Pioneer, Withdrawals	31001
Land	41001
Notes Payable	51001
Accounts Receivable	54001
Salaries Expense	59001

4. Refer to the information in the previous question. Suppose you needed to add the accounts listed below to the chart of accounts. Specify the range of numbers available for each of the new accounts to be added to the chart of accounts. Assume expenses are listed alphabetically.

   Notes Receivable

   Automobile

   Supplies

   Supplies Expense

   Unearned Revenue

   Service Revenue

Solutions appear at the end of this chapter and on MyAccountingLab

SPECIAL JOURNALS

The journal entries illustrated so far have been made in the **general journal**. However, it is not efficient to record all transactions in the general journal, so we use special journals. A **special journal** is an accounting journal designed to record one specific type of transaction.

Exhibit 7–5 diagrams a typical accounting system for a merchandising business. The remainder of this chapter describes how this system works.

While companies can create as many special journals as they like, most transactions fall into one of five categories, so accountants use at least five different journals. This system saves time and money, as we will see. The payroll journal will be discussed later in the text in Chapter 11. The five types of transactions, the special journals used, and the posting abbreviations are as follows:

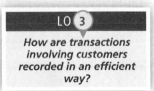

LO 3

How are transactions involving customers recorded in an efficient way?

KEY POINTS

Special journals are labour-saving devices: They are not mandatory, but they serve a useful purpose by summarizing similar transactions. However, a business need not use *any* special journals.

KEY POINTS

Transactions are recorded in either the general journal or a special journal, but not in both.

Transaction	Special Journal	Posting Abbreviation
1. Sale of merchandise on account	Sales journal	S
2. Cash receipt	Cash receipts journal	CR
3. Purchase on account	Purchases journal	P
4. Cash payment	Cash payments journal	CP
5. All others	General journal	G

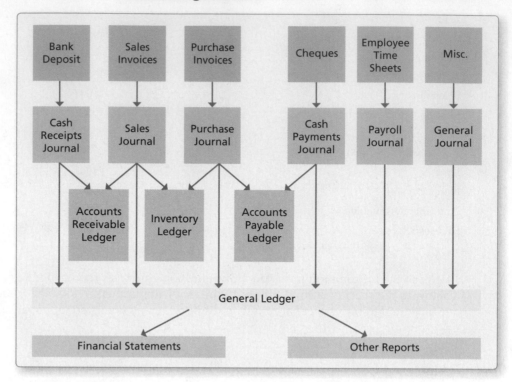

The Sales Journal

Most merchandisers sell inventory on account. These *credit sales* are recorded in the **sales journal**. Credit sales of assets other than inventory—for example, buildings—occur infrequently and may be recorded in the general journal.

Exhibit 7–6 illustrates a sales journal (Panel A) and the related posting to the ledgers (Panel B) of Slopes Ski Shop, a small ski shop we introduced in Chapter 5. Each entry in the Accounts Receivable Dr/Sales Revenue Cr column of the sales journal in Exhibit 7–6 is a debit (Dr) to Accounts Receivable and a credit (Cr) to Sales Revenue, as the heading above this column indicates. For each transaction, the accountant enters the following:

- Date
- Invoice number
- Customer name and number
- Transaction amount

This streamlined way of recording sales on account saves a vast amount of time that, in a manual system, would be spent entering account titles and dollar amounts in the general journal for every transaction.

In recording credit sales in the previous chapters, we did not record the names of credit-sale customers. In practice, the business must know the amount receivable from each customer. How else can the company identify who owes it money, when payment is due, and how much?

Consider the first transaction in Panel A. On November 2, 2017, Slopes Ski Shop sold ski equipment on account to Claudette Cabot for $935. The invoice number is 422. All this information appears on a single line in the sales journal. No explanation is necessary. The transaction's presence in the sales journal means that it is a credit sale, debited to Accounts Receivable—Claudette Cabot and credited to Sales Revenue. To gain any additional information about the transaction, we would look at the actual invoice.

KEY POINTS

Only credit sales of merchandise are recorded in the sales journal.

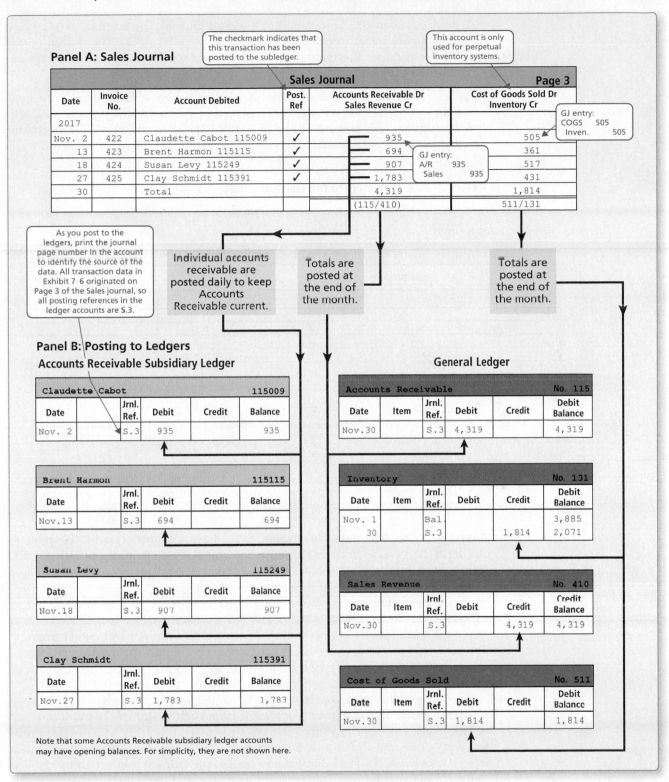

Recall from Chapter 5 that Slopes uses a *perpetual* inventory system. When recording the sale, Slopes also records the cost of goods sold and the decrease in inventory. The far-right column of the sales journal records the cost of goods sold and inventory amount—$505 for the goods sold to Claudette Cabot. If Slopes used a *periodic* inventory system, it would not record cost of goods sold or the decrease in inventory at the time of sale. The sales journal would need only one column to debit Accounts Receivable and to credit Sales Revenue for the amount of the sale.

Additional data can be recorded in the sales journal. For example, a company may add a column to record sale terms, such as 2/10, n/30. The design of the journal depends on the managers' needs for information. Special journals are flexible—they can be tailored to meet any special needs of a business.

Posting to the General Ledger   The only ledger we have used so far is the **general ledger**, which holds the accounts reported in the financial statements. We will soon introduce other ledgers. Exhibit 7–7 uses Panel A from Exhibit 7–6 to explain how the accounts are posted to the general ledger at the end of each month.

EXHIBIT 7–7 | Posting to the General Ledger

Panel A: Sales Journal

Sales Journal					Page 3
Date	Invoice No.	Account Debited	Post. Ref	Accounts Receivable Dr Sales Revenue Cr	Cost of Goods Sold Dr Inventory Cr
2017					
Nov. 2	422	Claudette Cabot 115009	✓	935	505
13	423	Brent Harmon 115115	✓	694	361
18	424	Susan Levy 115249	✓	907	517
27	425	Clay Schmidt 115391	✓	1,783	431
30		Total		4,319	1,814
				(115/410)	511/131

Showing these account numbers here indicates that $4,319 has been posted to these two accounts (Accounts Receivable and Sales Revenue) at the end of the month.

These account numbers indicate that $1,814 has been posted to the Cost of Good Sold and Inventory accounts at the end of the month.

KEY POINTS

The purpose of an Accounts Receivable subsidiary ledger account is to provide detail of a customer's account or history to facilitate billing and collection.

KEY POINTS

Posting to the subsidiary ledger and to the general ledger is *not* double posting since the subsidiary ledger is *not* part of the general ledger and will *not* appear on the trial balance. Posting to both is necessary to keep the two in balance.

Posting to the Accounts Receivable Subsidiary Ledger   The $4,319 debit to Accounts Receivable does not identify the amount receivable from any specific customer. A business may have many customers. For example, *SkiNews* has a customer account for each of its many subscribers.

Businesses must create an account for each customer in a subsidiary ledger called the accounts receivable subsidiary ledger. A **subsidiary ledger** is a book or file of the individual accounts that make up a total for a general ledger account. The customer accounts in the subsidiary ledger are usually arranged in alphabetical order, but they often have a customer number as well so that reports can be created by name or by customer number.

Amounts in the sales journal are posted to the subsidiary ledger *daily* to keep a current record of the amount receivable from each customer. The amounts are debits. Daily posting allows the business to answer customer inquiries promptly. Suppose Claudette Cabot telephones Slopes on November 11 to ask how much money she owes. The subsidiary ledger readily provides that information: $935 in Exhibit 7–6, Panel B:

Accounts Receivable Subsidiary Ledger					
Claudette Cabot					115009
Date		Jrnl. Ref.	Debit	Credit	Balance
Nov. 2		S.3	935		935

To simplify the process, when each transaction amount is posted to the subsidiary ledger in a manual system, a check mark or some other notation is printed in the posting reference column of the sales journal to indicate that the subsidiary ledger has been updated (see Exhibit 7–7). A general ledger account number would not be used here because it refers to the Accounts Receivable control account in the general ledger, which is the total of all the subsidiary ledger account balances.

Balancing the Ledgers The arrows in Exhibit 7–6 indicate the direction of the information. The arrows show the links between the individual customer accounts in the subsidiary ledger and the Accounts Receivable account. The Accounts Receivable debit balance in the general ledger should equal the sum of the individual customer balances in the subsidiary ledger, as follows. This is called balancing or **proving** the ledgers as shown below:

Accounts Receivable debit balance in the general ledger:	
Accounts Receivable	$4,319
Data from the Accounts Receivable Subsidiary Ledger	
SLOPES SKI SHOP	
Schedule of Accounts Receivable	
November 30, 2017	
115009 Claudette Cabot	$ 935
115115 Brent Harmon	694
115249 Susan Levy	907
115391 Clay Schmidt	1,783
Total accounts receivable	$4,319

Control account

After all postings, the balance in the control account should equal the sum of all the subsidiary accounts.

Lists the individual customer accounts and balances from the subsidiary ledger.

The Cash Receipts Journal

Cash transactions are common in most businesses because cash receipts from customers are vital to keep a business going. To record a large number of cash receipt transactions, accountants use the **cash receipts journal**.

Exhibit 7–8, Panel A, illustrates the cash receipts journal. The related posting to the ledgers is shown in Panel B. The exhibit illustrates November 2017 transactions for Slopes Ski Shop.

Every transaction recorded in this journal is a cash receipt, so the first column is for debits to the Cash account. The next column is for debits to Sales Discounts on collections from customers. In a typical merchandising business, the main sources of cash are collections on account and cash sales.

The cash receipts journal has credit columns for Accounts Receivable, Sales Revenue, and Other Accounts. The Other Accounts columns list sources of cash other than cash sales and collections on account and are also used to record the names and account numbers of customers from whom cash is received on account.

In Exhibit 7–8, cash sales occurred on November 6, 19, and 28. Observe the debits to Cash and the credits to Sales Revenue ($517, $853, and $1,802).

On November 25, Slopes collected $762 of interest revenue. The account credited, Interest Revenue, must be written in the Other Accounts column. The November 12 and 25 transactions illustrate a key fact about business. Different entities have different types of transactions, and they design their special journals to meet their particular needs for information. In this case, Slopes uses the Other Accounts Credit column as a catch-all to record all non-routine cash receipt transactions.

MyAccountingLab

MyAccountingLab has a DemoDoc that demonstrates posting using the cash receipts journal. The process is the same for other special journals.

KEY POINTS

Every entry in the cash receipts journal includes a debit to Cash. *Cash* sales are recorded here; *Credit* sales are recorded in the sales journal.

EXHIBIT 7-8 | Cash Receipts Journal (Panel A) and Posting to the Ledgers (Panel B) under the Perpetual Inventory System

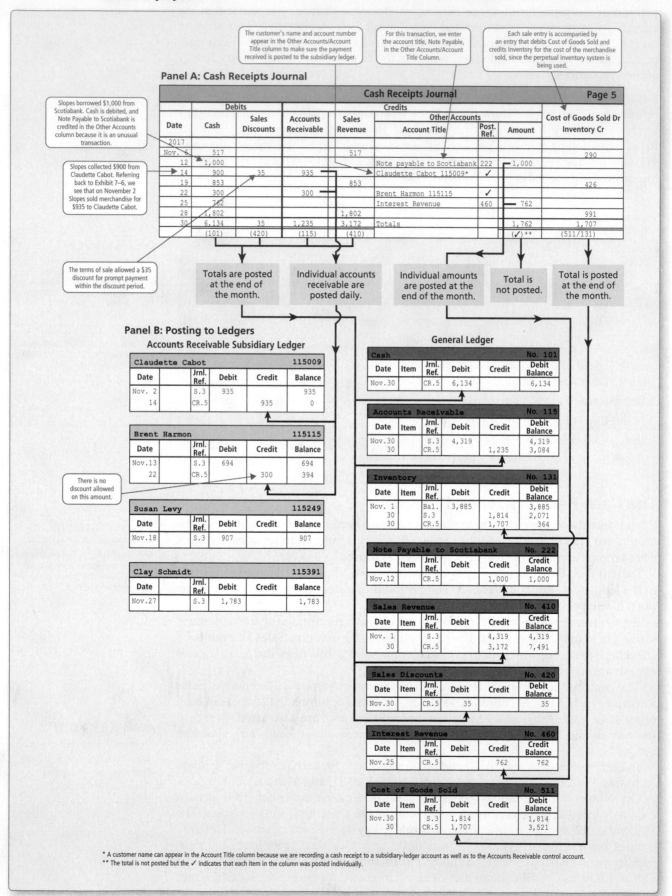

Panel A: Cash Receipts Journal

> The customer's name and account number appear in the Other Accounts/Account Title column to make sure the payment received is posted to the subsidiary ledger.

> For this transaction, we enter the account title, Note Payable, in the Other Accounts/Account Title Column.

> Each sale entry is accompanied by an entry that debits Cost of Goods Sold and credits Inventory for the cost of the merchandise sold, since the perpetual inventory system is being used.

> Slopes borrowed $1,000 from Scotiabank. Cash is debited, and Note Payable to Scotiabank is credited in the Other Accounts column because it is an unusual transaction.

> Slopes collected $900 from Claudette Cabot. Referring back to Exhibit 7-6, we see that on November 2 Slopes sold merchandise for $935 to Claudette Cabot.

> The terms of sale allowed a $35 discount for prompt payment within the discount period.

Cash Receipts Journal — Page 5

| | Debits | | | | Credits | | | Cost of Goods Sold Dr |
Date	Cash	Sales Discounts	Accounts Receivable	Sales Revenue	Other Accounts — Account Title	Post. Ref.	Amount	Inventory Cr
2017								
Nov. 6	517			517				290
12	1,000				Note payable to Scotiabank	222	1,000	
14	900	35	935		Claudette Cabot 115009*	✓		
19	853			853				426
22	300		300		Brent Harmon 115115	✓		
25	762				Interest Revenue	460	762	
28	1,802			1,802				991
30	6,134	35	1,235	3,172	Totals		1,762	1,707
	(101)	(420)	(115)	(410)		(✓)**		(511/131)

- Totals are posted at the end of the month.
- Individual accounts receivable are posted daily.
- Individual amounts are posted at the end of the month.
- Total is not posted.
- Total is posted at the end of the month.

Panel B: Posting to Ledgers

Accounts Receivable Subsidiary Ledger

Claudette Cabot — 115009

Date	Jrnl. Ref.	Debit	Credit	Balance
Nov. 2	S.3	935		935
14	CR.5		935	0

Brent Harmon — 115115

Date	Jrnl. Ref.	Debit	Credit	Balance
Nov. 13	S.3	694		694
22	CR.5		300	394

> There is no discount allowed on this amount.

Susan Levy — 115249

Date	Jrnl. Ref.	Debit	Credit	Balance
Nov. 18	S.3	907		907

Clay Schmidt — 115391

Date	Jrnl. Ref.	Debit	Credit	Balance
Nov. 27	S.3	1,783		1,783

General Ledger

Cash — No. 101

Date	Item	Jrnl. Ref.	Debit	Credit	Debit Balance
Nov. 30		CR.5	6,134		6,134

Accounts Receivable — No. 115

Date	Item	Jrnl. Ref.	Debit	Credit	Debit Balance
Nov. 30		S.3	4,319		4,319
30		CR.5		1,235	3,084

Inventory — No. 131

Date	Item	Jrnl. Ref.	Debit	Credit	Debit Balance
Nov. 1		Bal.	3,885		3,885
30		S.3		1,814	2,071
30		CR.5		1,707	364

Note Payable to Scotiabank — No. 222

Date	Item	Jrnl. Ref.	Debit	Credit	Credit Balance
Nov. 12		CR.5		1,000	1,000

Sales Revenue — No. 410

Date	Item	Jrnl. Ref.	Debit	Credit	Credit Balance
Nov. 1		S.3		4,319	4,319
30		CR.5		3,172	7,491

Sales Discounts — No. 420

Date	Item	Jrnl. Ref.	Debit	Credit	Debit Balance
Nov. 30		CR.5	35		35

Interest Revenue — No. 460

Date	Item	Jrnl. Ref.	Debit	Credit	Credit Balance
Nov. 25		CR.5		762	762

Cost of Goods Sold — No. 511

Date	Item	Jrnl. Ref.	Debit	Credit	Debit Balance
Nov. 30		S.3	1,814		1,814
30		CR.5	1,707		3,521

* A customer name can appear in the Account Title column because we are recording a cash receipt to a subsidiary-ledger account as well as to the Accounts Receivable control account.

** The total is not posted but the ✓ indicates that each item in the column was posted individually.

Total debits must equal total credits in the cash receipts journal. This equality holds for each transaction and for the monthly totals. For the month in Exhibit 7–8, total debits equal total credits, as shown:

Debit Columns		Credit Columns	
Cash	$6,134	Accounts Receivable	$1,235
Sales Discounts	35	Sales Revenue	3,172
*Cost of Goods Sold	1,707	Other Accounts	1,762
		*Inventory	1,707
Total	$7,876	Total	$7,876

*Only applies to the perpetual inventory system.

Posting to the General Ledger   The column totals are usually posted monthly. Trace the posting to Cash and the other accounts from the cash receipts journal to the general ledger In Exhibit 7–8.

The column total for Other Accounts is *not* posted. Instead, these credits are posted individually. In Exhibit 7–8, the November 12 transaction reads "Note Payable to Scotiabank." This account's number (222) in the Post. Ref. column indicates that the transaction amount was posted individually. The November 25 collection of interest revenue is also posted individually. These amounts can be posted to the general ledger at the end of the month, but their date in the ledger accounts should be their actual date in the journal to make it easy to trace each amount back to the cash receipts journal. The check mark (✓), instead of an account number, below the column total means that the column total was not posted because individual items above were posted.

Posting to the Subsidiary Ledger   Amounts from the cash receipts journal are posted to the accounts receivable subsidiary ledger *daily* to keep the individual balances up to date. The postings to the accounts receivable ledger are credits. For example, trace the $935 credit to Claudette Cabot's account. It reduces the balance in her account to zero. The $300 receipt from Brent Harmon reduces his accounts receivable balance to $394.

Balancing the Ledgers   After posting, the sum of the individual balances that remain in the accounts receivable subsidiary ledger equals the general ledger balance in Accounts Receivable.

SLOPES SKI SHOP Accounts Receivable Debit Balance in the General Ledger	
Accounts Receivable	$3,084

Subsidiary Ledger: Customer Accounts Receivable SLOPES SKI SHOP Schedule of Accounts Receivable November 30, 2017	
115115 Brent Harmon	$ 394
115249 Susan Levy	907
115391 Clay Schmidt	1,783
Total accounts receivable	$3,084

Slopes's list of account balances from the subsidiary ledger helps it follow up on slow-paying customers if it determines how long each customer's accounts receivable balance has been unpaid. (This is covered in Chapter 9.) Good accounts receivable records help a business manage its cash.

> Try It!

5. Refer to the Slopes Ski Shop information given in this chapter. Suppose you worked in the accounting department of the company. If Slopes did not use an accounts receivable subsidiary ledger and Claudette Cabot asked you for her account balance in the middle of the month, could you answer her?

6. Sidney Company experienced the following transactions during February 2017:

Feb.	2	Issued invoice no. 291 for a sale on account to Limpert Design Ltd., $400. Sidney's cost of this inventory was $240.
	3	Purchased inventory on credit terms of 1/10, n/30 from Dunning Co., $2,600. The invoice was dated February 3.
	4	Sold inventory for cash, $300 (cost, $204).
	5	Issued cheque no. 45 to Office Depot to purchase office furniture for cash, $1,400.
	8	Received payment on account, $200. The discount period had expired.
	10	Purchased inventory from Mega Corp. for cash, $1,300, issuing cheque no. 46.
	13	Received $400 cash from Limpert Design Ltd. in full settlement of its account receivable.
	13	Issued cheque no. 47 to pay Dunning Co. the net amount owed from February 3.
	14	Purchased supplies on account from Office Corp., $500. Payment is due in 30 days. The invoice was dated February 14.
	15	Sold inventory on account to Frankie's Diner, issuing invoice no. 292 for $800 (cost, $550).
	20	Purchased inventory on credit terms of net 30 from Super Sales Ltd., $1,600. The invoice was dated February 19.
	22	Issued cheque no. 48 to pay for insurance coverage, debiting Prepaid Insurance for $2,000.
	25	Issued cheque no. 49 to pay utilities, $450.
	28	Sold goods for $550 cash (cost, $325).

a. Which of these transactions would be recorded in the sales journal? Record those transactions in a sales journal using the format shown in Exhibit 7–6.

b. Which of these transactions would be recorded in the cash receipts journal? Record those transactions in a cash receipts journal using the format shown in Exhibit 7–8.

7. Identify the effect caused by each of the following transactions on the accounts receivable subsidiary ledger:

	Debit, Credit, or No Effect
a. Sale of merchandise on account	_____
b. Payment to supplier for goods	_____
c. Accrued rent owing at the end of the month	_____
d. Purchase of inventory on account	_____

Solutions appear at the end of this chapter and on MyAccountingLab

The Purchases Journal

A merchandising business like Slopes Ski Shop purchases inventory and supplies frequently. Such purchases are usually made on account. The **purchases journal** is designed to account for all purchases of inventory, supplies, and other assets *on account*. It can also be used to record expenses incurred *on account*. Cash purchases are normally paid by cheque and are recorded in the cash payments journal.

Exhibit 7–9 illustrates Slopes's purchases journal (Panel A) and posting to the ledgers (Panel B).[1] The purchases journal in Exhibit 7–9 has amount columns for

- Credits to Accounts Payable
- Debits to Inventory, Supplies, and Other Accounts

The Other Accounts columns record purchases of assets other than inventory and supplies. Each business designs its purchases journal to meet its own needs for information and efficiency. Accounts Payable is credited for all transactions recorded in the purchases journal.

On November 2, Slopes purchased ski poles inventory costing $700 from JVG Canada Inc. The supplier's name (JVG Canada Inc.) and account number are entered in the Supplier Account Credited column. The purchase terms of 3/15, n/30 are also entered in the Terms column to help identify the due date and the discount available. Accounts Payable is credited and Inventory is debited for the transaction amount. On November 19, a purchase of supplies on account is entered as a debit to Supplies and a credit to Accounts Payable.

Note the November 9 purchase of equipment from City Office Supply Co. The purchases journal contains no column for Equipment, so the Other Accounts debit column is used. Because this was a credit purchase, the accountant enters the supplier name (City Office Supply Co.) and account number in the Supplier Account Credited column and writes "Equipment" in the Other Accounts/Account Title column.

The total credits in the purchases journal ($2,876) must equal the total debits ($1,706 + $103 + $1,067 = $2,876).

Accounts Payable Subsidiary Ledger To pay debts on time, a company must know how much it owes to each supplier, the date of the invoice, and the payment terms. The Accounts Payable account in the general ledger shows only a single total for the amount owed on account. It does not indicate the amount owed to each supplier. Companies keep an accounts payable subsidiary ledger that is similar to the accounts receivable subsidiary ledger.

The accounts payable subsidiary ledger lists suppliers in alphabetical order, including account numbers if used, along with the amounts owed to them. Exhibit 7–9, Panel B, shows Slopes's accounts payable subsidiary ledger, which includes accounts for Audio Electronics Inc., City Office Supply Co., and others. After the daily and period-end postings are done, the total of the individual balances in the subsidiary ledger equals the balance in the Accounts Payable control account in the general ledger.

Posting from the Purchases Journal Posting from the purchases journal is similar to posting from the sales journal and the cash receipts journal. Exhibit 7–9, Panel B, illustrates the posting process.

Individual accounts payable in the purchases journal are posted daily to the *accounts payable subsidiary ledger*, and column totals and other amounts are usually posted to the *general ledger* at the end of the month. The column total for Other Accounts is not posted; each account's number in the Post. Ref. column indicates that the transaction amount was posted individually.

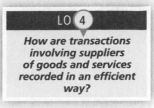

LO 4

How are transactions involving suppliers of goods and services recorded in an efficient way?

KEY POINTS

The source document for entries in the purchases journal is the supplier's (creditor's) invoice or bill.

REAL WORLD EXAMPLE

Companies design journals to meet their special needs. A repair service might not use a Supplies column but might need a Small Tools column for frequent purchases of tools.

---

[1] This is the only special journal that we illustrate with the credit column placed to the left and the debit columns to the right. This arrangement of columns focuses on Accounts Payable, which is credited for each entry to this journal, and on the individual supplier to be paid.

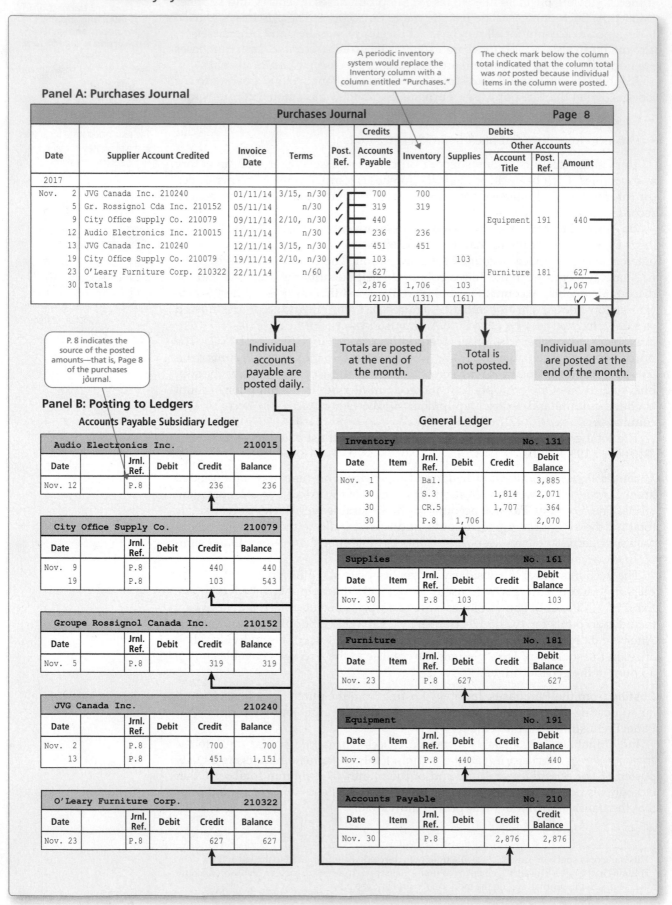

Panel A: Purchases Journal

A periodic inventory system would replace the Inventory column with a column entitled "Purchases."

The check mark below the column total indicated that the column total was *not* posted because individual items in the column were posted.

					Credits	Debits				
Purchases Journal										Page 8
Date	Supplier Account Credited	Invoice Date	Terms	Post. Ref.	Accounts Payable	Inventory	Supplies	Other Accounts		
								Account Title	Post. Ref.	Amount
2017										
Nov. 2	JVG Canada Inc. 210240	01/11/14	3/15, n/30	✓	700	700				
5	Gr. Rossignol Cda Inc. 210152	05/11/14	n/30	✓	319	319				
9	City Office Supply Co. 210079	09/11/14	2/10, n/30	✓	440			Equipment	191	440
12	Audio Electronics Inc. 210015	11/11/14	n/30	✓	236	236				
13	JVG Canada Inc. 210240	12/11/14	3/15, n/30	✓	451	451				
19	City Office Supply Co. 210079	19/11/14	2/10, n/30	✓	103		103			
23	O'Leary Furniture Corp. 210322	22/11/14	n/60	✓	627			Furniture	181	627
30	Totals				2,876	1,706	103			1,067
					(210)	(131)	(161)			(✓)

P. 8 indicates the source of the posted amounts—that is, Page 8 of the purchases journal.

Individual accounts payable are posted daily.

Totals are posted at the end of the month.

Total is not posted.

Individual amounts are posted at the end of the month.

Panel B: Posting to Ledgers

Accounts Payable Subsidiary Ledger

General Ledger

Audio Electronics Inc.				210015
Date	Jrnl. Ref.	Debit	Credit	Balance
Nov. 12	P.8		236	236

City Office Supply Co.				210079
Date	Jrnl. Ref.	Debit	Credit	Balance
Nov. 9	P.8		440	440
19	P.8		103	543

Groupe Rossignol Canada Inc.				210152
Date	Jrnl. Ref.	Debit	Credit	Balance
Nov. 5	P.8		319	319

JVG Canada Inc.				210240
Date	Jrnl. Ref.	Debit	Credit	Balance
Nov. 2	P.8		700	700
13	P.8		451	1,151

O'Leary Furniture Corp.				210322
Date	Jrnl. Ref.	Debit	Credit	Balance
Nov. 23	P.8		627	627

Inventory					No. 131
Date	Item	Jrnl. Ref.	Debit	Credit	Debit Balance
Nov. 1		Bal.			3,885
30		S.3		1,814	2,071
30		CR.5		1,707	364
30		P.8	1,706		2,070

Supplies					No. 161
Date	Item	Jrnl. Ref.	Debit	Credit	Debit Balance
Nov. 30		P.8	103		103

Furniture					No. 181
Date	Item	Jrnl. Ref.	Debit	Credit	Debit Balance
Nov. 23		P.8	627		627

Equipment					No. 191
Date	Item	Jrnl. Ref.	Debit	Credit	Debit Balance
Nov. 9		P.8	440		440

Accounts Payable					No. 210
Date	Item	Jrnl. Ref.	Debit	Credit	Credit Balance
Nov. 30		P.8		2,876	2,876

The accounts receivable and accounts payable subsidiary ledgers are two of the most common subsidiary ledgers, but they are not the only subsidiary ledgers. Companies can create subsidiary ledgers for any accounts they like. For example, many companies use an inventory control account and an inventory subsidiary ledger.

The Cash Payments Journal

Businesses make most cash payments by cheque for control purposes, and all payments by cheque are recorded in the **cash payments journal**. This special journal is also called the *cheque register* or the *cash disbursements journal*. Like the other special journals, it has multiple columns for recording cash payments that occur frequently.

Exhibit 7–10, Panel A, illustrates the cash payments journal, and Panel B shows the posting to the ledgers of Slopes Ski Shop. This cash payments journal has two debit columns—Other Accounts and Accounts Payable. It has two credit columns—one for purchase discounts, which are credited to the Inventory account in a perpetual inventory system, and one for Cash. This special journal also has columns for the date, cheque number, and payee of each cash payment.

All entries in the cash payments journal include a credit to Cash. Payments on account are debits to Accounts Payable. On November 15, Slopes paid JVG Canada Inc. on account, with credit terms of 3/15, n/30 (for details, see the first transaction in Exhibit 7–9). Therefore, Slopes took the 3 percent discount and paid $679 ($700 less the $21 discount). The discount is credited to the Inventory account.

The Other Accounts column is used to record debits to accounts for which no special column exists. For example, on November 3 Slopes paid rent expense of $1,200.

As with all the other journals, the total debits ($3,461 + $819 = $4,280) must equal the total credits ($21 + $4,259 = $4,280).

Posting from the Cash Payments Journal Posting from the cash payments journal is similar to posting from the cash receipts journal. Individual creditor amounts are posted daily. Column totals and Other Accounts are usually posted at the end of the month. Exhibit 7–10, Panel B, illustrates the posting process.

To review their accounts payable, companies list the individual supplier balances in the accounts payable subsidiary ledger. This is called balancing or proving the ledger:

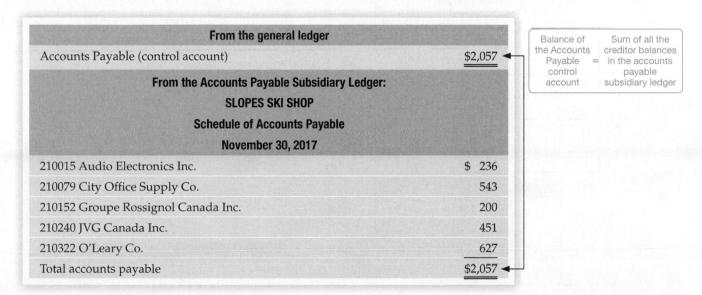

From the general ledger	
Accounts Payable (control account)	$2,057
From the Accounts Payable Subsidiary Ledger:	
SLOPES SKI SHOP	
Schedule of Accounts Payable	
November 30, 2017	
210015 Audio Electronics Inc.	$ 236
210079 City Office Supply Co.	543
210152 Groupe Rossignol Canada Inc.	200
210240 JVG Canada Inc.	451
210322 O'Leary Co.	627
Total accounts payable	$2,057

Balance of the Accounts Payable control account = Sum of all the creditor balances in the accounts payable subsidiary ledger

This total agrees with the Accounts Payable balance in Exhibit 7–10. Agreement of the two amounts indicates that the resulting account balances are correct.

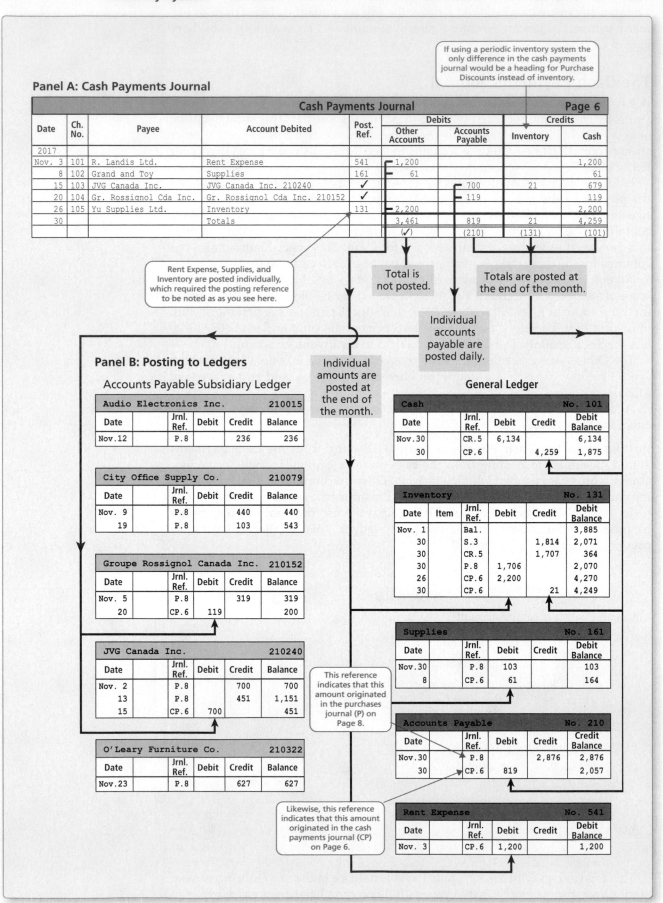

Panel A: Cash Payments Journal

If using a periodic inventory system the only difference in the cash payments journal would be a heading for Purchase Discounts instead of inventory.

Cash Payments Journal							Page 6
				Post. Ref.	Debits		Credits
Date	Ch. No.	Payee	Account Debited		Other Accounts	Accounts Payable	Inventory	Cash
2017								
Nov. 3	101	R. Landis Ltd.	Rent Expense	541	1,200			1,200
8	102	Grand and Toy	Supplies	161	61			61
15	103	JVG Canada Inc.	JVG Canada Inc. 210240	✓		700	21	679
20	104	Gr. Rossignol Cda Inc.	Gr. Rossignol Cda Inc. 210152	✓		119		119
26	105	Yu Supplies Ltd.	Inventory	131	2,200			2,200
30			Totals		3,461	819	21	4,259
					(✓)	(210)	(131)	(101)

Rent Expense, Supplies, and Inventory are posted individually, which required the posting reference to be noted as as you see here.

Total is not posted.

Totals are posted at the end of the month.

Individual accounts payable are posted daily.

Panel B: Posting to Ledgers

Individual amounts are posted at the end of the month.

Accounts Payable Subsidiary Ledger

General Ledger

Audio Electronics Inc.				210015
Date	Jrnl. Ref.	Debit	Credit	Balance
Nov.12	P.8		236	236

Cash				No. 101
Date	Jrnl. Ref.	Debit	Credit	Debit Balance
Nov.30	CR.5	6,134		6,134
30	CP.6		4,259	1,875

City Office Supply Co.				210079
Date	Jrnl. Ref.	Debit	Credit	Balance
Nov. 9	P.8		440	440
19	P.8		103	543

Inventory					No. 131
Date	Item	Jrnl. Ref.	Debit	Credit	Debit Balance
Nov. 1		Bal.			3,885
30		S.3		1,814	2,071
30		CR.5		1,707	364
30		P.8	1,706		2,070
26		CP.6	2,200		4,270
30		CP.6		21	4,249

Groupe Rossignol Canada Inc.				210152
Date	Jrnl. Ref.	Debit	Credit	Balance
Nov. 5	P.8		319	319
20	CP.6	119		200

Supplies				No. 161
Date	Jrnl. Ref.	Debit	Credit	Debit Balance
Nov.30	P.8	103		103
8	CP.6	61		164

JVG Canada Inc.				210240
Date	Jrnl. Ref.	Debit	Credit	Balance
Nov. 2	P.8		700	700
13	P.8		451	1,151
15	CP.6	700		451

This reference indicates that this amount originated in the purchases journal (P) on Page 8.

Accounts Payable				No. 210
Date	Jrnl. Ref.	Debit	Credit	Credit Balance
Nov.30	P.8		2,876	2,876
30	CP.6	819		2,057

O'Leary Furniture Co.				210322
Date	Jrnl. Ref.	Debit	Credit	Balance
Nov.23	P.8		627	627

Likewise, this reference indicates that this amount originated in the cash payments journal (CP) on Page 6.

Rent Expense				No. 541
Date	Jrnl. Ref.	Debit	Credit	Debit Balance
Nov. 3	CP.6	1,200		1,200

The payroll register is a special form of cash payments journal and is discussed in Chapter 11.

> Try It!

8. Refer to the Sidney Company transactions in Try It #6 on page 392. Which of those transactions would be recorded in the purchases journal? Record those transactions in a purchases journal using the format shown in Exhibit 7–9.

9. Refer to the Sidney Company transactions in Try It #6 on page 392. Which of those transactions would be recorded in the cash payments journal? Record those transactions in a cash payments journal using the format shown in Exhibit 7–10.

10. Identify the effect caused by each of the following transactions on the accounts payable subsidiary ledger.

	Debit, Credit, or No Effect
a. Purchase of merchandise on credit	_____
b. Sales of merchandise on credit	_____
c. Purchase of office supplies on credit	_____
d. Receipt of cash from credit customer	_____
e. Payment to supplier	_____

Solutions appear at the end of this chapter and on MyAccountingLab

THE ROLE OF THE GENERAL JOURNAL

Special journals save much time in recording repetitive transactions and posting to the ledgers. But some transactions do not fit into any of the special journals. Examples include merchandise returns and allowances or adjustments such as the amortization of buildings and equipment, the expiration of prepaid insurance, and the accrual of salary payable at the end of the period.

Even the most sophisticated accounting information system needs a general journal. The adjusting entries and the closing entries that we illustrated in Chapters 3 through 5 are recorded in the general journal, along with other non-routine transactions.

Let's turn now to sales returns and allowances and the related business document, the *credit memo*.

The Credit Memo—The Business Document for Recording Sales Returns and Allowances

As we saw in Chapter 5, customers sometimes return merchandise to the seller, and sellers grant sales allowances to customers because of product defects and for other reasons. The effect of sales returns and sales allowances is the same—they decrease net sales and accounts receivable in the same way sales discounts do. The document issued by the seller for a credit to the customer's account receivable is called a **credit memo**, because the company gives the customer credit for the returned merchandise. When a company issues a credit memo, it debits Sales Returns and Allowances and credits Accounts Receivable. If the returned merchandise is in good condition and can be resold in the future, the company also debits Inventory and credits Cost of Goods Sold for the *cost* of the merchandise.

On November 27, Slopes Ski Shop sold four high-end ski outfits from their Whistler location for $1,783 on account to Clay Schmidt. Later, Schmidt discovered

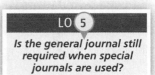

LO **5**

Is the general journal still required when special journals are used?

KEY POINTS

The *originator* of the credit memo is "crediting" Accounts Receivable. The *receiver* of the credit memo debits Accounts Payable.

that they were the wrong size and returned the outfits. Slopes then issued a credit memo to Schmidt like the one in Exhibit 7–11.

EXHIBIT 7–11 | Credit Memo

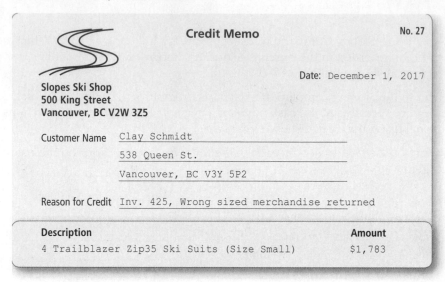

To record the *sale return* and receipt of the outfits from customer Clay Schmidt, Slopes would make the following entries in the general journal:

LEARNING TIPS

Two postings are needed for Accounts Receivable because the control account (115) and the customer account must both be updated. This is noted in the general journal with a posting reference like 115/✓.

General Journal				Page 9
Date 2017	**Accounts**	**Post Ref.**	**Debit**	**Credit**
Dec. 1	Sales Returns and Allowances	430	1,783	
	Accounts Receivable—Clay Schmidt 115391	115/✓		1,783
	Credit memo no. 27.			
Dec. 1	Inventory	131	431	
	Cost of Goods Sold	511		431
	Received wrong-sized goods from customer.			

Records Slopes' receipt of the inventory from the customer. The outfits cost Slopes $431, and Slopes, like all other merchandisers, records its inventory at cost.

Focus on the first entry. The debit side of the entry is posted to Sales Returns and Allowances. After posting, its account number (430) is written in the Posting Reference column. The credit side of the entry requires two $1,783 postings, one to Accounts Receivable, the *control account* in the general ledger (account number 115), and the other to Clay Schmidt's *individual account* in the accounts receivable subsidiary ledger, account number 115391. These credit postings explain why the document is called a *credit memo*.

A business with a high volume of sales returns, such as a department store chain, may use a special journal for sales returns and allowances.

The Debit Memo—The Business Document for Recording Purchase Returns and Allowances

Purchase returns occur when a business returns goods to the seller. The procedures for handling purchase returns are similar to those dealing with sales returns.

The purchaser gives the merchandise back to the seller and receives either a cash refund, a credit memo as in the case above, or replacement goods.

When a business returns merchandise to the seller, it may also send a business document known as a **debit memo**. This document states that the buyer no longer owes the seller for the amount of the returned purchases. The buyer debits the Accounts Payable account to the seller and credits Inventory for the cost of the goods returned to the seller.

Many businesses record their purchase returns in the general journal. Slopes would record its return of the ski outfits to JVG Canada Inc. as follows:

General Journal				Page 9
Date 2017	**Accounts**	**Post Ref.**	**Debit**	**Credit**
Dec. 2	Accounts Payable—JVG Canada Inc. 210240	210/✓	431	
	Inventory	131		431
	Debit memo no. 16.			

> When using a periodic inventory system, the Purchase Returns and Allowances account will be credited so that cost of goods sold can be calculated properly.

When using a perpetual inventory system, Inventory must be kept up to date for returns of goods to the seller. Therefore, Inventory is credited because the items are no longer on hand.

When you first learn about special journals, it may be confusing to remember which special journal to use for a transaction. Exhibit 7–12 summarizes a process you can follow to choose the special journal to use for a transaction.

EXHIBIT 7–12 | A Method of Choosing the Special Journal to Use for a Transaction

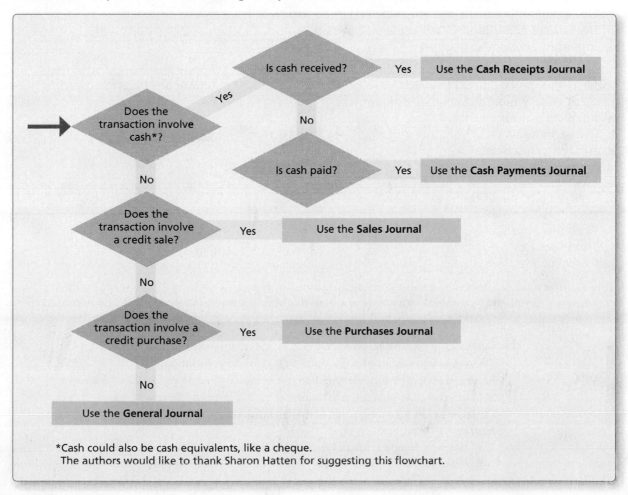

*Cash could also be cash equivalents, like a cheque.
The authors would like to thank Sharon Hatten for suggesting this flowchart.

Remember these four important points when recording transactions using special journals and subsidiary ledgers:

- Transactions are entered into one of the four special journals (or modules in a computerized system) or the general journal, but *not both*.

- Entries involving accounts receivable or accounts payable and inventory that are recorded in a special journal or the general journal must be posted to both the subsidiary ledger account and the related general ledger control account.

- At the end of the month or more often, a schedule of subsidiary ledger accounts must be reconciled or proved to the related control account in the general ledger to ensure the sum of all the amounts in the subsidiary ledger equals the balance in the control account.

- The trial balance and financial statements are created using the general ledger account balances at the end of the month or period. Using special journals does not affect this process.

> Try It!

11. In which journal would a business record each transaction?
    a. Six months' building rent paid in cash
    b. Sale of land for note receivable
    c. Bank lends a business cash
    d. Business purchases a personal computer for owner for cash
    e. Purchase of supplies on credit
    f. Accrue salary payable
    g. Closing of withdrawals account at the end of the year
    h. Investment of additional cash in the business
    i. Providing services on account
    j. Cash sale of office supplies, at cost, to another business

12. Indicate the special journal in which you would find the following column headings (the heading could appear in more than one special journal):
    a. Interest Revenue Cr
    b. Sales Discounts Dr
    c. Accounts Receivable Cr
    d. Supplies Dr
    e. Cash Dr
    f. Cost of Goods Sold Dr
    g. Accounts Payable Dr
    h. Accounts Payable Cr
    i. Purchases Dr
    j. Cash Cr

13. The Culinary Book Shop uses a sales journal, a purchases journal, a cash receipts journal, a cash payments journal, and a general journal. Journalize the May transactions that should be recorded in the general journal, assuming a perpetual inventory system.

May	1	Purchased merchandise on account for $6,500 from Woolley Inc., terms 2/10, n/30.
	8	The owner invested in a fridge worth $1,000 for demonstrations.
	15	Returned $500 of unsuitable merchandise to Woolley Inc. from the May 1 purchase.
	22	Sold merchandise on account to Ginko for $2,400, terms n/30; cost $1,200.
	30	Ginko returned $200 (cost $100) of merchandise sold on May 22; the merchandise was returned to inventory.
	31	The company bought raffle tickets from an employee and won $500.

Solutions appear at the end of this chapter and on MyAccountingLab

Objective of Financial Reporting

Quite simply, *accounting information systems* exist to make recording a company's transactions much simpler, more accurate, and timely. The accounting framework lists the characteristics of financial reports. One of those characteristics is reliability. If using an accounting information system allows a company to organize its transactions accurately, then the financial reports will be reliable. This in turn helps the company to achieve the objective of communicating useful information to users.

SUMMARY PROBLEM FOR YOUR REVIEW

Taylor Company, a furniture supplier, completed the following selected transactions during March 2017:

Key Fact: Merchandiser using a perpetual inventory system

Accounting Period: Month of March 2017

Mar.	1	Sold $1,300 of lighting to Jen Zrilladich, terms n/30, invoice 310 (cost, $850).
	3	Purchased inventory on credit terms of 1/10, n/60 from Lane Corp., $4,000.
	4	Received $1,000 from a cash sale to a customer (cost $638).
	6	Received $120 on account from Jim Bryant. The full invoice amount was $130, but Bryant paid within the discount period to earn the $10 discount.
	9	Received $2,160 on a note receivable from Lesley Cliff. This amount includes the $2,000 note receivable plus $160 of interest revenue.
	10	Purchased lighting from an artisan, $300, issuing cheque no. 401.
	15	Sold $2,500 of outdoor seating to Pajo's Restaurant, terms n/30, invoice 311 (cost, $1,700).
	15	Received $1,600 from a cash sale to a customer (cost, $1,044).
	24	Borrowed $4,400 by signing a note payable to Scotiabank.
	27	Received $2,400 on account from Lance Au. Payment was received after the discount period lapsed.
	29	Paid Lane Corp. for the purchase made on May 3, cheque no. 402.

The general ledger showed the following balances at February 28, 2017: Cash, $2,234; Accounts Receivable, $5,580; Note Receivable—Lesley Cliff, $2,000; Inventory, $3,638; Jim Taylor, Capital, $13,452. The accounts receivable subsidiary ledger at February 28 contained debit balances as follows: Lance Au, $3,680; Melinda Fultz, $1,770; Jim Bryant, $130.

Required

1. Record the transactions in the cash receipts journal (page 7), cash payments journal (page 5), sales journal (page 8), and purchases journal (page 4). Taylor Company uses a perpetual inventory system. Disregard GST and PST in this question.

2. Compute column totals at March 31, 2017, in all the special journals. Show that total debits equal total credits in each of the special journals.

3. Post to the general ledger, the accounts receivable subsidiary ledger, and the accounts payable subsidiary ledger. Use complete posting references, including the following account numbers: Cash, 11; Accounts Receivable, 12; Note Receivable—Lesley Cliff, 13; Inventory, 14; Accounts Payable, 20; Note Payable—Bank of Nova Scotia, 22; Jim Taylor, Capital, 30; Sales Revenue, 41; Sales Discounts, 42; Interest Revenue, 46; and Cost of Goods Sold, 51. Insert Bal. in the Posting Reference column (Jrnl. Ref.) for each February 28 account balance.

4. Create a schedule of accounts receivable to balance the accounts receivable subsidiary ledger with Accounts Receivable in the general ledger. Create a schedule of accounts payable to balance the accounts payable subsidiary ledger with Accounts Payable in the general ledger.

SOLUTION

Requirements 1 and 2

> Items recorded in the Other Accounts columns must be listed and posted individually.

> These accounts are used because the company is using a perpetual system.

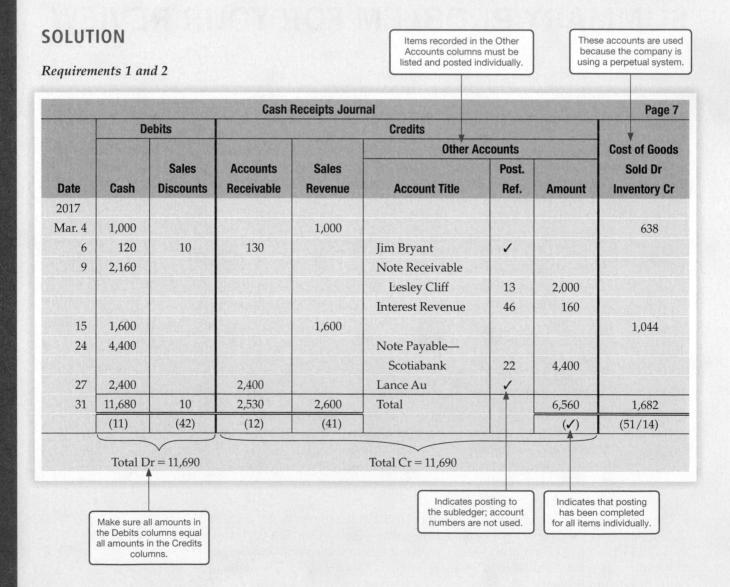

Cash Receipts Journal								Page 7
	Debits			**Credits**				
					Other Accounts			**Cost of Goods**
Date	**Cash**	**Sales Discounts**	**Accounts Receivable**	**Sales Revenue**	**Account Title**	**Post. Ref.**	**Amount**	**Sold Dr Inventory Cr**
2017								
Mar. 4	1,000			1,000				638
6	120	10	130		Jim Bryant	✓		
9	2,160				Note Receivable			
					Lesley Cliff	13	2,000	
					Interest Revenue	46	160	
15	1,600			1,600				1,044
24	4,400				Note Payable—			
					Scotiabank	22	4,400	
27	2,400		2,400		Lance Au	✓		
31	11,680	10	2,530	2,600	Total		6,560	1,682
	(11)	(42)	(12)	(41)			(✓)	(51/14)

Total Dr = 11,690

Total Cr = 11,690

> Make sure all amounts in the Debits columns equal all amounts in the Credits columns.

> Indicates posting to the subledger; account numbers are not used.

> Indicates that posting has been completed for all items individually.

Selected transactions are explained more fully:

Mar. 4 and 15: For each of these sales transactions, the cost of goods sold and inventory reduction are also recorded.

Mar. 6: The debit columns include the $120 cash received (invoice amount less the discount) and the $10 discount. Accounts Receivable is credited for $130, and Jim Bryant is entered in the Other Accounts/Account Title column so that his accounts receivable subsidiary ledger account balance is reduced by $130.

Mar. 9: This is an example of a compound entry with infrequently used accounts. Therefore, the Note Receivable— Lesley Cliff and Interest Revenue accounts are listed in the Other Accounts columns.

> Note that the Inventory column under the Credits heading is used to record the reduction in inventory when cash discounts are taken. This is different from the March 10 purchase of inventory for cash, which is recorded in the Other Accounts column and posted separately.

Cash Payments Journal — Page 5

Date	Chq. No.	Accounts Debited	Post. Ref.	Debits — Other Accounts	Debits — Accounts Payable	Credits — Inventory	Credits — Cash
2017							
Mar. 10	401	Inventory	14	300			300
29	402	Lane Corp.	✓		4,000		4,000
31				300	4,000		4,300
				✓	(20)		(11)

Total Dr = $4,300   Total Cr = $4,300

> Recall that Taylor Company uses the perpetual inventory system. As a result, record the cost of the goods sold and the inventory reduction for each sale transaction. Taylor's sales journal has a column at the far right for this purpose.

Sales Journal — Page 8

Date	Invoice No.	Accounts Debited	Post. Ref.	Account Receivable Dr	Sales Revenue Cr	Cost of Goods Sold Dr Inventory Cr
2017						
Mar. 1	310	J. Zrilladich	✓	1,300	1,300	850
15	311	Pajo's Restaurant	✓	2,500	2,500	1,700
31				3,800	3,800	2,550
				(12)	(41)	(51/14)

Total Dr = $3,800   Total Cr = $3,800

> For each transaction, make sure all amounts in the Debits columns equal all amounts in the Credits columns.

Purchases Journal — Page 4

Date	Account Credited	Invoice Date	Terms	Post. Ref.	Credits — Accounts Payable	Debits — Inventory	Debits — Other Accounts — Account Title	Debits — Other Accounts — Post. Ref.	Debits — Other Accounts — Amount
2017									
Mar. 3	Lane Corp.	03/03/14	1/10, n/60	✓	4,000	4,000			
31					4,000	4,000			
					(20)	(14)			

Total Cr = $4,000   Total Dr = $4,000

Requirement 3

Accounts Receivable Subsidiary Ledger

Lance Au

Date 2017	Item	Jrnl. Ref.	Debit	Credit	Balance
Feb. 28		Bal.			3,680
Mar. 27		CR. 7		2,400	1,280

Jim Bryant

Date 2017	Item	Jrnl. Ref.	Debit	Credit	Balance
Feb. 28		Bal.			130
Mar. 6		CR. 7		130	0

Melinda Fultz

Date 2017	Item	Jrnl. Ref.	Debit	Credit	Balance
Feb. 28		Bal.			1,770

Pajo's Restaurant

Date 2017	Item	Jrnl. Ref.	Debit	Credit	Balance
Mar. 15		S. 8	2,500		2,500

Jen Zrilladich

Date 2017	Item	Jrnl. Ref.	Debit	Credit	Balance
Mar. 1		S. 8	1,300		1,300

Accounts Payable Subsidiary Ledger

Lane Corp.

Date 2017	Item	Jrnl. Ref.	Debit	Credit	Credit Balance
Mar. 3		P. 4		4,000	4,000
Mar. 29		CP. 5	4,000		0

Recall that subsidiary ledger postings occur on the date of the transaction. General ledger postings occur at the end of the month. Both types of posting use a journal reference to indicate which journal was the source of the entry.

General Ledger

Cash — No. 11

Date 2017	Item	Jrnl. Ref.	Debit	Credit	Debit Balance
Feb. 28		Bal.			2,234
Mar. 31		CR. 7	11,680		13,914
31		CP. 5		4,300	9,614

Note Payable — Scotiabank — No. 22

Date 2017	Item	Jrnl. Ref.	Debit	Credit	Credit Balance
Mar. 24		CR. 7		4,400	4,400

Accounts Receivable — No. 12

Date 2017	Item	Jrnl. Ref.	Debit	Credit	Debit Balance
Feb. 28		Bal.			5,580
Mar. 31		CR. 7		2,530	3,050
31		S. 8	3,800		6,850

Jim Taylor, Capital — No. 30

Date 2017	Item	Jrnl. Ref.	Debit	Credit	Credit Balance
Feb. 28		Bal.			13,452

Note Receivable—Lesley Cliff — No. 13

Date 2017	Item	Jrnl. Ref.	Debit	Credit	Debit Balance
Feb. 28		Bal.			2,000
Mar. 9		CR. 7		2,000	0

Sales Revenue — No. 41

Date 2017	Item	Jrnl. Ref.	Debit	Credit	Credit Balance
Mar. 31		CR. 7		2,600	2,600
31		S. 8		3,800	6,400

Inventory — No. 14

Date 2017	Item	Jrnl. Ref.	Debit	Credit	Debit Balance
Feb. 28		Bal.			3,638
Mar. 10		CP. 5	300		3,938
31		CR. 7		1,682	2,256
31		S. 8		2,550	(294)
31		P. 4	4,000		3,706

Sales Discounts — No. 42

Date 2017	Item	Jrnl. Ref.	Debit	Credit	Debit Balance
Mar. 31		CR. 7	10		10

Interest Revenue — No. 46

Date 2017	Item	Jrnl. Ref.	Debit	Credit	Credit Balance
Mar. 9		CR. 7		160	160

Accounts Payable — No. 20

Date 2017	Item	Jrnl. Ref.	Debit	Credit	Credit Balance
Mar. 31		P. 4		4,000	4,000
31		CP. 5	4,000		0

Cost of Goods Sold — No. 51

Date 2017	Item	Jrnl. Ref.	Debit	Credit	Debit Balance
Mar. 31		CR. 7	1,682		1,682
31		S. 8	2,550		4,232

Requirement 4

<table>
<tr><th colspan="2">From the general ledger:</th></tr>
<tr><td>Accounts Receivable</td><td>$6,850</td></tr>
<tr><td colspan="2" align="center">From the accounts receivable subsidiary ledger:
TAYLOR COMPANY
Schedule of Accounts Receivable
March 31, 2017</td></tr>
<tr><td>Lance Au</td><td>$1,280</td></tr>
<tr><td>Melinda Fultz</td><td>1,770</td></tr>
<tr><td>Pajo's Restaurant</td><td>2,500</td></tr>
<tr><td>Jen Zrilladich</td><td>1,300</td></tr>
<tr><td>Total accounts receivable</td><td>$6,850</td></tr>
</table>

At month end, customer account balances from the accounts receivable subsidiary ledger are listed and compared to the general ledger control account.

At March 31, 2017, the Accounts Payable balance in the general ledger is nil. All accounts in the accounts payable subsidiary ledger are nil, so both the control account and subsidiary ledger are in balance.

Note: If Taylor Company had used the periodic inventory system, account No. 51, Cost of Goods Sold, would not exist, so there would be no Cost of Goods Sold column in the cash receipts journal. As well, there would be no $1,682 credit posting to Inventory originating from the cash receipts journal. The same is true for the Cost of Goods Sold and Inventory columns in the sales journal.

SUMMARY

LEARNING OBJECTIVE **1** Describe an effective accounting information system

What is an effective accounting system?   Pg. 378

An effective accounting information system captures and summarizes transactions to provide timely, accurate information to users and decision makers. The five major features are as follows:

- Control over operations
- Compatibility with the particular features of the business
- Flexibility in response to changes In the business
- Reports that meet users' needs
- A favourable cost–benefit relationship, with benefits outweighing costs

LEARNING OBJECTIVE **2** Understand the elements of computerized and manual accounting systems

How do accounting systems work?   Pg. 380

- Computerized systems process inputs faster than manual systems do and can generate more types of reports. However, the knowledge of a manual system enables the user to understand how the data are processed in any system.
- Account numbers play a bigger role in the operation of computerized systems than they do in manual systems because computers classify accounts by account numbers. Both computerized and manual accounting systems require transactions to be classified by type.
- Computerized systems use a menu structure to organize accounting functions.
- The computerized accounting system can be designed so that data are entered and the computer does the rest: posting, trial balances, financial statements, and closing procedures.
- Computerized accounting systems are integrated so that the different modules of the system are updated automatically.
- Computers cannot fix data entry errors, but accounting programs can reduce the chance of data errors by highlighting unbalanced or unusual journal entries.
- At the end of the period, general ledger account balances are listed on a trial balance to ensure total debits equal total credits.

How are transactions involving customers recorded in an efficient way?   Pg. 385
- Many accounting systems use special journals to record transactions by category.
- Credit sales are recorded in a sales journal, and cash receipts in a cash receipts journal.
- Posting from these journals is to both the general ledger and to the accounts receivable subsidiary ledger, which lists each customer and the amount receivable from that customer.
- The accounts receivable subsidiary ledger is the main device for ensuring that the company collects from customers.
- Accounts receivable subsidiary ledger customer account balances are totalled and compared or proved to the Accounts Receivable control account in the general ledger.

How are transactions involving suppliers of goods and services recorded in an efficient way?   Pg. 393
- Credit purchases are recorded in a purchases journal, and cash payments in a cash payments journal.
- Posting from these journals is to both the general ledger and the accounts payable subsidiary ledger.
- The accounts payable subsidiary ledger helps the company stay current in payments to suppliers and take advantage of purchase discounts.
- Accounts payable subsidiary ledger supplier account balances are totalled and compared or proved to the Accounts Payable control account in the general ledger.

Is the general journal still required when special journals are used?   Pg. 397
- Transactions that do not fit into any of the special journals are recorded in the general journal. Examples include sales returns and allowances, year-end adjusting entries for amortization, accruals, deferrals, and prepaids, as well as the period-end closing entries.
- A credit memo is the document used for recording sales returns and allowances.
- A debit memo is the document used for recording purchase returns and allowances.
- Most returns are recorded in the general journal and posted individually to the respective accounts. If a company has many returns, it may establish a special journal for this purpose.

Check **Accounting Vocabulary** for all key terms used in Chapter 7 and the **Glossary** at the back of the book for all key terms used in the textbook.

MORE CHAPTER REVIEW MATERIAL

MyAccountingLab

DemoDec covering Using the Cash Receipts Journal

Student PowerPoint Slides

Audio Chapter Summary

Note: All MyAccountingLab resources can be found in the Chapter Resources section and the Multimedia Library.

ACCOUNTING VOCABULARY

Accounting information system (AIS)   The combination of personnel, records, and procedures that a business uses to meet its need for financial data (*p. 378*).

Batch processing   Computerized accounting for similar transactions in a group or batch (*p. 383*).

Cash payments journal   A special journal used to record cash payments made by cheque (*p. 395*).

Cash receipts journal   A special journal used to record all types of cash receipts (*p. 389*).

Cloud computing   A subscription-based service where an external company provides software, processing capability,

and data storage that the customer accesses using the Internet. Customers gain the software capabilities without investing in the hardware and software themselves (*p. 379*).

Control account   An account whose balance equals the sum of the balances in a group of related accounts in a subsidiary ledger (*p. 379*).

Credit memo   The document issued by a seller for a credit to a customer's account receivable (*p. 397*).

Database   A computerized storehouse of information that can be systematically assessed in a variety of report forms (*p. 380*).

Debit memo The document issued by a buyer to reduce the buyer's account payable to a seller *(p. 399)*.

Enterprise resource planning (ERP) A computer system that integrates all company data into a single data warehouse *(p. 384)*.

General journal The journal used to record all transactions that do not fit into one of the special journals *(p. 385)*.

General ledger Ledger of accounts that are reported in the financial statements *(p. 388)*.

Hardware Electronic equipment that includes computers, disk drives, monitors, printers, and the network that connects them *(p. 379)*.

Menu A list of options for choosing computer functions *(p. 383)*.

Module Separate compatible units of an accounting package that are integrated to function together *(p. 383)*.

Network The system of electronic linkages that allow different computers to share the same information *(p. 379)*.

Online processing Computerized processing of related functions, such as the recording and posting of transactions, on a continuous basis *(p. 383)*.

Proving The process of ensuring the balance in the general ledger equals the sum of the individual balances in the subsidiary ledgers *(p. 389)*.

Purchases journal A special journal used to record all purchases of inventory, supplies, and other assets on account *(p. 393)*.

Real-time processing Computerized processing of related functions, such as the recording and posting of transactions, on a continuous basis. Also called *online processing (p. 383)*.

Sales journal A special journal used to record credit sales *(p. 386)*.

Server The main computer in a network where the program and data are stored *(p. 379)*.

Software A set of programs or instructions that cause the computer to perform the desired work *(p. 379)*.

Special journal An accounting journal designed to record one specific type of transaction *(p. 385)*.

Subsidiary ledger The book of accounts that provides supporting details on individual balances, the total of which appears in a general ledger account *(p. 388)*.

SIMILAR ACCOUNTING TERMS

Accounts payable subsidiary ledger	Accounts payable ledger, accounts payable subledger
Accounts receivable subsidiary ledger	Accounts receivable ledger, accounts receivable subledger
Balancing the ledgers	Proving the ledgers, reconciling the ledgers, reconciling receivables and payables
Cash payments journal	Cash disbursements journal, cheque register
CP	Cash payments journal
CR	Cash receipts journal
Credit memo	Credit memorandum
Debit memo	Debit memorandum
ERP	Enterprise resource planning
Online processing	Real-time processing
P	Purchases journal
Prove	Proving
S	Sales journal
Subsidiary ledger	Subledger

SELF-STUDY QUESTIONS

Test your understanding of the chapter by marking the correct answer for each of the following questions:

1. Why does a jewellery store need an accounting system that is different from what a physician uses? *(p. 378)*
   a. They have different kinds of employees.
   b. They have different kinds of journals and ledgers.
   c. They have different kinds of business transactions.
   d. They work different hours.

2. Which feature of an effective information system is most concerned with safeguarding assets? *(p. 378)*
   a. Control
   b. Flexibility
   c. Compatibility
   d. Reports that meet users' needs
   e. Favourable cost–benefit relationship

3. The account number 211031 most likely refers to (*pp. 381–382*)
   a. Liabilities
   b. Current liabilities
   c. Accounts payable
   d. An individual supplier

4. A company uses a sales journal, a purchases journal, a cash receipts journal, a cash payments journal, and a general journal. A sales return for credit would be recorded in the (*p. 382*)
   a. Sales journal
   b. General journal
   c. Sales return and allowances journal
   d. Cash payments journal
   e. Accounts payable subsidiary ledger

5. Special journals help most by (*p. 385*)
   a. Limiting the number of transactions that have to be recorded
   b. Reducing the cost of operating the accounting system
   c. Improving accuracy in posting to subsidiary ledgers
   d. Easing the preparation of the financial statements

6. Centex Sound Systems purchased inventory costing $8,000 from Sony on account. Where should Centex record this transaction, and what account is credited? (*p. 393*)
   a. Cash payments journal; credit Cash
   b. Sales journal; credit Sales Revenue
   c. Purchases journal; credit Accounts Payable
   d. General journal; credit Inventory

7. Every transaction recorded in the cash receipts journal includes a (*p. 389*)
   a. Credit to Cash
   b. Debit to Accounts Receivable
   c. Debit to Sales Discounts
   d. Debit to Cash

8. Entries in the purchases journal are posted to the (*p. 393*)
   a. General ledger only
   b. General ledger and the accounts payable subsidiary ledger
   c. General ledger and the accounts receivable subsidiary ledger
   d. Accounts receivable subsidiary ledger and the accounts payable subsidiary ledger

9. Every transaction recorded in the cash payments journal includes a (*p. 395*)
   a. Debit to Accounts Payable
   b. Debit to an Other Account
   c. Credit to Inventory
   d. Credit to Cash

10. The individual accounts in the accounts receivable subsidiary ledger identify (*p. 388*)
    a. Payees
    b. Debtors
    c. Amounts to be paid
    d. Suppliers

ASSIGNMENT MATERIAL

QUESTIONS

1. Describe the five criteria of an effective accounting system and give an example of each.

2. Distinguish batch computer processing from online computer processing.

3. What accounting categories correspond to the account numbers 1, 2, 3, 4, and 5 in the chart of accounts in a typical computerized accounting system?

4. Describe the benefits of a computerized accounting system versus a manual accounting system.

5. Why might the number 112 be assigned to Accounts Receivable and the number 1120708 to Carl Erickson, a customer?

6. Describe the function of menus in a computerized accounting system.

7. Name four special journals used in accounting systems. For what type of transaction is each designed?

8. Describe the two advantages that special journals have over recording all transactions in the general journal.

9. What is a control account, and how is it related to a subsidiary ledger? Name two common control accounts.

10. Graff Company's sales journal has amount columns headed Accounts Receivable Dr and Sales Revenue Cr. In this journal, 86 transactions are recorded. How many posting references or (✓) appear in the journal? State what each posting reference represents.

11. The accountant for Bannister Co. posted all amounts correctly from the cash receipts journal to the general ledger. However, she failed to post three credits to customer accounts in the accounts receivable subsidiary ledger. How would this error be detected?

12. At what two times is posting done from a special journal? What items are posted at each time?

13. What is the purpose of balancing, proving, or reconciling the ledgers?

14. Posting from the journals of McKedrick Realty is complete. But the total of the individual balances in the accounts payable subsidiary ledger does not equal the balance in the Accounts Payable control account in the general ledger. Does this necessarily indicate that the trial balance is out of balance? Explain.

15. Assume that posting is completed. The trial balance shows no errors, but the sum of the individual accounts payable does not equal the Accounts Payable control balance in the general ledger. What two errors could cause this problem?

MyAccountingLab   Make the grade with MyAccountingLab: The Starters, Exercises, and Problems marked in red can be found on MyAccountingLab. You can practise them as often as you want, and most feature step-by-step guided instructions to help you find the right answer.

STARTERS

Starter 7–1   Suppose you have invested your life savings in a company that prints rubberized logos on T-shirts. The business is growing fast, and you need a better accounting information system. Consider the features of an effective system, as discussed on pages 378–379. Which do you regard as most important? Why? Which feature must you consider if your financial resources are limited?

Features of an effective information system

Starter 7–2   Match each component of a computerized accounting information system with an example. Components may be used more than once.

Defining components of an accounting information system

Example	Component
1. Server	A. Source documents and input devices
2. Bank cheques	B. Processing and storage
3. Reports	C. Outputs
4. Keyboard	
5. Software	
6. Financial statements	
7. Bar code scanner	

Starter 7–3   Identify each of the following items as an element of a computerized accounting system (c), a manual accounting system (m), or both (b).

Identifying the elements of computerized and manual accounting systems

1. The trial balance transferred to or entered on the worksheet
2. Automatic posting to the general ledger
3. The use of UPC codes for inventory
4. Printing financial statements
5. Closing the accounts by debiting Income Summary and crediting expenses
6. Starting the cycle with account balances in the general ledger

Starter 7–4 Complete the crossword puzzle.

Across:

2. Electronic linkage that allows different computers to share the same information

3. Main computer in a networked system

7. Cost–_____ relationship must be favourable

Down:

1. Managers need _____ over operations to authorize transactions and safeguard assets

3. Programs that drive a computer

4. Electronic computer equipment

5. A _____ ible information system accommodates changes as the organization evolves

6. The opposite of debits

Starter 7–5 Indicate whether the items described below are inputs (I), outputs (O), or neither input nor output (N) of a computerized or manual accounting system.

1. Bank statement _____

2. Sales invoice _____

3. Cheque from customer _____

4. Cheque payable to supplier _____

5. Bank deposit slip _____

6. Inventory printout _____

7. Balance sheet _____

8. Debit memo from supplier _____

9. Post-closing trial balance _____

10. Unadjusted trial balance _____

11. Auditor's report _____

Starter 7–6 From the list below, identify the headings and the account names of LP Gas Co. Assign an account number to each account.

Assets   LP, Capital

Current Assets   LP, Withdrawals

Inventory   Revenues

Accounts Payable   Selling Expenses

Numbers from which to choose:

151	301
191	311
201	411
281	531

Starter 7–7 Given the following unidentified journal, write an explanation for each transaction.

	Debits				Credits			
Date	Cash	Sales Dis.	Acc. Rec.	Sales Rev.	Other Acct.	Amount	COGS Dr Inv. Cr
Aug. 8	3,000			3,000			1,250
10	2,500				Ruff, Capital	2,500	
15	340		340		Lucille Adams		
27	490	10	500		Marshall Field		
31	6,330	10	840	3,000	Totals	2,500	1,250

Starter 7–8 Use the sales journal and the related ledger accounts in Exhibit 7–6, page 387, to answer these questions about Slopes Ski Shop.

1. How much inventory did Slopes have on hand at the end of November? Where can you get this information?
2. What amount did Slopes post to the Sales Revenue account? When did Slopes post to the Sales Revenue account? Assume a manual accounting system.
3. After these transactions, how much does Susan Levy owe Slopes? Where did you obtain this information? Be specific.
4. If there were no discounts, how much would Slopes hope to collect from all its customers? Where is this amount stored in a single figure?

Using the sales journal and the related ledgers
(3)

Starter 7–9

1. A business that sells on account must have good accounts receivable records to ensure collection from customers. What is the name of the detailed record of amounts collectible from individual customers?
2. Where does the total amount receivable from all the customers appear? Be specific.
3. A key control feature of Slopes Ski Shop's accounting system lies in the agreement between the detailed customer receivable records and the summary total in the general ledger. Use the data in Exhibit 7–6, page 387, to reconcile Slopes's accounts receivable records at November 30, 2017.

Using accounts receivable records and balancing the ledgers
(3)

Starter 7–10 The cash receipts journal of Slopes Ski Shop appears in Exhibit 7–8, page 390, along with the company's various ledger accounts. Use the data in Exhibit 7–8 to answer the following questions raised by Steve Austin, owner of the business.

1. How much were total cash receipts during November?
2. How much cash did Slopes collect on account from customers? How much in total discounts did customers earn by paying quickly? How much did Slopes's accounts receivable decrease because of collections from customers during November?
3. How much were cash sales during November?
4. How much did Slopes borrow during November? Where else could you look to determine whether Slopes has paid off part of the loan?

Using cash receipts data
(3)

Starter 7–11 Use Slopes Ski Shop's purchases journal (Exhibit 7–9, page 394) to address these questions that Steve Austin, the owner of the business, is faced with.

1. How much were Slopes's total purchases of inventory during November?
2. Suppose it is December 1 and Slopes wishes to pay the full amount that Slopes owes on account. Examine only the purchases journal. Then make a general journal entry to record payment of the correct amount on December 1. Include an explanation. What other entry would have to be made to keep the ledgers in balance?

Using the purchases journal
(4)

Using the purchases journal and
the cash payments journal
④

1. Increase in accounts payable,
$2,876

Starter 7–12 Refer to Slopes Ski Shop's purchases journal (Exhibit 7–9, page 394) and cash payments journal (Exhibit 7–10, page 396). Steve Austin, the owner, has raised the following questions about the business.

1. By how much did total credit purchases of inventory, supplies, equipment, and furniture increase Slopes's accounts payable during November?
2. How much of the accounts payable balance did Slopes pay off during November?
3. At November 30, after all purchases and all cash payments, how much does Slopes owe JVG Canada Inc.? How much in total does Slopes owe on account?

Using all the journals
③ ④

2. Net sales revenue, $7,456

Starter 7–13 Answer the following questions about the November transactions of Slopes Ski Shop. You will need to refer to Exhibits 7–6 through 7–10, which begin on page 387.

1. How much cash does Slopes have on hand at November 30?
2. Determine Slopes's gross sales revenue and net sales revenue for November.
3. How did Slopes purchase furniture—for cash or on account? Indicate the basis for your answer.
4. From whom did Slopes purchase supplies on account? How much in total does Slopes owe this company on November 30?

Using the journals
③ ④ ⑤

Starter 7–14 Use the following abbreviations to indicate the journal in which you would record transactions a through o:

G = General journal   P = Purchases journal

S = Sales journal   CP = Cash payments journal

CR = Cash receipts journal

Transactions:

a. _____ Cash sale of inventory
b. _____ Payment of rent
c. _____ Amortization of computer equipment
d. _____ Purchases of inventory on account
e. _____ Collection of accounts receivable
f. _____ Expiration of prepaid insurance
g. _____ Sale on account
h. _____ Payment on account
i. _____ Cash purchase of inventory
j. _____ Collection of dividend revenue earned on an investment
k. _____ Prepayment of insurance
l. _____ Borrowing money on a long-term note payable
m. _____ Purchase of equipment on account
n. _____ Cost of goods sold along with a credit sale
o. _____ Return of merchandise

Identifying journals
③ ④ ⑤

Starter 7–15 Identify all the journals in which the following accounts would be debited or credited. Use P for purchases journal, S for sales journal, CP for cash payments journal, CR for cash receipts journal, and G for general journal. Some accounts may be used in more than one journal. Assume a perpetual inventory system.

1. Cost of goods sold   _____

2. Accounts payable   _____

3. Amortization expense   _____

4. Cash   _____

5. Accounts payable   _____

6. Sales revenue   _____

7. Sales returns and allowances _____

8. Inventory   _____

Starter 7–16 Journalize the transactions below that should be recorded in the general journal. If a transaction should not be recorded in the general journal, identify the special journal that should be used. Assume the company uses the perpetual inventory system.

Recording transactions in a general journal
(5)

Mar.	2	Sold merchandise inventory on account to B. Kielman, issuing invoice no. 501 for $300 (cost, $230).
	6	Issued credit memo to B. Kielman for $300 for merchandise returned to business by customer. Also accounted for receipt of the merchandise inventory at cost.
	21	Purchased merchandise inventory on credit terms of 2/10, n/30 from Poloskey Co., $500.
	28	Returned damaged merchandise inventory to Poloskey Co., issuing a debit memo for $500.

*Starter 7–17 Answer the following questions about Slopes Ski Shop's special journals.

Effects of taxes and the periodic inventory system on special journals
(3)(4)(A1)

1. Refer to Slopes Ski Shop's sales journal in Exhibit 7–6 on page 387. How would it look different if Slopes used the periodic inventory system and all credit sales transactions were subject to PST and GST? Give the headings for all new columns.
2. Refer to Slopes Ski Shop's cash receipts journal in Exhibit 7–8 on page 390. How would it look different if Slopes used the periodic inventory system and all cash sales transactions were subject to PST and GST? Give the headings for all new columns.
3. Refer to Slopes Ski Shop's purchases journal in Exhibit 7–9 on page 394. How would it look different if Slopes used the periodic inventory system and all purchases on account were subject to GST? Give the headings for all new columns.
4. Refer to Slopes Ski Shop's cash payments journal in Exhibit 7–10 on page 397. How would it look different if Slopes used the periodic inventory system and most cash payments were subject to GST? Give the headings for all new columns.

---

*This Starter covers Chapter 7 Appendix topics. The Appendix can be found on MyAccountingLab.

EXERCISES

MyAccountingLab

Exercise 7–1

The head office of Worldwide Circuits wants to "go green" and reduce paper use and unnecessary reports. Which features of an effective accounting information system will allow for this initiative? Discuss.

Features of an effective accounting information system
(1)

Exercise 7–2

It is very important to set up a properly numbered chart of accounts, especially in a computerized accounting system. Use account numbers 101 through 106, 201, 221, 301, 321, 401, 501, and 521 to correspond to the following selected accounts from the general ledger of Welluck Map Company. List the accounts and their account numbers in proper order, starting with the most liquid current asset.

Setting up a chart of accounts
(2)

Randy Welluck, Capital	Amortization Expense—Computer Equipment
Accounts Receivable	Cost of Goods Sold
Cash	Note Payable, Long-Term
Accounts Payable	Randy Welluck, Withdrawals
Computer Equipment	Inventory
Supplies	Sales Revenue
Accumulated Amortization—Computer Equipment	

Exercise 7–3

Refer to Exhibit 7–4 on page 383. Which steps are automatic in a computerized accounting system as compared to a manual accounting system?

Exercise 7–4

The following accounts and sums of accounts in the computerized accounting system of Zinn Supplies show some of the company's adjusted balances before closing:

Total assets..	?
Current assets	$16,800
Long-term assets	40,200
Total liabilities...	?
Sam Zinn, Capital...	$40,800
Sam Zinn, Withdrawals.......................................	15,000
Total revenues..	54,000
Total expenses..	33,000

Compute the missing amounts. You must also compute ending owner's equity.

Exercise 7–5

The sales and cash receipts journals of Jiajng Electronics include the following entries:

Sales Journal					
Date	Invoice No.	Account Debited	Post. Ref.	Accounts Receivable Dr Sales Revenue Cr	Cost of Goods Sold Dr Inventory Cr
May 7	671	I. Pax	✓	220	72
10	672	W. Singh	✓	120	58
10	673	F. Zehr	✓	120	50
12	674	J. Legg	✓	240	120
31		Total		700	300

Cash Receipts Journal								
	Debits			**Credits**				
					Other Accounts			Cost of Goods Sold Dr Inventory Cr
Date	Cash	Sales Discounts	Accounts Receivable	Sales Revenue	Account Title	Post. Ref.	Amount	
May 16					I. Pax	✓		
19					F. Zehr	✓		
24	600			600				380
30					W. Singh	✓		

Required   Complete the cash receipts journal for those transactions indicated. There are no sales discounts. Also, total the journal and show that total debits equal total credits.

Exercise 7-6

The cash receipts journal of Faubert Sports follows:

Using the sales and cash receipts journals (perpetual inventory system)
③

Cash Receipts Journal							Page 7
Debits			**Credits**				
					Other Accounts		
Date	**Cash**	**Sales Discounts**	**Accounts Receivable**	**Sales Revenue**	**Account Title**	**Post. Ref.**	**Amount**
Jan. 2	790	40	830		Magna Corp.	(a)	
9	490		490		Big Fish Inc.	(b)	
19	4,480				Note Receivable	(c)	4,000
					Interest Revenue	(d)	480
30	310	20	330		J T Richards	(e)	
31	4,230			4,230			
31	10,300	60	1,650	4,230	Totals		4,480
	(f)	(g)	(h)	(i)		(j)	

Faubert Sports's chart of accounts (general ledger) includes the following selected accounts, along with their account numbers:

Number	Account		Number	Account
110	Cash		510	Sales Revenue
120	Accounts Receivable		512	Sales Discounts
125	Note Receivable		515	Sales Returns
140	Land		520	Interest Revenue

Required

Indicate whether each posting reference (a) through (j) should be

- A check mark (✓) for a posting to a customer account in the accounts receivable subsidiary ledger
- An account number for a posting to an account in the general ledger. If so, give the account number
- A letter (X) for an amount not posted

Exercise 7-7

During February, Bryant Corporation had the following transactions:

Recording transactions in the sales journal
③
2. Accounts Receivable Dr, Sales Revenue Cr column total, $1,465

Feb.	1	Sold merchandise inventory on account to Curtis Co., $1,025. Cost of goods, $780. Invoice no. 401.
	6	Sold merchandise inventory for cash, $860 (cost, $640).
	12	Collected interest revenue of $80.
	15	Received cash from Curtis Co. in full settlement of its account receivable. There was no discount.
	20	Sold merchandise inventory on account to Delgado Co., issuing invoice no. 402 for $440 (cost, $330).
	22	Sold merchandise inventory for cash, $560 (cost $420).
	26	Sold office supplies to an employee for cash of $80.
	28	Received $431 from Delgado Co. in full settlement of its account receivable. Delgado earned a discount by paying early. Terms are 2/10, n/15.

Required

1. Prepare headings for the company's sales journal. Journalize the transactions that should be recorded in the sales journal. (Round the sales discount to a whole dollar.) Assume the company uses a perpetual inventory system.
2. Total each column of the sales journal.

Recording transactions in the cash receipts journal

(3)

2. Accounts Receivable Cr column total, $1,465

Exercise 7–8

Refer to the information in Exercise 7–7.

Required

1. Prepare headings for a cash receipts journal. Journalize the transactions that should be recorded in the cash receipts journal.
2. Total each column of the cash receipts journal.

Recording transactions in the cash receipts journal, sales journal, and general journal

(3)

Exercise 7–9

M and N Sporting Goods reported these selected transactions for the month of July:

Jul. 9	Issued invoice no. 159 for a sale on account to Evans Company, $4,600, terms 1/10, n/30. The cost of the merchandise was $2,700.
10	Issued invoice no. 160 for a sale on account to Sails and Boats, $5,700, terms 2/15, n/45. The cost of the merchandise was $2,450.
12	Sold $3,000 of merchandise to Bruce Services for cash. The cost of the merchandise was $1,250.
16	Owner invested $3,400 into the business.
18	Collected $580 from Lucille Adams on account.
20	Issued a credit memo to Sails and Boats for $2,800 for merchandise returned. The cost of the returned merchandise was $1,200.

Required Record the above transactions in either the sales journal, the cash receipts journal, or the general journal, using Exhibits 7–6 and 7–8 as templates. M and N Sporting Goods uses a perpetual inventory system.

Posting from the cash receipts journal and the sales journal

(3)

Exercise 7–10

Using the information in the following unidentified journals, state how the numbers identified as a) through h) would be posted using the selections below:

1. Posted to a general ledger account as a debit
2. Posted to a general ledger account as a credit
3. Posted to a subsidiary ledger account as a debit
4. Posted to a subsidiary ledger account as a credit
5. Posted to the general ledger as a debit and a credit
6. Not posted

Date	Account Debited	Acc. Rec. Dr Sales Rev. Cr	Cost of Goods Sold Dr Inventory Cr
Feb. 9	Jones Company	3,540	2,300
10	Sails and Boats	10,900	b) 5,550
26	Davis Enterprises	c) 7,000	g) 3,250
28	Totals	a) 21,440	11,100

Date	Cash	Debits Sales Dis.	Acc. Rec.	Credits Sales Rev.	Other Acct.	Amount	COGS Dr Inv. Cr
Sep. 8	3,000			3,000			1,750
10	2,500				Ross, Capital	2,500	
13	50				Int. Revenue	50	
15	582	18	600		Jane Gibson		
30	e) 6,132	d) 18	600	3,000	Totals	f) 2,550	h) 1,750

a) 21,440 _____
b) 5,550 _____
c) 7,000 _____
d) 18 _____
e) 6,132 _____
f) 2,550
g) 3,250 _____
h) 1,750 _____

Exercise 7–11

A customer account in the accounts receivable subsidiary ledger of Kettle Office Supplies follows:

Identifying transactions from postings to the accounts receivable subsidiary ledger

③

Date	Beaver Valley Lumber Inc. Jrnl. Ref.	Dr	Cr	112590 Debit Balance
Nov. 1				1,600
9	S.5	4,720		6,320
18	J.8		760	5,560
30	CR.9		2,800	2,760

Required Describe the three posted transactions.

Exercise 7–12

The purchases journal of Lightning Snowboards follows:

Posting from the purchases journal, balancing the ledgers

④

3. Total Accounts Payable, $2,990

									Other Accounts Dr			Page 7
Data	Account Credited	Invoice Date	Terms	Post. Ref.	Accounts Payable Cr	Inventory Dr	Supplies Dr		Acct. Title	Post. Ref.	Amt. Dr	
Sep. 2	Brotherton Inc.	02/09	n/30		800	800						
5	Rolf Office Supply	05/09	n/30		340		340					
13	Brotherton Inc.	13/09	2/10, n/30		1,400	1,400						
26	Marks Equipment Company	25/09	n/30		450				Equipment		450	
30	Totals				2,990	2,200	340				450	

Required

1. Open three-column general ledger accounts for Inventory (account #131), Supplies (account #141), Equipment (account #171), and Accounts Payable (account #210). Post to these accounts from the purchases journal. Use dates and posting references in the ledger accounts.

2. Open accounts in the accounts payable subsidiary ledger for Brotherton Inc., Rolf Office Supply, and Marks Equipment Company. Post from the purchases journal. Use dates and journal references in the ledger accounts.

3. Balance the Accounts Payable control account in the general ledger with the total of the balances in the accounts payable subsidiary ledger.

4. Does Lightning Snowboards use a perpetual or a periodic inventory system?

Exercise 7–13

Using the cash payments journal

④

3. Total credit to Cash, $37,790

During February, Dean Products had the following transactions:

Feb.	3	Paid $490 on account to Marquis Corp. net of a $10 discount for an earlier purchase of inventory.
	6	Purchased inventory for cash, $3,800.
	11	Paid $300 cash for supplies.
	15	Purchased inventory on account from Monroe Corporation, $1,548.
	16	Paid $24,100 on account to LaGrange Ltd.; there was no discount.
	21	Purchased furniture for cash, $2,800.
	26	Paid $3,900 on account to Graff Software Ltd. for an earlier $4,000 purchase of inventory. The purchase discount was $100.
	28	Made a semi-annual interest payment of $2,400 on a long-term note payable. The entire payment was for interest. (Assume none of the interest had been accrued previously.)

Required

1. Prepare a cash payments journal similar to the one illustrated in this chapter. Omit the payee column.
2. Record the transactions in the cash payments journal. Which transaction should not be recorded in the cash payments journal? In what journal does it belong?
3. Total the amount columns of the cash payments journal. Determine that the total debits equal the total credits.

Exercise 7–14

Identifying transactions from postings to the T-accounts

③ ④

Better Mousetrap Consulting makes most of its sales and purchases on account. It uses the five journals described in this chapter (sales, cash receipts, purchases, cash payments, and general journal). Identify the journal most likely used to record the postings for the transactions indicated by numbers in the following T-accounts.

	Cash		
1.	5,000	400	2.

	Prepaid Supplies		
	1,000	600	3.

	Accounts Receivable		
4.	10,000	5,000	5.

	Accounts Payable		
6.	400	2,000	7.
		200	12.

	Inventory	
8.	2,000	

	Service Revenue	
		10,000	9.

	Supplies Expense	
10.	600	

	Delivery Expense	
11.	200	

Exercise 7–15

Special journals perpetual inventory system

③ ④

Total debit to Cash from cash receipts journal, $8,000

Bright's Patio Shop sells garden and patio furniture. Record the following transactions in the appropriate special journals using the special journal formats shown in Exhibit 7A–1 found in the online Appendix. Total each special journal at May 31.

May	1	Sold $2,600 of patio furniture to Jen Williams, terms n/30, invoice 310 (cost, $1,700).
	2	Purchased inventory on credit terms of 1/10, n/60 from Sisco Corp., $8,000. Invoice date is May 2.
	5	Sold inventory for cash, $400 (cost, $220).
	10	Purchased $600 of patio lanterns from an artisan. Issued cheque no. 401.
	15	Sold $5,000 of outdoor seating to Pat's Restaurant, terms n/30, invoice 311 (cost, $3,400).
	22	Received payment from Jen Williams (May 1).
	26	Received payment from Pat's Restaurant (May 15).
	29	Paid Sisco Corp. for the purchase made on May 2, cheque no. 402.

Exercise 7–16

During April, Xitang Company completed the following credit purchase transactions:

Apr.	5	Purchased supplies, $400, from Central Co.
	11	Purchased inventory, $1,200, from McDonald Ltd. Xitang Company uses a perpetual inventory system.
	14	Issued cheque to pay Central Co.
	19	Purchased equipment, $4,300, from Baker Corp.
	20	Issued cheque to pay Baker Corp.
	22	Purchased inventory, $2,210, from Khalil Inc.

Required Record these transactions first in the general journal—with explanations—and then in the purchases journal. Omit credit terms, posting references, and invoice dates. After setting up the purchases journal form, which procedure for recording transactions is quicker? Why?

Recording purchase transactions in the general journal and purchases journal

④ ⑤

Purchases journal: Total credit to Accounts Payable, $8,110

Exercise 7–17

The following documents describe two business transactions:

Using business documents to record purchases, sales, and returns

⑤

Eddie's: Credit Cash for $1,835

Invoice		
Date:	March 14, 2017	
Sold to:	Eddie's Bicycle Shop	
Sold by:	Schwinn Company	
Terms:	2/10, n/30	
Items Purchased	Bicycles	
Quantity	Price	Total
8	$152	$1,216
2	112	224
10	96	960
Total...................		$2,400

Debit Memo		
Date:	March 20, 2017	
Issued to:	Schwinn Company	
Issued by:	Eddie's Bicycle Shop	
Items Returneed	Bicycles	
Quantity	Price	Total
2	$152	$304
2	112	224
Total....................		$528
Reason:	Damaged in shipment	

Required

1. Use the general journal to record these transactions and Eddie's Bicycle Shop's cash payment on March 21. Record the transactions first on the books of Eddie's Bicycle Shop and then on the books of Schwinn Company, which makes and sells bicycles. Both Eddie's Bicycle Shop and Schwinn Company use a perpetual inventory system. Schwinn Company's cost of the bicycles sold to Eddie's Bicycle Shop was $1,280. Schwinn Company's cost of the returned

merchandise was $256. Round to the nearest dollar. Explanations are not required. Set up your answer in the following format:

| Date | Eddie's Bicycle Shop Journal Entries | Schwinn Journal Entries |

2. How would your answer be different if both of these companies used the periodic inventory system?

Special journals using PST and GST for Saskatchewan, perpetual inventory system

③ ④ Ⓐ1

Total debit to Cash from cash receipts journal, $8,800

*Exercise 7–18

Refer to the Bright's Patio Shop transactions in Exercise 7–15. Assume that the company is located in Saskatchewan, and all of its sales are subject to 5 percent provincial sales tax and 5 percent GST; all of its purchases are subject to 5 percent GST. Record the transactions in the appropriate special journals, using the special journal formats shown in Exhibit 7A–1 found in the online Appendix. Total each special journal at May 31.

Special journals using PST and GST for Ontario, perpetual inventory system

③ ④ Ⓐ1

Total debit to Cash from cash receipts journal, $9,040

*Exercise 7–19

Refer to the Bright's Patio Shop transactions in Exercise 7–15. Assume that the company is located in Ontario, and all of its sales and purchases are subject to 13 percent HST. Record the transactions in the appropriate special journals. Total each special journal at May 31. Round all dollar amounts to the nearest dollar.

———————

*These Exercises cover Chapter 7 Appendix topics. The Appendix can be found on MyAccountingLab.

SERIAL EXERCISE

Accounting for both merchandising and service transactions under the perpetual inventory system using special journals

③ ④ ⑤

4. Adjusted trial balance total, $52,183

This exercise continues the Lee Management Consulting situation from Exercise 6–20 of Chapter 6. If you did not complete Exercise 6–20 you can still complete Exercise 7–20 as it is presented.

Exercise 7–20

Lee Management Consulting had the following post-closing trial balance at June 30, 2016. Also shown are the account numbers for each account, including the revenue and expense accounts.

	LEE MANAGEMENT CONSULTING		
	Post-Closing Trial Balance		
	June 30, 2016		
101	Cash	$23,750	
102	Accounts receivable	1,900	
103	Inventory	0	
104	Supplies	100	
105	Prepaid rent	0	
110	Equipment	1,000	
115	Accumulated amortization—equipment		$ 42
120	Furniture	5,000	
125	Accumulated amortization—furniture		167
201	Accounts payable		5,000
202	Salary payable		500
205	Unearned revenue		1,200
301	Michael Lee, capital		24,841
	Total	$31,750	$31,750

(Continued)

(Continued)

302	Michael Lee, withdrawals
401	Service revenue
402	Sales revenue
501	Cost of goods sold
511	Rent expense
513	Utilities expense
515	Salary expense
521	Amortization expense—equipment
522	Amortization expense—furniture
530	Supplies expense

Consider the July 2016 transactions for Lee Management Consulting that are shown below that were presented in Chapter 6. Cost of goods sold, which was calculated using the moving-weighted-average-cost method in a perpetual inventory system, is shown in brackets after each sale.

Jul.	2	Completed a consulting engagement and received cash of $7,200.
	2	Prepaid three months' office rent, $9,000.
	7	Purchased 100 units of software inventory on account, $1,900, plus owed the manufacturer freight-in of $100.
	16	Paid employee salary, $2,000. (Note previous year-end accrual of $500.)
	18	Sold 70 software units on account, $3,100 (cost, $1,400).
	19	Consulted with a client for a fee of $900 on account.
	21	Paid on account, $2,000, for the July 7 purchase.
	22	Purchased 200 units of software inventory on account, $4,600.
	24	Paid utilities, $300 cash.
	28	Sold 100 units of software for cash, $4,000 (cost, $2,261).
	31	Recorded the following adjusting entries:
		Accrued salary expense, $1,000
		Prepaid rent used, $3,000
		Amortization of office furniture, $167, and of equipment, $42
		Physical count of inventory, 120 units, $2,713

Required

1. Open three-column ledger accounts for all the accounts listed in the June 30, 2016, post-closing trial balance, and for the withdrawals, revenue, and expense accounts listed below it. Use the account numbers shown. Insert the June 30, 2016, balances as the opening balances for July 1, 2016.

2. Journalize the July 2016 transactions in the following special journals: cash receipts journal (Page 1), cash payments journal (Page 1), sales journal (Page 1), purchases journal (Page 1), and general journal (Page 6). Total each special journal at July 31, 2016.

3. Post the special journals totals to the three-column ledger accounts using the special journal posting references used in this chapter.

4. Prepare a trial balance in the Trial Balance columns of a worksheet. Record the July 31, 2016, adjusting entries on the worksheet, then complete the Adjusted Trial Balance columns of the worksheet for the month ended July 31, 2016.

5. Journalize and post the adjusting entries. Explanations are not required.

CHALLENGE EXERCISE

Exercise 7–21

1. Slopes Ski Shop's special journals in Exhibits 7–6 through 7–10 (pp. 387–396) provide the manager with much of the data needed for preparing the financial statements. Slopes uses the *perpetual* inventory system, so the amount of cost of goods sold is simply the ending balance in that account. The manager needs to know the business's gross margin for November. Compute the gross margin.

2. Suppose Slopes used the *periodic* inventory system. In that case, the business must compute cost of goods sold by the following formula:

Cost of goods sold:	
Beginning inventory	$ 3,885
+ Net purchases	XXX
= Cost of goods available for sale	XXX
− Ending inventory	(4,249)
= Cost of goods sold	$ XXX

Perform this calculation of cost of goods sold for Slopes. Does this computation of cost of goods sold agree with your answer to Requirement 1?

BEYOND THE NUMBERS

Beyond the Numbers 7–1

Queen Technology Associates creates and sells cutting-edge network software. Queen's quality control officer estimates that 20 percent of the company's sales and purchases of inventory are returned for additional debugging. Queen needs special journals for

- Sales returns and allowances
- Purchase returns and allowances

Required

1. Design on paper or on a computer the two special journals. For each journal, include a column for the appropriate business document.

2. Enter one transaction in each journal, using the Slopes Ski Shop transaction data illustrated on pages 398 and 399. Show all posting references, including those for column totals. In the purchase returns and allowances journal, assume debit memo number 14.

ETHICAL ISSUE

On a recent trip to Brazil, Lou Delgado, sales manager of Cyber Systems, took his wife along for a vacation and included her airfare and meals on his expense report, which he submitted for reimbursement. Donna Alliksar, vice-president of sales and Delgado's boss, thought his total travel and entertainment expenses seemed excessive. However, Alliksar approved the reimbursement because she owed Delgado a favour. Alliksar, well aware that the company president routinely reviews all expenses recorded in the cash payments journal, had the accountant record the expenses of Delgado's wife in the general journal as follows:

Sales Promotion Expense	9,000	
Cash		9,000

Required

1. Does recording the transaction in the general journal rather than in the cash payments journal affect the amounts of cash and total expenses reported in the financial statements?

2. Why did Alliksar want this transaction recorded in the general journal?

3. What is the ethical issue in this situation? What role does accounting play in the ethical issue?

PROBLEMS (GROUP A)　　　MyAccountingLab

Problem 7–1A

Sally Green has recently been hired as the CEO for a startup Internet-based retail store, ShopCan.ca. Her main job duties include responsibility for the information technology and computer systems of the business. Sally was reviewing the security of customer data and realized that customer service representatives had access to all customer data, including credit card information and billing addresses.

Safeguarding customer data
①

Required

1. What should Sally do?

2. Can you think of any real-world breaches that happened to retail chains where customer data was stolen or released? What were the consequences to the company?

Problem 7–2A

Winnie Lu is in the process of setting up the chart of accounts for a company that is converting its manual system to a computerized accounting system. Below is a proposed chart of accounts:

Computerized accounting system
②

T. Pioneer, Capital	30001
Advertising Expense	51001
Building	17001
Accounts Payable	21001
Sales Revenue	41001
Miscellaneous Expenses	59001
Cash	11001
T. Pioneer, Withdrawals	21002
Land	18001
Notes Payable	25001
Accounts Receivable	12001
Salaries Expense	54001

Required

1. Can you see a problem with the numbering system that has be decided upon by Winnie? How would this affect the financial reports?

2. What could happen during the closing process?

Problem 7–3A

The cash receipts journal shown below contains five entries. All five entries are for legitimate cash receipt transactions, but the journal contains some errors in recording the transactions. In fact, only one entry is correct, and each of the other four entries contains one error.

Correcting errors in the cash receipts journal (perpetual inventory system)
③

Corrected cash receipts journal: Total debit to Cash, $83,000

Cash Receipts Journal — Page 22

Date	Cash (Debits)	Sales Discounts	Accounts Receivable	Sales Revenue	Account Title (Other Accounts)	Post. Ref.	Amount	Cost of Goods Sold Dr Inventory Cr
Jan. 4		4,200		4,200				2,030
7	6,000	220			Debbie Hughes	✓	6,220	
13	57,400				Note Receivable	13	53,900	
					Interest Revenue	45	3,500	
20				4,620				2,100
30	15,400		10,780					
31	78,800	4,420	10,780	8,820	Totals		63,620	4,130
	(11)	(42)	(12)	(41)			(✓)	(51/13)

Total Dr = $83,220   Total Cr = $83,220

Required

1. Identify the correct entry in the cash receipts journal above.
2. Identify the error in each of the other four entries.
3. Using the following format, prepare a corrected cash receipts journal. All column totals are correct in the cash receipts journal that follows.

Cash Receipts Journal — Page 22

Date	Cash (Debits)	Sales Discounts	Accounts Receivable	Sales Revenue	Account Title (Other Accounts)	Post. Ref.	Amount	Cost of Goods Sold Dr Inventory Cr
Jan. 4								
7					Debbie Hughes	✓		
13					Note Receivable	13		
					Interest Revenue	45		
20								
30								
31	83,000	220	17,000	8,820	Totals		57,400	4,130
	(11)	(42)	(12)	(41)			(✓)	(51/13)

Total Dr = $83,220   Total Cr = $83,220

Problem 7–4A

Using all the journals, the accounts receivable subsidiary ledger, and the accounts payable subsidiary ledger

③ ④ ⑤

McMillan Distributors, which uses the perpetual inventory system and makes all credit sales on terms of 2/10, n/30, completed the following transactions during July. McMillan records all sales returns and all purchase returns in the general journal.

Jul. 2   Issued invoice no. 913 for sale on account to Teranishi Inc., $12,300. McMillan's cost of this inventory was $5,400.

3   Purchased inventory on credit terms of 3/10, n/60 from Chicosky Corp., $7,401. The invoice was dated July 3.

5   Sold inventory for cash, $3,231 (cost, $1,440).

5	Issued cheque no. 532 to purchase furniture for cash, $6,555.
8	Collected interest revenue of $3,325.
9	Issued invoice no. 914 for sale on account to Bell Ltd., $16,650 (cost, $6,930).
10	Purchased inventory for cash, $3,429, issuing cheque no. 533.
12	Received cash from Teranishi Inc. in full settlement of its account receivable from the sale on July 2.
13	Issued cheque no. 534 to pay Chicosky Corp. the net amount owed from July 3.
13	Purchased supplies on account from Manley Inc., $4,323. Terms were net end of month. The invoice was dated July 12.
15	Sold inventory on account to M. O. Brown, issuing invoice no. 915 for $1,995 (cost, $720).
17	Issued credit memo to M. O. Brown for $1,995 for merchandise sent in error and returned by Brown. Also accounted for receipt of the inventory.
18	Issued invoice no. 916 for credit sale to Teranishi Inc., $1,071 (cost, $381).
19	Received $16,317 from Bell Ltd. in full settlement of its account receivable from July 9.
20	Purchased inventory on credit terms of net 30 from Burgess Distributing Ltd., $6,141. The invoice was dated July 20.
22	Purchased furniture on credit terms of 3/10, n/60 from Chicosky Corp., $1,935. The invoice was dated July 22.
22	Issued cheque no. 535 to pay for insurance coverage, debiting Prepaid Insurance for $3,000.
24	Sold supplies to an employee for cash of $162, which was the cost of the supplies.
25	Issued cheque no. 536 to pay utilities, $3,359
28	Purchased inventory on credit terms of 2/10, n/30 from Manley Inc., $4,025. The invoice was dated July 28.
29	Returned damaged inventory to Manley Inc., issuing a debit memo for $2,025.
29	Sold goods on account to Bell Ltd., issuing invoice no. 917 for $1,488 (cost, $660).
30	Issued cheque no. 537 to pay Manley Inc. $1,323.
31	Received cash in full on account from Teranishi Inc.
31	Issued cheque no. 538 to pay monthly salaries of $7,041.

Required Use the following abbreviations to indicate the journal in which you would record each of the July transactions. Key each transaction by date. Also indicate whether the transaction would be recorded in the accounts receivable subsidiary ledger or the accounts payable subsidiary ledger.

G = General journal	P = Purchases journal
S = Sales journal	CP = Cash payments journal
CR = Cash receipts journal	

Problem 7–5A

The general ledger of Cannin Distributors includes the following selected accounts, along with their account numbers:

Cash..	11	Land	18
Accounts Receivable........................	12	Sales Revenue	41
Inventory..	13	Sales Discounts..................................	42
Notes Receivable	15	Sales Returns and Allowances	43
Supplies	16	Cost of Goods Sold...........................	51

Using the sales, cash receipts, and general journals (with the perpetual inventory system)

③ ⑤

1. Cash receipts journal: Total debit to Cash, $142,872

All credit sales are on the company's standard terms of 2/10, n/30. Transactions in July that affected sales and cash receipts were as follows:

Jul. 2   Sold inventory on credit to Fortin Inc., $2,800. Cannin's cost of these goods was $1,600.

4   As a favour to a competitor, sold supplies at cost, $3,100, receiving cash.

7   Cash sales of merchandise for the week totalled $7,560 (cost, $6,560).

9   Sold merchandise on account to A. L. Price, $29,280 (cost, $20,440).

10   Sold land that cost $50,000 for cash of $50,000.

11   Sold goods on account to Sloan Forge Ltd., $20,416 (cost, $14,080).

12   Received cash from Fortin Inc. in full settlement of its account receivable from July 2.

14   Cash sales of merchandise for the week were $8,424 (cost, $6,120).

15   Sold inventory on credit to the partnership of Wilkie & Blinn, $14,600 (cost, $9,040).

18   Received inventory sold on July 9 to A. L. Price for $2,400. The goods shipped were the wrong size. These goods cost Cannin $1,760.

20   Sold merchandise on account to Sloan Forge Ltd., $2,516 (cost, $1,800).

21   Cash sales of merchandise for the week were $3,960 (cost, $2,760).

22   Received $8,000 cash from A. L. Price in partial settlement of his account receivable.

25   Received cash from Wilkie & Blinn for its account receivable from July 15.

25   Sold goods on account to Olsen Inc., $6,080 (cost, $4,200).

27   Collected $10,500 on a note receivable.

28   Cash sales of merchandise for the week were $15,096 (cost, $9,840).

29   Sold inventory on account to R. O. Bankston Inc., $968 (cost, $680).

30   Received goods sold on July 25 to Olsen Inc. for $160. The wrong items were shipped. The cost of the goods was $100.

31   Received $18,880 cash on account from A. L. Price.

Required

1. Use the appropriate journal to record the above transactions: a sales journal (omit the Invoice No. column), a cash receipts journal, or a general journal. Cannin Distributors records sales returns and allowances in the general journal.

2. Total each column of the sales journal and the cash receipts journal. Show that total debits equal total credits.

3. Show how postings would be made from the journals by writing the account numbers and check marks in the appropriate places in the journals.

Problem 7–6A

Using the purchases, cash payments, and general journals

(4) (5)

1. Cash payments journal: Total credit to Cash, $19,981

The general ledger of Katie's Supplies includes the following accounts:

Cash	111	Furniture	187
Inventory	131	Accounts Payable	211
Prepaid Insurance	161	Rent Expense	564
Supplies	171	Utilities Expense	583

Transactions in August that affected purchases and cash payments were as follows:

Aug. 1   Purchased inventory on credit from Stiples Corp., $6,900. Terms were 2/10, n/30. The invoice was dated August 1.

1   Paid monthly rent, debiting Rent Expense for $2,000.

5   Purchased supplies on credit terms of 2/10, n/30 from Bella Supply Ltd., $450. The invoice date was August 5.

8   Paid electricity bill, $600.

9   Purchased furniture on account from Rite Office Supply, $9,100. Payment terms were net 30. The invoice date was August 8.

10	Returned the furniture to Rite Office Supply. It was the wrong colour.
11	Paid Stiples Corp. the amount owed on the purchase of August 1.
12	Purchased inventory on account from Wynne Inc., $4,400. Terms were 3/10, n/30. The invoice was dated August 12.
13	Purchased inventory for cash, $650.
14	Paid a semi-annual insurance premium, debiting Prepaid Insurance, $1,200.
15	Paid the account payable to Bella Supply Ltd. from August 5.
18	Paid gas and water bills with cash, $100.
21	Purchased inventory on credit terms of 1/10, n/45 from Cyber Software Ltd., $5,200. The invoice was dated August 21.
21	Paid account payable to Wynne Inc. from August 12.
22	Purchased supplies on account from Favron Sales, $2,740. Terms were net 30. The invoice was dated August 21.
25	Returned $1,200 of the inventory purchased on August 21 to Cyber Software Ltd.
31	Paid Cyber Software Ltd. the net amount owed from August 21.

Required

1. Katie's Supplies records purchase returns in the general journal. Use the appropriate journal to record the above transactions: a purchases journal, a cash payments journal (omit the Cheque No. column), or a general journal.

2. Total each column of the special journals. Show that total debits equal total credits in each journal.

3. Show how postings would be made from the journals by writing the account numbers and check marks in the appropriate places in the journals.

Problem 7–7A

Callahan Distributors, which uses the perpetual inventory system and makes all credit sales on terms of 1/10, n/30, completed the following transactions during July:

Using all the journals, posting, balancing the ledgers
③ ④ ⑤
6. Total Accounts Receivable, $2,976; total Accounts Payable, $26,152

Jul. 2	Issued invoice no. 913 for sale on account to Ishikawa Inc., $24,600. Callahan's cost of this inventory was $10,800. Credit sales terms are 1/10, n/30.
3	Purchased inventory on credit terms of 3/10, n/60 from Nakkach Corp., $14,802. The invoice was dated July 3.
5	Sold inventory for cash, $6,462 (cost, $2,880).
5	Issued cheque no. 532 to purchase furniture for cash, $13,110.
8	Collected interest revenue of $6,650.
9	Issued invoice no. 914 for sale on account to Bell Ltd., $33,300 (cost, $13,860). Credit sales terms are 1/10, n/30.
10	Purchased inventory for cash, $6,858, issuing cheque no. 533.
12	Received cash from Ishikawa Inc. in full settlement of its account receivable from the sale on July 2.
13	Issued cheque no. 534 to pay Nakkach Corp. the net amount owed from July 3. (Round to the nearest dollar.)
13	Purchased supplies on account from Manley Inc., $8,646. Terms were net end of month. The invoice was dated July 13.
15	Sold inventory on account to M. O. Brown, issuing invoice no. 915 for $3,990 (cost, $1,440). Credit sales terms are 1/10, n/30.
17	Issued credit memo to M. O. Brown for $3,990 for merchandise sent in error and returned by Brown. Also accounted for receipt of the inventory.
18	Issued invoice no. 916 for credit sale to Ishikawa Inc., $2,142 (cost, $762). Credit sales terms are 1/10, n/30.

19	Received $32,967 from Bell Ltd. in full settlement of its account receivable from July 9.
20	Purchased inventory on credit terms of net 30 from Burgess Distributing Ltd., $12,282. The invoice was dated July 20.
22	Purchased furniture on credit terms of 3/10, n/60 from Nakkach Corp., $3,870. The invoice was dated July 22.
22	Issued cheque no. 535 to pay for insurance coverage, debiting Prepaid Insurance for $6,000.
24	Sold supplies to an employee for cash of $324, which was the cost of the supplies.
25	Issued cheque no. 536 to pay utilities, $6,718.
28	Purchased inventory on credit terms of 2/10, n/30 from Manley Inc., $8,050. The invoice date was July 28.
29	Returned damaged inventory to Manley Inc., issuing a debit memo for $4,050.
29	Sold goods on account to Bell Ltd., issuing invoice no. 917 for $2,976 (cost, $1,320). Credit sales terms are 1/10, n/30.
30	Issued cheque no. 537 to pay Manley Inc. $2,646.
31	Received cash in full on account from Ishikawa Inc.
31	Issued cheque no. 538 to pay monthly salaries of $14,082.

Required

1. Open the following three-column general ledger accounts using the account numbers given:

Cash	111	Sales Revenue	411
Accounts Receivable	112	Sales Discounts	412
Supplies	116	Sales Returns and Allowances	413
Prepaid Insurance	117	Interest Revenue	419
Inventory	118	Cost of Goods Sold	511
Furniture	151	Salaries Expense	531
Accounts Payable	211	Utilities Expense	541

2. Open these accounts in the subsidiary ledgers: accounts receivable subsidiary ledger—Bell Ltd., M. O. Brown, and Ishikawa Inc.; accounts payable subsidiary ledger—Nakkach Corp., Manley Inc., and Burgess Distributing Ltd.

3. Enter the transactions in a sales journal (Page 7), a cash receipts journal (Page 5), a purchases journal (Page 10), a cash payments journal (Page 8), and a general journal (Page 6), as appropriate.

4. Post daily to the accounts receivable subsidiary ledger and to the accounts payable subsidiary ledger. Post the individual amounts to the general ledger on the date recorded in the journal; post column totals to the general ledger on July 31.

5. Total each column of the special journals. Show that total debits equal total credits in each journal.

6. Balance or reconcile the accounts receivable subsidiary ledger and Accounts Receivable in the general ledger. Do the same for the accounts payable subsidiary ledger and Accounts Payable in the general ledger.

*Problem 7–8A

Foxey Distributors had the following transactions for the month of April 2017:

Apr.	1	Sold $3,000 of merchandise to James Moss, terms n/30. Inventory had a cost of $1,340. The sale was subject to 7 percent PST and 5 percent GST.
	3	Purchased $28,500 of merchandise from MNO Suppliers Ltd., terms net 30, subject to 5 percent GST. The invoice was dated April 2.

Understanding how manual accounting systems are used, using the cash receipts journal and the cash payments journal with GST and PST (perpetual inventory system)

② ③ ④ (A1)

2. Cash receipts journal: Total debit to Cash, $10,304

*This Problem covers Chapter 7 Appendix topics. The Appendix can be found on MyAccountingLab.

6	Paid for the purchase of April 3 (MNO Suppliers Ltd.), cheque no. 12.
7	Paid $6,500 wages to employee, cheque no. 13.
9	Owner withdrew $15,000 for personal use, cheque no. 14.
11	Collected the amount owed by James Moss (April 1).
13	Purchased equipment from MB Machinery Ltd., $28,500 plus 5 percent GST, terms n/30. The invoice was dated April 12.
14	Issued a debit memo to MB Machinery Ltd. (April 13) for $1,500 plus 5 percent GST of equipment returned as defective.
15	Sold $4,000 of merchandise to St. Boniface School for cash. Inventory cost was $2,500. The sale was subject to 7 percent PST and 5 percent GST.
16	Paid the account owing to MB Machinery Ltd., cheque no. 15.
17	Purchased equipment from Dearing Equipment Inc. for $37,500 plus 5 percent GST, terms net 60. The invoice was dated April 17.
22	Paid a $9,000 note due to Commercial Bank, plus interest of $900, cheque no. 16.
24	Sold $2,200 of merchandise for cash; inventory cost was $1,500. The sale was subject to 7 percent PST and 5 percent GST.
25	Paid $1,500 to Canada Revenue Agency for income taxes owing from December 31, 2016, cheque no. 17.
26	Returned $8,500 plus 5 percent GST of the merchandise purchased from MNO Suppliers Ltd.
28	Purchased inventory for $6,000 plus 5 percent GST from Artois Ltd., promising to pay in 30 days. The invoice is dated April 28.
30	Recorded the adjusting journal entries for the month of April.

Required

1. For each date, indicate which journal would be used to record the transaction assuming Foxey Distributors uses a general journal, a sales journal, a cash receipts journal, a purchases journal, and a cash payments journal.

2. Record the appropriate transactions in the cash receipts journal and the cash payments journal using the special journal formats shown in Exhibit 7A–1 found in the online Appendix.

PROBLEMS (GROUP B)   MyAccountingLab

Problem 7–1B

Josh Gruen has recently been hired as the CEO for an online vitamin startup, VitaCan.ca. His main job duties include responsibility for the information technology and computer systems of the business. Josh was reviewing the security of customer data and realized that customer service representatives had access to all customer data and health records, including credit card information and billing addresses.

Safeguarding customer data
(1)

Required

1. What should Josh do?

2. Can you think of any real-world breaches that happened to retail chains where customer data was stolen or released? What were the consequences to the company? (Hint: Think of the Canada Revenue Agency in 2014.)

Problem 7–2B

Computerized accounting system
②

Hanna Na is in the process of setting up the chart of accounts for a company that is convert-ing their manual system to a computerized accounting system. Below is a proposed chart of accounts:

T. Forgere, Capital...	30001
Advertising Expense..	51001
Building	17001
Accounts Payable..	21001
Sales Revenue	41001
Miscellaneous Expenses..	59001
Cash...	11001
T. Forgere, Withdrawals	31002
Land	18001
Notes Payable..	25001
Accounts Receivable...	12001
Salaries Expense	54001
Net Income..	60000

Required

1. Can you see a problem with the numbering system that Hanna has decided on?
2. How would this affect the financial reports?

Problem 7–3B

Correcting errors in the cash receipts journal (perpetual inventory system)
③

The cash receipts journal below contains five entries. All five entries are for legitimate cash receipt transactions, but the journal contains some errors in recording the transactions. In fact, only one entry is correct, and each of the other four entries contains one error.

					Cash Receipts Journal			Page 16
	Debits			**Credits**				
					Other Accounts			
Date	**Cash**	**Sales Discounts**	**Accounts Receivable**	**Sales Revenue**	**Account Title**	**Post. Ref.**	**Amount**	**Cost of Goods Sold Dr Inventory Cr**
May. 3	7,110	340	7,450		Alcon Labs Ltd.	✓		
9			3,460	3,460	Carl Ryther	✓		
10	110,000			110,000	Land	19		
19	730							440
30	10,600			11,330				6,310
31	128,440	340	10,910	124,790	Totals			6,750
	(11)	(42)	(12)	(41)			✓	(51/13)

Total Dr = $128,780   Total Cr = $135,700

Required

1. Identify the correct entry in the cash receipts journal above.
2. Identify the error in each of the other four entries.
3. Using the following format, prepare a corrected cash receipts journal. All column totals are correct in the cash receipts journal that follows.

Cash Receipts Journal								Page 16
	Debits		Credits					
					Other Accounts			
Date	Cash	Sales Discounts	Accounts Receivable	Sales Revenue	Account Title	Post. Ref.	Amount	Cost of Goods Sold Dr Inventory Cr
May. 3					Alcon Labs Ltd.	✓		
9					Carl Ryther	✓		
10					Land	19		
19								
30								
31	131,900	340	10,910	11,330	Totals		110,000	6,750
	(11)	(42)	(12)	(41)			✓	(51/13)

Total Dr = $132,240   Total Cr = $132,240

Problem 7–4B

Butala Sales Company, which uses the perpetual inventory system and makes all credit sales with terms 1/10, n/30, had the following transactions during January. Butala records all sales returns and all purchase returns in the general journal.

Using all the journals and the accounts receivable and accounts payable subsidiary ledgers
③ ④ ⑤

Jan. 2	Issued invoice no. 191 for sale on account to Wooten Design Ltd., $9,400. Butala's cost of this inventory was $5,560.
3	Purchased inventory on credit terms of 1/10, n/60 from Delwood Co., $23,600. The invoice was dated January 3.
4	Sold inventory for cash, $3,232 (cost, $2,040).
5	Issued cheque no. 473 to purchase furniture for cash, $14,348.
8	Collected interest revenue of $10,760.
9	Issued invoice no. 192 for sale on account to Vachon Inc., $25,000 (cost, $13,200).
10	Purchased inventory for cash, $3,104, issuing cheque no. 474.
12	Received $9,212 cash from Wooten Design Ltd. in full settlement of its account receivable.
13	Issued cheque no. 475 to pay Delwood Co. net amount owed from January 3.
13	Purchased supplies on account from Lehigh Corp., $5,756. Terms were net end of month. The invoice date was January 13.
15	Sold inventory on account to Franklin Ltd., issuing invoice no. 193 for $2,972 (cost, $1,640).
17	Issued credit memo to Franklin Ltd. for $2,972 for merchandise sent in error and returned to Butala by Franklin. Also accounted for receipt of the inventory.
18	Issued invoice no. 194 for credit sale to Wooten Design Ltd., $7,300 (cost, $3,880).
19	Received $24,500 from Vachon Inc. in full settlement of its account receivable from January 9.
20	Purchased inventory on credit terms of net 30 from Jasper Sales Ltd., $5,600. The invoice was dated January 19.
22	Purchased furniture on credit terms of 1/10, n/60 from Delwood Co., $13,100. The invoice was dated January 22.
22	Issued cheque no. 476 to pay for insurance coverage, debiting Prepaid Insurance for $5,380.

24	Sold an old computer to an employee for cash of $1,344, which was the value of the computer.
25	Issued cheque no. 477 to pay utilities, $4,552.
28	Purchased inventory on credit terms of 1/10, n/30 from Lehigh Corp., $1,684. The invoice was dated January 28.
29	Returned damaged inventory to Lehigh Corp., issuing a debit memo for $1,684.
29	Sold goods on account to Vachon Inc., issuing invoice no. 195 for $5,268 (cost, $3,256).
30	Issued cheque no. 478 to pay Lehigh Corp. on account from January 13.
31	Received cash in full on account from Wooten Design Ltd. for credit sale of January 18. There was no discount.
31	Issued cheque no. 479 to pay monthly salaries of $17,400.

Required Use the following abbreviations to indicate the journal in which you would record each of the January transactions. Key each transaction by date. Also indicate whether the transaction would be recorded in the accounts receivable subsidiary ledger or the accounts payable subsidiary ledger.

G = General journal   P = Purchases journal

S = Sales journal   CP = Cash payments journal

CR = Cash receipts journal

Problem 7–5B

Using the sales, cash receipts, and general journals (with the perpetual inventory system)

The general ledger of Beauchamp Supply includes the following accounts:

Cash	111	Land	142
Accounts Receivable	112	Sales Revenue	411
Notes Receivable	115	Sales Discounts	412
Inventory	131	Sales Returns and Allowances	413
Equipment	141	Cost of Goods Sold	511

All credit sales are on the company's standard terms of 1/10, n/30. Transactions in November that affected sales and cash receipts were as follows:

Nov.	1	Sold inventory on credit to Ijri Ltd., $4,000. Beauchamp Supply's cost of these goods was $2,228.
	5	As a favour to another company, sold new equipment for its cost of $23,080, receiving cash in this amount.
	6	Cash sales of merchandise for the week totalled $8,400 (cost, $5,400).
	8	Sold merchandise on account to Izzo Ltd., $14,320 (cost, $11,854).
	9	Sold land that cost $64,000 for cash of $64,000.
	11	Sold goods on account to Dryer Builders Inc., $12,198 (cost, $7,706).
	11	Received cash from Ijri Ltd. in full settlement of its account receivable from November 1.
	13	Cash sales of merchandise for the week were $7,980 (cost, $5,144).
	15	Sold inventory on credit to Rapp and Howe, a partnership, $3,200 (cost, $2,068).
	18	Received inventory sold on November 8 to Izzo Ltd. for $480. The goods shipped were the wrong colour. These goods cost Beauchamp Supply $292.
	19	Sold merchandise on account to Dryer Builders, $14,400 (cost, $11,854).
	20	Cash sales of merchandise for the week were $9,320 (cost, $6,296).
	21	Received $6,400 cash from Izzo Ltd. in partial settlement of its account receivable. There was no discount.

22	Received payment in full from Rapp and Howe for its account receivable from November 15.
22	Sold goods on account to Diamond Inc., $8,088 (cost, $5,300).
25	Collected $6,400 on a note receivable.
27	Cash sales of merchandise for the week totalled $8,910 (cost, $5,808).
27	Sold inventory on account to Littleton Corporation, $7,580 (cost, $5,868).
28	Received goods sold on November 22 to Diamond Inc. for $2,720. The goods were shipped in error, so were returned to inventory. The cost of these goods was $1,920.
28	Received $7,440 cash on account from Izzo Ltd.

Required

1. Use the appropriate journal to record the above transactions: a sales journal (omit the Invoice No. column), a cash receipts journal, and a general journal. Beauchamp Supply records sales returns and allowances in the general journal.
2. Total each column of the sales journal and the cash receipts journal. Show that total debits equal total credits.
3. Show how postings would be made from the journals by writing the account numbers and check marks in the appropriate places in the journals.

Problem 7–6B

The general ledger of Argyle Supply Company includes the following accounts:

Using the purchases, cash payments, and general journals
④ ⑤

Cash	111	Equipment	189
Inventory	131	Accounts Payable	211
Prepaid Insurance	161	Rent Expense	562
Supplies	171	Utilities Expense	565

Transactions in November that affected purchases and cash payments were as follows:

Nov.	1	Paid monthly rent, debiting Rent Expense for $17,000.
	3	Purchased inventory on credit from Sylvania Ltd., $4,000. Terms were 2/15, n/45. The invoice was dated November 3.
	4	Purchased supplies on credit terms of 2/10, n/30 from Harmon Sales Ltd., $1,600. The invoice was dated November 4.
	7	Paid utility bills, $1,812.
	10	Purchased equipment on account from Epee Corp., $12,200. Payment terms were 2/10, n/30. The invoice was dated November 10.
	11	Returned the equipment to Epee Corp. It was defective.
	12	Paid Sylvania Ltd. the amount owed on the purchase of November 3.
	12	Purchased inventory on account from Epee Corp., $42,000. Terms were 2/10, n/30. The invoice was dated November 12.
	14	Purchased inventory for cash, $3,200.
	15	Paid an insurance premium, debiting Prepaid Insurance, $4,832.
	16	Paid the account payable to Harmon Sales Ltd. from November 4.
	17	Paid electricity bill with cash, $1,400.
	20	Paid the November 12 account payable to Epee Corp., less the purchase discount.
	21	Purchased supplies on account from Master Supply Ltd., $15,080, terms net 30. The invoice was dated November 20.
	22	Purchased inventory on credit terms of 1/10, n/30 from Linz Brothers Inc., $6,800. The invoice was dated November 22.
	26	Returned $1,000 of inventory purchased on November 22 to Linz Brothers Inc.
	30	Paid Linz Brothers Inc. the net amount owed.

Required

1. Use the appropriate journal to record the above transactions: a purchases journal, a cash payments journal (do not use the Cheque No. column), or a general journal. Argyle Supply Company records purchase returns in the general journal.
2. Total each column of the special journals. Show that total debits equal total credits in each journal.
3. Show how postings would be made from the journals by writing the account numbers and check marks in the appropriate places in the journals.

Problem 7–7B

Using all the journals, posting, balancing the ledgers (perpetual inventory system)
③ ④ ⑤

Zwicky Sales Company, which uses the perpetual inventory system and makes all credit sales with terms 1/10, n/30, had these transactions during January:

Jan.	2	Issued invoice no. 191 for sale on account to Wooten Design Ltd., $9,400. Zwicky's cost of this inventory was $5,560. Credit sales terms are 1/10, n/30.
	3	Purchased inventory on credit terms of 3/10, n/60 from Delwood Co., $23,600. The invoice was dated January 3.
	4	Sold inventory for cash, $3,232 (cost, $2,040).
	5	Issued cheque no. 473 to purchase furniture for cash, $4,348.
	8	Collected interest revenue of $10,760.
	9	Issued invoice no. 192 for sale on account to Piver Inc., $25,000 (cost, $13,200). Credit sales terms are 1/10, n/30.
	10	Purchased inventory for cash, $3,104, issuing cheque no. 474.
	12	Received $9,306 cash from Wooten Design Ltd. in full settlement of its account receivable.
	13	Issued cheque no. 475 to pay Delwood Co. net amount owed from January 3.
	13	Purchased supplies on account from Lehigh Corp., $5,756. Terms were net end of month. The invoice was dated January 13.
	15	Sold inventory on account to Cradick Ltd., issuing invoice no. 193 for $2,972 (cost, $1,640). Credit sales terms are 1/10, n/30.
	17	Issued credit memo to Cradick Ltd. for $2,972 for merchandise sent in error and returned to Zwicky by Cradick. Also accounted for receipt of the inventory.
	18	Issued invoice no. 194 for credit sale to Wooten Design Ltd., $7,300 (cost, $3,880). Credit sales terms are 1/10, n/30.
	19	Received $24,750 from Piver Inc. in full settlement of its account receivable from January 9.
	20	Purchased inventory on credit terms of net 30 from Jasper Sales Ltd., $5,600. The invoice was dated January 19.
	22	Purchased furniture on credit terms of 3/10, n/60 from Delwood Co., $13,100. The invoice was dated January 22.
	22	Issued cheque no. 476 to pay for insurance coverage, debiting Prepaid Insurance for $5,380.
	24	Sold supplies to an employee for cash of $1,344, which was the value of the supplies.
	25	Issued cheque no. 477 to pay utilities, $4,552.
	28	Purchased inventory on credit terms of 2/10, n/30 from Lehigh Corp., $1,684. The invoice was dated January 28.
	29	Returned damaged inventory to Lehigh Corp., issuing a debit memo for $1,684.
	29	Sold goods on account to Piver Inc., issuing invoice no. 195 for $5,268 (cost, $3,256). Credit sales terms are 1/10, n/30.
	30	Issued cheque no. 478 to pay Lehigh Corp. on account from January 13.

| 31 | | Received cash in full on account from Wooten Design Ltd. for credit sale of January 18. There was no discount. |
| 31 | | Issued cheque no. 479 to pay monthly salaries of $7,400. |

Required

1. For Zwicky Sales Company, open the following three-column general ledger accounts using the account numbers given:

Cash	111	Sales Revenue	411
Accounts Receivable	112	Sales Discounts	412
Supplies	116	Sales Returns and Allowances	413
Prepaid Insurance	117	Interest Revenue	419
Inventory	118	Cost of Goods Sold	511
Furniture	151	Salaries Expense	531
Accounts Payable	211	Utilities Expense	541

2. Open these accounts in the subsidiary ledgers: accounts receivable subsidiary ledger—Piver Inc., Cradick Ltd., and Wooten Design Ltd.; accounts payable subsidiary ledger—Delwood Co., Lehigh Corp., and Jasper Sales Ltd.

3. Enter the transactions in a sales journal (Page 8), a cash receipts journal (Page 3), a purchases journal (Page 6), a cash payments journal (Page 9), and a general journal (Page 4), as appropriate. Disregard PST and GST in this question.

4. Post daily to the accounts receivable subsidiary ledger and to the accounts payable subsidiary ledger. Post the individual amounts to the general ledger on the date recorded in the journal; post column totals to the general ledger on January 31.

5. Total each column of the special journals. Show that total debits equal total credits in each journal.

6. Balance or reconcile the accounts receivable subsidiary ledger and Accounts Receivable in the general ledger. Do the same for the accounts payable subsidiary ledger and Accounts Payable in the general ledger.

*Problem 7–8B

Lively Home Products had the following transactions for the month of June 2017:

Jun.	1	Sold $4,000 of merchandise to Thomas Chase, terms n/30. Inventory had a cost of $2,248. The sale was subject to 7 percent PST and 5 percent GST.
	3	Purchased $9,000 of merchandise from STU Suppliers Inc., terms net 30, subject to 5 percent GST. The invoice was dated June 3.
	6	Paid for the purchase of June 3 (STU Suppliers Inc.), cheque no. 12.
	7	Paid $8,500 wages to employee, cheque no. 13.
	9	Owner withdrew $22,500 for personal use, cheque no. 14.
	11	Collected the amount owed by Thomas Chase (June 1).
	13	Purchased equipment from DE Machinery Inc. for $25,000 plus 5 percent GST, terms n/30. The invoice was dated June 12.
	14	Issued a debit memo to DE Machinery Inc. (June 13) for $3,000 plus 5 percent GST of equipment returned as defective.
	15	Sold merchandise to DePloy Construction Ltd. for cash of $7,500 plus 7 percent PST and 5 percent GST. Inventory had a cost of $4,500.
	16	Paid the account owing to DE Machinery Inc. (June 13, 14), cheque no. 15.
	17	Purchased equipment from Alfreds Equipment Inc. for $21,000 plus 5 percent GST, terms net 60. The invoice was dated June 16.
	22	Paid a $15,000 note due to Commercial Bank, plus interest of $1,500, cheque no. 16.
	24	Sold $5,200 of merchandise for cash; inventory cost was $3,000. The sale was subject to 7 percent PST and 5 percent GST.

Understanding how manual accounting systems are used, using the cash receipts journal and the cash payments journal with GST and PST (perpetual inventory system)
② ③ ④ A1

---

*This Problem covers Chapter 7 Appendix topics. The Appendix can be found on MyAccountingLab.

25	Paid $2,250 to Canada Revenue Agency for income taxes owing for the year 2016, cheque no. 17.
26	Returned merchandise purchased from STU Suppliers Inc., $1,500 plus 5 percent GST.
28	Purchased inventory for $9,000 plus 5 percent GST from Damon Ltd., promising to pay in 30 days. The invoice was dated June 28.
30	Recorded the adjusting journal entries for the month of June.

Required

1. For each date, indicate which journal would be used to record the transaction assuming Lively Home Products uses a general journal, a sales journal, a cash receipts journal, a purchases journal, and a cash payments journal.
2. Record the appropriate transactions in the cash receipts journal and the cash payments journal using the special journal formats shown in Exhibit 7A–1 found in the online Appendix.

CHALLENGE PROBLEMS

Problem 7–1C

Advantage of an effective accounting information system ①

An accounting information system that provides timely, accurate information to management is an important asset of any organization. This is especially true as organizations become larger and move into different parts of the world. The integration of computers into many organizations' information systems has enhanced their usefulness to the organization.

Required Assume your older sister is a pharmacist. She regards an information system as simply an accounting system that keeps track of her company's revenues and expenses. Explain to her how an effective accounting information system can make her a more effective pharmacist.

Problem 7–2C

Providing advice about a computerized accounting system ②

Information technology is increasingly sophisticated, and everyone wants the latest technology. Your brother has asked you about installing this "wonderful" computer system in his car dealership and auto repair business. The salesperson has promised your brother that the system "will do everything he wants and then some." Your brother has come to you for advice about acquiring this new computerized accounting information system. At present he uses Sage 50 with only the general ledger module.

Required Provide the advice your brother wants, focusing on the costs of the new computerized accounting information system; your brother has been told all the positive aspects of purchasing the system.

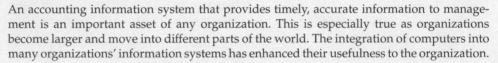

EXTENDING YOUR KNOWLEDGE

DECISION PROBLEMS

Reconstructing transactions from amounts posted to the accounts receivable subsidiary ledger ③

Cash receipts journal: Total debit to Cash, $31,632

Decision Problem 1

A fire destroyed some accounting records of Critter Hollow Company. The owner, Jennifer Chu, asks for your help in reconstructing the records. *She needs to know the beginning and ending balances of Accounts Receivable and the credit sales and cash receipts on account from customers during March.* All Critter Hollow Company sales are on credit, with payment terms of 2/10, n/30. All cash receipts on account reached Critter Hollow Company within the

10-day discount period, except as noted. The only accounting record preserved from the fire is the accounts receivable subsidiary ledger, which follows:

Adam Chi					
Date		Jrnl. Ref.	Debit	Credit	Balance
Mar. 1	Balance				0
8		S.6	15,000		15,000
16		S.6	3,000		18,000
18		CR.8		15,000	3,000
19		J.5		600	2,400
27		CR.8		2,400	0

Anna Fowler					
Date		Jrnl. Ref.	Debit	Credit	Balance
Mar. 1	Balance				3,300
5		CR.8		3,300	0
11		S.6	1,200		1,200
21		CR.8		1,200	0
24		S.6	12,000		12,000

Norris Associates Ltd.					
Date		Jrnl. Ref.	Debit	Credit	Balance
Mar. 1	Balance				9,000
15		S.6	9,000		18,000
29		CR.8		8,700*	9,300

*Cash receipt did not occur within the discount period.

Robertson Inc.					
Date		Jrnl. Ref.	Debit	Credit	Balance
Mar. 1	Balance				1,500
3		CR.8		1,500	0
25		S.6	12,000		12,000
29		S.6	3,600		15,600

Decision Problem 2

The external auditor must ensure that the amounts shown on the balance sheet for Accounts Receivable represent actual amounts that customers owe the company. Each customer account in the accounts receivable subsidiary ledger must represent an actual credit sale to the person or company indicated, and the customer's balance must not have been collected. This auditing concept is called *validity*, or *validating* the existence of the accounts receivable.

The auditor must also ensure that all amounts that the company owes are included in Accounts Payable and other liability accounts. For example, all credit purchases of inventory made by the company (and not yet paid) should be included in the balance of the Accounts Payable account. This auditing concept is called *completeness*.

Required Suggest how an auditor might test a customer's Account Receivable balance for validity. Indicate how the auditor might test the balance of the Accounts Payable account for completeness.

Understanding an accounting system

1. C

2. The feature of an effective accounting information system most compromised in this example would be compatibility. The new system is not compatible with the old system, and the new system would have to have other valuable features or qualities to consider changing to it. To solve this dilemma, it might be possible to change the job-order numbers to "-1" instead of the alpha character, assuming the new system would accept this. For example, instead of job number 1645a, you could use job number 1645-1.

3.

T. Pioneer, Capital	30001
Advertising Expense	51001
Building	17001
Accounts Payable	21001
Sales Revenue	41001
Miscellaneous Expenses	59001
Cash	11001
T. Pioneer, Withdrawals	31001
Land	18001
Notes Payable	25001
Accounts Receivable	12001
Salaries Expense	54001

Note that the expenses are assumed to be listed in the chart of accounts in alphabetical order. They could also be listed in another order, with Salaries Expense having account number 51001 and Advertising Expense having account number 54001. However, Miscellaneous Expense is always listed last on an income statement and would typically have the final account number of the expenses, although this may not always be the case.

4. Possible ranges of account numbers in the chart of accounts are:

Notes Receivable	12002 to 17000, although likely in the middle part of the range since Supplies are more liquid and an Automobile is less liquid than Notes Receivable
Automobile	12002 to 17000, although likely in the end part of the range since Supplies and Notes Receivable are more liquid than an Automobile
Supplies	12002 to 17000, although likely in the earlier part of the range since Supplies are more liquid than Notes Receivable and an Automobile
Supplies Expense	54002 to 59000, since alphabetically this account would follow Salaries Expense
Unearned Revenue	21002 to 25000 or 25002 to 29999, depending on how soon Unearned Revenue would be earned compared to Notes Payable being paid
Service Revenue	41002 to 49999

5. If Slopes Ski Shop did not use an accounts receivable subsidiary ledger and Claudette Cabot asked you for her account balance, it would be difficult to answer her. A subsidiary ledger is needed for ready access to the data for each customer. The inefficient alternative is to look through all transactions in the general journal for the ones involving Claudette Cabot—definitely an error-prone and time-consuming alternative.

6. a. The sales journal records sales on account. The transactions on February 2 and 15, 2017, were sales on account and are shown in the sales journal below.
   b. The cash receipts journal records cash received from all sources. The transactions on February 4, 8, 13, and 28, 2017, were cash receipts from all sources and are shown in the cash receipts journal below.

Sales Journal						Page 2
Date 2017	Invoice No.	Account Debited	Post. Ref.	Accounts Receivable Dr Sales Revenue Cr		Cost Of Goods Sold Dr Inventory Cr
Feb. 2	291	Limpert Design Ltd.		400		240
15	292	Frankie's Diner		800		550
28				1,200		790

Cash Receipts Journal								Page 5
	Debits			Credits				
					Other Accounts			
Date 2017	Cash	Sales. Disc	Accounts Receivable	Sales Revenue	Account Title	Post. Ref.	Amount	Cost Of Goods Sold Dr Inventory Cr
Feb. 4	300			300				204
8	200	0	200					
13	400	0	400		Limpert Design Ltd.			
28	550			550				325
28	1,450	0	600	850				529

7. a. Debit
   b. No Effect
   c. No Effect
   d. No Effect

8. The purchases journal records all purchases made on account. The transactions on February 3, 14, and 20, 2017, were purchases on account and are shown in the purchases journal below.

					Credits		Debits		
Purchases Journal									**Page 9**
							Other Accounts		
Date 2017	Supplier Account Credited	Invoice Date	Terms	Post Ref.	Accounts Payable	Inventory	Account Title	Post. Ref.	Amount
Feb. 3	Dunning Co.	03/02/17	1/10, n/30		2,600	2,600			
14	Office Corp.	14/02/17	n/30		500		Supplies		500
20	Super Sales Ltd.	19/02/17	n/30		1,600	1,600			
28					4,700	4,200			500

9. The cash payments journal records all cash payments paid by cheque. The transactions on February 5, 10, 13, 22, and 25, 2017, were cash payments paid by cheque and are shown in the cash payments journal below.

				Debits		Credits	
Cash Payments Journal							**Page 6**
Date 2017	Chq. No.	Payee/Accounts Debited	Post Ref.	Other Accounts	Accounts Payable	Inventory	Cash
Feb. 5	45	Office Depot/Office Furniture		1,400			1,400
10	46	Mega Corp./Inventory		1,300			1,300
13	47	Dunning Co.			2,600	26	2,574
22	48	Insurance/Prepaid Insurance		2,000			2,000
25	49	Utilities/Utilities Expense		450			450
28				5,150	2,600	26	7,724

10. a. Credit
    b. No Effect
    c. No Effect
    d. Debit
    e. Debit

11. a. Cash payments journal
    b. General journal
    c. Cash receipts journal
    d. Cash payments journal
    e. Purchases journal
    f. General journal
    g. General journal
    h. Cash receipts journal
    i. Sales journal
    j. Cash receipts journal

12. a. Cash receipts journal
    b. Cash receipts journal
    c. Cash receipts journal
    d. Purchases journal
    e. Cash receipts journal
    f. Sales journal, Cash receipts journal
    g. Cash payments journal
    h. Purchases journal
    i. Purchases journal
    j. Cash payments journal

13.

May 8	Store Equipment	1,000	
	Owners' Capital		1,000
15	Accounts Payable, Woolley	500	
	Inventory		500
30	Sales Returns and Allowances	200	
	Accounts Receivable, Ginko		200
30	Inventory	100	
	Cost of Goods Sold		100

COMPREHENSIVE PROBLEM FOR PART 1

1. COMPLETING A MERCHANDISER'S ACCOUNTING CYCLE

3. Net income, $14,700
Total assets, $139,305

The end-of-month trial balance of Skelly Building Materials at January 31, 2017, is shown below.

		Balance	
	SKELLY BUILDING MATERIALS Trial Balance January 31, 2017		
Account Number	**Account**	**Debit**	**Credit**
110	Cash	$ 8,215	
120	Accounts receivable	9,545	
130	Inventory	30,200	
140	Supplies	1,350	
150	Building	64,085	
151	Accumulated amortization—building		$ 18,000
160	Fixtures	22,800	
161	Accumulated amortization—fixtures		2,900
170	Land	30,000	
200	Accounts payable		11,650
205	Salary payable		0
210	Interest payable		0
240	Unearned sales revenue		3,280
250	Note payable, long-term		41,000
300	S. Skelly, capital		72,490
311	S. Skelly, withdrawals	4,600	
400	Sales revenue		93,985
402	Sales discounts	2,400	
430	Sales returns and allowances	2,820	
500	Cost of goods sold	51,500	
600	Selling expense	10,760	
700	General expense	5,030	
705	Interest expense	0	
	Total	$243,305	$243,305

a. Supplies consumed during the month, $750. One-half is selling expense, and the other half is general expense.

b. Amortization for the month: building, $2,000; fixtures, $2,400. One-quarter of amortization is selling expense, and three-quarters is general expense.

c. Unearned sales revenue still unearned, $600.

d. Accrued salaries, a general expense, $1,825.

e. Accrued interest expense, $1,640.

f. Inventory on hand, $29,360. Skelly Building Materials uses the perpetual inventory system.

Required

1. Using three-column ledger accounts, open the accounts listed on the trial balance, inserting their unadjusted balances. Also open account number 312, Income Summary. Date the balances of the following accounts January 1: Supplies; Building; Accumulated Amortization—Building; Fixtures; Accumulated Amortization—Fixtures; Land; Unearned Sales Revenue; and S. Skelly, Capital. Date the balance of S. Skelly, Withdrawals January 31.

2. Enter the trial balance on a worksheet and complete the worksheet for the month ended January 31, 2017. Skelly Building Materials groups all operating expenses under two accounts, Selling Expense and General Expense. Leave two blank lines under Selling Expense and three blank lines under General Expense.

3. Prepare the company's multi-step income statement and statement of owner's equity for the month ended January 31, 2017. Also prepare the balance sheet at that date in report form.

4. Journalize the adjusting and closing entries at January 31, 2017, using Page 3 of the general journal.

5. Post the adjusting and closing entries, using dates and posting references.

6. Compute Skelly Building Materials's current ratio and debt ratio at January 31, 2017, and compare these values with the industry averages of 1.9 for the current ratio and 0.57 for the debt ratio. Compute the gross margin percentage and the rate of inventory turnover for the month (the inventory balance at the end of December 2016 was $33,250) and compare these ratio values with the industry averages of 0.36 for the gross margin ratio and 1.7 times for inventory turnover. Does Skelly Building Materials appear to be stronger or weaker than the average company in the building materials industry?

2. COMPLETING THE ACCOUNTING CYCLE FOR A MERCHANDISING ENTITY

Note: This problem can be solved with or without special journals. See Requirement 2.

Azizi Distributors closes its books and prepares financial statements at the end of each month. Azizi uses the perpetual inventory system. The company completed the following transactions during August 2017:

5. Net loss, $1,057
Total assets, $59,293

Aug.	1	Issued cheque no. 682 for August office rent, $1,000 (debit Rent Expense).
	2	Issued cheque no. 683 to pay salaries of $1,620, which includes salary payable of $465 from July 31. Azizi does not use reversing entries.
	2*	Issued invoice no. 503 for sale on account to R. T. Loeb, $300. Azizi's cost of this merchandise was $95.
	3	Purchased inventory on credit terms of 1/15, n/60 from Grant Ltd., $700. The invoice was dated August 3.
	4	Received net amount of cash on account from Fullam Corp., $2,058, within the discount period.
	4	Sold inventory for cash, $1,165 (cost, $552).
	5	Received from Park-Hee Inc. merchandise that had been sold earlier for $275 (cost, $87). The wrong merchandise had been sent.
	5	Issued cheque no. 684 to purchase supplies for cash, $390.
	6	Collected interest revenue of $550.
	7	Issued invoice no. 504 for sale on account to K. D. Skipper Inc., $1,200 (cost, $380).
	8	Issued cheque no. 685 to pay Fayda Corp. $1,300 of the amount owed at July 31. This payment occurred after the end of the discount period.

11	Issued cheque no. 686 to pay Grant Ltd. the net amount owed from August 3.
12*	Received cash from R. T. Loeb in full settlement of her account from August 2. R. T. Loeb notified Azizi that only one-quarter of the goods ordered had been received, but agreed to pay now if Azizi held the remaining goods in the Azizi warehouse until September.
16	Issued cheque no. 687 to pay salary expense of $620.
19	Purchased inventory for cash, $425, issuing cheque no. 688.
22	Purchased furniture on credit terms of 3/15, n/60 from Beaver Corporation, $255. The invoice was dated August 22.
23	Sold inventory on account to Fullam Corp., issuing invoice no. 505 for $4,983 (cost, $1,576).
24	Received $2,193 of the July 31 amount receivable from K. D. Skipper Inc.—after the end of the discount period.
25	Issued cheque no. 689 to pay utilities, $1,216.
26	Purchased supplies on credit terms of 2/10, n/30 from Fayda Corp., $90. The invoice was dated August 26.
30	Returned damaged inventory to company from whom Azizi made the cash purchase on August 19, receiving cash of $425.
30	Granted a sales allowance of $88 to K. D. Skipper Inc.
31	Purchased inventory on credit terms of 1/10, n/30 from Suncrest Supply Ltd., $5,165. The invoice was dated August 31.
31	Issued cheque no. 690 to Mona Azizi, owner of Azizi, for $850.

Required

1. Open the following three-column ledger accounts with their account numbers and July 31 balances in the ledgers indicated.

General Ledger		
101	Cash	$ 2,245
102	Accounts Receivable	12,280
104	Interest Receivable	0
105	Inventory	20,900
109	Supplies	670
117	Prepaid Insurance	1,100
140	Note Receivable, Long-term	5,500
160	Furniture	18,635
161	Accumulated Amortization—Furniture	5,275
201	Accounts Payable	5,300
204	Salary Payable	465
207	Interest Payable	2,160
208	Unearned Sales Revenue	0
220	Note Payable, Long-term	21,000

(Continued)

---

*Azizi Distributors sold inventory on account to R. T. Loeb on August 2 and collected in full on August 12. Loeb indicated that the shipment was incomplete and arranged with Azizi to have the goods shipped to Loeb in September. At August 31, $225 of unearned sales revenue needs to be recorded and the cost of this merchandise ($71) needs to be removed from Cost of Goods Sold and returned to Inventory.

(Continued)

301	Mona Azizi, Capital	27,130
303	Mona Azizi, Withdrawals	0
400	Income Summary	0
401	Sales Revenue	0
402	Sales Discounts	0
403	Sales Returns and Allowances	0
410	Interest Revenue	0
501	Cost of Goods Sold	0
510	Salary Expense	0
513	Rent Expense	0
514	Amortization Expense—Furniture	0
516	Insurance Expense	0
517	Utilities Expense	0
519	Supplies Expense	0
523	Interest Expense	0

Accounts receivable subsidiary ledger: Fullam Corp., $2,100; R. T. Loeb, $0; Park-Hee Inc., $5,795; K. D. Skipper Inc., $4,385.

Accounts payable subsidiary ledger: Beaver Corporation, $0; Fayda Corp., $5,300; Grant Ltd., $0; Suncrest Supply Ltd., $0.

2. Ask your professor for directions. Journalize the August transactions either in the general journal (Page 9; explanations not required) or, as illustrated in this chapter, in a series of special journals: a sales journal (Page 4), a cash receipts journal (Page 11), a purchases journal (Page 8), a cash payments journal (Page 5), and a general journal (Page 9). Azizi makes all credit sales on terms of 2/10, n/30.

3. Post daily to the accounts receivable subsidiary ledger and the accounts payable subsidiary ledger. On August 31, 2017, post to the general ledger.

4. Prepare a trial balance in the Trial Balance columns of a worksheet and use the following information to complete the worksheet for the month ended August 31, 2017:

   a. Accrued interest revenue, $500

   b. Supplies on hand, $495

   c. Prepaid insurance expired, $275

   d. Amortization expense, $115

   e. Accrued salary expense, $515

   f. Accrued interest expense, $660

   g. Unearned sales revenue, $225 (refers to August 2 transaction)

   h. Inventory on hand, $23,850

5. Prepare Azizi's multi-step income statement and statement of owner's equity for August 2017. Prepare the balance sheet at August 31, 2017 (account format).

6. Journalize and post the adjusting and closing entries.

7. Prepare a post-closing trial balance at August 31, 2017. Also, balance the total of the customer accounts in the accounts receivable subsidiary ledger against the Accounts Receivable balance in the general ledger. Do the same for the accounts payable subsidiary ledger and Accounts Payable in the general ledger.

8 INTERNAL CONTROL AND CASH

CONNECTING CHAPTER 8

MyAccountingLab   The **Summary** for Chapter 8 appears on page 474. This lists all of the MyAccountingLab resources. **Accounting Vocabulary** with definitions for this chapter's material appears on page 475.

One would think that theft by internal associates only happens at large, for-profit corporations. But not-for-profit organizations, charities, and clubs can become victims, too. Any organization can be at risk when employees—or even volunteers—are given the power to manage large sums of money with little or no supervision. In many cases the money is never recovered, even if the thief is charged.

This is exactly what happened to Vancouver-based International Centre for Criminal Law Reform (ICCLR), which is housed in Allard Hall at the University of British Columbia. Founded in 1991, ICCLR is a joint initiative of governments, universities, and the International Society for the Reform of Criminal Law. The goal of the organization is to promote the rule of law, good governance, and human rights both at home and around the world. In 2013, however, nine charges of fraud were laid against an accountant, Janet Mercedes Bayda, for allegedly embezzling over $1 million from the law centre over several years by creating false payments for entries in the account records.

Although $425,000 was recovered in January and February 2012 with Bayda's cooperation, the organization was still hit hard by the theft. The ICCLR is not a large operation, with only four full-time employees and 2012 revenues of $650,000. The money recovered allowed the centre to remain operational, but they had to cut some staff to do so.[1]

The use of strong internal controls and procedures likely would have prevented this large theft. This chapter discusses the importance of internal controls, especially over cash, and how companies can create good internal control policies.

---

[1] Ming Wong, "Accountant Allegedly Embezzled $1 Million from UBC-Based Law Centre," *The Ubyssey*, May 3, 2013, http://ubyssey.ca/news/accountant-allegedly-embezzled-1-million-from-ubc-based-law-centre. Reprinted with permission of *The Ubyssey*. ICCLR, "About Us," http://icclr.law.ubc.ca/about-us.

> Every company, especially an expanding company, faces similar challenges:

- How will the company safeguard its assets?
- How will the company make sure its managers and employees follow policies that are best for the company?

This chapter discusses **internal control**—the organizational plan that companies use to protect their assets and records. Internal controls are important to *all* managers, not just the accounting manager, because assets in every department throughout the company need to be protected. The chapter applies internal control techniques mainly to cash, because cash is an attractive asset for unethical employees to steal. The chapter also provides a framework for making ethical judgments in business. The material covered in this chapter is some of the most important in all of business; however, it is sometimes overlooked, as in the example of ICCLR in the chapter-opening vignette.

Cash—which includes cash on hand in funds such as *petty cash*, cash on deposit in banks and trust companies (both Canadian cash and cash in other currencies), and cash equivalents, such as term deposits or **Treasury bills** (very safe, short-term financial instruments issued by the federal government)—is the most liquid asset an organization has. Accordingly, it is usually the first item under the heading "Current Assets" on the balance sheet and can also be called "Cash and Cash Equivalents." Cash does *not* include **postdated cheques** (which are cheques that can only be cashed on a future date) or **stale-dated cheques** (cheques that are more than six months old) since banks will not include them as part of a company's cash balance. Cash's liquidity is an advantage because it is easily exchangeable for other assets. However, cash's liquidity is also a disadvantage because it is the most attractive asset to steal, and therefore it must be protected with good internal controls and risk management policies. The next section will explain how organizations strive to protect their cash by using internal controls.

INTERNAL CONTROL

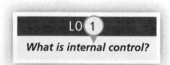

What is internal control?

One of a business owner's key responsibilities is to control operations. The owners set goals, hire managers to lead the way, and expect employees to carry out the plan.

Both in Canada (in the *CPA Canada Handbook*) and internationally, **internal control** consists of the process designed and put in place by management to provide reasonable assurance that the organization will achieve its objectives of reliable financial reporting, effective and efficient operations, and compliance with applicable laws and regulations. You may see examples of these controls when you are processing transactions at a bank or a retail store, such as when the teller at a bank may need a supervisor to authorize a transaction. Internal control is designed and put in place to address risks that threaten the achievement of any of the organization's objectives. Key internal control objectives are:

- **Encouraging operational efficiency.** A company must optimize the use of resources, minimize expenses, and ensure management's business policies are implemented and followed while operating in agreement with regulations and reporting requirements.

- **Preventing and detecting error and fraud.** Companies must prevent and detect error and fraud, which lead to a waste of company resources.

- **Safeguarding assets and records.** A company must protect its assets so that company resources are not wasted needlessly. Safeguarding records ensures they are accurate and complete when needed for decision making.

- **Providing accurate, reliable information.** A company must provide accurate, reliable information, including accounting records. This is essential for decision making.

REAL WORLD EXAMPLE

One of the auditor's first steps in auditing a business is to understand and evaluate its internal controls. If a company has good controls, then misstatements are minimized and are usually corrected before the financial statements are prepared. If the control system is weak, then misstatements can go undetected, as mentioned in the chapter-opening vignette.

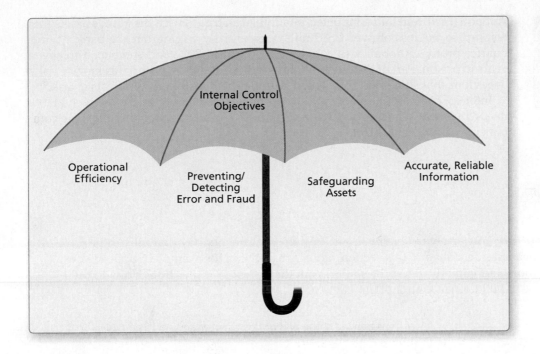

Companies cannot afford to waste resources. In the chapter-opening vignette, the accountant allegedly took money from the ICCLR and hid the theft. She stole a charity's resources. A company must safeguard its assets, or it could experience the type of fraud illustrated in this story and waste its resources.

Accurate, reliable records are essential. Without reliable records, a manager cannot tell what investments to make or how much to charge for products, and banks cannot determine whether to make a loan.

How critical are internal controls? They are so important that the US Congress passed a law that requires public companies (those that sell their shares of stock to the public) to maintain a system of internal controls.

The Sarbanes-Oxley Act and the Dodd-Frank Act

In 2005, the former chief executive officer of WorldCom, Edmonton-born Bernie Ebbers, was convicted of securities fraud and sentenced to 25 years in prison. Up until 2008, the WorldCom scandal was the largest accounting scandal in US history.

As the scandals unfolded in the United States, many people asked "How can these things happen? Where were the auditors?" To address public concern, Congress passed the Sarbanes-Oxley Act of 2002 (SOX). SOX revamped the way corporations were directed and controlled in the United States and changed the requirements for those connected in any way with US companies or stock exchanges as well as the accounting profession. The Dodd-Frank Act amended SOX, granting authority to the Public Company Accounting Oversight Board (PCAOB) to inspect foreign auditing firms that practise in the United States. Basically, the act requires that foreign firms comply with SOX when they are employed by US public companies that list on a US stock exchange.[2] The details of these proposed changes are still in the discussion phase as of 2015.

A real-world example of why this type of oversight is necessary occurred in 2011. In September of that year, the Swiss bank UBS announced that Kweku

---

[2] American Institute of CPAs, "U.S. Sweeping Financial Reform Act Has Implications around the Globe," February 8, 2011, www.aicpa.org/news/featurednews/pages/ ussweepingfinancialreformacthasimplicationsaroundtheglobe.aspx. © 2011, AICPA. All rights reserved. Used by permission.

Adoboli (pictured) had conducted unauthorized trades with the bank's assets that resulted in the loss of over US$2 billion, essentially wiping out the bank's third-quarter profits. Adoboli was convicted of fraud in 2012 and sentenced to seven years in prison. Part of the intent of the Dodd-Frank Act is to stop this kind of risky behaviour that some firms engage in, putting their customers' interests at risk.[3]

Internal controls enable people to do business securely and effectively. How does a business achieve good internal control? The next section identifies the components of internal control.

> Try It!

1. Internal controls do not only apply to "big business." We do things every day that mirror the four internal control measures described in this section. Consider your car, for example. Suppose you always lock the doors and you buy gas at the station with the lowest price per litre. How do these personal acts relate to an internal control plan?

Solutions appear at the end of this chapter and on MyAccountingLab

THE COMPONENTS OF INTERNAL CONTROL

LO 2

What should we think about when designing an internal control system?

A business can achieve its internal control objectives by applying five components, which can be remembered by the acronym CRIME:

- Control procedures/environment
- Risk assessment
- Information system   CRIME
- Monitoring of controls
- Environmental controls

Control Environment   This is the "tone at the top" of the business. It starts with the owner and the top managers. They must have goal-oriented rules and processes and they must behave in a way that sets a good example for company employees. For example, managers who cheat on expense claims and brag about it will likely have employees that do the same. Examples of good control procedures include assigning responsibilities, separating duties, and using security devices to protect assets.

Risk Assessment   This is identifying a company's risks. Some risks are controllable, such as retaining good employees, while others are not, such as weathering the ups and downs of the economy. For example, companies could face big problems if a key employee/owner dies, supply chain disruptions occur, or the firm's home currency is devalued. All firms should have policies in place to deal with such risks. Credit risks and operational risks such as legal liability and lawsuits are also cause for concern without strong risk management policies.

Information System   A good information communications system is critical and provides the owner of a business with accurate information to keep track of assets, track receivables, and measure profits and losses.

---

[3] Adrienne Carter and Ben Protess, "UBS Scandal Is a Reminder about Why Dodd-Frank Came to Be," *New York Times,* September 19, 2011, http://dealbook.nytimes.com/2011/09/19/ubs-scandal-is-reminder-of-why-dodd-frank-came-to-be/?_r=0.

Monitoring of Controls   Companies should hire external auditors to express an opinion on the company's internal controls. In large companies, internal auditors monitor company controls to safeguard assets, whereas in small companies the managers and the owner ensure controls are operating as they should. Exhibit 8–1 diagrams the components of internal control, using car ownership as an example.

EXHIBIT 8–1 | The Components of Internal Control (Applied to Car Ownership)

Control Environment: Owner takes responsibility for the car and its operation

Monitoring of Controls: Checking engine lights that go on; checking when the car alarm is activated

Risk Assessment: Checking road conditions in winter before heading out

Information System: Gas gauge and all other gauges and displays on the dashboard; technician's scope

Control Procedures: Getting a driver's licence; car alarm for security

Environmental Controls   Governments, organizations, and individuals have measures in place that help ensure that the business world runs honestly and efficiently. Governments have rules and regulations often called red tape, organizations have codes of ethics and rules of professional conduct (e.g., CPA Canada oversees the members and students within the accounting profession), and individuals rely on personal self-control measures such as "the golden rule." It is the hope of organizations that these environmental influences in conjunction with the other measures discussed ensure that owners and employees take responsibility for problems as they occur.

Internal control is a management priority, not merely a part of the accounting system. Thus, it is a responsibility not only of accountants but also of managers in all functional areas throughout the organization.

In annual reports, top managers take responsibility for the financial statements and the related system of internal control. A typical report states "Management is responsible for establishing and maintaining adequate internal control over financial reporting to provide reasonable assurance regarding the reliability of financial reporting and the preparation of financial statements for external purposes in accordance with GAAP."

Let's examine in detail how businesses create an effective system of internal control.

Internal Control Procedures

Whether the business is a large multinational company or a local department store, an effective system of internal controls has the procedures or characteristics discussed below.

Competent, Reliable, and Ethical Personnel   Companies must hire qualified, well-educated, and skilled employees and pay them fairly. Companies must also train employees to do their job and must supervise their work. This will help build a competent staff. Internal controls are most effective when employees at all levels and in all areas adopt the organization's goals and ethical standards.

Assignment of Responsibilities   In a business with good internal controls, each employee has certain responsibilities and access to only certain information. For example, two important duties are writing cheques and doing the accounting. In a large company, the **treasurer** is responsible for cash management whereas the **controller** is the chief accounting officer. The controller approves invoices (bills) for payment and the treasurer signs the cheques. Both the treasurer and the controller report to the president, as shown below.

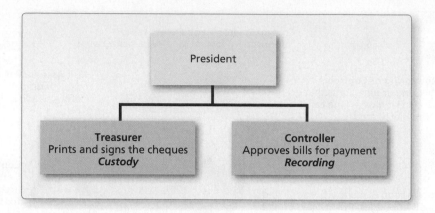

In small companies, a clerk prepares invoices for payment and adjusts the accounting records, but the controller or owner signs the cheques. With clearly assigned responsibilities, all duties are carried out.

Separation of Duties   Smart management divides the responsibilities for transactions between two or more people or departments. *Separation of duties* (also called *segregation of duties*) limits the chances for fraud and promotes the accuracy of accounting records by dividing up the three tasks of authorization, recording, and custody. Separation of duties can be divided into three parts:

1. *Separate operations from accounting.* Accounting should be completely separate from operating departments, such as production and sales. Sales figures could be inflated, and top managers wouldn't know how much the company actually sold unless an impartial department records the information.

2. *Separate the custody of assets from accounting.* Accountants must not handle cash, and cashiers must not have access to the accounting records. If one employee has both cash-handling and accounting duties, as in the chapter-opening vignette about the ICCLR, theft is encouraged.

   Likewise, only warehouse employees with no accounting duties should have custody of inventory. If they were allowed to account for the inventory, they could steal it and make fake journal entries so that inventory disappears from the accounting records without actually being sold.

3. *Separation of the authorization of transactions from the custody of related assets.* Persons who authorize transactions should not handle the related asset. For example, the same individual should not authorize the payment of a supplier's invoice and also sign the cheque to pay the invoice.

Even the smallest businesses should have internal controls and some separation of duties. For example, if the bookkeeper writes all cheques and keeps the general ledger records, the owner should sign all cheques and reconcile the monthly bank statement.

Proper Authorization   An organization generally has written rules that outline approved procedures. Any deviation from policy requires *proper authorization*. For example, managers or assistant managers of retail stores often ask for ID when verifying payment by a customer or approving returns.

Internal and External Audits   External audits provide users of financial information and management with reasonable assurance that the financial statements fairly present the financial position of an organization and the results of its operations. An **audit** is an examination of the organization's financial statements and the accounting systems, controls, and records that produced them.

Audits can be internal or external. *Internal auditors* are employees of the organization. They strive to ensure that other employees are following company policies and that operations are running efficiently. Internal auditors also determine whether the company is following legal requirements, such as privacy protection.

External auditors are completely independent of the organization. They are hired to determine that the organization's financial statements have been prepared in accordance with generally accepted accounting principles. Auditors can also be from other agencies, such as tax auditors from the Canada Revenue Agency. Both internal and external auditors should be independent of the operations they examine, and both should suggest improvements that can help the business run efficiently. Although proprietorships do not require external audits, proprietorships may have external audits completed to satisfy bankers or other financial statement users.

Use of Documents and Records   Business *documents and records* provide the details of business transactions. Such documents include sales invoices and purchase orders, and records include journals and ledgers. Documents should be prenumbered because a gap in the numbered sequence draws attention to a possible missing document.

In a bowling alley, for example, a key document is the score sheet. The manager can check on cashiers by comparing the number of games scored with the amount of cash received. By multiplying the number of games by the price per game to estimate the revenue and comparing this amount with each day's cash receipts, the manager can see whether the business is collecting all of its revenues.

Use of Electronic Devices and Computer Controls   Businesses use electronic devices to protect assets. For example, retailers like Winners control their inventories by attaching an *electronic sensor* to merchandise. The cashier removes the sensor at checkout. If a customer tries to remove an item from the store with the sensor attached an alarm sounds. According to Checkpoint Systems, which manufactures electronic sensors, these devices reduce loss due to theft by as much as 50 percent.

Other Controls   Businesses of all types keep cash and important documents in *fireproof vaults*. *Burglar alarms* protect buildings, and *security cameras* protect other property. *Loss-prevention specialists* train employees to spot suspicious activity.

Retailers receive most of their cash from customers on the spot. To safeguard cash, they use *point-of-sale terminals* that serve as a cash register and also record each transaction. Several times each day a supervisor removes the cash for deposit in the bank. Regular data backups help businesses reduce the risk of losing important information from theft or accidents.

Employees who handle cash might have an opportunity to steal it. Some businesses purchase **fidelity bonds** on cashiers; we say cashiers are "bonded." The bond is an insurance policy that reimburses the company for any losses from the employee's theft. Before issuing a fidelity bond, the insurance company investigates the employee's record.

Mandatory vacations and *job rotation* are also important internal controls. Vancity Credit Union, for example, moves employees from job to job. This improves morale by giving employees a broad view of the business. Also, knowing that someone else will be doing that job next month keeps an employee honest. Fraud is often

REAL WORLD EXAMPLE

In some audits, procedures and even the audit itself may occur as a surprise to the employees so that they cannot cover up fraud or weaknesses in the system.

REAL WORLD EXAMPLE

The Personal Information Protection and Electronic Documents Act is legislation requiring companies to safeguard private information about individuals. There are 10 principles of fair information practices. As an example, principle #7 states:

Safeguards: Protect personal information against loss or theft; safeguard the information from unauthorized access, disclosure, copying, use or modifications; protect personal information regardless of the format in which it is held.

REAL WORLD EXAMPLE

If a clerk in a retail store makes a mistake on the sales receipt, the receipt is not destroyed but is marked VOID. Most businesses use prenumbered sales receipts, so a missing receipt would be noticed.

discovered when someone takes vacation or is hospitalized unexpectedly because the person is not there to cover up the fraudulent activities, and the person filling in questions those activities.

Internal Controls for Ecommerce

Ecommerce creates its own unique types of risks. Hackers may gain access to confidential information, such as account numbers and passwords, that would normally be unavailable in face-to-face transactions. Confidentiality is a significant challenge for companies doing business online. To convince people to buy online, companies must ensure security of customer data.

Pitfalls Ecommerce pitfalls include the following:

- Stolen credit card numbers
- Computer viruses and Trojans
- Phishing expeditions and identity theft

Wireless networks (Wi-Fi) are creating new security hazards. There have been cases of companies potentially exposing their customers' financial data to outsiders because of a breach in their Internet security systems. For example, Target was hacked just before the busiest selling season—Christmas—in 2013. Hackers installed malware in the security and payments systems just before Thanksgiving of that year, when the Christmas selling season really starts to ramp up. The malware kicked in when customers swiped their credit card at any of Target's 1,797 US stores, capturing the customer's credit card number and storing it on a Target server that had been taken over by the hackers. This was the largest attack on a retailer in US history.[4]

Below is a list of some of the most common security pitfalls of ecommerce:

- *Computer viruses and Trojans.* A **computer virus** is a malicious program that (1) enters program code without consent and (2) performs destructive actions. A **Trojan** hides inside a legitimate program and works like a virus. Viruses can destroy or alter data, make bogus calculations, and infect files.

- *Phishing expeditions.* **Phishing** is when thieves create legitimate-sounding bogus websites to attract lots of visitors that the thieves use to obtain account numbers and passwords from the unsuspecting visitors. The thieves use the data for illicit purposes.

- *Identity theft.* Identity theft occurs when thieves obtain and control your personal data to steal your assets, make purchases, or obtain loans in your name without your knowledge or permission. This can often have devastating effects on a person's finances by leaving them with no assets or large debts or by ruining their credit record. This is a problem for companies as well, and the advice that applies to individuals also applies to companies: Never give private information or personal identification numbers (PINs) to companies or people you don't know, especially over the Internet.

Security Measures To address the risks posed by ecommerce, companies have devised a number of security measures, including encryption and firewalls.

- *Encryption.* The server holding confidential information should always be secure, but sometimes hackers try to enter a server to get access to customer data. One technique for protecting customer data is encryption. **Encryption** rearranges messages by a mathematical process. The encrypted message cannot

---

[4] Michael Riley, "Missed Alarms and 40 Milllion Stolen Credit Card Numbers: How Target Blew It," *Bloomberg Business*, March 13, 2014, www.bloomberg.com/bw/articles/2014-03-13/target-missed-alarms-in-epic-hack-of-credit-card-data.

be read by anyone who does not know the process. An accounting example uses check-sum digits for account numbers. Each account number has its last digit equal to the sum of the previous digits, for example, Customer Number 2237, where 2 + 2 + 3 = 7. Any account number that fails this test triggers an error message.

- *Firewalls.* **Firewalls** limit access to a local network. Network members can access the network, but non-members cannot. Usually several firewalls are built into the system. At the point of entry, passwords, PINs, and signatures are used to restrict entry. More sophisticated firewalls are used deeper in the network.

The Limitations of Internal Control

Unfortunately, most internal controls can be circumvented or overcome by two limitations: collusion and the cost–benefit constraint. **Collusion**—where two or more people work as a team—can beat internal controls. Consider the Classic Theatre. Geoff and Lana can design a scheme in which Geoff sells the tickets and pockets the cash from 10 customers. Lana, the ticket taker, admits 10 customers without tickets. Geoff and Lana then split the cash. To prevent this situation, the manager must take additional steps, such as counting the people in the theatre and matching that figure against the number of ticket stubs retained. But that takes time away from other duties.

However, the stricter the internal control system, the more it costs. A complex system of internal control may strangle the business with red tape. How tight should the controls be? Internal controls must be judged in the light of the costs and benefits. An example of a good **cost–benefit constraint** is a security guard at a store, who costs about $28,000 a year. On average, each guard prevents about $50,000 of theft. The net benefit to the store is $22,000.

Indigo Books and Music's management acknowledges the limitations of internal controls on page 23 in their 2014 Annual Report:

> All internal control systems, no matter how well designed, have inherent limitations. Therefore, even those systems determined to be effective can provide only reasonable assurance with respect to consolidated financial statements preparation and presentation. Additionally, management is necessarily required to use judgment in evaluation controls and procedures.[5]

A control system, no matter how well conceived or operated, can provide only reasonable, not absolute, assurance that the objectives of the system are met.

> **2.** Geoff works the late movie shift at Classic Theatre. Occasionally Geoff must sell tickets *and* take the tickets as customers enter the theatre. Standard procedure requires that Geoff tear the tickets, give one-half to the customer, and keep the other half. To control cash receipts, the manager compares each night's cash receipts with the number of ticket stubs on hand.
>
>   a. How could Geoff take money from the theatre's cash receipts and hide the theft? What additional steps should the manager take to strengthen the internal control over cash receipts?
>
>   b. What is the internal control weakness in this situation? Explain the weakness.
>
>   c. What electronic device is often used at concerts and events to ensure legitimate tickets are presented by the patrons?

(Continued)

---

[5] From Indigo Books and Music Inc. 2014 Annual Report (page 37), http://static.indigoimages.ca/2014/corporate/Indigo_FY14AnnualReport.pdf.

(Continued)

3. What problems can result when a sales clerk can also grant credit approval and record the sales in addition to handling the cash?

4. Match each of these terms with its description:

_____ Computer virus	a. Collecting passwords and personal data using bogus websites
_____ Encryption	b. Using passwords and PINs to limit access to a local network
_____ Trojan	c. Rearranging messages and data so they cannot be read during transmission over the Internet
_____ Firewall	d. A malicious and destructive program that enters program code without consent
_____ Phishing	e. A malicious program that hides inside a legitimate program to corrupt data

Solutions appear at the end of this chapter and on MyAccountingLab

THE BANK ACCOUNT AS A CONTROL DEVICE

LO 3

What do we do when the bank statement balance and the cash account balance are not the same?

Cash is the most liquid asset because it is the fundamental medium of exchange used in our society—it is the currency used to pay for goods and services that are bought and sold. Cash is easy to conceal, easy to move, and relatively easy to steal. As a result, most businesses create specific controls for cash.

Keeping cash in a *bank account* helps because banks have established practices for safeguarding customers' money. Banks also provide customers with detailed records of their transactions. To take full advantage of these control features, a business should deposit all cash receipts in the bank and make all cash payments through the bank rather than paying for things out of the cash register. An exception is petty cash, which we look at later.

The documents related to the use of a bank account include the following:

- Signature cards and electronic signatures on file
- Deposit books or slips
- Cheques
- Bank statements
- Bank reconciliations

Signature Card Banks require each person authorized to transact business through an account to sign a *signature card*. The signature card shows each authorized person's signature. This helps protect against forgery. The teller sees an electronic copy of this card when processing a transaction on the account.

Deposit Slip Banks supply standard forms such as *deposit slips* or *deposit books*. The customer fills in the dollar amount of each deposit. As proof of the transaction, the customer keeps a deposit receipt. A bank machine also gives a receipt, but even the smallest business should use deposit books or deposit slips to ensure proper documentation.

Cheque To pay from a bank account, the company writes a **cheque**, which is the document that tells the bank to pay the designated person or company a specified amount of money. There are three people or organizations involved with every cheque:

- The *maker*, who signs the cheque
- The *payee*, to whom the cheque is paid
- The *bank* on which the cheque is drawn

Exhibit 8–2 shows a cheque drawn on the bank account of Business Research Inc., the maker. The cheque has two parts: the cheque itself and the **remittance advice**, an optional attachment that tells the payee the reason for payment.

EXHIBIT 8–2 | Cheque with Remittance Advice

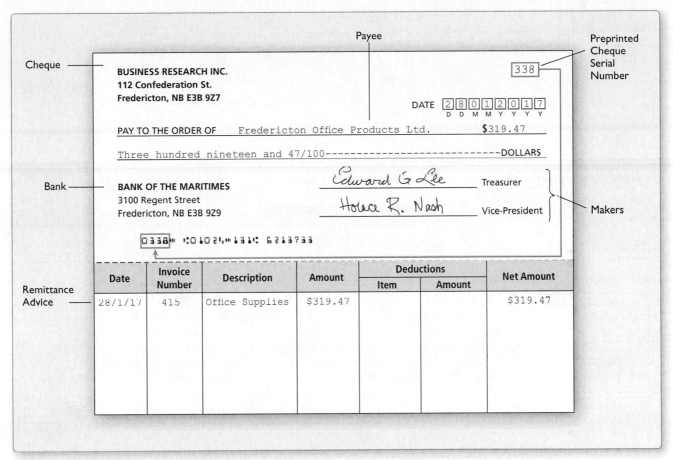

Bank Statement Banks often send monthly statements to their customers, or they can be downloaded online as needed. A **bank statement** reports what the bank did with the customer's cash. The statement shows the account's beginning and ending balances for the period, and lists cash receipts and payments transacted through the bank. Included with the statement are either the maker's *cancelled cheques* that have been cashed by the payee or copies of these cheques. The statement also lists deposits and other changes in the account. Exhibit 8–3 is the bank statement of Business Research Inc. for the month ended January 31, 2017.

Electronic funds transfer (EFT) moves cash by electronic communications rather than by paper documents. It is much cheaper for a company to pay employees by EFT (**direct deposit**) than by issuing hundreds of payroll cheques. Also, like many people, companies make mortgage, rent, insurance, credit card, and other payments, and many of these are made through automatic withdrawals, which are EFTs. The bank statement lists EFT deposits and payments, and the bank statement is the only way the company knows about EFT deposits.

One method of transferring funds electronically is through the use of a *debit card*. When a customer makes a purchase from a store and pays with a debit card, the customer authorizes the bank to immediately withdraw the money for the purchase from the customer's bank account and deposit it into the store's bank

EXHIBIT 8–3 | Bank Statement

Bank of the Maritimes
3100 REGENT STREET
FREDERICTON, NEW BRUNSWICK
E3B 9Z9

BUSINESS RESEARCH INC.
112 CONFEDERATION ST.
FREDERICTON, NB

E3B 9Z7

For Current Interest Rates:	Statement of Account		Statement From – To	
CALL OUR INFOLINE 1-800-386-2093 QUEBEC 1-800-386-1600 TORONTO 416-987-7735	**Branch No.**	**Account No.**	JAN 01/17 JAN 31/17	
	1024	1316213733	**Page** 1 **of** 1	

DESCRIPTION	WITHDRAWALS	DEPOSITS	DATE	BALANCE
BALANCE FORWARD			Jan01	6,556.12
DEPOSIT		1,112.00	Jan04	
NSF CHEQUE	52.00		Jan04	
NSF CHARGE	25.00		Jan04	7,591.12
CHQ#00256	100.00		Jan06	
CHQ#00334	100.00		Jan06	7,391.12
DEPOSIT		194.60	Jan08	7,585.72
CHQ#00335	100.00		Jan08	7,485.72
CHQ#00332	3,000.00		Jan12	
CHQ#00333	150.00		Jan12	4,335.72
EFT RENT COLLECTION		900.00	Jan17	5,235.72
EFT INSURANCE	361.00		Jan20	4,874.72
BANK COLLECTION		2,114.00	Jan26	6,988.72
CHQ#00336	1,100.00		Jan31	
SERVICE CHARGES	14.25		Jan31	
INTEREST CREDIT		28.01	Jan31	5,902.48
	5,002.25	4,348.61		

To the bank, your deposit account is a liability (a credit balance account). The bank owes your money to you because you can withdraw it or write cheques on it at any time.

The opposite is true for a bank loan, which to a bank is a receivable (a debit balance account).

account. The customer will see the amount of the withdrawal on his or her monthly bank statement, passbook, or online record, and the store will see the amount of the deposit on its monthly bank statement. Debit cards and bank cards will be discussed more fully in Chapter 9.

The Bank Reconciliation

A business might assume that the amount of cash in its bank account is the same as the amount of cash in its accounting records. However, this is rarely the case, so the two amounts must be compared and reconciled. There are two records of the business's cash:

1. The Cash account in the company's general ledger. Exhibit 8–4 shows that Business Research Inc.'s January 31 ending cash balance is $3,294.21.

EXHIBIT 8–4 | Cash Records of Business Research Inc.

General Ledger:

ACCOUNT Cash No. 1100

Date	Item	Jrn. Ref.	Debit	Credit	Balance
2017					
Jan. 1	Balance	✓			6,556.12 Dr
2	Cash receipt	CR. 9	1,112.00		7,668.12 Dr
7	Cash receipt	CR. 9	194.60		7,862.72 Dr
31	Cash payments	CP. 17		6,160.14	1,702.58 Dr
31	Cash receipt	CR. 10	1,591.63		3,294.21 Dr

Cash Payments from the Cash Payments Journal (CP; refer to Chapter 7):

Date	Cheque No.	Cash
Jan. 3	332	$3,000.00
5	333	510.00
5	334	100.00
6	335	100.00
10	336	1,100.00
11	337	286.00
15	338	319.47
20	339	83.00
25	340	203.14
28	341	458.53
	Total	$6,160.14

2. The bank statement, which shows the cash receipts and payments transacted through the bank during the month of January. In Exhibit 8–3, the bank shows an ending balance of $5,902.48 for Business Research Inc.

The books and the bank statement usually show different cash balances. Differences arise because of a time lag in recording transactions, called a **timing difference**. Three examples of timing differences follow:

- When companies write a cheque, they immediately deduct the amount of the cheque from their Cash account balance. But the bank does not subtract this amount from the company's account until the bank pays it. That may take days, even weeks, if the payee waits to cash the cheque.

REAL WORLD EXAMPLE

In this course, you have learned that debits to cash are increases and credits are deductions from the cash balance. In banking, the opposite is true:
- Debits are decreases to cash
- Credits are increases to cash

- Likewise, companies immediately add the amount of the cash receipt for each deposit that they make to their account. But it may take a day or more for the bank to add deposits to the company's balance.
- Any EFT payments and cash receipts are recorded by the bank before companies learn of them.

To ensure accurate cash records, companies need to update their records—either online or after they receive their bank statement. As part of this updating process a document called the **bank reconciliation** is prepared by the company (not the bank), usually monthly. The bank reconciliation accomplishes the following:

- It explains the differences between the company's cash records and the bank balance
- It ensures that all cash transactions have been accounted for
- It establishes that the bank and book records of cash are correct

The person who prepares the bank reconciliation should have no other cash duties. Otherwise, he or she could steal cash and manipulate the bank reconciliation to hide the theft.

Items on the Bank Reconciliation   Exhibit 8–5 lists the items that appear on a bank reconciliation. They all cause differences between the bank balance and the book balance. (We refer to the company's cash records as the "Book" records.) The items are defined and explained in the annotations.

EXHIBIT 8–5 | Items that Appear on the Bank Reconciliation

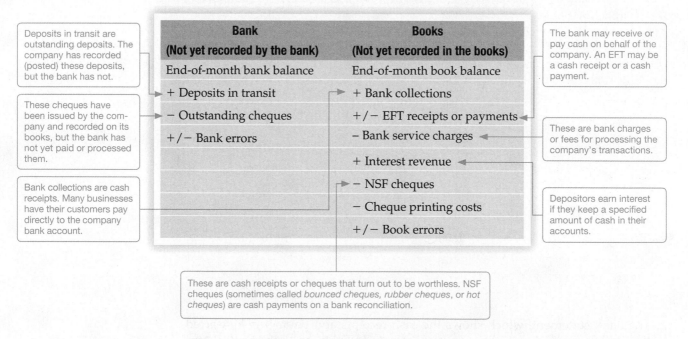

Deposits in transit are outstanding deposits. The company has recorded (posted) these deposits, but the bank has not.

These cheques have been issued by the company and recorded on its books, but the bank has not yet paid or processed them.

Bank collections are cash receipts. Many businesses have their customers pay directly to the company bank account.

Bank (Not yet recorded by the bank)	Books (Not yet recorded in the books)
End-of-month bank balance	End-of-month book balance
+ Deposits in transit	+ Bank collections
− Outstanding cheques	+/− EFT receipts or payments
+/− Bank errors	− Bank service charges
	+ Interest revenue
	− NSF cheques
	− Cheque printing costs
	+/− Book errors

The bank may receive or pay cash on behalf of the company. An EFT may be a cash receipt or a cash payment.

These are bank charges or fees for processing the company's transactions.

Depositors earn interest if they keep a specified amount of cash in their accounts.

These are cash receipts or cheques that turn out to be worthless. NSF cheques (sometimes called *bounced cheques*, *rubber cheques*, or *hot cheques*) are cash payments on a bank reconciliation.

Preparing the Bank Reconciliation

The steps in preparing the bank reconciliation are as follows and address the items listed in Exhibit 8–5:

1. After setting up your bank reconciliation form, start with two figures, the balance in the business's Cash account in the general ledger (*balance per books*) and the balance shown on the bank statement (*balance per bank*) on the same

date. Using Exhibit 8–3, the balance per bank would be $5,902.48, and using Exhibit 8–4 the balance per books would be $3,294.21. These two amounts are different because of the timing differences discussed earlier.

2. Add to or subtract from the *bank* balance those items that appear correctly on the books but not on the bank statement (refer to Exhibit 8–5):

   a. Add **deposits in transit** to the bank balance. Deposits in transit are identified by comparing the deposits listed on the bank statement for that month to the business's list of cash receipts (based on the deposit book). They appear as cash receipts on the books but not as deposits on the bank statement. Normally they will be deposits on the bank statement within days, so they are added to the bank balance.

   b. Subtract **outstanding cheques** from the bank balance. Outstanding cheques are identified by comparing the cancelled cheques returned with the bank statement to the business's list of cheques written. Outstanding cheques appear as cash payments on the books (CP) but not as paid cheques on the bank statement. Since they will normally be paid by the bank very soon, they are subtracted from the bank balance. If cheques were outstanding on the bank reconciliation for the preceding month and have still not been cashed, add them to the list of outstanding cheques on this month's bank reconciliation. There are often a lot of outstanding cheques and they are usually the most numerous item on a bank reconciliation.

3. Add to or subtract from the *book* balance those items that appear on the bank statement but not on the company books (refer to Exhibit 8–5):

   a. Add to the book balance (1) **bank collections**, (2) EFT cash receipts, and (3) interest revenue earned on the money in the bank. These items are identified by comparing the deposits listed on the bank statement with the business's list of cash receipts. They show up as cash receipts on the bank statement but not on the books.

   b. Subtract from the book balance (1) EFT cash payments, (2) service charges, (3) the cost of printed cheques, and (4) other bank charges (e.g., service charges for handling **nonsufficient funds (NSF) cheques** or stale-dated cheques). These items are identified by comparing the other charges listed on the bank statement to the cash payments recorded on the business's books. They appear as subtractions on the bank statement but not as cash payments on the books.

4. Compute the *adjusted bank balance* and *adjusted book balance*. The two adjusted balances should be equal.

5. Journalize each item in step 3, that is, each item listed on the book portion of the bank reconciliation. These items must be recorded on the business's books because they are cash amounts that have increased or decreased the cash in the bank account, but they have not been recorded in the accounting records. This will make the Cash balance equal to the reconciled bank balance.

6. Correct all book errors with journal entries and notify the bank of any errors the bank has made.

Bank Reconciliation Illustrated (Steps 1–4) The bank statement in Exhibit 8–3 (page 456) indicates that the January 31, 2017, bank balance of Business Research Inc. is $5,902.48. However, the company's Cash account has a balance of $3,294.21, as shown in Exhibit 8–4. This situation calls for a bank reconciliation. Exhibit 8–6, Panel A, lists the reconciling items for easy reference, and Panel B shows the completed reconciliation. The bank reconciliation can be prepared using a side-by-side format as shown in Exhibit 8–6 or in a vertical format as shown in the solution to the Summary Problem for Your Review on page 472. The format is important and should look neat and organized, but there is no standard presentation since this is an internal company document.

> *Who doesn't know about this item yet?* is a question to ask to help determine whether to add or subtract from the bank balance or the book balance. For example, for deposits in transit, the bank does not know about the transactions, so the bank's side of the reconciliation is updated.

KEY POINTS

Errors can be made by the bank or on the books. The balance that is adjusted for the error depends on where the error occurred. If the bank makes the error, the bank statement balance is adjusted. If the error is on the books, the book balance is adjusted.

EXHIBIT 8–6 | Bank Reconciliation

PANEL A: Reconciling Items

① Deposit in transit, $1,591.63

② Bank error: The bank deducted $100 for a cheque written by another company. Add $100 to bank balance.

③ Outstanding cheques: no. 337, $286.00; no. 338, $319.47; no. 339, $83.00; no. 340, $203.14; no. 341, $458.53

④ EFT receipt of rent revenue, $900.00

⑤ Bank collection of note receivable, $2,114.00, including interest revenue of $114.00

⑥ Interest earned on bank balance, $28.01

⑦ Book error: cheque no. 333 for $150.00 paid to Brown Corp. on account was recorded as $510.00

⑧ Bank service charges, $39.25 ($25.00 + $14.25)

⑨ NSF cheque from L. Ross, $52.00

⑩ EFT payment of insurance expense, $361.00

Note that additions are summarized first to avoid dealing with negative numbers.

PANEL B: Bank Reconciliation

BUSINESS RESEARCH INC.
Bank Reconciliation
January 31, 2017

Bank			Books		
Bank Balance, January 31, 2017		$5,902.48	Book Balance, January 31, 2017		$3,294.21
Add: ◄			Add:		
① Deposit of January 31 in transit		1,591.63	④ EFT receipt of rent revenue		900.00
② Correction of bank error—Business Research Associates cheque erroneously charged against company account		100.00	⑤ Bank collection of note receivable, including interest revenue of $114.00		2,114.00
		$7,594.11	⑥ Interest revenue earned on bank balance		28.01
			⑦ Correction of book error—overstated amount of cheque no. 333		360.00
③ Less: outstanding cheques					6,696.22
No. 337	$286.00		Less:		
338	319.47		⑧ Service charges	$ 39.25	
339	83.00		⑨ NSF cheque	52.00	
340	203.14		⑩ EFT payment of insurance expense	361.00	(452.25)
341	458.53	(1,350.14)			
Adjusted bank balance		**$6,243.97**	**Adjusted book balance**		**$6,243.97**

Amounts should agree

Each reconciling item is treated in the same way in every situation. Here is a summary of how to treat the various reconciling items:

BANK BALANCE—ALWAYS

- *Add* deposits in transit.
- *Subtract* outstanding cheques.
- *Add* or *subtract* corrections of bank errors.

BOOK BALANCE—ALWAYS

- *Add* bank collections, interest revenue, and EFT receipts.
- *Subtract* service charges, NSF cheques, and EFT payments.
- *Add* or *subtract* corrections of book errors.

Journalizing Transactions from the Reconciliation (Steps 5 and 6) The bank reconciliation is an accountant's tool that is separate from the company's journals and ledgers. It explains the effects of all cash receipts and all cash payments through the bank. But the bank reconciliation does *not* enter any transactions into the journals. To ensure that the transactions are entered into the accounts, we must make journal entries for the reconciling items on the books side of the bank reconciliation and post to the ledger to update the Cash account. These journal entries are made on January 31, 2017, and are shown in Exhibit 8–7. The numbers in circles correspond to the reconciling items listed in Exhibit 8–6, Panel A and shown in Panel B.

EXHIBIT 8–7 | Business Research Inc. Journal Entries Resulting from the Bank Reconciliation

General Journal				Page 11
Date 2017	**Accounts**	**Post Ref.**	**Debit**	**Credit**
④ Jan. 31	Cash		900.00	
	Rent Revenue			900.00
	Receipt of monthly rent.			
⑤ Jan. 31	Cash		2,114.00	
	Notes Receivable			2,000.00
	Interest Revenue			114.00
	Note receivable collected by bank.			
⑥ Jan. 31	Cash		28.01	
	Interest Revenue			28.01
	Interest earned on bank balance.			
⑦ Jan. 31	Cash		360.00	
	Accounts Payable—Brown Corp.			360.00
	Correction of cheque no. 333.			
⑧ Jan.31	Bank Charges Expense		39.25	
	Cash			39.25
	Bank service charges ($25.00 NSF + $14.25).			
⑨ Jan. 31	Accounts Receivable—L. Ross		52.00	
	Cash			52.00
	NSF cheque returned by bank.			
⑩ Jan. 31	Insurance Expense		361.00	
	Cash			361.00
	Payment of monthly insurance.			

LEARNING TIPS

This is an example of the journal entries for the NSF cheque in ⑨ from Exhibit 8–7.

First, record the payment by customer L. Ross to Business Research Inc.:

Cash	52	
Accounts Rec.—		52
L. Ross		

L. Ross did not have enough cash in his chequing account to cover the cheque, so the bank removed the cash from Business Research's account as a withdrawal.

Second, Business Research must reverse the original entry as shown in ⑨ in Exhibit 8–7.

Business Research has set up the receivable again and must now try to collect it. At this point an additional charge could also be administered by the company for the default.

The journal entries in Exhibit 8–7 update the company's books once they are posted.

Online and Telephone Banking Canadian banks offer online and telephone banking, where customers use their computers or telephones to effect transactions such as paying bills, transferring money from one account to another, or arranging a loan. Businesses can now even take a picture of a received cheque and deposit the amount electronically, with some restrictions. With online banking, customers use a computer and an Internet connection to effect transactions. The bank supplies a confirmation number on the customer's computer screen to show that the transaction has occurred, and the transaction is confirmed by its appearance on a

MyAccountingLab

Video: Performing a Bank Reconciliation

subsequent bank statement or printout from the online banking website. There is no other "paper trail" as evidence of the transaction. Businesses must implement additional procedures to carefully track and record these transactions.

Since bank statements are usually received monthly, a bank reconciliation is often performed only once a month. However, with online access to bank account information, you are able to print your bank account history at any time. Thus, companies and individuals could prepare bank reconciliations more frequently than once a month.

How Owners and Managers Use the Bank Reconciliation

The bank reconciliation can be a powerful control device, as the following example illustrates.

Randy Vaughn is a CPA in Regina, Saskatchewan. Vaughn owns several apartment complexes that are managed by his cousin, Alexis Vaughn. His accounting practice keeps him busy, so he has little time to devote to the properties. Vaughn's cousin approves tenants, collects the monthly rent cheques, arranges custodial and maintenance work, hires and fires employees, writes the cheques, and performs the bank reconciliation. This concentration of duties in one person is terrible from an internal control standpoint—Vaughn's cousin could be stealing from him. As a CPA he is aware of this possibility, so Vaughn exercises some internal controls over his cousin's activities:

1. Periodically, he drops by his properties to see whether the apartments are in good condition.

2. To control cash, Vaughn uses a bank reconciliation. On an irregular basis, he examines the bank reconciliations as prepared by his cousin. He matches every cheque that cleared the bank to the journal entry on the books. Vaughn would know immediately if his cousin were writing cheques to herself. Vaughn sometimes prepares his own bank reconciliation to see whether it agrees with his cousin's work.

3. To keep his cousin on her toes, Vaughn lets her know that he periodically checks her work.

4. Vaughn has a simple method for controlling cash receipts. He knows the occupancy level of his apartments. He also knows the monthly rent he charges, and he requires all tenants to pay by cheque. He multiplies the number of apartments—say 100—by the monthly rent (which averages $500 per unit) to arrive at an expected monthly rent revenue of $50,000. By tracing the $50,000 revenue to the bank statement, Vaughn can tell that his rent money went into his bank account.

Control activities such as these (often referred to as **executive controls**) are critical in small businesses. With only a few employees, a separation of duties may not be feasible. The owner must oversee and, if possible, become involved in the operations of the business, or the assets may disappear.

> Try It!

5. List the three items that can appear on the bank side of a bank reconciliation. Why does the company *not* need to record the reconciling items that appear on the bank side of the bank reconciliation?

6. Jonas Company's July 31, 2017, bank statement balance is $9,000 and shows a service charge of $30, interest earned of $10, and an NSF cheque for $600. Deposits in transit total $2,400, and outstanding

(Continued)

(Continued)

cheques are $1,150. The bookkeeper incorrectly recorded as $152 a cheque of $125 in payment of an account payable. The company's book balance at July 31, 2017, was $10,843.

a. Prepare the bank reconciliation for Jonas Company at July 31, 2017. Calculate the adjusted bank balance first, then calculate the adjusted book balance below it. Draw an arrow to show that both adjusted balances agree.

b. Prepare the journal entries needed to update the company's books.

Solutions appear at the end of this chapter and on MyAccountingLab

INTERNAL CONTROL OVER CASH RECEIPTS

Internal control over cash receipts (also includes credit card receipts and debit card payments) ensures that all cash receipts are deposited daily. Companies receive cash over the counter, electronically, and through the mail. Each source of cash has its own security measures.

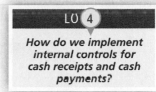

LO 4

How do we implement internal controls for cash receipts and cash payments?

Controls over Cash Receipts

Cash Receipts over the Counter   Consider a Canadian Tire store. The cash register, which is often a computer terminal, is positioned so that customers can see the amounts the cashier scans into the terminal. No person willingly pays more than the marked price for an item, so the customer helps prevent the sales clerk from overcharging. For each transaction, Canadian Tire issues a receipt to ensure that each sale is recorded.

The cash drawer opens only when the clerk enters a transaction and the machine records it. At the end of the day, a manager ensures the amount of cash is correct by comparing the cash in the drawer against the machine's record of sales. This step helps prevent theft by the clerk.

At the end of the day—or several times a day if business is brisk—the cashier or another employee with cash-handling duties records all the cash on a deposit slip and deposits the cash in the bank. The machine tape or digital information then goes to the accounting department as the basis for the journal entry to record sales revenue. These security measures, coupled with oversight by a manager, discourage theft.

It is important to deposit *all* the cash received at least daily to know the amount of total cash sales. Neither managers nor employees should use cash received to make purchases or other cash payments. In some rare circumstances where records are destroyed or missing, the bank statement can be used to reconstruct transactions.

Electronic Cash Receipts   Many companies receive payments via the Internet. For example, the online payment service PayPal enables small businesses to send electronic payments without a credit card and receive electronic payments without a merchant account. PayPal can connect to the company bank account for both sending and receiving payments, but businesses still need to be aware of the safety and security of this system.

Cash Receipts by Mail   Many companies receive payments (cheques and credit card authorizations) by mail. Exhibit 8–8 shows how large companies with many staff members segregate duties and control payments received by mail.

❶ All incoming mail is opened by a mailroom employee who sends all customer payments to the treasurer.

❷ The treasurer has the cashier deposit the money in the bank.

EXHIBIT 8–8 | Cash Receipts by Mail

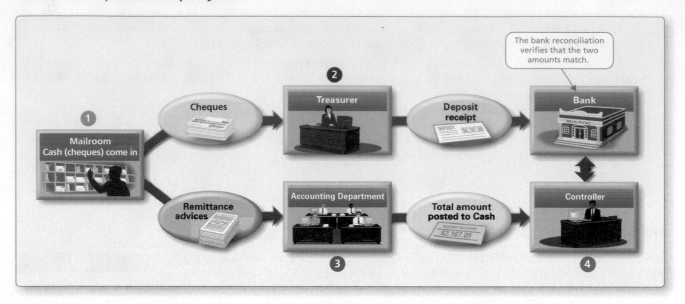

❸ The remittance advices, or records of payment, go to the accounting department so that journal entries can be recorded in the Cash and customers' accounts.

❹ As a final step, the controller compares the records of the day's cash receipts (step ❷ to step ❸) to ensure that they match. The debit to Cash should equal the amount deposited in the bank. All cash receipts are safe in the bank, and the company books are up to date.

In small companies with few staff members, the manager or owner should check the mail clerk's work or make the cash deposit to ensure the procedures are working properly when it's not possible to segregate duties.

Some companies use a lock-box system. Customers send their cheques to a post office box belonging to the bank; the bank deposits the cheques directly to the company's bank account. Internal control is tight because company personnel never touch incoming cash. This process is also evolving into a digital format as **cheque truncation**, or taking a picture of the cheque to be deposited is becoming the norm.

Cash Short and Over

When the recorded cash balance exceeds cash on hand, we have a *cash short* situation. When the actual cash exceeds the recorded Cash balance, we have a *cash over* situation. Suppose the tapes from a cash register at Little Short Stop convenience store indicated sales revenue of $15,000, but the cash received was $14,980. To record the day's sales for that register, the store would make this entry:

LEARNING TIPS

The Cash Short and Over account can have a debit or credit balance depending on the final balance in the account. A credit balance would be classified as Other Revenue. Since customers tend to notify the cashier when they don't receive enough change, Cash Short and Over is more likely to have a debit balance.

Dec. 18	Cash	14,980	
	Cash Short and Over	20	
	Sales Revenue		15,000
	Daily cash sales.		

In this entry, **Cash Short and Over** is an expense account because sales revenue exceeds cash receipts. This account is credited when cash receipts exceed sales. The Cash Short and Over account's balance should be small. The debits and credits for cash shorts and overs collected over an accounting period tend to cancel each other out. A large balance signals the accountant to investigate. For example, too large a debit balance may mean an employee is stealing. Cash Short and Over, then, acts as an internal control device.

Exhibit 8–9 summarizes the internal controls over cash receipts.

EXHIBIT 8–9 | Internal Controls over Cash Receipts

Internal Control Procedures	Internal Controls over Cash Receipts
Competent, reliable, ethical personnel	Screen employees for undesirable personality traits. Create effective training programs.
Assignment of responsibilities	Specific employees are designated as cashiers, supervisors, and accountants.
Proper authorization	Only designated employees can approve cheque cashing above a certain amount, approve purchases on credit, etc.
Separation of duties	Cashiers and mailroom employees who handle cash do not have access to the accounting records. Accountants who record cash receipts do not handle cash.
Internal audits	Internal auditors examine company transactions for agreement with management policies.
Documents and records	Customers receive receipts as transaction records. Bank statements list cash receipts for deposit. Customers who pay by mail with a cheque include a remittance advice showing the amount of cash they sent to the company.
Electronic devices and computer controls	Cash registers serve as transaction records. Also, each day's receipts are matched with customer remittance advices for the cheques received and with the day's deposit slip with the bank.
Other controls	Cashiers are bonded (fidelity bond). Cash is stored in vaults and banks. Employees are rotated among jobs and are required to take vacations.

INTERNAL CONTROL OVER CASH PAYMENTS

Cash payments are as important as cash receipts. It is therefore critical to control cash payments for goods and services by cheque. Prior to issuing the cheque, authorization for payment would be required. Companies often also pay small amounts from a petty cash fund.

Controls over Payments by Cheque

Payment by cheque is an important internal control:

- The cheque provides a record of the payment.
- The cheque must be signed by an authorized official. An even better control is to require two signatures.
- Before signing the cheque, the official should verify the evidence supporting the payment.

As noted in our discussion on internal controls, companies need a good separation of duties among ordering goods, possession of goods, updating the accounting records, and writing cheques for cash payments.

Controls over Purchase and Payment To illustrate the internal control over cash payments, let's suppose the business is paying for merchandise inventory. The purchasing and payment process follows these steps, as outlined in Exhibit 8–10:

EXHIBIT 8–10 | Cash Payments by Cheque

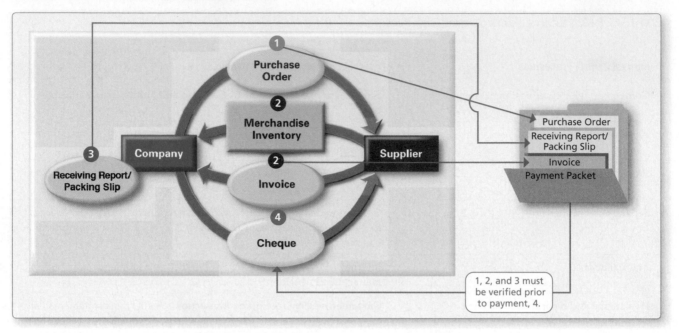

❶ The company sends an authorized *purchase order* to the supplier.

❷ The supplier ships the merchandise and mails the *invoice,* or bill. (We introduced the invoice in Chapters 2 and 5.)

❸ The company receives the goods. The receiving department checks the goods for damage and either checks off the items received on the packing slip that accompanies the goods or prepares a list of the goods received on a *receiving report*.

❹ After the accounting department checks and confirms all the forgoing documents using a *payment packet* or voucher, the company sends a *cheque* to the supplier only for the goods received.

For good internal control, the purchasing agent should neither receive the goods nor approve the payment. If these duties are not separated, a purchasing agent could buy goods and have them shipped to his or her home. Or the purchasing agent could increase the price of purchases, approve the payment, and then split the price increase with the supplier.

After payment, the cheque signer should punch a hole through the payment packet or otherwise mark the packet and its contents as paid. These actions alert the company that it has paid the bill. Dishonest employees and suppliers have been known to present a bill for cash payment two or more times.

Streamlined Procedures Technology is streamlining payment procedures, especially for large companies. **Evaluated Receipt Settlement (ERS)** compresses the approval process into a single step: comparing the receiving report with the purchase order. If the two documents match, that proves that the company received the merchandise it ordered. Then the company pays the supplier.

An even more streamlined process bypasses people and documents altogether. In **Electronic Data Interchange (EDI)**, Canadian Tire's computers can communicate directly with the computers of suppliers like General Tire, Rubbermaid, and Procter & Gamble. When Canadian Tire's inventory of automobile tires reaches a certain (low) level, the computer sends a purchase order to General Tire. General

Tire ships the tires and invoices Canadian Tire electronically. General Tire receives funds directly from Canadian Tire's bank via an EFT.

Exhibit 8–11 summarizes the internal controls over cash payments.

EXHIBIT 8–11 | Internal Controls over Cash Payments

Element of Internal Control	Internal Controls over Cash Payments
Competent, reliable, ethical personnel	Cash payments are entrusted to high-level employees.
Assignment of responsibility	Specific employees approve purchase documents for payment. Executives examine approvals, then co-sign cheques.
Proper authorization	Large expenditures must be authorized by company officials.
Separation of duties	Computer operators and other employees who handle cheques have no access to the accounting records. Accountants who record cash payments have no opportunity to handle cash. Purchasing should be separate from payment.
Internal audits	Internal auditors examine company transactions for agreement with management policies. External auditors may also be hired to review compliance to specific policies, like expense claims (the recent Canadian Senate spending scandal illustrates the need for external auditors sometimes).
Documents and records	Bank statements list cash payments (cheques and EFT payments) for reconciliation with company records. Cheques are prenumbered and used in sequence to account for payments.
Electronic devices, computer controls, and other controls	Evaluated Receipt Settlement (ERS) streamlines the cheque approval process. Machines stamp the amount on a cheque in indelible ink. Paid invoices are punched or otherwise mutilated to avoid duplicate payment.

> Try It!

7. When cash is received by mail, what keeps the mailroom employee from pocketing a customer cheque and destroying the remittance advice?

8. Suppose the tapes from the cash registers at a Burger King restaurant indicated sales revenue of $7,252, but the cash received was $7,262. Journalize the day's sales.

9. Two officers' signatures are required for cheques over $1,000. One officer is going on vacation and presigns several cheques. The cheques are locked in the vault. What is the internal control feature in this scenario, and is it effective?

Solutions appear at the end of this chapter and on MyAccountingLab

INTERNAL CONTROL OVER PETTY CASH

It is wasteful to write a cheque for an employee's taxi fare (while on company business), or the delivery of a package across town. To meet these needs, companies keep cash on hand to pay small amounts. This fund is called **petty cash**.

Even though petty cash payments are small, employee theft is often seen with this fund. Therefore, internal controls are important to enforce in this area, such as the following:

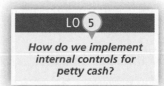
LO 5

How do we implement internal controls for petty cash?

- Designate a **custodian** of the petty cash fund.
- Keep a specific amount of cash on hand in a secure location.

- Support all fund payments for expenses with a **petty cash ticket or voucher**.
- Do surprise audits of the fund to ensure receipts and cash total the assigned amount.

Creating the Petty Cash Fund

The petty cash fund is opened when a cheque is written for the designated amount. The cheque is made payable to the employee responsible for petty cash. Banks do not like to cash cheques made out to "Cash" or "Petty Cash" unless they know the customer. Assume that on February 28 the business creates a petty cash fund of $400.

The petty cash custodian cashes a $400 cheque and places the money in the fund (a locked metal box or other secure location). Starting the fund is recorded as follows:

Feb. 28	Petty Cash	400	
	Cash		400
	To open the petty cash fund.		

For each petty cash payment, the custodian prepares a *petty cash ticket* or *petty cash voucher* like the one illustrated in Exhibit 8–12. Prior to replenishment of the fund, each petty cash voucher should have a receipt, invoice, or other documentation to support the payment.

EXHIBIT 8–12 | Petty Cash Ticket

PETTY CASH TICKET

Date ___Mar. 25, 2017___   No. _45_

Amount ___$34.00___

For ___Payment for delivery of contract.___

Debit ___Delivery Expense, Acct. No. 545___

Received by _Lewis Wright_   Fund Custodian _MAR_

KEY POINTS

The Petty Cash account only changes when the fund is established or when it is changed. Replenishment does not affect the Petty Cash account.

Signatures (or initials) identify the recipient of the cash (Lewis Wright) and the fund custodian (MAR). Requiring both signatures reduces fraudulent payments. The custodian keeps all the prenumbered petty cash tickets in the petty cash fund box or location. The sum of the cash plus the total of the ticket amounts should equal the opening balance ($400) at all times. Also, the Petty Cash account keeps its $400 balance at all times. As the use of company debit cards increases, the use of Petty Cash accounts is decreasing.

No journal entries are made for petty cash payments until the fund is replenished. At that time, all petty cash payments will be recorded in a summary entry. This procedure avoids the need to journalize many payments for small amounts.

Maintaining the Petty Cash account at its designated balance is the nature of an **imprest system**. This system clearly identifies the amount of cash for which the fund custodian is responsible and is the system's main internal control feature. Petty cash is often the first place an employee will steal funds from, so it is important to keep track of these funds. Imprest systems are also used for branch offices that keep cash for the office in a fund. Payments reduce the cash in the fund, so the fund must be replenished periodically.

Replenishing the Petty Cash Fund

On March 31, the petty cash fund holds

- $230 in petty cash
- $164 in petty cash tickets

We can see that $6 is missing:

Fund balance	$400
Cash on hand	$230
Petty cash tickets	164
Total accounted for	$394
Amount of cash missing	$ 6

To replenish the petty cash fund, we need to bring the cash on hand up to $400. The company writes a cheque, payable to the fund custodian, for $170 ($400 – $230). The fund custodian cashes this cheque and puts $170 back into the fund. Now the fund holds $400 cash, as it should.

The petty cash tickets identify the accounts to debit, as shown in the entry to replenish the fund (items are assumed for this illustration):

Mar. 31	Office Supplies	46	
	Delivery Expense	34	
	Cash Short and Over	6	
	Selling Expense	84	
	Cash		170
	To replenish the petty cash fund.		

> Notice that replenishing the fund does not affect the Petty Cash account balance.

The cash payments appear to have exceeded the sum of the tickets, since the fund was short $6, so Cash Short and Over was debited for the missing amount ($6). If the sum of the tickets exceeds the payment, Cash Short and Over is credited. Petty Cash keeps its $400 balance at all times.

The petty cash fund *must* be replenished, especially prior to year end. Otherwise, the income statement will understate the expenses listed on the petty cash tickets.

The Petty Cash account in the general ledger is debited only when the fund is started (see the February 28 entry) or when its amount is changed. In our illustration, suppose the business decides to raise the fund amount from $400 to $500 because of increased demands for petty cash. This step would require a $100 debit to the Petty Cash account and a $100 credit to the Cash account.

 **Try It!**

10. Leitch Design Studios established a $300 petty cash fund. James C. Brown (JCB) is the fund custodian. At the end of the first week, the petty cash fund contains the following:

    1. Cash: $163
    2. Petty cash tickets:

No.	Amount	Issued to	Signed by	Account Debited
1	$14	B. Jarvis	B. Jarvis and JCB	Office Supplies
2	39	S. Bell	S. Bell	Delivery Expense
4	43	R. Tate	R. Tate and JCB	—
5	33	G. Blair	G. Blair and JCB	Travel Expense

(Continued)

(Continued)

a. Identify three internal control weaknesses revealed in the given data.

b. Prepare the general journal entries to record the following:

   i. January 1. Establishment of the petty cash fund

   ii. June 30: Replenishment of the fund. Assume petty cash ticket no. 4 was issued for the purchase of office supplies

c. What is the balance in the Petty Cash account immediately before replenishment? Immediately after replenishment?

Solutions appear at the end of this chapter and on MyAccountingLab

> Why It's Done This Way ▲

Objective of Financial Reporting

Cash, the subject of this chapter, is always reported at its fair value, simply by virtue of what cash is. The accounting framework presented in Exhibit 1–5 in Chapter 1 (and on the inside back cover of this book) describes the elements of the financial statements, one of which is assets. Cash is an asset, since it is controlled by a company and it has an expected future benefit.

This chapter mentioned that postdated cheques received are not included in the cash balance. This is because the cash is not available to the company and it would be misleading to include postdated cheques in the cash balance since it would overstate the amount of cash the company has that is expected to produce a future benefit.

ETHICS AND ACCOUNTING

LO 6

Are there steps we can follow when making ethical business judgments?

Robert Schad, former president and CEO of Husky Injection Molding Systems Ltd. in Bolton, Ontario, said, "Ethical practice is, quite simply, good business." The late Anita Roddick, British founder of The Body Shop, said "Being good is good business." Both Roddick and Schad were in business long enough to recognize the danger in unethical behaviour. Sooner or later unethical conduct comes to light, as was true in our chapter-opening vignette about the ICCLR. Moreover, ethical behaviour wins out in the end because it is the right thing to do.

Corporate and Professional Codes of Ethics

Most companies have a code of ethics to encourage employees to behave ethically. But codes of ethics are not enough by themselves. Owners and managers must set a high ethical tone. They must make it clear that the company will not tolerate unethical conduct.

Accountants have additional incentives to behave ethically. As professionals, they are expected to maintain higher standards than society in general. Their ability to attract business depends entirely on their reputation.

Chartered Professional Accountants (CPAs) must adhere to the code of ethics and the rules of professional conduct set out by CPA Canada. These documents set minimum standards of conduct for members. Unacceptable actions can result in expulsion from the organization, which makes it impossible for the person to remain a professional accountant.

Ethical Issues in Accounting

In many situations the ethical choice is easy. For example, stealing money, as in the chapter-opening vignette, is illegal and unethical. In other cases, the choices are more difficult. But in every instance ethical judgments are a personal decision. What should I do in a given situation? Let's consider an ethical issue in accounting.

Sonja Kleberg is preparing the income tax return of a client who earned more income than expected. On January 2, the client pays for advertising to run in late January and asks Sonja to backdate the expense to the preceding year. Backdating would decrease the client's taxable income of the earlier year and postpone a few dollars in tax payments. No big deal, right? After all, there is a difference of only two days between January 2 and December 31. This client is important to Kleberg. What should she do?

**She should refuse the request because the
transaction took place in January of the new year.**

What internal control device could prove that Kleberg behaved unethically if she backdated the transaction in the accounting records? A Canada Revenue Agency audit could prove that the expense occurred in January rather than in December by reviewing the documentation. Falsifying tax returns is both illegal and unethical.

Weighing tough ethical judgments requires a decision framework. A framework is shown in the box below. Consider the six questions shown there as general guidelines; they will guide you through answering tough ethical questions.

MyAccountingLab

Video: Real World Accounting

Decision Guidelines: Making Ethical Judgments

Decision	Guideline
1. What are the facts?	1. *Determine the facts.*
2. What is the ethical issue, if any?	2. *Identify the ethical issues.* The root word of *ethical* is *ethics*, which the *Canadian Oxford Dictionary* defines as "the science of morals in human conduct; moral philosophy; moral principles in human conduct; moral correctness."
3. What are the alternatives?	3. *Specify the alternatives.* "Do nothing" is always an alternative.
4. Who is involved in the situation?	4. *Identify the stakeholders,* the people involved.
5. What are the possible consequences of each alternative in question 3?	5. *Assess the possible outcomes of each alternative.*
6. What should be done?	6. *Make a decision.*

> Try It!

11. Suppose David Duncan, the lead external auditor for Axiom Corporation, thinks Axiom may be understating its liabilities on the balance sheet. Axiom's transactions are very complex, and outsiders may never figure this out. Duncan asks his firm's standards committee how he should handle the situation. They reply, "Require Axiom to report all its liabilities." Axiom is Duncan's most important client, and Axiom is pressuring Duncan to certify the liabilities. Duncan tries to rationalize that Axiom's reported amounts are okay. What should Duncan do? To make his decision, Duncan could follow the decision guidelines outlined in this chapter. Apply those guidelines to David Duncan's situation.

Solutions appear at the end of this chapter and on MyAccountingLab

SUMMARY PROBLEM FOR YOUR REVIEW

The Cash account of Cambridge Dental Associates at February 28, 2017, follows:

Cash

Feb. 1	Bal.	7,990	Feb. 3		800
6		1,600	12		6,200
15		3,600	19		2,200
23		2,200	25		1,000
28		4,800	27		1,800
28	Bal.	8,190			

Cambridge Dental Associates receives the February 2017 bank statement data in the first week of March 2017 (negative amounts appear in parentheses):

Bank Statement for February 2017				
Description	**Withdrawals**	**Deposits**	**Date**	**Balance**
Balance Forward			Feb01	$ 7,990
Deposits		1,600	Feb07	9,590
Cheques total for day	800		Feb08	8,790
Deposits		3,600	Feb15	12,390
Cheques total for day	6,200		Feb16	6,190
Cheques total for day		2,200	Feb23	3,990
Deposits	2,200		Feb24	6,190
NSF cheque, M. E. Crown	1,400		Feb24	4,790
Bank collection of note receivable		2,000*	Feb26	6,790
EFT rent expense	660		Feb28	6,130
Service charge	20		Feb28	6,110
Interest		5	Feb28	6,115
	11,280	9,405		

*Includes principal of $1,762 plus interest of $238.

Required

1. Prepare the bank reconciliation of Cambridge Dental Associates at February 28, 2017.
2. Journalize the entries based on the bank reconciliation.

SOLUTION

Requirement 1

Bank	
Bank Balance, February 28, 2017	$ 6,115
Add: Deposit of February 28 in transit	4,800
	10,915
Less: Outstanding cheques issued on Feb. 25 ($1,000) and Feb. 27 ($1,800)	(2,800)
Adjusted bank balance, February 28, 2017	$ 8,115

Books		
Book Balance, February 28, 2017		$ 8,190
Add: Bank collection of note receivable, including interest of $238		2,000
Add: Interest earned on bank balance		5
		10,195
Less: Service charge	$ 20	
NSF cheque	1,400	
EFT—Rent expense	660	(2,080)
Adjusted book balance, February 28, 2017		$ 8,115

Before creating the bank reconciliation, compare the Cash account and the bank statement. Cross out all items that appear in both places. The items that remain are the reconciling items.

Begin with the ending balance on the bank statement.

- Add deposits (debits) from the Cash account not on the bank statement.
- Deduct cheques (credits) from the Cash account not on the bank statement.

Begin with the ending balance in the Cash general ledger account.

- Add money received by the bank on behalf of the company (increases to the bank statement balance).
- Deduct bank charges, NSF cheques, or preauthorized payments (decreases to the bank statement balance).

Requirement 2

Feb.	28	Cash	2,000	
		Note Receivable		1,762
		Interest Revenue		238
		Note receivable collected by bank ($2,000 – $238).		
	28	Cash	5	
		Interest Revenue		5
		Interest earned on bank balance.		
	28	Bank Charges Expense	20	
		Cash		20
		Bank service charge.		
	28	Accounts Receivable—M. E. Crown	1,400	
		Cash		1,400
		NSF cheque returned by bank.		
	28	Rent Expense	660	
		Cash		660
		Monthly rent expense.		

Prepare journal entries for all reconciling items from the "books" section of the bank reconciliation.

SUMMARY

LEARNING OBJECTIVE (1) Define internal control

What is internal control?   pg. 446

- Internal control is the organizational plan and all related measures adopted by an entity to meet the following management objectives:
  - Encouraging operational efficiency
  - Prevention and detection of fraud and error
  - Safeguarding assets and records
  - Providing accurate, reliability information
- The Sarbanes-Oxley Act and the Dodd-Frank Act are controls implemented in the United States that affect Canadian companies listed on US stock exchanges.

LEARNING OBJECTIVE (2) List and describe the components of internal control and control procedures

What should we think about when designing an internal control system?   pg. 448

- Internal control objectives can be achieved by applying these components:
  - **C**ontrol procedures/environment
  - **R**isk assessment
  - **I**nformation system   **CRIME**
  - **M**onitoring of controls
  - **E**nvironmental controls
- An effective system of internal control has these procedures or characteristics:
  - Competent, reliable, and ethical personnel
  - Clear assignment of responsibilities
  - Separation of duties
  - Proper authorization
  - Internal and external audits
  - Documents and records
  - Electronic devices and computer controls
- Other controls companies also make use of include fireproof vaults, point-of-sale terminals, fidelity bonds, mandatory vacations, surveillance cameras, and job rotation.

LEARNING OBJECTIVE (3) Prepare a bank reconciliation and the related journal entries

What do we do when the bank statement balance and the cash account balance are not the same?   pg. 454

- Businesses use the *bank statement* and the *bank reconciliation* to account for banking transactions.
- The bank reconciliation explains the reasons for the difference between the company's cash balance in its accounting records and the cash balance in its bank account.

MyAccountingLab **Video:** Concepts of Bank Reconciliation

MyAccountingLab **Video:** Performing a Bank Reconciliation

LEARNING OBJECTIVE (4) Apply internal controls to cash receipts and cash payments

How do we implement internal controls for cash receipts and cash payments?   pg. 463

- To control cash receipts over the counter, companies use point-of-sale terminals that customers can see and require cashiers to provide customers with receipts.
- A duplicate tape inside the machine or a link to a central computer records each sale and cash transaction.
- To control cash receipts by mail:
  - A mailroom employee should be assigned the responsibility for opening the mail as an essential separation of duties—the accounting department should not open the mail.
  - At the end of the day, the controller compares the two records of the day's cash receipts: the bank deposit amount from the cashier and the debit to Cash from the accounting department.
- To control cash payments, cheques should be issued and signed only when supporting documents, including the purchase order, invoice (bill), and receiving report (all with appropriate signatures), have been reviewed.

How do we implement internal controls for petty cash?   pg. 467

- Even though petty cash payments are small, a business still needs controls over it, such as the following:
  - Designate an employee or custodian of the petty cash fund.
  - Keep a specific amount of cash on hand in a secure location.
  - Support all fund payments for expenses with a petty cash ticket or voucher.
  - Perform unannounced checks or audits on the petty cash fund to count the balance.

LEARNING OBJECTIVE Make ethical business judgments

Are there steps we can follow when making ethical business judgments?   pg. 470

- To make ethical decisions, businesspeople should follow six guidelines:
  1. Determine the facts
  2. Identify the ethical issues
  3. Specify the alternatives
  4. Identify the stakeholders
  5. Assess the possible outcomes of each alternative
  6. Make the decision
  MyAccountingLab **Video:** Real World Accounting

Check **Accounting Vocabulary** for all key terms used in Chapter 8 and the **Glossary** at the back of the book for all key terms used in the textbook.

MORE CHAPTER REVIEW MATERIAL

MyAccountingLab

DemoDoc covering Bank Reconciliations and Internal Control over Cash Receipts

Student PowerPoint Slides

Audio Chapter Summary

Note: All MyAccountingLab resources can be found in the Chapter Resources section and the Multimedia Library.

ACCOUNTING VOCABULARY

Audit The examination of financial statements by outside accountants. The conclusion of an audit is the accountant's professional opinion about the financial statements (*p. 451*).

Bank collection Collection of money by the bank on behalf of a depositor (*p. 459*).

Bank reconciliation The process of explaining the reasons for the difference between a depositor's records and the bank's records about the depositor's bank account (*p. 458*).

Bank statement A document for a particular bank account showing its beginning and ending balances and listing the month's transactions that affected the account (*p. 455*).

Cash The most liquid asset an organization has; includes cash on hand, cash on deposit in banks and trust companies, and cash equivalents (*p. 446*).

Cash short and over When the recorded cash balance does not match the actual amount counted (*p. 464*).

Cheque A document that instructs the bank to pay the designated person or business a specified amount of money (*p. 454*).

Cheque truncation The conversion of a physical cheque into an electronic format (i.e., taking a picture) for processing through the banking system to save time and resources (*p. 464*).

Collusion When two or more people work as a team to beat internal controls and steal from a company (*p. 453*).

Computer virus A malicious computer program that reproduces itself, gets included in program code without consent, and destroys program code (*p. 452*).

Controller The chief accounting officer of a company (*p. 450*).

Cost–benefit constraint An accounting constraint that says the benefits of the information produced should not exceed the costs of producing the information *(p. 453)*.

Custodian A person designated to be responsible for something of value, like the petty cash fund *(p. 467)*.

Deposit in transit A deposit recorded by the company but not yet by its bank *(p. 459)*.

Direct deposit Funds that are deposited and transferred directly to a bank account, such as employee payroll *(p. 455)*.

Electronic Data Interchange (EDI) The transfer of structured data by electronic means and standards between organizations from one computer system to another without human intervention *(p. 466)*.

Electronic funds transfer (EFT) A system that transfers cash by digital communication rather than paper documents *(p. 455)*.

Encryption The process of rearranging plain-text messages by some mathematical formula to achieve confidentiality *(p. 452)*.

Evaluated Receipt Settlement (ERS) A streamlined payment procedure that compresses the approval process into a single step: comparing the receiving report with the purchase order *(p. 466)*.

Executive controls Management involvement in internal controls *(p. 462)*.

Fidelity bond An insurance policy that reimburses the company for any losses due to the employee's theft. Before hiring, the bonding company checks the employee's background *(p. 451)*.

Firewall Barriers used to prevent entry into a computer network or a part of a network. Examples include passwords, personal identification numbers (PINs), and fingerprints *(p. 453)*.

Imprest system A way to account for petty cash by maintaining a constant balance in the Petty Cash account, supported by the fund (cash plus disbursement tickets) totalling the same amount *(p. 468)*.

Internal control The organizational plan and all the related measures adopted by an entity to meet management's objectives of discharging statutory responsibilities, profitability, prevention and detection of fraud and error, safeguarding assets, reliability of accounting records, and timely preparation of reliable financial information *(p. 446)*.

Nonsufficient funds (NSF) cheque A "bounced" cheque, one for which the maker's bank account has insufficient money to pay the cheque *(p. 459)*.

Outstanding cheque A cheque issued by the company and recorded on its books but not yet paid by its bank *(p. 459)*.

Petty cash A fund containing a small amount of cash that is used to pay minor expenditures *(p. 467)*.

Petty cash ticket (voucher) A document indicating that money has been removed from the petty cash fund and a receipt is required to verify the expense *(p. 468)*.

Phishing A method of gathering account numbers and passwords from people who visit legitimate-sounding bogus websites. The data gathered are then used for illicit purposes *(p. 452)*.

Postdated cheques Cheques that are written for a future date *(p. 446)*.

Remittance advice An optional attachment to a cheque that tells the payee the reason for payment *(p. 455)*.

Stale-dated cheques Cheques that are older than six months and need to be reissued *(p. 446)*.

Timing difference A time lag in recording transactions *(p. 457)*.

Treasurer The person in a company responsible for cash management *(p. 450)*.

Treasury bill A financial instrument issued by the federal government that has a term of one year or less. It is sold at a discount and matures at par. The difference between the cost and maturity value is the purchaser's income *(p. 446)*.

Trojan A computer virus that does not reproduce but gets included into program code without consent and performs actions that can be destructive *(p. 452)*.

SIMILAR ACCOUNTING TERMS

Cash receipts	Cash, cheques, and other negotiable instruments received
EDI	Electronic Data Interchange
EFT	Electronic funds transfer
ERS	Evaluated Receipt Settlement
Invoice	Bill
NSF (non-sufficient funds) cheques	Bounced cheques, rubber cheques, hot cheques
Separation of duties	Segregation of duties, division of duties

SELF-STUDY QUESTIONS

Test your understanding of the chapter by marking the correct answer for each of the following questions:

1. Which of the following is an objective of internal control? (*p. 446*)
   a. Safeguarding assets
   b. Providing information for decision making while maintaining reliable records and control systems
   c. Encouraging operating efficiency and optimizing the use of resources
   d. Preventing and detecting fraud and error
   e. All of the above are objectives of internal control

2. Janice Gould receives cash from customers. Her other assigned job is to post the collections to customer accounts receivable. Her company has weak (*p. 450*)
   a. Ethics
   b. Assignment of responsibilities
   c. Computer controls
   d. Separation of duties

3. What internal control function is performed by auditors? (*p. 451*)
   a. Objective opinion on the fair presentation of the financial statements
   b. Assurance that all transactions are accounted for correctly
   c. Communication of the results of the audit to regulatory agencies
   d. Guarantee that company employees have behaved ethically

4. Encryption (*pp. 452–453*)
   a. Creates firewalls to protect data
   b. Cannot be broken by hackers
   c. Avoids the need for separation of duties
   d. Rearranges messages by a special process

5. The bank account serves as a control device over (*p. 454*)
   a. Cash receipts
   b. Cash payments
   c. Both of the above
   d. None of the above

6. Which of the following items appears on the bank side of a bank reconciliation? (*p. 458*)
   a. Book error
   b. Outstanding cheque
   c. NSF cheque
   d. Interest revenue earned on bank balance

7. Which of the following items appears on the book side of a bank reconciliation? (*p. 458*)
   a. Outstanding cheques
   b. Deposits in transit
   c. Both of the above
   d. None of the above

8. Which of the following reconciling items requires a journal entry on the books of the company? (*p. 461*)
   a. Book error
   b. Outstanding cheque
   c. NSF cheque
   d. Interest revenue earned on bank balance
   e. All of the above except (b)
   f. None of the above

9. The internal control feature that is specific to petty cash is (*p. 468*)
   a. Separation of duties
   b. Assignment of responsibility
   c. Proper authorization
   d. The imprest system

10. Ethical judgments in accounting and business (*pp. 470–471*)
    a. Require employees to break laws to get ahead
    b. Force decision makers to think about what is good and bad
    c. Always hurt someone
    d. Are affected by internal controls but not by external controls

Answers to Self-Study Questions

1. e   2. d   3. a   4. d   5. c   6. b   7. d   8. e   9. d   10. b

ASSIGNMENT MATERIAL

QUESTIONS

1. Which of the features of effective internal control is the most fundamental? Why?

2. Which company employees bear primary responsibility for a company's financial statements and for maintaining the company's system of internal control? How do these individuals carry out this responsibility?

3. Identify at least seven characteristics of an effective system of internal control. What is one inherent limit/weakness of any internal control system?

4. Separation of duties may be divided into three parts. What are they?

5. What is an audit? Identify the two types of audit and the differences between them.

6. Why are documents and records a feature of internal control systems?

7. What is Evaluated Receipt Settlement (ERS) and how does it streamline payment procedures?

8. Why should the same employee not write the code used to account for cash payments, sign cheques, and mail the cheques to payees?

9. Briefly state how each of the following serves as an internal control measure over cash: bank account, signature card, deposit slip, and bank statement.

10. Are internal control systems designed to be foolproof and perfect? What is a fundamental constraint in planning and maintaining systems?

11. How can internal control systems be circumvented?

12. Each of the items in the following list must be accounted for in the bank reconciliation. Next to each item, enter the appropriate letter from the following possible treatments: (a) bank side of reconciliation—add the item; (b) bank side of reconciliation—subtract the item; (c) book side of reconciliation—add the item; and (d) book side of reconciliation—subtract the item.

_____ Outstanding cheque

_____ NSF cheque

_____ Bank service charge

_____ Cost of printed cheques

_____ EFT receipt

_____ Bank error that decreased the bank balance

_____ Deposit in transit

_____ Bank collection

_____ EFT payment

_____ Customer cheque returned because of unauthorized signature

_____ Book error that increased balance of Cash account

13. What purpose does a bank reconciliation serve?

14. What role does a cash register play in an internal control system?

15. Describe internal control procedures for cash received by mail.

16. Discuss the specific characteristics of an effective internal control system for cash receipts over the counter.

17. What documents make up the payment packet? Describe three procedures that use the payment packet to ensure that each payment is appropriate.

18. What balance does the Petty Cash account have at all times? Does this balance always equal the amount of cash in the fund? When are the two amounts equal? When are they unequal?

19. Suppose a company has six bank accounts, two petty cash funds, and three certificates of deposit that can be withdrawn on demand. How many cash amounts would this company likely report separately on its balance sheet?

20. Why should accountants adhere to a higher standard of ethical conduct than many other members of society do?

21. "Our managers know that they are expected to meet budgeted profit figures. We don't want excuses. We want results." Discuss the ethical implications of this policy.

STARTERS

Definition of internal control

Starter 8–1 Internal controls are designed to safeguard assets; encourage employees to follow company policies; promote operational efficiency; provide accurate, reliable information; and ensure accurate records. Which objective mentioned must the internal controls accomplish for the business to survive? Give your reason.

Starter 8–2 How does the Dodd-Frank amendment of the Sarbanes-Oxley Act of 2002 affect Canadian companies with regard to internal controls? Be specific.

Applying the definition of internal controls
①

Starter 8–3 Explain in your own words why separation of duties is often described as the cornerstone of internal control for safeguarding assets. Describe what can happen if the same person has custody of an asset and also accounts for the asset.

Applying the definition of internal controls
①

Starter 8–4 How do external auditors differ from internal auditors? How does an external audit differ from an internal audit? How are the two types of audits similar?

Characteristics of an effective system of internal control
②

Starter 8–5 Answer the following questions about the bank reconciliation:

1. Is the bank reconciliation a journal, a ledger, an account, or a financial statement? If it is none of these, what is it?
2. What is the difference between a bank statement and a bank reconciliation?

Aspects of a bank reconciliation
③

Starter 8–6 In the month of July, The Red Apple Co. wrote and recorded cheques in the amount of $4,520. In August, the company wrote and recorded cheques in the amount of $6,340. Of these cheques, $3,760 were paid by the bank in July and $2,580 were paid in August. What is the amount of the outstanding cheques at the end of July and at the end of August?

Calculating aspects of a bank reconciliation
③

Starter 8–7 The Cash account of Hunter Security Systems reported a balance of $4,960 at May 31, 2017. There were outstanding cheques totalling $1,800 and a May 31 deposit in transit of $400. The bank statement, which came from Royal Bank, listed a May 31 balance of $7,600. Included in the bank balance was a collection of $1,260 on account from Kelly Brooks, a Hunter customer who pays the bank directly. The bank statement also shows a $40 service charge and $20 of interest revenue that Hunter earned on its bank balance. Prepare Hunter's bank reconciliation at May 31, 2017.

Preparing a bank reconciliation
③
Adjusted balance, $6,200

Starter 8–8 After preparing Hunter Security Systems' bank reconciliation in Starter 8–7, journalize the company's transactions that arise from the bank reconciliation. Date each transaction May 31, 2017, and include an explanation with each entry.

Recording transactions from a bank reconciliation
③

Starter 8–9 Dogtopia sells pet supplies and food and handles all sales with a cash register. The cash register displays the amount of the sale. It also shows the cash received and any change returned to the customer. The register also produces a customer receipt but keeps no internal record of the transactions. At the end of the day, the clerk counts the cash in the register and gives it to the cashier for deposit in the company bank account.

Apply internal controls to cash receipts
④

Required

1. Identify the internal control weakness over cash receipts.
2. What could Dogtopia do to correct the weakness?

Starter 8–10 Francois sells furniture for Monet Furniture Company. He is having financial problems and takes $300 that he received from a customer. He recorded the sale through the cash register. What will alert Giles DuBois, the owner, that something is wrong?

Control over cash receipts
④

Starter 8–11 Review the internal controls over cash receipts by mail. Exactly what is accomplished by the final step in the process, performed by the controller?

Control over cash receipts by mail
④

Starter 8–12 A purchasing agent for Napai Auto receives the goods that he purchased and also approves payment for the goods. How could this purchasing agent cheat his company? How could Napai avoid this internal control weakness?

Internal control over payments by cheque
④

Petty cash
(5)

April 30, Credit Cash Short and
Over for $6

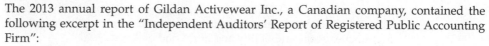

Starter 8–13 Record the following petty cash transactions of Lexite Laminated Surfaces in general journal form (explanations are not required):

Apr. 1   Established a petty cash fund with a $200 balance.
30   The petty cash fund has $19 in cash and $187 in petty cash tickets that were issued to pay for office supplies ($117) and entertainment expenses ($70). Replenished the fund with $181 of cash and recorded the expenses.

Making an ethical judgment
(6)

Starter 8–14 Angela Brennan, an accountant for Dublin Co., discovers that her supervisor, Barney Stone, made several errors last year. Overall, the errors overstated the company's net income by 15 percent. It is not clear whether the errors were deliberate or accidental. What should Brennan do?

EXERCISES   MyAccountingLab

Exercise 8–1

Internal control and the United
States
(1)

The 2013 annual report of Gildan Activewear Inc., a Canadian company, contained the following excerpt in the "Independent Auditors' Report of Registered Public Accounting Firm":

> We also have audited, in accordance with the standards of the Public Company Accounting Oversight Board (United States), the company's internal control over the financial reporting as at September 29, 2013 …

Why is this a requirement of a Canadian company?

Exercise 8–2

Identifying and correcting an
internal control weakness
(2)

Yorkshire Bike Shop has a liberal return policy. A customer can return any product for a full refund within 14 days of purchase. When a customer returns merchandise, Yorkshire policy specifies the following:

• Store clerk issues a prenumbered return slip, refunds cash from the cash register, and keeps a copy of the return slip for review by the manager.

• Store clerk places the returned goods back on the shelf or on the floor as soon as possible.

Yorkshire uses a periodic inventory system.

Required

1. How can a dishonest store clerk steal from Yorkshire? What part of company policy enables the store clerk to steal without getting caught?

2. How can Yorkshire improve its internal controls to prevent this theft?

Exercise 8–3

Correcting an internal control
weakness
(2)

UK trader Nick Leeson worked for Baring Securities (Singapore) Limited (BSS) as the general manager and head trader. Due to his experience in operations, he also acted as head of the "back office" that does the record keeping and tracks who owes what to whom. Leeson appeared to be making huge profits by speculating on Japan's Nikkei stock market—until he fled Singapore, leaving behind a loss of £827,000,000 hidden in an unused error account on the Barings balance sheet. As a result of this situation, Barings Bank collapsed.

What internal control weaknesses at BSS allowed this loss to grow so large? How could Barings have avoided or limited the size of the loss?

Exercise 8–4

Identifying internal control
strengths and weaknesses
(2)

The following situations suggest either a strength or a weakness in internal control. Identify each as a *strength* or a *weakness* and give your reason for each answer.

a. Top managers delegate all internal control procedures to the accounting department.

b. The accounting department orders merchandise and approves invoices for payment.

c. Cash received over the counter is controlled by the clerk, who enters the sale and places the cash in the register. The clerk matches the total recorded by the register to each day's cash sales.

d. The vice-president, who signs cheques, assumes the accounting department has matched the invoice with other supporting documents and therefore does not examine the payment packet.

Exercise 8–5

Identify the missing internal control procedure in the following situations:

Identifying internal controls

a. In the course of auditing the records of a company, you find that the same employee orders merchandise and approves invoices for payment.

b. Business is slow at the Vogue Theatre on Tuesday, Wednesday, and Thursday nights. To reduce expenses, the owner decides not to use a ticket taker on those nights. The ticket seller (cashier) is told to keep the tickets as a record of the number sold.

c. The same trusted employee has served as cashier for 10 years.

d. When business is brisk, Hasties Convenience Store deposits cash in the bank several times during the day. The manager at the convenience store wants to reduce the time employees spend delivering cash to the bank, so he starts a new policy. Cash will build up over weekends, and the total will be deposited on Monday.

e. Grocery stores such as No Frills and Walmart purchase large quantities of their merchandise from a few suppliers. At one grocery store, the manager decides to reduce paperwork. He eliminates the requirement that a receiving department employee prepare a receiving report, which lists the quantities of items received from the supplier.

f. The treasurer of the Beta Soccer Association was elected for a third term to manage all the financial affairs of the club. The president and secretary have signing authority, so sound internal controls are in place.

g. A pancake breakfast is held every year to raise funds (over $10,000) for charity. The organizers 15-year-old daughter is hired to sell tickets and handle the funds collected.

Exercise 8–6

The following questions pertain to internal control. Consider each situation separately.

Explaining the role of internal control

1. Wong Company requires that all documents supporting a cheque be cancelled (stamped Paid) by the person who signs the cheque. Why do you think this practice is required? What might happen if it were not?

2. Separation of duties is an important consideration if a system of internal control is to be effective. Why is this so?

3. Cash may be a relatively small item on the financial statements. Nevertheless, internal control over cash is very important. Why is this true?

4. Many managers think that safeguarding assets is the most important objective of internal control systems, while auditors emphasize internal control's role in ensuring reliable accounting data. Explain why managers are more concerned about safeguarding assets and auditors are more concerned about the quality of the accounting records.

Exercise 8–7

Skinner & Sons owns the following assets at the balance sheet date:

Calculating bank reconciliation items

Cash in bank—chequing account	$3,250
Treasury bills..	3,000
Postdated cheques from customers..	500
Cash in bank—savings account	5,000
Cash on hand in cash register	250
Cash refund due from Canada Revenue Agency....................	2,000
US dollar bank account converted to Canadian dollars........	500

What amount of cash should be reported on the balance sheet?

Exercise 8–8

Classifying bank reconciliation items

③

The following items could appear on a bank reconciliation:

a. Outstanding cheques

b. Deposits in transit for current month

c. NSF cheque

d. Bank collection of a note receivable on the company's behalf

e. Bank credit memo for interest earned on bank balance

f. Bank debit memo for service charge

g. Book error: We credited Cash for $200. The correct credit was $2,000

h. Bank error: The bank decreased our account for a cheque written by another customer

i. Outstanding cheques from the previous month that are still outstanding

j. EFT payment by a customer

k. Bank error in recording a deposit for $464 should have been $446

Required

1. Classify each item as (1) an addition to the book balance, (2) a subtraction from the book balance, (3) an addition to the bank balance, or (4) a subtraction from the bank balance.

2. Indicate (a) the items that will result in an adjustment to the company's records, and (b) why the other items do not require an adjustment.

Exercise 8–9

Preparing a bank reconciliation
③
Adjusted balance, $14,560

Adams Enterprises began operations on January 2, 2017, depositing $40,000 in the bank. During this first month of business, the following transactions occurred that affected the Cash account in the general ledger:

Date	Description	Dr	Cr
Jan. 2	Deposit	$40,000	
5	Payment, cheque 001		$12,000
8	Payment, cheque 002		16,000
9	Cash sales	16,000	
15	Payment, cheque 003		10,000
18	Cash sales	12,000	
20	Bank loan	50,000	
26	Equipment purchase, cheque 004		74,000
30	Payment on account, cheque 005		17,000
31	Cash sales	25,600	

Shortly after the end of January the company received its first bank statement:

Description	Withdrawals	Deposits	Date	Balance
Balance Forward			Jan01	0
Deposit		40,000	Jan02	40,000
Chq#001	12,000		Jan07	28,000
Deposit		16,000	Jan09	44,000
Chq#002	16,000		Jan13	28,000
Deposit		12,000	Jan18	40,000
Bank Loan		50,000	Jan20	90,000
Chq#004	74,000		Jan28	16,000
Deposit		2,000	Jan29	18,000
Service Charge	48		Jan31	17,952
Interest		8	Jan31	17,960
	102,048	120,008		

In preparing to do the bank reconciliation, Adams Enterprises noticed that the $2,000 deposit on January 29 was a bank error and informed the bank. The bank will correct the error on the next bank statement.

Required   Prepare Adams Enterprises' bank reconciliation at January 31, 2017.

Exercise 8–10

Inkameep Travel's general ledger Cash account showed the following transactions during October 2017:

Preparing a bank reconciliation
③
Adjusted balance $19,334

Date	Description	Dr	Cr	Balance
Oct. 1	Opening balance			$ 2,800
2	Deposit	$20,000		22,800
5	Payment, cheque 233		$ 6,000	16,800
8	Payment, cheque 234		18,000	(1,200)
9	Deposit	18,000		16,800
15	Payment, cheque 235		5,000	11,800
18	Deposit	5,200		17,000
26	Payment, cheque 236		3,300	13,700
30	Payment, cheque 237		4,750	8,950
31	Deposit	10,500		19,450

The bank statement for the month ending October 31, 2017, is shown below:

Description	Withdrawals	Deposits	Date	Balance
Balance Forward			Oct01	2,800
Deposit		20,000	Oct02	22,800
Chq#00233	6,000		Oct07	16,800
Deposit		18,000	Oct09	34,800
Chq#00234	18,000		Oct10	16,800
Deposit		5,200	Oct18	22,000
Chq#00235	5,000		Oct18	17,000
Service Charge	120		Oct31	16,880
Service Charge	120		Oct31	16,760
Interest		4	Oct31	16,764
	29,240	43,204		

Inkameep Travel informed its bank that the bank charged a service charge twice. The bank has agreed to reverse one of the bank charges on the next month's bank statement.

Required   Prepare Inkameep Travel's bank reconciliation at October 31, 2017.

Exercise 8–11

Preparing a bank reconciliation

(3)

Adjusted balance, $17,356

Bobbie Brown's chequebook lists the entries shown here:

Date	Cheque No.	Item	Cheque	Deposit	Balance
Jul. 1					$ 3,868
4	622	West Coast Sports	$ 208		3,660
9		Dividends received		$ 400	4,060
13	623	TELUS	304		3,756
14	624	Chevron	276		3,480
18	625	Cash	268		3,212
26	626	JDRF	132		3,080
28	627	Belfour Apartments	2,932		148
31		Paycheque		17,332	17,480

Brown's July bank statement is shown below:

Balance			$3,868
Add: Deposits			400
Deduct cheques:	No.	Amount	
	622	$ 208	
	623	304	
	624	316*	
	625	268	(1,096)
Other charges:			
Printed cheques		$ 52	
Service charge		32	(84)
Balance			$3,088

*This is the correct amount of cheque number 624

Required Prepare Bobbie Brown's bank reconciliation at July 31, 2017. How much cash does Brown actually have on July 31?

Exercise 8–12

Preparing a bank reconciliation

(3)

Adjusted balance, $61,568

Roger Snieder operates two gas stations. He has just received the monthly bank statement at May 31 from Royal Bank, and the statement shows an ending balance of $46,880. Listed on the statement are an EFT rent collection of $3,200, a service charge of $120, two NSF cheques totalling $2,760, and a $200 charge for printed cheques. In reviewing his cash records, Snieder identifies outstanding cheques totalling $1,432 and a May 31 deposit in transit of $16,120. During May, he recorded an $880 cheque for the salary of a part-time employee by debiting Salary Expense and crediting Cash for $288. Snieder's Cash account shows a May 31 balance of $62,040. Prepare the bank reconciliation at May 31, 2017.

Exercise 8–13

Making journal entries from a
bank reconciliation

(3)

Using the data from Exercise 8–12, record the entries that Snieder should make in the general journal on May 31, 2017. Include an explanation for each of the entries.

Exercise 8–14

In the months of February and March, Apex Ski Shop wrote and journalized cheques in the amount of $6,532 and $9,764, respectively. Of these cheques, $5,220 cleared the bank in February and $8,223 cleared the bank in March. What is the amount of outstanding cheques at the end of February and at the end of March?

Calculating bank reconciliation items

Exercise 8–15

Winfray Co. records all cash receipts on the basis of its cash register tapes. Winfray Co. discovered during January 2017 that one of its sales clerks had stolen an undetermined amount of cash receipts when she took the daily deposits to the bank. The following data have been gathered for January:

Bank reconciliation, detecting theft, and internal controls

Note collection...	$ 2,500
Bank service charges..	80
Interest earned...	500
Outstanding cheques as of January 31, 2017..........................	6,450
Cash in the bank per the general ledger account..................	31,000
Cash according to the January 31, 2017, bank statement......	36,938

There were no outstanding deposits on January 31, 2017.

Required

1. Determine the amount of cash receipts stolen by the sales clerk.
2. What accounting controls would have prevented or detected this theft?

Exercise 8–16

A jury convicted the treasurer of GTX Company of stealing cash from the company. Over a three-year period, the treasurer allegedly took almost $100,000 and attempted to cover the theft by manipulating the bank reconciliation.

Applying internal controls to the bank reconciliation

Required What is a likely way that a person would manipulate a bank reconciliation to cover a theft? Use the data from Exercise 18–15 to illustrate how $1,000 could be stolen and covered up. What internal control arrangement could have avoided this theft?

Exercise 8–17

When you pay for goods at Trent's Discount Store, the cash register displays the amount of the sale, the cash received, and any change returned to you. Suppose the register also produces a customer receipt but keeps no record of the sales transactions. At the end of the day, the clerk counts the cash in the register and gives it to the cashier for deposit in the company bank account.

Evaluating internal control over cash receipts

Required Write a memo to Trent Simon, the owner. Identify the internal control weakness over cash receipts, and explain how the weakness gives an employee the opportunity to steal cash. State how to prevent such a theft.

Exercise 8–18

Gary's Motors purchases high-performance auto parts from a Winnipeg vendor. Joel Sieben, the accountant for Gary's, verifies receipt of merchandise and then prepares, signs, and mails the cheque to the vendor.

Evaluating internal control over cash payments

Required

1. Identify the internal control weakness over cash payments in this scenario.
2. What could the business do to correct the weakness?

Exercise 8–19

Apply internal controls to cash payments

The petty cash fund had the following petty cash ticket:

Toner for a printer	$ 42
Freight to deliver goods sold	39
Freight on inventory purchased	112
Miscellaneous expense	10
Postage expense	25
	$228

Assume that the business has established a petty cash fund in the amount of $250 and that the amount of cash in the fund at the time of replenishment is $20. The business uses a perpetual inventory system.

Prepare the entry to replenish the fund on February 28.

Exercise 8–20

Petty cash, cash short and over

Record the following selected transactions of Kelly's Fine Foods in general journal format (explanations are not required):

2017

Jun. 1 Established a petty cash fund with a $200 balance.

2 Journalized the day's cash sales. Cash register tapes show a $4,875 total, but the cash in the register is $4,885.

10 The petty cash fund had $56.50 in cash and $134.00 in petty cash tickets issued to pay for office supplies ($21.00), delivery expenses ($69.50), and entertainment expenses ($43.50). Replenished the fund.

Exercise 8–21

Control over petty cash

5

3. Petty Cash balance, $300

1. Explain how an *imprest* petty cash system works.

2. Atlantic Press maintains an imprest petty cash fund of $300, which is under the control of Gladys Yu. At November 30, the fund holds $80 cash and petty cash tickets for $140 of office supplies and $100 of delivery expenses.

   Journalize (a) the establishment of the petty cash fund on November 1 and (b) the replenishment of the fund on November 30.

3. Prepare a T-account for Petty Cash and post to the account. What is Petty Cash's balance at all times?

Exercise 8–22

Accounting for petty cash

5

Maritime Distributors created a $500 imprest petty cash fund. During the first month of use, the fund custodian authorized and signed petty cash tickets as shown below.

Ticket No.	Item	Account Debited	Amount
1	Delivery of flyers to customers	Delivery Expense	$228.80
2	Stamp purchase	Postage Expense	85.98
3	Newsletter	Supplies Expense	60.40
4	Key to closet	Miscellaneous Expense	9.52
5	Staples	Supplies Expense	14.72

Required Make general journal entries to (a) create the petty cash fund and (b) record its replenishment. Cash in the fund totals $97.58. Include explanations.

Exercise 8–23

Refer to the Maritime Distributors petty cash fund data in Exercise 8–22. Suppose, one month later, the company decided to decrease the petty cash fund by $100 due to theft and break-ins in the area. Journalize the decrease in the petty cash fund.

Accounting for petty cash

Exercise 8–24

You have a part-time job in a local coffee shop, which is part of a chain of cafés. You received the job through your parent's friendship with Tina Presley, the coffee shop manager. The job is going well, but you are puzzled by the actions of Tina and her husband, Sean. Each day, one or both of them fills takeout orders and takes them to Tina's office. Later you notice Sean and Tina enjoying the takeout orders, sometimes with friends. You know the orders were not rung through the checkout counter. When you ask a co-worker about the practice, you are told that Tina is the boss and can do as she wishes, and besides, many employees help themselves to meals.

Evaluating the ethics of conduct by a manager

Required   Apply the decision guidelines for ethical judgments outlined in the box on page 471 to decide whether a manager of a coffee shop should help herself or himself to meals on a regular basis and not pay for what she or he takes.

SERIAL EXERCISE

This exercise continues the Lee Management Consulting situation from Exercise 7–20 of Chapter 7. If you did not complete Exercise 7–20 you can still complete Exercise 8–25 as it is presented below for the month of October.

Exercise 8–25

Lee Management Consulting performs systems consulting. Lee Management Consulting's bank statement dated October 31, 2016, follows:

Preparing a bank reconciliation
3
1. Adjusted balance, $39,802

Description	Withdrawals	Deposits	Date	Balance
Balance Forward			Sep30	$32,850
Deposit		750"	Oct01	33,600
EFT to Cheap Cheques	17		Oct02	33,583
Chq 206	1,250*		Oct02	32,333
Deposit		2,500	Oct08	34,833
Deposit		3,000	Oct14	37,833
Chq 207	4,000		Oct17	33,833
Chq 209	1,415		Oct18	32,418
EFT Hot Houses (a customer)		500	Oct20	32,918
Deposit		4,800	Oct22	37,718
EFT to Internet Service	125		Oct28	37,593
Chq 208	795		Oct28	36,798
Bank Service Charge	13		Oct28	36,785
Interest Credit		7	Oct31	36,792
	7,615	11,557		

*This was a reconciling item on the September 2016 bank reconciliation.

Lee's October Cash from its general ledger appears below:

Cash

Sep.	30	Bal.	32,350	chq. 207	4,000	Oct.	1
Oct.	6		2,500	chq. 208	795	Oct.	14
Oct.	13		3,000	chq. 209	1,415	Oct.	14
Oct.	20		4,800	chq. 210	190	Oct.	28
Oct.	27		3,600	chq. 211	400	Oct.	28
Oct.	28	Unadj. Bal.	39,450				

Required

1. Prepare the October 2016 bank reconciliation.
2. Journalize and post any transactions required from the bank reconciliation. Key all items by date. Compute each account balance, and denote the balance as *Bal.*

CHALLENGE EXERCISES

Exercise 8–26

Bank reconciliation items
③
1. Sep. 30, $2,338

The accounting records of Abacus Supplies showed the following:

Outstanding cheques:

- The July 31 bank reconciliation reported outstanding cheques of $489. In the month of August, the Abacus accounting records showed that cheques in the amount of $14,089 were written. Total cheques that cleared the bank according to the bank statement were $13,089 in August.
- In September, cash payments from the accounting records were $19,349 and the total cheques that cleared the bank were $18,500.

Outstanding deposits:

- The July 31 bank reconciliation reported that deposits outstanding totalled $889. In August, the cash account (according to the ledger) showed deposits of $18,322, but the bank statement listed the total deposits of $17,322.
- In September, the bank statement listed deposits of $16,766 and the deposits recorded in the cash receipts journal totalled $15,667.

Required

1. What was the amount of outstanding cheques at August 31 and at September 30?
2. What was the amount of outstanding deposits at August 31 and at September 30?

Exercise 8–27

Bank reconciliation items
③
4. $2,780

Eldorado Mining had the following information available from a November 2017 bank reconciliation: outstanding cheques totalling $2,890 and outstanding deposits totalling $2,140. The November 30 reconciled cash balance per the bank and books was $9,210.

Additional December information:

a. The December bank statement shows the following amounts and charges:
   i. Credit item—note collection, $1,105, plus interest, $23
   ii. Debit item—NSF cheque from B. Jones, $242
   iii. Service charges in the amount of $20

b. Cheques that cleared the bank in December totalled $30,212.

c. Deposits from the December bank statement, not including the credit item above, totalled $27,402.

d. Eldorado wrote and recorded cheques in the amount of $30,102.

e. Eldorado recorded collections and deposits of $34,370.

Required

Calculate the following at December 31, 2017:

1. The unadjusted balance in the Cash account
2. The unadjusted balance in the bank account
3. Deposits in transit
4. Outstanding cheques
5. Reconciled bank balance
6. Reconciled book balance

BEYOND THE NUMBERS

Beyond the Numbers 8–1

Theta Construction Company, headquartered in Calgary, built a Roadway Inn in High River, 64 kilometres south of Calgary. The construction foreman, whose name was Slim, moved into High River in March to hire the 40 workers needed to complete the project. Slim hired the construction workers, had them fill out the necessary tax forms, and sent the employment documents to the home office, which opened a payroll file for each employee.

Correcting an internal control weakness

Work on the motel began on April 1 and ended September 1. Each Thursday evening Slim filled out an electronic time card that listed the hours worked by each employee during the five-day workweek that ended at 5:00 p.m. on Thursday. Slim emailed the time sheets to the home office, which prepared the payroll cheques on Friday morning. A courier delivered the payroll cheques to Slim, and at 5:00 p.m. on Friday he distributed the payroll cheques to the workers.

Required

1. Describe in detail the internal control weakness in this situation. Specify what negative result(s) could occur because of the internal control weakness.
2. Describe what you would do to correct the internal control weakness.

ETHICAL ISSUE

Arjun Samji owns apartment buildings in Ontario. Each property has a manager who collects rent, arranges for repairs, and runs advertisements in the local newspaper. The property managers transfer cash to Samji monthly and prepare their own bank reconciliations.

The manager in Hamilton has been stealing large sums of money. To cover the theft, she understates the amount of outstanding cheques on the monthly bank reconciliation. As a result, each monthly bank reconciliation appears to balance. However, the balance sheet reports more cash than Samji actually has in the bank. In negotiating the sale of the Hamilton property, Samji is showing the balance sheet to prospective investors.

Required

1. Identify two parties other than Samji who can be harmed by this theft. In what ways can they be harmed?
2. Discuss the role accounting plays in this situation.

PROBLEMS (GROUP A)

MyAccountingLab

Define internal control

(1)

Problem 8–1A

An employee of Ellerback Event Planning recently stole thousands of dollars of the company's cash. The company has decided to install a new system of internal controls.

Required As controller of Ellerback Event Planning, write a memo to the owner, Nick Flewelling, explaining what internal controls are and how they can benefit the company.

Identifying the characteristics of an effective internal control system

(1) (2)

Problem 8–2A

Use the information in Problem 8–1A to explain how separation of duties helps to safeguard assets.

Problem 8–3A

Identifying internal control weaknesses

(2)

Each of the following situations has an internal control weakness:

a. Syspro Software Associates sells accounting software. Recently, the development of a new software program stopped while the programmers redesigned Syspro Software Associates' accounting system. Syspro Software Associates' own accountants could have performed this task.

b. Judy Sloan has been your trusted employee for 30 years. She performs all cash-handling and accounting duties. She has just purchased a new Lexus and a new home in an expensive suburb. As the owner of the company, you wonder how she can afford these luxuries because you pay her $35,000 per year and she has no sources of outside income.

c. Sanchez Hardwoods Ltd., a private corporation, falsified sales and inventory figures to get a large loan. The company prepared its own financial statements. The company received the loan but later went bankrupt and couldn't repay the loan.

d. The office supply company from which The Family Shoe Store purchases sales receipts recently notified Family that the last shipped receipts were not prenumbered. Louise Bourseault, the owner of Family, replied that she never uses the receipt numbers, so the omission is not important.

e. Discount stores such as Dollar Mart make most of their sales for cash, with the remainder in debit card and credit card sales. To reduce expenses, one store manager ceases purchasing fidelity bonds on the cashiers.

Required

1. Identify the missing internal control characteristic in each situation.
2. Identify the potential problem that could be caused by each control weakness.
3. Propose a solution to each internal control problem.

Problem 8–4A

Excel Spreadsheet Template

Using the bank reconciliation as a control device

(3)

1. Adjusted balance, $28,060

The cash receipts and the cash payments of Silver Hills Estates Development for November 2017 are as follows:

Cash Receipts (Posting Reference is CR)		Cash Payments (Posting Reference is CP)	
Date	**Cash Debit**	**Cheque No.**	**Cash Credit**
Nov. 5	$ 3,436	1221	$ 1,819
7	470	1222	1,144
13	1,723	1223	429
15	1,065	1224	111
19	441	1225	816
24	10,875	1226	109
30	2,598	1227	4,468
Total	$20,608	1228	998
		1229	330
		1230	2,724
		Total	$12,948

The Cash account of Silver Hills Estates shows a balance of $26,983 on November 30, 2017. Outstanding amounts from the previous month's bank reconciliation were cheque #1219 for $500, cheque #1218 for $400, and an October 31 deposit in the amount of $2,000. On December 3, 2017, Silver Hills Estates received this bank statement:

Bank Statement for November 2017				
Description	Withdrawals	Deposits	Date	Balance
Balance Forward			Nov01	18,223
Deposit		2,000	Nov01	20,223
EFT Rent Collection		880	Nov01	21,103
Deposit		3,436	Nov06	24,539
NSF Cheque	433		Nov08	24,106
Chq#001221	1,819		Nov09	22,287
Deposit		470	Nov10	22,757
Chq#001222	1,144		Nov13	21,613
Chq#001223	429		Nov14	21,184
Deposit		1,723	Nov14	22,907
Chq#001224	111		Nov15	22,796
Deposit		1,065	Nov15	23,861
EFT Insurance	275		Nov19	23,586
Deposit		441	Nov20	24,027
Chq#001225	816		Nov22	23,211
Deposit		10,875	Nov25	34,086
Chq#001226	109		Nov29	33,977
Chq#001227	4,968		Nov30	29,009
Bank Collection		1,430	Nov30	30,439
Chq#001219	500		Nov30	29,939
Service Charge	25		Nov30	29,914
	10,629	22,320		

Explanations: EFT—electronic funds transfer, NSF—nonsufficient funds

Additional data for the bank reconciliation is as follows:

a. The EFT deposit was a receipt of monthly rent. The EFT debit was payment for monthly insurance.

b. The NSF cheque was received late in October from a customer.

c. The $1,430 bank collection of a note receivable on November 30 included $100 interest revenue.

d. The correct amount of cheque #1227, a payment on account, is $4,968. (The Silver Hills Estates Development accountant mistakenly recorded the cheque for $4,468.)

Required

1. Prepare the bank reconciliation of Silver Hills Estates Development at November 30, 2017.
2. Describe how a bank account and the bank reconciliation help Silver Hills' managers control the business's cash.
3. How are outstanding items from the previous month's bank reconciliation that clear on the November bank statement dealt with?

Problem 8–5A

Spottify Electronics had a computer failure on October 1, 2017, that resulted in the loss of data, including the balance of its Cash account and its bank reconciliation from September 30, 2017. The accountant, Matt Vincent, has been able to obtain the following information from the records of the company and its bank:

a. An examination showed that two cheques (#244 for $305.00 and #266 for $632.50) had not been cashed as of October 1. Vincent recalled that there was only one deposit in transit on the September 30 bank reconciliation but was unable to recall the amount.

b. The cash receipts and cash payments journals contained the following entries for October 2017:

Cash Receipts:		Cash Payments:	
Amounts		Cheque #	Amount
$ 908.50		275	$ 310.50
1,748.00		276	448.50
3,726.00		277	466.90
1,975.00		278	811.90
736.00		279	577.30
$9,093.50		280	3,886.90
		281	void
		282	488.50
		283	1,058.00
			$8,048.50

c. The company's bank provided the following statement as of October 31, 2017:

Date		Cheques and Other Debits		Deposits and Other Credits		Balance
Oct.	1	#276	448.50		2,346.00	6,520.50
	2	#266	632.50			5,888.00
	5	#277	466.90			5,421.10
	8				908.50	6,329.60
	14	#275	310.50		1,196.00	7,215.10
	17	EFT	529.00			6,686.10
	19			EFT	414.00	7,100.10
	22	#279	577.30		1,748.00	8,270.80
	22	#280	3,976.90	EFT	1,196.00	5,489.90
	24			EFT	471.50	5,961.40
	27	NSF	805.00		3,726.00	8,882.40
	28	SC	20.00			8,862.40
	31	#283	1,058.00		1,975.00	9,779.40

d. The deposit made on October 14 was for the collection of a note receivable ($1,100.00) plus interest.

e. The electronic funds transfers (EFTs) had not yet been recorded by Spottify Electronics because the bank statement was the first notification of them.

  • The October 17 EFT was for the monthly payment on an insurance policy for Spottify Electronics.

  • The October 19 and 24 EFTs were collections on accounts receivable.

  • The October 22 EFT was in error—the transfer should have been to Spottify Auto Parts.

f. The NSF cheque on October 27 was received from a customer as payment for electronics purchased for $805.00.

g. Cheque #280 was correctly written for $3,976.90 for the purchase of inventory (assume a periodic system) but incorrectly recorded by the cash payments clerk.

Required

1. Prepare a bank reconciliation as of October 31, 2017, including the calculation of the book balance of October 31, 2017.
2. Prepare all journal entries that would be required by the bank reconciliation.

Problem 8–6A

The October 31, 2017, bank statement of Jazzera Distributors has just arrived. To prepare Jazzera Distributors' bank reconciliation, you gather the following data:

a. The October 31 bank balance is $38,212.

b. The bank statement includes two deductions for NSF cheques from customers. One was for $168 and the other was for $370.

c. The following Jazzera Distributors' cheques are outstanding at October 31:

Cheque No.	Amount
312	$1,098
522	1,086
534	114
539	112
540	416
541	894

d. A few customers pay their accounts by EFT. The October bank statement lists a $12,732 deposit against customer accounts.

e. The bank statement includes two special deposits: $1,766, which is the amount of GST refund the bank received on behalf of Jazzera Distributors, and $160, the interest revenue Jazzera earned on its bank balance during October.

f. Jazzera's owner wrote a cheque for $818 for the purchase of auction equipment items. The cheque was processed by the bank, but the owner did not notify his accounting staff until they discovered the blank cheque stub, so the cheque was not recorded until after October 31.

g. On October 31, the company deposited $932, but this deposit does not appear on the bank statement.

h. The bank statement includes an $818 deduction for a cheque drawn by Jazz Communications. Jazzera promptly notified the bank of its error.

i. The bank statement lists a $132 subtraction for the bank service charge.

j. Jazzera's Cash account shows a balance of $23,072 on October 31.

Required

1. Prepare the bank reconciliation for Jazzera Distributors at October 31, 2017.
2. Record in general journal form the entries necessary to bring the book balance of Cash into agreement with the adjusted book balance on the reconciliation. Include an explanation for each entry.

Problem 8–7A

Calibre Interiors makes all sales on credit. Cash receipts arrive by mail, usually within 30 days of sale. Sarah Romano opens envelopes and separates the cheques from the accompanying remittance advices. Romano forwards the cheques to another employee, who makes the daily bank deposit but has no access to the accounting records. Romano sends the remittance advices, which show the amount of cash received, to the accounting department for entry in the accounts. Her only other duty is to grant sales allowances to customers. (Recall that a *sales allowance* decreases the amount that the customer must pay.) When she receives a customer cheque for less than the full amount of the invoice, she records the sales allowance and forwards the document to the accounting department.

Required You are a new management employee of Calibre Interiors. Write a memo to the company president, Mary Briscoll, identifying the internal control weakness in this situation. State how to correct the weakness.

Problem 8–8A

Applying internal controls to cash payments, including petty cash transactions

④ ⑤

A-1 Machines is located in Saskatoon, Saskatchewan, with a sales territory covering the entire province.

The company has established a large petty cash fund to handle small cash payments and cash advances to the salespeople to cover frequent sales trips.

The controller, Margaret Hamm, has decided that two people (Anne Bloom and Tom Hurry) should be in charge of the fund since money is often needed when one person may be out for coffee or lunch. Hamm also feels this will increase internal control, as the work of one person will serve as a check on that of the other.

Regular small cash payments are handled by either Bloom or Hurry, who make the payment and have the person receiving the money sign a sheet of paper listing the date and reason for the payment. Whenever a salesperson requires an advance for a trip, he or she simply signs a receipt for the money received. The salespeople later submit receipts for the cost of the trip to either Bloom or Hurry to offset the cash advance.

Hamm is puzzled that the fund is almost always out of balance and either over or short.

Required Comment on the internal control procedures of A-1 Machines. Suggest changes that you think would improve the system.

Problem 8–9A

Accounting for petty cash transactions

⑤

2. Fund should hold $23.50

Suppose that, on June 1, Devine Design creates a petty cash fund with an imprest balance of $400. During June, Lucie Chao, the fund custodian, signs the following petty cash tickets:

Ticket No.	Item	Amount
101	Office supplies	$26.64
102	Cab fare for executive	60.00
103	Delivery of package across town	29.32
104	Dinner money for sales manager entertaining a customer	133.34
105	Office supplies	127.20

On June 30, prior to replenishment, the fund contains these tickets plus $34.40. The accounts affected by petty cash payments are Office Supplies Expense, Travel Expense, Delivery Expense, and Entertainment Expense.

Required

1. Explain the characteristics and internal control features of an imprest fund.
2. On June 30, how much cash should the petty cash fund hold before it is replenished?
3. Make general journal entries to (a) create the fund and (b) replenish it. Include explanations.
4. Make the July 1 entry to increase the fund balance to $500. Include an explanation, and briefly describe what the custodian does in this case.

Problem 8–10A

Making ethical business judgments

⑥

Jennifer Black, CPA, is the controller of Arc Industries, a large manufacturing company. Company president, Allen Arc, informed Jennifer that if the company failed to report a "healthy bottom line" this year the bank would turn down its application for a $1,000,000 loan. The company has suffered losses for the past two years, and current economic conditions have caused a downturn in demand for the company's product. Arc suggested that Jennifer use "creative accounting" if necessary to ensure the company reported a profit. As a reward Jennifer would receive a substantial year-end bonus. If you were Jennifer, how would you respond to the president?

PROBLEMS (GROUP B)   MyAccountingLab

Problem 8–1B

Kyanoga Real Estate prospered during the past 10 years. Business was so good that the company bothered with few internal controls. The recent decline in the local real estate market, however, has caused Kyanoga to experience a shortage of cash. John Flannigan, the company owner, is looking for ways to save money.

Define internal control

Required   As controller of the company, write a memorandum to convince John Flannigan of the company's need for a good system of internal control. Include the definition of internal control, and briefly discuss key internal control objectives.

Problem 8–2B

Using the information from Problem 8–1B, briefly discuss the characteristics of internal control, beginning with competent, reliable, and ethical personnel.

Identifying the characteristics of an effective internal control system

Problem 8–3B

Each of the following situations has an internal control weakness:

Identifying internal control weaknesses

a. Upside-Down Applications develops custom programs to customer's specifications. Recently, development of a new program stopped while the programmers redesigned Upside-Down's accounting system. Upside-Down's accountants could have performed this task.

b. Norma Rottler has been your trusted employee for 24 years. She performs all cash-handling and accounting duties. Ms. Rottler just purchased a new Lexus and a new home in an expensive suburb. As owner of the company, you wonder how she can afford these luxuries because you pay her only $30,000 a year and she has no source of outside income.

c. Izzie Hardwoods, a private company, falsified sales and inventory figures in order to get an important loan. The loan went through, but Izzie later went bankrupt and could not repay the bank.

d. The office supply company where Pet Grooming Goods purchases sales receipts recently notified Pet Grooming Goods that its documents were not prenumbered. Howard Mustro, the owner, replied that he never uses receipt numbers.

e. Discount stores such as Cusco make most of their sales in cash, with the remainder in credit card sales. To reduce expenses, one store manager ceases purchasing fidelity bonds on the cashiers.

f. Cornelius' Corndogs keeps all cash receipts in a shoebox for a week because he likes to go to the bank on Tuesdays when Joann is working.

Required

1. Identify the missing internal control characteristic in each situation.

2. Identify the problem that could be caused by each control weakness.

3. Propose a solution to each internal control problem.

Problem 8–4B

The cash receipts and the cash payments of Ace Hardware for January 2017 are as follows:

Cash Receipts (Posting Reference is CR)		Cash Payments (Posting Reference is CP)	
Date	**Cash Debit**	**Cheque No.**	**Cash Credit**
Jan. 3	$20,988	311	$ 3,672
8	1,480	312	1,668
10	1,980	313	12,562
16	7,788	314	2,584
22	20,736	315	8,588
29	2,404	316	3,900
31	1,428	317	1,304
Total	$56,804	318	6,268
		319	800
		320	12,664
		Total	$54,010

The Cash account of Ace Hardware shows a balance of $39,478 at January 31, 2017.

Ace Hardware received the following bank statement on January 31, 2017:

Bank Statement for January 2017				
Description	**Withdrawals**	**Deposits**	**Date**	**Balance**
Balance Forward			Jan01	36,684
EFT Dividend Collection		1,052	Jan01	37,736
Deposit		20,988	Jan04	58,724
Chq#00311	3,672		Jan07	55,052
Deposit		1,480	Jan09	56,532
Deposit		1,980	Jan12	58,512
Chq#00313	12,436		Jan13	46,076
NSF Cheque	3,456		Jan14	42,620
Chq#00312	1,668		Jan15	40,952
Deposit		7,788	Jan17	48,740
Chq#00314	2,584		Jan18	46,156
EFT Insurance	1,316		Jan21	44,840
Bank Collection		12,744	Jan22	57,584
Deposit		20,736	Jan23	78,320
Chq#00315	8,588		Jan26	69,732
Chq#00316	3,900		Jan30	65,832
Service Charge	40		Jan31	65,792
	37,660	66,768		

Additional data for the bank reconciliation:

a. The EFT deposit was a receipt of monthly rent. The EFT debit was payment of monthly insurance.

b. The NSF cheque was received from A. Levine.

c. The $12,744 bank collection of a note receivable on January 22 included $200 interest revenue.

d. The correct amount of cheque #313, a payment on account, is $12,436. (Ace Hardware's accountant mistakenly recorded the cheque for $12,562.)

Required

1. Prepare the Ace Hardware bank reconciliation at January 31, 2017.

2. Describe how a bank account and the bank reconciliation help Ace Hardware's owner control the business's cash.

3. How would you handle items that were outstanding (bank side) from the previous month's bank reconciliation?

Problem 8–5B

Excel Communications had a computer failure on August 1, 2017, which resulted in the loss of data, including the balance of its Cash account and its bank reconciliation from July 31, 2017. The accountant, Brad Eyers, has been able to obtain the following information from the records of the company and its bank:

Preparing a bank reconciliation and related journal entries

③

a. An examination showed that two cheques (#461 for $645.00 and #492 for $225.00) had not been cashed as of August 1. Eyers recalled that there was only one deposit in transit on the July 31 bank reconciliation, but was unable to recall the amount.

b. The cash receipts and cash payments journal contained the following entries for August 2017:

Cash Receipts:		Cash Payments:	
Amounts		**Cheque #**	**Amount**
$ 876.00		499	$ 678.00
1,230.00		500	651.00
1,545.00		501	2,578.50
612.00		502	846.00
2,460.00		503	327.00
$6,723.00		504	820.00
		505	void
		506	314.00
		507	543.00
			$6,757.50

c. The bank provided the following statement as of August 31, 2017:

Date		Cheques and Other Debits		Deposits and Other Credits		Balance
Aug.	1	#500	651.00		660.00	3,579.00
	3	#492	225.00			3,354.00
	5	#501	2,578.50			775.50
	8				876.00	1,651.50
	16	#499	678.00		585.00	1,558.50
	17	EFT	442.50			1,116.00
	19			EFT	720.00	1,836.00
	21	#503	327.00		1,230.00	2,739.00
	22	#504	860.00	EFT	336.50	2,215.50
	24			EFT	471.00	2,686.50
	26	NSF	1,792.50		1,545.00	2,439.00
	27	SC	37.50			2,401.50
	31	#507	543.00		612.00	2,470.50

d. The deposit made on August 16 was for the collection of a note receivable ($540.00) plus interest.

e. The EFTs had not yet been recorded by Excel Communications since the bank statement was the first notification of them.

- The August 17 EFT was for the monthly payment on an insurance policy for Excel Communications.

- The August 19 and 24 EFTs were collections on accounts receivable.

- The August 22 EFT was in error—the transfer should have been to Accel Communications.

f. The NSF cheque on August 26 was received from a customer as payment of $1,792.50 for installation of a satellite purchased from Excel.

g. Cheque #504 was correctly written for $860.00 for the purchase of inventory (assume a perpetual system), but incorrectly recorded by the cash payments clerk.

Required

1. Prepare a bank reconciliation as of August 31, 2017, including the calculation of the book balance of August 31, 2017.

2. Prepare all journal entries that would be required by the bank reconciliation.

Excel Spreadsheet Template

Preparing a bank reconciliation and the related journal entries

③

Problem 8–6B

The June 30, 2017, bank statement of Copps Shoes has just arrived from the Royal Bank. To prepare the Copps Shoes bank reconciliation, you gather the following data:

a. The Copps Shoes Cash account shows a balance of $39,518 on June 30.

b. The bank statement includes two charges for returned cheques from customers. One is a $3,558 cheque received from Trinity Western and deposited on June 20, returned by Trinity Western's bank with the imprint "Unauthorized Signature." The other is an NSF cheque in the amount of $988 received from Mavis Jones. This cheque had been deposited on June 17.

c. Copps Shoes pays rent ($5,650), utilities ($2,000), and cellphone charges ($120) each month by EFT.

d. The following Copps Shoes' cheques are outstanding at June 30:

Cheque No.	Amount
291	$ 306
322	1,074
327	4,312
329	82
330	3,096
331	432
332	1,860

e. The bank statement includes a deposit of $11,466, collected by the bank on behalf of Copps Shoes. Of the total, $11,208 is collection of a note receivable and the remainder is interest revenue.

f. The bank statement shows that Copps Shoes earned $26 in interest on its bank balance during June. This amount was added to Copps Shoes' account by the bank.

g. The bank statement lists a $144 subtraction for the bank service charge.

h. On June 30, the Copps Shoes accountant deposited $3,378, but this deposit does not appear on the bank statement.

i. The bank statement includes a $4,200 deposit that Copps Shoes did not make. The bank had erroneously credited the Copps Shoes' account for another bank customer's deposit.

j. The June 30 bank balance is $50,534.

Required

1. Prepare the bank reconciliation for Copps Shoes at June 30, 2017.

2. Record in general journal form the entries that bring the book balance of Cash into agreement with the adjusted book balance on the reconciliation. Include an explanation for each entry.

Problem 8–7B

Inno Bakery makes all sales of its bread to retailers on account. Cash receipts arrive by mail, usually within 30 days of the sale. Gary Cho opens envelopes and separates the cheques from the accompanying remittance advices. Cho forwards the cheques to another employee, who makes the daily bank deposit but has no access to the accounting records. Cho sends the remittance advices, which show the amount of cash received, to the accounting department for entry in the accounts. Cho's only other duty is to grant sales allowances to customers. (Recall that a *sales allowance* decreases the amount that the customer must pay.) When he receives a customer cheque for less than the full amount of the invoice, he records the sales allowance and forwards the document to the accounting department.

Required   You are the new controller of Inno Bakery. Write a memo to the company president, John Senick, identifying the internal control weakness in this situation. State how to correct the weakness.

 Identifying internal control weaknesses in cash receipts
④

Problem 8–8B

MEI Distributors is located in Moncton, New Brunswick, with a sales territory covering the Maritime provinces and Newfoundland. Employees live in New Brunswick and all report to work at the company's offices in Moncton.

The company has established a large petty cash fund to handle cash payments and cash advances to its salespeople to cover trips to and from New Brunswick on sales calls.

The controller, Jelisa Valji, has decided that two people (Sarah Wong and Martha Dekinder) should be in charge of the petty cash fund, since money is often needed when one person is out of the office. Valji also feels this will increase internal control, because the work of one person will serve as a check on that of the other.

Regular small cash payments are handled by either Wong or Dekinder, who make the payment and have the person receiving the money sign a sheet of paper giving the date and reason for the payment. Whenever a salesperson requires an advance for a sales trip, that person simply signs a receipt for the money received. The salesperson later submits receipts covering the costs incurred to either Wong or Dekinder to offset the cash advance.

Valji, a family friend as well as the controller, doesn't think the system is working and, knowing you are studying accounting, has asked for your advice.

Required   Write a memo to Valji commenting on the internal control procedures of MEI. Suggest changes that you think would improve the system.

 Applying internal controls to cash payments, including petty cash transactions
④ ⑤

Problem 8–9B

Suppose that on September 1, Lavene Motors opens a new showroom in Napanee, Ontario, and creates a petty cash fund with an imprest balance of $400. During September, Lisa Manfield, the fund custodian, signs the petty cash tickets shown below:

 Accounting for petty cash transactions
⑤

Ticket No.	Item	Amount
1	Courier for package received	$ 49.67
2	Refreshments for showroom opening	101.00
3	Computer disks	88.07
4	Office supplies	7.50
5	Dinner money for sales manager entertaining a customer	87.50

On September 30, prior to replenishment, the fund contains these tickets plus $61.34. The accounts affected by petty cash payments are Office Supplies Expense, Entertainment Expense, and Delivery Expense.

Required

1. Explain the characteristics and the internal control features of an imprest fund.
2. On September 30, how much cash should this petty cash fund hold before it is replenished?
3. Make the general journal entries to (a) create the fund and (b) replenish it. Include explanations.
4. Due to the risk of robbery, make the entry on October 1 to decrease the fund balance to $300. Include an explanation.

Problem 8–10B

Making an ethical judgment

Hans Bozzell is a vice-president of the Western Bank in Markham, Ontario. Active in community affairs, Bozzell serves on the board of directors of Orson Tool & Dye. Orson is expanding rapidly and is considering relocating its factory. At a recent meeting, board members decided to try to buy 20 hectares of land on the edge of town. The owner of the property is Sherri Fallon, a customer of Western Bank. Fallon is a recent widow. Bozzell knows that Fallon is eager to sell her local property. In view of Fallon's anguished condition, Bozzell believes she would accept almost any offer for the land. Realtors have appraised the property at $4 million.

Required Apply the ethical judgment framework outlined in the box on page 471 to help Bozzell decide what his role should be in Orson's attempt to buy the land from Fallon.

CHALLENGE PROBLEMS

Problem 8–1C

Management's role in internal control

"Effective internal control must begin with top management."

"The 'tone at the top' is a necessary condition if an organization is to have an effective system of internal control."

Statements such as these are becoming a more important part of internal control literature and thought.

The chapter lists a number of characteristics that are important for an effective system of internal control. Many of these characteristics have been part of the internal control literature for years.

Required Explain why you think a commitment to good internal control by top management is fundamental to an effective system of internal control.

Problem 8–2C

Applying internal controls to cash transactions

4

1. Many companies require some person other than the person preparing the bank reconciliation to review the reconciliation.

2. Organizations routinely require cheques over a certain amount to be signed by two signing officers.

3. The purchasing department orders goods, but the receiving department receives the goods.

Required All of the above situations have a common thread. What is that common thread and why is it important?

EXTENDING YOUR KNOWLEDGE

DECISION PROBLEM

Stratford Tech Solutions has poor internal control over cash. Recently Sanjay Gupda, the owner, has suspected the cashier of stealing. Details of the business's cash position at April 30, 2017, follow:

a. The Cash account in the ledger shows a balance of $12,900.

b. The April 30 bank statement shows a balance of $8,600. The bank statement lists a $400 credit for a bank collection, a $20 debit for the service charge, and an $80 debit for an NSF cheque. C. J. Ellis, the Stratford Tech Solutions accountant, has not recorded any of these items on the books.

c. At April 30 the following cheques are outstanding:

Cheque No.	Amount
402	$200
527	600
531	1,200
561	400

d. There is a $6,000 deposit in transit at April 30, 2017.

e. Cindy Bing, the cashier, handles all incoming cash and makes bank deposits. She also writes cheques and reconciles the monthly bank statement.

   Gupda asks you to determine whether Bing has stolen cash from the business and, if so, how much. Perform a bank reconciliation, using the format illustrated in Exhibit 8–6 on page 460. There are no bank or book errors. Gupda also asks you to evaluate the internal controls and recommend any changes needed to improve them.

> Using the bank reconciliation to detect a theft
> ③
> Adjusted bank balance, $12,200

FINANCIAL STATEMENT CASES

Financial Statement Case 1

Review Indigo Books and Music Inc.'s (Indigo's) 2014 annual report, given in Appendix A at the end of this book and on MyAccountingLab. Answer the following questions about Indigo's internal controls and cash position:

1. What is the name of Indigo's outside auditing firm? What is the date of the annual report? Who is the president of Indigo Books and Music Inc.?

2. Who bears primary responsibility for the financial statements? How can you tell?

3. Who bears primary responsibility for internal controls?

4. Examine the independent auditor's report. What standard of auditing did the outside auditors use in examining Indigo's financial statements? By what accounting standards were the statements evaluated?

5. What are cash equivalents?

6. By how much did Indigo's cash position change during fiscal 2014?

> Audit opinion, management responsibility, internal controls, and cash
> ①
> 6. Decreased by $52,984,000

Financial Statement Case 2

Study the report of the independent registered public accounting firm in the TELUS annual report given on MyAccountingLab and answer the following questions about TELUS's internal controls and cash position:

1. What is the name of TELUS's outside auditing firm? What office of this firm signed the auditor's report? How long after TELUS's year end did the auditors issue their opinion?

2. Who bears responsibility for the financial statements? How can you tell?

> Audit opinion, management responsibility, internal controls, and cash
> ①
> 5. $229,000,000 increase

3. Does the auditor guarantee that internal controls are effective? Explain.

4. What standard of auditing did the outside auditors use in examining TELUS's financial statements? By what accounting standards were the statements evaluated?

5. By how much did TELUS's cash position change during 2013?

> Try It! SOLUTIONS FOR CHAPTER 8

1. Internal controls do not only apply to "big business." Locking your car door is an example of safeguarding assets. Finding the lowest price per litre of gas is an example of operational efficiency.

2. a. Geoff could issue no ticket and keep the customer's cash. Management could physically count the number of people watching a movie and compare that number with the number of ticket stubs retained.

   Geoff could destroy some tickets and keep the customer's cash. Management could account for all ticket stubs by serial number. Missing serial numbers raise questions.

   b. The internal control weakness is lack of separation of duties. Geoff receives cash and also controls the tickets, so he could destroy tickets to cover a theft of cash.

   c. Most entertainment events issue tickets with bar codes and use a scanner at the door that electronically reads the ticket to ensure it is valid.

3. A number of problems can result when a sales clerk can also grant credit approval and record the sales in addition to handling the cash. The clerk could grant credit approval to friends and others who do not meet the credit standards; the clerk could also steal merchandise and hide the theft in the accounting records. In addition, the clerk could fail to do all three jobs well and make mistakes, or forget to perform a task when the sales floor is busy.

4. _d_ Computer virus

   _c_ Encryption

   _e_ Trojan

   _b_ Firewall

   _a_ Phishing

5. The three items that can appear on the bank side of a bank reconciliation are deposits in transit, outstanding cheques, and corrections of bank errors. The company does *not* need to record the reconciling items that appear on the bank side of the bank reconciliation because those items have already been recorded on the company books or are errors of the bank that should not be entered on the company books.

6. a.

JONAS COMPANY	
Bank Reconciliation	
July 31, 2017	
Bank	
Bank balance, July 31, 2017	$ 9,000
Add: Deposits in transit	2,400
	$11,400
Less: Outstanding cheques	1,150
Adjusted bank balance	**$10,250**
Books	
Book balance, July 31, 2017	$10,843
Add: Interest revenue earned	10
Correction of book error—overstated a cheque	27
	$10,880
Less: Bank charges	30
NSF cheque	600
Adjusted book balance	**$10,250**

b. Journal entries to update the company's books:

Cash	10	
Interest Revenue		10

To record interest earned during July 2017.

Cash	27	
Accounts Payable		27

To correct a cheque recorded as $152 that should have been recorded as $125 ($152 − $125 = $27).

Bank Charges Expense	30	
Cash		30

To record bank service charge for July 2017.

Accounts Receivable	600	
Cash		600

To reinstate the account receivable for an NSF cheque.

7. When cash is received by mail, a mailroom employee cannot pocket a customer cheque and destroy the remittance advice because the customer will notify the company. If a customer gets a statement from the company listing the invoice and amount a second time, the customer can show the paid cheque to prove that he or she has already paid. That would indicate that the company has a dishonest employee.

8. The journal entry for the day's sales would be:

Cash	7,262	
Sales Revenue		7,252
Cash Short and Over		10

To record the day's sales, along with the cash overage.

9. The internal control feature in this scenario is proper authorization. Two signatures are required to ensure that no unauthorized expenditures are made. Presigning the cheques defeats the control and should be discouraged.

10. a. The three internal control weaknesses are
   - Petty cash ticket no. 3 is missing. There is no indication of what happened to this ticket. The company should investigate.
   - The petty cash custodian (JCB) did not sign petty cash ticket no. 2. This omission may have been an oversight on his part. However, it raises the question of whether he authorized the payment. Both the fund custodian and the recipient of the cash should sign the ticket.
   - Petty cash ticket no. 4 does not indicate which account to debit and presumably has no receipt attached. What did Tate do with the money, and what account should be debited? At worst, the funds have been stolen. At best, asking the custodian to reconstruct the transaction from memory is haphazard. Since we are instructed in requirement (b) to assume petty cash ticket no. 4 was issued for the purchase of office supplies, debit Office Supplies.

   A fourth control weakness is that, after only one week, the fund is already short $8. This implies a lack of control over petty cash disbursements.
      While it is not specifically asked for in this question, always check for the following when reviewing a petty cash fund:
   - Ensure the cash in the fund plus the total of all petty cash ticket amounts equal the opening balance of the petty cash fund ($300 in this case).
   - Sequence all petty cash tickets by their ticket number and ensure all ticket numbers in the sequence are accounted for.
   - Ensure all transaction details are filled in on each petty cash ticket and that receipts are attached.
   - Ensure the fund custodian signs each petty cash ticket.
   - Investigate any significant cash short and over amounts.

   b. Petty cash journal entries
   i. Entry to establish the petty cash fund:

Jan. 1	Petty Cash	300	
	Cash		300

To open the petty cash fund.

This journal entry is only made once, when the petty cash fund is created. Funds are transferred from one Cash account to another Cash account.

ii. Entry to replenish the fund:

Jun. 30	Office Supplies ($14 + $43)	57	
	Delivery Expense	39	
	Travel Expense	33	
	Cash Short and Over	8	
	Cash		137

To replenish the petty cash fund.

Ensure the cash in the fund ($163) plus the total of all petty cash ticket amounts ($129) equal the opening balance of the petty cash fund ($300). If the total is less than $300, the fund is short. If the total is greater than $300, the fund is over.

c. The balance in Petty Cash is *always* its specified balance, in this case $300, as shown by posting the above entries to the account.

Petty Cash	
(i) 300	

The Petty Cash account is only affected when the petty cash fund is created or when the petty cash fund balance is later increased or decreased.

11. Each step of the framework for making ethical judgments is answered below for David Duncan's situation:
   1. *Determine the facts.* The facts are given in the situation description.
   2. *Identify the ethical issues.* Duncan's ethical dilemma is to decide what he should do with the information he has uncovered.
   3. *Specify the alternatives.* For Duncan, the alternatives include (a) go along with Axiom's liabilities as reported (i.e., do nothing), or (b) force Axiom's management to report liabilities at more correct amounts.
   4. *Identify the stakeholders.* Individuals who could be affected include Duncan, the partners and staff of his auditing firm, the management and employees at Axiom, Axiom's investors, Axiom's creditors, the federal and various provincial governments.
   5. *Assess the possible outcomes of each alternative.*
      (a) If Duncan certifies Axiom's present level of liabilities—and if no one ever objects—Duncan will keep this valuable client. But if Axiom's actual liabilities turn out to be higher than reported, Axiom's investors and creditors may lose money and take Duncan to court. That would damage his reputation as an auditor and hurt his firm.
      (b) If Duncan follows the policy suggestion of his company, he must force Axiom to increase its reported liabilities. That will anger Axiom, and Duncan and his firm may get fired as Axiom's auditor. In this case Duncan will save his reputation, but it will cost him and his firm business in the short run.
   6. *Make a decision.* In the end, Duncan went along with Axiom and he certified Axiom's liabilities. He went directly against his firm's policies. Axiom later admitted understating its liabilities, Duncan had to retract his audit opinion, and Duncan's firm collapsed soon after. Duncan should have followed company policy. Rarely is one person smarter than a team of experts. Not following company policy cost him and many others dearly.

9 RECEIVABLES

LEARNING OBJECTIVE (A1) Discount a note receivable

Is it possible to receive cash from a note receivable prior to the note's maturity date?
Discounting (Selling) a Note Receivable, page 527

MyAccountingLab   The **Summary** for Chapter 9 appears on page 528. This lists all of the MyAccountingLab resources. **Accounting Vocabulary** with definitions for this chapter's material appears on page 530.

Rogers Communications Inc. is one of Canada's largest communications companies. It owns radio and television stations, magazines, cable and wireless businesses, the Rogers Centre in Toronto, a portion of the Toronto Blue Jays baseball team, and other Canadian businesses.

You may recognize this company because you might receive monthly cellphone bills from Rogers or one of its subsidiaries, such as Fido or Koodo. When a person signs up for a cellphone contract, their credit history is evaluated to see if they are likely to pay their bills. The credit department at Fido decides which customers are allowed to have an account.

While a company like Rogers does its best to carefully choose customers, it recognizes that not all customers pay their bills. Why doesn't Rogers ask all customers to prepay their accounts? Sales increase when people are allowed to pay later. But if they eventually don't pay, this creates a loss for the business.

To keep the accounting records accurate, Rogers has to make an estimate of how much they might not get paid. According to the Rogers' 2014 annual report, which includes all of their businesses and not just the wireless division, they estimated that they might not get paid $98 million of accounts receivable. This chapter will look at how all businesses estimate and report accounts receivable and other types of receivables.

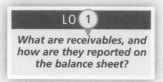

Rogers Communications' business grows, so do its revenues and receivables. This chapter demonstrates how to account for receivables.

RECEIVABLES: AN INTRODUCTION

LO 1

What are receivables, and how are they reported on the balance sheet?

A *receivable* arises when a business (or person) sells goods or services to another party on credit. The receivable is the seller's claim for the amount of the transaction. A receivable also arises when one person or business lends money to another. Each credit transaction involves at least two parties:

- The **creditor**, who sells something and obtains a receivable, which is an asset
- The **debtor**, who makes the purchase and has a payable, which is a liability

A receivable is an asset, just as cash is. But the receivable is slightly different: It's very close to cash, but it's not cash yet.

This chapter focuses on accounting for receivables by the seller (the creditor).

Types of Receivables

Receivables are monetary claims against others. The three major types of receivables are:

- Accounts receivable
- Notes receivable
- Other receivables

Accounts Receivable Accounts receivable, also called *trade receivables*, are amounts to be collected from customers. Accounts receivable are *current assets*. The Accounts Receivable account in the general ledger serves as a *control account* because it summarizes the total of the receivables from all customers. As we saw in Chapter 7, companies also keep a *subsidiary ledger* of the receivable from each customer. This is illustrated as follows:

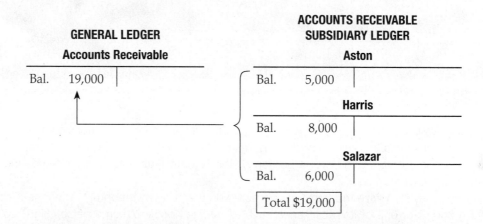

Notes Receivable *Notes receivable* are more formal than accounts receivable. The debtor promises in writing to pay the creditor a definite sum at a definite future date. A written document known as a *promissory note* serves as the evidence of the receivable. Notes receivable due within one year, or one operating cycle if longer than one year, are current assets. Notes due beyond one year are *long-term* notes receivables and are classified as long-term assets.

Other Receivables *Other receivables* is a miscellaneous category that may include loans to employees or shareholders (called Shareholder Loans). Usually these are long-term receivables, but that portion that is due within one year or less is classified as a current asset. Receivables can be reported as shown in Exhibit 9–1, where they are bolded for emphasis (amounts assumed).

EXHIBIT 9–1 | Receivables on the Balance Sheet

EXAMPLE COMPANY Partial Balance Sheet—Assets Section Date		
Assets		
Current assets:		
Cash		$ 1,000
Accounts receivable	**$20,000**	
Less: Allowance for doubtful accounts	1,500	18,500
Notes receivable, short-term*		5,000
Inventories		7,000
Prepaid expenses		1,500
Total current assets		33,000
Investments and long-term receivables:		
Investments	6,000	
Notes receivable, long-term	16,000	
Other receivables	4,000	
Total non-current assets		26,000
Property, plant, and equipment, net		15,000
Total assets		$74,000

* This balance could also include the short-term portion of long-term receivables.
   Note: If there is a credit balance for any customers, it is reported as a liability.

Accounts Receivable

Selling on credit (on account) creates an account receivable. The related journal entries (amounts and the perpetual method are assumed) are as follows:

Service Company			
Feb. 14	Accounts Receivable	10,000	
	Service Revenue		10,000
	Performed service on account.		

Merchandiser			
Feb. 14	Accounts Receivable	10,000	
	Sales Revenue		10,000
	Sold goods on account.		
Feb. 14	Cost of Goods Sold	4,000	
	Merchandise Inventory		4,000
	Cost of goods sold on account.		

The business collects cash for most receivables and makes this entry:

Mar. 3	Cash	10,000	
	Accounts Receivable		10,000
	Collected cash on account.		

ACCOUNTING FOR UNCOLLECTIBLE ACCOUNTS

Selling on credit provides both a benefit and a cost to the selling company.

- *The benefit:* The business increases sales revenues and profits by making sales to a wide range of customers. Customers can buy now but pay later.
- *The cost:* The company will be unable to collect from some customers, and that creates an expense. The expense is called **bad debt expense**, **uncollectible account expense**, or **doubtful account expense**. Bad-debt expense is an operating expense, the same as salaries expense and amortization expense.

There is no single indicator that an account has become delinquent and will not be paid. Some clues would be:

- Receivable is past due
- Customer does not respond to company calls or attempts to collect
- Customer files for bankruptcy
- Company finds out that the business has closed
- The customer has left town or cannot be located

Bad debt expense varies from company to company. The older the receivable, the less valuable it is because of the decreasing likelihood of collection. If a customer doesn't pay and there is a chance of recovering some or all of the balance, then the receivable can be turned over to a collection agency. If the customer doesn't pay and there is no chance any amount will be received, then the balance would be worthless.

How do companies account for these uncollectible accounts? They use the allowance method or, in certain limited cases, the direct write-off method. We begin the next section with the allowance method because it is required when reporting under ASPE.

The Allowance Method

Most companies use the **allowance method** to measure bad debts. The key concept is to record bad debt expense in the same period as the sales revenue, which is an application of the *matching objective*. The business doesn't wait to see which customers will not pay. Instead, it records bad debt expense on the basis of estimates developed from past experience or professional judgment.

The business records bad debt expense for the estimated amount and sets up **Allowance for Doubtful Accounts** (or **Allowance for Uncollectible Accounts**), a contra account to Accounts Receivable. The allowance is the amount of receivables that the business expects *not* to collect. Subtracting the allowance from Accounts Receivable yields the net amount that the company does expect to collect, as shown in the following partial balance sheet (using assumed numbers):

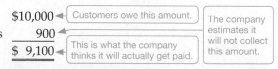

Accounts receivable	$10,000
Less: Allowance for doubtful accounts	900
Accounts receivable, net	$ 9,100

In this example, $9,100 is the **net realizable value (NRV)** of the accounts receivable.

Many Canadian companies do not provide information on their gross receivables and allowance for doubtful accounts; rather, they simply report the net receivable. They sometimes report the details in the notes to the financial statements. Gildan Activewear Inc., a Canadian marketer and manufacturer of quality branded basic family apparel, including T-shirts, fleece, sport shirts, underwear, socks, hosiery, and shapewear, presented the following information about their accounts receivable (in thousands of US dollars) on the balance sheet of their 2014 annual report:

	October 5, 2014	September 29, 2013
Trade accounts receivable (note 7)	354,265	255,018

© Gildan Activewear Inc. 2014.

In the notes to the financial statement, it provides this additional information:

7. Trade Accounts Receivable:

	October 5, 2014	September 29, 2013
Trade accounts receivable	$358,688	$258,685
Allowance for doubtful accounts	(4,423)	(3,667)
	$354,265	$255,018

The movement in the allowance for doubtful accounts in respect of trade receivables was as follows:

	2014	2013
Balance, beginning of year	$(3,667)	$(4,495)
Bad debt expense	(2,420)	(713)
Write-off of trade accounts receivable	1,834	1,607
Increase due to business acquisitions (note 5)	(170)	(66)
Balance, end of year	$(4,423)	$(3,667)

Estimating Uncollectibles

How are bad debts estimated? Companies base estimates on their past experience. There are three ways to estimate uncollectibles:

- Percent-of-sales method
- Aging-of-accounts-receivable method
- Percent-of-accounts-receivable method

The three approaches all normally require an adjusting entry at the end of the period.

Percent-of-Sales Method The **percent-of-sales method** computes bad debt expense as a percent of net credit sales. This method is called an **income statement approach** because the estimate is based on credit sales for the period (an income-statement figure). Assume it is December 31, 2017, and the accounts have these balances *before the year-end adjustments:*

Accounts Receivable		Allowance for Doubtful Accounts	
100,000			1,000

Based on prior experience, the company's bad debt expense is 2 percent of net credit sales, which were $500,000 in 2017.

> **Percent-of-Sales Method:**
> **Bad Debt Expense = Net credit sales × estimated %**

The adjusting entry to record bad debt expense for 2017 and to update the allowance is:

2017			
Dec. 31	Bad Debt Expense	10,000	
	Allowance for Doubtful Accounts		10,000
	To record bad debt expense for the year ($500,000 × 0.02).		

After posting, the accounts are ready for reporting on the 2017 balance sheet.

Accounts Receivable			Allowance for Doubtful Accounts		
100,000					1,000
			Adj.		10,000
					11,000

Net accounts receivable, $89,000

Now the allowance for doubtful accounts is realistic. The balance sheet will report accounts receivable at the net amount of $89,000 ($100,000 – $11,000). The income statement will report the estimated bad debt expense of $10,000, along with revenue and other operating expenses for the period.

Aging-of-Accounts-Receivable Method Another method for estimating uncollectible accounts is the **aging-of-accounts-receivable method**. This method is called a **balance sheet approach** because it focuses on accounts receivable, a balance sheet account.

In the aging-of-accounts-receivable method, the company groups each customer account (Baring Tools Co., etc.) according to how long amounts due have been outstanding. All accounting software offers reports that can sort customer accounts by age. Exhibit 9–2 shows an aging schedule. Notice that the percentage uncollectible increases as a customer account gets older.

EXHIBIT 9–2 | Accounts Receivable Aging Schedule, December 31, 2017

Customer Name	Age of Account				Total Balance
	1–30 Days	31–60 Days	61–90 Days	Over 90 Days	
Baring Tools Co.	$20,000				$ 20,000
Calgary Drills Ltd.	10,000				10,000
Red Deer Pipe Corp.		$3,000	$ 5,000		8,000
Seal Coatings Inc.			9,000	$1,000	10,000
Other accounts*	30,000	2,000	12,000	8,000	52,000
Totals	$60,000	$5,000	$26,000	$9,000	$100,000
Estimated percent uncollectible	× 1%	× 2%	× 5%	× 90%	
Allowance for Doubtful Accounts	$ 600	$ 100	$ 1,300	$8,100	$ 10,100 ← Target balance

*Each of the "Other accounts" would appear individually.

Customers owe the company $100,000, but the company expects *not* to collect $10,100 of this amount.

How the Aging-of-Accounts-Receivable Method Works The aging-of-accounts-receivable method starts with a calculation of what the credit balance of the allowance account needs to be—$10,100 in this case.

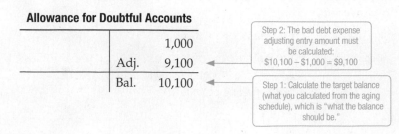

Allowance for Doubtful Accounts		
		1,000
Adj.		9,100
Bal.		10,100

Step 2: The bad debt expense adjusting entry amount must be calculated: $10,100 – $1,000 = $9,100

Step 1: Calculate the target balance (what you calculated from the aging schedule), which is "what the balance should be."

To adjust the allowance, the company makes this adjusting entry at the end of the period:

2017			
Dec. 31	Bad Debt Expense	9,100	
	Allowance for Doubtful Accounts		9,100
	To update the Allowance account to its target balance ($10,100 – $1,000) and record bad debt expense for the period.		

After posting, the accounts are ready for reporting on the balance sheet at net realizable value ($89,900) because that is the amount the company expects to realize, or collect in cash.

Accounts Receivable	Allowance for Doubtful Accounts
100,000	1,000
	Adj. 9,100
	Bal. 10,100

Net accounts receivable, $89,900

The income statement reports the bad debt expense—in this case, $9,100.

Percent-of-Accounts-Receivable Method   Another balance sheet–based method of determining the allowance for doubtful accounts is the **percent-of-accounts-receivable method**. This method is similar to the aging-of-accounts-receivable method; companies can determine what the credit balance of the Allowance account needs to be by calculating it as a percent of the Accounts Receivable balance.

For example, assume Accounts Receivable are $100,000 and Allowance for Doubtful Accounts has a credit balance of $1,000 at December 31, 2017, *before the year-end adjustment*. Based on experience, the company determines that the allowance should be 5 percent of Accounts Receivable, or $5,000. This is the target balance. The adjusting entry is calculated as follows:

Allowance for Doubtful Accounts	
	1,000
Adj.	4,000
Bal.	5,000

Step 2: The bad debt expense adjusting entry amount must be calculated:
$5,000 – $1,000 = $4,000

Step 1: Calculate the target balance as a percentage of the total receivable balance outstanding. In this case it is $100,000 x .05 = $5,000

To adjust the allowance, the company makes this adjusting entry at the end of the period:

2017			
Dec. 31	Bad Debt Expense	4,000	
	Allowance for Doubtful Accounts		4,000
	To update the Allowance account to its target balance ($5,000 – $1,000) and record bad debt expense for the period.		

What if There Is a Debit Balance in the Allowance Account before Adjustments?
This would happen when a company has written off more accounts receivable than expected during the year. In this case, let's assume there is a $500 debit balance in the Allowance for Doubtful Accounts prior to adjustment and the balance in this account should be $5,000, like in the previous example:

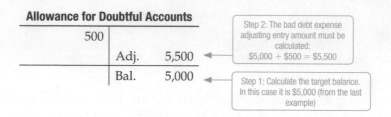

Allowance for Doubtful Accounts		
500		
	Adj.	5,500
	Bal.	5,000

Step 2: The bad debt expense adjusting entry amount must be calculated: $5,000 + $500 = $5,500

Step 1: Calculate the target balance. In this case it is $5,000 (from the last example)

The expense for the period and the increase to the Allowance account would be recorded as $5,500.

Using the Allowance Methods Together In practice, many companies use the percent-of-sales and the aging-of-accounts-receivable or the percent-of-accounts-receivable methods together.

MyAccountingLab

Video: Concepts of Allowance for Bad Debts

- For *interim statements* (monthly or quarterly), companies use the percent-of-sales method because it is easier to apply. The percent-of-sales method focuses on the amount of bad debt *expense*, calculated by multiplying sales by a chosen percent.

- At the end of the year, these companies use the aging-of-accounts-receivable method or the percent-of-accounts-receivable method to ensure that Accounts Receivable is reported at *expected net realizable value*. These two methods focus on the amount of the receivables—the *asset*—that is uncollectible.

Exhibit 9–3 summarizes and compares the three methods.

EXHIBIT 9–3 | Comparing the Percent-of-Sales, the Aging-of-Accounts-Receivable, and the Percent-of-Accounts-Receivable Methods for Estimating Uncollectibles

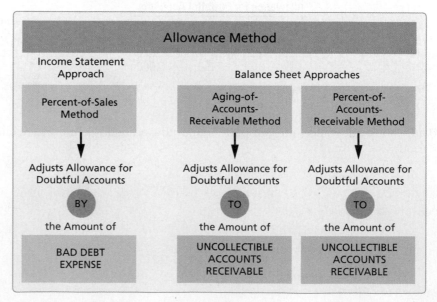

Writing Off Uncollectible Accounts

Let's assume that during early 2018 the company collects on most of its $100,000 of accounts receivable and records the cash receipts as follows:

2018			
Jan.–Mar.	Cash	80,000	
	Accounts Receivable		80,000
	To record collections on account.		

Suppose that, after repeated attempts to collect, the company's credit department determines that it cannot collect a total of $1,200 from customers Auger ($900) and Kirsh ($300). The company then **writes off** or removes the balances of these customers from the Accounts Receivable control account and subsidiary ledger:

2018			
Mar. 31	Allowance for Doubtful Accounts	1,200	
	Accounts Receivable—Auger		900
	Accounts Receivable—Kirsh		300
	To write off uncollectible accounts.		

> Notice the new account name convention here? This is how individual customer accounts within the control account are identified.

Since Allowance for Doubtful Accounts is a contra-asset account, the write-off of uncollectible accounts has no effect on total assets, liabilities, or equity:

	Assets	=	Liabilities	+	Owner's Equity
Allowance	+1,200	=	0	+	0
Accounts Receivable	−1,200				

A write-off of uncollectible accounts affects neither an expense account nor the net amount of receivables.

These written off customers must be eliminated from the accounts receivable records because the company does not want to waste time and money pursuing collections from them. In other words, they need to be removed from the list of customers we expect to pay their invoices (Accounts Receivable) and they need to be removed from the list of people we estimate may not pay their invoices (Allowance for Doubtful Accounts)—because we now know for sure that nothing will be paid. However, a record of these customers will still be retained in the system or by the credit department for future reference and possible future credit applications.

Recovery of Accounts Previously Written Off

When an account receivable is written off as uncollectible, the customer still owes the money. However, the company may stop pursuing collection.

Some companies turn delinquent receivables over to a lawyer or a collection agency to help recover some of the cash. If the lawyer or collection agency is able to get cash from the customer and pay it to the company it is called a **recovery**.

Let's see how to record the recovery of an account that we wrote off earlier. Recall that on March 31, 2018, the company wrote off the $900 receivable from customer Auger. Suppose it is now October 4, 2018, and the company unexpectedly receives $900 from Auger. To account for this recovery, the company makes two journal entries to (1) reverse the earlier write-off and (2) record the cash collection, as follows:

2018			
❶ Oct. 4	Accounts Receivable—Auger	900	
	Allowance for Doubtful Accounts		900
	Reinstated Auger's account receivable.		
❷ Oct. 4	Cash	900	
	Accounts Receivable—Auger		900
	To record collection on account.		

Follow through the entries to Auger's subsidiary ledger account, shown in the T-account below: first the credit sale, then the write-off, then the reversal of the write-off, and finally the credit to the account when Auger pays in full. The customer's subsidiary account shows the complete credit history—an important feature of the subsidiary ledger system and one of the reasons why both steps are shown separately in the journals—so there is a detailed record of what happened with each customer.

Accounts Receivable—Auger

Sale – 2016	900	900	Write-off – Mar. 31, 2017
❶ Reinstate – Oct. 4, 2017	900	900	❷ Collection – Oct. 4, 2017

> Try It!

1. Acadia Building Supplies is a chain of hardware and building supply stores concentrated in the Maritimes. The company's year-end balance sheet on December 31, 2016, reported:

Accounts receivable	$4,000,000
Less: Allowance for doubtful accounts	175,000

a. Journalize, without explanations, year 2017 entries for Acadia Building Supplies:
   i. Estimated bad debt expense was $140,000 for the first three-quarters of the year, based on the percent-of-sales method.
   ii. Write-offs of Accounts Receivable totalled $160,000.
   iii. December 31, 2017, aging of receivables indicates, using estimated amounts, that $192,000 of total receivables are uncollectible.
b. Post all three transactions to the T-account for Allowance for Doubtful Accounts, as follows:

Allowance for Doubtful Accounts

2017 Write-offs	?	Dec. 31, 2016, Bal.	175,000
		2017 Expense	?
		Bal. before Adj.	?
		Dec. 31, 2017, Adj	?
		Dec. 31, 2017, Bal.	192,000

c. Report Acadia Building Supplies' receivables and related allowance on the December 31, 2017, balance sheet. Accounts Receivable at that date totals $4,155,000.

d. What is the expected net realizable value of receivables at December 31, 2017? How much is bad debt expense for 2017?

2. Poco Supplies wrote off the following accounts receivable as uncollectible for the year ended December 31, 2017:

Carl Rogers $3,250, Vince Tran $4,100, Dan Saerose $2,200, Total = $9,550

The company prepared the following aging schedule for its accounts receivable on December 31, 2017:

Aging Class	Receivables Balance on December 31, 2017	Estimated Percent Uncollectible
0 – 30 days	$115,000	1%
31 – 60 days	55,000	2%
61 – 90 days	35,000	20%
91 – 120 days	15,000	30%
Over 120 days	10,000	50%

a. Journalize the write-offs and the year-end adjusting entry for 2017 using the allowance method. Assume that Allowance for Doubtful Accounts had a beginning credit balance of $15,000 on January 1, 2017, and the company uses the aging method.

b. Determine the net realizable value of accounts receivable on December 31, 2017.

Solutions appear at the end of this chapter and on MyAccountingLab

THE DIRECT WRITE-OFF METHOD

There is another way to account for uncollectible receivables—the **direct write-off method**. It is not appropriate for most companies because it does not follow generally accepted accounting principles (GAAP).

Under the direct write-off method, the company waits until it decides that a customer's account receivable is uncollectible to record the expense. The company writes off the customer's account receivable by debiting Bad Debt Expense and crediting the customer's Account Receivable, as follows (using assumed data):

LO 3
What is the direct write-off method?

2017			
Mar. 6	Bad Debt Expense	2,000	
	Accounts Receivable—Sterling		2,000
	Wrote off an uncollectible account from Dec. 10, 2016, sale.		

The direct write-off method is inferior to the allowance method for two reasons:

- It does not set up an Allowance for Doubtful Accounts. As a result, the direct write-off method always reports the receivables at their full amount. Assets are then overstated on the balance sheet, since the business likely does not expect to collect the full amount of accounts receivable.

- It does not match the bad debt expense against revenue very well. In this example, the company made the sale to Sterling in 2016 and should have estimated and recorded the bad debt expense during 2016, matching the bad debt expense to its related sales revenue. That is the only way to measure net income properly. By recording the bad debt expense in 2017, the company overstates net income in 2016 and understates net income in 2017. Both years' net income amounts are incorrect.

The direct write-off method is acceptable only if uncollectibles are immaterial (very low) in amount or if the difference between using an allowance method and the direct write-off method is immaterial. It works for retailers such as small neighbourhood stores or bakeries, because those companies report almost no receivables.

> Try It!

3. Cersei Crowley is a home decorator. She uses the direct write-off method to account for uncollectible receivables. At January 31, 2017, Cersei's accounts receivable totalled $15,000. During February, she reported $18,000 of sales on account and collected $19,000 on account. She wrote off one account with Jane Eyre in the amount of $1,800 on February 26, 2017.
   a. Journalize the write-off. No explanation is required.
   b. What is Cersei's accounts receivable balance at the end of February?

Solutions appear at the end of this chapter and on MyAccountingLab

OTHER PAYMENT METHODS

Credit Card Sales

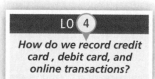

LO 4

How do we record credit card , debit card, and online transactions?

Credit card sales are common in both traditional and online retailing. American Express, VISA, and MasterCard are popular. The customer presents the credit card to pay for purchases. The credit card company pays the seller and then bills the customer, who pays the credit card company.

Credit cards offer the convenience of buying without having to pay the cash immediately. A VISA customer receives a monthly statement from VISA, detailing each of the customer's credit card transactions. The customer can write one cheque or make an online payment to cover the total of these credit card purchases.

Retailers accept credit cards from customers to increase revenue. Not only are credit cards more convenient for the customer, but research shows that customers purchase more with credit cards than with cash only. This transaction is essentially a sale of the receivable to the credit card company. The credit card company previously performed the credit check and now assumes the risk of uncollectible accounts. Hence, retailers do not have to keep accounts receivable records, and they do not have to collect cash from customers.

These benefits to the seller do not come free. The seller pays a fee to the credit card company and, therefore, receives less than the full amount of the sale. The credit card company takes a fee of 1 to 5 percent[1] on the sale. Accounting for credit card sales differs for bank credit cards and for non-bank credit cards.

Bank Credit Cards VISA, MasterCard, and American Express are popular *bank credit cards*. With bank credit cards, the seller uses chip technology to immediately process credit transactions that are electronically deposited into the merchant's bank account. Smaller retailers may still need to bundle and deposit the VISA or MasterCard receipts at the bank for processing. Suppose you and your family have lunch at The Keg restaurant. You pay the bill—$100—with a VISA card. The

---

[1] The rate varies among companies and over time.

Keg's entry to record the $100 VISA card sale, subject to the credit card company's (assumed) 2 percent discount, which is an *expense* to The Keg for a credit card transaction, is as follows:

2017			
Mar. 2	Cash	98	
	Credit Card Discount Expense	2	
	Sales Revenue		100
	Recorded VISA credit card sale less a 2 percent credit card discount expense.		

Non-bank Credit Cards Credit cards other than VISA, MasterCard, and American Express are known as *non-bank credit cards* and are rarely seen in the marketplace. With non-bank credit cards, the seller mails the credit card receipts to the credit card company and awaits payment, less the credit card company's fee. Suppose instead that you pay the bill at The Keg—$100—with a Diners Club card, a non-bank credit card. The Keg's entry to record the $100 non-bank credit card sale is subject to the credit card company's (assumed) 2 percent discount:

Mar. 2	Accounts Receivable	98	
	Credit Card Discount Expense	2	
	Sales Revenue		100
	Recorded Diners Club credit card sale less a 2 percent credit card discount expense.		

In both the bank credit card and the non-bank credit card examples, the customer pays either VISA or Diners Club the $100 after later receiving the monthly statement from the credit card company. The Keg receives $98 from the credit card company, and the credit card company keeps $2 for this transaction.

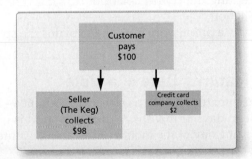

Debit Card Sales

Debit cards are fundamentally different from credit cards. Using a *debit card* is like paying with cash, except that you don't have to carry cash or write a cheque. All banks issue debit cards. When a business makes a sale, the customer "swipes" her debit card through an Interac or similar card reader and enters her personal identification number (PIN). The bank deducts the cost of the purchase from the customer's account immediately and transfers the purchase amount, less a debit card service fee for processing the transaction, into the business's account. The journal entry for the business is almost the same as the journal entry for a bank credit card sale. For example, suppose you buy groceries at a grocery store for a total cost of $56.35. The grocery store records the sale as follows:

Mar. 31	Cash	55.85	
	Debit Card Service Fee	0.50	
	Sales Revenue		56.35
	To record a debit card sale.		

Online Payments

PayPal ®, Apple Pay ®, and other providers of online payment solutions are usually accounted for the same way as bank debit and credit card transactions. Payments are deposited directly into a company's bank account at the time of the transaction, less a percentage discount and sometimes an additional transaction fee.

> Try It!

4. Restaurants do a large volume of business by customer credit cards and debit cards. Suppose a Swiss Chalet restaurant had these transactions on a Thursday in May:

MasterCard credit card sales	$15,000
Non-bank credit card sales	3,000
Debit card sales	5,000

Suppose MasterCard charges merchants 2 percent, the non-bank credit card companies charge 3 percent, and the debit card transactions incur a charge of 2.5 percent. Record these sale transactions for this Swiss Chalet restaurant on June 12.

Solutions appear at the end of this chapter and on MyAccountingLab

ACCOUNTING FOR NOTES RECEIVABLE

LO 5

What are notes receivable, and how do we account for these assets?

Notes receivable are more formal than accounts receivable. The debtor signs a promissory note accepting the conditions of borrowing. The note also serves as evidence of the transaction.

Exhibit 9–4 illustrates a promissory note and explains the special terms used for notes receivable.

Identifying the Maturity Date of a Note

LEARNING TIPS

You need to know the following: September, April, June, and November have 30 days. All the rest have 31, except February, which has 28 and one day more every four years.

Some notes specify the maturity date, as shown in Exhibit 9–4. Other notes state the period of the note in days or months. When the period is given in months, the note matures on the same day of the month as the date the note was issued. A six-month note dated February 16 matures on August 16.

A 120-day note dated September 14, 2016, matures on January 12, 2017, as shown below:

Month		Number of Days	Cumulative Total
Sep.	2016	16*	16
Oct.	2016	31	47
Nov.	2016	30	77
Dec.	2016	31	108
Jan.	2017	12	120

*30 – 14 = 16

EXHIBIT 9–4 | A Promissory Note

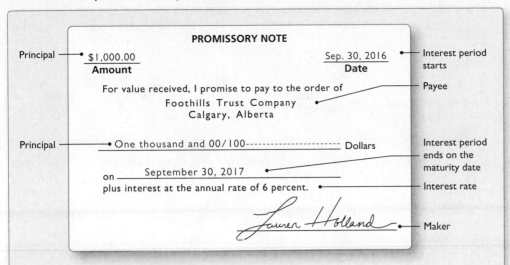

Promissory note: A written promise to pay a specified sum of money at a particular future date.

Maker of the note (*debtor*): The entity that signs the note and promises to pay the required amount; the maker of the note is the *debtor*.

Payee of the note (*creditor*): The entity to whom the maker promises future payment; the payee of the note is the *creditor*.

Principal: The amount lent by the payee and borrowed by the maker of the note.

Interest: The revenue to the payee for lending the money; interest is an expense to the debtor.

Interest period: The period of time during which interest is to be computed, extending from the original date of the note to the maturity date; also called the **note term** or simply the **time period**.

Interest rate: The percentage rate of interest specified by the note, always stated for a period of one year; therefore, a 6 percent note means that the amount of interest for *one year* is 6 percent of the note's principal amount.

Maturity date (also called **due date**): The date on which final payment of the note is due.

Maturity value: The sum of the principal plus interest due at maturity.

When the period is given in days, the maturity date is determined by counting the days from date of issue. The 120-day note dated September 14, 2016, would have to be *repaid* by January 12, 2017. In counting the days remaining for a note, remember to:

MyAccountingLab

Video: Determining Maturity Date

- Count the maturity date
- Omit the date the note was issued

Computing Simple Interest on a Note

Since most of these notes are for a period of less than one year, simple interest is used to focus on the concepts and journal entries rather than formulae. The formula for computing simple interest is:

> **Amount of simple interest = Principal × Interest rate × Time**

KEY POINTS
Time means interest period.

Using the data in Exhibit 9–4, Foothills Trust Company computes its interest revenue for one year on its note receivable as follows:

Amount of simple interest $60	=	Principal $1,000	×	Interest rate 0.06	×	Time 1 (year)

The maturity value of the note is $1,060 ($1,000 principal + $60 interest). The time element is one (1) because the note's term is one year.

Interest on a $2,000 note at 10 percent per year for three months is computed as follows:

When the term of a note is stated in months, we compute the interest based on the 12-month year.

Amount of simple interest $50	=	Principal $2,000	×	Interest rate 0.10	×	Time $3/12$

The interest on a $5,000 note at 12 percent for 60 days is computed as follows:

When the interest period of a note is stated in days, we usually compute interest based on a 365-day year.

Amount of simple interest $98.63	=	Principal $5,000	×	Interest rate 0.12	×	Time $60/365$

MyAccountingLab

Video: Computing Interest and Maturity Values
Interactive Figure: Interact with Amount of Interest
Video: Real World Accounting

Keep in mind that interest rates are stated as an annual rate. Therefore, the time in the interest formula should also be expressed in terms of a year.

Recording Notes Receivable

Notes Receivable is not a common account. There are a limited number of situations where the account might be used. Each is discussed below.

Note Received in Return for Cash Consider the loan agreement shown in Exhibit 9–4. After Lauren Holland signs the note and presents it to Foothills Trust Company, the trust company gives her $1,000 cash. At the maturity date, Holland pays the trust company $1,060 ($1,000 principal + $60 interest). The trust company's entries (assuming it has a September 30 year end) are as follows:

2016				
Sep. 30	Note Receivable—L. Holland		1,000	
	Cash			1,000
	Lent money at 6% for 1 year.			
2017				
Sep. 30	Cash		1,060	
	Note Receivable—L. Holland			1,000
	Interest Revenue			60
	Collected note at maturity with interest (Interest revenue = $1,000 × 0.06 × 1)			

Note Received as Payment for Sale Some companies sell merchandise in exchange for notes receivable. This arrangement often occurs when the payment term extends beyond the customary accounts receivable period, which ranges from 30 to 60 days, as indicated by the company's credit terms of 2/10, net 30 or net 60.

Suppose that, on October 20, 2017, Midland Plumbing services a boiler for $15,000 at Western Builders' head office. Western signs a 90-day promissory note at 10 percent interest. Midland's entries to record the service and collection from Western (Midland's year end is June 30) are as follows:

2017			
Oct. 20	Note Receivable—Western Builders	15,000.00	
	Service Revenue		15,000.00
	To record service provided. Note at 10% for 90 days.		
2018			
Jan. 18	Cash	15,369.86	
	Note Receivable—Western Builders		15,000.00
	Interest Revenue		369.86
	To record collection at maturity with interest. (Interest revenue = $15,000 \times 0.10 \times {}^{90}/_{365}$)		

Note Received in Exchange for an Account Receivable A company may accept a note receivable from a trade customer who fails to pay an account receivable on time. The customer signs a promissory note and gives it to the creditor.

Suppose Clifford Sales sees that it will not be able to pay off its account payable with Fridoris Supply, which is due in 15 days. Fridoris Supply may accept a 12-month, $6,000 note receivable with 9 percent interest from Clifford Sales on October 1, 2017. Fridoris Supply's entry is as follows:

2017			
Oct. 1	Note Receivable—Clifford Sales	6,000	
	Accounts Receivable—Clifford Sales		6,000
	Received a note at 9% for 12 months.		

Accruing Interest Revenue

A note receivable may be outstanding at the end of the accounting period. The interest revenue earned on the note up to the year end is part of that year's earnings. Recall that interest revenue is earned over time, not just when cash is received. We saw in Chapter 3, on pages 130–131, that accrued revenue creates an asset for the amount that has been earned but not received.

Let's continue with the Fridoris Supply note receivable from Clifford Sales. Fridoris Supply's accounting period ends December 31.

How much of the total interest revenue does Fridoris Supply earn in 2017 (for October, November, and December)?

$$\$6,000 \times 0.09 \times {}^{3}/_{12} = \$135$$

Fridoris Supply makes this adjusting entry to accrue interest revenue at December 31, 2017:

2017			
Dec. 31	Interest Receivable	135	
	Interest Revenue		135
	To accrue interest revenue earned in 2017 but not yet received ($6,000 \times 0.09 \times {}^{3}/_{12}$).		

How much interest revenue does Fridoris Supply earn in 2018 (for January through September)?

$$\$6{,}000 \times 0.09 \times {}^{9}/_{12} = \$405$$

On the note's maturity date, Fridoris Supply makes this entry:

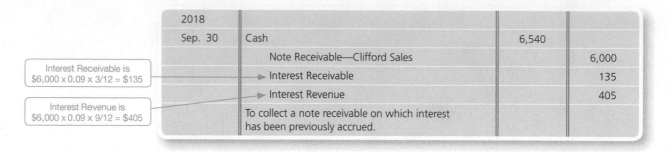

2018			
Sep. 30	Cash	6,540	
	Note Receivable—Clifford Sales		6,000
	Interest Receivable		135
	Interest Revenue		405
	To collect a note receivable on which interest has been previously accrued.		

Interest Receivable is $6,000 x 0.09 x 3/12 = $135

Interest Revenue is $6,000 x 0.09 x 9/12 = $405

The entries for accrued interest at December 31, 2017, and for collection in 2018 assign the correct amount of interest revenue to each year.

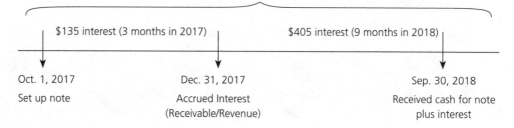

$540 total interest revenue ($6,000 × 0.09 × 1 year)

$135 interest (3 months in 2017) $405 interest (9 months in 2018)

Oct. 1, 2017	Dec. 31, 2017	Sep. 30, 2018
Set up note	Accrued Interest (Receivable/Revenue)	Received cash for note plus interest

A company holding a note may need cash before the note matures. A procedure for selling the note, called discounting a note receivable, appears in the Chapter 9 Appendix beginning on page 527.

Dishonoured Notes Receivable

If the maker of a note does not pay a note receivable at maturity, the maker **dishonours** or **defaults on the note**. Because the note has expired, it is no longer in force. However, the debtor still owes the payee. The payee must transfer the note receivable amount to Accounts Receivable since Notes Receivable contains only notes that have not yet matured.

Suppose Whitehorse Hardware has a six-month, 10 percent note receivable for $5,000 from Northern Cabinets. On the February 3 maturity date, Northern Cabinets defaults. Whitehorse Hardware would record the default as follows:

Feb. 3	Accounts Receivable—Northern Cabinets	5,250	
	Note Receivable—Northern Cabinets		5,000
	Interest Revenue		250
	To record the default on a note receivable.		

$5,250 [$5,000 + ($5,000 x 0.10 x 6/12)]

$250 ($5,000 x 0.10 x 6/12)

Whitehorse Hardware would pursue collection from Northern Cabinets for this account receivable and would account for the receivable in the normal way. Further accrual of interest from this point until payment is received could only be recorded if collection is likely, according to the revenue recognition criterion.

KEY POINTS

According to the recognition criteria for revenues, the accrual of interest beyond the default date is valid only if collection is likely.

> Try It!

5. On April 1, 2016, Mediterranean Importers loaned $20,000 cash to Bud Shriver on a one-year, 7 percent note. Record the loan transaction and any year-end transactions for Mediterranean.

6. Refer to the previous question. The loan was repaid on April 1, 2017, with its related interest. Record the repayment for Mediterranean, assuming no reversing entries were used.

7. Refer to Try It #5. Suppose Shriver defaulted on the note at maturity instead of repaying it. How would Mediterranean Importers record the default?

Solutions appear at the end of this chapter and on MyAccountingLab

> Why It's Done This Way

Accountants and users have agreed that a company should *estimate* its bad debts, and this chapter presented various methods that companies can use to do that.

In terms of the accounting framework, is this a good idea? We need to focus on the characteristics of financial information that make it beneficial to users. Think about relevance and reliability. Reporting an allowance for doubtful accounts is less *reliable* than either waiting to record the revenue until cash payment is received or waiting for a bad debt to be confirmed.

It does, however, add *relevance* to the financial statements: It allows revenue to be recorded in the period it occurred and allows accounts receivable to not be overstated by setting up an Allowance for Doubtful Accounts to reflect the possibility that some accounts will not be collected.

While neither situation is perfect, the trade-off between using an estimate to make information more relevant and losing some reliability seems appropriate in this situation, leading to financial statements that communicate useful information to users.

USING ACCOUNTING INFORMATION FOR DECISION MAKING

The relationships between assets, liabilities, and revenues provide new information about how well a business and its managers are doing. Let's examine two important ratios using the accounts presented in Exhibit 9–5.

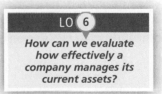

LO 6

How can we evaluate how effectively a company manages its current assets?

Acid-Test (or Quick) Ratio

Corporate stakeholders, investors, managers, government, and other readers of financial reports use ratios for decision making. In Chapter 4, for example, we discussed the current ratio, which indicates the ability to pay current liabilities with current assets. A more stringent measure of the ability to pay current liabilities is the **acid-test ratio** (or **quick ratio**). The acid-test ratio tells whether the entity could pay all its current liabilities if they came due immediately.

EXHIBIT 9–5 | ABC Ltd.'s Partial Financial Statement Information

Partial Balance Sheet	2017	2016
Current Assets		
Cash	$ 19,796	$ 10,000
Accounts receivable	63,175	57,308
Inventories	68,117	74,742
Prepaid expenses	2,060	1,945
Supplies	3,363	2,702
Total current assets	$156,511	$146,697
Current Liabilities		
Accounts payable and accrued expenses	$ 33,298	$ 38,061
Income taxes payable	2,017	5,037
Total current liabilities	$ 35,315	$ 43,098
Sales revenue from the income statement	$512,037	

For ABC Ltd. from Exhibit 9–5:

$$\text{Acid-test ratio} = \frac{\text{Cash + Short-term investments + Net current receivables}}{\text{Total current liabilities}}$$

$$2017: \frac{\$19{,}796 + \$0 + \$63{,}175}{\$35{,}315} = 2.35$$

$$2016: \frac{\$10{,}000 + \$0 + \$57{,}308}{\$43{,}098} = 1.56$$

The higher the acid-test ratio, the better able the business is to pay its current liabilities. ABC's ratio in 2017 is 2.35, showing excellent liquidity. There is more than twice as much in assets coming in to the company as opposed to leaving the company. A comparison of 2017 to 2016 indicates that the ratio has improved from 1.56 to 2.35.

What is an acceptable acid-test ratio value? In general, an acid-test ratio of 1.00 is considered safe. However, the answer depends on the industry. Automobile dealers can operate smoothly with an acid-test ratio of 0.20. The acid-test ratio for most department stores clusters about 0.80, while travel agencies average 1.10.

Days' Sales in Receivables

After a business makes a credit sale, the next critical event in the business cycle is collection of the receivable. Several financial ratios centre on receivables. **Days' sales in receivables**, also called *days sales uncollected* or the **collection period**, indicates how many days it takes to collect the average level of receivables. The shorter the collection period, the more quickly the organization has cash to use for operations. The longer the collection period, the less cash is available to pay bills and expand. Days' sales in receivables can be computed in two steps, as follows:

$$❶ \text{ One day's sales} = \frac{\text{Net sales}}{\text{365 days}}$$

Day's sales in average accounts receivable	=	Average net accounts receivable / One day's sales	=	(Beginning net receivables + Ending net receivables) / 2 / One day's sales

For ABC Ltd. from Exhibit 9–5, the days' sales in receivables for 2017 is:

❶ One day's sales $= \dfrac{\$512,037}{365} = \$1,403$ per day

❷ Day's sales in average accounts receivable $= \dfrac{(\$57,308 + \$63,175)/2}{\$1,403} = 42.9$ days

On average, it takes ABC Ltd. about 43 days to collect its accounts receivable. The length of the collection period depends on the credit terms of the sale and the terms that are common in a particular industry. For example, sales on net 30 terms should be collected within approximately 30 days. When there is a discount, such as 2/10, net 30, the collection period may be shorter. Terms of net 45 result in a longer collection period. If the terms are net 45, then 43 days is good; however, if the terms are net 30, 43 days to collect is not an efficient collection result and should be improved.

A company should watch its collection period closely. Whenever the collection period lengthens, the business must find other sources of financing, such as borrowing. During recessions customers pay more slowly, and a longer collection period may be unavoidable. Cash flow or lack thereof is a serious issue since companies need cash to operate. This is covered in more detail in Chapters 17 and 18.

LEARNING TIPS

Refer to Chapter 5, page 253, if you need help recalling these terms.

REAL WORLD EXAMPLE

When the days' sales in receivables result is lower than the industry standard, this may mean that credit is too tight and potential sales might be lost.

> **Try It!**

8. Use the data in Exhibit 9–5 to compute ABC Ltd.'s current ratio at December 31, 2017. Then compare ABC Ltd.'s current ratio and acid-test ratio. Why is the current ratio higher?

9. Can days' sales in receivables be computed in one step instead of two? If so, what would be the formula?

Solutions appear at the end of this chapter and on MyAccountingLab

THE IMPACT OF IFRS ON ACCOUNTS RECEIVABLE

LO 7

How does IFRS affect accounts receivable?

ASPE	IFRS

Assets categorized as current, including accounts receivable, are essentially reported at their fair values. How do we know this? We subtract the allowance for doubtful accounts from the gross receivables and show the anticipated amount that a company will be able to collect. Because of this deduction, we are really presenting the account at its estimated collectible amount, or its fair value.

Accounts Receivable is the usual term used.	Trade Receivables is the usual term used.

SUMMARY PROBLEM FOR YOUR REVIEW

Akerlof Investigations has an Accounts Receivable balance of $34,000 and an Allowance for Doubtful Accounts credit balance of $3,000 at the December 31, 2015, fiscal year end.

Required:

Record the journal entries for the following Akerlof Investigations transactions. No explanations are needed.

2016

Apr.	1	Lent $20,000 to Blatchford Agencies. Received a six-month, 10 percent note.
Jun.	21	J. Schiller called to say there was no way he could pay his $1,000 balance and Akerlof should stop calling.
Oct.	1	Collected the Blatchford Agencies' note at maturity.
Nov.	30	Lent $15,000 to Fane Industries on a three-month, 12 percent note.
Dec.	31	Accrued interest revenue on the Fane Industries' note.
Dec.	31	Recorded estimated uncollectible as 1 percent of the $550,000 of credit sales.

2017

Feb.	28	Collected the Fane Industries' note at maturity.
Mar.	3	J. Shiller wanted to do further business with Akerlof Investigations and paid the $1,000 balance from 2016.

SOLUTION

2016			
Apr. 1	Note Receivable—Blatchford Agencies	20,000	
	Cash		20,000
June 21	Allowance for Doubtful Accounts	1,000	
	Accounts Receivable—J. Schiller		1,000
Oct. 1	Cash	21,000	
	Note Receivable—Blatchford Agencies		20,000
	Interest Revenue		1,000
Nov. 30	Note Receivable—Fane Industries	15,000	
	Cash		15,000
Dec. 31	Interest Receivable	150	
	Interest Revenue		150
Dec. 31	Bad Debt Expense	5,500	
	Allowance for Doubtful Accounts		5,500
2017			
Feb. 28	Cash	15,450	
	Note Receivable—Fane Industries		15,000
	Interest Receivable		150
	Interest Revenue		300
Mar. 3	Accounts Receivable—J. Schiller	1,000	
	Allowance for Doubtful Accounts		1,000
Mar. 3	Cash	1,000	
	Accounts Receivable—J. Schiller		1,000

All notes receivable in this company are stated in terms of months, so interest is calculated based on 12 months in a year (not 365 days in a year).

($20,000 × 0.10 × $^{6}/_{12}$) Accrue interest for only one month. This is how much time has passed.

($15,000 × 0.12 × $^{1}/_{12}$)

($550,000 × .01)

$15,000 + ($15,000 × 0.12 × $^{3}/_{12}$)

($15,000 × 0.12 × $^{2}/_{12}$) The revenue is reported for the two months that the loan was outstanding in 2017.

CHAPTER 9 APPENDIX

DISCOUNTING (SELLING) A NOTE RECEIVABLE

A payee of a note receivable may need cash before the maturity date of the note. When this occurs, the payee may sell the note, a practice called **discounting a note receivable**. The price to be received for the note is determined by a present-value calculation. We discuss these concepts in detail in Chapter 15. The transaction between the seller and the buyer of the note can take any form agreeable to the two parties. Here we illustrate one procedure used for discounting short-term notes receivable. To receive cash immediately, the seller is willing to accept a lower price than the note's maturity value.

LO A1

Is it possible to receive cash from a note receivable prior to the note's maturity date?

Proceeds Are More than the Note   To illustrate, suppose EMCO Ltd. lent $15,000 to Dartmouth Builders on October 20, 2016. The maturity date of the 90-day, 10 percent Dartmouth note is January 18, 2017. Suppose EMCO discounts the Dartmouth Builders note at the National Bank on December 9, 2016, when the note is 50 days old. The bank applies a 12 percent annual interest rate in computing the discounted value of the note.

The bank will use a discount rate that is higher than the interest rate on the note in order to earn some interest on the transaction. EMCO may be willing to accept this higher rate in order to get cash quickly. The discounted value, called the *proceeds*, is the amount EMCO receives from the bank. The proceeds can be computed in five steps, as shown in Exhibit 9–1A. At maturity the bank collects $15,370 from the maker of the note and earns $202 interest revenue from holding the note.

EXHIBIT 9–1A | Discounting (Selling) a Note Receivable: EMCO Ltd. Discounts the Dartmouth Builders Note

Steps	Computations		
1. Compute the original amount of interest on the note receivable.	$15,000 × 0.10 × $^{90}/_{365}$	=	$370
2. Maturity value of note = Principal + Interest	$15,000 + $370	=	$15,370
3. Determine the period (number of days, months, or years) the bank will hold the note (the discount period).	Dec. 9, 2016, to Jan. 18, 2017	=	40 days
4. Compute the bank's discount on the note. This is the bank's interest revenue from holding the note.	$15,370 × 0.12 × $^{40}/_{365}$	=	$202
5. Seller's proceeds from discounting the note receivable* = Maturity value of note – Bank's discount on the note	$15,370 – $202	=	$15,168

*(Buyer's cost of purchasing)

EMCO Ltd.'s entry to record discounting (selling) the note on December 9, 2016, is:

2016			
Dec. 9	Cash	15,168	
	Note Receivable—Dartmouth Builders		15,000
	Interest Revenue		168
	To record discounting a note receivable.		

> $370 total interest on note
> − $202 bank's interest revenue
> $168 left for EMCO as revenue

Proceeds Are Less than the Note   When the proceeds from discounting a note receivable are less than the principal amount of the note, the payee records a debit to Interest Expense for the amount of the difference. For example, EMCO could discount the note receivable for cash proceeds of $14,980. The entry to record this transaction would be:

2016			
Dec. 9	Cash	14,980	
	Interest Expense	20	
	Note Receivable—Dartmouth Builders		15,000

In the discounting of the note receivable just described, interest revenue accrued from the original date of the note (October 20, 2016) to the date of discounting (December 9, 2016) was not recognized because the discount fee was greater than the amount of interest earned between October 20 and December 9. The company incurred an additional $20 plus the forgone interest revenue of $370 that it could have earned if held to maturity. The bank will collect $15,370 from Dartmouth and the bank paid EMCO $14,980, thereby earning a profit of $390 on discounting this note.

10. If a 60-day note dated April 16 is discounted on May 2, what is the discount period?

Solutions appear at the end of this chapter and on MyAccountingLab

SUMMARY

LEARNING OBJECTIVE ① Define common types of receivables, and report receivables on the balance sheet

What are receivables, and how are they reported on the balance sheet?   Pg. 506

- A *receivable* arises when a business (or person) sells goods or services to another party on credit.
- The receivable is the seller's claim for the amount of the transaction.
- A receivable also arises when one person lends money to another.
- Each credit transaction involves two parties: the *creditor*, who sells something and obtains a receivable, which is an asset, and the *debtor*, who makes the purchase and has a payable, which is a liability.
- All accounts receivable, notes receivable, and allowance accounts appear in the balance sheet in the current asset section when they are due within one year.

LEARNING OBJECTIVE ② Use the allowance method to account for uncollectibles, and estimate uncollectibles by the percent-of-sales, aging-of-accounts-receivable, and the percent-of-accounts-receivable methods

Why would companies estimate their uncollectible accounts receivable, and how could they do that?   Pg. 508

- The *allowance method* matches expenses to sales revenue and also results in a more realistic measure of net accounts receivable.
- The *percent-of-sales method*, the *aging-of-accounts-receivable method*, and the *percent-of-accounts-receivable method* are the main approaches to estimating bad debts under the allowance method.
- Here is where each of the journal entries is recorded in the T-accounts and the order in which they usually occur:

Accounts Receivable		Allowance for Doubtful Accounts	
1. Sales on credit	2. Customer payments on account		3. Estimate of uncollectible
	4. Write off uncollectible	4. Write off uncollectible	
5. Recovery of account reinstated			5. Recovery of account reinstated

MyAccountingLab **Video:** Concepts of Allowance for Bad Debts

LEARNING OBJECTIVE ③ Use the direct write-off method to account for uncollectibles

What is the direct write-off method?   Pg. 515

- Businesses using the *direct write-off method* only recognize bad debts when they are writing them off. This is easy to apply, but it fails to match the bad debt expense to the corresponding sales revenue.
- Accounts Receivable are reported at their full amount, which is misleading because it suggests that the company expects to collect all its accounts receivable.

LEARNING OBJECTIVE (4) Account for credit card, debit card, and online sales

How do we record credit card, debit card, and online payment transactions?   Pg. 516

- When customers pay for their purchases using a *credit card*, the credit card company pays the vendor and collects from the customer.
- Non-bank credit cards, such as Diners Club, reimburse vendors at a later date, creating a receivable for the vendor until payment is received from the credit card company.
- When a customer pays with a *debit card,* the issuer removes the amount of the purchase from the customer's bank account and puts it into the vendor's account.
- The vendor pays a fee to the credit card company or to the bank for each credit card and debit card transaction.
- Online payments through PayPal or other providers are accounted for like credit and debit card transactions.

LEARNING OBJECTIVE (5) Account for notes receivable

What are notes receivable, and how do we account for these assets?   Pg. 518

- *Notes receivable* are formal credit agreements.
- The formula used for computing interest on most notes receivable is as follows:

$$\text{Amount of simple interest} = \text{Principal} \times \text{Interest rate} \times \text{Time}$$

MyAccountingLab **Video:** Computing Interest and Maturity Values
Interactive Figure: Interact with Amount of Interest
Video: Real World Accounting
Video: Determining Maturity Date

LEARNING OBJECTIVE (6) Use the acid-test ratio and days' sales in receivables to evaluate a company

How can we evaluate how effectively a company collects its accounts receivable?   Pg. 523

- The *acid-test ratio* measures a company's ability to pay current liabilities from the most liquid current assets:

$$\text{Acid-test ratio} = \frac{\text{Cash} + \text{Short-term investments} + \text{Net current receivables}}{\text{Total current liabilities}}$$

- *Days' sales in receivables* indicates how long it takes to collect the average level of receivables:

$$\text{Days' sales in average accounts receivable} = \frac{\text{Average net accounts receivable}}{\text{One day's sales}} = \frac{(\text{Beginning net receivables} + \text{Ending net receivables}) / 2}{\text{One day's sales}}$$

LEARNING OBJECTIVE (7) Understand the impact on accounts receivable of International Financial Reporting Standards (IFRS)

How does IFRS affect accounts receivable?   Pg. 525

- Receivables are reported at fair value. Both sets of standards are essentially *converged*.
- There is one presentation difference—IFRS report Accounts Receivable as "Trade Receivables."

LEARNING OBJECTIVE (A1) Discount a note receivable

Is it possible to receive cash from a note receivable prior to the note's maturity date?   Pg. 527

- The payee of a note receivable will sometimes discount, or sell, the note to a bank or other third party before the maturity date of the note.

Check **Accounting Vocabulary** on page 530 for all key terms used in Chapter 9 and the **Glossary** at the back of the book for all key terms used in the textbook.

ACCOUNTING VOCABULARY

Acid-test ratio   Ratio of the sum of cash plus short-term investments plus net current receivables to current liabilities. Tells whether the entity could pay all its current liabilities if they came due immediately. Also called the *quick ratio*   (p. 523).

Aging-of-accounts-receivable method   A way to estimate bad debts by analyzing individual accounts receivable according to the length of time they have been due   (p. 510).

Allowance for Doubtful Accounts   A contra account, related to accounts receivable, that holds the estimated amount of collection losses. Also called *allowance for uncollectible accounts*   (p. 508).

Allowance for Uncollectible Accounts   Another name for *allowance for doubtful accounts*   (p. 508).

Allowance method   A method of recording collection losses based on estimates made prior to determining that the business will not collect from specific customers   (p. 508).

Bad debt expense   The cost to the seller of extending credit. Arises from the failure to collect from credit customers. Also called *doubtful accounts expense* or *uncollectible accounts expense*   (p. 508).

Balance sheet approach   Another name for the *aging-of-accounts-receivable method* of estimating uncollectibles   (p. 510).

Collection period   Another name for *days' sales in receivables*   (p. 524).

Creditor   The party to a credit transaction who sells a service or merchandise and obtains a receivable   (p. 506).

Days' sales in receivables   Ratio of average net accounts receivable to one day's sales. Indicates how many days' sales remain in Accounts Receivable awaiting collection. Also called the *collection period*   (p. 524).

Debtor   The party to a credit transaction who makes a purchase and creates a payable   (p. 506).

Default on a note   Failure of the maker of a note to pay at maturity. Also called *dishonour of a note*   (p. 522).

Direct write-off method   A method of accounting for bad debts by which the company waits until the credit department decides that a customer's account receivable is uncollectible and then debits Bad Debt Expense and credits the customer's Account Receivable   (p. 515).

Discounting a note receivable   Selling a note receivable before its maturity date   (p. 527).

Dishonour a note   Failure of the maker of a note to pay a note receivable at maturity. Also called *default on a note*   (p. 522).

Doubtful account expense   Another name for *bad debt expense*   (p. 508).

Due date   The date on which the final payment of a note is due. Also called the *maturity date*   (p. 519).

Income statement approach   Another name for the *percent-of-sales method* of estimating uncollectibles   (p. 509).

Interest   The revenue to the payee for loaning out the principal, and the expense to the maker for borrowing the principal   (p. 519).

Interest period   The period of time during which interest is to be computed, extending from the original date of the note to the maturity date. Also called the *note term* or the *time period*   (p. 519).

Interest rate   The percentage rate that is multiplied by the principal amount to compute the amount of interest on a note   (p. 519).

Maker of a note   The person or business that signs the note and promises to pay the amount required by the note agreement. The maker is the *debtor*   (p. 519).

Maturity date   The date on which the final payment of a note is due. Also called the *due date*   (p. 519).

Maturity value   The sum of the principal and interest due at the maturity date of a note   (p. 519).

Net realizable value (NRV)   Accounts receivable minus allowance for doubtful accounts equals the amount of accounts receivable the company hopes to realize, or collect   (p. 508).

Note term   Another name for the *interest period* of a note   (p. 519).

Payee of a note   The person or business to whom the maker of a note promises future payment. The payee is the *creditor*   (p. 519).

Percent-of-accounts-receivable method   A method of estimating uncollectible receivables by determining the balance of Allowance for Doubtful Accounts based on a percentage of accounts receivable   (p. 511).

Percent-of-sales method   A method of estimating uncollectible receivables as a percent of the net credit sales (or net sales). Also called the *income statement approach*   (p. 509).

Principal The amount loaned out by the payee and borrowed by the maker of a note *(p. 519)*.

Promissory note A written promise to pay a specified amount of money at a particular future date *(p. 519)*.

Quick ratio Another name for the *acid-test ratio* *(p. 523)*.

Receivable A monetary claim against a business or an individual, acquired mainly by selling goods and services and by lending money *(p. 506)*.

Recovery When a previously written off receivables amount is collected *(p. 513)*.

Time period Another name for the *interest period* *(p. 519)*.

Uncollectible accounts expense Another name for *bad debt expense* *(p. 508)*.

Write-off Remove the balance of the customer's account from the Accounts Receivable control account and subsidiary ledger in the accounting records since the customer will not pay what it owes *(p. 513)*.

SIMILAR ACCOUNTING TERMS

Acid-test ratio	Quick ratio
Aging-of-accounts-receivable method (of estimating uncollectibles)	Balance sheet approach (of estimating uncollectibles)
Allowance for Doubtful Accounts	Allowance for Uncollectible Accounts; Allowance for Bad Debts
Bad debt expense	Uncollectible accounts expense; Doubtful accounts expense
Days' sales in receivables	Collection period, days' sales uncollected
Dishonour a note	Default on a note
Interest period	Note period; Note term; Time
Maturity date	Due date
Percent-of-Accounts-Receivable Method (of estimating uncollectibles)	Balance sheet approach (of estimating uncollectibles)
Percent-of-Sales Method (of estimating uncollectibles)	Income statement approach (of estimating uncollectibles)
Trade receivables	Accounts receivable

SELF-STUDY QUESTIONS

Test your understanding of the chapter by marking the correct answer for each of the following questions:

1. The party that holds a receivable is called the *(p. 506)*
   a. Creditor
   b. Debtor
   c. Maker
   d. Security holder

2. Which of the following assets is listed first on a balance sheet? *(p. 507)*
   a. Accounts receivable
   b. Notes receivable
   c. Cash
   d. Inventory

3. The function of the credit department is to *(p. 508)*
   a. Collect accounts receivable from customers
   b. Report bad credit risks to other companies
   c. Evaluate customers who apply for credit
   d. Write off uncollectible accounts receivable

4. Keady Marina made the following general journal entry related to uncollectibles:

Bad Debt Expense	700	
Allowance for Doubtful Accounts		700

   The purpose of this entry is to *(p. 510–511)*
   a. Write off uncollectibles
   b. Close the expense account
   c. Age the accounts receivable
   d. Estimate and record bad debt expense

5. The credit balance in Allowance for Doubtful Accounts is $12,600 prior to the adjusting entries at the end of the period. The aging of the accounts indicates that an allowance of $81,200 is needed. The amount of expense to record is *(pp. 510–511)*
   a. $12,600
   b. $68,600
   c. $81,200
   d. $93,800

6. Keady Marina also made this general journal entry:

Allowance for Doubtful Accounts   1,800

    Accounts Receivable (detailed)   1,800

The purpose of this entry is to (p. 513)
a. Write off uncollectibles
b. Close the expense account
c. Age the accounts receivable
d. Record bad debt expense

7. Keady Marina also made this general journal entry:

Accounts Receivable (detailed)   640

    Allowance for Doubtful Accounts   640

The purpose of this entry is to (pp. 513–514)
a. Write off uncollectibles
b. Close the expense account
c. Reverse the write-off of receivables
d. Record bad debt expense

8. A six-month, $40,000 note specifies interest of 8 percent. The full amount of interest on this note will be (p. 519)
a. $400
b. $800
c. $1,600
d. $3,200

9. The maturity value of a note is equal to the (p. 519)
a. Principal plus total interest due
b. Face value of the note
c. Principal minus total interest due
d. Principal times the interest rate

10. The note in Self-Study Question 8 was issued on August 31, and the company's accounting year ends on December 31. The year-end balance sheet will report interest receivable of (pp. 520–521)
a. $533
b. $1,067
c. $1,600
d. $3,200

11. The best acid-test ratio among the following is (p. 524)
a. 0.10
b. 0.80
c. 1.0
d. 1.2

12. Cottage Canoes holds a $40,000, 10 percent, 120-day note receivable from Painter's Hall. Prior to maturity, Cottage Canoe discounts the note and sells it for proceeds of $41,000. The journal entry to record the discounting of the note would include (p. 527)
a. A debit to notes receivable of $40,000
b. A credit to notes receivable of $41,000
c. A debit to interest expense of $1,000
d. A credit to interest revenue of $1,000

ASSIGNMENT MATERIAL

QUESTIONS

1. Name the two parties to a receivable/payable transaction. Which party has the receivable? Which has the payable? The asset? The liability?

2. List three categories of receivables. State how each category is classified for reporting on the balance sheet.

3. Name the two methods of accounting for uncollectible receivables. Which method is easier to apply? Which method is consistent with GAAP?

4. Which of the two methods of accounting for uncollectible accounts—the allowance method or the direct write-off method—is preferable? Why?

5. Identify the accounts debited and credited to account for uncollectibles under (a) the allowance method, and (b) the direct write-off method.

6. What is another name for Allowance for Doubtful Accounts? What are two other names for Bad Debt Expense?

7. Which entry decreases net income under the allowance method of accounting for uncollectibles: the entry

to record bad debt expense or the entry to write off an uncollectible account receivable?

8. Suppose a company records a credit sale to a new customer in 2016. In 2017, the company discovers the customer is bankrupt; the company will be unable to collect its receivable from the customer. The bad debt expense for this customer is recorded in 2017. What are the accounting problems with this situation? Is recording the bad debt expense in 2017 incorrect?

9. Identify and briefly describe the three ways to estimate bad debt expense and uncollectible accounts.

10. Briefly describe how a company may use both the percent-of-sales method and aging-of-accounts-receivable method (or the percent-of-accounts-receivable method) to account for uncollectibles.

11. a. How accurately does the direct write-off method measure income?

    b. How accurately does the direct write-off method value accounts receivable?

12. How does a credit balance arise in a customer's account receivable? How does the company report this credit balance on its balance sheet?

13. Show three ways to report Accounts Receivable of $50,000 and Allowance for Doubtful Accounts of $1,400 Cr on the balance sheet or in the related notes.

14. What are the benefits of credit card sales to a retailer? What is the cost to the retailer? How is the cost of a credit card sale recorded?

15. Use the terms *maker, payee, principal, maturity date, promissory note,* and *interest* in an appropriate sentence or two describing a note receivable.

16. Name three situations in which a company might receive a note receivable. For each situation, show the account debited and the account credited to record receipt of the note.

17. For each of the following notes receivable, compute the amount of interest revenue earned during 2017:

	Principal	Interest Rate	Interest Period	Maturity date
a. Note #1	$ 10,000	4%	60 days	Nov. 30, 2017
b. Note #2	50,000	6	3 months	Sep. 30, 2017
c. Note #3	100,000	4	1/2 year	Dec. 31, 2017
d. Note #4	15,000	8	90 days	Jan. 15, 2018

*This Question covers Chapter 9 Appendix topics.

18. When the maker of a note dishonours the note at maturity, what accounts does the payee debit and credit?

19. Why does the payee of a note receivable usually need to make adjusting entries for interest at the end of the accounting period?

20. Yellowknife Hardware has a policy of charging 2 percent interest on overdue (past 60 days) accounts receivable. Northern Cabinets has declared bankruptcy, and it is unlikely that full payment on this account will be collected. Should Yellowknife charge additional interest on the Northern Cabinets account receivable?

21. Why is the acid-test ratio a more stringent measure of the ability to pay current liabilities than is the current ratio?

22. Which measure of days' sales in receivables is preferable, 30 or 40? Give your reason.

*23. Why would a payee sell a note receivable before its maturity date?

STARTERS

Starter 9–1 From the following alphabetical list of adjusted account balances, prepare the current assets section of Versi-Vista Berries' September 30, 2017, balance sheet. Use a multi-column format, as shown in Exhibit 9–1.

Account Title	Debit	Credit
Accounts receivable	75,000	
Allowance for doubtful accounts		2,800
Bad debt expense	500	
Cash	112,000	
Farm equipment	122,000	
Office supplies	1,200	
Prepaid rent	650	

Reporting receivables on the balance sheet

①

Current assets, $186,050

Starter 9–2 During its first year of operations, Spring Break Travel earned revenue of $700,000 on account. Industry experience suggests that Spring Break's bad debts will amount to 1 percent of revenues. At December 31, 2016, accounts receivable total $80,000. The company uses the allowance method to account for uncollectibles.

1. Journalize Spring Break Travel's bad debt expense using the percent-of-sales method.

2. Show how Spring Break should report accounts receivable on its balance sheet at December 31, 2016.

Applying the allowance method (percent of sales) to account for uncollectibles

②

2. Accounts Receivable, net, $73,000

Applying the allowance method
(percent of sales) to account for
uncollectibles

(2)

4. Bad Debt Expense, $8,000

Starter 9–3   This exercise continues the situation of Starter 9–2, in which Spring Break Travel ended 2016 with Accounts Receivable at $80,000 and Allowance for Doubtful Accounts at $7,000.

During 2017, Spring Break Travel completed these transactions:

1. Service revenue on account, $800,000 (assume no cost of goods sold).
2. Collections on account, $840,000.
3. Write-offs of uncollectibles, $6,000.
4. Bad debt expense, 1 percent of service revenue.

Journalize Spring Break Travel's 2017 transactions and show the updated balance sheet totals.

Starter 9–4   Harrison Real Estate reported the following information for 2017:

Accounts receivable, Jan. 1, 2017	$18,000
Allowance for doubtful accounts, Dec. 31, 2017, prior to adjustment	600
Net credit sales during 2017	195,000
Collections on account during 2017	87,000
Cash sales during 2017	27,000

1. If uncollectible accounts are determined by the percent-of-sales method to be 3 percent of net credit sales, what is the bad debt expense for 2017?
2. If uncollectible accounts are determined by the aging of receivables to be $3,450, what is the amount of net accounts receivable after adjusting entries for 2017?

Applying the direct
write-off method to account
for uncollectibles

(3)

1. Bad Debt Expense, $6,000

Starter 9–5   Tolco Importers Inc. had the following balances at December 31, 2017, before the year-end adjustments:

Accounts Receivable		Allowance for Doubtful Accounts	
148,000			4,000

The aging of accounts receivable yields these data:

	Age of Accounts Receivable		
	0–60 Days	**Over 60 Days**	**Total Receivables**
Accounts receivable	$140,000	$8,000	$148,000
Percent uncollectible	3%	20%	

1. Journalize Tolco Importers Inc.'s entry to adjust the Allowance account to its correct balance at December 31, 2017.
2. Prepare the T-account for Allowance for Doubtful Accounts.
3. Repeat question 1 assuming that, instead of aging the accounts, the allowance is calculated as 3.5 percent of the Accounts Receivable balance.

Starter 9–6   Branson Shipping uses the direct write-off method in dealing with uncollectible accounts because it is highly unusual that the business ever has bad debts, and when they do they are not material in relation to total sales.

2016

Oct. 15   Shipped goods for Marine Specialties on account, $2,200.

2017

May 15   Received notice of bankruptcy from Marine Specialties and wrote off the amount they owed from the October 15 sale.

1. Journalize the transactions.
2. What is the major flaw in using the direct write-off method as opposed to the allowance method?

Starter 9–7

Larry Libbey is a lawyer in Calgary. He uses the direct write-off method to account for uncollectible receivables because he rarely has delinquent accounts.

At May 31, Libbey's accounts receivable totalled $32,000. During June, he earned revenue of $40,000 on account and collected $36,000 on account. He also wrote off uncollectible receivables of $6,000 on June 12.

1. Use the direct write-off method to journalize Libbey's write-off of the uncollectible receivables.
2. What is Libbey's balance of Accounts Receivable at June 30? Does he expect to collect the full amount? Explain.

Applying the direct write-off method to account for uncollectibles
③
1. Bad Debt Expense, $6,000

Starter 9–8

University Cycle Shop had trouble collecting its account receivable from Matt Reid. On January 19, University finally wrote off Reid's $2,400 account receivable. University turned the account over to a lawyer, who pursued Reid for payment for the rest of the year. On December 31, Reid sent a $2,400 cheque to University Cycle Shop with a note that said, "Here's your money. Please call off your bloodhound!"

Journalize the following transactions for University Cycle Shop:

Jan. 19   Write-off of Reid's account against Allowance for Doubtful
          Accounts.
Dec. 31   Reinstatement of Reid's account.
     31   Collection of cash from Reid.

Collecting a receivable previously written off
③

Starter 9–9

Northern Consultants accepts MasterCard credit cards from its customers. Assume Northern makes a sale of $2,000 and the credit card company charges a 3 percent fee. Provide the journal entry on June 22 to record the sales revenue.

Recording credit card sales
④

Starter 9–10

Gas stations do a large volume of business by customer credit cards and debit cards. Suppose an Esso station had these transactions on July 17:

VISA credit card sales $20,000
Non-bank credit card sales 5,000
Debit card sales... 16,000

Suppose VISA charges merchants 3 percent, non-bank credit card companies charge 4 percent, and the bank charges 2 percent for debit card transactions. Record these sale transactions for the Esso station.

Recording credit card and debit card sales
④
Debit cards, Cash, $15,680

Starter 9–11

For each of the following notes receivable, compute the amount of interest revenue earned during 2017. Use a 365-day year or base your calculations on the number of months, depending on how the interest period is stated, and round only your answer to the nearest dollar.

Computing interest amounts on notes receivable
⑤
Note #1, $8,000

	Principal	Interest Rate	Interest Period During 2017
Note 1	$200,000	8%	6 months
Note 2	30,000	4	75 days
Note 3	20,000	9	60 days
Note 4	100,000	5	3 months

Starter 9–12

HSBC Bank lent $200,000 to Johann Schroeder on a 90-day, 4 percent note. Record the following transactions for HSBC, rounding to the nearest dollar (explanations are not required):

1. Lending the money on May 6.
2. Collecting the principal and interest at maturity. Specify the date. For the computation of interest, use a 365-day year.

Accounting for a note receivable
⑤
2. Debit Cash, $201,973

Starter 9–13

Portage Planners accepted a $12,900 note receivable from M. Bonicalzi in settlement of an old account receivable. The 4 percent note was dated October 2, 2016, and was due in four months.

1. What is the journal entry on Portage Planners' books on October 2, 2016?
2. Assume that Portage Planners' year end is December 31. How much interest revenue is accrued on December 31, 2016?
3. What is the amount of interest revenue in 2017?

Accounting for notes receivable
⑤
3. $43

Using the acid-test ratio and
days' sales in receivables to
evaluate a company

a. 0.78

Starter 9–14 Vision Electronics, which makes DVD players, reported the following items at February 28, 2017 (amounts in thousands, with last year's—2016—amounts also given as needed):

Accounts Payable...........	$1,796	Accounts Receivable, net:	
Cash..................................	860	February 28, 2017	$ 440
Inventories:		February 29, 2016	300
February 28, 2017 ...	380	Cost of Goods Sold.................	4,800
February 29, 2016	320	Short-term investments..........	330
Net sales revenue	7,720	Other current assets	180
Long-term assets	820	Other current liabilities	290
Long-term liabilities........	20		

Compute for 2017 Vision Electronics' (a) acid-test ratio, (b) days' sales in average receivables, (c) current ratio, (d) debt ratio, (e) gross margin percent, (f) inventory turnover. Evaluate each ratio value as strong or weak. Assume Vision Electronics sells on terms of net 30.

Computing key ratios
for a company and
assessing their meaning

Starter 9–15 Surfwood Co. and Berry's Bait Inc. are similar companies that operate within the same industry. The following information is available:

	Industry Average	Surfwood Co.			Berry's Bait		
		2017	2016	2015	2017	2016	2015
Days' sales in receivables	32	28.3	31.8	33.9	36.7	30.5	29.9

Which company has the greater number of days in uncollected accounts in 2017? Is the days' sales in receivables generally favourable or unfavourable? Which company is showing an unfavourable trend in terms of managing accounts receivable?

Starter 9–16 In determining how accounts should be presented, accountants are concerned about the values being both relevant and reliable. Is the accounts receivable value presented on the balance sheet both relevant and reliable under IFRS?

EXERCISES

MyAccountingLab

Exercise 9–1

From the following list of adjusted account balances, prepare the current asset section of Delainey's Hardscaping for December 31, 2017. Assume all accounts have normal balances.

Accounts receivable	$51,000	Inventory	$22,000
Bad debt expense..........................	1,200	Cash..	15,000
Notes receivable, due		Accumulated Amortization,	
August 31, 2018..........................	12,000	Equipment.................................	5,000
		Allowance for doubtful	
Supplies	1,440	accounts...	3,500
Notes receivable, due			
August 31, 2020..........................	5,300	Equipment......................................	25,000

Exercise 9–2

BooBoo's Home Health Care has the following adjusted account balances at April 30, 2017. All accounts have normal balances. Prepare the current asset section of BooBoo's balance sheet.

Account Title	Balance
Accounts receivable	$ 51,000
Accumulated amortization—furniture	8,500
Allowance for doubtful accounts	2,500
Bad debt expense	4,100
Cash	98,700
Furniture	22,000
Inventory	122,750
Notes receivable, due July 1, 2017	41,000
Notes receivable, due November 1, 2020	68,000
Prepaid expenses	2,100

Exercise 9–3

On February 28, Big White Ski Equipment had a $25,500 debit balance in Accounts Receivable. During March, the company had sales of $65,500, which included $60,000 in credit sales. March collections were $53,000, and write-offs of uncollectible receivables totalled $1,250. Other data include:

a. February 28 credit balance in Allowance for Doubtful Accounts is $1,300.
b. Bad debt expense is estimated as 3 percent of credit sales.

Using the allowance (percent-of-sales) method for bad debts

2. Accounts Receivable, net $29,400

Required

1. Prepare journal entries to record sales, collections, write-offs of uncollectibles during March, and bad debt expense by the allowance method (using the percent-of-sales method). Use March 31 as the journal entry date. Explanations are not required.

2. Prepare T-accounts to show the ending balances in Accounts Receivable and Allowance for Doubtful Accounts. Compute *net* Accounts Receivable at March 31. How much does Big White expect to collect?

Exercise 9–4

Lui Dental began operations in January 2017 selling dental appliances to dentists. The following transactions occurred during the first six months of operations:

Using the allowance (aging-of-accounts-receivable) method for bad debts

Jan.	15	Sold appliances to Dr. Hall on account for $15,750; cost $6,400.
Feb.	22	Received payment in full from Dr. Hall.
Mar.	4	Sold merchandise to Dr. Evans on account for $4,400; cost $1,250.
Apr.	20	Sold merchandise to Dr. Murray on account for $6,700; cost $2,990.
May	31	Sold merchandise to Dr. Kim on account for $3,200; cost $1,100.
Jun.	28	Received $3,000 on account from Dr. Evans.

Required

1. Complete the following aged listing of customer accounts as of June 30, 2017:

	Age of Account				
Customer	1–30 days	31–60 days	61–90 days	Over 90 days	Total
Dr. Evans					
Dr. Hall					
Dr. Kim	3,200				3,200
Dr. Murray					

2. Estimate the Allowance for Doubtful Accounts required at June 30, 2017, assuming the following uncollectible rates: 30 days, 2%; 60 days, 5%; 90 days, 15%; >90 days, 50%.

3. Show how Lui Dental would report its accounts receivable on its June 30, 2017, balance sheet. What amounts would be reported on an income statement prepared for the six-month period ended June 30, 2017?

4. If Dr. Evans's account needed to be written off in September 2017, how accurate is Lui Dental at estimating its bad debts?

Excel Spreadsheet
Template
Using the aging approach
to estimate bad debts
and reporting receivables
on the balance sheet

2. Accounts Receivable,
net, $288,500

Exercise 9–5

At December 31, 2017, the Accounts Receivable balance of Stenner's Electronics is $300,000. The Allowance for Doubtful Accounts has an $8,900 credit balance. Accountants for Stenner's Electronics prepare the following aging schedule for its accounts receivable:

Accounts Receivable	Age of Accounts			
	1–30 Days	31–60 Days	61–90 Days	Over 90 Days
$300,000	$140,000	$80,000	$70,000	$10,000
Estimated percent uncollectible	0.5%	2.0%	6.0%	50.0%

Required

1. Journalize the adjusting entry for doubtful accounts based on the aging schedule. Show the T-account for the allowance at December 31, 2017.

2. Show how Stenner's Electronics will report Accounts Receivable on its December 31, 2017, balance sheet.

3. Suppose all the facts of this situation are the same except that Allowance for Doubtful Accounts has a $900 debit balance. Calculate the amount of the adjusting entry.

Exercise 9–6

Using the allowance method to account for uncollectibles

②

5. Accounts receivable, net, $40,711

Angel Landscaping Services started the year 2017 with an Accounts Receivable balance of $40,500 and an Allowance for Doubtful Accounts balance of $4,310. During the year, $4,290 of accounts receivable were identified as uncollectible. Sales revenue for 2017 was $429,000, including credit sales of $422,400. Cash collections on account were $415,600 during the year.

The aging of accounts receivable yields these data:

	Age of Accounts				
	0–30 Days	31–60 Days	61–90 Days	Over 90 Days	Total Receivables
Amount of receivable	$26,400	$6,600	$5,500	$4,510	$43,010
Percent uncollectible	1%	1%	3%	40%	

You are the accountant preparing the December 31, 2017, year-end entries.

Required

1. Journalize Angel's (a) credit sales, (b) cash collections on account, (c) write-off of the accounts receivable identified as uncollectible, and (d) bad debt expense based on 0.5 percent of credit sales.

2. Prepare a T-account for the Accounts Receivable and Allowance for Doubtful Accounts accounts.

3. Calculate the balance in Allowance for Doubtful Accounts based on the aging-of-accounts-receivable method.

4. Make any adjustment required to the Allowance for Doubtful Accounts based on your calculation in Requirement 3.

5. Show how Angel Landscaping Services should report Accounts Receivable on the balance sheet.

Sales, write-offs, and bad debt recovery using the allowance method and the direct write-off method

② ③

3. Accounts Receivable, ending bal., $100,000

Exercise 9–7

Acme Cell Phones had a debit balance in Accounts Receivable of $100,000 on January 1, 2017. Acme sold $80,000 of merchandise to Brodie Trucking Company on account. Brodie paid only $56,000 of the account receivable. After repeated attempts to collect, Acme finally wrote off its accounts receivable from Brodie. Six months later, Acme received Brodie's cheque for $24,000 with a note apologizing for the late payment.

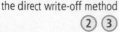

Required

1. Journalize the following for Acme Cell Phones:
   a. Sale on account, $80,000 (ignore cost of goods sold).
   b. Collection of $56,000 on account.
   c. Write-off of the remaining portion of the Brodie account receivable. Acme Cell Phones uses the allowance method for uncollectibles.
   d. Reinstatement of Brodie's account receivable.
   e. Collection in full from Brodie, $24,000.

2. Repeat (c), (d), and (e) using the direct write-off method.

3. What amount of net Accounts Receivable would Acme Cell Phones report on its December 31, 2017, balance sheet under the direct write-off method? Does Acme expect to collect this much of the receivable? Give your reasons.

Interpreting amounts from T-accounts resulting from the allowance method
② ③

Exercise 9–8

Wellington Corp. summarized its accounts receivable activity in the following two T-accounts:

Accounts Receivable					Allowance for Doubtful Accounts		
Dec. 31, 2016 Bal.	80,000					6,000	Dec. 31, 2016 Bal.
	320,000	350,000				500	
		5,800			5,800	4,900	
	500	500					
Dec. 31, 2017 Bal.	44,200					5,600	Dec. 31, 2017 Bal.

Required Analyze the information presented in the T-accounts and identify the amount related to each of the following:

a. Credit sales during the period.
b. Collection of credit sales during the period.
c. Write-off of a delinquent account.
d. Recovery of an account previously written off.
e. Adjusting entry to estimate bad debts.

Exercise 9–9

Return to the example of accounting for uncollectibles that begins under the heading "Writing Off Uncollectible Accounts" on page 513. Suppose past experience indicates that the company will fail to collect 2 percent of net credit sales, which totalled $100,000 during the three-month period January through March of 2018.

Contrasting the allowance method and the direct write-off method to account for uncollectibles
② ③
a. Bad Debt Expense, $2,000

Required

1. Record bad-debt expense for the three-month period January through March under:
   a. The percent-of-sales method (allowance method).
   b. The direct write-off method. (You don't need to identify individual customer accounts. Use the data given for Auger and Kirsh on page 513.)

2. Which method of accounting for uncollectibles is better? What makes this preferred method better? Mention accounting concepts and principles in your answer.

Exercise 9–10

Record the following transactions in the journal of Seaview Supplies, which ends its accounting year on November 30:

Recording notes receivable and accruing interest revenue
⑤
Nov. 30 Interest Revenue, $310.02

Oct.	1	Lent $88,000 cash to Joe Lazarus on a one-year, 2 percent note.
Nov.	3	Sold goods to Highwater Inc., receiving a 100-day, 4 percent note for $3,162.50. Cost of the goods was $2,000.00. Seaview uses a perpetual inventory system.
	16	Received a $2,200, six-month, 8 percent note on account from STM Inc. when the receivable for that amount could not be paid on time.
	30	Accrued interest revenue on all notes receivable.

Hint: Recall that you divide by days or months depending on the terms of the note.

Record the following transactions in the general journal of Jesse's Quick Clean Service. Assume Scotiabank charges merchants $0.50 per debit card transaction and MasterCard charges 4 percent of sales as service fees.

Mar.	31	Scotiabank debit card sales of $22,000, consisting of 1,500 transactions.
	31	MasterCard credit card sales of $33,000.
Mar.	31	FleetPlan card accepted for $2,800 of payments. This card requires that receipts are submitted for payment manually. A 2 percent fee applies.
April	10	Payment was received from FleetPlan.

Exercise 9–12

Franklin Ltd., a gift store, reported the following amounts in its 2017 financial statements. The 2016 figures are given for comparison.

		2017		2016
Current assets:				
Cash		$ 12,000		$ 26,000
Short-term investments		46,000		22,000
Accounts receivable	$120,000		$148,000	
Less: Allow. for uncollectibles	20,000	100,000	18,000	130,000
Inventory		384,000		378,000
Prepaid insurance		4,000		4,000
Total current assets		$ 546,000		$ 560,000
Total current liabilities		$ 218,000		$ 224,000
Net sales		$1,460,000		$1,464,000

Required

1. Determine whether Franklin Ltd.'s acid-test ratio improved or deteriorated from 2016 to 2017. How does Franklin Ltd.'s acid-test ratio compare with the industry average of 0.90?

2. Compare the days' sales in receivables measure for 2017 with the company's credit terms of net 30. What action, if any, should Franklin Ltd. take?

3. Indicate the most likely effect of the following changes in credit policy on the days' sales in receivables (+ for increase, – for decrease, and NE for no effect):

   a. Granted credit to people with poor credit history.

   b. Increased collection techniques or methods.

   c. Granted credit with discounts for early payment.

Exercise 9–13

Tropical North Company, which has a December 31 year end and uses a periodic inventory system, completed the following transactions during 2016 and 2017:

2016

Oct.	14	Sold merchandise to OFTR Racing, receiving a 60-day, 6 percent note for $5,000.
Nov.	16	Sold merchandise to Sunshine Racing receiving a 72-day, 4 percent note for $7,500.
Dec.	13	Received amount due from OFTR Racing.
Dec.	31	Accrued interest on the Sunshine Racing note.

2017

Jan.	27	Collected in full from Sunshine Company.

Required Prepare the necessary journal entries to record the above transactions. Assume that a 365-day year is used for calculations.

Exercise 9–14

Swift Media Sign Company sells on account. Recently, Swift reported these figures:

Collection period for receivables
(6)
1. 25 days

	2017	2016
Net sales	$600,060	$570,000
Receivables at year end	42,800	38,200

Required

1. Compute Swift Media Sign Company's days' sales in average receivables for 2017.
2. Suppose Swift's normal credit terms for a sale on account are 2/10, net 30. How well does Swift's collection period compare to the company's credit terms? Is this good or bad for Swift? Explain.

*Exercise 9–15

Suncare Corporation installs switching systems and receives its pay in the form of notes receivable. It installed a system for the city of Edson, Alberta, receiving a nine-month, 10 percent, $200,000 note receivable on May 31, 2017. To obtain cash quickly, Suncare discounted the note with HSBC Bank on June 30, 2017. The bank charged a discount rate of 11 percent.

Compute Suncare's cash proceeds from discounting the note. Follow the five-step procedure outlined in Exhibit 9–1A on page 527. Round to the nearest dollar.

Discounting a note receivable
(A1)
Cash proceeds, $199,233

*Exercise 9–16

Use your answers to Exercise 9–15 to journalize Suncare Corporation's transactions as follows (round to the nearest dollar):

Accounting for notes receivable, including a discounted note
(5) (A1)
Jun. 30 debit to Cash, $199,233

May	31	Sold a telecommunications system, receiving a nine-month, 10 percent, $200,000 note from the city of Edson, Alberta. Suncare Corporation's cost of the system was $131,250.
Jun.	30	Received cash for interest revenue for one month.
	30	Discounted the note to HSBC Bank at a discount rate of 11 percent.

*Exercise 9–17

Bonavista Outdoors Store sells on account. When a customer account becomes three months old, Bonavista Outdoors Store converts the account to a note receivable and immediately discounts the note to a bank. During 2017, Bonavista Outdoors Store completed these transactions:

Accounting for notes receivable, including a discounted note
(5) (A1)
Sep. 1 debit to Cash, $7,440

May	29	Sold goods on account to Raj Diwali, $9,600.
Sep.	1	Received an $8,000, 60-day, 8 percent note and cash of $1,600 from Raj Diwali in satisfaction of his past-due account receivable.
	1	Sold the Diwali note by discounting it to a bank for proceeds of $7,440.

Required Record the transactions in Bonavista Outdoors Store's journal.

---

*These Exercises cover Chapter 9 Appendix topics.

SERIAL EXERCISE

This exercise continues the Lee Management Consulting situation from Exercise 8–25 in Chapter 8. If you did not complete any Serial Exercises in earlier chapters, you can still complete Exercise 9–18 as it is presented.

Receivables transactions

Nov. 1 Bad Debt Expense, $1,575

Exercise 9–18

Lee Management Consulting wants to follow generally accepted accounting principles and use the allowance method for receivables. Michael Lee, owner of Lee Management Consulting, has decided that the best way to estimate uncollectibles would be to calculate 3.5 percent of credit sales. He has operated for several months and has not done this yet.

On November 10, 2016, Michael reviewed the list of outstanding accounts. He has identified that Gene is not going to pay his $900 receivable from July 19.

On November 16, 2016, Michael offered another client, Jin Lo, the opportunity to turn the unpaid account into a $1,000 note receivable. The note would incur 6 percent interest and be paid in three months.

Required

1. Journalize the entry on November 1, 2016, to record and establish the allowance for doubtful accounts using the percent-of-sales method for prior months' credit sales, which totalled $45,000.

2. Journalize the entry to record Gene's bad debt.

3. Journalize the establishment of the note receivable.

4. Prepare the journal entry that will be recorded on the date the note is settled (assuming it is settled on the maturity date).

CHALLENGE EXERCISES

Exercise 9–19

Evaluating credit card sales for profitability

Net income with bank credit cards, $489,200

Trendy Fashions provides store credit and manages its own receivables. Average experience for the past three years has been as follows:

	Cash	Credit	Total
Sales	$1,040,000	$700,000	$1,740,000
Cost of Goods Sold	624,000	420,000	1,044,000
Bad Debt Expense	—	38,000	38,000
Other Expenses	115,600	106,000	221,600

Helen Tran, the owner, is considering whether to accept bank credit cards and discontinue providing store credit. Typically, the availability of bank credit cards increases credit sales by 15 percent. But the bank credit card companies charge approximately 4 percent of credit card sales. If Tran switches to bank credit cards, she can save $5,000 on accounting and other expenses and will eliminate bad debt expense. She figures that cash customers will continue buying in the same volume regardless of the type of credit the store offers.

Required Should Trendy Fashions start offering bank credit card service and discontinue providing store credit? Show the computations of net income under the present plan and under the bank credit card plan.

BEYOND THE NUMBERS

Beyond the Numbers 9–1

Bhatti Communications' cash flow statement reported the following *cash* receipts and *cash* payments (the amount in brackets) for the year ended August 31, 2017:

Reporting receivables on the balance sheet

①

Aug. 31, 2017, Accounts Receivable, $126,250

BHATTI COMMUNICATIONS	
Cash Flow Statement	
For the Year Ended August 31, 2017	
Cash flows from operating activities:	
Cash receipts from customers	$827,500
Interest received	2,300
Cash flows from investing activities:	
Loans made on notes receivable	(13,750)
Collection of loans on notes receivable	27,500

Bhatti's balance sheet one year earlier—at August 31, 2016—reported Accounts Receivable of $93,750 and Notes Receivable of $20,750. Credit sales for the year ended August 31, 2017, totalled $860,000, and the company collects all of its accounts receivable because uncollectibles rarely occur.

Bhatti Communications needs a loan, and the manager is preparing the company's balance sheet at August 31, 2017. To complete the balance sheet, the owner needs to know the balances of Accounts Receivable and Notes Receivable at August 31, 2017. Supply the needed information; T-accounts are helpful.

ETHICAL ISSUE

Miagi's auto showroom sells cars. Miagi's bank requires the company to submit quarterly financial statements in order to keep its line of credit. Notes Receivable and Accounts Receivable are 60 percent of current assets. Therefore, Bad Debt Expense and Allowance for Doubtful Accounts are important accounts.

Miagi's president, Ed Edwards, likes net income to increase in a smooth pattern rather than to increase in some periods and decrease in other periods. To report smoothly increasing net income, Edwards underestimates bad debt expense in some accounting periods. In other accounting periods, Edwards overestimates the expense. He reasons that the income overstatements roughly offset the income understatements over time.

Required Is Miagi's practice of smoothing income ethical? Give your reasons, mentioning any accounting principles that might be violated.

PROBLEMS (GROUP A)   MyAccountingLab

Problem 9–1A

The September 30, 2017, balance sheet of Nelson Products reported the following:

Using the percent-of-sales and aging-of-accounts-receivable approaches for uncollectibles

②

3. Accounts Receivable, net in 2017, $319,361

Accounts Receivable	$310,000
Allowance for Doubtful Accounts (credit balance)	10,000

During the last quarter of 2017, Nelson Products completed the following selected transactions:

Dec. 30   Wrote off the following accounts receivable as uncollectible: Barry White, $2,500; Carlos Media, $2,200; and Doug Zabellos, $1,100.

31   Recorded bad debt expense based on the aging of accounts receivable, as follows:

Accounts Receivable	Age of Accounts			
	1–30 Days	31–60 Days	61–90 Days	Over 90 Days
Total = $328,500	$179,000	$95,000	$37,500	$17,000
Estimated percent uncollectible	0.1%	0.3%	5.0%	40.0%

Required

1. Record the transactions in the general journal.

2. Open the Allowance for Doubtful Accounts three-column ledger account and post entries affecting that account. Keep a running balance.

3. Most companies report two-year comparative financial statements. If Nelson Products' Accounts Receivable balance was $320,000 and the Allowance for Doubtful Accounts stood at $12,000 at December 31, 2016, show how the company will report its Accounts Receivable in a comparative balance sheet for 2017 and 2016.

4. Suppose, on December 31, the bad debt expense was based on an estimate of 4 percent of the accounts receivable balance rather than on the aging of accounts receivable. Record the December 31, 2017, entry for bad debt expense in the general journal.

Problem 9–2A

Matiere Co. completed the following transactions during 2016 and 2017:

Use the percent-of-sales, aging-of-accounts-receivable, and percent-of-accounts-receivable methods for uncollectibles

②

3. Net Accounts Receivable, $129,282.50

2016

Dec.   31   Estimated that bad debt expense for the year was 3 percent of credit sales of $385,000 and recorded that amount as expense.

31   Made the closing entry for bad debt expense.

2017

Mar.   26   Sold inventory to Mabel Sanders, $10,037.50, on credit terms of 2/10, n/30. Ignore cost of goods sold.

Sep.   15   Wrote off Mabel Sanders's account as uncollectible after repeated efforts to collect from her.

Nov.   10   Received $5,500 from Sanders, along with a letter stating her intention to pay her debt in full within 30 days. Reinstated her account in full.

Dec.   5   Received the balance due from Sanders.

31   Made a compound entry to write off the following accounts as uncollectible: Curt Major, $2,200; Bernadette Lalonde, $962.50; Ellen Smart, $1,470.

31   Estimated that bad debt expense for the year was 2 percent of credit sales of $490,000 and recorded the expense.

31   Made the closing entry for bad debt expense.

Required

1. Open three-column general ledger accounts for Allowance for Doubtful Accounts and Bad Debt Expense. Keep running balances.

2. Record the transactions in the general journal and post to the ledger accounts.

3. The December 31, 2017, balance of Accounts Receivable is $146,000. Show how Accounts Receivable would be reported at that date.

4. Assume that Matiere Co. begins aging accounts receivable on December 31, 2017. The balance in Accounts Receivable is $146,000, the credit balance in Allowance for Doubtful Accounts is $16,717.50 (use your calculations from Requirement 3), and the company estimates that $19,900 of its accounts receivable will prove uncollectible.

   a. Make the adjusting entry for uncollectibles.

   b. Show how Accounts Receivable will be reported on the December 31, 2017, balance sheet after this adjusting entry.

Problem 9–3A

Hollingsworth Personnel started business on January 1, 2017. The company produced monthly financial statements and had total sales of $500,000 (of which $400,000 was on account) during the first four months.

On April 30, Accounts Receivable had a balance of $236,400 (no accounts have been written off to date), which was made up of the following accounts aged according to the date of the sale:

Using the allowance method of accounting for uncollectibles, estimating uncollectibles using the aging-of-accounts method, reporting receivables on the balance sheet

① ②

2. a. Accounts Receivable, net May 31, $262,104

	Month of Sale			
Customer	**January**	**February**	**March**	**April**
Netpac Distributors	$ 3,600	$ 1,000	$ 2,000	$ 1,800
PG Courier	1,000	1,200	3,400	2,400
Vent Axia Transport	5,000	14,000	8,000	4,000
Natures Design	2,000	7,400	8,120	28,400
Other Accounts Receivable	23,760	16,360	53,480	49,480
	$35,360	$39,960	$75,000	$86,080

The following accounts receivable transactions took place in May 2017:

May 12   Decided the PG Courier account was uncollectible and wrote it off.

15   Collected $6,600 from Netpac Distributors for sales made in the first three months.

21   Decided the Vent Axia Transport account was uncollectible and wrote it off.

24   Collected $2,000 from Natures Design for sales made in the month of January.

26   Received a cheque from Vent Axia Transport for $18,200 plus four cheques of $3,200 each, postdated to June 26, July 26, August 26, and September 26.

31   Total sales in the month were $380,000; 90 percent of these were on account, and 75 percent of the sales on account were collected in the month.

Required

1. Hollingsworth Personnel has heard that other companies in the industry use the allowance method of accounting for uncollectibles, with many of these estimating the uncollectibles through an aging of accounts receivable.

   a. Journalize the adjustments that would have to be made on April 30 (for the months of January through April), assuming the following estimates of uncollectibles:

Age of Accounts Receivable	Percent Estimated Uncollectible
From current month	3%
From prior month	4
From two months prior	5
From three months prior	20
From four months prior	45

   (Round your total estimate to the nearest whole dollar.)

   b. Journalize the transactions of May 2017.

   c. Journalize the month-end adjustment, using the information from the table that appears in Requirement 1a.

2. For the method of accounting for the uncollectibles used above, show:

   a. The balance sheet presentation of the accounts receivable.

   b. The overall effect of the uncollectibles on the income statement for the months of April and May 2017.

Problem 9–4A

On March 31, 2017, Summitt Manufacturing had a $290,000 debit balance in Accounts Receivable. During April, the business had sales revenue of $1,050,000, which included $990,000 in credit sales. Other data for April include the following:

a. Collections on accounts receivable, $910,000.

b. Write-offs of uncollectible receivables, $4,500.

Accounting for uncollectibles by the direct write-off and allowance methods

② ③

4. Net Accounts Receivable, allowance method, $361,300

Required

1. Record bad debt expense for April by the direct write-off method. Use T-accounts to show all April activity in Accounts Receivable and Bad Debt Expense.

2. Record bad debt expense and write-offs of customer accounts for April by the allowance method. Use T-accounts to show all April activity in Accounts Receivable, Allowance for Doubtful Accounts, and Bad Debt Expense. The March 31 unadjusted balance in Allowance for Doubtful Accounts was $1,200 (debit). Bad debt expense was estimated at 1 percent of credit sales.

3. What amount of bad debt expense would Summitt report on its April income statement under the two methods? Which amount better matches expense with revenue? Give your reason.

4. What amount of *net* accounts receivable would Summitt report on its April 30 balance sheet under the two methods? Which amount is more realistic? Give your reason.

Problem 9–5A

Accounting for notes receivable, including accruing interest revenue

⑤

1. Note (a), $9,090.00

A company received the following notes during 2017:

Note	Date	Principal Amount	Interest Rate	Term
(a)	Aug. 30	$ 9,000	4%	3 months
(b)	Nov. 19	12,000	3	60 days
(c)	Dec. 1	15,000	5	1 year
(d)	Dec. 1	20,000	6	2 years

Required

1. Determine the due date and maturity value of each note. Compute the interest for each note. Round all interest amounts to the nearest cent.

2. Journalize a single adjusting entry at December 31, 2017, to record accrued interest revenue on the notes. An explanation is not required.

3. Journalize the collection of principal and interest on note (b). Explanations are not required.

4. Show how these notes will be reported on December 31, 2017.

Problem 9–6A

Accounting for credit card sales, notes receivable, dishonoured notes, and accrued interest revenue

④ ⑤

Jan. 20, 2017, debit Cash, $18,118.36

Record the following selected transactions in the general journal of WM Gaming Supplies. Explanations are not required.

2016

Nov.	21	Received an $18,000, 60-day, 4 percent note from Barb Nuefield on account.
	30	Recorded VISA credit card sales of $26,000. VISA charges 3 percent of sales.
Dec.	31	Made an adjusting entry to accrue interest on the Nuefield note.
	31	Made an adjusting entry to record bad debt expense based on 3 percent of credit sales of $1,950,000.
	31	Made a compound closing entry for Interest Revenue and Bad Debt Expense (ignore credit card sales and charges).

2017

Jan.	20	Collected the maturity value of the Nuefield note.
Mar.	14	Lent $20,000 cash to Morgan Supplies, receiving a six-month, 5 percent note.
	30	Received a $5,600, 30-day, 10 percent note from Quin Carson on his past-due account receivable.
May	29	Carson dishonoured (failed to pay) his note at maturity; after attempting to collect his note for one month, wrote off the account as uncollectible.
Sep.	14	Collected the maturity value of the Morgan Supplies note.
	30	Wrote off as uncollectible the accounts receivable of Sue Parsons, $3,250 and Mac Gally, $5,200.

Problem 9–7A

Assume that Penske Tire, a large tire distributor, completed the following selected transactions:

Journalizing uncollectible notes receivable and accrued interest revenue

④ ⑤

Dec. 31, 2016, debit Bad Debt Expense, $8,700

2016

Dec.	1	Sold tires to Select Movers Inc., receiving a $40,000, six-month, 5 percent note. Ignore cost of goods sold.
	31	Made an adjusting entry to accrue interest on the Select Movers note.
	31	Made an adjusting entry to record bad debt expense based on an aging of accounts receivable. The aging analysis indicates that $56,200 of accounts receivable will not be collected. Prior to this adjustment, the credit balance in Allowance for Doubtful Accounts is $47,500.

2017

Jun.	1	Collected the maturity value of the Select Movers note.
	30	Sold tires for $16,000 on MasterCard. MasterCard charges 1.75 percent.
Jul.	21	Sold merchandise to Marco Donolo, receiving a 45-day, 3 percent note for $11,200. Ignore cost of goods sold.
Sep.	4	Donolo dishonoured (failed to pay) his note at maturity; converted the maturity value of the note to an account receivable.
Nov.	11	Sold merchandise to Solomon Tractor for $9,600, receiving a 120-day, 5 percent note. Ignore cost of goods sold.
Dec.	2	Collected in full from Donolo.
	31	Accrued the interest on the Solomon Tractor note.

Required Record the transactions in the general journal. Explanations are not required. Round interest amounts to the nearest cent.

Problem 9–8A

Eastern Supply uses the allowance method in accounting for uncollectible accounts with the estimate based on the aging-of-accounts-receivable method. The company had the following account balances on August 31, 2017:

Using the allowance method of accounting for uncollectibles, estimating uncollectibles by the percent-of-sales and the aging-of-accounts-receivable methods, accounting for notes receivable

② ⑤

2. Bad Debt Expense, debit, $48,960

Accounts Receivable	$687,000
Allowance for Doubtful Accounts (credit balance)	72,600

The following transactions took place during September 2017:

Sep.	2	Elbow Inc., which owes $48,000, is unable to pay on time and has given a 25-day, 8 percent note in settlement of the account.
	6	Received from Irma Good the amount owed on an August 7 dishonoured note, plus extra interest for 30 days at 4 percent computed on the maturity value of the note ($12,600). This dishonoured note had been converted to an account receivable on August 7.
	9	Received notice that a customer (Tony Goad) has filed for bankruptcy. Goad owes $19,200. The courts will confirm the amount recoverable at a later date.
	11	Determined the account receivable from Kay Walsh ($9,120) was uncollectible and wrote it off.
	18	Received a cheque from the courts in the amount of $15,000 as final settlement of Goad's account.
	27	Elbow Inc. paid the note received on September 2.
	27	Determined the account receivable for Dave Campbell ($5,040) was uncollectible and wrote it off.
	30	Sales for the month totalled $720,000 (of which 85 percent were on account) and collections on account totalled $601,200.
	30	Eastern Supply did an aging of accounts receivable that indicated that $75,000 is expected to be uncollectible. The company recorded the appropriate adjustment.

Required

1. Record the above transactions in the general journal.
2. What would be the adjusting entry required on September 30 if the company used the percent-of-sales method with an estimate of uncollectibles equal to 8 percent of credit sales?
3. Which of the two methods of estimating uncollectible accounts would normally be more accurate? Why?

Excel Spreadsheet Template

Using ratio data to evaluate a company's financial position

(6)

For 2017: a. 1.52

Problem 9–9A

The comparative financial statements of Sopa Company for 2017, 2016, and 2015 included the following selected data:

	2017	2016	2015
	(in thousands)		
Balance Sheet			
Current assets:			
Cash	$ 80	$ 80	$ 40
Short-term investments	280	400	240
Receivables, net	760	600	480
Inventories	1,680	1,520	1,360
Prepaid expenses	120	120	80
Total current assets	$ 2,920	$ 2,720	$ 2,200
Total current liabilities	$ 1,920	$ 1,640	$ 1,520
Income Statement			
Sales revenue	$10,400	$10,000	$ 7,600

Required

1. Compute these ratios for 2017 and 2016:

   a. Current ratio

   b. Acid-test ratio

   c. Days' sales in receivables

2. Write a brief memo explaining to Tony Crane, owner of Sopa Company, which ratio values showed improvement from 2016 to 2017 and which ratio values deteriorated. Discuss whether this trend is favourable or unfavourable for the company.

*Problem 9–10A

Discounting notes receivable

(A1)

2. Proceeds from discounting: Note (a), $20,063.16

A company received the following notes during 2017. The notes were discounted on the dates and at the rates indicated.

Note	Date	Principal Amount	Interest Rate	Term	Date Discounted	Discount Rate
(a)	Jun. 15	$20,000	8%	60 days	Jul. 15	12%
(b)	Aug. 1	9,000	10	90 days	Aug. 27	12
(c)	Nov. 21	12,000	15	90 days	Dec. 4	15

Required   Identify each note by letter, compute interest using a 365-day year for all notes, round all interest amounts to the nearest cent, and present entries in general journal form. Explanations are not required.

1. Determine the due date and maturity value of each note.
2. Determine the discount and proceeds from the sale (discounting) of each note.
3. Journalize the discounting of notes (a) and (b).

---

*This Problem covers Chapter 9 Appendix topics.

PROBLEMS (GROUP B)   MyAccountingLab

Problem 9–1B

The November 30, 2017, balance sheet of Thyme Company reported the following:

Using the percent-of-sales, aging-of-accounts-receivable, and percent-of-accounts-receivable methods for uncollectibles

②

Accounts Receivable	$358,000
Allowance for Doubtful Accounts (credit balance)	7,700

At the end of each quarter, Thyme estimates bad debt expense to be 2 percent of credit sales. At the end of the year, the company ages its accounts receivable and adjusts the balance in Allowance for Doubtful Accounts to correspond to the aging schedule. During the last month of 2017, Thyme completes the following selected transactions:

Dec. 9   Made a compound entry to write off the following uncollectible accounts: M. Yang, $710; Tory Ltd., $315; and S. Roberts, $1,050.

18   Wrote off as uncollectible the $1,360 account receivable from Acme Ltd. and the $790 account receivable from Data Services.

31   Recorded bad debt expense based on credit sales of $420,000.

31   Recorded bad debt expense based on the following summary of the aging of accounts receivable:

	Age of Accounts			
Accounts Receivable	1–30 Days	31–60 Days	61–90 Days	Over 90 Days
Total = $341,900	$188,400	$78,500	$40,500	$34,500
Estimated percent uncollectible	0.15%	0.5%	7.0%	35.0%

Required

1. Record the transactions in the general journal.

2. Open the Allowance for Doubtful Accounts three-column ledger account and post entries affecting that account. Keep a running balance.

3. Most companies report two-year comparative financial statements. If Thyme Company's Accounts Receivable balance was $299,500 and the Allowance for Doubtful Accounts stood at $9,975 on December 31, 2016, show how the company will report its accounts receivable on a comparative balance sheet for 2017 and 2016.

4. Suppose, on December 31, 2017, the bad debt expense was based on an estimate of 3 percent of the accounts receivable balance, rather than on the aging of accounts receivable. Record the December 31, 2017, entry for bad debt expense in the general journal.

Problem 9–2B

Choices Clothing completed the following selected transactions during 2016 and 2017:

Using the percent-of-sales and aging-of-accounts methods for uncollectibles

②

2016

Dec. 31   Estimated that bad debt expense for the year was 3 percent of credit sales of $748,000 and recorded that amount as expense.

31   Made the closing entry for bad debt expense.

2017

Feb. 17   Sold inventory to Bruce Jones, $1,412, on credit terms of 2/10, n/30. Ignore the cost of goods sold.

Jul. 29   Wrote off Jones's account as uncollectible after repeated efforts to collect from the customer.

Sep. 6   Received $1,150 from Jones, along with a letter stating his intention to pay his debt in full within 45 days. Reinstated the account in full.

Oct. 21   Received the balance due from Jones.

Dec. 31   Made a compound entry to write off the following accounts as uncollectible: Sean Rooney, $1,610; Sargent Ltd., $3,075; and Linda Lod, $11,580.

31   Estimated that bad debt expense for the year was 3 percent of credit sales of $860,000 and recorded the expense.

31   Made the closing entry for the bad debt expense.

Required

1. Open three-column general ledger accounts for Allowance for Doubtful Accounts and Bad Debt Expense. Keep running balances.

2. Record the transactions in the general journal and post to the two ledger accounts.

3. The December 31, 2017, balance of Accounts Receivable is $501,000. Show how Accounts Receivable would be reported at that date.

4. Assume that Choices Clothing begins aging its accounts on December 31, 2017. The balance in Accounts Receivable is $501,000, the credit balance in Allowance for Doubtful Accounts is $31,975, and the company estimates that $32,000 of its accounts receivable will prove uncollectible.

   a. Make the adjusting entry for uncollectibles.

   b. Show how Accounts Receivable will be reported on the December 31, 2017, balance sheet.

Problem 9–3B

Using the allowance method of accounting for uncollectibles, estimating uncollectibles using the aging-of-accounts-receivable method, reporting receivables on the balance sheet

Airdrie Services Inc. started business on March 1, 2017. The company produces monthly financial statements and had total sales of $600,000 (of which $570,000 were on account) during the first four months.

On June 30, the Accounts Receivable account had a balance of $210,000 (no accounts have been written off to date), which was made up of the following accounts aged according to the date the services were provided:

Customer	Month of Service			
	March	April	May	June
Torrance Trucks	$ 2,520	$ 1,200	$ 1,800	$ 1,440
Vesuvus Ltd.	1,500	1,140	1,632	4,344
Lou Del Rio	6,876	4,464	9,168	7,908
Mort Black	6,408	3,468	12,624	15,912
Other Accounts Receivable	14,760	23,916	31,380	57,540
	$32,064	$34,188	$56,604	$87,144

The following accounts receivable transactions took place in July 2017:

Jul. 12 Determined the account of Vesuvus Ltd. was uncollectible and wrote it off.

15 Collected $4,200 from Torrance Trucks for services in the first three months.

21 Decided the account of Lou Del Rio was uncollectible and wrote it off.

24 Collected $6,408 from Mort Black for services in the month of March.

26 Received a cheque from Lou Del Rio for $9,600 plus two cheques, of $9,408 each, postdated to September 10 and November 10.

31 Total sales of service in the month were $162,000; 90 percent of these were on on account and 60 percent of the sales on account were collected in the month.

Required

1. Airdrie Services Inc. has heard that other companies in the industry use the allowance method of accounting for uncollectibles, with many of these estimating the uncollectibles through an aging of accounts receivable.

   a. Journalize the adjustments that would have to be made on June 30 (for the months of March through June), assuming the following estimates of uncollectibles:

Age of Accounts Receivable	Estimated Percent Uncollectible
From current month	1%
From prior month	3
From two months prior	6
From three months prior	20
From four months prior	40

   (Round your total estimate to the nearest whole dollar.)

   b. Journalize the transactions of July 2017.

   c. Journalize the month-end adjustment, using the information from the table that appears in Requirement 1a.

2. For the method of accounting for the uncollectibles used above, show:

   a. The balance sheet presentation of the accounts receivable.

   b. The overall effect of the uncollectibles on the income statement for the months of June and July 2017.

Problem 9–4B

On June 30, 2017, Alberta Wireless had a $100,000 debit balance in Accounts Receivable. During July, the company had sales revenue of $150,000, which included $140,000 in credit sales. Other data for July include:

a. Collections of accounts receivable, $120,000.

b. Write-offs of uncollectible receivables, $4,000.

Accounting for uncollectibles by the direct write-off and allowance methods

①②③

Required

1. Record bad debt expense for July by the direct write-off method. Use T-accounts to show all July activity in Accounts Receivable and Bad Debt Expense.

2. Record bad debt expense and write-offs of customer accounts for July by the allowance method. Use T-accounts to show all July activity in Accounts Receivable, Allowance for Doubtful Accounts, and Bad Debt Expense. The June 30 unadjusted balance in Allowance for Doubtful Accounts was $3,000 (credit). Bad debt expense was estimated at 2 percent of credit sales.

3. What amount of bad debt expense would Alberta Wireless report on its July income statement under the two methods? Which amount better matches expense with revenue? Give your reason.

4. What amount of *net* accounts receivable would Alberta Wireless report on its July 31 balance sheet under the two methods? Which amount is more realistic? Give your reason.

Problem 9–5B

Speedy Loans issued the following notes during 2017:

Accounting for notes receivable, including accruing interest revenue

⑤

Note	Date	Principal Amount	Interest Rate	Term
(a)	Oct. 31	$33,000	6%	6 months
(b)	Nov. 10	12,000	5	60 days
(c)	Dec. 1	21,000	7	1 year

Required

1. Determine the due date and maturity value of each note. Compute the interest for each note. Round all interest amounts to the nearest cent.

2. Journalize a single adjusting entry at December 31, 2017, to record accrued interest revenue on all three notes. An explanation is not required.

3. Journalize the collection of principal and interest on note (b). Explanations are not required.

4. Show how these notes will be reported on December 31, 2017.

Problem 9–6B

Record the following selected transactions in the general journal of J&S Event Planners. Explanations are not required.

Accounting for debit card sales, notes receivable, dishonoured notes, and accrued interest revenue

④⑤

2016

Dec.	12	Received a $5,775, 120-day, 8 percent note from Jacques Alard to settle his $5,775 account receivable balance.
	31	Made an adjusting entry to accrue interest on the Alard note.
	31	Made an adjusting entry to record bad debt expense in the amount of 4 percent of credit sales of $288,200.
	31	Recorded $88,000 of debit card sales. Royal Bank's debit card service fee is 2 percent.
	31	Made a compound closing entry for sales revenue, interest revenue, bad debt expense, and debit card service fees.

2017

Apr.	11	Collected the maturity value of the Alard note.
Jun.	1	Lent $16,500 cash to Mercury Inc., receiving a six-month, 7 percent note.
Oct.	31	Received a $3,025, 60-day, 8 percent note from Jay Nakashi on his past-due account receivable.
Dec.	1	Collected the maturity value of the Mercury Inc. note.
	30	Jay Nakashi dishonoured (failed to pay) his note at maturity as it was confirmed that he had moved; wrote off the receivable as uncollectible, debiting Allowance for Doubtful Accounts.
	31	Wrote off as uncollectible the account receivable of Art Pierce, $853, and of John Grey, $623.

Problem 9–7B

Journalizing credit card sales, uncollectibles, notes receivable, and accrued interest revenue

④ ⑤

HyLooi Food Products completed the following selected transactions:

2016

Nov.	1	Sold goods to NoExtras Foods, receiving a $300,000, six-month, 5 percent note. Ignore cost of goods sold.
Dec.	5	Recorded VISA credit card sale of $30,000. VISA charges a 4 percent fee.
	31	Made an adjusting entry to accrue interest on the NoExtras note.
	31	Made an adjusting entry to record bad debt expense based on an aging of accounts receivable. The aging analysis indicates that $154,000 of accounts receivable will not be collected. Prior to this adjustment, the credit balance in Allowance for Doubtful Accounts is $140,000.

2017

May	1	Collected the maturity value of the NoExtras note.
	15	Received a 60-day, 8 percent, $7,200 note from Sherwood Market on account.
Jun.	23	Sold merchandise to Meadows Foods, receiving a 30-day, 6 percent note for $18,000. Ignore cost of goods sold.
Jul.	14	Collected the maturity value of the Sherwood Market note.
	23	Meadows Foods dishonoured (failed to pay) its note at maturity; converted the maturity value of the note to an account receivable.
Nov.	16	Lent $25,000 cash to Urban Provisions, receiving a 120-day, 8 percent note.
Dec.	5	Collected in full from Meadows Foods.
	31	Accrued the interest on the Urban Provisions note.

Required Record the transactions in the general journal. Explanations are not required.

Problem 9–8B

Using the allowance method of accounting for uncollectibles, estimating uncollectibles by the percent-of-sales and the aging-of-accounts-receivable methods, accounting for notes receivable

② ⑤

Barrie Supplies uses the allowance method for accounting for uncollectible accounts with the estimate based on an aging of accounts receivable. The company had the following account balances on September 30, 2017:

Accounts Receivable	$498,000
Allowance for Doubtful Accounts (credit balance)	56,000

The following transactions took place during the month of October 2017:

Oct.	2	Albert Morrison, who owes $40,000, is unable to pay on time and has given a 20-day, 8 percent note in settlement of the account.
	6	Received from Al Klassen the amount owed on a September 6 dishonoured note, plus extra interest for 30 days at 4 percent computed on the maturity value of the note ($15,300). This dishonoured note had been converted to an account receivable on September 6.
	9	Received notice that a customer (Will Wong) has filed for bankruptcy. Wong owes $35,000. The courts will confirm the amount recoverable at a later date.
	11	Determined the account receivable for Susan Knight ($7,200) was uncollectible and wrote it off.
	18	Received a cheque from the courts in the amount of $23,000 as final settlement of Wong's account.
	22	Morrison paid the note received on October 2.

25   Determined the account receivable for Donald Purcell ($8,200) was uncollectible and wrote it off.

31   Sales for the month totalled $743,000 (of which 95 percent were on account) and collections on account totalled $520,000.

31   Barrie Supplies did an aging of accounts receivable that indicated that $60,000 is expected to be uncollectible. The company recorded the appropriate adjustment.

Required

1. Record the above transactions in the general journal.

2. What would be the adjusting entry required on October 31 if the company used the percent-of-sales method with an estimate of uncollectibles equal to 4 percent of sales on account?

3. Which of the two methods of estimating uncollectible accounts would normally be more accurate? Why?

Problem 9–9B

The comparative financial statements of Harbour View for 2017, 2016, and 2015 included the selected data shown below:

Excel Spreadsheet Template
Using ratio data to evaluate a company's financial position

	2017	2016	2015
		(in millions)	
Balance Sheet			
Current assets:			
Cash	$ 580	$ 560	$ 520
Short-term investments	280	340	252
Receivables, net	560	520	488
Inventories	720	680	600
Prepaid expenses	100	40	80
Total current assets	$ 2,240	$ 2,140	$1,940
Total current liabilities	$ 1,160	$ 1,200	$1,320
Income Statement			
Sales revenue	$11,680	$10,220	$8,400

Required

1. Compute these ratios for 2017 and 2016:

   a. Current ratio

   b. Acid-test ratio

   c. Days' sales in receivables

2. Write a memo explaining to Jack Dodds, owner of Harbour View, which ratio values showed improvement from 2016 to 2017, and which ratio values showed deterioration. Discuss whether these factors convey a favourable or an unfavourable impression about the company.

*Problem 9–10B

A company received the following notes during 2017. The notes were discounted on the dates and at the rates indicated.

Discounting notes receivable

Note	Date	Principal Amount	Interest Rate	Term	Date Discounted	Discount Rate
(a)	Aug. 18	$10,000	11%	6 months	Nov. 18	13%
(b)	Jul. 15	9,000	9	90 days	Jul. 26	12
(c)	Sep. 1	16,000	10	180 days	Nov. 2	13

*This Problem covers Chapter 9 Appendix topics.

Required Identify each note by letter, compute interest for each note, round all interest amounts to the nearest cent, and present entries in general journal form. Explanations are not required.

1. Determine the due date and maturity value of each note.
2. Determine the discount and proceeds from the sale (discounting) of each note.
3. Journalize the discounting of notes (a) and (b).

CHALLENGE PROBLEMS

Problem 9–1C

Understanding accounts receivable management

New Market Builders Supply is a six-store chain of retail stores selling home renovation materials and supplies mainly on credit; the company has its own credit card and does not accept other cards. New Market Builders Supply had a tendency to institute policies that conflicted with each other. Management rarely became aware of these conflicts until they became serious.

Recently, the owner, Angela Kim, who has been reading all the latest management texts, has instituted a new bonus plan. All managers are to be paid bonuses based on the success of their department. For example, the bonus for George Tatulis, the sales manager, is based on how much he can increase sales. The bonus for Sonia Petrov, the credit manager, is based on reducing the bad debt expense.

Required Describe the conflict that the bonus plan has created for the sales manager and the credit manager. How might the conflict be resolved?

Problem 9–2C

Explaining days' sales in accounts receivable

(6)

Days' sales in receivables is a good measure of a company's ability to collect the amounts owed to it. You have owned shares in Stapler Office Ltd. for some years and follow the company's progress by reading the annual report. You noticed the most recent report indicated that the days' sales in receivables had increased over the previous year, and you are concerned.

Required Suggest reasons that may have resulted in the increase in the number of days' sales in receivables.

EXTENDING YOUR KNOWLEDGE

DECISION PROBLEMS

Decision Problem 1

Comparing the allowance and direct write-off methods for uncollectibles

2. $40,260

Hamed Hazara Advertising has always used the direct write-off method to account for uncollectibles. The company's revenues, bad debt write-offs, and year-end receivables for the most recent year follow.

Year	Revenues	Write-Offs	Receivables at Year End
2017	$187,000	$3,300	$44,000

Hamed Hazara is applying for a bank loan, and the loan officer requires figures based on the allowance method of accounting for bad debts. Hazara estimates that bad debts run about 2 percent of revenues each year.

Required

Hamed Hazara must give the banker the following information:

1. How much more or less would net income be for 2017 if Hazara were to use the allowance method for bad debts?

2. How much of the receivables balance at the end of 2017 does Hazara expect to collect?

Compute these amounts, and then explain for Hazara why net income is more or less for 2017 using the allowance method versus the direct write-off method for uncollectibles.

Decision Problem 2

Cholowsky Camping Products sells its products either for cash or on notes receivable that earn interest. The business uses the direct write-off method to account for uncollectible accounts. Paul Cholowsky, the owner, has prepared Cholowsky Camping Products' financial statements. The most recent comparative income statements, for 2017 and 2016, are as follows:

Uncollectible accounts and evaluating a business

(2) (3)

1. 2017 net income, $243,336

	2017	2016
Total revenue	$528,000	$468,000
Total expenses	282,600	252,000
Net income	$245,400	$216,000

Based on the increase in net income, Cholowsky seeks to expand his operations. He asks you to invest $60,000 in the business. You and Cholowsky have several meetings, at which you learn that notes receivable from customers were $120,000 at the end of 2016 and $540,000 at the end of 2017. Also, total revenues for 2017 and 2016 include interest at 12 percent on the year's ending notes receivable balance. Total expenses include bad debt expense of $7,200 each year, based on the direct write-off basis. Cholowsky estimates that bad debt expense would be 2 percent of sales revenue if the allowance method were used.

Required

1. Prepare for Cholowsky Camping Products a comparative single-step income statement that identifies sales revenue, interest revenue, bad debt expense, and other expenses, all computed in accordance with ASPE.

2. Is Cholowsky Camping Products' future as promising as Cholowsky's income statement makes it appear? Give the reason for your answer.

FINANCIAL STATEMENT CASES

Financial Statement Case 1

Indigo Books & Music Inc. (Indigo)—like all other businesses—makes adjusting entries prior to year end to measure assets, liabilities, revenues, and expenses properly.

Examine Indigo's balance sheet in Appendix A at the back of this book and on MyAccountingLab to answer the questions below.

Trade receivables and related uncollectibles

(2) (6)

Required

1. Indigo has accounts receivable of $5,582,000. What types of customers account for these receivables? (Hint: Most of this information can be found in Note 19, specifically in the section Credit Risk.)

2. How many days' sales are in Accounts Receivable at March 29, 2014? Show all calculations. What does this ratio mean to the company?

Financial Statement Case 2

Answer the following questions using the financial statements for TELUS Corporation that appear on MyAccountingLab.

Accounts receivable and related uncollectibles

(2) (7)

2. 2013, 53 days

1. What is the total Accounts Receivable at December 31, 2013? What was the total Accounts Receivable at December 31, 2012?

2. What is TELUS's Allowance for Doubtful Accounts balance, and how is the estimate calculated? (See Note 4.)

3. Does TELUS age its accounts receivable? (Hint: See Note 4.)

4. How much did TELUS write off as doubtful accounts expense during 2013? (Again, see Note 4.)

5. How many days' sales are in Accounts Receivable at December 31, 2013? Discuss these results.

IFRS MINI-CASE

Effects of IFRS on ratios

Janice Sampson is a financial analyst who has worked for a large Canadian brokerage firm for the past five years. Part of her job is to review as much information as she can for manufacturing companies in the fashion industry, especially the financial statements of a company. She also analyzes economic information about the industry and the general economy. Based on her expectations about the company's future financial performance, Janice then advises the firm's clients whether or not to invest in a certain company.

Although not an accountant, Janice is very familiar with the financial reports issued by manufacturing companies in the fashion industry. A key focus is analyzing the current assets of a company. She is particularly interested in the accounts receivable turnover and the inventory turnover; she has found that these two ratios typically provide good information about anticipated trends and might signal upcoming cash flow concerns.

Starting in 2011, the companies Janice analyzed had to report their results under IFRS. Although she was aware that reporting current assets under IFRS was not much different from reporting under ASPE, Janice was interested in knowing about any differences that might exist, and how the change to IFRS might impact her analysis of accounts receivable turnover and inventory turnover.

Required   Prepare a brief report outlining the differences in reporting accounts receivable and inventory under IFRS and ASPE. Will the change to IFRS have any impact on the calculation of accounts receivable turnover and inventory turnover? (Recall that inventory turnover is calculated as Cost of Goods Sold ÷ Average Inventory, where Average Inventory = [(Beginning Inventory + Ending Inventory) ÷ 2].)

>Try It! SOLUTIONS FOR CHAPTER 9

1. a. i.

| Bad Debt Expense | 140,000 | |
| Allowance for Doubtful Accounts | | 140,000 |

ii.

| Allowance for Doubtful Accounts | 160,000 | |
| Accounts Receivable | | 160,000 |

iii.

| Bad Debt Expense | 37,000 | |
| Allowance for Doubtful Accounts | | 37,000 |

Recall that write-offs reduce the Allowance for Doubtful Accounts and Accounts Receivable. They do *not* affect the bad debt expense.

b.

Allowance for Doubtful Accounts

		Dec. 31, 2016, Bal.	175,000
2017 Write-offs (ii)	160,000	2017 Expense Estimate (i)	140,000
		Bal. before Adj.	155,000
		Dec. 31, 2017, Adj. (iii)	37,000
		Dec. 31, 2017, Bal.	192,000

First, determine the balance in Allowance for Doubtful Accounts by filling in this T-account. Add the expense amount from (a) i. and deduct the write-offs from (a) ii.

The final balance in Allowance for Doubtful Accounts must be $192,000 (given in (a) iii.). The balance in the T-account before the adjustment is already $155,000 (calculated above). Therefore, Bad Debt Expense and Allowance for Doubtful Accounts must be increased by the difference of $37,000.

c.

Accounts receivable	$4,155,000
Less: Allowance for doubtful accounts	192,000
Accounts receivable, net	$3,963,000

d. Expected realizable value of receivables at

| December 31, 2017 ($4,155,000 − $192,000) | $3,963,000 |
| Bad debt expense for 2017 ($140,000 + $37,000) | $ 177,000 |

2. a.

Dec. 31	Allowance for doubtful accounts	9,550	
	Accounts Receivable—Carl Rogers		3,250
	Accounts Receivable—Vince Tran		4,100
	Accounts Receivable—Dan Saerose		2,200
Dec. 31	Bad Debt Expense	24,200*	
	Allowance for Doubtful Accounts		24,200

Balance in account should be 115,000 × 0.01 + 55,000 × 0.02 + 35,000 × 0.20 + 15,000 × 0.30 + 10,000 × 0.50 = $18,750

Allowance for Doubtful Accounts

	15,000	Opening Balance
Write-off	9,550	X
	18,750	Calculated Balance

*X = 18,750 − 9,550 + 15,000 = 24,200
This is the journal entry amount.

b.	Accounts Receivable	$ 230,000	
	Allowance for Doubtful Accounts	18,750	
	Net Realizable Value	$ 211,250	

3. a.

Feb. 26	Bad Debt Expense	1,800	
	Accounts Receivable—Jane Eyre		1,800

b. Balance in Accounts Receivable = $15,000 + $18,000 − $19,000 − $1,000 = $12,200

4.

Jun. 12	Cash	14,700	
	Credit Card Discount Expense	300	
	Sales Revenue		15,000
	To record MasterCard credit card sales for the day less a 2 percent credit card discount expense.		
Jun. 12	Accounts Receivable—credit card company	2,910	
	Credit Card Discount Expense	90	
	Sales Revenue		3,000
	To record non-bank credit card sales for the day less a 3 percent credit card discount expense.		
Jun. 12	Cash	4,875	
	Debit Card Service Fee	125	
	Sales Revenue		5,000
	To record debit card sales for the day less a 2.5 percent service fee.		

5.

2016			
Apr. 1	Note Receivable—Bud Shriver	20,000	
	Cash		20,000
	Loaned money at 7% for 1 year.		
Dec. 31	Interest Receivable	1,050	
	Interest Revenue		1,050
	To accrue interest revenue earned in 2016 but not yet received ($20,000 × 7% × 9/12 = $1,050).		

6.

2017			
Apr. 1	Cash	21,400	
	Note Receivable—Bud Shriver		20,000
	Interest Receivable		1,050
	Interest Revenue		350
	To record collection of note receivable from Bud Shriver on which interest has been accrued previously. Interest Receivable is $350 ($20,000 × 7% × 3/12 = $350).		

7.

2017			
Apr. 1	Accounts Receivable Bud Shriver	21,400	
	Note Receivable—Bud Shriver		20,000
	Interest Receivable		1,050
	Interest Revenue		350
	To record default on the note receivable from Bud Shriver on which interest has been accrued previously. Interest Receivable is $350 ($20,000 × 7% × 3/12 = $350).		

8. Current ratio = $\dfrac{\text{Total current assets}}{\text{Total current liabilities}}$

   = $156,511 ÷ $35,315

   = 4.43

   Acid-test ratio = $\dfrac{\text{Cash and cash equivalents} + \text{Accounts receivable}}{\text{Total current liabilities}}$

   = ($19,796 + $63,175) ÷ $35,315

   = 2.35

   The current ratio is higher because it includes all the current assets and not just cash, short-term investments, and receivables.

9. Yes. By inserting the "one day's sales" formula into the "days' sales in average accounts receivable" formula, the single formula becomes:

   Days' sales in average accounts receivable

   = $\dfrac{\text{Average net accounts receivable}}{\text{Net sales}} \times 365$

10. The discount period is 44 days. Method: Compute the number of days the note was held prior to discounting (April 16 to May 2 is 16 days). Subtract the days held from the length of the note (60 − 16 = 44). This method eliminates the necessity of determining the maturity date and then having to count from the discount date to the maturity date.

CONNECTING CHAPTER 10

MyAccountingLab   The **Summary** for Chapter 10 appears on page 584. This lists all of the MyAccountingLab resources. **Accounting Vocabulary** with definitions for this chapter's material appears on page 586.

Kawartha Dairy Limited is a 100% Canadian-owned ice cream and dairy processor located in Bobcaygeon, Ontario, and is still operated by the same family that started it back in 1937. As a business, it is different from many in the food industry because it not only operates its own production facility, but also runs a chain of eight of its own retail stores. It also wholesales its Kawartha Dairy-branded products to other businesses, who in turn offer the products in their own stores. In addition to ice cream and milk, it produces specialized products like buttermilk for the baking industry and private-label items for other companies.

A firm like this has a huge investment in assets. Kawartha Dairy owns buildings, land, production equipment, and office furniture that it uses to run the business. It also has a fleet of trucks to deliver its goods to its own retail outlets, independent specialty shops, grocery stores, and institutional customers.

How does the company record the purchase of these trucks in their accounting records? Do they expense them or set them up as assets? Because they help the company earn revenue over several periods, they are reported as assets.

How should Kawartha Dairy account for the use of the trucks? They record amortization over each truck's useful life. Managers estimate how long they can use the truck and how much they can sell it for when it is taken out of service. They don't amortize this last amount because they get it back when they sell the truck or trade it in for a new one.

Because most companies keep assets for as long as they can, they also need to make repairs and maintain the trucks. *How do you decide when work done on the truck is part of the cost or considered a repair?* Professional judgment is just as important in these decisions as are the generally accepted accounting principles. Managers at Kawartha and other companies need to know how to account for these assets.

This chapter covers these and other matters about property, plant, and equipment, the long-term tangible assets that a business uses to operate, such as airplanes for Air Canada and automobiles for Discount Car and Truck Rentals. It also looks at *intangibles*—those assets with no physical form, such as trademarks and copyrights, and finally, this chapter shows how to account for natural resources such as oil and timber.

>Property,

 plant, and equipment are **identifiable tangible assets**. They are often referred to by their initials PPE. On many financial statements, these are a major component of the total assets owned by a company. These assets have some special characteristics:

- You hold them for use in the business—not to sell as inventory—and they are *tangible*, which means you can touch them. Other assets are *intangible*, and we will explore those later in the chapter.
- They are relatively expensive and their cost can be a challenge to determine.
- They last a long time—usually for several years. If these assets wear out or become obsolete, you need to amortize them.
- They may be sold or traded in.

LO 1

What are property, plant, and equipment (PPE), and how do we measure their cost?

MEASURING THE COST OF PPE

The *cost principle of measurement* directs a business to carry an asset on the balance sheet at its cost—the amount paid for the asset, or the market value if the asset is transferred into the business.

> The cost of an asset = **The sum of all the costs incurred to bring the asset to its intended purpose, net of all discounts**

The cost of *property, plant, and equipment* is the purchase price plus taxes plus other acquisition costs, including commissions, and all other *necessary* costs incurred to ready the asset for its intended use. In Chapter 5 we applied this principle to determine the cost of inventory. The goods and services tax (GST) and the harmonized sales tax (HST), which are paid on the purchase, are never included as part of the cost since these amounts are recoverable by the purchaser. Provincial sales tax (PST) *is* included in the cost of a tangible capital asset. We discuss this in more detail in Chapter 11.

Property

Generally speaking, the *property* portion of long-lived tangible assets refers to land and land improvements. We will review each category separately.

Land

The cost of land includes the following costs paid (or to be paid) by the purchaser:

- The purchase price
- The brokerage commission
- The closing costs (which may include the survey, legal, registration, title, and transfer fees)
- Any property taxes in **arrears**
- The cost for grading and clearing the land
- The costs for demolishing or removing any unwanted buildings

Suppose Kawartha Dairy pays $500,000 to purchase 100 hectares of land. The company also pays $30,000 in brokerage commission, $10,000 in transfer taxes, $5,000 for removal of an old building, $2,000 for a new advertising sign saying "Coming Soon!" and a $1,000 survey fee. What is the cost of this land? Exhibit 10–1 shows all the *necessary* costs incurred to bring the land to its intended use.

EXHIBIT 10-1 | Measuring the Cost of Land

Purchase price of land		$500,000
Add related costs:		
Brokerage commission	$30,000	
Transfer taxes	10,000	
Removal of building	5,000	
Survey fee	1,000	
Total land costs		46,000
Total cost of land		$546,000

Kawartha's entry to record the purchase of the land is as follows:

Feb. 1	Land	546,000	
	Cash		546,000

We would say that Kawartha Dairy **capitalized** the cost of the land at $546,000. This means that the company debited an asset account (Land) for $546,000. The advertising sign cost would be expensed since it was not a necessary cost to ready the land for use.

Land Improvements

Land and Land Improvements are two separate asset accounts because one is amortized and one is not. Land improvements are amortized over their useful lives and include the following:

- Lighting
- Signs
- Fences

- Paving
- Sprinkler systems
- Landscaping

Suppose Kawartha Dairy spent $35,000 for the construction of fences around the land it had purchased above. The entry to record the expenditure is as follows:

Mar. 7	Land Improvements	35,000	
	Cash		35,000

It could be argued that decorative items such as trees and shrubs should be classified as land, since they may have an infinite useful life. The accountant would need to use professional judgment to determine the proper classification. (This is a situation where there are not always rules for all decisions.)

Plant (Buildings)

Plant refers to buildings a company owns such as manufacturing facilities, stores, and offices.

The cost of constructing a building includes the following:

- Architectural fees
- Building permits

- Contractors' charges
- Payments for materials, labour, and overhead

The time to complete a new building can be many months, even years, and the separate expenditures can be numerous. If the company constructs its own assets, the cost of the building may also include the cost of interest on money borrowed to finance the construction.

LEARNING TIPS

Capitalize has nothing to do with the Capital (or equity) account. In this case, it means the amount paid is added to the cost of the asset.

The cost of land is not amortized because it does not wear out. Since there is an *infinite useful life*, no adjustment is made to its reported value.

When an existing building is purchased, its cost includes all the costs to repair and renovate the building for its intended use.

Equipment

There are several different types of assets that fall under this category.

Machinery and Equipment The equipment category includes the productive assets a company builds or acquires to produce, store, manage, or distribute the products it sells. There are many different types of equipment. WestJet has baggage-handling equipment and planes, FedEx Kinko's has copy equipment, and Purolator has delivery trucks.

The cost of machinery and equipment includes the following:

- Purchase price (less any discounts)
- Purchase commission
- Transportation charges
- Installation costs
- Insurance while in transit
- Cost of testing the asset before it is used
- Provincial sales tax (PST)

After the asset is set up, tested, and ready to be used, we stop capitalizing these costs to the Machinery and Equipment account. Thereafter, insurance, taxes, and maintenance costs are recorded as expenses.

Furniture and Fixtures This category includes desks, chairs, filing cabinets, and display racks.

Computers Depending on the type of business, computers might be reported as equipment (when they control machinery), furniture and fixtures (as part of the office), or their own separate account (if there are a lot of them).

Leasehold Improvements

The Leasehold Improvements account includes alterations to assets the company is leasing. For example, suppose TELUS Corporation, known for its Fido and Koodo wireless businesses, leases some of its store locations. The company might renovate the stores to include a lockable storage room. This improvement of the leased space is an asset for TELUS even though the company does not own the store itself. The cost of leasehold improvements should be amortized over the term of the lease including the renewal option or the useful life of the leased asset, whichever is shorter.

LUMP-SUM PURCHASE OF ASSETS

A company may pay a single price for several assets purchased as a group—a "basket purchase." For example, suppose a company pays one price for land and an office building. For accounting purposes, the company must identify the cost of each asset in its own account.

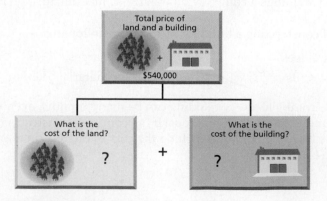

Suppose Kawartha Dairy purchases land and a building in Barrie to be used as a warehouse. The combined purchase price of the land and building is $540,000. An **appraisal**, which is an expert assessment of the value of an asset, indicates that the land's market value is $200,000 and the building's market value is $400,000. Notice that the appraisal is more than what was paid for the land and building—a good deal. It is also possible for an appraisal to come in at a lower value. The issue is that the appraisal amounts and the purchase price are not the same, so we need to determine what value to assign to each asset.

Relative-Fair-Value Method   The **relative-fair-value method** is a cost allocation technique where the total cost is divided among the assets according to their relative fair market values.

❶ Calculate the ratio of each asset's market value to the total market value of both assets combined. Total appraised value is $200,000 + $400,000 = $600,000. Thus, the land, valued at $200,000, is one-third, or 33.33 percent, of the total market value. The building's appraised value is two-thirds, or 66.67 percent, of the total.

❷ Apply that ratio to the total purchase price.

The cost of each asset is determined as follows:

Asset	Market Value	Fraction of Total Value ❶	Total Purchase Price ❷		Cost of Each Asset
Land	$200,000	$200,000 ÷ $600,000 = $^1/_3$ ×	$540,000	=	$180,000
Building	$400,000	$400,000 ÷ $600,000 = $^2/_3$ ×	$540,000	=	$360,000
Total	$600,000				$540,000

Suppose Kawartha Dairy pays cash. The entry to record the purchase of the land and building is as follows:

Apr. 6	Land		180,000	
	Building		360,000	
	Cash			540,000

BETTERMENTS VERSUS REPAIRS

When a company spends money on a capital asset it already owns, it must decide whether to debit an asset account for *betterments* or an expense account for *repairs*.

Betterments are debited to an asset account because they:

- Increase the capacity or efficiency of the asset, or
- Extend its useful life.

For example, the cost of a major engine overhaul that extends a Kawartha Dairy truck's useful life is a betterment. The amount of the expenditure, said to be *capitalized*, is a debit to the asset account Truck.

Repairs, such as maintenance expenses and truck repair expenses, do not extend the asset's capacity or efficiency but merely maintain the asset in working order. These expenses are matched against revenue. Examples could include repainting a truck, repairing a dented fender, and replacing tires. These costs are debited to Repair and Maintenance Expense.

The distinction between betterments (or capitalizing an asset) and repairs requires judgment:

- Does the cost extend the life of the asset (a betterment), or does it only maintain the asset in good order (a repair)?

EXHIBIT 10–2 | Delivery Truck Expenditures—Betterment or Repair?

Betterment: Debit an Asset Account	Repair: Debit Repair and Maintenance Expense
Betterments	Repairs
Major engine overhaul	Repair of headlights or other mechanism
Modification of truck for new use	Oil change, lubrication, and so on
Addition to storage capacity of truck	Replacement tires or windshield
Painting logo on truck	Repainting (to fix rust or damage)

- What about the materiality constraint? Most companies have a minimum dollar limit for betterments. For example, a $400 betterment to a truck would be expensed if the company had a $500 minimum dollar limit for betterments.

Exhibit 10–2 illustrates the distinction between betterments (capital expenditures) and repairs (expenses) for several delivery truck expenditures.

ETHICAL ISSUES

When there are choices to be made in accounting, such as whether a cost should be expensed or capitalized or how to allocate costs using the relative-fair-value method, accountants may face an ethical dilemma. On the one hand, companies want to save on taxes. This motivates companies to expense as many costs as possible or include more costs to assets other than land (which is not amortized) to decrease taxable income. But they also want their financial statements to look as good as possible, with high net income and high reported amounts for assets, which means they want to capitalize as many costs as possible.

In most cases, whether a cost is capitalized or expensed for tax purposes it must be treated the same way for accounting purposes in the financial statements. What, then, is the ethical path? Accountants should follow this general guideline for capitalizing a cost:

Capitalize all costs that provide a future benefit for the business and expense all other costs.

Many companies have gotten into trouble by capitalizing costs that really should have been expensed. They made their financial statements look better than the facts warranted. WorldCom committed this type of accounting fraud (among others), and its former top executives are now in prison as a result.

> Try It!

1. Which of the following would you include in the cost of machinery? (Note: There can be more than one correct answer.)
   a. Installation charges
   b. Testing of the machine
   c. Repair to machinery necessitated by installer's error
   d. First-year maintenance cost
2. How would a Tim Hortons franchise owner divide a $600,000 lump-sum purchase price for land, building, and equipment with estimated market values of $108,000, $432,000, and $180,000, respectively?
3. Classify each of the following as a betterment or a repair (assume all costs are material in amount):
   a. Installing new tires on a cement truck
   b. Repainting a delivery truck that was damaged in an accident
   c. Replacing the motor in a delivery truck
   d. Installing an elevating device in a delivery truck
   e. Safety test on a delivery truck when the licence is renewed
   f. Installing carrying racks on the roof of the delivery truck

Solutions appear at the end of this chapter and on MyAccountingLab

AMORTIZATION

As we have seen in Chapter 3, **amortization**[1] is defined as the allocation of the cost of property, plant, and equipment (except for land) less salvage value or residual value to expense over its useful life. Amortization matches the asset's cost (expense) against the revenue earned by the asset. Thus, the primary purpose of amortization accounting is to measure income correctly in each period.

LO 2
How do we calculate and account for amortization?

Suppose Kawartha Dairy buys a reefer truck (one with a refrigerated trailer). Kawartha believes it will get 20 years' service from the truck. Using the straight-line amortization method, Kawartha Dairy expenses 1/20th of the asset's cost in each of its 20 years' use.

Let's contrast what amortization *is* with what it *is not*.

- *Amortization is not a process of valuation.* Businesses do not record amortization based on the market (fair) value of their property, plant, and equipment; they use their actual cost.

- *Amortization does not mean that the business sets aside cash to replace assets as they become fully amortized*

- *Amortization is sometimes related to physical wear and tear.* All assets except land wear out. For some tangible assets, physical wear and tear creates the need to amortize their value. For example, physical factors wear out the trucks that Kawartha Dairy drives. The same is true of Winners' store fixtures.

- *Amortization is sometimes related to obsolescence.* Assets such as computers or jet aircraft may become obsolete before they wear out. An asset is obsolete when another asset can do the job more efficiently. Thus an asset's useful life may be shorter than its physical life. Accountants usually amortize computers over a short period of time—perhaps two to four years—even though they know the computers could be used much longer. This is because computers are typically replaced with newer models before they wear out. In all cases, the asset's cost is amortized over its *expected useful life*.

Property, plant, and equipment, goodwill, and intangible assets have their own terminology. Exhibit 10–3 shows which expense or loss applies to each category

EXHIBIT 10–3 | **Property, Plant, and Equipment, Goodwill, and Intangible Assets and Their Related Expenses**

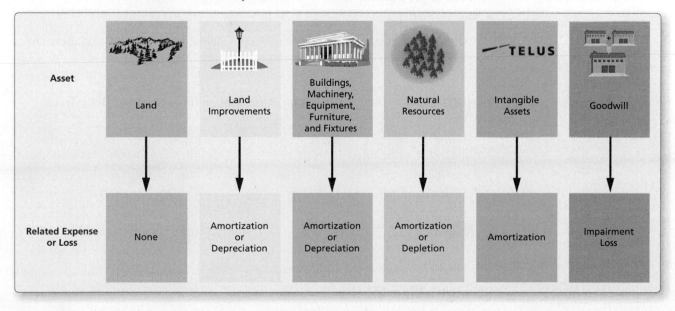

Asset	Land	Land Improvements	Buildings, Machinery, Equipment, Furniture, and Fixtures	Natural Resources	Intangible Assets	Goodwill
Related Expense or Loss	None	Amortization or Depreciation	Amortization or Depreciation	Amortization or Depletion	Amortization	Impairment Loss

---

[1] This is the term used in Part II (ASPE), Section 3061, *CPA Canada Handbook*.

and when to use the terms *amortization*, *depreciation*, *depletion*, and *impairment*. We will look at each of these in turn.

Amortization Methods

Amortization for a capital asset is based on three factors about the asset:

- Cost
- Estimated useful life
- Estimated residual value

The asset's cost is known. The other two factors must be estimated, so amortization itself is an estimated amount. It is important that these estimates be as accurate as possible because they have an impact on the amount of net income reported in each period that the asset is used.

Estimated useful life is the length of the service period expected from the asset. Useful life may be expressed in years, units of output, kilometres, or other measures. For example, a building's useful life is stated in years, a bookbinding machine's in the number of books the machine can bind, and a delivery truck's in kilometres.

Estimated residual value—also called salvage value—is the asset's expected cash value at the end of its useful life. Scrap value is the asset's value at the end of its physical life. For example, a business may believe that a machine's useful life (and physical life) will be seven years. After that time, the company expects to sell the machine as scrap metal. The expected cash receipt is the machine's residual value. Estimated residual value is *not* amortized because the business expects to receive this amount when the machine is sold.

A company stops recording amortization once the asset's book value is equal to the **amortizable cost**.

KEY POINTS

Note that the residual value is the portion of the asset's cost that will *not* be consumed or used; therefore, it should *not* be amortized.

KEY POINTS

It is impossible to quantify the exact amount of the useful life of an asset that has been used up during the period, but there is no doubt that a portion of the asset has been consumed. An estimate of the amount must be made using one of the amortization methods. Without this expense, there would be no *matching* of the cost of the asset with the revenues generated during the time the asset is used.

> **Cost − Residual value = Amortizable cost**

Three methods are widely used in Canada for computing amortization:

- Straight line
- Units of production
- Declining balance

Exhibit 10–4 presents the data we will use to illustrate amortization for a Kawartha Dairy delivery truck.

EXHIBIT 10–4 | Data for Recording Amortization for a Kawartha Dairy Truck

Cost of truck	$65,000
Estimated residual value	5,000
Amortizable cost	$60,000
Estimated useful life:	
Years	5 years
Units of production	400,000 units (kilometres)

Straight-Line Method

The **straight-line method** allocates an equal amount of amortization to each year of asset use. This method was introduced in Chapter 3. The equation for straight-line amortization expense applied to the Kawartha Dairy delivery truck data from Exhibit 10–4 is:

$$\text{Straight-line amortization} = \frac{\text{Cost} - \text{Residual value}}{\text{Useful life in years}}$$

$$= \frac{\$65,000 - \$5,000}{5}$$

$$= \$12,000 \text{ per year}$$

The entry to record each year's amortization is:

Dec. 31	Amortization Expense—Delivery Truck	12,000	
	Accumulated Amortization—Delivery Truck		12,000

> Notice that when there is more than one asset being amortized in a business, we update the account names to include the specific asset information.

Assume that this truck was purchased on January 1, 2017, and the business's fiscal year ends on December 31. A *straight-line* **amortization schedule** is presented in Exhibit 10–5. Spreadsheets are usually used to prepare these schedules.

Sometimes the formula for straight-line amortization is restated to show the useful life as a rate or percentage, known as the **amortization rate**. For example, if an asset has a five-year useful life, then $1/5$ or 20 percent is amortized each year. The formula can then be restated as follows:

$$\text{Straight-line amortization} = (\text{Cost} - \text{Residual value}) \times \frac{1}{\text{Useful life in years}}$$

$$= \text{Amortizable cost} \times \text{Amortization rate}$$

The final column of Exhibit 10–5 shows the asset's *book value* (also referred to as the *carrying value*), which is cost less accumulated amortization. The bolded amounts show that at the end of the second year, the asset's book value is $41,000, calculated as cost less accumulated amortization, or $65,000 − $24,000.

As an asset is used, accumulated amortization increases and the asset's book value decreases.

The partial balance sheet presentation at December 31, 2018, showing the book value of $41,000 would be:

Delivery truck	$65,000
Less: Accumulated amortization—delivery truck	24,000
Delivery truck, net	$41,000

EXHIBIT 10–5 | Straight-Line Amortization for a Truck

Date	Asset Cost	Amortization for the Year			Amortization Expense	Accumulated Amortization	Asset Book Value
		Amortization Rate		Amortizable Cost			
Jan. 1, 2017	$65,000						$65,000
Dec. 31, 2017		$1/5$	×	$60,000	=	$12,000	$12,000	53,000
Dec. 31, 2018		$1/5$	×	60,000	=	12,000	24,000	41,000
Dec. 31, 2019		$1/5$	×	60,000	=	12,000	36,000	29,000
Dec. 31, 2020		$1/5$	×	60,000	=	12,000	48,000	17,000
Dec. 31, 2021		$1/5$	×	60,000	=	12,000	60,000	5,000 ← Residual value

Units-of-Production Method

The **units-of-production (UOP) method** allocates a fixed amount of amortization to each unit of output produced by the asset. Think of this as a two-step process:

❶ Calculate amortization cost per unit.

❷ Multiply the cost per unit by the number of units produced or used in the period.

The equation for the UOP method, applied to the Exhibit 10–4 data, is:

$$
\begin{aligned}
\text{❶ Units-of-production amortization per unit of output} &= \frac{\text{Cost} - \text{Residual value}}{\text{Useful life in units of production}} \\[2mm]
&= \frac{\$65{,}000 - \$5{,}000}{400{,}000 \text{ kilometres}} \\[2mm]
&= \$0.15 \text{ per kilometre}
\end{aligned}
$$

This truck was driven 90,000 kilometres in the first year, 120,000 in the second, 100,000 in the third, 60,000 in the fourth, and 30,000 in the fifth. The amount of UOP amortization per period varies with the number of units the asset produces. Exhibit 10–6 shows the UOP amortization schedule for this asset.

EXHIBIT 10–6 | Units-of-Production Amortization for a Truck

Date	Asset Cost	Amortization Per Kilometre	❷	Number of Kilometres		Amortization Expense	Accumulated Amortization	Asset Book Value
				Amortization for the Year				
Jan. 1, 2017	$65,000							$65,000
Dec. 31, 2017		$0.15	×	90,000	=	$13,500	$13,500	51,500
Dec. 31, 2018		0.15	×	120,000	=	18,000	31,500	33,500
Dec. 31, 2019		0.15	×	100,000	=	15,000	46,500	18,500
Dec. 31, 2020		0.15	×	60,000	=	9,000	55,500	9,500
Dec. 31, 2021		0.15	×	30,000	=	4,500	60,000	5,000 ← Residual value

Double-Declining-Balance Method

The **double-declining-balance (DDB) method** computes annual amortization expense by multiplying the asset's book value by a constant percentage, which is two times (double) the straight-line amortization rate. This is an *accelerated* amortization model. It records a higher amount of amortization in the earlier years. DDB rates are computed as follows:

❶ Compute the straight-line amortization rate per year, for example, for the truck: (1 ÷ 5 years = 20% per year).

❷ Multiply the straight-line rate by 2 to get the **DDB rate**. For the truck example, the DDB rate is 20% × 2 = 40%; or you can think of it as the annual rate of one-fifth, which is then doubled to $^2/_5$, which is 40%.

❸ Multiply the asset's book value (cost less accumulated amortization) at the beginning of the year by the DDB rate. Ignore residual value except for the last year. The first year's amortization for the truck in Exhibit 10-4 is as follows:

> To do the calculation in one step, compute 2 ÷ Useful life in years. Express the result as a fraction or a percent, then multiply by the book value at the beginning of the period.

$$\begin{aligned}\text{DDB amortization} &= \text{Asset book value of the period} \times \text{DDB rate}\\ &= \$65,000 \times 0.40\\ &= \$26,000\end{aligned}$$

The same approach is used to compute DDB amortization for all later years, except for the final year.

The final year's amortization is the amount needed to reduce the asset's book value to its residual value. In the DDB amortization schedule in Exhibit 10–7, the fifth and final year's amortization is $3,424—the $8,424 book value less the $5,000 residual value.

Since amortization is an estimate, accountants usually round the final answer for calculations to the nearest whole dollar.

KEY POINTS

With declining-balance amortization, the asset's book value will rarely equal its residual value in the final year. Amortization expense in the final year is a "plug" figure. Use the amount that will reduce the asset's book value to the residual value.

EXHIBIT 10–7 | Double-Declining-Balance Amortization for a Truck

Date	Asset Cost	Amortization for the Year				Accumulated Amortization	Asset Book Value
		DDB Rate		Asset Book Value			
					Amortization Expense		
Jan. 1, 2017	$65,000						$65,000
Dec. 31, 2017		0.40	×	$65,000 =	$26,000	$26,000	39,000
Dec. 31, 2018		0.40	×	39,000 =	15,600	41,600	23,400
Dec. 31, 2019		0.40	×	23,400 =	9,360	50,960	14,040
Dec. 31, 2020		0.40	×	14,040 =	5,616	56,576	8,424
Dec. 31, 2021				=	3,424*	60,000	5,000 ← Residual value

*Amortization in 2021 is the amount needed to reduce the asset's book value to the residual value of $5,000 ($8,424 − $5,000 = $3,424).

The DDB method differs from the other methods in two ways:

- Residual value is ignored until the last period. In the first year, amortization is calculated on the asset's full cost.
- Final-year amortization is the amount needed to bring the asset's book value to the residual value. It is a "plug" figure.

LEARNING TIPS

The DDB formula is unique. Rather than use amortizable cost (as the other methods do), the formula for DDB is *book value* × DDB rate. Residual value is not used in the DDB formula until the final year's amortization calculation.

Comparing Amortization Methods

Let's compare the three methods we have just discussed. Each method allocates different amounts of amortization expense to each period, but they all result in the same amortization over the life of the asset.

	Amount of Amortization per Year		
Year	Straight Line	Units of Production	Double Declining Balance
2017	$12,000	$13,500	$26,000
2018	12,000	18,000	15,600
2019	12,000	15,000	9,360
2020	12,000	9,000	5,616
2021	12,000	4,500	3,424
Total	$60,000	$60,000	$60,000

Which method is best? That depends on the asset. For managers, it is the one that best represents the situation. A business should match an asset's expense against the revenue that the asset produces. A company can use different methods for different assets.

Method	Asset Characteristics	Effect on Amortization	Example
Straight line	Generates revenue evenly over time	Equal each period	Office furniture
Units of Production	Wears out because of physical use rather than obsolescence	More usage causes larger amortization	Airplane, machinery (hours)
Double Declining Balance	Produces more revenue or is more productive in early years	Higher expense in early years, less later	Computerized equipment

Exhibit 10–8 graphs the relationship between annual amortization amounts for the three methods.

EXHIBIT 10–8 | Amortization Expense Patterns for the Various Methods

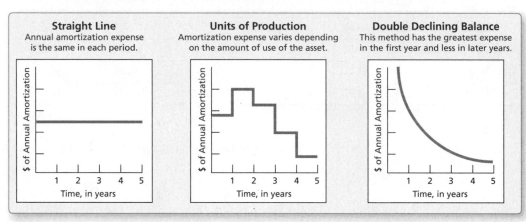

> Try It!

4. Sonoma Industrial Products purchased equipment on January 2, 2017, for $176,000. The expected life of the equipment is 10 years or 100,000 units of production, and its residual value is $16,000. Using three amortization methods, the annual amortization expense and total accumulated amortization at the end of 2017 and 2018 are as follows:

	Method A		Method B		Method C	
	Annual Amortization Expense	Accumulated Amortization	Annual Amortization Expense	Accumulated Amortization	Annual Amortization Expense	Accumulated Amortization
2017	$16,000	$16,000	$35,200	$35,200	$ 4,800	$ 4,800
2018	16,000	32,000	28,160	63,360	22,400	27,200

a. Identify the amortization method used in each instance and show the equation and computation for each. (Round off to the nearest dollar.)

b. Assume continued use of the same method through the year 2019. Determine the annual amortization expense, accumulated amortization, and book value of the equipment for 2017 through 2019 under each method, assuming 12,000 units of production in 2019.

Solutions appear at the end of this chapter and on MyAccountingLab

OTHER ISSUES IN ACCOUNTING FOR PPE

Amortization usually differs depending on whether it is being calculated for accounting or income tax purposes. At certain times amortization must be calculated for partial years; it also happens that amortization assumptions have to be revised. This section covers these topics.

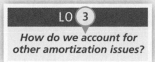

LO 3

How do we account for other amortization issues?

Amortization and Income Taxes

Most companies use the straight-line method for reporting capital asset values and amortization expense to their owners and creditors on their financial statements. Businesses often keep a separate set of records for calculating the amortization expense they claim on their tax returns because the Canada Revenue Agency (CRA) specifies the maximum amortization taxpayers can deduct for income tax purposes. This amount is usually different from amortization expense reported on the income statement.

Capital Cost Allowance The CRA allows corporations as well as individuals with business or professional income to compute deductions from income to recognize the consumption or use of capital assets. The deductions are called **capital cost allowance (CCA)**, the term the CRA uses to describe amortization for tax purposes. The CRA specifies the *maximum* rates allowed for each asset class, called *CCA rates*. A taxpayer may claim anything from zero to the maximum CCA allowed in a year. Most taxpayers claim the maximum CCA since this provides the largest deduction from taxable income as quickly as possible. This is because CCA is an accelerated method—similar to DDB. Claiming the maximum CCA reduces taxable income and thus tax payable, leaving more cash available for investment or other business uses.

Some CRA rates and classes in effect at the time of publication are as follows:

	Rate	Class
Automobiles costing over $30,000	30%	10.1
Most buildings bought after 1987	4%	1
Computer software	100%	12
Office furniture and fixtures	20%	8
Computers	55%	50

The CRA allows the taxpayer to claim only 50 percent of the normal CCA rate in the year of acquisition. This is referred to as the **half-year rule**. However, there are some exceptions, and Class 12 is one of them. Class 12 assets have a full 100 percent CCA rate in the year of acquisition.

The CCA rate is applied to the balance in the asset class at the end of the year (cost minus accumulated CCA claimed to date) in the same manner as the DDB method.

CCA is studied more fully in advanced accounting and tax courses.

Amortization for Partial Years

Companies purchase property, plant, and equipment whenever they need them—for example, on February 8 or August 17. They do not wait until the beginning of a year or a month. Therefore, companies develop policies to compute amortization for partial years. Suppose a company purchases a building as a maintenance shop on April 1, 2017, for $600,000. The building's estimated life is 18 years and its estimated residual value is $60,000. The company's fiscal year ends on December 31. How does the company compute amortization for the year ended December 31, 2017?

Many companies compute partial-year amortization by first calculating a full year's amortization. They then multiply full-year amortization by the fraction of

REAL WORLD EXAMPLE

Each company must make its own policies to ensure consistent treatment of partial years. Professional judgment is used rather than there being specific guidance available.

the year during which they used the asset. In this case, the company needs to record nine months' amortization, for April to December. Assuming the straight-line method, the 2017 amortization for the maintenance shop is $22,500, computed as follows:

$$\text{Full-year amortization: } \frac{\$600,000 - \$60,000}{18 \text{ years}} = \$30,000$$

$$\text{Partial-year amortization: } \$30,000 \times 9/12 = \$22,500$$

Another possible policy would be:

- Record a full month's amortization on an asset bought on or before the 15th of the month.
- Record no amortization on assets purchased after the 15th of the month.

If the company purchased the building above on August 17, then it would record no amortization for August. In this case, the year's amortization for four months (September to December) would be $10,000 ($30,000 $\times$ $^4/_{12}$).

Partial-year amortization is computed under the DDB amortization method in the same way—by applying the appropriate percentage of the year during which the asset is used.

For the UOP amortization method, partial-year and full-year amortization are calculated the same way because amortization is based on the number of units produced. Amortization for the UOP method is *not* a function of time, so partial-year amortization is not an issue as it is for the other amortization methods.

Spreadsheets or custom software can calculate amortization to the level of detail required by any company.

Change in the Useful Life of an Amortizable Asset

Estimating the useful life of property, plant, and equipment subject to amortization poses an accounting challenge. As previously discussed, a business must estimate the useful life of these assets to compute amortization. This prediction is the most difficult part of accounting for amortization. As the asset is used, the business may change the asset's estimated useful life based on experience and new information. Such a change is called a *change in accounting estimate*.

Accounting changes like these are infrequent despite the fact that no business has perfect foresight. To *record* a change in an accounting estimate, the asset's remaining amortizable book value is spread over its adjusted, or new, remaining useful life. The change is accounted for **prospectively**, meaning from this point on into the future.

The equation for revised straight-line amortization is:

$$\text{Revised straight-line amortization} = \frac{\text{Cost + Betterments} - \text{Accumulated amortization} - \text{New residual value}}{\text{Estimated remaining useful life in years}}$$

Assume that an ice cream–making machine owned by Kawartha Dairy cost $400,000, and the company originally believed the asset had a 16-year useful life with no residual value. The company uses the straight-line method and has used the machine for four years. There were no betterments during this time.

$$400,000 \div 16 \text{ years} = \$25,000 \text{ amortization per year}$$

$$\$25,000 \times 4 \text{ years} = \$100,000 \text{ accumulated amortization}$$

From its experience with the asset during the first four years, management believes the asset will remain useful for the next 20 years and at that time have no residual value. At the start of Year 5, the company would compute a revised annual amortization amount and record it as follows:

$$\text{Revised Annual Amortization} = \frac{\$400,000 + \$0 - \$100,000 - \$0}{20} = \$15,000$$

The yearly amortization entry based on the new estimated useful life is:

Dec. 31	Amortization Expense—Machine	15,000	
	Accumulated Amortization—Machine		15,000

Using Fully Amortized Assets

A *fully amortized asset* is one that has reached the end of its *estimated* useful life. No more amortization is recorded for the asset. If the asset is no longer useful, it is disposed of. But the asset may still be useful, and the company may continue using it. The asset account and its accumulated amortization remain on the books, but no additional amortization is recorded.

5. On April 17, 2017, Logan Services purchased a used crane for $65,000. The company expects the crane to remain useful for four years (600 hours of use) and to have a residual value of $5,000. The company expects the crane to be used for 130 hours until December 31, 2017, the company's year end. Compute the amortization expense for 2017 using the following amortization methods: (a) straight line, (b) UOP, and (c) DDB.

6. On January 10, 1997, ABC Co. purchased for $800,000 a building that had an estimated residual value of $50,000 and a useful life of 40 years. On January 13, 2017, a $200,000 addition to the building increased its residual value by $50,000. Calculate straight-line amortization expense for 2017.

Solutions appear at the end of this chapter and on MyAccountingLab

DISPOSING OF PPE

Eventually, an amortizable asset no longer serves its purpose. The asset may be worn out, obsolete, or no longer useful to the business for some other reason. The owner may sell the asset or exchange it. If the asset cannot be sold or exchanged, then it is discarded, or **junked**. While each situation is accounted for differently, there are some common steps that occur. In all cases, the business should:

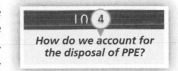

How do we account for the disposal of PPE?

❶ Bring amortization up to date. If the disposal occurs partway through the year, a partial year's amortization must be recorded to update accumulated amortization.

❷ Calculate whether there is a loss/gain on the disposal.

❸ Remove the asset and contra asset accounts from the books with a journal entry:

- Debit the asset's accumulated amortization account
- Credit the asset account
- Record any gain or loss
- Record payment and/or trade-in (if applicable)

Discarding PPE

When an asset is discarded, there is no cash received. Let's look at the journal entries, which vary depending on whether the asset is fully amortized or not.

Discarding Assets at Book Value Suppose Kawartha Dairy is disposing of an ice cream cone machine and the final year's amortization expense has just been recorded on December 31. The cost was $60,000, and there is no residual value. The machine's accumulated amortization totals $60,000. Assume this asset cannot be sold or exchanged, so it is discarded or junked.

❶ Amortization is up to date because this is recorded at year end. No further adjustment is needed.

❷ There is no gain or loss because the net book value is zero.

❸ The entry to record its disposal is:

Dec. 31	Accumulated Amortization—Machinery	60,000	
	Machinery		60,000
	To dispose of a fully amortized machine.		

Now both accounts have zero balances, as shown in the T-accounts below:

Machinery			
Dec. 31	60,000	Dec. 31	60,000

Accumulated Amortization—Machinery			
Dec. 31	60,000	Dec. 31	60,000

Discarding Assets at a Loss If assets are discarded before being fully amortized, the company records a loss equal to the asset's book value. Let's now suppose Kawartha Dairy's store fixtures that cost $40,000 are junked. If the accumulated amortization is $30,000, the book value is therefore $10,000.

❶ Amortization is up to date because this is recorded at year end.

❷ There is a loss because there is a book value of $10,000 but no payment received for it.

❸ Disposal of these store fixtures generates a loss, as follows:

KEY POINTS

A Gain or Loss on Disposal of Property, Plant, and Equipment is reported on the income statement in the "other gains and losses" section.

Dec. 31	Accumulated Amortization—Store Fixtures	30,000	
	Loss on Disposal of Property, Plant, and Equipment	10,000	
	Store Fixtures		40,000
	To dispose of store fixtures.		

Selling PPE

Let's use the following information from Kawartha Dairy for the next example about selling surplus office furniture:

Sales date:	September 30, 2017
Selling price:	$50,000 cash
Original cost:	$100,000
Purchased:	January 1, 2014

The furniture has been amortized on a straight-line basis with a 10-year useful life and no residual value.

❶ Bring the amortization up to date. If Kawartha Dairy uses the calendar year as its accounting period, partial amortization must be recorded for nine months from January 1, 2017, to the sale date of September 30. The straight-line amortization entry for nine months at September 30, 2017, is:

Sep. 30	Amortization Expense—Furniture	7,500	
	Accumulated Amortization—Furniture		7,500
	To update amortization ($100,000 ÷ 10 years × 9/12).		

After this entry is posted, the Furniture and the Accumulated Amortization—Furniture accounts appear as follows:

Furniture		Accumulated Amortization—Furniture	
Jan. 1, 2014 100,000		Dec. 31, 2014 10,000*	
		Dec. 31, 2015 10,000	
		Dec. 31, 2016 10,000	
		Sep. 30, 2017 7,500	
		Balance 37,500	

Book value = $62,500

*Annual amortization = ($100,000 cost – $0 residual value) ÷ 10 years = $10,000

❷ Calculate if there is a gain or loss on the sale. The loss is computed as follows:

Cash received from selling the asset		$50,000
Book value of asset sold:		
Cost	$100,000	
Accumulated amortization up to date of sale	37,500	62,500
Gain (loss) on sale of the asset		($12,500)

❸ Record the journal entry to remove the balances in the asset and its contra account. Kawartha Dairy's entry to record the sale of the furniture for $50,000 cash is:

Sep. 30	Cash	50,000	
	Loss on Disposal of Property, Plant, and Equipment	12,500	
	Accumulated Amortization—Furniture	37,500	
	Furniture		100,000
	To dispose of furniture.		

LEARNING TIPS

When disposing an asset, make sure to adjust both the asset and its accumulated amortization account balances to zero.

If the sale price had been $70,000, Kawartha Dairy would have had a gain of $7,500 (Cash, $70,000 – Asset book value, $62,500). The entry to record this gain would be as follows:

Sep. 30	Cash	70,000	
	Accumulated Amortization—Furniture	37,500	
	Furniture		100,000
	Gain on Disposal of Property, Plant, and Equipment		7,500
	To dispose of furniture.		

Gains/Losses   A gain is recorded when an asset is disposed of for more than book value. A loss is recorded when the sale price or exchange or disposal amount is less than book value. Gains increase net income and losses decrease net income. All gains and losses are reported on the income statement in the "other gains and losses" section.

Exchanging PPE

Businesses often exchange old tangible assets (property, plant, and equipment) for newer, more efficient assets. The most common exchange transaction is a *trade-in*.

The first thing to determine in any exchange transaction is whether the transaction has commercial substance.[2] **Commercial substance** exists when the entity's future cash flows from the new asset received will differ in risk, timing, or amount from the cash flows from the old asset given up in the exchange. This is almost always the case. Exhibit 10–9 summarizes the accounting treatment for exchanges.

EXHIBIT 10–9 | Accounting for Exchanges of Non-Monetary Assets

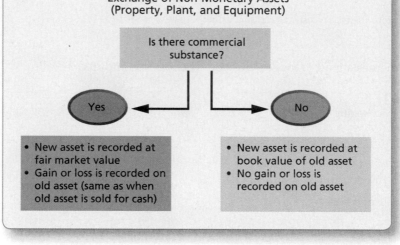

Suppose Kawartha Dairy owns a milk truck that it purchased for $42,000 on January 2, 2013. The old truck was expected to last seven years and was amortized on a straight-line basis. On January 2, 2018, Kawartha Dairy exchanged this truck for a newer truck that had a fair market value of $53,000. Kawartha Dairy received a trade-in allowance of $8,000 for the old truck and paid the seller $45,000 cash. Kawartha Dairy will receive better gas mileage with the new truck and will be able to save delivery expenses by delivering more with the new truck. Therefore, *this exchange of assets has commercial substance*. The entry to record this exchange would be as follows:

Jan. 2	New Truck	53,000	
	Loss on Exchange of Assets	4,000	
	Accumulated Amortization—Old Truck	30,000	
	Cash		45,000
	Old Truck		42,000
	To record exchange of the old milk truck and cash for a new milk truck. Accumulated amortization on the old truck was 5 × $6,000 = $30,000.		

---

[2] Part II, Section 3831, of the *CPA Canada Handbook*, "Non-monetary Transactions," guides the accounting treatment of tangible asset exchanges because property, plant, and equipment are defined as non-monetary assets.

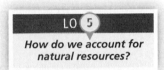

> Try It!

7. ABC Catering Service purchased equipment on January 8, 2015, for $58,500. The equipment is expected to last six years and to have a residual value of $4,500.

    a. Suppose ABC sold the equipment for $43,000 on December 29, 2017. Journalize the sale of the equipment, assuming straight-line amortization is used.

    b. Suppose ABC sold the equipment for $23,000 on December 29, 2017. Journalize the sale of the equipment, assuming straight-line amortization is used.

8. In January 2015, Luk's Catering purchased a portable food heater for $3,100 cash. The journal entry to record the purchase included a debit to Catering Equipment. During 2015 and 2016, Luk's Catering recorded total amortization of $2,200 on the heater. On January 2, 2017, Luk's Catering traded in the old food heater for a new one that is more efficient, paying $2,900 cash. This exchange transaction has commercial substance. Journalize Luk's Catering's exchange of equipment.

Solutions appear at the end of this chapter and on MyAccountingLab

ACCOUNTING FOR NATURAL RESOURCES

Natural resources are tangible capital assets that are often called *wasting assets* because they are used up in the process of production. Examples include iron ore, coal, oil, gas, and timber. Natural resources are like inventories in the ground (coal) or on top of the ground (timber). Natural resources are expensed through amortization. Some companies use the word **depletion** to describe amortization of natural resources. Amortization expense, or *depletion expense*, is that portion of the cost of natural resources that is used up in a particular period. It is computed the same way as the units-of-production (UOP) method:

> **LO 5**
> *How do we account for natural resources?*

> **1** Amortization per unit of resource $= \dfrac{\text{Cost} - \text{Residual value}}{\text{Estimated total units of natural resource}}$
>
> **2** Amortization expense $=$ Amortization per unit of resource $\times$ Number of units of resource

An oil well may cost $300,000 and contain an estimated 10,000 barrels of oil. (Natural resources usually have no residual value.) If 3,000 barrels are extracted during the first year, amortization expense is calculated as follows:

> **1** Amortization per unit of resource $= \dfrac{(\$300,000 - \$0)}{10,000 \text{ barrels/day}} = \$30$ **per barrel**
>
> **2** Amortization expense $= \$30/\text{barrel} \times 3,000$ **barrels extracted**
> $= \$90,000$

The journal entry to record the amortization for the year would be shown as follows:

Dec. 31	Amortization Expense—Oil	90,000	
	Accumulated Amortization—Oil		90,000

Accumulated Amortization for natural resources is a contra account similar to Accumulated Amortization for property, plant, and equipment. Natural resource assets can be reported on the balance sheet, as is shown for oil in the following example. See Exhibit 4–14 on page 193 to see how this fits into the rest of the balance sheet.

Property, plant, and equipment:			
Land			$ 120,000
Buildings	$ 800,000		
Less: accumulated amortization	305,000	$ 495,000	
Equipment	160,000		
Less: accumulated amortization	105,000	55,000	
			550,000
Oil and gas properties:			
Oil		**300,000**	
Less: Accumulated amortization		**90,000**	
Net oil and gas properties			210,000
Property, plant, and equipment, net			$ 880,000

Future Removal and Site Restoration Costs

There is increasing concern on the part of individuals and governments about the environment. In the past, a company exploiting natural resources, such as a mining company, would simply abandon the site once the ore body was mined completely. Now there is legislation in most jurisdictions requiring a natural resource company to remove buildings, equipment, and waste and to restore the site once a location is to be dismantled and abandoned.

The *CPA Canada Handbook* refers to future removal and site restoration costs as an **asset retirement obligation**, which is estimated at the time the asset is acquired or the obligation becomes known. The liability (a credit) for the asset retirement obligation is measured at the end of each period at the best estimate of the future expenditures. This estimate is determined by the judgment of management, supplemented by experience of similar transactions and perhaps reports from independent experts. The same amount is recorded as an asset retirement cost (a debit) and added to the carrying amount of its related asset (such as a mine). The asset retirement cost must then be expensed using an amortization method and time frame that matches that of the related asset.

Asset retirement obligations are reviewed at each balance sheet date and adjusted to reflect the current best estimate.

9. Suppose West Fraser Timber Co. Ltd. purchases, for $600,000, land that contains an estimated 400,000 fbm (foot-board measures) of timber. West Fraser harvests 200,000 fbm in the year of purchase, how much amortization should be recorded?

Solutions appear at the end of this chapter and on MyAccountingLab

LO 6

How do we account for intangible assets and goodwill?

INTANGIBLE ASSETS AND GOODWILL

As we discussed earlier in this chapter, **intangible assets** have no physical form. Instead, these assets convey special rights from ownership of patents, copyrights, trademarks, franchises, leaseholds, and goodwill.

In our technology-driven economy, intangibles are very important. Consider the online auctioneer eBay Inc. The company has no physical products—only the software it uses to provide the service that helps people buy and sell everything from toys to bathroom tiles millions of times each month.

The **intellectual capital** of eBay or a company like BlackBerry Ltd. is difficult to measure, but when one company buys another we get a glimpse of the value of the acquired intellectual capital. Intangibles can account for most of a company's market value, so companies must value their purchased intangibles just as they do their physical and financial assets.

Intangibles are expensed as they expire through amortization. Amortization is computed over the lesser of the asset's legal life or estimated useful life. Obsolescence often shortens an intangible asset's useful life. Amortization expense for intangibles can be written off directly against the intangible asset account with *no accumulated amortization account*. The residual value of most intangibles is zero.

Specific Intangibles

Patents   **Patents** are federal government grants conveying an exclusive right for 20 years to produce and sell an invention. The invention may be a product or a process. Patented products include Bombardier Ski-Doos and the BlackBerry Ltd.'s BlackBerry. Suppose BlackBerry Ltd. pays $2,000,000 to acquire a patent, and it believes the expected useful life of the patent is five years. Amortization expense is $400,000 per year ($2,000,000 ÷ 5 years). The company's entries for this patent are as follows:

Jan. 1	Patent	2,000,000	
	Cash		2,000,000
	To record purchase of a patent.		
Dec. 31	Amortization Expense—Patent	400,000	
	Patent		400,000
	To amortize the cost of a patent ($2,000,000 ÷ 5).		

At the end of the first year, BlackBerry would report the patent on the balance sheet at $1,600,000 ($2,000,000 minus the first year's amortization of $400,000).

Copyrights   **Copyrights** are exclusive rights to reproduce and sell software, a book, a musical composition, a film, or some other creative work. Issued by the federal government, copyrights extend 50 years beyond the end of the creator's life. A company may pay a large sum to purchase an existing copyright from the owner. For example, the publisher Penguin Random House (Canada) may pay the author of a popular novel tens of thousands of dollars or more for the book's copyright. The useful life of a copyright for a popular book may be two or three years; on the other hand, some copyrights, especially of musical compositions, such as works by the Beatles, seem to remain valuable over several decades.

Trademarks and Brand Names   **Trademarks** and **brand names** (or **trade names**) are distinctive identifiers of products or services. For example, The Sports Network (better known as TSN) has its distinctive logo of the red letters *TSN* on a white background, and the Edmonton Oilers and Toronto Blue Jays have insignia that identify their respective teams. Molson Canadian, Swiss Chalet chicken, WestJet, and Roots are everyday trade names. Advertising slogans such as Speedy Muffler's "At Speedy You're a Somebody" are also legally protected for a period of 15 years (which can be renewed). More recently, *soundmarks* (distinctive sounds used to perform the same function as a trademark, such as the THX sound system sound at the movies and the Intel sound in its commercials) are also being protected. The cost of a trademark or trade name is amortized over its useful life.

Franchises and Licences **Franchises** and **licences** are privileges granted by a private business or a government to sell a product or service in accordance with specified conditions. The Winnipeg Jets hockey organization is a franchise granted to its owners by the National Hockey League. Tim Hortons and Re/Max Ltd. are other well-known franchises. The acquisition cost of a franchise or licence is amortized over its useful life.

Leaseholds A **leasehold** is a right arising from a prepayment that a lessee (tenant) makes to secure the use of an asset from a lessor (landlord). For example, most malls lease the space to the mall stores and shops that you visit. Often, leases require the lessee to make this prepayment in addition to monthly rental payments. The prepayment is a debit to an intangible asset account entitled Leaseholds. This amount is amortized over the life of the lease by debiting Rent Expense and crediting Leaseholds.

Sometimes lessees modify or improve the leased asset. For example, a lessee may construct a fence on leased land. The lessee debits the cost of the fence to a separate intangible asset account, **Leasehold Improvements**, and amortizes its cost over the lesser of the term of the lease and its useful life.

Goodwill

Goodwill is a truly unique asset. *Goodwill* in accounting is a more limited term than in everyday use, as in "friendly or cooperative feelings." In accounting, **goodwill** is the excess of the cost to purchase a company over the market value of its net assets (assets minus liabilities). Why might an acquiring company pay an amount greater than the market value of net assets acquired when purchasing a business? The business being acquired might have good customer relations, a unique software code, a good location, efficient operations, a monopoly in the marketplace, strong sources of financing, and other factors that make it more valuable than just the net assets being acquired.

Suppose Purolator acquires Regional Express Ltd. at a cost of $10 million. The market value of Regional Express' assets is $9 million, and its liabilities total $1 million. In this case, Purolator paid $2 million for goodwill, computed as follows:

LEARNING TIPS

Another way to think about this calculation is that there is goodwill of $2 million because the payment of $10 million is more than the market value of $8 million.

Purchase price paid for Regional Express Ltd.		$10 million
Sum of the market value of Regional Express' assets	$9 million	
Less: Regional Express' liabilities	1 million	
Market value of Regional Express' net assets		8 million
Excess is called *goodwill*		$ 2 million

Purolator's entry to record the acquisition of Regional Express Ltd., including its goodwill, would be

June 30	Assets (Cash; Receivables; Inventories; Property, Plant, and Equipment; all at market value)	9,000,000	
	Goodwill	2,000,000	
	Liabilities		1,000,000
	Cash		10,000,000
	Purchased Regional Express Ltd.		

Goodwill has the following special features:

- Goodwill is recorded at its cost only by the company that purchases another company. A purchase transaction provides objective evidence of the value of the goodwill.

- Goodwill has an indefinite life, so it is not amortized like other intangibles. According to ASPE, the purchaser must assess the goodwill every year and, if its value is **impaired** (if the fair value falls below the carrying value in the accounting records), the goodwill must be written down to reflect the *impairment*. The write-down amount is accounted for as a loss in the year of the write-down. For example, suppose the goodwill—purchased above—is worth only $1,500,000 at the end of the first year due to a strike or some bad publicity at Regional Express. In that case, Purolator would make this entry:

MyAccountingLab

Video: Real World Accounting

Dec. 31	Loss on Goodwill (or Impairment Loss)	500,000	
	Goodwill		500,000
	Recorded loss on goodwill ($2,000,000 − $1,500,000).		

Purolator would then report this goodwill on the balance sheet at its current value of $1,500,000.

> Goodwill can be written down, but it cannot be written up if there is a reversal of circumstances.

> Why It's Done This Way

Objective of Financial Reporting

The accounting framework provides guidance on how to record transactions. We can focus on two principles: *recognition* and *measurement*. When an asset such as equipment is acquired by a business, a financial transaction has occurred and we should record it (*recognition*). We can determine the cost of the equipment easily, so we have satisfied the *cost principle of measurement*.

Next, into which account should the equipment be placed? Is it an asset or is it an expense? The framework also discusses elements. *Assets* are economic resources controlled by an entity that are expected to benefit the entity in the future. Does this equipment fit that description? It seems to, since the company expects to receive benefits from having the equipment for at least 10 years.

Part of its economic benefit is used up each year and needs to be *expensed*. We calculate amortization expense and, through that account, we recognize part of the cost of the equipment each year. In this way, we *match* the expense of the asset to the period of economic benefit—10 years. This supports *the matching objective*, which we learned is an expense recognition criteria.

> Try It!

10. Suppose a company paid $650,000 on January 5, 2017, to acquire a patent that it believes will have a five-year useful life. The company's year end is December 31.
    a. Journalize the purchase of the patent and the amortization entry at year end.
    b. Suppose this same patent was acquired on May 13, 2017. Journalize the purchase of the patent and the amortization entry at year end.

11. Suppose TELUS Corporation acquires Novel Networks, a small company that produces specialized computer programs, for $2,000,000. Novel Networks' assets have a book value of $500,000 and a market value of $400,000. Its liabilities have a market value of $300,000. Record the acquisition of Novel Networks by TELUS Corporation.

Solutions appear at the end of this chapter and on MyAccountingLab

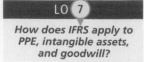

THE IMPACT OF IFRS ON PPE, INTANGIBLES, AND GOODWILL

ASPE	IFRS
Property, Plant, and Equipment (PPE)	
Amortization is the term often used for tangible and intangible assets.	*Depreciation* is the term often used for tangible assets, whereas *amortization* is often used for intangible assets.
There is no guidance on the level of detail required in reporting PPE.	After an asset has been capitalized, companies must capitalize replacement parts and **derecognize** the parts that are replaced. In other words, each part of an item of PPE that is significant relative to the total cost of the asset must be depreciated separately. This is called **componentization**. If a company purchases a building, it has to depreciate the significant components (roof, heating) of the building separately.
Cost is measured at acquisition. Follow historic cost principle and show this cost in later years unless there is an impairment.	In the years following acquisition, companies have the *option* to follow a **revaluation method**. Under the revaluation approach, the carrying amount of the PPE is its fair value at the date of revaluation. PPE must be tested for impairment annually and depreciation revised for future periods.
PPE must be tested for impairment when it is apparent.	To assess impairment under IFRS, assets may be looked at individually or they can be divided into **cash generating units (CGUs)**, the smallest identifiable group of assets that generates cash flows that are largely independent of the cash flows from other assets. The recoverable amount of the asset is compared annually with the carrying value to assess whether or not there is any write-down needed.
Assets that were written down *cannot* have their impairment reversed.	Assets that were written down *can* have their impairment reversed in a future period.
Intangible Assets and Goodwill	
Only purchased intangible assets can be reported and amortized.	*Internally generated* intangible assets must be analyzed to determine whether they will provide a future benefit to the company. If they will, they can be capitalized and amortized.
Companies may only use the historic cost principle to value assets.	Companies have the option of using a cost model or the revaluation model to determine the carrying amount of the intangible asset.

SUMMARY PROBLEMS FOR YOUR REVIEW

Problem 1

Uhuru Industrial Products purchased equipment on January 2, 2017, for $176,000. The expected life of the equipment is 10 years, or 100,000 units of production, and its residual value is $16,000. Management has amortized the equipment using the DDB method. On July 2, 2019, Uhuru sold the equipment for $100,000 cash.

Required

Record Uhuru Industrial Products' amortization for 2019 using the DDB method and the sale of the equipment on July 2, 2019.

Problem 2

Meben Logistics purchased a building at a cost of $500,000 on January 2, 2013. Meben has amortized the building by using the straight-line method, a 35-year useful life, and a residual value of $150,000. On January 2, 2017, the business changed the useful life of the building from 35 years to 25 years from the date of purchase. The fiscal year of Meben Logistics ends on December 31.

Required

Record amortization for 2017 assuming no change in the building's residual value.

SOLUTIONS

Problem 1

	Double Declining Balance		
Year	Annual Amortization Expense	Accumulated Amortization	Book Value
Start			$176,000
2017	$35,200	$ 35,200	140,800
2018	28,160	63,360	112,640
2019	22,528	85,888	90,112

2019			
Jul. 2	Amortization Expense—Equipment	11,264	
	Accumulated Amortization—Equipment		11,264
	To record amortization expense for the period Jan. 1, 2019, to Jun. 30, 2019. ($112,640 × 0.20* × $^1/_2$)		
Jul. 2	Cash	100,000	
	Accumulated Amortization—Equipment**	74,624	
	Loss on Sale of Equipment	1,376	
	Equipment		176,000
	To record sale of equipment.		

*10-year amortization using DDB = 1/10 × 2, or 0.20
**$35,200 + $28,160 + $11,264 = $74,624.

Amortization expense must first be recorded for the portion of the year that the asset was used before it was sold.

If Cash > Book value, then record a gain on disposal.

If Cash < Book value, then record a loss on disposal.

Problem 2

The equation for revised straight-line amortization is:

$$\text{Revised straight-line amortization} = \frac{\text{Cost + Betterments − Accumulated amortization − New residual value}}{\text{Estimated remaining useful life in years}}$$

Notice that these solutions are rounded to the nearest dollar. This is commonly done, but please check with your instructor to see if rounding to two decimal places is more appropriate for your course.

Calculating estimated remaining useful life in years can cause confusion. In this case, the expected useful life changed from 35 years to 25 years. Since amortization has already been expensed for the first four years, 21 years remain in the building's new 25-year useful life.

Cost = $500,000 (given)

Betterments = $0 (given)

Accumulated amortization = [($500,000 − $150,000) ÷ 35 years] × 4 years
= $40,000

New residual value = $150,000 (the same as old residual value)

Estimated remaining useful life in years = 25 − 4 = 21 years

Therefore,

$$\text{Revised straight-line amortization} = \frac{\$500,000 + \$0 - \$40,000 - \$150,000}{21 \text{ years}} = \$14,762 \text{ per year, rounded}$$

2017			
Dec. 31	Amortization Expense—Building	14,762	
	Accumulated Amortization—Building		14,762
	To record annual amortization for 2017.		

SUMMARY

LEARNING OBJECTIVE ① Measure the cost of property, plant, and equipment

What are property, plant, and equipment (PPE), and how do we measure their cost? Pg. 560

- Property, plant, and equipment (PPE) are tangible, long-lived assets that the business uses in its operations.
  - The cost is the purchase price plus applicable provincial taxes (but not GST or HST), purchase commissions, and all other necessary amounts incurred to acquire the asset and to prepare it for its intended use.
  - Capitalize only those costs that add to the asset's usefulness or its useful life.
  - Expense all other costs as maintenance or repairs.

LEARNING OBJECTIVE ② Calculate and account for amortization

How do we calculate and account for amortization? Pg. 565

- Straight-line method:

$$\text{Straight-line amortization} = \frac{\text{Cost} - \text{Residual value}}{\text{Useful life in years}}$$

- Units-of-production (UOP) method:

$$\text{Units-of-production amortization per unit of output} = \frac{\text{Cost} - \text{Residual value}}{\text{Useful life in units of production}}$$

- Double-declining-balance (DDB) method:

$$\text{DDB amortization} = \text{Asset book value} \times \text{DDB rate}$$

- Use the method that best matches amortization expense against the revenues produced by the asset.

LEARNING OBJECTIVE **3** Account for other issues: Amortization for income tax purposes, partial years, and revised assumptions

How do we account for other amortization issues? **Pg. 571**
- Amortization for financial statement purposes and income tax purposes often differs. This is both legal and ethical.
- CRA allows companies and individuals to claim capital cost allowance (CCA) against taxable income.
- When assets are purchased or sold during the year, calculate partial-year amortization.
- When significant changes occur to an asset's cost, residual value, or useful life, annual amortization expense must be revised for all future years to reflect the changes.

$$\text{Revised straight-line amortization} = \frac{\text{Cost + Betterments} - \text{Accumulated amortization} - \text{New residual value}}{\text{Estimated remaining useful life in years}}$$

MyAccountingLab **Interactive Figure:** Interact with Straight-Line Depreciation (Amortization)
Interactive Figure: Interact with Revised Depreciation (Amortization)

LEARNING OBJECTIVE **4** Account for the disposal of property, plant, and equipment

How do we account for the disposal of PPE? **Pg. 573**
- When disposing of PPE, always follow these three steps:
  1. Update amortization to date of sale, disposal, or trade.
  2. Calculate the gain or loss on disposal and report the gain or loss on the income statement.
  3. Remove the book balances from the asset account and its related accumulated amortization account.

LEARNING OBJECTIVE **5** Account for natural resources

How do we account for natural resources? **Pg. 577**
- Natural resources are expensed through amortization (depletion) on a UOP basis.

LEARNING OBJECTIVE **6** Account for intangible assets and goodwill

How do we account for intangible assets and goodwill? **Pg. 578**
- Intangible assets are assets that have no physical form.
  - They give their owners a special right to current and expected future benefits.
  - The major types of intangible assets are patents, copyrights, trademarks, franchises, leaseholds, and licences.
  - Amortization is computed on a straight-line basis over the lesser of the legal life or the useful life.
  - Goodwill is not amortized, but its carrying value is assessed annually and written down if its market value is less than its carrying value.

MyAccountingLab **Video:** Real World Accounting

LEARNING OBJECTIVE **7** Describe the impact of IFRS on property, plant, and equipment, intangible assets, and goodwill

How does IFRS apply to PPE, intangible assets, and goodwill? **Pg. 582**
- ASPE and IFRS are converged in many aspects, but there are a few differences:
  - Under IFRS, each part of an item of PPE that is significant relative to the total cost of the asset must be amortized separately. This is known as componentization.
  - IFRS allows fair market valuation of PPE assets at each balance sheet date subsequent to acquisition if the company so chooses. Depreciation is then revised.
  - ASPE and IFRS allow impairment assessment each year, but under IFRS assets may be looked at individually or they can be divided into cash generating units (CGUs).
  - IFRS allows assets that were written down to have the impairment reversed in a future period, while this is not possible under ASPE.
  - Under IFRS, internally generated intangible assets can be capitalized and amortized if they will provide a future benefit to the company.

Check **Accounting Vocabulary** on page 586 for all key terms used in Chapter 10 and the **Glossary** at the back of the book for all key terms used in the textbook.

ACCOUNTING VOCABULARY

Amortizable cost   The asset's cost minus its estimated residual value (p. 566).

Amortization   The systematic charging of the cost of a capital asset. It is often called depletion when applied to natural resources. The term is also used to describe the writing off to expense of capital assets (p. 565).

Amortization rate   The amount of amortization written off to expense stated as a percentage (p. 567).

Amortization schedule   A table or chart that shows the amortization expense and asset values by period (p. 567).

Appraisal   An expert assessment of the value of an asset (p. 563).

Arrears   A legal term for debt that is overdue because of at least one missed payment (p. 560).

Asset retirement obligation   A liability that records the future cost to settle a present obligation, such as future removal and site restoration costs (p. 578).

Betterment   An expenditure that increases the capacity or efficiency of an asset or extends its useful life. Capital expenditures are debited to an asset account (p. 563).

Brand name   A distinctive identification of a product or service (p. 579).

Capital cost allowance (CCA)   Amortization allowed for income tax purposes by the Canada Revenue Agency; the rates allowed are called capital cost allowance rates (p. 571).

Capitalize   To record as an asset (p. 561).

Cash generating unit (CGU)   Under IFRS, the smallest identifiable group of assets that generates cash flows that are largely independent of the cash flows from other assets (p. 582).

Commercial substance   In an exchange of tangible capital assets, commercial substance exists when an entity's future cash flows from the new asset received will differ in risk, timing, or amount from the cash flows from the old asset given up (p. 576).

Componentization   Under IFRS, recording each identifiable component of an asset separately to calculate depreciation on each part (p. 582).

Copyright   The exclusive right to reproduce and sell software, a book, a musical composition, a film, or other creative work. Issued by the federal government, copyrights extend 50 years beyond the creator's life (p. 579).

DDB rate   Double-declining-balance percentage applied to an asset to calculate its amortization or depreciation. It is twice the straight-line amortization rate (p. 568).

Depletion   Another word to describe the amortization of natural resources or wasting assets (p. 577).

Derecognize   Under IFRS, to remove an asset from the accounting records because it has been replaced (p. 582).

Double-declining-balance (DDB) method   A type of amortization method that expenses a relatively larger amount of an asset's cost nearer the start of its useful life than does the straight-line method (p. 568).

Estimated residual value   The expected cash value of an asset at the end of its useful life. Also called *residual value*, *scrap value*, or *salvage value* (p. 566).

Estimated useful life   Length of the service that a business expects to get from an asset; may be expressed in years, units of output, kilometres, or other measures (p. 566).

Franchise   Privileges granted by a private business or a government to sell a product or service in accordance with specified conditions (p. 580).

Goodwill   Excess of the cost of an acquired company over the sum of the market values of its net assets (assets minus liabilities) (p. 580).

Half-year rule   The Canada Revenue Agency allows businesses to claim only 50 percent of the normal CCA rate in the year an asset is acquired (p. 571).

Identifiable tangible asset   An asset that is physical—it can be seen and touched—and can be separated from other assets; used to describe property, plant, and equipment (p. 560).

Impaired   When the fair value falls below the carrying value in the accounting records (p. 581).

Intangible asset   An asset with no physical form that conveys a special right to current and expected future benefits (p. 578).

Intellectual capital   The knowledge of the people who work in a business (p. 579).

Junked   Discarded (p. 573).

Leasehold   A right arising from a prepayment that a lessee (tenant) makes to secure the use of an asset from a lessor (landlord) (p. 580).

Leasehold improvements   Changes to a leased asset that are amortized over the term of the lease or the useful life of the asset, whichever is shorter (p. 580).

Licence   Privileges granted by a private business or a government to sell a product or service in accordance with special conditions (p. 580).

Patent   A federal government grant giving the holder the exclusive right for 20 years to produce and sell an invention (p. 579).

Prospectively   In the future (p. 572).

Relative-fair-value method The allocation of the cost of assets according to their fair market value *(p. 563)*.

Repair An expenditure that merely maintains an asset in its existing condition or restores the asset to good working order. Repairs are expensed (matched against revenue) *(p. 563)*.

Revaluation method Under IFRS, when an asset's value is restated in the accounting records to reflect the asset's current market value *(p. 582)*.

Straight-line method An amortization method in which an equal amount of amortization expense is assigned to each year (or period) of asset use *(p. 566)*.

Trademark Distinctive identifications of a product or service. Also called *trade name (p. 579)*.

Trade name Another term for trademark *(p. 579)*.

Units-of-production (UOP) method An amortization method by which a fixed amount of amortization is assigned to each unit of output produced by the capital asset *(p. 568)*.

SIMILAR ACCOUNTING TERMS

Amortization	Depreciation (for assets such as property, plant, and equipment); Depletion (for natural resources)
Book value	Carrying value
Brand name	Trade mark; Trade name
CCA	Capital cost allowance
CGU	Cash generating unit
CRA	Canada Revenue Agency
DDB	Double-declining-balance method of amortization
Fair value	Market value
Junked	Scrapped
Natural resources	Wasting assets
PPE	Property, plant, and equipment
Property, plant, and equipment	Long-lived assets; Long-term assets; Capital assets
Residual value	Salvage value; Scrap value
Trade name	Brand name, trademark
UOP	Units-of-production method of amortization

SELF-STUDY QUESTIONS

Test your understanding of the chapter by marking the correct answer for each of the following questions:

1. Which of the following payments is *not* included in the cost of land? *(p. 560)*
   a. Removal of old building
   b. Legal fees
   c. Property taxes in arrears paid at acquisition
   d. Cost of fencing and lighting

2. Niall Home Builders plans to build a custom home. In the first quarter, they spent the following amounts:

Land purchase	$70,000
Surveys and legal fees	2,800
Land clearing	3,000
Install fences around the property	3,100
Install lighting and signage	400

   What amount should be recorded as the land cost? *(p. 561)*

   a. $78,900
   b. $76,200
   c. $75,800
   d. $79,300

3. Willard Windows paid $150,000 for two machines valued at $120,000 and $60,000. Willard will record these machines at costs of *(p. 563)*
   a. $120,000 and $60,000
   b. $75,000 each
   c. $100,000 and $50,000
   d. $90,000 and $60,000

4. Which of the following items is a repair? *(p. 563)*
   a. New brakes for delivery truck
   b. Paving of a company parking lot
   c. Cost of a new engine for a truck
   d. Building permit paid to construct an addition to an existing building

5. Which of the following definitions fits amortization? *(p. 565)*
   a. Allocation of the asset's market value to expense over its useful life
   b. Allocation of the asset's cost to expense over its useful life
   c. Decreases in the asset's market value over its useful life
   d. Increases in the fund set aside to replace the asset when it is worn out

6. Which amortization method's amounts are not computed based on time? (*p. 566*)
   a. Straight line
   b. Units of production (UOP)
   c. Double declining balance (DDB)
   d. All are based on time

7. Which amortization method gives the greatest amount of expense in the early years of using the asset? (*pp. 568–569*)
   a. Straight line
   b. Units of production
   c. Double declining balance
   d. All are equal

8. A company paid $900,000 for a building and was amortizing it by the straight-line method over a 40-year life, with estimated residual value of $60,000. After 10 years it became evident that the building's *remaining* useful life would be 40 years with a residual value of $50,000. Amortization for the 12th year is (*p. 567*)

a. $16,000	b. $17,250
c. $21,000	d. $28,000

9. PEI Products scrapped a delivery truck that cost $28,000 and had a book value of $2,500. The entry to record this disposal is (*p. 574*)

   a. Loss on Disposal of Truck 2,500
         Delivery Truck   2,500
   b. Accumulated Amortization 28,000
         Delivery Truck   28,000
   c. Accumulated Amortization 25,500
         Delivery Truck   25,500
   d. Accumulated Amortization 25,500
         Loss on Disposal of Truck 2,500
           Delivery Truck   28,000

10. Amortization of a natural resource is computed in the same manner as which amortization method? (*p. 577*)
    a. Straight line
    b. UOP
    c. Double declining balance
    d. CCA

11. On March 1, 2016, Gregor Goldfields purchased a mineral deposit for $400,000 that is expected to be in operation for 10 years. A geological report estimated the mineral deposit contained 125,000 tonnes of gold. Management expects the asset to have a zero residual value when fully amortized. During 2016, 34,000 tonnes of gold were mined. What is the amount of amortization expense at the company's year end, December 31, 2016? (*p. 577*)
    a. $33,333
    b. $40,000
    c. $75,000
    d. $108,800

12. Vasdev Company paid $1,100,000 to acquire Gentech Systems. Gentech's assets had a market value of $1,800,000 and its liabilities were $800,000. In recording the acquisition, Vasdev will record goodwill of (*p. 580*)
    a. $100,000
    b. $1,000,000
    c. $1,100,000
    d. $0

ASSIGNMENT MATERIAL

QUESTIONS

1. Describe how to measure the cost of property, plant, and equipment. Would an ordinary cost of repairing the asset after it is placed in service be included in the asset's cost?

2. Suppose land with a building on it is purchased for $1,050,000. How do you account for the $65,000 cost of removing this unwanted building?

3. When assets are purchased as a group for a single price and no individual asset cost is given, how is each asset's cost determined?

4. Distinguish a betterment from a repair. Why are they treated differently for accounting purposes?

5. Define amortization. What are common misconceptions about amortization?

6. To what types of assets does amortization expense apply under ASPE?

7. Which amortization method does each of the graphs at the bottom of the page characterize: straight line, UOP, or DDB?

8. Explain the concept of accelerated amortization. Which of the three amortization methods results in the most amortization in the first year of the asset's life?

9. The level of business activity fluctuates widely for Orillia Schoolbus Co., reaching its slowest time in July and August each year. At other times, business is brisk. What amortization method is most appropriate for the company's fleet of school buses? Why?

10. Shania Data Centre uses the most advanced computers available to keep a competitive edge over other data service centres. To maintain this advantage, the company usually replaces its computers before they are worn out. Describe the major factors affecting the useful life of a property, plant, and equipment asset, and indicate which seems more relevant to this company's computers.

11. Which amortization method does not consider estimated residual value in computing amortization during the early years of the asset's life?

12. What is capital cost allowance (CCA)?

13. Does amortization affect income taxes? How does amortization affect cash provided by operations?

14. Describe how to compute amortization for less than a full year and how to account for amortization for less than a full month.

15. Hudson Company paid $25,000 for office furniture. The company expected it to remain in service for six years and to have a $1,000 residual value. After two years' use, company accountants believe the furniture will last for the next seven years. How much amortization

will Hudson record for each of these last seven years, assuming straight-line amortization and no change in the estimated residual value? (Round your answer to the nearest dollar.)

16. When a company sells property, plant, and equipment before the year's end, what must it record before accounting for the sale?

17. Describe how to determine whether a company experiences a gain or a loss when an existing piece of equipment is exchanged for a new piece of equipment.

18. What expense applies to natural resources? By which amortization method is this expense computed?

19. How do intangible assets differ from most other assets? Why are they assets at all? What expense applies to intangible assets?

20. Why is the cost of patents and other intangible assets often expensed over a shorter period than the legal life of the asset?

21. Your company has just purchased another company for $1,000,000. The market value of the other company's net assets is $700,000. What is the $300,000 excess called? What type of asset is it? How is this asset amortized under ASPE?

22. Woodstock Industrial Products Inc. is recognized as a world leader in the manufacture of industrial products. The company's success has created vast amounts of business goodwill. Would you expect to see this goodwill reported on Woodstock's financial statements? Why, or why not?

23. To which types of assets does amortization expense apply under IFRS?

24. Under IFRS, companies need to calculate amortization separately for the major components of an amortizable asset. Does this provide better information for the users of financial information?

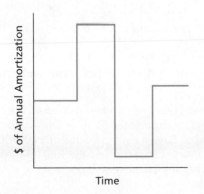

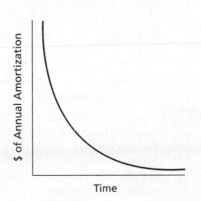

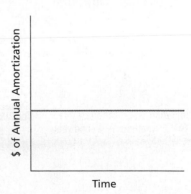

STARTERS

Starter 10–1 This chapter lists the costs included for the acquisition of land. First is the purchase price of the land, which is obviously included in the cost of the land. The reasons for including the other costs are not so obvious. For example, the removal of a building looks more like an expense. State why the costs listed are included as part of the cost of the land. After the land is ready for use, will these costs be capitalized or expensed?

Starter 10–2 Wishbone Landscapers bought land, a building, and equipment for a lump sum of $550,000. Following are the appraised fair market values of the newly acquired assets: Land $97,500, Building $390,000, and Equipment $162,500. Calculate the cost of each asset to be reported on the balance sheet.

Starter 10–3 Suppose you make a lump-sum purchase of land, building, and equipment on April 30. At the time of your purchase, the land has a current market value of $240,000, the building's market value is $350,000, and the equipment's market value is $175,000. Journalize the lump-sum purchase of the three assets for a total cost of $680,000. You sign a note payable for this amount.

Starter 10–4 FlyFast Airways repaired one of its Boeing 767 aircraft at a cost of $600,000, which FlyFast paid in cash. FlyFast erroneously capitalized this cost as part of the cost of the plane. How will this accounting error affect FlyFast's net income? Ignore amortization.

Starter 10–5 Give the amortization method(s) described by the following statements:

a. Amortization Expense declines over the life of the asset
b. Book value declines over the life of the asset
c. Amortization expense fluctuates with use
d. Amortization expense is the same each period
e. This method best fits an asset that amortizes because of physical use
f. This method best fits an asset that generates revenue evenly each period
g. This method is the most common
h. This method records the most amortization over the life of the asset

Starter 10–6 At the beginning of 2017, FlyFast Airways purchased a used Boeing jet at a cost of $50,000,000. FlyFast expects the plane to remain useful for five years (6,000,000 miles) and to have a residual value of $4,000,000. FlyFast expects the plane to be flown 750,000 miles the first year. (Note: "Miles" is the unit of measure used in the airline industry.)

1. Compute FlyFast's first-year amortization on the jet using the following methods:
   a. Straight line   b. UOP   c. DDB
2. Show the jet's book value at the end of the first year under the straight-line method.

Starter 10–7 At the beginning of 2017, FlyFast Airways purchased a used Boeing aircraft at a cost of $50,000,000. FlyFast expects the plane to remain useful for five years (6,000,000 miles) and to have a residual value of $4,000,000. FlyFast expects the plane to be flown 750,000 miles the first year and 500,000 miles the second year. Compute second-year amortization on the plane using the following methods:

a. Straight line   b. UOP   c. DDB

Starter 10–8 This exercise uses the FlyFast Airways data from Starter 10–6. FlyFast is comparing the CCA method used for income tax purposes with the straight-line amortization method.

1. Calculate the amount of CCA, at a rate of 25 percent, that FlyFast will be able to claim in its first year.
2. Why does the Government of Canada, through the CCA, regulate the amount of amortization that a company can claim for income tax purposes?

Starter 10-9 On March 31, 2017, JetHapppy Airways purchased a used Boeing jet at a cost of $40,000,000. JetHappy expects to fly the plane for six years and expects it to have a residual value of $4,000,000. Compute JetHappy's amortization on the plane for the year ended December 31, 2017, using the straight-line method.

Partial-year amortization
③

Starter 10-10 Assume the Goldeyes Baseball Club paid $60,000 for a hot dog stand with a 10-year useful life and no residual value. After using the hot dog stand for four years, the club determines that the asset will remain useful for only two more years. Record amortization on the hot dog stand for Year 5 on December 31. The company uses the straight-line method for amortizing assets.

Computing and recording amortization after a change in useful life
③

Starter 10-11 Red Pine Printers purchased equipment on January 1, 2013, for $250,000. The estimated residual value is $25,000 and the estimated useful life is 15 years. Red Pine Printers uses the straight-line method for amortization of its equipment. On January 1, 2016, Red Pine Printers revised the useful life to be nine more years rather than 12. How much amortization would be recorded on December 31, 2016?

Revised amortization
③
2016, $20,000

Starter 10-12 A fully amortized asset has a cost of $100,000 and zero residual value.
1. What is the asset's accumulated amortization? What is its carrying value?
2. The asset cost $100,000. Now suppose its residual value is $10,000. How much is its accumulated amortization if it is fully amortized?

Using fully amortized assets
③

Starter 10-13 Return to the Kawartha Dairy delivery truck example in Exhibits 10-4 and 10-5 on pages 566-567. Suppose Kawartha Dairy sold the truck on December 31, 2019, for $31,000 cash after using the truck for three full years. Amortization for 2019 has already been recorded. Make the journal entry to record Kawartha Dairy's sale of the truck under straight-line amortization.

Recording a gain or loss on disposal
④
Gain on sale, $2,000

Starter 10-14 In 2015, Global Millwrights purchased a milling machine for $4,000, debiting Milling Equipment. During 2015 and 2016, Global recorded total amortization of $2,000 on the machine. In January 2017, Global traded in the machine for a new one with a fair market value of $4,200, paying $2,700 cash. This exchange transaction has commercial substance. Journalize Global Millwrights' exchange of machines on January 15.

Exchanging property, plant, and equipment assets
④
Loss on exchange, $500

Starter 10-15 Suppose Quik Trip Stores' comparative income statement for two years included these items (dollars in thousands):

Understanding a gain/loss on the sale of PPE
④

	2017	2016
Net sales	$7,200	$6,800
Income from operations	49	65
Gain on sale of store facilities	28	—
Income before income taxes	$ 77	$ 65

Which was the better year for Quik Trip: 2017 or 2016? Explain.

Starter 10-16 EnCana, the giant oil company, holds huge reserves of oil and gas assets. Assume that at the end of 2017 EnCana's cost of oil and gas assets totalled approximately $18 billion, representing 2.4 billion barrels of oil and gas reserves in the ground.
1. Which amortization method does EnCana use to compute its annual amortization expense for the oil and gas removed from the ground?
2. Suppose EnCana removed 0.8 billion barrels of oil during 2017. Record EnCana's amortization expense for 2017.

Accounting for the amortization of natural resources
⑤
2. Amortization Expense, $6.0 billion

Accounting for goodwill

⑥

1. Goodwill, $200,000

Starter 10–17 Media-related companies have little in the way of property, plant, and equipment. Instead, their main asset is goodwill. When one media company buys another, goodwill is often the most costly asset acquired. Assume that Media Watch paid $800,000 on March 22 to acquire *The Thrifty Dime*, a weekly advertising paper. At the time of the acquisition, *The Thrifty Dime's* balance sheet reported total assets of $1,300,000 and liabilities of $600,000. The fair market value of *The Thrifty Dime's* assets was $1,200,000.

1. How much goodwill did Media Watch purchase as part of the acquisition of *The Thrifty Dime*?
2. Journalize Media Watch's acquisition of *The Thrifty Dime*.

Accounting for a patent

⑥

$4,500

Starter 10–18 Blue Consultants purchased a patent at a cost of $45,000 on June 30, 2016. It is estimated that the patent has a remaining useful life of five years in spite of the fact that it will expire in seven years from the date of purchase. Record the amortization for the December 31, 2016, year end.

Accounting for patents and for research and development cost

⑥

Net income, $700,000

Starter 10–19 InnoTech Applications paid $1,300,000 in research costs for a new software program. InnoTech also paid $1,000,000 to acquire a patent on other software. After readying the software for production, InnoTech's sales revenue for the first year totalled $3,400,000. Cost of goods sold was $400,000, and selling expenses were $800,000. All of these transactions occurred during 2017. InnoTech expects the patent to have a useful life of five years. Prepare InnoTech Applications' single-step income statement for the year ended December 31, 2017, complete with a heading.

Componentization

⑦

Starter 10–20 Under IFRS, companies need to calculate amortization separately for the major components of an amortizable asset. Does this provide better information for the users of financial information? Why or why not?

Internally generated assets under IFRS

⑦

Starter 10–21 Suppose your publicly traded company has developed a process that will make the manufacture of a product more efficient and will streamline costs. The only costs associated with this internally generated patent are the legal costs of registering the patent. Your company immediately sells the patent to another publicly traded company for about 100 times the cost of the patent. How would your company value the patent before it is sold? How will the acquiring company record the acquisition of the patent?

EXERCISES

MyAccountingLab

Exercise 10–1

Determining the cost of property, plant, and equipment

①

Land, $375,000

The accounting firm of Smith Schoefield, CPAs purchased land, paying $350,000 cash. In addition, the company paid property tax in arrears of $3,000, a legal fee of $1,500, and a $20,500 charge for levelling the land and removing an unwanted building. The company constructed an office building on the land at a cost of $1,200,000. It also paid $30,000 for a fence around the boundary of the property, $8,500 for the company sign near the entrance to the property, and $11,500 for special lighting of the grounds. During installation of the fence, $2,000 of damage to the fence was incurred. Determine the cost of the company's land, land improvements, and building.

Exercise 10–2

Allocating cost to assets acquired in a lump-sum purchase

①

Truck 1, $21,600

India Trucking bought three used trucks for $60,000. An independent appraisal of the trucks produced the following figures:

Truck No.	Appraised Value
1	$24,000
2	22,000
3	20,000

India Trucking paid $21,000 in cash and signed a note for the remainder. Record the purchase in the general journal on February 1 identifying each truck's individual cost in a separate Truck account.

Exercise 10–3

Classify each of the following expenditures related to the cost of a machine:

Measuring the cost of an asset, distinguishing betterments from repairs

	Cost or Betterment	Repair or Expense	Other
a. Purchase price			
b. Provincial sales tax paid on the purchase price			
c. Transportation and insurance while the machine is in transport from seller to buyer			
d. Installation			
e. Training of personnel for initial operation of the machine			
f. Special reinforcement to the machine platform			
g. Income tax paid on income earned from the sale of products manufactured by the machine			
h. Major overhaul to extend the machine's useful life by three years			
i. Ordinary recurring repairs to keep the machine in good working order			
j. Lubrication before the machine is placed in service			
k. Periodic lubrication after the machine is placed in service			
l. GST on the purchase price			

Exercise 10–4

Firestone Shoes is a family-owned retail shoe operation with two stores. Assume that early in Year 1 Firestone Shoes purchased computerized point-of-sale and operating systems costing $150,000. Bob Firestone expects this equipment will support the inventory and accounting requirements for four years. Because of technology obsolescence, no residual value is anticipated. Through error, Firestone Shoes accidentally expensed the entire cost of the equipment at the time of the purchase. Firestone Shoes' accounting policy for equipment amortization is the straight-line amortization method. The company is operated as a sole proprietorship, so it pays no corporate income tax.

Capitalizing versus expensing, measuring the effect of an error

Required

Compute the overstatement or understatement in these accounts immediately after purchasing the equipment:

1. Equipment
2. Net income

Exercise 10–5

On January 1, 2017, Murray Demolition, a Hamilton, Ontario, company specializing in blasting and removing buildings, purchased and took delivery of a new dump truck to add to its growing fleet. Murray Demolition has a high-class reputation and uses only the best and newest equipment on their worksites. The business spent $140,000 plus HST on the truck, which is expected to be useful to the business for four years, at which time it should be able to be sold for $60,000. Murray Demolition has always used the straight-line basis of calculating amortization. The new owners want to see the amortization schedules for the straight-line, UOP, and DDB methods just to be sure this makes sense. The business expects the truck to be useful for 200,000 kilometres—60,000 kilometres in Year 1, 50,000 kilometres in each of Years 2 and 3, and 40,000 kilometres in Year 4.

Calculate amortization three ways

Exercise 10–6

Zhang Machine & Dye bought a machine on January 2, 2017, for $460,000. The machine was expected to remain in service for three years and produce 2,000,000 parts. At the end of its useful life, company officials estimated that, due to technological changes, the machine's residual value would only be $10,000. The machine produced 700,000 parts in the first year, 660,000 in the second year, and 650,000 in the third year.

Required

1. Prepare a schedule of *amortization expense* per year for the machine using the straight-line, UOP, and DDB amortization methods. Assume that in all cases the machine is valued at $10,000 at the end of the third year, and the third-year amortization is adjusted (set as a plug) to ensure this happens.

2. Which amortization method results in the highest net income in the second year? Does this higher net income mean the machine was used more efficiently under this method?

3. Which method tracks the wear and tear on the machine most closely? Why?

4. After one year under the DDB method, the company switched to the straight-line method. Prepare a schedule of amortization expense for this situation, showing all calculations.

Exercise 10–7

On January 1, 2015, SCI Marketing bought a company car for $20,000. It has estimated residual value of $2,000 and an estimated useful life of five years. The company uses double-declining-balance amortization. Prepare an amortization schedule for the car using Exhibit 10-7 as a guide.

Exercise 10–8

In 2016, Maxwell Inc. paid $625,000 for equipment that is expected to have a five-year life. In this industry, the residual value is estimated to be 5 percent of the asset's cost. Maxwell Inc. plans to use straight-line amortization for accounting purposes. For income tax purposes, Maxwell chooses to use the maximum CCA rate of 20 percent and is subject to the half-year rule in 2016. The half-year rule allows only half the normal CCA to be claimed in the year of purchase.

Required

1. Calculate the amortization expense in 2016 and 2017 for accounting and tax purposes.

2. Why does the federal government regulate the amount of amortization a company can deduct when calculating income for income tax purposes?

Exercise 10–9

Jacoby Legal Services purchased land and a building for $1,100,000. The land had a fair value of $300,000 and the building $800,000. The building was amortized on a straight-line basis over a 50-year period. The estimated residual value was $50,000. After using the building for 20 years, the company realized that wear and tear on the building would force the company to replace it before 50 years. Starting with the 21st year, the company began amortizing the building over a revised *total* life of 40 years with zero residual value. Record amortization expense on the building for years 20 and 21.

Exercise 10–10

On January 13, 2016, Yeung's Gifts purchased store fixtures for $65,000 cash, expecting the fixtures to remain in service for 10 years. Yeung's Gifts has amortized the fixtures on a DDB basis with an estimated residual value of $5,000. On September 30, 2017, Yeung's Gifts sold the fixtures for $19,150 cash because they were not "green" technology. Record the amortization expense on the fixtures for the years ended December 31, 2016, and 2017, and the sale of the fixtures on September 30, 2017. Round all calculations to the nearest dollar.

Exercise 10–11

Prepare journal entries for the following transactions. Explanations are not required.

Purchase and sale of assets
(2) (4)
Loss on sale, $2,200

2016

Jan.	1	Purchased a bulldozer for $64,000 cash, $4,000 residual value, 20-year expected life, double-declining-balance amortization.
May	1	Purchased office furniture for $15,000 cash, $3,000 residual value, 10-year expected life, straight-line amortization.
Dec.	31	Recorded amortization on the bulldozer and furniture.

2017

| June | 30 | Sold the furniture for $11,000 cash. (Record amortization to date for 2017 before selling the furniture.) |
| Dec. | 31 | Recorded amortization on the bulldozer. |

Exercise 10–12

Measuring the cost of property, plant, and equipment using UOP amortization, trading in a used asset
(1) (2) (4)
Gain on exchange of trucks, $123,000

Triad Freight is a large warehousing and distribution company that operates throughout Eastern Canada. Triad Freight uses the UOP method to amortize its trucks because its managers believe UOP amortization best measures the wear and tear on the trucks. Triad Freight trades in used trucks often to keep driver morale high and to maximize fuel efficiency. Consider these facts about one Mack truck in the company's fleet:

When acquired in 2013, the tractor/trailer rig cost $585,000 and was expected to remain in service for eight years, or 1,500,000 kilometres. Estimated residual value was $60,000. The truck was driven 150,000 kilometres in 2014, 195,000 kilometres in 2015, and 235,000 kilometres in 2016. After 100,000 kilometres in 2017, the company traded in the Mack truck for a Freightliner rig with a fair market value of $510,000 on August 15. Triad Freight paid cash of $40,000. This trade-in will bring in significantly more income to Triad Freight by reducing operating costs. Determine Triad Freight's cost of the new truck. Prepare the journal entry to record the trade-in.

Exercise 10–13

Recording natural resources and amortization
(5)
c. Amortization Expense, $212,550

Beau Lac Mining Ltd. paid $900,000 for the right to extract ore from a 300,000-tonne mineral deposit. In addition to the purchase price, the company also paid a $1,000 filing fee, a $5,000 licence fee to the province of Quebec, and $75,000 for a geological survey. Because Beau Lac Mining Ltd. purchased the rights to the minerals only, the company expected the asset to have zero residual value when fully depleted. During the first year of production, the company removed 65,000 tonnes of ore. Make general journal entries to record (a) purchase of the mineral rights (debit Mineral Asset) on January 1, 2017; (b) payment of fees and other costs on January 1, 2017; and (c) amortization for first-year production as at December 31, 2017.

Exercise 10–14

Recording intangibles, amortization, and a change in the asset's useful life
(3) (6)
3. Amortization for Year 3, $420,000

Biikman Company manufactures flat screen monitors for the graphics industry and has recently purchased for $525,000 a patent for the design of a new monitor. Although it gives legal protection for 20 years, the patent is expected to provide Biikman Company with a competitive advantage for only 10 years. After using the patent for two years, Biikman Company learns at an industry trade show that another company is designing a more effective monitor. Based on this new information, Biikman Company decides to amortize the remaining cost of the patent over the current year, giving the patent a total useful life of three years.

Required

1. Prepare the journal entry to record the purchase of the patent.
2. Assume straight-line amortization is used. Record the journal entry for amortization in Year 1.
3. Record amortization for Year 3.

Exercise 10–15

Measuring goodwill

⑥

2. Goodwill, $12 million

Bolton Industries acquired companies with assets with a market value of $45 million and liabilities of $30 million. Bolton paid $27 million for these acquisitions during the year ended December 31, 2017.

Required

1. How would a value be assigned to the net assets acquired?
2. What value would be assigned to goodwill?
3. Will the goodwill be amortized? If so, by how much?

Exercise 10–16

Accounting for goodwill

⑥

1. Goodwill, $22,900

The financial statements of Niall's Foods for the year ended December 31, 2016, reported the following details of acquisitions (adapted):

	In thousands
Assets:	
Cash	$ 3,400
Accounts receivable	8,400
Equipment	72,000
Intangibles	700
	$84,500
Liabilities:	
Long-term debt	$16,400

Niall's Foods paid $91,000 cash for the acquisitions. Assume that the book value of the assets is equal to their fair value.

Required

1. How much goodwill did Niall's Foods purchase as part of the 2016 acquisitions?
2. Prepare the summary journal entry to record the acquisition at December 31, 2016.
3. Assume that, in 2017, the annual review of goodwill at December 31 identified a 15 percent impairment of the goodwill acquired in 2016. Prepare the journal entry required to record this impairment.

Exercise 10–17

Computing and recording goodwill

⑥

1. Goodwill, $700,000

In 2017, Camden Electronics purchased Raytheon Electronics, paying $2.0 million in a note payable. The market value of Raytheon Electronics' assets was $3.1 million, and Raytheon Electronics had liabilities of $1.8 million.

Required

1. Compute the cost of the goodwill purchased by Camden Electronics.
2. Record the purchase by Camden Electronics.
3. At 2017 year end, the annual review of goodwill value indicated no impairment of goodwill. Record the entry Camden will make for goodwill at December 31, 2017.
4. At 2018 year end, the annual review of goodwill value indicated a 40 percent impairment of the Raytheon Electronics goodwill. Record the entry for the goodwill impairment at December 31, 2018.

Exercise 10–18

IFRS depreciation calculation

⑦

Under IFRS, components of an asset may have different depreciation methods. Prime Printers Ltd. shows the following information about its special printing unit for banners on a spreadsheet that tracks its assets:

Banner Printer					
Component	Purchase Date	Cost	Estimated Residual	Depreciation Method	Estimated Life
Monitor	Jan. 1, 2017	$ 1,800	$ 0	Straight line	4 years
Base Unit	Jan. 1, 2017	75,000	5,000	UOP	200,000 copies
CPU	Jan. 1, 2017	4,700	200	Straight line	3 years
Printer trays	Jan. 1, 2017	15,000	2,000	Straight line	10 years
		96,500			

Required Compute depreciation for the banner printer for the year ended December 31, 2017. Assume that 17,000 copies were made during the year.

Exercise 10–19

IFRS terms and concepts

Note 1 of the notes to the financial statements (page 58) of the Loblaw 2013 Annual Report reads as follows:

> For the purpose of impairment testing, assets are grouped together into the smallest group of assets that generate cash inflows from continuing use that are largely independent of cash inflows of other assets or groups of assets. This grouping is referred to as a cash generating unit ("CGU"). The Company has determined that each location is a separate CGU for purposes of impairment testing.

Required

1. What is the "cash generating unit" for Loblaw?
2. How is this different from when the company followed the previous Canadian GAAP rules, which were similar to those described in this chapter?

SERIAL EXERCISE

This exercise continues the Lee Management Consulting situation from earlier chapters. If you did not complete any Serial Exercises in earlier chapters, you can still complete Exercise 10–20 as it is presented.

Exercise 10–20

In Chapter 2, on page 98, we learned that Lee Management Consulting had paid $1,000 cash for a Dell computer on June 3, 2016. The computer is expected to be useful for four years. On June 4, 2016, Lee Management Consulting purchased office furniture on account for $5,000. The furniture was expected to last for five years. Looking back through his records, Michael Lee sees that he recorded $42 of amortization for the equipment and $167 of amortization for the furniture in June. Both assets are assumed to have no residual value at the end of their useful life. Lee is not sure how this was calculated, so he needs some help figuring out the entry required for July 31, 2016.

Computing and journalizing amortization

1. July 2016 Amortization Expense—Furniture, $167

Required

1. Calculate the amount of amortization for each asset for the month ended July 31, 2016, under the straight-line and double-declining-balance methods in order to figure out what method is being used for the journal entries. Round only the total amounts to the nearest dollar.
2. Which method results in the highest expense?
3. Is the method that results in the highest expense used? What reason would Michael Lee use to justify the choice of method?
4. Journalize the entry to record the amortization expense to July 31, 2016, using the double-declining-balance method results. Use a compound entry.

5. If in December it was learned that the furniture's estimated useful life is really not correct and it should actually last an additional six years from now, what would the December 31, 2016 journal entry look like? Assume all amortization was recorded up to November 30. Round only the journal entry to the nearest dollar.

CHALLENGE EXERCISE

Exercise 10–21

Reconstructing transactions from the financial statements

② ④

1. $118,000

Great Lake Furniture Limited's 2017 financial statements reported these amounts (in thousands of dollars):

| | December 31 | | | |
| | 2017 | | 2016 | |
	Cost	Accumulated Amortization	Cost	Accumulated Amortization
Land	$ 41,378	—	$ 35,073	—
Buildings	116,832	$ 51,566	105,325	$ 46,981
Equipment	17,940	11,712	16,575	10,678
Vehicles	13,994	11,533	13,513	10,680
Computer hardware and software	6,869	4,335	5,885	3,614
Leasehold improvements	26,178	7,461	21,081	6,220
	$223,191	$ 86,607	$197,452	$ 78,173
Net book value		$136,584		$119,279

In the 2017 annual report, Great Lake Furniture Limited reported amortization expense of $8,552,000. In addition, the company reported it had disposed of certain property, plant, and equipment assets and acquired others. The gain on disposal of property, plant, and equipment was $56,000.

Required

1. What was the accumulated amortization of the assets disposed of during 2017?
2. Assume that Great Lake Furniture Limited acquired assets costing $27,681,000 during 2017. What was the cost price of the assets sold during the year?
3. Write the journal entry to record the disposal of the property, plant, and equipment during the year.

BEYOND THE NUMBERS

Beyond the Numbers 10–1

The following questions are unrelated except that they apply to property, plant, and equipment:

1. Julian Lyon, the owner of Lyon's Actuarial Services, regularly debits the cost of repairs and maintenance of amortizable assets to Property, Plant, and Equipment. Why would he do that, since he knows he is violating ASPE?
2. It has been suggested that, since many intangible assets have no value except to the company that owns them, they should be valued at $1 or zero on the balance sheet. Many accountants disagree with this view. Which view do you support? Why?
3. Jasmine Singh, the owner of Lakeshore Motors, regularly buys property, plant, and equipment and debits the cost to Repairs and Maintenance Expense. Why would she do that, since she knows this action violates ASPE?

ETHICAL ISSUE

Canam Group Developers purchased land and a building for a lump sum of $8.0 million. To get the maximum tax deduction, Canam's owner allocated 85 percent of the purchase price to the building and only 15 percent to the land. A more realistic allocation would have been 75 percent to the building and 25 percent to the land.

Required

1. Explain the tax advantage of allocating too much to the building and too little to the land.
2. Was Canam Group Developers' allocation ethical? If so, state why. If not, why not? Identify who was harmed.

PROBLEMS (GROUP A)   MyAccountingLab

Problem 10–1A

The board of directors of Mabel's Montessori is having its regular quarterly meeting. Accounting policies are on the agenda, and amortization is being discussed. Marcia Goodwin, a new board member, has some strong opinions about two aspects of amortization policy. She argues that amortization must be coupled with a fund to replace company assets. Otherwise, she argues, there is no substance to amortization. Goodwin also challenges the five-year estimated life over which Mabel's Montessori is amortizing the centre's computers. She notes that the computers will last much longer and should be amortized over at least 10 years.

Required Write a paragraph or two to explain the concept of amortization to Goodwin and to answer her arguments.

Explaining the concept of amortization

Problem 10–2A

On January 5, 2017, Paige Construction purchased a used crane at a total cost of $200,000. Before placing the crane in service, Paige spent $12,500 transporting it, $4,800 replacing parts, and $11,400 overhauling the engine. Karen Paige, the owner, estimates that the crane will remain in service for four years and have a residual value of $42,000. The crane's annual usage is expected to be 2,400 hours in each of the first three years and 2,200 hours in the fourth year. In trying to decide which amortization method to use, Mary Blundon, the accountant, requests an amortization schedule for each of the following generally accepted amortization methods: straight line, UOP, and DDB.

Excel Spreadsheet Template
Computing amortization by three methods

1. Book value, Dec. 31, 2019: Straight line $88,675; UOP $85,696; DDB $42,000

Required

1. Assuming Paige Construction amortizes this crane individually, prepare an amortization schedule for each of the three amortization methods listed, showing asset cost, amortization expense, accumulated amortization, and asset book value. Assume a December 31 year end.
2. Paige Construction prepares financial statements for its bankers using the amortization method that maximizes reported income in the early years of asset use. Identify the amortization method that meets the company's objective.

Problem 10–3A

Stefano Distributors incurred the following costs in acquiring land and a building, making land improvements, and constructing and furnishing an office building for its own use:

Identifying the elements of property, plant, and equipment's cost; partial-year amortization
2. Amortization Expense: Land Improvements, $5,333 Office Building, $28,771

a. Purchase price of 2 hectares of land, including an old building that will be used for storage of maintenance equipment (land appraised market value is $1,300,000; building appraised market value is $300,000)	$1,150,000
b. Real estate taxes in arrears on the land to be paid by Stefano Distributors	6,000

c.	Additional dirt and earth moving	6,000
d.	Legal fees on the land acquisition	4,500
e.	Fence around the boundary of the land	70,000
f.	Building permit for the office building	1,000
g.	Architect fee for the design of the office building	40,000
h.	Company signs near front and rear approaches to the company property	14,000
i.	Renovation of the storage building	150,000
j.	Concrete, wood, steel girders, and other materials used in the construction of the office building	700,000
k.	Masonry, carpentry, roofing, and other labour to construct the office building	550,000
l.	Parking lots and concrete walks on the property	31,500
m.	Lights for the parking lot, walkways, and company signs	12,500
n.	Salary of construction supervisor (90 percent to office building and 10 percent to storage building)	100,000
o.	Office furniture for the office building	125,000
p.	Transportation of furniture from seller to the office building	2,000

Stefano Distributors amortizes buildings over 40 years, land improvements over 20 years, and furniture over 6 years, all on a straight-line basis with zero residual value.

Required

1. Set up columns (or T-accounts) for Land, Land Improvements, Office Building, Storage Building, and Furniture. Show how to account for each of Stefano's costs by listing the cost under the correct account. Determine the total cost of each asset.

2. Assuming that all construction was complete and the assets were placed in service on February 25, record amortization for the year ended December 31. Round figures to the nearest dollar.

Problem 10–4A

Recording property, plant, and equipment transactions; exchanges; changes in useful life
① ② ③ ④

Dec. 31, 2017, Amortization Expense—Buildings, $700,000

Accurate Research surveys Canadian opinions. The company's balance sheet reports the following assets under Property, Plant, and Equipment: Land, Buildings, Office Furniture, Communication Equipment, and Video Equipment. The company has a separate Accumulated Amortization account for each of these assets except land. Assume that the company completed the following transactions during 2017:

Feb.	2	Traded in communication equipment with a book value of $26,000 (cost of $202,000) for similar new equipment with a fair market value of $196,000. The seller gave Accurate a trade-in allowance of $36,000 on the old equipment, and the company paid the remainder in cash. This transaction meets the criteria for commercial substance.
Jul.	19	Sold a building that had cost $1,050,000 and had accumulated amortization of $740,000 through December 31, 2016. Amortization is computed on a straight-line basis. The building has a 30-year useful life and a residual value of $90,000. Accurate received $150,000 cash and a $1,300,000 note receivable.
Oct.	21	Purchased used communication and video equipment from the A.C. Neilsen Company of Canada Ltd. Total cost was $200,000 paid in cash. An independent appraisal valued the communication equipment at $170,000 and the video equipment at $80,000.
Dec.	31	Equipment is amortized by the DDB method over a six-year life. Amortization on the equipment purchased on February 2 and on October 21 is recorded separately.

600 **Part 2** Accounting for Assets and Liabilities

Amortization on buildings is computed by the straight-line method. The company had assigned buildings an estimated useful life of 30 years and a residual value that is 30 percent of cost. After using the buildings for 10 years, the company has come to believe that their *total* useful life will be 20 years. Residual value remains unchanged. The buildings cost $15,000,000. Amortization for the year must be recorded.

Required   Record the transactions in the journal of Accurate Research.

Problem 10–5A

Assume that Rees Warehousing completed the following transactions:

Journalizing property, plant, and equipment transactions; asset exchanges; betterments versus repairs
① ② ③ ④
Dec. 31, 2017, Amortization Expense, $3,600

2016

Mar.	3	Paid $8,000 cash for a used forklift.
	5	Paid $1,500 to have the forklift engine overhauled.
	7	Paid $1,000 to have the forklift modified for specialized moving of large flat-screen televisions.
Nov.	3	Paid $550 for an oil change and regular maintenance.
Dec.	31	Used the DDB method to record amortization on the forklift. (Assume a three-year life and no residual value.)

2017

Feb.	13	Replaced the forklift's broken fork for $400 cash, the deductible on Rees Warehousing's insurance. The new fork will not increase the useful life of the forklift.
Jul.	10	Traded in the forklift for a new forklift costing $18,000. The dealer granted a $3,000 allowance on the old forklift, and Rees Warehousing paid the balance in cash. Recorded 2017 amortization for the year to date and then recorded the exchange of forklifts. This transaction has commercial substance.
Dec.	31	Used the DDB method to record amortization on the new forklift. (Assume a five-year life and no residual value.)

Rees Warehousing's amortization policy indicates that the company will take a full month's amortization on purchases occurring up to and on the 15th day of the month and will not take any amortization for the month if the transaction occurs after the 15th day of the month.

Required   Record the transactions in the general journal, indicating whether each transaction amount should be capitalized as an asset or expensed. Round all calculations to the nearest dollar.

Problem 10–6A

Pride Parts Co. has a fiscal year ending December 31. The company completed the following selected transactions:

Identifying the elements of property, plant, and equipment's cost; accounting for amortization by two methods; accounting for disposal of property, plant, and equipment; distinguishing betterments from repairs
① ② ③ ④
2. Total Property, Plant, and Equipment, $590,727

2016

July   2   Paid $640,000 plus $20,000 in legal fees (pertaining to all assets purchased) to purchase the following assets from a competitor that was going out of business:

Asset	Appraised Value	Estimated Useful Life	Estimated Residual Value
Land	$360,000	—	—
Buildings	240,000	8 years	$20,000
Equipment	120,000	3 years	2,000

Pride Parts Co. plans to use the straight-line amortization method for the building and for the equipment.

Sep.	2	Purchased a delivery truck with a list price of $39,000 for $36,000 cash. The truck is expected to be used for three years and driven a total of 280,000 kilometres; it is then expected to be sold for $4,000. It will be amortized using the UOP method.
	3	Paid $3,000 to paint the truck with the company's colours and logo.
Dec.	31	Recorded amortization on the assets. The truck had been driven 20,000 kilometres since it was purchased.
2017		
May	4	Pride Parts Co. paid $11,000 to Gill Services Ltd. for work done on the equipment. The job consisted of annual maintenance ($1,200) and the addition of automatic controls ($9,800) that allow the equipment to remain useful for the next five years and increases its expected residual value by $1,000.
Nov.	25	Sold the truck for $23,600. The truck had an odometer reading of 140,000 kilometres.
Dec.	31	Recorded amortization on the assets.

Required

1. Record the above transactions of Pride Parts Co. Round all amounts to the nearest dollar.
2. Show the balance sheet presentation of the assets at December 31, 2017.

Problem 10–7A

Accounting for natural resources

 (5)

Amortization Expense, $994,975

Oilco Canada Limited sells refined petroleum products. The company's balance sheet includes reserves of oil assets.

Suppose Oilco paid $15 million cash for an oil lease that contained an estimated reserve of 1,990,000 barrels of oil. Assume that the company paid $550,000 for additional geological tests of the property and $170,000 to prepare the surface for drilling. Prior to production, the company signed a $120,000 note payable to have a building constructed on the property. Because the building provides onsite headquarters for the drilling effort and will be abandoned when the oil is depleted, its cost is debited to the Oil Properties account and included in amortization charges. During the first year of production, Oilco removed 125,000 barrels of oil, which it sold on credit for $75 per barrel.

Required

1. Make general journal entries to record all transactions related to the oil and gas property, including amortization and sale of the first-year production. Dates are not required.
2. Show the accounts and amounts that would be presented on the balance sheet.

Problem 10–8A

Accounting for intangibles and goodwill (6)

Part 1 CTS Canada provides telephone service to most of Canada. Assume that CTS Canada purchased another company that had the following totals on its financial statements:

Book value of assets	$1,536,000
Market value of assets	1,800,000
Liabilities	540,000

Required

1. Make the general journal entry to record CTS Canada's purchase of the other company for $1,620,000 cash on April 3.
2. How should CTS Canada account for goodwill at year end and in the future? Explain in detail.

Part 2 Suppose BlackBerry Ltd. purchased a patent for $1,400,000 on January 1. Before using the patent, BlackBerry incurred an additional cost of $250,000 for a lawsuit to defend the company's right to purchase it. Even though the patent gives BlackBerry legal protection for 20 years, company management has decided to amortize its cost over an 8-year period because of the industry's fast-changing technologies.

Required

1. Make general journal entries to record the patent transactions, including straight-line amortization for one year at December 31.

2. Show the accounts and amounts that would be presented on the balance sheet.

PROBLEMS (GROUP B)   MyAccountingLab

Problem 10–1B

The board of directors of Mauger Real Estate Ltd. is reviewing the 2017 annual report. A new board member, a dermatologist with little business experience, questions the company accountant about the amortization amounts. The dermatologist wonders why amortization expense has decreased from $250,000 in 2015, to $230,000 in 2016, to $215,000 in 2017. He states that he could understand the decreasing annual amounts if the company had been disposing of properties each year, but that has not occurred. Further, he notes that growth in the city is increasing the values of company properties. Why is the company recording amortization when the property values are increasing?

Explaining the concept of amortization
②

Required   Write a short response to explain the concept of amortization to the dermatologist and to answer his questions.

Problem 10–2B

On January 5, 2017, Priestly Corp. paid $438,000 for equipment used in manufacturing computer equipment. In addition to the basic purchase price, the business paid $2,200 transportation charges, $600 insurance for the goods in transit, $35,200 provincial sales tax, and $20,000 for a special platform on which to place the equipment in the plant. Priestly Corp.'s owner estimates that the equipment will remain in service for four years and have a residual value of $10,000. The equipment will produce 85,000 units in the first year, with annual production decreasing by 10,000 units during each of the next three years (that is, 75,000 units in Year 2, 65,000 units in Year 3, and so on). In trying to decide which amortization method to use, owner Janice Priestly has requested an amortization schedule for each of three generally accepted amortization methods: straight line, UOP, and DDB.

Excel Spreadsheet Template
Computing amortization by three methods
②

Required

1. For each of the amortization methods listed above, prepare an amortization schedule showing asset cost, amortization expense, accumulated amortization, and asset book value. Assume a December 31 year end.

2. Priestly Corp. prepares financial statements for its creditors using the amortization method that maximizes reported income in the early years of asset use. Identify the amortization method that meets the business's objective.

Problem 10–3B

The owner of Cheetle Moving and Storage incurred the following costs in acquiring land, making land improvements, and constructing and furnishing the company's office building in the year ended December 31, 2017:

Identifying the elements of property, plant, and equipment's cost
① ② ③

a. Purchase price of 4 hectares of land, including an old building that will be used for a garage (land appraised market value is $450,000; building appraised market value is $50,000)	$ 400,000
b. Additional dirt and earth moving	8,000
c. Fence around the boundary of the land	25,000
d. Legal fee for title search on the land	2,000
e. Real estate taxes in arrears on the land to be paid by Cheetle Moving and Storage	4,800
f. Company signs at front of the company property	4,000
g. Building permit for the office building	2,000
h. Architect fee for the design of the office building	75,000

i.	Masonry, carpentry, roofing, and other labour to construct office building	850,000
j.	Concrete, wood, steel girders, and other materials used in the construction of the office building	650,000
k.	Renovation of the garage	30,000
l.	Flowers and plants	15,000
m.	Parking lot and concrete walks on the property	48,500
n.	Lights for the parking lot, walkways, and company signs	14,500
o.	Salary of construction supervisor (95 percent to office building and 5 percent to garage renovation)	100,000
p.	Office furniture for the office building	160,000
q.	Transportation and installation of office furniture	2,500

Cheetle Moving and Storage amortizes buildings over 35 years, land improvements over 15 years, and furniture over 5 years, all on a straight-line basis with zero residual value.

Required

1. Set up columns for Land, Land Improvements, Office Building, Garage Building, and Furniture. Show how to account for each of Cheetle Moving and Storage's costs by listing the cost under the correct account. Determine the total cost of each asset.

2. Assuming that all construction was complete and the assets were placed in service on June 30, record amortization for the year ending December 31, 2017. Round figures to the nearest dollar.

Problem 10–4B

Recording property, plant, and equipment transactions; exchanges; changes in useful life
① ② ③ ④

Belkin Freight provides general freight service in Canada. The business's balance sheet includes the following assets under Property, Plant, and Equipment: Land, Buildings, and Motor Carrier Equipment. Belkin Freight has a separate accumulated amortization account for each of these assets except land.

Assume that Belkin Freight completed the following transactions during 2017:

Feb. 6 Traded in motor carrier equipment with a book value of $86,000 (cost of $280,000) for similar new equipment with a fair market value of $330,000. Belkin Freight received a trade-in allowance of $120,000 on the old equipment and paid the remainder in cash. This transaction met the criteria for commercial substance.

Jun. 3 Sold a building that had cost $1,250,000 and had accumulated amortization of $577,500 through December 31, 2016. Amortization is computed on a straight-line basis. The building has a 40-year useful life and a residual value of $150,000. Belkin Freight received $300,000 cash and a $1,000,000 note receivable.

Sep. 25 Purchased land and a building for cash for a single price of $790,000. An independent appraisal valued the land at $250,000 and the building at $375,000.

Dec. 31 Motor carrier equipment has an expected useful life of four years and an estimated residual value of 6 percent of cost. Amortization is computed using the DDB method.

Amortization on buildings is computed by the straight-line method. The company had assigned to its older buildings, which cost $3,900,000, an estimated useful life of 30 years with a residual value equal to 30 percent of the asset cost. However, the owner of Belkin Freight has come to believe that the buildings will remain useful for a total of 35 years. Residual value remains unchanged. The company has used all its buildings, except for the one purchased on September 25, for 10 years. The new building carries a 35-year useful life and a residual value equal to 30 percent of its cost. Make separate entries for amortization on the building acquired on September 25 and the other buildings purchased in earlier years.

Required Record the transactions in Belkin Freight's general journal.

Problem 10–5B

Assume that Luxury Limousines completed the following transactions:

Journalizing property, plant, and equipment transactions; betterments versus repairs
①②③④

2016

Jan.	5	Paid $40,000 cash for a used limousine.
	6	Paid $4,000 to have the engine overhauled.
	9	Paid $1,500 to repair damage to the limousine as it sat in the parking lot.
Jun.	15	Paid $600 for a minor tune-up after the limousine was put into use.
Dec.	31	Recorded amortization on the limousine by the DDB method. (Assume a five-year life.)

2017

Mar.	9	Traded in the limousine for a new limousine costing $75,000. The dealer granted a $25,000 allowance on the old limousine, and the company paid the balance in cash. Recorded year 2017 amortization for the year to date and then recorded the exchange of the limousines. This transaction has commercial substance.
Aug.	9	Repaired the new limousine's damaged fender for $2,500 cash.
Dec.	31	Recorded amortization on the new limousine by the DDB method. (Assume an eight-year life and a residual value of $20,000.)

Luxury Limousines' amortization policy states that the company will take a full month's amortization on purchases occurring up to and on the 15th day of the month and will not take any amortization for the month if the purchase occurs after the 15th day of the month.

Required Record the transactions in the general journal, indicating whether each transaction amount should be capitalized as an asset or expensed. Round all calculations to the nearest dollar.

Problem 10–6B

Megatron Inc owns a television station in the interior of British Columbia. Its year end is June 30. The company completed the following transactions:

Identifying the elements of property, plant, and equipment's cost; accounting for amortization by two methods; accounting for disposal of property, plant, and equipment; distinguishing betterments from repairs
①②③④

2017

Apr.	1	Paid $2,175,000 plus $75,000 in legal fees (pertaining to all assets purchased) to purchase the following assets from a competitor that was going out of business:

Asset	Appraised Value	Estimated Useful Life	Estimated Residual Value
Land	$600,000	—	—
Buildings	960,000	30 years	$120,000
Equipment	840,000	5 years	80,000

Megatron Inc. plans to use the straight-line amortization method for the building and for the equipment.

May	1	Purchased a mobile broadcast unit truck with a list price of $295,000 for $245,000 cash. It is expected that the truck will be used for seven years and driven a total of 200,000 kilometres; it is then expected to be sold for $55,000. It will be amortized using the UOP method.
	3	Paid $10,000 to paint the truck with the station's colours and logo.
Jun.	30	Recorded amortization on the assets. The mobile unit had been driven 12,500 kilometres since it was purchased.
Dec.	30	Megatron Inc. paid $25,500 to Maxwell Maintenance for work done on the equipment. The job consisted of annual maintenance ($1,500) and the addition of automatic controls ($24,000) that allow the equipment to remain useful for another six years and increase its expected residual value by $10,000.

2018

Jun.	1	Sold the mobile unit truck for $200,000. The truck had an odometer reading of 82,000 kilometres.
	30	Recorded amortization on the assets.

Required

1. Record the above transactions of Megatron Inc. Round all amounts to the nearest dollar.

2. Show the balance sheet presentation of the assets at June 30, 2018.

Problem 10–7B

Accounting for natural resources
⑤

Kitkan Inc. is a global producer and marketer of rolled aluminum products.

Suppose Kitkan Inc. paid $4.4 million cash for a lease giving the firm the right to work a mine that contained an estimated 400,000 tonnes of bauxite. Assume that the company paid $30,000 to remove unwanted buildings from the land and $130,000 to prepare the surface for mining. Further assume that Kitkan Inc. signed a $140,000 note payable to a landscaping company to return the land surface to its original condition after the lease ends. During the first year, Kitkan Inc. removed 37,000 tonnes of bauxite, which it sold on account for $40 per tonne.

Required

1. Make general journal entries to record all transactions related to the bauxite, including amortization and sale of the first year's production.

2. Show the accounts and amounts that would be presented on the balance sheet.

Problem 10–8B

Accounting for goodwill and intangibles
⑥

Part 1 The Roasted Bean Ltd. operates franchised coffee shops. Assume that The Roasted Bean Ltd. purchased another company that carried these figures:

Book value of assets	$3.6 million
Market value of assets	4.4 million
Liabilities	2.2 million

Required

1. Make the general journal entry to record The Roasted Bean Ltd.'s purchase of the other company for $2.5 million cash on March 31.

2. How should The Roasted Bean Ltd. account for goodwill at year end and in the future? Explain in detail.

Part 2 Suppose Susan McMillan purchased a Roasted Bean franchise licence for $250,000 on January 1. In addition to the basic purchase price, McMillan also paid a lawyer $8,000 for assistance with the negotiations. McMillan believes the appropriate amortization period for the cost of the franchise licence is 10 years.

Required

1. Make general journal entries to record the franchise transactions, including straight-line amortization for one year at December 31.

2. Show the accounts and amounts that would be presented on the balance sheet.

CHALLENGE PROBLEMS

Problem 10–1C

Understanding amortization and betterments and repairs
① ②

The owner of newly formed Lake of the Woods Air Taxi, a friend of your family, knows you are taking an accounting course and asks for some advice. Mr. Linden tells you that he is pretty good at running the company but doesn't understand accounting. Specifically, he has two concerns:

1. The company has just paid $400,000 for two used float planes. His accountants tell him that he should use accelerated amortization for his financial statements, but he understands that straight-line amortization will result in lower charges to expense in the early years. He wants to use straight-line amortization.

2. A friend told him that Lake of the Woods Air Taxi should capitalize all repairs to the planes and "spread the cost out over the life of the planes." He wonders if there is anything wrong with this advice.

Required   Respond to Mr. Linden's questions using your understanding of amortization and betterments and repairs.

Problem 10–2C

Due to a computer crash, some accounting data were corrupted at Ace Industries. For the Furniture account, only some of the data were still accessible. The balance in the Accumulated Amortization—Furniture account was $75,000. The furniture had been amortized a total of 60 percent of its original cost. Prior notes indicate that the double-declining-balance method was used for all furniture. The estimated useful life was eight years, and its residual value is expected to be 20 percent of its original cost.

Required   Determine the age of the furniture to the nearest month.

Solve for missing information
③

Problem 10–3C

Courtnell Mining Corp. is a new company that has been formed to mine for nickel in Northern Ontario. The ore body is estimated to contain 100,000 tonnes of pure nickel for which the world price is $15,000 per tonne. The costs of mine development are estimated to be $80,000,000.

Required   Calculate the costs that would be charged against the nickel production in the form of amortization on a per-tonne basis. Estimate any costs you think should also be included. Do not include the costs to mine and refine the ore, or shipping and selling costs.

Accounting for natural resources
⑤

EXTENDING YOUR KNOWLEDGE

DECISION PROBLEM

Suppose you are considering investing in two businesses, Zastre Associates and Chen Co. The two companies are virtually identical, and both began operations at the beginning of 2017. During the year, each company purchased inventory as follows:

Jan.	10	12,000	units at $ 7 =	$ 84,000
Mar.	11	5,000	units at $ 9 =	45,000
Jul.	9	10,000	units at $10 =	100,000
Oct.	12	12,000	units at $11 =	132,000
Totals		39,000		$361,000

During 2017, both companies sold 30,000 units of inventory.

In early January 2017, both companies purchased equipment costing $400,000 that had a five-year estimated useful life and a $40,000 residual value. Zastre Associates uses

Measuring profitability based on different inventory and amortization methods
②
1. Net income: Zastre Associates, $116,000

the first-in, first-out (FIFO) method for its inventory and straight-line amortization for its equipment. Chen Co. uses the weighted-average method for inventory and DDB amortization. Both companies' trial balances at December 31, 2017, included the following:

Sales revenue	$560,000
Operating expenses (excluding amortization expense)	110,000

Required

1. Prepare both companies' income statements.
2. Write an investment newsletter to address the following questions for your clients: Which company appears to be more profitable? Which company will have more cash to invest in promising projects? Which company would you prefer to invest in? Why?

FINANCIAL STATEMENT CASES

Financial Statement Case 1

Property, plant, and equipment and intangible assets ② ④ ⑥

Refer to Indigo Books & Music Inc.'s financial statements in Appendix A at the end of this book and on MyAccountingLab to answer the following questions:

1. With respect to PPE, which amortization/depreciation method does Indigo use for the purpose of reporting to shareholders and creditors in the financial statements? What rates are used, and where did you find your answer?
2. What was the total amount of depreciation expense for 2014 as shown in Note 8?
3. Indigo lists intangible assets on the balance sheet. Where do you find more information about them? What types of intangible assets does Indigo have?
4. Note 4, "Significant Accounting Policies" in the notes to the financial statements includes the subsection "Impairment Testing." Explain the meaning of this subsection, and give an example of when it is used.

Financial Statement Case 2

Property, plant, and equipment and intangible assets ② ④ ⑥

2. Amortization expense 2013, $423,000,000

Refer to the financial statements of TELUS Corporation on MyAccountingLab to answer the following questions:

1. Which amortization method does TELUS use for property, plant, and equipment for the purpose of reporting to shareholders and creditors in the financial statements? What rates are used? Where did you find your answer?
2. What were the total amounts of depreciation and amortization expense for fiscal 2013? For fiscal 2012?
3. According to Note 16, how much was spent on network assets (additions) during 2013?
4. What types of intangible assets does TELUS have listed on the 2013 financial statements?

IFRS MINI-CASE

Based on the information from the Air Canada 2015 Annual Report shown below, identify differences between the accounting for PPE using IFRS (used by Air Canada) and ASPE (as shown in the chapter). Create a chart, and list each asset and its accounting treatment.

Summary of Significant Accounting Policies—Section T, Property and Equipment

Property and equipment is recognized using the cost model. . . . The Corporation allocates the amount initially recognized in respect of an item of property and equipment to its significant components and depreciates separately each component. Property and equipment are depreciated to estimated residual values based on the straight-line method over their estimated service lives. Aircraft and flight equipment are componentized into airframe, engine, and cabin interior equipment and modifications. Airframes and engines are depreciated over 20 to 25 years, with 10% to 20% estimated residual values. Spare engines and related parts ("rotables") are depreciated over the average remaining useful life of the fleet to which they relate with 10% to 20% estimated residual values. Cabin interior equipment and modifications to aircraft on operating leases are amortized over the term of the lease. Major maintenance of airframes and engines, including replacement spares and parts, labour costs, and/or third party maintenance service costs, are capitalized and amortized over the average expected life between major maintenance events.

Major maintenance events typically consist of more complex inspections and servicing of the aircraft.

>Try It! SOLUTIONS FOR CHAPTER 10

1. Include (a) installation charges and (b) testing of the machine in the cost of machinery because these costs are incurred to bring the machine to its intended purpose. However, do not include (c) repair to machinery necessitated by installer's error and (d) first-year maintenance cost because they maintain the asset once it is put in to use.

2.

Asset	Fair Value	Percentage of Total Value	Record as Cost
Land	$108,000	$108,000 ÷ $720,000 − 15.0% × $600,000	= $ 90,000
Building	432,000	$432,000 ÷ $720,000 = 60.0% × $600,000	= 360,000
Equipment	180,000	$180,000 ÷ $720,000 = 25.0% × $600,000	= 150,000
Total	$720,000	100.0%	$600,000

3. a. Installing new tires on a cement truck—repair
   b. Repainting a delivery truck that was damaged in an accident—repair
   c. Replacing the motor in a delivery truck—betterment
   d. Installing an elevating device in a delivery truck—betterment
   e. Safety test on a delivery truck when the licence is renewed—repair
   f. Installing carrying racks on the roof of the delivery truck—betterment

4. a. One approach is to look for patterns in the annual amortization expenses for each method, then check your guesses by calculating the expenses using the data given. Equal annual expenses indicate the straight-line method. A random pattern indicates the units of production method. Declining annual expenses indicate the double-declining-balance method.

   Method A: Straight-line method
   Amortizable cost = $160,000 ($176,000 − $16,000)
   Each year: $160,000 ÷ 10 years = $16,000

   Method B: Double-declining-balance method
   Rate = 100% ÷ 10 years = 10%; 10% × 2 = 20%
   2017: 0.20 × $176,000 = $35,200
   2018: 0.20 × ($176,000 − $35,200) = $28,160

   Method C: Units-of-production method
   Calculating the number of units for 2017 and 2018 is not necessary, but it helps you prepare for the calculation you'll make in Requirement b.

   Amortization per unit = ($176,000 − $16,000) ÷ 100,000 units = $1.60
   2017: $1.60 × 3,000 units = $4,800 (since $4,800 ÷ $1.60 = 3,000 units)
   2018: $1.60 × 14,000 units = $22,400 (since $22,400 ÷ $1.60 = 14,000 units)

4. b. Use the amortization rates calculated in Requirement a for the 2019 computations.

Method A		
Straight-Line Method		
Year	Annual Amortization Expense	Accumulated Amortization	Book Value
---	---	---	---
Start			$176,000
2017	$16,000	$16,000	160,000
2018	16,000	32,000	144,000
2019	16,000	48,000	128,000

Method B		
Double-Declining-Balance Method		
Year	Annual Amortization Expense	Accumulated Amortization	Book Value
---	---	---	---
Start			$176,000
2017	$35,200	$35,200	140,800
2018	28,160	63,360	112,640
2019	22,528	85,888	90,112

Method C		
Units-of-Production Method		
Year	Annual Amortization Expense	Accumulated Amortization	Book Value
---	---	---	---
Start			$176,000
2017	$ 4,800	$ 4,800	171,200
2018	22,400	27,200	148,800
2019	19,200	46,400	129,600

Computations for 2019:

Straight line:	$160,000 ÷ 10 years = $16,000	
Double declining balance:	0.20 × $112,640 = $22,528	
Units of production:	$1.60 × 12,000 units = $19,200	

5. a. Straight-line: ($65,000 − $5,000) ÷ 4 years = $15,000 per year
For 8 months (May–December 2017), $15,000 × 8/12 = $10,000

  b. Units-of-production: ($65,000 − $5,000) ÷ 600 hours = $100 per hour
For the period April 17–December 31, 2017, 130 hours × $100/hour = $13,000

  c. Double-declining-balance: Amortization rate = 2 × 25% = 50%
50% × $65,000 = $32,500 for full first year
For 8 months (May–December 2017), $32,500 × 8/12 = $21,667

6. Calculate the new book value:

Cost ($800,000 old + $200,000 new addition)	$1,000,000
Less: Accumulated amortization (20 years × $18,750/year*)	375,000
Revised book value	$ 625,000

Revised straight-line amortization:
= ($625,000 − $100,000**) ÷ 20
= $26,250 per year

*($800,000 − $50,000) ÷ 40 years = $18,750 per year amortization
**$50,000 old residual value + $50,000 additional residual value = $100,000

7. a. First take amortization for 2017. Annual amortization is ($58,500 − 4,500) ÷ 6 = $9,000 per year.

Cash received from selling the equipment:	$43,000
Book value of the equipment:	
Cost	$ 58,500
Less: Accumulated amortization at sale date (3 years × $9,000/year)	27,000 31,500
Gain on sale of equipment	$11,500

2017

Dec. 29	Cash	43,000	
	Accumulated Amortization— Equipment	27,000	
	Equipment		58,500
	Gain on Sale of Equipment		11,500
	To record the sale of equipment.		

b. First take amortization for 2017. Annual amortization is ($58,500 − 4,500) ÷ 6 = $9,000 per year.

Cash received from selling the equipment:	$23,000
Book value of the equipment:	
Cost	58,500
Less: Accumulated amortization at sale date (3 years × $9,000/year)	27,000 31,500
Gain (loss) on sale of equipment	($8,500)

2017

Dec. 29	Cash	23,000	
	Accumulated Amortization— Equipment	27,000	
	Loss on Sale of Equipment	8,500	
	Equipment		58,500
	To record the sale of equipment.		

8.

2017

Jan. 2	Catering Equipment (new)	2,900	
	Accumulated Amortization—Catering Equipment (old)	2,200	
	Loss on Sale of Catering Equipment	900	
	Catering Equipment (old)		3,100
	Cash		2,900
	To record the exchange of catering equipment.		

9. The amount of amortization expense to be recorded is:

$$\frac{\text{Cost} - \text{Residual value}}{\text{Estimated total units}} \times \text{Number of units produced}$$
= ($600,000 ÷ 400,000 fbm) × 200,000 fbm
= $1.50/fbm × 200,000 fbm
= $300,000

10. a.

2017

Jan. 5	Patent	650,000	
	Cash		650,000
	To record the purchase of a patent with an expected useful life of five years.		

2017

Dec. 31	Amortization Expense—Patent	130,000	
	Patent		130,000
	To record one year's amortization of patent ($650,000 ÷ 5 = $130,000).		

b.

2017			
May 13	Patent	650,000	
	Cash		650,000
	To record the purchase of a patent with an expected useful life of five years		

2017			
Dec. 31	Amortization Expense—Patent	86,667	
	Patent		86,667
	To record 2017 partial-year amortization of patent ($650,000 ÷ 5 = $130,000; $130,000 × 8/12 = $86,667).		

11.

Assets (all assets acquired, at market value)	400,000	
Goodwill	1,900,000	
Liabilities		300,000
Cash		2,000,000
To record purchase of Novel Networks.		

11 CURRENT LIABILITIES AND PAYROLL

CONNECTING CHAPTER 11

MyAccountingLab   The **Summary** for Chapter 11 appears on page 644. This lists all of the MyAccountingLab resources.
Accounting Vocabulary with definitions for this chapter's material appears on page 646.

Safari Condo is a Canadian innovator in the recreational vehicle (RV) market. They build both motorhomes and travel trailers. The picture here shows their Alto R series model with a retractable roof. It is a small, all-aluminum travel trailer made from recyclable materials that is aerodynamic and lightweight. It is designed so that it can be towed by vehicles that are smaller in size than what is typically required to pull a travel trailer.

Even though their product is unique, their accounting isn't. RV manufacturers have many of the same current liabilities as other businesses. They owe money to suppliers for goods and services provided, to the government for payroll and sales taxes, and they likely have loans outstanding.

In addition, manufacturers may have some liabilities they must estimate. RV manufacturers offer warranties on their products—a guarantee for a period of time that specific problems with their product will be fixed. But because Safari Condo does not know for certain if there will even be any warranty claims, how do they record a liability for an unknown amount? They make an *estimate* based on their own experience and the experience of others in their industry. Safari Condo might use the information found supplied by Warranty Week to estimate an amount for warranty expense. How much is reasonable? According to a study of American RV companies,[1] 1.7 percent of revenues is a reasonable estimate. Is this the right amount for Safari Condo to use in their accounting records? Given that they have high construction standards and use aluminum, they may record a different amount.

This chapter will look at how companies like Safari Condo record known liabilities and those that must be estimated.

[1] Warranty Week, "New Home & RV Warranty Report," May 21, 2015, www.warrantyweek.com/archive/ww20150521.html.

> Current

liabilities are obligations due within one year or within the company's operating cycle if it is longer than one year. Obligations due beyond that period of time are *long-term liabilities*. We discussed current liabilities and long-term liabilities in Chapter 4, page 191. Showing current liabilities separate from long-term liabilities is important for users of financial statements. If current liabilities are not recorded correctly (or worse, not recorded at all), this would affect the decisions made by users thinking of investing in a company. In this chapter we will see how companies account for their current liabilities, which include product warranties, accounts payable, sales taxes, and payroll, among others. Exhibit 11–12 on page 641 shows how they are presented in a balance sheet.

CURRENT LIABILITIES OF A KNOWN AMOUNT

LO 1

What are current liabilities and how do we account for them?

The amounts of most current liabilities are known. A few current liabilities must be estimated. Let's begin with current liabilities of known amount.

Accounts Payable

Amounts owed for products or services that are purchased on account are *accounts payable*. Because they are typically due in 30 days, they are current liabilities. We have seen many accounts payable examples in previous chapters. Accounts payable occur because the business receives the goods or services before the payment has been made.

If Safari Condo purchased $600 of inventory, the transaction would be recorded as follows:

Nov. 22	Inventory	600	
	Accounts Payable		600
	To record purchase of inventory on account.		

The payment of the amount owing to the supplier would be shown as:

Dec. 5	Accounts Payable	600	
	Cash		600
	To record payment of account.		

Short-Term Notes Payable

Short-term notes payable are a common form of financing. Short-term notes payable are promissory notes that must be paid with interest within one year. The following entries are typical for a short-term note payable that Safari Condo might have issued in 2016 to purchase inventory:

2016			
Oct. 31	Inventory	16,000	
	Note Payable, Short-Term		16,000
	Purchase of inventory by issuing a one-year, 10 percent note payable.		

At year end, it is necessary to accrue interest expense for two months. You may recall from Chapter 3 that the term *accrued expense* refers to an expense that the business has incurred but has not yet recorded, so it creates a liability.

2016				
Dec. 31	Interest Expense		267	
	Interest Payable			267
	Accrued interest expense at year end ($16,000 × 0.10 × 2/12).			

At maturity (the end of the loan), the note is paid back with interest:

2017				
Oct. 31	Note Payable, Short-Term		16,000	
	Interest Payable		267	
	Interest Expense		1,333	
	Cash			17,600
	Paid a note payable and interest at maturity. Interest expense is $1,333 ($16,000 × 0.10 × 10/12). Cash paid is $17,600 [$16,000 + ($16,000 × 0.10)].			

Remember that the calculation for interest is Principal × Interest rate × Time.

LEARNING TIPS

No longer a liability, the amount previously accrued must be eliminated with a debit to Interest Payable.

Interest expense of $267 was correctly allocated to the year ended December 31, 2016. Safari Condo's interest expense for 2017 will be $1,333. At maturity, Safari Condo will pay a full year's interest, $1,600, allocated as shown in Exhibit 11–1.

EXHIBIT 11–1 | Matching Objective: Putting Interest in the Correct Fiscal Year

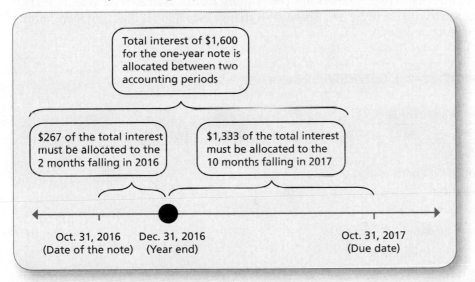

Short-Term Bank Loans and Operating Lines of Credit

Short-term bank loans are similar to short-term notes payable. They are arranged with a bank or other financial institution and are for a fixed time period at an interest rate negotiated between the bank and the borrower. If the bank loan is due in less than one year or less than the company's operating cycle, it is considered short term. Interest expense is recorded separately from the loan, and interest expense on a bank loan is accrued at the end of the year in the same way as for a note payable.

Many companies, and many people as well, arrange an operating **line of credit** with a financial institution to have cash available in case of a temporary cash shortfall. A line of credit is like a bank loan that is negotiated once, then used when needed. Interest is payable monthly only on the amount of the line of credit actually used—if the line of credit is not used, no interest is payable. Interest paid on a line of credit is recorded as interest expense. While most lines of credit are payable on demand (the bank can demand immediate repayment at any time), banks rarely demand repayment without warning. Typically, the amount of the principal to be repaid each month is flexible, often with a minimum repayment required every month.

Many lines of credit are *secured,* meaning that assets are **pledged as security** in case the borrower cannot repay the loan. Unsecured lines of credit do not have assets pledged as security. However, they often charge a higher rate of interest than secured lines of credit because there is a greater risk the financial institution will not receive the money it lent when there are no assets to be sold to recover the funds.

Goods and Services Tax, Harmonized Sales Tax, and Sales Tax Payable

There are two basic consumption taxes levied on purchases in Canada that are *visible* to consumers: the goods and services tax (GST) levied by the federal government and the provincial sales taxes (PST) levied by some provinces. In some provinces these two taxes are combined into a harmonized sales tax (HST). There are also excise or luxury taxes, which are a form of sales tax levied by the federal and provincial governments on products such as cigarettes, gasoline, jewellery, and alcoholic beverages; these taxes are *hidden* in that they are collected by the manufacturer and consumers do not see it as a separate tax on their invoice. The focus of discussion in this section will be on the visible consumption taxes; GST, HST, and PST will be discussed in turn below.

A summary of basic rates in effect on January 1, 2015, is presented in Exhibit 11–2. Rates vary with the item sold. These rates change on a regular basis but were correct at the time of writing.

EXHIBIT 11–2 | GST/HST/PST Rates

Province or Territory	2015 Rates			Notes
	GST	HST	PST	
Alberta	5%	—	—	
British Columbia	5%	—	7%	
Manitoba	5%	—	8%	
New Brunswick	—	13%	—	= 5% GST + 8% PST
Newfoundland and Labrador	—	13%*	—	= 5% GST + 8% PST
Northwest Territories	5%	—	—	
Nova Scotia	—	15%	—	= 5% GST + 10% PST
Nunavut	5%	—	—	
Ontario	—	13%	—	= 5% GST + 8% PST
Quebec	5%	—	9.975%	Called QST, not PST
Prince Edward Island	—	14%	—	= 5% GST + 9% PST
Saskatchewan	5%	—	5%	
Yukon	5%	—	—	

*Expected to rise to 15% in January 2016

Goods and Services Tax (GST) The federal government, through the Canada Revenue Agency (CRA), collects the GST on *most* goods and services consumed in Canada.

There are three categories of goods and services with respect to the GST:

- **Zero-rated supplies,** such as basic groceries, prescription drugs, goods and services exported from Canada to nonresidents, and medical devices
- **Exempt supplies,** such as educational services, health care services, and financial services
- **Taxable supplies,** which basically includes everything that is not zero-rated or exempt

The tax is collected by the individual or business (called the **registrant**) selling the taxable good or service (called *taxable supplies*). Businesses who supply taxable goods and services have to pay tax on their purchases. However, they are able to deduct the amount of GST paid (called an **input tax credit,** or **ITC**) from the GST they have collected from their sales in calculating the amount due. The GST return and the net tax must be remitted quarterly for most registrants and monthly for larger registrants.

For example, Mary Janicek, who lives in Whitehorse, Yukon, where there is no provincial tax, purchased a new sound system on July 2, 2017, with the intention of earning money by working as a disc jockey at weddings and local nightclubs.[2] The equipment cost $2,400 plus GST in the amount of $120. Because Janicek is planning to use the equipment exclusively to perform at special events, she could recover the $120. Assuming she were a registrant, she would have to charge all her customers the 5 percent GST for her services and remit it to the government. During the first three months of business, Janicek earned revenue of $4,000 and collected $200 of GST. She spent $105: $100 plus GST of $5 on advertising supplies. The entries to record these transactions would be as follows:

2017			
Jul. 2	Equipment	2,400	
	GST Recoverable	120	
	Cash		2,520
	To record purchase of a new sound system.		
Jul.–Sep.	Advertising Expense	100	
	GST Recoverable	5	
	Cash		105
	To record advertising costs for the period.		
Jul.–Sep.	Cash	4,200	
	Disc Jockey Revenue		4,000
	GST Payable		200
	To record revenue from various events.		

When Janicek remits her first quarterly GST payment, she sends $75 to the Receiver General. The entry would be as follows:

Oct. 31	GST Payable	200	
	GST Recoverable		125
	Cash		75
	To record payment of GST payable net of input tax credits to the Receiver General.		

---

[2] If a business earns less than $30,000 per year it does not have to be registered for GST or HST purposes. If this were the case, the owner would neither charge GST or HST to his or her clients nor be able to claim an input tax credit. This scenario assumes that Janicek plans to make over $30,000 per year. A business is only *required* to become a GST or HST registrant if taxable revenues exceed $30,000 for the last four consecutive quarters.

In the Mary Janicek example, we used two accounts—GST Recoverable and GST Payable—to illustrate input tax credits and GST collections to be remitted to the Receiver General. Some registrants use only one account—GST Payable—to record input tax credits *and* GST collections. When the GST return is sent to the Receiver General, the final account balance in the GST Payable account is remitted if the balance is a credit, or a refund is requested if the balance is a debit. However, since the CRA wants a report of both amounts, we will continue to use the two-account approach to illustrate input tax credits and GST collections.

Most companies include GST Payable as a current liability and report GST Recoverable as a current asset on their balance sheets. One can be netted against the other on the balance sheet if a company prefers to show it as one amount.

Harmonized Sales Tax (HST)   Several provinces have combined their respective provincial sales taxes with the GST to create a harmonized sales tax (HST). While GST is consistent at 5 percent, the amount of provincial sales tax varies. See Exhibit 11–2 on page 616 for rates in each province.

The entries to record HST collection and remittance to the CRA would be the same as the GST entries shown above except the amounts would differ. Let's assume that Mary Janicek lives in Ontario, which has HST of 13 percent, and look at the same transactions again:

2017			
Jul. 2	Equipment	2,400	
	HST Recoverable	312	
	Cash		2,712
	To record purchase of a new sound system.		
Jul.–Sep.	Advertising Expense	100	
	HST Recoverable	13	
	Cash		113
	To record advertising costs for the period.		
Jul.–Sep.	Cash	4,520	
	Disc Jockey Revenue		4,000
	HST Payable		520
	To record revenue from various events.		

In Ontario, Janicek would be required to remit $195 ($520 – $312 – $13) as her first quarterly payment. The entry would be as follows:

Oct. 31	HST Payable	520	
	HST Recoverable		325
	Cash		195
	To record payment of HST payable net of input tax credits to Receiver General.		

Provincial Sales Tax (PST)   Some provinces levy a tax on sales to the final consumers of products; sales tax is not levied on sales to wholesalers or retailers (unless they are the final consumers of the product, such as office supplies). The final sellers charge their customers the PST in addition to the price of the item sold. PST is often referred to as an **end-user tax** for this reason.

LEARNING TIPS

PST is charged on the price of the item before GST.

Consider Super Stereo Products, an electronics superstore located in Winnipeg. Super Stereo does not pay PST on its purchase of a TV set from Panasonic because it is inventory for resale, but you, as a consumer, would have to pay the province of Manitoba's 8 percent PST to Super Stereo when you buy a Panasonic TV from the store. Super Stereo pays the PST it collected from you to the provincial government. You would also have to pay the 5 percent GST on the purchase, and Super Stereo would have to remit it to the federal government.

Suppose on Saturday, September 16, sales at the Super Stereo store totalled $20,000. The business would record that day's sales as follows:

Sep. 16	Cash	22,600	
	Sales Revenue		20,000
	GST Payable		1,000
	Sales Tax Payable		1,600
	To record cash sales of $20,000 and the related taxes. GST = $20,000 × .05 = $1,000 PST = $20,000 × .08 = $1,600		

Companies forward the sales tax they collect on behalf of the government to the taxing authority at regular intervals (typically monthly for large companies and quarterly for small companies), at which time they debit Sales Tax Payable and credit Cash.

Current Portion of Long-Term Debt

Some long-term notes payable and bonds payable are paid in instalments, which means that portions of the principal are repaid at specific time intervals. The **current portion of long-term debt** is the amount of the principal that is payable within one year—a current liability. The remaining portion of the long-term debt is a long-term liability.

To illustrate, suppose Safari Condo borrowed $100,000 on January 1, 2017. This loan is to be repaid in instalments of $10,000 per year for 10 years on December 31 each year. On December 31, 2017, the first principal repayment of $10,000 is made (ignore interest), leaving a loan balance of $90,000.

The December 31, 2017, balance sheet reports the $10,000 portion due to be repaid on December 31, 2018, as a current liability and reports the remaining $80,000 portion as long-term debt. On December 31, 2017, the company *may* make an adjusting entry to shift the current instalment of the long-term debt to a current liability account as follows:

2017			
Dec. 31	Long-Term Debt	10,000	
	Current Portion of Long-Term Debt		10,000
	To transfer the portion of long-term debt due in 2018 to the current liability account.		

The reason we say *may* make the adjusting entry is that this is a reporting requirement on the balance sheet. A company could just show this on the balance sheet without making the actual journal entry. This example shows that accounting includes both *recording* transactions properly and *reporting* the information on the financial statements, which highlights that reporting is every bit as important as recording.

KEY POINTS

A current liability is due within one year, or within the company's operating cycle if it is longer than one year. The portion of a long-term debt payable within the year is classified as a current liability. The interest payable is classified separately from the principal.

The liabilities for the current portion of long-term debt do not include any accrued interest payable. The account, Current Portion of Long-Term Debt, represents only the appropriate portion of the *principal amount owed*. Interest Payable is a separate account for a different liability—the interest that must be paid.

What would be the effect if a company reported its full liability as all long term? Two ratios that would have been distorted by this accounting error are the current ratio and the acid-test ratio. Reporting a liability as long term could mislead external users because it understates current liabilities, overstating these two ratios and reporting an overly positive view of the company.

Accrued Expenses (Accrued Liabilities)

An **accrued expense** is an expense that has not yet been paid. An accrued expense creates a liability, which explains why accrued expenses are also called **accrued liabilities**. We introduced accrued expenses in Chapter 3, page 129.

Typical accrued expenses include the following:

- Salaries payable
- Payroll liabilities payable
- Interest payable
- Property taxes payable

We illustrated the accounting for interest payable on page 615. The second half of this chapter covers accounting for payroll liabilities.

Unearned Revenues

Unearned revenues are also called *deferred revenues* and *revenues collected in advance*. As we saw in Chapter 3, pages 130 and 131, an unearned revenue is a liability because it represents an obligation to provide a good or service. Each of these account titles indicates that the business has received cash from its customers before it has earned the revenue. Gift cards, concert tickets, and airline tickets are examples of prepayments that the company must record as a liability. The company has an obligation to provide goods or services to the customer. Let's consider an example.

Canadian Business magazine may be purchased individually or by means of a subscription (16 issues per year). When subscribers pay in advance to have *Canadian Business* delivered to their home or business, Rogers Media Inc. incurs a liability to provide future service. The liability account is called Unearned Subscription Revenue (which could also be titled Unearned Subscription Income or Deferred Subscription Income).

Assume that Rogers Media charges $20 (ignore taxes) for Bob Baylor's one-year subscription to *Canadian Business*. Rogers Media's entries would be:

2017			
Sep. 3	Cash	20	
	Unearned Subscription Revenue		20
	To record receipt of cash at the start of a one-year subscription.		

After receiving the cash on September 3, Rogers Media owes its customer magazines that it will provide over the next 12 months. Rogers Media's liability is:

Unearned Subscription Revenue		Cash	
	20	20	

During 2017, Rogers Media delivers four of the magazines and earns $5 ($20 × 4/16) of the subscription revenue. At December 31, 2017, it makes the following adjusting entry to decrease (debit) the liability Unearned Subscription Revenue and increase (credit) Subscription Revenue:

2017			
Dec. 31	Unearned Subscription Revenue	5	
	Subscription Revenue		5
	Earned revenue that was collected in advance ($20 × 4/16).		

After posting, Rogers Media still owes the subscriber $15 for magazines to be delivered during 2018 (this is unearned revenue for Rogers). Rogers Media has earned $5 of the revenue, as follows:

Unearned Subscription Revenue					Subscription Revenue		
Dec. 31	5	Sep. 3	20		Dec. 31	5
		Bal.	15			

Customer Deposits Payable

Some companies require cash deposits from customers as security on borrowed assets. These amounts are called Customer Deposits Payable because the company must refund the cash to the customer under certain conditions. Utility companies and businesses that lend tools and appliances commonly demand a deposit as protection against damage and theft. Certain manufacturers of products sold through individual dealers, such as Avon or Mary Kay, require deposits from the dealers who sell their products; the deposit is usually equal to the cost of the sample kit provided to the dealer. Companies whose products are sold in returnable containers collect deposits on those containers. Because the deposit is returned to the customer, the amount collected represents a liability.

> Try It!

1. Suppose Magnus' Private Tutoring in Victoria, British Columbia, made cash sales of $3,000 in April subject to 5 percent GST and 7 percent PST. Record sales and the related consumption taxes. Also record payment of the PST to the provincial government and the GST to the Receiver General on May 10. Assume input tax credits amount to $69.

2. On September 1, 2016, Snippy Hair Salons borrowed $20,000. A portion of the loan is to be paid back each year on September 1 as follows: in 2017, $6,000; in 2018, $5,000; in 2019, $4,000; in 2020, $3,000; and in 2021, $2,000. Interest of 5 percent on the outstanding amount is paid on August 31 each year. At December 31, 2016, Snippy Hair Salons reported the long-term debt payable as follows:

Current Liabilities (in part)	
Portion of long-term debt due within one year	$6,000
Interest payable*	333
Long-Term Liabilities (in part)	
Long-term debt	$14,000

Assuming the company makes the loan repayments as scheduled, show how Snippy Hair Salons would report its loan liability on the year-end balance sheet one year later—December 31, 2017.

*Calculated as $20,000 × 0.05 × $^4/_{12}$

Solutions appear at the end of this chapter and on MyAccountingLab

CURRENT LIABILITIES THAT MUST BE ESTIMATED

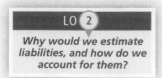

LO 2

Why would we estimate liabilities, and how do we account for them?

KEY POINTS

A warrantied product may be sold in one year but repaired in another year. When should the repair be expensed—in the year the product is sold or in the year the product is repaired? The matching objective requires matching the warranty expense with the revenue from the sale in the year of the sale.

A business may know that a liability exists but not know the exact amount. It cannot simply ignore the liability. This liability must be reported on the balance sheet.

Estimated Warranty Payable

Many companies guarantee their products against defects under **warranty** agreements. At the time of the sale, the company does not know the exact amount of warranty expense, but the business must estimate its warranty expense and the related liability.

The matching objective leads us to record the *warranty expense* in the same period we record the revenue. The expense occurs when you make a sale, not when you pay the warranty claim.

BlackBerry Ltd. explains its treatment of product warranties:

> The Company's estimates of costs are based upon historical experience and expectations of future return rates and unit warranty repair costs. If the Company experiences increased or decreased warranty activity, or increased or decreased costs associated with servicing those obligations, revisions to the estimated warranty liability would be recognized in the reporting period when such revisions are made.[3]

Assume that Collico Fabricating made sales in 2016 of $80 million that are subject to warranty. In Note 2, "Significant Accounting Policies," Collico indicates that the company provides warranty coverage for its products for one year from the date of sale. Assume that, in the past, the warranty provision and actual warranty cost was 1 percent of fabricating sales. Further, assume the company believes that 1 percent of the value of products sold in 2016 is the appropriate estimate of the cost of warranty work to be performed in the future. The company would record the sales of $80 million and the warranty expense of $800,000 ($80,000,000 × 0.01) in the same period as follows:

2016			
Various	Accounts Receivable	80,000,000	
dates	Sales Revenue		80,000,000
	Sales on account.		
Dec. 31	Warranty Expense	800,000	
	Estimated Warranty Payable		800,000
	To accrue warranty expense on $80 million of sales.		

Assume that the costs paid to repair defective merchandise during 2017 total $700,000. If Collico repairs the defective products, Collico makes this journal entry:

2017			
Various	Estimated Warranty Payable	700,000	
dates	Cash		700,000
	To pay repair costs for defective products sold under warranty.		

---

[3] BlackBerry Ltd.'s Notes to the Consolidated Financial Statements, 2014.

If Collico replaces the defective products rather than repairs them, Collico makes this journal entry:

2017			
Various	Estimated Warranty Payable	700,000	
dates	Inventory		700,000
	To replace defective products sold under warranty.		

After paying these warranty claims, Collico's liability account would have a credit balance of $100,000 at the December 31, 2017, year end:

Estimated Warranty Payable

2017 Adj.	700,000	800,000	Dec. 31, 2016
		100,000	Dec. 31, 2017, Bal.

Notice there is a balance left in the account. There is no adjustment made at this time. The accountants for Collico Fabricating will decrease their next estimate based on the fact that there was a lower amount of warranty claims than their previous estimate. If there were a debit balance in this account, then the next year's estimate would be increased.

While warranty expense is often calculated as a percent of sales dollars, it can also be calculated as a percent of units of product sold. For example, suppose a tire company sells 50,000 tires in one year. It estimates, based on experience, that 0.5 percent of them, or 250 tires, will need to be replaced in the future. If the tires cost $50 each, the warranty expense is estimated to be $12,500 (250 × $50). The accounts used in the journal entry to record the warranty expense are the same as those shown above.

Estimated Vacation Pay Liability

All Canadian companies are required by law to grant paid vacations to their employees. The employees receive this benefit when they take their vacation, but they earn the compensation by working the other days of the year. The law requires most employers to provide a minimum number of weeks' holiday per year (usually two, but sometimes more based on the number of years worked). To match expense with revenue properly, the company accrues the vacation pay expense and liability for each of the 50 workweeks of the year. Then, the company records payment during the two-week vacation period. Employee turnover, terminations, and ineligibility (e.g., no vacation allowed until one full year has been worked) force companies to estimate the vacation pay liability and accrue vacation expense incurred.

Suppose a company's January payroll is $100,000 and vacation pay adds 4 percent, or $4,000. In January, the company records the vacation pay accrual as follows:

> Two weeks of annual vacation divided by 50 workweeks in a year results in a rate of 4 percent.

Jan. 31	Vacation Pay Expense	4,000	
	Estimated Vacation Pay Liability		4,000
	To record vacation accrual for January.		

Each month thereafter, the company makes a similar entry.

If an employee takes a two-week vacation in August, his or her $2,000 monthly salary, made up of vacation and regular pay, is recorded as follows:

Aug. 31	Estimated Vacation Pay Liability	1,000	
	Salaries Expense	1,000	
	Various Withholding Accounts and Cash*		2,000
	To record payment of salary and vacation pay.		

*The various payroll accounts are discussed later in the chapter.

Employees are often encouraged to take vacation to eliminate large balances accumulating in these liability accounts.

Income Tax Payable (for a Corporation)

Corporations pay income tax in the same way as individual taxpayers do. Corporations file their income tax returns with the Canada Revenue Agency (CRA) and their provincial governments after the end of the fiscal year, so they must estimate their income tax payable for reporting on the balance sheet. During the year, corporations make monthly tax instalments (payments) to the government(s) based on their estimated tax for the year. A corporation with an estimated tax liability of $1,200,000 for the year would record each month's payment of the instalment as shown here for September:

Sep. 30	Income Tax Expense	100,000	
	Cash		100,000
	To pay monthly income tax instalment.		

If the corporation has a December 31 year end, then the last monthly payment would be made as usual, and then a reconciliation would be performed. If at that point the *actual* tax expense for the year was calculated to be $1,240,000, then the corporation would accrue an additional $40,000. On December 30, the corporation pays the last monthly instalment of $100,000. It will have reported $1,200,000 of income tax expense for the year.

Then, at December 31, the corporation calculates *actual* tax expense for the year to be $1,240,000. It must accrue the additional $40,000:

Dec. 31	Income Tax Expense	40,000	
	Income Tax Payable		40,000
	To accrue income tax at year end.		

The corporation will pay off the balance of this tax liability during the next year when it files its federal and provincial tax returns, so Income Tax Payable is a current liability.

CONTINGENT LIABILITIES

A **contingent liability** is a potential liability that depends on a *future* event arising out of past events. For example, Packenham town council may sue North Ontario Electric Supply Ltd., the company that installed new street lights in Packenham, claiming that the electrical wiring is faulty. The past transaction is the street-light installation. The future event is the court case that will decide the suit. North Ontario Electric Supply Ltd. thus faces a contingent liability, which may or may not become an actual obligation.

The *CPA Canada Handbook* generally requires *contingent losses* to be accrued or disclosed in the financial statements but does not allow *contingent gains* to be recognized *until* they are realized. The accounting treatment for contingencies requires the application of judgment, which follows the principle of *conservatism*. The accounting profession divides contingent liabilities into three categories. Each category indicates a likelihood that a contingency will cause a loss and become an actual liability. The three categories of contingent liabilities, along with how to report them, are shown in Exhibit 11–3.

EXHIBIT 11–3 | Contingent Liabilities: Three Categories

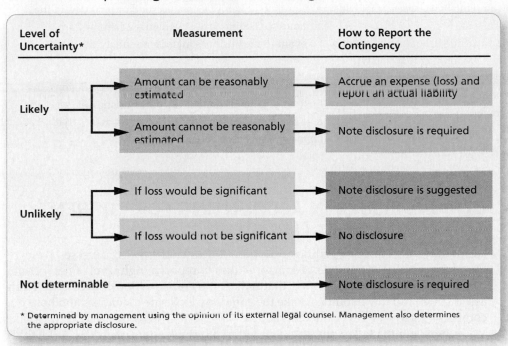

* Determined by management using the opinion of its external legal counsel. Management also determines the appropriate disclosure.

Accrue As shown earlier in this chapter, an accrual is a journal entry. Increase (debit) an expense account and increase (credit) a liability account so that the future payment is reported on the balance sheet.

Disclosure The *disclosure principle* of accounting (see Chapter 6, page 336) requires a company to report any information deemed relevant to outsiders of the business for decision making. The notes to the financial statements provide some of this information. BlackBerry Ltd. discusses how it deals with contingencies in Note 10. Commitments and Contingencies, (c) Litigation, of its 2014 annual report:

> As of March 1, 2014, there are claims outstanding for which the Company has assessed the potential loss as both probable to result and reasonably estimable, therefore an accrual has been made that is not material to the Company's financial statements. Further, there are claims outstanding for which the Company has assessed the potential loss as reasonably possible to result, however an estimate of the amount of loss cannot reasonably be made.
>
> . . .
>
> Though the Company does not believe the . . . legal proceedings will result in a significant loss, and does not believe they are claims for which the outcomes are determinable or where the amounts of the loss can be reasonably estimated, the Company has included . . . summaries of certain of its legal proceedings that it believes may be of interest to its investors.

This chapter is a great example of how the framework for financial reporting influences decisions about recording and reporting transactions.

- A company may purchase inventory that is received on the first day of the month, but the invoice does not have to be paid until the end of the month. In this case, the company has a liability because it has received the inventory (*recognition*) at an agreed-upon amount (*measurement*) that will be paid in the near future.
- Suppose you purchase an airline ticket from WestJet for a flight from Toronto to Winnipeg that you will take at the end of the semester. You have paid for the flight, so why shouldn't WestJet simply recognize your payment as revenue? Because WestJet still owes you the flight. If, for some reason, WestJet cannot fulfill the contract with you, it must refund your

fare. Thus, WestJet's unearned revenue for your flight is a liability until it provides the flight.
- Warranties and vacation pay are expenses that are estimated in order to be able to record an expense at the time the revenue is recognized (*matching objective*).
- Contingent liabilities are accrued or included in the notes to the financial statements when they are relevant to the business in order to satisfy the *disclosure principle*.

Of course, by recording all of these transactions the business complies with the characteristics of *relevance* and *reliability*, leading to financial statements that *communicate useful information to users*.

ETHICAL ISSUES IN ACCOUNTING FOR CURRENT AND CONTINGENT LIABILITIES

Accounting for current liabilities poses an ethical challenge. Businesses want to look as successful as possible. A company likes to report a high level of net income on the income statement because that makes the company look successful. High asset values and low liabilities make the company look safe to lenders and help the company borrow at lower interest rates.

Owners and managers may be tempted to overlook some expenses and liabilities at the end of the period. For example, a company can fail to accrue warranty expense or employee vacation pay. This will cause total expenses to be understated and net income to be overstated on the income statement. These omissions also affect the ratios, such as the current ratio and the acid-test ratio.

Contingent liabilities also pose an ethical challenge. Because contingencies are potential liabilities, they are easy to overlook. But a contingent liability can be very important. A business with a contingent liability walks a tightrope between (1) disclosing enough information to enable outsiders to evaluate the company realistically, and (2) not giving away too much information, which could harm the company.

Ethical business owners ensure their accounting records are complete and accurate. Falsifying financial statements can ruin one's reputation in the business community and lead to criminal convictions. In addition to legal repercussions, missing liabilities such as warranty liabilities, accrued liabilities, and contingent liabilities can be detrimental to proper financial disclosure and can have serious consequences for the all the stakeholders involved.

> Try It!

3. Chez Nous Limited, a new company, made sales (all on account) of $400,000. The company estimated warranty repairs at 3 percent of sales. Chez Nous' actual warranty payments were $9,000. Record sales, warranty expense, and warranty payments on December 31. How much is Chez Nous' estimated warranty payable at the end of the period?

(Continued)

(Continued)

> **4.** Chez Nous Limited, a new company, made sales (all on account) of 20,000 units at a cost of $40 per unit. The company offers a one-year warranty that replaces any defective units with a new one. The company estimated warranty replacements at 3 percent of units sold. Chez Nous' actual warranty replacements were 475 units. Record sales, warranty expense, and warranty payments on December 31. How much is Chez Nous' estimated warranty payable at the end of the period?

Solutions appear at the end of this chapter and on MyAccountingLab

ACCOUNTING FOR PAYROLL

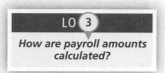

Payroll is a major expense of many businesses. For service organizations—such as public accounting firms and real estate brokers—payroll is *the* major expense. Salaries, wages, and related employment expenses usually cause an accrued liability at year end.

Labour costs require special calculations that are repeated, so most businesses develop or purchase a special payroll system or use the payroll module of their accounting software. This software is updated regularly by the software manufacturer to ensure that the tax rates and any changes in laws are kept current in the system.

Employee compensation can be provided in a number of different forms:

Salary	Pay stated at an annual, monthly, or weekly rate, such as $48,000 per year, $4,000 per month, or $1,000 per week.
Wages	Pay amounts stated at an hourly rate, such as $20 per hour.
Straight time	Base rate for a set period of time.
Overtime	Higher rate of pay for additional hours worked.
Commission	Pay stated as a percentage of a sale amount, such as a 5 percent commission on a sale. A realtor thus earns $5,000 on a $100,000 sale of real estate.
Piecework	Pay based on the number of pieces produced by the employee, such as number of trees planted or shirts sewn.
Bonus	Pay over and above base salary (wage or commission). A bonus is usually paid for exceptional performance—often a single amount after year end.
Benefits	Extra compensation items that aren't paid directly to the employee. Benefits could include health, life, and disability insurance. The employer pays the insurance company, which then provides coverage for the employee. Another type of benefit, a pension, sets aside money for the employee for his or her retirement.

MyAccountingLab

Interactive Figure: Interact with Bonus

Let's take a moment to see how overtime pay is calculated. Lucy Guild is an administrator and bookkeeper for MicroAge Electronics Inc. Lucy earns $20 per hour for **straight time** (40 hours). The company pays *time and a half* for **overtime**. That rate is 150 percent (1.5 times) the straight-time rate. Thus Lucy earns $30 for each hour of overtime ($20 × 1.5 = $30). For working 42 hours during a week, she earns $860, computed as follows:

Straight-time pay for 40 hours	$800
Overtime pay for two overtime hours (2 × $30.00)	60
Gross or total pay	$860

Gross Pay and Net Pay

Two pay amounts are important for accounting purposes:

- **Gross pay** is the total amount of salary, wages, commission, piecework, and bonus earned by the employee during a pay period. Gross pay is the amount before income taxes or any other deductions. Gross pay is the employer's expense. In the preceding example, Lucy Guild's gross pay was $860.

- **Net pay**, also called *take-home pay*, is the amount the employee keeps. Net pay equals gross pay minus all *deductions*. The employer writes a paycheque to each employee or makes an electronic funds transfer to each employee's bank account for his or her net pay.

Exhibit 11–4 illustrates gross and net pay.

EXHIBIT 11–4 | Gross Pay and Net Pay

Payroll Deductions

Payroll deductions create the difference between gross pay and net pay. They are **withheld** from employees' pay and fall into two categories:

- *Required* (or *statutory*) *deductions.* The federal government and most provincial governments require by law that employers act as collection agents for employee's income taxes, Canada Pension Plan (CPP) or Quebec Pension Plan (QPP) contributions, and Employment Insurance (EI) premiums, which are deducted from employee paycheques.

- *Optional deductions.* These deductions include union dues (which may be automatic deductions for all unionized employees), insurance premiums, charitable contributions to organizations such as the United Way, and other amounts that are withheld at the employee's request.

After being withheld, payroll deductions become current liabilities of the employer, which assumes responsibility for paying the outside party. For example, the employer pays the government the employee income tax withheld and pays the union the employee union dues withheld.

Required Payroll Deductions

Employees' Income Tax Payable For most employees, this deduction is the largest. The amount withheld depends on the employee's gross pay and on the amount of nonrefundable tax credits the employee claims. Each employee files both a provincial and a federal Personal Tax Credits Return (Form TD1), which is used by employers to determine how much income tax to withhold from an employee's gross pay. Factors on the TD1 that affect the amount of income tax to withhold include dependents, age, and student fees.

The employer accumulates both federal and provincial taxes withheld in the Employee Income Tax Payable account. The payable is eliminated when the employer pays (remits) these taxes to the government.

Employees' Canada (or Quebec) Pension Plan Contributions Payable The **Canada Pension Plan (CPP)** or **Quebec Pension Plan (QPP)** provides retirement, disability, and death benefits to employees who are covered by it. Employers are required to deduct premiums from each employee required to make a contribution (basically all employees between 18 and 70 years of age).

The federal government, through the CRA, determines annually the maximum pensionable earnings level (which is the maximum for deducting CPP), the basic annual exemption, and the contribution rate. In early 2015, the following information was applicable:

KEY POINTS

Divide the annual exemption of $3,500 by the number of pay periods in a year to ensure the correct amount of CPP exemption is calculated. For weekly pay periods, divide by 52; for two-week pay periods, divide by 26.

Maximum pensionable earnings	$ 53,600
Basic annual exemption	3,500
Maximum contributory earnings ($53,600 – $3,500)	50,100
Contribution rate	× 4.95%
Maximum employee contribution for the year	$ 2,479.95

The CRA provides tables that the employer uses to calculate the amount to deduct from each employee's pay; the tables take into account the basic exemption of $3,500 of income but also assume that the employee will be working for 12 months. The CRA also provides a free **Payroll Deductions Online Calculator (PDOC)** that provides more accurate calculations in a user-friendly format.

Once the employee reaches the maximum contribution of $2,479.95, the employer stops deducting CPP from the employee for that year. Some employees may have had more than one employer in a year; for example, you may have had a job for the summer and now have a part-time job while you are back at school. You recover any overpayment when you file your income tax return for the year.

Employees' Employment Insurance Premiums Payable The Employment Insurance Act requires employers to deduct **Employment Insurance (EI)** premiums from each employee each time that employee is paid until the employee reaches the maximum. The purpose of EI is to provide assistance to contributors to the fund who cannot work for a variety of reasons. The most common reason is that the employee has been laid off; another reason is maternity leave or parental leave. As with the CPP, the CRA requires every employer to deduct EI premiums from every eligible employee. Those who are self-employed or related to the employer are not eligible.

The federal government, through the CRA, establishes annually the maximum annual insurable earnings level and the EI premium rate. In early 2015, the following information was applicable:

Maximum insurable earnings	$49,500
Premium rate	× 1.88%
Maximum employee contribution	$930.60

The CRA provides tables and a Payroll Deductions Online Calculator that the employer uses to calculate the amount to deduct from each employee's gross pay each pay period, although this is easy to calculate manually. For example, if you earned $2,000 per month, $37.60 ($2,000 × 1.88%) would be deducted for EI each month.

If an employee exceeds the maximum contribution, for example, by having multiple employers, the overpayment can be recovered when he or she files an income tax return.

Remittance The employer must remit the income tax, CPP (or QPP) contributions, and EI premiums withheld and the employer's share, discussed below, to the CRA. The amount of withholdings determines how often the employer submits payroll payments. Most employers remit to the government at least monthly. Larger employers must remit two or four times a month depending on the total amounts withheld.

Other Payroll Deductions

As a convenience to their employees, many companies make optional payroll deductions and disburse cash according to employee instructions. Insurance payments, registered pension plan or retirement savings plan payments, payroll savings plans, and donations to charities such as the United Way are examples.

Some employees have union dues as a required deduction. They would be recorded in an account such as Employee Union Dues Payable.

Employer Payroll Costs

Employers also incur expenses for at least three payroll costs:

- CPP (or QPP) contributions
- EI premiums
- Workers' compensation plan premiums

REAL WORLD EXAMPLE

A new additional deduction for employees in Ontario who do not have a company pension plan will start in 2017. It is called the **Ontario Retirement Pension Plan (ORPP)**. At the time of printing, the contribution rate for 2017 was set at 1.9 percent of earnings subject to the same basic exemption as the CPP.

Employer Canada (or Quebec) Pension Plan Contributions In addition to being responsible for deducting and remitting the employee contribution to the CPP (or QPP), the employer must also pay into the program at the same time. The employer must match exactly the employee's contribution. Every employer must do so whether or not the employee also contributes elsewhere. Unlike the employee, the employer may not obtain a refund for overpayment.

Employer Employment Insurance Premiums The employer calculates the employee's EI premium and remits it together with the employer's share, which is generally 1.4 times the employee's premium, to the CRA. The maximum dollar amount of the employer's contribution would be 1.4 times the maximum employee's contribution of $930.60, which amounts to $1,302.84.

Workers' Compensation Premiums Unlike the previous two programs, which are administered by the federal government (the Quebec government for the QPP), **workers' compensation** plans are administered provincially. The purpose of the program is to provide financial support for workers injured on the job. The cost of the coverage is borne by the employer; the employee does not pay a premium to the fund. Workers' compensation payments are remitted quarterly.

In Manitoba, for example, almost all employees are covered by the program. There are over 70 different categories that the Workers Compensation Board uses to determine the cost of coverage. The category a group of workers is assigned to is based on the risk of injury to workers in that group, which is based on that group's and similar groups' experience. The employer pays a premium equal to the rate assessed times the employer's gross payroll, up to a maximum assessable.

Additional Provincial Payroll Taxes Certain provinces levy taxes on employers to pay for provincial health care, while others levy a combined health care and post-secondary education tax to pay for provincial health care and post-secondary education.

Payroll Withholding Tables

We have discussed the rates that employers use in calculating the withholdings that must be made from employees' wages for income taxes, CPP (or QPP) contributions, and EI premiums. Exhibit 11–5 provides excerpts of all four tables for a resident of Saskatchewan for 2015. The CRA provides tables for weekly, bi-weekly (every two weeks), semi-monthly, and monthly pay periods. The PDOC allows for more pay periods.

Suppose an employee, Lynne Graham, is paid a salary of $2,000 twice a month (semi-monthly). Graham's TD1 form for both federal and provincial taxes indicates a claim code of 0.

Graham's deductions each pay are as follows:

- $284.75—federal income taxes from Panel A
- $209.80—Saskatchewan income taxes from Panel B
- $91.78—CPP from Panel C
- $37.60—EI from Panel D

Graham's employer would keep track, as we will demonstrate later in the chapter, of Graham's CPP and EI deductions and, when they reached the maximums of $2,479.95 and $930.60, respectively, would stop deducting premiums from Graham's pay.

The employer's share would be $91.78 for CPP (matches employee's share), while the employer's share for EI would be $52.64 (1.4 times employee share) for this pay.

EXHIBIT 11–5 | Payroll Withholding Tables

Panel A

SASKATCHEWAN
Federal Tax Deductions
Effective January 1, 2015
Semi-Monthly: 24 Pay Periods Per Year

Pay	Federal claim codes										
	0	**1**	**2**	**3**	**4**	**5**	**6**	**7**	**8**	**9**	**10**
From Less than	Deduct from each pay										
1927 – 1945	269.65	198.85	192.05	178.55	165.00	151.50	137.95	124.45	110.90	97.40	83.85
1945 – 1963	273.40	202.60	195.85	182.35	168.80	155.30	141.75	128.25	114.70	101.20	87.65
1963 – 1981	277.20	206.40	199.65	186.10	172.60	159.05	145.55	132.00	118.50	104.95	91.45
1981 – 1999	280.95	210.15	203.40	189.90	176.35	162.85	149.30	135.80	122.25	108.75	95.20
1999 – 2017	284.75	213.95	207.20	193.65	180.15	166.60	153.10	139.55	126.05	112.50	99.00

Panel B

SASKATCHEWAN
Provincial Tax Deductions
Effective January 1, 2015
Semi-Monthly: 24 Pay Periods Per Year

Pay	Provincial claim codes										
	0	**1**	**2**	**3**	**4**	**5**	**6**	**7**	**8**	**9**	**10**
From Less than	Deduct from each pay										
1979 – 1997	207.60	135.90	131.30	122.05	112.85	103.60	94.40	85.15	75.95	66.70	57.50
1997 – 2015	209.80	138.10	133.50	124.30	115.05	105.80	96.60	87.35	78.15	68.90	59.70
2015 – 2033	212.00	140.30	135.70	126.50	117.25	108.05	98.80	89.60	80.35	71.10	61.90
2033 – 2051	214.20	142.55	137.90	128.70	119.45	110.25	101.00	91.80	82.55	73.35	64.10
2051 – 2069	216.40	144.75	140.10	130.90	121.65	112.45	103.20	94.00	84.75	75.55	66.30

Panel C
Canada Pension Plan Contributions
Semi-Monthly (24 pay periods per year)

Pay		CPP
From	To	
1998.46 – 1998.65		91.71
1998.66 – 1998.86		91.72
1998.87 – 1999.06		91.73
1999.07 – 1999.26		91.74
1999.27 – 1999.46		91.75
1999.47 – 1999.66		91.76
1999.67 – 1999.87		91.77
1999.88 – 2000.07		91.78
2000.08 – 2000.27		91.79

Panel D
Employment Insurance Premiums
Semi-Monthly (24 pay periods per year)

Insurable Earnings		EI
From	To	Premium
1997.55 – 1997.07		37.54
1997.08 – 1997.60		37.55
1997.61 – 1998.13		37.56
1998.14 – 1998.67		37.57
1998.68 – 1999.20		37.58
1999.21 – 1999.73		37.59
1999.74 2000.26		37.60
2000.27 – 2000.79		37.61
2000.80 – 2001.32		37.62

Source: Reproduced with the permission of the Minister of Public Works and Government Services Canada, 2015.

Payroll Deductions Online Calculator (PDOC)

As mentioned earlier, the CRA provides an online tool employers can use to calculate the required deductions. Exhibit 11–6 shows a screenshot of the same employee as the one we just discussed. Notice that the amounts are different; the PDOC is more accurate.

EXHIBIT 11–6 | The CRA's Payroll Deductions Online Calculator (PDOC)

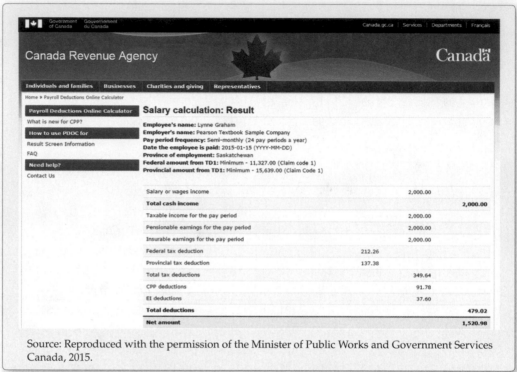

Source: Reproduced with the permission of the Minister of Public Works and Government Services Canada, 2015.

Exhibit 11–7 shows the disbursement of Graham's payroll costs by her Saskatchewan employer, assuming she pays $20 of union dues each pay period and has a workers' compensation premium to be paid by the employer of $15.00.

EXHIBIT 11–7 | Disbursement of Lynne Graham's Payroll Costs by an Employer Using the PDOC (Saskatchewan)

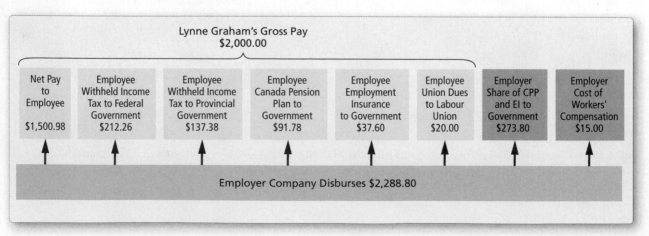

5. Use the tables in Exhibit 11–5 to determine federal tax, Saskatchewan provincial tax, CPP, and EI withholdings for the following employees who are paid semi-monthly:

a. Agatha Cross is paid $1,998.50 each pay period, with a federal and provincial claim code of 4.
b. Peter Simpson is paid $1,999.50 each pay period, with a federal and provincial claim code of 2.
c. Lana Morris is paid $2,000.25 each pay period, with a federal and provincial claim code of 3.

Solutions appear at the end of this chapter and on MyAccountingLab

PAYROLL ENTRIES

The journal entries in this section show an employer's entries to record a monthly payroll of $60,000 (all amounts are assumed for illustration purposes only).

The first journal entry records the employer's salary expense, which is the gross salary of all employees ($60,000) for a month. The liabilities are separated into different accounts because they are paid to different entities.

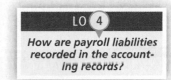

LO 4

How are payroll liabilities recorded in the accounting records?

Mar. 31	Salary Expense (or Wages or Commission Expense)	60,000	
	Employee Income Tax Payable		8,100
	Canada Pension Plan Payable		2,970
	Employment Insurance Payable		1,120
	Employee Union Dues Payable		1,532
	Salaries Payable		46,278
	To record salary expense and employee withholdings		

To the government
To outside organizations
To the employee

The second journal entry represents the employer's share of CPP and EI. Remember, the employer's share is 1.0 times the employee's share of CPP and 1.4 times the employee's share of EI.

Mar. 31	Employee Benefits Expense	4,538	
	Canada Pension Plan Payable		2,970
	Employment Insurance Payable		1,568
	To record employer's share of CPP (1.0 × $2,970) and EI (1.4 × $1,120).		

KEY POINTS

Payroll liabilities are accrued liabilities. These liabilities are separate liability accounts because each liability is paid to a different entity.

A third journal entry might record employee benefits paid by the employer. This company has a dental benefits plan for its employees for which it pays the premiums.

Mar. 31	Employee Dental Benefits Expense	1,092	
	Employee Benefits Payable		1,092
	To record employee benefits payable by employer.		

There would also be workers' compensation, which, you will recall, is paid completely by the employer, and other costs depending on the province in which the company operates.

Mar. 31	Workers' Compensation Expense	1,098	
	Workers' Compensation Payable		1,098
	To record workers' compensation premiums payable by employer.		

The final journal entries record the subsequent payment of the employee withholdings and the employer expenses to the CRA and other parties that provide employee benefits. Each payment that requires a separate cheque also requires a separate journal entry (dates are assumed).

Apr. 8	Employee Income Tax Payable	8,100	
	Canada Pension Plan Payable	2,970	
	Employment Insurance Payable	1,120	
	Canada Pension Plan Payable	2,970	
	Employment Insurance Payable	1,568	
	Cash		16,728
	To record payment to the CRA for federal and provincial income tax withholdings, CPP and EI withholdings for both the employee and employer portions; Cheque #XX1		
Apr. 8	Employee Union Dues Payable	1,532	
	Cash		1,532
	To record payment to Workers' Union for union dues withheld from employees; Cheque #XX2.		
Apr. 8	Employee Benefits Payable	1,092	
	Cash		1,092
	To record payment to Mega Dental for employee benefits; Cheque #XX3.		
Apr. 8	Workers' Compensation Payable	1,098	
	Cash		1,098
	To record payment for workers' compensation premium; Cheque #XX4		

Independent Contractors A company's payments to people who are not employees—outsiders called **independent contractors**—are *not* company payroll expenses. Consider two technical writers, Elena and Scott. Elena is the company's technical writer; Scott is a contractor hired to help Elena during the busy season. Elena is an employee of the company, and her compensation is a debit to Salaries Expense. Scott, however, performs writing services for many clients, and the company debits Contract Labour when it pays the invoice he presents for the work completed. Any payment for services performed by a person outside the company is recorded with a debit to an expense account other than payroll.

> Try It!

6. Record the payroll, payroll deductions, and employer payroll costs given the following information about an Ontario company at March 31:

Gross pay	$190,000
Employee withheld income tax	22,800
Employee withheld CPP	9,300
Employee withheld EI	3,500
Union dues	2,945
Registered Retirement Savings Plan (RRSP) contribution	10,000

Pension plan paid by employer only = 1.0 percent of gross pay

Solutions appear at the end of this chapter and on MyAccountingLab

THE PAYROLL SYSTEM

Good business practice requires paying employees accurately and on time. A payroll system accomplishes these goals. The components of the payroll system are:

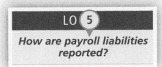

LO 5

How are payroll liabilities reported?

- A payroll register
- Payroll cheques
- Employee earnings records

Many accounting packages have a payroll module that records the entries, creates the register, and prints the cheques and other payroll documents. There are also companies that specialize in providing payroll and human resource information services. Ceridian Canada Ltd. is an example of a company that will provide payroll registers, cheques, earnings records, and other payroll documents.

Payroll Register

Each pay period the company organizes payroll data in a special journal called the *payroll register.* The payroll register is like a cash payments journal (see Chapter 7) and serves as a cheque register for recording payroll cheques.

Exhibit 11–8 is a payroll register for Leduc Petroleum. The payroll register has columns for each employee's gross pay, deductions, and net pay. This record gives the employer the information needed to record salary expense for the pay period as follows:

2015			
Dec. 31	Office Salaries Expense	4,464.00	
	Sales Salaries Expense	9,190.00	
	Employee Income Tax Payable		2,858.90
	Canada Pension Plan Payable		402.70
	Employment Insurance Payable		235.12
	United Way Payable		155.00
	Salaries Payable		10,002.28
	To record payroll expenses for the pay period ended December 31, 2015.		
Dec. 31	Employee Benefits Expense	731.87	
	Canada Pension Plan Payable		402.70
	Employment Insurance Payable		329.17
	To record the cost of employer's portion of payroll expenses for the pay period ended December 31, 2015. Employment Insurance Payable is calculated as $235.12 × 1.4		

Payroll Cheques

Companies pay employees by cheque or by electronic funds transfer (EFT). A *payroll cheque* has an attachment, or stub, that details the employee's gross pay, payroll deductions, and net pay. Employees paid by EFT must receive a statement of earnings with the same information on it. These amounts come from the payroll register. Exhibit 11–9 shows payroll cheque number 1622, issued to C.L. Drumm for net pay of $416.06 earned during the pay period ended December 31, 2015. To practise using payroll data, trace all amounts on the cheque attachment to the payroll register in Exhibit 11–8.

EXHIBIT 11-8 | Payroll Register for Leduc Petroleum

					Pay period ended December 31, 2015										
		A	B	C	D	E	F	G	H	I	J	K	L	M
		Gross Pay			Deductions						Net Pay		Account Debited	
Employee Name	Hours	Straight Time	Overtime	Total	Federal Income Tax	Prov. Inc. Tax (Alberta)	CPP	EI	United Way	Total	(c – i) Amount	Cheque No.	Office Salaries Expense	Sales Salaries Expense
Chen, W.L.*	40	500.00		500.00	33.20	11.30	21.42	9.15	2.00	77.07	422.93	1621	500.00	
Drumm, C.L.	46	400.00	90.00	490.00	31.50	10.55	16.85	8.97	2.00	73.94	416.06	1622		490.00
Elias, M.	41	560.00	21.00	581.00	44.65	16.85	25.43	10.63		97.56	483.44	1623	581.00	
Vokovich, E.A.**	40	1,360.00		196.40	93.90				15.00	305.30	1,054.70	1641		1,360.00
Total		12,940.00	714.00	13,654.00	1,966.18	892.72	402.70	235.12	155.00	3,651.72	10,002.28		4,464.00	9,190.00

* W.L. Chen earned gross pay of $500. His net pay was $422.93, paid with cheque number 1621. Chen is an office worker, so his salary is debited to Office Salaries Expense.

** E.A. Vokovich has exceeded maximum pensionable earnings of $53,600, so he has had the Canada Pension Plan maximum, $2,479.95, already deducted. Vokovich has also exceeded the maximum insurable Employment Insurance earnings of $49,500, so he has already had the maximum, $930.60, deducted.

EXHIBIT 11–9 | Payroll Cheque

Leduc Petroleum									1622	

Leduc Petroleum
Payroll Account
Red Deer, Alberta

1622

January 4, 2016

Pay to the
Order of ___ C.L. Drumm ___ $ 416.06

Four hundred and sixteen ---------------------- 6/100 ___ Dollars

The Bank of Nova Scotia
Red Deer
Alberta

Anna Figaro
Treasurer

⑈111900031⑈ 0787⑈500004454⑈

Pay			Deductions						Net Pay	Cheque No.
Straight Time	Over-time	Gross	Federal Income Tax	Prov. Income Tax	CPP	Employ-ment Ins.	United Way	Total		
400.00	90.00	490.00	31.50	10.55	20.92	8.97	2.00	73.94	416.06	1622

Recording Cash Payments for Payroll

Companies record at least three cash disbursements: for payments of net pay to employees, for payments of payroll withholdings to the government, and for payments to third parties for employee benefits. We saw these earlier in the chapter, but now let's review them briefly for use with the payroll register in Exhibit 11–8.

Net Pay to Employees   Reconciling the bank account can be time consuming because of the large number of paycheques that may be outstanding. Some companies use one bank account strictly for payroll purposes. This helps to keep the payroll charges and outstanding cheques separate from the company's day-to-day business charges and cheques, making each account's reconciliation easier and reducing the chance for errors. The company would make the following entry to record in early January the cash payment (column J in Exhibit 11-8) for the December 31, 2015, weekly payroll if it were paying a payroll company or if they were transferring the funds into a separate bank account for payroll:

2016			
Jan. 4	Salaries Payable	10,002.28	
	Cash		10,002.28
	Cash payment for December 31, 2015 weekly payroll.		

Payroll Withholdings to the Government and Other Organizations   The employer must send income taxes withheld from employees' pay and the employee deductions and employer's share of CPP (or QPP) contributions and EI premiums to the Canada Revenue Agency (or the Quebec government in the case of QPP). The payment for a given month is due on or before the 15th day of the following month. In addition, the employer has to remit any withholdings for union dues, charitable donations, and the like; the payment would probably be made in the following month.

Assume that for the first three weeks of December the following amounts appeared on the payroll register:

Federal income tax	$6,972.80
Province of Alberta income tax	$2,567.40
Employee CPP contributions	$1,645.02
Employee EI contributions	$997.02
United Way contributions	$465.00

Based on those amounts and columns D through H in Exhibit 11–8, the business would record payments to the CRA and the United Way for the month of December 2015 as follows:

2016			
Jan. 10	Employee Income Tax Payable	12,399.10	
	Canada Pension Plan Payable	4,095.44	
	Employment Insurance Payable	2,957.14	
	Cash		19,451.68
	To record payment to the CRA for December 2015 withholdings. Income Tax Payable = $6,972.80 + $1,966.18 + $2,567.40 + $892.72 CPP Payable = $1,645.02 + $402.70 + $1,645.02 + $402.70 EI Payable = $997.02 + $235.12 + [1.4 × ($997.02 + $235.12)]		
Jan. 10	United Way Payable	620.00	
	Cash		620.00
	To record payment to United Way for December 2015 withholdings ($465.00 + $155.00).		

Earnings Record The employer must file Summary of Remuneration Paid returns with the CRA on a calendar-year basis and must provide the employee with a Statement of Remuneration Paid, Form T4, by February 28 of the following year. Therefore, employers maintain an earnings record for each employee. (These earnings records are also used for EI claims.) Exhibit 11–10 is a five-week excerpt from the earnings record of employee Jason C. Jenkins.

The employee earnings record is not a journal or a ledger. It is an accounting tool—like the worksheet—that the employer uses to prepare payroll withholdings reports. The information provided on the employee earnings record with respect to year-to-date earnings also indicates when an employee has earned $53,600, the point at which the employer should stop withholding CPP contributions. (Unlike the employee, the employer may not obtain a refund for overpayment of CPP.) The same is true for EI deductions: the employer stops withholding EI contributions after the employee has earned $49,500. There is no maximum income tax deduction.

Exhibit 11–11 is the Statement of Remuneration Paid, Form T4, for employee Jason C. Jenkins. The employer prepares this form for each employee, as well as a form called a T4 Summary—Summary of Remuneration Paid, which summarizes the information on all the T4s issued by the employer for that year. The employer sends the T4 Summary and one copy of each T4 to the CRA by February 28 each year. The CRA uses the documents to ensure that the employer has correctly paid to the government all amounts withheld on its behalf from employees, together with the employer's share. The employee gets two copies of the T4; one copy must be filed with the employee's income tax return, while the second copy is for the employee's records.

The CRA matches the income on the T4 filed by the employer against the income reported on the employee's income tax return, filed by the employee, to ensure that the employee properly reported his or her income from employment.

EXHIBIT 11-10 | Employee Earnings Record for 2014

Employee Name and Address:
Jenkins, Jason C.
XX Camousen Crescent
Victoria, BC

Social Insurance No.: 111 111 111
Marital Status: Married
Net Claims Code: 4
Pay Rate: $700 per week; overtime $26.25 per hour
Job Title: Admin. Assistant

| Week Ended | Gross Pay | | | | Deductions | | | | | | Net Pay | |
	Hours	Straight Time	Overtime	Total	To Date	Federal Income Tax	Province of BC Income Tax	CPP	EI	United Way	Total	Amount	Cheque No.
Jan. 4	40	700.00		700.00	700.00	47.60	18.16	31.32	13.16	2.00	112.24	587.76	403
Dec. 3	40	700.00		700.00	35,437.50	47.60	18.16	31.32	13.16	2.00	112.24	587.76	1525
Dec. 10	40	700.00		700.00	36,137.50	47.60	18.16	31.32	13.16	2.00	112.24	587.80	1548
Dec. 17	44	700.00	105.00	805.00	36,942.50	62.28	25.27	36.52	15.13	2.00	141.20	663.80	1574
Dec. 24	48	700.00	210.00	910.00	37,852.50	81.48	32.99	41.71	17.11	2.00	175.29	734.71	1598
Dec. 31	46	700.00	157.50	857.50	38,710.00	70.47	29.13	39.11	16.12	2.00	156.83	700.67	1632
Total		36,400.00	2,310.00	38,710.00	38,710.00	2,798.16	1,082.28	1,742.83	727.80	104.00	6,455.12	32,254.88	

EXHIBIT 11–11 | Employee Statement of Remuneration Paid (Form T4)

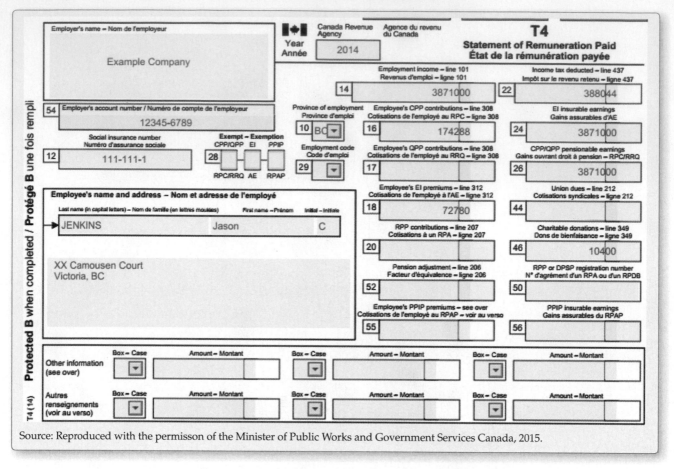

Source: Reproduced with the permisson of the Minister of Public Works and Government Services Canada, 2015.

Employers and employees can use the internet to file T4 information for reporting as well as to file tax information.

> Try It!

7. The payroll register for Quesnel Quarries showed the information below for the weekly pay period ending July 10, 2015. Use this information to record the payroll expenses for the week and the employer's portion of payroll expenses for the week.

Straight-time wages	$21,840
Overtime wages	2,500
Deductions:	
Federal income tax	1,850
Provincial income tax	980
Canada Pension Plan	1,200
Employment Insurance	445
Union Dues	420

8. From the following information, determine whether the accounts are current or long-term liabilities. Show how the current liabilities would be presented on the balance sheet at December 31, 2016, assuming a separate line on the balance sheet for each item. Perform any calculations that may be required.

   a. A one-year, 3 percent note payable for $3,000 was issued on November 3, 2016.

   b. A $10,000, 180-day, 5 percent bank loan was arranged and effective on September 17, 2016.

(Continued)

(Continued)

c. A $10,000, two-year, 3 percent bank loan was arranged and effective on September 17, 2016. The loan must be repaid in full on September 17, 2018.

d. A $10,000, two-year, 5 percent bank loan was arranged and effective on January 2, 2016. Half of the loan must be repaid on January 2, 2017, and the remainder repaid on January 2, 2018.

e. Of the $5,000 unearned subscription revenue that was recorded during the year, $4,200 was earned by December 31.

f. The company expects to pay future warranty costs of 3 percent of sales for the $350,000 of goods sold during 2016.

Solutions appear at the end of this chapter and on MyAccountingLab

REPORTING CURRENT LIABILITIES

Exhibit 11–12 illustrates the presentation of current liabilities in the liabilities section of a balance sheet. Large corporations may include less information on their balance sheet and put additional, more detailed information in the notes to the financial statements.

EXHIBIT 11–12 | Partial Balance Sheet as at December 31, 2017

SASHY'S FLOWERS Balance Sheet May 31, 2017		
Liabilities		
Current Liabilities		
Accounts payable	$ 97,000	
Salaries payable	61,000	
Estimated warranty payable	21,250	
Current portion of long-term debt	10,000	
GST payable	19,447	
Interest payable	661	
Employee income tax payable	8,100	
Canada Pension Plan payable	2,970	
Employment Insurance payable	1,120	
Contingent liability (Note 17)	25,000	
Other current liabilities	1,500	
Total current liabilities		$248,048
Long-Term Liabilities		
Notes payable	100,000	
Less: Current portion of long-term debt	10,000	
Total long-term liabilities		90,000
Total liabilities		$338,048

MyAccountingLab

Video: Real World Accounting

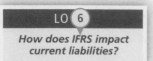

THE IMPACT OF IFRS ON CURRENT LIABILITIES

ASPE	IFRS
Where the Canadian standard is substantially the same as the international standard, we say that the standards are converged. This is the case with current liabilities. For example, both IFRS and ASPE require that liabilities are carried at their fair value.	
Accounts payable and *accrued liabilities* are the usual terms used.	*Trade payables* and *provisions* are the more common terms.
A contingent liability must be *likely* to occur in order to be recognized.	A contingent liability has a slightly lower standard for when it should be recognized; it must be *probable* that it will occur.

The following illustration highlights the differences in interpretation:

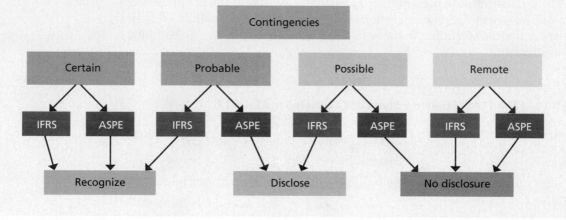

SUMMARY PROBLEM FOR YOUR REVIEW

Best Threads, a clothing store in Moose Jaw, Saskatchewan, employs one salesperson, Sheila Kingsley. Her straight-time pay is $420 per week. She earns time and a half for hours worked in excess of 35 per week. For Kingsley's wage rate and net claim code on her Personal Tax Credits Return (TD1), the federal income tax withholding rate is approximately 11.5 percent, and the provincial rate is 7.7 percent. CPP is 4.95 percent on income until the maximum total contribution of $2,479.95 is reached, while EI premiums are 1.88 percent until the maximum total contribution of $930.60 is reached. In addition, Best Threads pays Kingsley's Blue Cross supplemental health insurance premiums of $31.42 a month and dental insurance premiums of $18.50 a month.

During the week ended March 31, 2015, Kingsley worked 48 hours.

Required

1. Compute Kingsley's gross pay and net pay for the week.

2. Record the following payroll entries that Best Threads would make:

a. Expense for Kingsley's wages including overtime pay (ignore the basic CPP exemption)

b. Cost of employer's share of Kingsley's withholdings (ignore the basic CPP exemption)

c. Expense for medical and dental benefits

d. Payment of cash to Kingsley in April

e. Payment Best Threads must make to the CRA in April

f. Payment of medical and dental benefits in April

3. How much total payroll expense did Best Threads incur for the week? How much cash did the business spend on its payroll?

4. What payroll-related accounts and amounts would appear on the balance sheet at March 31, 2015, if all payments were made in April 2015?

SOLUTION

Requirement 1

Gross pay:		
Straight-time pay for 35 hours		$420.00
Overtime pay		
Rate per hour ($420 ÷ 35 = $12/hour × 1.5)	$18.00	
Hours (48 − 35)	× 13	234.00
		$654.00
Net pay:		
Gross pay		$654.00
Less: Withheld federal income tax ($654 × 0.115)	$ 75.21	
Withheld provincial income tax ($654 × 0.077)	50.36	
Withheld CPP ($654 × 0.0495)	32.37	
Withheld EI ($654 × 0.0188)	12.30	170.24
Net pay		483.76

To compute gross pay, first separate hours worked into straight-time and overtime hours. Then multiply each by the appropriate hourly pay rate.

Compute the amount of each withholding, either using the information given or by consulting tax, CPP, and EI tables or by entering the information in the PDOC. (Not using the rates provided will result in some differences to the totals.)

Gross pay − Total withholdings = Net pay

Requirement 2

a.	Sales Salary Expense	654.00	
	Employee Income Tax Payable		125.57
	Canada Pension Plan Payable		32.37
	Employment Insurance Payable		12.30
	Wages Payable		483.76
	To record expense for S. Kingsley's wages.		
b.	Employee Benefits Expense	49.59	
	Canada Pension Plan Payable		32.37
	Employment Insurance Payable		17.22
	To record cost of employer's portion of S. Kingsley's wages.		
	CPP is $32.37 ($32.37 × 1). EI is $17.22 ($12.30 × 1.4).		

This journal entry uses the gross pay, withholdings, and net pay amounts calculated in Requirement 1.

Add federal and provincial taxes ($75.21 + $50.36) to show one amount for Employee Income Tax Payable.

"Wages Payable" is the amount of net pay.

Remember that the employer's EI expense is 1.4 times the employee's EI withholding.

(*Continued*)

Requirement 2 (Continued)

c.	Medical and Dental Expense	49.92	
	Employee Benefits Payable		49.92
	To record expense of benefits ($31.42 + $18.50).		
d.	Wages Payable	483.76	
	Cash		483.76
	To record payment of wages to S. Kingsley.		
e.	Employee Income Tax Payable	125.57	
	Canada Pension Plan Payable	64.74	
	Employment Insurance Payable	29.52	
	Cash		219.83
	To record payment to the CRA. CPP = $32.37 + $32.37; EI = $12.30 + $17.22		
f.	Employee Benefits Payable	49.92	
	Cash		49.92
	To record payment of monthly benefits.		

This journal entry issues the paycheque or sends the funds by EFT to the employee's bank account.

Employers pay to the CRA:
- Federal and provincial taxes withheld from the employee
- EI premiums withheld from employee + paid by employer
- CPP (or QPP) withholdings from employee + paid by employer

Total payroll expense = Gross salary + EI expense + CPP expense + benefits

Total cash paid = Net pay + CRA payment + benefits payment (everyone who was sent a cheque)

Requirement 3

Best Threads incurred *total payroll expense* of $753.51 (gross salary of $654.00 + employer's cost of CPP of $32.37 + employer's cost of EI of $17.22 + benefits of $49.92). See entries (a) to (c).

Best Threads paid cash of $753.51 on payroll (Kingsley's net pay of $483.76 + payment to the CRA of $219.83 + benefits of $49.92). See entries (d) to (f).

Requirement 4

The accounts and amounts that would appear on the March 31, 2015, balance sheet are as follows:

Employee Income Tax Payable	$125.57
Canada Pension Plan Payable	64.74
Employment Insurance Payable	29.52
Employee Benefits Payable	49.92
Wages Payable	483.76

SUMMARY

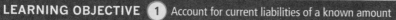

LEARNING OBJECTIVE ❶ Account for current liabilities of a known amount

What are current liabilities and how do we account for them? Pg. 614

- Current liabilities may be divided into those of *known amount* and those that must be *estimated*. Trade accounts payable, short-term notes payable, interest payable, GST payable, HST payable, PST payable, employee benefits payable, and unearned revenues are current liabilities of known amount.

LEARNING OBJECTIVE ② Account for current liabilities that must be estimated

Why would we estimate liabilities, and how do we account for them? Pg. 622
- Current liabilities that must be estimated include warranties payable, vacation pay, and the corporation's income tax payable.
- *Contingent liabilities* are not actual liabilities but potential liabilities that may arise in the future.
- Contingent liabilities, like current liabilities, may be of known amounts or indefinite amounts. The likelihood of the contingency and the ability to estimate the amount determine whether the contingency is recorded as a liability, recorded in the notes to the financial statements, or not recorded at all.

LEARNING OBJECTIVE ③ Compute payroll amounts

How are payroll amounts calculated? Pg. 627
- *Payroll* accounting handles the expenses and liabilities arising from compensating employees.
- Employers must withhold federal and provincial income taxes, CPP (or QPP) contributions, and EI premiums from employees' pay and send these *withholdings* together with the employer's share of the latter two to the appropriate government agency.
- Many employers allow their employees to pay for insurance and union dues and to make gifts to charities through payroll deductions.
- An employee's net pay is the gross pay less all withholdings and optional deductions.

MyAccountingLab **Interactive Figure:** Interact with Bonus

LEARNING OBJECTIVE ④ Record basic payroll transactions

How are payroll liabilities recorded in the accounting records? Pg. 633
- An *employer's* payroll expenses include the employer's share of CPP (or QPP) contributions and EI premiums; employers also pay provincial health care and post-secondary education taxes in those provinces that levy them, as well as workers' compensation.
- Employers may provide their employees with fringe benefits, such as dental coverage and retirement pensions.

LEARNING OBJECTIVE ⑤ Report payroll and other current liabilities on the balance sheet

How are payroll liabilities reported? Pg. 635
- A basic *payroll system* consists of a payroll register, a payroll bank account, payroll cheques or EFTs, and an earnings record for each employee.
- The company reports on the balance sheet all current liabilities that it owes: current liabilities of known amount, including payroll liabilities, and current liabilities that must be estimated.

MyAccountingLab **Video:** Real World Accounting

LEARNING OBJECTIVE ⑥ Describe the impact of IFRS on current liabilities

How does IFRS impact current liabilities? Pg. 642
- Under IFRS, the usual terms are *trade payables* and *provisions* for *accounts payable* and *accrued liabilities*, but these terms are optional for Canadian companies reporting under ASPE.

Check **Accounting Vocabulary** on page 646 for all key terms used in Chapter 11 and the **Glossary** at the back of the book for all key terms used in the textbook.

MORE CHAPTER REVIEW MATERIAL

MyAccountingLab

DemoDoc covering General Current Liabilities

Student PowerPoint Slides

Audio Chapter Summary

Note: All MyAccountingLab resources can be found in the Chapter Resources section and the Multimedia Library.

ACCOUNTING VOCABULARY

Accrued expense   An expense that has been incurred but not yet paid in cash; also called an *accrued liability* (p. 620).

Accrued liability   Another name for an *accrued expense* (p. 620).

Canada (or Quebec) Pension Plan (CPP or QPP)   All employees and self-employed persons in Canada (except in Quebec, where the pension plan is the Quebec Pension Plan) between 18 and 70 years of age are required to contribute to the Canada Pension Plan administered by the Government of Canada (p. 628).

Contingent liability   A potential liability from a past event that depends on an uncertain future event not within the business's control (p. 624).

Current portion of long-term debt   The amount of the principal that is payable within one year (p. 619).

Employee compensation   Payroll, a major expense of many businesses (p. 627).

Employment Insurance (EI)   Most employees and employers in Canada must contribute to the Employment Insurance fund, which provides assistance to unemployed workers (p. 629).

End-user tax   A consumption tax that is only paid by the final consumer (p. 618).

Exempt supplies   Goods and services that are not required to have GST or HST charged on them (p. 617).

Gross pay   Total amount of salary, wages, commissions, or any other employee compensation before taxes and other deductions are taken out (p. 627).

Independent contractors   Individuals who do work for a business but are not employees. They invoice the business for their contracted work (p. 634).

Input tax credit (ITC)   The sales tax that will be refunded by the government (p. 617).

Line of credit   Similar to a bank loan, it is negotiated once then drawn upon when needed. Interest is paid monthly only on the amount of the line of credit actually used (p. 615).

Net pay   Gross pay minus all deductions; the amount of employee compensation that the employee actually takes home (p. 627).

Ontario Retirement Pension Plan (ORPP)   Employees in Ontario without a company pension plan are required to contribute to the provincial pension plan in addition to their Canada Pension Plan contributions (effective 2017) (p. 629).

Overtime   For additional hours above the standard, employees are paid at a higher rate (p. 627).

Payroll   Employee compensation, a major expense of many businesses (p. 627).

Payroll Deductions Online Calculator (PDOC)   An online tool provided by the Canada Revenue Agency for calculating federal and provincial payroll deductions for all provinces (except Quebec) and territories (p. 629).

Pledged as security   A phrase that indicates an asset is held as collateral for a loan. In other words, if the loan is not paid, the asset will be taken as payment for the outstanding debt (p. 616).

Recoverable   In terms of accounting for taxes, this term means that the tax is refunded by the government (p. 617).

Registrant   A business or individual that is registered with the government to collect and remit sales taxes (p. 617).

Short-term note payable   A note payable that is due within one year, a common form of financing (p. 614).

Straight time   A set period during which the base rate is paid to an employee (p. 627).

Taxable supplies   Goods and services that, when sold, have GST or HST charged on them (p. 617).

Warranty   When a business guarantees its products or services against defects (p. 622).

Withheld   Deducted from pay and kept by the employer to be remitted to another party (p. 628).

Workers' compensation   A provincially administered plan that is funded by contributions by employers and that provides financial support for workers injured on the job (p. 630).

Zero-rated supplies   Goods and services that have a GST or HST rate of zero percent (p. 617).

SIMILAR ACCOUNTING TERMS

Accounts payable	Trade payables
Accrued expense	Accrued liability; Provisions
Accrued liabilities	Provisions; Accrued expenses
CPP	Canada Pension Plan
CRA	Canada Revenue Agency
Current portion of long-term debt	Current maturity
Deduction	Withholding
EI	Employment Insurance
GST	Goods and services tax
HST	Harmonized sales tax
ITC	Input tax credit

Net pay	Take-home pay
ORPP	Ontario Retirement Pension Plan
Payroll register	Payroll journal; Payroll record
PDOC	Payroll Deductions Online Calculator
PST	Provincial sales tax
QPP	Quebec Pension Plan
QST	Quebec (provincial) sales tax
T4	Statement of Remuneration Paid
TD1	Personal Tax Credit Return
Unearned revenues	Deferred revenues; Revenues collected in advance; Customer prepayments

SELF-STUDY QUESTIONS

Test your understanding of the chapter by marking the correct answer for each of the following questions:

1. A $10,000, 9 percent, one-year note payable was issued on July 31. The balance sheet at December 31 will report interest payable of (pp. 614–615)
   a. $0 because the interest is not due yet
   b. $522.74
   c. $375
   d. $900

2. Suppose Super Tires estimates that warranty costs will equal 1 percent of tire sales. Assume that November tire sales totalled $900,000, and the company's outlay in replacement tires and cash to satisfy warranty claims was $7,400. How much warranty expense should the November income statement report? (pp. 622–623)
   a. $1,600
   b. $7,400
   c. $9,000
   d. $16,400

3. Your company sells $180,000 (selling price) of goods and collects 5 percent GST. What current liability does the sale create? (p. 617)
   a. GST payable of $9,000
   b. Sales revenue of $189,000
   c. Unearned revenue of $9,000
   d. GST payable of $171,000

4. Liabilities that exist but whose exact amount is not known must be (p. 622)
   a. Estimated
   b. Ignored. Record them when they are paid
   c. Treated as a contingent liability
   d. Reported in the notes to the financial statements

5. A contingent liability that is likely and can be reasonably estimated should be (p. 625)
   a. Accrued as an expense and reported as a liability
   b. Only disclosed in a note to the financial statements
   c. Either disclosed in a note or accrued with a journal entry depending on the amount
   d. Ignored until the liability materializes

6. Nouvou Diet Systems Company is a defendant in a lawsuit that claims damages of $55,000. On the balance sheet date, it appears unlikely that the court will render a judgment against the company. How should Nouvou Diet Systems Company report this event in its financial statements? (p. 625)
   a. Omit mention because no judgment has been rendered
   b. Disclose the contingent liability in a note
   c. Report the loss on the income statement and the liability on the balance sheet.
   d. Do both b and c

7. Which of the following liabilities creates no expense for the company? (pp. 616–619)
   a. Interest
   b. Sales tax
   c. Employment Insurance
   d. Warranty

8. Darcy Renick's weekly pay for 40 hours is $400 plus time and a half for overtime. The federal tax rate, based on her income level and deductions, is 10.5 percent, the provincial rate is 8.8 percent, the QPP rate is 4.95 percent on her weekly earnings, and the EI rate is 1.88 percent on her weekly earnings. What is Darcy's take-home pay for a week in which she works 50 hours? (pp. 627–629)
   a. $426.34
   b. $460.97
   c. $428.42
   d. $406.28

9. Which of the following represents a cost to the employer? (p. 629)
   a. Withheld income tax
   b. Canada Pension Plan
   c. Employment Insurance
   d. Both b and c

10. Which of the following items is reported as a current liability on the balance sheet? (p. 641)
    a. Short-term notes payable
    b. Estimated warranties
    c. Payroll withholdings
    d. All of the above

ASSIGNMENT MATERIAL

QUESTIONS

1. What distinguishes a current liability from a long-term liability? What distinguishes a contingent liability from an actual liability?

2. A company purchases a machine by signing a $50,000, 4 percent, one-year note payable on June 30. Interest is to be paid at maturity. What two current liabilities related to this purchase does the company report on its December 31 balance sheet? What is the amount of each current liability?

3. Explain how GST that is paid by consumers is a liability of the store that sold the merchandise. To whom is GST paid?

4. Why is it important for a business to separate the current portion of long-term debt from the long-term debt?

5. What is meant by the term *current portion of long-term debt*, and how is this item reported in the financial statements?

6. Why is an accrued expense a liability?

7. Describe the similarities and differences between an account payable and a short-term note payable.

8. At the beginning of the school term, what type of account is the tuition that your college or university collects from students? What type of account is the tuition at the end of the school term?

9. Why is a customer deposit a liability? Give an example.

10. Murray Company warrants its products against defects for two years from date of sale. During the current year, the company made sales of $1,000,000. Management estimated warranty costs on those sales would total $50,000 over the two-year warranty period. Ultimately, the company paid $35,000 cash on warranties. What is the company's warranty expense for the year? What accounting principle or objective governs this answer?

11. Identify one contingent liability of a definite amount and one contingent liability of an indefinite amount.

12. What are the two basic categories of current liabilities? Give an example of each.

13. Why is payroll expense relatively more important to a service business such as a public accounting firm than it is to a merchandising company such as Canadian Tire?

14. Two people are studying Husky Company's manufacturing process. One person is Husky Company's factory supervisor, and the other person is an outside consultant who is an expert in the industry. Which person's salary is the payroll expense of Husky Company? Identify the expense account that Husky Company would debit to record the pay of each person.

15. What are two elements of an employer's payroll expense in addition to salaries, wages, commissions, and overtime pay?

16. What determines the amount of income tax that is withheld from employee paycheques?

17. What is the Canada (or Quebec) Pension Plan? Who pays contributions toward it? What are the funds used for?

18. Identify three required deductions and two optional deductions from employee paycheques.

19. Identify the employee benefit expenses an employer pays.

20. Who pays EI premiums? What are these funds used for?

21. Briefly describe a basic payroll accounting system's components and their functions.

22. How much EI has been withheld from the pay of an employee who has earned $52,288 during the current year? What is the employer's EI expense for this employee?

23. Why do some companies use a special payroll bank account?

24. Under IFRS, what is the standard that must be met to report a contingent liability? Is it a higher or lower standard than under ASPE?

STARTERS

Starter 11-1 On July 31, 2016, Mission Corp. purchased $32,000 of inventory on a one-year, 6-percent note payable. Journalize the company's (a) accrual of interest expense on December 31, 2016, and (b) payment of the note plus interest on July 31, 2017.

Accounting for a note payable
①
b. Credit Cash for $33,920

Starter 11-2 Refer to the data in Starter 11-1. Show what Mission Corp. reports for the note payable and related interest payable on its balance sheet at December 31, 2016, and on its income statement for the year ended on that date.

Reporting a short-term note payable and the related interest
①
Interest Expense, $800

Starter 11-3 Mosaic Music has a current ratio of 2.0 ($240,000 current assets ÷ $120,000 current liabilities). For each of the following transactions, determine whether the current ratio will increase, decrease, or remain the same:

a. Borrowed $20,000 from a local bank to be paid in 60 days.
b. Accrued wages in the amount of $50,000.
c. Paid accounts payable in the amount of $10,000.
d. Bought inventory on credit for $15,000.

Effect on current ratio
①

Starter 11-4 Grayson River Rafting has the following liabilities:

a. Accounts payable
b. Note payable due in three years
c. Salaries payable
d. Note payable due in six months
e. Sales tax payable
f. Unearned revenue

Indicate whether each liability would be considered a current liability (CL) or long-term liability (LTL).

Determining current versus long-term liabilities
①

Starter 11-5 On July 10, Keller Company, a business located in Alberta, purchased $15,000 of inventory for resale on account. On July 25, Keller recorded the sale of that merchandise on account for $20,000 plus tax. On August 10, Keller remitted GST to the Receiver General. They had no other sales or input tax credits. Journalize all three transactions.

Recording GST
①

Starter 11-6 On July 1, *Quill & Quire* magazine collected cash of $5,000 for annual subscriptions (12 issues per year) starting on August 1. Journalize the transaction to record the collection of cash on July 1 and the transaction required at December 31, the magazine's year end, assuming no revenue has been recorded so far. (Round the adjustment to the nearest whole dollar.)

Recording unearned revenue
①

Starter 11-7 On December 31, 2016, Jabot purchased $16,000 of equipment on a one-year, 9 percent note payable. Journalize the company's purchase of equipment, the accrual of interest expense on May 31, 2017 (its fiscal year end), and the payment of the note plus interest on December 31, 2017.

Accounting for a note payable
①

Starter 11-8 Western Yard Equipment offers warranties on all its lawn mowers. It estimates warranty expense at 1.4 percent of sales. At the beginning of 2016, the Estimated Warranty Payable account had a credit balance of $2,200. During the year, Western Yard Equipment had $580,000 of sales and had to pay out $8,950 in warranty payments for repairs.

1. Prepare the required journal entries to record warranty expense and payments. Use December 31 for the journal entry date.

2. What is the balance of the warranty liability at the end of 2016? Indicate whether the balance is a debit or a credit.

Warranty journal entries
②
Warranty expense, $8,120

Accounting for warranty expense and warranty payable

②

2. Estimated Warranty Payable bal., $8,000

Starter 11–9 Patagonia Corporation guarantees its snowmobiles for three years. Company experience indicates that warranty costs will be 3 percent of sales.

Assume that a Patagonia dealer made sales totalling $600,000 during 2017, its first year of operations. The company received cash for 30 percent of the sales and notes receivable for the remainder. Warranty payments totalled $10,000 during 2017.

1. Record the sales, warranty expense, and warranty payments for Patagonia Corporation.
2. Post to the Estimated Warranty Payable T-account. At the end of 2017, what is the Estimated Warranty Payable balance for Patagonia Corporation?

Reporting warranties in the financial statements

②

Starter 11–10 Refer to the data given in Starter 11–9.

What amount of warranty expense will Patagonia Corporation report during 2017? Does the warranty expense for the year equal the year's cash payments for warranties? Which accounting principle or objective addresses this situation?

Interpreting an actual company's contingent liabilities

②

Starter 11–11 Harley-Davidson, Inc., the motorcycle manufacturer, used to include the following note (adapted) in its annual report:

Notes to Consolidated Financial Statements

7 (in Part): Commitments and Contingencies (Adapted)

The Company self-insures its product liability losses in the United States up to $3 million.

Catastrophic coverage is maintained for individual claims in excess of $3 million up to $25 million.

---

1. Why are these *contingent* (versus real) liabilities?
2. How can a contingent liability become a real liability for Harley-Davidson? What are the limits to the company's product liabilities in the United States?

Computing payroll amounts

Net pay, $2,980

Starter 11–12 Suppose you work for an accounting firm all year and earn a monthly salary of $4,000. There is no overtime pay. Your withheld deductions are 20 percent of gross pay. In addition to payroll deductions, you choose to contribute 4 percent monthly to your pension plan. Your employer also deducts $60 monthly for your payment of the health insurance premium.

Compute your net pay for November.

Computing an employee's total pay

2. Net pay, $845.12

Starter 11–13 Mike Klyn is paid $840 for a 40-hour workweek and time and a half for hours worked above 40.

1. Compute Klyn's gross pay for working 50 hours during the first week of February.
2. Klyn is single, and his income tax withholding is 20 percent of total pay. His only payroll deductions are taxes withheld, CPP of 4.95 percent, and EI of 1.88 percent. Compute Klyn's net pay for the week.

Computing the payroll expense of an employer

③

Total expense, $1,317.31

Starter 11–14 Return to the Mike Klyn payroll situation in Starter 11–13. Klyn's employer, Jones Golf Corp., pays all the standard payroll expenses plus benefits for employee pensions (5 percent of gross pay), BC health insurance ($60 per employee per month), and disability insurance ($8 per employee per month). Assume February has four pay periods.

Compute Jones Golf Corp.'s total expense of employing Mike Klyn for the 50 hours that he worked during the first week of February. Carry amounts to the nearest cent.

Making payroll entries

a. Salary Expense, $1,155

Starter 11–15 After solving Starters 11-13 and 11-14, journalize for Jones Golf Corp. the following expenses related to the employment of Mike Klyn on February 17:

a. Salary expense
b. Benefits
c. Employer payroll expenses

Round all amounts to the nearest cent.

Starter 11–16 After solving Starters 11-13, 11-14, and 11-15, journalize for Jones Golf Corp. the remittance of this payroll to the CRA on March 15.

Making payroll entries

Starter 11–17 Refer to the payroll information in Starters 11-13, 11-14, and 11-15.

1. How much was the company's total salary expense for the week for Mike Klyn?
2. How much cash did Mike Klyn take home for his work?
3. How much did the *employee* pay this week for
   a. Income tax?
   b. CPP and EI?
4. How much expense did the *employer* have this week for
   a. CPP and EI?
   b. Benefits?

Making payroll entries

1. Total Salary Expense $1,317.31

Starter 11–18 GC Company has employees who are paid on a monthly basis. Payroll information for August of the current year is given below.

Employee salaries	$155,000
Union dues	1,050
Charitable contributions	375
Employee CPP contributions	7,320
Employee EI contributions	2,836
Employee income tax withheld	31,250

Prepare the journal entries to record the August 30 payroll payment and the payroll benefits expense for GC Company for August. Also prepare the entries to record the payment of payroll withholdings to the government and other agencies on September 15. Explanations are not required.

Payroll journal entries

Employee benefits expense, $11,290.40

Starter 11–19 Identify the proper classification of each item below. In the space beside each item, write C for a current liability, L for long-term liability, or N if it is not a liability.

Reporting liabilities on the balance sheet

_____ a. Bank loan payments due in the next 12 months
_____ b. Income taxes payable
_____ c. Estimated property taxes
_____ d. Warranty liability
_____ e. Unearned revenue
_____ f. Note payable in 120 days
_____ g. Mortgage payable payments do not start for 13 months
_____ h. Bank overdraft

EXERCISES

MyAccountingLab

Exercise 11–1

Prepare the journal entries for Passport Merchandising, assuming that Passport Merchandising uses a perpetual inventory system. Passport Merchandising charges GST on all its sales at the rate of 5 percent and pays GST on all its purchases at the rate of 5 percent. Explanations are not required.

Recording GST on a series of transactions

May 8	Purchased inventory, on account, FOB destination, from Seguin Wholesale. $2,000 plus applicable GST.
10	Returned defective merchandise to Seguin, $300 plus applicable GST.
12	Sold merchandise to Dainty Store on account for $3,000 plus applicable GST. Cost of the merchandise sold was $1,300.
28	Collected balance on account from Dainty Store.
30	Paid balance on account to Seguin.
June 15	Prepare the remittance payment of GST based on only the above transactions in May.

Recording note payable
transactions

June 1, 2017, Credit Cash,
$91,160

Exercise 11–2

Record the following note payable transactions of Lambda Company in the company's general journal. Explanations are not required.

2016

Jun. 1 Purchased delivery truck costing $86,000 by issuing a one-year, 6 percent note payable.

Dec. 31 Accrued interest on the note payable.

2017

Jun. 1 Paid the note payable at maturity.

Exercise 11–3

Recording sales tax and GST

June 30, Debit Cash, $129,950

Make general journal entries to record the following transactions of Mehta Products for a two-month period:

Jun. 30 Recorded cash sales of $115,000 for the month plus PST of 8 percent collected on behalf of the province of Manitoba and GST of 5 percent. Record the two taxes in separate accounts.

Jul. 6 Sent June PST and GST to the appropriate authorities (Minister of Finance for PST and Receiver General for GST). Assume no GST input tax credits.

Exercise 11–4

Current portion of long-term
debt

2014: Current portion of long-term debt, $500,000; Interest payable, $80,000

Suppose Detweiler Technologies borrowed $2,000,000 on December 31, 2013, by issuing 4 percent long-term debt that must be paid in four equal annual instalments plus interest commencing January 2, 2015.

Required Insert the appropriate amounts in the following excerpts from the company's partial balance sheet to show how Detweiler Technologies should report its current and long-term liabilities for this debt.

	December 31,			
	2014	**2015**	**2016**	**2017**
Current liabilities:				
Current portion of long-term debt	$_____	$_____	$_____	$_____
Interest payable	$_____	$_____	$_____	$_____
Long-term liabilities:				
Long-term debt	$_____	$_____	$_____	$_____

Exercise 11–5

Recording current liabilities

The management of Epsot Marketing Services examines the following company accounting records at August 29, immediately before the end of the year, August 31:

Total current assets....................................	$ 325,000
Property, plant, and equipment	1,079,500
	$1,404,500
Total current liabilities............................	$ 192,500
Long-term liabilities.................................	247,500
Owner's equity...	964,500
	$1,404,500

Epsot's banking agreement with Royal Bank requires the company to keep a current ratio (current assets ÷ current liabilities) of 2.0 or better. How much in current liabilities should Epsot pay off within the next two days in order to comply with its borrowing agreements?

Exercise 11–6

The law firm Garner & Brown received from a large corporate client an annual retainer fee of $60,000 on January 2, 2017. The fee is based on anticipated monthly services of $5,000.

Required

1. Using the account title Retainer Fees for unearned revenue, journalize (a) Garner & Brown's receipt of retainer fees, and (b) the provision of services in the month of January 2017.
2. Post the journal entries in Requirement 1 to the unearned revenue account (Retainer Fees) T-account. What is the value of services to be provided to the client in the remaining 11 months?

Accounting for unearned revenue

① ②

2. Services to be provided, $55,000

Exercise 11–7

Assume the *National Post* completed the following transactions for one subscriber during 2017:

Oct. 1 Sold a six-month subscription, collecting cash of $100 plus PST of 8 percent and GST of 5 percent.

Nov. 15 Remitted (paid) the PST to the Province of Manitoba and the GST to the Receiver General. Remember: Write two cheques.

Dec. 31 Made the necessary adjustment at year end to record the amount of subscription revenue earned during the year.

Required

1. Using the account title Unearned Subscription Revenue, journalize the transactions above.
2. Post the entries to the Unearned Subscription Revenue T-account. How much does the *National Post* owe the subscriber at December 31, 2017?
3. How would the entries in Requirement 1 be different if the *National Post* were in a different province that uses a 12 percent HST rate? Record the entries.

Accounting for unearned revenue

① ②

2. Unearned subscription revenue, $50.00

Exercise 11–8

The accounting records of Harroy Industries included the following at January 1, 2017:

Estimated Warranty Payable

	Jan. 1, 2017 24,800

In the past, Harroy Industries' warranty expense has been 3 percent of sales. During 2017, Harroy Industries made sales of $1,038,000 and paid $27,900 to satisfy warranty claims.

Required

1. Record Harroy Industries' warranty expense and warranty payments during 2017. Explanations are not required.
2. What balance of Estimated Warranty Payable will Harroy Industries report on its balance sheet at December 31, 2017?

Accounting for warranty expense and the related liability

②

2. Estimated Warranty Payable bal., $28,040

Exercise 11–9

Ludeman Security Systems is a defendant in lawsuits brought against the monitoring service of its installed systems. Damages of $1,000,000 are claimed against Ludeman Security Systems, but the company denies the charges and is vigorously defending itself. In a recent newspaper interview, the president of the company stated that he could not predict the outcome of the lawsuits. Nevertheless, he said management does not believe that any actual liabilities resulting from the lawsuits will significantly affect the company's financial position.

Required Describe what, if any, disclosure Ludeman Security Systems should provide of this contingent liability. Total liabilities are $4.0 million. If you believe note disclosure is required, write the note to describe the contingency.

Reporting a contingent liability

②

Exercise 11–10

Accruing a contingency

Refer to the Ludeman Security Systems situation in Exercise 11-9. Suppose that Ludeman Security Systems' lawyers advise that a preliminary judgment of $300,000 has been rendered against the company. The company will appeal the decision.

Required   Describe how to report this situation in the Ludeman Security Systems' financial statements. Journalize any entry required under ASPE. Explanations are not required.

Exercise 11–11

Accounting for income taxes

Blue Water Dredging recorded $10,000 in estimated taxes on the last day of each month and made the payment on the 15th of the following month. On December 31, 2016, Blue Water's year end, it was determined that total income tax expense for the year was $126,000. Record the final instalment on December 31 and its payment on January 15, 2017.

Exercise 11–12

Computing net pay

③

Net pay, $3,848.18

Sylvia Chan is a clerk in the shoe department of the Hudson's Bay store in Winnipeg. She earns a base monthly salary of $1,875 plus a 7 percent commission on her sales. Through payroll deductions, Chan donates $50 per month to a charitable organization and pays benefit premiums of $49.15. Compute Chan's gross pay and net pay for December, assuming her sales for the month are $50,000. The income tax rate on her earnings is 20 percent, the CPP contribution rate is 4.95 percent (account for the $3,500 basic annual exemption), and the EI premium rate is 1.88 percent. Chan has not yet reached the CPP or EI maximum earning levels.

Excel Spreadsheet Template

Computing and recording gross pay and net pay

1. Net pay, $297.54

Exercise 11–13

Brad Jackson works for a Bob's Burgers takeout for straight-time earnings of $10.50 per hour with time and a half for hours in excess of 35 per week. Jackson's payroll deductions include income tax of 25 percent, CPP of 4.95 percent on earnings (account for the $3,500 basic annual exemption), and EI of 1.88 percent on earnings. In addition, he contributes $10 per week to his Registered Retirement Savings Plan (RRSP). Assume Jackson worked 40 hours during the week. He has not yet reached the CPP or EI maximum earning levels.

Required

1. Compute Jackson's gross pay and net pay for the week.
2. Make a June 14 general journal entry to record the restaurant's wage expense for Jackson's work, including his payroll deductions and the employer payroll costs. Round all amounts to the nearest cent. An explanation is not required.

Exercise 11–14

Recording a payroll

③ ④

Total of CPP and EI Expense, $7,202.90

Natural Step Manufacturing incurred salary expense of $95,000 for September. The company's payroll expense includes CPP of 4.95 percent and EI of 1.4 times the employee payment, which is 1.88 percent of earnings. Also, the company provides the following benefits for employees: dental insurance (cost to the company of $5,723.09), life insurance (cost to the company of $441.09), and pension benefits through a private plan (cost to the company of $1,745.60). Record Natural Step Manufacturing's payroll expenses for CPP, EI, and employee benefits on September 30. Ignore the CPP basic exemption.

Exercise 11–15

Using a payroll system to compute total payroll expense

Total payroll expense, $43,947.30

Study the Employee Earnings Record for Jason C. Jenkins in Exhibit 11–10, page 639. In addition to the amounts shown in the exhibit, the employer also paid all employee benefits plus (a) an amount equal to 5 percent of gross pay into Jenkins's pension retirement account, and (b) dental insurance for Jenkins at a cost of $35 per month and parking of $10 per month. Compute the employer's total payroll expense for employee Jason C. Jenkins during 2015. Carry all amounts to the nearest cent.

Exercise 11–16

Reporting current and long-term liabilities

① ⑤

Total current liabilities, $597,671

Assume Salem Electronics completed these selected transactions during December 2016:

1. Music For You Inc., a chain of music stores, ordered $105,000 worth of CD players. With its order, Music For You Inc. sent a cheque for $105,000. Salem Electronics will ship the goods on January 3, 2017.

2. The December payroll of $600,000 is subject to employee withheld income tax of 16 percent, CPP expenses of 4.95 percent for the employee and 4.95 percent for the employer, EI deductions of 1.88 percent for the employee and 1.4 times the employee rate of 1.88 percent for the employer. On December 31, Salem Electronics pays employees but accrues all tax amounts. Employees have not reached CPP or EI maximums.

3. Sales of $30,000,000 are subject to estimated warranty cost of 1 percent. This was the first year the company provided a warranty, and no warranty claims have been recorded or paid.

4. On December 2, Salem Electronics signed a $50,000 note payable that requires annual payments of $10,000 plus 5 percent interest on the unpaid balance each December 2. Salem calculates interest on this note based on days, not months.

Required Report these items on Salem Electronics' balance sheet at December 31, 2016.

SERIAL EXERCISE

This exercise continues the Lee Management Consulting situation from earlier chapters. If you did not complete any Serial Exercises in earlier chapters, you can still complete Exercise 11–17 as it is presented.

Exercise 11–17

In Chapter 2, on page 99, we learned that Lee Management Consulting hired a part-time office manager to be paid $2,000 salary per month. She started work on Monday, June 25. The following additional payroll information is available for the June 29 pay date:

Recording a payroll
③ ④
1. Net pay, $1,639.59

Federal income tax to be withheld	$138.55
Provincial income tax to be withheld	99.70
CPP	84.56
EI	37.60

Required

1. Compute the office manager's gross pay and net pay for the month.
2. Make one general journal entry to record Lee Management Consulting's salary expense for the office manager, including her payroll deductions and the employer payroll costs. Round all amounts to the nearest cent.

CHALLENGE EXERCISES

Exercise 11–18

Suppose the balance sheets of a corporation for two years reported these figures:

Accounting for and reporting current liabilities
① ⑤
1. Current ratios:
2017, 2.10
2016, 1.52

	Billions	
	2017	**2016**
Total current assets	$ 24.50	$ 22.92
Property, plant, and equipment, net	44.74	40.96
Total assets	$ 69.24	$ 63.88
Total current liabilities	$ 11.66	$ 15.12
Long-term liabilities	29.92	23.32
Shareholders' equity	27.66	25.44
Total liabilities and shareholders' equity	$ 69.24	$ 63.88

The notes to the 2017 financial statements report that because of some refinancing arrangements, the corporation was able to reclassify $7.0 billion from current liabilities to long-term liabilities during 2017.

Required

1. Compute the corporation's current ratio (current assets ÷ current liabilities) at the end of each year. Describe the change between the years that you observe.
2. Suppose that the corporation had not refinanced and not been able to reclassify the $7.0 billion of current liabilities as long term during 2017. Recompute the current ratio for 2017 to include the $7.0 billion. Why do you think the corporation decided to reclassify the liabilities as long term?

Exercise 11–19

Analyzing current liability accounts

① ⑤

1. Payment of notes payable, $55 mil.

Vallarta Company recently reported notes payable and accrued payrolls and benefits as follows:

	December 31,	
	2017	**2016**
	(in millions of dollars)	
Current liabilities (partial):		
Notes payable	$ 26	$ 78
Accrued payrolls and benefits	270	298

Assume that, during 2017, Vallarta Company borrowed $3.0 million on notes payable. Also assume that Vallarta paid $250 million for employee compensation and benefits during 2017.

Required

1. Compute Vallarta Company's payment of notes payable during 2017.
2. Compute Vallarta Company's employee compensation expense for 2017.

BEYOND THE NUMBERS

Beyond the Numbers 11–1

Suppose a large manufacturing company is the defendant in numerous lawsuits claiming unfair trade practices. The company has strong incentives not to disclose these contingent liabilities. However, ASPE requires companies to report their contingent liabilities.

Required

1. Why would a company prefer not to disclose its contingent liabilities?
2. Describe how a bank could be harmed if a company seeking a loan did not disclose its contingent liabilities.
3. What is the ethical tightrope that companies must walk when they report their contingent liabilities?

Beyond the Numbers 11–2

The following questions are independent of each other.

a. A warranty is like a contingent liability in that the amount to be paid is not known at year end. Why are warranties payable shown as a current liability, whereas contingent liabilities are often reported in the notes to the financial statements?

b. A friend comments that he thought that liabilities represented amounts owed by a company. He asks why unearned revenues are shown as a current liability. How would you respond?

c. Auditors have procedures for determining whether they have discovered all of a company's contingent liabilities often called "a search for unrecorded liabilities." These procedures differ from the procedures used for determining that accounts payable are stated correctly. How would an auditor identify a client's contingent liabilities?

ETHICAL ISSUE

Many companies, such as Wall Financial Corporation, a real estate developer located in Vancouver, borrowed heavily during the past 20 years to exploit the advantage of financing operations with debt. At first, companies were often able to earn operating income higher than their interest expense and were, therefore, quite profitable. However, when the business cycle turned down, their debt burdens caused problems for creditors. In extreme cases, operating income was less than debt servicing or interest expense.

Required   Is it unethical for managers to commit a company to a high level of debt? Or is it just risky? Who could be hurt by a company's taking on too much debt? Discuss.

PROBLEMS (GROUP A)   MyAccountingLab

Problem 11–1A

The following selected transactions of Truestar Communications, a Manitoba company, occurred during 2016 and 2017. The company's year end is December 31.

Journalizing liability-related transactions

2016

Jan.	3	Purchased a machine at a cost of $350,000 plus 5 percent GST, signing a 5 percent, 180-day note payable for that amount.
	29	Recorded the month's sales of $1,570,000 (excludes PST and GST), 80 percent on credit and 20 percent for cash. Sales amounts are subject to 8 percent PST and 5 percent GST.
Feb.	5	Paid January's PST and GST to the appropriate authorities.
	28	Borrowed $3,000,000 on a 3 percent note payable that calls for annual instalment payments of $300,000 principal plus interest.
Jul.	3	Paid the six-month, 5 percent note at maturity.
Nov.	30	Purchased inventory for $150,000 plus GST, signing a six-month, 5 percent note payable.
Dec.	31	Accrued warranty expense, which is estimated at 2 percent of annual sales of $8,000,000.
	31	Accrued interest on all outstanding notes payable. Make a separate interest accrual entry for each note payable.

2017

Feb.	28	Paid the first instalment and interest for one year on the long-term note payable.
May	31	Paid off the 5 percent note plus interest at maturity.

Required   Record the transactions in the company's general journal. Use days in any interest accrual calculations, not months. Round all amounts to the nearest whole dollar. Explanations are not required.

Problem 11–2A

Austin Motors is located in Victoria, British Columbia, and is the only Austin dealer in Western Canada. The dealership repairs and restores Austin vintage cars. Hal Irwin, the general manager, is considering changing insurance companies because of a disagreement with Len Legrew, an agent for the Dominion of Canada Insurance Company. Dominion is doubling Austin Motors' liability insurance cost for the next year. In discussing insurance coverage with you, a trusted business associate, Legrew brings up the subject of contingent liabilities.

Identifying contingent liabilities

Required   Write a memorandum to inform Austin Motors of specific contingent liabilities arising from the business. In your discussion, define a contingent liability.

The partial monthly records of Westwood Golf Shop show the following figures:

Employee Earnings		Employment Insurance	$ 478
Regular employee earnings	$19,947	Medical insurance	541
Overtime pay	a	Total deductions	7,947
Total employee earnings	b	Net pay	17,595

Deductions and Net Pay		Accounts Debited	
Withheld income tax	6,379	Salaries Expense	d
Canada Pension Plan	c	Wages Expense	6,938
		Sales Commission Expense	1,681

Required

1. Determine missing amounts a, b, c, and d.
2. Prepare the general journal entry to record Westwood Golf Shop's payroll on August 31. Credit Payroll Payable for net pay. No explanation is required.

Problem 11–4A

Assume that Raji Patel is a vice-president in Maple Capital's leasing operations. During 2015 she worked for the company all year at a $7,500 monthly salary. She also earned a year-end bonus equal to 10 percent of her salary.

Patel's federal income tax withheld during 2015 was $2,398 per month. Also, there was a one-time federal withholding tax of $4,512 on her bonus cheque. She paid $356.85 per month into the CPP until she had paid the maximum of $2,479.95. In addition, Patel paid $157.50 per month EI through her employer until the maximum of $930.60 had been reached. She had authorized Maple Capital to make the following payroll deductions: RRSP contribution of $55 per month and United Way donation of $37.50 per month.

Maple Capital incurred CPP expense equal to the amount deducted from Patel's pay and EI expense equal to 1.4 times the amount Patel paid. In addition, Maple Capital paid dental and drug insurance of $38 per month and pension benefits of 7 percent of her base salary.

Required

1. Compute Patel's gross pay, payroll deductions, and net pay for the full year 2015. Round all amounts to the nearest cent.
2. Compute Maple Capital's total 2015 payroll expense for Patel.
3. Prepare Maple Capital's general journal entries (explanations are not required) to record its expense for the following:

   a. Patel's total earnings for the year, her payroll deductions, and her net pay. Debit Salary Expense and Bonus Expense as appropriate for salary and bonus. Credit liability accounts for the payroll deductions and Cash for net pay.

   b. Employer payroll expenses for Patel. Credit the appropriate liability accounts.

   c. Benefits provided to Patel. Credit Health Insurance Payable and Company Pension Payable.

Excel Spreadsheet
Template

Using a payroll register, recording a payroll

(3) (4) (5)

1. Total net pay, $2,154,49

Problem 11–5A

The payroll records of Radii Video Productions Inc. provide the following information for the weekly pay period ended September 21:

Employee	Hours Worked	Hourly Earnings Rate	Income Tax	Canada Pension Plan	Employ-ment Insurance	United Way	Year-to-Date Earnings at End of Previous Week
Molly Dodge	43	$30	$474.10	$ 0	$ 0	$25	$51,500
Tally Allard	40	13	67.60	22.41	9.52	2	19,760
George White	49	10	63.70	23.15	9.79	2	20,250
Luigi Valenti	42	20	352.00	39.24	0	5	49,950

Tally Allard and George White work in the office, and Molly Dodge and Luigi Valenti work in sales. All employees are paid time and a half for hours worked in excess of 40 hours per week. Assume that the company contributes an amount equal to 8 percent of each employee's gross pay to a retirement program. Each employee also accrues 4 percent vacation pay based on the gross pay. Show computations.

Required

1. Enter the appropriate information in a payroll register similar to Exhibit 11–8.
2. Record the payroll information in the general journal, crediting net pay to Cash.
3. The employer's payroll costs include matching each employee's CPP contribution and paying 1.4 times the employees' EI premium. Record the employer's payroll costs in the general journal.
4. Why was there no deduction of CPP or EI for Dodge and no deduction of EI for Valenti?
5. What would be the vacation pay liability for Radii Video Productions Inc.?

Problem 11–6A

The following information about the payroll for the week ended April 27, 2017, was obtained from the records of Eastport Construction in St. John's, Newfoundland. This is a standard week that does not change unless directed by management.

Accounting for current liabilities, making basic payroll entries, reporting current liabilities

① ② ④

5. May 4 net pay, $168,014

Salaries:		Deductions:	
Sales salaries	$167,000	Income taxes withheld	$49,686
Jobsite salaries	27,000	CPP withheld	12,900
Office salaries	58,000	EI withheld	3,800
	$252,000	RRSP contribution	7,600
		Blue Cross insurance	10,000
			$83,986

Required Eastport's employees are paid at the end of every week, and they work a five-day workweek. Journalize the following transactions:

1. Record the payroll entry on April 27, 2017.
2. Record the employer's payroll deductions on April 27, 2017.
3. Record the accrual of the year-end payroll entries on April 30, 2017 (assume one day was worked).
4. Record the accrual of the employer's payroll deduction entries on April 30, 2017.
5. Record the payroll entry on May 4, 2017 (assume reversing entries were not used).
6. Record the employer's payroll deductions on May 4, 2017.
7. Record the CRA remittance on May 15, 2017, assuming the only week worked was the last week of April. Include the year-end accrual.
8. Record the remittances on May 31, 2017, to the insurance company and the financial institution for the Blue Cross and RRSP contributions. Each remittance is for the April pay periods listed above.

Problem 11–7A

The general ledger of Shell Storage Units at June 30, 2017, the end of the company's fiscal year, includes the following account balances before adjusting entries:

Journalizing, posting, and reporting liabilities

① ② ③ ④ ⑤

3. Total liabilities, $559,591

Notes Payable, Short-Term	$ 20,000	Employee Insurance	
Accounts Payable	235,620	Benefits Payable	_____
Current Portion of Long-Term Debt Payable	_____	Estimated Vacation Pay Liability	$ 12,360
Interest Payable	_____	Sales Tax and GST Payable	5,972
Salaries Payable	_____	Unearned Rent Revenue	18,000
Employee Income Tax Payable	_____	Long-Term Debt Payable	250,000
Employer Payroll Costs Payable	_____		

The additional data needed to develop the adjusting entries at June 30 are as follows:

a. The $20,000 short-term note payable was issued on February 28. It matures six months from date of issuance and bears interest at 6 percent.

b. The long-term debt is payable in annual instalments of $50,000 with the next instalment due on August 31. On that date, Shell Storage Units will also pay one year's interest at 3 percent. Interest was last paid on August 31 of the preceding year.

c. Gross salaries for the last payroll of the fiscal year were $6,328. Of this amount, employee payroll withholdings payable were $1,365, and salary payable was $4,963.

d. Employer Payroll Costs Payable was $820, and Shell Storage Units' liability for employee health insurance was $991.

e. Shell Storage estimates that vacation pay expense is 6 percent of gross salaries of $147,500 (the $147,500 includes the last payroll of the fiscal year).

f. On March 1, the company collected one year's rent of $18,000 in advance.

g. At June 30, Shell Storage is the defendant in a $200,000 lawsuit, which the company expects to win. However, the outcome is uncertain.

Required

1. Open T-accounts for the listed accounts, inserting their unadjusted June 30, 2017, balances.

2. Post the June 30, 2017, adjusting entries to the T-accounts opened. Round all amounts to the nearest whole dollar.

3. Prepare the liability section of Shell Storage Units' balance sheet at June 30, 2017.

Problem 11–8A

Reporting current liabilities

⑤

Following are five pertinent facts about events during the current year at Babcock's Fly and Tackle, a Manitoba fisheries supply company:

a. Sales of $911,000 were covered by Babcock's Fly and Tackle's product warranty. At January 1 the estimated warranty payable was $14,600. During the year, Babcock's recorded warranty expense of 2 percent of sales and paid warranty claims of $15,600.

b. On August 31, Babcock's Fly and Tackle signed a six-month, 6 percent note payable to purchase supplies costing $45,000. The note requires payment of principal and interest at maturity.

c. On November 30, Babcock's Fly and Tackle received rent of $36,000 in advance from a subtenant in its building. This rent will be earned evenly over three months.

d. December sales totalled $80,000 and Babcock's Fly and Tackle collected GST of 5 percent plus PST of 8 percent on these sales. These taxes will be sent to the appropriate authorities early in January.

e. Babcock's Fly and Tackle owes $150,000 on a long-term note payable. At December 31, $30,000 of this principal plus 5 percent accrued interest since September 30 are payable within one year.

Required For each item, indicate the account and the related amount to be reported as a *current* liability on Babcock's Fly and Tackle's December 31 (year-end) balance sheet. Round all amounts to the nearest whole dollar.

Problem 11–9A

Accounting for current liabilities, accounting for contingent liabilities, reporting current liabilities

① ② ⑤

2. Total current liabilities, $32,540

Beaufort Explorations produces and sells customized mining equipment in New Brunswick. The company offers a 60-day, all parts and labour—and an extra 90-day, parts-only—warranty on all of its products. The company had the following transactions in 2017:

Jan. 31   Sales for the month totalled $80,000 (not including HST), of which 90 percent were on credit. The company collects 13 percent HST on all sales and estimates its warranty costs at 4 percent of sales.

       31   Based on last year's property tax assessment, the company estimated that the property taxes for the year would be $60,000 (3 percent of last year's $2,000,000 assessed value). Recorded the estimated property taxes for the month; credited Property Taxes Payable.

Feb. 4   Completed repair work for a customer. The parts ($500) and labour ($850) were all covered under the warranty. Record the labour as Wages Expense.

     7   Sent a cheque for the appropriate HST for the month of January (the company had paid $3,700 of HST on purchases in January).

    28   Recorded the estimated property taxes for the month of February.

    28   Sales for the month totalled $92,000 (not including HST), of which 85 percent were on credit. The company estimates its warranty costs at 4 percent of sales.

Mar. 7   Sent a cheque for the appropriate HST amount for the month of February (the company had paid $4,750 of HST on purchases in February).

     8   Beaufort Explorations received notice that it was being sued by a customer for an accident resulting from the failure of its product. The company's lawyer was reluctant to estimate the likely outcome of the lawsuit, but another customer indicated that a similar case had resulted in a $500,000 settlement.

    15   Completed repair work for a customer. The parts ($2,500) and labour ($1,200) were all covered under the warranty.

    21   Completed repair work for a customer. The parts ($750) were covered by the warranty, but the labour ($500) was not. Payment from the customer is due for the labour in 30 days.

    31   Sales for the month totalled $88,000 (not including HST), of which 90 percent were on credit. The company estimates its warranty costs at 4 percent of sales.

    31   Received the property tax assessment for 2017. It showed the assessed value of the property to be $2,200,000 and a tax rate of 3 percent of the assessed value. The company made the appropriate adjustment and used the Property Taxes Payable account. Property tax will be paid on December 31, 2017.

Required

1. Journalize the above transactions.
2. Show the appropriate financial statement presentation for all liabilities at March 31, 2017.

PROBLEMS (GROUP B)   MyAccountingLab

Problem 11–1B

The following transactions of Drumheller Technology of Calgary, Alberta, occurred during 2016 and 2017. The company's year end is December 31.

Journalizing liability-related transactions

2016

Mar. 3   Purchased a machine for $66,000 plus 5 percent GST, signing a six-month, 3 percent note payable.

    31   Recorded the month's sales of $134,500, one-quarter of which were for cash, and three-quarters were on credit. All sales amounts are subject to 5 percent GST, to be calculated on the sales of $134,500.

Apr. 7   Paid March's GST to the Receiver General.

May 31   Borrowed $75,000 with a 5 percent note payable that calls for annual instalment payments of $15,000 principal plus interest.

Sep. 3   Paid the six-month, 3 percent note at maturity.

    30   Purchased inventory at a cost of $25,000 plus GST, signing a 5 percent, 180-day note payable for that amount.

Dec. 31   Accrued warranty expense, which is estimated at 3 percent of annual sales of $1,445,000.

    31   Accrued interest on all outstanding notes payable. Make a separate interest accrual entry for each note payable.

2017

Mar. 31   Paid off the 5 percent inventory note, plus interest, at maturity.

May 31   Paid the first instalment and interest for one year on the long-term note payable.

Required Record the transactions in the company's general journal. Explanations are not required. Use days in any interest accrual calculations, not months. Round all amounts to the nearest whole dollar.

Problem 11–2B

Identifying contingent liabilities

Alessandra Gesso provides skating lessons for children ages 8 through 15. Most students are beginners. Gesso rents ice time from the local arena. Because this is a new business venture, Gesso wants to save money and does not want to purchase insurance. She seeks your advice about her business exposure to liabilities.

Required Write a memorandum to inform Gesso of specific contingent liabilities that could arise from the business. It will be necessary to define a contingent liability because she is a professional skater, not a businessperson. Propose a way for Gesso to limit her exposure to these possible liabilities.

Problem 11–3B

Computing and reporting payroll amounts

The partial monthly records of KSell Products show the following figures:

Employee Earnings

Regular earnings	a	Dental and drug insurance	$ 1,556
Overtime pay	$13,994	Total deductions	c
Total employee earnings	b	Net pay	140,810

Deductions and Net Pay		**Accounts Debited**	
Withheld income tax	$31,704	Salaries Expense	66,468
Canada Pension Plan	9,200	Wages Expense	d
Employment Insurance	3,492	Sales Commission Expense	59,356

Required

1. Determine missing amounts a, b, c, and d.

2. Prepare the general journal entry on October 31 to record KSell Products' payroll for the month. Credit Payroll Payable for net pay. No explanation is required.

Excel Spreadsheet Template

Computing and recording payroll amounts

Problem 11–4B

Assume that Marcy Jones is a marketing director in Metro Mobility's head office in Toronto. During 2015 she worked for the company all year at a $6,500 monthly salary. She also earned a year-end bonus equal to 20 percent of her salary.

Jones's monthly income tax withholding for 2015 was $1,762.28. Also, she paid a one-time withholding tax of $4,095.11 on her bonus cheque. She paid $307.31 per month toward the CPP until the maximum ($2,479.95) had been withheld. In addition, Jones's employer deducted $106.50 per month for EI until the maximum ($930.60) had been withheld. Jones authorized the following deductions: 1.5 percent per month of her monthly pay to Metro's charitable donation fund and $68 per month for life insurance.

Metro Mobility incurred CPP expense equal to the amount deducted from Jones's pay. EI cost the company 1.4 times the amount deducted from Jones's pay. In addition, the company provided Jones with the following benefits: dental and drug insurance at a cost of $65 per month, and pension benefits to be paid to Jones upon retirement. The pension contribution is based on her income and was $5,350 in 2015.

Required

1. Compute Jones's gross pay, payroll deductions, and net pay for the full year 2015. Round all amounts to the nearest cent.

2. Compute Metro Mobility's total 2015 payroll cost for Jones.

3. Prepare Metro Mobility's summary general journal entries (explanations are not required) to record its expense for the following:

a. Jones's total earnings for the year, her payroll deductions, and her net pay. Debit Salary Expense and Executive Bonus Compensation as appropriate. Credit liability accounts for the payroll deductions and Cash for net pay.

b. Employer payroll expenses for Jones. Credit the appropriate liability accounts.

c. Benefits provided to Jones. Credit Health Insurance Payable and Company Pension Payable.

Problem 11–5B

Excel Spreadsheet Template
Using a payroll register, recording a payroll
③ ④ ⑤

Assume that payroll records of a branch of Indigo Books provided the following information for the weekly pay period ended December 18, 2015:

Employee	Hours Worked	40-Hour Weekly Earnings	Income Tax	Canada Pension Plan	Employ- ment Insurance	United Way	Year-to-Date Earnings at End of Previous Week
Lucy Bourdon	45	$440	$ 62.85	$22.53	$ 9.56	$16	$19,130.00
Maura Wells	50	500	73.25	30.70	12.58	16	28,400.00
Carl Boyd	49	850	184.10	0.00	0.00	40	56,380.00
Maurice Lamont	40	380	42.60	15.48	6.95	4	8,966.00

Lucy Bourdon and Maurice Lamont work in the office, and Maura Wells and Carl Boyd are sales staff. All employees are paid time and a half for hours worked in excess of 40 hours per week. Show computations. Explanations are not required for journal entries.

Required

1. Enter the appropriate information in a payroll register similar to Exhibit 11–8.
2. Record the payroll information in the general journal, crediting net pay to Cash.
3. The employer's payroll costs are calculated by matching each employee's CPP contribution and paying 1.4 times the employees' EI premium. Record the employer's payroll costs in the general journal.
4. Why is no CPP or EI deducted for Boyd?

Problem 11–6B

Accounting for current liabilities, making basic payroll entries, reporting current liabilities
① ② ④

The following information about the payroll for the week ended April 27, 2015, was obtained from the records of St. Lawrence Construction of Ontario. Assume that this is a standard week and does not change unless management approves.

Salaries:		Deductions:	
Sales salaries	$334,000	Income taxes withheld	$ 99,372
Jobsite salaries	54,000	CPP withheld	25,800
Office salaries	116,000	EI withheld	7,600
	$504,000	RRSP contributions	15,200
		Blue Cross insurance	20,000
			$167,972

Required St. Lawrence's employees are paid at the end of every week, and they work a five-day workweek. Journalize the following transactions:

1. Record the payroll entry on April 27, 2015.
2. Record the employer's payroll deductions on April 27, 2015.
3. Record the accrual of the year-end payroll entries on April 30, 2015. Assume one day was worked.
4. Record the accrual of the employer's payroll deduction entries on April 30, 2015.
5. Record the payroll entry on May 4, 2015 (assume reversing entries were not used).
6. Record the employer's payroll deductions on May 4, 2015.
7. Record the CRA remittance on May 15, 2015, assuming the only week worked was the last week of April. Include the year-end accrual.

8. Record the remittances on May 31, 2015, to the insurance company and financial institution for the Blue Cross and RRSP contributions. Each remittance is for the April pay periods.

Problem 11–7B

Journalizing, posting, and reporting liabilities
①②③④⑤

Uptown Hardware's general ledger at June 30, 2017, the end of the company's fiscal year, includes the following account balances before adjusting entries.

Note Payable, Short-Term	$ 74,000	Employee Insurance	
Accounts Payable	355,680	Benefits Payable	$_____
Current Portion of Long-Term Debt Payable	_____	Estimated Vacation Pay Liability	7,896
Interest Payable	_____	GST Payable	4,900
Salaries Payable	_____	Property Tax Payable	9,284
Employee Withholdings Payable	_____	Unearned Service Revenue	18,000
Employer Payroll Costs Payable	_____	Long-Term Debt Payable	300,000

The additional data needed to develop the adjusting entries at June 30 are as follows:

a. The $74,000 short-term note payable was issued on July 31, 2016; it matures one year from the date of issuance and bears interest at 5 percent.

b. The long-term debt is payable in annual instalments of $60,000, with the next instalment due February 28, 2018. On that date, Uptown Hardware will also pay one year's interest at 5.5 percent. Interest was last paid on February 28, 2017.

c. Gross salaries for the last payroll of the fiscal year were $21,446. Of this amount, employee withholdings were $4,756 and salaries payable were $16,690.

d. Employer payroll costs were $2,788, and Uptown Hardware's liability for employee life insurance was $300.

e. Uptown Hardware estimates that vacation pay is 6 percent of gross salaries of $240,000 (the $240,000 includes the last payroll of the fiscal year).

f. On March 1, 2017, the company collected one year's service contract revenue of $18,000 in advance. It will earn the revenue evenly during the year.

g. At June 30, 2017, Uptown Hardware is the defendant in a $100,000 lawsuit, which the store expects to win. However, the outcome is uncertain.

Required

1. Open T-accounts for the listed accounts, inserting their unadjusted June 30, 2017, balances.

2. Post the June 30, 2017, adjusting entries to the accounts opened. Round all amounts to the nearest whole dollar.

3. Prepare the liability section of Uptown Hardware's balance sheet at June 30, 2017. Show total current liabilities and total liabilities.

4. Is there a contingent liability? If yes, write the note to describe it and indicate where it should appear.

Problem 11–8B

Reporting current liabilities
①②⑤

Following are six pertinent facts about events during the year at Assinaboine Manufacturing, a farm equipment company:

a. On June 30, Assinaboine Manufacturing signed a nine-month, 5 percent note payable to purchase a machine costing $120,000. The note requires payment of principal and interest at maturity.

b. Sales of $2,103,000 were covered by Assinaboine Manufacturing's product warranty. At January 1, estimated warranty payable was $29,300. During the year, Assinaboine Manufacturing recorded warranty expense of 3 percent of sales and paid warranty claims of $55,700.

c. On November 15, Assinaboine Manufacturing received $10,000 on deposit for a tractor. The tractor will be delivered in March of next year.

d. December sales totalled $323,000 and Assinaboine Manufacturing collected GST of 5 percent on these sales. This amount will be sent to the appropriate authority early in January.

e. Assinaboine Manufacturing owes $200,000 on a long-term note payable. At December 31, 4 percent interest for the year plus $40,000 of this principal are payable within one year.

Required For each item, indicate the account and the related amount to be reported as a *current* liability on Assinaboine Manufacturing's December 31 (year-end) balance sheet. Round all amounts to the nearest whole dollar.

Problem 11–9B

Sundial Technologies produces and sells customized network systems in New Brunswick. The company offers a 60-day, all software and labour—and an extra 90-day, parts-only— warranty on all of its products. The company had the following transactions in 2016:

Accounting for current liabilities, accounting for contingent liabilities, reporting current liabilities
①②⑤

Jan. 31 Sales for the month totalled $350,000 (not including HST), of which 95 percent were on credit. The company collects 13 percent HST on all sales and estimates its warranty costs at 2 percent of sales.

31 Based on last year's property tax assessment, the company estimated that the property taxes for the year would be $114,000 (6 percent of last year's $1,900,000 assessed value). Recorded the estimated property taxes for the month; credit Property Taxes Payable.

Feb. 4 Completed repair work for a customer. The software ($3,000) and labour ($3,250) were all covered under the warranty.

7 Remitted the appropriate HST for the month of January (the company had paid $15,610 HST on purchases in January).

28 Recorded the estimated property taxes for the month of February.

28 Sales for the month totalled $325,000 (not including HST), of which 90 percent were on credit. The company estimates its warranty costs at 2 percent of sales.

Mar. 7 Remitted the appropriate HST for the month of February (the company had paid $18,648 HST on purchases in February).

8 Sundial Technologies received notice that it was being sued by a customer for an error resulting from the failure of its product. The company's lawyer was reluctant to estimate the likely outcome of the lawsuit, but another customer indicated that a similar case had resulted in a $100,000 settlement.

15 Completed repair work for a customer. The software ($3,500) and labour ($2,750) were all covered under the warranty.

21 Completed repair work for a customer. The software ($1,500) was covered by the warranty, but the labour ($1,650) was not. Payment for the labour is due from the customer in 30 days.

31 Sales for the month totalled $315,000 (not including HST), of which 80 percent were on credit. The company estimates its warranty costs will increase to 4 percent of sales.

31 Received the property tax assessment for 2016. It showed the assessed value of the property to be $2,300,000 and a tax rate of 5.6 percent of the assessed value. The company made the appropriate adjustment and used the Property Taxes Payable account. Property tax will be paid on December 31, 2016.

Required

1. Journalize the above transactions.
2. Show the appropriate financial statement presentation for all liabilities.

CHALLENGE PROBLEMS

Problem 11–1C

Public accounting firms acting as auditors of companies are very careful to ensure that all of the company's accounts payable are recorded in the proper period. In other words, they want to ensure that all payables relating to the year under review are recorded as a liability at year end.

Verifying the completeness of liabilities
①

Accounting for estimated liabilities

Problem 11–2C

There is no consensus on the proper amount for airlines to record with respect to frequent-flyer expense. Two alternative scenarios are presented below:

a. The person claiming a ticket under the frequent-flyer program would use a seat that otherwise would be empty.

b. The person claiming a ticket under the frequent-flyer program would use a seat that otherwise would be used by a full-fare-paying passenger.

Required

1. Recommend to an airline how much it should record as a liability under each of the scenarios. Which amount would you suggest the airline record, given that it doesn't know which will occur?

2. Write a response to the person who states that, since it is not known if the frequent-flyer miles will be used, the liability is contingent and need not be expensed until the passenger actually uses the frequent-flyer miles. This person suggests that because the liability is contingent, not actual, it should be disclosed in the notes.

EXTENDING YOUR KNOWLEDGE

DECISION PROBLEM

Understanding contingent liabilities

Soft-Sell is the defendant in numerous lawsuits claiming unfair trade practices. Soft-Sell has strong incentives to not disclose these contingent liabilities. However, GAAP requires that companies report their contingent liabilities.

Required

1. Why would a company prefer not to disclose its contingent liabilities?
2. Describe how a bank could be harmed if a company seeking a loan did not disclose its contingent liabilities.
3. What ethical tightrope must companies walk when they report contingent liabilities?

FINANCIAL STATEMENT CASES

Financial Statement Case 1

Current and contingent liabilities
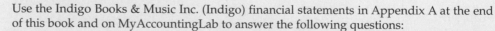

Use the Indigo Books & Music Inc. (Indigo) financial statements in Appendix A at the end of this book and on MyAccountingLab to answer the following questions:

1. Give the breakdown of Indigo's current liabilities at March 29, 2014.
2. In Note 3, Basis of Preparation, Indigo defines "provisions." What is their definition of a provision?

3. Does Indigo have any contingent liabilities or provisions outstanding? Describe the main types of contingencies, and discuss where you found this information.

Financial Statement Case 2

Use the TELUS Corporation (TELUS) financial statements on MyAccountingLab to answer the following questions:

Current and contingent liabilities
① ②

1. Give the breakdown of TELUS's current liabilities at December 31, 2013.

2. TELUS has "short-term borrowings." Describe what these obligations are.

3. Did TELUS have any contingent liabilities in 2013? If so, where did you find information about them? Describe these contingent liabilities.

IFRS MINI-CASE

Brian Lulay is a professional accountant who has his own firm. He provides advice on accounting matters to various companies, both publicly accountable companies that report under IFRS and private companies that report under ASPE. He was recently approached by two clients who are seeking advice on contingent liabilities.

The first client is a *large publicly traded company*, Merit Resources, which reports under IFRS. The company is seeking Brian's advice on *two situations*:

- The first situation involves a tract of land owned by the company. The land is required to complete an access road, so it is about to be expropriated by the provincial government. Merit has had several discussions with the government and feels confident that they will receive fair value for the property from the government. If so, the company will have an accounting gain of $3,000,000.

- In the second situation, Merit is being sued for breach of contract by a supplier. The company feels that it is probable that the lawsuit will be successful and that Merit will have to pay between $800,000 and $1,200,000 to the supplier.

The second client is a *private company*, Harris Distribution Inc., which reports under ASPE. It, too, has been told by the provincial government that some of its property will be expropriated, and the company will be compensated at fair value. If so, Harris Distribution will record an accounting gain of $500,000. Both companies are approaching their year ends and have asked for Brian's advice on how to account for and report the transactions.

Required Assume the role of Brian Lulay and prepare a brief report on how you would report Merit's two situations and Harris's situation in each company's year-end financial statements.

⟩Try It! SOLUTIONS FOR CHAPTER 11

1.

Separate journal entries are required for GST and PST payments because cheques are sent to two different governments.

April	Cash	3,360	
	Sales Revenue		3,000
	GST Payable		150
	Sales Tax Payable		210
	To record cash sales and related GST and PST. GST Payable is $150 ($3,000 × 0.05). Sales Tax Payable is $210 ($3,000 × 0.07).		

May 10	GST Payable	150	
	Cash		81
	GST Recoverable		69
	To pay GST to the Receiver General, less the input tax credit.		
May 10	Sales Tax Payable	210	
	Cash		210
	To pay sales tax to the provincial government.		

2. Snippy Hair Salons' balance sheet at December 31, 2017, would be as follows:

Current Liabilities (in part)

Portion of long-term debt due within one year	$5,000
Interest payable*	233

Long-Term Debt (in part)

Long-term debt	$9,000

*Calculated as $14,000 \times 0.05 \times 4/12$, rounded to the nearest dollar

Total long-term debt amount at Dec. 31, 2017, is $14,000 ($5,000 current portion payable in 2018 + $9,000 long-term portion)

3.

Dec. 31	Accounts Receivable	400,000	
	Sales Revenue		400,000
	To record sales made on account during the year.		
Dec. 31	Warranty Expense	12,000	
	Estimated Warranty Payable		12,000
	To record warranty expense, calculated as $400,000 \times 0.03$.		
Dec. 31	Estimated Warranty Payable	9,000	
	Cash		9,000
	To record payments for repairs under warranty.		

Estimated Warranty Payable

9,000	12,000
	Bal. 3,000

4.

Dec. 31	Accounts Receivable	800,000	
	Sales Revenue		800,000
	To record sales made on account during the year (20,000 units × $40 per unit).		
Dec. 31	Warranty Expense	24,000	
	Estimated Warranty Payable		24,000
	To record warranty expense for the year (3% × 20,000 units × $40 per unit).		
Dec. 31	Estimated Warranty Payable	19,000	
	Inventory		19,000
	To record replacements of units under warranty (475 units × $40 per unit).		

Estimated Warranty Payable

19,000	24,000
	Bal. 5,000

5. a. Agatha Cross: $1,998.50 claim code 4

   Federal tax: $176.35
   Provincial tax: $115.05
   CPP: $91.71
   EI: $37.57

   b. Peter Simpson: $1,999.50 claim code 2

   Federal tax: $207.20
   Provincial tax: $133.50
   CPP: $91.76
   EI: $37.59

   c. Lana Morris: $2,000.25, claim code 3

   Federal tax: $193.65
   Provincial tax: $124.30
   CPP: $91.79
   EI: $37.60

6.

Mar. 31	Salary expense	190,000	
	Employee Income Tax Payable		22,800
	Canada Pension Plan (CPP) Payable.		9,300
	Employment Insurance (EI) Payable		3,500
	Union Dues Payable		2,945
	RRSP Contribution Payable		10,000
	Salaries Payable		141,455
	To record payroll for the period.		
Mar. 31	Employee Benefits Expense	14,200	
	Canada Pension Plan (CPP) Payable		9,300
	Employment Insurance (EI) Payable		4,900
	To record employer payroll costs.		
Mar. 31	Pension Expense	1,900	
	Employee Benefits Payable		1,900
	To record pension plan expense.		

7.

July 10	Wages Expense*	24,340	
	Employee Federal Income Tax Payable		1,850
	Employee Provincial Income Tax Payable		980
	Canada Pension Plan (CPP) Payable		1,200
	Employment Insurance (EI) Payable		445
	Union Dues Payable		420
	Wages Payable		19,445
	To record payroll for the week.		
	* $21,840 + $2,500 = $24,340		
July 10	Employee Benefits Expense	1,823	
	Canada Pension Plan (CPP) Payable		1,200
	Employment Insurance (EI) Payable**		623
	To record employer payroll costs for the week.		
	** $445 × 1.4 = $623		

8. The *current liabilities* section would appear as follows:
   a. A one-year, 6 percent note payable for $3,000 was issued on November 3, 2016.

Note Payable, Short Term	$3,000
Interest Payable*	14
* $3,000 × 0.03 × 58/365 = $14.30 (rounded to $14 for presentation on balance sheet)	

   b. A $10,000, six-month, 5 percent bank loan was arranged and effective on September 17, 2016.

Bank Loan Payable	$10,000
Interest Payable*	144
* $10,000 × 0.05 × 105/365 = $143.84 (rounded to $144 for presentation on balance sheet)	

   c. A $10,000, two-year, 3 percent bank loan was arranged and effective on September 17, 2016. The loan must be repaid in full on September 17, 2018.

Interest Payable*	$86
* $10,000 × 0.03 × 105/365 = $86.30 (rounded to $86 for presentation on balance sheet)	

The loan would be listed as a long-term liability.

   d. A $10,000, two-year, 5 percent bank loan was arranged and effective on January 2, 2016. Half of the loan must be repaid on January 2, 2017, and the remainder repaid on January 2, 2018.

Bank Loan Payable	$5,000
Interest Payable*	497
* $10,000 × 0.05 × 363/365 = $497.26 (rounded to $497 for presentation on balance sheet)	

The remainder of the loan, $5,000, would be listed as a long-term liability.

   e. Of the $5,000 unearned subscription revenue that was recorded during the year, $4,200 was earned by December 31.

Unearned Subscription Revenue	$ 800

   f. The company expects to pay future warranty costs of 3 percent of sales for the $350,000 of goods sold during 2016.

Estimated Warranty Payable	$10,500

COMPREHENSIVE PROBLEM FOR PART 2

COMPARING TWO BUSINESSES

Suppose you are ready to invest in a small resort property. Two locations look promising: Nootka Resort in Victoria, British Columbia, and Critter Cove Resort in Nova Scotia. Each place has its appeal, but Nootka Resort wins out. The main allure is that the price is better. The property owners provide the following data:

	Nootka Resort	Critter Cove Resort
Cash	$ 18,250	$ 34,150
Accounts receivable	10,950	9,800
Inventory	39,700	36,600
Land	144,750	358,000
Buildings	960,000	1,048,600
Accumulated amortization—buildings	(63,772)	(440,100)
Furniture and fixtures	401,500	499,150
Accumulated amortization—furniture and fixtures	(120,500)	(286,400)
Total assets	$1,390,878	$1,259,800
Total liabilities	$ 601,500	$ 539,550
Owner's equity	789,378	720,250
Total liabilities and owner's equity	$1,390,878	$1,259,800

Income statements for the last three years report total net income of $284,100 for Nootka Resort and $151,400 for Critter Cove Resort.

Inventories Nootka Resort uses the FIFO inventory method, and Critter Cove Resort uses the weighted-average method. If Nootka Resort had used weighted-average, its reported inventory would have been $3,750 lower. If Critter Cove Resort had used FIFO, its reported inventory would have been $3,200 higher. Three years ago there was little difference between weighted-average and FIFO amounts for Nootka, and between weighted-average and FIFO amounts for Critter Cove.

Property, Plant, and Equipment Nootka Resort uses the straight-line amortization method and an estimated useful life of 35 years for buildings and 7 years for furniture and fixtures. Estimated residual values are $216,000 for buildings and $0 for furniture and fixtures. Nootka Resort's buildings and furniture and fixtures are three years old.

Critter Cove Resort uses the double-declining-balance method and amortizes buildings over 35 years with an estimated residual value of $245,000. The furniture and fixtures, now two years old, are being amortized over seven years with an estimated residual value of $45,450.

Accounts Receivable Nootka Resort uses the direct write-off method for uncollectibles. Critter Cove Resort uses the allowance method. The Nootka Resort owner estimates that $1,075 of the company's receivables are doubtful. Prior to the current year, uncollectibles were insignificant. Critter Cove Resort's receivables are already reported at net realizable value.

Required

1. To compare the two resorts, convert Nootka Resort's net income to the accounting methods and the estimated useful lives used by Critter Cove Resort.

2. Compare the two resorts' net income after you have revised Nootka Resort's figures. Which resort looked better at the outset? Which resort looks better when they are placed on equal footing?

Appendix A

Portions of Indigo's 2014 Annual Report are reproduced here. The information here is needed to complete each chapter's Financial Statement Case 1. To download your own copy of the full annual report, please go to the Chapter Resources section of MyAccountingLab. In addition, the TELUS 2013 Annual Report is available there, which is needed to complete the Financial Statement Case 2 in each chapter.

ANNUAL REPORT
FOR THE 52-WEEK PERIOD ENDED MARCH 29, 2014

"We are what we repeatedly do. Excellence, then, is not an act, but a habit."

Aristotle

Indigo

Enrich your life™

Indigo   Chapters   Coles   indigo.ca

Report of the CEO

Dear Shareholder,

In this note last year, I confirmed that we were in the early stages of a journey that is taking us from our position as Canada's leading bookseller to our vision of becoming the world's first cultural department store. 2013/14 was the year in which we made a very meaningful financial commitment to accelerate our transformation, positioning ourselves for real growth in the years ahead.

Over the course of this year we launched 37 Indigotech™ shops and meaningfully enhanced the lifestyle merchandising in almost all of our large format stores. At the same time, we made effective advances in the merchandising of our book experience reinforcing our commitment to booklovers, writers and publishers who are, without doubt, at the very core of our business.

This was also the year in which we focused investment on the digital side of our business, expanding our digital marketing and merchandising capabilities and launching a five-star rated mobile app.

Finally, just after the end of the year, we launched our first two American Girl® shops within IndigoKids, reinforcing our commitment to being the leading specialty kids' book and toy retailer in the country.

Contrary to last year, when we had the benefit of the biggest blockbuster in book history as well as some very strong performing titles, this year was one in which we had no single breakout book. We also experienced some important learning curves in our lifestyle business which impacted margin in the second half of the year.

The combination of the very significant operating investments, the pressure on margin, and some non-cash accounting requirements impacting us, result in a challenged bottom line.

I want to highlight that we are focused and committed to returning to full growth and profitability; that said, I am fully convinced that both the decisions we made and the learning in the Company are key ingredients to achieve these objectives.

In a time of industry transformation, investing to reposition is the key to success. It is also satisfying to know that as we invest in our future, we have the strength on our balance sheet to comfortably support our efforts. Even with these significant operating investments Indigo remains in a very healthy financial position.

As the year came to a close and even more so now that we are into our new year – there are several key indicators that our strategy is gaining real traction. For the first time since the advent of eReading we are seeing growth in our core book business – and not driven by a big hit but rather by efforts from our book team to create a great experience for readers both in our stores and online. We are also seeing growth in every one of our lifestyle categories (gift, paper and toys) both in sales and in margin. It is truly energizing to see our customers responding so well to what we are doing.

That said, going through a transformation is no easy task. It requires a clear vision, tenacity, incredible dedication from everyone on the team, and the willingness to take risks, make mistakes, course correct and push forward. We are totally up to the challenge.

We have a clear path forward and firm conviction that we are on the right track – one which will see Indigo grow customer affection and deliver meaningfully to both our shareholders and our employees.

As always, we have, over the course of the year, continued to support the tremendous work of the Indigo Love of Reading Foundation. This year brings to over $15.5 million the amount we have invested in high needs schools across Canada. This is a very special initiative for us – and for those we touch. It is work in which we take great pride and to which we remain fully committed. I want to thank our customers who directly, and through their support of us, allow us to change forever the lives of the children we touch.

In closing, I want to take this opportunity to thank everyone on our team for the creativity and tremendous effort which you bring to work every day. I also want to thank our Directors and Shareholders for their continued support.

I look forward to reporting on our progress quarter-over-quarter and in this Letter next year.

Heather Reisman

Heather Reisman
Chair and Chief Executive Officer

Management's Responsibility for Financial Reporting

Management of Indigo Books & Music Inc. ("Indigo") is responsible for the preparation and integrity of the consolidated financial statements as well as the information contained in this report. The following consolidated financial statements of Indigo have been prepared in accordance with International Financial Reporting Standards, which involve management's best judgments and estimates based on available information.

Indigo's accounting procedures and related systems of internal control are designed to provide reasonable assurance that its assets are safeguarded and its financial records are reliable. In recognizing that the Company is responsible for both the integrity and objectivity of the consolidated financial statements, management is satisfied that the consolidated financial statements have been prepared according to and within reasonable limits of materiality and that the financial information throughout this report is consistent with these consolidated financial statements.

Ernst & Young LLP, Chartered Accountants, Licensed Public Accountants, serve as Indigo's auditors. Ernst & Young's report on the accompanying consolidated financial statements follows. Their report outlines the extent of their examination as well as an opinion on the consolidated financial statements. The Board of Directors of Indigo, along with the management team, have reviewed and approved the consolidated financial statements and information contained within this report.

Heather Reisman
Chair and Chief Executive Officer

Kay Brekken
Chief Financial Officer

Independent Auditors' Report

We have audited the accompanying consolidated financial statements of Indigo Books & Music Inc., which comprise the consolidated balance sheets as at March 29, 2014, March 30, 2013, and April 1, 2012, and the consolidated statements of earnings (loss) and comprehensive earnings (loss), changes in equity and cash flows for the 52 week periods then ended March 29, 2014 and March 30, 2013 and a summary of significant accounting policies and other explanatory information.

Management's responsibility for the consolidated financial statements

Management is responsible for the preparation and fair presentation of these consolidated financial statements in accordance with International Financial Reporting Standards, and for such internal control as management determines is necessary to enable the preparation of consolidated financial statements that are free from material misstatement, whether due to fraud or error.

Auditors' responsibility

Our responsibility is to express an opinion on these consolidated financial statements based on our audits. We conducted our audits in accordance with Canadian generally accepted auditing standards. Those standards require that we comply with ethical requirements and plan and perform the audit to obtain reasonable assurance about whether the consolidated financial statements are free from material misstatement.

An audit involves performing procedures to obtain audit evidence about the amounts and disclosures in the consolidated financial statements. The procedures selected depend on the auditors' judgment, including the assessment of the risks of material misstatement of the consolidated financial statements, whether due to fraud or error. In making those risk assessments, the auditors consider internal control relevant to the entity's preparation and fair presentation of the consolidated financial statements in order to design audit procedures that are appropriate in the circumstances, but not for the purpose of expressing an opinion on the effectiveness of the entity's internal control. An audit also includes evaluating the appropriateness of accounting policies used and the reasonableness of accounting estimates made by management, as well as evaluating the overall presentation of the consolidated financial statements.

We believe that the audit evidence we have obtained in our audits is sufficient and appropriate to provide a basis for our audit opinion.

Opinion

In our opinion, the consolidated financial statements present fairly, in all material respects, the financial position of Indigo Books & Music Inc. as at March 29, 2014, March 30, 2013 and April 1, 2012 and its financial performance and its cash flows for the 52 week periods then ended March 29, 2014 and March 30, 2013 in accordance with International Financial Reporting Standards.

Ernst & Young LLP

Toronto, Canada
May 27, 2014

Chartered Accountants
Licensed Public Accountants

Consolidated Balance Sheets

(thousands of Canadian dollars)	As at March 29, 2014	As at March 30, 2013 restated (notes 4 and 22)	As at April 1, 2012 restated (notes 4 and 22)
ASSETS			
Current			
Cash and cash equivalents (note 6)	157,578	210,562	206,718
Accounts receivable	5,582	7,126	12,810
Inventories (note 7)	218,979	216,533	229,199
Prepaid expenses	5,184	4,153	3,692
Total current assets	387,323	438,374	452,419
Property, plant and equipment (note 8)	58,476	58,903	66,928
Intangible assets (note 9)	21,587	22,164	22,810
Equity investment (note 20)	598	968	961
Deferred tax assets (note 10)	44,604	48,731	48,633
Total assets	512,588	569,140	591,751
LIABILITIES AND EQUITY			
Current			
Accounts payable and accrued liabilities (note 19)	136,428	150,177	173,416
Unredeemed gift card liability (note 19)	46,827	47,169	42,711
Provisions (note 11)	928	2,168	232
Deferred revenue	12,860	13,733	11,234
Income taxes payable	–	11	65
Current portion of long-term debt (notes 12 and 18)	584	773	1,060
Total current liabilities	197,627	214,031	228,718
Long-term accrued liabilities (note 19)	2,896	4,004	5,800
Long-term provisions (note 11)	164	78	460
Long-term debt (notes 12 and 18)	227	705	1,141
Total liabilities	200,914	218,818	236,119
Equity			
Share capital (note 13)	203,812	203,805	203,373
Contributed surplus (note 14)	8,820	8,128	7,039
Retained earnings	99,042	138,389	145,220
Total equity	311,674	350,322	355,632
Total liabilities and equity	512,588	569,140	591,751

See accompanying notes

On behalf of the Board:

Heather Reisman

Heather Reisman
Director

Michael Kirby

Michael Kirby
Director

26 Consolidated Financial Statements and Notes

Consolidated Statements of Earnings (Loss) and Comprehensive Earnings (Loss)

(thousands of Canadian dollars, except per share data)	52-week period ended March 29, 2014	52-week period ended March 30, 2013 restated (notes 4 and 22)
Revenues	867,668	878,785
Cost of sales	(493,955)	(495,099)
Gross profit	373,713	383,686
Operating, selling and administrative expenses (notes 8, 9 and 15)	(403,693)	(383,319)
Operating profit (loss)	(29,980)	367
Interest on long-term debt and financing charges	(95)	(101)
Interest income on cash and cash equivalents	2,377	2,609
Share of earnings from equity investment (note 20)	789	1,315
Earnings (loss) before income taxes	(26,909)	4,190
Income tax recovery (expense) (note 10)		
Current	37	–
Deferred	(4,127)	98
Net earnings (loss) and comprehensive earnings (loss) for the period	(30,999)	4,288
Net earnings (loss) per common share (note 16)		
Basic	$(1.21)	$0.17
Diluted	$(1.21)	$0.17

See accompanying notes

Consolidated Statements of Changes in Equity

(thousands of Canadian dollars)	Share Capital	Contributed Surplus	Retained Earnings	Total Equity
Balance, March 31, 2012	203,373	7,039	145,220	355,632
Earnings for the 52-week period ended March 30, 2013	–	–	4,288	4,288
Exercise of options (notes 13 and 14)	417	(85)	–	332
Directors' deferred share units converted (note 13)	15	(15)	–	–
Stock-based compensation (note 14)	–	743	–	743
Directors' compensation (note 14)	–	446	–	446
Dividends paid (note 13)	–	–	(11,119)	(11,119)
Balance, March 30, 2013	203,805	8,128	138,389	350,322
Balance, March 30, 2013	203,805	8,128	138,389	350,322
Loss for the 52-week period ended March 29, 2014	–	–	(30,999)	(30,999)
Exercise of options (notes 13 and 14)	7	–	–	7
Directors' deferred share units converted (note 13)	–	–	–	–
Stock-based compensation (note 14)	–	1,242	–	1,242
Directors' compensation (note 14)	–	425	–	425
Dividends paid (note 13)	–	–	(8,348)	(8,348)
Repurchase of options (note 14)	–	(975)	–	(975)
Balance, March 29, 2014	203,812	8,820	99,042	311,674

See accompanying notes

Consolidated Statements of Cash Flows

(thousands of Canadian dollars)	52-week period ended March 29, 2014	52-week period ended March 30, 2013 restated (notes 4 and 22)
CASH FLOWS FROM OPERATING ACTIVITIES		
Net earnings (loss) for the period	(30,999)	4,288
Add (deduct) items not affecting cash		
Depreciation of property, plant and equipment (note 8)	16,358	17,638
Amortization of intangible assets (note 9)	11,123	10,245
Net impairment of capital assets (note 8)	2,604	250
Loss on disposal of capital assets	302	65
Stock-based compensation (note 14)	1,242	743
Directors' compensation (note 14)	425	446
Deferred tax assets (note 10)	4,127	(98)
Other	(206)	(482)
Net change in non-cash working capital balances (note 17)	(19,196)	1,089
Interest on long-term debt and financing charges	95	101
Interest income on cash and cash equivalents	(2,377)	(2,609)
Income taxes received	26	32
Share of earnings from equity investment (note 20)	(789)	(1,315)
Cash flows from (used in) operating activities	(17,265)	30,393
CASH FLOWS FROM INVESTING ACTIVITIES		
Purchase of property, plant and equipment (note 8)	(18,700)	(9,441)
Addition of intangible assets (note 9)	(10,546)	(9,621)
Distributions from equity investment (note 20)	1,159	1,308
Interest received	2,463	2,691
Cash flows used in investing activities	(25,624)	(15,063)
CASH FLOWS FROM FINANCING ACTIVITIES		
Notes payable (note 21)	–	190
Repayment of long-term debt	(814)	(1,200)
Interest paid	(110)	(160)
Proceeds from share issuances (note 13)	7	332
Dividends paid (note 13)	(8,348)	(11,119)
Repurchase of options (note 14)	(975)	–
Cash flows used in financing activities	(10,240)	(11,957)
Effect of foreign currency exchange rate changes on cash and cash equivalents	145	471
Net increase (decrease) in cash and cash equivalents during the period	(52,984)	3,844
Cash and cash equivalents, beginning of period	210,562	206,718
Cash and cash equivalents, end of period	157,578	210,562

See accompanying notes

Notes to Consolidated Financial Statements

March 29, 2014

1. CORPORATE INFORMATION

Indigo Books & Music Inc. (the "Company" or "Indigo") is a corporation domiciled and incorporated under the laws of the Province of Ontario in Canada. The Company's registered office is located at 468 King Street West, Toronto, Ontario, M5V 1L8, Canada. The consolidated financial statements of the Company comprise the Company, its equity investment in Calendar Club of Canada Limited Partnership ("Calendar Club"), and its wholly-owned subsidiary, Soho Inc. The Company is the ultimate parent of the consolidated organization.

2. NATURE OF OPERATIONS

Indigo is Canada's largest book, gift and specialty toy retailer and was formed as a result of an amalgamation of Chapters Inc. and Indigo Books & Music, Inc. under the laws of the Province of Ontario, pursuant to a Certificate of Amalgamation dated August 16, 2001. The Company operates a chain of retail bookstores across all ten provinces and one territory in Canada, including 95 superstores (2013 – 97) under the *Chapters*, *Indigo* and the *World's Biggest Bookstore* names, as well as 131 small format stores (2013 – 134) under the banners *Coles*, *Indigo*, *Indigospirit*, *SmithBooks*, and *The Book Company*. Subsequent to year end, the Company closed the *World's Biggest Bookstore*. In addition, the Company operates *indigo.ca*, an e-commerce retail destination which sells books, gifts, toys, and paper products. The Company also operates seasonal kiosks and year-round stores in shopping malls across Canada through Calendar Club.

The Company's operations are focused on the merchandising of products and services in Canada. As such, the Company presents one operating segment in its consolidated financial statements.

Indigo also has a separate registered charity under the name Indigo Love of Reading Foundation (the "Foundation"). The Foundation provides new books and learning material to high-needs elementary schools across the country through donations from Indigo, its customers, suppliers, and employees.

3. BASIS OF PREPARATION

Statement of compliance

These consolidated financial statements have been prepared in accordance with International Financial Reporting Standards ("IFRS") as issued by the International Accounting Standards Board ("IASB") and using the accounting policies described herein.

These consolidated financial statements were approved by the Company's Board of Directors on May 27, 2014.

Use of judgment

The preparation of the consolidated financial statements in conformity with IFRS requires the Company to make judgments, apart from those involving estimation, in applying accounting policies that affect the recognition and measurement of assets, liabilities, revenues, and expenses. Actual results may differ from the judgments made by the Company. Information about judgments that have the most significant effect on recognition and measurement of assets, liabilities, revenues, and expenses are discussed below. Information about significant estimates is discussed in the following section.

Impairment

An impairment loss is recognized for the amount by which the carrying amount of an asset or a cash-generating unit ("CGU") exceeds its recoverable amount. The Company uses judgment when identifying CGUs and when assessing for indicators of impairment.

Intangible assets

Initial capitalization of intangible asset costs is based on the Company's judgment that technological and economic feasibility are confirmed and the project will generate future economic benefits by way of estimated future discounted cash flows that are being generated.

Leases

The Company uses judgment in determining whether a lease qualifies as a finance lease arrangement that transfers substantially all the risks and rewards incidental to ownership.

Deferred tax assets

The recognition of deferred tax assets is based on the Company's judgment. The assessment of the probability of future taxable income in which deferred tax assets can be utilized is based on management's best estimate of future taxable income that the Company expects to achieve from reviewing its latest forecast. This estimate is adjusted for significant non-taxable income and expenses and for specific limits to the use of any unused tax loss or credit. Deferred tax assets are recognized to the extent that it is probable that taxable profit will be available against which the deductible temporary differences and the carryforward of unused tax credits and unused tax losses can be utilized. Any difference between the gross deferred tax asset and the amount recognized is recorded on the balance sheet as a valuation allowance. If the valuation allowance decreases as the result of subsequent events, the previously recognized valuation allowance will be reversed. The recognition of deferred tax assets that are subject to certain legal or economic limits or uncertainties are assessed individually by the Company based on the specific facts and circumstances.

Use of estimates

The preparation of the consolidated financial statements in conformity with IFRS requires the Company to make estimates and assumptions in applying accounting policies that affect the recognition and measurement of assets, liabilities, revenues, and expenses. Actual results may differ from the estimates made by the Company, and actual results will seldom equal estimates. Information about estimates that have the most significant effect on the recognition and measurement of assets, liabilities, revenues, and expenses are discussed below.

Revenues

The Company recognizes revenue from unredeemed gift cards ("gift card breakage") if the likelihood of gift card redemption by the customer is considered to be remote. The Company estimates its average gift card breakage rate based on historical redemption rates. The resulting revenue is recognized over the estimated period of redemption based on historical redemption patterns commencing when the gift cards are sold.

The Indigo plum rewards program ("Plum") allows customers to earn points on their purchases. The fair value of Plum points is calculated by multiplying the number of points issued by the estimated cost per point. The estimated cost per point is based on many factors, including the expected future redemption patterns and associated costs. On an ongoing basis, the Company monitors trends in redemption patterns (redemption at each reward level), historical redemption rates (points redeemed as a percentage of points issued) and net cost per point redeemed, adjusting the estimated cost per point based upon expected future activity. Points revenue is included with total revenues in the Company's consolidated statements of earnings (loss) and comprehensive earnings (loss).

Inventories

The future realization of the carrying amount of inventory is affected by future sales demand, inventory levels, and product quality. At each balance sheet date, the Company reviews its on-hand inventory and uses historical trends and current inventory mix to determine a reserve for the impact of future markdowns which will take the net realizable value of inventory on-hand below cost. Inventory valuation also incorporates a write-down to reflect future losses on the disposition of obsolete merchandise. The Company reduces inventory for estimated shrinkage that has occurred between physical inventory counts and the end of the fiscal year based on historical experience as a percentage of sales. In addition, the Company records a vendor settlement accrual to cover any disputes between the Company and its vendors. The Company estimates this reserve based on historical experience of settlements with its vendors.

Share-based payments

The cost of equity-settled transactions with counterparties is based on the Company's estimate of the fair value of share-based instruments and the number of equity instruments that will eventually vest. The Company's estimated fair value of the share-based instruments is calculated using the following variables: risk-free interest rate; expected volatility; expected time until exercise; and expected dividend yield. Risk-free interest rate is based on Government of Canada bond yields, while all other variables are estimated based on the Company's historical experience with its share-based payments.

Impairment

To determine the recoverable amount of an impaired asset, the Company estimates expected future cash flows at the CGU level and determines a suitable discount rate in order to calculate the present value of those cash flows. In the process of measuring expected future cash flows, the Company makes assumptions about future sales, gross margin rates, expenses, capital expenditures, and working capital investments which are based upon past and expected future performance. Determining the applicable discount rate involves estimating appropriate adjustments to market risk and to Company-specific risk factors.

Property, plant and equipment and intangible assets (collectively, "capital assets")

Capital assets are depreciated over their useful lives, taking into account residual values where appropriate. Assessments of useful lives and residual values are performed annually and take into consideration factors such as technological innovation, maintenance programs, and relevant market information. In assessing residual values, the Company considers the remaining life of the asset, its projected disposal value, and future market conditions.

4. SIGNIFICANT ACCOUNTING POLICIES

The accounting policies set out below have been applied consistently to all periods presented in these consolidated financial statements.

Basis of measurement

The Company's consolidated financial statements are prepared on the historical cost basis of accounting, except as disclosed in the accounting policies set out below.

Basis of consolidation

The consolidated financial statements comprise the financial statements of the Company and entities controlled by the Company. Control exists when the Company is exposed to, or has the right to, variable returns from its involvement with the controlled entity and when the Company has the current ability to affect those returns through its power over the controlled entity. When the Company does not own all of the equity in a subsidiary, the non-controlling interest is disclosed as a separate line item in the consolidated balance sheets and the earnings accruing to non-controlling interest holders is disclosed as a separate line item in the consolidated statements of earnings (loss) and comprehensive earnings (loss).

The financial statements of the subsidiary are prepared for the same reporting period as the parent company, using consistent accounting policies. Subsidiaries are fully consolidated from the date of acquisition, being the date on which the Company obtains control, and continue to be consolidated until the date that such control ceases. All intercompany balances and transactions and any unrealized gains and losses arising from intercompany transactions are eliminated in preparing these consolidated financial statements.

Equity investment

The equity method of accounting is applied to investments in companies where Indigo has the ability to exert significant influence over the financial and operating policy decisions of the company but lacks control or joint control over those policies. Under the equity method, the Company's investment is initially recognized at cost and subsequently increased or decreased to recognize the Company's share of earnings and losses of the investment, and for impairment losses after the initial recognition date. The Company's share of losses that are in excess of its investment are recognized only to the extent that the Company has incurred legal or constructive obligations or made payments on behalf of the company. The Company's share of earnings and losses of its equity investment are recognized through profit or loss during the period. Cash distributions received from the investment are accounted for as a reduction in the carrying amount of the Company's equity investment.

Cash and cash equivalents

Cash and cash equivalents consist of cash on hand, balances with banks, and highly liquid investments that are readily convertible to known amounts of cash with maturities of three months or less at the date of acquisition. Cash is considered to be restricted when it is subject to contingent rights of a third-party customer, vendor, or government agency.

Inventories

Inventories are valued at the lower of cost, determined on a moving average cost basis, and market, being net realizable value. Costs include all direct and reasonable expenditures that are incurred in bringing inventories to their present location and condition. Net realizable value is the estimated selling price in the ordinary course of business. When the Company permanently reduces the retail price of an item and the markdown incurred brings the retail price below the cost of the item, there is a corresponding reduction in inventory recognized in the period. Vendor rebates are recorded as a reduction in the price of the products, and corresponding inventories are recorded net of vendor rebates.

Prepaid expenses

Prepaid expenses include store supplies, rent, license fees, maintenance contracts, and insurance. Store supplies are expensed as they are used while other costs are amortized over the term of the contract.

Income taxes

Current income taxes are the expected taxes payable or receivable on the taxable earnings or loss for the period. Current income taxes are payable on taxable earnings for the period as calculated under Canadian taxation guidelines, which differs from taxable earnings under IFRS. Calculation of current income taxes is based on tax rates and tax laws that have been enacted, or substantively enacted, by the end of the reporting period. Current income taxes relating to items recognized directly in equity are recognized in equity and not in the consolidated statements of earnings (loss) and comprehensive earnings (loss).

Deferred income taxes are calculated at the reporting date using the liability method based on temporary differences between the carrying amounts of assets and liabilities and their tax bases. However, deferred tax assets and liabilities on temporary differences arising from the initial recognition of goodwill, or of an asset or liability in a transaction that is not a business combination, will not be recognized when neither accounting nor taxable profit or loss are affected at the time of the transaction.

Deferred tax assets arising from temporary differences associated with investments in subsidiaries are provided for if it is probable that the differences will reverse in the foreseeable future and taxable profit will be available against which the tax assets may be utilized. Deferred tax assets on temporary differences associated with investments in subsidiaries are not provided for if the timing of the reversal of these temporary differences can be controlled by the Company and it is probable that reversal will not occur in the foreseeable future.

Deferred tax assets and liabilities are calculated, without discounting, at tax rates that are expected to apply to their respective periods of realization, provided they are enacted or substantively enacted by the end of the reporting period. Deferred tax assets and liabilities are offset only when the Company has the right and intention to set off current tax assets and liabilities from the same taxable entity and the same taxation authority.

Deferred tax assets are recognized to the extent that it is probable that taxable profit will be available against which the deductible temporary differences and the carryforward of unused tax credits and unused tax losses can be utilized. Any difference between the gross deferred tax asset and the amount recognized is recorded on the balance sheet as a valuation allowance. If the valuation allowance decreases as the result of subsequent events, the previously recognized valuation allowance will be reversed.

Property, plant and equipment

All items of property, plant and equipment are initially recognized at cost, which includes any costs directly attributable to bringing the asset to the location and condition necessary for it to be capable of operating in the manner intended by the Company. Subsequent to initial recognition, property, plant and equipment assets are shown at cost less accumulated depreciation and any accumulated impairment losses.

Depreciation of an asset begins once it becomes available for use. The depreciable amount of an asset, being the cost of an asset less the residual value, is allocated on a straight-line basis over the estimated useful life of the asset. Residual value is estimated to be zero unless the Company expects to dispose of the asset at a value that exceeds the estimated disposal costs. The residual values, useful lives, and depreciation methods applied to assets are reviewed annually based on relevant market information and management considerations.

The following useful lives are applied:

Furniture, fixtures and equipment	5 – 10 years
Computer equipment	3 – 5 years
Equipment under finance leases	3 – 5 years
Leasehold improvements	over the lease term and probable renewal periods to a maximum of 10 years

Items of property, plant and equipment are assessed for impairment as detailed in the accounting policy note on impairment and are derecognized either upon disposal or when no future economic benefits are expected from their use. Any gain or loss arising on derecognition is included in earnings when the asset is derecognized.

Leased assets

Leases are classified as finance leases when the terms of the lease transfer substantially all the risks and rewards related to ownership of the leased asset to the Company. At lease inception, the related asset is recognized at the lower of the fair value of the leased asset or the present value of the lease payments. The corresponding liability amount is recognized as long-term debt.

Depreciation methods and useful lives for assets held under finance lease agreements correspond to those applied to comparable assets which are legally owned by the Company. If there is no reasonable certainty that the Company will obtain ownership of the financed asset at the end of the lease term, the asset is depreciated over the shorter of its estimated useful life or the lease term. The corresponding long-term debt is reduced by lease payments less interest paid. Interest payments are expensed as part of interest on long-term debt and financing charges on the consolidated statements of earnings (loss) and comprehensive earnings (loss) over the period of the lease. As at March 29, 2014, computer equipment assets are the only type of asset leased under finance lease arrangements.

All other leases are treated as operating leases. Payments on operating lease agreements are recognized as an expense on a straight-line basis over the lease term. Associated costs, such as maintenance and insurance, are expensed as incurred.

The Company performs quarterly assessments of contracts which do not take the legal form of a lease to determine whether they convey the right to use an asset in return for a payment or series of payments and therefore need to be accounted for as leases. As at March 29, 2014, the Company had no such contracts.

Leased premises

The Company conducts all of its business from leased premises. Leasehold improvements are depreciated over the lesser of their economic life or the initial lease term plus renewal periods where renewal has been determined to be reasonably assured ("lease term"). Leasehold improvements are assessed for impairment as detailed in the accounting policy note on impairment. Leasehold improvement allowances are depreciated over the lease term. Other inducements, such as rent-free periods, are amortized into earnings over the lease term, with the unamortized portion recorded in current and long-term accounts payable and accrued liabilities. As at March 29, 2014, all of the Company's leases on premises were accounted for as operating leases. Expenses incurred for leased premises include base rent, taxes, and contingent rent based upon a percentage of sales.

Intangible assets

Intangible assets are initially recognized at cost, if acquired separately, or at fair value, if acquired as part of a business combination. After initial recognition, intangible assets are carried at cost less accumulated amortization and any accumulated impairment losses.

Amortization commences when the intangible assets are available for their intended use. The useful lives of intangible assets are assessed as either finite or indefinite. Intangible assets with finite lives are amortized over their useful economic life. Intangible assets with indefinite lives are not amortized but are reviewed at each reporting date to determine whether the indefinite life continues to be supportable. If not, the change in useful life from indefinite to finite is made on a prospective basis. Residual value is estimated to be zero unless the Company expects to dispose of the asset at a value that exceeds the estimated disposal costs. The residual values, useful lives and amortization methods applied to assets are reviewed annually based on relevant market information and management considerations.

The following useful lives are applied:

Computer application software	3 – 5 years
Internal development costs	3 years

Intangible assets are assessed for impairment as detailed in the accounting policy note on impairment. An intangible asset is derecognized either upon disposal or when no future economic benefit is expected from its use. Any gain or loss arising on derecognition is included in earnings when the asset is derecognized.

Computer application software

When computer application software is not an integral part of a related item of computer hardware, the software is treated as an intangible asset. Computer application software that is integral to the use of related computer hardware is recorded as property, plant and equipment.

Internal development costs

Costs that are directly attributable to internal development are recognized as intangible assets provided they meet the definition of an intangible asset. Development costs not meeting these criteria are expensed as incurred. Capitalized development costs include external direct costs of materials and services and the payroll and payroll-related costs for employees who are directly associated with the projects.

Impairment testing

Capital assets

For the purposes of assessing impairment, capital assets are grouped at the lowest levels for which there are largely independent cash inflows and for which a reasonable and consistent allocation basis can be identified. For capital assets which can be reasonably and consistently allocated to individual stores, the store level is used as the CGU for impairment testing. For all other capital assets, the corporate level is used as the group of CGUs. Capital assets and related CGUs or groups of CGUs are tested for impairment at each reporting date and whenever events or changes in circumstances indicate that the carrying amount may not be recoverable. Events or changes in circumstances which may indicate impairment include a significant change to the Company's operations, a significant decline in performance, or a change in market conditions which adversely affects the Company.

An impairment loss is recognized for the amount by which the carrying amount of a CGU or group of CGUs exceeds its recoverable amount. To determine the recoverable amount, management uses a value in use calculation to determine the present value of the expected future cash flows from each CGU or group of CGUs based on the CGU's estimated growth rate. The Company's growth rate and future cash flows are based on historical data and management's expectations. Impairment losses are charged pro rata to the capital assets in the CGU or group of CGUs. Capital assets and CGUs or groups of CGUs are subsequently reassessed for indicators that a previously recognized impairment loss may no longer exist. An impairment loss is reversed if the recoverable amount of the capital asset, CGU, or group of CGUs exceeds its carrying amount, but only to the extent that the carrying amount of the asset does not exceed the carrying amount that would have been determined, net of depreciation or amortization, if no impairment loss had been recognized.

Financial assets

Individually significant financial assets are tested for impairment on an individual basis. The remaining financial assets are assessed collectively in groups that share similar credit risk characteristics. Financial assets are tested for impairment at each reporting date and whenever events or changes in circumstances indicate that the carrying amount may not be recoverable. Evidence of impairment may include indications that a debtor or a group of debtors are experiencing significant financial difficulty, default or delinquency in interest or principal payments, and observable data indicating that there is a measurable decrease in the estimated future cash flows.

A financial asset is deemed to be impaired if there is objective evidence that one or more loss events having a negative effect on future cash flows of the financial asset occurs after initial recognition and the loss can be reliably measured. The impairment loss is measured as the difference between the carrying amount of the financial asset and the present value of the estimated future cash flows, discounted at the original effective interest rate. The impairment loss is recorded as an allowance and recognized in net earnings. If the impairment loss decreases as the result of subsequent events, the previously recognized impairment loss is reversed.

Provisions

Provisions are recognized when the Company has a present legal or constructive obligation as a result of past events, for which it is probable that the Company will be required to settle the obligation and a reliable estimate of the settlement can be made. The amount recognized as a provision is the best estimate of the consideration required to settle the present obligation at the end of the reporting period, taking into account risks and uncertainties of cash flow. Where the effect of discounting to present value is material, provisions are adjusted to reflect the time value of money. Examples of provisions include legal claims, onerous leases, and decommissioning liabilities.

Borrowing costs

Borrowing costs are primarily comprised of interest on the Company's long-term debt. Borrowing costs are capitalized using the effective interest rate method to the extent that they are directly attributable to the acquisition, production, or construction of qualifying assets that require a substantial period of time to get ready for their intended use or sale. All other borrowing costs are expensed as incurred and reported in the consolidated statements of earnings (loss) and comprehensive earnings (loss) as part of interest on long-term debt and finance charges.

Total equity

Share capital represents the nominal value of shares that have been issued. Retained earnings include all current and prior period retained profits. Dividend distributions payable to equity shareholders are recorded as dividends payable when the dividends have been approved by the Board of Directors prior to the reporting date.

Share-based awards

The Company has established an employee stock option plan for key employees. The fair value of each tranche of options granted is estimated on grant date using the Black-Scholes option pricing model. The Black-Scholes option pricing model is based on variables such as: risk-free interest rate; expected volatility; expected time until exercise; and expected dividend yield. Expected stock price volatility is based on the historical volatility of the Company's stock for a period approximating the expected life. The grant date fair value, net of estimated forfeitures, is recognized as an expense with a corresponding increase to contributed surplus over the vesting period. Estimates are subsequently revised if there is an indication that the number of stock options expected to vest differs from previous estimates. Any consideration paid by employees on exercise of stock options is credited to share capital with a corresponding reduction to contributed surplus.

Revenues

The Company recognizes revenue when the substantial risks and rewards of ownership pass to the customer. Revenue is measured at the fair value of consideration received or receivable by the Company for goods supplied, inclusive of amounts invoiced for shipping, and net of sales discounts, returns and amounts deferred related to the issuance of Plum points. Return allowances are estimated using historical experience. Revenue is recognized when the amount can be measured reliably, it is probable that economic benefits associated with the transaction will flow to the Company, the costs incurred or to be incurred can be measured reliably, and the criteria for each of the Company's activities (as described below) have been met.

Retail sales

Revenue for retail customers is recognized at the time of purchase.

Online sales

Revenue for online customers is recognized when the product is shipped.

Commission revenue

The Company earns commission revenue through partnerships with other companies and recognizes revenue once services have been rendered and the amount of revenue can be measured reliably.

Gift cards

The Company sells gift cards to its customers and recognizes the revenue as gift cards are redeemed. The Company also recognizes gift card breakage if the likelihood of gift card redemption by the customer is considered to be remote. The Company determines its average gift card breakage rate based on historical redemption rates. Once the breakage rate is determined, the resulting revenue is recognized over the estimated period of redemption based on historical redemption patterns, commencing when the gift cards are sold. Gift card breakage is included in revenues in the Company's consolidated statements of earnings (loss) and comprehensive earnings (loss).

Indigo irewards loyalty program

For an annual fee, the Company offers loyalty cards to customers that entitle the cardholder to receive discounts on purchases. Each card is issued with a 12-month expiry period. The fee revenue related to the issuance of a card is deferred and amortized into earnings over the expiry period, based upon historical sales volumes.

Indigo plum rewards program

Plum is a free program that allows members to earn points on their purchases in the Company's stores and enjoy member pricing at the Company's online website. Members can then redeem points for discounts on future purchases of store merchandise.

When a Plum member purchases merchandise, the Company allocates the payment received between the merchandise and the points. The payment is allocated based on the residual method, where the amount allocated to the merchandise is the total payment less the fair value of the points. The portion of revenue attributed to the merchandise is recognized at the time of purchase. Revenue attributed to the points is recorded as deferred revenue and recognized when points are redeemed.

The fair value of the points is calculated by multiplying the number of points issued by the estimated cost per point. The estimated cost per point is determined based on a number of factors, including the expected future redemption patterns and associated costs. On an ongoing basis, the Company monitors trends in redemption patterns (redemption at each reward level), historical redemption rates (points redeemed as a percentage of points issued) and net cost per point redeemed, adjusting the estimated cost per point based upon expected future activity. Points revenue is included with total revenues in the Company's consolidated statements of earnings (loss) and comprehensive earnings (loss).

Interest income

Interest income is reported on an accrual basis using the effective interest method.

Vendor rebates

The Company records cash consideration received from vendors as a reduction to the price of vendors' products. This is reflected as a reduction in cost of goods sold and related inventories when recognized in the consolidated financial statements. Certain exceptions apply where the cash consideration received is a reimbursement of incremental selling costs incurred by the Company, in which case the cash received is reflected as a reduction in operating and administrative expenses.

Earnings per share

Basic earnings per share is determined by dividing the net earnings attributable to common shareholders by the weighted average number of common shares outstanding during the period. Diluted earnings per share are calculated in accordance with the treasury stock method and are based on the weighted average number of common shares and dilutive common share equivalents outstanding during the period. The weighted average number of shares used in the computation of both basic and fully diluted earnings per share may be the same due to the anti-dilutive effect of securities.

Financial instruments

Financial assets and financial liabilities are recognized when the Company becomes a party to the contractual provisions of the financial instrument. Financial assets are derecognized when the contractual rights to the cash flows from the financial asset expire, or when the financial asset and all substantial risks and rewards are transferred. A financial liability is derecognized when it is extinguished, discharged, cancelled, or expires. Where a legally enforceable right to offset exists for recognized financial assets and financial liabilities and there is an intention to settle the liability and realize the asset simultaneously, or to settle on a net basis, such related financial assets and financial liabilities are offset.

For the purposes of ongoing measurement, financial assets and liabilities are classified according to their characteristics and management's intent. All financial instruments are initially recognized at fair value. The following methods and assumptions were used to estimate the initial fair value of each type of financial instrument by reference to market data and other valuation techniques, as appropriate:

(i) The fair values of cash and cash equivalents, accounts receivable, and accounts payable and accrued liabilities approximate their carrying values given their short-term maturities; and

(ii) The fair value of long-term debt is estimated based on the discounted cash payments of the debt at the Company's estimated incremental borrowing rates for debt of the same remaining maturities. The fair value of long-term debt approximates its carrying value.

Embedded derivatives are separated and measured at fair value if certain criteria are met. Management has reviewed all material contracts and has determined that the Company does not currently have any significant embedded derivatives that require separate accounting and disclosure.

After initial recognition, financial instruments are subsequently measured as follows:

Financial assets

(i) Loans and receivables – These are non-derivative financial assets with fixed or determinable payments that are not quoted in an active market. These assets are measured at amortized cost, less impairment charges, using the effective interest method. Gains and losses are recognized in earnings through the amortization process or when the assets are derecognized.

(ii) Financial assets at fair value through profit or loss – These assets are held for trading if acquired for the purpose of selling in the near term or are designated to this category upon initial recognition. These assets are measured at fair value, with gains or losses recognized in earnings.

(iii) Held-to-maturity investments – These are non-derivative financial assets with fixed or determinable payments and fixed maturities which the Company intends, and is able, to hold until maturity. These assets are measured at amortized cost, less impairment charges, using the effective interest method. Gains and losses are recognized in earnings through the amortization process or when the assets are derecognized.

(iv) Available-for-sale financial assets – These are non-derivative financial assets that are either designated to this category upon initial recognition or do not qualify for inclusion in any of the other categories. These assets are measured at fair value, with unrealized gains and losses recognized in Other Comprehensive Income until the asset is derecognized or determined to be impaired. If the asset is derecognized or determined to be impaired, the cumulative gain or loss previously reported in Accumulated Other Comprehensive Income is included in earnings.

Financial liabilities

(i) Other liabilities – These liabilities are measured at amortized cost using the effective interest rate method. Gains and losses are recognized in earnings through the amortization process or when the liabilities are derecognized.

(ii) Financial liabilities at fair value through profit or loss – These liabilities are held for trading if acquired for the purpose of selling in the near term or are designated to this category upon initial recognition. These liabilities are measured at fair value, with gains or losses recognized in earnings.

The Company's financial assets and financial liabilities are generally classified and measured as follows:

Financial Asset/Liability	Category	Measurement
Cash and cash equivalents	Loans and receivables	Amortized cost
Accounts receivable	Loans and receivables	Amortized cost
Accounts payable and accrued liabilities	Other liabilities	Amortized cost
Long-term debt	Other liabilities	Amortized cost

All other balance sheet accounts are not considered financial instruments.

All financial instruments measured at fair value after initial recognition are categorized into one of three hierarchy levels for disclosure purposes. Each level reflects the significance of the inputs used in making the fair value measurements.

Level 1: Fair value is determined by reference to quoted prices in active markets.
Level 2: Valuations use inputs based on observable market data, either directly or indirectly, other than the quoted prices.
Level 3: Valuations are based on inputs that are not based on observable market data.

As at March 29, 2014, there are no financial instruments classified into these levels. The Company measures all financial instruments at amortized cost.

Retirement benefits

The Company provides retirement benefits through a defined contribution retirement plan. Under the defined contribution retirement plan, the Company pays fixed contributions to an independent entity. The Company has no legal or constructive obligations to pay further contributions after its payment of the fixed contribution. The costs of benefits under the defined contribution retirement plan are expensed as contributions are due and are reversed if employees leave before the vesting period.

Foreign currency translation

The consolidated financial statements are presented in Canadian dollars, which is the functional currency of the Company. Sales transacted in foreign currencies are aggregated monthly and translated using the average exchange rate. Transactions in foreign currencies are translated at rates of exchange at the time of the transaction. Monetary assets and liabilities denominated in foreign currencies which are held at the reporting date are translated at the closing consolidated balance sheet rate. Non-monetary items are measured at historical cost and are translated using the exchange rates at the date of the transaction. Non-monetary items measured at fair value are translated using exchange rates at the date when fair value was determined. The resulting exchange gains or losses are included in earnings.

Accounting Standards Implemented in Fiscal 2014

Adoption of these amendments and standards in fiscal 2014 impacted the Company's results of operations, financial position, and disclosures as follows:

- Joint Arrangements ("IFRS 11") replaces IAS 31, "Interests in Joint Ventures" ("IAS 31") and SIC-13, "Jointly-controlled Entities – Non-monetary Contributions by Venturers," and requires that a party in a joint arrangement assess its rights and obligations to determine the type of joint arrangement and account for those rights and obligations accordingly. Previously, the Company accounted for its interest in Calendar Club under IAS 31 using proportionate consolidation. However, the Company concluded that its interest in Calendar Club does not meet the definition of a joint arrangement under IFRS 11 and needs to be accounted for under "Investments in Associates and Joint Ventures" ("IAS 28") as a significant investment using the equity method. The Company has retrospectively restated its comparative financial statements to reclassify pro-portionately consolidated Calendar Club operating results into a single equity investment line. These restatements have no impact to the Company's total net earnings (loss) or cash flows. The impact of reclassification on the Company's financial statements is as follows:

(thousands of Canadian dollars)	52-week period ended March 30, 2013
Decrease in revenues	(15,272)
Decrease in expenses	(13,957)
Increase in equity investment	1,315

(thousands of Canadian dollars)	As at March 30, 2013	As at April 1, 2012
Decrease in assets	(2,074)	(1,746)
Increase in equity investment	968	961
Decrease in liabilities	(1,106)	(785)

- Amendments to Investments in Associates and Joint Ventures ("IAS 28") impact accounting for associates and joint ventures held for sale and changes in interests held in associates and joint ventures; and
- Disclosure of Interests in Other Entities ("IFRS 12") includes all of the disclosures that were previously in IAS 27, "Separate Financial Statements," IAS 31 and IAS 28, "Investments in Associates." These disclosures relate to an entity's interests in subsidiaries, joint arrangements, associates, and structured entities.

Adoption of the following amendments and standards in fiscal 2014 did not have an impact on the Company's results of operations, financial position, or disclosures:

- Amendments to Presentation of Financial Statements ("IAS 1") require companies to group together items within other comprehensive earnings which may be reclassified to net earnings. The amendments are effective for annual periods beginning on or after July 1, 2012 and were applied retrospectively;
- Amendments to Financial Instruments: Disclosures ("IFRS 7") regarding the offsetting of financial instruments. These amendments were applied retrospectively and are effective for annual periods beginning on or after January 1, 2013 and interim periods within those annual periods;
- Fair Value Measurement ("IFRS 13") provides guidance to improve consistency and comparability in fair value measurements and related disclosures through a fair value hierarchy. This standard was applied prospectively and is effective for annual periods beginning on or after January 1, 2013;
- Amendments to Separate Financial Statements ("IAS 27") remove all requirements relating to consolidated financial statements. This standard was applied retrospectively and is effective for annual periods beginning on or after January 1, 2013; and
- Consolidated Financial Statements ("IFRS 10") replaces portions of IAS 27, "Consolidated and Separate Financial Statements," supersedes SIC-12, "Consolidation – Special Purpose Entities," and establishes standards for the presentation and preparation of consolidated financial statements when an entity controls one or more entities. This standard was applied retrospectively and is effective for annual periods beginning on or after January 1, 2013.

5. NEW ACCOUNTING PRONOUNCEMENTS

Impairment of Assets ("IAS 36")

In May 2013, the IASB issued amendments to IAS 36 which require disclosures about assets or CGUs for which an impairment loss was recognized or reversed during the period. The Company will apply the amendments to IAS 36 as of the first quarter of its 2015 fiscal year. Additional information will be disclosed through notes to financial statements.

Levies ("IFRIC 21")

The IASB has issued IFRIC 21, an interpretation which provides guidance on when to recognize a liability for a levy imposed by a government, both for levies that are accounted for in accordance with IAS 37, "Provisions, Contingent Liabilities and Contingent Assets," and those where the timing and amount of the levy is certain. A levy is an outflow of resources embodying economic benefits that is imposed by governments on entities in accordance with legislation. This interpretation is applicable for annual periods beginning on or after January 1, 2014 and must be applied retrospectively. The Company will apply these amendments beginning in the first quarter of fiscal 2015. The Company is assessing the impact of the new interpretation on its consolidated financial statements.

Financial Instruments: Presentation ("IAS 32")

The IASB has issued amendments to IAS 32 that clarify its requirements for offsetting financial instruments. These amendments must be applied retrospectively and are effective for annual periods beginning on or after January 1, 2014. The Company will apply these amendments beginning in the first quarter of fiscal 2015. The Company does not expect implementation of these amendments to have a significant impact on its consolidated financial statements.

Financial Instruments ("IFRS 9")

The IASB has issued a new standard, IFRS 9, which will ultimately replace IAS 39, "Financial Instruments: Recognition and Measurement" ("IAS 39"). The replacement of IAS 39 is a multi-phase project with the objective of improving and simplifying the reporting for financial instruments. Issuance of IFRS 9 provides guidance on the classification and measurement of financial assets and financial liabilities. Due to the incomplete status of the project, the mandatory effective date of this standard has not been determined. The Company will evaluate the overall impact on its consolidated financial statements when the final standard, including all phases, is issued.

6. CASH AND CASH EQUIVALENTS

Cash and cash equivalents consist of the following:

(thousands of Canadian dollars)	March 29, 2014	March 30, 2013	April 1, 2012
Cash	57,098	88,268	86,199
Restricted cash	3,369	470	487
Cash equivalents	97,111	121,824	120,032
Cash and cash equivalents	157,578	210,562	206,718

Restricted cash represents cash pledged as collateral for letter of credit obligations issued to support the Company's purchases of offshore merchandise.

7. INVENTORIES

The cost of inventories recognized as an expense was $495.1 million in fiscal 2014 (2013 – $499.5 million). Inventories consist of the landed cost of goods sold and exclude online shipping costs, inventory shrink and damage reserve, and all vendor support programs. The amount of inventory write-downs as a result of net realizable value lower than cost was $8.6 million in fiscal 2014 (2013 – $3.9 million), and there were no reversals of inventory write-downs that were recognized in fiscal 2014 (2013 – nil). The amount of inventory with net realizable value equal to cost was $1.8 million as at March 29, 2014 (March 30, 2013 – $1.4 million; April 1, 2012 – $1.7 million).

8. PROPERTY, PLANT AND EQUIPMENT

(thousands of Canadian dollars)	Furniture, fixtures and equipment	Computer equipment	Leasehold improvements	Equipment under finance leases	Total
Gross carrying amount					
Balance, March 31, 2012	56,273	15,756	58,773	6,146	136,948
Additions	4,296	2,439	2,706	465	9,906
Transfers/reclassifications	(4)	(411)	415	–	–
Disposals	(161)	(20)	(110)	(2,976)	(3,267)
Assets with zero net book value	(5,113)	(3,279)	(5,015)	–	(13,407)
Balance, March 30, 2013	55,291	14,485	56,769	3,635	130,180
Additions	10,008	3,451	5,241	137	18,837
Transfers / reclassifications	16	(465)	449	–	–
Disposals	(478)	(217)	(208)	(948)	(1,851)
Assets with zero net book value	(2,719)	(6,174)	(7,922)	–	(16,815)
Balance, March 29, 2014	62,118	11,080	54,329	2,824	130,351
Accumulated depreciation and impairment					
Balance, March 31, 2012	25,953	8,895	31,240	3,932	70,020
Depreciation	5,208	3,092	8,129	1,209	17,638
Transfers/reclassifications	–	5	(5)	–	–
Disposals	(130)	(9)	(109)	(2,976)	(3,224)
Net impairment losses and reversals	–	–	250	–	250
Assets with zero net book value	(5,113)	(3,279)	(5,015)	–	(13,407)
Balance, March 30, 2013	25,918	8,704	34,490	2,165	71,277
Depreciation	5,422	2,631	7,495	810	16,358
Transfers / reclassifications	–	5	(5)	–	–
Disposals	(216)	(197)	(188)	(948)	(1,549)
Net impairment losses and reversals	1,007	60	1,537	–	2,604
Assets with zero net book value	(2,719)	(6,174)	(7,922)	–	(16,815)
Balance, March 29, 2014	29,412	5,029	35,407	2,027	71,875
Net carrying amount					
April 1, 2012	30,320	6,861	27,533	2,214	66,928
March 30, 2013	29,373	5,781	22,279	1,470	58,903
March 29, 2014	32,706	6,051	18,922	797	58,476

Capital assets are assessed for impairment at the CGU level, except for those capital assets which are considered to be corporate assets. As certain corporate assets cannot be allocated on a reasonable and consistent basis to individual CGUs, they are tested for impairment at the corporate level.

A CGU has been defined as an individual retail store, as each store generates cash flows that are largely independent from the cash flows of other stores. CGUs and groups of CGUs are tested for impairment if impairment indicators exist at the reporting date. Recoverable amounts for CGUs being tested are based on value in use, which is calculated from discounted cash flow projections over the remaining lease terms, plus any renewal options where renewal is likely. Corporate asset testing calculates discounted cash flow projections over a five-year period plus a terminal value.

The key assumptions from the value in use calculations are those regarding growth rates and discount rates. The cash flow projections are based on both past and forecasted performance and are extrapolated using long-term growth rates which are calculated separately for each CGU being tested. Average long-term growth rates for impairment testing ranged from 0.0% to 3.0% (2013 – 0.0% to 3.0%). Management's estimate of the discount rate reflects the current market assessment of the time value of money and the risks specific to the Company. The pre-tax and post-tax discount rates used to calculate value in use for store assets were 20.3% and 12.0%, respectively (2013 – 21.9% and 14.0%, respectively).

Impairment indicators were identified during fiscal 2014 for Indigo's retail stores and corporate assets. Accordingly, the Company performed impairment testing, which resulted in the recognition and reversal of impairment losses for Indigo's retail stores only. Impairment losses recognized were $2.6 million in fiscal 2014 (2013 – $1.3 million) and are spread across a number of CGUs. The impairment losses relate to CGUs whose carrying amounts exceed their recoverable amounts. In all cases, impairment losses arose due to stores performing at lower-than-expected profitability. There were no capital asset impairment reversals recognized in fiscal 2014 (2013 – $1.0 million). Impairment reversals arose due to improved store performance and the likelihood of lease term renewals.

9. INTANGIBLE ASSETS

(thousands of Canadian dollars)	Computer application software	Internal development costs	Total
Gross carrying amount			
Balance, March 31, 2012	23,929	12,078	36,007
Additions	5,936	3,685	9,621
Transfers / reclassifications	266	(266)	–
Disposals	(5)	(21)	(26)
Assets with zero net book value	(4,890)	(2,999)	(7,889)
Balance, March 30, 2013	25,236	12,477	37,713
Additions	6,609	3,937	10,546
Transfers / reclassifications	(203)	203	–
Disposals	–	–	–
Assets with zero net book value	(4,361)	(3,471)	(7,832)
Balance, March 29, 2014	27,281	13,146	40,427
Accumulated amortization and impairment			
Balance, March 31, 2012	8,408	4,789	13,197
Amortization	6,567	3,678	10,245
Disposals	(2)	(2)	(4)
Assets with zero net book value	(4,890)	(2,999)	(7,889)
Balance, March 30, 2013	10,083	5,466	15,549
Amortization	7,071	4,052	11,123
Disposals	–	–	–
Assets with zero net book value	(4,361)	(3,471)	(7,832)
Balance, March 29, 2014	12,793	6,047	18,840
Net carrying amount			
April 1, 2012	15,521	7,289	22,810
March 30, 2013	15,153	7,011	22,164
March 29, 2014	14,488	7,099	21,587

Impairment testing for intangible assets is performed using the same methodology, CGUs, and groups of CGUs as those used for property, plant and equipment. The key assumptions from the value in use calculations for intangible asset impairment testing are also identical to the key assumptions used for property, plant and equipment testing. Impairment and reversal indicators were identified during fiscal 2014 for Indigo's retail stores. Accordingly, the Company performed impairment and reversal testing but there were no intangible asset impairment losses or reversals in fiscal 2014 (2013 – no impairment losses or reversals).

10. INCOME TAXES

Deferred tax assets are recognized to the extent that it is probable that taxable profit will be available against which the deductible temporary differences and the carryforward of unused tax credits and unused tax losses can be utilized. As at March 29, 2014, the Company has recorded $56.2 million in gross value of deferred tax assets with a valuation allowance of $11.6 million based on management's best estimate of future taxable income that the Company expects to achieve from reviewing its latest forecast. If the valuation allowance decreases as the result of subsequent events, the previously recognized valuation allowance will be reversed.

Deferred income taxes reflect the net tax effects of temporary differences between the carrying amounts of assets and liabilities for financial reporting purposes and the amounts used for income tax purposes. Significant components of the Company's deferred tax assets are as follows:

(thousands of Canadian dollars)	March 29, 2014	March 30, 2013	April 1, 2012
Deferred tax assets			
Reserves and allowances	2,032	2,990	3,343
Tax loss carryforwards	23,562	22,648	25,620
Corporate minimum tax	1,354	1,354	1,354
Book amortization in excess of cumulative eligible capital deduction	249	267	285
Book amortization in excess of capital cost allowance	29,002	21,472	18,031
Deferred tax assets before valuation allowance	56,199	48,731	48,633
Valuation allowance	(11,595)	–	–
Net deferred tax assets	44,604	48,731	48,633

The Company has recorded deferred tax assets of $44.6 million pertaining to tax loss carryforwards and other deductible temporary differences based on the probable use of the deferred tax assets.

Significant components of income tax expense (recovery) are as follows:

(thousands of Canadian dollars)	52-week period ended March 29, 2014	52-week period ended March 30, 2013
Current income tax recovery		
Adjustment for prior periods	(37)	–
	(37)	–
Deferred income tax expense (recovery)		
Origination and reversal of temporary differences	(7,164)	(6,174)
Increase in valuation allowance	11,595	–
Deferred income tax expense relating to utilization of loss carryforwards	–	7,745
Adjustment to deferred tax assets resulting from increase in substantively enacted tax rate	(261)	(1,636)
Change in tax rates due to change in expected pattern of reversal	(44)	(32)
Other, net	1	(1)
	4,127	(98)
Total income tax expense (recovery)	4,090	(98)

The reconciliation of income taxes computed at statutory income tax rates to the effective income tax rates is as follows:

(thousands of Canadian dollars)	52-week period ended March 29, 2014	%	52-week period ended March 30, 2013	%
Earnings (loss) before income taxes	(26,909)		4,190	
Tax at combined federal and provincial tax rates	(7,110)	26.4%	1,102	26.3%
Tax effect of expenses not deductible for income tax purposes	246	(0.9%)	388	9.3%
Increase in valuation allowance	11,595	(43.1%)	–	–
Adjustment to deferred tax assets resulting from increase in substantively enacted tax rate	(261)	1.0%	(1,636)	(39.0%)
Change in tax rates due to change in expected pattern of reversal	(44)	0.2%	(32)	(0.8%)
Other, net	(336)	1.2%	80	1.9%
	4,090	(15.2%)	(98)	(2.3%)

The combined federal and provincial income tax rate used for fiscal 2014 is 26.4% (2013 – 26.3%). The rate has increased due to higher provincial income tax rates.

As at March 29, 2014, the Company has combined non-capital loss carryforwards of approximately $89.1 million for income tax purposes that expire in 2031 if not utilized.

11. PROVISIONS

Provisions consist primarily of amounts recorded in respect of decommissioning liabilities, onerous lease arrangements, and legal claims. Activity related to the Company's provisions is as follows:

(thousands of Canadian dollars)	52-week period ended March 29, 2014	52-week period ended March 30, 2013
Balance, beginning of period	2,246	692
Charged	230	1,814
Utilized / released	(1,384)	(260)
Balance, end of period	1,092	2,246

12. COMMITMENTS AND CONTINGENCIES

(a) Commitments

As at March 9, 2014, the Company had the following commitments:

(i) Operating lease obligations

The Company had operating lease commitments in respect of its stores, support office premises and certain equipment. The leases expire at various dates between 2014 and 2022, and may be subject to renewal options. Annual store rent consists of a base amount plus, in some cases, additional payments based on store sales. The Company expects to generate $10.9 million of revenues from subleases related to these operating leases over the next seven fiscal years.

(ii) Finance lease obligations

The Company entered into finance lease agreements for certain equipment. The obligations under these finance leases is $0.8 million as at March 29, 2014 (March 30, 2013 – $1.5 million; April 1, 2012 – $2.2 million), of which $0.6 million (March 30, 2013 – $0.8 million; April 1, 2012 – $1.1 million) is included in the current portion of long-term debt. The remainder of the finance lease obligations have been included in the non-current portion of long-term debt.

The Company's minimum contractual obligations due over the next five fiscal years and thereafter are summarized below:

(millions of Canadian dollars)	Operating leases	Finance leases	Total
2015	57.6	0.6	58.2
2016	49.6	0.2	49.8
2017	40.1	–	40.1
2018	31.8	–	31.8
2019	19.8	–	19.8
Thereafter	6.9		6.9
Total obligations	205.8	0.8	206.6

(b) Legal claims

In the normal course of business, the Company becomes involved in various claims and litigation. While the final outcome of such claims and litigation pending as at March 29, 2014 cannot be predicted with certainty, management believes that any such amount would not have a material impact on the Company's financial position or financial performance, except for those amounts which have been recorded as provisions on the Company's consolidated balance sheets.

13. SHARE CAPITAL

Share capital consists of the following:

Authorized

Unlimited Class A preference shares with no par value, voting, convertible into common shares on a one-for-one basis at the option of the shareholder

Unlimited common shares, voting

	52-week period ended March 29, 2014		52-week period ended March 30, 2013	
	Number of shares	Amount C$ (thousands)	Number of shares	Amount C$ (thousands)
Balance, beginning of period	25,297,389	203,805	25,238,414	203,373
Issued during the period				
Directors' deferred share units converted	–	–	1,075	15
Options exercised	850	7	57,900	417
Balance, end of period	25,298,239	203,812	25,297,389	203,805

During fiscal 2014, the Company did not issue any common shares (2013 – 1,075 common shares) in exchange for Directors' deferred share units ("DSUs").

During fiscal 2014, the Company distributed dividends per share of $0.33 (2013 – $0.44).

14. SHARE-BASED COMPENSATION

The Company has established an employee stock option plan (the "Plan") for key employees. The number of common shares reserved for issuance under the Plan is 3,294,736. Most options granted between May 21, 2002 and March 31, 2012 have a ten-year term and have one fifth of the options granted exercisable one year after the date of issue with the remainder exercisable in equal instalments on the anniversary date over the next four years. Subsequently, most options granted after April 1, 2012 have a five-year term and have one third of the options granted exercisable one year after the date of issue with the remainder exercisable in equal instalments on the anniversary date over the next two years. A small number of options have special vesting schedules that were approved by the Board. Each option is exercisable into one common share of the Company at the price specified in the terms of the option agreement.

During the first quarter of fiscal 2014, the Company offered a one-time cash repurchase to holders of stock options above a specified value. The repurchase was approved by the Board of Directors and by the Company's shareholders; repurchased options were subsequently cancelled by the Company. As part of this transaction, the Company immediately recorded the remaining unamortized expense of $0.5 million for repurchased options. The Company repurchased and cancelled 870,500 options and made a cash payment to option holders of $1.0 million.

The Company uses the fair value method of accounting for stock options, which estimates the fair value of the stock options granted on the date of grant, net of estimated forfeitures, and expenses this value over the vesting period. During fiscal 2014, the pre-forfeiture fair value of options granted was $2.8 million (2013 – $0.7 million). The weighted average fair value of options issued in fiscal 2014 was $1.97 per option (2013 – $1.54 per option).

The fair value of the employee stock options is estimated at the date of grant using the Black-Scholes option pricing model with the following weighted average assumptions during the periods presented:

	52-week period ended March 29, 2014	52-week period ended March 30, 2013
Black-Scholes option pricing assumptions		
Risk-free interest rate	1.3%	1.2%
Expected volatility	35.4%	37.1%
Expected time until exercise	3.0 years	3.0 years
Expected dividend yield	3.4%	5.0%
Other assumptions		
Forfeiture rate	26.7%	24.9%

A summary of the status of the Plan and changes during both periods is presented below:

	52-week period ended March 29, 2014		52-week period ended March 30, 2013	
	Number #	Weighted average exercise price C$	Number #	Weighted average exercise price C$
Outstanding options, beginning of period	1,627,000	12.64	1,372,400	13.64
Granted	1,401,000	10.25	430,000	8.63
Forfeited / repurchased	(1,347,000)	13.77	(117,500)	12.97
Expired	(4,000)	4.45	–	–
Exercised	(850)	8.00	(57,900)	5.74
Outstanding options, end of period	1,676,150	9.75	1,627,000	12.64
Options exercisable, end of period	245,900	8.88	722,500	14.52

Options outstanding and exercisable

	March 29, 2014				
	Outstanding			Exercisable	
Range of exercise prices C$	Number #	Weighted average exercise price C$	Weighted average remaining contractual life (in years)	Number #	Weighted average exercise price C$
7.20 – 8.06	313,650	7.74	3.1	143,700	7.61
8.07 – 9.72	366,500	8.36	4.3	43,900	8.66
9.73 – 10.80	910,000	10.70	4.3	23,800	10.70
10.81 – 14.05	78,500	12.79	6.9	30,000	12.88
14.06 – 15.21	7,500	15.21	6.6	4,500	15.21
7.20 – 15.21	1,676,150	9.75	4.2	245,900	8.88

Directors' compensation

The Company has established a Directors' Deferred Share Unit Plan ("DSU Plan"). Under the DSU Plan, Directors receive their annual retainer fees and other Board-related compensation in the form of deferred share units ("DSUs"). The number of shares reserved for issuance under this plan is 500,000. The Company issued 43,757 DSUs with a value of $0.4 million during fiscal 2014 (2013 – 46,409 DSUs with a value of $0.4 million). The number of DSUs to be issued to each Director is based on a set fee schedule. The grant date fair value of the outstanding DSUs as at March 29, 2014 was $3.3 million (March 30, 2013 – $2.9 million; April 1, 2012 – $2.5 million) and was recorded in contributed surplus. The fair value of DSUs is equal to the traded price of the Company's common shares on grant date.

15. SUPPLEMENTARY OPERATING INFORMATION

Supplemental product line revenue information:

	52-week period ended March 29, 2014	52-week period ended March 30, 2013
Print[1]	585,239	613,626
General merchandise[2]	240,237	207,520
eReading[3]	24,743	35,898
Other[4]	17,449	21,741
Total	867,668	878,785

1 Includes books, calendars, magazines, and newspapers.
2 Includes lifestyle, paper, toys, music, DVDs, and electronics.
3 Includes eReaders, eReader accessories, and Kobo revenue share.
4 Includes cafés, irewards, gift card breakage, and Plum breakage.

Supplemental operating and administrative expenses information:

(thousands of Canadian dollars)	52-week period ended March 29, 2014	52-week period ended March 30, 2013
Wages, salaries and bonuses	157,904	150,469
Short-term benefits expense	18,321	17,598
Termination benefits expense	4,945	3,482
Retirement benefits expense	1,286	1,224
Stock-based compensation	1,242	743
Total employee benefits expense	183,698	173,516

Termination benefits arise when the Company terminates certain employment agreements.

Minimum lease payments recognized as an expense during fiscal 2014 were $63.5 million (2013 – $62.7 million). Contingent rents recognized as an expense during fiscal 2014 were $1.0 million (2013 – $1.3 million).

16. EARNINGS PER SHARE

Earnings per share is calculated based on the weighted average number of common shares outstanding during the period. In calculating diluted earnings per share amounts under the treasury stock method, the numerator remains unchanged from the basic earnings per share calculations as the assumed exercise of the Company's stock options do not result in an adjustment to net earnings. The reconciliation of the denominator in calculating diluted earnings per share amounts for the periods presented is as follows:

(thousands of shares)	52-week period ended March 29, 2014	52-week period ended March 30, 2013
Weighted average number of common shares outstanding, basic	25,601	25,529
Effect of dilutive securities		
Stock options	47	34
Weighted average number of common shares outstanding, diluted	25,648	25,563

As at March 29, 2014, 1,246,000 (March 30, 2013 – 1,505,500; April 1, 2012 – 1,293,000) options could potentially dilute basic earnings per share in the future, but were excluded from the computation of diluted net earnings per common share in the current period as they were anti-dilutive.

17. STATEMENTS OF CASH FLOWS

Supplemental cash flow information:

(thousands of Canadian dollars)	52-week period ended March 29, 2014	52-week period ended March 30, 2013
Net change in non-cash working capital balances:		
Accounts receivable	1,544	5,494
Inventories	(2,446)	12,666
Income taxes recoverable	(37)	(86)
Prepaid expenses	(1,031)	(461)
Accounts payable and accrued liabilities	(14,857)	(25,035)
Unredeemed gift card liability	(342)	4,458
Provisions	(1,154)	1,554
Deferred revenue	(873)	2,499
	(19,196)	1,089
Assets acquired under finance leases	137	465

18. CAPITAL MANAGEMENT

The Company's main objectives when managing capital are to safeguard its ability to continue as a going concern while maintaining adequate financial flexibility to invest in new business opportunities that will provide attractive returns to shareholders. The primary activities engaged by the Company to generate attractive returns include construction and related leasehold improvements of stores, the development of new business concepts, and investment in information technology and distribution capacity to support the online and retail networks. The Company's main sources of capital are its current cash position, cash flows generated from operations, and long-term debt. On June 12, 2013, the Company cancelled its revolving line of credit. Cash flow is used to fund working capital needs, capital expenditures and debt service requirements.

In order to maintain sufficient capital resources to fund the Company's transformation, management and the Company's Board of Directors decided to suspend quarterly dividend payments beyond December 3, 2013. The Company primarily manages its capital by monitoring its available cash balance to ensure that sufficient funds are available for long-term debt and interest payments over the next year.

The following table summarizes selected capital structure information for the Company:

(thousands of Canadian dollars)	March 29, 2014	March 30, 2013	April 1, 2012
Current portion of long-term debt	584	773	1,060
Long-term debt	227	705	1,141
Total debt	811	1,478	2,201
Total equity	311,674	350,322	355,632
Total capital under management	312,485	351,800	357,833

19. FINANCIAL RISK MANAGEMENT

The Company's activities expose it to a variety of financial risks, including risks related to foreign exchange, interest rate, credit, and liquidity.

Foreign exchange risk

The Company's foreign exchange risk is largely limited to currency fluctuations between the Canadian and U.S. dollars. Decreases in the value of the Canadian dollar relative to the U.S. dollar could negatively impact net earnings since the purchase price of some of the Company's products are negotiated with vendors in U.S. dollars, while the retail price to customers is set in Canadian dollars. The Company did not use any forward contracts to manage foreign exchange risk in fiscal 2014 (2013 – no forward contracts).

As the Company expands its product selection to include a greater number of non-book items, foreign exchange risk has increased due to more purchases being denominated in U.S. dollars. A 10% appreciation or depreciation in the U.S. and Canadian dollar exchange rates during fiscal 2014 would have had an impact of $3.9 million (2013 – $3.9 million) on net earnings (loss) and comprehensive earnings (loss).

In fiscal 2014, the effect of foreign currency translation on net earnings (loss) and comprehensive earnings (loss) was a loss of $0.4 million (2013 – gain of $0.2 million).

Interest rate risk

On June 12, 2013, the Company cancelled its revolving line of credit. As such, the Company's interest rate risk is largely limited to its long-term debt, for which interest rates are fixed at the time a contract is finalized. The Company's interest income is also sensitive to fluctuations in Canadian interest rates, which affect the interest earned on the Company's cash and cash equivalents. The Company has minimal interest rate risk and does not use any interest rate swaps to manage its risk.

Credit risk

The Company is exposed to credit risk resulting from the possibility that counterparties may default on their financial obligations to the Company. The Company's maximum exposure to credit risk at the reporting date is equal to the carrying value of accounts receivable. Accounts receivable primarily consists of receivables from retail customers who pay by credit card, recoveries of credits from suppliers for returned or damaged products, and receivables from other companies for sales of products, gift cards and other services. Credit card payments have minimal credit risk and the limited number of corporate receivables is closely monitored.

Liquidity risk

Liquidity risk is the risk that the Company will be unable to meet its obligations relating to its financial liabilities. The Company manages liquidity risk by preparing and monitoring cash flow budgets and forecasts to ensure that the Company has sufficient funds to meet its financial obligations and fund new business opportunities or other unanticipated requirements as they arise.

The contractual maturities of the Company's current and long-term liabilities as at March 29, 2014 are as follows:

(thousands of Canadian dollars)	Payments due in the next 90 days	Payments due between 90 days and less than a year	Payments due after 1 year	Total
Accounts payable and accrued liabilities	109,671	26,757	–	136,428
Unredeemed gift card liability	46,827	–	–	46,827
Provisions	–	928	–	928
Current portion of long-term debt	–	584	–	584
Long-term accrued liabilities	–	–	2,896	2,896
Long-term provisions	–	–	164	164
Long-term debt	–	–	227	227
Total	156,498	28,269	3,287	188,054

20. EQUITY INVESTMENT

The Company holds a 50% equity ownership in its associate, Calendar Club, to sell calendars, games, and gifts through seasonal kiosks and year-round stores in Canada. The Company uses the equity method of accounting to record Calendar Club results. In fiscal 2014, the Company received $1.2 million (2013 – $1.3 million) of distributions from Calendar Club.

The following tables represent financial information for Calendar Club along with the Company's share therein:

(thousands of Canadian dollars)	Total			Company's share		
	March 29, 2014	March 30, 2013	April 1, 2012	March 29, 2014	March 30, 2013	April 1, 2012
Cash and cash equivalents	1,185	2,278	1,766	593	1,139	883
Total current assets	2,565	3,316	2,798	1,283	1,658	1,399
Total long-term assets	658	831	1,071	329	416	536
Total current liabilities	2,027	2,212	1,948	1,014	1,106	974

(thousands of Canadian dollars)	Total		Company's share	
	52-week period ended March 29, 2014	52-week period ended March 30, 2013	52-week period ended March 29, 2014	52-week period ended March 30, 2013
Revenue	31,003	30,543	15,502	15,272
Expenses	(29,425)	(27,914)	(14,713)	(13,957)
Net earnings	1,578	2,629	789	1,315

Changes in the carrying amount of the investment were as follows:

(thousands of Canadian dollars)	Carrying value
Balance, March 31, 2012	961
Equity income from Calendar Club	1,315
Distributions from Calendar Club	(1,308)
Balance, March 30, 2013	968
Equity income from Calendar Club	789
Distributions from Calendar Club	(1,159)
Balance, March 29, 2014	598

21. RELATED PARTY TRANSACTIONS

The Company's related parties include its key management personnel, shareholders, defined contribution retirement plan, equity investment in Calendar Club, and subsidiary. Unless otherwise stated, none of the transactions incorporate special terms and conditions and no guarantees were given or received. Outstanding balances are usually settled in cash.

Transactions with key management personnel

Key management of the Company includes members of the Board of Directors as well as members of the Executive Committee. Key management personnel remuneration includes the following expenses:

(thousands of Canadian dollars)	52-week period ended March 29, 2014	52-week period ended March 30, 2013
Wages, salaries, bonus and consulting	4,654	4,085
Short-term benefits expense	242	246
Termination benefits expense	457	450
Retirement benefits expense	60	66
Stock-based compensation	789	443
Directors' compensation	425	446
Total remuneration	6,627	5,736

Transactions with shareholders

During fiscal 2014, Indigo purchased goods and services from companies in which Mr. Gerald W. Schwartz, who is the controlling shareholder of Indigo, holds a controlling or significant interest. In fiscal 2014, Indigo paid $5.3 million for these goods and services (2013 – $0.2 million). As at March 29, 2014, Indigo had less than $0.1 million payable to these companies under standard payment terms and $2.8 million of restricted cash pledged as collateral for letter of credit obligations issued to support the Company's purchases of merchandise from these companies (March 30, 2013 and April 1, 2012 – no amounts payable and no restricted cash). All transactions were in the normal course of business for both Indigo and the related companies.

Transactions with defined contribution retirement plan

The Company's transactions with the defined contribution retirement plan include contributions paid to the retirement plan as disclosed in note 15. The Company has not entered into other transactions with the retirement plan.

Transactions with associate

The Company's associate, Calendar Club, is a seasonal operation which is dependent on the December holiday sales season to generate revenues. During the year, the Company loans cash to Calendar Club for working capital requirements and Calendar Club repays the loans once profits are generated in the third quarter. The net amount of these transactions for fiscal 2014 was nil (2013 – nil), as Calendar Club has repaid all loans as at March 29, 2014. In fiscal 2013, Calendar Club repaid an outstanding $0.2 million note payable to Indigo.

22. COMPARATIVE CONSOLIDATED FINANCIAL STATEMENTS

The comparative consolidated financial statements have been reclassified from statements previously presented to conform to the presentation of the current year audited consolidated financial statements.

Five Year Summary of Financial Information

For the years ended (millions of Canadian dollars, except share and per share data)	IFRS March 29, 2014	March 30, 2013	March 31, 2012	April 2, 2011	Canadian GAAP April 3, 2010
SELECTED STATEMENTS OF EARNINGS INFORMATION					
Revenues					
Superstores	617.8	626.6	656.5	667.6	670.5
Small format stores	127.4	137.6	145.2	149.4	159.3
Online	102.0	91.9	91.3	90.6	92.2
Other	20.5	22.7	27.2	33.9	46.1
Total revenues	867.7	878.8	920.2	941.5	968.1
Adjusted EBITDA[1]	0.1	28.5	25.0	54.8	76.1
Earnings (loss) before income taxes	(26.9)	4.2	(29.3)	25.8	49.8
Net earnings (loss) and comprehensive earnings (loss)	(31.0)	4.3	66.2	(19.4)	34.9
Dividends per share	$0.33	$0.44	$0.44	$0.44	$0.40
Net earnings (loss) per common share	$(1.21)	$0.17	$3.68	$(0.23)	$1.42
SELECTED BALANCE SHEET INFORMATION					
Working capital	189.7	224.3	223.7	101.1	106.4
Total assets	512.6	569.1	591.8	510.3	519.8
Long-term debt (including current portion)	0.8	1.5	2.2	3.3	3.0
Total equity	311.7	350.3	355.6	267.4	259.0
Weighted average number of shares outstanding	25,601,260	25,529,035	25,201,127	24,874,199	24,549,622
Common shares outstanding at end of period	25,298,239	25,297,389	25,238,414	25,140,540	24,742,915
STORE OPERATING STATISTICS					
Number of stores at end of period					
Superstores	95	97	97	97	96
Small format stores	131	134	143	150	151
Selling square footage at end of period (in thousands)					
Superstores	2,200	2,235	2,235	2,235	2,217
Small format stores	370	379	400	413	417
Comparable store sales					
Superstores	(0.9%)	(4.6%)	(1.9%)	(0.3%)	0.6%
Small format stores	(5.0%)	(2.4%)	(0.8%)	(3.2%)	(2.2%)
Sales per selling square foot					
Superstores	281	280	294	299	302
Small format stores	344	362	363	362	382

1 Earnings before interest, taxes, depreciation, amortization, impairment, and equity investment. Also see "Non-IFRS Financial Measures".

Appendix B

TYPICAL CHART OF ACCOUNTS FOR SERVICE PROPRIETORSHIPS (ASPE)

ASSETS	LIABILITIES	OWNER'S EQUITY
Cash	Accounts Payable	Owner, Capital
Petty Cash	Notes Payable, Short-Term	Owner, Withdrawals
Accounts Receivable	Salaries Payable	
Allowance for Doubtful Accounts	Wages Payable	**REVENUES AND GAINS**
Notes Receivable, Short-Term	Goods and Services Tax Payable	Service Revenue
Goods and Services Tax Recoverable	Harmonized Sales Tax Payable	Interest Revenue
Harmonized Sales Tax Recoverable	Employee Income Tax Payable	Gain on sale of Land (or Furniture,
Interest Receivable	Employment Insurance Payable	Equipment, or Building)
Supplies	Canada Pension Plan Payable	
Prepaid Rent	Quebec Pension Plan Payable	**EXPENSES AND LOSSES**
Prepaid Insurance	Employee Benefits Payable	Amortization Expense—Furniture
	Interest Payable	Amortization Expense—Equipment
Furniture	Unearned Service Revenue	Amortization Expense—Building
Accumulated Amortization—	Estimated Warranty Payable	Amortization Expense—Land
Furniture	Estimated Vacation Pay Liability	Improvements
Equipment	Current Portion of Long-term Debt	Bad Debt Expense
Accumulated Amortization—		Bank Charge Expense
Equipment		Cash Short & Over
Building		Credit Card Discount Expense
Accumulated Amortization—	Notes Payable, Long-Term	Debit Card Service Fee
Building		Delivery Expense
Land Improvements		Employee Benefits Expense
Accumulated Amortization—Land		Interest Expense
Improvements		Insurance Expense
Leasehold Improvements		Miscellaneous Expense
Land		Property Tax Expense
Notes Receivable, Long-Term		Rent Expense
Patents		Supplies Expense
Goodwill		Utilities Expense
		Vacation Pay Expense
		Warranty Expense
		Loss on Sale (or Exchange) of Land
		(or Furniture, Equipment, or
		Buildings)

GLOSSARY

2/15, n30 Credit terms offered by some merchandisers, meaning that if the invoice is paid within 15 days of the invoice date (the *discount period*), a 2 percent discount may be taken. If not, the full amount (net) is due in 30 days (p. 253).

Account The detailed record of the changes that have occurred in a particular asset, liability, or item of owner's equity during a period (p. 13).

Accounting The system that measures business activities, processes that information into reports and financial statements, and communicates the findings to decision makers (p. 4).

Accounting cycle The process by which accountants produce an entity's financial statements and update the financial reports for a period of time (p. 60).

Accounting equation The most basic tool of accounting: Assets = Liabilities + Owner's Equity (proprietorship) or Assets − Liabilities + Shareholders' Equity (corporation) (p. 12).

Accounting information system (AIS) The combination of personnel, records, and procedures that a business uses to meet its need for financial data (p. 378).

Accounting period The time frame, or period of time, covered by financial statements and other reports (p. 60).

Accounting Standards for Private Enterprises (ASPE) Created by the Accounting Standards Board, guidelines for reporting the financial results of nonpublicly accountable enterprises in Canada (p. 10).

Account payable The oral or implied promise to pay off debts arising from credit purchases. A liability that is backed by the general reputation and credit standing of the debtor (p. 14).

Account receivable An asset; a promise to receive cash in the future from customers to whom the business has sold goods or services (p. 13).

Accrual-basis accounting Accounting that recognizes (records) the impact of a business event as it occurs, regardless of whether the transaction affected cash (p. 121).

Accrued expense An expense that has been incurred but not yet paid in cash; also called an *accrued liability* (p. 129, 620).

Accrued liability Another name for an *accrued expense* (p. 620).

Accrued revenue A revenue that has been earned but not yet received in cash (p. 131).

Accumulated amortization The cumulative sum of all amortization expense from the date of acquiring a capital asset (p. 127).

Acid-test ratio Ratio of the sum of cash plus short-term investments plus net current receivables to current liabilities. Tells whether the entity could pay all its current liabilities if they came due immediately. Also called the *quick ratio* (p. 523).

Adjusted trial balance A list of all the ledger accounts with their adjusted balances (p. 134).

Adjusting entry An entry made at the end of the period to assign revenues to the period in which they are earned and expenses to the period in which they are incurred. Adjusting entries help measure the period's income and bring the related asset and liability accounts to correct balances for the financial statements (p. 122).

Aging-of-accounts-receivable method A way to estimate bad debts by analyzing individual accounts receivable according to the length of time they have been due (p. 510).

Allowance for Doubtful Accounts A contra account, related to accounts receivable, that holds the estimated amount of collection losses. Also called *allowance for uncollectible accounts* (p. 508).

Allowance for Uncollectible Accounts Another name for *allowance for doubtful accounts* (p. 508).

Allowance method A method of recording collection losses based on estimates made prior to determining that the business will not collect from specific customers (p. 508).

Amortizable cost The asset's cost minus its estimated residual value (p. 566).

Amortization The term the *CPA Canada Handbook* uses to describe the writing off that occurs to expense the cost of capital assets; also called *depreciation* or *depletion* when applied to natural resources (pp. 126, 565).

Amortization rate The amount of amortization written off to expense stated as a percentage (p. 567).

Amortization schedule A table or chart that shows the amortization expense and asset values by period (p. 567).

Appraisal An expert assessment of the value of an asset (p. 563).

Arrears A legal term for debt that is overdue because of at least one missed payment (p. 560).

Asset An economic resource a business owns that is expected to be of benefit in the future (p. 13).

Asset retirement obligation A liability that records the future cost to settle a present obligation, such as future removal and site restoration costs (p. 578).

Audit The examination of financial statements by outside accountants. The conclusion of an audit is the accountant's professional opinion about the financial statements (pp. 6, 451).

Bad debt expense The cost to the seller of extending credit. Arises from the failure to collect from credit customers. Also called *doubtful accounts expense* or *uncollectible accounts expense* (p. 508).

Balance sheet A list of an entity's assets, liabilities, and owner's equity (proprietorship) or shareholders' equity (corporation) as of a specific date. Also called the *statement of financial position* (p. 22).

Balance sheet approach Another name for the *aging-of-accounts-receivable method* of estimating uncollectibles (p. 510).

Bank cheque A document that instructs the bank to pay the designated person or business the specified amount of money (p. 67).

Bank collection Collection of money by the bank on behalf of a depositor (p. 459).

Bank deposit slip A document that shows the amount of cash deposited into a person's or business's bank account (p. 67).

Bank reconciliation The process of explaining the reasons for the difference between a depositor's records and the bank's records about the depositor's bank account (p. 458).

Bank statement A document for a particular bank account showing its beginning and ending balances and listing the month's transactions that affected the account (p. 455).

Batch processing Computerized accounting for similar transactions in a group or batch (p. 383).

Betterment An expenditure that increases the capacity or efficiency of an asset or extends its useful life. Capital expenditures are debited to an asset account (p. 563).

Bill Another term for *invoice* (p. 252).

Book value The asset's cost less accumulated amortization. Also called *carrying value* (p. 127).

Bookkeeping A procedural element of accounting; the keeping of the financial records and the recording of financial information (p. 4).

Brand name A distinctive identification of a product or service (p. 579).

Business One or more individuals selling goods or services with the intent of making a profit (p. 4).

Canada (or Quebec) Pension Plan (CPP or QPP) All employees and self-employed persons in Canada (except in Quebec, where the pension plan is the Quebec Pension Plan) between 18 and 70 years of age are required to contribute to the Canada Pension Plan administered by the Government of Canada (p. 628).

Capital Another name for the *owner's equity* of a business (p. 14).

Capital cost allowance (CCA) Amortization allowed for income tax purposes by the Canada Revenue Agency; the rates allowed are called capital cost allowance rates (p. 571).

Capitalize To record as an asset (p. 561).

Carrying value (of property, plant, and equipment) The asset's cost less accumulated amortization Also called *book value* (p. 127).

Cash The most liquid asset an organization has; includes cash on hand, cash on deposit in banks and trust companies, and cash equivalents (p. 446).

Cash-basis accounting Accounting that records only transactions in which cash is received or paid (p. 121).

Cash discount Another name for a *purchase discount* (p. 253).

Cash flow statement Reports cash receipts and cash payments classified according to the entity's major activities: operating, investing, and financing (p. 23).

Cash generating unit (CGU) Under IFRS, the smallest identifiable group of assets that generates cash flows that are largely independent of the cash flows from other assets (p. 582).

Cash payments journal A special journal used to record cash payments made by cheque (p. 395).

Cash receipts journal A special journal used to record cash receipts (p. 389).

Cash short and over When the recorded cash balance does not match the actual amount counted (p. 464).

Chart of accounts A list of all the accounts and their account numbers in the ledger (p. 61).

Chartered Professional Accountant (CPA) An accountant who has met the examination and experience requirements of the CPA Canada (p. 6).

Cheque A document that instructs the bank to pay the designated person or business a specified amount of money (p. 454).

Cheque truncation The conversion of a physical cheque into an electronic format (i.e., taking a picture) for processing through the banking system to save time and resources (p. 464).

Classified balance sheet A balance sheet that places each asset and liability into a specific category (p. 190).

Closing entries Entries that transfer the revenue, expense, and owner withdrawal balances from these respective accounts to the Capital account (p. 185).

Closing the accounts A step in the accounting cycle at the end of the period that prepares the accounts for recording the transactions of the next period. Closing the accounts consists of journalizing and posting the closing entries to set the balances of the revenue, expense, and owner withdrawal accounts to zero (p. 185).

Cloud computing A subscription-based service where an external company provides software, processing capability, and data storage that the customer accesses using the Internet. Customers gain the software capabilities without investing in the hardware and software themselves (p. 379).

Collection period Another name for *days' sales in receivables* (p. 524).

Collusion When two or more people work as a team to beat internal controls and steal from a company (p. 453).

Commercial substance In an exchange of tangible capital assets, commercial substance exists when an entity's future cash flows from the new asset received will differ in risk, timing, or amount from the cash flows from the old asset given up (p. 576).

Comparability A characteristic of accounting information that states business must use the same accounting methods and procedures from period to period or disclose a change in method (p. 336).

Comparable A qualitative characteristic of accounting information that says financial statements should be able to be measured against results in previous years or other businesses in the same industry (p. 11).

Componentization Under IFRS, recording each identifiable component of an asset separately to calculate depreciation on each part (p. 582).

Compound journal entry A journal entry with more than one debit and credit (p. 74).

Computer virus A malicious computer program that reproduces itself, gets included in program code without consent, and destroys program code (p. 452).

Conservatism An accounting concept by which the least favourable figures are presented in the financial statements (p. 336).

Contingent liability A potential liability from a past event that depends on an uncertain future event not within the business's control (p. 624).

Contra account An account that always has a companion account and whose normal balance is opposite that of the companion account (p. 127).

Control account An account whose balance equals the sum of the balances in a group of related accounts in a subsidiary ledger (p. 379)

Controller The chief accounting officer of a company (p. 450).

Copyright The exclusive right to reproduce and sell software, a book, a musical composition, a film, or other creative work. Issued by the federal government, copyrights extend 50 years beyond the creator's life (p. 579).

Corporation A business owned by shareholders that begins when the federal or provincial government approves its articles of incorporation. A corporation is a legal entity, an "artificial person," in the eyes of the law (p. 8).

Cost of goods sold The cost of the inventory that the business has sold to customers; the largest single expense of most merchandising businesses. Also called *cost of sales* (p. 248).

Cost of sales Another name for *cost of goods sold* (p. 248).

Cost principle of measurement States that assets and services are recorded at their purchase cost and that the accounting record of the asset continues to be based on cost rather than current market value (p. 12).

Cost–benefit constraint An accounting constraint that says the benefits of the information produced should not exceed the costs of producing the information (pp. 12, 453).

Credit The right side of an account (p. 63).

Credit memo The document issued by a seller for a credit to a customer's account receivable (p. 397).

Creditor The party to a credit transaction who sells a service or merchandise and obtains a receivable (p. 506).

Creditors Businesses or individuals to which payment is owed (p. 5).

Current asset An asset that is expected to be converted to cash, sold, or consumed during the next 12 months, or within the business's normal operating cycle if longer than a year (p. 190).

Current liability A debt due to be paid within one year or one of the entity's operating cycles if the cycle is longer than a year (p. 191).

Current portion of long-term debt The amount of the principal that is payable within one year (p. 619).

Current ratio Current assets divided by current liabilities. Measures the company's ability to pay current liabilities from current assets (p. 194).

Current then non-current A balance sheet format that reports current assets before long-term assets, and current liabilities before long-term liabilities and equity. This format may be used for reporting under both ASPE and IFRS (p. 196).

Custodian A person designated to be responsible for something of value, like the petty cash fund (p. 467).

Database A computerized storehouse of information that can be systematically assessed in a variety of report forms (p. 380).

Days' sales in receivables Ratio of average net accounts receivable to one day's sales. Indicates how many days' sales remain in Accounts Receivable awaiting collection. Also called the *collection period* (p. 524).

DDB rate Double-declining-balance percentage applied to an asset to calculate its amortization or depreciation. It is twice the straight-line amortization rate (p. 568).

Debit The left side of an account (p. 63).

Debit memo The document issued by a buyer to reduce the buyer's account payable to a seller (p. 399).

Debtor The party to a credit transaction who makes a purchase and creates a payable (p. 506).

Debt ratio Ratio of total liabilities to total assets. Gives the proportion of a company's assets that it has financed with debt (p. 194).

Default on a note Failure of the maker of a note to pay at maturity. Also called *dishonour of a note* (p. 522).

Deferred revenue Another name for *unearned revenue* (p. 128).

Depletion Another word to describe the amortization of natural resources or wasting assets (p. 577).

Deposit in transit A deposit recorded by the company but not yet by its bank (p. 459).

Derecognize Under IFRS, to remove an asset from the accounting records because it has been replaced (p. 582).

Designated accountants Accountants who have met the education, examination, and experience requirements of an accounting body (p. 6).

Direct deposit Funds that are deposited and transferred directly to a bank account, such as employee payroll (p. 455).

Direct write-off method A method of accounting for bad debts by which the company waits until the credit department decides that a customer's account receivable is uncollectible and then debits Bad Debt Expense and credits the customer's Account Receivable (p. 515).

Disclosure principle An accounting concept that states a business's financial statements must report enough information for outsiders to make knowledgeable decisions about the business (p. 336).

Discounting a note receivable Selling a note receivable before its maturity date (p. 527).

Discount period The time period during which a cash discount is available and a reduced payment can be made by the purchaser (p. 253).

Dishonour a note Failure of the maker of a note to pay a note receivable at maturity. Also called *default on a note* (p. 522).

Dividends Distributions by a corporation to its shareholders (p. 15).

Double-declining-balance (DDB) method A type of amortization method that expenses a relatively larger amount of an asset's cost nearer the start of its useful life than does the straight-line method (p. 568).

Doubtful account expense Another name for *bad debt expense* (p. 508).

Due date The date on which the final payment of a note is due. Also called the *maturity date* (p. 519).

Economic entity assumption The accounting assumption that an organization or a section of an organization stands apart from other organizations and individuals as a separate economic unit for accounting purposes. (p. 11).

Electronic Data Interchange (EDI) The transfer of structured data by electronic means and standards between organizations from one computer system to another without human intervention (p. 466).

Electronic funds transfer (EFT) A system that transfers cash by digital communication rather than paper documents (p. 455).

Employee compensation Payroll, a major expense of many businesses (p. 627).

Employment Insurance (EI) Most employees and employers in Canada must contribute to the Employment Insurance fund, which provides assistance to unemployed workers (p. 629).

Encryption The process of rearranging plain-text messages by some mathematical formula to achieve confidentiality (p. 452).

End-user tax A consumption tax that is only paid by the final consumer (p. 618).

Enterprise resource planning (ERP) A computer system that integrates all company data into a single data warehouse (p. 384).

eom A credit term that means an invoice amount is due by the end of the month (p. 253).

Estimated residual value The expected cash value of an asset at the end of its useful life. Also called *residual value*, *scrap value*, or *salvage value* (p. 566).

Estimated useful life Length of the service that a business expects to get from an asset; may be expressed in years, units of output, kilometres, or other measures (p. 566).

Ethics Rules of behaviour based on what is good or bad (p. 7).

Evaluated Receipt Settlement (ERS) A streamlined payment procedure that compresses the approval process into a single step: comparing the receiving report with the purchase order (p. 466).

Executive controls Management involvement in internal controls (p. 462).

Exempt supplies Goods and services that are not required to have GST or HST charged on them (p. 617).

Expenses Costs incurred when running a business (or the using up of assets). Decrease in owner's equity that occurs in the course of delivering goods or services to customers or clients (p. 14).

External users Readers of financial information who do not work for the business (p. 5).

Fidelity bond An insurance policy that reimburses the company for any losses due to the employee's theft. Before hiring, the bonding company checks the employee's background (p. 451).

Financial accounting The branch of accounting that provides information to people outside the business (p. 5).

Financial statements Business documents that report financial information about an entity to persons and organizations outside the business (p. 4).

Firewall Barriers used to prevent entry into a computer network or a part of a network. Examples include passwords, personal identification numbers (PINs), and fingerprints (p. 453).

First-in, first-out (FIFO) method An inventory costing method by which the first costs into inventory are the first costs out to cost of goods sold. Ending inventory is based on the costs of the most recent purchases (p. 329).

Fiscal year An accounting year of any 12 consecutive months that may or may not coincide with the calendar year (p. 119).

FOB destination Legal title passes to the buyer only when the inventory reaches the destination (i.e., the seller pays the freight) (p. 255).

FOB shipping point Legal title passes to the buyer as soon as the inventory leaves the seller's place of business—the shipping point (p. 255).

Franchise Privileges granted by a private business or a government to sell a product or service in accordance with specified conditions (p. 580).

Freight-in The transportation costs on purchased goods (i.e., from the wholesaler to the retailer) (p. 256).

Freight-out The transportation costs on goods sold (i.e., from the retailer to the customer) (p. 256).

General journal The journal used to record all transactions that do not fit into one of the special journals (p. 385).

General ledger Ledger of accounts that are reported in the financial statements (p. 388).

Generally accepted accounting principles (GAAP) Accounting guidelines, formulated by the Accounting Standards Board, that govern how businesses report their results in financial statements to the public (p. 9).

Going concern assumption An accounting assumption that the business will continue operating in the foreseeable future (p. 11).

Goodwill Excess of the cost of an acquired company over the sum of the market values of its net assets (assets minus liabilities) (p. 580).

Gross margin Excess of sales revenue over cost of goods sold. Also called *gross profit* (p. 248).

Gross margin method A way to estimate inventory based on a rearrangement of the cost of goods sold model: Beginning inventory + Net purchases = Cost of goods available for sale. Cost of goods available for sale − Cost of goods sold = Ending inventory. Also called the *gross profit method* (p. 342).

Gross margin percentage Gross margin divided by net sales revenue. A measure of profitability (p. 268).

Gross pay Total amount of salary, wages, commissions, or any other employee compensation before taxes and other deductions are taken out (p. 627).

Gross profit method Another name for the *gross margin method* (p. 342).

Half-year rule The Canada Revenue Agency allows businesses to claim only 50 percent of the normal CCA rate in the year an asset is acquired (p. 571).

Hardware Electronic equipment that includes computers, disk drives, monitors, printers, and the network that connects them (p. 379).

Identifiable tangible asset An asset that is physical—it can be seen and touched—and can be separated from other assets; used to describe property, plant, and equipment (p. 560).

Impaired When the fair value falls below the carrying value in the accounting records (p. 581).

Impairment A write-down in value that occurs when an asset, such as inventory, becomes worth less than its cost (p. 338).

Impairment reversal A write-up in value that occurs when an asset that had been written down, such as inventory, increases in value up to the amount of the original write-down (p. 338).

Imprest system A way to account for petty cash by maintaining a constant balance in the Petty Cash account, supported by the fund (cash plus disbursement tickets) totalling the same amount (p. 468).

Income from operations Another name for *operating income* (p. 265).

Income statement A list of an entity's revenues, expenses, and net income or net loss for a specific period. Also called the *statement of earnings* or *statement of operations* (p. 21).

Income statement approach Another name for the *percent-of-sales method* of estimating uncollectibles (p. 509).

Income Summary A temporary "holding tank" account into which the revenues and expenses are transferred prior to their final transfer to the Capital account (p. 185).

Independence In accounting, this refers to there being no financial interest outside of the current business relationship. Auditors and other accountants must not be influenced by personal or professional gain from their auditing or accounting decisions (p. 6).

Independent contractors Individuals who do work for a business but are not employees. They invoice the business for their contracted work (p. 634).

Inflation A rise in the general level of prices (p. 12).

Input tax credit (ITC) The sales tax that will be refunded by the government (p. 617).

Intangible asset An asset with no physical form giving a special right to current and expected future benefits (p. 126).

Intellectual capital The knowledge of the people who work in a business (p. 579).

Interest The revenue to the payee for loaning out the principal, and the expense to the maker for borrowing the principal (p. 519).

Interest period The period of time during which interest is to be computed, extending from the original date of the note to the maturity date. Also called the *note term* or the *time period* (p. 519).

Interest rate The percentage rate that is multiplied by the principal amount to compute the amount of interest on a note (p. 519).

Internal control The organizational plan and all the related measures adopted by an entity to meet management's objectives of discharging statutory responsibilities, profitability, prevention and detection of fraud and error, safeguarding assets, reliability of accounting records, and timely preparation of reliable financial information (p. 446).

Internal users Readers of financial information who either own the business or are employed by it (p. 5).

International Accounting Standards Board (IASB) The body that sets International Financial Reporting Standards (p. 10).

International Financial Reporting Standards (IFRS) The accounting standards that specify the generally accepted accounting principles that must be applied by publicly accountable enterprises in Canada and over 130 countries (p. 10).

Inventory All goods that a company owns and expects to sell in the normal course of operation (p. 246).

Inventory turnover The ratio of cost of goods sold to average inventory. Measures the number of times a company sells its average level of inventory during a year (p. 269).

Investors A person or business that provides capital (usually money) to a business with the expectation of receiving financial gain (p. 5).

Invoice A seller's request for cash from the purchaser (p. 252).

Journal The chronological accounting record of an entity's transactions (p. 61).

Junked Discarded (p. 573).

Leasehold A right arising from a prepayment that a lessee (tenant) makes to secure the use of an asset from a lessor (landlord) (p. 580).

Leasehold improvements Changes to a leased asset that are amortized over the term of the lease or the useful life of the asset, whichever is shorter (p. 580).

Ledger The book (or printout) of accounts (p. 61).

Legacy designation The accounting designation of CPAs who joined as part of the initial merger of accounting bodies. It is the name of their prior accounting designation that must be used in conjunction with the CPA designation for a period of 10 years (p. 6).

Legal title The legal ownership of property (p. 255).

Liability An economic obligation (a debt) payable to an individual or an organization outside the business (p. 14).

Licence Privileges granted by a private business or a government to sell a product or service in accordance with special conditions (p. 580).

Limited-liability partnership (LLP) A form of partnership in which each partner's personal liability for the business's debts is limited to a certain amount (p. 8).

Limited personal liability The owner's legal and financial liability is limited to the amount he or she invested into the business (p. 9).

Line of credit Similar to a bank loan, it is negotiated once then drawn upon when needed. Interest is paid monthly only on the amount of the line of credit actually used (p. 615).

Liquidity A measure of how quickly an item can be converted to cash (p. 190).

Long-term asset An asset not classified as a current asset (p. 191).

Long-term liability A liability not classified as a current liability (p. 191).

Lower-of-cost-and-net-realizable-value (LCNRV) Requires that an asset be reported in the financial statements at the lower of its historical cost or its market value (current replacement cost for inventory) (p. 338).

Maker of a note The person or business that signs the note and promises to pay the amount required by the note agreement. The maker is the *debtor* (p. 519).

Management accounting The branch of accounting that generates information for internal decision makers of a business (p. 5).

Manufacturing entity A company that earns its revenue by making products (p. 191).

Matching objective The basis for recording expenses. Directs accountants to identify all expenses incurred during the period, measure the expenses, and match them against the revenues earned during that same span of time (p. 120).

Materiality The accounting constraint that says information should be reported if it is material to the user—that is, if knowing it might affect a decision maker's decision (p. 12).

Materiality constraint An accounting concept that states a company must perform strictly proper accounting only for items and transactions that are significant to the business's financial statements (p. 336).

Maturity date The date on which the final payment of a note is due. Also called the *due date* (p. 519).

Maturity value The sum of the principal and interest due at the maturity date of a note (p. 519).

Measurement The process of determining the amount at which an item is included in the financial statements (p. 12).

Menu A list of options for choosing computer functions (p. 383).

Merchandising business A business that resells products previously bought from suppliers (p. 17).

Merchandising entity A company that earns its revenue by selling products rather than services (p. 191).

Module Separate compatible units of an accounting package that are integrated to function together (p. 383).

Moving-weighted-average-cost method A weighted average-cost method where unit cost is changed to reflect each new purchase of inventory (p. 331).

Multi-step income statement An income statement format that contains subtotals to highlight significant relationships. In addition to net income, it also presents gross margin and income from operations (p. 266).

Net earnings Excess of total revenues over total expenses. Also called *net income* or *net profit* (p. 21).

Net income Excess of total revenues over total expenses. Also called *net earnings* or *net profit* (p. 21).

Net loss Excess of total expenses over total revenues (p. 21).

Net pay Gross pay minus all deductions; the amount of employee compensation that the employee actually takes home (p. 627).

Net profit Excess of total revenues over total expenses. Also called *net earnings* or *net income* (p. 21).

Net purchases Purchases plus freight-in and less purchase discounts and purchase returns and allowances (p. 256).

Net realizable value (NRV) Accounts receivable minus allowance for doubtful accounts equals the amount of accounts receivable the company hopes to realize, or collect (p. 508).

Net sales Sales revenue less sales discounts and sales returns and allowances (p. 248).

Network The system of electronic linkages that allow different computers to share the same information (p. 379).

Nominal account Another name for a *temporary account* (p. 185).

Non-current then current A balance sheet format that may be used for companies reporting under IFRS. Accounts are reported in the reverse order of liquidity, for example, long-term assets before current assets (p. 196).

Nonsufficient funds (NSF) cheque A "bounced" cheque, one for which the maker's bank account has insufficient money to pay the cheque (p. 459).

Normal balance The balance that appears on the side of an account—debit or credit—where we record increases (p. 66).

Note payable A liability evidenced by a written promise to make a future payment (p. 19).

Note receivable An asset evidenced by another party's written promise that entitles you to receive cash in the future (p. 13).

Note term Another name for the *interest period* of a note (p. 519).

Online processing Computerized processing of related functions, such as the recording and posting of transactions, on a continuous basis (p. 383).

Ontario Retirement Pension Plan (ORPP) Employees in Ontario without a company pension plan are required to contribute to the provincial pension plan in addition to their Canada Pension Plan contributions (effective 2017) (p. 629).

Operating cycle The time span during which cash is paid for goods and services that are sold to customers who then pay the business in cash (p. 190).

Operating expense Expense, other than cost of goods sold, that is incurred in the entity's major line of business: rent, amortization, salaries, wages, utilities, property tax, and supplies expense (p. 265).

Operating Income Gross margin minus operating expenses plus any other operating revenues. Also called *income from operations* (p. 265).

Other expense Expense that is outside the main operations of a business, such as a loss on the sale of capital assets (p. 265).

Other revenue Revenue that is outside the main operations of a business, such as a gain on the sale of capital assets (p. 265).

Outstanding cheque A cheque issued by the company and recorded on its books but not yet paid by its bank (p. 459).

Overdraw To remove more money from a bank account than exists in the bank account. This puts the bank account into a negative balance. This becomes a loan from the bank (p. 66).

Overtime For additional hours above the standard, employees are paid at a higher rate (p. 627).

Owner withdrawals Amounts removed from the business by an owner (p. 14).

Owner's equity In a proprietorship, the claim of an owner of a business to the assets of the business. Also called *capital* (p. 14).

Partners' equity The name for owner's equity when there is more than one owner. In this case, the owners are called partners (p. 14).

Partnership An unincorporated business with two or more owners (p. 8).

Patent A federal government grant giving the holder the exclusive right for 20 years to produce and sell an invention (p. 579).

Payee of a note The person or business to whom the maker of a note promises future payment. The payee is the *creditor* (p. 519).

Payroll Employee compensation, a major expense of many businesses (p. 627).

Payroll Deductions Online Calculator (PDOC) An online tool provided by the Canada Revenue Agency for calculating federal and provincial payroll deductions for all provinces (except Quebec) and territories (p. 629).

Percent-of-accounts-receivable method A method of estimating uncollectible receivables by determining the balance of Allowance for Doubtful Accounts based on a percentage of accounts receivable (p. 511).

Percent-of-sales method A method of estimating uncollectible receivables as a percent of the net credit sales (or net sales). Also called the *income statement approach* (p. 509).

Periodic inventory system A type of inventory accounting system in which the business does not keep a continuous record of the inventory on hand. Instead, at the end of the period the business makes a physical count of the on-hand inventory and applies the appropriate unit costs to determine the cost of the ending inventory (p. 249).

Permanent account An asset, liability, or owner's equity account that is not closed at the end of the period. Also called a *real account* (p. 185).

Perpetual inventory system A type of accounting inventory system in which the business keeps a continuous record for each inventory item to show the inventory on hand at all times (p. 250).

Petty cash A fund containing a small amount of cash that is used to pay minor expenditures (p. 467).

Petty cash ticket (voucher) A document indicating that money has been removed from the petty cash fund and a receipt is required to verify the expense (p. 468).

Phishing A method of gathering account numbers and passwords from people who visit legitimate-sounding bogus websites. The data gathered are then used for illicit purposes (p. 452).

Pledged as security A phrase that indicates an asset is held as collateral for a loan. In other words, if the loan is not paid, the asset will be taken as payment for the outstanding debt (p. 616).

Post-closing trial balance A list of the ledger accounts and their balances at the end of the period after the closing entries have been journalized and posted. The last step of the accounting cycle, it ensures that the ledger is in balance for the start of the next accounting period (p. 188).

Postdated cheques Cheques that are written for a future date (p. 446).

Posting Transferring of amounts from the journal to the ledger (p. 69).

Posting reference A column in the journal that indicates to the reader to which account the journal entry has been posted (p. 78).

Prepaid expense A category of assets that are paid for first, then expire or get used up in the near future (pp. 13, 123).

Principal The amount loaned out by the payee and borrowed by the maker of a note (p. 519).

Private accountants Accountants that only work for one employer that is not a public accounting firm (p. 6).

Private enterprise A corporation that does not offer its shares for sale to the public (p. 10).

Professional designations Acknowledgement of educational achievement from an agency to assure qualification to perform a job. (p. 6).

Profit Excess of total revenues over total expenses. Also called *net earnings, net income,* or *net profit* (p. 4).

Promissory note A written promise to pay a specified amount of money at a particular future date (pp. 13, 519).

Property, plant, and equipment (PPE) Long-lived tangible capital assets, such as land, buildings, and equipment, used to operate a business (p. 126).

Proprietorship An unincorporated business with a single owner (p. 7).

Prospectively In the future (p. 572).

Proving The process of ensuring the balance in the general ledger equals the sum of the individual balances in the subsidiary ledgers (p. 389).

Public accountants Designated accountants that provide services to clients in the practice of public accounting (p. 6).

Publicly accountable enterprise A corporation that has its shares traded on a stock exchange or for which a strong public interest exists (p. 10).

Purchase discount A reduction in the purchase price granted to the purchaser for paying within the discount period. Also called a *cash discount* (p. 253).

Purchase invoice A document from a vendor that shows a customer what was purchased, when it was purchased, and how much it cost (p. 67).

Purchase order A legal document that represents a business's intention to buy goods (p. 252).

Purchases journal A special journal used to record all purchases of inventory, supplies, and other assets on account (p. 393).

Quantity discount A reduction in the purchase price of an item based on the quantity of the item purchased; the greater the quantity purchased, the lower the price per item (p. 252).

Quick ratio Another name for the *acid-test ratio* (p. 523).

Real account Another name for a *permanent account* (p. 185).

Real-time processing Computerized processing of related functions, such as the recording and posting of transactions, on a continuous basis. Also called *online processing* (p. 383).

Receivable A monetary claim against a business or an individual, acquired mainly by selling goods and services and by lending money (p. 506).

Recognition criteria for revenues The basis for recording revenues; tells accountants when to record revenue and the amount of revenue to record (p. 119).

Recoverable In terms of accounting for taxes, this term means that the tax is refunded by the government (p. 617).

Recovery When a previously written off receivables amount is collected (p. 513).

Registrant A business or individual that is registered with the government to collect and remit sales taxes (p. 617).

Relative-fair-value method The allocation of the cost of assets according to their fair market value (p. 563).

Relevant Information that might influence a decision (p. 10).

Reliable A qualitative characteristic of accounting information that stays financial information is only useful if it accurately represents the impact of transactions—that is, it is free of error and bias (p. 11).

Remittance advice An optional attachment to a cheque that tells the payee the reason for payment (p. 455).

Repair An expenditure that merely maintains an asset in its existing condition or restores the asset to good working order. Repairs are expensed (matched against revenue) (p. 563).

Residual value The expected cash value of an asset at the end of its useful life (p. 126).

Retail method A method of estimating ending inventory based on the total cost and total selling price of opening inventory and net purchases (p. 342).

Revaluation method Under IFRS, when an asset's value is restated in the accounting records to reflect the asset's current market value (p. 582).

Revenue Amounts earned from delivering goods or services to customers. The increase in owner's equity that is earned by delivering goods or services to customers or clients (p. 14).

Reversing entry An entry that switches the debit and the credit of a previous adjusting entry. The reversing entry is dated the first day of the period following the adjusting entry (p. 202).

Sales Another name for *sales revenue* (p. 247).

Sales discount A reduction in the amount receivable from a customer offered by the seller as an incentive for the customer to pay promptly. A contra account to sales revenue (p. 258).

Sales invoice A seller's request for cash from the purchaser. This document gives the seller the amount of revenue to record (p. 67).

Sales journal A special journal used to record credit sales (p. 386).

Sales returns and allowances A decrease in the seller's receivable from a customer's return of merchandise or from granting the customer an allowance from the amount the customer owes the seller. A contra account to sales revenue (p. 258).

Sales revenue The amount that a merchandiser earns from selling inventory before subtracting expenses. Also called *sales* (pp. 17, 247).

Security An asset that will become the property of the lender if the debt that is owed to the lender is not paid (p. 13).

Server The main computer in a network where the program and data are stored (p. 379).

Service proprietorship An unincorporated business with one owner that earns income from selling services (p. 14).

Service revenue The amount of revenue that a business earns from selling services (p. 17).

Shareholder A person or company who owns one or more shares of stock in a corporation (p. 8).

Shareholders' equity The account name for owner's equity when the business is a corporation. In this case, the owners are called shareholders (p. 14).

Short-term note payable A note payable due within one year, a common form of financing (p. 614).

Shrinkage A reduction in the amount of inventory due to theft, spoilage, or error (p. 261).

Single-step income statement An income statement format that groups all revenues together and then lists and deducts all expenses together without drawing any subtotals (p. 266).

Slide A type of error in which one or several zeros are added or deleted in a figure; for example, writing $30 as $300 (p. 81).

Software A set of programs or instructions that cause the computer to perform the desired work (p. 379).

Source document A document that is evidence of a transaction, such as an invoice (p. 67).

Special journal An accounting journal designed to record one specific type of transaction (p. 385).

Specific identification method Another name for the *specific-unit-cost method* (p. 327).

Specific-unit-cost method An inventory costing method based on the specific cost of particular units of inventory. Also called the *specific identification method* (p. 327).

Stable monetary unit assumption Accountants' basis for ignoring the effect of inflation and making no adjustments for the changing value of the dollar (p. 12).

Stale-dated cheques Cheques that are older than six months and need to be reissued (p. 446).

Statement of earnings Another name for the *income statement* (p. 21).

Statement of financial position Another name for the *balance sheet* (p. 22).

Statement of operations Another name for the *income statement*. Also called the *statement of earnings* (p. 21).

Statement of owner's equity A summary of the changes in an entity's owner's equity during a specific period (p. 22).

Straight time A set period during which the base rate is paid to an employee (p. 627).

Straight-line method An amortization method in which an equal amount of amortization expense is assigned to each year (or period) of asset use (pp. 126, 566).

Subsidiary ledger The book of accounts that provides supporting details on individual balances, the total of which appears in a general ledger account (p. 388).

Tangible capital asset Physical assets expected to be used beyond the current accounting period. Examples include land, building, and equipment (p. 126).

Taxable supplies Goods and services that, when sold, have GST or HST charged on them (p. 617).

Temporary account The revenue and expense accounts that relate to a particular accounting period and are closed at the end of the period. For a proprietorship, the owner withdrawals account is also temporary. Also called a *nominal account* (p. 185).

Three-column format One common type of ledger format that includes three columns for dollar amounts—one for debit amounts, one for credit amounts, and the other for a running balance (p. 78).

Time period Another name for the *interest period* (p. 519).

Time period assumption Ensures that accounting information is reported at regular intervals (p. 119).

Timing difference A time lag in recording transactions (p. 457).

Trademark Distinctive identifications of a product or service. Also called *trade name* (p. 579).

Trade name Another term for *trademark* (p. 579).

Transaction An event that has a financial impact on a business and that can be reliably measured (p. 15).

Transposition A type of error in which two digits in a number are shown in reverse order (p. 81).

Treasurer The person in a company responsible for cash management (p. 450).

Treasury bill A financial instrument issued by the federal government that has a term of one year or less. It is sold at a discount and matures at par. The difference between the cost and maturity value is the purchaser's income (p. 446).

Trial balance A list of all the ledger accounts with their balances (p. 61).

Trojan A computer virus that does not reproduce but gets included into program code without consent and performs actions that can be destructive (p. 452).

Uncollectible accounts expense Another name for *bad debt expense* (p. 508).

Understandable A qualitative characteristic of accounting information that says users should be able to understand the information in financial statements (p. 11).

Unearned revenue A liability created when a business collects cash from customers in advance of doing work for the customer. The obligation is to provide a product or a service in the future. Also called *deferred revenue* (p. 128).

Units-of-production (UOP) method An amortization method by which a fixed amount of amortization is assigned to each unit of output produced by the capital asset (p. 568).

Unlimited personal liability When the debts of a business are greater than its resources, the owner is (owners are) responsible for their payment (p. 9).

Warranty When a business guarantees its products or services against defects (p. 622).

Weighted-average-cost method An inventory costing method used for the periodic inventory system where the average cost is calculated at the end of the period. Weighted-average cost is determined by dividing the cost of goods available for sale by the number of units available for sale (p. 335).

Withheld Deducted from pay and kept by the employer to be remitted to another party (p. 628).

Workers' compensation A provincially administered plan that is funded by contributions by employers and that provides financial support for workers injured on the job (p. 630).

Worksheet A columnar document designed to help move data from the trial balance to the financial statements (p. 177).

Write-off Remove the balance of the customer's account from the Accounts Receivable control account and subsidiary ledger in the accounting records since the customer will not pay what it owes (p. 513).

Zero-rated supplies Goods and services that have a GST or HST rate of zero percent (p. 617).

INDEX

transaction (Cont.)
  personal transactions, 18–19
  processing transactions in accounting systems, 382–383
  recording in journal, 67–68
  source documents, 67
transportation costs, 255–257, 274
transposition, 81
treasurer, 450
Treasury bills, 446
trial balance, 61, 80–81
  adjusted trial balance, 134–136, 179, 183–184
  correction of trial balance errors, 80–81
  post-closing trial balance, 188–189
  preparation of, 400
  unadjusted trial balance, 80, 122
  vs. balance sheet, 80
Trojan, 452
TSN, 579
2/15, n/30, 253

U

UBS, 447
unadjusted trial balance, 80, 122
unclassified balance sheet, 191
uncollectible account expense, 508
  see also uncollectible receivables
uncollectible receivables
  accounting for uncollectible accounts, 508–514
  aging-of-accounts-receivable method, 510–511, 512

allowance method, 508–509
debit balance in Allowance Account before adjustments, 512
direct write-off method, 515–516
estimating uncollectibles, 509–512, 523
percent-of-accounts-receivable method, 511, 512
percent-of-sales method, 509–510, 512
recovery of accounts previously written off, 513–514
using the allowance methods together, 512
writing off uncollectible accounts, 513
understandable, 11
unearned revenues, 128–129, 143, 620–621
unit cost, 327
United States
  depreciation, 126
  Dodd-Frank Act, 447–448
  Public Company Accounting Oversight Board (PCAOB), 447
  Sarbanes-Oxley Act, 447–448
United Way, 629
units-of-production (UOP) method, 568, 569–570, 572, 577
Universal Product Code (UPC), 381
unlimited personal liability, 9
use of documents and records, 451
use of electronic devices and computer controls, 451

users of accounting information, 5, 76

V

vacation pay liability, 622–623
Vancity Credit Union, 451
VIA Rail Canada, 380
VISA, 379, 516
voucher, 466

W

wages, 627
warranty, 622–623
warranty expense, 622
Warranty Week, 613
weighted-average cost method, 328, 329
weighted-average-cost method, 334–335
WestJet Airlines Ltd., 9, 562, 579
Winners, 451
Winnipeg Jets, 580
wireless networks (Wi-Fi), 452
withdrawals, 14
  see also owner withdrawals
withheld, 628, 637–638
workers' compensation, 630
worksheet, 176, 177–180, 276–277
WorldCom, 447
write-off, 513

Z

zero-rated supplies, 617